Psychology

AF770741

Concepts and Applications

4th Edition

Jeffrey S. Nevid

CENGAGE Learning®

Australia • Brazil • Japan • Korea • Mexico • Singapore • Spain • United Kingdom • United States

CENGAGE Learning

Psychology: Concepts and Applications, 4th Edition

Senior Project Development Manager:
Linda deStefano

Market Development Manager:
Heather Kramer

Senior Production/Manufacturing Manager:
Donna M. Brown

Production Editorial Manager:
Kim Fry

Sr. Rights Acquisition Account Manager:
Todd Osborne

Printed in the United States of America

Psychology: Concepts and Applications, 4th Edition
Jeffrey S. Nevid

© 2013 Cengage Learning. All rights reserved.

ALL RIGHTS RESERVED. No part of this work covered by the copyright herein may be reproduced, transmitted, stored or used in any form or by any means graphic, electronic, or mechanical, including but not limited to photocopying, recording, scanning, digitizing, taping, Web distribution, information networks, or information storage and retrieval systems, except as permitted under Section 107 or 108 of the 1976 United States Copyright Act, without the prior written permission of the publisher.

For product information and technology assistance, contact us at
Cengage Learning Customer & Sales Support, 1-800-354-9706
For permission to use material from this text or product,
submit all requests online at **cengage.com/permissions**
Further permissions questions can be emailed to
permissionrequest@cengage.com

This book contains select works from existing Cengage Learning resources and was produced by Cengage Learning Custom Solutions for collegiate use. As such, those adopting and/or contributing to this work are responsible for editorial content accuracy, continuity and completeness.

Compilation © 2013 Cengage Learning

ISBN-13: 978-1-285-92212-6

ISBN-10: 1-285-92212-3

Cengage Learning
5191 Natorp Boulevard
Mason, Ohio 45040
USA

Cengage Learning is a leading provider of customized learning solutions with office locations around the globe, including Singapore, the United Kingdom, Australia, Mexico, Brazil, and Japan. Locate your local office at: **international.cengage.com/region.**

Cengage Learning products are represented in Canada by Nelson Education, Ltd.
For your lifelong learning solutions, visit **www.cengage.com/custom.**
Visit our corporate website at **www.cengage.com.**

This text is dedicated to the thousands of psychology instructors who share their excitement and enthusiasm for the field of psychology with their students and seek to help them better understand the many contributions of psychology to our daily lives and to our understanding of ourselves and others. I consider myself fortunate to have the opportunity to be one of them.

About the Author

Dr. Jeffrey Nevid is Professor of Psychology at St. John's University in New York. He received his doctorate from the State University of New York at Albany and completed a post-doctoral fellowship in evaluation research at Northwestern University.

Dr. Nevid has conducted research in many areas of psychology, including health psychology, clinical and community psychology, social psychology, gender and human sexuality, adolescent development, and teaching of psychology. His research publications have appeared in such journals as *Health Psychology, Journal of Consulting and Clinical Psychology, Journal of Community Psychology, Journal of Youth and Adolescence, Behavior Therapy, Psychology & Marketing, Professional Psychology, Teaching of Psychology, Sex Roles,* and *Journal of Social Psychology*, among others. Dr. Nevid also served as Editorial Consultant for the journals *Health Psychology* and *Psychology and Marketing* and as Associate Editor for *Journal of Consulting and Clinical Psychology*. He continues exploring new ways of helping students learn through an ongoing pedagogy research program he directs at St. John's University.

Dr. Nevid has coauthored several other college texts, including *HLTH*, published by Cengage Learning, 4LTR Press, *Abnormal Psychology in a Changing World* and *Human Sexuality in a World of Diversity*, published by Pearson Education, and *Psychology and the Challenges of Life: Adjustment and Growth*, published by John Wiley & Sons. He has also authored several books on AIDS and sexually transmitted diseases published by Allyn and Bacon, including *A Student's Guide to AIDS and Other Sexually Transmitted Diseases* and *Choices: Sex in the Age of AIDS*. He lives in New York with his wife Judy and his children Michael and Daniella.

Brief Contents

Contents

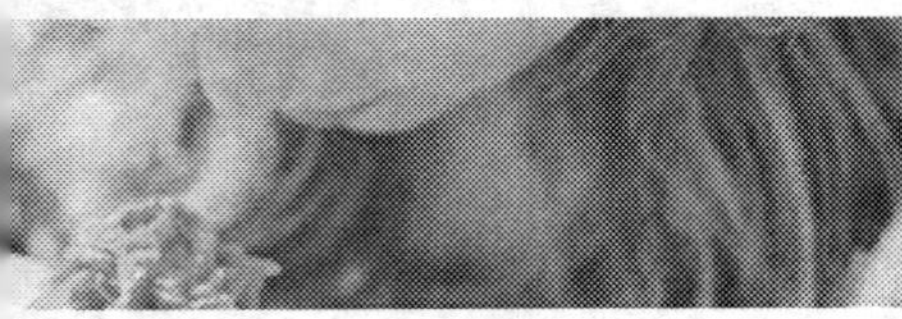

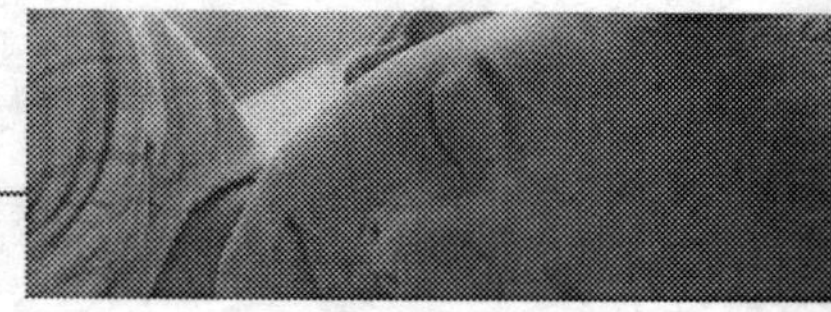

Chapter 4
Consciousness 136

Chapter 5
Learning 178

Chapter 6
Memory 214

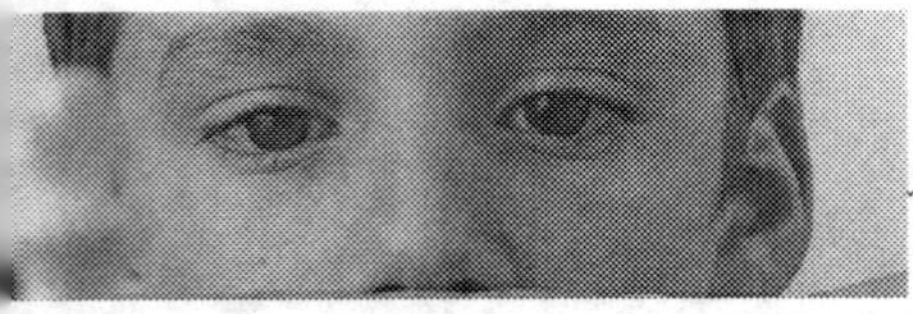

Chapter 7
Thinking, Language, and Intelligence 250

Chapter 8
Motivation and Emotion 286

Chapter 9
Child Development 326

Chapter 10
Adolescence and Adult Development 370

Chapter 11
Gender and Sexuality 408

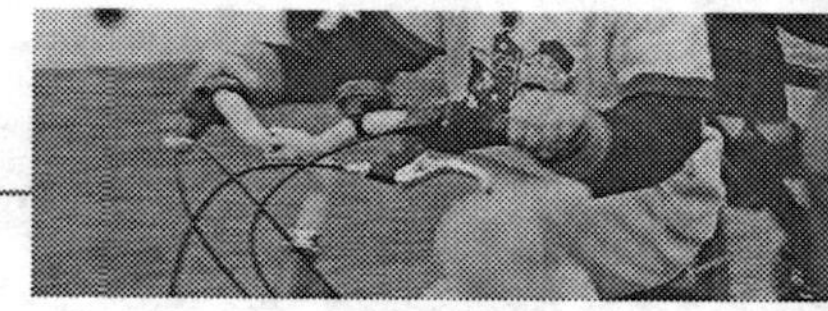

Chapter 12
Psychology and Health 446

Chapter 13
Personality 478

Chapter 14

Social Psychology 518

Chapter 15

Psychological Disorders 560

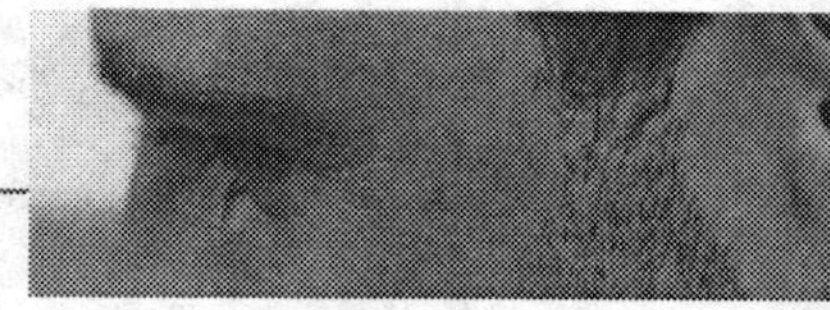

Chapter 16
Methods of Therapy 600

Features

Concept Charts

Try This Out

Application Modules

Preface

Welcome to the 4th edition of *Psychology: Concepts and Applications*. As instructors, we are challenged to help our students succeed in today's learning environment. I approached the task of writing this text with this fundamental challenge in mind. The pedagogical framework of this text is grounded in basic research on learning and memory and supplemented by research on textbook pedagogy I have conducted with my students.[1]

Overview of the Text

The text provides a broad perspective on psychology that covers the history, methods of research, major theories, and research findings of the discipline, as well as applications of knowledge gained from contemporary research to the problems and challenges we face in today's world. Psychology is a vibrant, dynamic discipline, and I try to bring to this writing the same enthusiasm and vigor that psychologists bring to their research, teaching, and professional work every day.

An effective textbook needs to be more than just a compendium of information. It needs to be an effective learning tool that helps students master complex concepts and principles. I set out to accomplish three major objectives in writing this text:

1. To make the study of psychology accessible and engaging to the beginning student in psychology.
2. To provide students with a solid grounding in the knowledge base in psychology.
3. To help students succeed in the course.

[1]Nevid, J. S., & Carmony, T. M (2002). Traditional versus modular format in presenting textual material in introductory psychology. *Teaching of Psychology, 29*, 237–238.
Nevid, J. S., & Lampmann, J. L. (2003). Effects on content acquisition of signaling key concepts in text material *Teaching of Psychology, 30*, 227–229
Nevid, J. S., & Forlenza, N. (2005). Graphing psychology: An analysis of the most commonly used graphs in introductory psychology textbooks. *Teaching of Psychology, 32*, 253–256.
Nevid, J. S. (2006, February). In pursuit of the "perfect lecture." *American Psychological Society Observer*, 19(2), 35–36, 42.
Nevid, J. S., & Mahon, K. (2009). Mastery quizzing as a signaling device to cue attention to lecture material. *Teaching of Psychology, 36*, 29–32.
Nevid, J. S. (2009/2010, Winter). Reaching and teaching millennial students. *Psychology Teacher Network, 19*(4), pp. 1, 3, 4.
Nevid, J. S. (2011, March). *A new IDEA in course assessment: Using active learning verbs to measure learning outcomes.* Invited presentation at the 18th Midwest Institute for Students and Teachers of Psychology (MISTOP), Glen Ellyn, IL.
Nevid, J. S. (2011, May/June). Teaching the millennials. *APS Observer, 24*(5), 53–56.
Nevid, J.S., McClelland, N., & Pastva, A. (2011, August). *Using action verbs as learning outcomes in introductory psychology*. Poster presentation at the meeting of the American Psychological Association, Washington, DC.

To accomplish these objectives, I adopted a learning-centric approach designed to help students encode and retain key concepts in psychology. The keystones of this approach include the following pedagogical tools:

- **Concept Signaling** Concept signaling does for key concepts what a running glossary does for key terms. Key concepts, not just key terms, are identified and highlighted in the margins to help students encode and retain core concepts. Students can gauge that they are understanding key concepts as they make their way through the text. Although some students easily extract key concepts from text material, others struggle with encoding important information. They may come away knowing a few isolated facts, but miss many of the major concepts that form the basic building blocks of knowledge in the field. Or they may feel "lost" in the middle of a chapter and become frustrated.

  Our research shows that concept signaling helps students grasp key concepts, but it is not a substitute for reading the entire chapter (Nevid & Lampmann, 2003). Our research reinforces what instructors have known for years—that students should not rely on pedagogical aids (whether they be chapter summaries, running glossaries, study breaks, interim quizzes, or cued concepts) as substitutes for reading the text in its entirety.

- **Concept-Based Modules** The text is organized in individualized study units called modules. Each module is a cohesive study unit organized around a set of key concepts relating to a particular topic. Many students juggle part-time jobs, families, and careers. Tight for time, they need to balance studying with other life responsibilities. The modular approach helps busy students organize their study efforts by allowing them to focus on one module at a time rather than trying to tackle a whole chapter at once.

  In our research, we found the majority of students preferred the modular format over a traditional format. We also found that students who preferred the modular format performed significantly better when material was presented in this format than in the traditional format (Nevid & Carmony, 2002). It stands to reason that when students prefer a particular format, they will become more engaged in reading texts based on that format—an outcome that may translate into improved performance in classroom situations.

- **Concept Charts** These built-in study charts offer "at-a-glance" summaries of key concepts to reinforce new knowledge.

- **Concept Links** This feature highlights connections between key concepts across chapters. Concept Links are integrated with the cued concepts in the margins, so students can see how basic concepts are applied across different areas of psychology.
- **Concept Maps for Psychology** This unique visual learning tool helps students visualize connections between key concepts in the text. These maps are schematic diagrams comprising key concepts, represented in boxed shapes called nodes, that are connected by links, which generally take the form of verbs or conjunctions. Unlike other study charts, concept maps can be read either across or down the page to express a coherent thought structure. To encourage active learning, concept maps are presented in an interactive (fill-in-the-blanks) format to engage students in the process of completing these knowledge structures. Concept Maps and the fill-in-the-blank answers are available on Psychology Coursemate.

Changes in the New Edition

Integrated Course Assessment: Introducing the IDEA Model™ of Course Assessment

The **IDEA Model™** is a unique course assessment tool that maps skills we expect students to acquire in their introductory psychology course to the set of learning goals and outcomes contained in the APA guidelines for the undergraduate major in psychology.

In August 2006, the APA Council of Representatives approved *The APA Guidelines for the Undergraduate Psychology Major*. These guidelines identify 10 major goals and suggested learning outcomes organized within the major categories of knowledge, skills, and values.

Knowledge in psychology develops through a series of courses in the psychology curriculum that provide the contexts in which students develop relevant skills and perspectives. The introductory course in psychology enables students to acquire a knowledge base relating to basic concepts, theoretical perspectives, and historical developments in the field, consistent with Goal 1 of the Guidelines. But introductory psychology also provides a first exposure to other learning goals in the Guidelines, including research methods in psychology, critical thinking, applications, values, information and technological literacy, communication skills, sociocultural and international awareness, personal development, and career planning and development.

The APA guidelines encourage the use of active learning verbs linked to learning outcomes in order to determine the skills students acquire in the course. Each chapter of the text begins with a listing of learning objectives expressed in the form of active learning verbs tied to measurable learning outcomes. The evaluation model is based on the simple acronym, **IDEA**, which comprises four types of acquired skills:

Identifying . . . key figures in the history of psychology, parts of nervous system, etc.

Defining or Describing . . . key concepts and theoretical principles

Evaluating or Explaining . . . underlying processes and mechanisms of behavior and mental processes

Applying . . . psychological concepts to examples

The IDEA model™ completes the circle of course assessment by keying test items from the accompanying test item file to specific learning objectives in each chapter, enabling instructors to evaluate skills their students acquire in their first exposure to psychology—the ability to *Identify, Define* or *Describe, Evaluate* or *Explain*, and *Apply* knowledge of psychology.

Making Classrooms Bloom

The IDEA Model™ is integrated with the widely used taxonomy of educational objectives developed by the educational researcher Benjamin Bloom. The taxonomy identifies educational objectives that vary in cognitive complexity, from knowledge and understanding at the lower levels to application of knowledge in the middle level and to analysis, synthesis, and evaluation at the highest level. The action verbs in the IDEA acronym (identify, define or describe, evaluate or explain, and apply) represent a hierarchical ordering of skills consistent with Bloom's taxonomy. The action verbs **define, describe**, and **identify** represent basic level cognitive skills in Bloom's taxonomy (i.e., knowledge and comprehension, or remembering and understanding in the later revised taxonomy). The verb **apply** assesses intermediate level skills representing the application of psychological concepts to life examples. Finally, the verbs **evaluate** and **explain** assess higher-order, more complex skills involved in analysis, synthesis, and evaluation of psychological knowledge (or analyzing and evaluating domains as represented in the revised taxonomy). Consequently, instructors can measure not just the types of skills students acquire, but the level of cognitive complexity these skills represent.

Slice of Life

This edition introduces a "Slice of Life" icon to identify personal stories and vignettes that bring the study of psychology to life and illustrate how psychological concepts relate to life experiences. This feature draws upon many sources, including biographies of prominent figures in psychology and anecdotes from my own life experiences as well as personal examples and stories from fellow psychology instructors.

Earlier Placement of Social Psychology

Traditionally, introductory psychology texts have placed social psychology at the end of the line-up, a practice dictated more by tradition than sound pedagogy. In this edition, we place the study of social psychology (now Chapter 14) directly after the chapter on personality, such that the study of social influences on behavior directly follows the chapter on individual differences in behavior.

The Four E's of Effective Learning: Helping Students Become More Effective Learners

The learning system adopted in this text is based on a broader pedagogical framework I call the *Four E's of Effective Learning*:

- Engaging interest
- Encoding information
- Elaborating meaning
- Evaluating progress

The accompanying figure shows the particular features in the text that help students become more effective learners. Here, let me briefly review how these features are represented in the underlying pedagogy in the text:

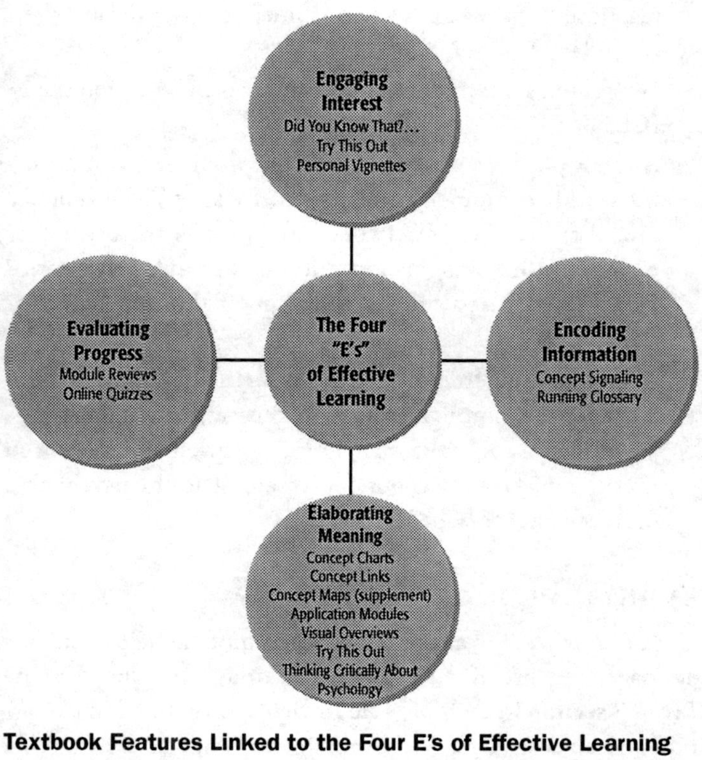

Textbook Features Linked to the Four E's of Effective Learning

Engaging Student Interest

Meaningful learning begins with focused attention. A textbook can only be an effective learning tool if it succeeds in engaging and retaining student interest. The use of personal vignettes and life examples draws the reader into the material and illustrates how psychological concepts relate to personal experiences. In addition, two distinctive pedagogical features further engage student interest:

1) Did You Know That... These chapter-opening questions whet students' appetite for the material covered in the chapter and encourage them to read further. Some questions debunk common myths and misconceptions, whereas others highlight interesting historical anecdotes or bring recent research developments into sharper focus. Accompanying page numbers provide easy cross-referencing to the pages in which the information is discussed. Here is a small sampling:

Did You Know That...

- A major school of psychology was inspired by the view from a train? (Ch. 1)
- Roy G. Biv is one of the most famous names learned by psychology students, but he is not a real person? (Ch. 3)
- Albert Einstein used mental imagery in developing his theory of relativity? (Ch. 7)
- The "Big Five" is not the name of a new NCAA basketball conference but the label used to describe the leading trait theory of personality today? (Ch. 13)
- In our society, it pays to be tall—literally? (Ch. 14)
- Stimulant drugs are used to help hyperactive children? (Ch. 16)

2) *Try This Out* These "hands-on" exercises encourage students to apply psychological concepts to their own experiences. Whether the topic involves trying to read a magazine sideways, breaking through the "Magic 7" barrier, reading emotions in facial expressions, or performing a personal experiment on lucid dreaming, students work through problems, generate solutions, and test out concepts and principles. They can participate in *active learning* activities by directly applying concepts in the text to real-life situations, rather than simply reading about them.

Try This Out activities also emphasize *service learning* through participation in research and volunteer experiences. This feature also includes self-scoring questionnaires offering students the opportunity to evaluate their own behavior and attitudes in light of the concepts discussed in the text (e.g., Are You an Optimist or a Pessimist?)

Encoding Information

Textbooks have long used the signaling device of highlighting key terms to help students acquire technical vocabulary. This text expands the use of signaling techniques to help students learn key concepts as well as key terms.

Running Glossary Key terms are highlighted in the text and defined in the margins. Students do not need to interrupt their reading to thumb through a glossary at the end of the text whenever they encounter an unfamiliar term. [A full glossary is presented at the end of the text as well.]

Concept Signaling Concept signaling helps students encode and retain key concepts by extracting and highlighting them in the margins of the text. Cued concepts are signposts students can use to gauge that they are getting the main points as they make their way through their reading. Here are some examples of keyed concepts:

CONCEPT 3.2
Sensory receptors convert sources of sensory stimuli, such as light and sound, into neural impulses the brain can use to create sensations.

CONCEPT 6.1
The three basic processes that make memory possible are encoding, storage, and retrieval.

CONCEPT 9.7
Infants may seem to do little more than eat and sleep, but a closer look reveals they are both active learners and active perceivers of their environment.

Elaborating Meaning

Information must first be encoded to be learned, but new learning needs to be strengthened to ensure long-term retention. Deeper processing in the form of ***elaborative rehearsal,*** such as applying concepts to life experiences, helps make fresh memories more enduring. This text provides several pedagogical features designed to facilitate elaborative rehearsal:

Concept Charts These study charts summarize key concepts in tabular form, reinforcing knowledge of major concepts and helping students make relational connections between concepts.

Concept Links This feature illustrates how concepts are linked together across different areas of psychology.

Visual Overviews This end-of-chapter feature provides a visual summary of many of the key concepts discussed in the chapter to strengthen new learning and understanding of connections between key concepts.

Annotated Diagrams Complex figures include numbered annotations to help students decipher diagrams, especially the more daunting anatomical diagrams.

Application Modules The final module in each chapter is an application module that illustrates how psychologists apply knowledge they gain from research studies to real-life problems. Students also see how the concepts discussed in the chapter may apply to their own lives. See the Features section on page xix for a chapter-by-chapter listing of the application modules in the text. Examples of these application modules include *Psychology and Pain Management* (Ch. 3), *Putting Reinforcement into Practice* (Ch. 5), *Becoming a Creative Problem Solver* (Ch. 7), and *Taking the Distress Out of Stress* (Ch. 12).

Try This Out These exercises not only engage student interest, but also encourage students to apply concepts discussed in the text to their own experiences.

Critical Thinking Features The *Think About It* section in each Module Review poses critical thinking questions to encourage students to think more deeply about concepts discussed in the chapter. The *Thinking Critically About Psychology* exercise at the end of each chapter helps students sharpen their critical thinking skills. Here we pose challenging questions that require students to analyze problems and evaluate claims in light of material discussed in the chapter. Students can then compare their own answers to sample responses provided in Appendix A.

The Brain Loves a Puzzle is a unique critical thinking feature that engages student interest and further encourages critical thinking. These thought-provoking puzzles challenge students to think more deeply about information in the text and to find related content in the chapter needed to solve them. Examples include:

- Why is it impossible to tickle yourself? Try it out for yourself. Why does tickling yourself fail to elicit the same tickling response that occurs when someone else tickles you? (Chapter 2)
- How could something as unpleasant as pain be a good thing? (Chapter 3)
- A young physicist was working on the problem of connecting the world's computers. After some false starts, he invented a model of a computer network based on how the brain does memory. What was this invention that changed the world? How was it based on the workings of the human brain? (Chapter 6)
- A man suffering from panic attacks seeks help from a psychiatrist. After a thorough evaluation, the psychiatrist prescribes an antidepressant. The man appears puzzled and says, "You must be mistaken. I'm not depressed." Did the psychiatrist make a mistake? (Chapter 16)

Evaluating Progress

The ***Module Review*** at the end of each module helps students evaluate their progress as they read through the chapter. The *Recite It* section in each Module Review is structured in a question-and-answer (Q & A) format to encourage active learning.

The questions correspond to the set of survey questions that introduce each module. This type of summary better fits the SQ3R model of encouraging recitation of answers to survey questions than a traditional narrative summary. Students can recite their answers to the questions and then compare them to sample answers presented in the text.

The *Recall It* section encourages students to test their knowledge by taking a short quiz on key concepts in the module. The answers are given in the appendix. In addition, students can complete online self-scoring quizzes in multiple-choice format that include factual and conceptual questions.

Expanded and Updated Coverage

The field of psychology is continually changing, and instructors and textbooks authors are challenged to keep pace. As you thumb through the pages of this edition, you will find hundreds of citations of research findings and theoretical developments appearing in the scientific literature in the past two or three years. Here is but a small sampling of the new research included in this edition:

- Findings from a recent research study that showed how physical warmth influences judgments of interpersonal warmth (Ch. 1)
- Recent findings showing that inert placebos work even when research participants know they are receiving a placebo (Ch. 1)
- New research using a reinforcement technique to train fish to tap a particular target shape (Ch. 1)
- Gender difference in handedness (Ch. 2)
- Recent evidence indicating that pleasurable excitement associated with falling in love involves release of dopamine in the brain (Ch. 2)
- New research on functions of glial cells (Ch. 2)
- New research on role of oxytocin in maternal bonding to infants and development of trust in other people (Ch. 2)
- New findings showing that men were rated as more attractive when they were wearing the color red (Ch. 3)
- New research on possible human pheromones (Ch. 3)
- New research on top-down and bottom-up types of processing of sounds (Ch. 3)
- New findings on distracted driving (Ch. 4)
- New findings on length of sleep in relation to risk of catching a cold after exposure to a cold virus (Ch. 4)
- New research that used an iPhone app to show that a wandering mind is not a happy mind (Ch. 4)
- New investigation of the true identity of "Little Albert" (Ch. 5)
- New discussion of insight learning, using a famous quote from Louis Pasteur (Ch.5)
- New research on working memory (Ch. 6)
- New research on the role of the hippocampus in memory formation (Ch.6)
- New research on genetic contributions to intelligence (Ch. 7)
- New research on gesturing as a form of human pre-speech (Ch. 7)
- New research on role of brain chemicals in regulating hunger (Ch. 8)
- New research on role of media exposure to heavily muscularized models on the self-image of young boys (Ch. 8)
- New research suggesting that facial expressions of emotion are hard-wired into the brain rather than learned as the result of visual experience (Ch. 8)
- New research on adjustment of children of lesbian and gay parents (Ch. 9)
- New data on the proportion of mothers who work outside the home (Ch. 9)
- New data on the number of hours of TV viewing by young children (Ch.9)
- New research on adjustment of later-maturing boys and girls (Ch.10)
- New research on the still-maturing adolescent brain (Ch. 10)
- New findings on trends in marital rates in the United States (Ch. 10)
- New data on life expectancy in the U.S. (Ch. 10)
- Latest findings on gender differences in math performance (Ch. 11)
- Major findings from the new nationally representative survey of sexual behaviors among adult Americans (Ch. 11)
- Update on HIV/AIDS and other sexually transmitted diseases (Ch. 11)
- Results of nationwide 2010 survey of the emotional health of first-year college students (Ch. 12)
- New findings from the 2010 APA Stress in America survey (Ch. 12)
- New research findings on acculturative stress (Ch. 12)
- New research on effects of perceived discrimination on psychological and physical health (Ch. 12)
- New findings on use of Facebook features in relation to Big Five personality traits (Ch. 13)
- New research findings on outcomes associated with Big Five personality factors (Ch. 13)
- New findings on changes in personality through the lifespan (Ch. 13)
- New findings on stereotype threat with respect to the "girls can't do math" stereotype (Ch. 14)
- New findings showing that adopting a power pose increases risk taking and testosterone levels in men and women (Ch. 14)

- New findings from a partial replication of Milgram's famous experiment (Ch. 14)
- New findings on the prevalence of psychological disorders (Ch. 15)
- New research findings on the role of the amygdala in anxiety disorders (Ch. 15)
- New research on brain abnormalities in schizophrenia (Ch. 15)
- New research on genetic underpinnings of mood disorders and schizophrenia (Ch. 15)
- New research on psychotherapy effectiveness (Ch. 16)
- Use of new technologies, such as "tweets," to monitor symptoms and behaviors of people with psychological disorders (Ch. 16)
- New research on the relative effectiveness of antidepressants compared to placebos in treating mild to moderate depression (Ch. 16)

Additional Features of the Text

Built-In Study Method: SQ3R+

The *survey, question, read, recite, review* (SQ3R) study method is a widely used technique for encouraging students to adopt a more active role in the learning process. This text expands upon the traditional model by adding a "+" in the form of an additional feature, the *Think About It* questions at the end of each module.

- *Survey and Question* Survey methods are incorporated within the chapter and modular structure. Learning objectives are identified at the beginning of each chapter. Each chapter opens with a preview section showing the contents and organization of the chapter (including a numbered list of modules presented in the chapter). The material covered in the chapter is also described in the introductory section preceding the first module. In addition, the use of survey questions at the beginning of each module encourages students to use questions as advance organizers for studying text material.
- *Read* The writing style has been carefully developed for reading level, content, and style. Students are often addressed directly to engage them in the material and encourage them to examine how the information relates to their own experiences.
- *Recite and Review* Each module ends with a review section that contains a *Recite It* feature that encourages students to recite answers to the survey questions that introduced the module and a *Recall It* feature in which students test their knowledge by completing a brief quiz comprising various types of questions (e.g., multiple-choice, fill-in, matching, short answers). *Concept Charts* in each module provide further opportunities for students to review the knowledge they have acquired.
- *Think About It* The text goes beyond review and recitation by posing thought-provoking questions in each module review. This feature encourages critical thinking and reflection on how text material relates to personal experiences.

Integrating Diversity

A primary objective of this text is to raise student awareness of the importance of issues relating to diversity in psychology. Discussion of cultural and gender issues is integrated within the main body of the text rather than relegated to boxed features. For a reference guide to the integrated coverage of gender and sociocultural issues in the text, see the complete listings available in the online *Instructor's Manual for Psychology: Concepts and Applications.*

Focus on Neuroscience

Neuroscientists are making important contributions to our understanding of brain-behavior relationships. In this text, students learn about current research developments in neuroscience that inform our understanding of the biological underpinnings of behavior, including brain abnormalities in schizophrenia and other psychological disorders, how drugs work in the brain, and even the puzzle of why people cannot tickle themselves. A tabbed listing of neuroscience content in the text is found in the online *Instructor's Manual.*

Focus on Positive Psychology

Positive psychology is a major contemporary movement within psychology that continues to grow in momentum. The text introduces students to many areas of interest in positive psychology, including the study of optimism, love, self-esteem, helping behavior, and personal happiness. For a full listing of positive psychology coverage, including such topics as love, optimism, and happiness, see the tabbing guide in the accompanying *Instructor's Manual.*

Ancillaries

Even the most comprehensive text is incomplete without ancillaries. Those accompanying *Psychology: Concepts and Applications* help make it a complete teaching package.

Teacher Ancillaries

Instructor's Resource Manual The Instructor's Resource Manual (IRM) contains a variety of resources to aid instructors in preparing and presenting text material in a manner that meets their personal preferences and course needs. The IRM begins with a comprehensive preface, which covers preparation, pitfalls, planning, execution, resources, and best practices for both new and seasoned instructors. Each chapter provides a preview and a goals and activity planner to help organize classes. In addition, each chapter of the IRM contains a detailed outline, lecture suggestions, topics for discussion, classroom and individual activities with handouts, and ideas for writing assignments.

Test Bank This test bank contains over 2,400 multiple-choice and essay questions, organized by chapter and module. Each chapter contains a total of about 150 questions, some 145 multiple choice questions and five essay questions. To facilitate exam construction, multiple choice questions are labeled by type (factual, conceptual, applied), learning objectives, module reference number, and page reference.

Unique to this text, test bank questions are keyed to learning objectives in the IDEA Model™ framework, which in turn is mapped to specific learning goals in the APA guidelines for the undergraduate major in psychology (see page xxii). This course evaluation model is built around the acronym IDEA, which specifies four types of acquired skills: (1) "*Identifying*" key figures in the history of psychology, parts of nervous system, etc.; (2) "*Defining or Describing*" major concepts and theoretical principles; (3) "*Evaluating or Explaining*" underlying processes and mechanisms of behavior and mental processes; and (4) "*Applying*" psychological concepts to examples.

PowerLecture The fastest, easiest way to build customized, media-rich lectures, PowerLecture™ provides a collection of newly-designed, book-specific Microsoft® PowerPoint® lecture slides. The slides reflect instructional design principles that define how humans best process information—combining text (including talking point examples not cited in the text), visuals, and one-click links to narrated animations—to engage students and optimize their learning.

WebTutor Jumpstart your course with customizable, rich, text-specific content within your Course Management System. Whether you want to Web-enable your class or put an entire course online, WebTutor™ delivers. WebTutor offers a wide array of resources, including integrated eBook, media assets, quizzing, and more! Visit webtutor.cengage.com to learn more.

CourseMate Cengage Learning's new *Psychology CourseMate* includes interactive teaching and learning tools including an integrated eBook, quizzes, flashcards, videos, concept maps, and more. It also features Engagement Tracker, a first-of-its-kind tool that monitors student engagement in the course.

CengageNOW CengageNOW is an online teaching and learning resource that gives you more control in less time and delivers better outcomes–NOW. Students have access to an integrated eBook, interactive quizzing and practice, videos, and other multimedia tools to help them get the most out of your course.

Aplia Founded in 2000 by economist and Stanford professor Paul Romer, Aplia™ is dedicated to improving learning by increasing student effort and engagement. Aplia is an online, auto-graded homework solution that keeps your students engaged and prepared for class and has been used by almost 2,000,000 students at over 1,700 institutions. Visit www.cengage.com/aplia for more details.

Student Ancillaries

Psychology CourseMate The more you study, the better the results. Make the most of your study time by accessing everything you need to succeed in one place. Read your textbook, take notes, review flashcards, watch videos, work through concept maps, and take practice quizzes—all online with Psychology CourseMate.

Acknowledgments

First, I am indebted to the thousands of psychologists and other scientists whose work has informed the writing of both this edition and the first edition of the text. Thanks to their efforts, the field of psychology has had an enormous impact in broadening our understanding of ourselves and enhancing the quality of our lives. On a more personal level, I owe a debt of gratitude to the many colleagues and publishing professionals who helped shape this manuscript into its present form. Let me begin by thanking my professional colleagues who reviewed this edition:

Annette Towler, DePaul University
Sue Frantz, Highline Community College
Jack Shilkret, Anne Arundel Community College
Diane Urban, Manhattan College
Ruth Hannon, Bridgewater State University
Kristina Schaefer, Moorpark College
Pete Peterson, Johnson County Community College
Ken Koenigshofer, University of Maryland

Thank you to my colleagues who contributed *Slice of Life* features used in this edition:

Jeffrey Stowell, Eastern Illinois University
Fred L. Nesbit, Sauk Valley Community College
Diane Urban, Manhattan College

I also thank the colleagues and professionals who reviewed previous editions of *Psychology: Concepts and Applications*, and helped me refine it through several stages of development:

Patricia Abbott, D'Youville College

Denise M. Arehart, University of Colorado, Denver
James E. Arruda, Mercer University
David R. Barkmeier, Northeastern University
Howard Berthold, Lycoming College
Kathleen Bey, Palm Beach Community College
Cheryl Bluestone, Queensborough Community College/CUNY
Reba M. Bowman, Tennessee Temple University
John W. Bouseman, Hillsborough Community College
Deborah S. Briihl, Valdosta State University
Charles Brodie, Georgia Perimeter College
John P. Broida, University of Southern Maine
Winfield Brown, Florence Darlington Technical College
Lawrence R. Burns, Grand Valley State University
Adam Butler, University of Northern Iowa
Bernard J. Carducci, Indiana University Southeast
Elaine Cassel, Marymount University, Lord Fairfax Community College
Hank Cetula, Adrian College
Matthew G. Chin, University of Central Florida
Sharon Church, Highland Community College
Saundra K. Ciccarelli, Gulf Coast Community College
Russell D. Clark, University of North Texas
Wanda Clark, South Plains College
Susan Clayton, The College of Wooster
Sandra Cole, New Hampshire Community Technical College
Larry J. Cology, Owens Community College
Robert S. Coombs, Southern Adventist University
Mary Webber Coplen, Hutchinson Community College
Richard S. Coyle, California State University, Chico
George J. Demakis, Elmhurst College
Robin DesJardin, John Tyler Community College
Victor Duarte, North Idaho College
Mary H. Dudley, Howard College
Vera Dunwoody, Chaffey College
Gianna Durso-Finley, New England Institute of Technology
Steven I. Dworkin, University of North Carolina, Wilmington
Rebecca F. Eaton, The University of Alabama, Huntsville
Tami Eggleston, McKendree College
Julie Felender, Fullerton College
Oney D. Fitzpatrick, Lamar University
William F. Ford, Bucks County Community College
Lenore Frigo, College of Southern Idaho
Grace Galliano, Kennesaw State University
David Griese, State University of New York, Farmingdale
Frank Hager, Allegany College of Maryland
Lynn Haller, Morehead State University
Amanda M. Maynard, State University of New York at New Paltz
Janet R. Pascal, DeVry Institute of Technology, Kansas City
Christine M. Paynard, University of Detroit Mercy
Lillian M. Range, University of Southern Mississippi
Darren R. Ritzer, George Mason University
Benjamin Wallace, Cleveland State University
Nancy White, Coastal Carolina Community College
David Yells, Utah Valley State College
Jeanette Youngblood, Arkansas State University, Newport
Michael J. Zeller, Minnesota State University
Otto Zinser, East Tennessee State University

Second, I would like to thank the many instructors and students who participated in our extensive market research conducted in the early stages of the text's development—including the instructors and students at Valencia Community College and the University of Central Florida, who provided us with great insight into their introductory psychology courses; the instructors who participated in the teleconference sessions and raised many important issues that impacted the day-to-day challenges of this course; and the 700-plus respondents who participated in our national survey on introductory psychology and the development of this text. The overwhelming response we received from these professionals proved to be a rich resource throughout the development of the text.

Third, I would like a special thanks to Dr. Celia Reaves of Monroe Community College for her helpful suggestions of several cartoons that convey psychological concepts in a medium that is both informative and entertaining.

This is the first edition of the text that was developed at its new publishing home, Cengage Learning. The people at Cengage are consummate publishing professionals and I am very thankful for the supportive way in which they have welcomed me and worked so closely with me to update and strengthen the text to make it an ever more effective learning platform designed to engage students in the study of psychology and help them succeed in the course. In particular I would like to thank my editor, Timothy Matray, for his guidance and support; my developmental editor, Tangelique Williams, for her many (too many to count) helpful comments and suggestions throughout the text; and my marketing manager, Elisabeth Rhoden, for her strong commitment to the text and her many creative ideas to bring the message of the book to instructors and students.

Jeff Nevid
New York, New York

Please feel free to contact me with your comments and suggestions at jeffnevid@gmail.com

The IDEA Model™ of Course Assessment: Mapping Skills Acquired to Learning Goals

GOAL 1 Knowledge Base of Psychology

Demonstrate familiarity with the major concepts, theoretical perspectives, empirical findings, and historical trends in psychology.

Specific Goals in "APA Guidelines for the Undergraduate Psychology Major"	Related Content in Text and Ancillaries	IDEA Model™ of Course Assessment: Skills Acquired *Identify. . . Define or Describe. . . Evaluate or Explain. . . Apply*
1.1 Characterize the nature of psychology as a discipline.	**Module 1.1**	**Define** psychology and **explain** why psychology is a science.
1.2 Demonstrate knowledge and understanding representing appropriate breadth and depth in selected content areas of psychology, including the following: (a) theory and research representing general domains: **(i)** learning and cognition **(ii)** individual differences, psychometrics, personality, and social processes, including those related to sociocultural and international dimensions **(iii)** biological bases of behavior and mental processes **(iv)** developmental processes	1.2.a *i. Learning and Cognition* **Module 5.1**	**Define** learning in psychological terms. **Describe** the process of classical conditioning and explain how conditioned responses are acquired. **Identify** key figures in the development and application of classical conditioning and **describe** their contributions. **Explain** how conditioned responses can be strengthened. **Apply** a cognitive perspective to understanding classical conditioning. **Apply** principles of classical conditioning to real-life examples.
	Module 5.2	**Identify** the major figures in the development and application of operant conditioning and **describe** their contributions. **Explain** the differences between different types of reinforcement and different schedules of reinforcement, and between reinforcement and punishment. **Explain** the differences between escape learning and avoidance learning. **Apply** principles of operant conditioning to real-life examples.
	Module 5.3	**Define** cognitive learning. **Describe** several forms of cognitive learning. **Apply** principles of cognitive learning to real-life examples. **Apply** principles of reinforcement to daily life.
	Module 6.1	**Identify** and **describe** the basic processes and stages of memory. **Describe** types of long-term memory. **Explain** the roles of the semantic network model and levels-of-processing theory in memory. **Explain** the difference between maintenance rehearsal and elaborative rehearsal. **Apply** constructionist theory to explain memory distortions. **Evaluate** the reliability of eyewitness testimony. **Explain** why the concept of recovered memory is controversial.
	Module 6.2	**Identify** and **describe** the major theories and factors in forgetting. **Identify** different methods of measuring memory. **Describe** the two major types of amnesia.
	Module 7.1	**Define** thinking. **Describe** the roles of mental imagery, concept formation, problem solving, and creativity in thinking. **Explain** the difference between logical and natural concepts. **Describe** mental strategies we can use to solve problems more effectively. **Apply** your knowledge of mental roadblocks and cognitive biases to how these factors affect problem solving and decision making. **Describe** the basic processes of creative thought and **explain** the difference between divergent and convergent thinking.
	Module 7.2	**Identify** the basic components of language and the milestones in language development. **Explain** the factors involved in language development. **Evaluate** whether language is unique to humans. **Evaluate** the linguistic relativity hypothesis in light of evidence.
	Module 7.3	**Define** intelligence and **identify** the major figures in the development of intelligence tests. **Describe** different tests of intelligence and **evaluate** the characteristics of a good test of intelligence. **Describe** the characteristics of the two extremes of intelligence. **Describe** the major theories of intelligence and **identify** the major theorists. **Evaluate** the roles of heredity and environment in intelligence. **Apply** skills of problem solving to become a creative problem solver.

Continued on following page

GOAL 1 Knowledge Base of Psychology, (*Continued*)

Demonstrate familiarity with the major concepts, theoretical perspectives, empirical findings, and historical trends in psychology.

Specific Goals in "APA Guidelines for the Undergraduate Psychology Major"	Related Content in Text and Ancillaries	IDEA Model™ of Course Assessment: Skills Acquired *Identify. . . Define or Describe. . . Evaluate or Explain. . . Apply*
	ii. Individual differences and social processes:	
	Module 13.1	**Define** the concept of personality. **Identify** and **describe** the three levels of consciousness and three mental structures or entities in Freud's psychoanalytic theory. **Identify** the stages of psychosexual development in Freud's theory and **describe** the features of each stage. **Describe** the personality theories of Jung, Adler, and Horney.
	Module 13.2	**Describe** the trait theories of Allport, Cattell, Eysenck, and the Big Five model. **Evaluate** the genetic basis of personality traits.
	Module 13.3	**Describe** the social-cognitive theories of Rotter, Bandura, and Mischel.
	Module 13.4	**Describe** the humanistic theories of Carl Rogers and Abraham Maslow. **Explain** the roles of collectivism and individualism in self-identity.
	Module 13.5	**Identify** different types of personality tests and **describe** their features. **Evaluate** self-report (MMPI) and projective personality tests (Rorschach, TAT).
	Module 14.1	**Identify** the major influences on first impressions and **explain** why first impressions often become lasting impressions. **Identify** two major types of causal attributions and **apply** this knowledge to examples. **Describe** the components and sources of attitudes. **Evaluate** pathways and factors involved in persuasion.
	Module 14.2	**Identify** and **describe** factors that influence attraction. **Identify** and **describe** factors linked to helping behavior and **apply** this knowledge to examples. **Explain** how prejudice develops and how it can be reduced. **Identify** and **describe** factors that contribute to human aggression.
	Module 14.3	**Explain** differences between social identity and personal identity. **Describe** the classic Asch study and **identify** factors that influence conformity. **Apply** knowledge of factors involved in compliance to resisting persuasive sales techniques **Evaluate** the findings and significance of Milgram's experiments. **Define** social facilitation and social loafing and **explain** how they affect performance. **Define** groupthink and **explain** how it can lead to wrong decisions. **Describe** factors involved in job satisfaction and ways in which the workplace is changing.
	iii. Biological bases of behavior and mental processes:	
	Module 2.1	**Identify** the parts of the neuron, **describe** the functions of these parts, and **explain** how neurons communicate with each other. **Identify** key neurotransmitters and **describe** their functions. **Explain** how an action potential is generated. **Explain** the difference between agonists and antagonists and **describe** the effects of these types of drugs on particular neurotransmitters.
	Module 2.2	**Describe** how the nervous system is organized and the functions of its various parts.
	Module 2.3	**Identify** major brain structures and **describe** how the brain is organized and the roles that particular brain structures play in behavior.
	Module 2.4	**Identify** and **describe** the methods scientists use to study the workings of the brain.
	Module 2.5	**Explain** how the two halves of the brain differ in their functions.
	Module 2.6	**Apply** knowledge of the endocrine system to the roles of hormones in behavior.

Continued on following page

GOAL 1 Knowledge Base of Psychology, (*Continued*)

Demonstrate familiarity with the major concepts, theoretical perspectives, empirical findings, and historical trends in psychology.

Specific Goals in "APA Guidelines for the Undergraduate Psychology Major"	Related Content in Text and Ancillaries	IDEA Model™ of Course Assessment: Skills Acquired *Identify. . . Define or Describe. . . Evaluate or Explain. . . Apply*
	Module 2.7	**Identify** and **describe** the methods scientists use to study roles of genes and environment in behavior.
	Module 2.8	**Apply** knowledge of brain-scanning techniques to detecting memory circuits, measuring personality traits, screening job applicants, shopping, marketing, and diagnosis.
	Module 6.3	**Identify** key brain structures involved in memory and **explain** the roles of neuronal networks and long-term potentiation. **Describe** the genetic bases of memory.
	iv. *Developmental processes:*	
	Module 9.2	**Identify** and **describe** the stages of prenatal development. **Apply** knowledge of teratogens to the threats faced during prenatal development.
	Module 9.3	**Identify** the major reflexes present at birth. **Describe** how the infant's motor skills change through the first year of life. **Describe** the infant's sensory, perceptual, and learning abilities.
	Module 9.4	**Identify** and **describe** the major types of temperament and attachment styles. **Identify** and **describe** the major styles of parenting and apply this knowledge to outcomes associated with these types. **Identify** Erikson's stages of psychosocial development in childhood and **describe** the central challenge of each stage.
	Module 9.5	**Describe** the characteristics of each stage in Piaget's theory of cognitive development and **evaluate** his legacy. **Describe** Vygotsky's psychosocial theory of cognitive development.
	Module 9.6	**Evaluate** the effects of television viewing on children's behavior and cognitive development. **Apply** knowledge of responsible television viewing to steps parents can take to foster this behavior in their children.
	Modules 10.1, 10.2, 10.3	**Describe** the physical and psychological changes that occur during puberty and **evaluate** the effects of pubertal timing on boys and girls. **Describe** changes in cognitive and psychosocial development during adolescence. **Identify** and **describe** Kohlberg's stages of moral reasoning and evaluate his theoretical model. **Describe** changes in physical, cognitive, psychosocial, and emotional development from early to late adulthood. **Identify** and **describe** Erickson's stages of psychosexual development in adolescence and adulthood and **apply** this knowledge to our understanding of the major psychosocial challenges we face through the lifespan. **Identify** qualities associated with successful aging. **Identify** and **describe** the stages of dying in Kübler-Ross's model.
	Module 10.4	**Apply** research findings to living longer and healthier lives.
(b) history of psychology	**1.2b *History of psychology:*** **Module 1.1**	**Identify** early schools of psychology and the important contributors to these schools. **Describe** the major concepts associated with each school.
(c) relevant levels of analysis	***1.2c Relevant levels of analysis: cellular, individual, group/ systems, society/culture***	**Cellular:** See Module 2.1 above. **Individual:** See Modules 13.1 to 13.5 above. **Group/Systems:** See Module 14.3 above. **Society/Culture:** See Modules 13.4, 14.1, 14.2, 14.3 above.
(d) overarching themes, persistent questions, or enduring conflicts in psychology	***1.2d Overarching themes: The interaction of heredity and environment: Module 2.7***	**Describe** how psychologists study the roles of genes and environment in behavior. **Evaluate** how genetics influences personality and behavior.
	Free will versus determinism: Modules 13.3, 13.4	**Describe** the social-cognitive theories of Rotter, Bandura, and Mischel. **Describe** the humanistic theories of Carl Rogers and Abraham Maslow.

Continued on following page

GOAL 1 Knowledge Base of Psychology, *(Continued)*

Demonstrate familiarity with the major concepts, theoretical perspectives, empirical findings, and historical trends in psychology.

Specific Goals in "APA Guidelines for the Undergraduate Psychology Major"	Related Content in Text and Ancillaries	IDEA Model™ of Course Assessment: Skills Acquired *Identify. . . Define or Describe. . . Evaluate or Explain. . . Apply*
	Interaction of mind and body: Modules 11.2, 12.1, 12.2, 12.3	**Define** stress in psychological terms. **Describe** the effects of stress on the body. **Identify** and **describe** the major sources of stress. **Identify** and **describe** different types of psychological conflicts. **Identify** the stages of the general adaptation syndrome and **describe** the changes that occur in the body during each stage. **Identify** and **describe** psychological factors that buffer the effects of stress. **Identify** psychological factors linked to coronary heart disease. **Evaluate** the relationship between emotions and the heart. **Identify** psychological factors linked to cancer. **Identify** different types of sexually transmitted diseases and **describe** their means of transmission, symptoms, and treatments. **Apply** knowledge of the transmission of sexually transmitted disease to steps we can take to protect ourselves from these diseases. **Apply** stress management techniques to daily life.
(e) relevant ethical issues	***1.2e Relevant ethical issues:***	
	Module 1.3	**Describe** the ethical standards that govern research in psychology.
	Module 14.3	**Evaluate** the findings and significance of Milgram's experiments.
1.3 Use the concepts, language, and major theories of the discipline to account for psychological phenomena.	**Early schools of psychology and contemporary perspectives Module 1.1**	**Describe** the major concepts associated with each of the early schools of psychology. **Identify** and **describe** the major contemporary perspectives in psychology.
	Theories of sleep, dreaming, and hypnosis: Modules 4.2, 4.3	**Describe** the functions of sleep. **Describe** the major theories of dreaming. **Describe** the major theories of hypnosis.
	Learning theories	See **Modules 5.1, 5.2,** and **5.3** above.
	Theories of intelligence: Module 7.3	**Describe** the major theories of intelligence.
	Theories of motivation: Module 8.1	**Identify** and **describe** biological and psychological sources of motivation. **Identify** and **describe** the levels in Maslow's need hierarchy.
	Theories of emotion: Module 8.3	**Describe** the major theories of emotions.
	Theories of cognitive and psychosocial development: Modules 9.3, 9.4	**Apply** Erikson's stages of psychosocial development to the challenges we face through the lifespan. **Describe** the characteristics of Piaget's stages of cognitive development and evaluate his legacy. **Describe** Vygotsky's psychosocial theory of cognitive development.
	Modules 10.1, 10.2 10.3	**Describe** and **evaluate** Kohlberg's stages of moral reasoning.
	Module 11.1	**Explain** the development of gender role behavior in terms of psychological, biological, and sociocultural theories.
	Module 11.2	**Evaluate** evidence concerning the origins of sexual orientation.
	Theories of personality	See **Modules 13.1, 13.2, 13.3, 13.4** above
1.4 Explain major perspectives of psychology (e.g., behavioral, biological, cognitive, evolutionary, humanistic, psychodynamic, and sociocultural).	**Early schools of psychology and contemporary perspectives in psychology**	See **Module 1.1** above

GOAL 2 Research Methods in Psychology

Understand and apply basic research methods in psychology, including research design, data analysis, and interpretation.

	Related Content in Text and Ancillaries
2.1 Describe the basic characteristics of the science of psychology.	**Modules 1.1, 1.3** **Module 1.3**: The Scientific Method **Module 9.1**: Studying Human Development: Key Questions and Methods of Study
2.2 Explain different research methods used by psychologists.	**Module 1.3**: Research Methods **Module 1.3**: Anatomy of a Research Study **Module 1.2**: Classic Study in Psychology (The Clarks' doll study) **Module 5.1**: Classic Study in Psychology (Little Albert) **Module 5.3**: Classic Study in Psychology (Bandura's Bobo doll study) **Module 6.1**: Classic Study in Psychology (Loftus's study on the misinformation effect) **Module 14.3**: Classic Study in Psychology (Asch's study on obedience to authority) **Module 14.3**: Classic Study in Psychology (Milgram's study on obedience to authority) **Module 14.3**: Classic Study in Psychology: Zimbardo's "prison experiment"
2.3 Evaluate the appropriateness of conclusions derived from psychological research.	**Module 1.3**: Anatomy of a Research Study **Statistics Appendix**
2.4 Design and conduct basic studies to address psychological questions using appropriate research methods.	**Module 1.3** **Module 9.1**
2.5 Follow the APA Ethics Code in the treatment of human and nonhuman participants in the design, data collection, interpretation, and reporting of psychological research.	**Module 1.3**
2.6 Generalize research conclusions appropriately based on the parameters of particular research methods.	**Module 1.3**

GOAL 3 Critical Thinking Skills in Psychology

Respect and use critical and creative thinking, skeptical inquiry, and, when possible, the scientific approach to solve problems related to behavior and mental processes.

	Related Content in Text and Ancillaries
3.1 Use critical thinking effectively.	**Module 1.4**: Exposes students to the features of critical thinking to help them develop critical thinking skills to evaluate claims made by others and online information ***Thinking Critically about Psychology*** sections challenge students to apply critical thinking skills to evaluate claims ***Think About It*** features in each Module Review encourage critical thinking about issues raised in the text **Interactive Concept Maps** included in Psychology CourseMate engage students in an active learning exercise in which they complete concept maps showing relational connections between key concepts
3.2 Engage in creative thinking.	***The Brain Loves a Puzzle*** features throughout the text (one per chapter) encourage students to use critical thinking skills to extract information from the chapter to solve puzzles **Module 7.1** discusses processes involved in creative thinking **Interactive Concept Maps** (see above)
3.3 Use reasoning to recognize, develop, defend, and criticize arguments and other persuasive appeals.	**Module 1.4** (see above) *Thinking Critically about Psychology* (see above)

GOAL 4 Application of Psychology

Understand and apply psychological principles to personal, social, and organizational issues.

	Related Content in Text and Ancillaries
4.1 Describe major applied areas (e.g., clinical, counseling, industrial/organizational, school, etc.) and emerging applied areas (e.g., health, forensics, media, military, etc.) of psychology.	**Module 1.2**
4.2 Identify appropriate applications of psychology in solving problems, including the following: **a.** The pursuit and effect of healthy lifestyles **b.** Origin and treatment of abnormal behavior **c.** Psychological tests and measurements **d.** Psychology-based interventions in clinical, counseling, educational, industrial/organizational, community, and other settings and their empirical evaluation **e.** The resolution of interpersonal and intercultural conflicts	**Module 2.8** **Module 3.6** **Module 4.5** **Module 7.3** **Module 10.4** **Modules 12.1, 12.2, 12.3** **Modules 15.2, 15.3, 15.4, 15.5, 15.6** **Module 13.5** **Module 16.2**
4.3 Articulate how psychological principles can be used to explain social issues and inform public policy.	**Module 14.3**
4.4 Apply psychological concepts, theories, and research findings as these relate to everyday life.	**Application Modules** **Module 1.4**: Becoming a Critical Thinker **Module 2.8**: Application: Looking Under the Hood: Scanning the Human Brain **Module 3.6**: Psychology and Pain Management **Module 4.5**: Getting Your Zs **Module 5.4**: Putting Reinforcement into Practice **Module 6.4**: Powering Up Your Memory **Module 7.4**: Becoming a Creative Problem Solver **Module 8.4**: Managing Anger **Module 10.4**: Living Longer, Healthier Lives **Module 12.3**: Taking the Distress Out of Stress **Module 13.6**: Building Self-Esteem **Module 14.4**: Psychology Goes to Work **Module 15.7**: Suicide Prevention **Module 16.4**: Getting Help

GOAL 5 Values in Psychology

Value empirical evidence, tolerate ambiguity, act ethically, and reflect other values that are the underpinnings of psychology as a science.

	Related Content in Text and Ancillaries
5.1 Recognize the necessity of ethical behavior in all aspects of the science and practice of psychology.	**Module 1.3**
5.2 Demonstrate reasonable skepticism and intellectual curiosity by asking questions about causes of behavior.	**Module 1.4**: Becoming a Critical Thinker ***Thinking Critically About Psychology*** feature in each chapter ***Think About It*** feature in each Module Review
5.3 Seek and evaluate scientific evidence for psychological claims.	**Evidence-based** evaluation of psychological claims integrated throughout text **Module 1.3**: Anatomy of a Research Study **Module 1.4**: Becoming a Critical Thinker ***Thinking Critically About Psychology*** feature in each chapter ***Think About It*** feature in each Module Review
5.4 Tolerate ambiguity and realize that psychological explanations are often complex and tentative.	**Modules 4.2, 4.4, 6.1, 7.3, 15.2, 15.3, 15.4, 15.5, 15.6** (e.g., functions of sleep and dreaming, nature of intelligence, causes of substance use and abuse, repressed memories, causes of psychological disorders)
5.5 Recognize and respect human diversity.	Integrated throughout text
5.6 Assess and justify their engagement with respect to civic, social, and global responsibilities.	***Try This Out*** service learning features
5.7 Understand the limitations of their psychological knowledge and skills.	***Thinking Critically About Psychology*** feature in each chapter ***Think About It*** feature in each Module Review

GOAL 6 Information and Technological Literacy

Demonstrate information competence and the ability to use computers and other technology for many purposes.

	Related Content in Text and Ancillaries
6.1 Demonstrate information competence.	**Module 1.3**: Introduction to parts of a scientific study in formal research papers (Anatomy of a Research Study) **Module 1.4**: Thinking Critically about Online Information (sourcing appropriate material)
6.2 Use appropriate software to produce understandable reports of the psychological literature, methods, and statistical and qualitative analyses in APA or other appropriate style, including graphic representations of data.	**Module 1.3**: Citing References (Introduction to APA reference style) **Statistics Appendix**
6.3 Use information and technology ethically and responsibly.	**Module 1.4**: Thinking Critically about Online Information

GOAL 7 Communication Skills

Communicate effectively in a variety of formats.

	Related Content in Text and Ancillaries
7.1 Demonstrate effective writing skills in various formats (e.g., essays, correspondence, technical papers, note taking) and for various purposes (e.g., informing, defending, explaining, persuading, arguing, teaching).	**Module 1.3**: Introduction to parts of a research study **Study Skills (Preface)**
7.2 Demonstrate effective oral communication skills in various formats (e.g., group discussion, debate, lecture) and for various purposes (e.g., informing, defending, explaining, persuading, arguing, teaching).	**Instructor's Manual**: Suggestions for group discussion
7.3 Exhibit quantitative literacy.	**Statistics Appendix** Graphs used to illustrate research findings throughout text
7.4 Demonstrate effective interpersonal communication skills (e.g., attending to nonverbal behaviors, adapting communication to diverse ethnic and cultural partners).	**Module 8.3**: Cultural differences and gender differences in emotional expression **Module 8.3**: Reading emotions in facial expressions **Module 14.1**: Cultural differences in self-disclosure **Module 14.1**: Stereotyping in interpreting nonverbal behavior

GOAL 8 Sociocultural and International Awareness

Recognize, understand, and respect the complexity of sociocultural and international diversity.

	Related Content in Text and Ancillaries
8.1 Interact effectively and sensitively with people of diverse abilities, backgrounds, and cultural perspectives.	**Module 2.5**: Learning through volunteering **Module 8.3**: Cultural differences in emotional expression **Module 14.1**: Cultural differences in impression formation **Module 15.5**: Exploring the Human Side of Abnormal Behavior
8.2 Examine the sociocultural and international contexts that influence individual differences.	**Modules 13.4, 14.1**: Collectivistic versus individualistic cultures **Module 11.2**: Cultural differences in attitudes toward homosexuality **Module 12.1**: Acculturative stress faced by immigrant groups **Module 14.2**: Sociocultural factors in aggression **Module 14.3**: Social identity **Module 14.3**: Sociocultural factors in conformity **Module 16.2**: Multicultural factors in psychotherapy
8.3 Explain how individual differences influence beliefs, values, and interactions with others and vice versa.	**Module 13.4**: Culture and self-identity **Module 14.1**: Cultural differences in self-serving bias **Modules 14.1, 14.2**: Effects of stereotyping **Module 14.2**: Individual differences in prejudice
8.4 Understand how privilege, power, and oppression may affect prejudice, discrimination, and inequity.	**Module 14.2**: Racism, prejudice, and discrimination **Module 1.2**: Classic study by the Clarks on self-esteem of African American children **Module 14.2**: Effects of stereotyping on stereotyped groups
8.5 Recognize prejudicial attitudes and discriminatory behaviors that might exist in themselves and in others.	**Module 14.2**: Roots of prejudice and discrimination **Module 14.2**: Methods of reducing prejudice **Module 14.2**: Examining prejudice

GOAL 9 Personal Development

Develop insight into their own and others' behavior and mental processes and apply effective strategies for self-management and self-improvement.

	Related Content in Text and Ancillaries
9.1 Reflect on their experiences and find meaning in them.	**Module 4.1**: Savoring Your Food **Module 8.3**: Tracking Your Emotions **Module 8.1**: Are You a Sensation Seeker? **Module 12.1**: Are You Type A? **Module 12.1**: Are You an Optimist or a Pessimist? **Module 12.1**: How Stressful Is Your Life? **Module 13.2**: Sizing Up Your Personality **Module 15.4**: Self-Screening for Depression **Module 13.5**: What Should I Become? **Module 14.2**: Examining Prejudice
9.2 Apply psychological principles to promote personal development.	**Module 5.4**: Putting Reinforcement into Practice **Module 6.4**: Powering Up Your Memory **Module 7.4**: Becoming a Creative Problem Solver **Module 13.4**: Examining Your Self-Concept **Module 13.6**: Building Self-Esteem **Module 14.3**: Fending off Manipulative Sales Tactics **Module 16.2**: Replacing Distorted Thoughts with Rational Alternatives
9.3 Enact self-management strategies that maximize healthy outcomes.	**Module 3.6**: Psychology and Pain Management **Module 4.5**: Getting Your Z's **Module 8.4**: Managing Anger **Module 10.4**: Living Longer, Healthier Lives **Module 11.4**: Combating Rape and Sexual Harassment **Module 12.2**: Suggestions for Quitting Smoking **Module 12.2**: Preventing STDs **Module 12.3**: Taking the Distress out of Stress **Module 15.7**: Suicide Prevention **Module 16.4**: Getting Help

GOAL 10 Career Planning and Development

Pursue realistic ideas about how to implement their psychological knowledge, skills, and values in occupational pursuits in a variety of settings that meet personal goals and societal needs.

	Related Content in Text and Ancillaries
10.1 Apply knowledge of psychology (e.g., decision strategies, life span processes, psychological assessment, types of psychological careers) when formulating career choices.	**Module 1.2**: Subfields in Psychology **Module 2.5**: Learning Through Volunteering **Module 7.4**: Becoming a Creative Problem Solver **Module 8.1**: Achievement Motivation versus Avoidance Motivation **Module 8.3**: Emotional Intelligence **Module 10.1**: Erickson's Concept of Identity Crisis
10.2 Identify the types of academic experience and performance in psychology and the liberal arts that will facilitate entry into the workforce, postbaccalaureate education, or both.	**Module 1.2**: Subfields in Psychology **Study Tips for Getting the Most from This Course** (and your other courses) (Preface)

A Message to Students

Study Tips for Getting the Most from This Course (and your other courses)

I often hear students say that they spend many hours reading their textbooks and attending classes, but their grades don't reflect the work that they do. I agree. Success is not a function of the time you put into your courses, but how well you use that time. Developing more effective study skills can help you become a more effective learner and get the most from this course as well as your other courses. Let's begin by discussing four key steps toward becoming an effective learner, which I call the Four E's: (1) engaging interest; (2) encoding information; (3) elaborating meaning; and (4) evaluating progress.

The Four E's of Effective Learning

1. Engaging Interest Paying close attention is the first step toward becoming an effective learner. The brain does not passively soak up information like a sponge. When your attention is divided, it is difficult to process new information at a level needed to understand the complex material required in college-level courses and to retain this newly acquired knowledge. If you find your mind wandering during class or while studying, bring your attention back to the lecture or study material. Becoming an active note-taker during class and while reading the text helps you remain alert and focused and avoid spacing out. Keep a notepad handy while reading the text and jot down key points as you read through the material.

2. Encoding Information Encoding is the process of bringing information into memory. To encode important information from your classes or assigned readings, make it a practice to stop and ask yourself, "What's the main point or idea? What am I hearing or reading? What am I expected to know?" Jot down the major concepts or ideas and review them later. Use the built-in study tools in your textbook, including key terms and concepts highlighted in the margins, and the module reviews and visual overviews at the end of each chapter, to identify main points and themes you need to learn.

3. Elaborating Meaning New learning is a fragile thing. Rehearsing or repeating information to yourself in the form of rote memorization may help reinforce newly acquired knowledge, but a more effective way of strengthening new learning and building more enduring memories is working with new concepts and ideas by elaborating their meaning, such as by linking them to real-life examples and using them to solve problems. Your teachers and parents in grade school may have encouraged you to demonstrate your understanding of new vocabulary words by using them in a sentence. When you learned formulas and other math skills in class, your teachers may have asked you to demonstrate this knowledge by using it to solve math problems in your textbooks or workbooks. Apply this principle to learning psychology. For every concept you read about in this text or learn in class, connect it to a real-life example or life experience. Your textbook authors and instructors provide many examples of concepts they use, but you can take this a step further by connecting these concepts to your own life experiences.

4. Evaluating Progress Keep track of your progress in the course. Most texts, including this one, have quizzes you can use to test yourself on the material you have just read. This text also offers online quizzes divided into conceptual and factual questions. Taking quizzes helps you gauge how you are doing and which areas you need to review further to improve your performance. Another built-in study tool to help you evaluate your progress is the Module Review section at the end of each module. Here you'll find sample answers to the survey questions that began the module. In the *Recite It* section of the Module Review, recite the answers to the survey questions to yourself before glancing at the sample answers in the text. Reciting answers gives you an opportunity to demonstrate your understanding of the material, rather than merely passively reading the sample answers. Then test your knowledge further by taking the brief quiz in the *Recall It* section of the Module Review.

Tips for Succeeding in Class

Read the Syllabus Think of the syllabus as a road map or a pathway for succeeding in the course. Take note of the course assignments, grading system, and other course requirements or expectations. Use your course syllabus as a guide to planning your semester, making entries in your calendar for examination dates and required papers and other course assignments.

Prepare for Class by Completing the Assigned Reading Instructors have good reasons for wanting you to read the assigned chapter or readings before coming to class. They know that students are better prepared for lectures when they have some familiarity with the topics discussed in class. When students have a working knowledge of the material before they come to class, instructors have more freedom to use class time exploring topics in greater depth and breadth, rather than simply reviewing basic concepts. However, lectures may not make much sense to students who lack basic knowledge about the material because they haven't kept up with their readings.

Attend Class One of the most important steps to succeeding in college is attending classes regularly. Missing classes can quickly lead to falling behind. If you do need to miss a class, notify your instructor beforehand and ask for any assignments you may miss. Then ask a classmate for the notes you missed, but only approach someone whom you believe is a good note-taker.

Be Punctual There may be nothing more distracting to your instructor and classmates than students who come late to class. Though your instructor may not say anything directly, coming late to class creates a poor impression. It also makes it difficult to keep up with lecture material because it puts you in the position of playing catch-up. You wouldn't think of arriving at a movie theater in the middle of a movie, so why should you expect to be able to follow a lecture when you arrive after it starts? If you occasionally arrive late due to traffic congestion or some other pressing demand, drop your instructor a note of apology explaining the circumstances. All of us, including instructors, occasionally face similar situations. However, if you have trouble regularly arriving on time, talk to your instructor or advisor about arranging a schedule that works better for you, or consider taking online courses that don't require regular class attendance.

Ask Questions Don't hesitate to ask questions in class. Failing to ask your instructor to clarify a particular point you don't understand can lead you to feel lost or confused during class. Also, make sure to ask your instructor about the material that will be covered on the exam, as well as the format used for the exam, such as essay, short-answer, or multiple-choice questions.

Become an Active Note-Taker Don't try to write down everything the instructor says or every word that pops up on a PowerPoint slide or an overhead. Very few people can write that fast. Besides, trying to copy everything verbatim can quickly lead you to fall behind. Attempting to write everything down also distracts you from thinking more deeply about material discussed in class. A better idea is to listen attentively and write down key points as clearly and concisely as you can as well as examples the instructor uses to illustrate these points. No one has perfect recall, so don't expect to remember every important point or concept discussed during a lecture. Write them down so that you can review them later.

Some instructors use PowerPoint slides as a guide to organizing the material discussed in class. Think of PowerPoint slides as a table of contents for the class. The bullet points in the slides are merely starting points for material your instructor plans to discuss. Your instructor will likely expand upon each point. If you spend class time simply copying bullet points, you will probably miss important information the instructor discusses about each point. Become an active note-taker, not a copy machine. Listen attentively and write down the main concepts and ideas and any examples the instructor may give.

Rephrase and Review Your Notes An effective way of reinforcing new learning is typing your class notes into a computer file for later review. But rather than typing them word for word, rephrase them in your own words. Reworking your notes in this way encourages deeper processing of the material, which is a key factor in strengthening memory of newly learned information. The more you think about the material, the more likely you'll remember it when exam time comes around.

Building Effective Study Skills

Where to Study Select a quiet study space that is neat, clean, and as free of distractions as possible.

When to Study

- *Prevent procrastination.* Schedule regular study times and keep to your schedule.
- *Plan to study at times of the day you are most likely to be alert and best able to concentrate.* Don't leave it until the very end of the day when you are feeling tired or sleepy. Avoid studying directly after a big meal. Give your body time to digest your food. Likewise, avoid studying at a time of day when you're likely to be distracted by hunger pangs.
- *Avoid cramming for exams.* Cramming causes mental fatigue that can interfere with learning and retention. Establish a weekly study schedule to ensure you are well prepared for exams. Plan to review or brush up on the required material the day or two before the exam.

How to Study

- *Plan study periods of 45 or 50 minutes.* Very few people can maintain concentration for longer than 45 minutes or so. Take a 5- or 10-minute break between study periods. Give your mind and body a break by getting up, stretching your legs, and moving around.
- *Establish clear study goals for each study period.* Goals can include topics you want to cover, pages in the textbook you want to read or review, questions you need to answer, problems you need to solve, and so on.

- *Sit properly to maintain concentration.* Sit upright and avoid reclining or lying down to prevent nodding off or losing focus. If your mind begins to wander, bring your thoughts back to your work. Or break the tendency to daydream by getting yourself out of your chair, gently stretch your muscles, take a quick walk around the room, and then return to studying.

How Much to Study A convenient rule of thumb to use is to study two hours per week for each hour of class time. Like most rules of thumb, you may need to adjust it according to the amount of work you need to complete.

Read for Understanding Slow down the pace of your reading so that you can pay close attention to the material you are trying to learn.

- Stop for a moment after every paragraph and pose questions to yourself about what you have just read (What did I just read? What were the main points?, etc.). Jot down your answers to the questions to reinforce your new learning.
- After reading a section of text, take a brief break and then review any concepts you don't fully understand to make sure you get the main points before moving to the next section or chapter. Yes, active reading takes more time and effort than just skimming, but it will make the time you spend reading more productive.

Reach Out for Help If you struggle to understand something, don't give up out of frustration. Ask your instructor for help.

Form Study Groups Reach out to other students to form study groups. Studying as part of a group may induce you to hit the books more seriously.

Using This Textbook as a Study Tool

You are about to embark on a journey through the field of psychology. As with any journey, it is helpful to have markers or road signs to navigate your course. This text provides a number of convenient markers to help you know where you've been and where you're headed. Take a moment to familiarize yourself with the terrain you'll encounter in your journey. It centers on the unique organizational framework of the text—the *concept-based modular format.*

Use Concept-Based Modules to Organize Your Study Time This text is organized in instructional units called *modules* to help you structure your study time more efficiently. The modules in each chapter break down the chapter into these smaller instructional units. Rather than try to digest an entire chapter at once, you can chew on one module at a time. Each module is organized around a set of key concepts. As you make your way through a module, you will be learning a set of basic concepts and how they relate to the theoretical and research foundations of the field of psychology.

Use Concept Signaling as at Tool to Learning Key Concepts Key concepts in each module are highlighted or signaled in the margins of the text to help ensure you learn the main points and ideas as you make your way through the text. Ii is important that you read all the surrounding material in the text, not just the material highlighted in the concept boxes in the margins. Your exams will likely test your knowledge of all the assigned material in the text.

Keep Notes as You Read Taking notes in your own words strengthens deeper, more durable learning. Avoid underlining or highlighting whole sections of text. Let your brain—not your fingers—do the work. Highlight only the important sections of text you want to review further.

Use the Running Glossary to Learn Key Terms Key terms are highlighted (boldfaced) in the text and defined in the margins for easy reference. To ensure you understand the meaning of these terms in context, see how they are used in the adjacent paragraphs of the text.

Review Your Progress Each module begins with a set of survey or study questions. Jot down these questions in a notebook or computer file and try to answer them as you read along. Check your answers against the sample answers in the *Recite It* sections of the Module Review at the end of each module. Then test yourself by taking the brief quizzes you'll find in the *Recall It* section of the Module Reviews. If you find you are struggling with the quiz questions, review the corresponding sections of the text to strengthen your knowledge and then test yourself again.

Use Additional Study Aids Use online study tools, which include Psychology Coursemate learning tools.

Get the Study Edge with the SQ3R+ Study Method The text includes a built-in study system called the SQ3R+ study method that is designed to help students develop more effective study habits. SQ3R is an acronym that stands for five key study skills: *survey, question, read, recite,* and *review.* The text also includes adds an additional feature, the "*Think About It* sections in the Module Reviews, which is the "+" in the SQ3R+ study method. Here's how the SQ3R+ study method works:

1. **Survey** Preview each chapter before reading it. Get a sense of how the chapter is organized, the modules it contains, and the range of material it covers.

2. **Question** Each module begins with a set of survey or study questions that highlight key issues addressed in the module. To become a more active learner, jot down these questions in a notebook or computer file so that you can answer them as you read along, and generate additional questions you can answer yourself.
3. **Read** Read the module carefully, stopping after every paragraph or so to review what you've read. Answer the survey questions to ensure you grasp the key concepts and related information. To strengthen your understanding of text material, you may find it helpful to read each module a second or third time before an exam.
4. **Recite** When you reach the end of the module, gauge how well you understand the material by using the Module Review section to evaluate your progress. Remember to recite the answers to the survey questions before looking at the sample answers in the text. Hearing yourself speak the answers enhances retention of newly learned information.
5. **Review** Establish a study schedule for reviewing text material on a regular basis. Test yourself each time you review or reread the material to boost long-term retention. Use the brief quiz in the "*Recall It*" section of the Module Review and the online quizzes to test your knowledge.
6. **Think About It** The *Think About It* feature in the Module Review poses thought-provoking questions that encourage you to apply critical thinking skills and to reflect on how the material relates to your own experiences. Thinking more deeply about these concepts and relating them to life experiences strengthens new learning.

I hope this guide to a successful course will help you succeed not only in this course but in your other courses as well. I also hope you enjoy your journey through psychology. I began my own journey through psychology in my freshman year in college and have continued along this path with a sense of wonder and joy ever since.

Please e-mail your comments, questions, or suggestions to me at jeffnevid@gmail.com

Jeff Nevid
New York, NY

Psychology

Concepts and Applications

1 The Science of Psychology

You. Me. Us.

This may be your first course in psychology, but it is probably not your first encounter with many of the topics psychologists study. Your earliest exposure to the subject matter of psychology probably began many years ago. Perhaps it came as you first wondered about why people do what they do or how their personalities differ. Perhaps you wondered why your third-grade classmate just couldn't seem to sit still and often disrupted the class. Or perhaps you were curious about how people relate to each other and how they influence each other's behavior. Or maybe you wondered mostly about yourself, about who you are and why you do the things you do. Perhaps one of the reasons you are taking this course is to learn more about yourself.

Psychologists study behavior in all its forms. One way of thinking about psychology is to understand that it involves the study of *you* (the behavior of other people), *me* (one's own behavior), and *us* (how our behavior is affected by groups and social influences). Psychologists are interested in studying behavior in nonhuman species as well. Studies of behavior of other animals can shed light on basic principles of behavior and may help inform our understanding of our own behavior as well.

You may find answers to many of the questions you have about yourself and others in this introductory course in psychology. But you will probably not find all the answers you are seeking. There is still so much we do not understand, so much that remains to be explored. This text, like the field of psychology itself, is really about the process of exploration—the quest for knowledge about behavior and mental processes.

Psychology is a scientific discipline, but what makes it scientific? One answer is that being scientific means valuing evidence over opinion and tradition—even honored tradition or the opinions of respected scholars and thinkers. Psychologists don't dismiss opinion, tradition, or even folklore. Yet as scientists, they require that opinions, assumptions, beliefs, and theories be tested and scrutinized in the light of the available evidence. Psychologists seek answers to the questions they and others pose about human nature by using scientific methods of inquiry. Like other scientists, psychologists are professional skeptics. They have confidence only in theories that can be tied to observable evidence. As in all branches of science, investigators in the field of psychology gather evidence to test their theories, beliefs, and assumptions.

(*Continued on page 4*)

DID YOU KNOW THAT...

- One of the founders of modern psychology was such a poor student he was actually left back a grade in school? (p. 5)
- A movement that once dominated psychology believed that psychologists should turn away from the study of the mind? (p. 7)
- A major school of psychology was inspired by the view from a train? (p. 8)
- The school of psychology originated by Sigmund Freud holds that we are generally unaware of our true motives? (p. 9)
- Multiracial Americans are among the nation's fastest-growing population groups? (p. 12)
- The popularity of women's names influences the judgments people make about their physical attractiveness? (p. 32)
- You can obtain listings and abstracts of articles from major psychology journals by using the Internet (and much of it is free of charge)? (p. 41)

Learning Objectives

By reading this chapter you will be able to . . .

1 **PSYCHOLOGY** and explain why psychology is a science.

2 **IDENTIFY** the early schools of psychology and the important contributors to these schools.

3 **DESCRIBE** the major concepts associated with each of the early schools of psychology.

4 **IDENTIFY** and **DESCRIBE** the major contemporary perspectives in psychology.

5 **IDENTIFY** the specialty areas or subfields of psychology and **APPLY** your knowledge to the work that various types of psychologists do.

6 **IDENTIFY** the women and African-American pioneers in psychology and **DESCRIBE** their contributions to the field.

7 **DESCRIBE** the ethnic and gender characteristics of psychologists today and the changes that have occurred over time.

8 **IDENTIFY** and **DESCRIBE** the steps in the scientific method.

9 **IDENTIFY** and **DESCRIBE** research methods in psychology and **APPLY** this knowledge to the methods psychologists use to study love.

10 **EVALUATE** the strengths and weaknesses of research methods in psychology.

11 **DESCRIBE** the ethical standards that govern research in psychology.

12 **APPLY** critical thinking skills to evaluate claims made by others as well as online information.

© Tyler Olson/Shutterstock.com

Preview

(*Continued from page 2*)

Before we go further with our exploration of psychology, let us define what we mean by the term *psychology*. Though many definitions of psychology have been proposed, the one most widely used today defines psychology as the science of behavior and mental processes. But what do these terms mean—*behavior* and *mental processes*? Broadly speaking, anything an organism does is a form of behavior. Sitting in a chair is a form of behavior. Reading, studying, and watching TV are forms of behavior. Making yourself a sandwich and talking on the telephone are forms of behavior. Smiling, dancing, and raising your arm are also behaviors. Even thinking and dreaming are forms of behavior.

Mental processes are the private experiences that constitute our inner lives. These private experiences include thoughts, feelings, dreams and daydreams, sensations, perceptions, and beliefs that others cannot directly observe or experience. Among the challenges psychologists face is finding ways of making such inner experiences available to scientific study.

Before we begin exploring how psychologists study behavior and mental processes, let us take the story of psychology back to its origins to see how it developed as a scientific discipline and where it stands today.

MODULE 1.1

Foundations of Modern Psychology

- What is psychology?
- What are the origins of psychology?
- What were the major early schools of psychology?
- What are the major contemporary perspectives in psychology?

CONCEPT 1.1
Psychology is the scientific discipline that studies behavior and mental processes.

CONCEPT 1.2
Although psychology is a relatively young science, interest in understanding the nature of mind and behavior can be traced back to ancient times.

This first module in the text sets the stage for our study of psychology. It describes the development of psychology as a scientific discipline. How did psychology develop? What were the important influences that shaped its development as a scientific discipline? Here we address those questions by recounting a brief history of psychology. Let us begin by noting that although psychology is still a young science, its origins can be traced back to ancient times.

Origins of Psychology

The story of psychology has no clear beginning. We cannot mark its birth on any calendar. We can speculate that the story very likely began when early humans developed the capacity to reflect on human nature. Perhaps they were curious, as many of us are today, about what makes people tick. But what they may have thought or said about the nature of human beings remains unknown, as no record exists of their musings.

The word **psychology** is derived from two Greek roots: *psyche*, meaning "mind," and *logos*, meaning "study" or "knowledge." So it is fitting that we turn to the philosophers of

psychology The science of behavior and mental processes.

the classical period of ancient Greece, around 500 to 300 B.C. The ancient Greek philosophers who had the most profound influence on psychological thought were Socrates (ca. 469–399 B.C.), Plato (ca. 428–348 B.C.), and Aristotle (ca. 384–332 B.C.).

We know of Socrates through the writings of his most eminent pupil, Plato. Socrates, whose famous credo was "know thyself," emphasized the importance of self-examination and personal reflection. He believed the unexamined life is not worth living. His theme of self-exploration remains one of the most enduring in modern psychology. Plato had also learned from Socrates that we should not rely on our senses to acquire knowledge about the world, since the world that is given to us by our senses is an imperfect copy of reality. The notion that our senses are not to be trusted as windows to the truth resonates with modern psychologists who study how our senses can deceive us in the form of visual illusions (see Chapter 3). Like Socrates before him, Plato believed that to acquire true knowledge we should rely on thought and reason, not on information that comes to us through our imperfect senses.

Aristotle, Plato's most famous student, thought differently. He was trained as a naturalist, so it is not surprising he came to believe that knowledge could be acquired by the senses through careful observation. Aristotle held that the pursuit of knowledge should be based on experience with the world around us, not on pure thought or reasoning. Aristotelian thinking came to influence the development of the modern sciences, as can be seen in the emphasis those sciences place on experimentation and careful observation as pathways to knowledge.

While most ancient Greeks believed that the gods interfered in people's daily lives, Aristotle maintained that people should believe in what they can see and touch. He was one of the first to write about natural causes of human behavior rather than appealing to divine or supernatural explanations. Aristotle even explained the ways in which one thought leads to another; his ideas on the association of thoughts are still found in contemporary views of learning and thinking. Aristotle also said that people and lower animals are primarily motivated to seek pleasure and avoid pain. This view has become a mainstay of modern theories of motivation.

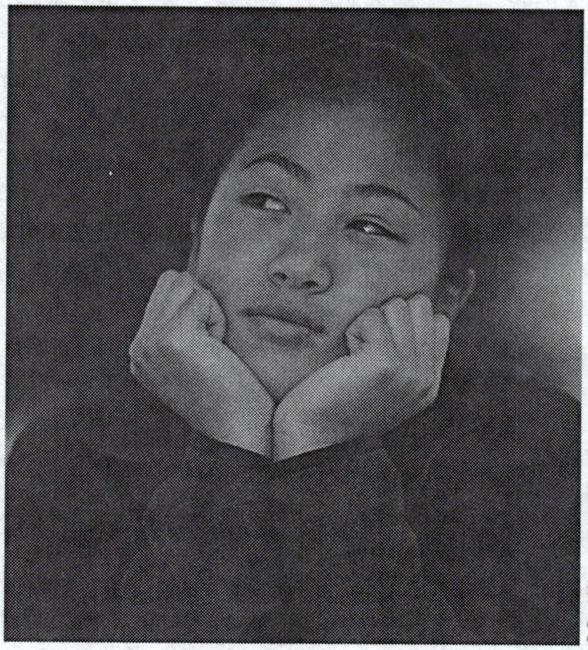

© David Young-Wolff/PhotoEdit

Psychologists study what we do and what we think, feel, dream, sense, and perceive. They use scientific methods to guide their investigations of behavior and mental processes.

Even as we consider the contributions of the ancient Greek philosophers, we shouldn't forget that other systems of thought about human nature were taking root elsewhere around the same time—in Africa, the Middle East, and the Far East, where the philosopher and essayist Confucius (ca. 551–479 B.C.) was to become the most influential and respected thinker in Chinese history. Confucius believed that people have an inborn capacity to do good and that evil is the product of a bad environment or a lack of education, not an evil nature. As we'll see, the belief that environmental influences play a key role in determining behavior finds expression in modern schools of thought in psychology. Confucius also believed that people should be governed by moral principles (rather than profit motives) and that they should cultivate their minds to the utmost. Contemporary psychologists have also turned their attention to issues of moral reasoning and moral development, as we'll see in Chapter 10.

Psychology remained largely an interest of philosophers, theologians, and writers for several thousand years. It did not begin to emerge as a scientific discipline until the nineteenth century. One of the first scientists to study psychological processes was the German physiologist Gustav Theodor Fechner (pronounced *feck-ner*) (1801–1887).

psychophysics The study of the relationships between features of physical stimuli, such as their intensity, and the sensations we experience in response to them.

introspection Inward focusing on mental experiences, such as sensations or feelings.

Fechner studied **psychophysics**, the branch of psychology that studies relationships between the intensity and other physical characteristics of light, sound, and other stimuli, and the sensations we experience in response to them (their brightness, loudness, and so on). In 1860, Fechner published his findings in his book *Elements of Psychophysics*. In the 1850s, another German physiologist, Hermann von Helmholtz (1821–1894), developed a theory of how people perceive color. We'll return to the contributions of Fechner and von Helmholtz when we consider processes of sensation and perception in Chapter 3.

The founding of psychology as an independent science is generally credited to a German scientist, Wilhelm Wundt (1832–1920). The credit is given to Wundt (pronounced *Voont*) because he established the first scientific laboratory dedicated to the study of psychology (Stout, 2008). With the founding of Wundt's laboratory in Leipzig, Germany, in 1879, psychology made the transition from philosophy to science (Benjamin, 2000).

SLICE OF LIFE Wundt was in some respects an unlikely candidate to found a new science. As a boy, he was a poor student and was even required to repeat a grade. The problem for young Wundt was that he tended to daydream in class. He would often be found sitting with an open book in his hand, staring off into space rather than reading his assigned text (a practice this author hopes you don't imitate when you open your psychology text). But he persevered, eventually graduating from medical school and, from there, launching a successful research career as a physiologist. Later, he would apply his scientific training to his true passion, the understanding of conscious experience. In establishing the first psychology laboratory, the man who had once been left back in school because he was so absorbed in his own thoughts became the first scientist of the mind.

Like any scientific discipline, the field of psychology is an unfolding story of exploration and discovery. In this text, you will encounter many of the explorers and discoverers who have shaped the continuing story of psychology. The bridge from ancient thought to the present starts with Wundt; there we encounter his disciple Edward Titchener and structuralism, the school of thought with which both men were associated. (See ■ Figure 1.1 for a timeline of the early days of psychology.)

1860	• Gustav Fechner publishes *Elements of Psychophysics*
1875	• William James gives first psychology lecture at Harvard
1878	• G. Stanley Hall receives first Ph.D. in psychology in the U.S.
1879	• Wilhelm Wundt establishes first psychology laboratory
1883	• First American psychology laboratory established at Johns Hopkins University by G. Stanley Hall
1887	• G. Stanley Hall initiates the *American Journal of Psychology*
1889	• James Mark Baldwin establishes first Canadian psychology laboratory at the University of Toronto
1890	• James writes first psychology text, *Principles of Psychology*
1892	• American Psychological Association (APA) formed; G. Stanley Hall first president
1894	• Margaret Floy Washburn is first woman to receive a Ph.D. in psychology
1895	• Sigmund Freud publishes first work on psychology
1896	• Lightner Witmer establishes the first psychology clinic in the U.S.
1900	• Freud publishes *The Interpretation of Dreams*
1905	• Two Frenchmen, Alfred Binet and Théodore Simon, announce development of the first intelligence test, which they describe as "a measuring scale of intelligence" • Mary Whiton Calkins becomes first woman president of APA
1908	• Ivan Pavlov's work on conditioning first appears in an American scientific journal
1910	• Max Wertheimer and colleagues begin research on Gestalt psychology
1913	• Watson publishes the behaviorist manifesto, *Psychology as the Behaviorist Views It*
1920	• Francis Sumner is first African American to receive a Ph.D. in psychology in the U.S. • Henry Alston is first African American to publish his research findings in a major psychology journal in the U.S.

Figure 1.1 Psychology, the Early Days: A Timeline

Wilhelm Wundt and Structuralism

Wilhelm Wundt was interested in studying mental experiences. He used a method called **introspection**, or careful self-examination and reporting of one's conscious experiences. For example, he would present subjects with an object, such as piece of fruit, and ask them to describe their impressions or perceptions of the object in terms of its shape, color, or texture and how the object felt when touched. Or subjects might be asked to sniff a scent and describe the sensations or feelings the scent evoked in them.

In this way, Wundt and his students sought to break down mental experiences into their component parts—sensations, perceptions, and feelings—and then find the rules determining how these elements come together to produce the full range of conscious experiences.

Edward Titchener (1867–1927), an Englishman who was a disciple of Wundt, brought Wundt's teachings and methods of introspection to the United States and other English-speaking countries. The school of psychology identified with Wundt and Titchener became known as **structuralism**, an approach that attempted to define the structure of the mind by breaking down mental experiences into their component parts.

The first American to work in Wundt's experimental laboratory was the psychologist G. Stanley Hall (1844–1924) (Johnson, 2000). In 1892, Hall founded the American Psychological Association (APA), now the largest organization of psychologists in the United States, and he served as its first president (Pate, 2000). Nine years earlier, in 1883, he had established the first psychology laboratory in the United States, which was housed at Johns Hopkins University (Benjamin, 2000). Although Hall played a pivotal role in the early days of psychology in the United States, Harvard psychologist William James is generally recognized as the father of American psychology.

© INTERFOTO/Alamy

Wilhelm Wundt (seated) with colleagues in the first psychological laboratory.

William James and Functionalism

William James (1842–1910) was trained as a medical doctor but made important contributions to both psychology and philosophy (Pate, 2000). Although he used introspection, he shifted the focus to the *functions* of behavior. Unlike the structuralists, he did not believe that conscious experience could be parceled into discrete elements. Rather, he believed that mental experience is best understood in terms of the functions or purposes it serves.

James founded **functionalism**, the school of psychology that focused on how behavior helps individuals adapt to demands placed upon them in the environment. Whereas structuralists were concerned with understanding the structure of the human mind, functionalists were concerned with the functions of mental processes (Willingham, 2007). Functionalists examined the roles or functions of mental processes—*why* we do *what* we do. For example, James believed we develop habits, such as the characteristic ways in which we use a fork or a spoon, because they enable us to perform more effectively in meeting the many demands we face in daily life.

John B. Watson and Behaviorism

In the early 1900s, a new force in psychology gathered momentum. It was called **behaviorism**, and its credo was that psychology should limit itself to the study of overt behavior that observers could record and measure. The problem with introspectionism, the behaviorists held, is that there is no way to directly observe another person's thoughts, feelings, or sensations. The founder of behaviorism, the American psychologist John Broadus Watson (1878–1958), argued that psychology would never advance as a science unless it dropped introspectionism as a method of study and eliminated mentalistic concepts like mind, consciousness, thinking, and feeling. With Watson and behaviorism, psychology became a science of behavior, not of mental processes (Tweney & Budzynski, 2000). In this respect, Watson and the other behaviorists shared with the ancient Greek philosopher Aristotle the belief that science should rely on observable events.

CONCEPT 1.3
Structuralism, the early school of psychology associated with Wundt and Titchener, used introspection as a method of revealing the fundamental structures of mental experience in the form of sensations, perceptions, and feelings.

CONCEPT 1.4
William James, the founder of functionalism, believed that psychology should focus on how our behavior and mental processes help us adapt to the demands we face in the world.

CONCEPT 1.5
Behaviorism was based on the belief that psychology would advance as a science only if it turned away from the study of mental processes and limited itself to the study of observable behaviors that could be recorded and measured.

structuralism The school of psychology that attempts to understand the structure of the mind by breaking it down into its component parts.

functionalism The school of psychology that focuses on the adaptive functions of behavior.

behaviorism The school of psychology that holds that psychology should limit itself to the study of overt, observable behavior.

Watson believed that the environment molds the behavior of humans and other animals. He even boasted that if he were given control over the lives of infants, he could determine the kinds of adults they would become:

> Give me a dozen healthy infants, well-formed, and my own specified world to bring them up in and I'll guarantee to take any one at random and train him to become any type of specialist I might suggest—doctor, lawyer, merchant-chief and, yes, even beggar-man and thief, regardless of his talents, penchants, tendencies, abilities, vocations, and the race of his ancestors. (Watson, 1924, p. 82)

No one, of course, took up Watson's challenge, so we never will know how "a dozen healthy infants" would have fared under his direction. Psychologists today, however, believe that human development is much more complex than Watson thought. Few would believe that Watson could have succeeded in meeting the challenge he posed.

By the 1920s, behaviorism had become the main school of psychology in the United States, and it remained the dominant force in American psychology for several generations. Its popularity owed a great deal to the work of the Harvard University psychologist B. F. Skinner (1904–1990). Skinner studied how behavior is shaped by rewards and punishments, the environmental consequences that follow specific responses. Skinner showed he could train animals to perform simple behaviors by rewarding particular responses. A rat could learn to press a bar and a pigeon to peck a button if they were rewarded for these responses by receiving pellets of food. Skinner also showed how more complex behaviors could be learned and maintained by manipulation of rewards, which he called *reinforcers.* In some of his more colorful demonstrations of the use of reinforcement, he trained a pigeon to play a tune on a toy piano and a pair of pigeons to play a type of Ping-Pong in which the birds rolled a ball back and forth between them. These methods can even be used to teach a raccoon to shoot a basketball and to train fish to tap a particular target shape (Carroll, 2009).

© JP Laffont Sygma/Corbis

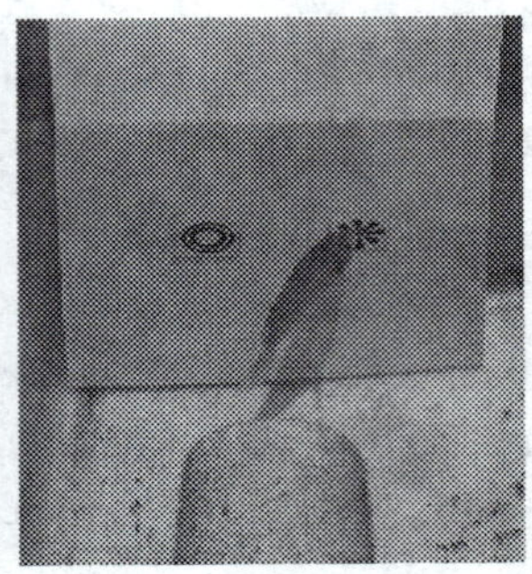

© Courtesy of Ulrike Siebeck

By reinforcing specific responses, we can teach a raccoon to shoot a basketball and a fish to peck at a particular shape. Still, the three-point shot might be beyond the raccoon's range.

Source: Courtesy of Ulrike Siebeck, reproduced with permission of *The Journal of Experimental Biology.* U. E. Siebeck, L. Litherland and G. M. Wallis, JEB 212, 2113-2119 (2009). http://jeb.biologists.org/cgi/content/full/212/13/2113.

Although Skinner studied mainly pigeons and rats, he believed that the same principles of learning he observed in laboratory animals could be applied to humans as well. He argued that human behavior is as much a product of environmental consequences as the behavior of other animals. Everything we do, from saying "excuse me" when we sneeze, to attending class, to making a sandwich, represents responses learned through reinforcement, even though we cannot expect to recall the many reinforcement occasions involved in acquiring and maintaining these behaviors.

CONCEPT 1.6

Gestalt psychology is based on the principle that the human brain organizes our perceptions of the world so that we perceive organized patterns or wholes, not individual bits and pieces of sense experiences added together.

→ Concept Link

Although the influences of Gestalt psychology extend to many areas of psychology, it is best known for its contributions to the study of perception. See Module 3.5.

Max Wertheimer and Gestalt Psychology

SLICE OF LIFE In 1910, at about the time Watson was appealing to psychologists to abandon the study of the mind, another young psychologist, Max Wertheimer (1880–1943), was traveling by train through central Germany on his way to a vacation in the Rhineland (Hunt, 1993). What he saw from the train would lead him to found a new movement in psychology. Called **Gestalt psychology,** it is the school of psychology that studies the ways in which the brain organizes and structures our perceptions of the world.

Gestalt psychology The school of psychology that holds that the brain structures our perceptions of the world in terms of meaningful patterns or wholes.

What had captured Wertheimer's attention on the train was the illusion that objects in the distance—telegraph poles, houses, and hilltops—appeared to be moving along with the train, even though they were obviously standing still. Countless other people had observed the same phenomenon of apparent movement but paid little if any attention to it. Wertheimer was intrigued to find out why the phenomenon occurred. He had the idea that the illusion was not a trick of the eye but reflected higher-level processes in the brain that create the perception of movement. He promptly canceled his vacation and began experimental studies of the phenomenon. The experiments he conducted with two assistants, Wolfgang Köhler (1887–1967) and Kurt Koffka (1886–1943), led to discoveries about the nature of perception—the processes by which we organize our sense impressions and form meaningful representations of the world around us.

© Archives of the History of American Psychology, The Center for the History of Psychology—The University of Akron

Max Wertheimer

The Gestalt psychologists rejected the structuralist belief that mental experience could be understood by breaking it down into its component parts. The German word **gestalt** can be roughly translated as "unitary form" or "pattern." Gestalt psychologists believe the brain organizes our perceptions of the world by grouping elements together into unified or organized wholes, rather than as individual bits and pieces of sense experience (Sayim, Westheimer, & Herzog, 2010). The well-known Gestalt maxim that the "whole is greater than the sum of the parts" expresses this core belief. As an example, when you look at the dots in ■ Figure 1.2, you are likely to see them forming an arrow, rather than perceiving them as a formless array of individual dots. When you see a large number of black objects flying overhead, you instantly recognize them as a flock of birds flying in formation. In other words, your brain interprets what your eyes see as organized patterns or wholes.

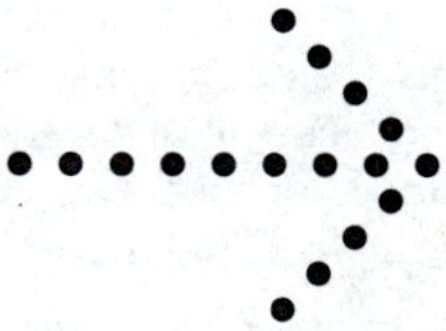

Figure 1.2 What Is This? A disorganized series of dots? Or an organized form—an arrow? The Gestalt psychologists taught that what the eyes see is not necessarily what the brain perceives.

Sigmund Freud and Psychoanalysis

Around the time that behaviorism and Gestalt psychology were establishing a foothold in organized psychology, a very different model of psychology was emerging. It was based on the writings of an Austrian physician named Sigmund Freud (1856–1939). Freud's psychology focused not only on the mind, but also on a region of the mind that lay beyond the reach of ordinary consciousness—a region he called the **unconscious**. Freud conceived of the unconscious as the repository of primitive sexual and aggressive drives or instincts and of the wishes, impulses, and urges that arise from those drives or instincts. He believed that the motives underlying our behavior involve sexual and aggressive impulses that lie in the murky depths of the unconscious, hidden away from our ordinary awareness of ourselves. In other words, we may do or say things without understanding the true motives that prompted these behaviors.

Freud also believed that early childhood experiences play a determining role in shaping our personalities and behavior, including abnormal behaviors like excessive fears or phobias. He held that abnormal behavior patterns are rooted in unconscious conflicts originating in childhood. These conflicts involve a dynamic struggle within the unconscious mind between unacceptable sexual or aggressive impulses striving for expression and opposing mental forces seeking to keep this threatening material out of conscious awareness. Thus, Freud's view of psychology, and that of his followers, is often called the **psychodynamic perspective**.

Unlike Wundt, James, and Watson, Freud was a therapist, and his main aim was to help people overcome psychological problems. He developed a form of psychotherapy

gestalt A German word meaning "unitary form" or "pattern."

unconscious In Freudian theory, the part of the mind that lies outside the range of ordinary awareness and that contains primitive drives and instincts.

psychodynamic perspective The view that behavior is influenced by the struggle between unconscious sexual or aggressive impulses and opposing forces that try to keep this threatening material out of consciousness.

CONCEPT 1.7
According to Freud, much of our behavior is determined by unconscious forces and motives that lie beyond the reach of ordinary awareness.

→ Concept Link
Freud's model of therapy, called psychoanalysis, is based on the belief that therapeutic change comes from uncovering and working through unconscious conflicts within the personality. See Module 16.2.

© Tips Italia/Antique Research Centre/PhotoLibrary

Sigmund Freud

psychoanalysis Freud's method of psychotherapy; it focuses on uncovering and working through unconscious conflicts he believed were at the root of psychological problems.

behavioral perspective An approach to the study of psychology that focuses on the role of learning in explaining observable behavior.

social-cognitive theory A contemporary learning-based model that emphasizes the roles of cognitive and environmental factors in determining behavior.

behavior therapy A form of therapy that involves the systematic application of the principles of learning.

CONCEPT 1.8

Although some early schools of psychology have essentially disappeared, contemporary perspectives in the field, including the behavioral, psychodynamic, humanistic, physiological, cognitive, and sociocultural perspectives, continue to evolve and to shape our understandings of behavior.

CONCEPT 1.9

Many psychologists today subscribe to a broad learning-based perspective, called social-cognitive theory, that emphasizes the environmental and cognitive influences on behavior.

→ Concept Link

Social-cognitive theorists believe that personality comprises not only learned behavior but also ways in which individuals think about themselves and the world around them. See Module 13.3.

or "talk therapy" that he called **psychoanalysis** (discussed in Chapter 16). Psychoanalysis is a type of mental detective work. It incorporates methods, such as analysis of dreams and of "slips of the tongue," that Freud believed could be used to gain insight into the nature of the underlying motives and conflicts of which his patients were unaware. Freud maintained that once these unconscious conflicts were brought into the light of conscious awareness, they could be successfully resolved, or "worked through," during the course of therapy.

Contemporary Perspectives in Psychology

What do we find when we look over the landscape of psychology today? For one thing, we find a discipline that owes a great debt to its founders but is constantly reinventing itself to meet new challenges. Not all schools of thought have survived the test of time. Structuralism, for one, has essentially disappeared from the landscape; others maintain small groups of devoted followers who remain true to the original precepts. But by and large, the early schools of psychology—functionalism, behaviorism, Gestalt psychology, psychoanalysis—have continued to evolve or have been consolidated within broader perspectives. Today, the landscape of psychology can be divided into six major perspectives: the behavioral, psychodynamic, humanistic, physiological, cognitive, and sociocultural.

The Behavioral Perspective

The linchpin of the **behavioral perspective**, which focuses on observable behavior and the important role of learning in behavior, is, of course, behaviorism. However, many psychologists believe that traditional behaviorism is too simplistic or limited to explain complex human behavior. Though traditional behaviorism continues to influence modern psychology, it is no longer the dominant force it was during its heyday in the early to mid-1900s.

Many psychologists today adopt a broader, learning-based perspective called **social-cognitive theory** (formerly called *social-learning theory*). This perspective originated in the 1960s with a group of learning theorists who broke away from traditional behaviorism (see Chapter 13). They believed that behavior is shaped not only by environmental factors, such as rewards and punishments, but also by *cognitive* factors, such as the value placed on different objects or goals (e.g., getting good grades) and expectancies about the outcomes of behavior ("If I do X, then Y will follow"). Social-cognitive theorists challenged their fellow psychologists to find ways to study these mental processes rather than casting them aside as unscientific, as traditional behaviorists would. Traditional behaviorists may not deny that thinking occurs, but they do believe that mental processes lie outside the range of scientific study.

The behavioral perspective led to the development of a major school of therapy, **behavior therapy**. Behavior therapy involves the systematic application of learning principles that are grounded in the behaviorist tradition of Watson and Skinner. Whereas the psychoanalyst is concerned with the workings of the unconscious mind, the behavior therapist helps people acquire more adaptive behaviors to overcome psychological problems such as fears and social inhibitions. Today, many behavior therapists subscribe to a broader therapeutic approach, called *cognitive-behavioral therapy,* which incorporates techniques for changing maladaptive thoughts as well as overt behaviors. (see Chapter 16).

The Psychodynamic Perspective

The psychodynamic perspective remains a vibrant force in psychology. Like other contemporary perspectives in psychology, it continues to evolve. As we'll see in Chapter 13, "neo-Freudians" (psychodynamic theorists who have followed in the Freudian tradition) tend to place less emphasis on basic drives like sex and aggression than Freud did and more emphasis on processes of self-awareness, self-direction, and conscious choice.

The influence of psychodynamic theory extends well beyond the field of psychology. Its focus on our inner lives—our fantasies, wishes, dreams, and hidden motives—has had a profound impact on popular literature, art, and culture. Beliefs that psychological problems may be rooted in childhood and that people may not be consciously aware of their deeper motives and wishes continue to be widely endorsed, even by people not formally schooled in Freudian psychology.

CONCEPT 1.10
The psychodynamic perspective focuses on the role of unconscious motivation (inner wishes and impulses of which we are unaware) and the importance of childhood experiences in shaping personality.

The Humanistic Perspective: A "Third Force" in Psychology

In the 1950s, another force began to achieve prominence in psychology. Known as **humanistic psychology**, it was a response to behaviorism and Freudian psychology, which were the two dominant perspectives in the field at that time. For that reason, humanistic psychology was called the "third force" in psychology. Humanistic psychologists, including the Americans Abraham Maslow (1908–1970) and Carl Rogers (1902–1987), rejected the deterministic views of behaviorism and psychodynamic psychology—beliefs that human behavior is determined by the environment (in the case of behaviorism) or by the interplay of unconscious forces and motives lying outside the person's awareness (in the case of Freudian psychology). Humanistic psychologists believe that free will and conscious choice are essential aspects of the human experience.

Psychologists who adopt a **humanistic perspective** believe that psychology should focus on conscious experiences, even if those experiences are subjective and cannot be directly observed and scientifically measured. Humanistic psychologists view each of us as individuals who possess distinctive clusters of traits and abilities and unique frames of reference or perspectives on life. They emphasize the value of self-awareness and of becoming an authentic person by being true to oneself. They also stress the creative potentials of individuals and their ability to make choices that imbue their lives with meaning and purpose.

humanistic psychology The school of psychology that believes that free will and conscious choice are essential aspects of the human experience.

humanistic perspective An approach to the study of psychology that applies the principles of humanistic psychology.

physiological perspective An approach to the study of psychology that focuses on the relationships between biological processes and behavior.

CONCEPT 1.11
Humanistic psychology emphasizes personal freedom and responsibility for our actions and the value of self-awareness and acceptance of our true selves.

The Physiological Perspective

The **physiological perspective** examines relationships between biological processes and behavior. It is identified not with any one contributor but, rather, with many psychologists and neuroscientists who focus on the biological bases of behavior and mental processes.

Sitting atop your shoulders is a wondrous mass of tissue—your brain—that governs virtually everything you do. The brain is the center of the nervous system, an incredibly complex living computer that allows you to sense the world around you, to think and feel, to move through space, to regulate heartbeat and other bodily functions, and to coordinate what you see and hear with what you do. Your nervous system also allows you to visualize the world and imagine worlds that never were. As we'll find

CONCEPT 1.12
The physiological perspective examines relationships between biological processes and behavior.

CONCEPT 1.13
Evolutionary psychology subscribes to the view that our behavior reflects inherited predispositions or tendencies that increased the likelihood of survival of our early ancestors.

© AP Photo/Ed Betz

Evolutionary psychologists believe that behavioral tendencies that had survival value to ancestral humans, such as aggressiveness, may have been passed down the genetic highway to modern humans. Even our penchant for aggressive sports might reflect these genetic undercurrents.

evolutionary psychology A branch of psychology that focuses on the role of evolutionary processes in shaping behavior.

throughout this text, physiological psychology has illuminated our understanding of the biological bases of behavior and mental processes, including the roles of heredity, hormones, and the nervous system.

Evolutionary psychology is a movement within modern psychology that applies principles from Charles Darwin's theory of evolution to a wide range of behavior in humans and other animals (Buss, 2008; Confer et al., 2010; Durrant, 2011; Gallup & Frederick, 2010). Darwin (1809–1882) believed that all life forms, including humans, evolved from earlier life forms by adapting over time to the demands of their natural environments.

Evolutionary psychologists believe that behavioral *tendencies* or *predispositions,* such as aggressive tendencies, might be rooted in our genes, having been passed along from generation to generation from ancestral times all the way down the genetic highway to us. These traits may have helped ancestral humans survive, even if they are no longer adaptive in modern society. Evolutionary psychologists examine behaviors in different species that they believe may be influenced by evolutionary processes, including aggression, mating, and even acts of altruism (i.e., self-sacrifice of the individual to help perpetuate the group). But they recognize that environmental factors, such as cultural and family influences, play an important role in determining whether these behavioral tendencies or predispositions lead to actual behavior (e.g., whether a person acts aggressively or not).

© Tribune Media Services, Inc. All Rights Reserved. Reprinted with Permission.

"I'm the gene that causes alcoholism. I figured I'd cut out the middle man."

The Cognitive Perspective

Cognitive psychologists study people's mental processes in an effort to understand how people gain knowledge about themselves and the world around them. The word *cognitive* comes from the Latin word *cognitio,* meaning "knowledge." Psychologists who adopt the **cognitive perspective** study the mental processes by which we acquire knowledge—how we learn, form concepts, solve problems, make decisions, and use language. Some cognitive psychologists apply principles of computer information processing (i.e., the methods by which computers process information to solve problems) to explain how humans process, store, retrieve, and manipulate information.

Cognitive psychologists make no apology for studying mental experience; they believe the methods they use to study cognition are well grounded in the scientific tradition. After all, no one has ever observed subatomic particles such as protons and neutrons, but that hasn't prevented physicists from conducting scientific studies that attempt to investigate their properties. Chapter 7 examines the intriguing research findings reported by cognitive psychologists.

The Sociocultural Perspective

cognitive perspective An approach to the study of psychology that focuses on the processes by which we acquire knowledge.

Psychologists who adopt a **sociocultural perspective** examine how behavior and attitudes are shaped by the social and cultural influences to which people are exposed. More specifically, they focus on the influences of age, ethnicity, gender, sexual orientation, lifestyle, income level, disability status, and culture on behavior and mental processes.

The sociocultural perspective leads us to pose a number of questions to which we shall return later in the text: Does susceptibility to visual illusions vary across cultures? Are there gender differences in basic abilities in math or verbal skills? How does culture influence concepts of the self? Are there ethnic differences in drug-use patterns, and if so, how might we account for them? Are there racial differences in intelligence, and if so, what do we make of them? What role does acculturation play in the psychological adjustment of immigrant groups?

sociocultural perspective An approach to the study of psychology that emphasizes the role of social and cultural influences on behavior.

This study of sociocultural factors in behavior is especially relevant today because of the increasing diversity of American society. Ethnic minority groups now comprise about one-third of the U.S. population and are expected to make up about half the population by the middle of the twenty-first century ("U.S. Minority Population," 2007). Moreover, multiracial Americans are among the nation's fastest-growing population groups, now comprising about 5.2 million people, including such high-profile individuals as President Barack Obama, golfer Tiger Woods, singer Mariah Carey, and baseball player Derek Jeter ("Multiracial America," 2009; Saulny, 2011). Traditional "racial" identities are also becoming more blurred as increasing numbers of people are identifying with nontraditional categories. For example, many Hispanics identify themselves as *moreno, trigueno,* or *indio*—terms that indicate ancestry and variations in skin tones.

CONCEPT 1.14
The cognitive perspective focuses on understanding the mental processes by which people gain knowledge about themselves and the world around them.

CONCEPT 1.15
The sociocultural perspective places behavior within a broad social context by examining the influences of ethnicity, gender, lifestyles, socioeconomic status, and culture.

Cons 3+4 Due 1

Why is it important to consider racial or ethnic distinctions at all? One reason is that ethnic and cultural groups often differ in values, customs, and traditions that influence their behavior. Consequently, taking differences of ethnicity and culture into account helps us gain a better understanding of human diversity. We need to recognize that diversity in psychology is not limited to differences in ethnicity and cultural background. It also relates to differences in age, gender, sexual orientation, and disability status.

Psychologists recognize that research samples need to be broadly representative of the populations to which they wish to generalize their findings. Much of the early research in psychology focused on white, middle-class samples, composed largely of male college students. We should not assume that findings based on narrowly defined groups of individuals necessarily generalize to other groups who have different life experiences.

positive psychology A contemporary movement within psychology that emphasizes the study of human virtues and assets, rather than weaknesses and deficits.

Summary of Contemporary Perspectives

It's important to realize that no one perspective is necessarily right and the others wrong. Each major perspective in contemporary psychology focuses on different aspects of behavior or psychological functioning. Each has something unique to offer to our understanding of human behavior, and none offers a complete view. Given the complexity of human behavior and experience, it is not surprising that psychology has spawned multiple pathways for approaching its subject matter. It is also not surprising that many psychologists today identify with an *eclectic* approach to understanding human behavior—one that draws on theories and principles representing different perspectives. We should recognize, too, that contemporary psychology is not divided as neatly into different schools of thought, as it seemed to be in its early days. There is considerable room for overlap among the different perspectives.

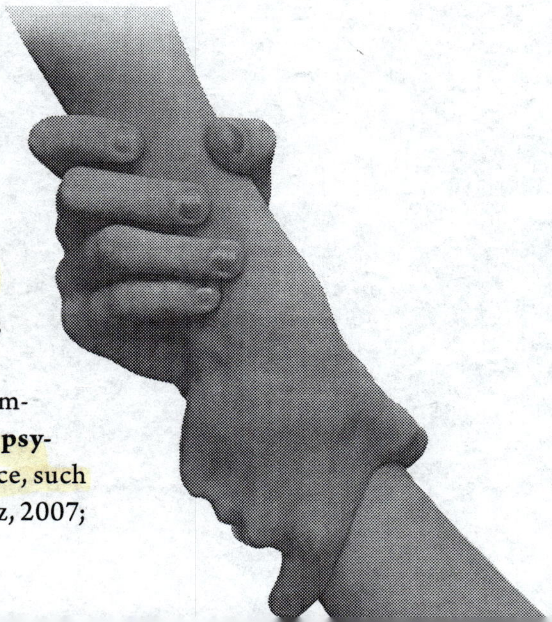
© vadim kozlovsky/Shutterstock.com

In addition to the six major perspectives that dot the landscape of contemporary psychology, a growing movement within psychology, called **positive psychology,** is directed toward the study of positive aspects of human experience, such as love, happiness, altruism, and hope (Seligman et al., 2005; Snyder & Lopez, 2007;

CONCEPT CHART 1.1 Contemporary Perspectives in Psychology: How They Differ

Perspective	General Questions	Questions About Specific Topics: Aggression	Depression	Obesity
Behavioral	How do early learning experiences shape our behavior as adults?	How is aggressive behavior learned? How is it rewarded or reinforced? Does exposure to violence in the media or among one's peers play a role?	How is depression related to changes in reinforcement patterns? What social skills are needed to establish and maintain social relationships that could serve as sources of reinforcement?	How might unhealthy eating habits lead to obesity? How might we change those habits?
Psychodynamic	How do unresolved conflicts from childhood affect adult behavior? How can people be helped to cope with these conflicts?	How is aggression related to unconscious impulses? Against whom are these impulses really directed?	How might depression be related to unresolved loss? Might it represent anger turned inward?	Might obesity relate to childhood conflicts revolving around unresolved needs for love and support? Might food have become a substitute for love?
Humanistic	How do people pursue goals that give their lives a sense of meaning and purpose?	Might violence be related to frustration arising when people are blocked from pursuing their goals? How might we turn this around to prevent violence?	Might depression be related to a lack of self-esteem or a threat to one's self-image? Might it stem from a sense of purposelessness or lack of meaning in life?	What sets the stage for obesity? Does food have a special meaning for obese people? How can we help them to find other sources of satisfaction?
Physiological	How do biological structures and processes make behavior possible? What roles do nature (heredity) and nurture (environment) play in such areas as intelligence, language development, and aggression?	What brain mechanisms control aggressive behavior? Might brain abnormalities explain violent behavior in some people?	How are changes in brain chemistry related to depression? What genetic links might there be?	Is obesity inherited? What genes may be involved? How would knowledge of a genetic basis lead to new approaches to treatment or prevention?
Cognitive	How do people solve problems, make decisions, and develop language?	What thoughts trigger aggressive responses? What beliefs do aggressive people hold that might increase their potential for violence?	What types of thinking patterns are related to depression? How might they be changed to help people overcome depression or prevent it from occurring?	How does obesity affect a person's self-concept? What thoughts lead to eating binges? How might they be changed?
Sociocultural	How do concepts of self differ across cultures? How do social and cultural influences shape behavior?	What social conditions give rise to drug use and aggressive behavior? Does our society condone or even reward certain forms of violence, such as sexual aggression against women or spousal abuse?	Is depression linked to social stresses, such as poverty or unemployment? Why is depression more common among certain groups of people, especially women? Does it have to do with their expected social roles?	Are some groups at greater risk of obesity than others? Do cultural differences in dietary patterns and customs play a role?

Vallea, Huebner, & Suldo, 2006). Psychologists have devoted a great deal of attention to understanding human weaknesses and deficits, including emotional problems, effects of traumatic stress, and problem behaviors such as violence and drug addiction. Founded by psychologist Martin Seligman, positive psychology balances the scale by focusing on our virtues and strengths, not our flaws. Throughout the text we discuss aspects of positive psychology, including love, helping behavior, optimism, successful aging, happiness, self-esteem, self-actualization, and creativity.

In Concept Chart 1.1, the first of many such charts in the text, you'll find examples of the kinds of general questions that psychologists from each of the major contemporary perspectives might ask, as well as the kinds of questions they might pose to learn more about specific topics. These topics are introduced here to help you distinguish among the various perspectives in contemporary psychology. They will be discussed further in later chapters.

1.1 MODULE REVIEW — Foundations of Modern Psychology

Recite It

What is psychology?

- Psychology is the science of behavior and mental processes.

What are the origins of psychology?

- Though systematic attempts to explain human behavior can be traced to philosophers in ancient times, psychology emerged as a scientific discipline in the nineteenth century with Wundt's founding of the first psychological laboratory in Leipzig, Germany, in 1879.

What were the major early schools of psychology?

- Structuralism is the earliest school of psychology. Identified with Wilhelm Wundt and Edward Titchener, it attempted to break down mental experiences into their component parts—sensations, perceptions, and feelings.
- Functionalism, the school of psychology founded by William James, attempts to explain our behavior in terms of the functions it serves in helping us adapt to the environment.
- Behaviorism, the school of psychology begun by James Watson, holds that psychology should limit itself to observable phenomena—namely, behavior.
- Gestalt psychology, the school of psychology founded by Max Wertheimer, is grounded in the belief that the brain structures our perceptions of the world in terms of organized patterns or wholes.
- Psychoanalysis, the school of thought originated by Sigmund Freud, emphasizes the role of unconscious motives and conflicts in determining human behavior.

What are the major contemporary perspectives in psychology?

- The behavioral perspective focuses on observable behavior and the influences of learning processes in behavior.
- The psychodynamic perspective represents the model of psychology developed by Freud and his followers. It holds that our behavior and personalities are shaped by unconscious motives and conflicts that lie outside the range of ordinary awareness.
- The humanistic perspective reflects the views of humanistic psychologists such as Carl Rogers and Abraham Maslow, who emphasized the importance of subjective conscious experience and personal freedom and responsibility.
- The physiological perspective examines the ways in which behavior and mental experience are influenced by biological processes such as heredity, hormones, and the workings of the brain and other parts of the nervous system.
- The cognitive perspective focuses on mental processes that allow us to gain knowledge about ourselves and the world.
- The sociocultural perspective examines how our behavior and attitudes are shaped by social and cultural influences.

Recall It

1. The scientist generally credited with the founding of psychology as an independent science was ________.
2. The early school of psychology called structuralism
   a. rejected the use of introspection as a research method.
   b. focused on overt behavior.
   c. investigated the structure of the mind.
   d. was concerned with the functions of behavior.
3. The school of psychology that believes psychology should be limited to the study of observable behavior is ________.
4. Gestalt psychology focuses on
   a. the organization of the mind.
   b. the ways in which the brain organizes and structures our perceptions of the world.
   c. the functions of behavior.
   d. the role of self-actualization in motivating behavior.
5. Humanistic psychologists rejected the notion that unconscious processes and environmental influences determine our behavior. Rather, they emphasized the importance of ________ in understanding behavior.
   a. conscious choice.
   b. heredity and physiological processes.
   c. classical and operant conditioning.
   d. the underlying structures of the mind.
6. Which psychological perspective originated with Sigmund Freud?

Answers to Recall It questions are placed in the appendix at the end of the text.

Think About It

- Suppose you wanted to explain behavior in terms of how people's habits help them adapt to the environmental demands they face. Which early school of psychology would you be adopting in your approach?
- Suppose you wanted to understand behavior in terms of underlying forces within the personality that influence behavior even though the person may not be aware of them. Which early school of psychology would this approach represent?
- Humanistic psychologists emphasize the importance of finding a purpose or meaning in life. What are your purposes in life? How can you make your life more meaningful?

MODULE 1.2

Psychologists: Who They Are and What They Do

- What are the various specialties in psychology?
- What changes have occurred in the ethnic and gender characteristics of psychologists over time?

When you think of a psychologist, do you form a mental image of someone working in a hospital or clinic and treating people with psychological problems? This image describes one particular type of psychologist—a clinical psychologist. But there are many other types. Psychology is a diverse profession because of the large number of areas in the field and because of the many different roles psychologists perform. Some psychologists teach and conduct research. Others provide psychological services to individuals or to organizations, such as schools or businesses. Psychologists are usually identified with one particular specialty or subfield within psychology—for example, experimental, clinical, developmental, educational, or social psychology.

Some psychologists conduct **basic research**—research that seeks to expand our understanding of psychological phenomena even if such knowledge does not lead directly to any practical benefits. These psychologists typically work for universities or government agencies. Some psychologists conduct **applied research**—research intended to find solutions to specific problems. For example, a psychologist might apply research on learning and memory to studying methods of enhancing the educational experiences of children with mental retardation. Still other psychologists work in applied areas of psychology in which they provide services to people or organizations. These include clinical, counseling, school, and industrial/organizational psychologists. Many applied psychologists also conduct research in the areas in which they practice. In this module, we take a closer look at the various types of psychologists.

THE BRAIN LOVES A PUZZLE

As you read ahead, use the information in the text to solve the following puzzle:

A student successfully completed all Ph.D. requirements at Johns Hopkins University but was refused a doctorate. Undeterred, the student went on to a distinguished research career in psychology, even formulating a new theory of color vision. Why had the university refused to grant the doctoral degree?

basic research Research focused on acquiring knowledge, even if such knowledge has no direct practical application.

applied research Research that attempts to find solutions to specific problems.

Specialty Areas of Psychology

All psychologists study behavior and mental processes, but they pursue this knowledge in different ways, in different settings, and from different perspectives. The following sections provide a rundown of some of the major specialty areas within the field of psychology and some emerging ones.

Most psychologists earn doctoral degrees in their area of specialization, such as experimental psychology, clinical psychology, or social psychology. The Ph.D. (Doctor of Philosophy), the most common doctoral degree, is awarded after completion of required graduate coursework and a dissertation, which involves an original research project. Some psychologists seeking practice careers may earn a Doctor of Psychology degree (Psy.D.), a doctoral degree that is focused more on practitioner skills than on research skills. Others may pursue graduate programs in schools of education and be awarded a Doctorate in Education (Ed.D.). In some specialty areas, such as school psychology and industrial/organization (I/O) psychology, the Master's degree is recognized as the entry-level degree for professional work in the field.

CONCEPT 1.16
The field of psychology consists of an ever-growing number of specialty areas.

Major Specialty Areas

Concept Chart 1.2 provides an overview of the major specialties in psychology discussed in this section. ■ Figure 1.3 shows the percentages of psychologists working in major specialty areas. ■ Figure 1.4 summarizes where psychologists work.

Experimental psychologists apply experimental methods to the study of behavior and mental processes such as learning, sensation and perception, and cognition. Some experimental psychologists, called **comparative psychologists**, seek to understand animal behavior for its own sake and possibly for what it might teach us about human behavior. Others, called **physiological psychologists** (also known as *biological psychologists*), study the biological bases of behavior.

Clinical psychologists evaluate and treat people with psychological disorders, such as mood disorders and anxiety disorders. They may use psychotherapy to help people overcome psychological problems or cope better with the stresses they face in their lives. They may administer psychological tests to better understand people's problems or to evaluate their intellectual abilities or personalities.

Many conduct research in the field or train future psychologists. Others work in hospitals or clinics, while still others work in private practice or university settings. As Figure 1.3 shows, clinical psychology is the largest specialty area in psychology.

experimental psychologists Psychologists who apply experimental methods to the study of behavior and mental processes.

comparative psychologists Psychologists who study behavioral similarities and differences among animal species.

physiological psychologists Psychologists who focus on the biological underpinnings of behavior.

clinical psychologists Psychologists who use psychological techniques to evaluate and treat individuals with mental or psychological disorders.

CONCEPT CHART 1.2 Specialty Areas of Psychology

Types of Psychologists	Major Focus	Typical Questions Studied
Experimental psychologists	Exploring processes of learning, cognition, sensation, and perception; biological bases of behavior; and animal behavior	How do various states of arousal affect learning? What brain centers are responsible for memory?
Clinical psychologists	Evaluating and treating psychological problems and disorders	How can we diagnose mood disorders? Is depression treated more effectively with psychotherapy or drug therapy?
Counseling psychologists	Helping people with adjustment problems	What kind of occupation would this student find fulfilling? Why does this person find it difficult to make friends?
School psychologists	Helping children in school with academic problems or special needs	Would this child profit from special education, or would he or she be better off in a regular classroom?
Educational psychologists	Developing psychological and educational tests (such as the SAT); improving course planning and instructional methods	Is this test a valid predictor of success in college? How can we teach algebra more efficiently?
Developmental psychologists	Examining physical, cognitive, social, and personality development across the life span	At what age do children begin to walk or speak? What types of crises do people face in middle or later adulthood?
Personality psychologists	Examining the psychological characteristics that make each of us unique	What is the structure of personality? How do we measure personality?
Social psychologists	Exploring the effects of the social environment on behavior	What are the origins of prejudice? Why do people do things as members of groups that they would not do as individuals?
Environmental psychologists	Examining how the physical environment affects people's behavior	What are the effects of city life on people? How does overcrowding affect people's health and behavior?
Industrial/organizational psychologists	Exploring the psychological aspects of work environments	How can we find out who would perform well in this position? How can we make hiring and promotion fairer? How can we enhance employees' motivation?
Health psychologists	Examining relationships between psychological factors and the prevention and treatment of physical illness	How can we help people avoid risky sexual behaviors? How can we help people quit smoking and start exercising?
Consumer psychologists	Exploring relationships between psychological factors and consumers' preferences and purchasing behavior	Why do people select particular brands? What types of people prefer a particular type of product?

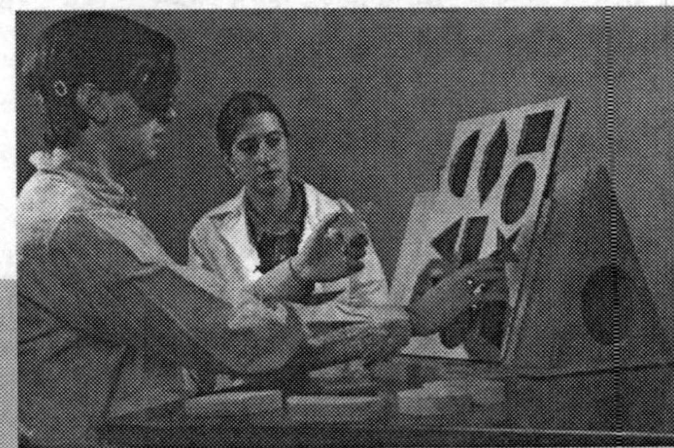

© Richard T. Nowitz / Photo Researchers, Inc.

What are the different specialty areas in psychology? What types of questions do the different types of psychologists study?

The professional roles of clinical psychologists in evaluating and treating psychological disorders often overlap with those of **psychiatrists**, medical doctors who complete residency training in the medical specialty of psychiatry. Unlike psychiatrists, however, psychologists cannot prescribe drugs. But even these lines may be blurring now that a small number of psychologists have been trained in a specialized program to prescribe drugs to treat psychological disorders (Bradshaw, 2008; Meyers, 2005).

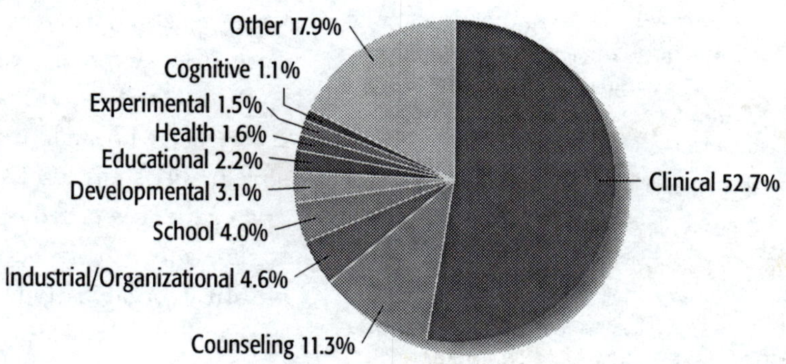

Figure 1.3 Psychologists' Areas of Specialization
Clinical psychologists make up the largest group of psychologists, followed by counseling psychologists and industrial/organizational psychologists.
Source: American Psychological Association, 2004.

Counseling psychologists help people who have adjustment problems that are usually not as severe as the kinds of problems treated by clinical psychologists. If you did not know what course of study to follow in college, or if you were having a difficult time adjusting to college, you might talk to a counseling psychologist about it. Counseling psychologists also help people make vocational decisions or resolve marital problems. Many work in college counseling centers or community-based counseling or mental health centers.

School psychologists work in school systems, where they help children with academic, emotional, and behavioral problems and evaluate students for placement in special-education programs. They are team players who work collaboratively with teachers and other professionals in providing a broad range of services for children.

Educational psychologists develop tests that measure intellectual ability or academic potential, help gear training approaches to students' learning styles, and create ways of helping students reach their maximum academic potential. Many also conduct research; among the issues they study are the nature of intelligence, how teachers can enhance the learning process, and why some children are more highly motivated than others to do well in school.

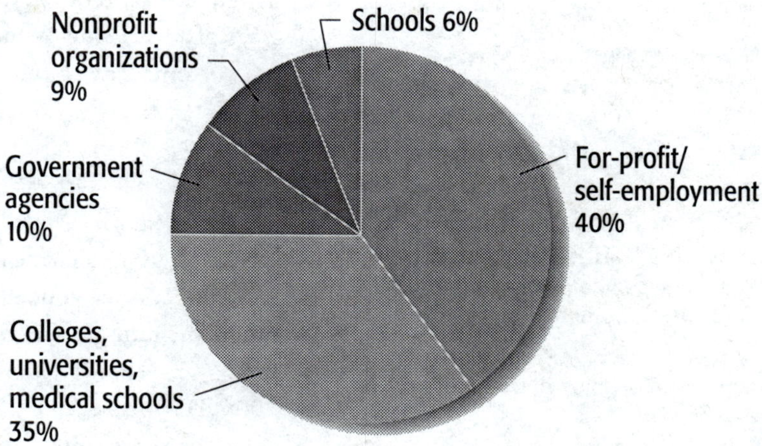

Figure 1.4 Where Psychologists Work
The largest grouping of psychologists are those who work in settings in which they provide psychological services. Many work in colleges and universities as teachers, researchers, administrators, or supervisors of psychologists in training. Some also work in schools or government agencies.
Source: American Psychological Association, 2003.

Developmental psychologists study people's physical, cognitive, social, and personality development throughout the life span. *Child psychologists* are developmental psychologists who limit their focus to child development.

Personality psychologists seek to understand the nature of personality—the cluster of psychological characteristics and behaviors that distinguishes us as unique individuals and leads us to act consistently over time. In particular, they study how personality is structured, and how it develops and changes.

Social psychologists study how group or social influences affect behavior and attitudes. Whereas personality psychologists look within the individual's psychological make-up to explain behavior, social psychologists focus on how groups affect individuals and, in some cases, how individuals affect groups.

Environmental psychologists study relationships between the physical environment and behavior. For example, they study the effects of outdoor temperature on aggression and the psychological impact of such environmental factors as air pollution, overcrowding, and noise (Stansfeld et al., 2009). Did you know that people's moods tend to fluctuate with seasonal weather patterns? In a recent study, environmental psychologists found that people tended to report more positive moods during pleasant

psychiatrists Medical doctors who specialize in the diagnosis and treatment of mental or psychological disorders.

counseling psychologists Psychologists who help people clarify their goals and make life decisions or find ways of overcoming problems in various areas of their lives.

school psychologists Psychologists who evaluate and assist children with learning problems or other special needs.

educational psychologists Psychologists who study issues relating to the measurement of intelligence and the processes involved in educational or academic achievement.

developmental psychologists Psychologists who focus on processes involving physical, cognitive, social, and personality development.

personality psychologists Psychologists who study the psychological characteristics and behaviors that distinguish us as individuals and lead us to act consistently over time.

social psychologists Psychologists who study group or social influences on behavior and attitudes.

environmental psychologists Psychologists who study relationships between the physical environment and behavior.

industrial/organizational (I/O) psychologists Psychologists who study people's behavior at work.

health psychologists Psychologists who focus on the relationship between psychological factors and physical health.

consumer psychologists Psychologists who study why people purchase particular products and brands.

neuropsychologists Psychologists who study relationships between the brain and behavior.

geropsychologists Psychologists who focus on psychological processes involved in aging.

spring weather, whereas the hotter weather during the summer was associated with reports of lower moods (Keller et al., 2005).

Industrial/organizational (I/O) psychologists study people at work. They are concerned with such issues as job satisfaction, personnel selection and training, leadership qualities, effects of organizational structure on productivity and work performance, and challenges posed by changes in the workplace. They may use psychological tests to determine the fit between applicants' abilities and interests and the jobs available within an organization or corporation (Chan, 2005). Some I/O psychologists perform human factors research, in which they examine ways of making equipment (e.g., airplane gauges and computer systems) more efficient and easier to use (Benson, 2006).

Health psychologists study how such psychological factors as stress, lifestyle, and attitude affect physical health. They apply this knowledge in developing disease prevention programs and interventions to improve the quality of life of patients with chronic diseases, such as heart disease, cancer, and HIV/AIDS.

Consumer psychologists are interested in understanding consumer behavior—why people purchase particular products and particular brands (Hawkins, Mothersbaugh, & Best, 2007). They examine consumers' attitudes toward different products, ways of advertising or packaging products, and even the choice of music stores play to put customers in a buying mood.

Emerging Specialty Areas

When G. Stanley Hall founded the American Psychological Association (APA) in 1892, it had 31 charter members (Benjamin, 1997); today, the membership exceeds 150,000. It's no wonder that psychology's interests and specialties cover so wide a range, including such emerging specialty areas as neuropsychology, geropsychology, forensic psychology, and sport psychology (e.g., Canter, 2011; Fernández-Ballesterosa, 2006; Harmison, 2006; Holt & Tamminen, 2010).

Neuropsychologists study relationships between the brain and behavior. While some neuropsychologists limit their activities to research, *clinical neuropsychologists* use specialized tests to evaluate the cognitive effects of brain injuries and strokes. These tests can help them pinpoint the particular areas of the brain affected by injury or disease. Clinical neuropsychologists may also work with rehabilitation specialists in designing programs to help people who have suffered various forms of brain damage regain as much of their functioning as possible.

© Photo by Sam Greenwood/Getty Images

Sport psychologists are playing an increasingly important role in helping athletes deal with the demands of athletic competition and working with them to improve their athletic performance.

Geropsychologists focus on psychological processes associated with aging. They may work with geriatric patients to help them cope with the stresses of later life, including retirement, loss of loved ones, and declining physical health.

Forensic psychologists work within the legal system. They may perform psychological evaluations in child custody cases, testify about the competence of defendants to stand trial, develop psychological profiles of criminal types, give expert testimony in court on psychological issues, or assist attorneys in selecting potential jury members.

Sport psychologists apply psychology to sports and athletic competition. They help athletes develop relaxation and mental-focusing skills to overcome performance anxiety and enhance their athletic performance. Some study personality traits associated with athletic performance, including the reasons that certain athletes "choke" in difficult situations. Some help athletes handle competitive pressures and balance travel, family, and life demands as well as team dynamics. Sport psychologists also counsel players who experience psychological difficulties adjusting to the rigors of competition.

forensic psychologists Psychologists involved in the application of psychology to the legal system.

sport psychologists Psychologists who apply psychology to understanding and improving athletic performance.

Diversity in Professional Psychology

CONCEPT 1.17
Women and minority members faced difficult obstacles in pursuing careers in psychology in the early days of the profession.

The early psychologists shared more than just a yearning to understand behavior: Almost all of them were white males of European background. The ranks of women in the early days of psychology were slim, and the ranks of racial and ethnic minorities even slimmer. Back then, women and minority members faced many barriers in pursuing careers in psychology, as they did in numerous other professions. The earliest woman pioneer in psychology was Christine Ladd-Franklin (1847–1930). She completed all the requirements for a Ph.D. at Johns Hopkins University in 1882, but the university refused to award her the degree because at that time it did not issue doctoral degrees to women. Nonetheless, she went on to pursue a distinguished research career in psychology, during which she developed a new theory of color vision. She finally received her Ph.D. in 1926.

SLICE OF LIFE Another woman pioneer was Mary Whiton Calkins (1863–1930). A brilliant student of William James, Calkins completed all her Ph.D. requirements at Harvard, but Harvard denied her a doctorate; like Johns Hopkins, it did not grant doctoral degrees to women. She was offered the doctorate through Radcliffe College, a women's academy affiliated with Harvard, but she refused it. Not easily deterred, she went on to a distinguished career in psychology—teaching and conducting important research on learning and short-term memory. In 1905, she became the first female president of the APA.

Margaret Floy Washburn (1871–1939) encountered similar discrimination when she pursued studies in psychology at Columbia University. In 1894, having found a more receptive environment at Cornell University, she became the first woman in the United States to earn a Ph.D. in psychology. She wrote an influential book, *The Animal Mind*, and in 1921 became the second female president of the APA.

In 1909, Gilbert Haven Jones (1883–1966), an African American, received a doctorate in psychology from a university in Germany. It wasn't until 1920, however, at Clark University in Worcester, Massachusetts, that Francis Sumner (1895–1954) became the first African American to receive a doctorate in psychology in the United States. Sumner went on to a distinguished career in teaching and research. He helped establish the psychology department at Howard University and served as its chairperson until his death in 1954.

In 1920, the same year Sumner earned his doctorate, J. Henry Alston became the first

© Wellesley College Archives/photo by Pastridge

Mary Whiton Calkins

© Archives of the History of American Psychology-The University of Akron

Margaret Floy Washburn

© Courtesy Wilberforce University/Archives & Special Collections

Gilbert Haven Jones

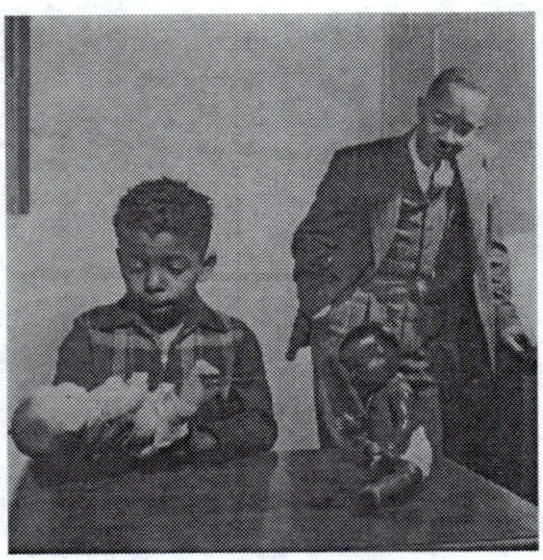

©Parks, Gordon, 1912-2006, photographer/Library of Congress

Psychologist Kenneth Clark observing as an African American child selects a white doll over a black doll to play with.

CONCEPT 1.18

Though the field of psychology has become more diverse, people of color are still underrepresented in professional psychology.

African American to publish his research findings (on the perception of warmth and cold) in a major U.S. psychology journal. It took another 50 years (until 1971) before the first—and, to this date, the only—African American psychologist, Kenneth Clark (1914–2005), was elected president of the APA. In 1999, Richard Suinn became the first Asian American psychologist to be elected president of the APA.

Clark's influential work on personality development of African American children extended beyond the field of psychology. His writings were cited in the U.S. Supreme Court in its landmark 1954 decision, *Brown* v. *Board of Education of Topeka, Kansas*, which held that separate schools were inherently unequal (Tomes, 2004). A classic study he conducted in 1939 with his wife, Mamie Phipps-Clark (1917–1983), showed that African American preschool children preferred playing with a white doll rather than a black one and attributed more positive characteristics to the white doll (Clark & Clark, 1939). The Clarks argued that African American children come to believe they must be inferior because they were prevented from attending school with white children.

The professional ranks of psychology have become more diverse, but people of color still remain underrepresented in the profession, especially at the doctoral level (Vasquez & Jones, 2006). Minority representation in psychology at the doctoral level remains at about half of what it is in the general society. ■ Figure 1.5 shows the ethnic make-up of persons holding doctorates in psychology. Representation among certain minority groups is especially limited. For example, there is but one Native American psychologist for every 30,000 Native Americans (Rabasca, 2000a).

A different picture emerges when we examine gender shifts in professional psychology. Women now account for more than two-thirds of all doctorate recipients

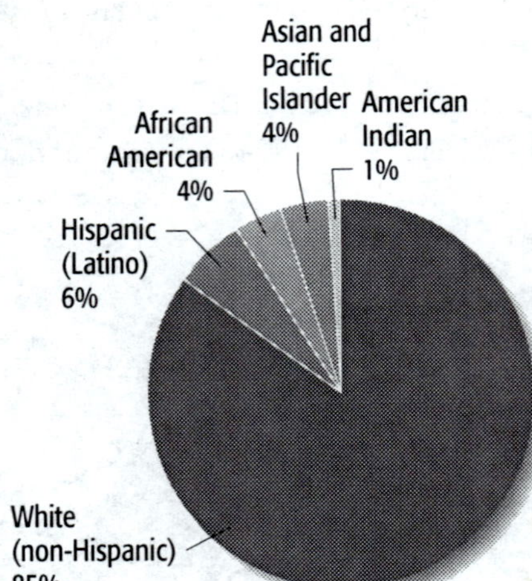

Figure 1.5 Ethnicities of Doctorate Recipients in Psychology
Though the percentages of minorities in the field of psychology have increased over the years, white Americans of European background still constitute the majority of new doctorate recipients in psychology.
Source: National Science Foundation, 2004.

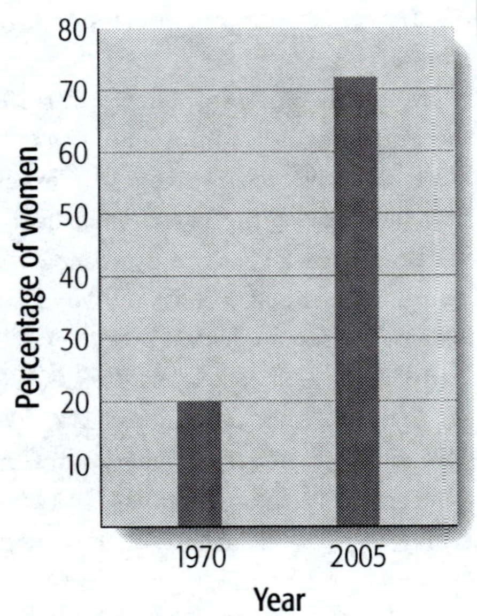

Figure 1.6 Women Ph.D. Recipients in Psychology
Women now represent more than two-thirds of new Ph.D.s in psychology, as compared to about one-fifth in 1970.
Source: Cynkar, 2007.

in psychology, as compared to one in five in 1970 (Cynkar, 2007; Gill, 2006) (see ■ Figure 1.6). This gender shift mirrors the increased representation of women in occupations traditionally dominated by men, including medicine and law. However, the gender shift is occurring at a faster rate in psychology than in other professions.

CONCEPT 1.19
The profession of psychology has undergone a major gender shift in recent years.

1.2 MODULE REVIEW Psychologists: Who They Are and What They Do

Recite It

What are the various specialties in psychology?

➤ These include major subfields such as clinical and counseling psychology, school psychology, and experimental psychology, as well as emerging specialty areas such as gero-psychology, forensic psychology, and sport psychology.

What changes have occurred in the ethnic and gender characteristics of psychologists over time?

➤ Though psychology is now a more diverse discipline, African Americans and other minority groups remain underrepresented in the professional ranks of psychologists.

➤ Unlike in the early days of the profession, when women were actively excluded from pursuing professional careers, they now constitute more than two-thirds of the new Ph.D.s in psychology.

Recall It

1. ________ research focuses on expanding our understanding and knowledge, whereas ________ research focuses on finding answers or solutions to particular problems.
2. Match the following types of psychologists with the type of work they do: (a) counseling psychologists; (b) developmental psychologists; (c) environmental psychologists; (d) consumer psychologists:
   - **i.** study changes in behaviors and attitudes throughout the life cycle.
   - **ii.** study effects of outdoor temperature on aggression.
   - **iii.** study psychological characteristics of people who buy particular products.
   - **iv.** help students adjust to college life.
3. A psychologist who works within the legal system is most likely to be a
   - **a.** social psychologist.
   - **b.** neuropsychologist.
   - **c.** forensic psychologist.
   - **d.** counseling psychologist.
4. The first African American to receive a doctorate in psychology in the United States was
   - **a.** Mary Whiton Calkins.
   - **b.** Francis Sumner.
   - **c.** Gilbert Haven Jones.
   - **d.** Kenneth Clark.

Think About It

➤ If you were uncertain about what career to pursue and wanted help sorting through the vocational choices best suited to you, what type of psychologist would you consult? Why?

➤ Suppose you read in a newspaper about a psychologist who was studying how people's behavior changes when they become part of an unorganized mob. What type of psychologist would this person likely be?

MODULE 1.3

Research Methods in Psychology

- What are the basic objectives of science?
- What is the scientific method, and what are its four general steps?
- What major research methods do psychologists use?
- What ethical guidelines must psychologists follow in their research?

Psychologists are trained to be skeptical of claims and arguments that are not grounded in evidence. They are especially skeptical of public opinion and folklore. What distinguishes psychology from other inquiries into human nature, including philosophy, theology, and poetry, is the use of scientific methods to gain knowledge. Psychologists adopt an **empirical approach**; that is, they base their beliefs on evidence gathered from experiments and careful observation.

empirical approach A method of developing knowledge based on evaluating evidence gathered from experiments and careful observation.

The Objectives of Science: To Describe, Explain, Predict, and Control

The basic objectives of science are to describe, explain, predict, and control events. As scientists dedicated to understanding behavior and mental processes and using that understanding for human betterment, psychologists share these major goals.

Description

Clear and accurate description is a cornerstone of science. Psychologists use methods of careful observation to make unbiased and accurate descriptions. But sometimes we mistake inferences for descriptions, as in the following example:

Imagine you are a student in an experimental psychology class. On the first day of class your professor, a distinguished woman of about 50, walks in, carrying a small wire-mesh cage containing a white rat. She smiles, removes the rat from the cage, and places the rat on the desk. She then asks the class to describe the rat's behavior.

As a serious student, you attend closely. The animal moves to the edge of the desk, pauses, peers over the edge, and seems to jiggle its whiskers at the floor below. It maneuvers along the edge of the desk, tracking the perimeter. Now and then it pauses and vibrates its whiskers downward in the direction of the floor. The professor picks up the rat and returns it to the cage. She asks the class to describe the animal's behavior.

A student responds, "The rat seems to be looking for a way to escape."

Another student: "It is reconnoitering its environment, examining it."

"Reconnoitering?," you think. That student has seen too many war movies.

The professor writes each response on the blackboard. Another student raises her hand. "The rat is making a visual search of the environment," she says. "Maybe it's looking for food."

The professor prompts other students for their descriptions.

"It's looking around," says one.

"Trying to escape," says another.

Your turn arrives. Trying to be scientific, you say, "We can't say what its motivation might be. All we know is that it's scanning its environment."

"How so?" the professor asks.

"Visually," you reply, confidently.

The professor writes the response and then turns to the class, shaking her head. "Each of you observed the rat," she said, "but none of you described its behavior. Each of you made certain inferences—that the rat was 'looking for a way down,' or 'scanning its environment,' or 'looking for food,' and the like. These are not unreasonable inferences, but they are inferences, not descriptions. They also happen to be wrong. You see, the rat is blind. It's been blind since birth. It couldn't possibly be looking around, at least not in a visual sense." (From Nevid, Rathus, & Greene, 2008, pp. 19–20)

The students inferred that the rat was "looking around" at its environment. But that is an **inference**, not an observation. Psychologists are trained to distinguish between observations and inferences—conclusions drawn from observations.

inference A conclusion drawn from observations.

Inferences do play an important role in science, enabling us to jump from the particular to the general, from what we observe about an individual's behavior to more general statements about what the behavior might mean or represent. But we need to distinguish between describing what we observe and making inferences based on those observations. Consider the question "Have you ever observed abnormal behavior?" The answer, scientifically speaking, is no. You can only observe behavior. Labeling behavior as abnormal (or normal) is an inference, not an observation.

How, then, might you accurately and objectively describe the rat's behavior? You might give a detailed account of the animal's movements, such as exactly how far it moves in each direction, how long it pauses before turning, how it moves its head from side to side, and so on. Careful observation and description of behavior provide data for developing theories that can help us better understand the phenomena we study and perhaps also predict future occurrences.

Explanation

If we were to limit ourselves to description, we would be left with a buzzing confusion of unconnected observations. Psychologists, like other scientists, construct theories to help them understand the phenomena they study. A **theory** is an explanation that organizes observations into meaningful patterns and accounts for relationships among observed events in terms of underlying mechanisms. Social-cognitive theory, for instance, attempts to explain behavior in terms of the influence of situational factors, such as rewards and punishments, and of cognitive factors, such as personal values and expectancies.

theory A formulation that accounts for relationships among observed events or experimental findings in ways that make them more understandable and predictable.

CONCEPT 1.20
Psychologists seek to explain events by developing theories that lead to predictions that can be tested through research and careful observation.

Theories are judged by how useful they are in accounting for a given set of observations or experimental findings. Scientists recognize that even the best of theories are but crude approximations of ultimate truth. They understand that alternative theories with even better explanations of the evidence derived from careful observation may come along later.

A combination of theories, rather than any one theory, may best account for a given set of facts. For example, as you'll discover in Chapter 3, the best available explanation of color vision combines elements of two competing theories.

Prediction

Scientists draw on their theoretical understanding of events to make predictions about future occurrences. Theories help make events more understandable. They also help us in making predictions about future occurrences and in suggesting ways of controlling them. Based on social-cognitive theory, for example, we might expect young people who have positive expectancies about alcohol or drug use—who believe these substances will make them more popular or have other desired outcomes—will be more likely to use them. By changing expectancies—by helping young people see the negative outcomes associated with alcohol or drug use—we may help them avoid using them.

A theory linking stress and depression might lead us to predict that stressful experiences, such as marital conflict or prolonged unemployment, would increase the risk of depression. If evidence supports this link (and it does; see Chapter 15), we might be able to prevent depression by providing counseling to people in times of stress.

To be sure, not all scientific predictions about future events are borne out by the evidence. But even when contrary findings occur, they help scientists reformulate or refine their theories, which may then enable them to make more accurate predictions.

Control

The fourth objective of science is control of events. The science of physics enabled people to harness nuclear power and to create the electronic superhighway, the Internet. Biological and medical sciences have enabled society to control many infectious diseases through vaccination programs and other public health initiatives, even to the extent of eradicating some historic scourges, such as smallpox.

Psychologists do not seek to control people or manipulate them to do their bidding. Rather, they find methods of using psychological knowledge to help people gain greater mastery and control over their own lives. Psychotherapy, for one, has helped people gain better control over negative emotional states, such as anxiety and depression; improve their relationships with others; and develop their unique potentials. Many other myths and misconceptions about psychology abound; Table 1.1 provides a sampling.

variables Factors or measures that vary within an experiment or among individuals.

Psychologists seek yet another kind of control—control over the **variables** they study. In an experiment, variables are factors the experimenter manipulates or varies systematically, such as the dosage level of an experimental drug the participants receive. In a memory study, a psychologist who is interested in factors that affect the ability to recall newly learned information might manipulate such variables as the length of time that research participants have to first learn the material.

CONCEPT 1.21

Control has two meanings in psychological research: control of the variables under study, and using knowledge gained from research to help people attain better control over their lives.

As we'll see later in this chapter, psychologists subscribe to a code of ethics that respects the dignity and welfare of their clients and those who participate in their research studies. This code recognizes that people have a basic right to make their own decisions and to exercise choices, including the choice of whether to participate in psychological research.

The Scientific Method: How We Know What We Know

scientific method A method of inquiry involving careful observation and use of experimental methods.

Like other scientific disciplines, psychology uses the scientific method in its pursuit of knowledge. The **scientific method** is a framework for acquiring knowledge based on careful observation and the use of experimental methods. It can be conceptualized in terms of four general steps that scientists use to test their ideas and to expand and refine

TABLE 1.1 Common Misconceptions About Psychology

Myth	Fact
Psychologists can read people's minds.	No, psychologists cannot read people's minds. As one prominent psychologist put it, "If you want to know what people are thinking, ask them. They just might tell you."
Psychology is not a true science.	Psychology is indeed a true science because it is grounded in the scientific method.
Psychologists manipulate people like puppets.	Psychologists help people change their behavior and achieve their goals. They do not manipulate or control people.
There can be only one true psychological theory; all the others must be false.	No one theory accounts for all forms of behavior. Theories are more or less useful to the degree they account for the available evidence and lead to accurate predictions of future behavior. Some theories account for some types of behavior better than others, but many have value in accounting for some forms of behavior.
Psychotherapy is useless.	A large body of evidence shows that psychotherapy is indeed effective (see Chapter 16).
People cannot change—they are what they are.	Evidence shows that people can indeed change their behavior and their ways of relating to others.

their knowledge: (1) developing a research question, (2) framing the research question in the form of a hypothesis, (3) gathering evidence to test the hypothesis, and (4) drawing conclusions about the hypothesis. ■ Figure 1.7 summarizes these steps.

1. *Developing a research question.* Psychologists generate research questions from many sources, including theory, careful observation, previous experience, and commonly held beliefs. For example, a researcher might be interested in the question "Does exposure to stress increase risk of the common cold?"
2. *Framing the research question in the form of a hypothesis.* An investigator reframes the research question in the form of a **hypothesis**—a precise prediction that can be tested through research. Hypotheses are often drawn from theory. For example, a researcher might theorize that stress weakens the immune system—the body's defense system against disease—leaving us more vulnerable to various kinds of illness, including the common cold. Based on this theoretical model, the investigator might frame the research question in the form of a testable hypothesis: "People who encounter high levels of stress in their lives are more likely to develop a common cold after exposure to cold viruses than are people with lower levels of stress."

CONCEPT 1.22
The scientific method is a framework for acquiring knowledge through careful observation and experimentation.

CONCEPT 1.23
Scientists use the scientific method to test out predictions derived from theory, observation, experience, and commonly held beliefs.

CONCEPT 1.24
Psychologists frame their research questions in the form of hypotheses, or specific predictions about the outcomes they expect to find.

hypothesis A precise prediction about the outcomes of an experiment.

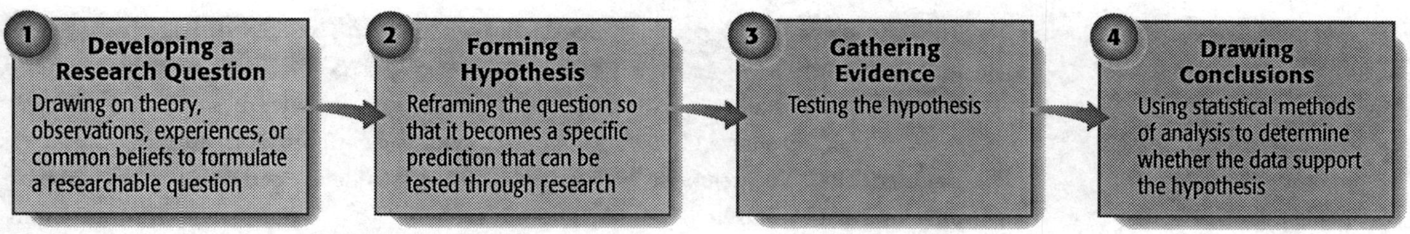

Figure 1.7 General Steps in the Scientific Method

CONCEPT 1.25
Psychologists gather evidence to test out their hypotheses.

CONCEPT 1.26
Psychologists evaluate the results of scientific studies by using statistical tests to determine whether relationships between variables or differences between groups are unlikely to be due to chance.

statistics The branch of mathematics involving the tabulation, analysis, and interpretation of numerical data.

replication The attempt to duplicate findings.

Investigators may also develop hypotheses based on common beliefs or assumptions about behavior. Consider the commonly held belief that "opposites attract." An opposing belief is that people are attracted to those similar to themselves—that "birds of a feather flock together." A specific hypothesis drawn from the latter belief might be phrased as follows: "Most people choose romantic partners who are similar in educational level."

3. *Gathering evidence to test the hypothesis.* The investigator develops a research design or strategy for gathering evidence to provide a scientific test of the hypothesis. The type of research method used depends on the nature of the problem. In the stress and common cold example, the investigator might classify people into high-stress and low-stress groups and then expose them (with their permission, of course) to cold viruses to see if the high-stress group is more likely to develop a common cold. Using this methodology, researchers found that people under high levels of chronic stress were more likely to develop a cold after exposure to a cold virus than were people in a low-stress comparison group (Cohen et al., 1998).
4. *Drawing conclusions about the hypothesis.* Investigators draw conclusions about their hypotheses based on the evidence their research has produced. To test their hypotheses, they turn to **statistics**, the branch of mathematics involving methods of tabulating and analyzing numerical data. Investigators use statistical methods to determine whether relationships between variables (e.g., stress and vulnerability to the common cold) or differences between groups (e.g., an experimental group that receives a treatment versus a control group that does not) are *statistically significant* (relatively unlikely to have been due to chance). A *variable* is a factor that varies in an experiment, such as the dosage level of an experimental drug or the scores that participants receive on a measure of interest.

When research findings do not support the study's hypotheses, scientists may adjust the theories from which the hypotheses were derived. Research findings may suggest new avenues of research or revision of the psychological theories themselves.

Another important factor in drawing conclusions is **replication**, the attempt to duplicate findings reported by others to determine whether they will occur again under the same experimental conditions. Scientists have more confidence in findings that can be reliably replicated by others.

© Brand X Pictures/Getty Images

Psychologists propose testable hypotheses that guide their research. For example, a psychologist might hypothesize that romantic partners with similar interests and attitudes are more likely to remain together than are couples with dissimilar interests and attitudes. Preferences for matching sweaters may have no bearing on the longevity of the relationship, however.

Research Methods: How We Learn What We Know

The scientific method is a framework psychologists use to take their ideas for a test ride. Now let's consider the particular methods they employ to acquire knowledge about behavior and mental processes: the case study, survey, naturalistic observation, correlational, and experimental methods.

The Case Study Method

case study method An in-depth study of one or more individuals.

The **case study method** is an in-depth study of one or more individuals. The psychologist draws information from interviews, observation, or written records. Sigmund Freud, for example, based much of his theory of personality and abnormal behavior on data from intensive observation and study of the patients he treated in his clinical practice. The Swiss scientist Jean Piaget (1896–1980) developed a theory of cognitive development by closely observing and interviewing a small number of children. Many of the early findings on brain function came from studies of brain-injured patients that matched the types of injuries they sustained with particular deficits in memory functioning and motor skills.

Problems with case studies can arise when investigators rely on people's memories of their past experiences, since memories can become distorted or filled with gaps. People may also withhold important information out of embarrassment or shame. To present a more favorable impression, some may even purposefully deceive the researcher. Interviewers may hear only what they expect or want to hear; observers may see only what they want or expect to see. In sum, though case studies can provide a treasure trove of information and lead to testable hypotheses, they lack the rigorous controls of scientific experiments.

The Survey Method

The **survey method** gathers information from target groups of people through the use of structured interviews or questionnaires. A **structured interview** is a questioning technique that follows a preset series of questions in a particular order. A **questionnaire** is a written set of questions or statements to which people can reply by marking responses on an answer form.

Psychologists and other researchers conduct survey research to learn about the characteristics, beliefs, attitudes, and behaviors of certain populations. In survey research, a **population** represents the total group of people who are the subjects of interest. For example, a population might consist of all persons 18 years of age or older in the United States, or perhaps all high school seniors. Generally speaking, it is impractical to study an entire population; an exception would be a very small population that could be studied in its entirety, such as the population of students living in a particular dormitory. In virtually all cases, however, surveys are conducted on **samples**, or segments, of populations.

To draw conclusions about a population based on the results of a sample, the sample must be representative of the target population. Representative samples allow researchers to *generalize*, or transfer, their results from a sample to the population it represents. To create representative samples, researchers use **random sampling**, a technique whereby individuals are selected at random from a given population for participation in a sample. This often entails the use of a computer program that randomly selects names of individuals or households within a given population. Political polls reported in the media typically use random samples of voters to predict outcomes of elections.

Like case studies, surveys may be limited by gaps in people's memories. Participants may also give answers that they believe are socially desirable rather than reflective of what they truly feel or believe. This response style results from what is called **social desirability bias**. For example, many people exaggerate how frequently they attend church (Espenshade, 1993). Social desirability may be especially strong in situations where people have a considerable stake in what others think of them (McGovern & Nevid, 1986). Another form of bias in survey research is **volunteer bias**. This arises when people who volunteer to participate in surveys or other research studies are not representative of the population from which they are drawn.

survey method A research method in which structured interviews or questionnaires are used to gather information about groups of people.

structured interview An interview in which a set of specific questions is asked in a particular order.

questionnaire A written set of questions or statements to which people reply by marking their responses on an answer form.

population All the individuals or organisms that constitute particular groups.

samples Subsets of a population.

random sampling A method of sampling in which each individual in the population has an equal chance of being selected.

social desirability bias The tendency to respond to questions in a socially desirable manner.

volunteer bias The type of bias that arises when people who volunteer to participate in a survey or research study possess characteristics that make them unrepresentative of the population from which they were drawn.

CONCEPT 1.27
Psychologists use a variety of research methods to learn about behavior and mental processes, including the case study, survey, naturalistic observation, correlational, and experimental methods.

CONCEPT 1.28
Case studies can provide a wealth of information and suggest testable hypotheses, but they lack the controls found in scientific experiments.

CONCEPT 1.29
Through survey research, psychologists can gather information about attitudes and behaviors of large numbers of people, but the information they obtain may be subject to memory gaps and biases.

The Naturalistic Observation Method

The **naturalistic observation method** takes the laboratory "into the field" to directly observe the behavior of humans or other animal species in their natural habitats or

naturalistic observation method A method of research based on careful observation of behavior in natural settings.

correlational method A research method used to examine relationships between variables, which are expressed in the form of a statistical measure called a correlation coefficient.

correlation coefficient A statistical measure of association between variables that can vary from –1.00 to +1.00.

CONCEPT 1.30
With the naturalistic observation method, researchers in the field can examine behavior as it unfolds, but they run the risk of influencing the behavior they are observing.

environments. The people or other animals serving as research participants may behave more "naturally" in their natural environments than they would in the artificial confines of the experimental laboratory. Psychologists have observed children at home with their parents to learn more about parent-child interactions and in schoolyards and classrooms to see how children relate to each other. Because people may act differently when they know they are being observed, the observers try to avoid interfering with the behaviors they are observing. To further minimize this potential bias, the observers may spend time allowing the subjects to get accustomed to them so that they begin acting more naturally before any actual measurement takes place. Observers may also position themselves so that the subjects can't see them.

Problems with this method may arise if observers introduce their own biases. For example, if observers have a preconceived idea about how a parent's interaction with a child affects the child's behavior, they may tend to see what they expect to see. To guard against this, pairs of observers may be used to check for consistency between observers. Experimenters may also make random spot checks to see that observers are recording their measurements accurately.

Animals in laboratory or zoolike environments may act differently than they do in their natural habitats. To learn more about chimp behavior, naturalist Jane Goodall lived for many years among chimpanzees in their natural environment. Gradually she came to be accepted by the chimps. Her observations disputed the long-held belief that only humans use tools. For example, she watched as chimps used a stick as a tool, inserting it into a termite mound to remove termites, which they then ate. Not only did chimpanzees use tools, but they also showed other humanlike behavior, such as kissing when greeting one another.

Though the method of naturalistic observation may lack the controls available in controlled experiments, it can provide important insights into behavior as it occurs under natural conditions.

The Correlational Method

Psychologists use the **correlational method** to examine relationships between variables. In Chapter 12, you will read about findings that show a *correlation*, or link, between optimism and better psychological adjustment among cancer patients. In Chapter 9, you will see that maternal smoking during pregnancy is correlated, unfortunately, with increased risk of sudden infant death syndrome (SIDS) in babies.

Naturalist Jane Goodall studied behavior of chimpanzees in their natural environment.

A **correlation coefficient** is a statistical measure of association between two variables. Correlation coefficients can vary from –1.00 to +1.00. Coefficients with a positive sign represent a positive correlation in which higher values on one variable are associated with higher values on the other variable (e.g., people with higher levels of education tend to earn higher incomes; see ■ Figure 1.8). A negative correlation, which is denoted by a negative sign, means the reverse: Higher values on one variable are associated with lower values on the other. For example, the longer people are deprived of sleep, the less alert they are likely to be. The size of the correlation expresses the strength or magnitude of the relationship between the variables. The stronger

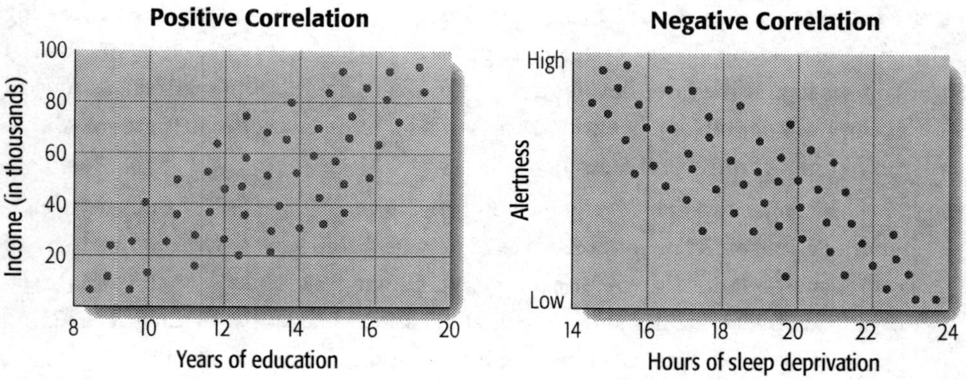

Generally speaking, people with higher levels of education tend to earn higher incomes.

Generally speaking, the longer a person is deprived of sleep, the less alert the person is likely to be.

Figure 1.8 Correlational Relationships These graphs display positive and negative correlations. For a positive correlation, increases in one variable (educational level) are associated with increases in another (income level). For a negative correlation, increases in one variable (sleep deprivation) are associated with decreases in another (alertness). Each dot in these graphs represents the point of intersection of an individual's scores on the two plotted variables.

the relationship, the closer the correlation coefficient will be to either +1.00 (for a positive correlation) or –1.00 (for a negative correlation).

Correlations are useful because they allow us to predict one variable on the basis of the other. A perfect correlation of +11.00 or –1.00 allows us to predict with certainty. Let's say we discovered a perfect correlation between certain genetic characteristics and the likelihood of developing a particular disease. If we knew you possessed these genetic characteristics, we would be able to predict with certainty whether you would develop the disease. However, virtually all of the relationships of interest to psychologists are less than perfect (i.e., they vary in strength between 0.00 and either +11.00 or –1.00). For example, although intelligence is correlated with academic achievement, not everyone with a high score on intelligence tests succeeds in school. A zero correlation means that there is no relationship between the two variables; thus, one variable is of no value in predicting the other.

CONCEPT 1.31
With the correlational method, we can examine how variables are related to each other but cannot determine cause-and-effect relationships.

You may have heard the expression "correlation is not causation." *The fact that two variables are correlated, even highly correlated, doesn't mean that one causes the other.* For example, shoe size in children correlates strongly with vocabulary. While you may argue that some people seem to have more smarts in their little toes than others have in their whole brain, I don't think you'd argue that a growing foot causes vocabulary to expand. Rather, shoe size and vocabulary are correlated because older children tend to have larger feet and a larger vocabulary than younger children. Another example is the strong correlation between ice cream sales and homicide rates. Before you infer that eating ice cream causes people to commit homicide, think of an alternative explanation (Hint: Ice cream sales rise in the warmer weather when people spend more time outside).

© David Young-Wolff/Photo Edit

Are your brains in your feet? Shoe size is correlated with vocabulary size in children, but we should not infer that foot size determines the size of a child's vocabulary.

Although we recognize that the correlational method is limited with respect to determining underlying causes, it does off several important benefits:

- *It offers clues to underlying causes.* Though correlational relationships cannot determine cause-and-effect relationships, they may point to possible causal factors that can be followed up in experimental research. For example, evidence of a correlation between smoking and lung cancer led to experimental studies with animals that showed that exposure to cigarette smoke induced the formation of cancerous lesions in the lungs.

- *It can identify groups of people at high risk for physical or behavioral problems.* Knowing that a relationship exists between the positive expectancies of adolescents toward alcohol use and the later development of problem drinking may direct us toward developing alcoholism prevention efforts that focus on changing attitudes of youngsters before drinking problems arise.
- *It increases understanding of relationships between variables or events.* Such an understanding is one of the major objectives of science. From time to time in this text, we explore such relationships. For example, in Chapter 11 we look at statistical relationships between gender and mathematical and verbal skills. In Chapters 12 and 15 we explore how stress is related to physical and psychological health.

CONCEPT 1.32
With the experimental method, researchers can explore cause-and-effect relationships by directly manipulating some variables and observing their effects on other variables under controlled conditions.

The Experimental Method

experimental method A method of scientific investigation involving the manipulation of independent variables and observation or measurement of their effects on dependent variables under controlled conditions.

independent variables Factors that are manipulated in an experiment.

dependent variables The effects or outcomes of an experiment that are believed to be dependent on the values of the independent variables.

With the **experimental method,** investigators directly explore cause-and-effect relationships by manipulating certain variables, called **independent variables,** and observing their effects on certain outcomes called **dependent variables**. Independent variables are manipulated, and their effects on the dependent variable or variables are measured. Depend ent variables are so-called because measures of these variables depend on the independent, or manipulated, variable. Experimenters attempt to hold constant all other factors or conditions to ensure that the independent variable alone is the cause of the observed effects on the dependent variable.

Consider an experiment that examined whether the popularity of women's names affects judgments of their physical attractiveness. The experimenter paired women's photographs with either a currently popular name, such as Jessica, Jennifer, or Christine, or a traditional name that had fallen out of favor, such as Harriet, Gertrude, and Ethel (Garwood et al., 1980). The investigators found that college student participants rated the women depicted in the photographs who were assigned popular names as more attractive than those given unfashionable names. The experimenter controlled the *independent variable* (popularity of female names) by assigning women's photographs randomly to either currently popular or old-fashioned names. They measured the effects of the independent variable on the *dependent variable* (ratings of attractiveness).

operational definition A definition of a variable based on the procedures or operations used to measure it.

Psychologists use **operational definitions** for defining the variables they study based on the operations or procedures they use to measure them. Operational definitions establish an objective basis for determining what the variables of interest mean. In the study of female names, investigators operationalized the independent variable of popularity of names by classifying names on the basis of whether they were currently popular or out-of-date. They operationalized the dependent variable of physical attractiveness on the basis of scores on an attractiveness rating scale.

control groups Groups of participants in a research experiment who do not receive the experimental treatment or intervention.

Experimenters typically use **control groups** to ensure that the effects of an independent variable are not due to other factors, such as the passage of time. For example, in a study examining the effects of alcohol intake on aggressive behavior, the experimental group would receive a dose of alcohol but the control group would not. The investigator would then observe whether the group given alcohol showed more aggressive behavior in a laboratory task than the control group.

random assignment A method of randomly assigning subjects to experimental or control groups.

In well-designed studies, experimenters use **random assignment** to place participants randomly in experimental groups or control groups. Random assignment balances experimental and control groups in terms of their backgrounds and personality characteristics. Random assignment gives us confidence that differences between the groups' performance on dependent measures are due to the independent variable or variables, not to the characteristics of the people making up the groups. However, random assignment is not always feasible or ethically responsible. For example, ethical experimenters would never randomly assign children to be exposed to abuse or neglect to see what effects these experiences might have on their development. They may rely on correlational methods to examine these relationships, even though such methods do not necessarily determine cause and effect.

Experimenters may wish to keep research participants and themselves in the dark concerning which groups receive which treatments. In drug studies, subjects are typically assigned to receive either an active drug or a **placebo**—an inert pill, or "sugar pill," made to resemble the active drug. The purpose is to control **placebo effects**—the positive outcomes that reflect a person's hopeful expectancies rather than the chemical properties of the drug. Say you took an antibiotic drug you mistakenly believed would produce an immediate effect. You might start feeling better within minutes or a few hours due to the placebo effect, even though medically the drug wouldn't start working for perhaps 12 to 24 hours.

placebo An inert substance or experimental condition that resembles the active treatment.

placebo effects Positive outcomes of an experiment resulting from a participant's positive expectations about the treatment rather than from the treatment itself.

The placebo effect is an example of the power of the human mind (Raz, Zigman, & de Jong, 2009). We can see this power at work in a study in which pain patients who were given placebos showed actual changes in how their brains responded to painful stimuli (Wager, 2005). Nonetheless, placebos tend to have stronger effects on subjective states, such as feelings of pain, than on objectively measured medical conditions, such as high blood pressure (Bailar, 2001). A recent study found that inert placebos work even when research participants *know* they are receiving a placebo (Boutron et al., 2010).

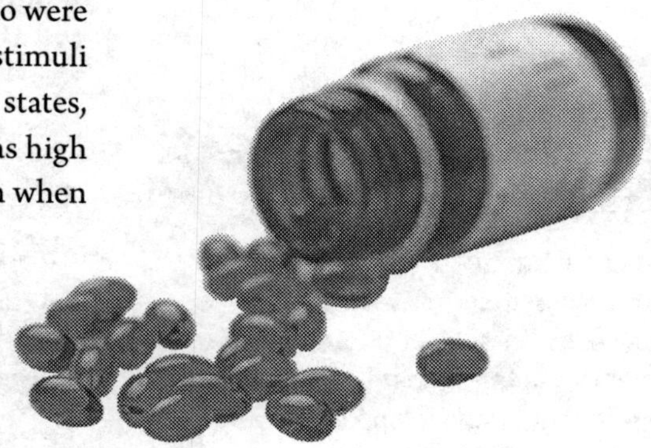

© Denis Larkin/Shutterstock.com

In drug studies, experimenters attempt to control for expectancy effects by preventing research participants from knowing whether they are receiving the active drug or a placebo. In **single-blind studies**, only the participants are kept in the dark. In **double-blind studies**, both the participants and the experimenters (prescribing physicians and other researchers) are "blinded" (kept uninformed) with respect to which participants are receiving the active drug. Keeping the experimenters "blind" helps prevent their own expectancies from affecting the results.

Unfortunately, the "blinds" in many double-blind studies are more like venetian blinds with the slats slightly open; that is, participants and experimenters are often able to tell whether a participant received a placebo or an active drug (Perlis et al., 2010; Schulz et al., 2010). Active drugs often have telltale side effects that give them away. Still, when conducted properly, the double-blind, randomized study is among the strongest research methods and is widely considered the "gold standard" when it comes to evaluating new medications (Perlis et al., 2010). To learn more about research methods, see the nearby *Try This Out.*

single-blind studies In drug research, studies in which subjects are kept uninformed about whether they are receiving the experimental drug or a placebo.

double-blind studies In drug research, studies in which both participants and experimenters are kept uninformed about which participants are receiving the active drug and which are receiving the placebo.

Anatomy of a Research Study: Do Warm Hands Make a Warm Heart?

Psychologists recognize that subtle cues in the environment influence our behavior, even if we are not fully aware of them. For example, we may suddenly feel warm feelings when exposed to environmental cues such as the whiff of a scent or the way light bounces off a ceiling, which could resemble cues associated with pleasant experiences in the past.

Do warm hands make for a warm heart? Yale University psychologists tested whether holding a warm object affects judgments people make about the warmth or coldness of a target person. What do you think they found?

Might having warm hands serve as a subtle cue for detecting a warm heart? Investigators Lawrence Williams and John Bargh at Yale University put the question to the test by examining whether the physical experience of warmth would influence a person's judgments about whether someone else is "warm" or "cold," even without the person's awareness of this influence. In other words, does holding a hot object affect how you perceive the warmth of another person? Here, we go under the hood to examine the workings of the experiment.

Study Hypothesis (What They Predicted Would Occur)

A scientific hypothesis is a predicted outcome, but it is far from a wild guess. Hypotheses are informed by a careful review of theory and prior research. Psychologists have long recognized that early life experiences of being warmly held and comforted by a parent or trusting caregiver forges a link between physical warmth and psychological warmth. The Yale psychologists hypothesized that the tactile experience of physical warmth would activate associated feelings of interpersonal warmth that would influence the judgments people make about the warmth of a target individual.

TRY THIS OUT
Getting Involved

You can learn about psychological research firsthand by volunteering as a research subject or a research assistant. Most psychology departments provide opportunities for students to participate in faculty research as subjects, research assistants, or both. Ask your instructor or department chairperson about how you can participate. Serving as a research assistant will provide you with a front-row view of cutting-edge developments in the field and with opportunities to obtain valuable research experience, which you may need when applying for jobs or admission to graduate school.

Procedure (What They Did and How They Did It)

The study sample consisted of 41 undergraduates who averaged 18.5 years of age. The investigators needed to create a ruse so that participants would not recognize that physical (tactile) warmth was the independent (experimental) variable of interest. The ruse involved priming participants by having them hold either a cup of hot coffee or a cup of iced coffee. To pull this off, a female lab assistant met each participant in the lobby of the psychology building. The assistant carried a cup of coffee (either hot or iced) along with a clipboard and two textbooks. Taking the elevator together to the fourth-floor laboratory, the assistant quite casually asked the participant to hold the cup for a second so she could free her hands to record the participant's name and time of participation. The assistant then took back the coffee cup.

Once the participant arrived at the laboratory, he or she was asked to complete a personality impression questionnaire based on a hypothetical "Person A" who was described as intelligent, skillful, industrious, determined, practical, and cautious. The participant then rated the hypothetical person on five personality traits associated with the psychological concept of warmth and on five other traits unrelated to psychological warmth. Participants rated these personality traits of the hypothetical person using a seven-point scale. Bear in mind that all participants completed the same questionnaire; the only difference was that some were first primed by holding a warm object (i.e., cup of hot coffee) while others were primed by holding a cold object (i.e., cup of iced coffee).

Results and Discussion (What They Found and What It Means)

The dependent variable was a composite (averaged) score of the five scales measuring the warm-cold dimension of personality. The independent variable was the manipulation of warmth based on holding either a cup of hot coffee or a cup of iced coffee. Consistent with the hypothesis, statistical analysis showed that participants who had held the hot coffee cup rated the target person as significantly warmer than did those who had held the cold coffee. The term "significantly" is used here in the statistical sense that differences in ratings between participants in the hot and cold coffee conditions were relatively unlikely to have been due to chance. The average (mean) score on the composite warmth measure was 4.71 (out of a possible 7) for those participants who had held the hot coffee, as compared with an average (mean) score of 4.25 for participants who had held the iced coffee (see ■ Figure 1.9).

The independent variable did not affect ratings on traits unrelated to the warm-cold dimension, which suggests that physical warmth did not simply boost positive ratings of personality overall but was limited to ratings of a person's warmth. In summary, the Yale investigators found that tactile warmth influences personality judgments of warmth without direct awareness of such influences.

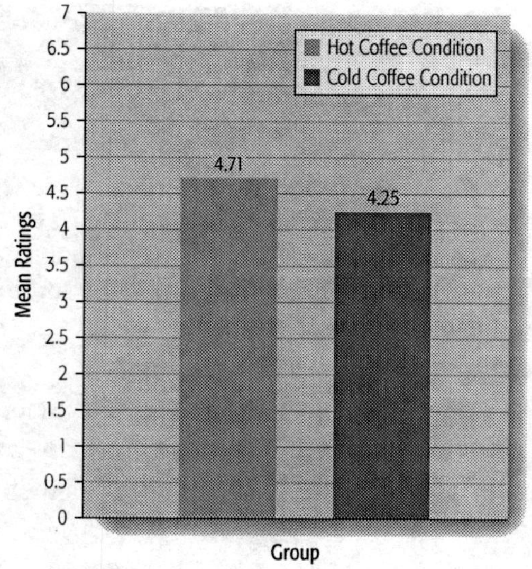

Figure 1.9 Composite Ratings of Warmth
Scores are based on a seven-point scale, with higher scores indicative of greater perceived warmth of a target person based on five dimensions indicative of warmth.

Citing References

Psychologists use a particular style for citing references that was developed by the American Psychological Association. ■ Figure 1.10 shows the reference style for journal articles, using the Yale study as an example.

Before you move on, review Concept Chart 1.3, which summarizes the research methods we have discussed.

Ethical Principles in Psychological Research

Psychologists subscribe to a code of ethics that respects the dignity and welfare of their clients and those who participate in their research studies. This code recognizes that people have a basic right to make their own decisions and to exercise choices, including the choice of whether to participate in psychological research. Ethical guidelines also prohibit psychologists from using methods that would harm research participants or clients (American Psychological Association, 2002).

People who participate in experiments may be harmed not only by physical interventions, such as experimental drugs that have adverse effects, but also by psychological interventions, such as being goaded into aggressive behavior that leads to feelings of guilt or shame. Invasions of privacy are another concern.

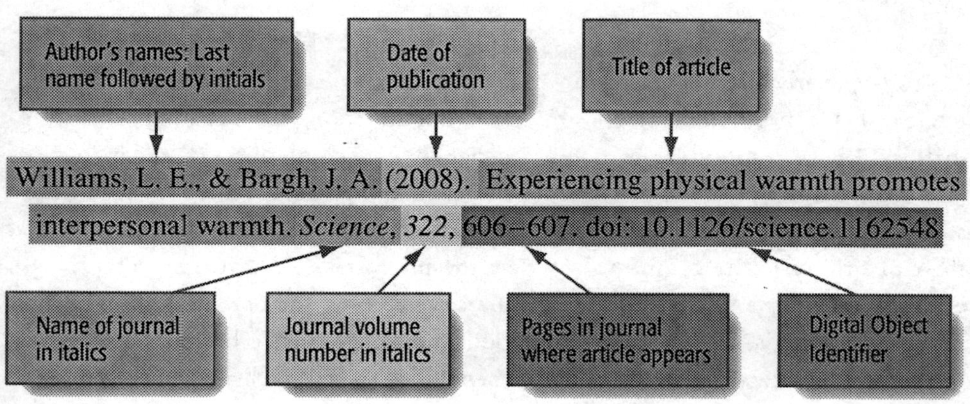

Figure 1.10 APA Reference Style

CONCEPT CHART 1.3 How Psychologists Do Research

What Researchers Do	Key Features/Limitations	Examples: Applying Research Methods to the Study of Love
Case study method: Researcher interviews or observes an individual (or small group of individuals) or examines historical records of the lives of particular individuals.	Accuracy may be jeopardized by gaps or errors in people's memories or attempts to leave a favorable impression on the researcher.	Psychologists might study the reasons people choose their mates by conducting in-depth interviews with married couples.
Survey method: Researcher uses questionnaires or interviews to obtain information about a particular group of people.	Results of surveys may be compromised by social desirability and volunteer biases.	Psychologists might use a questionnaire to survey thousands of people about the factors that influenced their choice of mates.
Naturalistic observation method: Researcher observes behavior in the field—that is, where it occurs naturally.	Special care is taken not to interfere with behaviors the researcher is observing. Researchers need to allow participants to become accustomed to their presence before beginning observations.	Psychologists might observe from a distance how lovers walk together and how they look at each other.
Correlational method: Researcher uses statistical methods to describe positive and negative relationships (correlations) between variables.	Correlational research may point to possible causal factors, but does not demonstrate cause-and-effect relationships.	Psychologists might study relationships between feelings of love, self-esteem, and sexual satisfaction.
Experimental method: Researcher manipulates one or more independent variables or factors and observes their effects on one or more dependent (measured) variables.	Used to establish cause-and-effect relationships between independent and dependent variables. Experimental groups receive an experimental treatment, whereas control groups do not. All other conditions are held constant. Random assignment helps ensure that groups do not differ in other characteristics that might affect the outcome.	Psychologists might expose dating partners to an arousing experience (experimental treatment), such as watching an emotionally powerful movie, and then measure the effects on partners' feelings toward each other. The control group might watch a neutral movie.

How do psychologists study love? Let us count the ways.

© AISPIX/Shutterstock.com

ethics review committees Committees that evaluate whether proposed studies meet ethical guidelines.

Today, nearly all institutions in which biomedical and behavioral research is conducted, such as hospitals, colleges, and research foundations, have **ethics review committees**. These committees, which are generally called institutional review boards (IRBs), are usually composed of professionals and laypersons. They must put their stamp of approval on all research proposals before the research can be carried out at their institutions. The committees review the proposals to see if they comply with ethical guidelines and advise the researchers concerning the potential harm of their proposed methods. In cases where individuals may experience harm or discomfort, the committees must weigh the potential benefits of the research against the potential harm. If the committees believe that the proposed research might be unacceptably harmful, they will withhold approval.

CONCEPT 1.33
Psychologists engaged in research must follow ethical guidelines that are designed to protect the welfare of research participants.

One of the foremost ethical requirements is that investigators obtain **informed consent** from research participants before they begin participating in the study. This means that participants must be given enough information about the study's methods and purposes to make an "informed" decision about whether they wish to participate. Participants must also be free to withdraw from the study at any time.

informed consent Agreement to participate in a study following disclosure of information about the purposes and nature of the study and its potential risks and benefits.

Many studies of historic importance in psychology, including the famous Milgram studies on obedience to authority (see Chapter 14), have required that subjects be deceived as to the true purposes of the study. The APA's *Ethical Principles of Psychologists and Code of Conduct* (American Psychological Association, 2002) specifies the conditions that psychologists must meet to use deceptive practices in research. These conditions include a determination that the research is justified by its scientific, educational, or practical value; that no nondeceptive alternative research strategy is possible; that research participants are not misled about any research that can reasonably be expected to result in physical harm or severe emotional distress; and that participants receive an explanation of the deception at the earliest time that it is feasible to do so.

Psychologists must also protect the *confidentiality* of the records of research participants and of the clients they treat (Fisher, 2008). That is, they must respect people's right to privacy. There are situations, however, when laws require psychologists to disclose confidential information acquired in research or clinical practice, as when a participant or a therapy client threatens to do physical harm to someone else.

Ethical guidelines also extend to the use of animals in psychological research. The design of research projects often precludes the use of human participants, and in such cases the researchers use animals as subjects. For example, to determine which behaviors are instinctive and which are not, scientists have reared birds and fish in isolation from other members of their species; such research could not be conducted with humans because of the harmful effects of separating infants from their families. Scientists routinely test experimental drugs on animals to determine harmful effects before human trials are begun. And those who study the brain may destroy parts of the brains of laboratory animals, such as rats and monkeys, to learn how these parts of the brain are connected with behavior. (In Chapter 8, you will see how the surgical destruction of particular parts of the brain causes laboratory animals to either overeat or stop eating completely.)

Issues concerning the ethical treatment of animals in research studies have risen to the fore in recent years. On one side of the debate are those who argue that significant advances in medicine and psychology could not have occurred without such research. Yet others argue that it is unethical to kill animals or expose them to pain, regardless of the potential benefits of the research to humans. According to APA ethical guidelines, animals may not be harmed or subjected to stress unless there is no alternative way to conduct the research and the goals of the research are justified by their intended scientific, educational, or practical value (American Psychological Association, 2002). Researchers must also obtain approval from their institutional review boards to ensure that ethical practices are followed.

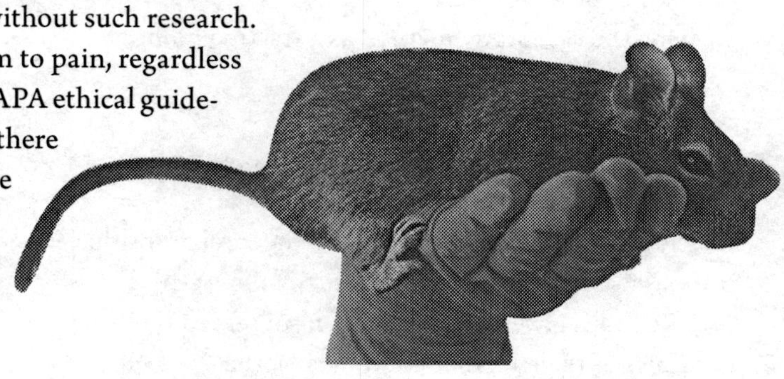

© cubephoto, 2009/Shutterstock.com

1.3 MODULE REVIEW Research Methods in Psychology

Recite It

What are the basic objectives of science?

- The basic objectives are description, explanation, prediction, and control of events or variables.

What is the scientific method, and what are its four general steps?

- The scientific method is a set of guiding principles that directs the scientific process.
- The scientific method comprises four general steps that guide research: (1) developing a research question, (2) formulating a hypothesis, (3) gathering evidence, and (4) drawing conclusions.

What major research methods do psychologists use?

- These include the case study method, the survey method, the naturalistic observation method, the correlational method, and the experimental method.

What ethical guidelines must psychologists follow in their research?

- Psychologists are committed to following ethical guidelines that promote the dignity of the individual, human welfare, and scientific integrity.
- Psychologists are precluded from using methods that harm research participants or clients and must receive approval of their research protocols from institutional review boards before undertaking research with humans or animals.

Recall It

1. Which of the following is *not* one of the four general steps in the scientific method?
   a. developing a research question.
   b. testing the hypothesis.
   c. using the case study method as a starting point of investigation.
   d. drawing conclusions.
2. A distinct advantage of the naturalistic observation method, when used correctly, is that it
   a. allows us to establish cause-and-effect relationships.
   b. does not require experimenters to follow ethical guidelines governing other forms of research.
   c. allows us to generate hypotheses on the basis of intensive study of a person's life experiences.
   d. provides a view of behavior that occurs in natural settings.
3. Which research method is best suited to providing evidence of cause-and-effect relationships?
4. In the study by Williams and Bargh, judgments of the warmth of a target person were influenced by
   a. perceptions of coldness.
   b. the method used to rate warmness.
   c. holding a coffee cup.
   d. tactile sensations of warmth.
5. Ethical guidelines in psychological research
   a. provide a set of rules that govern research when obtaining approval from ethics review committees would cause critical delays in a project.
   b. are designed to protect research participants from physical or psychological harm.
   c. permit researchers to violate the principle of informed consent when experiments cannot be performed in accordance with that principle.
   d. are a set of standards that apply to human research but not animal research.

Think About It

- Perhaps you won't be surprised by research findings that adolescents with tattoos are more likely to engage in riskier behavior than their nontattooed peers (Roberts & Ryan, 2002). Tattooed youth are more likely to smoke cigarettes, engage in binge drinking, use marijuana, and join gangs. But does tattooing cause these risky behaviors? Can you think of other possible explanations for links between tattooing and high-risk behavior?
- Can you think of another example in which two variables are correlated but not causally related?
- Suppose you were interested in studying the relationship between alcohol use and grades among college students, but you couldn't experimentally control whether students used alcohol or how much they used. How might you use correlational methods to study this relationship? What might be the value of this type of research? Would you be able to conclude that alcohol use affects grades? Why or why not?

Becoming a Critical Thinker

APPLICATION MODULE 1.4

CONCEPT 1.34
Critical thinking involves adopting a skeptical, questioning attitude toward commonly held beliefs and assumptions, and weighing arguments in terms of the available evidence.

critical thinking The adoption of a skeptical, questioning attitude and careful scrutiny of claims or arguments.

Critical thinking involves adopting a questioning attitude in which you weigh evidence carefully and apply thoughtful analysis in probing the claims and arguments of others. It is a way of evaluating information by maintaining a skeptical attitude toward what you hear and read—even what you read in the pages of this text.

Critical thinking requires a willingness to challenge conventional wisdom and common knowledge that many of us take for granted. When you think critically, you maintain an open mind and suspend belief until you can obtain and evaluate evidence that either supports or refutes a particular claim or statement. You find *reasons* to support your beliefs, rather than relying on impressions or "gut feelings." In this text, you'll be able to hone your critical thinking skills by answering the questions posed in the "Thinking Critically About Psychology" sections that appear at the end of every chapter.

Features of Critical Thinking

Critical thinkers maintain a healthy skepticism. They question assumptions and claims made by others and demand to see the evidence upon which conclusions are based. Here are some suggestions for thinking critically about psychology:

© -vector-illustration-/Shutterstock.com

1. *Question everything.* Critical thinkers do not blindly accept the validity of claims made by others, even claims made by authority figures, such as political or religious leaders, scientists, or even textbook authors. They keep an open mind and weigh the evidence on which claims are made.
2. *Clarify what you mean.* Whether a claim is true or false may depend on how we define the terms we use. Consider the claim "Stress is bad for you." If we define stress only in terms of the pressures and hassles of daily life, then perhaps there is some truth to that claim. But if we define stress more broadly to include any events that impose a pressure on us to adjust, even positive events such as the birth of a child or a promotion at work, then certain kinds of stress may actually be desirable (see Chapter 12). Perhaps we even need a certain amount of stress to be active and alert.
3. *Avoid oversimplifying.* Consider the claim "Alcoholism is inherited." In Chapter 4, we review evidence indicating that genetic factors may contribute to alcoholism. But the origins of alcoholism, as well as the origins of many other psychological and physical disorders, are more complex. Genetics alone does not tell the whole story. Many disorders involve the interplay of biological, psychological, and environmental factors, the nature of which we are only beginning to unravel.
4. *Avoid overgeneralizing.* People from China and Japan and other East Asian cultures tend to be more reserved about disclosing information about themselves

to strangers than are Americans or Europeans (see Chapter 14). Yet this doesn't mean that every person from these East Asian cultures is more withholding, or that every American or European is more disclosing.

5. *Don't confuse correlation with causation.* As you'll see in Chapter 10, girls who show earlier signs of puberty than their peers (e.g., early breast development) tend to have lower self-esteem, a more negative body image, and more emotional problems. But do physical changes associated with early puberty cause these negative psychological consequences, or might other factors be involved in explaining these links, such as how people react to these changes?
6. *Consider the assumptions on which claims are based.* Consider the claim that homosexuality is a psychological disorder. The claim rests in part on underlying assumptions about the nature of psychological disorders. What is a psychological disorder? What criteria are used to determine whether someone has a psychological disorder? Do gays, lesbians, or people with a bisexual sexual orientation meet these criteria? Is there evidence to support these assertions? In Chapter 15, you will see that mental health professionals no longer classify homosexuality as a psychological disorder.
7. *Examine sources of claims.* In their publications, scientists cite the sources on which they base their claims. (See this book's References section, which cites the sources used in its preparation.) When examining source citations, note such features as publication dates (to determine whether the sources are outdated or current) and the journals or other periodicals in which the sources have appeared (to see whether they are well-respected scientific journals or questionable sources). Source citations allow readers to check the original sources for themselves to see if the information provided is accurate.
8. *Question the evidence on which claims are based.* Are claims based on sound scientific evidence or on anecdotes and personal testimonials that cannot be independently verified? In Chapter 6, we consider the controversy over so-called recovered memories—memories of childhood sexual abuse that suddenly reappear during adulthood, usually during the course of psychotherapy or hypnosis. Are such memories accurate? Or might they be tales spun of imaginary thread?
9. *Consider alternative ways of explaining claims.* Do you believe in the existence of extrasensory perception (ESP)? Some people claim to have extrasensory skills that enable them, simply by using their minds, to read other people's minds, to transmit their thoughts to others, or to move objects or change their shapes. Are such claims believable? Or might more mundane explanations account for these strange phenomena, such as coincidence, deliberate fabrication, or sleight-of-hand? In Chapter 3, we consider the case of a psychic who claims to have relied on her extrasensory ability in finding a missing person. Was it ESP? Or might there be other explanations?

© sandy young / Alamy

Think critically about online information. Check out the credibility of the source of the material and be wary of information provided by companies or marketers seeking to promote or sell particular products or services.

Thinking Critically About Online Information

One of the features of the Internet is that any user can post information that others can access. Yet this freedom carries with it the risk that the information posted may be inaccurate. For example, investigators find that while most health information on health-related websites is generally accurate, it is often incomplete and difficult for many people to understand (Berland et al., 2001; Benotsch, Kalichman, & Weinhardt, 2004).

Critical thinkers don't suspend their skeptical attitude when they go online. They check out the credentials of the source by asking questions such as: Who is posting the material? Is the source a well-respected institution? Or is it an individual or group of individuals with no apparent credentials and perhaps with an axe to grind?

The most trustworthy online information comes from well-known scientific sources, such as leading scientific journals, government agencies like the National Institutes of Health, and major professional organizations like the American Psychological Association (APA) and the Association for Psychological Science (APS). One reason articles in scientific journals are so trustworthy is that they undergo a process of peer review in which independent scientists carefully scrutinize them before they are accepted for publication. Many leading scientific organizations provide links to abstracts (brief descriptions) of recent works. Much of this information is available without charge.

Sad to say, many people never question the information that comes to them on the printed page or on their computer screens. But as a critical thinker, you *can* evaluate assertions and claims for yourself. The critical thinking sections found at the end of each chapter give you an opportunity to sharpen your critical thinking skills.

Thinking Critically About Psychology

Here is the first critical thinking exercise you will encounter in this text. Based on your reading of the chapter, answer the following questions. Then, to evaluate your progress in developing critical thinking skills, compare your answers with the sample answers in Appendix A.

An experimenter claims that listening to a professor's lectures while you sleep can help improve your grades. The experimenter based this conclusion on the following data.

The experimenter invited students in a large introductory psychology class to participate in a study in which they would be given audiotapes of the professor's lectures and asked to play them back while they slept. Each of the 36 students who agreed to participate received a specially equipped audiotape player. Secured in the machine with tamper-proof sealing tape were recordings of each lecture given in the two weeks before the final examination. The tape played automatically two hours after the students went to bed. At other times, the play button was deactivated so that the students could not play the tape.

After the final examination, the experimenter compared the grades of the participating students with those of a group of students selected from the same class who had not participated in the study. The results showed that participating students achieved higher test grades.

1. Do you believe the experimenter's claims are justified? Why or why not?
2. What other factors might account for the observed differences in test scores between the two groups?
3. How might you design the study differently to strengthen the experimenter's conclusion?

Log in to CengageBrain to access the resources your instructor requires. For this book, you can access:

CourseMate

Psychology CourseMate brings course concepts to life with interactive learning, study, and exam preparation tools that support the printed textbook. A textbook-specific website, Psychology CourseMate includes an integrated interactive eBook and other interactive learning tools including quizzes, flashcards, videos, and more.

CENGAGENOW

CengageNow is an easy-to-use online resource that helps you study in less time to get the grade you want—NOW. Take a pre-test for this chapter and receive a personalized study plan based on your results that will identify the topics you need to review and direct you to online resources to help you master those topics. Then take a post-test to help you determine the concepts you have mastered and what you will need to work on. If your textbook does not include an access code card, go to CengageBrain.com to gain access.

Visit www.cengagebrain.com to access your account and purchase materials.

VISUAL OVERVIEW Chapter 1 The Science of Psychology

MODULE 1.1 Foundations of Modern Psychology

© INTERFOTO / Alamy

Wilhelm Wundt

Early Schools of Psychology

- **Wilhelm Wundt and Structuralism**: Breaking down mental experience into its components parts
- **William James and Functionalism**: Behavior tied to function
- **John Watson and Behaviorism**: Psychology as the science of observable behavior
- **Max Wertheimer and Gestalt Psychology**: "The whole is greater than the sum of the parts"
- **Sigmund Freud and Psychoanalysis**: Exploring the unconscious

Contemporary Perspectives in Psychology

- **Behavioral**: Focuses on role of learning in explaining observable behavior
- **Psychodynamic**: Explores unconscious influences of unconscious conflicts on behavior
- **Humanistic**: Focuses on conscious experience and self-awareness
- **Physiological**: Focuses on the biological underpinnings of behavior
- **Cognitive**: Explores the mental processes by which we acquire knowledge of the world
- **Sociocultural**: Explores how behavior is influenced by social and cultural factors

MODULE 1.2 Psychologists: Who They Are and What They Do

Specialty Areas of Psychology

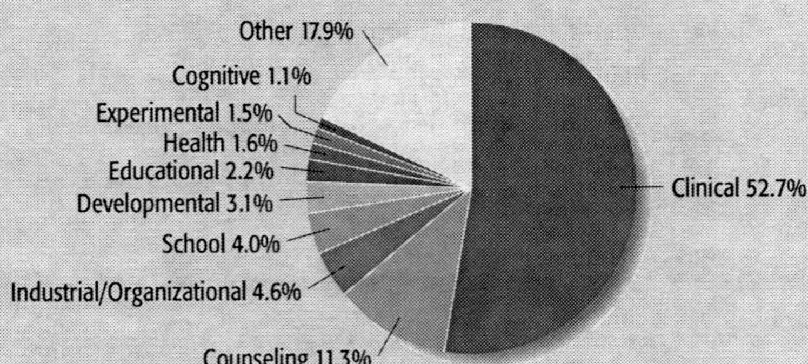

Ethnicities of Doctorate Recipients in Psychology:

Field becoming more diverse, but is still predominantly comprised of whites of European descent

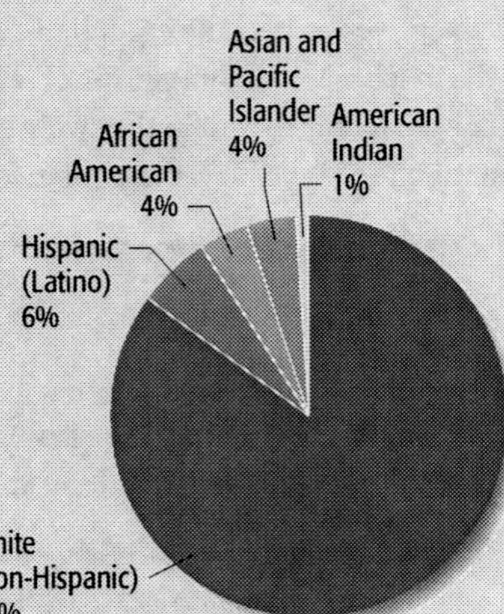

Emerging Specialty Areas

Neuropsychology
Geropsychology
Forensic psychology
Sport psychology

MODULE 1.3 Research Methods in Psychology

The Scientific Method

A framework for acquiring knowledge through careful observation and experimentation, comprising four general steps:

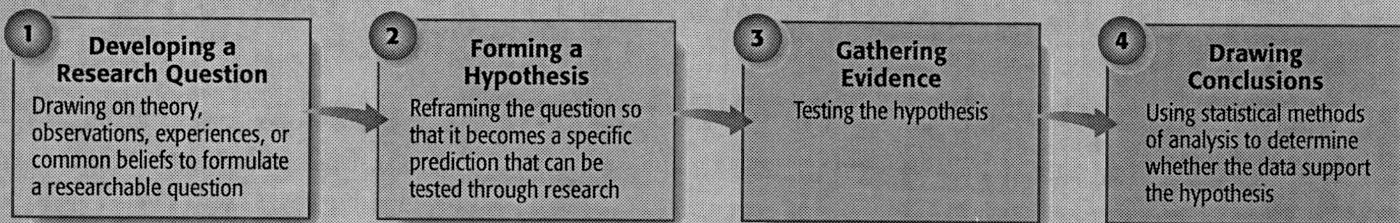

General Steps in the Scientific Method

Gathering Evidence: Types of Research Methods

- **Case Study Method**: Intensive study of individuals
- **Survey Method**: Measuring opinions and attitudes
- **Naturalistic Observation Method**: Taking research into the field
- **Correlational Method**: Examining relationships between variables
- **Experimental Method**: Exploring cause-and-effect relationships by manipulating independent variables and measuring their effects on dependent variables

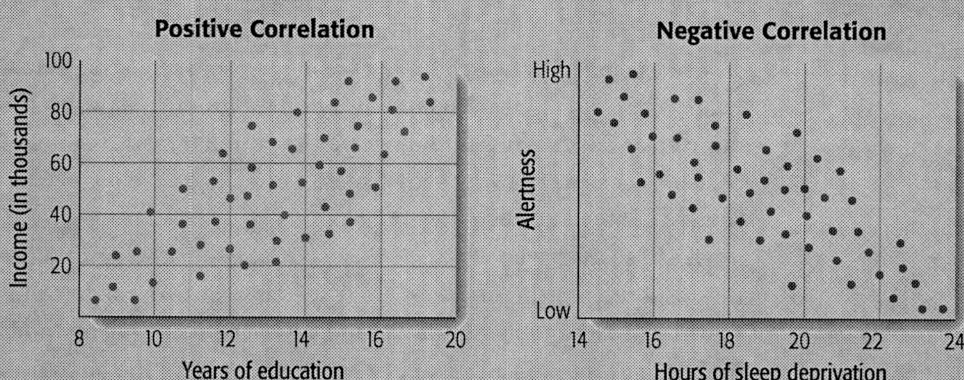

Generally speaking, people with higher levels of education tend to earn higher incomes.

Generally speaking, the longer a person is deprived of sleep, the less alert the person is likely to be.

Correlational Relationships

2 Biological Foundations of Behavior

Do You Have Shopping on the Brain?

An MRI scanner may be about as far removed from a shopping mall as you can imagine, but it was used in a kind of mock shopping mall in a recent study (Knutson et al., 2007). While participants were having their brains scanned, they were shown pictures of consumer products along with the prices, which were set at about 75 percent below retail value—a real bargain. The participants were then asked to think about whether they would like a chance to buy some of these products, using a $40 stash provided by the experimenters.

The investigators wanted to see what happens in the brain at the moment someone decides, "Yes, I want to buy that." They discovered that a particular cluster of nerve cells in the brain became active a moment before people made a conscious decision to buy a particular item. These brain cells form part of the brain's reward circuitry, a dense network of interconnected nerve cells that produce feelings of pleasure associated with many of life's pleasurable activities, such as consuming a good meal, partying, watching an exciting movie, or enjoying sexual relations. In effect, deciding to buy a desired product activates the same brain pathways as those involved in producing other states of pleasure. This may be why people often experience a feeling of pleasurable excitement when they shop.

Brain scans have long been used to evaluate pathological conditions affecting the brain, as we'll see later in this chapter. But now researchers are beginning to use advanced scanning methods to peer into the working brain to better understand the biological bases of ordinary behaviors such as shopping. We can even imagine the possibility, in the not-too-distant future, that scientists may discover ways of tamping down these reward networks to help people who pile up huge credit card bills exercise greater restraint whenever they visit the mall (Tierney, 2007).

In this chapter, we take an inward journey of discovery to explore the biological bases of behavior. We study the organization and workings of the human brain, the most remarkable feat of engineering ever achieved. It is small enough to hold in your hands and weighs a mere three pounds. The brain is a living

(*Continued on page 46*)

DID YOU KNOW THAT...

- The brain (and the rest of the nervous system) run on electricity? (p. 50)
- Nerve impulses don't actually jump from one nerve cell to another, but are ferried by chemical messengers? (p. 46)
- Our bodies produce natural painkillers that are chemically similar to morphine and other narcotic drugs? (p. 53)
- Sometimes it's better not to use our brains before we respond? (p. 56)
- The brain functions in a way that makes it impossible for you to tickle yourself? (p. 68)
- The likelihood of your hair swirling in a clockwise or counterclockwise direction is related to whether you are right-handed or left-handed? (p. 73)
- A man survived an accident in which a thick metal rod was driven through his skull, but his personality changed so much that people thought he no longer was himself? (p. 73)

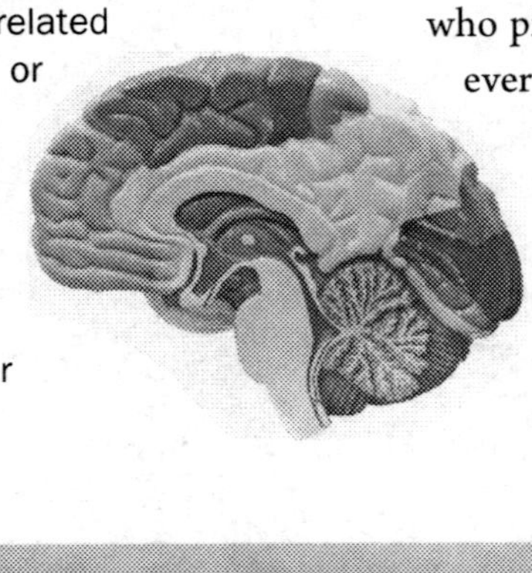

© DDCoral/BigStockPhoto.com

Learning Objectives

By reading this chapter you will be able to . . .

1 **IDENTIFY** the parts of the neuron, **DESCRIBE** the functions of these parts, and **EXPLAIN** how neurons communicate with each other.

2 **IDENTIFY** key neurotransmitters and **DESCRIBE** their functions.

3 **EXPLAIN** how an action potential is generated.

4 **EXPLAIN** the difference between agonists and antagonists and **DESCRIBE** the effects of these types of drugs on particular neurotransmitters.

5 **DESCRIBE** how the nervous system is organized and the functions of its various parts.

6 **IDENTIFY** major brain structures and **DESCRIBE** how the brain is organized and the roles that particular brain structures play in behavior.

7 **IDENTIFY** and **DESCRIBE** the methods scientists use to study the workings of the brain.

8 **EXPLAIN** how the two halves of the brain differ in their functions.

9 **APPLY** knowledge of the endocrine system to the roles of hormones in behavior.

10 **IDENTIFY** and **DESCRIBE** the methods scientists use to study the roles of genes and the environment in behavior.

11 **EVALUATE** the influence of genetics on personality and behavior.

12 **APPLY** knowledge of brain-scanning techniques to detecting memory circuits, measuring personality traits, screening job applicants, shopping, and solving problems.

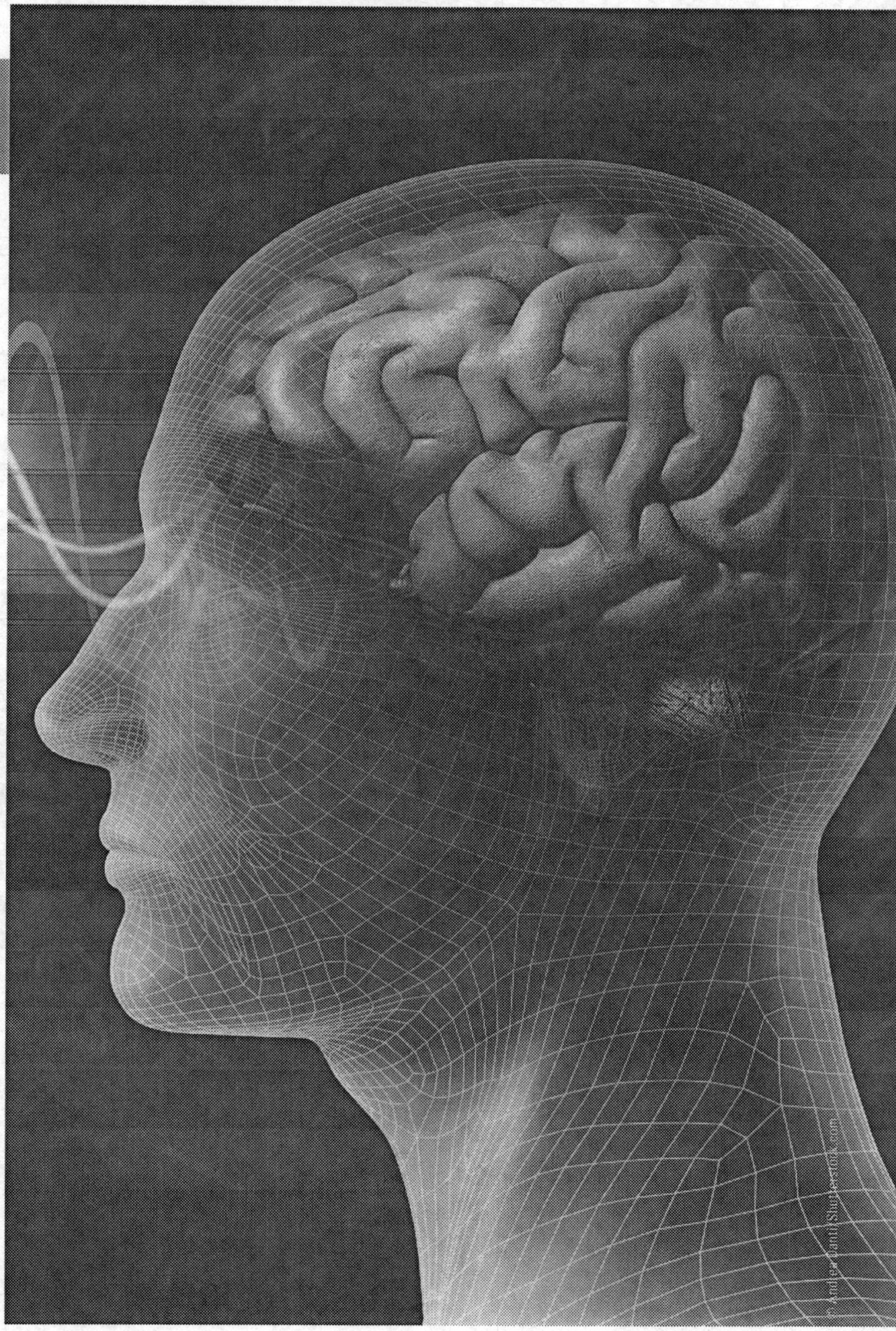

Preview

(*Continued from page 44*)

supercomputer, but one far more elegant and sophisticated than any machine Silicon Valley wizards could hope to create. Even the most advanced computers lack the capacity for basic insights and creativity performed by the human brain. What computer has written noteworthy music or a decent poem? What computer is aware of itself or aware that it even exists? Such wonders remain the stuff of science fiction. We begin this inward journey by first studying the structure and workings of the basic unit of the nervous system—the nerve cell, or *neuron*.

To perform its many functions, the brain needs to communicate with the senses and other parts of the body. It does so through an information superhighway that took millions of years to construct. This complex network, of which the brain is a part, is called the nervous system.

MODULE 2.1

Neurons: The Body's Wiring

- What is a neuron?
- What are the parts of a neuron?
- What are the types of neurons and types of cells found in the nervous system?
- How is a neural impulse generated and transmitted from one neuron to another?
- What roles do neurotransmitters play in psychological functioning?

neurons Nerve cells.

brain The mass of nerve tissue encased in the skull that controls virtually everything we are and everything we do.

Neurons do wondrous things, such as informing your **brain** when light strikes your eye and carrying messages from the brain that command your muscles to raise your arms and your heart to pump blood. They also enable you to think, plan, even to dream. They enable you to read this page and to wonder what will turn up in the next paragraph.

In this module, we first look at the structure of an individual neuron and then observe how neurons communicate with one another to transmit information within the nervous system.

The Structure of the Neuron

soma The cell body of a neuron that contains the nucleus of the cell and carries out the cell's metabolic functions.

axon The tubelike part of a neuron that carries messages away from the cell body toward other neurons.

CONCEPT 2.1
Neurons are the basic building blocks of the nervous system—the body's wiring through which messages are transmitted within the nervous system.

Neurons, the basic building blocks of the nervous system, are body cells that are specialized for transmitting information or messages. They transmit messages through the brain and nerve pathways of the body in the form of small electrical impulses. These electrical signals relay information from the sense organs to the brain and commands from the brain to muscles, glands, and other organs throughout the body.

Each neuron is a single cell, consisting of a cell body (or *soma*), an axon, and dendrites. ■ Figure 2.1 illustrates these structures; Concept Chart 2.1 summarizes their functions. The **soma** is the main body of the cell. It houses the cell nucleus, which contains the cell's genetic material and carries out the *metabolic*, or life-sustaining, functions of the cell. Each neuron also has an **axon**, a long cable that projects trunklike from the soma and conducts outgoing messages to other neurons.

The axons of the neurons in your brain may be only a few thousandths of an inch long. Other axons, such as those that run from your spinal cord to your toes, are several

Figure 2.1 The Neuron
① A neuron or nerve cell consists of a cell body, or soma, which houses the cell nucleus; an axon, which carries the neural message; and dendrites, which receive messages from adjacent neurons. ② Terminal buttons are swellings at the end of the axon from which neurotransmitter molecules are released to ferry the message to other neurons. ③ Axons of many neurons are covered with a myelin sheath, which is a type of insulating layer that helps speed transmission of neural impulses.

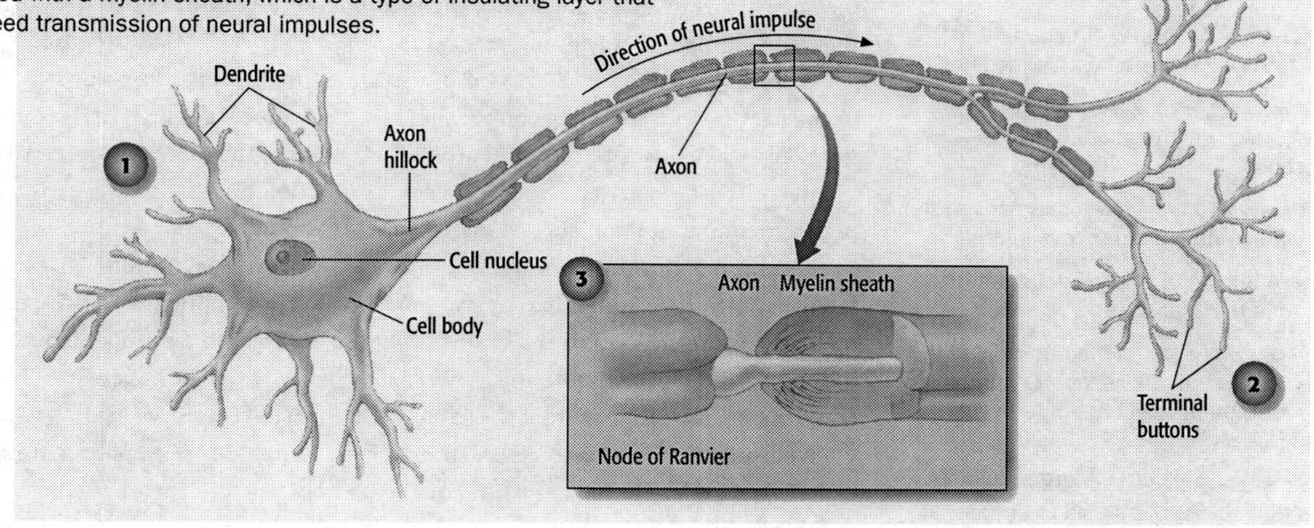

feet long. Axons may branch off like the stems of plants, fanning out in different directions. At the ends of these branches are knoblike swellings called **terminal buttons**. It is here that chemicals called **neurotransmitters** are stored and released. These chemicals are synthesized in the soma and ferry outgoing messages to neighboring neurons across the **synapse**, a tiny gap that separates one neuron from another (the word *synapse* comes from Greek roots meaning "joining together" or "clasping together").

Dendrites are treelike structures that project from the soma. Dendrites have receptor sites, or docking stations, that receive neurotransmitters carrying messages released by neighboring neurons. Each neuron may receive messages from thousands of other neurons through its dendrites (Priebe & Ferster, 2010).

The nervous system has three types of neurons: sensory neurons, motor neurons, and interneurons. These different types play specialized roles in the nervous system.

Sensory neurons (also called *afferent neurons*) transmit information about the outside world to the spinal cord and brain. This information first registers on your sensory organs. So when someone touches your hand, sensory receptors within the skin transmit the message through sensory neurons to the spinal cord and brain, where

terminal buttons Swellings at the tips of axons from which neurotransmitters are dispatched into the synapse.

neurotransmitters Chemical messengers that transport nerve impulses from one nerve cell to another.

synapse The small fluid-filled gap between neurons through which neurotransmitters carry neural impulses.

dendrites Rootlike structures at the end of axons that receive neural impulses from neighboring neurons.

sensory neurons Neurons that transmit information from sensory organs, muscles, and inner organs to the spinal cord and brain.

CONCEPT CHART 2.1 Parts of the Neuron

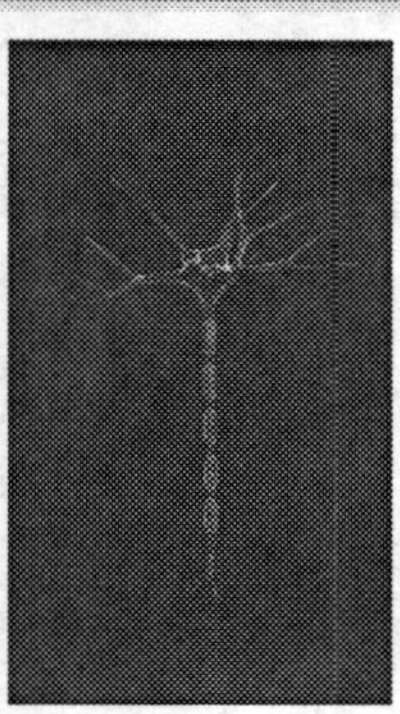
© sgame/Shutterstock.com

Part	Description	Functions
Soma	Cell body containing the nucleus	Performs metabolic, or life-sustaining, functions of the cell
Axon	Long cable projecting from the soma	Carries neural impulses to the terminal buttons
Terminal buttons	Swellings at ends of axons	Release chemicals, called neurotransmitters, that carry neural messages to adjacent neurons
Dendrites	Fibers that project from the soma	Receive messages from neighboring neurons

the information is processed, resulting in the feeling of touch. Sensory neurons also carry information from your muscles and inner organs to your spinal cord and brain.

motor neurons Neurons that convey nerve impulses from the central nervous system to muscles and glands.

glands Body organs or structures that produce secretions called hormones.

hormones Secretions from endocrine glands that help regulate bodily processes.

interneurons Nerve cells within the central nervous system that process information.

nerve A bundle of axons from different neurons that transmit nerve impulses.

glial cells Small but numerous cells in the nervous system that support neurons and form the myelin sheath found on many axons.

myelin sheath A layer of protective insulation that covers the axons of certain neurons and helps speed transmission of nerve impulses.

nodes of Ranvier Gaps in the myelin sheath that create noninsulated areas along the axon.

multiple sclerosis (MS) A disease of the central nervous system in which the myelin sheath that insulates axons is damaged or destroyed.

Motor neurons (also called *efferent neurons*) convey messages from the brain and spinal cord to the muscles that control the movements of your body. They also convey messages to your **glands**, causing them to release **hormones**—chemical substances that help regulate bodily processes.

Interneurons (also called *associative neurons*) are the most common type of neuron in the nervous system. They connect neurons to neurons. In the spinal cord, they connect sensory neurons to motor neurons. In the brain, they form complex assemblages of interconnected nerve cells that process information from sensory organs and control higher mental functions, such as planning and thinking.

A neuron is not the same thing as a nerve. A **nerve** is a bundle of axons from different neurons. An individual nerve—for example, the optic nerve, which transmits messages from the eyes to the brain—contains more than a million axons. Although individual axons are microscopic, a nerve may be visible to the naked eye. The cell bodies of the neurons that contain the axons are not part of the nerve itself.

Neurons are not the only cells in the nervous system. More numerous are small cells called **glial cells**. They act as a kind of glue to hold neurons together. The word *glial* is derived from the Greek word for "glue." Glial cells also support the nervous system by nourishing neurons, removing their waste products, and possibly may assist them in communicating with one another (Kriegstein & Alvarez-Buylla, 2009; Smith, 2010).

Glial cells serve yet another important function: They form the **myelin sheath**, a fatty layer of cells that—like the insulation that wraps around electrical wires—acts as a protective shield on many axons. The insulation provided by the myelin sheath helps speed transmission of neural impulses, allowing muscles to move more efficiently and smoothly (Newbern et al., 2011).

As shown in Figure 2.1, myelinated axons resemble a string of sausages that are pinched at various points, creating gaps called **nodes of Ranvier**. The neural impulse appears to jump from node to node as it speeds down the axon. Because myelin sheaths are white, parts of the nervous system that contain myelinated axons are referred to as "white matter."

Multiple sclerosis (MS) is a chronic and often crippling disease of the central nervous system, affecting about one in one thousand adults, that results in the eventual destruction of the myelin sheath (Ransohoff, 2007). It generally affects young adults between 20 and 40 years of age and is believed to be genetically influenced (Baranzini et al., 2010; Renoux et al., 2007). The loss of myelin slows the transmission of nerve impulses. This leads to a range of symptoms; in the most severe cases, the person loses the ability to speak, walk, write, or even breathe.

CONCEPT 2.2
The nervous system has three types of neurons: sensory neurons, motor neurons, and interneurons.

CONCEPT 2.3
The nervous system has two types of cells, neurons and glial cells.

CONCEPT 2.4
Many axons are covered with a protective coating, called a myelin sheath, that speeds the transmission of neural impulses.

How Neurons Communicate

The human brain is densely packed with more than one hundred billion neurons. From the time we are born and begin learning about the world around us, our brains become an increasingly complex network of billions upon billions of interlaced neurons. These complex assemblages of cells form intricate circuits in the brain that allow us to interpret the world around us and respond to external stimuli, as well as to organize our behavior, think, feel, make plans, and use language.

Neurons accomplish these tasks by sending messages to one another. Let us break down the process into smaller steps to see how it works.

Both inside and outside the neuron are electrically charged atoms and molecules called **ions**. Like the poles of a battery, ions have either a positive (+) or negative (–) charge. The movements of ions across the cell wall, or *cell membrane,* cause electrochemical changes in the cell that generate an electrical signal to travel down the cell's axon in the form of a neural impulse. The most important ions in this process are two types of positively charged ions, *sodium* ions and *potassium* ions. The movement of ions through the cell membrane is controlled by a series of gates, or tiny doors, that open to allow ions to enter the cell and close to shut them out.

When a neuron is at rest (not being stimulated), the gates that control the passage of sodium ions are closed. A greater concentration of positively charged sodium ions remains outside the cell, causing it to have a slightly negative charge, called a **resting potential**, relative to the surrounding fluid. The resting potential of a neuron is about –70 millivolts (mV) (a millivolt is one-thousandth of a volt). Like a charged battery sitting on a shelf, a neuron in the resting state holds a store of potential energy that can be used to generate, or "fire," a neural impulse in response to stimulation. It awaits a source of stimulation that will temporarily reverse the electrical charges within the cell, causing it to fire.

When the cell is stimulated—usually by neurotransmitters released from adjoining neurons—sodium gates at the base of the axon open. Positively charged sodium ions from the surrounding fluid then rush in, which causes the area inside the cell membrane at the point of excitation to become less negatively charged. This process is called **depolarization**. When stimulation is sufficiently strong, as when enough of a neurotransmitter is present, depolarization quickly spreads along the cell membrane (Calderon de Anda et al., 2005). As this wave of depolarization reaches a critical threshold, the neuron abruptly shifts from a negative charge to a positive charge of about +40 mV. The sudden reversal of electrical charge is called an **action potential**, or *neural impulse.* The action potential typically begins at the juncture between the soma and the axon, which is called the *axon hillock.* It then shoots down the entire length of the axon as a wave of changing electrical charges. We refer to this action as a "firing" of the neuron, or as a *spike* (see ■ Figure 2.2).

Once an action potential reaches the end of an axon, it causes the release of neurotransmitters from the terminal buttons that carry the neural message to the next neuron. Action potentials are generated according to the **all-or-none principle**. A neuron will fire completely (generate an action potential) if sufficient stimulation is available, or it will not fire; there is no halfway point. Different axons generate action potentials of different speeds depending on such characteristics as their thickness (generally the thicker

CONCEPT 2.5
The nervous system is a massive communication network that connects billions of neurons throughout your body.

CONCEPT 2.6
A neuron fires when a stimulus triggers electrochemical changes along its cell membrane that lead to a chain reaction within the cell.

ions Electrically charged chemical particles.

resting potential The electrical potential across the cell membrane of a neuron in its resting state.

depolarization A positive shift in the electrical charge in the neuron's resting potential, making it less negatively charged.

action potential An abrupt change from a negative to a positive charge of a nerve cell; also called a neural impulse.

all-or-none principle The principle by which neurons will fire only when a change in the level of excitation occurs that is sufficient to produce an action potential.

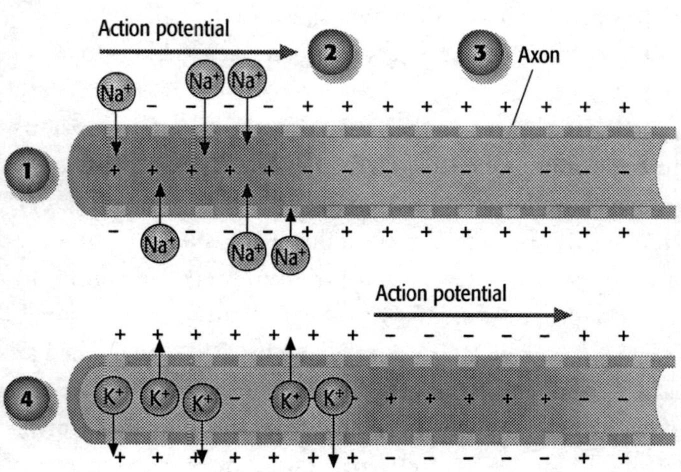

Figure 2.2 An Action Potential
Here we see how a neural impulse or action potential is generated. (1) When a neuron in a resting state is stimulated, sodium gates in the cell membrane open, allowing positively charged sodium ions to rush into the cell. (2) With sufficient stimulation, the cell suddenly shifts from a negative to a positive charge. (3) The sudden reversal of charge is called an action potential or neural impulse that shoots down the axon, momentarily reversing charges all along the cell membrane. Once the action potential passes, sodium gates close, preventing further inflows of positively charged sodium ions. (4) The cell then pumps out positively charged ions, restoring the cell's negatively charged state, allowing it to fire again in response to stimulation.

the axon, the faster the speed) and whether or not they are covered with a myelin sheath (which speeds transmission). Speeds of action potentials range from between two miles an hour to about 250 miles an hour. Even the fastest neural impulses are much slower than a speeding bullet, which travels at the rate of several hundred miles a minute. Even so, neural impulses race to their destinations at several hundred feet per second, which is certainly fast enough to pull your hand in an instant from a burning surface, but perhaps not fast enough to avoid a burn (Aamodt & Wang, 2008).

For about one-thousandth of a second (1 millisecond) after firing, a neuron busies itself preparing to fire again. Sodium gates along the cell membrane close, preventing further inflows of positively charged sodium ions. The cell pumps out positively charged ions, mostly potassium ions, and as it rids itself of these positive ions, the neuron's negatively charged resting potential is restored. Then, in a slower process, the cell restores the electrochemical balance by pumping out sodium ions and drawing in some potassium ions, making it possible for another action potential to occur. During the time these changes are occurring, called a **refractory period**, the neuron, like a gun being reloaded, is temporarily incapable of firing. But *temporarily* truly means *temporarily*, for a neuron can "reload" hundreds of times per second.

CONCEPT 2.7
An action potential is generated according to the all-or-none principle—it is produced only if the level of excitation is sufficient.

CONCEPT 2.8
When the neural impulse reaches the axon's terminal buttons, it triggers the release of chemicals that either increase or decrease the likelihood that neighboring cells will fire.

Neurotransmitters: The Nervous System's Chemical Messengers

Neurons don't actually touch. Recall that neurons are separated by the tiny fluid-filled gap called a synapse, which measures less than a millionth of an inch across. Neural impulses or messages cannot jump even this tiniest of gaps. They must be transferred by neurotransmitters, the chemical agents or messengers that carry the message across the synapse (Ottersen, 2005). When a neuron fires, tiny vesicles (or sacs) in the axon's terminal buttons release molecules of neurotransmitters into the synaptic gap (also called the *synaptic cleft*) like a flotilla of ships casting off into the sea (see ■ Figure 2.3). Neurotransmitters carry messages that control activities ranging from contraction of muscles that move our bodies, to stimulation of glands to release hormones, to the psychological states of thinking and emotion.

refractory period A temporary state in which a neuron is unable to fire in response to continued stimulation.

Each specific type of neurotransmitter has a particular chemical structure, or three-dimensional shape. It fits into only one kind of **receptor site**, like a key fitting into a lock. When neurotransmitters dock at receptor sites, they lock into place, causing chemical changes in the receiving (or *postsynaptic*) neuron. These changes have either an *excitatory effect* or an *inhibitory effect*. Excitatory effects make an action potential more likely to occur, whereas inhibitory effects make an action potential less likely to occur. Some neurotransmitters have excitatory effects, triggering the cell to fire, whereas others have inhibitory effects, putting the brakes on the action potential. Some neurotransmitters have both excitatory and inhibitory effects. The nervous system depends on a balance between excitation and inhibition—the turning on and turning off of neurons—in order to function smoothly and efficiently (Haider et al., 2006).

receptor site A site on the receiving neuron in which neurotransmitters dock.

Several processes normally prevent excitatory neurotransmitters from continuing to stimulate a receiving cell. One process, called **reuptake**, is nature's own version of recycling. Through reuptake, neurotransmitters not taken up by the receiving cell are reabsorbed by their vesicles to be used again. In another process, **enzymes** in the synapse break down neurotransmitters, which are then eliminated from the body in the urine. In yet another process, terminal buttons release **neuromodulators**, chemicals that either increase or decrease the sensitivity of the receiving neuron to neurotransmitters.

reuptake The process by which neurotransmitters are reabsorbed by the transmitting neuron.

enzymes Organic substances that produce certain chemical changes in other organic substances through a catalytic action.

neuromodulators Chemicals released in the nervous system that influence the sensitivity of the receiving neuron to neurotransmitters.

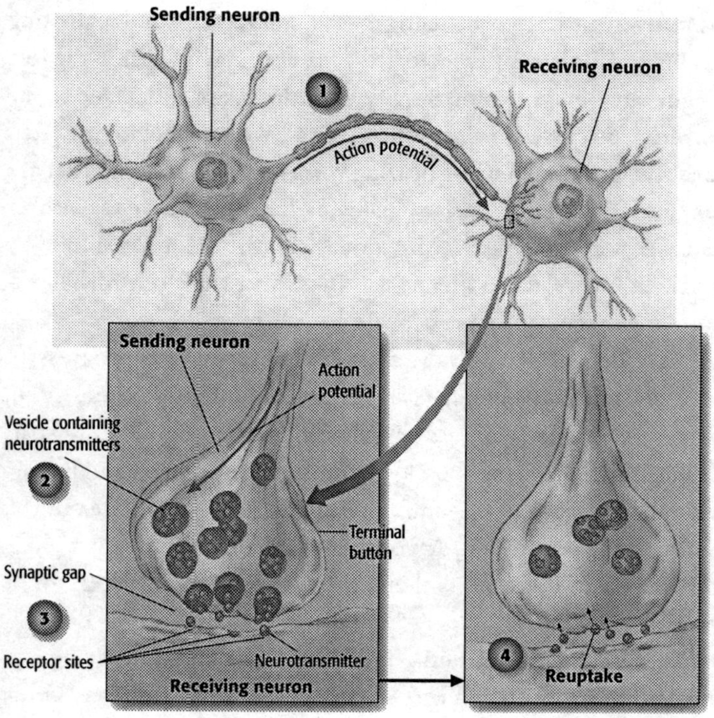

FIGURE 2.3 How Neurons Communicate
Neurons communicate with other neurons through the transmission of neural impulses.
1 The neural impulse, or action potential, travels along the axon of the sending or transmitting neuron toward the receiving neuron. 2 Neurotransmitters are released from vesicles in the axon terminal buttons of the sending neuron. 3 These chemical messengers then travel across the synaptic gap and are taken up by receptor sites on the dendrites of the receiving neuron. 4 Neurotransmitter molecules that do not dock at receptor sites are decomposed in the synaptic gap or are reabsorbed by the transmitting neuron in a process called reuptake.

Normal psychological functioning depends on the smooth transmission of messages among neurons in the brain. Your ability to think clearly, move your arms and legs at will, feel pain or emotions such as joy, fear, or anger—everything you do, feel, or think—depends on neurotransmitters. When the body produces too little or too much of a neurotransmitter, problems may occur. Sometimes receptor sites allow too many neurotransmitter molecules to dock, or they do not accept neurotransmitters properly. Excesses or deficits of particular neurotransmitters in the brain, or irregularities in how they function, are associated with many disorders. For example, irregularities in neurotransmitter functioning are linked to various psychological disorders, including anxiety disorders, mood disorders, eating disorders, and schizophrenia (see Chapters 8 and 15).

Antagonists and Agonists

Chemical substances have effects on neurotransmitter functioning. Some drugs attach to receptor sites, preventing particular neurotransmitters from docking. The neurotransmitter *acetylcholine* (ACh), for example, has an excitatory effect on skeletal muscles by triggering them to contract in response to commands from the brain. But if you were to prevent ACh from locking into its receptor sites, the skeletal muscles that control voluntary movements (raising your arm, for example) would be unable to contract. Some South American Indian cultures dip arrowheads in a poison called *curare* extracted from plants. When an arrow pierces an animal's skin, the poison enters the body, blocking receptor sites for ACh and locking it out, causing paralysis. The animal cannot use its muscles for breathing and dies from suffocation. ACh is also involved in other bodily functions, including memory formation and control of heartbeat. Patients with Alzheimer's disease have low levels of ACh in the brain, as the disease is associated with the death of ACh-producing cells (see Chapter 10).

Chemical substances (curare is one) that block actions of neurotransmitters by occupying their receptor sites are called **antagonists**. When they lock into these receptor sites, antagonists prevent transmission of messages carried by the neurotransmitter. An example

antagonists Drugs that block the actions of neurotransmitters by occupying the receptor sites in which the neurotransmitters dock.

CONCEPT 2.9
Normal psychological functioning depends on the delicate balance of neurotransmitter activity in the brain.

→ Concept Link
Irregularities in neurotransmitter functioning are implicated in many psychological disorders, including eating disorders, depression, and schizophrenia.

Eating disorders are discussed in Module 8.2, depression in Module 15.4, and schizophrenia in Module 15.5.

schizophrenia A severe and chronic psychological disorder characterized by disturbances in thinking, perception, emotions, and behavior.

hallucinations Perceptions experienced in the absence of corresponding external stimuli.

delusions Fixed but patently false beliefs, such as believing that one is being hounded by demons.

Parkinson's disease A progressive brain disease involving destruction of dopamine-producing brain cells and characterized by muscle tremors, shakiness, rigidity, and difficulty in walking and controlling fine body movements.

agonists Drugs that either increase the availability or effectiveness of neurotransmitters or mimic their actions.

stimulant A drug that activates the central nervous system, such as amphetamines and cocaine.

amphetamines A class of synthetically derived stimulant drugs, such as methamphetamine, or "speed."

antidepressants Drugs that combat depression by affecting the levels or activity of neurotransmitters.

© AP Photo/Mathaias Rietschel

Boxing legend Muhammad Ali developed Parkinson's disease, a degenerative brain disease that causes rigidity and tremors and affects the ability to control body movements.

is *dopamine*, a neurotransmitter involved in controlling muscle contractions and regulating learning, memory, and feelings of pleasure. Psychologists have a special interest in the role of dopamine because irregularities in dopamine activity in the brain are connected to the development of **schizophrenia** (discussed in Chapter 15). People with schizophrenia often experience **hallucinations** (the phenomenon of "hearing voices" or seeing things that are not there) and **delusions** (fixed, false ideas, such as believing that aliens have taken over their bodies). *Antipsychotic drugs* are chemicals that work as antagonists to dopamine by blocking receptor sites where the neurotransmitter docks. These drugs help control hallucinations and delusional thinking in schizophrenia patients (see Chapter 16).

Parkinson's disease is a degenerative brain disease that leads to a progressive loss of motor functions or physical movements (Dagher & Robbins, 2009; Lees et al., 2009). Parkinson's sufferers experience tremors (shakiness), muscle rigidity and stiffness, and difficulty walking and controlling the movements of their fingers and hands. These symptoms result from the death of dopamine-producing cells in an area of the brain involved in regulating body movement. According to one expert, "Dopamine is like the oil in the engine of a car... If the oil is there, the car runs smoothly. If not, it seizes up" (cited in Carroll, 2004).

Parkinson's affects an estimated 1.5 million Americans, including former heavyweight boxing champion Muhammad Ali and actor Michael J. Fox. We don't yet know what causes dopamine-producing cells to die off, but scientists believe that genetic factors are involved (Grayson, 2010; Hampton, 2010; Yang et al., 2009).

In contrast to antagonists that compete with neurotransmitters at the same receptor sites, other drugs, called **agonists**, enhance the activity of neurotransmitters. Agonists work by increasing either the availability or effectiveness of neurotransmitters or by binding to their receptor sites and mimicking their actions. As an example, the mild **stimulant** caffeine increases the availability of a neurotransmitter called *glutamate*. Glutamate is an excitatory neurotransmitter that keeps the central nervous system aroused and also plays a key role in the transmission of auditory signals from the inner ear to the brain (Weisz, Glowatzki, & Fuchs, 2009).

Stronger stimulants, such as **amphetamines** and cocaine, are agonists that increase the availability of the neurotransmitter dopamine in the brain by blocking its reuptake by the transmitting neuron. Dopamine plays many roles, among them carrying messages through neural pathways in the brain that produce feelings of pleasure (Burgdorf & Panksepp, 2006). Scientists believe that different types of drugs, including amphetamines and cocaine, as well as alcohol and opiates, work on the brain to produce states of pleasure or "highs" by increasing the availability of dopamine (Gallistel, 2006; Pierce & Kumaresan, 2006). (We'll return to this topic in Chapter 4.) Investigators also believe the pleasurable excitement associated with falling in love involves release of dopamine (and other chemicals) in the brain (Ortigue et al., 2010).

Alcohol and antianxiety drugs like Valium act as agonists by increasing the sensitivity of receptor sites to the neurotransmitter *gamma-aminobutyric acid (GABA)* (discussed in Chapter 4). GABA is the major *inhibitory* neurotransmitter in the adult brain; it helps regulate nervous system activity by preventing neurons from overly exciting their neighbors (Gel et al., 2006). Drugs that boost GABA's activity have calming or relaxing effects on the nervous system. Lower levels of GABA in the brain may play a role in emotional disorders in which anxiety is a core feature, such as panic disorder.

Neurotransmitter functioning is also implicated in depression (Carver, Johnson, & Joormann, 2009). Drugs that help relieve depression, called **antidepressants**, are agonists that increase the availability of the neurotransmitters norepinephrine and serotonin in the synapse. Norepinephrine (also called *noradrenaline*), a chemical cousin of the hormone *epinephrine* (also called *adrenaline*), does double duty as both a neurotransmitter and a hormone (see Module 2.6). Serotonin, which works largely as an inhibitory neurotransmitter in the brain, helps regulate mood states and sleep, as well as the feeling of fullness after meals. Serotonin also works as a kind of behavioral seat belt to curb impulsive behaviors, including impulsive acts of aggression (Crockett, 2009; Seo, Patrick, & Kennealy, 2008).

Did you know that the brain produces neurotransmitters that are chemical cousins to narcotic drugs like morphine and heroin? These natural chemicals, called **endorphins** (short for *endogenous morphine*—morphine that "develops from within"), are inhibitory neurotransmitters. They lock into the same receptors in the brain as the drug morphine. (Narcotics and other psychoactive drugs are discussed further in Chapter 4.)

endorphins Natural chemicals released in the brain that have pain-killing and pleasure-inducing effects.

Endorphins are the body's natural painkillers. Like morphine, heroin, and other narcotics, they deaden pain by fitting into receptor sites for chemicals that carry pain messages to the brain, thereby locking out pain messages. They also produce feelings of well-being and pleasure and may contribute to the "runner's high" experienced by many long-distance runners (Boecker et al., 2008). Morphine, heroin, and other narcotics are agonists, since they mimic the effects of naturally occurring endorphins in the body (Vetter et al., 2006).

© Juice Images/PhotoLibrary

"I'll have a tall iced agonist to go." The caffeine in coffee is an agonist that enhances the actions of the excitatory neurotransmitter glutamate. What is the difference between drugs that work as agonists and those that work as antagonists?

Why It Matters

Why does it matter if a drug is an agonist or antagonist? Let's say we learn that a psychological disorder is connected with an increased level of activity of a particular neurotransmitter. If you were seeking to develop a therapeutic drug to treat the disorder, would you be more likely to work on developing an agonist or an antagonist to this neurotransmitter?

The answer is that you'd probably work on an antagonist, a drug that blocks or interferes with the activity of this neurotransmitter. Blunting the actions of the neurotransmitter may help control troubling symptoms, as we discovered with antagonists that block the activity of dopamine in the treatment of schizophrenia.

2.1 MODULE REVIEW — Neurons: The Body's Wiring

Recite It

What is a neuron?

- A neuron is a nerve cell, the basic building block of the nervous system through which information in the form of neural impulses is transmitted.

What are the parts of a neuron?

- Like other cells, neurons have a cell body, or soma, that houses the cell nucleus and carries out the metabolic work of the cell. Each neuron also has an axon, a long cable that conducts outgoing messages (neural impulses) to other neurons, as well as dendrites, which are fibers that receive neural messages from other neurons. Terminal buttons are swellings at the ends of the axon that release neurotransmitters, which are chemical messengers that carry the message to adjacent neurons.

What are the types of neurons and types of cells found in the nervous system?

- The nervous system has three types of neurons: sensory neurons, which carry information from sensory organs and internal bodily organs and tissues to the spinal cord and brain; motor neurons, which carry messages from the central nervous system to the muscles and inner organs; and interneurons, which connect neurons with each other.
- The nervous system has two types of cells: neurons, the nerve cells that conduct neural impulses, and glial cells, which support and nourish neurons. Glial cells also form the myelin sheath that covers some axons and speeds transmission of neural impulses.

How is a neural impulse generated and transmitted from one neuron to another?

- Neural impulses are electrochemical events. When a neuron is stimulated beyond a threshold level, there is a rapid shift in its polarity from a negative to a positive charge. This reversal of charge, called an action potential or neural impulse, is generated along the length of the axon to the terminal buttons.
- When a neural impulse reaches the terminal buttons, it triggers the release of neurotransmitters, the chemical messengers that carry the message across the synapse to neighboring neurons. Neurotransmitters can have either excitatory or inhibitory effects on the neurons at which they dock.

What roles do neurotransmitters play in psychological functioning?

- Neurotransmitters are involved in such psychological processes as memory, learning, and emotional response. Irregularities in the functioning of particular neurotransmitters are implicated in various disorders, including schizophrenia and depression.

Recall It

1. When a neuron is at rest,
   a. the cell has a slightly positive charge (relative to surrounding fluid).
   b. a greater concentration of sodium ions lies outside the nerve cell.
   c. the state is known as an action potential.
   d. it is in a state of depolarization.
2. The part of the neuron that houses the cell nucleus is the ________.
3. What are the three types of neurons in the human body?
4. When a neuron is at rest,
   a. greater concentration of sodium ions remains outside the nerve cell.
   b. the cell has a slightly positive charge (relative to surrounding fluid).
   c. the state is known as an action potential.
   d. it is in a state of depolarization.
5. Although nerve cells don't actually touch each other, they communicate by means of
   a. electrical impulses that travel from dendrites to receptor sites on adjacent neurons.
   b. neurotransmitters that carry the neural impulse across the synapse.
   c. interneurons that serve as relay stations between neurons.
   d. nerve cells that function independently and have no need to communicate with each other.

Think About It

- How is a neuron in a resting state like a battery sitting on a shelf?
- What is an action potential? How is it generated? What happens when it reaches the end of an axon?
- A scientist develops a drug that blocks the actions of cocaine by locking into the same receptor sites as cocaine. So long as a person is taking the drug, cocaine will no longer produce a high. Would this drug be an antagonist or an agonist to cocaine? Why?

MODULE 2.2

The Nervous System: Your Body's Information Superhighway

- How is the nervous system organized?
- What are spinal reflexes?
- What are the somatic nervous system and autonomic nervous system?
- What is the relationship between the sympathetic and parasympathetic divisions of the autonomic nervous system?

nervous system The network of nerve cells and support cells for communicating and processing information from within and outside the body.

To perform its many functions, the brain needs to communicate with the sensory organs, muscles, and other parts of our body. It does so through a complex network of neurons, of which the brain is a part, called the **nervous system**. The nervous system is an intricate network of neurons that functions as a communication network that conducts information in the form of neural impulses. This information superhighway is divided into two major parts, the *central nervous system*, consisting of the brain and spinal cord, and the *peripheral nervous system*, which connects the central nervous system to other parts of the body (see ■ Figure 2.4). Concept Chart 2.2 (see page 56) shows the organization of the nervous system.

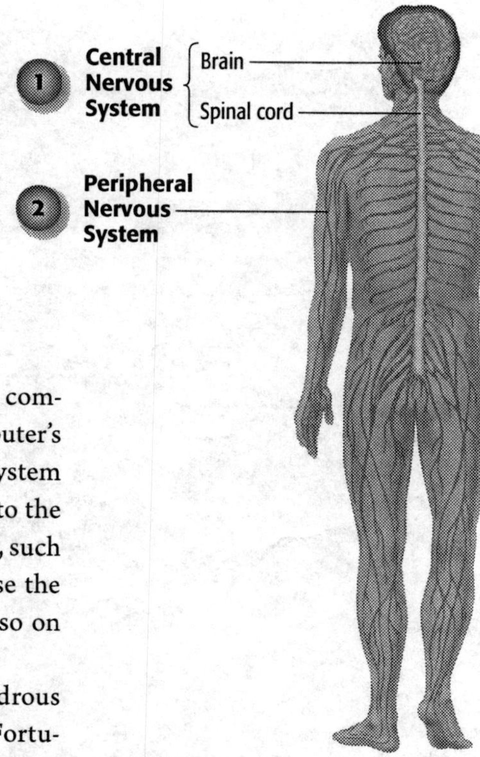

Figure 2.4 Parts of the Nervous System The nervous system has two major divisions, ① the central nervous system and ② the peripheral nervous system.

The Central Nervous System: Your Body's Master Control Unit

You can compare the **central nervous system** to the central processing unit of a computer—the "brains" of the computer etched into a chip that controls the computer's central processing functions. The central nervous system is a master control system that regulates everything in your body, from the rate at which your heart beats, to the movements of your eyes as you scan these words, to your higher mental processes, such as thinking and reasoning. The central nervous system also enables you to sense the world around you and experience sensations of sight, sound, touch, smell, and so on (see Chapter 3).

The crowning glory of your central nervous system is your brain, that wondrous organ that regulates life processes and enables you to think, plan, and create. Fortunately, this tender mass of tissue is cushioned in a hard, bony shell called the skull.

As you'll see in Module 2.3, one way of studying the brain is by exploring its three major parts: the hindbrain, or lower brain—the brain's "basement"; the midbrain; and the forebrain, the highest region, where thoughts and your sense of self "live." Here let us consider the other major part of the central nervous system, the spinal cord—the brain's link to the peripheral nervous system.

CONCEPT 2.10
The nervous system has two major parts: the central nervous system, which consists of the brain and spinal cord, and the peripheral nervous system, which consists of the nerves that connect the central nervous system to sensory organs, muscles, and glands.

The Spinal Cord

The **spinal cord**—a column of nerves nearly as thick as your thumb—is literally an extension of the brain. The spinal cord begins at the base of your brain and runs down the center of your back, ending just below the waist. It is a neural pathway that transmits information between the brain and the peripheral nervous system. It receives incoming information from your sense organs and other peripheral body parts and carries outgoing commands from your brain to muscles, glands, and organs throughout your body.

The spinal cord is encased in a protective bony column called the **spine**. Despite this protection, the spinal cord can suffer injury. In severe spinal cord injuries, such as the one the late actor Christopher Reeve sustained when he fell from a horse, signals cannot be transmitted between the brain and the peripheral organs, which may result in paralysis of the limbs and an inability to breathe on one's own. As a result of his injury, Reeve became quadriplegic (i.e., he lost control over his arms and legs). Also, because he lost the ability to breathe, he required an artificial respirator. (Before he died, Reeve regained some ability to breathe on his own.)

central nervous system The part of the nervous system that consists of the brain and spinal cord.

spinal cord The column of nerves that transmits information between the brain and the peripheral nervous system.

spine The protective bony column that houses the spinal cord.

reflex An automatic unlearned response to particular stimuli.

The spinal cord is not simply a conduit for neural transmission of signals between the brain and the peripheral nervous system. It also controls some *spinal reflexes* that let you respond as quickly as possible to particular types of stimuli. A **reflex** is an automatic, unlearned reaction to a stimulus; a **spinal reflex** is a reflex controlled at the level of the spinal cord—one that bypasses the brain. An example of a spinal reflex is the jerk your knee gives when a doctor who's examining you taps it lightly with a hammer. Some spinal reflexes, including the knee-jerk response, involve just two neurons—one sensory neuron

spinal reflex A reflex controlled at the level of the spinal cord that may involve as few as two neurons.

CONCEPT CHART 2.2 Organization of the Nervous System

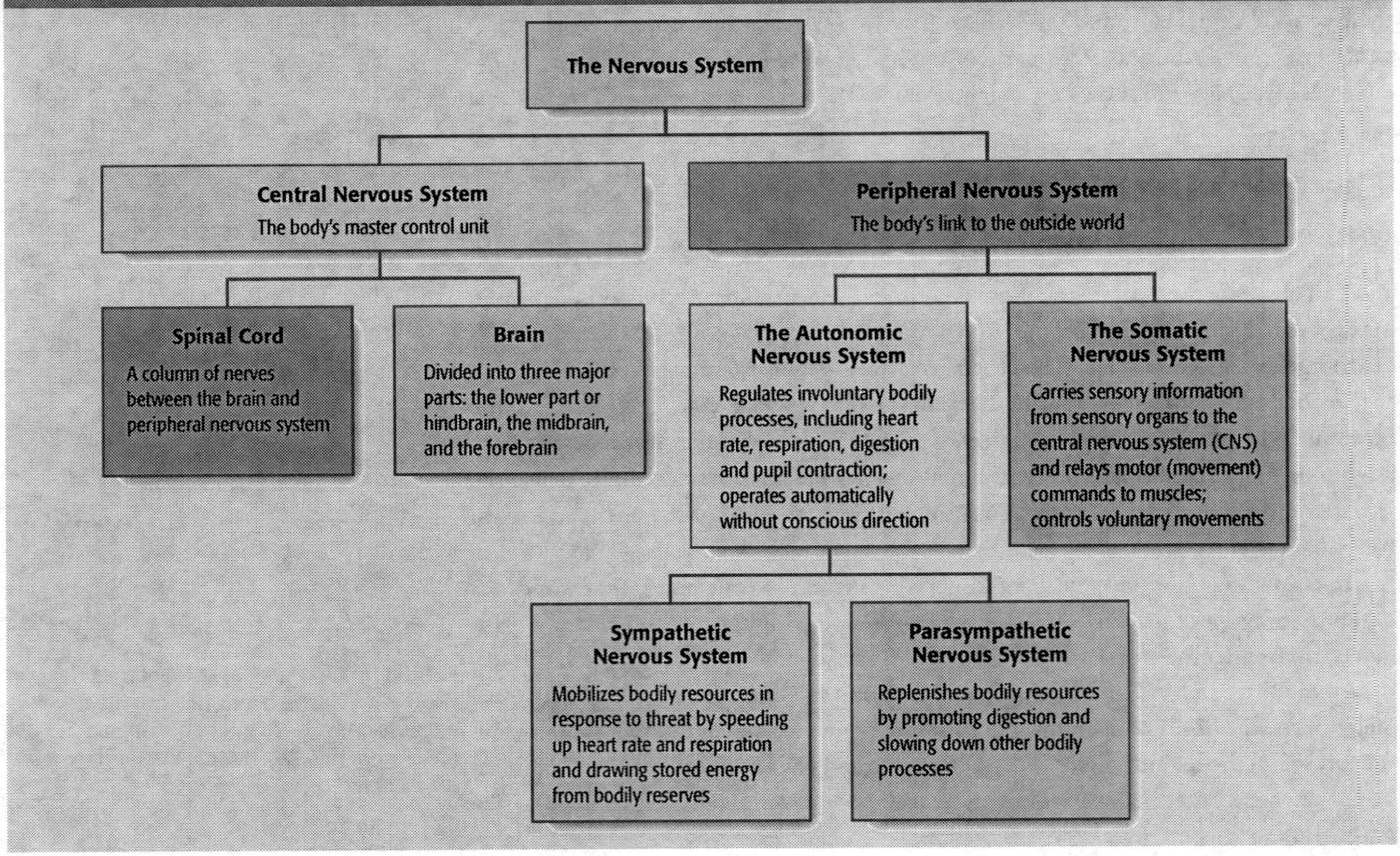

and one motor neuron (see ■ Figure 2.5). In other cases, such as the reflexive withdrawal of the hand upon touching a hot object, a third neuron in the spinal cord, an interneuron, transmits information from the incoming sensory neuron to the outgoing motor neuron.

Spinal reflexes allow us to respond almost instantly and with great efficiency to particular stimuli. The knee-jerk reflex takes a mere 50 milliseconds from the time the knee is tapped until the time the leg jerks forward (as compared with the hundreds of milliseconds it takes to voluntarily flex your leg). To appreciate the value of spinal reflexes, recall the times you've pulled your hand away from a hot stove or blinked when a gust of wind sent particles of debris hurtling toward your eyeballs. By saving the many milliseconds it would take to send a message to your brain, have it interpreted, and have a command sent back along the spinal highway to motor neurons, spinal reflexes can spell the difference between a minor injury and a serious one.

peripheral nervous system The part of the nervous system that connects the spinal cord and brain with the sensory organs, muscles, and glands.

CONCEPT 2.11
The spinal cord is an information highway that conducts information between the brain and the peripheral nervous system.

CONCEPT 2.12
Spinal reflexes are innate, automatic responses controlled at the level of the spinal cord that allow you to respond quickly to particular stimuli.

CONCEPT 2.13
The somatic nervous system is the part of the peripheral nervous system that controls voluntary movements of muscles and relays information between the central nervous system and sensory organs.

The Peripheral Nervous System: Your Body's Link to the Outside World

The central nervous system depends on the constant flow of information that it receives from your internal organs and sensory receptors, as well as on its ability to convey information to the muscles and glands that it regulates. These functions are performed by the **peripheral nervous system** (PNS), the part of the nervous system that connects your central nervous system with other parts of your body.

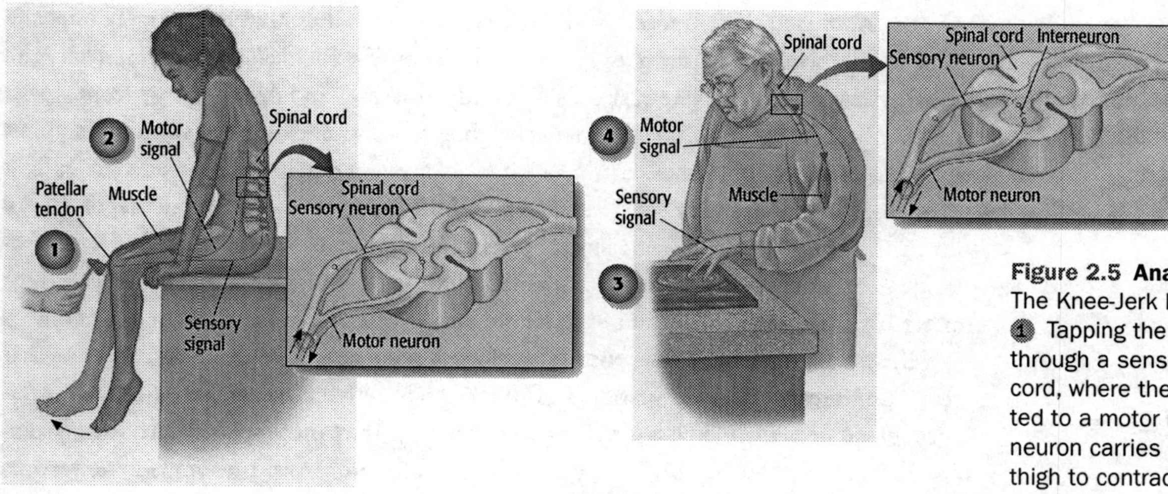

Figure 2.5 Anatomy of a Spinal Reflex
The Knee-Jerk Reflex
1 Tapping the knee sends a signal through a sensory neuron to the spinal cord, where the information is transmitted to a motor neuron. 2 The motor neuron carries signals to muscles in the thigh to contract, causing the leg to kick forward.
The Withdrawal Reflex
3 Touching a hot stove sends a signal through a sensory neuron to the spinal cord. 5 The information is relayed through an interneuron to a motor neuron, which signals muscles in the hand to contract, causing the hand to withdraw from the hot object.

Without the peripheral nervous system, your brain would be like a computer chip disconnected from the computer hardware—a marvelous feat of engineering but unable to function. Without information transmitted from your sensory organs—your eyes, ears, tongue, nose, and skin—you would be unable to perceive the world. Without commands sent to your muscles, you would be unable to act upon the world. The PNS is divided into two parts, the **somatic nervous system** and the **autonomic nervous system** (ANS).

The Somatic Nervous System

The somatic nervous system transmits messages between your central nervous system and your sensory organs and muscles. It not only enables you to perceive the world, but also ensures that your muscles will contract in response to an intentional command or a stimulus that triggers a reflex action. It also regulates subtle movements that maintain posture and balance.

The somatic nervous system is composed of sensory and motor neurons. As noted in Module 2.1, sensory neurons send messages from the sensory organs to the spinal cord and brain. In this way, information about stimuli that impinge upon our senses (light, sounds, odors, taste, pressure on our skin, and so on) is transmitted to the central nervous system. The brain then interprets these messages, allowing you to perceive a beautiful sunset or a threatening animal, distinguish a whisper from the rustling of the wind, determine whether you are sitting in a reclining or upright position, and experience sensations of warmth, cold, and pain.

The central nervous system processes the information it receives and sends messages back through motor neurons that control movements—such as walking and running, pulling your arm back reflexively upon touching a hot object, raising and lowering your arms at will—and the tiny, almost imperceptible, movements that regulate your balance and posture.

The Autonomic Nervous System

The autonomic nervous system (ANS) is the part of the peripheral nervous system that controls such internal bodily processes as heartbeat, respiration, digestion, and dilation of the pupils. The ANS does these tasks automatically, regulating these vital bodily processes without your having to think about them. (*Autonomic* means "automatic.") You can, however, exercise some voluntary control over some of these functions, as by intentionally breathing more rapidly or slowly.

somatic nervous system The part of the peripheral nervous system that transmits information between the central nervous system and the sensory organs and muscles; also controls voluntary movements.

autonomic nervous system The part of the peripheral nervous system that automatically regulates involuntary bodily processes, such as breathing, heart rate, and digestion.

CONCEPT 2.14
Like an automatic pilot, the autonomic nervous system, a division of the peripheral nervous system, automatically controls such involuntary bodily processes as heartbeat, respiration, and digestion.

CONCEPT 2.15
The autonomic nervous system is divided into two branches that have largely opposite effects: the sympathetic nervous system and the parasympathetic nervous system.

sympathetic nervous system The branch of the autonomic nervous system that accelerates bodily processes and releases stores of energy needed to meet increased physical demands.

parasympathetic nervous system The branch of the autonomic nervous system that regulates bodily processes, such as digestion, that replenish stores of energy.

The ANS is itself composed of two divisions, or branches, that have largely opposite effects, the *sympathetic nervous system* and the *parasympathetic nervous system*. The **sympathetic nervous system** speeds up bodily processes and draws energy from stored reserves. It serves as an alarm system that heightens arousal and mobilizes bodily resources in times of stress or physical exertion, or when defensive action might be needed to fend off a threat. It accelerates your heart rate and breathing rate and provides more fuel or energy for the body to use by releasing sugar (glucose) from the liver. Activation of the sympathetic nervous system is often accompanied by strong emotions, such as anxiety, fear, or anger. That is why we sense our hearts beating faster when we are anxious or angered.

The **parasympathetic nervous system** fosters bodily processes, such as digestion, that replenish stores of energy. Digestion provides the body with fuel by converting food into glucose (blood sugar), which cells use as a source of energy. The parasympathetic nervous system also helps conserve energy by slowing down other bodily processes. The sympathetic nervous system speeds up your heart; the parasympathetic slows it down. The sympathetic nervous system turns off (inhibits) digestive activity; the parasympathetic turns it on. The parasympathetic system is in command whenever you are relaxing or digesting a meal.

2.2 MODULE REVIEW The Nervous System: Your Body's Information Superhighway

Recite It

How is the nervous system organized?

➤ The major divisions of the nervous system are the central nervous system, which consists of the brain and spinal cord, and the peripheral nervous system, which connects the central nervous system to the rest of the body. The peripheral nervous system is divided into the somatic nervous system and autonomic nervous system.

What are spinal reflexes?

➤ Spinal reflexes are automatic, unlearned responses that are controlled at the level of the spinal cord. They may involve as few as two neurons.

What are the somatic nervous system and autonomic nervous system?

➤ The somatic nervous system and autonomic nervous system are the two branches of the peripheral nervous system (PNS), the part of the nervous system that connects your central nervous system with other parts of your body. The somatic nervous system relays messages between your central nervous system and your sensory organs and muscles. The autonomic nervous system (ANS) automatically controls vital bodily processes such as heartbeat, respiration, digestion, and dilation of the pupils. It is divided into the sympathetic and parasympathetic branches.

What is the relationship between the sympathetic and parasympathetic divisions of the autonomic nervous system?

➤ These two divisions have largely opposite effects. The sympathetic nervous system speeds up bodily processes that expend energy, while the parasympathetic system slows down some bodily processes and fosters others, such as digestion, that replenish stores of energy.

Recall It

1. The two major divisions in the human nervous system are the ________ nervous system and the ________ nervous system.
2. The brain and spinal cord constitute the ________ nervous system.
3. Which part of the nervous system triggers changes that prepare the body to cope with stress?
4. The parasympathetic nervous system
   a. slows some bodily activity and allows for the replenishment of energy.
   b. is part of the central nervous system.
   c. is also known as the "fight-or-flight" mechanism.
   d. draws energy from bodily reserves to meet stressful demands on the body.

Think About It

➤ As you're running to catch a bus, your breathing quickens and your heart starts pounding. Which part of your peripheral nervous system kicks into gear at such a time?

➤ Were there any times in your life when a spinal reflex prevented serious injury?

The Brain: Your Crowning Glory

MODULE 2.3

- How is the brain organized, and what are the functions of its various parts?
- How is the cerebral cortex organized?
- What are the major functions associated with the four lobes of the cerebral cortex?

Let us take a tour of the brain, beginning with the lowest level, the *hindbrain*—the part of the brain where the spinal cord enters the skull and widens. We then work our way upward, first to the *midbrain*, which lies above the hindbrain, and then to the *forebrain*, which lies in the highest part of the brain. Concept Chart 2.3 shows these major brain structures.

CONCEPT 2.16
The brain is divided into three major parts: the hindbrain, the midbrain, and the forebrain.

The Hindbrain

The lowest part of the brain, the **hindbrain**, is also the oldest part in evolutionary terms. The hindbrain includes the *medulla*, *pons*, and *cerebellum*. These structures control such basic life-support functions as breathing and heart rate.

hindbrain The lowest and, in evolutionary terms, oldest part of the brain; includes the medulla, pons, and cerebellum.

CONCEPT CHART 2.3 Major Structures of the Human Brain

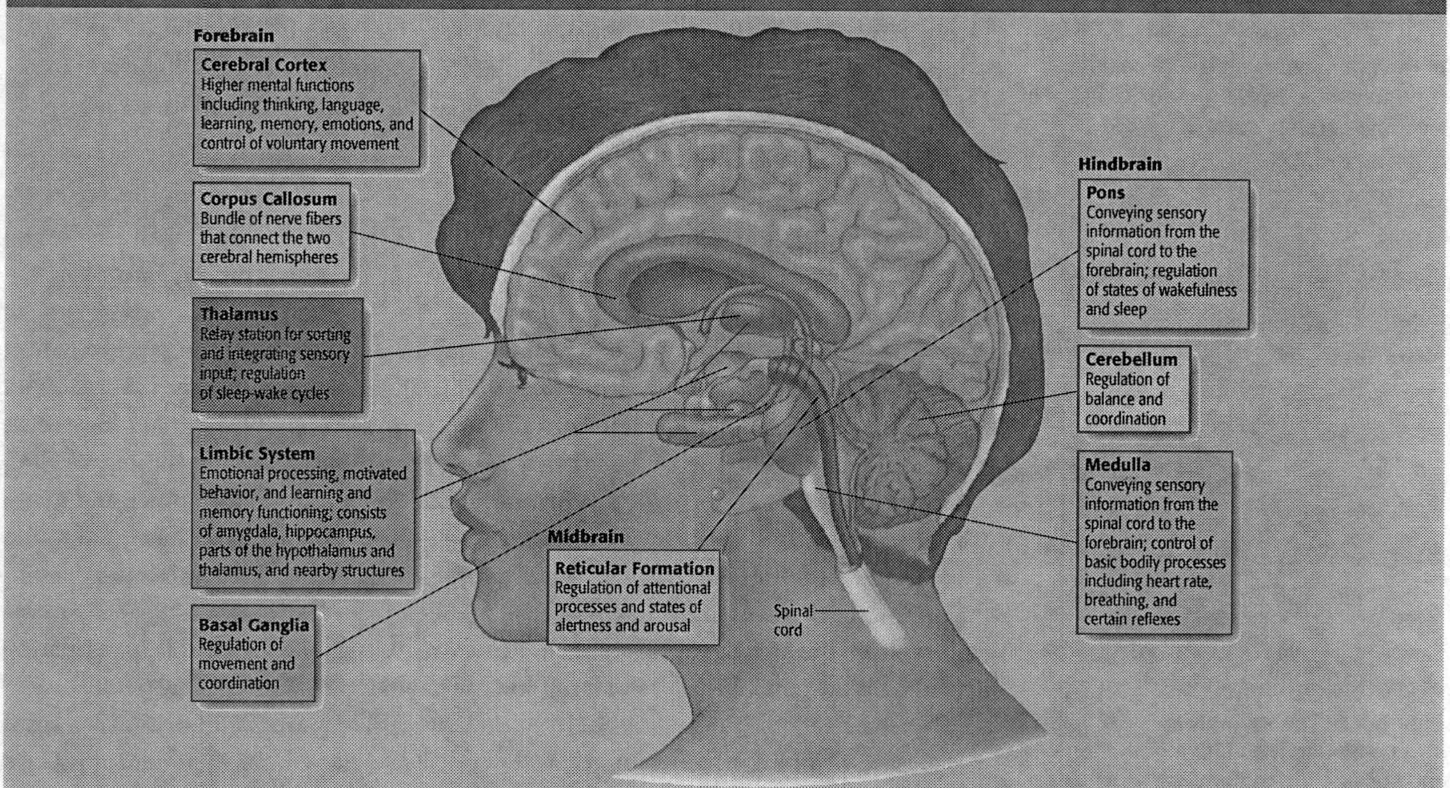

CONCEPT 2.17
The hindbrain, the lowest part of the brain, contains structures that control basic bodily functions, such as breathing and heart rate.

CONCEPT 2.18
The midbrain contains nerve pathways for relaying messages between the hindbrain and the forebrain, as well as structures that control some automatic movements.

medulla A structure in the hindbrain involved in regulating basic life functions, such as heartbeat and respiration.

pons A structure in the hindbrain involved in regulating states of wakefulness and sleep.

brainstem The "stalk" in the lower part of the brain that connects the spinal cord to higher regions of the brain.

cerebellum A structure in the hindbrain involved in controlling coordination and balance.

midbrain The part of the brain that lies on top of the hindbrain and below the forebrain.

reticular formation A weblike formation of neurons involved in regulating states of attention, alertness, and arousal.

forebrain The largest and uppermost part of the brain; contains the thalamus, hypothalamus, limbic system, basal ganglia, and cerebral cortex.

The **medulla** and **pons** contain sensory neurons that transmit information from the spinal cord to the forebrain. The medulla is the section of the hindbrain that lies closest to the spinal cord. It forms the marrow, or core, of the **brainstem**, the "stem" or "stalk" that connects the spinal cord to the higher regions of the brain (see ■ Figure 2.6). (*Medulla* is a Latin word meaning "marrow.") The medulla controls such vital bodily processes as heart rate and breathing, and such reflexes as swallowing, coughing, and sneezing. The pons lies directly above the medulla. It contains nerve fibers that conduct information from the spinal cord and lower parts of the brain through the midbrain to the forebrain. It also helps regulate states of wakefulness and sleep.

Located behind the pons, the **cerebellum** is involved in controlling balance and coordination (Glickstein, Strata, & Voogd, 2009; Strata, Thach, & Ottersen, 2009). Injury to the cerebellum can lead not only to problems with balance and coordination but also to difficulties in initiating voluntary movements, such as lifting an arm or a leg.

As we continue our brief tour of the brain, we come to the midbrain, the part of the brain that serves as a major relay station for information passing between the lower brain and the forebrain.

The Midbrain

The **midbrain**, which lies above the hindbrain, contains nerve pathways that connect the hindbrain with the forebrain. Structures in the midbrain perform important roles, including control of automatic movements of the eye muscles, which allows you to keep your eyes focused on an object as your head changes position in relation to the object. Parts of the midbrain make up the brainstem.

The **reticular formation** (also called the *reticular activating system*, or *RAS*) is a weblike network of neurons that rises from the hindbrain and passes through the midbrain to the thalamus in the forebrain. The reticular formation plays a key role in regulating states of attention, alertness, and arousal. It screens visual and auditory information, filtering out irrelevant information while allowing important information to reach the higher processing centers of the brain, even when we are asleep.

The Forebrain

The **forebrain**, located toward the top and front of the brain, is the largest part of the brain. The major structures in the forebrain are the *thalamus*, the *hypothalamus*, the *limbic system*, and the *cerebral cortex*.

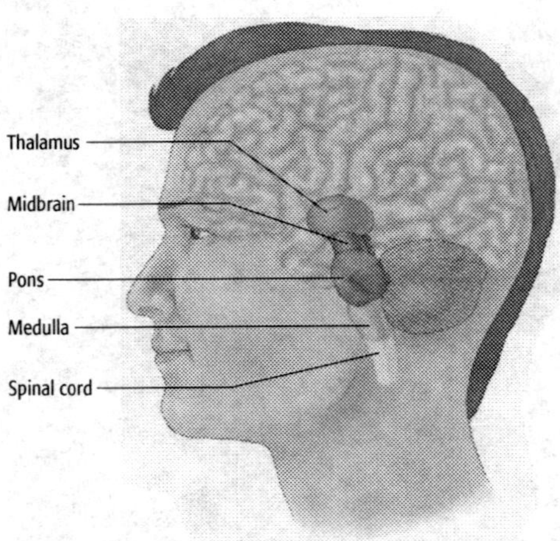

Figure 2.6 The Brainstem
The brainstem reaches from the top of the spinal cord up through the midbrain. It connects the spinal cord to the higher regions of the brain.

The **thalamus** is a relay station near the middle of the brain. It consists of a pair of egg-shaped structures that route information from sense receptors for touch, vision, hearing, and taste (but not smell) to the processing centers of the brain located in the cerebral cortex. The thalamus first sorts through sensory information, sending information about vision to one area, information about hearing to another, and so on. From these relay stations in the thalamus, the information is then transmitted to the appropriate parts of the cerebral cortex for processing. The thalamus also plays an important role in regulating states of sleep and wakefulness (Jan et al., 2009) and receives input from the **basal ganglia**, a cluster of nerve cells that plays a key role in regulating voluntary movement, such as walking and use of our hands (Chetrit et al., 2009).

Just beneath the thalamus is the **hypothalamus** (*hypo* meaning "under"), a pea-sized structure weighing a mere four grams. Despite its small size, the hypothalamus helps regulate many vital bodily functions, including hunger, thirst, daily sleep cycles, body temperature, bodily response to stress, reproductive processes, as well as emotional states and aggressive behavior. As we'll see in Module 2.6, the hypothalamus is part of the endocrine system, and it triggers release of hormones throughout the body. Electrical stimulation of particular parts of the hypothalamus in other mammals, such as rats, can generate, or "switch on," stereotypical behavior patterns that range from eating to attacking rivals, courting, mounting attempts, and caring for the young (Bandler, 2006).

The **limbic system** is a group of interconnected structures that includes the *amygdala, hippocampus,* parts of the *thalamus* and *hypothalamus,* and other nearby interconnected structures (see Concept Chart 2.3). The limbic system is much more evolved in mammals than in lower animals. It plays important roles in both memory and emotional processing.

Referring again to Concept Chart 2.3, we find within the limbic system the **amygdala**, a set of two almond-shaped structures (*amygdala* is derived from the Greek root for "almond"). Among its functions, the amygdala triggers the emotional response of fear when we encounter a threatening stimulus or situation (see Chapter 8) (Roy et al., 2009; Vuilleumier & Huang, 2009).

The **hippocampus** resembles a sea horse, from which it derives its name (the genus of sea horse is hippocampus). Located just behind the amygdala, the hippocampus plays an important role in the formation of new memories (Leutgeb, 2008; Reitz et al., 2009) (see Chapter 6).

Our journey through the brain now brings us to the uppermost part of the forebrain, the cerebral cortex. Because it is responsible for our ability to think, use language, calculate, organize, and create, we devote the entire next section to it.

The Cerebral Cortex: The Brain's Thinking, Calculating, Organizing, and Creative Center

The **cerebral cortex** forms the thin, outer layer of the largest part of the forebrain, which is called the **cerebrum**. The cerebrum consists of two large masses, the right and left **cerebral hemispheres**. The cerebral cortex covers the cerebrum like a cap and derives its name from the Latin words for brain ("cerebrum") and bark ("cortex"). A thick bundle of nerve fibers, called the **corpus callosum** (Latin for "thick body" or "hard body") connects the cerebral hemispheres and forms a pathway by which the hemispheres share information and communicate with each other. Structures in the brain that lie beneath the cerebral cortex are called *subcortical* structures (*sub* meaning "below" the cortex).

Though a mere one-eighth of an inch thick—no thicker than a napkin—the cerebral cortex accounts for more than 80 percent of the brain's total mass. The cortex owes its wrinkled or convoluted appearance to contours created by ridges and valleys. These contours enable its large surface area to be packed tightly within the confines of the skull (see Concept Chart 2.3). Its massive size in relation to the other parts of the brain reflects the amount of the brain devoted to higher mental functions, such as thinking, language use, and problem solving. Only in humans does the cortex account for so great a portion of the brain (see ■ Figure 2.7). The cortex also controls voluntary movement, states of motivation and emotional arousal, and processing of sensory information.

Each hemisphere of the cerebral cortex is divided into four parts, or *lobes*, as shown in ■ Figure 2.8. Thus, each lobe is represented in each hemisphere. The functions of the lobes are summarized in Table 2.1. Generally speaking, each of the cerebral hemispheres controls feeling and movement on the opposite side of the body.

The **occipital lobes**, located in the back of the head, process visual information, including visual cues that enable us to recognize faces (Connor, 2010). We experience sight when a source of light stimulates receptors in the eyes and causes neurons in the

CONCEPT 2.19
The largest part of the brain, the forebrain, controls higher mental functions, such as thinking, problem solving, use of language, planning, and memory.

thalamus A structure in the forebrain that serves as a relay station for sensory information and plays a key role in regulating states of wakefulness and sleep.

basal ganglia An assemblage of neurons lying in the forebrain that is important in controlling movement and coordination.

hypothalamus A pea-sized structure in the forebrain that helps regulate many vital bodily functions, including body temperature and reproduction, as well as emotional states, aggression, and responses to stress.

limbic system A formation of structures in the forebrain that includes the hippocampus, amygdala, and parts of the thalamus and hypothalamus.

amygdala A set of almond-shaped structures in the limbic system believed to play an important role in aggression, rage, and fear.

hippocampus A structure in the limbic system involved in memory formation.

cerebral cortex The wrinkled, outer layer of gray matter that covers the cerebral hemispheres; controls higher mental functions, such as thought and language.

cerebrum The largest mass of the forebrain, consisting of two cerebral hemispheres.

cerebral hemispheres The right and left masses of the cerebrum, which are joined by the corpus callosum.

corpus callosum The thick bundle of nerve fibers that connects the two cerebral hemispheres.

occipital lobes The parts of the cerebral cortex, located at the back of both cerebral hemispheres, that process visual stimuli.

CONCEPT 2.20
The limbic system plays an important role in the regulation of memory and emotions.

CONCEPT 2.21
The cerebrum is divided into two hemispheres and is covered by a thin, outer layer, the cerebral cortex, which is responsible for higher mental functions.

Figure 2.7 The Size of the Cerebral Cortex in Humans and Other Animals
The cerebral cortex accounts for a much greater portion of the brain in humans than in other animals.

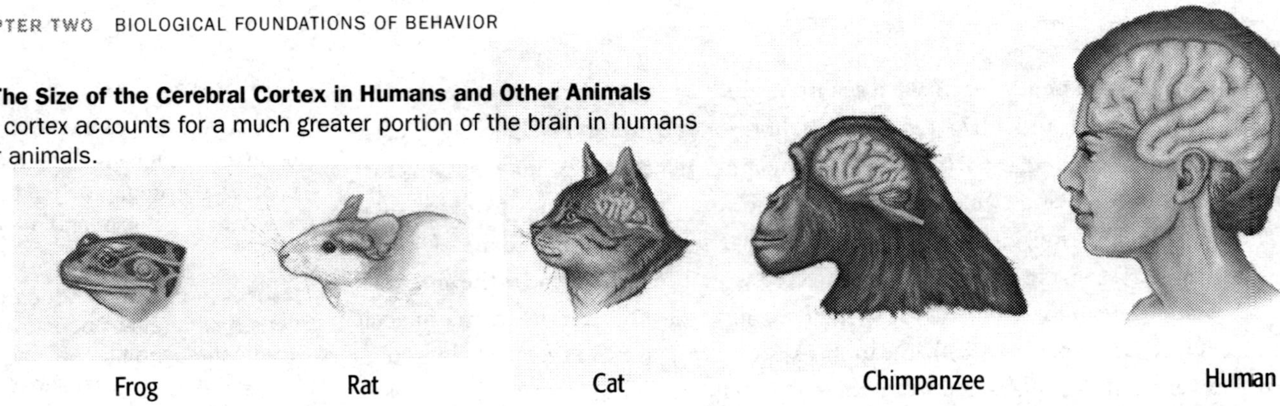

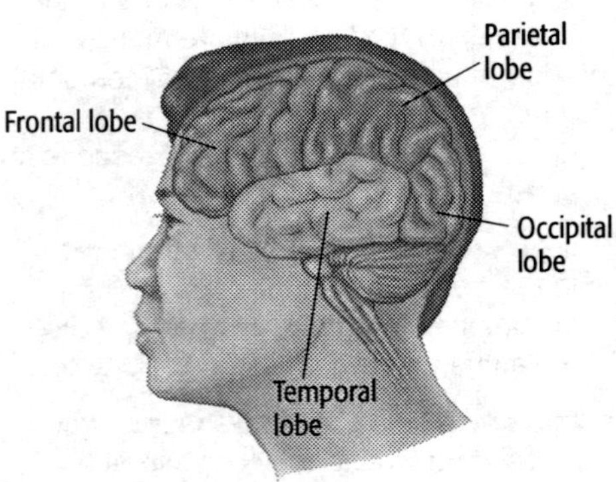

Figure 2.8 Lobes of the Cerebral Cortex
The cerebral cortex is divided into four parts, or lobes: the occipital, parietal, frontal, and temporal lobes.

parietal lobes The parts of the cerebral cortex, located on the side of each cerebral hemisphere, that process bodily sensations.

somatosensory cortex The part of the parietal lobe that processes information about touch and pressure on the skin, as well as the position of our body parts as we move about.

occipital lobes to fire (discussed further in Chapter 3). Even blows to the back of the head can stimulate the visual cortex, producing visual sensations such as "seeing stars."

The **parietal lobes** are located on the sides of the brain, directly above and in front of the occipital lobes. At the front of the parietal lobes lies a strip of nerve cells called the **somatosensory cortex**, which processes sensory information received from receptors in the skin, giving rise to our experience of touch, pressure, temperature (hotness or coldness), and pain. Like your eyes and ears, your skin is a sensory organ that provides information about the world. The somatosensory cortex also receives information from receptors in your muscles and joints to keep you aware of the position of the parts of your body as you move about.

■ Figure 2.9 illustrates how specific parts of the somatosensory cortex correspond to sensory information (touch, pressure, pain, and temperature) received from specific parts of the body. Electrical stimulation of particular parts of the somatosensory cortex can make it seem as though your shoulder or your leg were experiencing touch or pressure, for example.

The strange-looking "being" shown in ■ Figure 2.10 is not a creature from the latest *Star Wars* installment. Sensory information from some parts of the body is transmitted to larger areas of the somatosensory cortex than is sensory information from other parts. This is because the brain devotes more of its capabilities to parts of the body that require greater sensitivity or control, such as the hands. Nor are the parts of the body represented in the somatosensory cortex in a way that directly corresponds to the body itself. For example, sensory input from the genitals projects to an area that lies beneath the part receiving input from the toes, and the area that responds to stimulation of the tongue does not lie within the area that responds to stimulation of the lips. We don't know why this is so. But each of us knows the precise areas of our body that are touched. We know, for instance, when it is our lips that are touched and not our tongues, and vice versa.

TABLE 2.1 The Lobes of the Cerebral Cortex

Structure	Functions
Occipital lobes	Process visual information, giving rise to sensations of vision
Parietal lobes	Process information relating to sensations of touch, pressure, temperature (hot and cold), pain, and body movement
Frontal lobes	Control motor responses and higher mental functions, such as thinking, planning, problem solving, decision making, and accessing and acting on stored memories
Temporal lobes	Process auditory information, giving rise to sensations of sound

The **frontal lobes** are located in the front part of the brain, just behind the forehead. Scientists call the frontal lobes the "executive center" of the brain, because they believe they contain your "you"—the part that accesses your memories, mulls things over, has self-awareness, and decides that the red plaid shirt is just "too retro." Like the central processing unit of a computer, parts of the frontal lobes retrieve memories from storage, place them in active memory, manipulate them, and make decisions based on them (Gazzaniga, 1999). For example, your frontal lobes pull sensory memories about visual cues, sounds, odors, and even tastes from storage, so that the second time you see that oblong-shaped red pepper sitting innocently in your bowl of Kung Pao chicken, you remember not to bite into it. Your frontal lobes also allow you to solve problems, make decisions, plan actions, weigh evidence, and carry out coordinated actions.

Laboratory studies show that the frontal lobes are involved in processing emotional states, such as happiness and sadness (Davidson et al., 2002). In addition, they enable you to suppress tendencies to act on impulse, such as when you restrain yourself from telling your boss or professor what you really think of him or her.

The frontal lobes contain the **motor cortex**, which is located just across the border that separates them from the parietal lobes (see Figure 2.9). The motor cortex controls voluntary movements of specific parts of the body. For example, some neurons in the motor cortex control movements of the hands. When an electrode is used to stimulate a certain part of

© The Natural History Museum Picture Library, London.

Figure 2.10 A Creature from *Star Wars*? Actually, this is an artist's rendering of how we would appear if the size of our body parts were in proportion to the areas of the somatosensory cortex that process sensory information from these parts. Because much more cortex is devoted to the fingers and hands than to elbows or thighs, we can discern much finer differences in sensations of touch with our fingertips.

frontal lobes The parts of the cerebral cortex, located at the front of the cerebral hemispheres, that are considered the "executive center" of the brain because of their role in higher mental functions.

motor cortex A region of the frontal lobes involved in regulating body movement.

CONCEPT 2.22
The corpus callosum is a bundle of nerve fibers connecting the two hemispheres of the brain, allowing them to share information.

CONCEPT 2.23
Each cerebral hemisphere has four main parts, or lobes: the occipital, parietal, frontal, and temporal lobes.

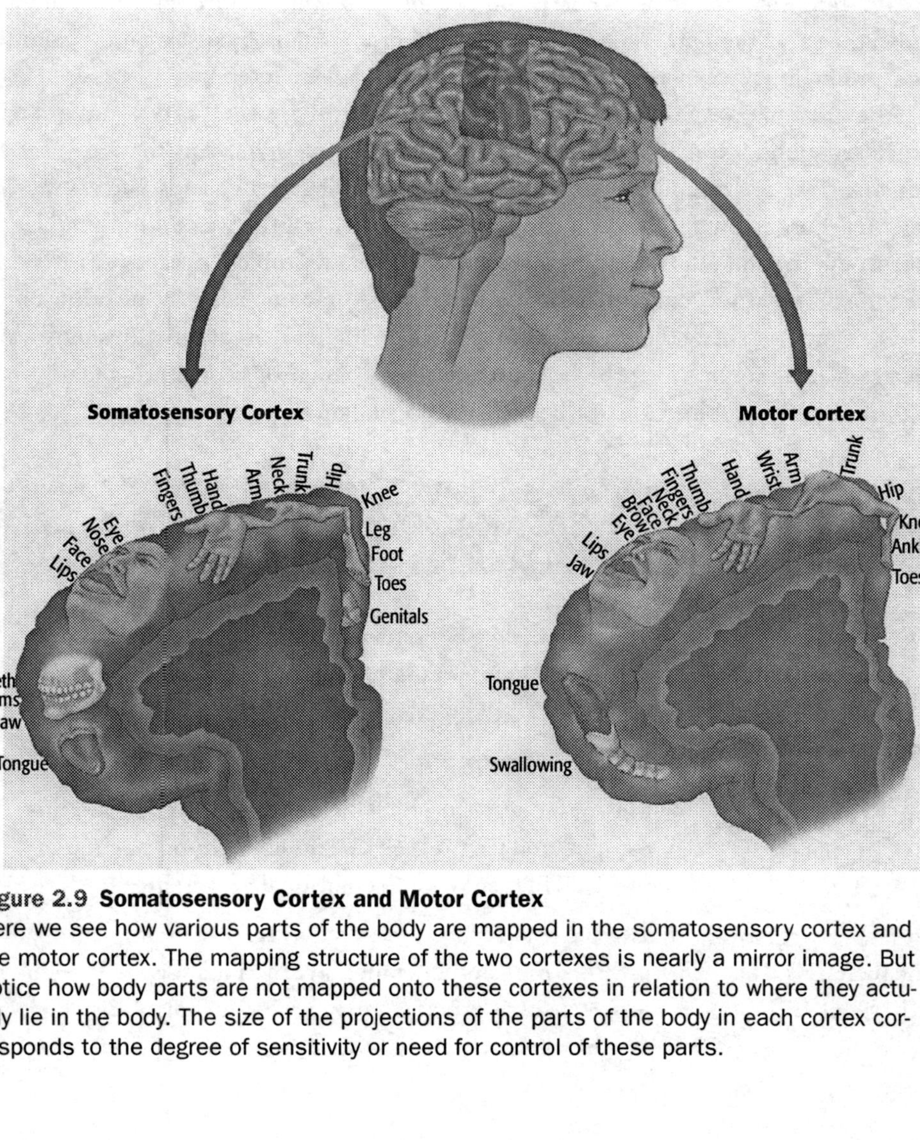

Figure 2.9 Somatosensory Cortex and Motor Cortex
Here we see how various parts of the body are mapped in the somatosensory cortex and the motor cortex. The mapping structure of the two cortexes is nearly a mirror image. But notice how body parts are not mapped onto these cortexes in relation to where they actually lie in the body. The size of the projections of the parts of the body in each cortex corresponds to the degree of sensitivity or need for control of these parts.

the motor cortex (a painless procedure sometimes used during brain surgery), muscles on the other side of the body contract. Depending on the electrode placement, the patient may lift a finger or tense a muscle in the leg. The representation of the body on the motor cortex is similar to that mapped out on the somatosensory cortex, as you can see in Figure 2.9.

Did you ever have the experience of grabbing the arms of your seat in a movie theater more tightly when you see characters on the screen doing the same in a scene in which they are bracing for the impact of an airplane crash? Did you head ever recoil when watching someone receive a jarring blow to the head in a movie? Scientists suspect they may have an explanation of these mirroring experiences. Experimental work with monkeys led to the discovery of specialized neurons in the motor cortex, called **mirror neurons**, that fired when the monkey performed a certain action, such as grabbing an object such as a peanut, and when they merely observed another monkey grab the same object (Decety & Cacioppo, 2010; Jaffe, 2007). The actions of these neurons "mirror" observed behaviors, just as though an observer were actually performing the action. In humans, neurons in the somatosensory cortex fire both when individuals are lightly touched and when they observe pictures of another person touched in the same spot (Keysers et al., 2004). Some scientists suspect that mirror neurons represent a neurological basis for forms of social behavior, such as imitative behavior and empathy, but we should caution that we lack sufficient evidence to support these views (see Decety & Cacioppo, 2010; Distein et al., 2008).

mirror neurons Neurons that fire both when an action is performed and when the same action is merely observed.

CONCEPT 2.24
Most of the cerebral cortex consists of association areas that are responsible for higher mental functions.

The **temporal lobes** lie beneath and somewhat behind the frontal lobes, directly above the ears. The temporal lobes receive and process sensory information from the ears, producing the experience of hearing (discussed in Chapter 3).

The great majority of cortex consists of **association areas**. The association areas, which are found in each lobe, are more highly developed in humans than in other organisms. They are responsible for performing higher mental functions, such as piecing together sensory input to form meaningful perceptions of the world, thinking, learning, producing and understanding speech, solving math problems, planning activities, creating masterworks of architecture, and perhaps even composing the next hit song.

temporal lobes The parts of the cerebral cortex lying beneath and somewhat behind the frontal lobes that are involved in processing auditory stimuli.

association areas Areas of the cerebral cortex that piece together sensory information to form meaningful perceptions of the world and perform higher mental functions.

We cannot identify the precise locations where higher mental functions occur. Association areas are linked within intricate networks of neurons connecting many parts of the brain, the architecture of which we are only beginning to comprehend.

2.3 MODULE REVIEW The Brain: Your Crowning Glory

Recite It

How is the brain organized, and what are the functions of its various parts?

- The brain has three major sections. The hindbrain, which houses the medulla, pons, and cerebellum, is involved in controlling basic bodily functions. The midbrain houses nerve bundles that relay messages between the hindbrain and the forebrain; it also houses structures that help regulate automatic movement. The forebrain is the largest part of the brain; its major structures are the thalamus, the hypothalamus, the limbic system, and the cerebral cortex.
- The thalamus relays sensory information to the cerebral cortex and helps regulate states of sleep and wakefulness.
- The hypothalamus plays a key role in controlling many vital bodily processes.
- The limbic system, which includes the amygdala, hippocampus, and parts of the thalamus and hypothalamus, is involved in memory and emotional processing.
- The cerebral cortex is responsible for processing sensory information, for higher mental functions such as thought, problem solving, and language, and for controlling voluntary movement, among other functions.

How is the cerebral cortex organized?

➤ Each hemisphere of the cerebral cortex has four lobes: the frontal, parietal, temporal, and occipital lobes. Each of the lobes is contained in each cerebral hemisphere. The corpus callosum is a nerve bundle that connects the two hemispheres.

What are the major functions associated with the four lobes of the cerebral cortex?

➤ The occipital lobes are primarily involved with vision; the parietal lobes, with somatosensory processing; the temporal lobes, with hearing; and the frontal lobes, with motor control and higher mental functions, including retrieving and acting on stored memories, solving problems, making decisions, and carrying out coordinated actions.

Recall It

1. The limbic system structure that resembles a sea horse and that plays an important role in memory functioning is
   a. the frontal cortex.
   b. the thalamus.
   c. the amygdala.
   d. the hippocampus.
2. Match the following parts of the brain with the functions they control: (a) medulla; (b) cerebellum; (c) thalamus; (d) cerebral cortex.
   i. balance and coordination
   ii. thinking and organizing
   iii. relay of sensory information to the cerebral cortex
   iv. heart rate and breathing
3. Which of the following is not correct? The cerebral cortex
   a. is the part of the brain most directly responsible for reasoning, language, and problem solving.
   b. is divided into four lobes.
   c. forms the outer layer of the cerebral hemispheres.
   d. accounts for a much smaller percentage of brain mass in humans than in other animals.
4. Which part of the cerebral cortex processes auditory information?

Think About It

➤ Why does the text refer to your brain as your "crowning glory"?

➤ A person suffers a serious fall and sustains severe damage to the back of the head. What sensory processes are most likely to be affected by the injury?

Methods of Studying the Brain

MODULE 2.4

- What recording and imaging techniques are used to study brain functioning?
- What experimental methods do scientists use to study brain functioning?

Scientists use various methods of studying brain structures and their functions. One method is to observe the effects of diseases or injuries on the brain. As a result of this type of observation, scientists have known for nearly two centuries that damage to the left side of the brain is connected with loss of sensation or movement on the right side of the body, and vice versa.

Over the years, scientists have also used invasive experimental methods to study the brain at work, including surgical procedures. Today, thanks to advanced technology, they have other, less invasive recording and imaging methods at their disposal. Concept Chart 2.4 summarizes both types of methods.

THE BRAIN LOVES A PUZZLE

As you read ahead, use the information in the text to solve the following puzzle:

Why is it impossible to tickle yourself? Try it out. Why does tickling yourself fail to elicit the same tickling response that occurs when someone else tickles you?

Recording and Imaging Techniques

Today, we have available a range of techniques that allow us to peer into the working brain and other parts of the body without invasive surgery. These techniques are used to diagnose brain diseases and examine brain damage, as well to expand our

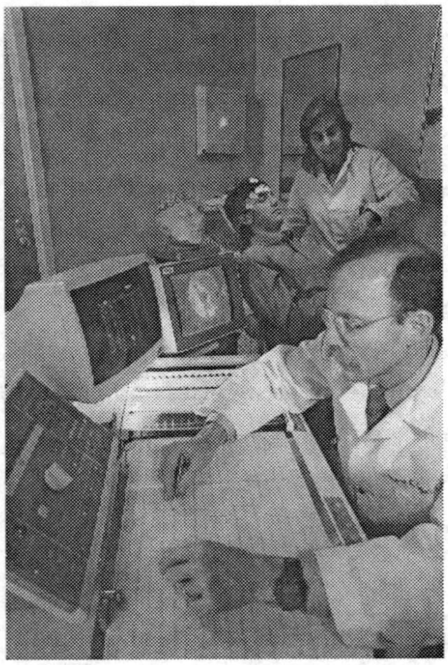
© Richard T. Nowitz/CORBIS

Figure 2.11 The Electroencephalograph (EEG)
The EEG is a device that records electrical activity in the brain in the form of brain wave patterns. It is used to study the brains of people with physical or psychological disorders and to explore brain wave patterns during stages of sleep.

understanding of brain functioning. Using these techniques, neuroscientists can examine the working brain while the subject is awake and alert.

The **EEG (electroencephalograph)** is an instrument that records electrical activity in the brain (see ■ Figure 2.11). Electrodes are attached to the scalp to measure the electrical currents, or *brain waves,* that are conducted between them. The EEG is used to study electrical activity in the brains of people with physical or psychological disorders and to explore brain wave patterns during stages of sleep.

The **CT (computed tomography) scan** (also called a *CAT* scan) is an imaging technique in which a computer measures the reflection of a narrow X-ray beam from various angles as it passes through the brain or other bodily structures; it thus produces a three-dimensional image of the inside of the body (see ■ Figure 2.12). The CT scan reveals brain abnormalities associated with structural problems such as blood clots, tumors, and brain injuries. We can also use it to explore structural abnormalities in the brains of people with schizophrenia or other severe psychological disorders.

Whereas the CT scan reveals information about the shape and size of structures in the brain, the **PET (positron emission tomography) scan** provides a computerized image of the brain and other organs at work. The subject receives an injection of a radioactive isotope that acts as a tracer in the bloodstream. How the tracer is metabolized (converted by cells into energy) in the brain reveals the parts of the brain that are more active than others. More active areas metabolize more of the tracer than less active ones (see ■ Figure 2.13). The PET scan can reveal which parts of the brain are most active when we are reading and writing, daydreaming, listening to music, or experiencing emotions. From these patterns, we can determine which parts of the brain are involved in particular functions.

CONCEPT CHART 2.4 Methods of Studying the Brain

Recording and Imaging Techniques	Description
EEG (electroencephalograph)	A device that uses electrodes attached to the skull to record brain wave activity
CT (computed tomography) scan	A computer-enhanced X-ray technique that can provide images of the internal structures of the brain
PET (positron emission tomography) scan	A method that can provide a computer-generated image of the brain, formed by tracing the amounts of glucose used in different parts of the brain during different types of activity
MRI (magnetic resonance imaging)	A method of producing computerized images of the brain and other body parts by measuring the signals they emit when placed in a strong magnetic field
Experimental Techniques	**Description**
Lesioning	Destruction of brain tissue in order to observe the effects on behavior
Electrical recording	Placement of electrodes in brain tissue to record changes in electrical activity in response to particular stimuli
Electrical stimulation	The use of a mild electric current to observe the effects of stimulating various parts of the brain

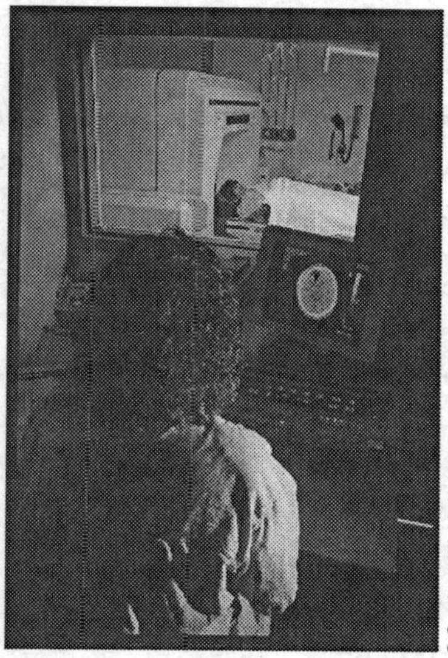
© Southern Illinois University/Photo Researchers, Inc.

Figure 2.12 CT Scan
The CT scan provides a three-dimensional X-ray image of bodily structures. It can reveal structural abnormalities in the brain that may be associated with blood clots, tumors, brain injuries, or psychological disorders, such as schizophrenia.

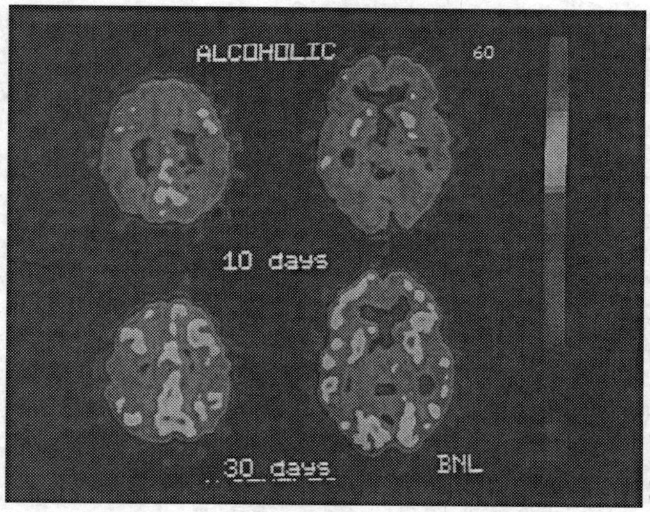

© Pascal Goetgheluck/Photo Researchers, Inc.

Figure 2.13 PET Scan
The PET scan measures the metabolic activity of the brain. More active regions are highlighted in yellow and red, whereas less active regions are shown in blue and green. Here we see PET scan images of the brain of an alcoholic patient during withdrawal. By comparing relative levels of brain activity following 10 days (top row) and 30 days (bottom row) of withdrawal, we can observe that the brain becomes more active with greater length of time without alcohol.

MRI (magnetic resonance imaging) provides a detailed image of the brain or other body parts. To produce a brain image, a technician places the person's head within a doughnut-shaped device that emits a strong magnetic field, aligning the atoms that spin in the brain. A burst of radio waves directed at the person disrupts the atoms, which release signals as they become realigned. A computer then integrates the signals into an image of the brain.

A new form of MRI, called *functional MRI* (fMRI), takes snapshots of the brain in action (see ■ Figure 2.14). Whereas traditional MRI is limited to mapping brain structures, functional MRI is used to study both the functions and the structure of the human brain. In Figure 2.14, we see fMRI images of the working brain in response to different tasks.

Investigators use fMRI to identify parts of the brain that "light up" or become activated when we perform particular tasks, such as seeing, hearing, remembering, using language, cooperating with others, and experiencing emotional states, even feelings of romantic love. However, a fuller account of psychological processes like memory and perception requires a better understanding of the workings of complex brain networks, not simply individual brain structures (Gonsalves & Cohen, 2010; Poldrack, 2010). PET scans also map functions of brain structures, but fMRI is less invasive in that it does not require injections of radioactive isotopes.

Functional MRI may well have helped clear up a longstanding scientific mystery—why it is impossible to tickle yourself (Provine, 2004). Using this method, British researchers peered into the brains of people as they tickled themselves and as they were being tickled by a mechanical device. The part of the brain that processes sensations of touch, the somatosensory cortex, showed more activity when people were being tickled than when they tickled themselves. When we move our fingers to tickle ourselves, the brain center that coordinates these types of complex movements, the cerebellum, sends a signal that blocks some of the activity of the somatosensory cortex, which processes touch. But being

CONCEPT 2.25
Modern technology provides ways of studying the structure and functions of the brain without the need for invasive techniques.

→ Concept Link
Brain scans are used to help us better understand the biological bases of schizophrenia and other psychological disorders. See Module 15.5.

EEG (electroencephalograph) A device that records electrical activity in the brain.

CT (computed tomography) scan A computer-enhanced imaging technique in which an X-ray beam is passed through the body at different angles to generate a three-dimensional image of bodily structures (also called a CAT scan, short for *computerized axial tomography*).

PET (positron emission tomography) scan An imaging technique in which a radioactive sugar tracer is injected into the bloodstream and used to measure levels of activity of various parts of the brain.

MRI (magnetic resonance imaging) A technique that uses a magnetic field to create a computerized image of internal bodily structures.

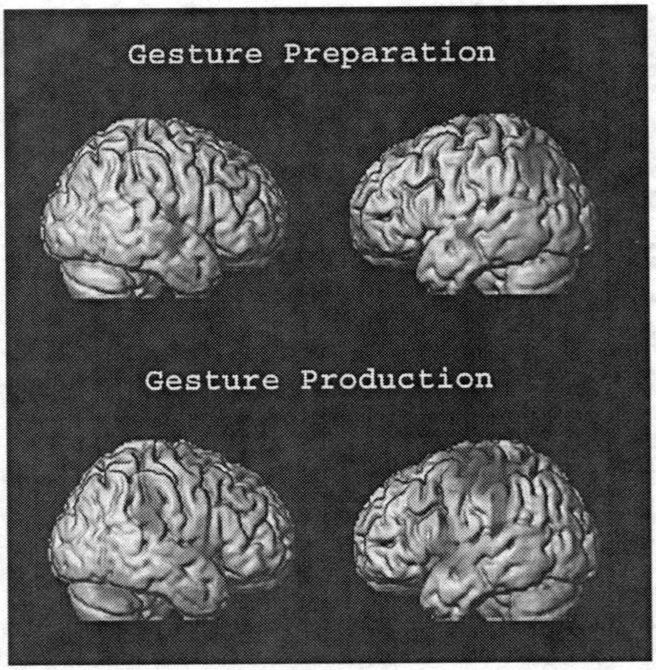

Figure 2.14 Functional Magnetic Resonance Imaging (fMRI) Here we see fMRI images of the brain when a person thinks about performing certain gestures (top), such as using a hammer or writing with a pen, and when actually performing these acts (bottom). The left hemisphere is depicted on the right side of the image, while the right hemisphere is shown on the left. Areas in red are associated with greater levels of brain activity.

tickled by an outside source comes as a surprise, so the cerebellum does not send a blocking signal to the cortex. Scientists believe this brain mechanism allows us to distinguish between stimuli we produce ourselves and unexpected outside stimuli that require closer attention by the cerebral cortex because they may pose a threat (Aamodt & Wang, 2008).

Experimental Methods

Scientists sometimes use invasive methods to investigate brain functioning. In one such method, called **lesioning**, the investigator destroys parts of the brain in experimental animals and then observes the effects. For example, destroying one part of a rhesus monkey's limbic system causes the animal to fly into a rage at the slightest provocation. But destroy another part of this system, and the monkey shows a placid response to all manner of provocation. Destroy one part of a rat's hypothalamus, and it gorges itself on food until it becomes extremely obese; destroy another part, and it stops eating. These experiments point to the parts of the brain engaged in these and other forms of behavior.

Other experimental techniques for studying brain function include *electrical recording* and *electrical stimulation*. In **electrical recording,** electrodes are implanted into particular neurons, groups of neurons, or nerves in specific parts of the brain. They provide a record of electrical changes in response to particular stimuli. Some experimental techniques are so refined that investigators can record electrical activity from a single brain cell. Using these methods, scientists discovered how individual neurons in the visual cortex respond to particular types of visual stimuli (see Chapter 3).

With the technique of **electrical stimulation,** investigators pass a mild electric current through particular parts of the brain and observe the effects. In this way, they can learn which parts of the brain are involved in controlling which behaviors. For example, we mentioned earlier how stimulation of parts of the hypothalamus in rats and other animals switches on stereotypical behavior patterns.

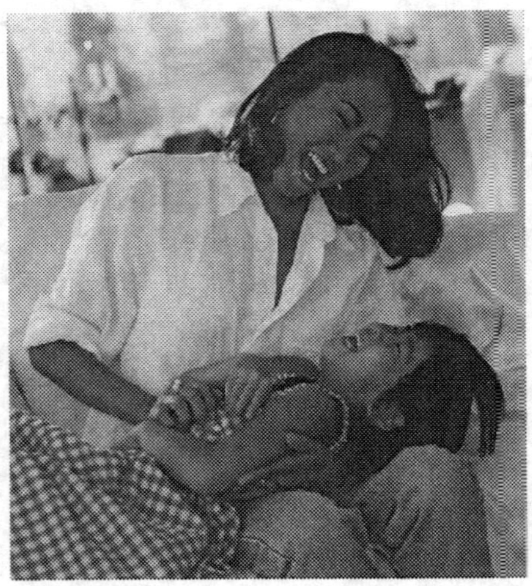

© Mark Richard/Photo Edit

Here's a ticklish question for you: Why is it that you can't tickle yourself? Researchers using a brain-imaging technique believe they have the answer.

lesioning In studies of brain functioning, the intentional destruction of brain tissue in order to observe the effects on behavior.

electrical recording As a method of investigating brain functioning, a process of recording the electrical changes that occur in a specific neuron or groups of neurons in the brain in relation to particular activities or behaviors.

electrical stimulation As a method of investigating brain functioning, a process of electrically stimulating particular parts of the brain to observe the effects on behavior.

CONCEPT 2.26
Experimental methods used to study brain functioning include lesioning, electrical recording, and electrical stimulation.

2.4 MODULE REVIEW Methods of Studying the Brain

Recite It

What recording and imaging techniques are used to study brain functioning?

- These techniques include the EEG, CT scan, PET scan, and MRI.

What experimental methods do scientists use to study brain functioning?

- Lesioning is a method that involves destroying certain parts of the brains of laboratory animals in order to observe the effects.

- Electrical recording involves implanting electrodes in the brain to record changes in brain activity associated with certain activities or behaviors.
- Electrical stimulation entails passing a mild electric current through the brain so that the effects on specific parts of the brain can be observed.

Recall It

1. Which of the following is a computer-enhanced imaging technique that uses X-ray beams to study structural abnormalities of the brain?
   a. fMRI **b.** PET scan **c.** CT scan **d.** MRI
2. Scientists who use the experimental technique of electrical recording to study brain functioning
   a. also make use of a radioactive isotope that can be detected in the bloodstream.
   b. implant electrodes in particular neurons, groups of neurons, or nerves in particular parts of the brain.
   c. send a narrow X-ray beam through the head.
   d. are unable to get precise measurements from a single brain cell.
3. Functional MRI (fMRI)
   a. is used to study both brain structure and brain functioning.
   b. involves an invasive technique known as lesioning.
   c. is a controversial procedure with ethical implications.
   d. is based on a sophisticated type of X-ray technique.
4. In the experimental technique for brain study called lesioning,
   a. parts of the brain of living organisms are destroyed.
   b. electrodes are surgically implanted in the brain.
   c. parts of the brain are electrically stimulated to observe the effects on behavior.
   d. connections between the brain and spinal cord are severed.

Think About It

- What brain-imaging techniques do scientists use to study the functioning of the brain? To study the structures of the brain?
- What is your opinion about using animals in experimental brain research? What safeguards do you think should be observed in this kind of research?

The Divided Brain: Specialization of Function

MODULE 2.5

- What are the major differences between the left and right hemispheres?
- What determines handedness?
- What can we learn about brain lateralization from studies of "split-brain" patients?

If you stub your left toe, cells in your right parietal lobe will "light up," producing sensations of pain. Conversely, a blow to your right toe will register in your left parietal lobe. This is because the sensory cortex in each hemisphere is connected to sensory receptors on the opposite sides of the body. Likewise, the motor cortex in your right frontal lobe controls the movements of the left side of your body, and vice versa. Thus, if we were to stimulate your left motor cortex in a certain spot, the fingers on your right hand would involuntarily contract. As we see next, evidence indicates that the right and left hemispheres are also specialized for certain types of functions.

CONCEPT 2.27
In most people, the left hemisphere is specialized for use of language and logical analysis, whereas the right hemisphere is specialized for spatial processing and other nonverbal tasks.

The Brain at Work: Lateralization and Integration

The term **lateralization** refers to the division of functions between the right and left hemispheres (see Concept Chart 2.5). Generally speaking, the left hemisphere in most people appears to be dominant for language abilities—speaking, reading, and

lateralization The specialization of the right and left cerebral hemispheres for particular functions.

CONCEPT CHART 2.5 Lateralization of Brain Functions

Areas of Left-Hemisphere Dominance	Areas of Right-Hemisphere Dominance
 © Yuri Arcurs/Shutterstock.com	 © Sergiy Zavgorondny/Shutterstock.com
Verbal functions (for most people), including spoken and written use of language, as well as logical analysis, problem solving, and mathematical computation	Nonverbal functions, including understanding spatial relationships (as presented, e.g., in jigsaw puzzles or maps), recognizing faces and interpreting gestures, perceiving and expressing emotion, and appreciating music and art

writing. The left hemisphere also appears to be dominant for tasks requiring logical analysis, problem solving, and mathematical computations. The right hemisphere in most people appears to be dominant for nonverbal processing, such as understanding spatial relationships (e.g., piecing together puzzles, arranging blocks to match designs, reading maps), recognizing faces, interpreting people's gestures and facial expressions, perceiving and expressing emotion, and appreciating music and art.

Despite these differences, we shouldn't think of people as either "left-brained" or "right-brained." The brain operates as a whole system. The functions of the left and right hemispheres largely overlap, and messages quickly zap back and forth between them across the corpus callosum.

Although one hemisphere may be dominant for a particular task, both hemispheres share the work in performing most tasks. Language dominance is associated with handedness (Hopkins & Cantalupo, 2008). The left hemisphere is dominant for language functions in about 95 percent of right-handed people and about 70 percent of left-handed people (Pinker, 1994; Springer & Deutsch, 1993). For about 15 percent of left-handed people, the right hemisphere is dominant for language functions. The other 15 percent of left-handers show patterns of mixed dominance.

© Andrey Pavlov/Shutterstock.com

The French surgeon Paul Broca (1824–1880) was one of the pioneers in the discovery of the language areas of the brain. His most important discovery involved a male patient, 51 years old, who was admitted to the ward suffering from gangrene in his leg. The patient was also nearly unable to speak. He understood clearly what he heard, but his verbal utterances were limited primarily to one meaningless sound (*tan*).

The patient died a few days after being admitted. While conducting an autopsy, Broca found that an egg-shaped part of the left frontal lobe of the patient's brain had degenerated. The surgeon concluded that this area of the brain, now known as **Broca's area** in his honor, is essential to the production of speech (see ■ Figure 2.15) (Sahin et al., 2009).

Broca's area is one of the brain's two vital language areas. The other, which is in the left temporal lobe, is **Wernicke's area** (see Figure 2.15). It is named after the German researcher Karl Wernicke (1848–1905). Wernicke's area is responsible for our ability to comprehend language in written or spoken form (Plaza, Gatignol, & Duffau, 2009). Wernicke's and Broca's areas are connected by nerve fibers, so that there is an ongoing interaction between understanding language and being able to produce it or express it. Significant damage to Broca's area or Wernicke's area, or to the nerve connections between them, can lead to different forms of **aphasia**—the loss or impairment of the ability to understand or express language.

Broca's area An area of the left frontal lobe involved in speech.

Wernicke's area An area of the left temporal lobe involved in processing written and spoken language.

aphasia Loss or impairment of the ability to understand or express language.

epilepsy A neurological disorder characterized by seizures that involve sudden, violent discharges of electrical activity in the brain.

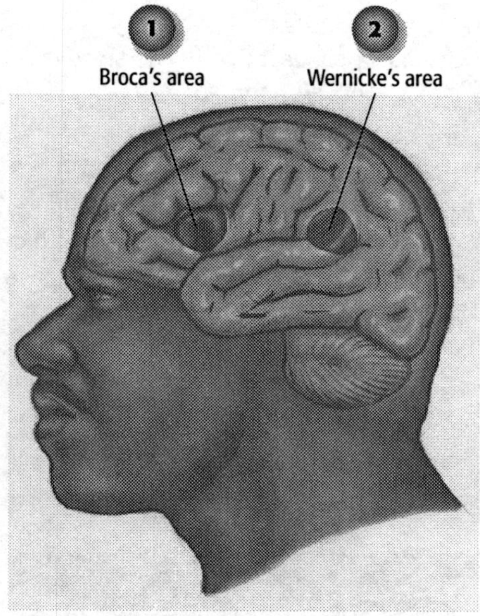

Figure 2.15 Broca's and Wernicke's Areas
1 Broca's area, an egg-shaped part of the frontal lobe, plays a key role in the production of speech. 2 Wernicke's area, located in the temporal lobe, enables us to understand written or spoken language.

Handedness: Why Are People Not More Even-Handed?

Though we may not be "right-brained" or "left-brained," most of us are primarily either right-handed or left-handed. About 90 percent of people are right-handed, with the remainder either left-handed or ambidextrous to some degree (Price, 2009a). Evidence points to genetics playing an important role in determining handedness (Klass, 2011; Scerri et al., 2010). Not surprisingly, handedness tends to run in families (see Table 2.2). However, since handedness differs in about one in five sets of identical twins (one twin may be right-handed, the other left-handed), other factors than genetics must also contribute to handedness. Social influences, such as family pressures on children to use their right hands for writing, may also play a part in determining handedness.

Men are more likely to be left-handed than women (Papadatou-Pastou et al., 2008). The explanation of this gender difference remains unclear, although scientists suspect that sex-linked genetic factors and perhaps prenatal exposure to the male sex hormone testosterone are possible causal factors (Price, 2009b). We do know that handedness preferences begin to develop before birth. In an ultrasound-based study of more than two hundred fetuses, researchers found that more than 95 percent of them sucked their right thumbs, whereas fewer than 5 percent sucked their left thumbs (Hepper, Shahidullah, & White, 1990). These percentages correspond closely to the distribution of right-handers and left-handers in the population.

Whatever the origins of handedness may be, forcibly imposing right-handedness on children may cause them to become secretive about using their left hands (e.g., by switching to the left hand when they are not being observed) and to develop emotional problems.

TABLE 2.2 Parents' Handedness and Child's Odds of Being Left-Handed

Parents Who Are Left-Handed	Child's Odds
Neither parent	1 in 50
One parent	1 in 6
Both parents	1 in 2

Source: Springer and Deutsch, 1993.

Split-Brain Research: Can the Hemispheres Go It Alone?

Epilepsy is a neurological disorder in which sudden, violent neural discharges of electrical activity in the brain cause seizures. In many cases, these discharges resemble a neural Ping-Pong match—the electrical discharges begin in one cerebral hemisphere and thunder into the other. As they bounce back and forth, they create a kind of wild electrical storm in the brain. Fortunately, most people with epilepsy are able to avoid or control seizures with medication.

When the disorder fails to respond to conventional forms of treatment, surgery may become an option. In the 1960s, neurosurgeons treated some severe cases of epilepsy by severing the corpus callosum. The purpose was to stop the neural storm in the brain by preventing the electrical activity in one hemisphere from crossing into the other. The surgery prevents communication between the cerebral hemispheres.

split-brain patients Persons whose corpus callosum has been surgically severed.

Remarkably, patients who undergo the cutting of the corpus callosum, whom we call **split-brain patients**, retain their intellectual competence and distinctive personalities following surgery. Yet the two hemispheres appear to be of two minds about some things (Gazzaniga, 1999). We might sometimes joke that it seems as if our left hand doesn't know what our right hand is doing. For split-brain patients, this strikes close to home, as illustrated in landmark research conducted by Nobel Prize winner Roger Sperry and his colleague Michael Gazzaniga.

CONCEPT 2.28
Scientists suspect that handedness is strongly influenced by genetics.

CONCEPT 2.29
The results of split-brain operations show that, under some conditions, the right hand literally doesn't know what the left hand is doing.

In one of these experiments, researchers placed a familiar object, such as a key, in the left hands of split-brain patients (Gazzaniga, 1992). When blindfolded, the patients could not name the object they were holding, although they were able to use the key to open a lock. The question is, *why*?

Recall that the somatosensory cortex in the right hemisphere processes sensory information from the left side of the body (the touch of a key placed in the left hand, for instance). Since the right hemisphere shares this information with the left hemisphere, speech centers in the left hemisphere can respond by naming the object that was felt. Thus, people whose brains function normally have no trouble naming a familiar object placed in their left hands even if they can't see it.

But in split-brain patients, the right hemisphere cannot transmit information to the speech centers in the left hemisphere, making it impossible to name the object being held in the left hand. The right hemisphere literally cannot "say" what the left hand is holding (Gazzaniga, 1995). But despite this lack of ability to name the object, the right hemisphere recognizes the object by touch and can demonstrate through hand movements how it is used.

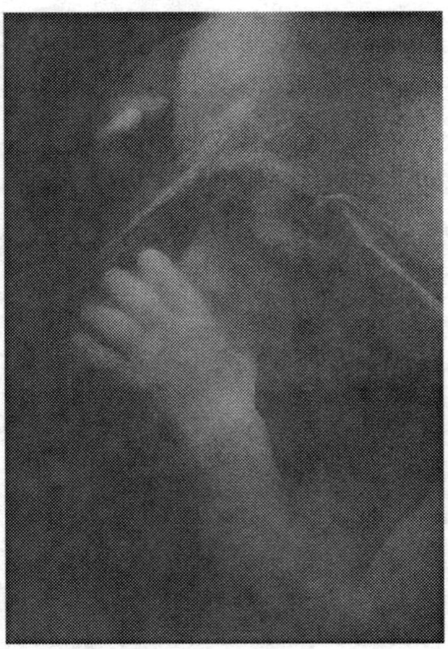

© Neil Bromhall, Photo Researchers, Inc.

The proportions of fetuses sucking their right or left thumbs parallel those of right-handed people in the population, suggesting that handedness preferences may begin to develop before birth.

In perception studies with split-brain patients, researchers briefly flash pictures of objects on a screen and then ask the patients to identify them by naming them or by selecting them from among a group of objects hidden behind the screen (see ■ Figure 2.16). The experimenters vary whether the stimuli are projected to the left or right visual cortex, which is located in the occipital lobes in the back of the head. If you look straight ahead and project a vertical line dividing your field of view into a right and a left half, the area to the left of the line represents your left visual field. Information presented to the left visual field crosses over and is processed by the right visual cortex. Conversely, information presented to the right of your field of view (to the right visual field) is projected to the left visual cortex. In people whose corpus callosum is intact, information is quickly exchanged between the hemispheres, but in split-brain patients, one hemisphere does not communicate with the other.

When an image is flashed to the right visual field of a split-brain patient, the left hemisphere processes the information, and the patient is able to name the object ("I saw a pencil"). This is not surprising when you consider that the left hemisphere in most people controls speech. But what happens when the picture of the object is flashed on the left side of the screen, which projects information to the right hemisphere, the one without language function? In this case, the patient cannot say what, if anything, is seen. The patient is likely to report, "I saw nothing." However, because the right

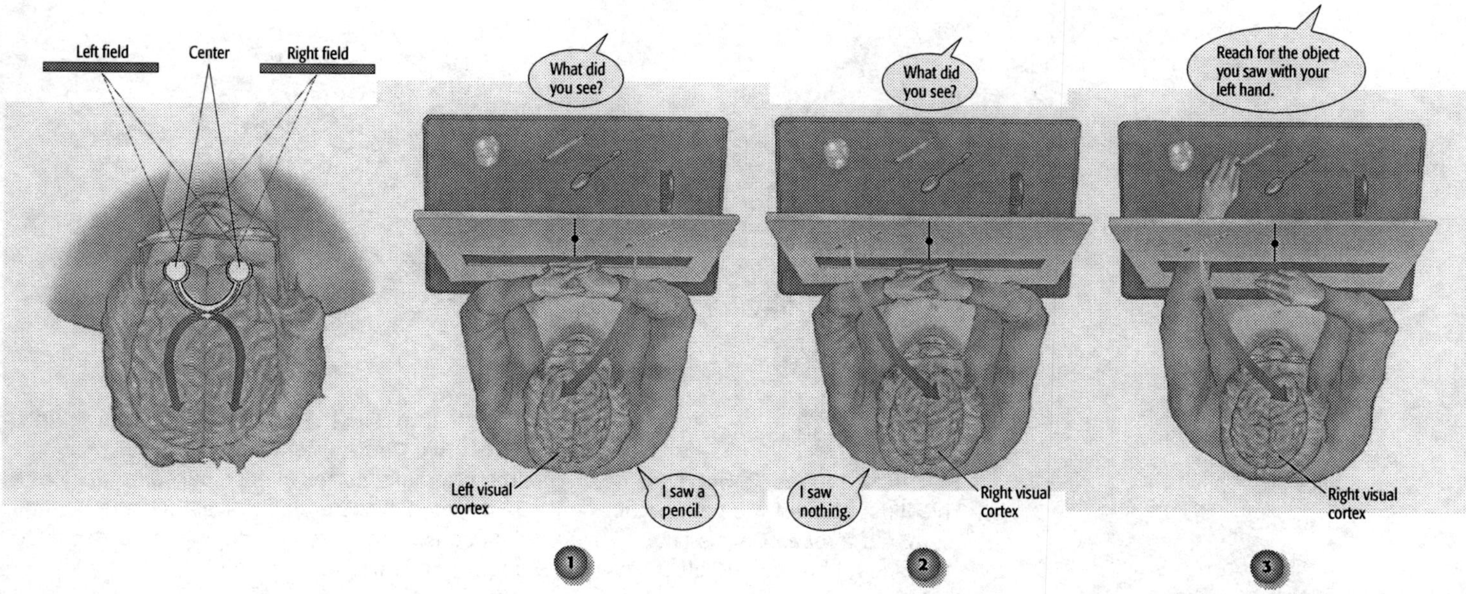

Figure 2.16 Split-Brain Study
The right part of this figure shows that information from the right half of the visual field is transmitted to the occipital cortex in the left hemisphere; conversely, information from the left half of the visual field goes to the right occipital cortex for processing. In split-brain patients, information received by one hemisphere cannot be transferred to the other.

In a typical study with split-brain patients, investigators present a visual stimulus to each hemisphere individually.

1. When an object, such as a pencil, is flashed in the right visual field, the visual information is transmitted to the patient's left hemisphere. Since the left hemisphere controls language, the patient can correctly name the object.
2. When visual information is presented to the nonverbal right hemisphere, the patient is unable to name it.
3. The patient is able to pick out the object by touch from a group of hidden objects when using the left hand, since the tactile information from the left hand projects to the right hemisphere, which has already "seen" the object.

hemisphere can recognize objects by touch, the patient is able to use the left hand to select the correct object from among those hidden behind the screen.

Findings from studies of split-brain patients provide additional evidence of the importance of the left hemisphere in speech and language production. Perhaps more revealing is the observation from the pioneering studies of split-brain patients that they appear to be quite normal in their outward behavior (Sperry, 1982). It seems as if their brains are able to adapt new strategies for processing information and solving problems that do not rely on communication between the hemispheres. As we will now see, this speaks to the remarkable ability of the human brain to adapt to new demands.

Brain Damage and Psychological Functioning

SLICE OF LIFE Many people have made remarkable recoveries from brain damage resulting from stroke or head trauma. Perhaps none is more remarkable than that of Phineas Gage, a nineteenth-century railroad worker whose case astounded the medical practitioners of his time. One day in 1848, Gage was packing blasting powder for a dynamite charge and accidentally set it off. The blast shot an inch-thick metal rod through his

TRY THIS OUT
Which Way Does Your Hair Swirl?

Are you looking for something to do while waiting out a long delay at the airport? Why not follow the lead of National Cancer Institute investigator Amar Klar and examine the swirls on people's heads? While observing people at airports and shopping malls, Klar noticed an interesting pattern in the swirl directions of the hair on their heads (Klar, 2003). More than 95 percent of right-handers had hair that swirled clockwise, whereas left-handers and people who were ambidextrous were equally likely to have swirls in either direction. Perhaps the same genes are involved in controlling both hair swirls and handedness.

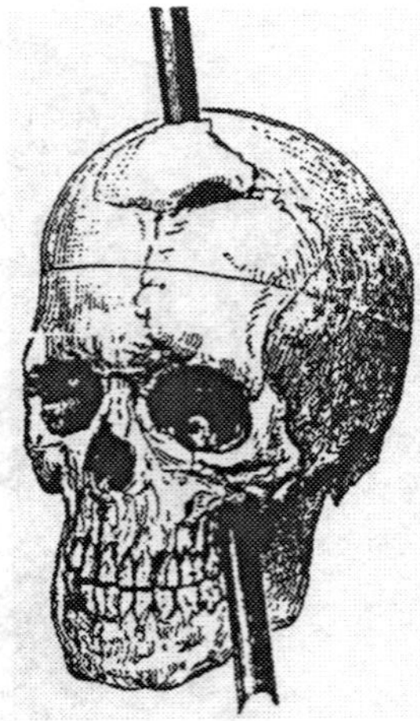

FIGURE 2.17 Yet He Survived
This illustration of the path of the metal rod through Gage's skull shows just how remarkable it was that he survived.

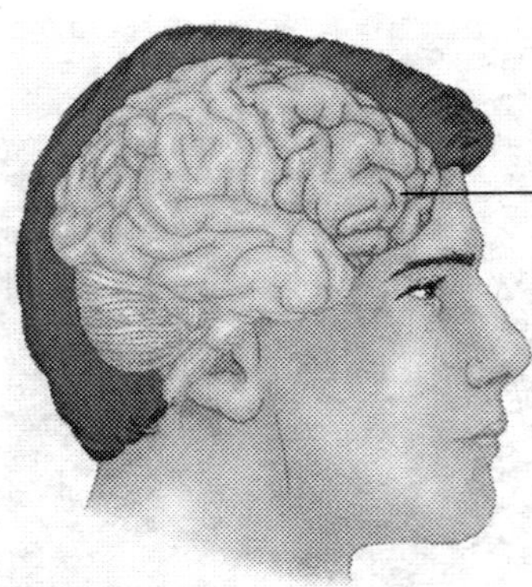

Figure 2.18 The Prefrontal Cortex: The Brain's Executive Control Center
The prefrontal cortex in each of the frontal lobes is the area of the brain involved in higher mental functions such as reasoning, planning, decision making, creative thinking, and restraining impulsive behavior

A more recent yet no less remarkable story of survival is that of Rep. Gabrielle Giffords, who was shot through the head by an assailant at point blank range. The bullet passed through the left side of her brain, sparing critical brain structures needed for survival, but affecting areas involved in speech and movement.

CONCEPT 2.30
Brain damage can result in subtle or profound consequences in physical and psychological functioning.

cheek and brain and out through the top of his head (Ratiu & Talos, 2004). Gage fell to the ground, but to the astonishment of his co-workers, he soon stood up, dusted himself off, and spoke to them. He was helped home, where his wounds were bandaged. Gage's wounds healed within two months, and he was able to function despite the massive head injury he had suffered. Then, however, changes in his personality began to appear, which suggests to us that he suffered from subtle forms of brain damage. The formerly polite and conscientious worker became irritable, rude, and irresponsible (Holden, 2009). He started brawling and drinking heavily. Those who knew him before the accident said, "Gage is no longer Gage."

Gage's skull is now on display at Harvard University. The trajectory of the metal rod is obvious (see ■ Figure 2.17). With near-surgical precision, it apparently missed the parts of the brain controlling vital bodily processes but damaged the **prefrontal cortex** (PFC), the area of the frontal lobe that lies in front of the motor cortex (see ■ Figure 2.18).

In the human brain, the PFC comprises about one-third of the entire cerebral cortex, which shouldn't surprise us given the central role it plays in many of the

TRY THIS OUT Raising Your Awareness About Disability

Volunteering at a rehabilitation center can help raise your awareness about the needs of people with disabilities. There are also things you can do on your own to become more aware of the challenges posed by sensory and motor disabilities. Here are some suggestions offered by Professors Stephen Wurst and Karen Wolford of SUNY Oswego:

(1) to simulate a hand (motor) disability, splinter two fingers together on your dominant hand and go about your daily routine (excepting any activities, like driving, where it might pose a risk);
(2) to simulate the challenge posed by mutism, try not talking for a specified period of time; and
(3) to simulate an auditory disability, use ear plugs such as those found at your local pharmacy (being careful to avoid any activities in which lack of hearing might pose a risk).

These exercises are merely simulations, but they can give you a glimpse into the kinds of challenges that people with disabilities face in their daily lives.

behaviors that make up what it is to be "human" (Huey, Krueger, & Grafman, 2006). We can think of the PFC as the "seat of intelligence" or the "executive control center" of the brain because it is involved is so many higher mental functions, including reasoning, decision making, weighing the consequences of our actions, creative thinking, planning, problem solving, and control of impulsive behavior (Reyna & Farley, 2006). Damage to the PFC, as in the case of Phineas Gage, may impair the person's ability to follow moral and social codes of conduct. Contemporary research also links damage to the PFC of the type suffered by Phineas Gage to changes in how people make moral decisions or judgments (Koenigs et al., 2007).

prefrontal cortex The area of the frontal lobe that lies in front of the motor cortex and is involved in higher mental functions, including thinking, planning, impulse control, and weighing the consequences of behavior.

laceration A type of brain trauma in which a foreign object, such as a bullet or a piece of shrapnel, pierces the skull and injures the brain.

concussion A jarring of the brain caused by a blow to the head.

plasticity The ability of the brain to adapt itself after trauma or surgical alteration.

Head Trauma

In a head trauma, the brain is injured by a blow to, or jarring of, the head or by the piercing of the skull by a foreign object. The injury Gage suffered is called a **laceration,** a form of head trauma that occurs when a foreign object (a metal rod in Gage's case) penetrates the skull and damages the brain. The effects of a laceration can range from mild impairment to immediate death, depending on the location and extent of the injury. Damage to the frontal lobes can also lead to a range of psychological effects, including changes of mood and personality, as was the case for Phineas Gage.

Another form of head trauma is a **concussion,** an injury to the brain resulting from a blow to the head that may result in momentary loss of consciousness. A mild concussion suffered on the football field is not likely to have lasting consequences. But a severe concussion or repeated concussions can lead to permanent brain damage, which may include memory and attention deficits, emotional instability, and slurred speech.

CONCEPT 2.31

The brain is capable of reorganizing itself to a certain extent to adapt to new functions, even in some cases in which half of it is surgically removed.

Brain Plasticity

In some cases of epilepsy and other neurological disorders, damage to one of the hemispheres is so severe that it must be surgically removed. Remarkably, most patients who undergo this radical procedure are able to function normally, at least when the operation is performed by the time the patient is about 13 years old. Until that age, the functions of the left and right hemispheres appear to be quite flexible, or "plastic." In younger children who have the left (language-dominant) hemisphere removed, the right hemisphere may reorganize itself and develop language functions (Hertz-Pannier et al., 2002). This is an amazing example of adaptability—perhaps even more amazing than the ability of a lizard to regenerate a lost limb.

The ability of the brain to adapt and reorganize itself following trauma or surgical alteration is called **plasticity.** When one part of the brain is damaged by injury or disease, another part of the brain may take over its functions to a certain extent. Seeking to capitalize on the brain's ability to heal itself, physicians are now stimulating healthy neurons in the brains of stroke victims, hoping that these neurons will take over the functions that stroke-damaged neurons are no longer able to serve (Carmichael, 2004).

As with patients who undergo surgical removal of one of their cerebral hemispheres, plasticity is greatest among young children whose brains are not fully lateralized. How the brain accomplishes these feats of reorganization—whether in building new circuitry or altering existing circuitry—remains uncertain. Yet, as in the case of many brain injuries, there are limits to how well the brain can compensate for damage to brain tissue.

TRY THIS OUT
Learning Through Volunteering

To learn first-hand about the effects of stroke and brain injuries, consider spending a few hours a week volunteering at a local rehabilitation center or clinic. Volunteers may assist occupational therapists, physical therapists, rehabilitation counselors, and other professionals. Or they may be asked to spend time with patients in the role of a companion or attentive listener. The work can be personally rewarding and give you the opportunity to see whether you might be well suited for a career in rehabilitation.

2.5 MODULE REVIEW The Divided Brain: Specialization of Function

Recite It

What are the major differences between the left and right hemispheres?

- In most people, the left hemisphere appears to play a larger role in verbal tasks, including the use of language and logic, whereas the right hemisphere is specialized for tasks involving nonverbal processing, such as understanding spatial relationships, recognizing faces, and appreciating music and art.

What determines handedness?

- Genetic factors appear to be a strong determinant of handedness, although hormonal factors and social and cultural influences may also play a role.

What can we learn about brain lateralization from studies of "split-brain" patients?

- Studies of split-brain patients, whose left and right cerebral hemispheres are surgically disconnected, can help us better understand the specialized functions of each cerebral hemisphere.

Recall It

1. One long-established fact about the brain is that
   a. it is completely lateralized with respect to functions.
   b. the left part of the brain controls language, but only in right-handed people.
   c. the right side of the brain controls functioning in the left part of the human body, and vice versa.
   d. the functions of the left and right cerebral hemispheres do not overlap.

2. Whereas for most people the ________ hemisphere appears to be dominant for language functions, the ________ hemisphere appears to be dominant for nonverbal functions.

3. The part of the brain directly involved in speech production is
   a. the corpus callosum. **c.** Broca's area.
   b. Wernicke's area. **d.** the anterior fissure.

4. The part of the brain directly involved in comprehending written or spoken language is
   a. the prefrontal cortex.
   b. Broca's area.
   c. the corpus callosum.
   d. Wernicke's area.

5. Which of the following is *not* true?
   a. Handedness runs in families.
   b. Handedness is determined entirely by genetic factors.
   c. Researchers have found that the great majority of fetuses suck their right thumbs.
   d. Imposing right-handedness on left-handed children can lead to emotional problems.

Think About It

- Why is it incorrect to say that someone is either right-brained or left-brained?
- What are the risks of trying to impose right-handedness on left-handed children?

MODULE 2.6 The Endocrine System: The Body's Other Communication System

- What are the major endocrine glands?
- What roles do hormones play in behavior?

The nervous system is not the only means by which parts of the body communicate with each other. The *endocrine system* is also a communication system, although it is vastly slower than the nervous system. The messages it sends are conveyed through blood vessels rather than a network of nerves. The messengers it uses are hormones, which, as you may recall from Module 2.1, are chemical substances that help regulate bodily processes. Here we explore the endocrine system and the role that it plays in behavior.

Endocrine Glands: The Body's Pumping Stations

The **endocrine system** is a grouping of glands located in various parts of the body that release secretions, called hormones, directly into the bloodstream. ■ Figure 2.19 shows the location of many of the major endocrine glands in the body. Concept Chart 2.6 summarizes the functions of the hormones they release.

The endocrine system regulates important bodily processes, such as growth, reproduction, and metabolism. To do so, it relies on hormones to communicate its messages to organs and other bodily tissues. (The word *hormone* is derived from Greek roots that mean "to stimulate" or "to excite.")

Like neurotransmitters, hormones lock into receptor sites on target cells to trigger changes in these cells. For example, *insulin,* a hormone produced by the **pancreas**, regulates the concentration of glucose (sugar) in the blood. Like a key fitting into a lock, insulin opens glucose receptors on cells, allowing sugar to pass from the bloodstream into the cells, where it is used as fuel. Unlike neurotransmitters, which are found only in the nervous system, hormones travel through the bloodstream to their destinations.

One important function of the endocrine system is helping to maintain an internally balanced state, or **homeostasis**, in the body. When the level of sugar in the blood exceeds a certain threshold, or set point—as may happen when you eat a meal rich in carbohydrates (sugars and starches)—the pancreas releases more insulin into the bloodstream. Insulin stimulates cells throughout the body to draw more glucose from the blood, which decreases the level of glucose in the body. As this level declines to its set point, the pancreas reduces the amount of insulin it secretes.

The two most important endocrine glands in the body, the hypothalamus and the **pituitary gland**, are located in the brain. The pituitary is often referred to as the "master gland" because it affects so many bodily processes. But even the so-called master gland operates under the control of another "master"—the hypothalamus.

The hypothalamus secretes hormones known as *releasing factors* that cause the nearby pituitary gland to release other hormones. For example, the hypothalamus releases *growth-hormone releasing factor (hGRF),* which stimulates the pituitary to release *growth hormone (GH),* which in turn promotes physical growth. Other pituitary hormones cause other glands, such as the testes in men and ovaries in women, to release their own hormones. The process is akin to a series of falling dominoes.

In addition to the hypothalamus and pituitary, the brain houses another endocrine gland, the **pineal gland**, which releases *melatonin,* a hormone that helps regulate sleep-wake cycles (see Chapter 4). The **adrenal glands** are a pair of glands that lie above the kidneys. They have an outer layer, called the *adrenal cortex,* and a core, called the *adrenal medulla.* The pituitary hormone *ACTH* stimulates the adrenal cortex to secrete hormones called *cortical steroids,* which promote muscle development and stimulate the liver to release stores of sugar in times of stress. More energy thus becomes available in response to stressful situations, such as emergencies in which the organism faces the imminent threat of a predator attack. Other stress hormones, *epinephrine* and

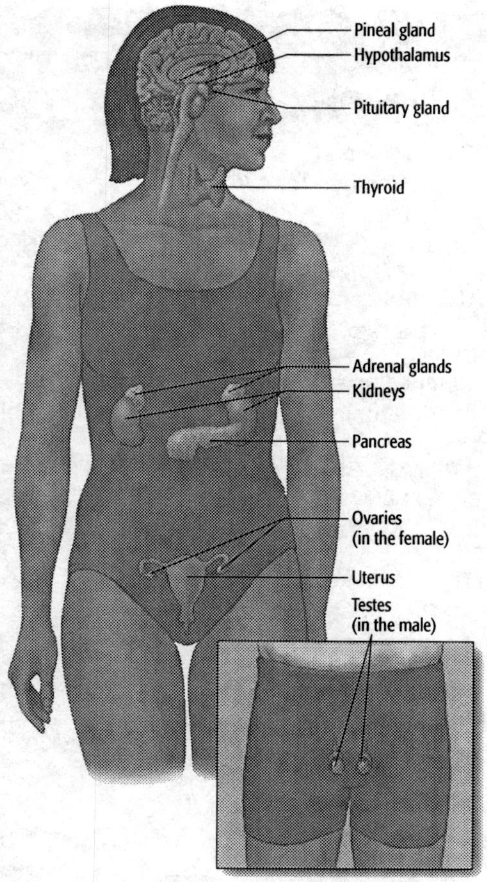

Figure 2.19 Major Glands of the Endocrine System
The endocrine system consists of glands that release secretions, called hormones, directly into the bloodstream.

endocrine system The body's system of glands that release secretions, called hormones, directly into the bloodstream.

pancreas An endocrine gland located near the stomach that produces the hormone insulin.

homeostasis The tendency of systems to maintain a steady, internally balanced state.

pituitary gland An endocrine gland in the brain that produces various hormones involved in growth, regulation of the menstrual cycle, and childbirth.

pineal gland A small endocrine gland in the brain that produces the hormone melatonin, which is involved in regulating sleep-wake cycles.

adrenal glands A pair of endocrine glands located just above the kidneys that produce various stress-related hormones.

CONCEPT CHART 2.6 The Endocrine System

Gland/Hormone	Function
Pituitary gland	
Growth hormone (GH)	Stimulates growth, especially of bones
ACTH	Stimulates adrenal cortex to secrete cortical steroids
Oxytocin	Stimulates uterine contractions during childbirth and release of milk following childbirth
Hypothalamus	
Releasing factors	Stimulate the pituitary gland to release other hormones, including growth hormone
Pineal gland	
Melatonin	Helps regulate sleep-wake cycles
Pancreas	
Insulin	Facilitates entry of blood glucose (sugar) into cells; involved in regulation of blood sugar levels
Thyroid gland	
Thyroid hormones	Involved in regulating metabolic rate, growth, and maturation
Adrenal glands	
Cortical steroids	Help body cope with stress; promote muscle development; stimulate the liver to release stores of sugar
Epinephrine (adrenaline) and Norepinephrine (noradrenaline)	Speeds up bodily processes, such as heart rate and breathing rate
Ovaries	
Estrogen	Fosters female sexual maturation; helps regulate menstrual cycle
Progesterone	Helps maintain pregnancy; helps regulate menstrual cycle
Testes	
Testosterone	Promotes sperm production; fosters male sexual differentiation during prenatal development; stokes sexual maturation in pubertal males

norepinephrine, are released by the adrenal medulla. They help prepare the body to deal with stress by speeding up bodily processes, such as heart rate and respiration rate.

As noted earlier in the chapter, some chemicals, like norepinephrine, do double duty: They function both as neurotransmitters in the nervous system and as hormones in the bloodstream. In the brain, norepinephrine—and to a lesser degree, epinephrine—function as neurotransmitters. Norepinephrine plays an important role in the nervous system in regulating mood, alertness, and appetite.

The **gonads** are the sex glands—**ovaries** in women and **testes** in men. The gonads produce the **germ cells**—egg cells in women and sperm in men. The ovaries also produce the female sex hormones *estrogen* and *progesterone,* which help regulate the menstrual cycle. Progesterone also stimulates growth of the female reproductive organs and helps the uterus maintain pregnancy.

The testes produce the male sex hormone, *testosterone,* which leads to the development of male sex organs in male fetuses. Following puberty in males, release of testosterone by the testes fosters growth of the male genitals, development of a beard, and deepening of the voice.

Though the nervous system and endocrine system are separate systems, they are closely intertwined. The brain regulates the activity of the endocrine system so that the body responds not as separate systems but as an integrated whole. The brain controls endocrine functions through the autonomic nervous system. In times of stress, for

CONCEPT 2.32
Endocrine glands distributed throughout the body help coordinate many bodily functions.

CONCEPT 2.33
Hormones are released by endocrine glands directly into the bloodstream. From there they travel to specific receptor sites on target organs and tissues.

CONCEPT 2.34
In concert with the nervous system, the endocrine system helps the body maintain a state of equilibrium, or homeostasis.

CONCEPT 2.35
The pituitary gland is often called the "master gland" because it helps regulate so many other endocrine glands.

example, the sympathetic nervous system transmits commands from the brain to the adrenal medulla, leading to the release of the stress hormones epinephrine and norepinephrine that help prepare the body to deal with stress (discussed further in Chapter 12).

gonads Sex glands (testes in men and ovaries in women) that produce sex hormones and germ cells (sperm in the male and egg cells in the female).

ovaries The female gonads, which secrete the female sex hormones estrogen and progesterone and produce mature egg cells.

testes The male gonads, which produce sperm and secrete the male sex hormone testosterone.

germ cells Sperm and egg cells from which new life develops.

Hormones and Behavior

Though human behavior is more strongly influenced by learning and experience than by hormones, hormones do play a role in our behavior. For example, the male sex hormone testosterone is linked to higher levels of dominance, competitiveness, and risk-taking (Miller & Maner, 2010). Testosterone is also linked to greater physical aggressiveness in both men and women (Archer, 2006). Testosterone is produced in both men's and women's bodies, but in lesser amounts in women.

Ingestion of anabolic steroids (synthetic testosterone), which some people use to build up muscle mass, is also linked to increased aggressive and belligerent behavior. We should recognize, however, that testosterone is perhaps one of many factors interacting in complex ways that lead to aggressive behavior in humans. Deficiencies of testosterone can also lead to loss of sexual desire in both men and women.

Oxytocin, a hormone released by the pituitary gland, is involved in regulating uterine contractions during childbirth and release of mother's milk during nursing. Evidence suggests that the hormone has effects on psychological factors involving social behaviors, including the mother's attachment to her infant child and the development of trust in other people (Mikolajczak et al., 2010; Rimmele et al., 2009; Seltzer, Ziegler, & Pollak, 2010; Wade, 2011).

Excesses and deficiencies in hormone levels are associated with many physical and psychological disorders. Thyroid hormones, produced by the **thyroid gland,** help regulate body metabolism, the rate at which the body turns food into energy. Excess thyroid hormones are associated with states of anxiety and irritability. Deficiencies of thyroid hormones can lead to sluggishness and weight gain and can retard intellectual development in children.

thyroid gland An endocrine gland in the neck that secretes the hormone thyroxin, which is involved in regulating metabolic functions and physical growth.

During the menstrual cycle, testosterone levels in women remain fairly stable, but levels of estrogen and progesterone shift dramatically. Most women, about three out of four, experience some form of **premenstrual syndrome (PMS)**—a constellation of physical and psychological symptoms in the days leading up to menstruation each month. These symptoms may include anxiety, depression, irritability, weight gain from fluid retention, and abdominal discomfort (Yonkers, O'Brien, & Eriksson, 2008). Nearly one in five women have PMS symptoms significant enough to affect daily functioning or cause significant emotional distress (Halbreich et al., 2006). Severe forms of PMS are associated with impaired work performance and increased absenteeism (Heinemann et al., 2010).

premenstrual syndrome (PMS) A cluster of physical and psychological symptoms occurring in the days preceding the menstrual flow.

The causes of PMS are unclear. We lack solid evidence that hormonal imbalances—too much or too little circulating estrogen or progesterone—are responsible for PMS. Scientists suspect that differences in sensitivity to these hormones, not their levels per se, may predispose some women to develop PMS (Kiesner, 2009).

PMS may also involve irregularities in the functioning of the neurotransmitter serotonin in the brain (Bäckström et al., 2003). Estrogen may also affect mood by way of influencing serotonin activity. Other factors—such as how women cope with menstrual symptoms, what their cultures teach them about menstruation, and their general mood states—may also influence the likelihood of a woman's experiencing PMS.

CONCEPT 2.36
Hormones are linked to a wide range of behaviors and mood states.

CONCEPT 2.37
Hormonal factors may be involved in explaining PMS, a syndrome affecting about three out of four women.

2.6 MODULE REVIEW The Endocrine System: The Body's Other Communication System

Recite It

What are the major endocrine glands?

- The major endocrine glands are the pituitary gland, hypothalamus, pineal gland, thyroid, adrenal glands, pancreas, and gonads (testes in males and ovaries in females).

What roles do hormones play in behavior?

- Excesses of thyroid hormones can cause anxiety and irritability, whereas too little can lead to sluggishness and weight gain and can retard intellectual development in children.
- Testosterone has been linked to aggressiveness.
- Female sex hormones appear to play a role in PMS.

Recall It

1. Although it is vastly slower than the nervous system, the ________ system is another communication system in the human body.
2. Which of the following do glands secrete directly into the body's bloodstream?
   a. neurotransmitters
   b. hormones
   c. neuromodulators
   d. glial cells
3. What term is used to describe an internally balanced state in the body?
4. The gland known as the "master gland" because of its role in regulating the activity of many other glands is the ________ gland.

Think About It

- Do you believe your behavior is influenced by your hormones? Why or why not?
- Why does the text refer to the endocrine system as the body's other communication system?

MODULE 2.7 Genes and Behavior: A Case of Nature and Nurture

- What roles do genetic factors play in behavior?
- What are the methods used to study genetic influences on behavior?

genotype An organism's genetic code.

genes Basic units of heredity that contain the individual's genetic code.

deoxyribonucleic acid (DNA) The basic chemical material in chromosomes that carries the individual's genetic code.

chromosomes Rodlike structures in the cell nucleus that house the individual's genes.

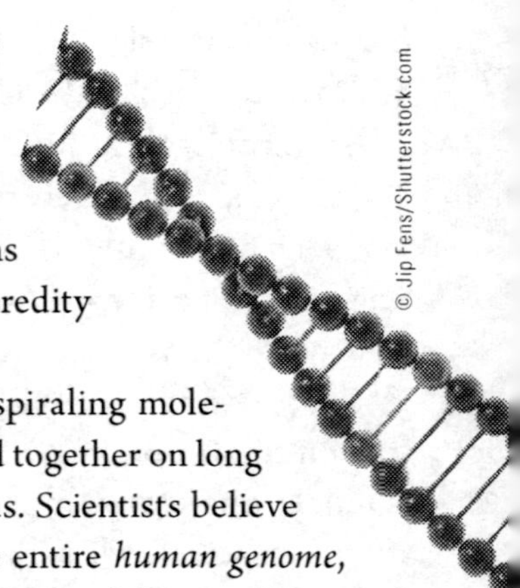

© Jip Fens/Shutterstock.com

Within every living organism is a set of inherited instructions that determines whether it will have lungs or gills, a penis or a vagina, blue eyes or green. This set of instructions, called a **genotype**, constitutes a master plan for building and maintaining a living organism. The genetic instructions are encoded in the organism's **genes**, the basic units of heredity that are passed along from parent to offspring.

Genes are composed of a complex, double-stranded, spiraling molecule called **deoxyribonucleic acid (DNA)**. They are linked together on long strands called **chromosomes** that reside in the cell nucleus. Scientists believe there are about 20,000 to 30,000 genes that compose the entire *human genome*, or human genetic code (Dermitzakis, 2011; Lupski, 2007). This full complement of genes is found in each body cell except for the germ cells (egg cells and sperm), which carry half of the person's genes. Children inherit half of their chromosomes and the genes they carry from their mothers and half from their fathers. During conception, the 23 chromosomes in the mother's egg cell unite with the 23 chromosomes in the father's sperm cell, forming the normal arrangement of 23 pairs of chromosomes in the cell nucleus. With the exception of identical twins, no two people share the same genetic code.

Having recently completed work on deciphering the human genome, scientists can now read the entire genetic script of a human being. They suspect that buried within the code are DNA sequences that play important roles in determining a person's risk of developing many physical and mental disorders (Kendler, 2005a,b). Scientists are focusing on understanding how genes work and tracking down the specific genes involved in particular physical and mental disorders. By further studying the human genome, they hope to gain insights into the genetic origins of disease and develop ways of blocking the actions of harmful genes and harnessing the actions of useful ones.

Genetic factors clearly determine physical characteristics such as eye color and hair color, but what about their role in behavior? Is our behavior a product of our genes, our environment, or both?

Genetic Influences on Behavior

Genes influence many patterns of behavior (Plomin et al., 2003). Some dogs are bold or placid in temperament; others are yappy. They all share enough genes to make them dogs and not cats, but they may differ greatly from one another in their behavior and physical traits. People have selectively bred animals to enhance specific behavior patterns as well as physical traits. But what about human behavior?

CONCEPT 2.38
The view held by most scientists today is that both heredity and environment interact in complex ways in shaping our personalities and intellectual abilities.

One of the oldest debates in psychology is the nature-nurture problem. Is our behavior governed by nature (genetics) or nurture (environment and culture)? Though the debate continues, most psychologists believe human behavior is influenced by a combination of genes and the environment. The contemporary version of the nature-nurture debate is more about the relative contributions of nature *and* nurture to particular behaviors than it is about nature *or* nurture.

CONCEPT 2.39
Genetic factors create predispositions that increase the likelihood that certain behaviors, abilities, or personality traits will emerge, but whether they do emerge depends largely on environmental influences and individual experiences.

→ Concept Link
Investigators believe that genetics influences many personality traits, from shyness to novelty seeking. See Module 13.2.

Virtually all of our behavioral traits are influenced to some degree by genetic factors (Johnson et al., 2009). Heredity influences many traits, including intelligence, shyness, impulsivity, aggressiveness, and sociability, as well as our aptitudes in music and art, whether we have a happy or sad disposition, the occupation we choose, and our tendency to be altruistic or helpful to others (e.g., Bouchard, 2004; Ellis & Bonin, 2003; Kelsoe, 2010; King & Suzman, 2008; Malouff, Rooke, & Schutte, 2008; Reuter et al., 2010).

Frank and Ernest

© 2007 Thaves. Reprinted with permission.

Genetic factors are also implicated in many psychological problems, including anxiety disorders, mood disorders, antisocial behavior, alcohol and drug dependence, and schizophrenia (e.g., Edvardsen et al., 2009; Malouff, Rooke, & Schutte, 2008; Treutlein et al., 2009). However, our genes do not dictate what our lives or personalities become. Who we are, how we act, and how we interact with others are determined by many factors, including environmental as well as genetic influences and the interactions among these influences (Champagne & Mashoodh, 2009; Larsen et al., 2010; Yang et al., 2009).

The genotype, or genetic code, is a kind of recipe that determines the features or traits of an organism. The extent to which the genotype becomes expressed in the organism's observable traits, or **phenotype**, depends on a complex interaction of genes and the environment. Psychological traits, such as shyness, intelligence, or a predisposition to schizophrenia or alcoholism, appear to be **polygenic traits**. These traits are influenced by multiple genes interacting with the environment in complex ways.

phenotype The observable physical and behavioral characteristics of an organism, representing the influences of the genotype and environment.

polygenic traits Traits that are influenced by multiple genes interacting in complex ways.

We should think of genetic factors as creating a *predisposition* or *likelihood*—not a certainty—that particular behaviors, abilities, personality traits, or psychological disorders will develop. Environmental factors, including family relationships, stress, and learning experiences, also play key roles in determining how, or even if, genetic factors become expressed in observable behaviors or psychological traits (Confer et al., 2010; Diamond, 2009). One lesson we can draw from understanding the interaction of genes and environment is that good parenting may help offset the influence of bad genes, including genes that increase the potential that adolescents will develop problems with substance abuse (Brody et al., 2009). Conversely, some people may possess certain genetic variations that render them more sensitive than others to harmful environmental influences, such as stressful life experiences or bad parenting (Caspi et al., 2010; Reiss, 2010).

Consider the landmark research of psychologist David Reiss and his colleagues (Reiss et al., 2000). They showed that the degree to which genetic influences on the personality trait of shyness become expressed in the overt behavior of children depends on the interactions they have with their parents and other important people in their lives. Parents who are overprotective of a shy child may accentuate an underlying genetic tendency toward shyness, whereas those who encourage more outgoing behavior may help the child overcome it.

But how can we separate the effects of environment from those of genetics? Let us consider several methods scientists use to untangle these effects.

Kinship Studies: Untangling the Roles of Heredity and Environment

CONCEPT 2.40
Scientists use three basic types of kinship studies to examine genetic influences on behavior: familial association studies, twin studies, and adoptee studies.

→ Concept Link
Similarities between identical twins as compared with fraternal twins provide evidence that genes contribute to intelligence. See Module 7.3.

Scientists rely on several methods to examine genetic contributions to behavior, including familial association studies, twin studies, and adoptee studies. Concept Chart 2.7 provides a summary of these three basic types of kinship studies.

Familial Association Studies

The more closely related people are, the more genes they have in common. Each parent shares 50 percent of his or her genes with his or her children, as do siblings with each other. More distant relatives, such as uncles, aunts, and cousins, have fewer genes in common. Therefore, if genes contribute to a given trait or disorder, we would expect to find more closely related people to be more likely to share the trait or disorder in question.

Familial association studies have been used to study family linkages in psychological disorders, such as schizophrenia. Consistent with a role for genetics in the development of this disorder, we find a greater risk of the disorder among closer blood relatives of schizophrenia patients than among more distant relatives. The risk among blood relatives rises from 2 percent among first cousins and uncles and aunts to 48 percent among identical twins. However, we should note a major limitation of this kind of study. The closer their blood relationship, the more likely people are to share common environments. Thus, researchers look to other types of studies, such as twin studies and adoptee studies, to help disentangle the relative contributions of heredity and environment.

familial association studies Studies that examine the degree to which disorders or characteristics are shared among family members.

identical twins Twins who developed from the same zygote and so have identical genes (also called *monozygotic*, or *MZ*, twins).

zygote A fertilized egg cell.

fraternal twins Twins who developed from separate zygotes and so have 50 percent of their genes in common (also called *dizygotic*, or *DZ*, twins).

twin studies Studies that examine the degree to which concordance rates between twin pairs for particular disorders or characteristics vary in relation to whether the twins are identical or fraternal.

Twin Studies

In the case of **identical twins** (also called *monozygotic*, or *MZ*, twins), a fertilized egg cell, or **zygote**, splits into two cells, and each one develops into a separate person. Because their genetic code had been carried in the single cell before it split in two, identical twins have the same genetic makeup. In the case of **fraternal twins** (also called *dizygotic*, or *DZ*, twins), the mother releases two egg cells in the same month. They are fertilized by different sperm cells, and each fertilized egg cell then develops into a separate person. Fraternal twins thus share only 50 percent of their genetic makeup, as do other brothers and sisters.

In **twin studies**, researchers compare **concordance rates**, or percentages of shared traits or disorders. A higher rate of concordance (percentage of times both twins have the same disorder or trait) among MZ twins than among DZ twins strongly suggests a genetic contribution to the disorder or trait (Price & Jaffee, 2008). Identical twins are more likely than fraternal twins to share many psychological traits and even such disorders as schizophrenia (Hamilton, 2008; Kendler, 2005a).

concordance rates In twin studies, the percentages of cases in which both members of twin pairs share the same trait or disorder.

Twin studies have a major limitation, however. The problem is that identical twins may be treated more alike than fraternal twins. Thus, environmental factors, not genes, may account for their higher rates of concordance. For example, identical twins may be encouraged to dress alike, take the same courses, even play the same musical instrument. Despite this limitation, twin studies provide useful information on genetic contributions to personality and intellectual development.

© Andi Berger/Shutterstock.com

Adoptee Studies

The clearest way to separate the roles of environment and heredity is to conduct **adoptee studies**. These studies (also called *adoption studies*) compare adopted children with both their adoptive parents and their biological parents. If they tend to be more like their adoptive parents in their psychological traits or the disorders they develop, we can

adoptee studies Studies that examine whether adoptees are more similar to their biological or adoptive parents with respect to their psychological traits or to the disorders they develop.

CONCEPT CHART 2.7 Types of Kinship Studies

Type of Study	Method of Analysis	Evaluation
Familial association study  © Andresr/Shutterstock.com	Analysis of shared traits or disorders among family members in relation to their degree of kinship	Provides supportive evidence of genetic contribution to behavior when concordance is greater among more closely related family members than among more distantly related ones; limited because the closer their blood relationship, the more likely people are to share similar environments
Twin study  © Kenneth Sponsler/Shutterstock.com	Analysis of differences in the rates of overlap (concordance) for a given trait or disorder between identical and fraternal twins	Provides strong evidence of the role of genetic factors in behavior when concordance rates are greater among identical twins than among fraternal twins; may be biased by greater environmental similarity between identical twins than fraternal twins
Adoptee study  © Yurchyks/Shutterstock.com	Analysis of similarity in traits or psychological or physical disorders between adoptees and their biological and adoptive parents, or between identical twins reared apart and those reared together	The clearest way of separating the roles of heredity and environment, but may overlook common environmental factors for reared-apart twins early in life

argue that environment plays the more dominant role. If they tend to be more like their biological parents, we may assume that heredity has a greater influence.

When identical twins are separated at an early age and reared apart in separate adoptive families, we can attribute any differences between them to environmental factors since their genetic makeup is the same. This natural experiment—separating identical twins at an early age—does not happen often, but when it does, it provides a special opportunity to examine the role of nature and nurture. One landmark study showed a high level of similarity between identical twins reared apart and those reared together across a range of personality traits (Tellegen et al., 1988). These findings suggest that heredity plays an important role in personality development. Yet studies of twins reared apart may overlook common environmental factors. Since twins are rarely adopted at birth, they may have shared a common environment during infancy. Many continue to meet periodically throughout their lives. Thus, twins reared apart may have opportunities to be influenced by others in their shared environments or to influence each other, quite apart from their genetic overlap.

2.7 MODULE REVIEW Genes and Behavior: A Case of Nature and Nurture

Recite It

What roles do genetic factors play in behavior?

- Genetic factors are major influences on animal behavior and temperament.
- In humans, genetic factors interact in complex ways with environmental influences in determining personality and intellectual development.

What are the methods used to study genetic influences on behavior?

- Three types of kinship studies are used to study the role of genetics in human behavior: familial association studies, twin studies, and adoptee studies.

Recall It

1. Scientists believe there are about ______ genes in the human genome.
   a. Fewer than 5,000
   b. 10,000
   c. 20,000 to 30,000
   d. More than 100,000
2. In the longstanding debate in psychology over the nature-nurture issue, the central question is
   a. How much of our genetic code do we have in common with others?
   b. Which is a more influential factor in human behavior: the genotype or the phenotype?
   c. Does heredity or environment govern human behavior?
   d. To what extent do rearing influences affect our genotype?
3. Polygenic traits are
   a. traits that are influenced by multiple genes.
   b. traits that are influenced by polygenic genes.
   c. traits that are determined by genetic defects.
   d. traits that are fully determined by combinations of genes.
4. What are the basic types of studies used to examine the influence of genetics on behavior?
5. Dizygotic (fraternal) twins result when
   a. a zygote is formed and then splits into two cells.
   b. two egg cells are fertilized by different sperm.
   c. two different sperm fertilize the same egg cell, which then divides in half.
   d. two zygotes are formed from the fertilization of the same egg cell.

Think About It

- What aspects of your personality, if any, do you believe were influenced by your genetic inheritance?
- What methods do researchers use to disentangle the influences of heredity and environment on behavior? What are the limitations of these methods?

Looking Under the Hood: Scanning the Human Brain

APPLICATION MODULE 2.8

Advances in cognitive neuroscience made possible by sophisticated brain-imaging techniques are broadening our understanding of how the brain works. Here we examine some cutting-edge applications of brain-scanning technology that allow us to better understand how the brain works by peering directly into the working brain.

Discovering Memory Circuits in the Brain

Using advanced scanning techniques, investigators identified circuits in the brains of laboratory animals that corresponded to the animals' past experiences (Bartho et al., 2004; Csicsvari et al., 2003). Research along these lines is still in its infancy, but it raises the possibility of pinpointing memory circuits in the human brain of hold the memories comprising the repository of our life experiences. Perhaps one day we'll be able to decode brain activity to detect a person's thoughts and memories on a moment-to-moment basis, just as though we were watching thoughts float by on a computer screen (Haynes & Rees, 2006) (see ■ Figure 2.20).

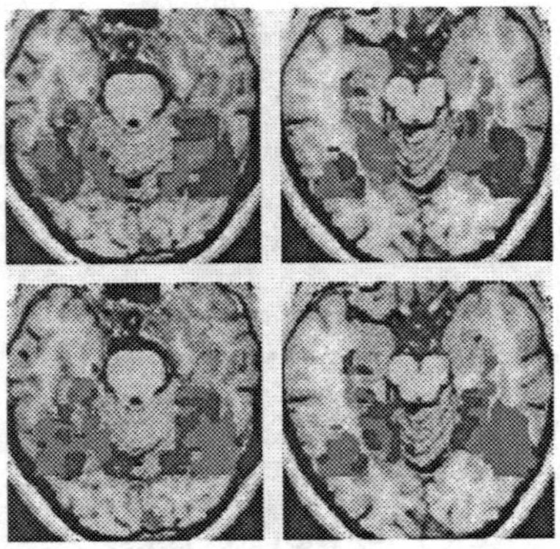

Figure 2.20 What's On Your Mind? Using fMRI responses, investigators can detect distinct brain signals occurring when individuals look at different stimuli. The red areas indicate parts of the brain in which signals are elevated when people are shown images of faces. The blue areas denote brain regions in which signals are elevated when people are shown pictures of buildings. Eventually, perhaps, we may be able to tell what a person is thinking by decoding their brain images.
Source: Haynes & Rees, 2006

Revealing Personality Traits

Brain scans may also reveal underlying personality traits. Recently, test subjects were shown a mix of positive and negative images, such as those in ■ Figure 2.21, while researchers tracked the neural activity in their brains using a high-tech imaging technique. The results showed differences in brain activity between people with different personality features or traits. In response to these positive and negative images, the brains of people who had personality traits of extraversion (were sociable, outgoing, and people-oriented) showed different patterns of activity than those who had traits of neuroticism (were anxious and worrisome). As the lead investigator, psychologist Turhan Canli put it, "If I know what the conditions are under which I see [a certain] activation pattern, I can make a good prediction as to what this person's personality traits are" (quoted in Pepper, 2005).

Screening Job Applicants

Brain scans may become a part of regular employment screenings. In addition to filling out traditional background and interest inventories, employers may someday peer inside the heads of job applicants (Pepper, 2005). Psychologist Turhan Canli has even begun testing how differences in brain activation patterns in response to pictures of positive and negative images might reveal which individuals are better suited for particular tasks.

Neuromarketing

neuromarketing An emerging field of marketing that explores brain responses to advertisements and brand-related messages.

Not only might brain scans reveal what happens in the brain when people see something they want to buy, but they might also predict how people respond to advertisements, as well as their likelihood of buying or using particular products. In the emerging field of **neuromarketing**, researchers probe brain wave patterns to measure the brain's response to advertisements and other brand-related stimuli (Nevid, 2010). Marketers hope to find these "whispers in the brain" that can be detected by EEG and other biometric tracking equipment so that they can learn which ads evoke the strongest attentional and emotional responses (Singer, 2010).

In a recent laboratory study, UCLA researchers scanned the brains of student volunteers in sunny California while they saw and listened to public service announcements touting

The Test Research participants are shown mixed "positive" anc "negative" images, like the images shown here. Meanwhile, brain scans track the differences in the patterns of activity among neurons in different parts of the brain.

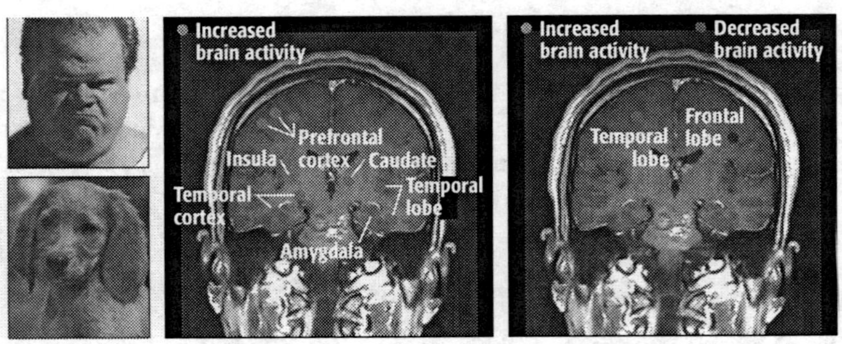

1. The Extrovert "Positive" images stimulate these areas in people who are more social and show positive emotions.

2. The Neurotic "Negative" images provoke these responses among people prone to anxiety and negative emotions.

Figure 2.21 Showing Personalities
The brains of people with different personality traits (extroversion vs. neuroticism) show different patterns of activity in response to positive and negative images. Research along these lines may help us learn more about relationships between brain functioning and personality types.
Source: Adapted from *Newsweek*, February 21, 2005, p. E.26.

the importance of using sunscreen (Falk et al., 2010). Students also indicated how much sunscreen they expected to use in the following week. A week later the students were contacted again and asked how often they had applied sunscreen during the preceding week. The findings showed that activation of a particular area in the prefrontal cortex was a reliable predictor of how much sunscreen students actually used, above and beyond the student's own expectations.

Advertisers take note. As scientists learn more about how neural markers relate to consumer behavior, marketers may begin applying this knowledge to develop more effective advertisements that tap directly into key brain responses. Still, the field of neuromarketing needs to first demonstrate that brain wave patterns actually predict purchasing behavior.

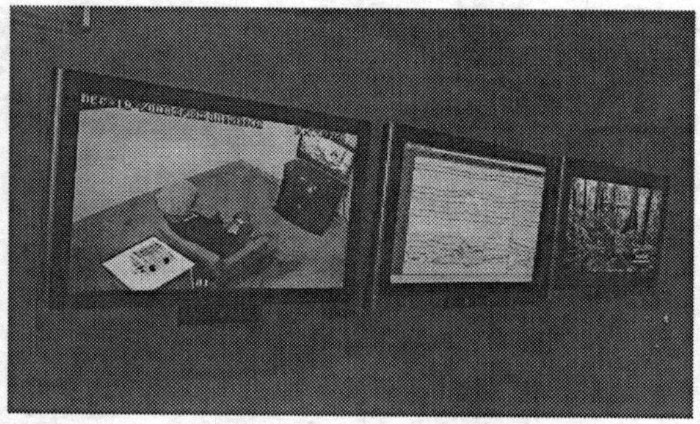

Courtesy of Neurofocus

Figure 2.22 How Your Brain Responds to TV Commercials
Marketing researchers are turning to the use of biometric measures to probe consumer responses to advertisements. Here, a volunteer wearing a fabric cap containing EEG sensors and an eye-tracking device is exposed to marketing images on a TV monitor.

Diagnosing Psychological Disorders

Brain scans may also come into general use in diagnosing psychological or psychiatric disorders. Teams of experimenters are actively engaged in research exploring the use of brain scans in detecting signs of abnormal behavior patterns such as bipolar disorder, schizophrenia, and attention-deficit hyperactivity disorder (ADHD). Investigators hope to uncover signs of psychological disorders through scanning techniques, in much the same ways that scanning techniques are presently used to reveal tumors and other physical disorders (Cyranoski, 2011; Raeburn, 2005). These techniques are presently limited to experimental use, but one day—perhaps one day soon—they may become as common as chest X-rays or even dental X-rays.

Thinking Critically About Psychology

Based on your reading of this chapter, answer the following questions. Then, to evaluate your progress in developing critical thinking skills, compare your answers to the sample answers found in Appendix A.

The case of Phineas Gage is one of the best-known case studies in the annals of psychology. In 1848, as you already know, Gage suffered an accident in which a metal rod pierced his cheek and brain and penetrated the top of his head. Yet not only did he survive this horrific accident, but he also managed to pick himself up and speak to workers who came to his aid. Though he survived his injuries, his personality changed—so much so that people would remark, "Gage is no longer Gage."

1. Why do you think Gage's injury affected his personality but not the basic life functions that the brain controls, such as breathing and heart rate?
2. How might the nature of the injury that Gage sustained explain why this once polite and courteous man became aggressive and unruly?

Log in to CengageBrain to access the resources your instructor requires. For this book, you can access:

CourseMate

Psychology CourseMate brings course concepts to life with interactive learning, study, and exam preparation tools that support the printed textbook. A textbook-specific website, Psychology CourseMate includes an integrated interactive eBook and other interactive learning tools including quizzes, flashcards, videos, and more.

CENGAGENOW

CengageNow is an easy-to-use online resource that helps you study in less time to get the grade you want—NOW. Take a pre-test for this chapter and receive a personalized study plan based on your results that will identify the topics you need to review and direct you to online resources to help you master those topics. Then take a post-test to help you determine the concepts you have mastered and what you will need to work on. If your textbook does not include an access code card, go to CengageBrain.com to gain access.

Visit www.cengagebrain.com to access your account and purchase materials.

VISUAL OVERVIEW Chapter 2 Biological Foundations of Behavior

MODULE 2.1 Neurons

Parts of the Neuron

- **Soma**: Cell body
- **Axon**: "Cable" that conducts outgoing messages or action potentials
- **Dendrites**: Rootlike projections that receive messages from neighboring neurons
- **Terminal Buttons**: Knoblike structures at the end of axons that release neurotransmitters into the synapse
- **Myelin Sheath**: Protective coating of axons

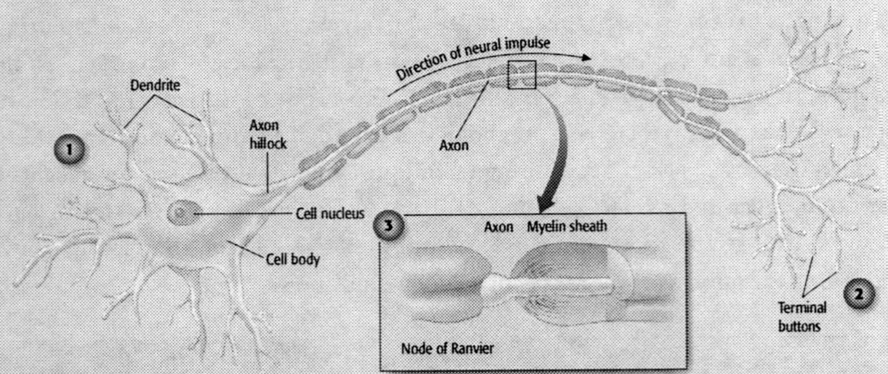

The Neuron

Transmission of Neural Impulses

- **Action Potentials**: Neural impulses or messages generated according to the "all-or-none" principle
- **Neurotransmitters**: Chemical messengers that carry messages to neighboring neurons

MODULE 2.2 The Nervous System

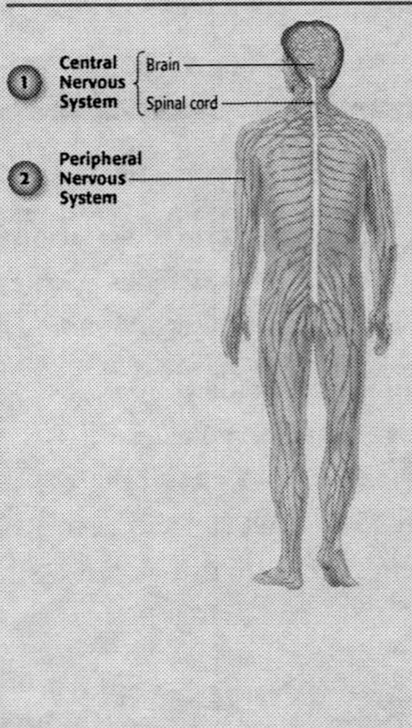

- **Central Nervous System (CNS)**: The brain and spinal cord
- **Peripheral Nervous System (PNS)**: The body's link to the outside world
- **Somatic Nervous System:** Part of PNS that relays sensory information from sensory organs to the CNS and motor (movement) commands from the CNS to muscles
- **Autonomic Nervous System (ANS)**: Controls automatic bodily functions and processes
- **Sympathetic and Parasympathetic Divisions of ANS**: Have largely opposing effects on bodily processes

MODULES 2.3–2.5 The Brain

- **Hindbrain**: Consists of the medulla, pons, and cerebellum; involved in vital bodily functions
- **Midbrain**: Nerve pathways connecting hindbrain and forebrain; includes the reticular formation
- **Forebrain**: Includes the thalamus, the hypothalamus, other parts of the limbic system, and the cerebral cortex—the outer covering of the brain comprising four parts or lobes responsible for voluntary movement and higher mental functions
- **Methods of Studying the Brain**: Imaging techniques (EEG, CT scan, PET scan, MRI) and experimental techniques (lesioning, brain recording, electrical stimulation)
- **Brain Lateralization**: Specialization of function of the two cerebral hemispheres

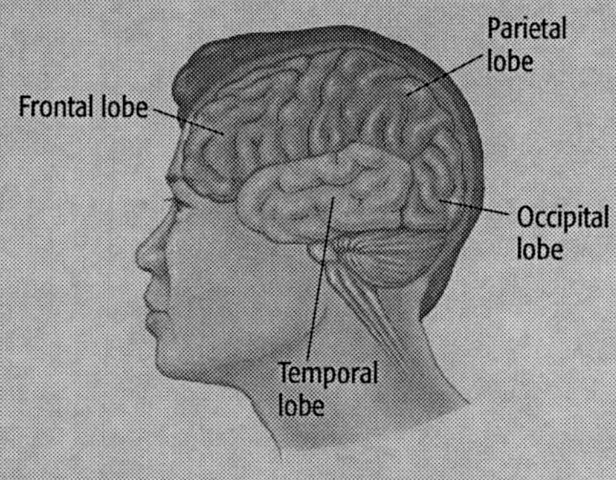

Lobes of the Cerebral Cortex

MODULE 2.6 The Endocrine System

Major Endocrine Glands and Hormones

- **Pituitary:** Growth hormone, ACTH, oxytocin
- **Hypothalamus:** Releasing factors
- **Pineal Gland:** Melatonin
- **Pancreas:** Insulin
- **Thyroid:** Thyroid hormones
- **Adrenals:** Cortical steroids, epinephrine, norepinephrine
- **Ovaries in Women:** Estrogen, progesterone
- **Testes in Men:** Testosterone

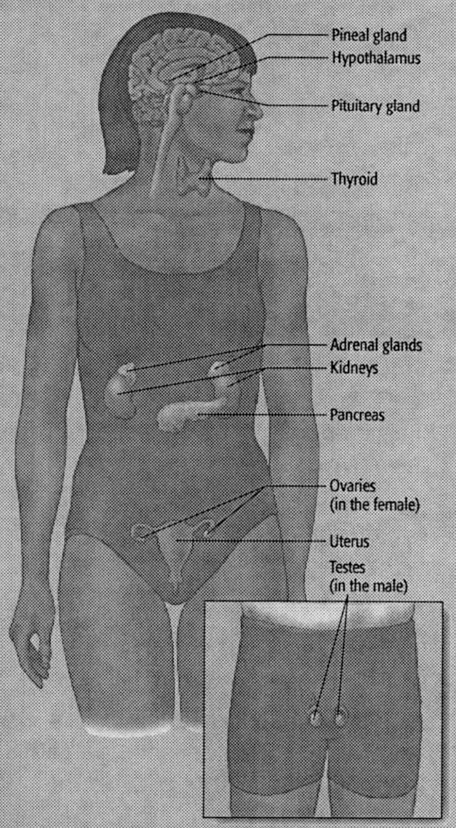

MODULE 2.7 Genes and Behavior

- **Genotype versus Phenotype:** Genetic coding versus observable traits
- **Types of Kinship Studies:** Familial association study, twin studies, adoptee studies

3 Sensation and Perception

My Daughter, the Giant

SLICE OF LIFE One day, my infant daughter Daniella turned into a giant. Or so it seemed. I was making a video recording of her fledgling attempts to crawl. All was going well until she noticed the camera. She then started crawling toward this funny man holding the camera—me. As she approached, her image in the viewfinder grew larger and larger, eventually so large that she blotted out all other objects in my view. The image of my daughter that was cast upon my eyes was of a large and ever-growing giant! But I didn't panic. Despite the information my eyes were transmitting to my brain, I understood my daughter was not morphing into a giant. Fortunately, we tend to perceive objects to be of their actual size despite changes in the size of the image they project on our eyes as they grow nearer. Yet the sensation of seeing your infant grow to be a giant before your eyes can be an unsettling experience, especially when the "giant" then attempts to mouth the camera.

DID YOU KNOW THAT...

- Our sense of smell may not be as keen as that of dogs, but humans can detect the presence of even one drop of perfume dispersed through a small house? (p. 92)
- Roy G. Biv is one of the most famous names learned by psychology students, but he is not a real person? (p. 96)
- The bending of hair cells in the inner ear makes hearing possible, but these cells are not real hairs? (p. 105)
- A meteoric rise in hearing loss is expected to occur over the next few decades, largely as the result of years of living loudly? (p. 106)
- Exposure to bodily secretions of the opposite sex may have subtle effects on our behavior, even if we are not consciously aware of it? (p. 110)
- Some people are born with a distaste for broccoli? (p. 111)
- The mechanism that makes motion pictures possible lies in the viewer, not the projector? (p. 125)

We are continually bombarded with stimuli from the outside world that impinge on our sensory organs. The world is a medley of lights and sounds that strike our eyes and ears, and of chemical substances that waft past our noses or land on our tongues as we consume food or drink liquids. In this chapter, you will see how your sense organs respond to external stimuli and transform these stimuli into sensory signals your brain uses to produce *sensations* of vision, hearing, touch, smell, and taste. You will learn how your brain assembles bits and pieces of sensory information into meaningful impressions of the world that are called *perceptions*. You will also learn how your brain senses changes in the position of your body, so you can move about without stumbling or losing your balance. Our sensory systems operate at blinding speeds, but the real marvel is how the brain processes all the information it receives from the body's sensory organs, making it possible for us not only to sense the world around us but also to make sense of it. As the example of my "giant" daughter illustrates, sensation and perception are different processes. What we perceive may not correspond to what we sense.

The study of sensation and perception is critical to psychology because our investigation of behavior and mental processes begins with input from the world around us and the way the senses and brain interpret that information. Let us proceed, first, to explore how our sensory systems operate. Then we will explore how the brain assembles the sensory information it receives to form perceptions that help us comprehend the colors and sounds that form the rich tapestry of sensory experience.

Learning Objectives

By reading this chapter you will be able to . . .

1. **EXPLAIN** the difference between sensation and perception.
2. **DEFINE** and **DESCRIBE** the following terms and **EXPLAIN** how they influence the process of sensation: absolute thresholds, difference thresholds, signal detection theory, sensory adaptation.
3. **DEFINE** psychophysics.
4. **IDENTIFY** the parts of the eye and the ear and **EXPLAIN** how vision, audition, and our other senses work.
5. **IDENTIFY** the sensory receptors for the body's senses and **DESCRIBE** what they do.
6. **EXPLAIN** how perception is influenced by attention, perceptual set, and modes of visual processing.
7. **IDENTIFY** and **DESCRIBE** the Gestalt principles of grouping objects into meaningful patterns or forms.
8. **DESCRIBE** the concept of perceptual constancy and **APPLY** this knowledge to the perception of shape, size, color, and brightness.
9. **DESCRIBE** cues we use to judge distance and perceive movement.
10. **DESCRIBE** some common visual illusions and **EXPLAIN** them in terms of cues used in depth perception.
11. **EVALUATE** evidence concerning the existence of subliminal perception and extrasensory perception.
12. **APPLY** knowledge of biological and psychological factors involved in the perception of pain to ways of helping people manage pain more effectively.

© loriklaszlo/Shutterstock.com

Preview

MODULE 3.1

Sensing Our World: Basic Concepts of Sensation

- What is sensation?
- What is the difference between absolute thresholds and difference thresholds?
- What factors contribute to signal detection?
- What is sensory adaptation?

sensation The process by which we receive, transform, and process stimuli from the outside world to create sensory experiences of vision, touch, hearing, taste, smell, and so on.

sensory receptors Specialized cells that detect sensory stimuli and convert them into neural impulses.

psychophysics The study of the relationship between features of physical stimuli, such as the intensity of light and sound, and the sensation we experience in response to these stimuli.

absolute threshold The smallest amount of a given stimulus a person can sense.

Sensation is the process by which we receive, transform, and process stimuli that impinge on our sensory organs into neural impulses, or signals, that the brain uses to create experiences of vision, hearing, taste, smell, touch, and so on.

Each of our sense organs contains specialized cells, called **sensory receptors,** that detect stimuli from the outside world, such as light, sound, and odors, and transform them into patterns of neural impulses the brain uses to create sensations of vision, hearing, and so on (DeWeese & Zador, 2006; Sharpee et al., 2006). Sensory receptors are found throughout the body, in such organs as the eyes, ears, nose, and mouth, and in less obvious locations, such as the joints and muscles of the body and the entirety of the skin. In this module, we examine how sensory receptors respond to external stimuli and how they convert these stimuli into messages the brain uses to create the experience of sensation.

Our exploration of the process of sensation has its roots in **psychophysics,** the study of how physical sources of stimulation—light, sound, odors, and so on—relate to our experience of these stimuli in the form of sensations. Psychophysics began with the work of the nineteenth-century German scientist Gustav Theodor Fechner. Though Wilhelm Wundt is credited with establishing the first psychological laboratory in 1879, some historians believe that the publication of Fechner's *Elements of Psychophysics* in 1860 signaled the beginning of the scientific approach to psychology.

We begin our study of sensation by examining the common characteristics that relate to the functioning of our sensory systems: thresholds, signal detection, and sensory adaptation.

CONCEPT 3.1
Sensation is the process by which physical stimuli that impinge on our sensory organs are converted into neural impulses the brain uses to create our experiences of vision, touch, hearing, taste, smell, and so on.

CONCEPT 3.2
Sensory receptors convert sources of sensory stimuli, such as light and sound, into neural impulses the brain can use to create sensations.

CONCEPT 3.3
Through the study of psychophysics, we learn how the properties of external stimuli relate to our sensations.

CONCEPT 3.4
Our sensory systems vary in the amounts of stimulation needed to detect the presence of a stimulus and the differences among stimuli.

Absolute and Difference Thresholds: Is Something There? Is Something *Else* There?

Our sensory receptors are remarkably sensitive to certain types of stimuli. On a clear, dark night we can detect a flickering candle 30 miles away. We can also detect about one drop of perfume spread through a small house. The **absolute threshold** is the smallest amount of a stimulus that a person can reliably detect. Table 3.1 lists absolute thresholds for the senses of vision, hearing, taste, smell, and touch.

People differ in their absolute thresholds. Some are more sensitive than others to certain kinds of sensory stimulation—for example, sounds or odors. Fechner sought to determine the absolute thresholds for various senses by presenting people with stimuli of different magnitudes, such as brighter and duller lights, and then asking them whether they could see them. According to this method, the absolute threshold

TABLE 3.1 Absolute Thresholds for Various Senses

Sense	Stimulus	Receptors	Threshold
Vision	Light energy	Rods and cones in the eyes	The flame from a single candle flickering about 30 miles away on a dark, clear night
Hearing	Sound waves	Hair cells in the inner ear	The ticking of a watch placed about 20 feet away from a listener in a quiet room
Taste	Chemical substances that contact the tongue	Taste buds on the tongue	About 1 teaspoon of sugar dissolved in 2 gallons of water
Smell	Chemical substances that enter the nose	Receptor cells in the upper nostrils	About one drop of perfume dispersed in a small house
Touch	Movement of, or pressure on, the skin	Nerve endings in the skin	The wing of a bee falling on the cheek from about 1 centimeter away

Source: Adapted from Galanter, 1962.

is defined as the minimal level of stimulus energy that people can detect 50 percent of the time. Stimuli detected less than 50 percent of the time are considered below the absolute threshold. Stimuli that can be detected more often are above the threshold.

The nineteenth-century German scientist Ernst Weber (1795–1878) (pronounced *Vay-ber*) studied the smallest differences between stimuli that people were able to perceive. The minimal difference between two stimuli that people can reliably detect is the **difference threshold,** or *just-noticeable difference (jnd).* Just-noticeable differences apply to each of our senses.

difference threshold The minimal difference in the magnitude of energy needed for people to detect a difference between two stimuli.

How do difference thresholds apply to the range of stimuli we perceive with our senses? Weber summarized his findings in what is now known as **Weber's law.** According to this law, the amount you must change a stimulus to detect a difference is given by a constant fraction or proportion (called a *constant*) of the original stimulus. For example, Weber's constant for noticing a difference in weights is about 1/50 (or 2 percent). This means that if you were lifting a 50-pound weight, you would probably not notice a difference unless the weight were increased or reduced by about 2 percent (or 1 pound). But if you were lifting a 200-pound weight, the weight would have to be increased by about 4 pounds (2 percent) for you to notice the difference. Though the absolute weight needed to detect a difference is about quadruple as you increase the initial weight from 50 pounds to 200, the fraction remains the same (1/50).

Weber's law The principle that the amount of change in a stimulus needed to detect a difference is given by a constant ratio or fraction, called a constant, of the original stimulus.

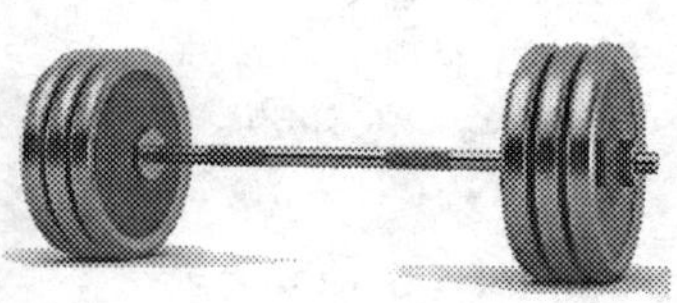

© SerhioGrey/Shutterstock.com

Weber found that the difference threshold differed for each of the senses. People are noticeably more sensitive to changes in the pitch of a sound than to changes in volume. They will perceive the difference if you raise or lower the pitch of your voice by about one-third of 1 percent (1/333). Yet they will not perceive a difference in the loudness of a sound unless the sound is made louder or softer by about 10 percent. Table 3.2 lists Weber's constants for various senses.

Weber's constants have practical applications. If you're going to sing, you had better be right on pitch (hit the note precisely) or people are going to groan. However, if you raise the volume on your stereo system just a little, your next-door neighbor might not notice any difference. Then, too, if your neighbor is complaining about the loudness, lowering the volume of the music by a notch may not be noticeable.

CONCEPT 3.5

The ability to detect a stimulus depends not only on the stimulus itself, but also on the perceiver and the level of background stimulation.

TABLE 3.2 Examples of Weber's Constants

Sensation	Weber's Constant (Approximate)
Saltiness of food	1/5
Pressure on skin	1/7
Loudness of sounds	1/10
Odor	1/20
Heaviness of weights	1/50
Brightness of lights	1/60
Pitch of sounds	1/333

Signal Detection: More Than a Matter of Energy

Scientists who study psychophysics describe sounds, flashes of light, and other stimuli as *signals*. According to **signal-detection theory,** the threshold for detecting a signal depends not only on the properties of the stimulus itself, such as its intensity—the loudness of a sound, for example—but also on the level of background stimulation, or noise, and, importantly, on the biological and psychological characteristics of the perceiver. The sensitivity or degree of sharpness of an individual's sensory systems (e.g., the acuity of your eyesight or hearing) partially determines whether a signal is detected. The organism's physical condition also plays a role. For instance, your sense of smell is duller when you have a cold and your nose is stuffed. Levels of fatigue or alertness also contribute to signal detection.

Psychological factors, including attention levels and states of motivation like hunger, also play important roles in signal detection. As you are walking down a darkened street by yourself late at night, you may be especially attentive to even the slightest sounds because they may signal danger. You may fail to notice the same sounds as you walk along the same street in broad daylight. If you haven't eaten for a while, you may be more likely to notice aromas of food wafting from a nearby kitchen than if you had just consumed a hearty meal.

signal-detection theory The belief that the detection of a stimulus depends on factors involving the intensity of the stimulus, the level of background stimulation, and the biological and psychological characteristics of the perceiver.

sensory adaptation The process by which sensory receptors adapt to constant stimuli by becoming less sensitive to them.

Sensory Adaptation: Turning the Volume Down

Through the process of **sensory adaptation,** sensory systems become *less* sensitive to constant or unchanging stimuli. When you are wearing a new wristwatch or ring, you may at first be aware of the sensation of pressure on your skin, but after a while you no longer notice it. We may be thankful for sensory adaptation when, after a few minutes of exposure, the water in a crisp mountain lake seems warmer or the odors in a locker room become less noticeable. However, sensory adaptation may not occur when we are repeatedly exposed to certain strong stimuli, such as the loud wail of a car alarm. In such cases, our sensory systems show no change in sensitivity to the stimulus. Concept Chart 3.1 reviews the basic concepts in sensation.

CONCEPT 3.6
Through the process of sensory adaptation, our sensory systems deal with repeated exposure to the same stimuli by becoming less sensitive to them.

CONCEPT CHART 3.1 Basic Concepts in Sensation

Sensation	The process of transforming stimuli that impinge on our sense organs into neural signals that the brain processes to create sensations of vision, touch, sound, taste, smell, and so on
Absolute threshold	The smallest amount of a stimulus that a person can reliably detect
Difference threshold	The minimal difference between two stimuli that people can reliably detect; also called *just-noticeable difference*
Weber's law	The amount of change in a stimulus needed to detect a difference, expressed as a constant ratio or fraction of the original stimulus
Signal-detection theory	The belief that the ability to detect a signal varies with the characteristics of the perceiver, the background, and the stimulus itself
Sensory adaptation	The process by which sensory systems adapt to constant stimuli by becoming less sensitive to them

3.1 MODULE REVIEW Sensing Our World: Basic Concepts of Sensation

Recite It

What is sensation?

➤ Sensation is the process of taking information from the world, transforming it into neural impulses, and transmitting these signals to the brain, where they are processed to produce experiences of vision, hearing, smell, taste, touch, and so on.

What is the difference between absolute thresholds and difference thresholds?

➤ An absolute threshold is the smallest amount of a stimulus that a person can sense. A difference threshold, or just-noticeable difference (jnd), is the minimal difference in magnitude of energy needed for people to detect a difference between two stimuli.

What factors contribute to signal detection?

➤ Factors affecting signal detection include the intensity of the stimulus; the level of background stimulation, or noise; the biological characteristics of the perceiver, such as the sharpness of the person's sensory system and levels of fatigue or alertness; and psychological factors, such as attention levels and states of motivation.

What is sensory adaptation?

➤ Sensory adaptation is the process by which sensory systems become less sensitive to unchanging stimuli.

Recall It

1. Specialized cells in the sense organs, which are geared to detect stimuli in the external environment, are called
   a. feature detectors.
   b. threshold detectors.
   c. sensory receptors.
   d. signal detectors.

2. The smallest amount of stimulation that a person can reliably detect is called a(n)
   a. minimal sensory field.
   b. absolute threshold.
   c. just-noticeable difference.
   d. vector of constants.

3. Jill notices the humming sound made by an air conditioner when she first enters the room, but within a few minutes she is no longer aware of the sound. What sensory process does this illustrate?

Think About It

➤ You've probably noticed that when you draw a bath it seems hotter at first than it does a minute or two later. Based on your reading of the text, explain this phenomenon.

➤ Let's say you're using a recipe that calls for 15 grams of salt. According to Weber's constant for saltiness, which is 1/5, how much more salt must you add to make the recipe noticeably saltier?

Vision: Seeing the Light

MODULE 3.2

- How do the eyes process light?
- What are feature detectors, and what role do they play in visual processing?
- What are the two major theories of color vision?
- What are the two major forms of color blindness?

Vision is the process by which light energy is converted into signals (neural impulses) that the brain interprets to produce the experience of sight. Our sense of vision allows us to receive visual information from a mere few inches away, as when we read from a book held close to our eyes, to many billions of miles away, as when we observe twinkling stars on a clear night. To understand vision, we first need to consider the source of physical energy that gives rise to vision: light.

CONCEPT 3.7
Vision is the process by which light energy is converted into neural impulses that the brain interprets to produce the experience of sight.

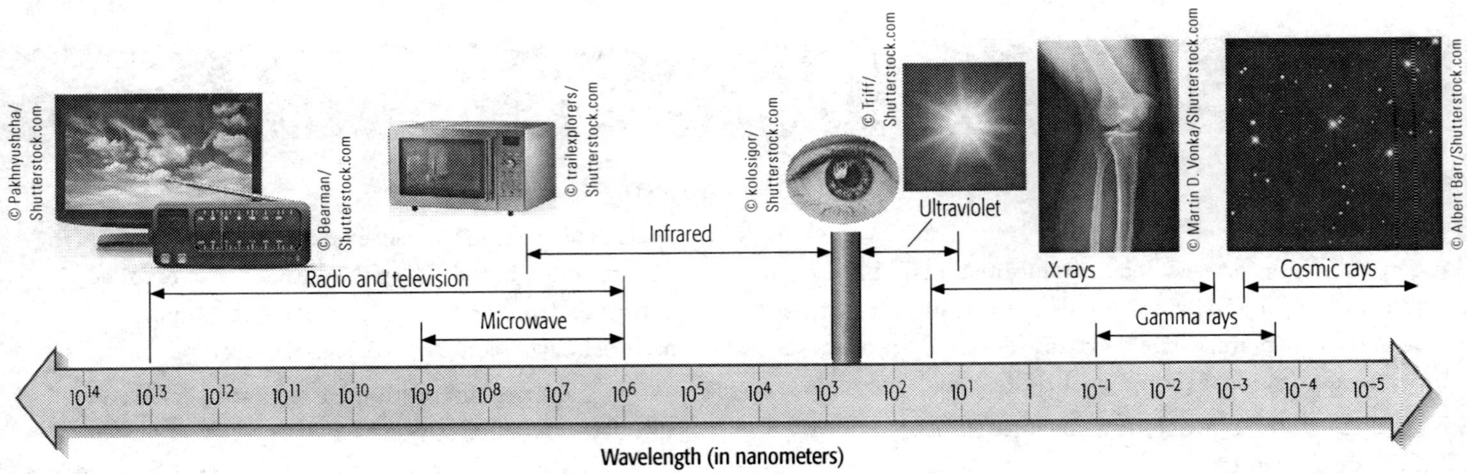

FIGURE 3.1 The Electromagnetic Spectrum
Visible light (represented by color bands) occupies only a small portion of the range of electromagnetic radiation that is called the electromagnetic spectrum.

cornea A transparent covering on the eye's surface through which light enters.

iris The pigmented, circular muscle in the eye that regulates the size of the pupil to adjust to changes in the level of illumination.

pupil The black opening inside the iris that allows light to enter the eye.

CONCEPT 3.8
Light, a form of physical energy, is the stimulus to which receptors in the eyes respond, giving rise to our sense of vision.

CONCEPT 3.9
When energy in the form of light comes into contact with the photoreceptor cells in the retina, it is converted into neural signals that are transmitted to the brain.

Light: The Energy of Vision

Light is physical energy in the form of electromagnetic radiation (electrically charged particles). X-rays, ultraviolet waves, and radio waves are other forms of electromagnetic energy. Visible light is the portion of the spectrum of electromagnetic radiation that gives rise to our sense of vision. As you can see ■ in Figure 3.1, the visible spectrum occupies only a small portion of the full spectrum of electromagnetic radiation. It consists of the wavelengths from approximately 300 to 750 nanometers (a nanometer is one billionth of a meter).

Different wavelengths within the visible spectrum give rise to the experience of different colors (see ■ Figure 3.2). Violet has the shortest wavelength (about 400 billionths of a meter long), and red has the longest (about 700 billionths of a meter). Psychology students are often told that they can remember the order of the colors of the spectrum by thinking of the name Roy G. Biv (standing for red, orange, yellow, green, blue, indigo, and violet).

The Eye: The Visionary Sensory Organ

The eye is the organ with receptor cells that respond to light. Light enters the eye through the **cornea,** a transparent covering on the eye's surface (see ■ Figure 3.3). A muscle called the **iris** contracts or expands to determine the amount of light that enters. The iris is colored, most often brown or blue, and gives the eye its color. The **pupil** of the eye is the black opening inside the iris. The iris increases or decreases the size of the pupil reflexively to adjust to the amount of light entering the eye. The brighter the light, the smaller the

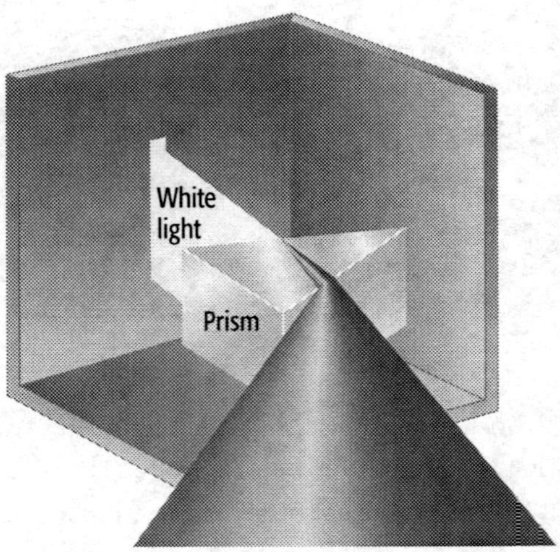

FIGURE 3.2 The Color Spectrum
A prism separates white light into the various hues that make up the part of the electromagnetic spectrum that is visible to humans.

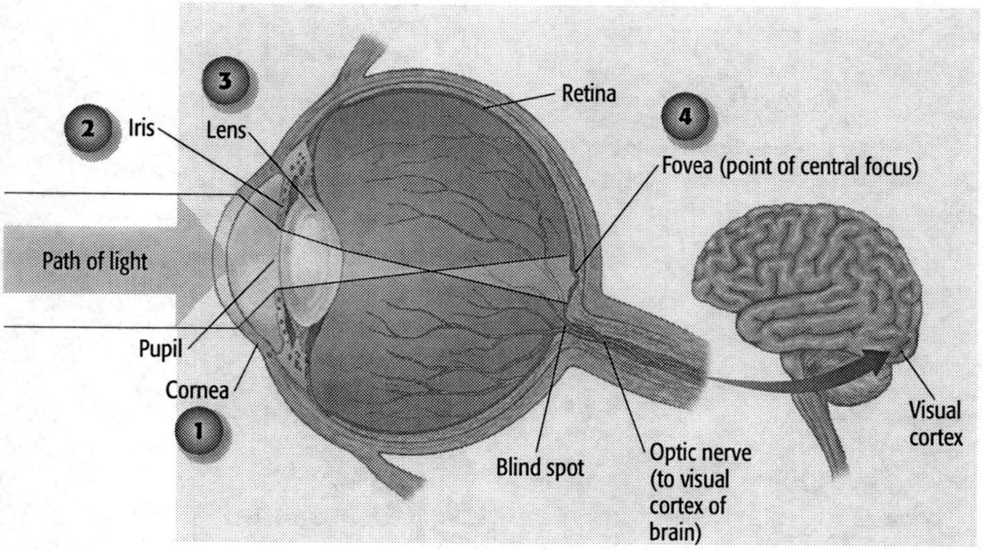

FIGURE 3.3 Parts of the Eye
1 Light enters the eye through the cornea. 2 The iris adjusts reflexively to control the size of the pupil. 3 The lens focuses the light on the retina, especially on the 4 fovea, the point of central focus that gives rise to clearest vision.

lens The structure in the eye that focuses light rays on the retina.

accommodation The process by which the lens changes its shape to focus images more clearly on the retina.

retina The light-sensitive layer of the inner surface of the eye that contains photoreceptor cells.

photoreceptors Light-sensitive cells (rods and cones) in the eye upon which light registers.

rods Photoreceptors that are sensitive only to the intensity of light (light and dark).

cones Photoreceptors that are sensitive to color.

CONCEPT 3.10
Rods, which are more sensitive to light than are cones, are responsible for peripheral vision and vision in dim light, whereas cones allow us to detect colors and to discern fine details of objects under bright illumination.

CONCEPT 3.11
Objects are seen most clearly when their images are focused on the fovea, a part of the retina that contains only cones.

iris makes the pupil. Under darkened conditions, the iris opens to allow more light to enter the pupil so that we can see more clearly. Because these are reflex actions, they happen automatically (you don't have to think about them).

Light enters the eye through the cornea and then passes through the pupil and **lens.** Through a process called **accommodation,** the lens changes its shape to adjust for the distance of the object, which helps focus the visual image on the inner surface of the eye called the **retina.** Like the film in a camera, the retina receives the image as light strikes it. But the retina is much more sophisticated than photographic film. It contains two kinds of **photoreceptors,** specialized receptor cells that are sensitive to light.

When light hits the retina, it comes into contact with these photoreceptors. Because of their shapes, they are called **rods** and **cones** (see ■ Figure 3.4). The normal eye has about 120 million rods and 6 million cones. The rods and cones convert the physical energy of light into neural signals that the brain processes to create visual sensations.

Have you ever noticed that when lighting is dim, you tend to make out the shapes of objects but not their colors? That's because cones are responsible for color vision but are less sensitive to light than rods are. Rods allow us to detect objects in low light but are sensitive only to the intensity or brightness of light. They are also responsible for *peripheral vision*—the ability to detect objects, especially moving objects, at the edges (sides, as well as the top and bottom) of our visual field. Cones allow us to detect colors, as well as to discern fine details of objects in bright light. Some animals, including some species of birds, have only cones in their eyes. They can see only during daylight hours when the cones are activated. Because they become totally blind at night, they must return to their roosts as evening approaches.

The neural signals produced by the rods and cones pass back through a layer of interconnecting cells called **bipolar cells** and then through a layer of neurons called **ganglion cells** (see ■ Figure 3.5). The axon projecting from each ganglion cell makes

bipolar cells A layer of interconnecting cells in the eye that connect photoreceptors to ganglion cells.

ganglion cells Nerve cells in the back of the eye that transmit neural impulses in response to light stimulation, the axons of which make up the optic nerve.

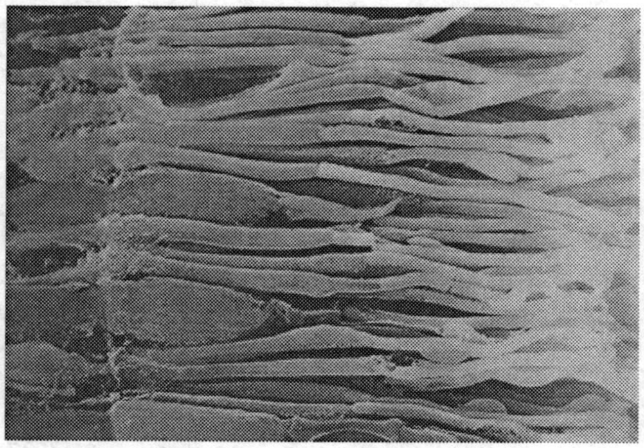

© Ralph C. Eagle, Jr/Photo Researchers, Inc.

FIGURE 3.4 Rods and Cones
This close-up image of a portion of the retina shows cones (large, reddish, cone-like objects on the left side of the photograph) and rods (more numerous rodlike objects).

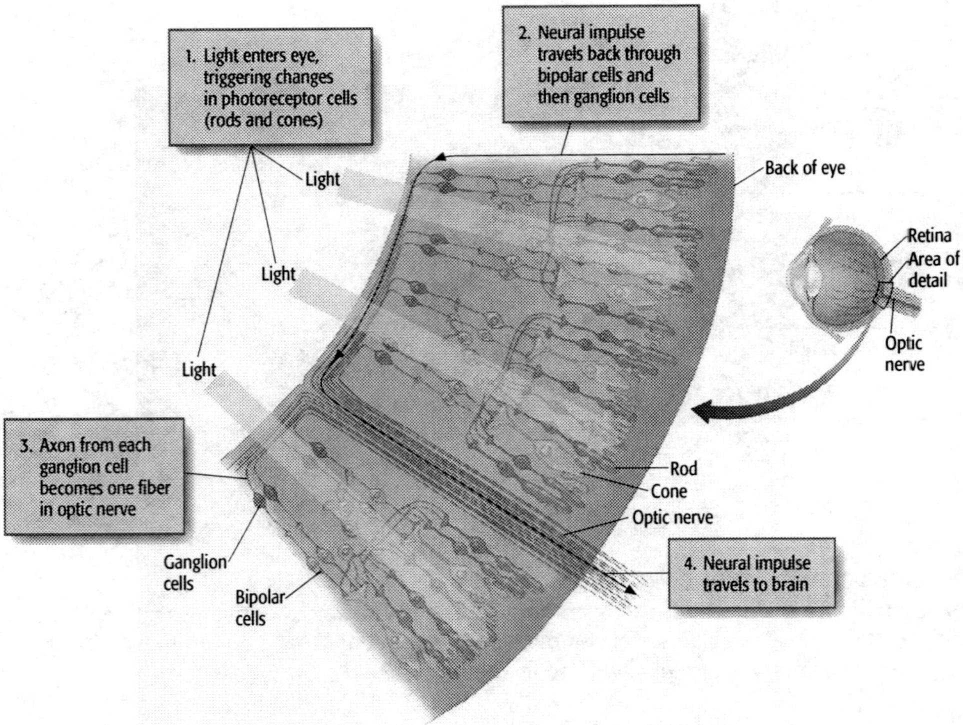

FIGURE 3.5 Conversion of Light into Neural Impulses
Light is converted into neural impulses that the brain uses to produce the sensation of vision.

optic nerve The nerve that carries neural impulses generated by light stimulation from the eye to the brain.

blind spot The area in the retina where the optic nerve leaves the eye and that contains no photoreceptor cells.

fovea The area near the center of the retina that contains only cones and that is the center of focus for clearest vision.

up one nerve fiber in the **optic nerve.** The optic nerve, which consists of a million or so ganglion axons, transmits visual information to the brain, where it is routed to the thalamus, a major relay station, and from there to the visual cortex. The visual cortex lies in the occipital lobes, the part of the cerebral cortex that processes visual information and produces the experience of vision.

The part of the retina where the optic nerve leaves the eye is known as the **blind spot** (see ■ Figure 3.6). Because it contains no photoreceptors (rods or cones), we do not see images that form on the blind spot. By contrast, the **fovea** is the part of the retina that corresponds to the center of our gaze and that gives rise to our sharpest vision (see Figure 3.3). It contains only cones. Focusing our eyes on an object brings its image to bear directly on the fovea.

FIGURE 3.6 Blind Spot
Because there are no receptor cells in the blind spot—no rods or cones—images formed on the blind spot cannot be seen. You can demonstrate this for yourself by closing your left eye and, while focusing on the dot, slowly move the book farther away to about a distance of a foot. You'll notice there is a point at which the stack of money disappears. We are not typically aware of our blind spots because our eyes are constantly moving and because they work together to compensate for any loss of vision when an image falls on the blind spot.

Farther away from the fovea, the proportion of cones decreases while the proportion of rods increases. Rods show the opposite pattern. They are few and far between close to the fovea and more densely packed farther away from the fovea. The far ends of the retina contain only rods (see *Try This Out*).

Visual acuity, or sharpness of vision, is the ability to discern visual details. Many of us have impaired visual acuity. People who need to be unusually close to objects to discern their details are *nearsighted.* People who need to be unusually far away from objects to see them clearly are *farsighted.* Nearsightedness and farsightedness result from abnormalities in the shape of the eye. Nearsightedness can occur when the eyeball is too long or the cornea is too curved. In either case, distant objects are focused in front of the retina. Farsightedness can occur when the eyeball is too short so that light from nearby objects is focused behind the retina.

TRY THIS OUT
Reading Sideways

Hold a book or magazine to the side and try reading it. Did you notice that the words were blurry, if you could make them out at all? How does the distribution of rods and cones in the retina explain this phenomenon?

Feature Detectors: Getting Down to Basics

In 1981, David Hubel and Torsten Wiesel received a Nobel Prize for unraveling a small piece of the puzzle of how we transform sensory information into rich visual experiences of the world around us. They discovered that the visual cortex contains nerve cells that respond only when an animal (in their studies, a cat) is shown a line with a particular orientation—horizontal, vertical, or diagonal (Hubel, 1988; Hubel & Wiesel, 1979). Some of these nerve cells respond only to lines that form right angles; others, to dots of light that move from right to left across the visual field; and yet others to dots of light that move from left to right. Hubel and Wiesel made their discoveries by implanting a tiny electrode in individual cells in the cat's visual cortex. They then flashed different visual stimuli on a screen within the cat's field of vision and observed which cells fired in response to which types of stimuli. Neurons that respond to specific features of a visual stimulus are called **feature detectors.**

feature detectors Specialized neurons in the visual cortex that respond only to particular features of visual stimuli, such as horizontal or vertical lines.

We do not see a world composed of scattered bits and pieces of sensory data, of lines, angles, and moving points of light. Somehow the visual cortex compiles information from various cells, combining them to form meaningful patterns. How do we go from recognizing specific features of a stimulus—its individual angles, lines, and edges—to discerning a meaningful pattern, such as letters, numbers, words, or the human face? Scientists believe that complex assemblages of neurons in the brain work together to analyze relationships among specific features of objects. Hubel and Wiesel opened a door to understanding the beginning steps in this process at the level of the individual feature detector. Yet we are still a long way from understanding how the brain transforms sensory stimulation into the rich visual world we experience.

CONCEPT 3.12
The brain's visual cortex contains cells so specialized that they fire only when they detect precise angles, lines, or points of light.

Color Vision: Sensing a Colorful World

To be able to perceive different colors, color receptors in the retina of the eye must transmit different messages to the brain when visible lights having different wavelengths stimulate them. How are these messages transmitted? Two nineteenth-century German scientists, Hermann von Helmholtz (1821–1894) and Ewald Hering (1834–1918), proposed different answers to this question.

Helmholtz contributed to many fields of science, but is perhaps best known to psychologists for his work on color vision. He was impressed by the earlier work on

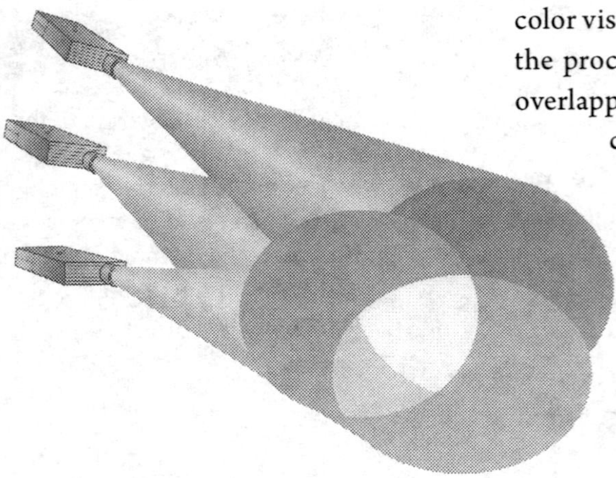

FIGURE 3.7 **Primary Colors**
The three primary colors of light—red, green, and blue-violet—combine to form white. Thomas Young showed that you could create any color of light by mixing these component colors and varying their brightness. For example, a combination of red and green light creates yellow.

color vision by the English scientist Thomas Young (1773–1829). Young had reversed the process by which a prism breaks light down into component colors. He shone overlapping lights of red, green, and blue-violet onto a screen and found that he could create light of any color on the spectrum by varying the brightness of the lights (see ■ Figure 3.7). Where all three lights overlapped, white light resulted—the color of sunlight.

Building on Young's work, Helmholtz proposed what is now known as the Young-Helmholtz theory, or **trichromatic theory** (from Greek roots meaning "three" and "color"). Helmholtz believed that Young's experimental results showed that our eyes have three types of color receptors—red, green, and blue-violet. We now call these color receptors *cones*. These three types of cones have differing sensitivities to different wavelengths of light. Blue-violet cones are most sensitive to short wavelengths; green cones, to middle wavelengths; and red cones, to long wavelengths. According to the trichromatic theory, the response pattern of these three types of cones allows us to see different colors. So when green cones are most strongly activated, we see green. But when a combination of different types of cones is activated, we see other colors, just as mixing paint of different colors produces yet other colors. For example, when red and green receptors are stimulated at the same time, we see yellow.

trichromatic theory A theory of color vision that posits that the ability to see different colors depends on the relative activity of three types of color receptors in the eye (red, green, and blue-violet).

afterimage The visual image of a stimulus that remains after the stimulus is removed.

Hering developed a different theory of color vision based on his work with *afterimages*. An **afterimage** is what you see if you gaze at a visual stimulus for a while and then look at a neutral surface, such as a sheet of white paper.

Pause for a demonstration. The flag in ■ Figure 3.8 has all the shapes in the American flag, but the colors are off. Instead of being red, white, and blue, this flag is green, black, and yellow. Now, although you may not particularly wish to defend this oddly colored flag, gaze at it for a full minute (time yourself). Then quickly shift your gaze to a white sheet of paper. You may well see a more familiar flag; this is because red is the afterimage of green, white is the afterimage of black, and blue is the afterimage of yellow.

Hering's work with afterimages led him to develop the **opponent-process theory** of color vision. Opponent-process theory, like trichromatic theory, suggests that our eyes have three types of color receptors. According to this theory, however, each type of receptor consists of a pair of opposing receptors. Rather than there being separate receptors for red, green, and blue-violet, some receptors are sensitive to red or green; others, to blue or yellow; and others, to black or white. The black-white receptors detect brightness or shades of gray; the red-green and blue-yellow pairs detect differences in colors.

FIGURE 3.8 **Afterimages**
The colors in the American flag shown here can be set right by performing a simple experiment. Stare at the dot in the center of the flag for about 60 seconds. Then quickly shift your gaze to a white wall or white sheet of paper. You will then see the more familiar colors of the American flag as afterimages.

Hering believed that color vision arises from pairs of opposing processes. According to his theory, red-green receptors do not simultaneously transmit messages for red and green. Rather, they transmit messages for either one or the other. When the red one is activated, the green one is blocked, or inhibited, and so we see red. Yet prolonged transmission of any one message, such as red or green, disturbs the balance of neural activity, making it more difficult to inhibit the opposing color receptor. Thus, according to Hering's theory, if you stare at the green, black, and yellow flag in Figure 3.8 for a minute or so, you will disturb the balance of neural activity, producing an *opponent process.* The afterimage of red, white, and blue you experience represents the eye's attempt to reestablish a balance between the two opposing receptors.

opponent-process theory Holds that the experience of color results from opposing processes involving two sets of color receptors, red-green receptors and blue-yellow receptors; another set of opposing receptors, black-white, detects differences in brightness.

Which model of color vision has it right—the trichromatic model or the opponent-process model? Contemporary research shows both theories are right to a certain extent (Hergenhahn, 1997; Jacobs & Nathans, 2009). The trichromatic theory is correct at the receptor level, since the photochemistry of cones responds in the way described by trichromatic theory—some are sensitive to red light; others to green light; and still others to blue-violet light. But Hering's opponent-process theory is correct in terms of the behavior of cells that lie between the cones and the occipital lobe of the cerebral cortex—including bipolar and ganglion cells. These cells operate in an opponent-process fashion. Some are turned on by red light but are prevented (inhibited) from firing by green light. Others are turned on by green light but are inhibited by red light. Most authorities today believe that color vision includes elements of both trichromatic and opponent-process theories.

CONCEPT 3.13
The major theories of color, trichromatic theory and opponent-process theory, may each partially account for color vision.

CONCEPT 3.14
The most common form of color blindness is red-green color blindness, in which people cannot tell reds from greens.

Psychologists have begun to look at how colors affect us. In one recent example, researchers found that men were rated as more attractive when they were wearing the color red (Elliot et al., 2010). In this study, men who were pictured wearing red shirts were perceived by women (but not by other men) as more attractive and sexually desirable than were men shown in photos in which they wore clothes of other colors. There may be an evolutionary basis to this "men look hot in red" effect. The color red in males of many other animal species signals higher status and power, which is a desirable mating attribute.

Trichromats are people with normal color vision who can discern all the colors of the visible spectrum—red, green, and blue-violet—as well as colors formed by various combinations of these hues.

trichromats People with normal color vision who can discern all the colors of the visual spectrum.

monochromats People who have no color vision and can see only in black and white.

dichromats People who can see some colors but not others.

About one out of every 40,000 people is completely color blind. We classify these individuals as **monochromats** because they can see only in black and white, as though they were watching an old movie or TV show. Because of a genetic defect, they have only one type of cone, so their brains cannot discern differences in wavelengths of light that give rise to perception of color. They can detect only brightness, so the world appears in shades of gray. Much more common are **dichromats**—people who lack one of the three types of color receptors or cones, making it difficult for them to distinguish between certain colors. About 8 percent of men and about 1 percent of women have some form of color blindness (Bennett, 2009). The most common form is red-green color blindness, a genetic defect that makes it difficult to tell red from green. Much less common is blue-yellow color blindness, in which the person has difficulty distinguishing blues from yellows. ■ Figure 3.9 shows a plate from a test commonly used to assess color blindness.

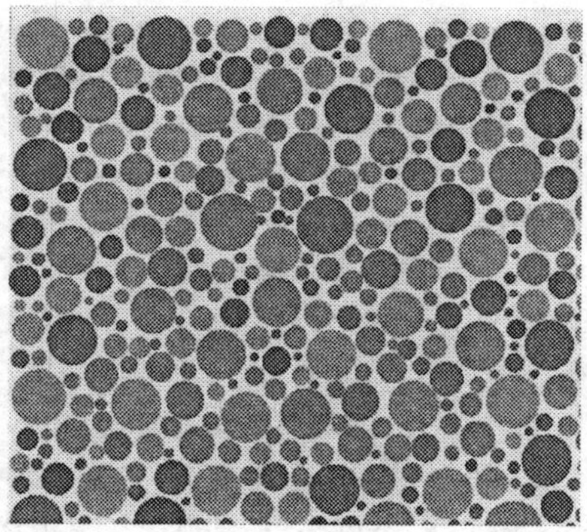

FIGURE 3.9 Color Blindness
What do you see? People with normal color vision will see the triangle in this array of dots. People with red-green color blindness will not perceive it.

People with red-green color blindness might put on one green sock and one red sock, as long as they were similar in brightness. But they would not confuse green with blue. Red-green color blindness appears to be a sex-linked genetic defect that is carried on the X sex chromosome. As noted, more males than females are affected by this condition. Because males have only one X chromosome whereas females have two, a defect on one X chromosome is more likely to be expressed in males than in females (Jacobs & Nathans, 2009). Concept Chart 3.2 provides an overview of vision.

CONCEPT CHART 3.2 Vision	
Source of sensory information	Visible light
Receptor organs	The eyes. Light enters through the cornea and pupil and is focused on the retina.
Receptor cells	The retina has two kinds of photoreceptors. Rods are sensitive to the intensity of light, which is the basis of our sense of light and dark. Cones are sensitive to differences in the wavelengths of light, which is the basis of color vision. Visual information is transmitted to the brain by means of the optic nerve.
Color vision	Two major theories of color vision have been proposed, the trichromatic theory and the opponent-process theory. Each theory appears to account for some aspects of color vision.

3.2 MODULE REVIEW Vision: Seeing the Light

Recite It

How do the eyes process light?

- Light enters the eye through the cornea and passes through the pupil and then the lens, which focuses the image on the retina.
- The light then stimulates photoreceptor cells, rods or cones, which convert the light energy into neural impulses that are carried first through bipolar cells and then to ganglion cells that terminate in the optic nerve.
- When we focus on an object, we bring its image to bear on the fovea, the cone-rich part of the retina in which we have our sharpest vision.
- Cones allow us to see colors but are less sensitive to light than rods are.
- Rods allow us to see objects in black and white in dim light; they are also responsible for peripheral vision.

What are feature detectors, and what role do they play in visual processing?

- Feature detectors are specialized cells in the visual cortex that respond only to specific features of visual stimuli, such as horizontal or vertical lines.

What are the two major theories of color vision?

- The trichromatic theory, or Young-Helmholtz theory, proposes that there are three kinds of color receptors (red, green, and blue-violet) and that all the colors in the spectrum can be generated by the simultaneous stimulation of a combination of these color receptors.
- The opponent-process theory developed by Ewald Hering proposes that there are three pairs of receptors (red-green, blue-yellow, black-white) and that opposing processes within each pair determine our experience of color.

What are the two major forms of color blindness?

- The two major forms of color blindness are complete color blindness (lack of any ability to discern colors) and partial color blindness (red-green or blue-yellow color blindness).

Recall It

1. Which of the following statements is true? Rods
   a. are most heavily concentrated around the fovea.
   b. are primarily responsible for color vision.
   c. allow us to discern fine details of objects under high illumination.
   d. are more sensitive to light than cones.
2. The photoreceptors in the retina that are responsible for peripheral vision and vision in dim light are called ______; those responsible for color vision and for discerning fine details in bright light are called ______.
3. The visual cortex lies in the ______ lobes.
4. Match the following parts of the eye with their respective functions: (a) iris; (b) pupil; (c) lens; (d) retina; (e) fovea; (f) blind spot.
   i. part of the eye that focuses the visual image on the retina.
   ii. inner surface of the eye in which the photoreceptors are found.
   iii. part of the retina from which the optic nerve leaves the eye.
   iv. muscle controlling the size of the pupil.
   v. area on the retina responsible for clearest vision.
   vi. opening through which light enters the eye.

Think About It

- Explain the phenomenon of afterimages by drawing upon Hering's opponent-process theory of color vision.
- Are you color blind? Do you know anyone who is? How has it affected your (or his or her) life, if at all?

Hearing: The Music of Sound

MODULE 3.3

- How does the ear enable us to hear sound?
- What determines our perception of pitch?
- What are the main types of and causes of deafness?

The chattering of birds, the voices of children, the stirring melodies of Tchaikovsky—we sense all these sounds by means of hearing, or **audition.** We hear by sensing sound waves, which result from changes in the pressure of air or water. Sound waves cause parts of the ear to vibrate. These vibrations are then converted into electrical signals that are sent to the brain.

audition The sense of hearing.

pitch The highness or lowness of a sound that corresponds to the frequency of the sound wave.

Sound: Sensing Waves of Vibration

Like visible light, sound is a form of energy that travels in waves. Yet while light can travel through the empty reaches of outer space, sound exists only in a medium, such as air, liquids, gases, or even solids (which is why you may hear your neighbor's stereo through a solid wall). A vibrating object causes molecules of air (or other substances, such as water) to vibrate. For example, your voice is produced when your vocal cords vibrate. The resulting vibrations spread outward from the source in the form of sound waves that are characterized by such physical properties as *amplitude* (the height of the sound wave, which is a measure of its energy) and *frequency* (the number of complete waves, or cycles, per second) (see ■ Figure 3.10).

CONCEPT 3.15
Sound vibrations are the stimuli transformed by receptors in the ears into signals the brain uses to let you experience the sounds of the world around you.

The amplitude of sound waves determines their perceived loudness and is measured in *decibels* (dB). For each 10-decibel increase, loudness of sound increases tenfold. Thus, a sound of 20 decibels is actually 10 times louder than a sound of 10 decibels, not two times louder.

Light travels at 186,000 miles per second. Sound is a slowpoke by comparison. Sound travels through air at only about 1,130 feet per second (or 770 miles per *hour*). Therefore, it may take about 5 seconds for thunder from a storm a mile away to reach your ears. But most of the sounds that matter to us—the voice of a teacher or a lover, the screeches and whines of cars and buses, and the sounds of music—are so close that they seem to reach us in no time at all.

Although sound travels more slowly than light, the vibrations that give rise to sound still occur many times a second. The frequency with which they occur per second provides information that the brain uses to produce perceptions of **pitch,** or how high or low a sound seems. The human ear senses sound waves that vary in frequency from about 20 to perhaps 20,000 cycles per second. Sound

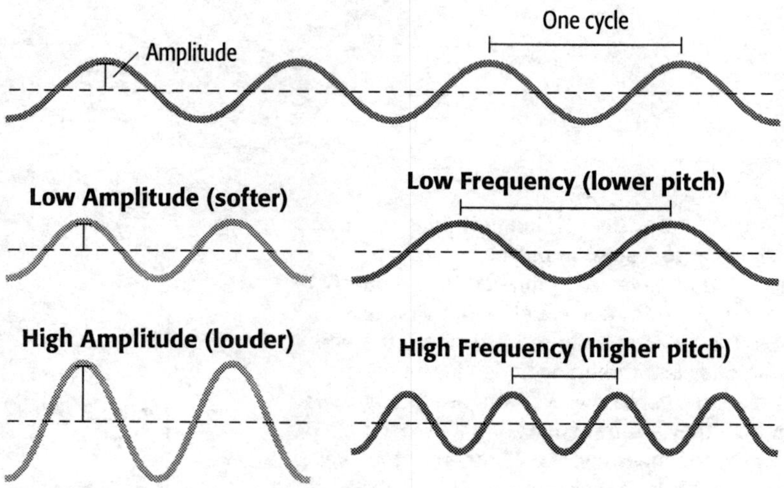

FIGURE 3.10 Sound Waves
Sound waves vary in such physical properties as amplitude, or height of the wave, and frequency, or number of complete cycles per second. Differences in amplitude give rise to perceptions of loudness, whereas differences in frequency lead to perceptions of pitch.

waves that are higher in frequency are perceived as being higher in pitch. Women's voices are usually higher than men's because their vocal cords tend to be shorter and thus to vibrate more rapidly (at a greater frequency). The shorter strings on a harp (or in a piano) produce higher notes than the longer strings because they vibrate more rapidly.

CONCEPT 3.16
Sound waves cause parts of the ear to vibrate; this mechanical vibration in turn affects sensory receptors in the inner ear, called hair cells, triggering the transmission of auditory messages to the brain.

The Ear: A Sound Machine

The ear is structured to capture sound waves, reverberate with them, and convert them into messages or electrical signals the brain can interpret (see ■ Figure 3.11). Here's how it works: The outer ear funnels sound waves to the **eardrum,** a tight membrane that vibrates in response to them. The vibrations are then transmitted through three tiny bones in the middle ear called the **ossicles** (literally "little bones"). The first of these to vibrate, the "hammer" (*malleus*), is connected to the eardrum. It strikes the "anvil" (*incus*), which in turn strikes the "stirrup" (*stapes*), causing it to vibrate. The vibration is transmitted from the stirrup to the **oval window,** a membrane to which the stirrup is attached. The oval window connects the middle ear to a snail-shaped bony tube in the inner ear called the **cochlea** (*cochlea* is the Greek word for "snail").

eardrum A sheet of connective tissue separating the outer ear from the middle ear that vibrates in response to auditory stimuli and transmits sound waves to the middle ear.

ossicles Three tiny bones in the middle ear (the hammer, anvil, and stirrup) that vibrate in response to vibrations of the eardrum.

oval window The membrane-covered opening that separates the middle ear from the inner ear.

cochlea The snail-shaped organ in the inner ear that contains sensory receptors for hearing.

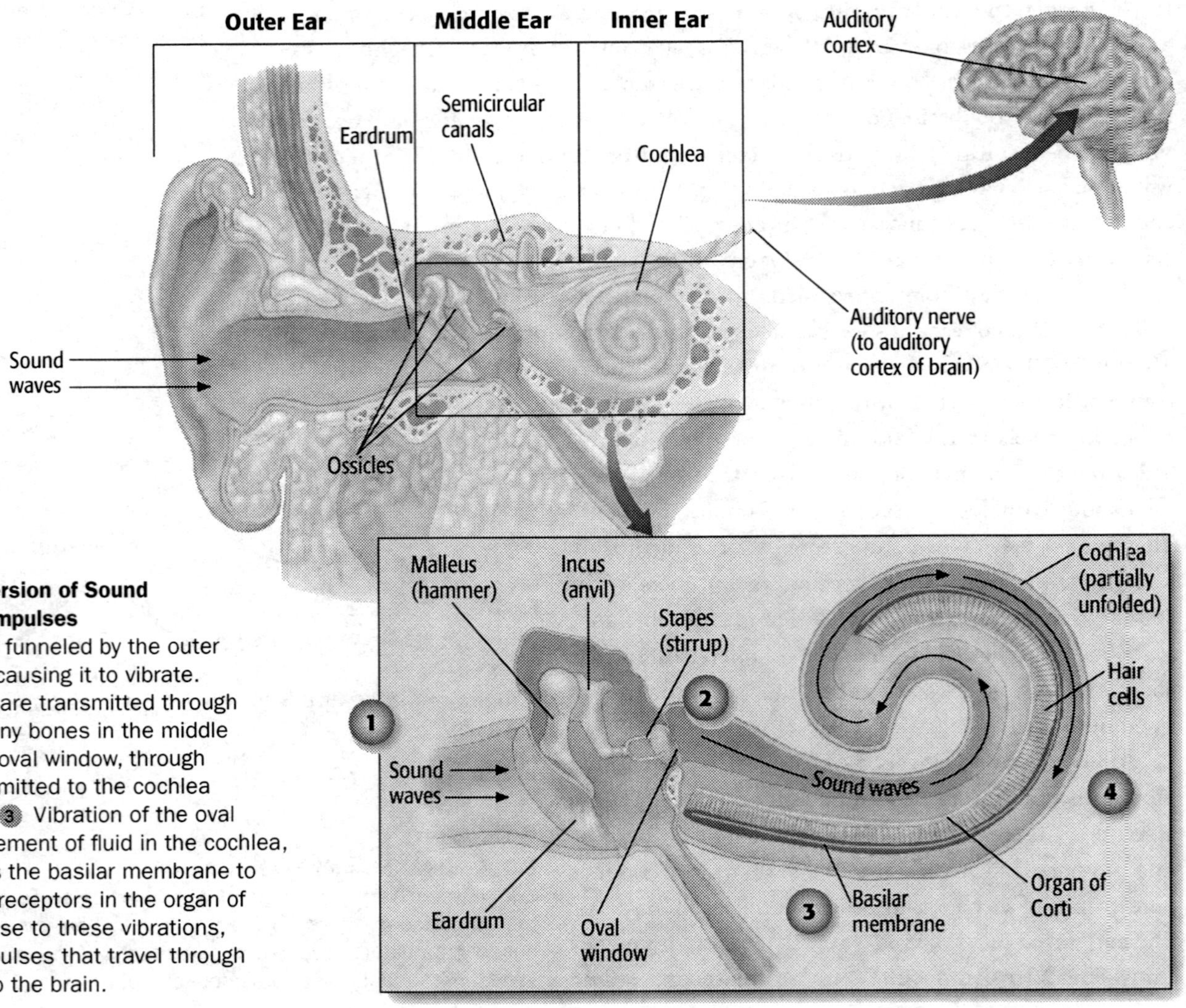

FIGURE 3.11 Conversion of Sound Waves into Neural Impulses
(1) Sound waves are funneled by the outer ear to the eardrum, causing it to vibrate. (2) These vibrations are transmitted through the ossicles, three tiny bones in the middle ear, and then to the oval window, through which they are transmitted to the cochlea within the inner ear. (3) Vibration of the oval window causes movement of fluid in the cochlea, which in turn causes the basilar membrane to vibrate. (4) Hair-cell receptors in the organ of Corti bend in response to these vibrations, triggering neural impulses that travel through the auditory nerve to the brain.

Vibrations of the oval window cause waves of motion in fluid within the cochlea. The motion of this fluid causes a structure within the cochlea, called the **basilar membrane,** to vibrate. The basilar membrane is attached to a gelatinous structure called the **organ of Corti,** which is lined with 15,000 or so **hair cells** that act as auditory receptors. These hair cells are not real hairs, but cells with 100 or so hair-like projections sticking out from their surfaces that bend in response to movements of the basilar membrane (Kros, 2005). These movements in turn trigger transmission of auditory messages to the auditory cortex in the brain via the **auditory nerve** (Gubbels et al., 2008). Located in the temporal lobes of the cerebral cortex, the auditory cortex processes auditory stimuli, producing the experience of sound.

basilar membrane The membrane in the cochlea that is attached to the organ of Corti.

organ of Corti A gelatinous structure in the cochlea containing the hair cells that serve as auditory receptors.

hair cells The auditory receptors that transform vibrations caused by sound waves into neural impulses that are then transmitted to the brain via the auditory nerve.

auditory nerve The nerve that carries neural impulses from the ear to the brain, which gives rise to the experience of hearing.

Unless sounds originate from sources equally distant from both ears—for example, exactly in front of or above you—they reach one ear before the other. Although you might not be able to say exactly how much sooner you hear a sound in one ear than in the other, your brain can detect a difference as small as one ten-thousandth of a second. It uses such information to help locate the source of a sound. More distant sounds tend to be softer (just as more distant objects look smaller), which provides yet another cue for locating sounds.

Perception of Pitch: Perceiving the Highs and Lows

How do people distinguish whether one sound is higher or lower in pitch than another? As with perception of color, more than one theory is needed to help us understand how we perceive pitch. Two theories, *place theory* and *frequency theory,* help explain how we detect high and low pitches, and a combination of the two, called the *volley principle,* helps explain how we detect mid-range pitches.

Place theory, originally developed by Hermann von Helmholtz, suggests that people perceive a sound to have a certain pitch according to the place along the basilar membrane that vibrates the most when sound waves of particular frequencies strike the ear. It is as though neurons line up along the basilar membrane like so many keys on a piano, standing ready to respond by producing sounds of different pitch when they are "struck" (Azar, 1996a).

place theory The belief that pitch depends on the place along the basilar membrane that vibrates the most in response to a particular auditory stimulus.

Georg von Békésy (1957) won a Nobel Prize for showing that high-frequency sounds cause the greatest vibration of hair cells close to the oval window, whereas those with lower frequencies cause the greatest vibration farther down the basilar membrane. Hair cells at the point of maximal vibration, like the crest of a wave, excite particular neurons that inform the brain about their location. The brain uses this information to code sounds for pitch. However, low-frequency sounds—those below about 4,000 cycles per second—cannot be coded for location because they do not cause the membrane to vibrate the most at any one spot. Yet we know that people can detect sounds with frequencies as low as 20 cycles per second.

CONCEPT 3.17

Perception of pitch may best be explained by a combination of place theory, frequency theory, and the volley principle.

Frequency theory may account for how we perceive the pitch of sounds of about 20 to 1,000 cycles per second. According to frequency theory, the basilar membrane vibrates at the same frequency as the sound wave itself. In other words, a sound wave with a frequency of 200 cycles per second would cause the basilar membrane to vibrate at that rate and generate a corresponding number of neural impulses to the brain. That is, there would be 200 neural impulses to the brain per second. But frequency theory also has its limitations. Most importantly, neurons cannot fire more frequently than about 1,000 times per second.

frequency theory The belief that pitch depends on the frequency of vibration of the basilar membrane and the volley of neural impulses transmitted to the brain via the auditory nerve.

volley principle The principle that relates the experience of pitch to the alternating firing of groups of neurons along the basilar membrane.

What, then, do we make of sounds with frequencies between 1,000 and 4,000 cycles per second? How do we bridge that gap? By means of the **volley principle.** In one of nature's many surprises, it seems that groups of neurons along the basilar membrane fire in volleys, or alternating succession. (Think of Revolutionary War or Civil War movies in which one group of soldiers stands and fires while an alternate group kneels and reloads.) By firing in rotation, groups of neurons combine their frequencies of firing to fill the gap.

In sum, frequency theory best explains pitch perception for low-frequency sounds, whereas place theory best explains pitch of high-frequency sounds. A combination of frequency and place theory, called the volley principle, suggests how we perceive the pitch of mid-range sounds.

Hearing Loss: Are You Protecting Your Hearing?

Nearly 30 million Americans suffer from hearing loss, and as many as 2 million are deaf. There are many causes of hearing loss and deafness, including birth defects, disease, advanced age, and injury, as well as exposure to loud music and noise. The number of hearing-impaired individuals is expected to mushroom to an astounding 78 million by 2030, largely as the result of years of living loudly, a by-product of listening to earsplitting music on personal music devices (Noonan, 2006).

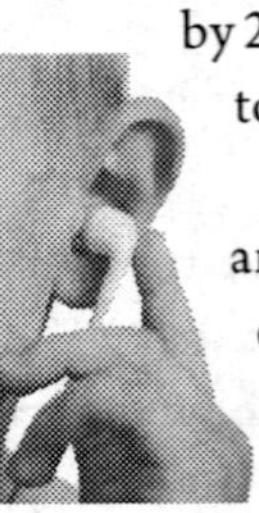

© iStockphoto.com/Ilya Andriyanov

Unfortunately, many young people, as well as many of their parents, are failing to heed warnings about the loudness of music piped through earbuds (see Table 3.3). A staggering proportion of teens—nearly one in five—show evidence of hearing loss, such as having difficulty discerning T's or K's (the word "talk" may sound like "aw") (Heffernan, 2011; Johnson, 2010). Exposure to loud music at concerts can also contribute to hearing loss, a problem unfortunately encountered by many aging rock musicians and frequent concertgoers (Kujawa & Liberman, 2006).

CONCEPT 3.18
Loud noise can lead to hearing loss and impair learning ability.

Prolonged exposure to noise of 85 decibels can cause hearing loss, as can brief exposure to sounds of 120 decibels or louder. ■ Figure 3.12 shows the decibel levels of many familiar sounds. The clamor at most bars and clubs reaches 110 to 120 decibels, and even headphones can register 100 decibels or more.

conduction deafness A form of deafness, usually involving damage to the middle ear, in which there is a loss of conduction of sound vibrations through the ear.

nerve deafness Deafness associated with nerve damage, usually involving damage to the hair cells or to the auditory nerve itself.

There are two main types of deafness: conduction deafness and nerve deafness. **Conduction deafness** is usually caused by damage to the middle ear. The eardrum may be punctured, or the three bones that amplify sound waves and conduct them to the inner ear may lose the ability to vibrate properly. People who experience conduction deafness may benefit from hearing aids that amplify sound waves.

Nerve deafness is usually caused by damage to the hair cells of the inner ear or to the auditory nerve. Exposure to loud sounds, disease, and aging can cause nerve

TABLE 3.3 Now Hear This: Teens and Hearing Problems

28% report having to turn up the volume on the television or radio to hear well.
29% report saying "what" or "huh" during normal conversations.
17% report having had tinnitus, or ringing of the ears.

Source: Teens not heeding headphone warning. (2006, March 14). Retrieved March 18, 2006, from http://www.cnn.com/2006/HEALTH/conditions/03/14/ipod.hearingrisk/index.html.

deafness. The ringing sensation that can follow exposure to loud noises may indicate damage to hair cells. Cochlear implants, or "artificial ears," are sometimes successful in transmitting sounds past damaged hair cells to the auditory nerve. They work by converting sounds into electrical impulses. But these implants cannot correct for damage to the auditory nerve itself. If the auditory nerve does not function, even sounds that cause the hair cells on the basilar membrane to dance frantically will not be sensed in the auditory cortex of the brain.

Hearing loss in later life is not inevitable. It is largely due to years of abuse from loud music and noise. Here are some suggestions to avoid exposure to excessive noise and to help prevent noise-induced hearing loss later in life:

- When you can't avoid excessive noise, as in worksites, wear hearing protectors or earplugs.
- Turn down the volume on your stereo, especially when using earphones, and avoid attending ear-splitting concerts.
- If you live in a particularly noisy area, organize your neighbors to pressure government officials to seek remedies.

Before moving on, you may wish to review the basic concepts in hearing that are outlined in Concept Chart 3.3.

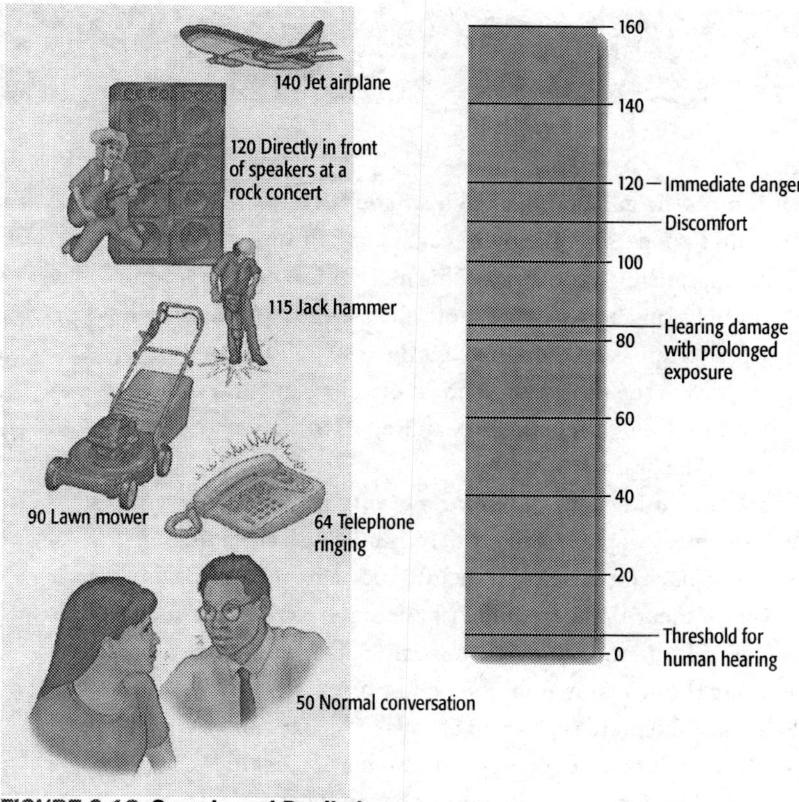

FIGURE 3.12 Sounds and Decibels
Permanent hearing loss may occur from prolonged exposure to sound over 85 decibels (dB). Exposure to 120 dB or higher creates an immediate danger to hearing. Most people can detect faint sounds at a decibel level just above 0 dB.

CONCEPT CHART 3.3 Hearing

Source of sensory information	Sound waves
Receptor organs 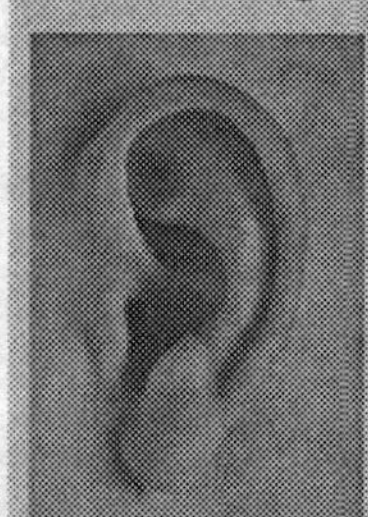 © Wolfgang Amri/Shutterstock.com	The ears. The outer ear funnels sound waves through the eardrum to the middle ear, where they are amplified by three tiny bones and transmitted through the oval window to the inner ear.
Receptor cells	Hair cells on the basilar membrane within the cochlea of the inner ear.
Pitch perception 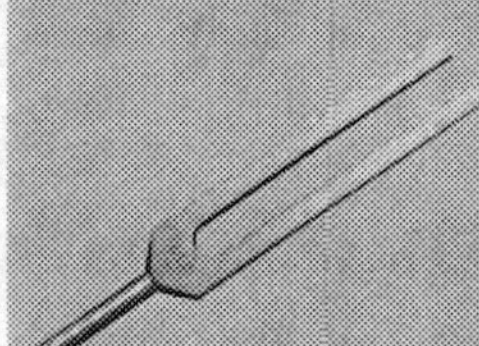 © Jason Nemeth/ Shutterstock.com	Three theories contribute to our understanding of pitch perception: frequency theory for lower-frequency sounds, the volley principle for middle-frequency sounds, and place frequency for higher-frequency sounds.

3.3 MODULE REVIEW Hearing: The Music of Sound

Recite It

How does the ear enable us to hear sound?

- Sound waves enter the outer ear and are funneled to the eardrum, causing it to vibrate. This mechanical energy is conveyed to tiny bones in the middle ear—the hammer, anvil, and stirrup—and then through the oval window to the cochlea in the inner ear. There, hair cells bend in response to the vibrations, triggering neural impulses that are transmitted to the brain.

What determines our perception of pitch?

- Perception of pitch is likely determined by a combination of the place on the basilar membrane of greatest vibration (place theory), the frequency of neural impulses (frequency theory), and the sequencing of firing of groups of neurons along the basilar membrane (volley principle).

What are the main types and causes of deafness?

- The main types of deafness are conduction deafness, usually caused by damage to the middle ear, and nerve deafness, usually caused by damage to the hair cells of the inner ear or to the auditory nerve.

Recall It

1. Which characteristics of sound waves give rise to the perception of loudness and pitch?
2. According to the frequency theory of pitch perception, our ability to detect differences in pitch is due to the rate of vibration of the ________ membrane.
3. Match these parts of the ear with the descriptions that follow: (a) eardrum; (b) ossicles; (c) cochlea; (d) basilar membrane; (e) organ of Corti; (f) hair cells.
   i. a membrane that separates the outer ear from the middle ear.
   ii. sensory receptors for hearing.
   iii. a gelatinous structure attached to the basilar membrane and lined with sensory receptors.
   iv. the membrane in the cochlea that moves in response to sound vibration.
   v. three small bones in the middle ear that conduct sound vibrations.
   vi. a snail-shaped bony tube in the inner ear in which fluid moves in response to the vibrations of the oval window.

Think About It

- What characteristics of sound waves give rise to the perception of loudness and pitch?
- What steps are you taking to protect your hearing from the damaging effects of noise? Are you doing enough?

MODULE 3.4 Our Other Senses: Chemical, Skin, and Body Senses

- How do we sense odors?
- How do we sense tastes?
- What are the skin senses?
- What are the kinesthetic and vestibular senses?

THE BRAIN LOVES A PUZZLE

As you read on, use the information in the text to solve the following puzzle:

How could something as unpleasant as pain be a good thing?

We usually think of five senses—sight, hearing, smell, taste, and touch. Yet there are actually many more. Here we take a look at the chemical, skin, and body senses. These sensory systems allow us to smell, taste, and touch and keep us informed about the position and movement of our bodies.

The nose and tongue are like human chemistry laboratories. Smell and taste are chemical senses because they are based on the chemical analysis of molecules of substances that waft past the nose or that land on the tongue. The chemical senses allow us to perform chemistry on the fly.

Olfaction: What Your Nose Knows

CONCEPT 3.20
The sense of smell depends on receptors in the nose that detect thousands of chemical substances and transmit information about them to the brain.

Our sense of smell, or **olfaction,** depends on our ability to detect shapes of molecules of odorous chemical substances that waft into our nose. The work of detecting these chemical shapes is performed by some 5 million or so odor receptors that line our nasal passageways. Though our olfactory system may not be as sensitive as that of dogs or cats, it is nonetheless exquisitely sensitive, allowing us to discern some 10,000 different substances on the basis of the shape of their molecules.

Molecules of different chemical substances fit into particular types of odor receptors as keys fit into locks, triggering olfactory messages that are carried to the brain by the **olfactory nerve.** This olfactory information is processed by the brain, giving rise to sensations of odors corresponding to these particular chemical stimuli (Miyamichi et al., 2010) (see ■ Figure 3.13). The intensity of an odor appears to be a function of the number of olfactory receptors that are stimulated simultaneously.

olfaction The sense of smell.

olfactory nerve The nerve that carries impulses from olfactory receptors in the nose to the brain.

olfactory bulb The area in the front of the brain above the nostrils that receives sensory input from olfactory receptors in the nose.

Smell is the only sense in which sensory information does not go through the thalamus on its way to the cerebral cortex. Instead, olfactory information travels through the olfactory nerve directly to the **olfactory bulb,** a structure in the front of the brain above the nostrils. This information is then routed to the olfactory cortex in the temporal lobe and to several structures in the limbic system, which, as noted in Chapter 2, are a set of brain structures with important roles in emotion and memory. The connections between the olfactory system and the limbic system may account for the close relationship between odors and emotional memories. A whiff of chocolate pudding simmering on the stove or of someone's perfume may bring back strong feelings associated with childhood experiences or a particular person.

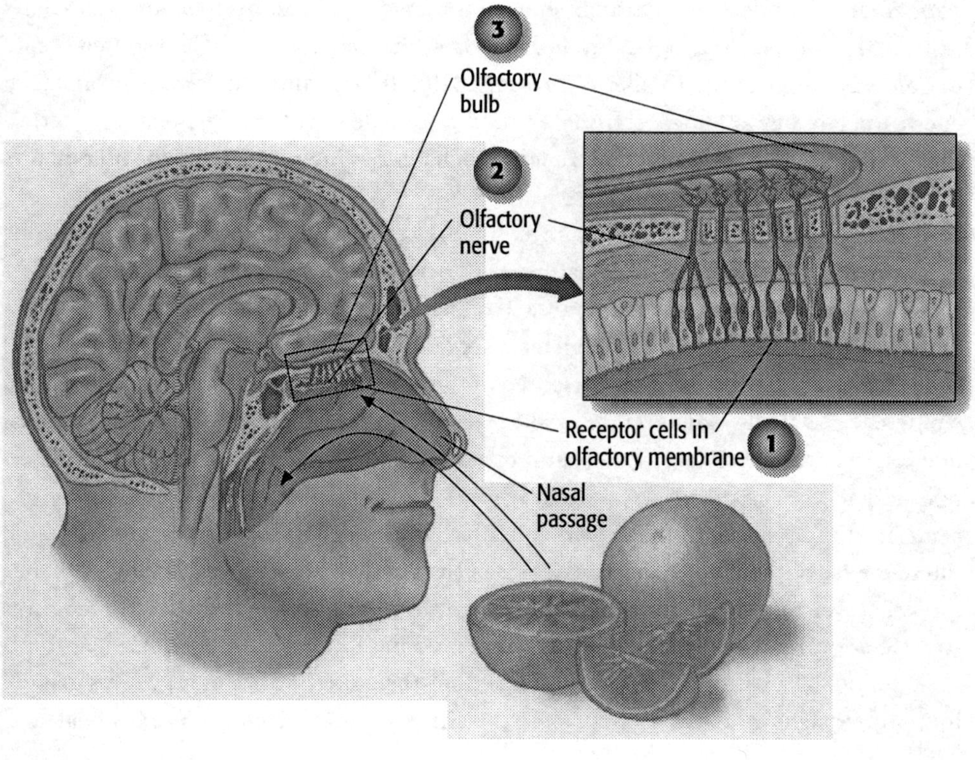

FIGURE 3.13 Olfaction
1 Receptor cells (odor receptors) in the upper nose respond to the molecular shapes of particular chemical substances that enter the nose. 2 Molecules fit particular odor receptors, triggering transmission of nerve impulses that travel through the olfactory nerve to 3 the olfactory bulb in the brain.

TRY THIS OUT
The Smell of Taste

Ever notice that food tastes bland when your nose is stuffed? To demonstrate how olfaction affects the sense of taste, try eating a meal while holding your nostrils closed. What effect does it have on your ability to taste your food? On your enjoyment of the meal?

© David Young-Wolff/Photo Edit

pheromones Chemical substances that are emitted by many species and that have various functions, including sexual attraction.

Olfaction is a key factor in the flavor of foods (see *Try This Out*). Without the sense of smell, the flavor of a steak might not be all that different from that of cardboard. An apple might taste the same as a raw potato. A declining sense of smell in later life may be the major reason many older people complain that food doesn't taste as good as it once did.

Our sensory organs were shaped over the course of millions of years of adaptation to the environment. Olfaction, among our other senses, is critical to our survival. It helps us avoid rotten and potentially harmful foods long before we put our tongue to them. In various animal species, olfaction serves other functions as well. Fur seals and many other animal species recognize their own young from the pack on the basis of smell. Salmon roam the seven seas but sniff out the streams of their birth at spawning time on the basis of a few molecules of water emitted by those streams.

Many animal species emit chemical substances, called **pheromones,** that play important roles in many behaviors, including those involved in attracting mates, marking territory, establishing dominance hierarchies, acting aggressively, gathering food, and bonding with young (Chamero et al., 2006; Nakagawa et al., 2005). Pheromones are found in bodily secretions, such as urine and vaginal secretions, and are detected by other members of the same species through the senses of smell and taste.

We know that pheromones influence sexual attraction in many species of animals and insects. But what about human behavior? Humans have receptors in the nose that may enable them to sense the presence of pheromones (Liberles & Buck, 2006). But whether these chemicals affect their behavior is something we don't yet know (Shepherd, 2006).

Suffice it to say that what the nose knows remains largely an open question. But an intriguing study in 2010 suggests that, hormonally speaking, men may be led around by their noses when exposed to the scent of a woman. Men in this study were asked to sniff a T-shirt previously worn by a woman. Some men smelled T-shirts that had been worn by women who were ovulating, which is the time of greatest female reproductive fertility. In many animal species, males show the greatest mating interest when females are at their peak fertility. Other men in the study sniffed T-shirts that had been worn by nonovulating women. The findings showed that men who had been exposed to scents of ovulating women had higher levels of testosterone than those who had sniffed scents of nonovulating women (Miller & Maner, 2010). This finding suggests that olfactory cues associated with female fertility are tied into male hormonal responses. Whether these influences actually affect men's sexual behavior or interest in women still remains to be determined.

Yet another intriguing study reported in 2011 exposed men to chemical secretions in a woman's tears (or in a control saline solution) while they were making judgments of the sex appeal of images of women presented on a computer screen (Gelstein et al., 2011; "Emotional Signals," 2011). Although tears are odorless, sniffing a woman's tears reduced the perceived sexiness that men attributed to the female images. Other men who sniffed women's tears while watching an emotional movie rated their level of sexual arousal lower, had lower physiological measures of sexual arousal, and even had lower testosterone levels—a hormone linked to sexual arousal—than did men exposed to saline control samples. It appears that women's tears contain chemical signals that dampen men's sexual interest, even without conscious awareness or the physical presence of a crying woman.

© Nagy-Bagoly Arpad/Shutterstock.com

Merely sniffing a woman's tears, even if a crying woman is not present, appears to be a sexual turn-off for men. Female tears may contain a chemical signal that is tantamount to saying, "Not tonight, dear."

Whatever role scents may play in sexual arousal in humans, we should recognize that we are primarily visual creatures when it comes to sexual arousal. As the prominent biological anthropologist Helen Fisher put the issue, "For humans . . . it's usually love at first sight, not love at first smell. . . . There are many factors to sex appeal, and romance and scent is among them. But from studying the brain, I would argue that our brains are largely built for visual stimuli" (cited in Sweeney, 2009).

CONCEPT 3.21
Pheromones are chemical substances that play various roles in animal behavior, but their functions in human behavior remain unclear.

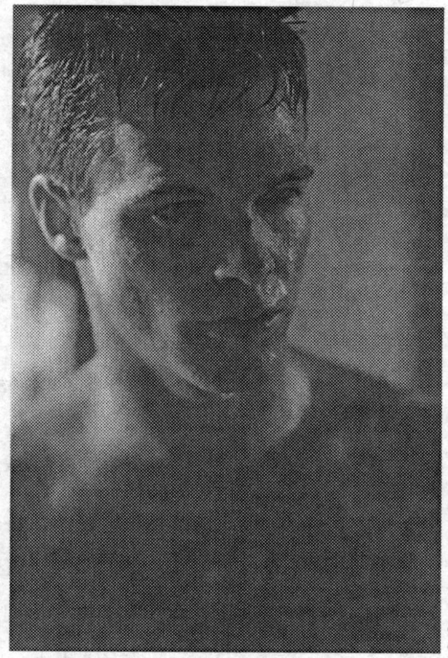

© iStockphoto.com/Bob Thomas

Whether there are naturally sexy scents that induce sexual attraction in men and women remains a question that scientists (as well as fragrance companies) continue to explore.

Taste: The Flavorful Sense

Taste, like our other senses, plays an important role in adaptation and survival. We rely on both taste and smell to discriminate between healthy, nutritious food and spoiled or rotten food. (The sense organs are not perfect, however; some poisonous substances are undetectable by smell or taste.)

There are thousands of different kinds of food and thousands of different flavors. Yet there are only four basic tastes: sweet, sour, salty, and bitter. The *flavor* of a food results from combinations of these taste qualities, the aroma of the food, its texture, and its temperature.

Tastes are sensed by receptors called **taste cells.** These are nerve cells located within pores or openings on the tongue called **taste buds.** Most taste buds are found near the edges and back of the tongue. Yet people without tongues can also sense taste because additional taste receptors are located on the roof of the mouth, inside the cheeks, and in the throat. In all, we have some 5,000 to 10,000 taste buds. Some taste receptors are more sensitive to a specific taste quality, such as bitterness or sweetness; others respond to several tastes. The brain decodes stimulation from virtually any part of the tongue containing taste receptors to produce any of the primary tastes (Sugita & Shiba, 2005). Taste receptors differ from other neurons in that they regenerate very quickly—within a week to 10 days. This is a good thing because people kill them off regularly by eating very hot food, such as pizza that is just out of the oven. But we also lose taste cells as we age, so that by our 20s we have lost about half of our taste cells. Foods still taste good, to be sure, but as adults we may not react as strongly to certain tastes as children do.

Why do some people like their food spicy, while others like it plain? Differences in cultural backgrounds play a part in taste preferences. For example, people from some cultures develop preferences for spicy foods. But why do people tend to sweat when they eat spicy foods? It turns out that the chemical that makes food spicy also activates receptors that detect warmth (Aamodt & Wang, 2008). These warmth receptors are found not only on the tongue but throughout the body. So when you chew into a hot chili paper, the brain senses warmth and produces a natural sweating response. No wonder we say spicy foods are hot.

CONCEPT 3.22
Like the sense of smell, the sense of taste depends on receptors that detect chemical substances and transmit information about them to the brain.

Genetic factors influence taste sensitivities (Reed, 2008; Sandell & Breslin, 2006). Some people who douse their meat with salt may be nearly taste-blind to salt as the result of a genetic trait. Others are genetically predisposed to be extremely sensitive to salt, pepper, and other spices. Some inherit a sensitivity to bitter tastes that turns them off to sharp-tasting vegetables like Brussels sprouts (Pearson, 2006). Preference for sugary foods (a "sweet tooth") is also influenced by genetic factors (Eny et al., 2008).

taste cells Nerve cells that are sensitive to tastes.

taste buds Pores or openings on the tongue containing taste cells.

Differences in taste sensitivities exist among different species. Cats appear to be taste-blind to sweetness, but pigs can sense sweetness. (It might be accurate to say that while humans may eat like pigs, pigs may also eat like humans.) About one in four people (more women than men) are "supertasters." They are born with a greater than average number of taste buds, making them more sensitive to certain tastes than other people (Bartoshuk, 2007). They may recoil at the sharp or bitter tastes of many fruits and vegetables, such as broccoli, or find sugary foods sickeningly sweet. Asian women are more likely to be supertasters than other groups, whereas Caucasian men are much less likely to have this tendency (Carpenter, 2000).

Concept Chart 3.4 reviews the chemical senses—olfaction and taste.

CONCEPT CHART 3.4 Chemical, Skin, and Body Senses

Chemical Senses	Olfaction	Source of sensory information	Molecules of the substance being sensed
		Receptor organ	The nose
		Receptor cells	Receptors in each nostril that can sense about 10,000 different substances on the basis of their molecular shapes
	Taste	Source of sensory information	Molecules of the substance being sensed
		Receptor organs	Mainly taste buds on the tongue, although there are additional receptors elsewhere in the mouth and throat
		Receptor cells	Taste cells located in taste buds are nerve cells that are sensitive to different tastes
Skin Senses	Skin Senses	Source of sensory information	Touch, pressure, warmth, cold, and pain
		Receptor organ	The skin (pain can also originate in many other parts of the body)
		Receptor cells	Receptors that code for touch, pressure, warmth, cold, and pain
Body Senses	Kinesthesis	Source of sensory information	Movement and relative position of body parts
		Receptor cells	Receptors located mainly in joints, ligaments, and muscles
	Vestibular Sense	Source of sensory information	Motion of the body and orientation in space
		Receptor organs	Semicircular canals and vestibular sacs in the inner ear
		Receptor cells	Hair-cell receptors that respond to the movement of fluid in the semicircular canals and to shifts in position of crystals in vestibular sacs

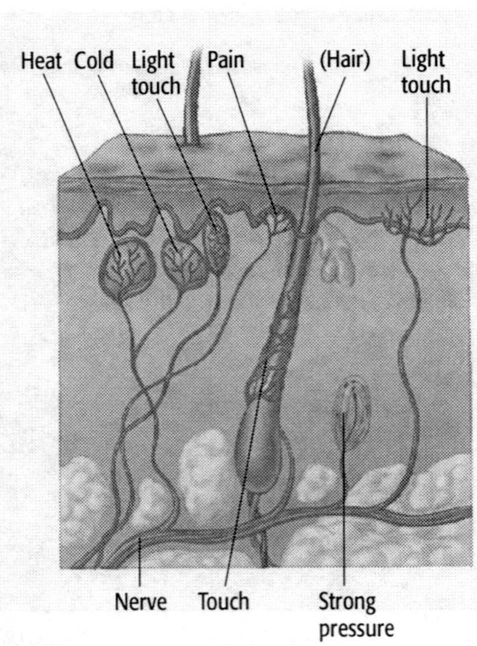

FIGURE 3.14 Your Largest Sensory Organ—Your Skin
The skin contains receptors that are sensitive to touch, pressure, warm and cold temperatures, and pain.

The Skin Senses: Your Largest Sensory Organ

You may not think of it as such, but your skin is actually your body's largest sensory organ. It contains receptors for the body's **skin senses** that code for sensations of touch, pressure, warmth, cold, and pain. Some skin receptors respond to just one type of stimulation, such as pressure or warmth. Others respond to more than one type of stimulation.

Nearly half a million receptors for touch and pressure are distributed throughout the body. They transmit sensory information to the spinal cord, which relays it to the *somatosensory cortex*, the part of the cerebral cortex that processes information from our skin receptors and makes us aware of how and where we have been touched. Many touch receptors are located near the surface of the skin (see ■ Figure 3.14). They fire when the skin is lightly touched—for example, caressed, stroked, or patted. Other receptors at deeper levels beneath the skin fire in response to pressure.

Receptors for temperature are also found just beneath the skin. Scientists generally agree that specific receptors exist for warmth and cold. In one of nature's more interesting surprises, sensations of hotness are produced by simultaneous stimulation of receptors for warmth and cold. If you were to clutch coiled pipes with warm and cold water circulating through them, you might feel as though your hand were being burned. Then, if the pipes were uncoiled, you would find that neither one by itself could give rise to sensations of heat.

Reflect for a moment about what it might mean if you did not experience pain. At first thought, not sensing pain might seem to be a good thing. After all, why go through life with headaches, toothaches, and backaches if you do not have to do so? Yet a life without pain could be a short one.

Pain is a sign that something is wrong. Without the experience of pain, you might not notice splinters, paper cuts, burns, and the many sources of injury, irritation, and infection that can ultimately threaten life if not attended to promptly. Pain is adaptive—that is, we use it to search for and do something about the source of the pain and learn to avoid those actions that cause it.

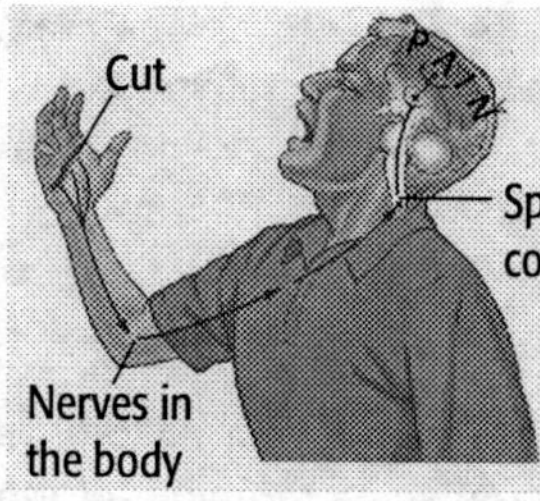

Figure 3.15 A Neural Pathway for Pain Pain messages are conveyed from the point of injury to the spinal cord and from there to the brain for processing.
Source: Adapted from Society for Neuroscience, 2005.

Pain receptors are located not just in the skin but also in other parts of the body, including muscles, joints, ligaments, and the pulp of the teeth—the source of tooth pain. We can feel pain in most parts of the body. Pain can be particularly acute where nerve endings are densely packed, as in the fingers and face.

People often try to control pain by rubbing or scratching a painful area or applying an ice pack. An explanation of why these methods may help involves a theory developed by psychologist Ronald Melzack and biologist Patrick Wall (1965, 1983). According to their gate-control theory of pain, a gating mechanism in the spinal cord opens and closes to let pain messages through to the brain or to shut them out. The "gate" is not an actual physical structure in the spinal cord but, rather, a pattern of nervous system activity that results in either blocking pain signals or letting them through. ■ Figure 3.15 illustrates a pathway for pain signals from the point of injury to the brain.

skin senses The senses of touch, pressure, warmth, cold, and pain that involve stimulation of sensory receptors in the skin.

CONCEPT 3.23
Sensory receptors in the skin are sensitive to touch, pressure, temperature, and pain, and transmit information about these stimuli to your brain.

Creating a bottleneck at the "gate" may block out pain signals. Signals associated with dull or throbbing pain are conducted through the neural gate by nerve fibers that are thinner and slower than the nerve fibers that carry sensory signals for warmth, cold, and touch. The signals carried by the faster and thicker nerve fibers can cause a bottleneck at the neural gate, thus blocking the passage of other messages. Rubbing or scratching an area in pain sends signals to the spinal cord through fast nerve fibers. Those signals may successfully compete for space with pain messages carried by thin fibers, which close the gate and temporarily block signals for dull and throbbing pain from reaching the brain. However, the first sharp pangs of pain you experience when you stub your toe or cut your finger are carried by large nerve pathways and apparently cannot be blocked out. This is a good thing, as it ensures that pain messages register quickly in the brain, alerting you instantly to the part of your body that has been injured.

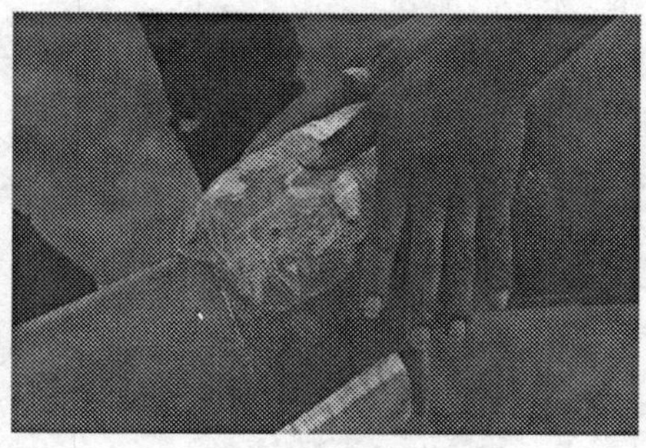

© Ralph R. Echtinaw/Shutterstock.com

Applying an ice pack to an injured area may help reduce pain. Based on your reading of the text, how would you explain this phenomenon?

An ice pack applied to the source of pain may help for several reasons. In addition to reducing inflammation and swelling—both of which contribute to the experience of pain—ice produces sensations of cold that help create a bottleneck at the gate in the spinal cord and thus, as in the earlier example, may temporarily block pain messages from reaching the brain.

The brain plays a critical role in controlling pain. In response to pain, the brain signals the release of *endorphins.* As you may recall from Chapter 2, endorphins are neurotransmitters that are similar in chemical composition to narcotic drugs, such as heroin. Like heroin, they have pain-killing effects. They lock into receptor sites in the spinal cord that transmit pain messages, thereby closing the "pain gate" and preventing pain messages from reaching the brain.

CONCEPT 3.24
The gate-control theory of pain proposes that the spinal cord contains a gating mechanism that controls the transmission of pain messages to the brain.

The release of endorphins may explain the benefits of a traditional Chinese medical practice called **acupuncture.** The acupuncturist inserts thin needles at "acupuncture points" on the body and then rotates them. According to traditional Chinese beliefs,

acupuncture An ancient Chinese practice of inserting and rotating thin needles in various parts of the body in order to release natural healing energy.

CONCEPT 3.25
Sensory receptors in your joints, ligaments, and muscles transmit information that the brain uses to keep you aware of the position and movement of parts of your body.

kinesthesia The body sense that keeps us informed about the movement of the parts of the body and their position in relation to each other.

vestibular sense The sense that keeps us informed about balance and the position of our body in space.

semicircular canals Three curved, tubelike canals in the inner ear that are involved in sensing changes in the direction and movement of the head.

vestibular sacs Organs in the inner ear that connect the semicircular canals.

CONCEPT 3.26
Sensory organs within your inner ears respond to movements of your head, which provides the brain with sensory information it needs to help you maintain your balance and sense the position and movement of your body in space.

© Andersen Ross/Blend Images/Getty Images

Can you sense the position of your hands while blindfolded? Of course you can, thanks to your kinesthetic sense. This body sense enables you to know the position of the parts of your body in relation to each other, even when blindfolded.

manipulation of the needles releases the body's natural healing energy. Although acupuncture helped reduce chronic back pain in research trials, it was no more effective than a sham (fake) acupuncture procedure in which needles were inserted superficially in non-acupuncture points in the body (Brinkhaus et al., 2006; Haake et al., 2007). Taken together with other recent evidence that acupuncture is no more effective for headache pain relief than sham (pseudo) treatments (e.g., Suarez-Almazor et al., 2010), investigators question whether the benefits of acupuncture involve anything more than a strong placebo effect (Cloud, 2011; Linde et al., 2009a; 2009b). For a summary of the skin senses, see Concept Chart 3.4.

The Kinesthetic and Vestibular Senses: Of Grace and Balance

Kinesthesia is the body sense that allows you to ride a bicycle without watching the movements of your legs, type without looking at the keyboard, and wash the back of your neck without checking yourself in the mirror. It also makes it possible to touch your nose or your ears with your eyes closed or while blindfolded, or to swat away a mosquito that lands on your hand, even in darkness ("Part of the Brain," 2010). Your kinesthetic sense keeps you continuously informed about the movements of the parts of your body and their positions in relation to one another (Gandevia et al., 2006). The sensory information that makes these tasks possible is processed by the brain based on information it receives from receptors in the joints, ligaments, tendons, skin, and muscles (Azañón et al., 2010).

You may occasionally watch what you are doing or think about what you are doing, but most of the time your movements are performed automatically based on this kinesthetic information.

Did you know there is a movement-sensing mechanism in your inner ear? The **vestibular sense** monitors the position and movement of your body in space and helps you maintain your balance. It allows you to know whether you are moving faster or slower and to sense the position and rotation of your head, as when you are tilting your head or spinning around (Day & Fitzpatrick, 2005). You rely on your vestibular sense to know when the train or car in which you are riding is speeding up, slowing down, coming to a stop, or reversing direction. Changes in the position of your head in space, such as when you rotate or tilt your head or move forward, backward, or sideways, causes movement of fluid within the **semicircular canals** in your inner ear, and shifts in the position of crystals in the **vestibular sacs** that connect the canals, which in turn stimulates tiny hair-cell receptors in your inner ear (see ■ Figure 3.16). These sensory receptors transmit messages to the brain that are decoded to allow you to sense the position and movement of your head in relation to the outside world (Day & Fitzpatrick, 2005).

If you spin around and around and come to an abrupt stop, you are likely to feel dizzy. The reason is that fluid in the semicircular canals in your inner ears keeps swirling about for a while after you stop, making it seem as if the world is still spinning. You may experience *motion sickness* when the vestibular and visual senses receive conflicting information about movement, as when you are riding in a car headed in one direction while observing a moving train headed in the other direction. For a summary of the kinesthetic and vestibular senses, see Concept Chart 3.4.

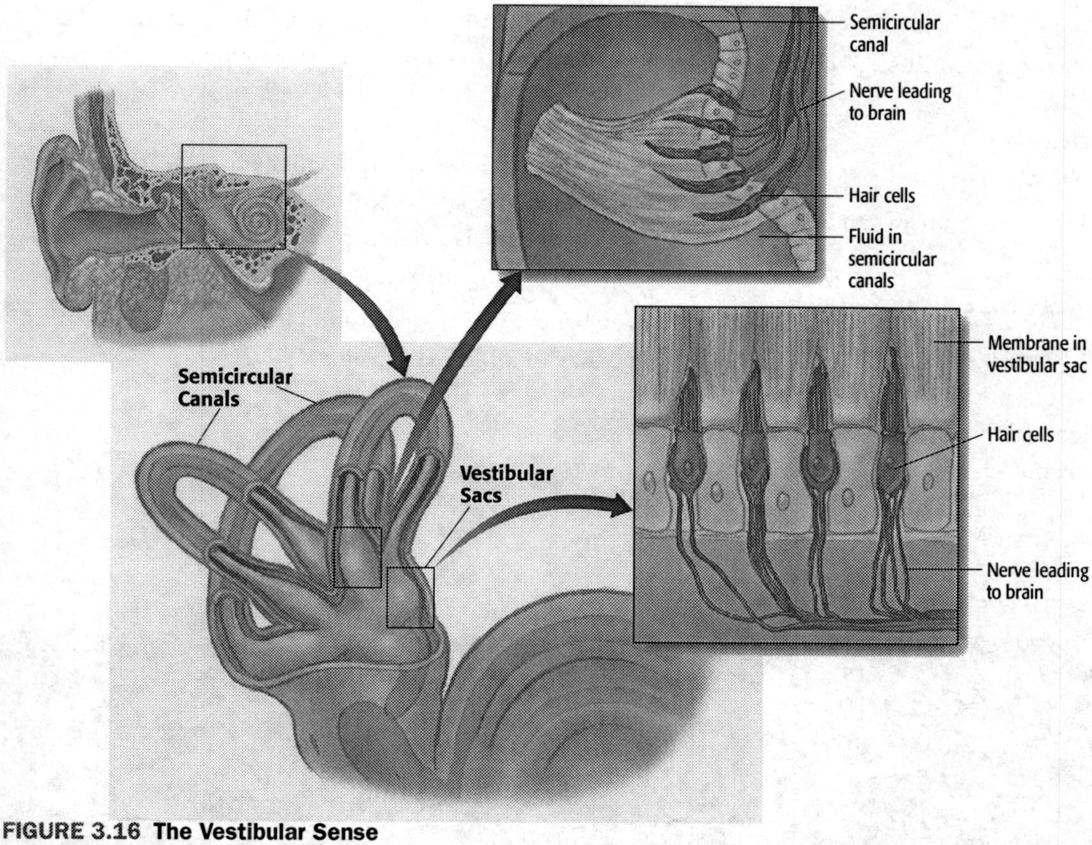

FIGURE 3.16 The Vestibular Sense
Hair-cell receptors in the inner ear bend in response to forces of gravity when we tilt our head and to movement of the head through space, triggering messages the brain uses to maintain our sense of balance and equilibrium and detect movement and orientation of our head in space.

3.4 MODULE REVIEW Our Other Senses: Chemical, Skin, and Body Senses

Recite It

How do we sense odors?

- Olfaction, or sense of smell, depends on receptors in the nostrils that are capable of sensing different chemical substances on the basis of their molecular shapes. This information is transmitted to the brain for processing, giving rise to the sensation of odor.

How do we sense tastes?

- The sense of taste involves stimulation of taste receptors located in taste buds, mostly on the tongue. Some taste receptors are sensitive to one basic type of taste (sweet, sour, salty, bitter), while others respond to several tastes.

What are the skin senses?

- The skin senses enable us to detect touch, pressure, temperature, and pain. Different receptors in the skin respond to these stimuli and transmit the information to the brain for processing.
- The gate-control theory of pain holds that there is a gating mechanism in the spinal cord that opens to allow pain messages through to the brain to signal that something is wrong and closes to shut them off.

What are the kinesthetic and vestibular senses?

- The kinesthetic sense enables you to sense the movement of various parts of your body and their positions in relation to one another. Receptors in the joints, ligaments, and muscles transmit information about body movement and position to the brain for processing.
- The vestibular sense is the sensory system that enables you to detect your body's position and maintain your balance. As the position of your head changes, messages are transmitted to the brain, which interprets them as information about the position of your body in space.

Recall It

1. Olfactory receptors in the nose recognize different chemical substances on the basis of their
   a. aromas. c. density.
   b. molecular shapes. d. vibrations.
2. Approximately how many different substances can our olfactory receptors sense?
3. Chemicals that function as sexual attractants are called ______.
4. What kinds of sensory receptors are found in the skin?
5. The receptors that provide sensory information that helps us maintain our balance are located in
   a. joints and ligaments. c. muscles.
   b. the back of the eye. d. the inner ear.
6. John is learning to swing a golf club. He relies on his ______ sense to know how far back he is swinging the club.

Think About It

- Selling cars is no longer simply a matter of performance, value, styling, and safety. Now, some cars are scented to attract customers. Do you think people will be led by their noses when buying their next car?
- Do you believe you are led around by your nose? How is your behavior affected by aromas?

MODULE 3.5

Perceiving Our World: Principles of Perception

- How is perception influenced by attention?
- How is perception influenced by perceptual set?
- What are the two general modes of processing visual stimuli?
- What are the Gestalt principles of perceptual organization?
- What is perceptual constancy?
- What cues do we use to perceive depth?
- What cues do we use to perceive movement?
- What are visual illusions?
- Does subliminal perception exist?
- Does evidence support the existence of ESP?

CONCEPT 3.27
Through the process of perception, the brain pieces together sensory information to form meaningful impressions of the world.

perception The process by which the brain integrates, organizes, and interprets sensory impressions to create representations of the world.

Perception is the process by which the brain interprets sensory information, turning it into meaningful representations of the external world. Through perception, the brain attempts to make sense of the mass of sensory stimuli that impinge on our sensory organs. Were it not for perception, the world would seem like a continually changing hodgepodge of disconnected sensations—a buzzing confusion of lights, sounds, and other sensory impressions. The brain brings order to the mix of sensations we experience, organizing them into coherent pictures of the world around us. To paraphrase Shakespeare, sensation without perception would be "full of sound and fury but signifying nothing."

Consider what you see on this page. When the dots of black ink register on your retina, your brain transforms these images into meaningful symbols you perceive as letters.

Perception enables us to make sense of the world, but it may not accurately reflect external reality. Look at the central circles in the left and right configurations in ■ Figure 3.17. Which of these two circles is larger? If you were to measure the diameter of each central circle with a ruler, you would find that they are exactly the same size. Yet you may perceive the central circle at the right to be larger than the one at the left. This is because the circle on the right is presented within an array of smaller circles, and your brain takes into account the context in which these shapes appear.

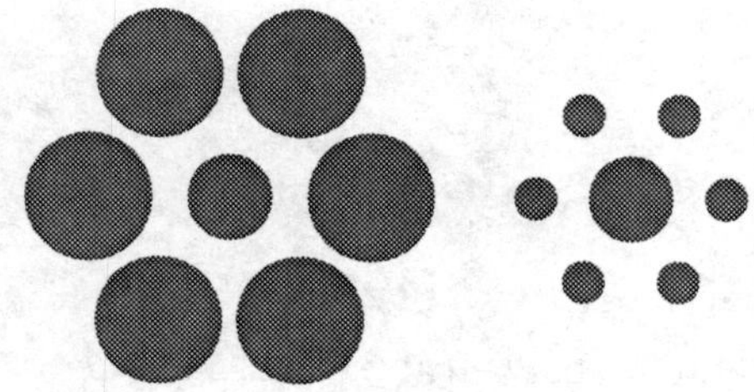

FIGURE 3.17 Perception versus Reality?
Which of the circles in the middle of these two groupings is larger?

With perception, what you see is not necessarily what you get. Take a quick look at the gender-ambiguous facial image in the nearby photograph. Do you perceive it be a man's face, or a woman's? The answer may depend on which part of your visual field the image appears. Investigators recently discovered that if a series of gender-ambiguous images like this one are presented in a particular area of the visual field, say the upper-right-hand corner, some people will perceive all the faces as male, whereas others will perceive the same faces as female (Afraz, Pashkam, & Cavanagh, 2010). We can't yet explain why the visual processing centers in the brain in some people respond differently to ambiguous images than those in other people. But the lesson here is that perceptual experiences of the same stimuli do vary from person to person.

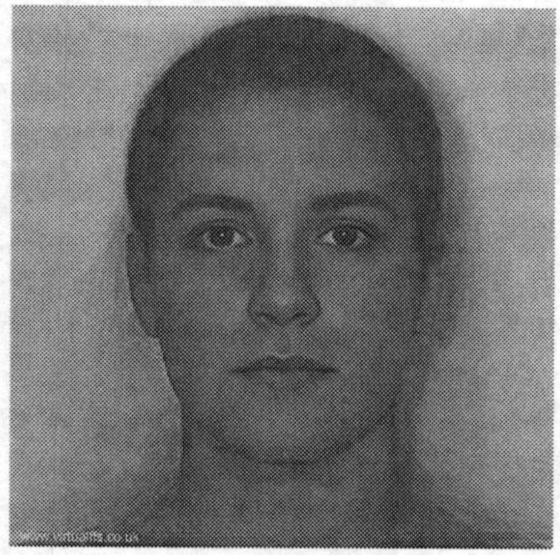

© Alexandra Hamer

Is this the face of a man or a woman? Your answer may depend on the part of your visual field in which the image is projected.

In this module, we explore basic concepts of perception, paying particular attention to visual perception—the area of perception that has captured the most research attention.

Attention: Did You Notice That?

Attention is the first step in perception. Through **selective attention**, you limit your attention to certain stimuli while filtering out other stimuli (Phelps, Ling, & Carrasco, 2006). Selective attention prevents you from being flooded with extraneous information. It explains why you may perceive certain stimuli but not others. It allows you to focus on the words you are reading but not perceive the sounds of a car passing outside the window or the feeling of your toes touching the inside of your shoes. We pay more attention to stimuli that are meaningful or emotionally significant. For example, a parent in a deep sleep may perceive the faint cry of an infant in the next room but be undisturbed by the wail of a siren from an ambulance passing just outside the house.

selective attention The process by which we attend to meaningful stimuli and filter out irrelevant or extraneous stimuli.

Our motivational states—whether we're hungry or thirsty, for example—play important roles in attention. When we are hungry, we are more likely than when we've just eaten to pay attention to odors wafting out of a restaurant. We also are more likely to notice billboards on the side of the road advertising nearby restaurants. I recall one professor who had the habit of dropping the words "midterm exam" into his lectures when he felt the class was nodding off. That seemed to motivate his students to pay closer attention.

CONCEPT 3.28
Many factors affect our attention to particular stimuli, including motivation and repeated exposure.

→ Concept Link
Our ability to divide our attention allows us to multitask—which can pose a risk, for instance when we combine driving with using a cell phone. See Module 4.1.

Repeated exposure may increase attention to particular stimuli. Prenatal auditory exposure may explain why three-day-old infants prefer the sounds of their mother's voice—as measured by head turning—to the voices of other women (Freeman, Spence, & Oliphant, 1993).

CONCEPT 3.29
Our interpretations of stimuli depend in part on what we expect to happen in particular situations.

On the other hand, exposure to a constant stimulus can lead us to become *habituated*, or accustomed, to it. When you first turn on an air conditioner or fan, you may notice the constant humming sound it makes. But after a time you no longer perceive it, even though the sound continues to impinge on the sensory receptors in your ears. Your brain has adapted to the constant stimulus by tuning it out. Habituation makes sense

FIGURE 3.18 What Do You See Here, the Letter B or the Number 13?
Your answer may depend on your perceptual set.

perceptual set The tendency for perceptions to be influenced by one's expectations or preconceptions.

from an evolutionary perspective, since constant stimuli are less likely than changing stimuli to require an adaptive response.

Perceptual Set: Seeing What You Expect to See

Perceptual set is the tendency for perceptions to be influenced by expectations or preconceptions. Do you see the number 13 or the letter B in ■ Figure 3.18? In a classic study, Jerome Bruner and A. Leigh Minturn (1955) showed this figure to research participants after they had seen either a series of numbers or a series of letters. Among those who had viewed the number series, 83 percent said the stimulus was the number 13. Of those who had seen the letter series, 93 percent said the stimulus was a B. When faced with ambiguous stimuli, people often base their perceptions on their expectations and preconceptions. We might speculate that devoted fans of science fiction would be more likely than others to perceive flickering lights in the night sky as a UFO. ■ Figure 3.19 shows another example of a perceptual set.

(a) (b) (c)

FIGURE 3.19 A Duck or a Rabbit?
The figure in *a* appears to be *a* duck when you see it after viewing the figure in *c*. But if you first observed the figure in *b*, then the figure in *a* appears to be a rabbit.
From H.R. Shiffman, "Sensation and Perception: An Integrated Approach." Copyright © 2000 by John Wiley & Sons, Inc. Used by permission.

bottom-up processing A mode of perceptual processing by which the brain recognizes meaningful patterns by piecing together bits and pieces of sensory information.

top-down processing A mode of perceptual processing by which the brain identifies patterns as meaningful wholes rather than as piecemeal constructions.

Modes of Visual Processing: Bottom-Up versus Top-Down

As noted earlier, Hubel and Wiesel's (1979) work on feature detectors showed that specialized receptors in the visual cortex respond only to specific visual features, such as straight lines, angles, or moving points of light. Two general modes of visual processing, *bottom-up processing* and *top-down processing*, help account for how the brain transforms visual stimuli into meaningful patterns.

In **bottom-up processing**, the brain assembles specific features of shapes, such as angles and lines, to form patterns that we can compare with stored images we have seen before. For example, the brain combines individual lines and angles to form a pattern we recognize as the number 4. Bottom-up processing may also be used to combine the individual elements of letters and words into recognizable patterns. But how is it that we can read handwriting in which the same letter is never formed twice in exactly the same way? This style of processing, called **top-down processing**, involves perceiving patterns as meaningful wholes—such as recognizing faces of people we know—without needing to piece together their component parts. We also use top-down and bottom-up processing for auditory stimulation (Tervaniemi et al., 2009). For example, we use bottom-up processing when trying to carefully discriminate between different musical instruments in orchestral music or listening intently for particular words in a song. We use top-down processing when listening to a melody or the blending of instruments in a symphony or of words and lyrics in a song.

CONCEPT 3.29
Our interpretations of stimuli depend in part on what we expect to happen in particular situations.

© Francis Roberts/Alamy

Do you see the arrow in the FedEx symbol? We typically perceive letters as figures and white space as ground. To perceive the arrow, try reversing figure and ground. (Hint: Look at the white space between the E and the X.)

Top-down processing is based on acquired experience and knowledge with patterns, but it is not perfect. You may have had the experience of thinking you recognized someone approaching you from a distance, only to find you were mistaken as you got a closer look at the person. You made the mistake because of the tendency to perceive faces on the basis of their whole patterns rather than building them up feature by feature (see ■ Figure 3.20). Despite the occasional miss, facial recognition is something the human brain does better than any computer system yet devised (Wagstaff, 2006). Can you think of other functions the human brain does better than computers?

We now turn to the contributions of Gestalt psychologists to help us understand how the brain organizes our visual perceptions.

FIGURE 3.20 Reversible Figure
Whether you see two profiles facing each other in this picture or a vase depends on your perception of figure and ground. See if you can shift back and forth between perceiving the profiles and the vase by switching the parts you take to be figure and those you take to be ground.

Gestalt Principles of Perceptual Organization

Max Wertheimer and the other early Gestalt psychologists conducted studies in which they observed the ways in which people assemble bits of sensory stimulation into meaningful wholes. On this basis, they formulated **laws of perceptual organization.** Here we consider laws of figure-ground perception and laws of grouping.

CONCEPT 3.30
The brain forms meaningful visual patterns using two different modes of processing visual stimuli: bottom-up processing and top-down processing.

laws of perceptual organization The principles identified by Gestalt psychologists that describe the ways in which the brain groups bits of sensory stimulation into meaningful wholes or patterns.

Figure and Ground

Look around as you are walking down the street. What do you see? Are there people milling about? Are there clouds in the sky? Gestalt psychologists have shown that people, clouds, and other objects are perceived in terms of *figure,* and the background against which the figures are perceived (the street, for the people; the sky, for the clouds) serves as the *ground.* Figures have definite shapes, but ground is shapeless (Kimchi & Peterson, 2008). We perceive objects as figures when they have shapes or other characteristics, such as distinctive coloring, which are set against a backdrop of the ground in which they appear (Peterson & Skow, 2008).

Sometimes, however, when we perceive an outline, it may be unclear as to what constitutes the figure and what constitutes the ground. Does Figure 3.20 show a vase, or does it show two profiles? Which is the figure, and which is the ground? Outline alone does not tell the tale, because the same outline describes a vase and human profiles. What other cues do you use to decide which is the figure and which is the ground?

Now consider ■ Figure 3.21, an ambiguous figure that can be perceived in different ways depending on how you organize your perceptions. What does the figure look like? Take a minute to focus on it before reading further.

Did you see an old woman or a young one? Are you able to switch back and forth? If you are struggling to switch between the two, here is a helpful hint: The old woman is facing forward and downward, while the young woman is facing diagonally away. Also, the old woman's nose is the young woman's chin, and her right eye is her counterpart's left ear. Whether you see an old woman or a young one depends on how you organize your perceptual experience—which parts you take to be the figure and which parts you take to be the ground. ■ Figure 3.22 provides an example in which figure and ground are less ambiguous.

TRY THIS OUT
Your Neighborhood Gestalt

Take a walk through your neighborhood or local area. Look around you. How many examples of the Gestalt laws of perceptual organization can you identify?

Gestalt Laws of Grouping

People tend to group bits and pieces of sensory information into unitary forms or wholes (see *Try This Out*). Gestalt psychologists described several principles of grouping, including *proximity, similarity, continuity, closure,* and *connectedness.*

FIGURE 3.21 Ambiguous Figure
Do you see an old woman or a young one? If you have trouble switching between the two, look at Figure 3.22, in which figure and ground are less ambiguous.

FIGURE 3.22 Old/Young Woman
The figure on the right shows the downward-looking "old woman" more clearly as figure than as ground, while the one on the left highlights the figural aspects of the "young woman" looking away from the perceiver. Now look back at Figure 3.21 and see if you can't switch back between the two impressions.

CONCEPT 3.31
Gestalt psychologists described how the brain constructs meaning from sensations by organizing them into recognizable patterns.

→ Concept Link
Gestalt therapy is a form of psychotherapy that helps individuals blend conflicting parts of the personality into an integrated whole, or "gestalt." See Module 16.2.

proximity The principle that objects that are near each other will be perceived as belonging to a common set.

similarity The principle that objects that are similar will be perceived as belonging to the same group.

continuity The principle that a series of stimuli will be perceived as representing a unified form.

closure The perceptual principle that people tend to piece together disconnected bits of information to perceive whole forms.

connectedness The principle that objects positioned together or moving together will be perceived as belonging to the same group.

■ Figure 3.23*a* illustrates **proximity**, or nearness. Most observers would perceive the figure as consisting of three sets of parallel lines rather than six separate lines, although six lines are sensed. That is, we use the relative closeness of the lines as a perceptual cue for organizing them into a group.

How would you describe Figure 3.23*b*? Do you perceive nine separate geometric shapes or two columns of X's and one column of ●'s? If you describe it in terms of X's and ●'s, you are using the principle of **similarity**—that is, grouping figures that are similar to one another (in this case, geometric figures that resemble each other). If you see four bare-chested young men at a football game who've painted their bodies in the colors of the home team, you are likely to perceive them as a group distinct from other fans.

Figure 3.23*c* represents another way we group stimuli, **continuity**, which is the tendency to perceive a series of stimuli as a unified form when the stimuli appear to represent a continuous pattern. Here we perceive two intersecting continuous lines, one curved and one straight, rather than four separate lines.

Now check Figure 3.23*d*. You sense a number of short lines, but do you perceive a meaningless array of lines or a broken triangle? If you perceive the triangle, your perception draws on the principle of **closure**—grouping disconnected pieces of information into a meaningful whole. You perceive a complete form even when there are gaps in the form. This illustrates the principle for which Gestalt psychologists are best known—that the whole is more than the sum of the parts.

Figure 3.23*e* gives an example of **connectedness**—the tendency to perceive objects as belonging together when they are positioned together or are moving together. Thus, you perceive three sets of connected triangles rather than six triangles with three interspersing lines. Perhaps you have noticed this tendency while watching two people walk down a street next to each other and being surprised when they suddenly walk off in different directions without saying goodbye. We tend to perceive the people as belonging together because they are moving together.

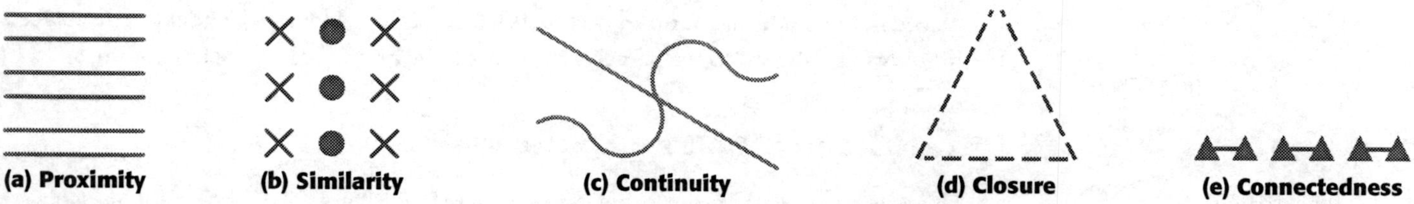

FIGURE 3.23 Gestalt Laws of Grouping
Gestalt psychologists recognized that people group objects according to certain organizational principles. Here we see examples of five such principles: proximity, similarity, continuity, closure, and connectedness.

Perceptual Constancies

CONCEPT 3.32
We tend to perceive objects as having a constant size, shape, color, and brightness even when the image they cast on our retinas changes.

Here we focus on perceptual constancy—the tendency to perceive the size, shape, color, and brightness of an object as remaining the same even when the image it casts on the retina changes. We could not adjust to our world very well without perceptual constancy. The world is constantly shifting before our eyes as we look at objects from different distances and perspectives. Just turning our heads changes the geometry of an object projected on the retina. Yet we don't perceive objects as changing before our eyes. We perceive them as constant—a good thing, because, of course, they are constant. For example, the ability to perceive that a tiger is a tiger and not a housecat regardless of the distance from which the animal is viewed could be a life-saving mechanism.

The tendency to perceive an object as being the same shape even when the object is viewed from different perspectives is **shape constancy**. If you observe a round bowl on a table from different angles, the image it casts on your retina changes shape. Nonetheless, you perceive the bowl as round. In other words, its shape remains constant despite the change in your angle of view. Similarly, you perceive a door as having an unchanging shape despite differences in the image it casts on your retina when it is open or closed (see ■ Figure 3.24).

Returning to the bowl, as you approach the bowl at eye level, its size—in terms of the size of the retinal image—grows. As you move farther away from it, the size of its retinal image decreases. Yet you continue to perceive the bowl as being the same size, just as I knew my daughter did not suddenly become a giant as she approached the camera. The tendency to perceive an object as retaining the same size despite changes in the size of the retinal image it casts is called **size constancy** (Combe & Wexler, 2010).

Experience teaches people about distance and perspective. We learn that an object seen at a distance will look smaller than when it is close, and that an object seen from different perspectives will appear to have different shapes. (If we are wrong, please send out an all-points bulletin for a runaway giant infant.)

People also perceive objects as retaining their color even when lighting conditions change. This tendency is called **color constancy**. For example, if your car is red, you perceive it to be red even though it may look grayish as evening falls. The tendency for perceived brightness or lightness of an object to remain relatively constant despite changes in illumination is called **brightness constancy** or *lightness constancy* (Wilcox & Duke, 2003). For example, a piece of white chalk

shape constancy The tendency to perceive an object as having the same shape despite differences in the images it casts on the retina as the viewer's perspective changes.

size constancy The tendency to perceive an object as having the same size despite changes in the images it casts on the retina as the viewing distance changes.

color constancy The tendency to perceive an object as having the same color despite changes in lighting conditions.

brightness constancy The tendency to perceive objects as retaining their brightness even when they are viewed in dim light.

FIGURE 3.24 Shape Constancy
Perception of an object's shape remains the same even when the image it casts on the retina changes with the angle of view. You perceive three rectangular doors, despite the fact that the image each projects on the retina is different.

placed in the shade on a sunny day reflects less light than does a black hockey puck placed directly in sunlight. Yet we perceive the chalk to be brighter than the hockey puck.

Cues to Depth Perception

CONCEPT 3.33
Our perception of depth depends on both monocular and binocular cues for judging distance.

How do we know that some objects are closer than others? The perception of distance, or depth perception, relies on cues involving both the individual eye (monocular cues) and both eyes working together (binocular cues) (Proffitt, 2006).

Binocular Cues for Depth

binocular cues Cues for depth that involve both eyes, such as retinal disparity and convergence.

retinal disparity A binocular cue for distance based on the slight differences in the visual impressions formed in both eyes.

Having two eyes also comes in handy for judging distance. Some cues for depth, called **binocular cues**, depend on both eyes. Our eyes are a few inches apart, so each eye receives slightly different images of the world (Farell, 2006). The brain interprets differences in the two retinal images—the **retinal disparity** between them—as cues to the relative distances of objects. The closer an object, the greater the retinal disparity.

You can see for yourself how retinal disparity works by holding a finger an inch in front of your nose. First close your left eye and look at the finger only with your right eye. The finger looks as if it is off to the left. Then close your right eye and look at the finger with your left eye. The finger seems off to the right. The finger appears to move from side to side as you open and close each eye. The distance between the two apparent fingers corresponds to the retinal disparity between the two images that form on your retina. Now hold a finger straight ahead at arm's length away from your eyes. Again close one eye and focus on the finger. Then close that eye and open the other. The finger may still seem to "move," but there will be less distance between the two "fingers" because retinal disparity is smaller at greater distances.

convergence A binocular cue for distance based on the degree of tension required to focus both eyes on the same object.

monocular cues Cues for depth that can be perceived by each eye alone, such as relative size and interposition.

Now let's try an experiment to illustrate the binocular cue of **convergence**, which depends on the muscular tension produced by turning both eyes inward to form a single image. Hold a finger once more at arm's length. Keeping both eyes open, concentrate on the finger so that you perceive only one finger. Now bring it slowly closer to your eyes, maintaining the single image. As you do, you will feel tension in your eye muscles. This is because your eyes are *converging*, or looking inward, to maintain the single image, as shown in ■ Figure 3.25. The closer the object—in this case, the finger—the greater the tension. Your brain uses the tension as a cue for depth perception.

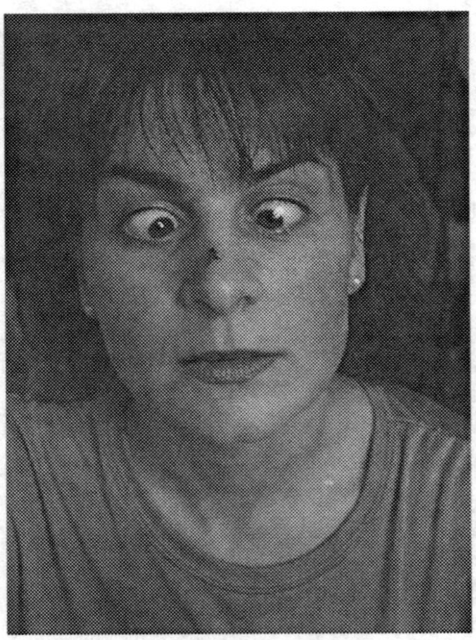

© Susan Van Etten/Photo Edit

FIGURE 3.25 Binocular Cues for Depth When we rely on binocular cues for judging the depth of a nearby object, our eyes must converge on the object, which can give us that cross-eyed look.

Monocular Cues for Depth

Monocular cues depend on one eye only. When people drive, they use a combination of binocular and monocular cues to judge the distance of other cars and of the surrounding scenery. Although there are advantages to using binocular cues, most people can get by relying only on monocular cues while driving, which include such cues as relative size, interposition, relative clarity, texture gradient, linear perspective, and shadowing.

- *Relative size.* When two objects are believed to be the same size, the one that appears larger is perceived to be closer (see ■ Figure 3.26*a*).
- *Interposition.* When objects block or otherwise obscure our view of other objects, we perceive the obscured object as farther away. Notice that in Figure 3.26*b* we perceive the horses in front to be closer than the ones that are partially blocked.
- *Relative clarity.* Smog, dust, smoke, and water droplets in the atmosphere create a "haze" that makes distant objects appear more blurry than nearer objects (see Figure 3.26*c*). You may have noticed how much closer faraway mountains appear on a really clear day.

© William Johnson/Stock Boston
© David Stoecklein/CORBIS
© Andy Dean Photography/Shutterstock.com
© Francis DeRichemond/The Image Works
© Mladen Mitrinovic, 2009/Shutterstock.com
© Aleksandr Petrunovskyi/Shutterstock.com

FIGURE 3.26 Monocular Cues for Depth
We use many different monocular cues to judge depth, including:
(a) Relative size
(b) Interposition
(c) Relative clarity
(d) Texture gradient
(e) Linear perspective
(f) Shadowing

- *Texture gradient.* The relative coarseness or smoothness of an object is used as a cue for distance. Closer objects appear to have a coarser or more detailed texture than more distant objects. Thus, the texture of flowers that are farther away is smoother than the texture of those that are closer (Figure 3.26*d*).
- *Linear perspective.* Linear perspective is the perception of parallel lines converging as they recede into the distance. As we look straight ahead, objects and the distances between them appear smaller the farther away they are from us. Thus, the road ahead of the driver, which consists of parallel lines, appears to grow narrower as it recedes into the distance (Figure 3.26*e*). It may even seem to end in a point.
- *Shadowing.* Patterns of light and dark, or shadowing, create the appearance of three-dimensional objects or curving surfaces. Shadowing can make an object appear to be concave or convex. Notice how the dents that appear in Figure 3.26*f* look like bumps when the image is turned upside down. We perceive objects that are lighter on top and darker on the bottom to be bumps, whereas the opposite is the case for dents (Gaulin & McBurney, 2001).

© 2004 Dan Piraro. Distributed by King Features Syndicate

"I have no depth perception. Is there a cop standing on the corner, or do you have a tiny person in your hair?"

Motion Perception

CONCEPT 3.34
We use two basic cues in perceiving movement: the path of the image as it crosses the retina and the changing size of the object.

We use various cues to perceive motion. One is the actual movement of an object across our field of vision as the image it projects moves from point to point on the retina. The brain interprets the swath that the image paints across the retina as a sign of movement (Derrington, 2004). Another cue is the changing size of an object. Objects appear

(a) Müller-Lyer Illusion **(b) Ponzo Illusion** **(c)** **(d)**

FIGURE 3.27 **Müller-Lyer Illusion and Ponzo Illusion**
Visual illusions involve misperceptions in which our eyes seem to be playing tricks on us.

larger when they are closer. When you are driving and you see the cars ahead suddenly looming much larger, you perceive that you are moving faster than they are—so fast you may need to apply the brakes to avoid a collision. When cars ahead grow smaller, they appear to be moving faster than you are.

Visual Illusions: Do Your Eyes Deceive You?

visual illusions Misperceptions of visual stimuli.

CONCEPT 3.35
Visual illusions are misperceptions of visual stimuli in which it seems that our eyes are playing tricks on us.

Our eyes sometimes seem to play tricks on us in the form of **visual illusions.** ■ Figure 3.27 shows two well-known visual illusions: the *Müller-Lyer illusion* (*a*) and the *Ponzo illusion* (*b*). In both cases, what you think you see isn't exactly what you get when you pull out a ruler. Although the center lines in (*a*) are actually the same length, as are the center lines in (*c*) and (*d*), the line on the right in (*a*) seems longer, as does the center line in (*d*) as compared to the one in (*c*). The figure with the inward wings creates the impression of an outward corner of a room that appears to be closer (*c*). In the Müller-Lyer illusion, the figure with the outward wings suggests the inner corner of a room (*d*), which makes the center line seem farther away.

Although no one explanation may fully account for the Müller-Lyer illusion, a partial explanation may involve how the brain interprets size and distance cues.

© Photofest/Twentieth Century-Fox Film Corporation

To create a three-dimensional effect, as in the movie *Avatar*, slightly different images are projected to each eye. The brain pieces together the information to give the impression of depth.

As you'll recall from the discussion of size constancy, people tend to perceive an object as remaining the same size even as the image it projects on the retina changes in relation to distance from the observer. But when two objects of the same size appear to be at different distances from the observer, the one that is judged to be farther away is perceived to be larger. In the Müller-Lyer illusion, the figure with the outward wings suggests the inner corner of a room, which makes the center line seem farther away. The figure with the inward wings creates the impression of an outward corner of a room that appears to be closer to the observer. Since both center lines actually create the same size image on the retina, the brain interprets the one that appears to be farther away as being longer.

Now consider the Ponzo illusion (also called the railroad illusion). Which of the two horizontal lines in Figure 3.27*b* looks longer? Why do you think people generally perceive the line at the top to be longer? Converging lines may create an impression of linear perspective, leading us to perceive the upper line as farther away. As with the Müller-Lyer illusion, since lines of equal length cast the same size image on the retina, the one perceived as farther away is judged to be longer.

Another type of illusion involves *impossible figures,* such as the one in ■ Figure 3.28. Impossible figures fool the brain into creating the impression of a whole figure when the figure is viewed from certain perspectives. An impossible figure appears to make sense when you look at parts of it, but not when you try to take into account the characteristics of the whole figure.

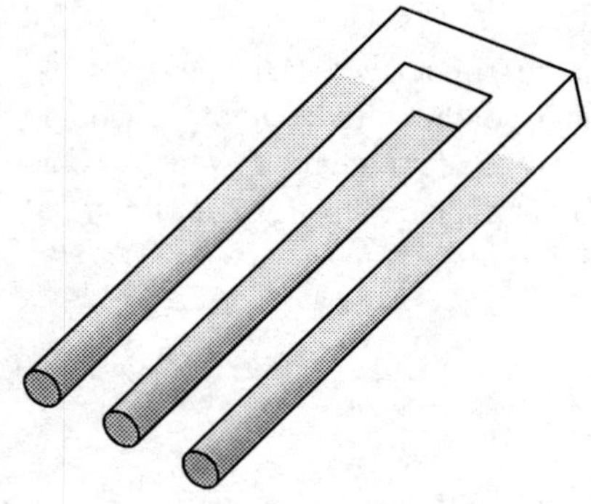

FIGURE 3.28 An Impossible Figure
Notice how the figure makes sense if you look at certain of its features, but not when you take all its features into account.

The well-known *moon illusion* has baffled people for ages (see ■ Figure 3.29). When a full moon appears near the horizon, it may seem enormous compared with its "normal" size—that is, its apparent size when it is high in the evening sky. Actually, the image the moon casts on the retina is the same size whether it sits high in the sky or just over the horizon. We don't have an entirely satisfactory explanation of this illusion. One leading theory, the *relative size hypothesis,* relates the phenomenon to the amount of space surrounding the perceived object (Baird, Wagner, & Fuld, 1990). When the moon is at the horizon, it appears larger by comparison with objects far off in the distance, such as tall trees and mountains. When the moon is high in the sky, there is nothing to compare it with except the vast featureless wastes of space, and this comparison makes it seem smaller.

stroboscopic movement A type of apparent movement based on the rapid succession of still images, as in motion pictures.

You can test out the moon illusion for yourself by looking at the full moon on the horizon. Then, to remove any distance cues, look again at the moon through a rolled-up magazine. You'll find that the moon appears to shrink in size. One problem with the relative size hypothesis is that it doesn't account for all cases in which the phenomenon is observed, including a planetarium in which the moon is depicted in the absence of intervening landscape cues (Suzuki, 1991).

We have discussed how we perceive actual movement, but there are also interesting examples of *apparent movement,* such as **stroboscopic movement** (see ■ Figure 3.30). Stroboscopic movement puts the motion in motion pictures. We perceive the rapid progression of illuminated still images to be a seamless "motion picture." The film itself contains a series of still images projected at more than 20 pictures, or "frames," per second. Each frame differs somewhat from the one shown before. This is nothing but a quick slide show; the "movie" mechanism lies within us—the viewers.

© Phyllis Picardi/Stock Boston

FIGURE 3.29 Moon Illusion
The moon illusion refers to the perception that the moon is larger when at the horizon than when it is high in the sky.

© Andrew Davidhazy/ Rochester Institute of Technology

FIGURE 3.30 Stroboscopic Movement
The perception of movement in "moving pictures" is a feature of the viewer, not the projector.

CONCEPT 3.36

The susceptibility to visual illusions is influenced by cultural factors, such as the types of structures to which people in a particular culture are accustomed.

Cultural Differences in Perceiving Visual Illusions

Suppose you lived in a culture in which structures with corners and angles were uncommon. Would you be as likely to experience the Müller-Lyer illusion as someone raised in, say, Cleveland or Dallas? To find out, Darhl Pedersen and John Wheeler (1983) tested two groups of Navajo Indians on the Müller-Lyer illusion. One group lived in rectangular houses that provided daily exposure to angles and corners. Another group lived in traditional rounded huts with fewer of these cues. Those living in the rounded huts were less likely to be deceived by the Müller-Lyer illusion, suggesting that prior experience plays a role in determining susceptibility to the illusion. Other studies have produced similar results. For example, the illusion was observed less frequently among the Zulu people of southern Africa, who also live in rounded structures (Segall, 1994).

carpentered-world hypothesis An attempt to explain the Müller-Lyer illusion in terms of the cultural experience of living in a carpentered, right-angled world like our own.

The **carpentered-world hypothesis** was put forth to account for cultural differences in susceptibility to the Müller-Lyer illusion (Segall, Campbell, & Herskovits, 1966). A carpentered world is one, like our own, that is dominated by structures (buildings, rooms, and furniture) in which straight lines meet at right angles. People living in noncarpentered worlds, which consist largely of rounded structures, are less prone to the illusion because of their limited experience with angular structures. Cultural experience, rather than race, seems the determinant. Zulus who move to cities where they become accustomed to seeing angular structures are more likely to be fooled by the illusion (Segall, Campbell, & Herskovits, 1963).

Studies with the Ponzo (railroad) illusion also show cultural differences. The illusion is less prominent among the people of Guam, an island with a hilly terrain and no long, uninterrupted highways or railroads (Leibowitz, 1971).

SLICE OF LIFE The lesson here goes beyond cultural differences in visual illusions. Perception is influenced not only by our sensory systems but also by our experience of living in a particular culture. People from different cultures may perceive the physical world differently. Consider a classic example offered by the anthropologist Colin Turnbull (1961). Turnbull took Kenge, an African pygmy guide, on his first trip outside the dense forest into the open plain. When Kenge saw buffalo several miles away on the plain, he took them to be insects. When he got closer to the animals and recognized them as buffalo, he was aghast at how the animals had been able to grow so quickly. Why would Kenge mistake a buffalo for an insect? In Kenge's culture, people lived in remote villages in a dense forest. He had never before had an unobstructed view of objects at a great distance. He lacked the experience needed to acquire size constancy for distant objects—to learn that objects retain their size even as the image they project on our eyes grows smaller.

Recent research shows that Westerners and East Asians tend to perceive the same visual scenes in different ways. Investigators found that Americans tend to focus more attention on objects in the foreground of visual scenes than do East Asians, whereas East Asians take in more of the background or contextual characteristics than do Americans (Chua, Boland, & Nisbett, 2005; Masuda & Nisbett, 2001). When it comes to West and East, Nisbett and his colleagues claim, we have two fundamentally different processing styles—a Western style of focusing on categorizing

© JJ pixs/Alamy

According to the carpentered-world hypothesis, people living in cultures in which right-angled structures are rare are less prone to the Müller-Lyer illusion.

specific objects versus a more holistic Eastern style of attending to contextual information and making judgments about relationships among objects rather than simply classifying them (Chua, Boland, & Nisbett, 2005).

Next we focus on two controversies in perception that have sparked a continuing debate within both the scientific community and society at large.

© Marilyn Genter/The Image Works

Americans tend to focus more than East Asians on focal objects, such as the large, brightly colored fish in this picture, whereas Asians take in more of the background information, such as rocks and smaller objects in the tank.

Controversies in Perception: Subliminal Perception and Extrasensory Perception

It created quite a stir in the U.S. presidential race back in 2000 when a campaign commercial for then candidate George W. Bush used what appeared to be a subliminal slur against his opponent, Vice President Al Gore ("Democrats Smell a Rat," 2000). The word *RATS* was flashed during an ad attacking Gore's health care plan. The producer of the ad claimed the message was not intended as a slur against Gore and simply represented a visual reminder of the word *bureaucrats* (*rats* being the last four letters of the word). Whether intended as a slur or not, it led people to wonder whether **subliminal perception** affects attitudes and behavior.

An even more controversial topic is **extrasensory perception (ESP)**—perception occurring without benefit of the known senses. Is it possible to read people's minds or to know the contents of a letter in a sealed envelope? Here we consider these longstanding controversies in light of scientific evidence.

subliminal perception Perception of stimuli that are presented below the threshold of conscious awareness.

extrasensory perception (ESP) Perception that occurs without benefit of the known senses.

Subliminal Perception: Did You See Something Flash By?

CONCEPT 3.37
Though we sometimes perceive things we are not conscious of perceiving, there is no evidence that subliminal cues have significant effects on our attitudes or behavior.

Does subliminal perception exist? Two-thirds of Americans think so (Onion, 2000). But does scientific evidence support this belief? The answer, researchers report, is *yes*, but it is a qualified yes.

Laboratory studies show that people can detect a wide range of subliminal stimuli (visual images, sounds, and even some odors) without being consciously aware of them (Bahrami, Lavie, & Rees, 2007; Ferguson & Zayas, 2009; W. Li et al., 2007; Pallier, Kouider, & De Gardelle, 2008). Subliminal exposure to certain brand names may have subtle effects on our behavior, even making us think more creatively. Investigators flashed images of the logos of Apple and IBM at speeds too fast to be detected consciously. The investigators had earlier found the Apple brand to be more strongly associated with creativity. In their experiment, people who were flashed images of the Apple logo showed more creative responses in a follow-up task than those exposed to either an IBM logo or no logo at all (Fitzsimons, Chartrand, & Fitzsimons, 2008; R. Walker, 2008). In another

© imagebroker/Alamy

© Bernd Pfeifer/Photo Library

In a test of the effects of subliminal cues, research participants demonstrated more creative responses after they were flashed subliminal images of the Apple brand as compared with others who were exposed to either an IBM logo or no logo at all.

CONCEPT 3.38
Claims of ESP remain just that—claims that have not met the rigorous tests of scientific inquiry.

recent study, subliminal exposure to fast food images increased the participants' reading speed in a later reading task (Zhong, 2010). The upshot is that we are influenced by some stimuli that whizz by us so quickly they don't register fully in consciousness.

A person's motivational state may influence the effects of subliminal perception. Investigators found that flashing a subliminal message containing a brand name of a particular drink (i.e., Lipton Ice) increased people's likelihood of choosing the brand from between two alternatives, but only for participants who were thirsty at the time (Karremans, Stroebe, & Claus, 2005).

How might we account for subliminal effects? One possibility is that people may be able to detect some features of a subliminally presented stimulus, even though they cannot report verbally what they have seen. Partial perception of a stimulus may help account for subliminal effects in laboratory studies, but we still lack any convincing evidence that subliminal messaging in advertising or motivational audiotapes actually influences purchase decisions, helps people become more successful in life, or has any meaningful impact on people's lives.

Extrasensory Perception: Is It for Real?

A man claims to be able to bend spoons with his mind. A woman claims to be able to find the bodies of crime victims aided by nothing more than a piece of clothing worn by the victim. Another woman claims to be able to foretell future events. The study of such *paranormal phenomena*—events that cannot be explained by known physical, psychological, or biological mechanisms—is called **parapsychology**. The major focus of paranormal psychology is *extrasensory perception*, the so-called "sixth sense" by which people claim they can perceive objects or events without using the known senses. The forms of paranormal phenomena most commonly identified with ESP are *telepathy, clairvoyance, precognition,* and *psychokinesis.*

parapsychology The study of paranormal phenomena.

telepathy Communication of thoughts from one mind to another that occurs without using the known senses.

clairvoyance The ability to perceive objects and events without using the known senses.

precognition The ability to foretell the future.

psychokinesis The ability to move objects by mental effort alone.

Telepathy refers to the purported ability to project one's thoughts into other people's minds or to read what is in their minds—to perceive their thoughts or feelings without using the known senses. **Clairvoyance** is the perception of events that are not available to the senses. The clairvoyant may claim to know what someone across town is doing at that precise moment or to identify the contents of a sealed envelope. **Precognition** is the ability to foretell the future. **Psychokinesis** (formerly called *telekinesis*) is the ability to move objects without touching them. Strictly speaking, psychokinesis is not a form of ESP since it does not involve perception, but for the sake of convenience it is often classified as such.

Critical thinkers maintain an appropriate skepticism about claims of ESP or other paranormal phenomena that seem to defy the laws of nature. Many claims have proven to be hoaxes, whereas others may be explained as random or chance occurrences, or mere statistical flukes (Hyman, 2010; Wagenmakers et al., 2011; Wiseman & Watt, 2006). Despite many decades of scientific study, we lack clear and convincing evidence supporting the existence of ESP that can withstand scientific scrutiny. As critical thinkers, we need to maintain a skeptical attitude and insist that claims of extrasensory abilities be reliably demonstrated under tightly controlled conditions before we are willing to accept them.

Concept Chart 3.5 provides an overview of many of the key concepts of perception discussed in this module.

CONCEPT CHART 3.5 Overview of Perception

Basic Concepts in Perception		Selective attention	The tendency to pay attention to types of sensory information that are important to us; such factors as motivational states and repeated exposure influence whether we attend to particular stimuli
		Perceptual set	The tendency for our expectations or preconceptions to influence our perceptions
		Perceptual constancy	The tendency to perceive objects as unchanging in size, shape, color, and brightness despite changes in perspective, distance, or lighting conditions
Modes of Perceptual Processing		Bottom-up	The process by which the brain forms perceptions by piecing together bits and pieces of sensory data to form meaningful patterns
		Top-down	The process by which the brain forms perceptions by recognizing whole patterns without first piecing together their component parts
Gestalt Principles of Perceptual Organization		Figure-ground	The tendency to perceive the visual environment in terms of figures (objects) that stand out from the surrounding background, or ground
	Principles of Grouping	Proximity	The tendency to perceive objects as belonging together when they are close to one another
		Similarity	The tendency to group objects that have similar characteristics
		Continuity	The tendency to perceive a series of stimuli as a unified form when they appear to represent a continuous pattern
		Closure	The tendency to group disconnected pieces of information into a meaningful whole
		Connectedness	The tendency to perceive objects as belonging together when they are positioned together or are moving together
Cues for Depth Perception	**Binocular Cues**	Retinal disparity	The disparity in the images of objects projected onto the retina, which the brain uses as a cue to the distance of the objects; nearby objects produce greater retinal disparity
		Convergence	Turning the eyes inward to focus on a nearby object, which creates muscular tension that the brain uses as a cue for depth perception; the closer the object, the more the eyes must converge to maintain the single image
	Monocular Cues	Relative size	An object that appears larger than another object believed to be of the same size is judged to be closer
		Interposition	Objects that are obscured by other objects are perceived as being farther away
		Relative clarity	Nearby objects are clearer than more distant objects
		Texture gradient	The details of nearby objects appear to have a coarser texture than those of distant objects
		Linear perspective	Objects and the spaces between them look smaller as they become more distant; thus, parallel lines appear to converge as they recede into the distance
		Shadowing	Shadows can create the appearance of curving surfaces or three dimensions, giving the impression of depth
Controversies in Perception		Subliminal perception	Perception of stimuli presented below the threshold of conscious awareness
		Extrasensory perception (ESP)	Perception occurring without the benefit of the known senses

3.5 MODULE REVIEW Perceiving Our World: Principles of Perception

Recite It

How is perception influenced by attention?

- Through the process of selective attention we focus on the most meaningful stimuli impinging upon us at any one time.
- Attention is influenced by such factors as motivational states and repeated exposure.

How is perception influenced by perceptual set?

- The tendency for perceptions to be influenced by expectations and preconceptions is known as a perceptual set.

What are the two general modes of processing visual stimuli?

- The two general modes of visual processing are bottom-up processing, which involves piecing together specific features of visual stimuli to form meaningful patterns, and top-down processing, which involves recognizing patterns as meaningful wholes without first piecing together their component parts.

What are the Gestalt principles of perceptual organization?

- The Gestalt principles of perceptual organization include laws of figure-ground perception and laws of grouping (proximity, similarity, continuity, closure, and connectedness).

What is perceptual constancy?

- Perceptual constancy is the tendency to perceive an object to be of the same shape, size, color, and brightness even when the images it casts on the retina change in response to changes in viewing perspective, distance, and lighting.

What cues do we use to perceive depth?

- Binocular cues include retinal disparity and convergence. Monocular cues include relative size, interposition, relative clarity, texture gradient, linear perspective, and shadowing.

What cues do we use to perceive movement?

- The movement of an object across our field of vision stimulates an array of points on the retina, which the brain interprets as movement. The changing size of the object is another cue for movement.

What are visual illusions?

- Visual illusions are misperceptions of visual stimuli in which our eyes seem to play tricks on us. Examples include the Müller-Lyer illusion, the Ponzo illusion, and the moon illusion.
- The brain may be fooled into perceiving apparent movement, as in the case of stroboscopic motion.

Does subliminal perception exist?

- Some limited forms of subliminal perception exist, but there is no evidence that exposure to subliminally presented messages in everyday life affects attitudes or behavior.

Does evidence support the existence of ESP?

- We lack clear and convincing evidence that proves the existence of various forms of ESP such as as telepathy, clairvoyance, precognition, and psychokinesis.

Recall It

1. The process by which the brain turns sensations into meaningful impressions of the external world is called ______.
2. The newborn infant's apparent preference for the sound of its mother's voice may be explained as a function of
   a. sensory facilitation.
   b. prenatal auditory exposure.
   c. inborn reflexes.
   d. the maximal adherence effect.
3. The term used to describe the tendency for our expectations and preconceived notions to influence how we perceive events is ______.
4. What Gestalt principle describes the tendency to perceive objects as belonging together when they are positioned together or moving together?
5. The monocular cue by which we perceive objects to be closer to us when they obscure objects that are behind them is called ______.
6. Which of the following is not a monocular cue for depth?
   a. convergence
   b. relative clarity
   c. interposition
   d. shadowing
7. Subliminal perception involves
   a. acquiring knowledge or insight without using the known senses.
   b. perceiving information presented below the level of conscious awareness.
   c. perceiving stimuli in an underwater environment.
   d. sensory systems that can transmit all of a stimulus's features.

Think About It

- Drawing upon your understanding of Gestalt principles of perceptual organization, explain how perceptions differ from photographic images.
- Have you ever had any unusual experiences that you believe involved ESP? Think critically. What alternative explanations might account for these experiences?

Psychology and Pain Management

APPLICATION MODULE 3.6

The brain is a marvel of engineering. By allowing us to experience the first pangs of pain, it alerts us to danger. Without such a warning, we might not pull our hand away from a hot object in time to prevent burns. Then, by releasing endorphins, the brain gradually shuts the gate on pain.

Though we all experience acute pain in response to injury, some 80 million Americans suffer from lingering, chronic pain, including back pain, headache, and pain associated with arthritis and other medical conditions (Edwards et al., 2009; Park, 2011). Not surprisingly, the management of chronic pain is a rapidly growing field. New technologies and approaches to pain management are being introduced to clinical practice every year. Although pain has a biological basis, psychological methods can help reduce the suffering of pain patients and assist them in coping with chronic pain (e.g., Cloud, 2011; Morley, Williams, & Hussain, 2008; Park, 2011). In this module, we focus on psychological factors in pain management. However, before attempting to treat pain yourself, consult a health professional to determine the source of the pain and the appropriate course of treatment.

CONCEPT 3.39
Psychological interventions may be helpful in managing pain.

→ Concept Link
Meditation is used to combat stress, relieve pain, and lower blood pressure. See Module 4.3.

Distraction

Distraction can help direct our attention away from pain. For example, when faced with a painful medical or dental procedure, you can help keep your mind off your pain by focusing on a pleasing picture on the wall or some other stimulus or by letting your mind become absorbed in a pleasant fantasy. Chronic pain sufferers may find they are better able to cope with the pain if they distract themselves by exercising or becoming immersed in a good book or video.

Creating a Bottleneck at the "Gate"

As noted earlier, the gate-control theory of pain holds that other sensory stimuli may temporarily block pain messages from passing through a neural gate in the spinal cord. You can attempt to create a "traffic jam" at the gate by lightly rubbing an irritated area. Interestingly, applying both heat and cold may help because each sends messages through the spinal cord that compete for attention. Cold packs have the additional advantage of reducing inflammation.

Changing Thoughts and Attitudes

What people say to themselves about their pain can affect how much pain they feel and how well they cope with it. Thinking pessimistic thoughts ("This will never get better") and catastrophic thoughts ("I can't take this anymore. I'm going to fall apart!")

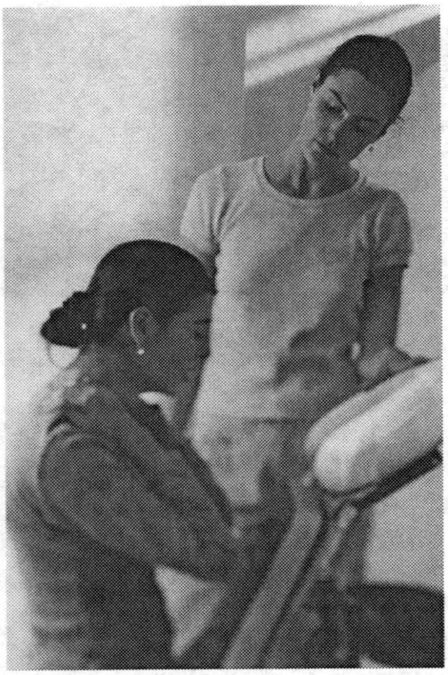
© Keith Brofsky/Photodosc/JupiterImages

What are some coping skills people can use to help manage pain more effectively?

can worsen the feelings of pain (Sullivan et al., 2006). Catastrophizing (thinking the worst) has been called the quintessential maladaptive response to coping with pain (Edwards et al., 2009). Findings from brain-scanning studies show higher levels of catstrophizing are associated with greater levels of pain-related brain activity (Edwards et al., 2009).

Negative thinking can also lead to perceptions of lack of control, which in turn can produce feelings of helplessness and hopelessness. Psychologists help pain sufferers examine their thoughts and replace negative or pessimistic self-evaluations with rational alternatives—thoughts like "Don't give in to hopelessness. Focus on what you need to do to cope with this pain." Psychologists find that helping pain patients alter catastrophic thinking reduces the intensity of the pain they experience and improves their daily functioning (Turner, Mancl, & Aaron, 2006). Even if changing thoughts and attitudes does not eliminate pain, it can help people cope more effectively in managing their pain symptoms.

Obtaining Accurate Information

One of the most effective psychological methods for managing pain is obtaining factual and thorough information about the source of the pain and the available treatments. Many people try to avoid thinking about pain and its implications. Obtaining information helps people take an active role in controlling the challenges they face.

Meditation and Biofeedback

Meditation can help relieve chronic pain (e.g., Grossman, 2008; Oz, 2003; Roemer & Orsillo, 2003). As we'll discuss in Chapter 4, meditation involves the narrowing or focusing of attention to induce a relaxed, contemplative state. There are different ways to meditate, but most involve narrowing attention by means of repeating a word, thought, or phrase or maintaining a steady visual focus on one object, such as a burning candle or the design on a vase.

Psychologists find that providing people with feedback about their internal bodily functions ("biofeedback") helps them gain greater awareness and some degree of voluntary control over their internal bodily processes. In **biofeedback training (BFT)**, individuals are attached to physiological monitoring equipment that provides them with a continual stream of information about their internal bodily states. A rising tone may indicate increasing heart rate or muscle tension, while a lower tone indicates changes in the opposite direction. People use these biofeedback signals as cues to help them learn to modify their heart rates, blood pressure, muscle tension, body temperature, brain wave patterns, and other physiological processes (e.g., Dalen et al., 2009; Moser, Franklin, & Handler, 2007; Nestoriuc & Martin, 2007).

One form of biofeedback training used to help relieve tension headache pain is **electromyographic (EMG) biofeedback** (Nestoriuc, Rief, & Martin, 2008). In EMG, electrodes placed on the forehead or elsewhere on the body monitor muscle tension. A tone is used to indicate increases or decreases in muscle tension. By learning to lower the tone, people can relax their forehead muscles, which can help reduce pain associated with tension headaches.

biofeedback training (BFT) A method of learning to control certain bodily responses by using information from the body transmitted by physiological monitoring equipment.

electromyographic (EMG) biofeedback A form of BFT that involves feedback about changes in the level of muscle tension in the forehead or elsewhere in the body.

migraine headache A prolonged, intense headache brought on by changes in blood flow in the brain's blood vessels.

thermal biofeedback A form of BFT that involves feedback about changes in temperature and blood flow in selected parts of the body; used in the treatment of migraine headaches.

Migraine headache sufferers may benefit from a biofeedback technique that helps them learn to modulate blood flow to their extremities. Migraines involve intense, pulsating pain on one side of the head that is associated with changes in blood flow to the brain (Durham, 2004; Linde et al., 2005). In **thermal biofeedback,** a temperature-sensing device is attached to a finger. The device beeps more slowly (or more rapidly, depending on the settings) as the temperature in the finger rises. Some people learn they can raise the temperature in their fingers simply by imagining a finger growing warmer. The temperature rises as more blood flows to the limbs and away from the head. This change in blood flow may help relieve migraine pain.

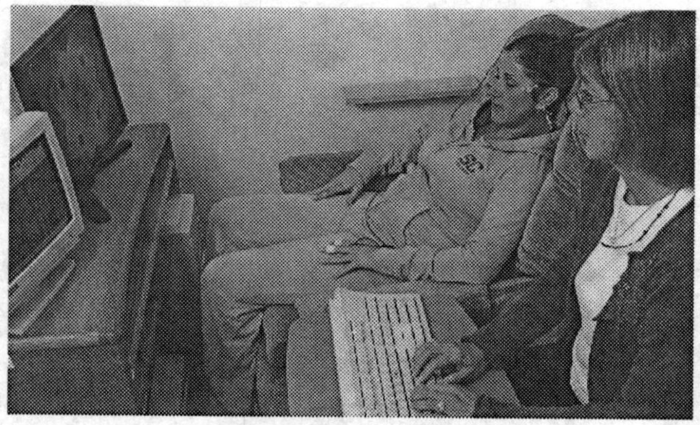
© Bonnie Kamin/PhotoEdit

Through biofeedback training, people can learn to alter some internal bodily processes, such as heart rate, blood pressure, muscle tension, body temperature, and certain types of brain wave patterns.

We should recognize, however, that at least some of the benefits of BFT in reducing pain or hypertension may be achieved through simpler forms of relaxation training that don't require expensive equipment, such as muscle relaxation techniques and deep breathing exercises. In Chapter 4 we discuss another psychological technique that can help control pain—hypnosis.

Thinking Critically About Psychology

Based on your reading of this chapter, answer the following questions. Then, to evaluate your progress in developing critical thinking skills, compare your answers to the sample answers found in Appendix A.

SLICE OF LIFE A few years ago, a police department asked a woman who claimed to have psychic abilities to help them locate an elderly man who had disappeared in a wooded area outside of town. Despite an extended search of the area, the police had been unable to locate the man. Working only from a photograph of the man and a map of the area, the woman circled an area of the map where she felt the man might be found. The police were amazed to discover the man's body in the area she had indicated. He had died of natural causes, and his body was hidden by a dense thicket of bushes.

Critical thinkers adopt a skeptical attitude toward claims of ESP. They evaluate the evidence and consider more plausible alternative explanations. Consider these questions:

1. Do you believe this case demonstrates the existence of ESP? Why or why not?
2. What, if any, additional information would you need to help you evaluate the woman's claims or to generate alternative explanations?

Log in to CengageBrain to access the resources your instructor requires. For this book, you can access:

CourseMate

Psychology CourseMate brings course concepts to life with interactive learning, study, and exam preparation tools that support the printed textbook. A textbook-specific website, Psychology CourseMate includes an integrated interactive eBook and other interactive learning tools including quizzes, flashcards, videos, and more.

CENGAGENOW

CengageNow is an easy-to-use online resource that helps you study in less time to get the grade you want—NOW. Take a pre-test for this chapter and receive a personalized study plan based on your results that will identify the topics you need to review and direct you to online resources to help you master those topics. Then take a post-test to help you determine the concepts you have mastered and what you will need to work on. If your textbook does not include an access code card, go to CengageBrain.com to gain access.

Visit www.cengagebrain.com to access your account and purchase materials.

VISUAL OVERVIEW Chapter 3 Sensation and Perception

MODULE 3.1 Basic Concepts of Sensation

- **Absolute Thresholds**: Is something there?
- **Difference Thresholds**: Is something different there?
- **Sensory Adaptation**: Getting duller with time
- **Signal Detection**: Picking up a signal

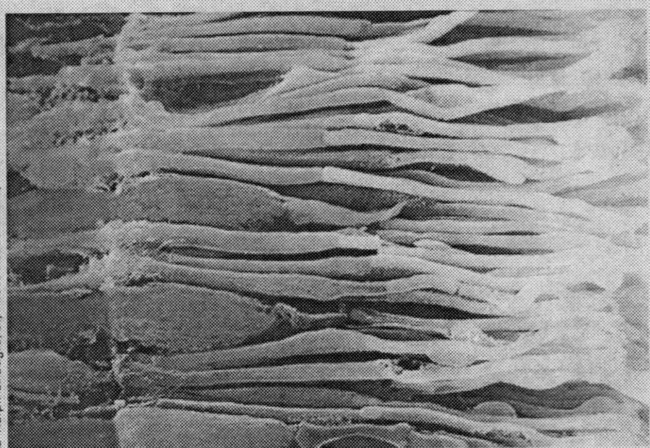

© Ralph C. Eagle, Jr/Photo Researchers, Inc.

Rods and Cones

Sensory Receptors

- Rods and cones for vision
- Hair cells for hearing
- Taste cells for taste
- Odor receptors for smell
- Skin receptors for skin senses
- Kinesthetic receptors in the joints, ligaments, and tendons
- Vestibular receptors in the inner ear

MODULES 3.2–3.4 Our Senses

The Senses

- **Vision**: Light energy → Receptor cells in retina → Neural impulses → Sight
- **Hearing:** Sound vibrations → Receptor cells in inner ear → Neural impulses along auditory nerve to auditory cortex → Sound
- **Chemical Senses:** Chemical substances → Transformed into neural impulses by receptors in nose and mouth→ Smell and taste
- **Skin Senses:** Tactile stimuli → Receptors in skin → Neural impulses transmitted to somatosensory cortex → Touch, pressure, temperature, and pain
- **Kinesthesis:** Body receptors in joints, ligaments, and muscles → Neural signals to brain → Sense of position and movement of parts of the body
- **Vestibular Sense:** Gravitational forces → Stimulate receptors in the inner ear → Neural signals to brain → Sense of position of the body in space and maintenance of balance

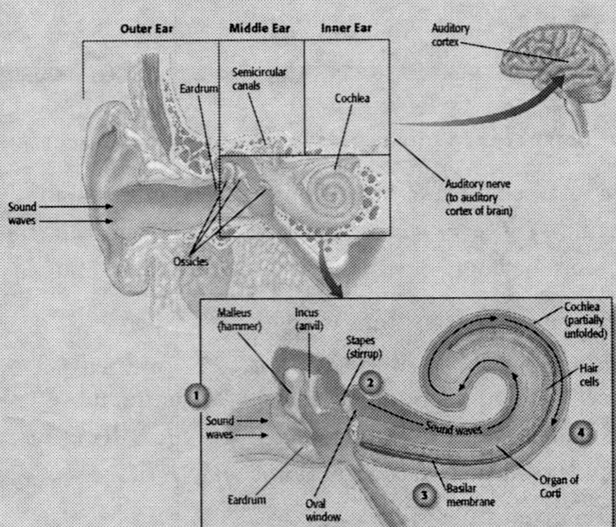

The Ear

MODULE 3.5 Perceiving Our World

Psychological Processes

- **Selective Attention:** Attending to important stimuli
- **Perceptual Set:** Expectations influence perceptions
- **Bottom-Up and Top-Down Processing:** Perceiving parts of patterns versus perceiving whole patterns
- **Gestalt Principles of Perceptual Organization:** Brain organizes sensations into recognizable wholes or patterns
- **Perceptual Constancy:** Objects retain their shapes and other properties even when the images they cast change with changing conditions

Perceptual Cues

- **Cues for Depth Perception:** *Monocular cues* depend on the individual eye (relative size, texture gradient, linear perspective, etc.). *Binocular cues* depend on both eyes working together (retinal disparity and convergence).
- **Cues for Motion Perception:** The two basic cues are the path of the image as it crosses the retina and changing size of the object.

Visual Illusions

- **When the Brain, Not the Eye, Plays Tricks on Us:** Examples include the Müller-Lyer illusion, the Ponzo illusion, the moon illusion, and apparent movement.

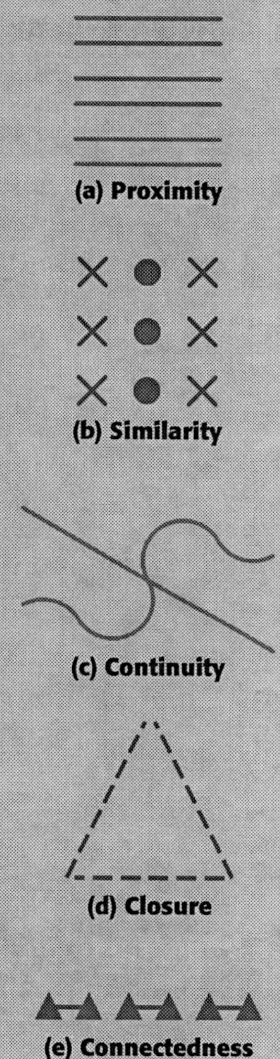

Gestalt Laws of Grouping

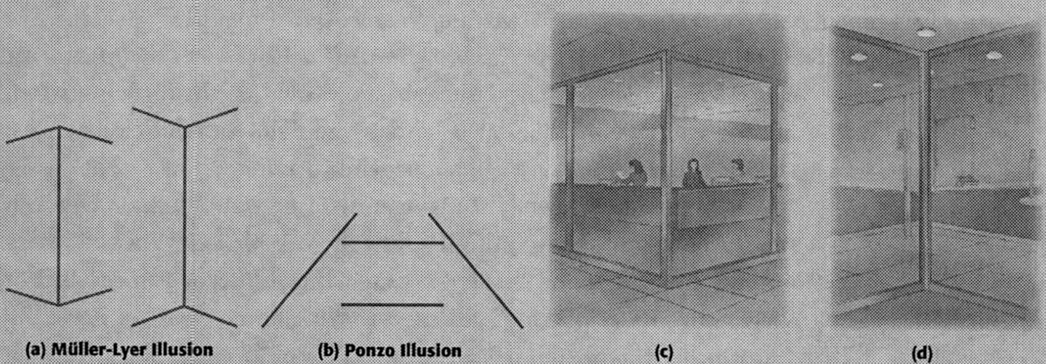

(a) Müller-Lyer Illusion (b) Ponzo Illusion

4 Consciousness

Are You a Multitasker?

Think about what you are doing right now. Is your attention fully absorbed by reading this page? Or is it divided between two or more tasks? As you are reading, are you also listening to music or perhaps musing about your plans for the weekend? We live in a multitasking world in which we keep one eye on one thing and another eye (or ear) on something else. The word *multitasking* entered the popular vocabulary with the introduction of computer systems that allowed users to perform two or more tasks at the same time, such as word processing and e-mailing. But with advances in technology, multitasking has spilled into our daily lives. We talk on cell phones while shopping and send e-mails or text our buddies while listening to the latest hit song we just downloaded.

Computers are becoming ever more sophisticated and capable of handling multiple tasks without a hitch, but what about the human brain? How well equipped is the brain when it comes to dividing attention between two or more tasks at once?

Multitasking may be a timesaver, but scientific findings back up the common perception that it is difficult to do two things well at the same time. Two thousand years before the introduction of cell phones and iPods, the Roman sage Publilius Syrus had this to say of what today we would call multitasking: "To do two things at once is to do neither."

The problem is that performing two tasks at the same time reduces the mental resources needed to perform either task well (Lien, Ruthruff, & Johnston, 2006). Multitasking may also be dangerous in some circumstances, such as when talking on a cell phone while driving.

Do you multitask while studying—dividing your attention between the textbook and the TV, the iPod, or the cell phone? When it comes to performing the many challenging mental tasks needed to succeed in college, such as deciphering a lecture, studying for an exam, or decoding basic principles of calculus or learning theory, multitasking can indeed take a toll on performance, which in turn may result in lower grades. But the very fact that we are capable of multitasking means that we can divide our consciousness or mental awareness between different activities. We can focus part of our awareness on one task while engaging another part on something else. But what is consciousness and how do our states of consciousness change through the course of the day?

In this chapter we set out on an inward exploration of human consciousness. We explore different states of consciousness and examine ways in which people seek to alter their ordinary waking states of consciousness, such as by practicing meditation, undergoing hypnosis, or using mind-altering drugs. We also consider the psychological and physiological effects of these drugs and the risks they pose.

© vita khorzhevska/Shutterstock.com

DID YOU KNOW THAT...

- You have a biological clock in your brain that regulates your sleep-wake cycle? (p. 143)
- Body temperature does not remain at a steady 98.6 degrees Fahrenheit throughout the day? (p. 143)
- In ancient Egypt, people practiced a form of meditation that involved staring at an oil-burning lamp, a custom that may have inspired the tale of Aladdin's lamp? (p. 154)
- Alcohol, not cocaine, heroin, or marijuana, remains the BDOC—the big drug on campus? (p. 162)
- It can be dangerous—indeed deadly—to let a person who blacks out from drinking too much "to just sleep it off"? (p. 163)
- Coca-Cola once contained cocaine? (p. 165)
- You may be hooked on a drug you have with breakfast every morning? (p. 167)

Learning Objectives

By reading this chapter you will be able to . . .

1 **DEFINE** consciousness.

2 **DESCRIBE** the different states of consciousness and **APPLY** your knowledge of these states to our daily experiences.

3 **EXPLAIN** how the sleep-wake cycle is regulated.

4 **DESCRIBE** the characteristics of each stage of sleep and **IDENTIFY** brain wave patterns associated with each stage.

5 **DESCRIBE** the functions of sleep.

6 **DESCRIBE** the major theories of dreaming.

7 **EVALUATE** the effects of sleep deprivation.

8 **IDENTIFY** different types of sleep disorders and **APPLY** your knowledge to understanding sleep problems people may encounter.

9 **DESCRIBE** the effects of meditation and hypnosis.

10 **DESCRIBE** the major theories of hypnosis.

11 **EXPLAIN** the differences between physiological and psychological dependence and between drug abuse and drug dependence.

12 **IDENTIFY** various types of psychoactive drugs and **DESCRIBE** their effects.

13 **EXPLAIN** the development of alcohol and drug abuse problems in terms of psychological, biological, and sociocultural factors.

14 **APPLY** behavioral techniques to developing healthier sleep habits.

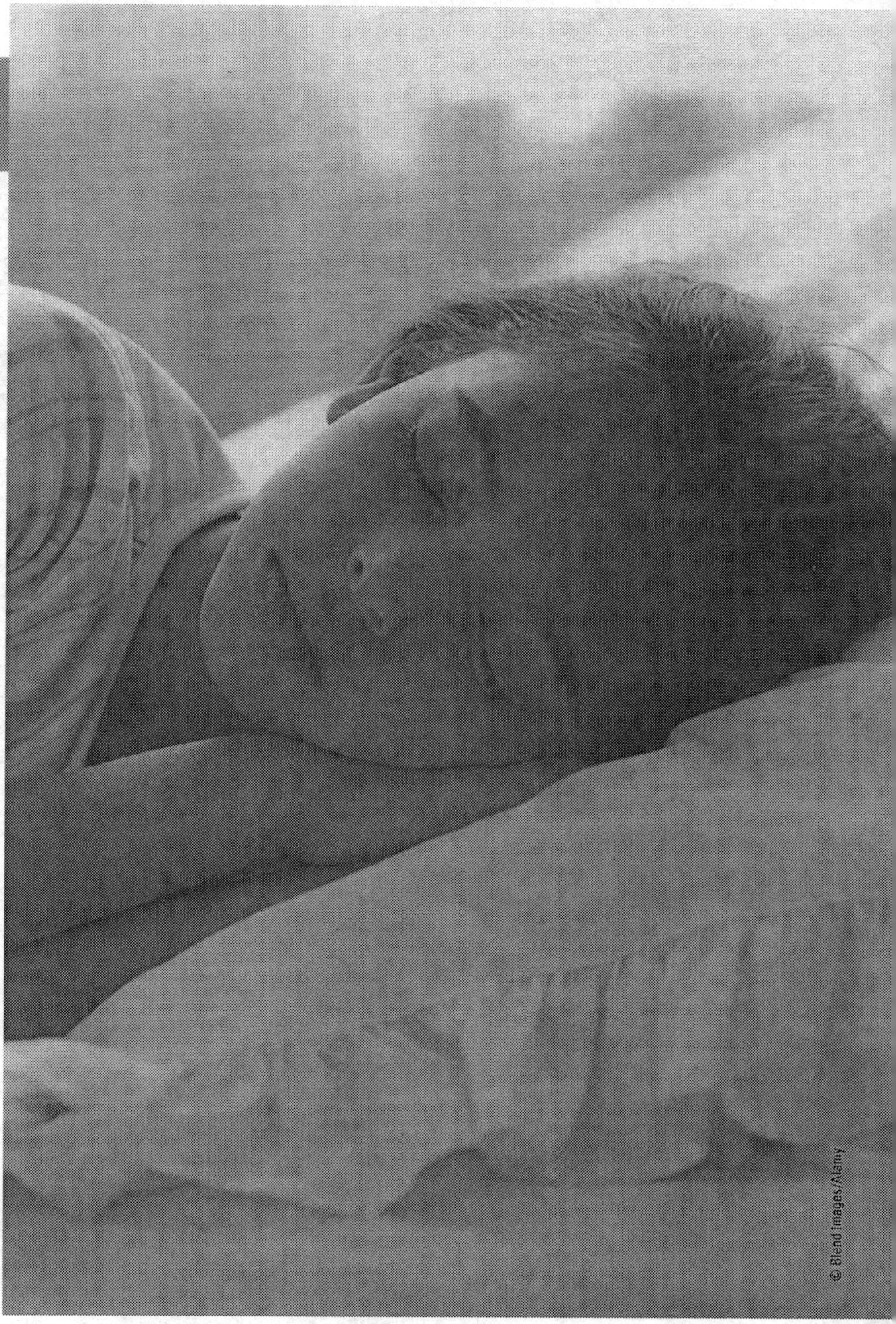

© Blend Images/Alamy

Preview

MODULE 4.1

States of Consciousness

■ What are different states of consciousness?

© Archives of the History of American Psychology, The Center for the History of Psychology—The University of Akron

William James
To James, consciousness is like an ever-flowing river of thoughts and mental experiences.

William James is widely regarded as the father of American psychology. He was such an early figure in the field that the first psychology lecture he ever attended was the one he gave himself (Hothersall, 1995). At the time (1875) there were no psychology textbooks. It would be another 15 years, in fact, before the first textbook on psychology would be written, by James himself, entitled *Principles of Psychology* (James, 1890/1970).

James was interested in the nature of **consciousness**, which he described as a stream of thoughts. To James, consciousness was not a fixed state or a collection of "chopped bits" of disconnected thoughts and experiences. Rather, it was a continuous process of thinking in which one thought flows into another, like water flowing continuously down a river (James, 1890/1970). Today, we view consciousness in much the same way James envisioned it, as a *state of awareness of ourselves and of the world around us.*

Your consciousness consists of whatever you happen to be aware of at any given moment in time—your thoughts, feelings, sensations, and perceptions of the outside world. Your awareness at this very moment is probably focused on reading these words. But your consciousness could quickly shift if, for example, you focused on the pressure of your backside against the chair in which you are sitting or listened carefully for a faint sound in the background.

CONCEPT 4.1
Waking consciousness varies during the course of a day from focused awareness to divided consciousness to drifting consciousness.

consciousness A state of awareness of ourselves and of the world around us.

states of consciousness Levels of consciousness ranging from alert wakefulness to deep sleep.

focused awareness A state of heightened alertness in which one is fully absorbed in the task at hand.

During the course of a day we experience different **states of consciousness**, or levels of awareness. At certain times of the day, we experience a state of focused awareness in which we are alert and absorbed in the task at hand. At other times, our consciousness follows a meandering or wandering course across a landscape of daydreams and fantasies. For perhaps a third of the day, we lapse into sleep, when our awareness of the external world is dimmed. In this module, we examine three states of consciousness you are likely to experience throughout the day: focused awareness, drifting consciousness, and divided consciousness. In the next module, we enter the realm of sleep and dreams.

Focused Awareness

CONCEPT 4.2
The selectivity of consciousness allows us to direct our attention to meaningful stimuli, events, or experiences while filtering out other stimuli.

→ Concept Link
Negative ways of thinking act like mental filters in our consciousness that put a slant on how we react to life events, which can set the stage for depression in the face of disappointing life experiences. See Module 15.4.

Consciousness is *selective*—we have the ability to direct our attention to certain objects, events, or experiences while filtering out extraneous stimuli. The selectivity of consciousness enables us to achieve a heightened state of alert wakefulness called **focused awareness**. In a state of focused awareness, we are wide awake, fully alert, and completely engrossed in the task at hand. We pay little if any heed to distracting external stimuli (traffic noises, rumbling air conditioners) or even disturbing internal stimuli (hunger pangs and nagging aches and pains). Focused awareness may be needed to perform tasks that require fixed attention, such as learning a new skill or studying for an exam (see *Try This Out* on p. 140).

Drifting Consciousness

CONCEPT 4.3
States of drifting consciousness are associated with mental meanderings called daydreams.

It is difficult to maintain a state of focused awareness for an extended period of time. Before long, your mind may start drifting from thought to thought. This state of **drifting consciousness** may lead to **daydreaming**, a form of consciousness during a waking state in which your mind wanders to dreamy thoughts or fantasies (Mason et al., 2007). Generally, daydreams involve mundane facets of everyday life; relatively few involve sexual or romantic adventures.

drifting consciousness A state of awareness characterized by drifting thoughts or mental imagery.

daydreaming A form of consciousness during a waking state in which one's mind wanders to dreamy thoughts or fantasies.

We tend to daydream more when bored or engaged in unstructured activities, such as waiting for a bus. Daydreaming in class, however, can disrupt recent memories, so it's best to maintain your focus if you want to remember the day's lecture (Delaney et al., 2010). We also tend to blink more when our mind wanders, which reduces the amount of information coming into the brain, making it more difficult for the brain to process information in class ("Out of Sight," 2010; Smile, Carriere & Cheyne, 2010).

Just how much time do we spend mind wandering or daydreaming? A recent Harvard University study provided participants with an iPhone app that texted them several times a day to report what they were doing, thinking, and feeling at the moment (Killingsworth & Gilbert, 2010). Data from more than 2,000 adults showed that, on average, people reported their minds wandering nearly half of the time (47%). The least frequent time spent mind wandering was (no surprise!) when participants were having sex. It appears that a wandering mind is not a happy mind. People tended to report unhappier moods at times when their minds were wandering than when they were focused on activities (Schenkman, 2010). The results of the Harvard study suggests we may find greater happiness by focusing on what we're doing at the moment, rather than escaping into mental fantasies. Even people whose minds wandered to pleasant activities were not any happier than those who were thinking about their current activity.

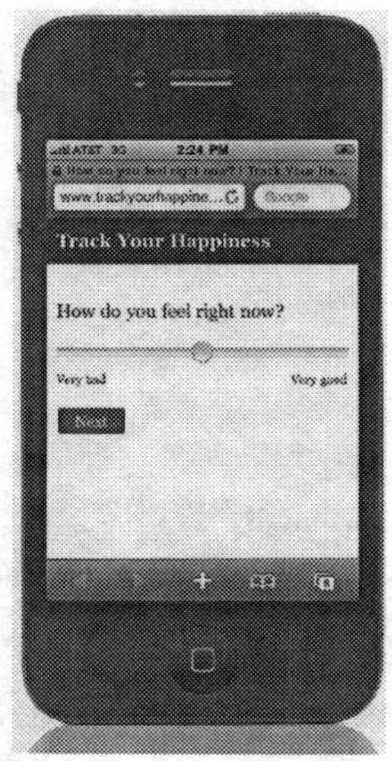

© iStockphoto.com/Tomasz Pietryszek

Harvard researchers used an iPhone app to track people's moods, thoughts, and daily activities. People who were thinking of other things were less happy than those who were focused on what they were doing at the moment.

Divided Consciousness

Learning a new skill typically requires focused awareness. When learning to drive, for example, you need to pay close attention to how far to turn the wheel when steering into a curve, how much pressure to apply to the brakes when stopping, and so on. But after a time, driving may become so routine that you experience a state of divided consciousness—dividing your attention between driving and other thoughts, such as trying to remember the words of a song or fantasizing about a vacation.

States of **divided consciousness** occur when we perform two different tasks at the same time, such as driving and listening to music, or doing the dishes and thinking about our plans for the weekend. For more routine tasks, such as washing dishes, part of our mind seems to operate on "automatic pilot" while the other part is free to think about other things.

divided consciousness A state of awareness characterized by divided attention to two or more tasks or activities performed at the same time.

Divided attention on the road can be dangerously distracting. Drivers who talk on a cell phone are four times more likely to have an accident than those who do not—about the same level of increased risk as drivers who are legally drunk (Parker-Pope, 2009). The problem is not simply that of fiddling with the phone. Using a hands-free cell phone doesn't eliminate the increased risk (Richtel, 2009). Evidence shows that use of either a hands-free or hand-held phone takes your attention off the road and leads to a serious loss of concentration called "inattention blindness" (Strayer & Drews, 2007).

TRY THIS OUT Savoring Your Food

How does mental focusing affect your experience of eating a meal? Try this out:

1. Focus your attention completely on your next meal. Avoid talking, watching TV, or reading while eating.
2. Notice the shape, color, and texture of the food.
3. Take a deep whiff of the aroma of the food before chewing.
4. Slowly chew each morsel, savoring the distinctive flavor of each bite.
5. Mix different foods together in your mouth to appreciate their distinctive flavors and how they blend together in a mélange of taste.

What differences do you notice between this experience and your usual dining experience?

Psychologist David Strayer, a leading researcher in the field, says, "It's not that your hands aren't on the wheel. . . . It's that your mind is not on the road" (cited in Parker-Pope, 2009). Ordinary conversations with passengers are not nearly as distracting as talking on a cell phone (Drews, Pasupathi, & Strayer, 2008; Strayer & Drews, 2007).

Why is cell phone use so dangerously distracting? The basic reason is that the human brain is limited in its capacity for performing two high-level tasks at the same time (Novotney, 2009). We may be able to work out on the treadmill while watching a show on TV, but performing more complex tasks like driving requires attentional resources that cannot be split effectively with other demanding tasks, such as using a cell phone. Talking on a cell phone is more attention demanding than ordinary conversation in part because the person on the other end is not physically present and so we lack the visual cues that are available with a conversant that we rely on to modulate the give-and-take in a conversation.

CONCEPT 4.4
Our ability to divide consciousness allows us to perform more than one activity at a time.

altered states of consciousness States of awareness during wakefulness that are different than the person's usual waking state.

© Radius Images/Jupiter Images

Multitasking may be an efficient use of attentional resources when performing routine or well-practiced tasks, such as washing the dishes or jogging along a familiar path. But when it comes to multitasking and studying, in a word, don't.

Texting during driving can be deadly, even more deadly than talking on a cell phone. A study of long-haul truck drivers showed that texting increased drivers' reaction times by an average of 30 percent and was associated with a twenty-three-fold greater risk of accidents (Drews et al., 2008; Richtel, 2009a). Using a driving simulator, investigators found that drivers who were texting were slower to respond to brake lights on cars ahead of them, had more difficulty staying in their lane, and had more crashes than did nontexting drivers and even drivers using cell phones (Drews et al., 2009).

Keeping your eyes and your mind on the road at all times can help save a life, quite possibly your own. The hazards of divided driving extend beyond the use of a cell phone (Conkle & West, 2008). Fussing with a child in the back seat, putting on make-up, and eating or drinking can all be dangerously distracting (see Table 4.1).

On the other hand, it might surprise you to learn that many tasks we routinely perform are performed better when we do them without consciously thinking about them. Think about daily tasks we perform without conscious direction, such as climbing stairs or typing (for the experienced typist) (Bargh & Morsella, 2008). These skills become so ingrained that we are able to perform them without conscious attention to them, which frees up mental resources needed for more important behaviors. We can thus think about what we are writing when we are typing, rather than focusing on the mechanics of hitting the correct keys.

Changes in the level of ordinary awareness in the waking state are called **altered states of consciousness**. Altered states of consciousness may occur when we daydream,

TABLE 4.1 Driving While Distracted

A Canadian survey asked drivers whether they had engaged in the behaviors below while driving and whether they had observed other drivers engaging in the same behaviors.

Behaviors	Yourself (%)	Another Driver (%)
Drinking beverages (e.g., coffee, soft drinks)	65	74
Eating	53	66
Using a cell phone	35	79
Arguing with passengers	27	41
Disciplining children	18	33
Reading	8	26
Putting on make-up, shaving, or combing hair	8	43
Using PDAs, laptops, or other high-tech devices	5	21

Source: Adapted from *2003 Nerves of Steel* survey, commissioned by the Steel Alliance and the Canada Safety Council. Retrieved from http://www.safety-council.org/info/traffic/distract.html.

© gazmandhu/Shutterstock.com

The ability to divide consciousness allows us to perform two tasks at once. But the combination of driving and using a phone is associated with a fourfold increase in the risk of motor vehicle accidents.

meditate or undergo hypnosis, or use mind-altering drugs like alcohol and marijuana. Repetitive physical activity, such as long-distance running or lap swimming, also may induce an altered state of consciousness—one in which the outside world seems to fade out of awareness. In some altered states, the person may experience changes in the sense of time (time may seem to stand still or speed up) and in sensory experiences (colors may seem more vibrant or, as in some drug-induced states, the person may hear voices or see visions). In Modules 4.2 to 4.4, we explore the range of human consciousness, from states of sleep and wakefulness to altered states of consciousness. Concept Chart 4.1 offers an overview of these different levels or states of consciousness.

© Betsy Streeter, Reproduction rights obtainable from www.CartoonStock.com

CONCEPT 4.5

Altered states of consciousness may be induced in different ways, such as by practicing meditation or undergoing hypnosis, or by using mind-altering drugs.

TRY THIS OUT Putting Multitasking to the Test

How distracting is multitasking during studying? Let's put it to the test. Read page 143 with full attention on your reading. Then jot down on a piece of paper or type into the computer everything you learned—concepts, definitions, key points, research findings—without looking back at the text. Then read the following page in the text while listening to one of your favorite musical groups while you are reading. After reading the page, jot down everything you learned. Then compare the two documents. Does the first provide a more complete and accurate account of the text material? To what extent did multitasking interfere with your ability to learn and remember what you were reading?

CONCEPT CHART 4.1 States of Consciousness

	States of Consciousness	Level of Alertness/Attention	Examples or Features
 © wrangler/ Shutterstock.com	Focused awareness	High; fully awake and alert	Learning a new skill; watching an engrossing movie
 © Yuri Arcurs/Shutterstock.com	Drifting consciousness	Variable or shifting	Daydreaming, or letting one's thoughts wander
 © Bochkarev Photography/ Shutterstock.com	Divided consciousness	Medium; attention split between two activities	Thinking of other things while exercising or driving a car
 © Gravicapa/ Shutterstock.com	Sleeping and dreaming	Low	During sleep, the person is generally unaware of external surroundings but may respond to certain stimuli
 © iStockphoto.com/ nicolas hansen	Waking states of altered consciousness	Variable	Changes in consciousness associated with hypnosis, meditation, and drug use

4.1 MODULE REVIEW States of Consciousness

Recite It

What are different states of consciousness?

➤ States of consciousness are different levels of awareness that may range during the course of the day from alert wakefulness to deep sleep.

➤ Altered states of consciousness are states of wakefulness that differ from one's usual waking state of awareness.

Recall It

1. The nineteenth-century psychologist William James likened consciousness to
   a. water flowing continuously down a river.
   b. a drifting cloud.
   c. a swirling ocean.
   d. a state of tranquility.

2. The ________ of consciousness makes it possible to focus on meaningful stimuli, events, and experiences.

3. The state of awareness in which we are completely alert and engrossed in a task is known as
   a. daydreaming.
   b. divided consciousness.
   c. altered consciousness.
   d. focused awareness.

Think About It

➤ What steps can you take to reduce your risk of driving while distracted? Did the discussion in the module change your views on the issue? Why or why not?

Sleeping and Dreaming

MODULE 4.2

- How are our sleep-wake cycles regulated?
- What are the stages of sleep?
- What functions does sleep serve?
- Why do we dream?
- What are sleep disorders?

We spend about a third of our lives sleeping. During sleep, we enter our own private theater of the mind—a realm of dreams in which the mind weaves tales ranging from the mundane and ordinary to the fantastic and bizarre. The laws of the physical world don't apply when we dream. Objects change shape, one person may be transformed into another, and scenes move abruptly without regard to the physical limits of time and place. Though we've learned much about sleeping and dreaming, many mysteries remain. We lack a consensus about such basic questions as "Why do we sleep?" and "Why do we dream?" In this module, we venture into the mysterious domain of sleep and dreams. We begin by examining the bodily mechanisms responsible for our sleep-wake cycles.

During sleep, we are relatively unaware of our external surroundings. Passing sounds do not register in our awareness unless they are very loud or blaring and interrupt our sleep. Despite the fact that our awareness of the world is dimmed while we sleep, we may still be responsive to certain types of stimuli that are personally meaningful or relevant. As noted in Chapter 3, people may sleep soundly through the wail of a passing ambulance but be awakened instantly by their child's soft cry.

CONCEPT 4.6
At the lower end of the continuum of awareness are states of sleeping and dreaming.

Sleep and Wakefulness: A Circadian Rhythm

Many bodily processes—sleep-wake cycles, as well as body temperature, hormonal secretions, blood pressure, and heart rate—fluctuate daily in a pattern called a **circadian rhythm**. The word *circadian* is derived from the Latin roots *circa* ("about") and *dies* ("day"). Circadian or daily rhythms are found in virtually all species, including organisms as varied as single-celled paramecia, fruit flies, humans, and even trees (Gallego et al., 2006; Meyer, Saez, & Young, 2006). These rhythms are synchronized with the 24-hour cycle of day and night. In humans, the sleep-wake cycle operates on a circadian rhythm that is about 24 hours in length.

circadian rhythm The pattern of fluctuations in bodily processes that occur regularly each day.

It may surprise you to learn that the human body does not maintain a steady 98.6-degree temperature. Body temperature follows a circadian rhythm, falling a few degrees during the middle of the night, then rising in the early morning hours and peaking at around midday.

CONCEPT 4.7
A clocklike mechanism in the hypothalamus is responsible for regulating our sleep-wake cycles.

A small area of the hypothalamus called the *suprachiasmatic nucleus* (SCN) regulates our sleep-wake cycles (Borgs et al., 2009). This internal body clock responds to light impinging on the retina. When light enters the eye, its energy is transformed into neural impulses that travel to the SCN. The SCN in turn regulates the pineal gland, which, as noted in Chapter 2, is a gland in the brain that releases the hormone *melatonin*. Melatonin helps synchronize the body's sleep-wake cycle by making us feel sleepy as day descends into night (Buscemi et al., 2006; Van der Heijden et al., 2007). Exposure to darkness during evening hours stimulates the brain's production of melatonin. During exposure

CONCEPT 4.8

Your internal body clock does not adjust easily to time shifts associated with changes in time zones or shift work.

jet lag A disruption of sleep-wake cycles caused by the shifts in time zones that accompany long-distance air travel.

to bright light, melatonin production falls off, helping us to stay awake and alert during daylight hours. (This might also explain why we often feel sleepy on cloudy days.)

Frequent time shifts can play havoc with the body's circadian rhythms (Sadeghniiat-Haghighi et al, 2008). If you've ever traveled by plane across several time zones, you've probably experienced jet lag. **Jet lag** occurs when a change in local time conflicts with your internal body clock, making it difficult to fall asleep earlier than usual or to stay awake later than usual, depending on whether you've lost time by traveling east or gained time by traveling west. Jet lag is associated not only with disruption of sleep-wake cycles but also with irritability, fatigue, and difficulty in concentrating.

The Stages of Sleep

CONCEPT 4.9

During sleep, your body cycles through four stages, followed by a period of REM sleep, in which most dreaming occurs.

The electroencephalograph (EEG) is one of several devices researchers use to determine how our bodies respond when we sleep. The EEG tracks brain waves, which vary in intensity or amplitude (height of the wave) and speed or frequency (wave cycles per second). When you are awake and alert, your brain wave pattern is dominated by fast, low-amplitude *beta waves.* As you close your eyes and relax in bed, you enter a state of relaxed wakefulness. In this state, your brain wave pattern is dominated by slower, rhythmic cycles called *alpha waves.* When people sleep, the EEG shows they progress through several distinct stages of sleep characterized by different brain wave patterns (see ■ Figure 4.1).

Stages 1 to 4: From Light to Deep Sleep

In Stage 1 sleep, brain waves become small and irregular, with varying frequencies. The sleeper can be easily awakened during this stage and may not even realize she or he had

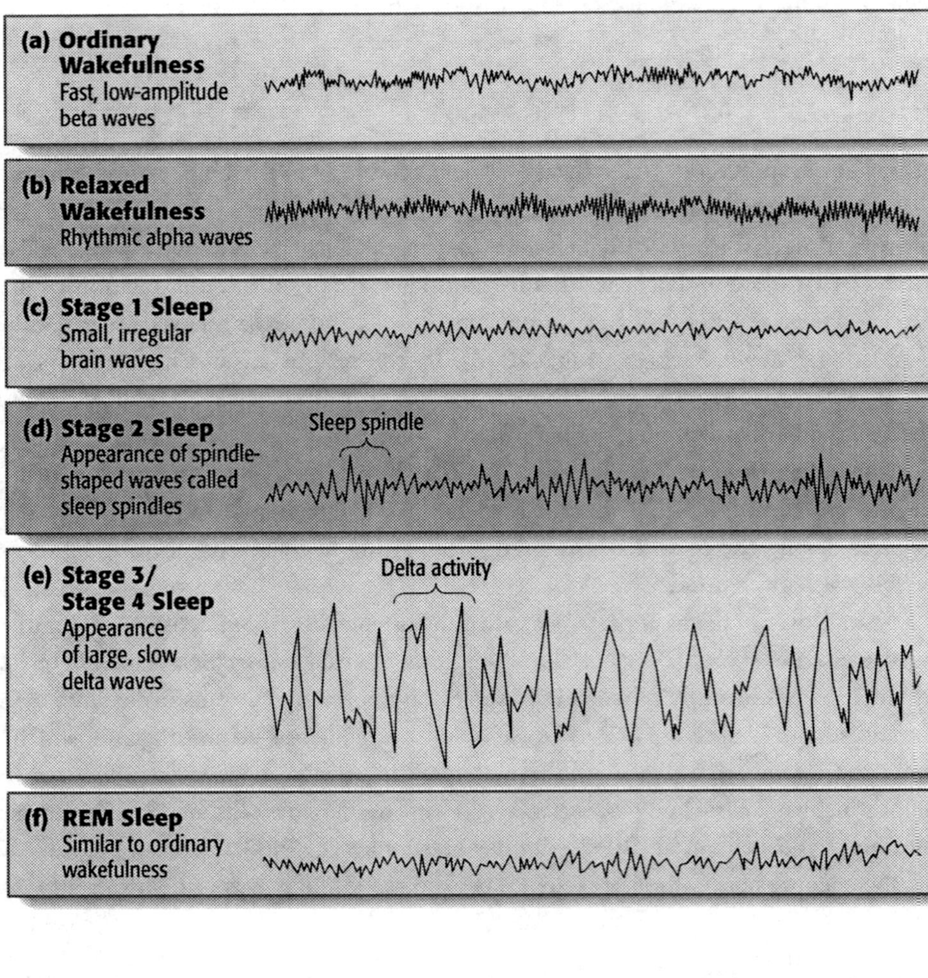

Figure 4.1 Brain Wave Patterns During Wakefulness and Sleep
Here we see the characteristic brain wave patterns associated with each stage of sleep. *(a)* Ordinary wakefulness: fast, low-amplitude beta waves; *(b)* relaxed wakefulness: rhythmic alpha waves; *(c)* Stage 1 sleep: small, irregular brain waves with varying frequencies; *(d)* Stage 2 sleep: sleep spindles; *(e)* Stage 3 and Stage 4 sleep: large, slow, delta waves; *(f)* REM sleep: rapid, active pattern similar to that in ordinary wakefulness.

been sleeping. Stage 2 sleep begins about two minutes after Stage 1 sleep and is characterized by bursts of brain wave activity represented by spindle-shaped waves called *sleep spindles.* People spend more than half of their sleep time in Stage 2 sleep. This is a deeper stage of sleep, but the person can still be readily awakened. Stages 3 and 4 of sleep, called *delta sleep* or *slow-wave sleep (SWS),* are characterized by the appearance of large, slow brain waves called *delta waves.* This is the period of deep sleep in which it is difficult to awaken the person. The distinction between Stage 3 and Stage 4 is based on the proportion of delta waves. In Stage 3, delta waves constitute 50 percent or fewer of the brain wave patterns; in Stage 4, they constitute more than 50 percent.

REM Sleep: The Stuff of Which Dreams Are Made

Rapid-eye-movement (REM) sleep is the stage of sleep in which one's eyes dart about under closed eyelids. After Stage 4 sleep, the sleeper briefly recycles through Stages 3 and 2 and from there enters REM sleep. REM is the stage of sleep most closely associated with dreaming. Dreams also occur during Stages 1 to 4—which are collectively called non-REM (NREM) sleep—but they are generally briefer, less frequent, and more thoughtlike than those experienced during REM sleep.

rapid-eye-movement (REM) sleep The stage of sleep that involves rapid eye movements and that is most closely associated with periods of dreaming.

The brain becomes more active during REM sleep, which is why it is sometimes called *active sleep.* As Robert Stickgold, a leading sleep researcher, explains, "During sleep, our brain is very active. Much of that activity helps the brain to learn, to remember, and to make connections" (cited in Stickgold & Wehrwein, 2009).

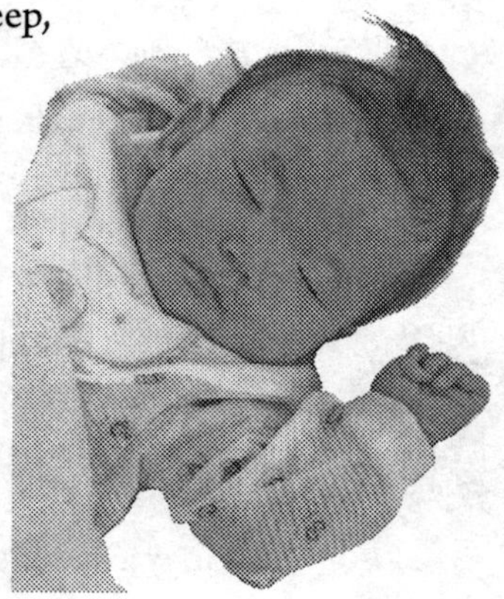

© grafica/Shutterstock.com

Brain wave patterns during REM sleep are similar to those during states of alert wakefulness. REM sleep is also called *paradoxical sleep.* What makes it paradoxical is that despite a high level of brain activity, muscle activity is blocked to the point that the person is practically paralyzed. This is indeed fortunate, as it prevents injuries that might occur if dreamers were to suddenly bolt out of bed and act out their dreams.

Sleep cycles generally repeat about every 90 minutes. The average person has about four or five sleep cycles during a night's sleep. It may take about an hour to reach Stage 4 sleep in the first cycle and then another 30 or 40 minutes to reach REM. As the night goes on, the amount of time spent in REM sleep increases (see ■ Figure 4.2). Moreover, Stage 4 sleep disappears during the course of the night, which means that we progress faster to REM sleep as the night wears on.

Concept Chart 4.2 summarizes the different states of wakefulness and stages of sleep.

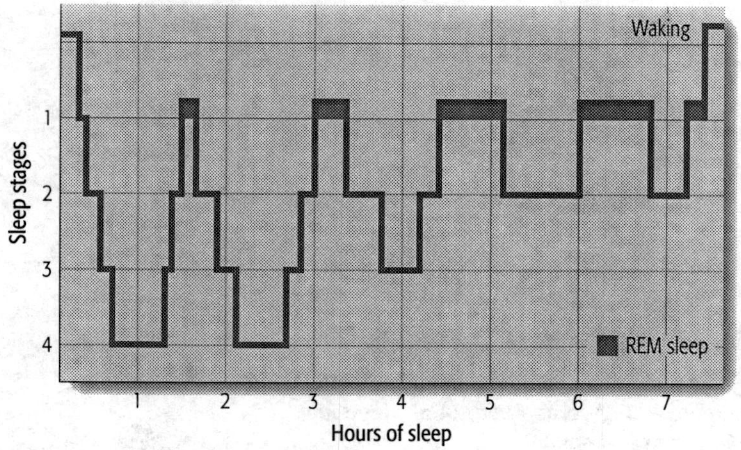

Figure 4.2 REM Sleep Through the Night
Notice how periods of REM sleep become longer as sleep progresses through the night.

Why Do We Sleep?

Humans and nearly all other animals sleep, although the average length of sleep varies across species (see ■ Figure 4.3). The near universality of sleep throughout the animal kingdom suggests that it serves an important function in the struggle to survive. Yet scientists still debate the functions of sleep (Walker & Stickgold, 2006). As one leading sleep

CONCEPT CHART 4.2 Wakefulness and Sleep

State of Wakefulness/ Stage of Sleep	Characteristic Brain Wave Pattern	Key Features
Alert wakefulness	Fast, low-amplitude beta waves	State of focused attention or active thought
Relaxed wakefulness	Slower, rhythmic alpha waves	State of resting quietly with eyes closed
Stage 1 sleep	Small, irregular brain waves with varying frequencies	Light sleep from which the person can be easily awakened
Stage 2 sleep	Sleep spindles	Deeper sleep, but the sleeper is still readily awakened
Stage 3 sleep	Large, slow delta waves	Deep sleep (called delta sleep or slow-wave sleep) from which it is difficult to arouse the sleeper
Stage 4 sleep	Dominance of delta waves	Deepest level of sleep
REM sleep	Rapid, active pattern, similar to that in alert wakefulness	Sleep in which the brain becomes more active but muscle activity is blocked (also called active sleep or paradoxical sleep); stage associated with dreaming

© Joy Brown/Shutterstock.com

researcher, Alan Rechtschaffen, put it, "If sleep doesn't serve an absolutely vital function, it is the biggest mistake evolution ever made" (cited in Azar, 2006, p. 55). Here we consider several of the leading theories of sleep.

One leading theory posits that sleep serves a *protective* function in keeping the organism out of harm's way. A sleeping animal may be less conspicuous to predators that roam about at night and less likely to suffer dangerous falls or accidents that could arise from moving about in the dark (Gaulin & McBurney, 2001).

Sleep may also help an organism conserve bodily energy (Gilestro, Tononi, & Cirelli, 2009; Miller, 2009). The lowering of body temperature during sleep may give warm-blooded animals, such as humans and other mammals, more energy to maintain the higher body temperature they need during the waking state.

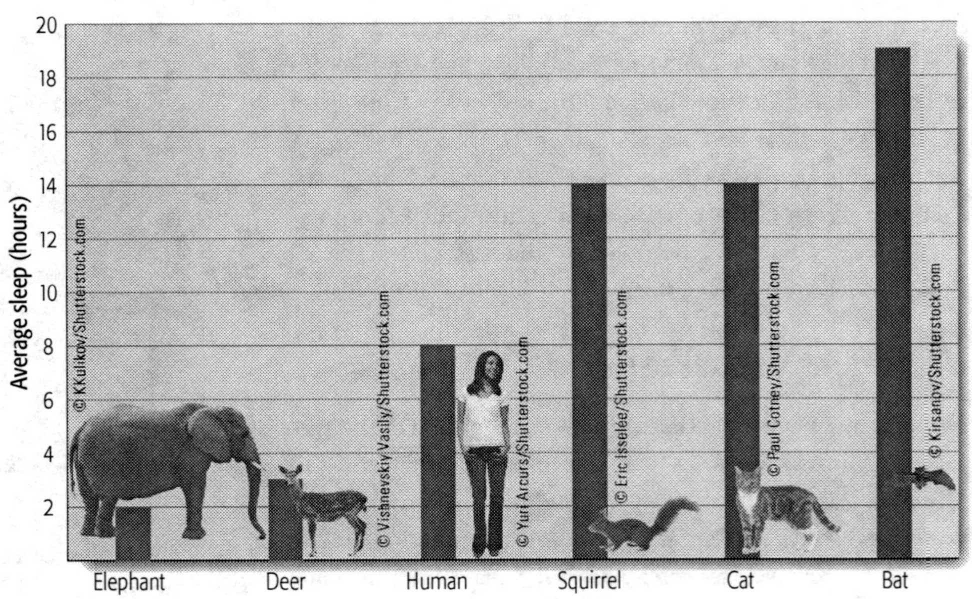

Figure 4.3 Average Length of Sleep in Different Mammals
The average amount of sleep varies among animal species.

Sleep may also serve a *restorative* function, helping the brain recover from daily wear and tear and replenishing vital proteins used by the body during the day's busy activities (Winerman, 2006). The restorative function of sleep may explain the subjective experience of feeling rested and mentally alert after a good night's sleep.

Sleep may play an important role in *consolidating* newly formed memories of daily experiences into more lasting ones (Arnold, 2011; Stickgold & Wehrwein, 2009). Recent evidence shows that the sleeping brain works on information acquired during the day to process and consolidate new memories (Wamsley et al., 2010; Wilhelm et al., 2011). Would you like to improve your ability to remember newly learned material? Here's a suggestion bolstered by recent research: sleep on it. In a recent study, participants who learned a word list in the evening and then went to sleep before being tested the following morning did better than others who learned the material in the morning but were tested later that evening before they had a chance to sleep (Ellenbogen et al., 2006).

CONCEPT 4.10
Sleep may serve many functions, including a protective function, an energy conservation function, a restorative function, and a memory consolidation function.

→ Concept Link
Newly learned material may be better retained when you have the chance to sleep on it. See Module 6.2.

Want to reduce your chances of catching the common cold? Get more sleep. Evidence suggests that sleep bolsters the body's ability to defend itself against disease-causing agents. In a recent study, investigators found that research participants who slept less than seven hours a night were nearly three times more likely to develop a cold after exposure to a cold virus than were those who slept eight hours or more (Cohen et al., 2009). As the study's lead researcher, psychologist Sheldon Cohen, pointed out, "Regular sleep habits may play an important role in your immune system's ability to fight off infectious disease" (cited in Reinberg, 2009). Not surprisingly, you may find yourself more susceptible to the common cold and other ailments when you've gone without your necessary quota of sleep.

CONCEPT 4.11
Though we all dream while asleep, the question of why we dream remains unanswered.

Dreams and Dreaming

Why do we dream? The short answer is that no one really knows. In all likelihood, dreaming has multiple functions, as sleep does. One of these functions may relate to memory consolidation. Evidence points to a role of REM sleep in memory consolidation, the process by which freshly formed memories are turned into lasting ones (Huber et al., 2004; Ribeiro & Nicolelis, 2004). Scientists suspect the brain may replay waking experiences during the dream state in order to strengthen new memories (Ji & Wilson, 2007; Miller, 2007).

Dreams may have other functions as well. Ernest Hartmann, a leading dream investigator, believes that dreams help us sort through possible solutions to everyday problems and concerns and work through emotional crises or traumas (Hartmann, 1998). Consistent with this view, the content of many dreams involves encountering difficulties while trying to perform a task (Maggiolini et al., 2010).

Another prominent view of dreaming, called the **activation-synthesis hypothesis** (Hobson, 1999), holds that dreams represent an attempt by the cerebral cortex to make sense of random discharges of electrical activity in the brain during REM sleep. The electrical activity arises from the brain stem, the part of the brain responsible for such basic functions as breathing and heart rate (see ■ Figure 4.4). According to this hypothesis, the cerebral cortex creates a story line based on the individual's storehouse of knowledge and memories to explain these random signals emanating from lower brain structures and the emotions and sensory experiences they generate.

activation-synthesis hypothesis The proposition that dreams represent the brain's attempt to make sense of the random discharges of electrical activity that occur during REM sleep.

Interestingly, there is decreased activity during REM sleep in parts of the cerebral cortex involved in logical thought. This may explain why many dreams seem to lack the

Figure 4.4 Activation-Synthesis Hypothesis
According to the activation-synthesis hypothesis, dreams arise when the cerebral cortex attempts to make sense of random electrical discharges emanating from the brain stem during REM sleep.

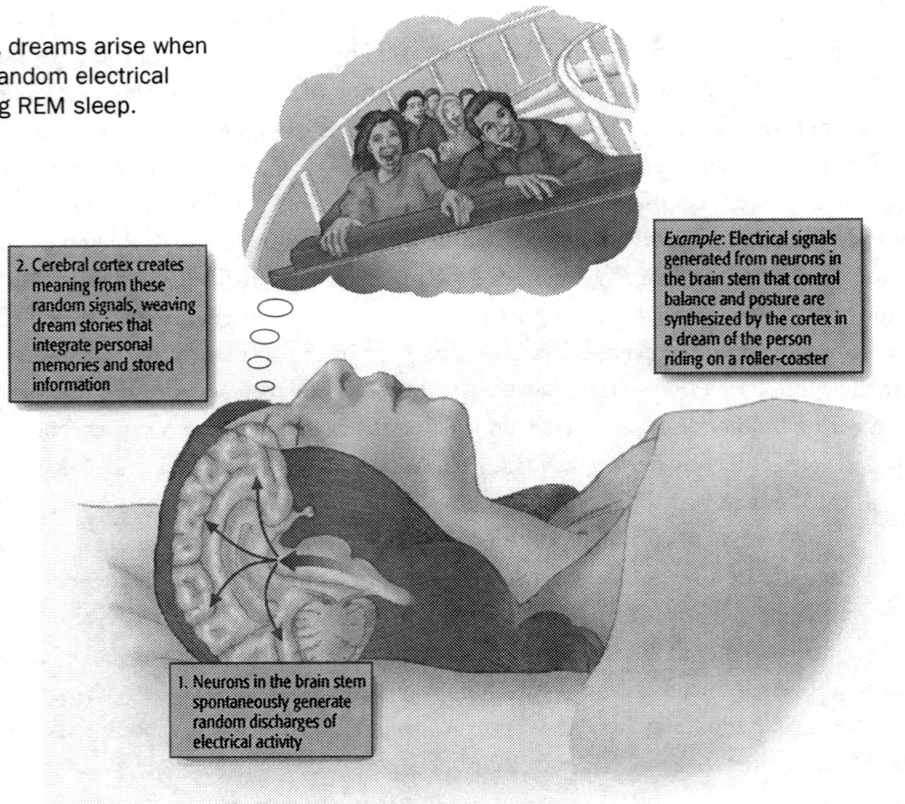

logical ordering of events of ordinary conscious thought—why they may form from bits and pieces of emotionally charged memories and vivid imagery that unfold in a chaotic sequence of events.

Even if dreams emanate from a hodgepodge of electrical discharges from the deep recesses of the brain, they may be filled with personal meaning since they are based on individual memories and associations. But what, if anything, do they mean?

Sigmund Freud (1900) had an answer to this question in arguing that dreams represent a form of *wish fulfillment.* According to Freud, dreams contain symbols that represent the sleeper's underlying wishes, usually of a sexual or aggressive nature. He called dreams the "royal road" to the unconscious mind, but he believed you needed a kind of psychological road map to interpret them because the dream symbols mask their true meanings. Freud distinguished between two types of dream content:

© Images.com/Corbis

Why do we dream? Although speculations about dreams abound, their meaning remains a mystery.

1. *Manifest content.* The manifest content refers to events that occur in the dream. You might dream, for example, of driving fast and getting a speeding ticket from a police officer.
2. *Latent content.* This is the true, underlying meaning of the dream, disguised in the form of dream symbols. The disguise conceals the dream's real meaning, thereby helping preserve sleep by preventing emotionally threatening material from waking you up. Driving fast might symbolize an unacceptable sexual wish. The police officer, a symbol of male authority, might represent your father punishing you for having the sexual wish.

In Freud's view, phallic objects such as trees, skyscrapers, snakes, and guns are symbols of male genitalia, whereas enclosed objects such as boxes, closets, and ovens symbolize female genitalia. But Freud believed we shouldn't rush to judgment when

TRY THIS OUT Dream a Little Dream for Me

Can you determine what you dream about? To find out, try this experiment:

1. Before retiring for the night, select a topic to dream about—for example, meeting a famous person or playing your favorite sport—and put a pen and pad within handy reach of your bed.
2. For 10 or 15 minutes before retiring, mentally rehearse the dream by fantasizing about the topic.
3. Upon retiring, say to yourself, "I think I'll dream some more about this."
4. As you grow sleepier, return to the fantasy, but don't resist letting your mind wander off.
5. When you awake, whether in the middle of the night or the next morning, lie still while you recollect what you dreamed about, then immediately reach for your pen and pad and write down the dream content.
6. Evaluate your results. Were you able to program your dream in advance?

interpreting dream symbols—that sometimes "a cigar is just a cigar." Freud also recognized that the same dream events might have different meanings for different people, so individual analysis is necessary to ferret out their particular meanings (Pesant & Zadra, 2004).

Dream interpretation makes for an interesting exercise, but how do we know that our interpretations are accurate? Unfortunately, although the meaning of dreams has been studied and debated for more than a century since Freud's initial work, we still lack any objective means of verifying the accuracy of dream interpretations. Nor do we have any evidence that dreams serve the function of preserving sleep, as Freud proposed. At the very least, we should credit Freud with raising our awareness that dreams may have a psychological meaning and may express underlying emotional issues.

Whatever the underlying meaning of dreams may be, investigators find that some people report **lucid dreams**—dreams in which the person is aware of dreaming (Erlacher & Schredl, 2008; Holzinger, LaBerge, & Levitan, 2006). However, relatively few people report experiencing lucid dreams regularly. We also lack evidence to support the claims of some lucid dreamers that they can determine beforehand what they will dream about or can consciously direct the action of a dream as it unfolds (see *Try This Out*).

lucid dreams Dreams in which the dreamer is aware that he or she is dreaming.

On the other hand, psychologists find that thinking about something shortly before sleep or trying not to think about something both increase the chances of dreaming about it (A. O'Connor, 2004b; Wegner, Wenzlaff, & Kozak, 2004). So trying to keep something out of mind can have the unintended consequence of making it more likely to pop up in your dreams. All the mental energy expended in suppressing a thought may actually tag the thought as something meaningful your brain incorporates in your dreams. Table 4.2 offers some answers to common questions people often ask about dreams.

Sleep Deprivation: Getting By on Less

Though people vary in their need for sleep, most require between seven and nine hours of sleep to feel fully refreshed and to function at their best. However, according to a recent national survey, nearly one in three Americans report sleeping six hours or less a night (CDC, 2008) (see ■ Figure 4.5). College students tend to be even sleepier, averaging only 6.0 to 6.9 hours sleep a night (Markel, 2003). Among high school students, only about 15 percent report sleeping the recommended 8.5 hours they need (Kantrowitz & Springen, 2003).

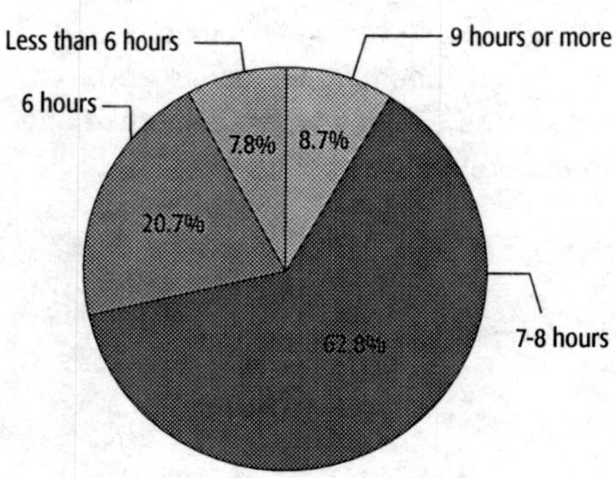

Figure 4.5 How Long We Sleep
Nearly one in three Americans fail to get the recommended seven to nine hours of sleep a night.
Source: CDC, National Health Interview Survey, 2008.

TABLE 4.2 Questions and Answers About Dreams

Question	Answer
Do dreams foretell the future?	People who believe they have had prophetic dreams may point to one or two "hits" (correspondences between dream events and real-life events). But they overlook the many times when they dreamed about an event that did not occur. No credible scientific evidence supports the belief that dreams foretell the future. Any correspondence between a dream event and the same event in real life may be mere coincidence.
Do we dream in color?	We cannot give a definitive answer, since we must rely on dream reports (people recalling their dreams upon awakening) rather than direct dream experience. But in laboratory-based sleep studies the great majority of people report that they dream in color.
Do animals dream?	Nonhuman animals cannot tell us if they dream, so the question is moot. But we know from laboratory studies that other mammals show similar brain activation patterns as humans do when they sleep. These brain responses indicate a kind of wordless dream state in other mammals when they sleep.
Do dreams occur in a flash?	Actually, dreams events unfold in near real time. Dreams typically last from about five to 45 minutes.
Do blind people dream?	People who have been blind since birth do dream, but they do not have visual images in their dreams. Their dreams involve other sense experiences, such as tactile, auditory, and bodily sensations. In effect, they feel or touch their dreams, rather than see them. People who lose their sight after about the age of seven do retain the capacity to have visual images when they dream, at least for some 20 or 30 years after losing their vision.
If you dream about falling from a high place, will you die if you fail to wake up in time?	Certainly not. Many people have dreams of falling and hitting the ground or even of dying, but they don't actually fall or die.

© Carlos Caetano/Shutterstock.com

Source: Hobson, 2002; Kerr & Homhoff, 2004; Schredl et al., 2008, among other sources.

CONCEPT 4.12
Though people vary in how much sleep they need, most people require seven to nine hours of sleep to feel refreshed and to perform at their best.

Newborn infants sleep about 16 hours a day. Infants also spend a greater proportion of sleep time in REM sleep than do older children and adults. The amount of REM sleep gradually declines during childhood and continues to decline throughout adulthood. Both total sleep and time spent in deep sleep also decline as we age, while periods of wakefulness increase. By late adulthood, most people report sleeping only about six or seven hours per night.

If you miss a few hours of sleep, you may feel a little groggy the next day but will probably be able to muddle through. However, sleep deprivation slows reaction times, impairs attention, concentration, and problem-solving ability, and makes it more difficult to remember recently learned information (Hampton, 2008; Lim & Dinges, 2010; Stickgold & Wehrwein, 2009). It's no surprise that many Americans are sleepy, considering that many of them don't get to bed until the wee small hours of the morning (see ■ Figure 4.6). As many as 15 percent of Americans don't get the sleep they need because of lifestyle factors, such as demanding work schedules and caregiving responsibilities (Minerd & Jasmer, 2006).

Not surprisingly, sleep deprivation is among the most common causes of motor vehicle accidents. Such accidents are most likely to occur in the early morning hours, when drivers are typically at their sleepiest. Nor should we be surprised that when extended work shifts among overworked medical interns are eliminated, the frequency of attentional failures during work shifts declines (Lockley et al., 2004).

It's not just the total amount of sleep that affects our functioning, but also the type of sleep. Lack of REM sleep impairs learning ability and memory (Greer, 2004b). REM sleep also helps boost creative problem-solving ability, which is yet another reason not to skimp on sleep (Mednick et al., 2009).

Although temporary periods of sleep deprivation are not linked to lasting ill effects, burning the candle at both ends is potentially hazardous to your health. Prolonged periods of sleep deprivation increase the risk of developing hypertension (high blood pressure), a serious cardiovascular disorder and potential killer (Bakalar, 2006a; Egan, 2006; Motivala & Irwin, 2007). However, we shouldn't become alarmed if we miss a few hours of sleep; rather, we should attempt to restore our normal sleep pattern the following night.

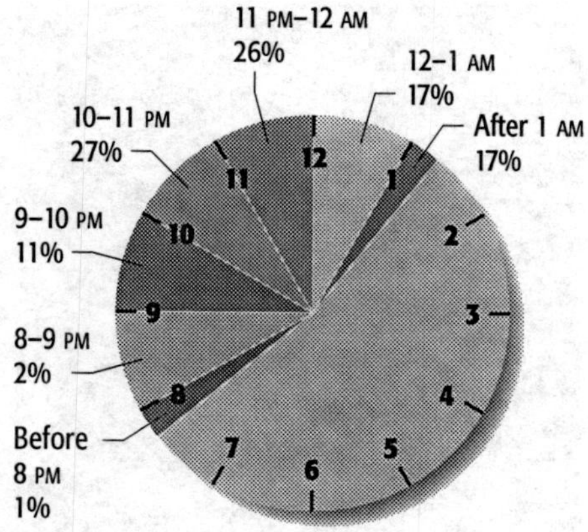

Note: Percentages do not sum to 100% due to rounding.

Figure 4.6 When America Goes to Bed Living in a "24/7" world in which we can watch movies and news all night long or even order a pizza at 2:00 a.m. has taken its toll on America's sleep habits. One reason that many Americans don't get enough sleep is that they are going to bed too late.

Source: Adapted from Sleepless in America, a survey conducted by the ACNielsen Company, April 2005, retrieved from http://us.acnielsen.com/news/20050404.shtml.

Sleep Disorders: When Normal Sleep Eludes Us

Sleep disorders are disturbances of sleep that interfere with getting a good night's sleep and remaining alert during the day. The most common sleep disorder is chronic insomnia, which affects about one in 10 U.S. adults (Smith & Perlis, 2006). People with insomnia have difficulty falling asleep, remaining asleep, or returning to sleep after nighttime awakenings. Insomnia prevents people from achieving restorative sleep—the type of sleep that leaves them feeling refreshed and alert in the morning.

Insomnia is caused by many factors, including substance abuse, physical illness, and psychological disorders like depression. If the underlying problem is resolved, chances are that sleep patterns will return to normal. Problem sleep habits, such as bringing daily worries and concerns to bed, may also lead to insomnia. Worrying is accompanied by increased bodily arousal, which can prevent normal sleep. Thinking it is absolutely necessary to get a full night's sleep can also bump up the person's anxiety level (Sánchez-Ortuño & Edinger, 2010). The harder the person tries to fall asleep, the more difficult it becomes. The lesson here is that sleep is a natural function that cannot be forced.

CONCEPT 4.13
The amount of REM sleep you get affects your ability to function at your best.

insomnia Difficulty falling asleep, remaining asleep, or returning to sleep after nighttime awakenings.

Narcolepsy, a sleep disorder afflicting some 150,000 Americans, is characterized by sudden, unexplained "sleep attacks" occurring during daytime hours (Siegel, 2004). A person with narcolepsy may be engaged in conversation one moment and collapse on the floor the next, fast asleep. In contrast to the normal sleep pattern in which REM sleep occurs after several stages of non-REM sleep, REM sleep usually begins almost immediately after the onset of a narcoleptic attack. The sleep episode lasts usually for about 15 minutes. In some cases, the sleep attack is preceded by frightening hallucinations that may involve several senses—visual, auditory, tactile, or kinesthetic (body movement).

CONCEPT 4.14
Sleep disorders are disturbances of sleep that prevent a person from getting a good night's sleep and remaining awake or alert during the day.

narcolepsy A disorder characterized by sudden unexplained "sleep attacks" during the day.

Sleep attacks can be very dangerous. Household accidents due to falls are common. Even more disturbing, some patients report narcoleptic attacks while driving. Genetics plays a role in narcolepsy, which is believed to be caused by a loss of brain cells in an area of the hypothalamus that produces a chemical needed to maintain wakefulness (Dauvilliers, Arnulf, & Mignot, 2007; Goel et al., 2010). The available

© iStockphoto.com/Pawel Gaul

Sleep deprivation does not just leave you feeling groggy; it also slows your reaction times and impairs your concentration, memory, and problem-solving ability.

treatments include daytime naps and use of stimulant drugs (amphetamines) to help maintain wakefulness.

People with **sleep apnea** may momentarily stop breathing many times during a night's sleep, even hundreds of times (Friedman, 2008; Kumar et al., 2008). (The word *apnea* means "without breath.") Sleep apnea affects an estimated 20 million Americans and is more common in men, especially middle-aged men, and among obese people.

Sleep apnea is caused by a structural defect, such as an overly thick palate or enlarged tonsils, that partially or fully blocks the flow of air through the upper airways. With complete blockage, people may stop breathing for perhaps 15 seconds or as long as 90 seconds. They usually awaken the next morning with no memory of these episodes. However, their fitful sleep patterns deprive them of solid sleep, so that they are sleepy during the day and have difficulty functioning at their best. For reasons that aren't clear, people with sleep apnea stand an increased risk of stroke and hypertension (high blood pressure) (Yaggi et al., 2005). They also snore very loudly (described as "industrial strength" snoring) because of their narrowed airways. The disorder may be treated with certain appliances, such as a nose mask that exerts pressure to keep the upper airway passages open during sleep, or with surgery that opens narrowed airways.

sleep apnea Temporary cessation of breathing during sleep.

nightmare disorder A sleep disorder involving a pattern of frequent, disturbing nightmares.

sleep terror disorder A sleep disorder involving repeated episodes of intense fear during sleep, causing the person to awake abruptly in a terrified state.

sleepwalking disorder A sleep disorder characterized by repeated episodes of sleepwalking.

People with **nightmare disorder** have frequent, disturbing nightmares. Children are especially prone to nightmare disorder. Nightmares are storylike dreams that contain threats to the dreamer's life or safety. The action of the nightmare may be vivid and intense—falling through space or fleeing from attackers or giant insects. Nightmares typically take place during REM sleep. People are usually more susceptible to nightmares when they are under emotional stress, have high fevers, or are suffering from sleep deprivation.

People with **sleep terror disorder** have frequent "night terrors," which are more intense than ordinary nightmares. Unlike nightmares, which occur mainly during REM sleep, night terrors occur during deep sleep. The disorder primarily affects children, and it affects boys more often than girls. Night terrors begin with a loud panicky scream. The child may sit up in bed, appear dazed and frightened, and be able to remember only fragmentary dream images, rather than the detailed dream stories that typically are remembered after nightmares. Most children outgrow the condition by adolescence.

Sleepwalking disorder is another sleep disorder that occurs more often in children than in adults. Occasional childhood sleepwalking episodes are normal, but persistent sleepwalking is indicative of a sleep disorder. In a sleepwalking episode, the person remains soundly asleep while walking about with eyes open and perhaps an expressionless look on his or her face. Though sleepwalkers generally avoid knocking into things, accidents do occur. The following morning, the sleepwalker usually remembers nothing of the nighttime wanderings. Sleepwalking typically occurs during deep, dreamless sleep. Despite the belief to the contrary, there is no harm in (gently) awakening a sleepwalker.

Sleep disorders are often treated with sleep medications that help induce sleep. However, sleep drugs can lead to physiological dependence and should be used for only a brief period of time, a few weeks at most (Pollack, 2004a). Alternatively, psychological techniques such as cognitive-behavioral therapy that focus on changing problem sleep habits (see Module 4.5 of this chapter) are just as effective as sleep medication in treating insomnia in the short term and more effective over the long term (Dolan et al., 2010; Ebben & Spielman, 2009; Morin, 2010; Perlis et al., 2008).

4.2 MODULE REVIEW Sleeping and Dreaming

Recite It

How are our sleep-wake cycles regulated?

➤ The suprachiasmatic nucleus (SCN), a clocklike mechanism in the hypothalamus, regulates our sleep-wake cycles according to a circadian rhythm that approximates the 24-hour day.

What are the stages of sleep?

➤ In addition to REM sleep, there are four non-REM stages of sleep (Stages 1 through 4); in these stages, sleep becomes increasingly deep. The brain is relatively active during REM sleep, which is when most dreaming occurs.

What functions does sleep serve?

➤ Though no one knows for sure, sleep experts suspect that sleep may serve several functions, including a protective function, an energy conservation function, a restorative function, and a memory consolidation function.

Why do we dream?

➤ Again, no one can say for sure, but theories include the belief that dreams are needed to consolidate memories and experiences that occur during the day; Hartmann's view that dreams help people work out their everyday problems; the activation-synthesis hypothesis; and Freud's view that dreaming helps preserve sleep by disguising potentially threatening wishes or impulses in the form of dream symbols.

What are sleep disorders?

➤ Sleep disorders are disturbances in the amount or quality of sleep. They include insomnia, narcolepsy, sleep apnea, nightmare disorder, sleep terror disorder, and sleepwalking. The most common sleep disorder is insomnia.

Recall It

1. The sleep-wake cycle operates according to a ______ cycle.
2. Deep sleep, which is characterized by delta brain wave patterns, occurs during
   a. Stages 1 and 2 of sleep.
   b. Stages 2 and 3 of sleep.
   c. Stages 3 and 4 of sleep.
   d. REM sleep.
3. Sleep may help the body replenish resources expended during wakefulness. What is this function of sleep called?
4. Match each of the sleep disorders listed on the left with the appropriate description on the right:

i. narcolepsy	a. frequent, frightening dreams that usually occur during REM sleep.
ii. sleep terror disorder	b. intense nightmares that occur during deep sleep and primarily affect children.
iii. sleep apnea	c. sudden, unexplained "sleep attacks" during the day.
iv. nightmare disorder	d. temporary cessation of breathing during sleep.

Think About It

➤ Have you experienced jet lag? How did it affect you? What might you do differently in the future to cope with it? One suggestion is to gradually alter your body clock by adjusting the time you go to bed by an hour a day for several days before your trip. If you will be away for only a brief time, you might be better off to follow your body clock as much as possible during the trip.

➤ Many college students disrupt their normal sleep-wake cycles by staying up all hours of the night and then napping during the day to catch up on missed sleep. They may feel as though they are continually suffering from jet lag. What would you suggest to help someone get his or her sleep cycle back on track?

➤ How would you rate your sleep habits? What specific changes can you make to improve them? (For some suggestions on developing healthier sleep habits, see Module 4.5.)

➤ Apply each of the major theories of dreaming—Hartmann's belief that dreams allow us to sort through potential solutions to everyday problems and concerns, Freud's wish-fulfillment theory, and the activation-synthesis hypothesis—to a particular dream or dreams you are able to recall. Which of these theories do you believe best accounts for your dream or dreams?

MODULE 4.3

Altering Consciousness Through Meditation and Hypnosis

- What is meditation?
- What is hypnosis?
- What are the major theories of hypnosis?

We venture now from considering states of ordinary wakefulness and sleep to considering states of altered consciousness. Some people use psychoactive drugs to achieve altered states of consciousness, whereas others may practice meditation or undergo hypnosis. You might not think of meditation and hypnosis as having much in common, but both involve rituals that focus on the narrowing of attention or concentration to achieve an altered state of consciousness.

Meditation: Achieving a Peaceful State by Focusing Your Attention

SLICE OF LIFE A group of Americans traveled to a remote village in India on a hopeful journey (Ornstein, 1973). They sought an audience with a venerable Indian guru (teacher) whom they hoped would invite them to participate in a secret initiation or share with them a magic word. Upon arriving in India, they travelled overland, walking over rugged hilly trails for many days until they finally arrived at their destination. At great length they told the guru of their long and arduous journey. They implored him to share his wisdom so that they too could achieve inner peace and harmony. The guru then turned to the travelers and said but a few words: "Sit, facing the wall, and count your breaths. This is all."

This is all, the travelers wondered? This was the secret of great wisdom for which they had trekked halfway around the world? They could have learned this at home! A few of them realized this was actually the point of the guru's lesson.

meditation A process of focused attention that induces a relaxed, contemplative state.

transcendental meditation (TM) A form of meditation in which practitioners focus their attention by repeating a particular mantra.

mantra A sound or phrase chanted repeatedly during transcendental meditation.

mindfulness meditation A form of meditation in which one adopts a state of nonjudgmental attention to the unfolding of experience on a moment-to-moment basis.

Counting your breaths is a form of **meditation**, a practice of narrowing consciousness so that ordinary demands and stresses of everyday life fade out of awareness. There are many forms of meditation, but they don't require a pilgrimage to a far-off destination to learn to practice them.

Meditation induces a relaxed, contemplative state through a process of narrowing attention. To remove all other thoughts from consciousness, practitioners of meditation narrow their attention to a single object or thought. The particular meditative technique used varies among cultures. In ancient Egypt, practitioners stared at an oil-burning lamp—a custom that may have inspired the tale of Aladdin's lamp. Yogis focus on the design of a vase or a graphic symbol. Other practitioners focus on a burning candle.

CONCEPT 4.15
Meditation involves practices that induce an altered state of consciousness through techniques of focused attention.

→ Concept Link
As a form of relaxation, meditation can help tone down the body's response to stress. See Module 12.3.

Practitioners of **transcendental meditation (TM)** focus their attention by repeating a phrase or sound (such as *ommm*), which is known as a **mantra**. In another form of meditation, **mindfulness meditation**, practitioners limit their attention to their unfolding experience on a moment-to-moment basis without bringing judgment to bear on their experience (Ludwig & Kabat-Zinn, 2008). Mindfulness is about being present in the moment rather than standing back and evaluating or judging the situation. The Dalai Lama, the Buddhist spiritual leader, likens mindfulness to "watching a river flow by" (Gyatso, 2003). Perhaps there is a meeting of the twain when it comes to East and West. Recall the Harvard iPhone app study discussed earlier in the chapter that suggests that focusing on the "here and now" may be linked to greater happiness (Killingsworth & Gilbert, 2010).

Some practitioners of meditation believe it does more than just relax the body and mind. They believe it expands their consciousness and allows them to experience a deeper state of awareness or a state of inner peace. Perhaps meditation achieves these effects by helping people tune out the outside world, thus allowing them more opportunity for inward focus. Yet many people practice meditation not to expand consciousness but to find relief from the stress of everyday life.

Many healthful benefits are associated with the practice of meditation, including combating effects of daily stress on the body, lowering blood pressure, and relieving chronic pain, insomnia, and even anxiety and depression (e.g., Kuyken et al., 2010; Manicavasgar, Parker, & Perich, 2011; Ong, Shapiro, & Manber, 2008; Segal et al., 2010; Treanor, 2011; Zeidan et al., 2011). Mindfulness meditation also produces physical changes in the brain linked to improved memory and better regulation of emotional states (Hölzela et al., 2011).

© Desmond Boylan/Reuters/Corbis

The Buddhist spiritual leader, the Dalai Lama, describes mindfulness as "watching a river flow by."

CONCEPT 4.16

Hypnosis is not sleep, but rather a relaxed state of focused attention in which a person may become more responsive to suggestions.

Hypnosis: You Are Now Getting Sleepier

Hypnosis is derived from the Greek word *hypnos*, meaning "sleep." Though definitions of **hypnosis** abound, it is most commonly defined as an altered state of consciousness characterized by focused attention, deep relaxation, and heightened susceptibility to suggestion. Techniques for inducing hypnosis vary, but they usually involve a narrowing of attention to the hypnotist's voice.

hypnosis An altered state of consciousness characterized by focused attention, deep relaxation, and heightened susceptibility to suggestion.

People who undergo hypnosis may feel sleepier, but they are not asleep. During a hypnotic induction, the hypnotist may ask the person to focus on an object, such as a swinging watch, and listen only to the sound of his or her voice. The hypnotist may also suggest that the person's eyelids are getting heavier and heavier and that the person is becoming sleepy.

Once the person becomes deeply relaxed, the hypnotist begins giving the person hypnotic suggestions that may lead to unusual experiences. These experiences include **hypnotic age regression** (reliving past events, usually from childhood) and **hypnotic analgesia** (loss of feeling or responsiveness to pain in certain parts of the body). Other hypnotic experiences include distortions of reality—seeing, hearing, or feeling something that is not present in reality (a *positive* hallucination), or not perceiving something, such as a pen or a chair, that truly does exist (a *negative* hallucination). Another kind of hypnotic experience in response to hypnotic suggestions is **posthypnotic amnesia**, an inability to recall what happened during hypnosis. Yet another type of hypnotic experience is **posthypnotic suggestion**, in which the hypnotist plants the idea that, after coming out of the hypnotic state, people will respond in particular ways (such as touching their ears or scratching their heads) when they hear a cue word—for example, *elephant*. A person may respond in the suggested way but deny any awareness of having performed the behavior.

hypnotic age regression A hypnotically induced experience that involves reexperiencing past events in one's life.

hypnotic analgesia A loss of feeling or responsiveness to pain in certain parts of the body occurring during hypnosis.

posthypnotic amnesia An inability to recall what happened during hypnosis.

posthypnotic suggestion A hypnotist's suggestion that the subject will respond in a particular way following hypnosis.

Theories of Hypnosis

Despite more than 100 years of scientific study, there is still no consensus about what hypnosis is or even how it should be defined (Vaitl et al., 2005). There is still an active debate about whether hypnosis involves anything more than a role a subject performs

CONCEPT 4.17
Two theoretical models that have guided recent research on hypnosis are the role-playing model and neodissociation theory.

in an attempt to please the hypnotist by following the hypnotist's every suggestion (Blakeslee, 2005). This point of view, called the *role-playing model*, proposes that hypnosis is a type of social interaction between a hypnotist and a subject willing to assume the role of a "good" hypnotic subject—one who faithfully follows the hypnotist's directions. This doesn't mean that hypnotic subjects are faking their responses, any more than you are faking your responses by playing the role of a good student, such as by raising your hand before speaking in class.

© Michael Newman/Photo Edit

The clinical use of hypnosis ranges from treating those with chronic pain to helping people stop smoking.

An alternative view of hypnosis is that it is a *trance state*—an altered state of awareness characterized by heightened *suggestibility*. Suggestibility is the readiness with which one complies with suggestions offered by others, such as a hypnotist. Yet many psychologists reject the view that hypnosis is a trance state, or even that it constitutes any altered state of consciousness (Kihlstrom, 2005; Lynn et al. 2008).

Some research supports the role-playing model. For example, when subjects are given a role-playing explanation of hypnosis before a hypnotic induction takes place, their later responses to hypnotic suggestions are either reduced or eliminated (Wagstaff & Frost, 1996). On the other hand, investigators find that patterns of brain activity in people who are hypnotized differ from those who are merely instructed to *act* as though they were hypnotized (Kosslyn et al., 2000). More research in this area is needed, but there appears to be something more to hypnosis than mere role playing (Bryant & Mallard, 2002).

neodissociation theory A theory of hypnosis based on the belief that hypnosis represents a state of dissociated (divided) consciousness.

hidden observer Hilgard's term for a part of consciousness that remains detached from the hypnotic experience but aware of everything that happens during it.

One leading theorist who believed that hypnosis is a special state of consciousness was the psychologist Ernest Hilgard (1977, 1994). His **neodissociation theory** rests on the belief that there are multiple levels of awareness that can be split off or dissociated from one another. Hypnosis induces a splitting of consciousness into two parts, a part that carries out the hypnotist's suggestions and another part, called the **hidden observer**, that stands apart, monitoring everything that happens. In hypnotic analgesia, for example, the person experiences a splitting off, or dissociation, of consciousness into one part that is aware of the pain (the hidden observer) and another part (the dissociated or hypnotized part) that is not.

The belief that hypnotists have special powers that give them control over the hypnotized subject may be part of the mystique of hypnosis, but it is not consistent with contemporary views. It is a widely held myth that hypnosis can cause people to commit murder or other immoral and illegal acts they wouldn't otherwise perform. On the contrary, hypnosis depends on the willingness of subjects to go along with imagining the alternate realities suggested by the hypnotist. In hypnotic age regression, for instance, people do not actually relive childhood incidents or experiences; they merely imagine themselves as children (T. X. Barber, 1999). The effects of hypnotic suggestion may have more to do with the efforts and skills of the people who are hypnotized than with those of the hypnotist (I. Kirsch & Lynn, 1995).

CONCEPT 4.18
The effectiveness of hypnosis may have more to do with the psychological characteristics of the hypnotized subject than with the skills of the hypnotist.

Though most people can be hypnotized to some extent, some are more hypnotizable, or susceptible to suggestions, than others. People who are highly hypnotizable tend to have a well-developed fantasy life, a vivid sense of imagination, a tendency to be forgetful, and a positive attitude toward hypnosis (T. X. Barber, 1999). These characteristics help them to think along with the hypnotist—to imagine whatever the hypnotist suggests, perhaps so vividly that it seems real to them.

The practice of hypnosis extends to the helping professions. Hypnosis is used to help people cope with pain and anxiety, lose excess weight, or quit smoking (e.g., Carmody et al., 2008; Hammond, 2007; Jensen, 2008). Hypnosis may even boost the body's

CONCEPT CHART 4.3 Altering Consciousness Through Meditation and Hypnosis

	Technique	Method of Induction	Key Points
 © Simon@naffarts.co.uk/ Shutterstock.com	Meditation	Narrowing attention to a single object, word, or thought or performing a repetitive ritual	Meditation relaxes the body and mind, helps combat stress, and can help people cope with pain. Some believe it leads to a sense of inner peace or spiritual enlightenment.
 © Tatiana Popova/Shutterstock.com	Hypnosis	Narrowing attention to the hypnotist's voice or a repetitive stimulus	Debate about the nature of hypnosis continues. Role-playing theory and neodissociation theory are major contemporary theories of hypnosis. All forms of hypnosis may actually involve self-hypnosis.

immune system to function better during times of stress (Kiecolt-Glaser et al., 2001; Patterson & Jensen, 2003). Though hypnosis may have therapeutic benefits, it should be used only as an additional or adjunctive treatment, not as a substitute for traditional treatment.

For a summary of altering consciousness through meditation and hypnosis, see Concept Chart 4.3.

4.3 MODULE REVIEW Altering Consciousness Through Meditation and Hypnosis

Recite It

What is meditation?

- Meditation is an altered state of consciousness induced by narrowing attention to a single object, word, or thought, or by performing a repetitive ritual.
- Meditation produces a relaxed state that may have therapeutic benefits in relieving stress and pain.

What is hypnosis?

- Although there is no consensus about the nature of hypnosis, it has traditionally been defined as an altered state of consciousness characterized by focused attention, deep relaxation, and heightened susceptibility to suggestion. Hypnosis is increasingly being used within mainstream psychology and medicine.

What are the major theories of hypnosis?

- The two major contemporary views of hypnosis are the role-playing model, which proposes that hypnosis is a form of social role playing, and neodissociation theory, which holds that hypnosis is a state of divided consciousness.

Recall It

1. The type of meditation in which practitioners focus their attention by repeating a mantra is called ________.
2. The loss of feeling or responsiveness to pain as a result of hypnotic suggestion is called ________.
3. The concept of a "hidden observer" is a central feature of which theory of hypnosis?

Think About It

- Have you ever practiced meditation? How did it affect your state of consciousness?
- Were you ever hypnotized? If so, what was the experience like? Whether or not you've experienced hypnosis, has reading this module changed any of your views about hypnosis? If so, how?
- Do you believe the concept of the "hidden observer" is an example of a special state of consciousness? Why or why not?

MODULE 4.4

Altering Consciousness Through Drugs

- When does drug use cross the line from use to abuse and dependence?
- What are depressants?
- What are stimulants?
- What are hallucinogens?
- What factors contribute to alcohol and drug abuse?
- What treatment alternatives are available to help people with drug problems?

Most people who want to change their states of waking consciousness don't turn to meditation or hypnosis. They are more likely to pop a pill, drink an alcoholic beverage, or smoke a joint.

Psychoactive drugs are chemical substances that act on the brain to affect emotional or mental states. They affect mood, thought processes, perceptions, and behavior. People use psychoactive drugs for many reasons: to change their level of alertness (stimulants to perk them up; depressants to relax them and make them drowsy so they can fall asleep), to alter their mental states by getting "high" or induce feelings of intense pleasure (a euphoric "rush"), to blunt awareness of the stresses and strains of daily life, or to seek some type of inner truth. Some psychoactive drugs, including heroin, cocaine, and marijuana, are illegal or *illicit*. Others, such as alcohol and nicotine (found in tobacco), are legally available, but restrictions are placed on their use or sale. Another legal psychoactive drug, caffeine, is so widely used that many people don't realize they are ingesting a psychoactive drug when they drink a caffeinated beverage or eat a chocolate bar (yes, chocolate contains caffeine).

Nearly half of adult Americans admit to having used an illicit drug at some point in their lives, with marijuana topping the list of the most widely used illicit substances (SAMHSA, 2010a) (see ■ Figure 4.7). Nearly one in 10 Americans (8.7% according to the latest available statistics) age 12 and older report currently using illicit drugs (CDC, 2010a; SAMHSA, 2010b). Troubling signs are on the horizon, as marijuana use among youths has been rising in recent years (Johnston et al., 2010a; Kuehn, 2011). However, use of illicit drugs pales in comparison to two psychoactive substances that adults may use legally—alcohol and tobacco. Alcoholic beverages contain the depressant drug alcohol and tobacco products such as cigarettes contain the stimulant drug nicotine. Despite the fact that all states prohibit drinking by persons under the age of 21, nearly three in four high school seniors (70%) have tried alcohol, as have more than one in three (37%) 8th graders (Johnston et al., 2010b). More than half of high school students report having been drunk at least once. One in five high school students smoke, and some 1,000 teenagers begin smoking on any given day, setting the stage for addiction, serious health consequences, and premature death (SAMHSA, 2010b).

In this module we examine the risks associated with drug use, the factors that may lead people to use and abuse drugs, and ways of helping people with substance abuse problems.

THE BRAIN LOVES A PUZZLE

As you read ahead, use the information in the text to solve the following puzzle:

> *How might being "able to hold your liquor" be a genetic risk factor for developing problems with alcohol?*

psychoactive drugs Chemical substances that affect a person's mental or emotional state.

CONCEPT 4.19
Psychoactive substances—depressants, stimulants, and hallucinogens—are drugs that alter the user's mental state.

Drug Abuse: When Drug Use Causes Harm

Drug use becomes *drug abuse* when repeated use causes or aggravates personal, occupational, or health-related problems (American Psychiatric Association, 2000). **Drug abuse** is maladaptive or dangerous use of a chemical substance. If drug use impairs a person's health or ability to function at home, in school, or on the job, or if it becomes associated with dangerous behavior such as drinking and driving, the person has crossed the line from use to abuse. If you repeatedly miss school or work because you are drunk or "sleeping it off," you are abusing alcohol. You may not admit you have a drug problem, but you do. People who abuse more than one drug at a time are called **polyabusers**.

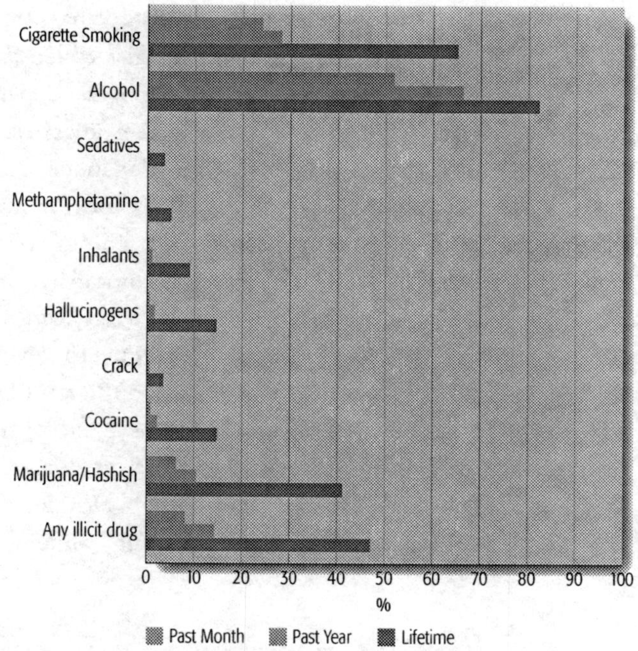

Figure 4.7 Reported Use of Illicit Drugs by U.S. Adults Nearly half of adult Americans admit to having used an illicit (illegal) drug at some point in their lives.
Source: Substance Abuse and Mental Health Services Administration (SAMSHA). Results from the 2008 National Survey on Drug Use and Health: National Findings, updated 2010; http://oas.samhsa.gov/NSDUH/2K8NSDUH/tabs/toc.htm.

Drug Dependence: When the Drug Takes Control

Drug abuse often leads to **drug dependence**, a severe drug-related problem characterized by impaired control over the use of a drug. People who become dependent on a drug feel compelled to use the drug or powerless to stop using it, even when they know the drug use is ruining their lives. About one in 10 adults in the United States develop a drug abuse or dependence disorder at some point in their lives (Compton et al., 2005).

Drug dependence is usually, but not always, associated with *physiological dependence* (also called *chemical dependence*). In **physiological dependence**, the result of repeated drug use, a person's body chemistry changes and comes to depend on a steady supply of the drug. When people with a drug dependence abruptly stop using the drug, they may experience a cluster of unpleasant and sometimes dangerous symptoms called a **withdrawal syndrome** (also called an *abstinence syndrome*). Another frequent sign of physiological dependence is **tolerance**, the need to increase the amount of a drug so that it has the same effect.

Professionals use the terms *drug abuse* and *drug dependence* to describe the different types of substance-use disorders. Laypeople more often use the term *drug addiction*,

© Don Mason/CORBIS

© Micah Hanson/Alamy

Many people use alcohol socially, but when does use cross over into abuse? According to mental health professionals, drug use becomes drug abuse when it leads to damaging or dangerous consequences.

CONCEPT 4.20
Drug use becomes abuse when it becomes maladaptive and either causes or contributes to personal, occupational, or health-related problems.

drug abuse Maladaptive or dangerous use of a chemical substance.

polyabusers People who abuse more than one drug at a time.

drug dependence A severe drug-related problem characterized by impaired control over the use of the drug.

physiological dependence A state of physical dependence on a drug caused by repeated usage that changes body chemistry.

withdrawal syndrome A cluster of symptoms associated with abrupt withdrawal from a drug.

tolerance A form of physical habituation to a drug in which increased amounts are needed to achieve the same effect.

CONCEPT 4.21
People who are psychologically dependent on drugs use them habitually or compulsively to cope with stress or to relieve negative feelings.

but it has different meanings to different people. Here, let us define **drug addiction** (also called *chemical addiction*) as a pattern of drug dependence accompanied by physiological dependence. By this definition, we consider people to be addicted when they feel powerless to control their use of the drug *and* have developed signs of physiological dependence—typically a withdrawal syndrome.

drug addiction Drug dependence accompanied by signs of physiological dependence, such as the development of a withdrawal syndrome.

Bear in mind that people may become *psychologically* dependent on a drug without becoming physiologically dependent on it. **Psychological dependence** is a pattern of compulsive or habitual use of a drug that serves a psychological need, such as lessening anxiety or escaping from stress. People who are psychologically dependent on a drug come to rely on it to counter unpleasant feelings or to cope with personal problems or conflicts with others. Some drugs, such as nicotine, alcohol, and heroin, can lead to both psychological and physiological dependence. Others, such as marijuana, can produce psychological dependence but are not known to produce physiological dependence.

psychological dependence A pattern of compulsive or habitual use of a drug to satisfy a psychological need.

Now let us turn to the major classes of psychoactive drugs: depressants, stimulants, and hallucinogens.

Depressants

Depressants are drugs that reduce central nervous system activity, which in turn depresses (slows down) such bodily processes as heart rate and respiration rate. The major types of depressants are alcohol, barbiturates and tranquilizers, and opioids. Psychologically, depressants induce feelings of relaxation and provide relief from states of anxiety and tension. Some depressants also produce a "rush" of pleasure. In high doses, depressants can kill by arresting vital bodily functions, such as breathing. Depressants are highly addictive and can be dangerous, even lethal, in overdose or when mixed with other drugs. The deaths of famed entertainers Marilyn Monroe and Judy Garland were blamed on the deadly mix of barbiturates and alcohol.

depressants Drugs, such as alcohol and barbiturates, that dampen central nervous system activity.

CONCEPT 4.22
Depressants are addictive drugs that can be deadly when used in high doses or when mixed with other drugs.

Alcohol: The Most Widely Used and Abused Depressant

Alcohol is an **intoxicant**—a chemical substance that produces a state of drunkenness. The more a person drinks, the stronger the intoxicating effects become. Table 4.3 summarizes how increasing blood alcohol levels affect behavior. Consuming even one alcoholic drink impairs driving ability. With heavier doses, the depressant effects of the drug on the central nervous system can induce a state of stupor, unconsciousness, and even death.

intoxicant A chemical substance that induces a state of drunkenness.

Women typically become intoxicated at lower doses of alcohol than men do. One reason is that women usually weigh less than men, and the less people weigh, the less alcohol it usually takes to produce intoxication. The rule of thumb is that a single drink for a woman is equal in its effects to two drinks for a man (Springen & Kantrowitz, 2004). Another reason for this gender difference is that women have less of an enzyme that breaks down alcohol in the stomach than men do and thus more pure alcohol reaches the bloodstream. Yet women's greater sensitivity to alcohol can work in their favor in that it may serve as a biological constraint on excessive drinking.

CONCEPT 4.23
Alcohol is a depressant drug that slows down central nervous system activity and affects higher cognitive functions, such as the ability to weigh the consequences of behavior.

→ Concept Link
Maternal use of alcohol during pregnancy can cause fetal alcohol syndrome, which is a leading cause of mental retardation. See Module 9.1.

Alcohol directly affects the brain, clouding judgment and impairing concentration and attention, as well as the ability to weigh the consequences of behavior. Thus, people may do or say things when they are drinking that they might not otherwise. They may take unnecessary risks without considering the consequences of their actions, which can have tragic results. The slogan from a recent public health campaign bears repeating: "First you get drunk. Then you get stupid. Then you get AIDS."

TABLE 4.3 Behavioral Effects of Blood Alcohol Levels

Blood Alcohol Concentration (%)	Behavioral Effects
.05	Lowered alertness; usually a "high" feeling; release of inhibitions; impaired judgment
.10	Slowed reaction times; impaired motor function; less caution
.15	Large, consistent decreases in reaction time
.20	Marked depression in sensory and motor capability; decidedly intoxicated
.25	Severe motor disturbance; staggering; sensory perceptions greatly impaired
.30	Stuporous but conscious; no comprehension of the external world
.35	Condition equivalent to surgical anesthesia; minimal level at which death occurs
.40	Death in about 50 percent of cases

Source: Ray & Ksir, 1990.

Alcohol has a releasing effect on inhibitions, which may lead to aggressive or impulsive behavior. Not everyone who drinks becomes aggressive or acts foolishly or recklessly, of course. Individual differences play a large role. Yet alcohol use is associated with many forms of aggressive behavior, from rape and spousal abuse to robbery, assault, and even homicide (Bartholow & Heinz, 2006; Buddie & Testa, 2005). We examine the relationship between alcohol and violent behavior in Chapter 14.

CONCEPT 4.24
Alcohol can reduce inhibitions, which may lead to aggressive or impulsive behavior.

An estimated 100,000 people in the United States die from alcohol-related causes each year, mostly from motor vehicle crashes and alcohol-related diseases (Society for Neuroscience, 2005). One reason that drinking and driving is so dangerous is that alcohol impairs depth perception, making it more difficult to judge distances between cars (Nawrot, Nordenstrom, & Olson, 2004).

© Image Source/Getty Images

Binge drinking is a major problem on many college campuses. What are the risks posed by binge drinking?

Alcohol-related accidents are the leading cause of death among young people in the 17- to 24-year-old age range (Ham & Hope, 2003). More than half a million college students between the ages of 18 and 24 are accidentally injured each year while driving under the influence (Dingfelder, 2005).

Overall, alcohol plays a role in about one in three suicides and accidental deaths in the United States (Dougherty et al., 2004; Sher, 2005). As noted above, many crimes of violence are also connected with the use of alcohol.

Alcoholism

Most people who drink alcohol do so in moderation. However, statistics show that about eight million Americans suffer from **alcoholism**, a form of chemical dependence in which the body becomes physically dependent on alcohol and the person is unable to control the use of the drug (Kranzler, 2006). Relatively few people suffering from alcoholism, perhaps only 5 percent, fit the stereotype of the "skid-row bum." Most have families and work for a living. They are the kinds of people you're likely to meet in your daily life—neighbors, coworkers, friends, and even family members. Yet alcoholism

alcoholism A chemical addiction characterized by impaired control over the use of alcohol and physiological dependence on it.

CONCEPT 4.25
Only a small percentage of people with alcoholism fit the stereotype of the "skid-row" bum.

is an equal opportunity destroyer, leading to devastating health problems, motor vehicle accidents, and ruined careers and marriages. Alcoholism typically begins in early adulthood, usually between the ages of 20 and 40, although it may develop earlier in life, even in some cases during childhood.

Alcohol abuse involving regular, heavy consumption of alcohol can damage nearly every major organ and body system. Heavy drinking often has its most damaging effects on the liver, the organ that primarily metabolizes (breaks down) alcohol. *Cirrhosis of the liver*, an irreversible scarring of liver tissue typically caused by alcohol abuse, accounts for some 30,000 deaths annually in the United States (Xiu et al., 2010).

Ironically, despite the health risks associated with heavy drinking, moderate use of alcohol (one to two drinks a day for men, one drink for women) is linked to a lower risk of heart disease and strokes and to lower death rates overall (e.g., Brien et al., 2011; Di Castelnuovo et al., 2006; Ronksley et al., 2011). However, health officials draw the line at encouraging moderate drinking because of concerns it may lead to heavier drinking, which clearly has unhealthy effects.

Binge Drinking: A Dangerous College Pastime

Alcohol, not cocaine, heroin, or marijuana, is the BDOC—big drug on campus. Two out of three college students drink alcohol at least once monthly, even though most of them are under the legal drinking age (see Table 4.4). College students tend to drink more than their peers who do not attend college (Slutske, 2005). Factors associated with college life, such as living away from home and being exposed to peers who drink, contribute to increased drinking during the first year of college (White et al., 2008).

© Ariel Skelley/Corbis

Which of these people suffers from alcoholism? The fact is that any one of these people might suffer from alcoholism. People struggling with alcoholism may be your neighbors, friends, or loved ones.

Excessive drinking on campus is also associated with the "Greek" culture of fraternities and sororities (Park, Sher, & Krull, 2008; Park et al., 2009). However, many fraternal organizations today either ban alcoholic behaviors or encourage more responsible drinking by their members. Still, drinking has become so ingrained in college life that it is virtually as much a part of the college experience as attending a dance or basketball game. Unfortunately, alcohol use and abuse are taking a significant toll on college campuses (see Table 4.5). Alcohol claims the lives of about 1,400 college students each year, with most of these deaths resulting from alcohol-related motor vehicle accidents (Sink, 2004).

TABLE 4.4 Alcohol Use Among College Students

86.6	Percentage who have used alcohol in their lifetime
83.2	Percentage who have used alcohol within the past year
67.4	Percentage who have used alcohol within the past 30 days
3.6	Percentage who have used alcohol daily within the past 30 days
39.3	Percentage who have had five or more drinks in a row during the last 2 weeks

Source: Johnston, O'Malley, & Bachman, 2001.

One of the major alcohol-related concerns on college campuses today is binge drinking. Binge drinking is on the rise among college students, with about 40% reporting binge drinking episodes during the previous 30 days (Hingson et al., 2009; Mitka, 2009). *Binge drinking* is usually defined as having five or more drinks (for men) or four or more drinks (for women) on one occasion. Binge drinking is not only damaging to a student's health, but it is also associated with negative academic performance, including missing class, falling behind in coursework, and receiving lower grades (Wechsler & Nelson, 2008).

For many college students, turning 21 (the legal drinking age) becomes an occasion for excessive and potentially dangerous drinking (Day-Cameron et al., 2009; Munsey, 2008). A recent survey at the University of Missouri showed about four of five students reported celebrating their 21st birthdays by drinking, with many drinking heavily to mark the occasion (Rutledge, Park, & Sher, 2008).

Heavy drinking is associated with lower GPAs, in part because students who drink heavily tend to get too little sleep (Singleton & Wolfson, 2009). Binge drinkers create additional risks for themselves, such as driving under the influence and engaging in unplanned sexual activities, which can result in unwanted pregnancies and sexually transmitted infections. Students who are strongly committed to academic achievement tend to be less likely to engage in binge drinking or other problem drinking behaviors than other students (Palfai & Weafer, 2006).

Binge drinking and related drinking games (e.g., beer chugging) are a serious concern primarily because they can place people at risk of coma and even death from alcohol overdose. Blackouts and seizures may also occur with consumption of large amounts of alcohol. Choking on one's own vomit is a frequent cause of alcohol-induced deaths. Although heavy drinking can cause people to vomit reflexively, the drug's depressant effects on the central nervous system interfere with the normal vomiting response. As a result, vomit accumulates in the air passages, which can lead to asphyxiation and death.

Prompt medical attention is needed if a person overdoses on alcohol. But how can you tell if a person has drunk too much? Table 4.6 lists some signs of alcohol overdose. A person who is unresponsive or unconscious should not be left alone. Don't simply assume that he or she will "sleep it off." You may think you have no right to interfere. You may have doubts about whether the person is truly in danger. But ask yourself, if you were in the place of a person who showed signs of overdosing on alcohol, wouldn't you want someone to intervene to save your life? Stay with the person until you or someone else can obtain medical attention. Most important, call a physician or local emergency number immediately and ask for advice.

Barbiturates and Tranquilizers

Barbiturates are calming or sedating drugs that have several legitimate medical uses. They are used to regulate high blood pressure, block pain during surgery, and control epileptic seizures. Yet they are also highly addictive and used illicitly as street drugs to induce states of euphoria and relaxation. Among the more widely used barbiturates are amobarbital, pentobarbital, phenobarbital, and secobarbital. Methaqualone (street names, "ludes" and "sopors") is a sedating drug with effects similar to those of barbiturates, and with similar risks.

Barbiturates can induce drowsiness and slurred speech and impair motor skills and judgment. Overdoses can lead to convulsions, coma, and death. The mixture of barbiturates or methaqualone with alcohol can be especially dangerous and potentially lethal. People who are physiologically dependent on barbiturates or methaqualone should withdraw under careful medical supervision, since abrupt withdrawal can cause convulsions and even death.

TABLE 4.5 Alcohol on Campus: The Annual Toll

600,000 physical assaults
500,000 injuries
70,000 sexual assaults
1,400 deaths due to overdose and accidents

Source: Hingson et al., 2002.

Note: These figures represent the estimated annual numbers of alcohol-related physical assaults, injuries, sexual assaults, and deaths among U.S. college students ages 18 to 24.

CONCEPT 4.26

Binge drinking is linked to increased risks of alcohol dependence, alcohol overdoses, unsafe or unplanned sex, and driving while impaired, among other problems.

© Sam Spady Foundation

Samantha Spady, a 19-year-old Colorado State University sophomore, died from alcohol poisoning after an evening of heavy drinking with her friends. At the time of her death, she had a blood alcohol concentration over five times the legal limit for driving.

TABLE 4.6 Signs of Alcohol Overdose
Failure to respond when talked to or shouted at
Failure to respond to being pinched, shaken, or poked
Inability to stand unaided
Failure to wake up
Purplish or clammy skin
Rapid pulse rate, irregular heart rhythm, low blood pressure, or difficulty breathing

narcotics Addictive drugs that have pain-relieving and sleep-inducing properties.

CONCEPT 4.27
Barbiturates and tranquilizers are depressants that help calm the nervous system, but they are addictive and potentially dangerous in high doses, especially when mixed with other drugs, such as alcohol.

CONCEPT 4.28
Opioids, such as morphine and heroin, are depressants that induce a euphoric high.

CONCEPT 4.29
Stimulants increase activity in the central nervous system, heightening states of alertness and in some cases producing a pleasurable "high."

→ **Concept Link**
Although stimulant drugs can become drugs of abuse, they are also used therapeutically in the treatment of attention-deficit hyperactivity disorder (ADHD). See Module 16.3.

stimulants Drugs that activate the central nervous system.

Tranquilizers are a class of depressants widely used to treat anxiety and insomnia. Though they are less toxic than barbiturates, they can be dangerous in high doses, especially if combined with alcohol or other drugs. They also carry a risk of addiction, so they should not be used for extended periods of time. The most widely used tranquilizers include Valium, Xanax, and Halcion, which are members of the *benzodiazepine* family of drugs. Benzodiazepines act by boosting the availability of the neurotransmitter GABA in the brain (see Chapter 2). GABA, an inhibitory neurotransmitter, reduces excess nervous system activity.

Opioids

Opioids (also called *opiates*) are **narcotics**—addictive drugs that have pain-relieving and sleep-inducing properties. They include morphine, heroin, and codeine, naturally occurring drugs derived from the poppy plant. Synthetic opioids, including Demerol, Percodan, and Darvon, are manufactured in a laboratory to have effects similar to those of natural opiates. Opiates produce a "rush" of pleasurable excitement and dampen awareness of personal problems, which are two main reasons for their popularity as illicit street drugs.

Opiates have legitimate medical uses as painkillers. They are routinely used to deaden postsurgical pain and for some other pain conditions. Because of their high potential for addiction, their medical use is strictly regulated. However, naturally occurring opiates like heroin and morphine, and synthetic opiates like OcyContin and Vicodin, are abused as street drugs when they are obtained and used illegally (Novak et al., 2004).

Opiates are similar in chemical structure to endorphins and lock into the same receptor sites in the brain. You'll recall from Chapter 2 that endorphins are neurotransmitters that block pain and regulate states of pleasure. Opiates mimic the actions of endorphins, our own "natural opioids," thereby stimulating brain centers that produce pleasurable sensations.

Approximately 3 million Americans have used heroin, the most widely used and abused opioid, and nearly 1 million are believed to be addicted (Krantz & Mehler, 2004). Heroin induces a euphoric rush that lasts perhaps five to 15 minutes. The rush is so intense and pleasurable that users liken it to orgasm. After the rush fades, a second phase sets in that is characterized by a relaxed, drowsy state. Worries and concerns seem to evaporate, which is why heroin often appeals to people seeking a psychological escape from their problems. This mellow state soon fades, too, leading the habitual user to seek another "fix" to return to the drugged state. Tolerance develops, and users begin needing higher doses, which can lead to dangerous overdoses. The life of the heroin addict is usually organized around efforts to obtain and use the drug. Many turn to crime or prostitution to support their habit.

Stimulants

Stimulants are drugs that heighten the activity of the central nervous system. They include amphetamines, cocaine, MDMA ("Ecstasy"), nicotine, and caffeine. Stimulants can produce both physiological and psychological dependence. Some of these drugs, like amphetamines and cocaine, can induce a pleasurable "high."

Amphetamines

Like the synthetic opioids, *amphetamines* are not found in nature; they are chemicals manufactured in a laboratory. They activate the sympathetic branch of the autonomic nervous system, causing heart rate, breathing rate, and blood pressure to rise. At low doses, they boost mental alertness and concentration, reduce fatigue, and lessen the need for sleep. At high doses, they can induce an intense, pleasurable rush.

Amphetamines act on the brain by boosting availability of the neurotransmitters norepinephrine and dopamine in the brain. Increased availability of these chemicals keeps neurons firing, which helps maintain high levels of arousal and alertness. Amphetamines also produce pleasurable feelings by directly stimulating the reward pathways in the brain—the circuitry responsible for feelings of pleasure.

CONCEPT 4.30
Cocaine is a highly addictive stimulant that induces a euphoric high by directly stimulating reward pathways in the brain.

The most widely used amphetamines are amphetamine sulfate (brand name, Benzedrine; street name, "bennies"), methamphetamine (Methedrine, or "speed"), and dextroamphetamine (Dexedrine, or "dexies"). They can be used in pill form, smoked in a relatively pure form of methamphetamine called "ice" or "crystal meth," or injected in the form of liquid methamphetamine.

More than 12 million Americans have used "meth," and some 1.5 million are regular users (Jefferson, 2005). Amphetamine overdoses, which often occur as users develop tolerance to the drug and keep increasing the amount they consume, can have dangerous, even fatal, consequences. In high doses, amphetamines can cause extreme restlessness, loss of appetite, tremors, and cardiovascular irregularities that may result in coma or death. High doses of amphetamines can also induce *amphetamine psychosis*, a psychotic reaction characterized by hallucinations and delusions that resembles acute episodes of schizophrenia. Brain-imaging studies show that "meth" can damage the brain, causing deficits in learning, memory, and other functions (P. M. Thompson et al., 2004; Toomey et al., 2003). Long-term use can also lead to stroke, liver damage, and other serious health problems.

Cocaine

Cocaine is a natural stimulant derived from the leaves of the coca plant. The drug can be administered in several ways: sniffed in powder form, smoked in a hardened form called *crack*, injected in liquid form, or ingested as a tea brewed from coca leaves. You may be surprised to learn that when Coca-Cola was introduced in 1886, it contained a small amount of cocaine and was soon being marketed as "the ideal brain tonic." (Cocaine was removed from Coca-Cola in the early twentieth century, but the beverage is still flavored with a nonpsychoactive extract from the coca plant.)

Cocaine produces states of pleasure primarily by working on the neurotransmitter dopamine, a brain chemical that directly stimulates reward or pleasure pathways in the brain (Flagel et al., 2011; Pierce & Kumaresan, 2006). These brain circuits provide reinforcement for behaviors essential to our survival. For example, when we are hungry and have something to eat, or thirsty and have something to drink, reward pathways in the brain become flooded with dopamine, leading to feelings of pleasure or satisfaction.

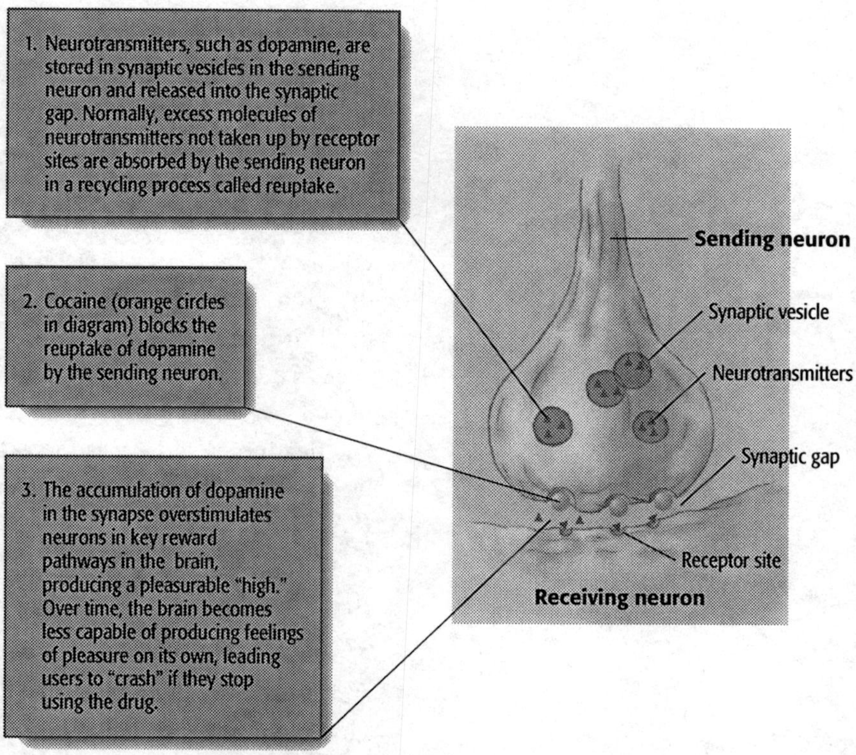

Figure 4.8 How Cocaine Works in the Brain
Cocaine blocks the normal recycling process of dopamine (the circles in the diagram), resulting in a buildup of the neurotransmitter in the synapse.
Source: National Institute on Drug Abuse, U.S. Department of Health and Human Services, National Institutes of Health, 2004.

As we can see in ■ Figure 4.8, cocaine blocks the reuptake of dopamine in the synapse between

© Bettmann/CORBIS

Coca-Cola has changed since it was first introduced in the late nineteenth century, and not just in its price. It originally contained an extract of cocaine and was promoted as a mental tonic to relieve exhaustion. Although cocaine was removed from the beverage more than 100 years ago, it now contains small amounts of the mild stimulant caffeine.

neurons. As a result, more dopamine molecules remain active in the synapse for longer periods of time, overstimulating neurons that produce states of pleasure, which may result in a euphoric drug high. Recent research suggests that dopamine also alerts us to objects we want, such as chocolate if we are chocolate lovers, and to objects we fear, such as creepy crawlers (Angier, 2009). So for example, a person with cocaine addiction may experience a rush of dopamine when a crack pipe is presented, making the drug and related paraphernalia more difficult to ignore.

Although amphetamines and cocaine have similar effects, the high induced by cocaine, especially in the form of crack, is typically shorter lived. Smoking crack delivers the drug almost instantaneously to the brain, producing an immediate, intense high. But the high fades within five or 10 minutes, leaving the user craving more.

Regular use of cocaine can have damaging effects on the heart and circulatory system and other body organs. High doses can result in life-threatening or fatal consequences. Prolonged use may also lead to psychological problems, such as anxiety, irritability, and depression. At high doses, cocaine can induce a type of psychosis, called *cocaine psychosis*, characterized by hallucinations and delusions of persecution (unfounded beliefs that one is being pursued by others or by mysterious forces).

Cocaine is highly addictive and can lead to a withdrawal syndrome involving intense cravings for the drug, feelings of depression, and an inability to experience pleasure in the activities of everyday life. People addicted to cocaine will often return to using the drug to gain relief from these unpleasant withdrawal symptoms. Tolerance also develops quickly—yet another sign of the physically addicting properties of cocaine. Users may also become psychologically dependent on the drug, using it compulsively to deal with life stress.

MDMA (Ecstasy)

MDMA (3,4-methylenedioxymethamphetamine), better known as *Ecstasy*, is an amphetamine-like drug synthesized in underground laboratories. MDMA produces mild euphoric and hallucinogenic effects. It is especially popular among high school and college students and is widely available in many late-night dance clubs in U.S. cities.

MDMA use can lead to undesirable psychological effects, such as depression, anxiety, insomnia, and even states of paranoia or psychotic symptoms. Heavy use of the drug is associated with cognitive deficits, including problems with memory functioning, learning ability, and attention (Eisner, 2005). The drug has physical effects as well, such as increased heart rate and blood pressure, a tense or chattering jaw, and feelings of body warmth and/or chills. High doses can lead to loss of consciousness, seizures, and death in severe cases (SAMHSA, 2005). Although the number of new users has begun to decline, more than 10 million Americans have used the drug at least once (SAMHSA, 2005).

Nicotine

CONCEPT 4.31
Nicotine, a stimulant, is an addictive substance found in tobacco.

Nicotine is a mild stimulant, but a highly addictive one. It is found naturally in tobacco, and users typically administer the drug by smoking, snorting, or chewing tobacco. Physiological dependence can begin within the first few weeks of cigarette smoking. Nicotine use can also lead to psychological dependence, as we see in people who smoke habitually as a means of coping with the stress of everyday life.

As a stimulant, nicotine speeds up the heart rate, dampens appetite, and produces a mild rush or psychological kick. It increases states of arousal, alertness, and concentration. But it may also have "paradoxical" effects, such as inducing feelings of relaxation or mental calmness. In fact, since nicotine causes the release of endorphins in the brain, it can produce states of pleasure and reduce pain.

You certainly are aware by now that smoking is dangerous. But just how dangerous? So dangerous that it is the leading cause of premature death in the United States and worldwide, accounting annually for nearly 450,000 deaths in the U.S. and about 4 million deaths throughout the world (CDC, 2009a; "Tobacco Use," 2010). Overall, smoking accounts for one in five deaths in the United States (Benowitz, 2010).

Smoking is responsible for nearly one in three cancer deaths in the United States, most of them due to lung cancer, the leading cancer killer of both men and women. It may surprise you to learn that more women die annually from lung cancer than from breast cancer. The toxic substances in cigarette smoke wend their way through the body, damaging virtually ever organ in the body (U.S. Surgeon General, 2010). The heartbreaking news about smoking is that it is also a major contributor to cardiovascular disease (heart and artery disease), the biggest killer of all. Smoking also causes other serious health problems, including emphysema and even cataracts. A British study reported that people who smoke have double the risk of dying during middle age (before age 70) (Doll et al., 2004). Another study found that heavy smoking during middle adulthood more than doubles the risk of developing Alzheimer's disease (Rusanen et al., 2010).

The good news is that smoking rates in the United States have declined dramatically over time to the lowest level in more than 50 years. Still, about one in five American adults today, and about the same proportion of 12th graders, smoke ("Adolescent Cigarette Smoking," 2010; "Tobacco Use," 2010). Unfortunately, smoking among teens is on the rise, portending more smoking-related illness and premature deaths in the years ahead. Smoking is more prevalent among men than women, among younger adults, and among less-educated people (CDC, 2009a).

Tobacco use often begins in adolescence and is difficult to eliminate once a pattern of regular use is established. Estimates that that about one in three young people who take up smoking each day will eventually die of a smoking-related disease.

Caffeine is the most widely used psychoactive drug. Most regular users can control their use of the drug despite being physiologically dependent on it.

Caffeine

Caffeine, a mild stimulant found in coffee, tea, cola drinks, chocolate, and other substances, is our most widely used psychoactive drug. Regular caffeine use leads to physiological dependence. If your daily routine includes one or more cups of coffee or caffeinated tea, and you feel on edge or have headaches when you go without your daily supply of caffeine, chances are you're physiologically dependent, or "hooked," on caffeine. Drinking just a cup or two of coffee or tea or even a few cans of caffeinated soft drinks each day can lead to dependence. The good news is that most caffeine users are able to maintain control over their use of the drug despite being physiologically dependent on it. In other words, they can limit their coffee or tea intake and can use the drug in moderation without it significantly interfering with their daily lives.

Fortunately, too, caffeine is not known to be associated with health risks (other than during pregnancy) when used in moderation. However, we recently learned that

CONCEPT 4.32
Caffeine, a mild stimulant found in coffee, tea, cola drinks, chocolate, and other substances, is the most widely used psychoactive drug.

coffee drinking, especially heavier drinking, is linked in some genetically predisposed individuals to an increased risk of heart attacks (Cornelis et al., 2006). Caffeine has some desirable effects, such as enhancing wakefulness and mental alertness, although negative effects, such as jitteriness or nervousness, can occur at higher dosages (from 200 to 600 milligrams).

Hallucinogens

hallucinogens Drugs that alter sensory experiences and produce hallucinations.

Hallucinogens are drugs that alter sensory perceptions, producing distortions or hallucinations in visual, auditory, or other sensory forms. They are also called *psychedelics*, a word that literally means "mind-revealing." Hallucinogens may induce feelings of relaxation and calmness in some users but cause feelings of paranoia or panic in others. Though they are not known to produce physiological dependence, they can lead to psychological dependence when users come to depend on them for help in coping with problems or stressful life experiences. Hallucinogens include LSD, mescaline, psilocybin, PCP, and marijuana. Of these, the two most widely used are LSD and marijuana.

CONCEPT 4.33
Hallucinogens alter or distort sensory perceptions and produce feelings of relaxation in some people but paranoid or panicky feelings in others.

LSD

LSD (lysergic acid diethylamide; street name, "acid") produces vivid hallucinations and other sensory distortions. The experience of using the drug is called a "trip," and it may last as long as 12 hours. More than a half million Americans reported using LSD (NIDA Notes, 2004).

LSD has various effects on the body, including pupil dilation and increases in heart rate, blood pressure, and body temperature. It may also produce sweating, tremors, loss of appetite, and sleeplessness. The psychological effects on the user are variable and unpredictable. Users often report distortions of time and space. Higher doses are likely to produce vivid displays of colors and outright hallucinations. The psychological effects depend not only on the amount used but also on the user's personality, expectancies about the drug, and the context in which it used. Some users experience "bad trips" in which they suffer intense anxiety or panic or have psychotic reactions, such as delusions of persecution. Others have flashbacks, which involve a sudden re-experiencing of some of the perceptual distortions of an LSD trip.

Mescaline, Psilocybin, and PCP

For centuries, Native Americans have used the hallucinogens *mescaline* (derived from the cactus plant) and *psilocybin* (derived from certain mushrooms) for religious purposes. *PCP* (phencyclidine), or "angel dust," is a synthetic drug that produces **delirium**, a state of mental confusion characterized by excitement, disorientation, and difficulty in focusing attention. PCP can produce distortions in the sense of time and space, feelings of unreality, and vivid, sometimes frightening, hallucinations. It may lead to feelings of paranoia and blind rage, and prompt bizarre or violent behavior. High doses can lead to coma and death.

delirium A mental state characterized by confusion, disorientation, difficulty in focusing attention, and excitable behavior.

Marijuana

Marijuana ("pot," "weed," "grass," "reefer," "dope") is derived from the cannabis plant. The psychoactive chemical in marijuana is THC (delta-9-tetrahydrocannabinol). The leaves of the plant are ground up and may be smoked in a pipe or rolled into "joints." The most potent form of the drug, called hashish ("hash"), is derived from the resin of the plant, which contains the highest concentration of THC. Though marijuana and hashish are usually smoked, some users ingest the drug by eating parts of the plant or foods into which the cannabis has been baked.

Marijuana is generally classified as a hallucinogen because it alters perceptions and can produce hallucinations, especially in high doses or when used by susceptible individuals. At lower doses, users may feel relaxed and mildly euphoric. It may seem as if time is passing more slowly. Bodily sensations may seem more pronounced, which can create anxiety or even panicky feelings in some users (e.g., a pronounced sense of the heartbeat may cause some users to fear they are having a heart attack). High doses can cause nausea and vomiting, feelings of disorientation, panic attacks, and paranoia.

Marijuana is the most widely used illicit drug in the United States and throughout the Western world (Yücel et al., 2008). More than 40 percent of adult Americans report having used marijuana at some point in their lives, and about 6 percent are current (past month) users (SAMHSA, 2006).

Whether marijuana leads to physiological dependence remains unclear. However, recent evidence points to a definable withdrawal syndrome in long-term heavy users of the drug who stop using it abruptly (Budney et al., 2004). It is certainly the case that marijuana use can lead to psychological dependence if people come to rely on it to deal with stress or personal difficulties. Marijuana use is also linked to later use of harder drugs such as heroin and cocaine (Kandel, 2003). Whether marijuana use plays a causal role in leading to harder drug use also remains an open question.

Marijuana use carries certain risks. It increases heart rate and possibly blood pressure, which can be potentially dangerous effects for people with cardiovascular problems. It impairs motor performance and coordination, which, together with causing perceptual distortions, makes marijuana and driving an especially dangerous combination. Long-term use may also lead to problems with learning and memory (Messinis et al., 2006; Puighermanal et al., 2009; Yücel et al., 2008).

Smoking marijuana introduces cancer-causing agents into the body and increases risks of respiratory diseases (Zickler, 2006). Marijuana use is also linked to greater risk of psychological problems, such as depression and anxiety, although we can't yet say whether marijuana use is a causal factor in the development of these problems (Patton et al., 2002; Rey & Tennant, 2002).

In Concept Chart 4.4, you'll find a listing of the major types of psychoactive drugs in terms of their potential for psychological and physiological dependence, major psychological effects, and major risks.

© Ann Marie Rousseau/ The Image Works

The hallucinogen LSD can produce vivid perceptual distortions and outright hallucinations. Some users experience "bad trips," which are characterized by panicky feelings and even psychotic states.

CONCEPT 4.34

Marijuana induces feelings of relaxation and mild euphoria at low doses, but it can produce hallucinations in high doses or when used by susceptible individuals.

Understanding Drug Abuse

People use drugs for many reasons, not simply to change their states of consciousness. To better understand the problems of drug use and abuse, we need to consider social, biological, and psychological factors. Pleasurable effects of drugs, peer pressure, and exposure to family members who smoke or use alcohol or other drugs are all important influences in leading young people to begin experimenting with these substances (Hu, Davies, & Kandel, 2006; Read et al., 2003).

CONCEPT 4.35

Drug abuse and dependence are complex problems arising from an interplay of social, biological, and psychological factors.

CONCEPT CHART 4.4 Major Types of Psychoactive Drugs

	Drug	Potential for Psychological/ Physiological Dependence	Major Psychological Effects	Major Risks
Depressants	Alcohol	Yes/Yes	Induces relaxation, mild euphoria, and intoxication; relieves anxiety; reduces mental alertness and inhibitions; impairs concentration, judgment, coordination, and balance	With heavy use, can cause liver disorders and other physical problems; in overdose, can cause coma or death
	Barbiturates and tranquilizers	Yes/Yes	Reduces mental alertness; induces relaxation and calm; may produce pleasurable rush (barbiturates)	High addictive potential; dangerous in overdose and when mixed with alcohol and other drugs
	Opioids	Yes/Yes	Induces relaxation and a euphoric rush; may temporarily blot out awareness of personal problems	High addictive potential; in overdose, may cause sudden death
Stimulants	Amphetamines	Yes/Yes	Boosts mental alertness; reduces need for sleep; induces pleasurable rush; causes loss of appetite	In high doses, can induce psychotic symptoms and cardiovascular irregularities that may lead to coma or death
	Cocaine	Yes/Yes	Effects similar to those of amphetamines but shorter lived	High addictive potential; risk of sudden death from overdose; in high doses, can have psychotic effects; risk of nasal defects from "snorting"
	MDMA ("Ecstasy")	Yes/Yes	Mild euphoria and hallucinogenic effects	High doses can be lethal; may lead to depression or other psychological effects; may impair learning, attention, and memory
	Nicotine	Yes/Yes	Increases mental alertness; produces mild rush but paradoxically may have relaxing and calming effects	Strong addictive potential; tobacco use causes cancer and contributes to cardiovascular disease and other health problems
	Caffeine	Yes/Yes	Increases mental alertness and wakefulness	In high doses, can cause jitteriness and sleeplessness; may increase risk of miscarriage during pregnancy
Hallucinogens	LSD	Yes/No	Produces hallucinations and other sensory distortions	Intense anxiety, panic, or psychotic reactions associated with "bad trips;" flashbacks
	Marijuana	Yes/?	Induces relaxation and mild euphoria; can produce hallucinations	In high doses, can cause nausea, vomiting, disorientation, panic, and paranoia; possible health risks from regular use

Young people who feel alienated from mainstream culture may identify with subcultures in which drug use is sanctioned or encouraged, such as the gang subculture. Though initiation into drug use may be motivated by the desire to "fit in" or appear "cool" in the eyes of peers, people generally continue using drugs because of their pleasurable or reinforcing effects . With prolonged use of a drug, the body comes to depend on a steady supply of it, leading to physiological dependence. As people become chemically dependent, they may continue using drugs primarily to avoid unpleasant withdrawal symptoms and cravings that occur when they stop using them.

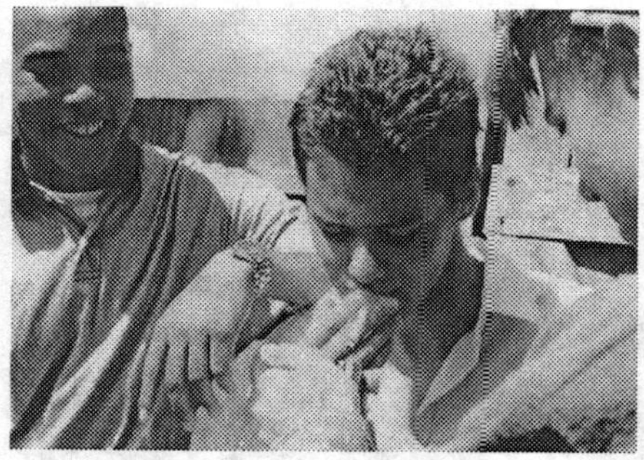

Peer pressure is an important influence on alcohol and drug use among young people.

Unemployment is another social factor linked to drug abuse. Yet this relationship may be two-sided: Drug abuse may increase the likelihood of unemployment, while unemployment may increase the likelihood of drug abuse.

Use of alcohol and other drugs is strongly affected by cultural norms. Cultural beliefs and customs may either encourage or discourage drinking. Some ethnic groups—Jews, Greeks, Italians, and Asians, for example—have low rates of alcoholism, largely because of tight social controls imposed on excessive and underage drinking. In traditional Islamic cultures, alcohol is prohibited altogether.

Gender and ethnic differences also need to be taken into account. According to a recent national survey, men are much more likely to have used alcohol and illicit drugs during the past month than are women (Maisto, Galizio, & Connors, 2008). Although recent use of alcohol was most frequent among whites, only small differences were found between whites, blacks, and Hispanics with respect to the likelihood of using any illicit drug during the past month.

Acculturation plays an important role in explaining drug use and abuse. Traditional Hispanic cultures place severe restrictions on women's use of alcohol, especially on heavy drinking. Not surprisingly, highly acculturated Hispanic American women who have been exposed to the loose constraints on female drinking in mainstream U.S. society are much more likely to drink heavily than are relatively unacculturated Hispanic American women (Caetano, 1987).

Genetic factors also contribute to our understanding of different forms of drug dependence, including alcoholism, heroin dependence, and even nicotine (smoking) dependence (Blomeyer et al., 2008; Chen et al., 2008; Kendler, et al., 2008; Uhl et al., 2008). Consistent with a genetic contribution, evidence shows that identical twins are much more likely to have alcoholism in common than are fraternal twins (Alterman et al., 2002; Liu et al., 2004).

No single gene is responsible for alcoholism or other forms of substance abuse or dependence. Rather, scientists believe that multiple genes acting together with environmental influences lead to alcohol and drug abuse and dependence (Kendler et al., 2008; Luczak, Glatt, & Wall, 2006). Some people may be genetically predisposed to reap greater pleasure from alcohol or other drugs, which raises their potential of abuse. Genetic factors may lead some people to drink more heavily when they are in the presence of friends who are drinking heavily (Larsen et al., 2010). Still others may have an inherited tendency making them more tolerant of alcohol's negative effects (the nausea and so on), which in turn may make it difficult for them "to know when to say when" (Corbett et al., 2005; Ehlers & Wilhelmsen, 2005; Radel et al., 2005). Ironically, having a greater ability to hold one's liquor appears to put one at greater risk of developing problems with alcohol (Edenberg et al., 2005).

People who inherit a greater sensitivity to the negative effects of alcohol—those whose bodies more readily "put the brakes" on excess drinking—may be less likely to develop problems with alcohol abuse or dependence. As noted, some people may also possess a genetically greater capacity for reaping pleasure from alcohol, thereby raising their risk of problem drinking.

We also need to consider the role of neurotransmitters. Many psychoactive drugs, including cocaine, amphetamines, alcohol, and opiates, produce pleasurable or euphoric effects by increasing the availability of the neurotransmitter dopamine in the brain—a neurotransmitter involved in activating the brain's reward or pleasure circuits (Borgland et al., 2006; Conner, 2010; Gallistel, 2006). Even the mere mention of words associated

© Corbis Photography/Veer

Many problem drinkers use alcohol as self-medication in the attempt to wash away their problems or troubling emotions.

with alcohol (such as "keg" or "binge") may activate brain circuits associated with pleasure or reward in people who suffer from alcohol dependence.

Drugs like cocaine, heroin, and amphetamines flood the brain's reward system with dopamine, temporarily producing intense states of pleasure. Yet, over time, regular use of these drugs can damage these brain circuits, impairing the brain's ability to produce dopamine on its own. As a result, the drug abuser may find it difficult to reap pleasure from ordinarily pleasurable activities, such as enjoying a good meal or socializing with others. The brain comes to depend on having these drugs available to produce any feelings of pleasure or to erase negative feelings, such as anxiety or depression. Without drugs, life may seem drab and unfulfilling, or even no longer worth living.

Drugs also have complex effects on other neurotransmitters, including endorphins. Opioids lock into the same receptor sites as endorphins. Over time, the brain becomes habituated to a supply of opiates and may suppress its natural production of endorphins. The person who is dependent on these drugs comes to rely on them to perform pain-relieving and pleasure-producing functions normally performed by endorphins. The habitual user who quits using the drugs may find that little aches and pains become magnified until the body resumes adequate production of endorphins.

Psychological factors, such as feelings of hopelessness, sensation-seeking and the desire to escape troubling emotions, are major contributors to the development of drug use and dependence. Young people from troubled backgrounds may turn to drugs out of a sense of futility and despair. People with a high need for sensation—those who become easily bored with the ordinary activities that fill most people's days—may come to rely on drugs to provide the stimulation they seek.

Some people use alcohol or other drugs as a form of self-medication to relieve anxiety or emotional pain, cope with negative experiences, or temporarily escape from life's problems (Tomlinson et al., 2006). Cognitive factors, such as holding positive attitudes toward drugs or positive expectancies about the effects they produce (e.g., making one more outgoing or socially confident), also contribute to drug use and abuse, especially among young people (Andrews et al., 2008; Gunn & Smith, 2010).

Drug Treatment

The most effective drug treatment programs use a variety of approaches in dealing with the wide range of problems faced by people with drug abuse problems (Grant et al., 2004; Litt et al., 2003). People with chemical dependencies may first need to undergo **detoxification**, a process in which their bodies are cleared of addictive drugs. To ensure that medical monitoring is available, detoxification usually requires a hospital stay. Follow-up services, including professional counseling, can assist people in remaining free of drugs by helping them confront the psychological problems that may underlie their drug abuse, such as depression and low self-esteem.

detoxification A process of clearing drugs or toxins from the body.

CONCEPT 4.36
Effective drug treatment requires a multifaceted approach to helping people free themselves of chemical dependence and develop more adaptive ways of coping with their problems.

Therapeutic drugs may be used in combination with psychological counseling to fight drug addiction. Some therapeutic drugs prevent opioids and alcohol from producing a high (Veilleux et al., 2010). Another type of drug, the synthetic opioid *methadone*, doesn't produce a rush or stuporous state associated with heroin use but can curb withdrawal symptoms when users stop taking heroin. When taken daily, it can help heroin abusers get their lives back on track (Marion, 2005). In addition, self-help programs, such as the 12-step program of Alcoholics Anonymous (AA), may motivate individuals to maintain abstinence and rebuild their lives free of drugs, especially those who commit themselves to abstinence goals (Ferri, Amato, & Davoli, 2006).

4.4 MODULE REVIEW Altering Consciousness Through Drugs

Recite It

When does drug use cross the line from use to abuse and dependence?

- Drug use becomes drug abuse when it involves the maladaptive or dangerous use of a drug (use that causes or aggravates personal, occupational, or physical problems).
- Drug dependence is a state of impaired control over the use of a drug. It is often accompanied by signs of physiological dependence. Drug abuse frequently leads to drug dependence.
- Physiological dependence means that the person's body has come to depend on having a steady supply of the drug. When psychologically dependent, people rely on a drug as a way of coping with anxiety, stress, and other negative feelings.

What are depressants?

- Depressants, such as alcohol, barbiturates, tranquilizers, and opioids, are addictive drugs that reduce the activity of the central nervous system. They have a range of effects, including reducing states of bodily arousal, relieving anxiety and tension, and, in the case of barbiturates and opioids, producing a pleasurable or euphoric rush.

What are stimulants?

- Stimulants, which include amphetamines, cocaine, MDMA ("Ecstasy"), nicotine, and caffeine, heighten the activity of the nervous system. Stimulants may induce feelings of euphoria, but they also can lead to physiological dependence. Cocaine directly stimulates reward pathways in the brain, producing states of euphoria, but it is a highly addictive and dangerous drug. MDMA is a chemical knockoff of amphetamines that can have serious psychological and physical consequences. Nicotine, a mild stimulant, is the addictive substance found in tobacco. Though regular use of caffeine may lead to psychological dependence, most users can maintain control over their consumption of it.

What are hallucinogens?

- Hallucinogens are drugs that alter sensory perceptions and produce hallucinations. They include LSD, mescaline, psilocybin, PCP, and marijuana. PCP ("angel dust") is a synthetic drug that produces delirium—a state of confusion and disorientation that may be accompanied by hallucinations and violent behavior. Marijuana, the most widely used illicit drug, has a range of effects depending on dosage level.

What factors contribute to alcohol and drug abuse problems?

- In addition to the reinforcing effects of the drugs themselves, social, biological, and psychological factors contribute to drug abuse. Among the contributing social factors are peer pressure and exposure to family members and friends who use drugs. Biological factors include high tolerance for negative drug effects. Psychological factors include feelings of hopelessness and the desire to escape troubling emotions.

What treatment alternatives are available to help people with drug problems?

- Approaches to treating people with drug problems include detoxification programs, professional counseling, the use of therapeutic drugs, and self-help programs such as Alcoholics Anonymous.

Recall It

1. Chemical substances that alter mental states are called ________ drugs.
2. When repeated use of a drug alters a person's body chemistry so that the body comes to rely on having a steady supply of the drug, the condition is called
   a. drug abuse.
   b. drug misuse.
   c. psychological dependence.
   d. physiological dependence.
3. Alcohol and heroin belong to which class of drugs?
4. The most widely used and abused type of depressant is
   a. nicotine. c. heroin.
   b. alcohol. d. caffeine.
5. ________ are drugs that are widely used in treating anxiety and insomnia but that can become addictive when used for extended periods of time.
6. Many psychoactive drugs induce pleasurable effects by increasing brain concentrations of the neurotransmitter ________.

Think About It

- What roles do positive and negative reinforcement play in problems of drug abuse and dependence?
- Should marijuana be legalized? Why or why not?

APPLICATION MODULE 4.5

Getting Your Zs

CONCEPT 4.37
Developing healthy sleep habits can help people overcome insomnia not caused by underlying physical or psychological problems.

Many people have difficulty falling asleep or getting enough sleep to feel refreshed upon awakening. Since insomnia may result from an underlying medical or psychological disorder, it is best to have the condition evaluated by a health professional. In many cases, however, insomnia reflects unhealthy sleep habits. Fortunately, people can change these problem habits by becoming more aware of their sleep patterns and making adaptive changes in their sleep behaviors and thinking patterns (Buysse et al., 2011; Dolan et al., 2010; Ebben & Spielman, 2009). Here are some suggestions for developing healthier sleep habits (adapted from J. E. Brody, 2006; Nevid & Rathus, 2010):

- *Adopt a regular sleep schedule.* Help get your internal body clock in sync by retiring and waking at about the same time every day, including weekends and holidays.
- *Don't try to force sleep.* Sleep is a natural process that cannot be forced. If you are wide-eyed and full of energy, allow your body and mind to wind down before going to bed.
- *Establish a regular bedtime routine.* Adopt a regular routine before going to bed. You may find that reading, watching TV, or practicing a relaxation or meditation technique helps prepare you for sleep.
- *Establish the proper cues for sleeping.* Make your bed a cue for sleeping by limiting as much as possible other activities in bed, such as eating, reading, watching TV, or talking on the telephone.
- *Avoid tossing and turning.* If you can't fall asleep within 20 minutes, don't continue tossing and turning. Get out of bed, move to another room, and achieve a state of relaxation by reading, listening to calming music, or meditating. When you are feeling relaxed, return to bed. Repeat this process as necessary until you are able to fall asleep.
- *Avoid daytime naps if you miss sleep.* Many people try to make up for nighttime sleeplessness by napping during the day. Napping can throw off your natural body clock, making it more difficult to fall asleep the following night.
- *Don't take your problems to bed.* Retiring to bed should be conducive to sleeping, not to mulling over your problems or organizing your daily schedule. Tell yourself you'll think about tomorrow, tomorrow. Or, before you go to bed, write reminder notes to yourself about the things you need to do the following day.
- *Use mental imagery.* Picturing relaxing scenes in your mind—for example, imagining yourself basking in the sun on a tropical beach or walking through a pristine forest—can help you slip from ordinary consciousness into the realm of sleep.
- *Adopt a regular exercise program.* Vigorous exercise can help relieve the stresses of daily life and prepare the body for restful sleep. But avoid exercising for several hours before sleep, since exercise increases states of bodily arousal.

© Simon Potter/Polka Dot/Jupiter Images

What's wrong with this picture? If you have a problem with insomnia, you might find it helpful to make your bed a stronger cue for sleep by limiting other activities in bed, such as eating, reading, watching TV, or talking on the phone.

- *Limit your intake of caffeine, especially in the afternoon.* The caffeine in coffee, tea, and other substances can increase states of bodily arousal for up to 10 hours. Also avoid smoking, not only because of its harmful effects on your health but also because tobacco contains nicotine, a mild stimulant.
- *Practice rational "self-talk."* Disturbing thoughts you silently mumble to yourself under your breath can lead to anxiety and worry that may keep you up well into the night. Replace such anxious "self-talk" with coping thoughts. For example, instead of thinking "I must get to sleep or I'll be a wreck tomorrow," substitute a thought like "I might not feel as sharp as usual but I'm not going to fall apart. I've gotten by with little sleep before and can do so again." Don't fall into the trap of blowing things out of proportion.

Thinking Critically About Psychology

Based on your reading of this chapter, answer the following questions. Then, to evaluate your progress in developing critical thinking skills, compare your answers to the sample answers found in Appendix A.

Do statistics lie? While statistics may not actually lie, they can certainly mislead if we don't apply critical thinking skills when interpreting them. Let's suppose we find a difference in the rates of illicit drug use (cocaine and marijuana, for example) among certain ethnic or racial groups. Let's say the rates of illicit drug use are higher in Group A than Group B. Apply your critical thinking skills to answer the following questions:

1. Would you say that ethnicity accounts for the differences in the rates of drug use between Group A and Group B? Why or why not?
2. What other explanations might account for these differences?

Log in to CengageBrain to access the resources your instructor requires. For this book, you can access:

CourseMate

Psychology CourseMate brings course concepts to life with interactive learning, study, and exam preparation tools that support the printed textbook. A textbook-specific website, Psychology CourseMate includes an integrated interactive eBook and other interactive learning tools including quizzes, flashcards, videos, and more.

CENGAGENOW

CengageNow is an easy-to-use online resource that helps you study in less time to get the grade you want—NOW. Take a pre-test for this chapter and receive a personalized study plan based on your results that will identify the topics you need to review and direct you to online resources to help you master those topics. Then take a post-test to help you determine the concepts you have mastered and what you will need to work on. If your textbook does not include an access code card, go to CengageBrain.com to gain access.

Visit www.cengagebrain.com to access your account and purchase materials.

VISUAL OVERVIEW Chapter 4 Consciousness

MODULE 4.1 States of Consciousness

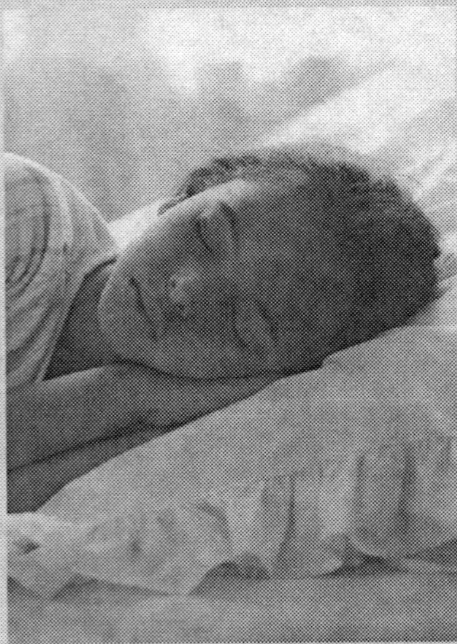

© Blend Images/Alamy

- **Focused Awareness**: Fully alert and absorbed
- **Drifting Consciousness**: Meandering thoughts
- **Divided Consciousness**: Dividing consciousness between two or more tasks
- **Sleeping and Dreaming**: Dimmed consciousness during sleep
- **Waking States of Altered Consciousness**: Changes in usual states of awareness during wakefulness

MODULE 4.2 Sleeping and Dreaming

Stages of Sleep

- **Non-REM Sleep (Stages 1 to 4)**: Changing brain wave patterns leading to slow wave sleep
- **REM Sleep**: Active brain wave patterns associated with dreaming

Functions of Sleep

- **Protective Function**: Keeping out of harm's way
- **Energy-Conservation Function**: Preserving energy needed to find food
- **Restorative Function**: Replenishing spent bodily resources
- **Memory Consolidation Function**: Converting fresh memories into more durable memories

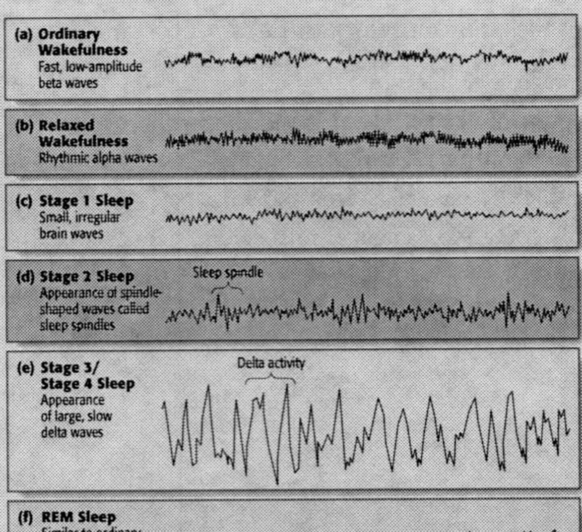

Brain Wave Patterns

Theories of Dreaming

- **Problem-Solving Hypothesis:** Dreams as attempts to solve problems of daily living
- **Activation-Synthesis Hypothesis:** The cortex trying to make sense of random electrical discharges from the brain stem
- **Wish-Fulfillment Hypothesis:** Freud's view of dreams as disguised sexual or aggressive wishes

Problems with Sleep

- **Sleep Deprivation:** Can cause significant problems if it becomes a pattern
- **Sleep Disorders**: Disturbances of normal sleep, including insomnia, narcolepsy, sleep apnea, nightmare disorder, sleep terror disorder, and sleepwalking disorder

MODULE 4.3 Altering Consciousness Through Meditation and Hypnosis

Types of Meditation

- **Transcendental Meditation**: Repeating a mantra to induce a meditative state
- **Mindfulness Meditation**: Passively attending to the flow of thoughts

Theories of Hypnosis

- **Role-Playing Theory**: Hypnosis as a social interaction
- **Neodissociation Theory**: Hypnosis as splitting of consciousness

© Michael Newman/Photo Edit

MODULE 4.4 Altering Consciousness Through Drugs

Types of Drugs

- **Depressants**: Alcohol, barbiturates, tranquilizers, opioids
- **Stimulants**: Amphetamine, cocaine, nicotine, caffeine
- **Hallucinogens**: LSD, mescaline, psilocybin, PCP, marijuana

Factors in Drug Use and Abuse (Multiple Factors Involved)

- **Social Factors**: Alienation, unemployment, cultural norms, acculturation
- **Biological Factors**: Genetic influences, effects on neurotransmitters in the brain
- **Psychological Factors**: Feelings of hopelessness, sensation seeking, desire to escape troubling emotions

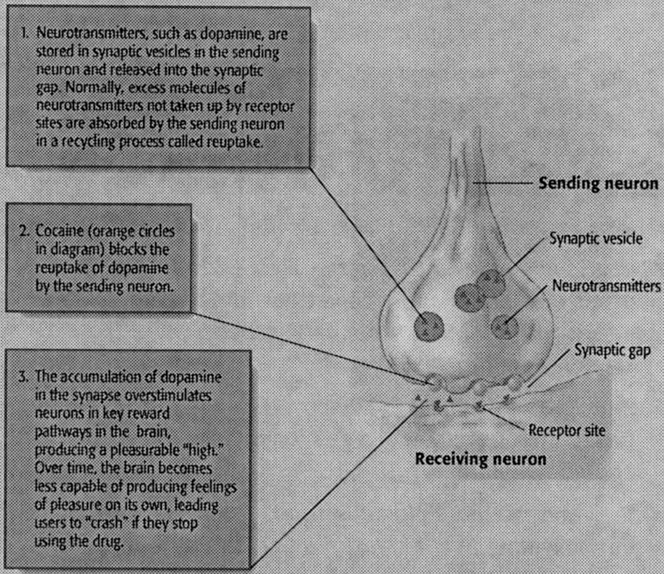

How Cocaine Works in the Brain

5 Learning

Confessions of an Egg Hater

SLICE OF LIFE I hate eggs. It's not just the taste of eggs I can't stand. The smell, the feel, the very sight of eggs is enough to make me sick. Watching other people eat eggs can make me nauseous. It's not that I'm allergic to eggs. I like all kinds of baked goods that are made with eggs. I'm fine with eggs as long as they are cooked into other foods so they are no longer recognizable as, well, eggs. But eggs themselves, especially runny eggs, fill me with disgust.

I wasn't born with a disgust for eggs. Nor did I always dislike eggs. My parents tell me I was actually quite fond of eggs as a young child. But somewhere along the line I acquired an aversion to eggs; chances are I had an unpleasant experience with them. No, I don't think I was chased around a barn by a clutch of crazed chickens. Most likely, I had an experience in which eating eggs sickened me. Or perhaps I was forced to eat eggs when I wasn't feeling well. In any event, I have no memory of it. All I know is that I hate eggs and have hated them for as long as I can recall.

I described my aversion to eggs to introduce you to the topic of learning. Some responses, such as pulling your hand away from a hot stove, are reflexive. We don't learn reflexive responses; we are biologically equipped to perform them automatically. Other behaviors develop naturally as the result of maturation. As a child's muscles mature, the child becomes capable of lifting heavier weights or throwing a ball a longer distance. But other responses, such as my aversion to eggs, are acquired through *experience*.

Psychologists take a broad view of the concept of learning. To psychologists, learning is more than just book learning or learning that takes place in a classroom. Psychologists generally define learning as a relatively permanent change in behavior that results from experience. It is through experience that we learn about the world and develop new skills, such as riding a bicycle or cooking a soufflé. Acquired taste preferences or aversions, including my aversion to eggs, are also learned behaviors. Note the use of the term *relatively permanent* in the definition of learning. For learning to occur, changes in behavior must be enduring. But change need not be permanent. It is possible to unlearn behavior. For example, you would need to unlearn the behavior of driving on the right side of the road if you wanted to drive in a country where people drive on the left side of the road.

© XAOC/Shutterstock.com

(*Continued on page 180*)

DID YOU KNOW THAT...

- Déjà-vu may be a learned response? (p. 183)
- In an early study, a young boy learned to fear a white rat after experimenters repeatedly made loud noises by banging steel bars behind his head while the rat was present? (p. 186)
- Principles of learning discovered by Ivan Pavlov based on his studies of digestion in dogs help explain phobias in humans? (p. 186)
- Salivating to the sound of a tone may not be harmful, but salivating at the sight of a Scotch bottle may well be dangerous to people battling alcoholism? (p. 187)
- The concept of a discriminative stimulus is a useful thing to keep in mind when asking someone for money or a favor? (p. 195)
- Principles of learning help explain how slot machines become "one-armed bandits"? (p. 197)
- Scheduling tests on specific days may inadvertently reinforce students to cram just before exams and to slack off afterward? (p. 198)

Learning Objectives

By reading this chapter you will be able to . . .

1. **DEFINE** learning in psychological terms.
2 **DESCRIBE** the process of classical conditioning and **EXPLAIN** how conditioned responses are acquired.
3 **IDENTIFY** key figures in the development and application of classical conditioning and **DESCRIBE** their contributions.
4 **EXPLAIN** how conditioned responses can be strengthened.
5 **APPLY** a cognitive perspective to understanding classical conditioning.
6 **APPLY** principles of classical conditioning to real-life examples.
7 **IDENTIFY** key figures in the development and application of operant conditioning and **DESCRIBE** their contributions.
8 **EXPLAIN** the differences between different types of reinforcement and different schedules of reinforcement, and between reinforcement and punishment.
9 **EXPLAIN** the differences between escape learning and avoidance learning.
10 **APPLY** principles of operant conditioning to real-life examples.
11 **DEFINE** cognitive learning.
12 **IDENTIFY** and **DESCRIBE** several forms of cognitive learning.
13 **APPLY** principles of cognitive learning to real-life examples.
14 **APPLY** principles of reinforcement to daily life.

© Arthur Tilley/Creatas/Jupiter Images

Preview

(*Continued from page 178*)

Learning is adaptive—it enables organisms to adapt their behavior to the demands they face in the environment. Through learning, organisms acquire behaviors that increase their chances of survival. Even taste aversions can be adaptive. They prevent animals, including humans, from eating foods that have sickened or poisoned them in the past. But not all learned responses are adaptive. My own aversion to eggs limits the range of foods I might enjoy. By and large, however, learning helps prepare organisms to meet the demands that their environments impose on them.

Psychologists study many forms of learning, including three major types that are the focus of this chapter: classical conditioning, operant conditioning, and cognitive learning.

MODULE 5.1

Classical Conditioning: Learning Through Association

- What is learning?
- What is classical conditioning?
- What roles do extinction and spontaneous recovery play in classical conditioning?
- What roles do stimulus generalization and discrimination play in classical conditioning?
- What stimulus characteristics strengthen conditioned responses?
- What is a cognitive perspective on classical conditioning?
- What are some examples of classical conditioning in humans?

Do your muscles tighten at the sound of a dentist's drill? Do you suddenly begin to salivate when passing by your favorite bakery? You weren't born with these responses—you learned them. But how does **learning** occur?

To understand how responses are learned, we need to consider the work of the Russian physiologist Ivan Pavlov (1849–1936). Pavlov discovered the form of learning we call **classical conditioning**. Pavlov, who at the time was studying digestive processes in dogs, made this discovery when he observed that dogs would salivate to sounds in his laboratory that had become associated with food, such as the sound of metal food carts being wheeled into his laboratory.

You can think of classical conditioning as *learning by association*. If you associate the sound of a dentist's drill with pain because of past dental treatment, the sound of the drill will probably cause you to respond with the muscle tension that is a natural reflex to pain. If you associate a certain bakery with a particularly tasty treat, you may find yourself salivating simply by driving by the bakery. In other words, you learn to connect or associate two stimuli—the sound of the dental drill and pain, for instance (Chance, 2009). Although classical conditioning is a relatively simple form of learning, it plays important roles in our lives—as you will see in this module.

THE BRAIN LOVES A PUZZLE

As you read ahead, use the information in the text to solve the following puzzle:

A recovering heroin addict in New York City was trying to get his life back on track. One day he took the subway to begin work at a new job site. Just as the subway doors opened at a particular station, he suddenly experienced intense cravings for heroin and shortly thereafter experienced a full-blown relapse. Why do you suppose he experienced these strong cravings at a particular subway stop? What principles of learning explain these cravings?

Principles of Classical Conditioning

Ivan Pavlov (right) in his laboratory

Pavlov performed many experiments in classical conditioning. In a typical experiment, he harnessed dogs in an apparatus similar to the one shown in ■ Figure 5.1. When food is placed on a dog's tongue, the dog naturally salivates. This reflexive behavior is called an **unconditioned response (UR** or **UCR)** (*unconditioned* means "unlearned"). A stimulus that elicits an unconditioned response—in this case, the dog's food—is called an **unconditioned stimulus (US** or **UCS)**.

■ Figure 5.2 outlines the steps involved in a Pavlovian experiment. As you can see in Figure 5.2b, the introduction of a **neutral stimulus (NS)**, such as the tone produced by striking a tuning fork or ringing a bell, does not initially elicit a response of salivation. It may produce other responses, however. A dog's ears may turn up in response to the sound, but the dog doesn't naturally salivate when it hears the sound. However, through repeated pairings of the neutral stimulus and the unconditioned stimulus (Figure 5.2c), the dog acquires a *learned* response: salivation in response to the neutral stimulus alone (Figure 5.2d). Salivation to a tone alone is an example of a **conditioned response (CR)**. A previously neutral stimulus becomes a **conditioned stimulus (CS)** when it is paired with an unconditioned stimulus and begins to elicit the conditioned response. In addition to showing that salivation (CR) could be made to occur in response to a stimulus that did not naturally elicit the response, Pavlov observed that the strength of the conditioned response (the amount of salivation) increased with the number of pairings of the CS and US.

Conditioned salivation has been demonstrated with a wide variety of animals, including cats, rats, and yes, even cockroaches. Rather than using a bell or a tone as a conditioned stimulus (CS), Japanese investigators Hidehiro Watanabe and Makoto Mizunami stimulated the antennae of cockroaches with a scent of peppermint (a CS) while they placed droplets

CONCEPT 5.1
Pavlov's discovery that dogs would salivate to particular sounds in his laboratory led him to identify a process of learning called classical conditioning.

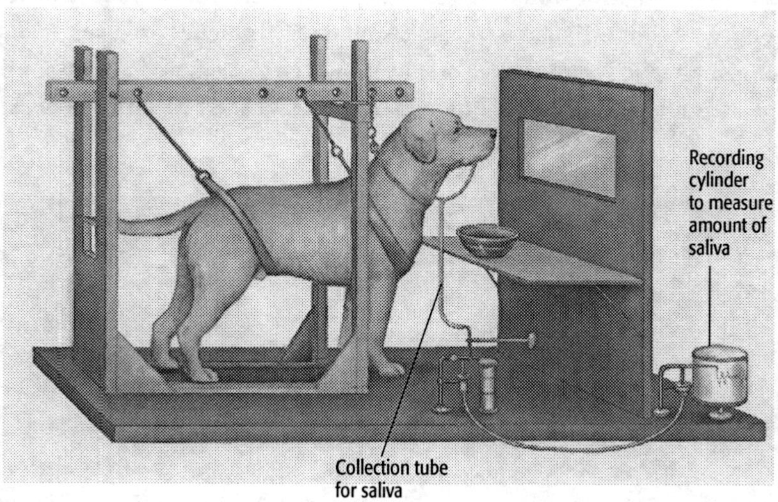

FIGURE 5.1 Apparatus Similar to One Used in Pavlov's Experiments on Conditioning
In Pavlov's studies, a research assistant positioned behind a mirror sounded a tone as food was placed on the dog's tongue. After several pairings of the tone and food, the dog acquired a conditioned response of salivation. The amount of saliva dripping through a tube to a collection vial was taken as the measure of the strength of the conditioned response.

learning A relatively permanent change in behavior acquired through experience.

classical conditioning The process of learning by which a previously neutral stimulus comes to elicit a response identical or similar to one that was originally elicited by another stimulus as the result of the pairing or association of the two stimuli.

unconditioned response (UR) An unlearned response to a stimulus.

unconditioned stimulus (US) A stimulus that elicits an unlearned response.

neutral stimulus (NS) A stimulus that before conditioning does not produce a particular response.

conditioned response (CR) An acquired or learned response to a conditioned stimulus.

conditioned stimulus (CS) A previously neutral stimulus that comes to elicit a conditioned response after it has been paired with an unconditioned stimulus.

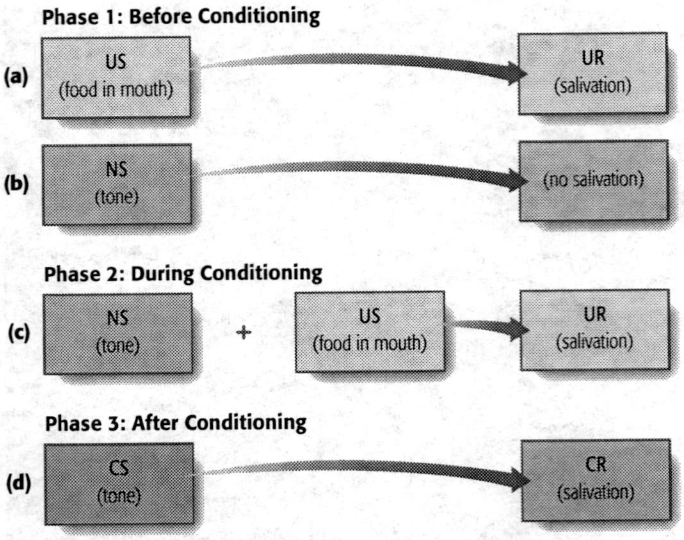

FIGURE 5.2 Diagramming Classical Conditioning
In classical conditioning, a neutral stimulus (the tone) is paired with an unconditioned stimulus (food) that normally elicits an unconditioned response (salivation). With repeated pairings, the neutral stimulus becomes a conditioned stimulus that elicits the conditioned response of salivation.

of a sugary substance (a US) on the insects' mouths (Watanabe & Mizunami, 2007). The insects naturally salivate (a UR) to sugary substances, but not to scents applied to their antennae. After a number of repetitions of this procedure, however, the insects salivated to the scent alone (a CR). Scientists hope that by studying simpler organisms like insects, they will learn more about the mechanisms of conditioning at the neuronal level (Fountain, 2007).

We next examine other characteristics of classical conditioning: extinction and spontaneous recovery, stimulus generalization and discrimination, and stimulus characteristics that strengthen conditioned responses.

Extinction and Spontaneous Recovery

Pavlov noticed that the conditioned response of salivation to the sound of a bell or a tuning fork would gradually weaken and eventually disappear when he repeatedly presented the sound in the absence of the US (food). This process is called **extinction** (see ■ Figure 5.3).

The extinguished response is not forgotten or lost to memory. It may return spontaneously at a later time when the animal is again exposed to the conditioned stimulus. This phenomenon is called **spontaneous recovery.** The recovered response will once again extinguish if the CS occurs in the absence of the US.

Pavlov discovered that when the CS and US are paired again after extinction has occurred, the response is likely to be learned more quickly than in the original conditioning. In many cases, the animal needs only one or two pairings. The process of relearning a conditioned response after extinction is called **reconditioning.**

CONCEPT 5.2
Through a process of extinction, conditioned responses gradually weaken and eventually disappear as the result of the repeated presentation of the conditioned stimulus in the absence of the unconditioned stimulus.

→ Concept Link
A therapy technique called gradual exposure makes use of the principle of extinction to help people overcome phobias. See Module 16.2.

CONCEPT 5.3
Extinguished responses are not forgotten but may return spontaneously in the future if the conditioned stimulus is presented again.

extinction The gradual weakening and eventual disappearance of a conditioned response.

spontaneous recovery The spontaneous return of a conditioned response following extinction.

reconditioning The process of relearning a conditioned response following extinction.

stimulus generalization The tendency for stimuli that are similar to the conditioned stimulus to elicit a conditioned response.

Stimulus Generalization and Stimulus Discrimination

Pavlov found that once animals were trained to salivate to a particular stimulus, such as a particular sound, they would also salivate, but less strongly, to a related sound that varied along a continuum, such as pitch. A sound with a higher or lower pitch than the original one might elicit some degree of salivation. The tendency of stimuli similar to the conditioned stimulus to elicit a conditioned response is called **stimulus generalization.**

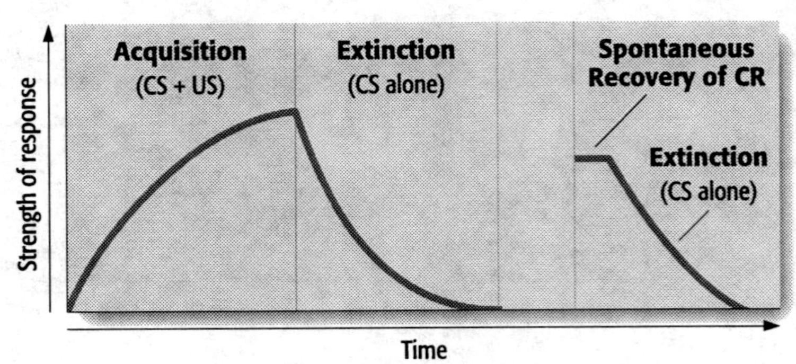

Figure 5.3 Strength of a Conditioned Response
With repeated pairings of the conditioned stimulus (CS) and unconditioned stimulus (US), the conditioned response (CR) increases in strength. When the CS is repeatedly presented alone, the CR gradually weakens and eventually is extinguished. After a period of time has elapsed, however, spontaneous recovery of the response may occur. But when the CS is again presented in the absence of the US, extinction re-occurs.

© Rich Diesslin and Rick London

Generally speaking, the greater the difference between the original stimulus and the related stimulus, the weaker the conditioned response. Were it not for stimulus generalization, the animal would need to be conditioned to respond to each stimulus no matter how slightly it varied from the original conditioned stimulus.

Stimulus generalization has survival value. It allows us to respond to a range of stimuli that are similar to an original threatening stimulus. Perhaps you were menaced or bitten by a large dog when you were young. Because of stimulus generalization, you may find yourself tensing up whenever you see a large dog approaching. Not all large dogs are dangerous, of course, but stimulus generalization helps prepare us just in case.

CONCEPT 5.4
Stimulus generalization has survival value by enabling organisms to generalize their learned responses to new stimuli that are similar to an original threatening stimulus.

Have you ever walked into a room and suddenly felt uncomfortable or anxious for no apparent reason? Your emotional reaction may be a conditioned response to generalized stimuli in the environment that are similar to cues associated with unpleasant experiences in the past. Perhaps, too, you have experienced déjà-vu—a feeling of having been in a place before when you've never actually been there. Stimulus generalization provides an explanation of these experiences. The feeling of familiarity in novel situations may be a conditioned response evoked by cues or stimuli in these novel environments that resemble conditioned stimuli encountered in other situations. A fleeting odor, the way light bounces off a ceiling, even the color of walls—all may be cues that evoke conditioned responses acquired in other settings.

© Andrew Yates Productions/Getty Images

In a case example, a man developed a conditioned fear of enclosed spaces (claustrophobia) after he became trapped behind a refrigerator and nearly suffocated while helping a friend move. Through stimulus generalization, the phobia generalized to related stimuli, including riding on small, crowded elevators. As the result of stimulus discrimination, however, he did not experience any fear of riding on larger, uncrowded elevators.

Stimulus discrimination, the ability to differentiate among related stimuli, represents the opposite side of the coin to stimulus generalization. This ability allows us to fine-tune our responses to the environment. Suppose, for example, an animal in a laboratory study receives a mild shock shortly after exposure to a CS (a tone) (Domjan, 2005). After a few pairings of the tone and shock, the animal shows signs of fear (e.g., cowering, urinating) to the tone alone. The tone is the CS, the shock is the US, and the pairing of the two leads to the acquisition of the conditioned response (CR) of fear to the tone alone. Now, let's say the pairings of the tone and the shock continue but are interspersed with a tone of a higher pitch that is not accompanied by a shock. The animal learns to discriminate between these two stimuli, responding with fear to the original tone but remaining calm when the higher-pitched tone is sounded.

stimulus discrimination The tendency to differentiate among stimuli so that stimuli that are related to the original conditioned stimulus, but not identical to it, fail to elicit a conditioned response.

Stimulus discrimination in daily life allows us to differentiate between threatening and nonthreatening stimuli. For example, through repeated noneventful encounters with certain breeds of dogs, we may learn to respond with fear to a large dog of an unfamiliar breed but not to the friendly Labrador that lives next door.

■ Figure 5.4 illustrates the processes of stimulus generalization and stimulus discrimination.

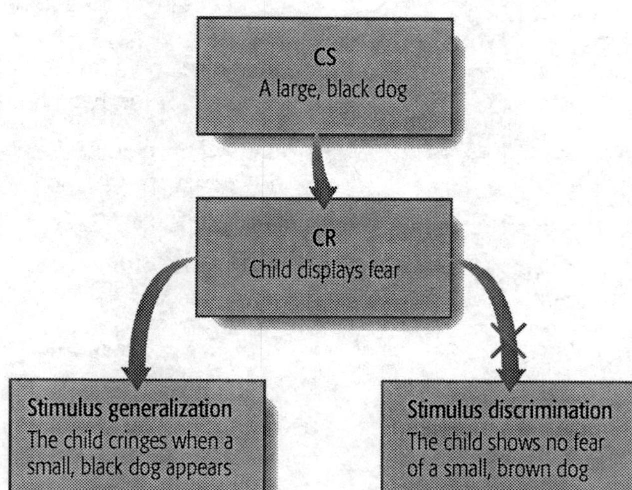

FIGURE 5.4 Stimulus Generalization and Discrimination
In stimulus generalization, a conditioned response generalizes to stimuli that are similar to the original conditioned stimulus. In stimulus discrimination, the organism differentiates between related stimuli.

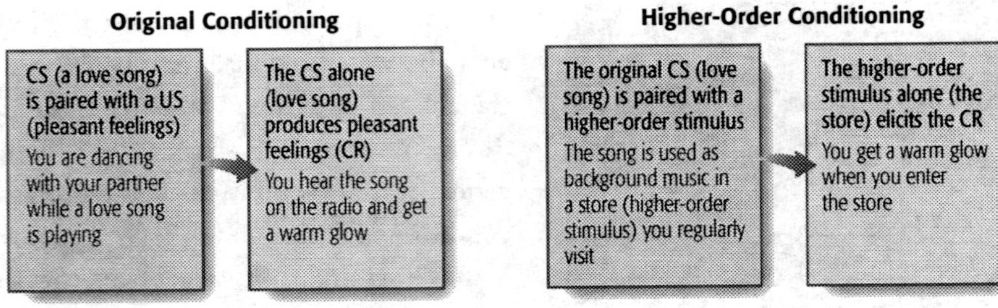

Figure 5.5 Higher-Order Conditioning
In higher-order conditioning, a previously neutral stimulus becomes a conditioned stimulus when it is paired with an already established conditioned stimulus.

CONCEPT 5.5
By learning to differentiate among related stimuli, we are able to fine-tune our responses to the environment.

higher-order conditioning The process by which a new stimulus comes to elicit a conditioned response as a result of its being paired with a conditioned stimulus that already elicits the conditioned response.

Higher-Order Conditioning

In **higher-order conditioning**, a new stimulus becomes a conditioned stimulus when it is paired with an established conditioned stimulus that already elicits the conditioned response (see ■ Figure 5.5). What is learned is the association between two conditioned stimuli, or a CS-CS connection. Consider, for example, a couple that has a favorite song that was previously associated with positive feelings they had towards one another when they first met or fell in love. The song becomes a conditioned stimulus (CS) that elicits these positive feelings (the CR). Other cues associated with the song, such as the jingle associated with the radio station that regularly played the song or even the name of the singer, may become conditioned stimuli that elicit a similar response. Concept Chart 5.1 presents an overview of the major concepts in classical conditioning.

Stimulus Characteristics That Strengthen Conditioned Responses

Psychologists have identified several key factors relating to the timing and intensity of stimuli that serve to strengthen conditioned responses:

1. *Frequency of pairings.* Generally, the more often the CS is paired with the US, the stronger and more reliable the CR will be. In some cases, however, even a single

CONCEPT CHART 5.1 Key Concepts in Classical Conditioning

Concept	Description	Example: Fear of Dentistry
Classical conditioning	The process of learning by which a response identical or similar to one originally elicited by an unconditioned stimulus (US) occurs following a conditioned stimulus (CS) as the result of the prior pairing of the two stimuli	The association of pain during dental procedures with environmental stimuli in the dentist's office leads to a learned fear response to the environmental cues alone.
Extinction	Gradual weakening and eventual disappearance of the conditioned response (CR) when the CS is repeatedly presented without the US	The use of anesthetics and painless dental techniques leads to the gradual reduction and elimination of fear of dentistry.
Spontaneous recovery	Spontaneous return of the CR some time after extinction occurs	Fear of dentistry returns spontaneously a few months or a few years after extinction.
Stimulus generalization	CR evoked by stimuli that are similar to the original CS	Person shows a fear response when visiting the office of a new dentist.
Stimulus discrimination	CR not evoked by stimuli that are related but not identical to the CS	Person shows a fear response to the sight of a dentist's drill but not to equipment used for cleaning teeth.

pairing can produce a strong CR. An airline passenger who experiences a sudden descent during a flight may develop an immediate and enduring fear of flying.

2. *Timing.* The strongest CRs occur when the CS is presented first and remains present throughout the administration of the US. Weaker CRs develop when the CS is presented first but is withdrawn before the US is introduced. Other timing sequences, such as the simultaneous presentation of the CS and US, produce even weaker CRs, if any at all.
3. *Intensity of the US.* A stronger US will typically lead to faster conditioning than a weaker one. For example, a puff of air (US) may be delivered shortly after a CS (e.g., a tone or a visual stimulus such as a light) is presented. The air puff produces a reflexive eyeblink response (UR). After a few pairings, a conditioned eyeblink (CR) occurs in response to the CS (tone or light) alone. A stronger air puff will lead to faster conditioning than a weaker one.

CONCEPT 5.6
The strength of a classically conditioned response depends on the frequency of pairings and the timing of the stimuli, as well as the intensity of the US.

A Cognitive Perspective on Classical Conditioning

Psychologist Robert Rescorla (1967, 1988, 2009) takes a cognitive perspective in explaining classical conditioning. He challenged the conventional behaviorist view that classical conditioning is based simply on repeated pairing of a previously neutral stimulus and an unconditioned stimulus. He argued that conditioning is a cognitive process by which the organism learns that a conditioned stimulus is a reliable signal for *predicting* the occurrence of the unconditioned stimulus. The tone or bell in Pavlov's experiments with dogs creates an expectancy that food is about to arrive, which in turn leads to salivation and other feeding behaviors, such as tail wagging. To Rescorla, humans and other animals actively seek information that helps them make predictions about important events in their environments. Conditioned stimuli are signals or cues organisms use to make these predictions. The more reliable the signal, the stronger the conditioned response.

CONCEPT 5.7
In Rescorla's view, classical conditioning involves a cognitive process by which organisms learn to anticipate certain events based on cues (conditioned stimuli) that reliably predict the occurrence of these events.

Rescorla's model has important survival implications. Dogs and other animals may be more likely to survive if they learn to respond with salivation to cues that food is present, since salivation prepares them to swallow food. Animals are also more likely to survive if they learn to respond with fear (heightened bodily arousal) to cues that reliably signal the presence of threatening stimuli. Consider an animal that hears a sound or gets a whiff of an odor (a CS) previously associated with the presence of a particular predator (a US). By responding quickly with heightened arousal to such a stimulus, the animal is better prepared to take defensive action if the predator appears. Thus, we can think of classical conditioning as a kind of built-in early-warning system.

Rescorla's model also explains why you are likely to develop a fear of dentistry more quickly if you experience pain during each dental visit than if you have pain only every now and then. In other words, the more reliably the CS (dental cues) signals the occurrence of the US (pain), the stronger the conditioned response is likely to be.

Why It Matters: Examples of Classical Conditioning

Pavlov's studies might merit only a footnote in the history of psychology if classical conditioning were limited to the salivary responses of dogs. However, classical conditioning helps us explain such diverse behaviors as phobias, drug cravings, and taste aversions. John B. Watson, the founder of behaviorism, believed that Pavlov's principles of

© Archives of the History of American, Psychology, The Center for the History of Psychology—The University of Akron
John Watson

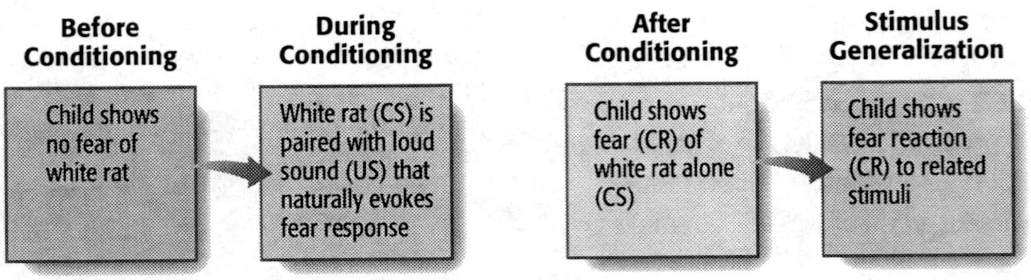

FIGURE 5.6 The Conditioning of "Little Albert"

conditioning could explain emotional responses in humans. In 1919, Watson set out with Rosalie Rayner, a student who was later to become his wife, to prove that a fear response could be acquired through classical conditioning. After taking a look at Watson and Rayner's experiment, we consider other examples of conditioning in humans.

Classical Conditioning of Fear Responses

conditioned emotional reaction (CER) An emotional response to a particular stimulus acquired through classical conditioning.

CONCEPT 5.8
Classical conditioning helps explain the development of conditioned emotional reactions, such as conditioned fear responses.

→ Concept Link
Clinicians apply principles of classical conditioning in explaining the development of excessive fear reactions, or phobias. See Module 15.2.

phobias Excessive fears of particular objects or situations.

As their subject, Watson and Rayner selected an 11-month-old boy whom they called Albert B., but who is better known in the annals of psychology as Little Albert (Watson & Rayner, 1920). Albert had previously shown no fear of a white rat that was placed near him and had even reached out to stroke the animal (see ■ Figure 5.6). In the experimental procedure, the rat was placed close to Albert, and as he reached for it, Watson banged a steel bar with a hammer just behind his head, creating a loud gong. Watson believed that loud sounds naturally make infants cringe and shudder with fear. Sure enough, Albert showed signs of fear when the bar was struck—crying and burying his face in the mattress. Watson and Rayner then repeatedly paired the rat and the loud sound, which resulted in Albert's developing a fear response to the sight of the rat alone. Such an acquired fear response is called a **conditioned emotional reaction (CER)**. Later experiments showed that Albert's fear response had generalized to other furry stimuli, including a dog, a rabbit, and even a Santa Claus mask that Watson had worn.

Let us examine the Watson and Rayner study by applying what we know about classical conditioning. Before conditioning, Albert showed no fear of the white rat; it was a neutral stimulus. The unconditioned stimulus (US) was the loud banging sound, a stimulus that naturally elicits a fear response (UR) in young children. Through repeated pairings of the white rat and the banging sound (US), the white rat alone (CS) came to elicit a fear response (CR).

Though the Little Albert experiment is among the most famous studies in psychology, it would not pass muster with the stricter ethical standards in place today. Exposing a child to intense fear, even with the parents' permission, fails to adhere to the responsibility investigators have to safeguard the welfare of research participants. In addition, Watson and Rayner made no attempt to undo or extinguish Albert's fears, as ethical codes would now require, although they did discuss techniques they might use to do so. We can't say for sure what became of Little Albert, but investigators report that, sadly, the child they believe may have been Albert succumbed to a childhood illness at the age of six (H. P. Beck, Levinson, & Irons, 2009).

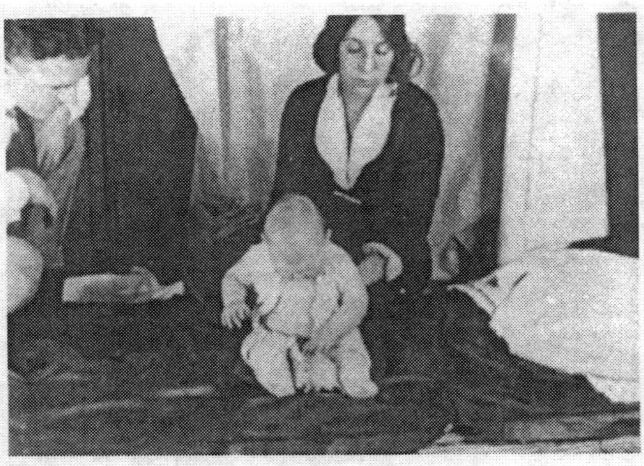

John Watson and Rosalie Rayner with Little Albert

© Archives of the History of American Psychology—The University of Akron.

Excessive fears, or **phobias**, such as Albert's fear of white rats or the fear of dentistry, can be acquired through classical conditioning (Field, 2006; J. J. Kim & Jung, 2006). In one case example, a 34-year-old woman had been terrified of riding on elevators ever since a childhood incident in which she and her grandmother were trapped on an elevator for hours. For her, the single pairing of previously neutral stimuli (cues associated with riding on elevators) and a traumatic experience was sufficient to produce an enduring phobia (fear of elevators). In some cases, the original conditioning experiences may be lost to memory, or have occurred even before language developed (as in Albert's case).

Early work on classical conditioning of fear responses set the stage for the development of **behavior therapy**, a form of therapy involving the systematic application of principles of learning to help people overcome phobias and change problem behaviors such as addictive behaviors and childhood behavior problems. We discuss specific applications of behavior therapy in Chapter 16.

CONCEPT 5.9
Feelings of nostalgia may be conditioned responses elicited by stimuli that were associated with pleasant experiences in the past.

behavior therapy A form of therapy that involves the systematic application of the principles of learning.

Classical Conditioning of Positive Emotions

It's not only negative emotions like fear that can be classically conditioned. Perhaps you've had the experience of hearing a certain song on the radio and suddenly smiling or feeling cheerful, or even experiencing a tinge of sexual arousal. Chances are the song evoked past experiences associated with pleasant emotions or sexual arousal. Similarly, feelings of nostalgia may be conditioned responses elicited by subtle cues in the environment that had come to be associated with pleasant experiences in the past. These cues—perhaps just a whiff of perfume or the mist in the air on a spring day—may induce nostalgic feelings.

Classical Conditioning of Drug Cravings

People with chemical dependencies frequently encounter drug cravings, especially when they undergo drug withdrawal or go "cold turkey." Though cravings may have a physiological basis (they constitute part of the withdrawal syndrome for addictive drugs), classical conditioning can also contribute to these strong desires. Cravings may be elicited by cues (conditioned stimuli) in the environment associated with prior drug use. People battling alcoholism may experience strong cravings for the drug when they are exposed to drug-related conditioned stimuli, such as the sight of a bottle of alcohol. Cravings may be elicited by conditioned stimuli long after withdrawal symptoms have passed, such as cues associated with a subway station where a drug abuser formerly bought drugs.

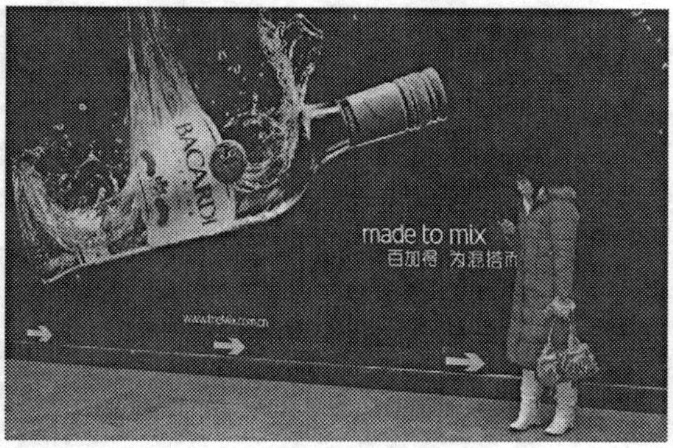

© Lou-Foto/Alamy

Drug cravings may be conditioned responses elicited by exposure to cues (conditioned stimuli) associated with drug-using behavior.

The conditioning model of drug cravings is supported by research that demonstrates that people with alcoholism salivate more at the sight and odor of alcohol than do nonalcoholic people (Monti et al., 1987). Salivating to the sound of a tone may be harmless enough, but salivating when looking at a picture of a Scotch bottle in a magazine can be dangerous to a person struggling with alcoholism. Not surprisingly, drug counselors encourage recovering drug and alcohol abusers to avoid cues associated with their former drug-use patterns.

© Tom Kitchin/Tom Stack & Associates

© John Garcia

In a field experiment by psychologist John Garcia (shown here), investigators left sheep carcasses on the range after injecting them with a nausea-producing chemical. After eating meat from these carcasses and becoming sickened, coyotes developed a conditioned taste aversion to sheep meat.

Classical Conditioning of Taste Aversions

conditioned taste aversions Aversions to particular tastes acquired through classical conditioning.

CONCEPT 5.10
Drug cravings and taste aversions may be acquired through classical conditioning.

The principles of classical conditioning can also be used to explain **conditioned taste aversions**, including my disgust for eggs (Ferreira et al., 2006; Garcia & Koelling, 2009; Limebeer & Parker, 2006). Psychologist John Garcia was the first to demonstrate experimentally the role of classical conditioning in the acquisition of taste aversions. Garcia and colleague Bob Koelling noticed something unusual in the behavior of rats that had been exposed to nausea-inducing radiation. The rats developed an aversion or "conditioned nausea" to flavored water sweetened with saccharin when the water was paired with the nausea-producing radiation (Garcia & Koelling, 1966). In classical conditioning terms, the radiation was the US; the nausea it produced was the UR; the flavored water was the CS; and the aversion (nausea) the CS elicited on its own was the CR.

In related work, Garcia demonstrated that aversion to particular foods could be classically conditioned by giving rats a nausea-inducing drug soon after they ate the foods (Garcia & Koelling, 1971). Moreover, taste aversions were acquired even when the CS (the taste of the food) was presented a few hours before the presentation of the US (the nausea-inducing stimulus) (Domjan, 2005). This discovery shocked Garcia's experimental colleagues, who believed that classical conditioning could occur only when the CS is followed almost immediately by the US. Moreover, Garcia and his team were able to demonstrate that conditioned taste aversions could be acquired on the basis of a single pairing of the flavor of a food or drink with a nausea-inducing stimulus.

SLICE OF LIFE Like other forms of classical conditioning, conditioned taste aversions have clear survival benefits. Our ancestors lived without the benefit of refrigeration or preservatives. Acquiring an aversion to foods whose rancid smells and tastes sickened them would have helped them avoid such foods in the future. In a classic study that literally applied the principles of classical conditioning on the range, John Garcia and his colleagues came up with an ingenious way to help sheep ranchers protect their sheep from coyotes (Gustavson & Garcia, 1974; Gustavson et al., 1974). At the time of the study, free-ranging coyotes were killing thousands of sheep, and ranchers seeking to protect their flocks were killing so many coyotes that their survival as a species was endangered. It was therefore important to find a way of stopping the coyotes' destructive behavior without killing them. As an experiment, the researchers injected sheep carcasses with a poison that would sicken but not kill the coyotes, and scattered the carcasses over the range. Not only did sheep killings decline, but some coyotes developed such an aversion to the taste of sheep meat that they ran away just at the sight or smell of sheep.

Conditioning the Immune System

immune system The body's system of defense against disease.

CONCEPT 5.11
Investigators have found that even immune-system responses can be classically conditioned.

In a landmark study, Robert Ader and Nicholas Cohen (1982) showed that classical conditioning even extends to the workings of the **immune system**. The immune system protects the body from disease-causing organisms. The researchers had laboratory rats ingest saccharin-sweetened water (CS) while simultaneously giving them a drug (US) that suppressed immune-system responses (UR). After several pairings of the CS and US, immune suppression (CR) occurred when the rats drank the sweetened water alone (CS).

Conditioned immune suppression can be made to occur in response to other conditioned stimuli, such as odors and sounds, as well as in humans (Kusnecov, 2001; Pacheco-Lopez et al., 2005). For example, a group of healthy people were given an immune-suppressant drug as an unconditioned stimulus, which was paired with a distinctively flavored drink as a conditioned stimulus during four separate sessions spread over three days (Goebel et al., 2002). Afterward, presenting the drink without the active drug succeeded in suppressing immune-system responses, thereby demonstrating the acquisition of a conditioned response.

The ability to acquire an immune-suppressant response through classical conditioning may have important health implications for humans. In people who receive organ transplants, the immune system attacks the transplanted organs as foreign objects. Perhaps classical conditioning can be used to suppress the tendency of the body to reject transplanted organs, lessening the need for immune-suppressant drugs. It is also conceivable that classical conditioning may be used to give the immune system a boost in its fight against disease, perhaps even to strengthen the body's ability to defend itself against cancer. However, we need further research to determine the value of classical conditioning in medical treatment.

5.1 MODULE REVIEW Classical Conditioning: Learning Through Association

Recite It

What is learning?

- Psychologists generally define learning as a relatively permanent change in behavior that results from experience.

What is classical conditioning?

- Classical conditioning is a process of learning in which the pairing of two stimuli leads to a response to one stimulus that is the same as or similar to the response previously elicited by the other stimulus.

What roles do extinction and spontaneous recovery play in classical conditioning?

- Extinction is the process by which learned responses gradually weaken and eventually disappear when the conditioned stimulus (CS) is presented repeatedly in the absence of the unconditioned stimulus (US).
- Spontaneous recovery is the return of the conditioned response some time after extinction.

What roles do stimulus generalization and discrimination play in classical conditioning?

- Stimulus generalization refers to the tendency of stimuli that are similar to the conditioned stimulus to elicit a conditioned response.
- Through stimulus discrimination, organisms learn to differentiate among stimuli so that stimuli that are related to the conditioned stimulus, but not identical to it, fail to elicit a conditioned response.

What stimulus characteristics strengthen conditioned responses?

- Factors related to the strength of conditioned responses include the frequency of the pairings of the conditioned stimulus and unconditioned stimulus, the timing of the presentation of the two stimuli, and the intensity of the unconditioned stimulus.

What is a cognitive perspective on classical conditioning?

- Developed by Robert Rescorla, the cognitive perspective on classical conditioning holds that conditioning depends on the informational value that the conditioned stimulus acquires in predicting the occurrence of the unconditioned stimulus. According to this model, humans and other animals actively seek information that helps them make predictions about important events in their environment; conditioned stimuli are cues that they use to make these predictions.

What are some examples of classical conditioning in humans?

- Examples include the acquisition of fear responses and taste aversions. Classical conditioning also plays a role in positive emotions, drug cravings, and immune-system responses.

Recall It

1. The process by which conditioned responses occur in response to stimuli that are similar to conditioned stimuli is called ________.
2. Which of the following does *not* affect the strength of conditioned responses?
   a. frequency of pairings of the CS with the US.
   b. timing of the presentation of the CS and US.
   c. intensity of the US.
   d. alternation of a US–CS presentation with a CR–UR presentation.

3. In classical conditioning terms, the radiation in Garcia's research on taste aversion is the ______.
   a. UR. b. CS. c. US. d. CR.
4. Rescorla's cognitive model of classical conditioning emphasizes the role of
   a. repeated pairings of the CS and US as the key factor in classical conditioning.
   b. the informational value of the CS as a signal or cue.
   c. the relationship between the strength of conditioning and the intensity of the US.
   d. the role of the US as a predictor of the CS.
5. In Watson and Rayner's study of "Little Albert," the child became frightened of a white rat and similar stimuli because
   a. children are naturally afraid of white rats.
   b. a loud noise occurred whenever the rat was in Albert's presence.
   c. the rat was repeatedly paired with a neutral stimulus.
   d. Albert had a traumatic experience with a rat.

Think About It

- Can you think of any examples of classical conditioning in your daily life? For example, some people experience emotional reactions when they hear certain music or sounds, or get a whiff of certain odors. How might you explain the origins of these responses in classical conditioning terms?
- What do you fear? Do these fears interfere with your daily life? Based on your reading of the chapter, what do you think might be the origin of these fears? How are you coping with them? Have you talked to anyone about them? Is there anyone you might contact to help you overcome them, such as a college health official or a health care provider in your area?

MODULE 5.2

Operant Conditioning: Learning Through Consequences

- What is Thorndike's Law of Effect?
- What is operant conditioning?
- What are the different types of reinforcers?
- What are the different schedules of reinforcement, and how are they related to learning?
- What are escape learning and avoidance learning?
- What is punishment, and why are psychologists concerned about its use?
- What are some applications of operant conditioning?

Classical conditioning can explain how we learn relatively simple, reflexive responses, such as salivation and eyeblinks, as well as emotional responses associated with fear and disgust. But classical conditioning cannot explain how we learn the more complex behaviors that are part and parcel of our experiences: getting up in the morning, dressing, going to work or school, preparing meals, taking care of household chores, running errands, completing homework, and socializing with friends, among countless other behaviors of daily life. To account for the process of learning such complex behaviors, we turn to a form of learning called *operant conditioning*. With classical conditioning, learning results from the association between stimuli before a response occurs. With operant conditioning, learning results from the association of a response with its consequences. With operant conditioning, responses are acquired and strengthened on the basis of the effects they produce in the environment.

Our study of operant conditioning focuses on two American psychologists: Edward Thorndike, whose Law of Effect was the first systematic attempt to describe how behavior is affected by its consequences, and B. F. Skinner, whose experimental work laid out many of the principles of operant conditioning.

CONCEPT 5.12
According to Thorndike's Law of Effect, we are more likely to repeat responses that have satisfying effects and are less likely to repeat those that lead to discomfort.

Thorndike and the Law of Effect

Edward Thorndike (1874–1947) studied learning in animals because he found them easier to work with than people. He constructed a device called a "puzzle box"—a cage in which the animal (usually a cat) had to perform a simple act (such as pulling a looped string or pushing a pedal) in order to make its escape and reach a dish of food placed within its view just outside the cage (see ■ Figure 5.7). The animal would first engage in seemingly random behaviors until it accidentally performed the response that released the door. Thorndike argued that the animals did not employ reasoning, insight, or any other form of higher intelligence to find their way to the exit. Rather, through a random process of *trial and error* they gradually eliminated useless responses and eventually chanced upon the successful behavior. Successful responses were then "stamped in" by the pleasure they produced and became more likely to be repeated in the future.

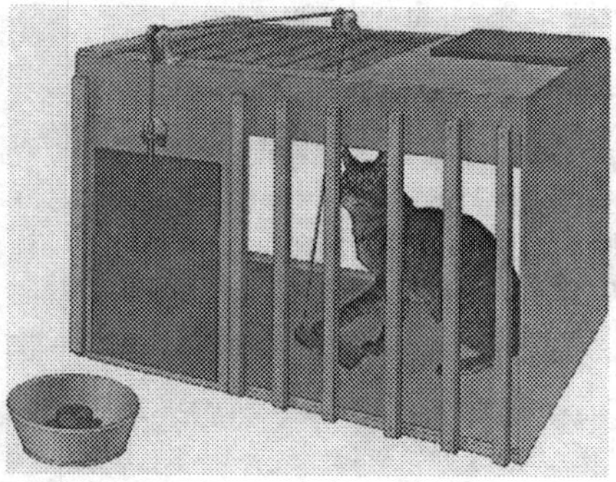

FIGURE 5.7 Thorndike's Puzzle Box
Cats placed in Thorndike's puzzle box learned to make their escape through a random process of trial and error.

Based on his observations, Thorndike (1905) proposed a principle that he called the **Law of Effect**, which holds that the tendency for a response to occur depends on the effects it has on the environment (P. L. Brown & Jenkins, 2009). Specifically, Thorndike's Law of Effect states that responses that have satisfying effects are strengthened and become more likely to occur again in a given situation, whereas responses that lead to discomfort are weakened and become less likely to recur. Modern psychologists call the first part of the Law of Effect *reinforcement* and the second part *punishment* (L. T. Benjamin, 1988).

Law of Effect Thorndike's principle that responses that have satisfying effects are more likely to recur, whereas those that have unpleasant effects are less likely to recur.

Thorndike went on to study how the principles of animal learning that he formulated could be applied to human behavior and especially to education. He believed that although human behavior is certainly more complex than animal behavior, it, too, can be explained on the basis of trial-and-error learning in which accidental successes become "stamped in" by positive consequences.

B. F. Skinner and Operant Conditioning

Thorndike laid the groundwork for an explanation of learning based on the association between responses and their consequences. It would fall to another American psychologist, B. F. Skinner (1904–1990), to develop a more formal model of this type of learning, which he called *operant conditioning.*

Skinner was arguably not only the most famous psychologist of his time but also the most controversial. What made him famous was his ability to bring behaviorist principles into the public eye through his books, articles in popular magazines, and public appearances. What made him controversial was his belief in *radical behaviorism*, which holds that behavior, whether animal or human, is completely determined by environmental and genetic influences. Free will, according to Skinner, is but an illusion or a myth. Though the staunch behaviorism he espoused was controversial in his own time

CONCEPT 5.13
B. F. Skinner believed that human behavior is completely determined by environmental and genetic influences and that the concept of free will is but an illusion or myth.

Skinner box An experimental apparatus developed by B. F. Skinner for studying relationships between reinforcement and behavior.

operant conditioning The process of learning in which the consequences of a response determine the probability that the response will be repeated.

operant response A response that operates on the environment to produce certain consequences.

reinforcer A stimulus or event that increases the probability that the response it follows will be repeated.

superstitious behavior In Skinner's view, behavior acquired through coincidental association of a response and a reinforcement.

and remains so today, there is no doubt that his concept of operant conditioning alone merits him a place among the pioneers of modern psychology.

Like Watson, Skinner was a strict behaviorist who believed that psychologists should limit themselves to the study of observable behavior. Because "private events," such as thoughts and feelings, cannot be observed, he believed they have no place in a scientific account of behavior. For Skinner, the mind was a "black box" whose contents cannot be illuminated by science.

Skinner allowed that some responses occur reflexively, as Pavlov had demonstrated. But classical conditioning is limited to explaining how new stimuli can elicit existing behaviors, such as salivation. It cannot account for new behaviors, such as the behavior of the experimental animals in Thorndike's puzzle box. Skinner found in Thorndike's work a guiding principle that behavior is shaped by its consequences. However, he rejected Thorndike's mentalistic concept that consequences influence behavior because they produce "satisfying effects." Skinner proposed that organisms learn responses that *operate* on the environment to produce consequences; he therefore called this learning process *operant conditioning.*

Skinner studied animal learning using a device we now call a **Skinner box**. The Skinner box is a cage that contains a food-release mechanism the animal activates when it responds in a certain way—for example, by pressing a lever or pushing a button.

Through **operant conditioning**, organisms learn responses, such as pressing a bar, that produce changes in the environment (release of food). In this form of learning, the consequences of a response determine the likelihood that the response will occur again. The response itself is called an **operant response** or, more simply, an "operant." Behaviors that produce rewarding effects are strengthened—that is, they become more likely to occur again. In effect, a well-trained operant response becomes a habit (Staddon & Cerutti, 2003). For example, if your teacher responds to a question only if you first raise your hand, you will become more likely to develop the habit of raising your hand before asking a question.

© Nina Leen/Time Life Pictures/Getty Images

B. F. Skinner with rat in Skinner Box

Operant conditioning is also called *instrumental learning* since the behavior is instrumental in bringing about rewarding consequences. The term **reinforcer** refers to a stimulus or event that increases the likelihood that the behavior it follows will be repeated. For example, the act of answering questions when students raise their hands is a reinforcer.

Skinner observed that the longer reinforcement is delayed, the weaker its effects will be. A rat or a pigeon in the Skinner box, or a child in the classroom, will learn the correct responses faster when reinforcement follows the response as quickly as possible. In general, learning progresses more slowly as the delay between response and reinforcement increases.

CONCEPT 5.14
Skinner showed how superstitious behavior can be learned through the coincidental pairing of responses and reinforcement.

Skinner also showed how operant conditioning could explain some forms of **superstitious behavior**. Consider a baseball player who hits a home run after a long slump and then wears the same pair of socks he had on at the time for good luck in every remaining game of the season. The superstitious behavior could be understood in terms of mistaking a mere coincidence between a response (wearing a particular pair of socks) and a reinforcement (home run) for a connection between the two.

Many commonly held superstitions—from not stepping on cracks in the sidewalk to throwing salt over one's shoulder for good luck—are part of our cultural heritage, handed down from generation to generation. Perhaps there was a time when these behaviors were accidentally reinforced, but they have become so much a part of our cultural tradition that people no longer recall their origins.

In the next sections, we review the basic principles of operant conditioning.

Principles of Operant Conditioning

Experimental work by Skinner and other psychologists established the basic principles of operant conditioning, including those we consider here: positive and negative reinforcement, primary and secondary reinforcers, discriminative stimuli, shaping, and extinction.

positive reinforcement The strengthening of a response through the introduction of a stimulus after the response occurs.

negative reinforcement The strengthening of a response through the removal of a stimulus after the response occurs.

Positive and Negative Reinforcement

Skinner distinguished between two types of reinforcement, *positive reinforcement* and *negative reinforcement.* In **positive reinforcement**, a response is strengthened by the introduction of a stimulus after the response occurs. This type of stimulus is called a *positive reinforcer* or *reward.* Examples of positive reinforcers include food, money, and social approval. You are more likely to continue working at your job if you receive a steady paycheck (a positive reinforcer) than if the checks stop coming. You are more likely to study hard for exams if your efforts are rewarded with good grades (another positive reinforcer) than if you consistently fail (see ■ Figure 5.8).

In **negative reinforcement**, a response is strengthened when it leads to the removal of an "aversive" (unpleasant or painful) stimulus. Negative reinforcers are aversive stimuli such as loud noise, cold, pain, nagging, or a child's crying. We are more likely to repeat behaviors that lead to their removal. A parent's behavior in picking up a crying baby to comfort it is negatively reinforced when the baby stops crying; in this case, the aversive stimulus of crying has been removed. Many people are confused about the meaning of negative reinforcement because the term "negative" implies punishment (Chance, 2009). However, remember that any form of reinforcement, whether positive or negative, actually strengthens behavior.

The difference is that in positive reinforcement, behaviors are strengthened when they are followed by the *introduction* or presentation of a stimulus, whereas in negative reinforcement, behaviors are strengthened when they lead to the *removal* of a stimulus. A positive reinforcer is typically a rewarding stimulus (e.g., food or praise), whereas a negative reinforcer is typically an unpleasant or aversive stimulus (e.g., pain or crying).

Negative reinforcement can be a two-way street. Crying is the only means infants have of letting us know when they are hungry or wet or have other needs. It is also an aversive stimulus to anyone within earshot. It is a negative reinforcer because parents will repeat behaviors that succeed in stopping the infant's crying. The baby's crying is

CONCEPT 5.15

In positive reinforcement, the introduction of a reward (positive reinforcer) after a response occurs strengthens the response. In negative reinforcement, the removal of an aversive stimulus (negative reinforcer) after a response occurs strengthens the response.

→ Concept Link

Negative reinforcement helps explain the avoidance of fearful stimuli or situations of people with phobias and the development of obsessive-compulsive disorder. See Module 15.2.

→ Concept Link

Behavior therapists use methods based on principles of reinforcement to strengthen desirable behaviors and weaken or eliminate undesirable behaviors. See Module 16.2.

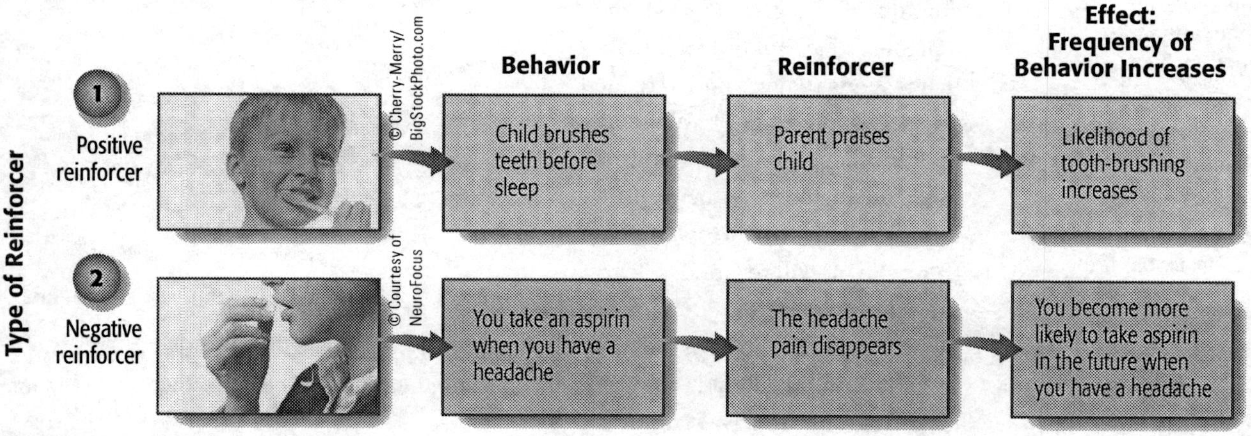

FIGURE 5.8 Types of Reinforcers
Positive and negative reinforcers strengthen the behaviors they follow. Can you think of examples of how positive and negative reinforcers influence your behavior?
Introducing a positive reinforcer strengthens the behavior it follows. The removal or elimination of a negative reinforcer also strengthens the preceding behavior.

© Bubbles/Loisjoy Thurston/Bubbles Photo Library

Reinforcement is not a one-way street. Who is reinforcing whom? Children and parents continually reinforce each other. By stopping a tantrum when she gets her way, the child negatively reinforces the parent. Unwittingly, perhaps, the parent positively reinforces tantrum-throwing behavior by giving in. How would you suggest the parent change these reinforcement patterns?

positively reinforced by the parents' responses. (Like Skinner's pigeons, parents may need to do some "pecking around" to find out what Junior wants: "Let's see, he's not wet, so he must be hungry.")

Negative reinforcement may have undesirable effects in some situations. Consider a child who throws a tantrum in a toy store when the parent refuses the child's request for a particular toy. The child may have learned from past experience that tantrums get results. In operant learning terms, when a tantrum does get results, the child is positively reinforced for throwing the tantrum (because the parent "gives in"), while the parent is negatively reinforced for complying with the child's demands because the tantrum stops. Unfortunately, this pattern of reinforcement only makes the recurrence of tantrums more likely.

Primary and Secondary Reinforcers

At 16 months of age, my daughter Daniella became intrigued with the contents of my wallet. It wasn't those greenbacks with the pictures of Washington and Lincoln that caught her eye. No, she ignored the paper money but was fascinated with the holograms on the plastic credit cards. The point here is that some stimuli, called **primary reinforcers**, are intrinsically rewarding because they satisfy basic biological needs or drives. Their reward or reinforcement value does not depend on learning. Primary reinforcers include food, water, sleep, relief from pain or loud noise, oxygen, sexual stimulation, and novel visual stimuli, such as holograms.

Other reinforcers, called **secondary reinforcers**, acquire their reinforcement value through a learning process by which they become associated with primary reinforcers (Chance, 2009). Money is a secondary reinforcer (also called a *conditioned reinforcer*). It acquires reinforcement value because we learn it can be exchanged for more basic reinforcers, such as food or clothing. Other examples of secondary reinforcers include good grades, awards, recognition, smiles, and praise. Much of our daily behavior is influenced by secondary reinforcers in the form of expressions of approval from others.

CONCEPT 5.16
Some reinforcers are rewarding because they satisfy basic biological needs; other reinforcers acquire reward value as the result of experience.

primary reinforcers Reinforcers, such as food or sexual stimulation, that are naturally rewarding because they satisfy basic biological needs or drives.

secondary reinforcers Learned reinforcers, such as money, that develop their reinforcing properties because of their association with primary reinforcers.

discriminative stimulus A cue that signals that reinforcement is available if the subject makes a particular response.

Discriminative Stimuli

Let's say you put a rat in a Skinner box and reinforce it with food when it presses a bar, but only if it makes that response when a light is turned on (see ■ Figure 5.9). When the light is off, it receives no reinforcement no matter how many times it presses the bar. How do you think the rat will respond? Clearly, the rate of response will be much higher when the light is on than when it is off. The light is an example of a **discriminative stimulus**, a cue that signals that reinforcement is available if the subject makes a particular response.

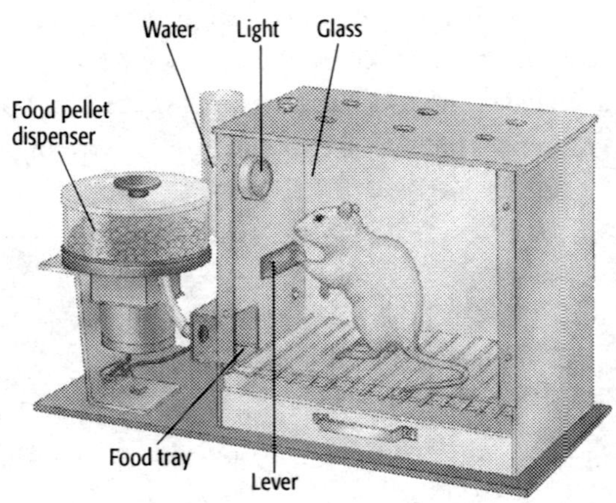

Figure 5.9 Discriminative Stimulus in a Skinner Box
Here we see a rat in a Skinner box, an apparatus used to study operant conditioning. When the rat presses the bar, it receives a pellet of food or a drop of water as a reinforcer. The light is a discriminative stimulus, a cue that signals that the reinforcer is available. The rat learns to press the lever only when the light is on.

CONCEPT 5.17
Discriminative stimuli set the stage for reinforcement, which is useful to know if you want to ask someone for a favor.

Our physical and social environment is teeming with discriminative stimuli. When is the better time to ask someone for a favor: When the person appears to be down in the dumps or is smiling and appears cheerful? You know the answer. The reason you know is that you have learned that a person's facial cues serve as discriminative stimuli that signal times when requests for help are more likely to be positively received. You also know that your professors are more likely to respond to your raising your hand if they are facing you than if their backs are turned. A green traffic light, another type of discriminative stimulus, signals that driving through an intersection is likely to be reinforced by a safe passage.

A green light is a discriminative stimulus signaling that driving through an intersection is likely to be reinforced by safe passage. People learn to respond to discriminative stimuli by performing behaviors that are reinforced in those situations.

Shaping

Rats don't naturally press levers or bars. If you place a rat in a Skinner box, it may eventually happen upon the correct response through trial and error. However, the experimenter can hasten the learning process by using the technique of **shaping**. Shaping involves learning in small steps through applying the *method of successive approximations,* in which the experimenter reinforces a series of ever-closer approximations of the target response (Kreuger & Dayan, 2009). The experimenter may at first reinforce the rat when it moves to the part of the cage that contains the bar. Once this behavior is established, reinforcement occurs only if the animal moves closer to the bar, then closer still, then touches the bar with its paw, and then actually presses the bar. If you have ever observed animal trainers at work, you will recognize how shaping is used to train animals to perform a complex sequence of behaviors.

shaping A process of learning that involves the reinforcement of increasingly closer approximations of the desired response.

CONCEPT 5.18
Organisms can learn complex behaviors through a process of shaping, or reinforcement of successive approximations to the desired behaviors.

We put the method of successive approximations into practice in our daily lives when we attempt to teach someone a new skill, especially one involving a complex set of behaviors. When teaching a child to swim, the instructor may deliver verbal reinforcement (telling the child he or she is doing "great") each time the child successfully performs a new step in the series of steps needed to develop proper form.

Extinction

You'll recall from Module 5.1 that extinction of classically conditioned responses occurs when the conditioned stimulus is repeatedly presented in the absence of the unconditioned stimulus. Similarly, in operant conditioning, extinction is the process by which responses are weakened and eventually eliminated when the response is repeatedly performed but is no longer reinforced. Thus, the bar-pressing response of a rat in the Skinner box will eventually be extinguished if reinforcement (food) is withheld. If you repeatedly raise your hand in class but aren't called upon, you will probably in time stop raising your hand.

CONCEPT 5.19
In operant conditioning, extinction is the weakening and eventual elimination of a response that occurs when the response is no longer reinforced.

Schedules of Reinforcement

In the Skinner box, an animal can be reinforced for each peck or bar press, or for some portion of pecks or bar presses. One of Skinner's major contributions was to show how these different **schedules of reinforcement**—predetermined plans for timing the delivery of reinforcement—influence learning.

schedules of reinforcement Predetermined plans for timing the delivery of reinforcement.

schedule of continuous reinforcement A system of dispensing a reinforcement each time a response is produced.

In a **schedule of continuous reinforcement**, reinforcement follows each instance of the operant response. The rat in the Skinner box receives a food pellet every time it presses the lever. Similarly, if a light comes on every time you flick a

CONCEPT 5.20
The schedule by which reinforcements are dispensed influences the rate of learning and resistance to extinction.

light switch, you will quickly learn to flick the switch each time you enter a darkened room. Operant responses are learned most rapidly under a schedule of continuous reinforcement. However, continuous reinforcement also leads to rapid extinction when reinforcement is withheld. How long will it take before you stop flicking the light switch if the light fails to come on because the bulb needs replacing? Just one or two flicks of the switch without results may be sufficient to extinguish the response. But extinction does not mean the response is forgotten or lost to memory. It is likely to return quickly once reinforcement is reinstated—that is, once you install a new bulb.

schedule of partial reinforcement A system of reinforcement in which only a portion of responses is reinforced.

Responses are more resistant to extinction under a **schedule of partial reinforcement** than under a schedule of continuous reinforcement. In a schedule of partial reinforcement, only a portion of responses is reinforced. Because this makes it more unlikely that an absence of reinforcement will be noticed, it takes longer for the response to fade out.

In daily life, schedules of partial reinforcement are much more common than schedules of continuous reinforcement. Think what it would mean to be reinforced on a continuous basis. You would receive a reinforcer (reward) each time you came to class, cracked open a textbook, or arrived at work on time. However desirable this rate of reinforcement might seem, it is no doubt impossible to achieve day to day. Fortunately, partial-reinforcement schedules produce overall high response rates and have the added advantage of greater resistance to extinction.

Partial reinforcement is administered under two general kinds of schedules: *ratio schedules* and *interval schedules*. In ratio schedules, reinforcement is based on the *number* of responses. In interval schedules, reinforcement is based on the *timing* of responses. For each type, reinforcement can be administered on either a *fixed* or *variable* basis.

Let's break this down further. ■ Figure 5.10 shows typical rates of response under different schedules of partial reinforcement. Notice how much faster response rates

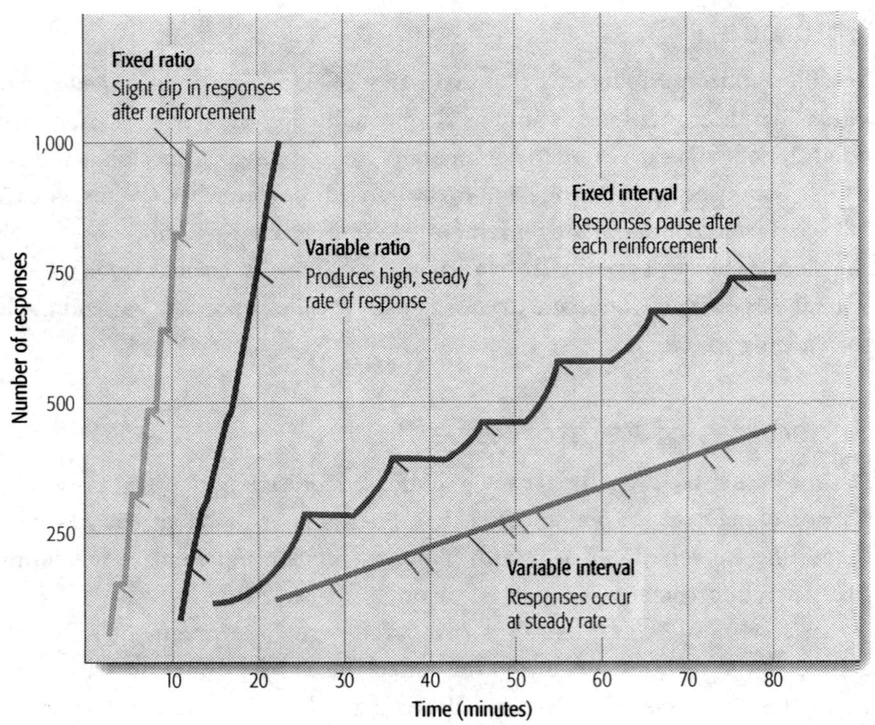

FIGURE 5.10 Rates of Response Under Different Schedules of Partial Reinforcement Here we see rates of response we typically find under different schedules of partial reinforcement. The diagonal lines that intersect with these response curves show the times at which reinforcement is given. Notice how ratio schedules produce much faster response rates than interval schedules. However, there is usually a short pause following each reinforced set of responses under fixed-ratio schedules. Fixed-interval schedules produce a "scalloped" effect with long pauses following each reinforcement, whereas variable-interval schedules typically produce a slow but steady rate of response.

Source: Adapted from Skinner, 1961.

are under ratio schedules than under interval schedules. To account for this difference, remember that in ratio schedules, reinforcement depends on the number of responses, not on the length of time elapsed since the last reinforcement, as is the case with interval schedules.

Fixed-Ratio (FR) Schedule

In a fixed-ratio (FR) schedule, reinforcement is given after a specified number of correct responses. For example, in an "FR-6" schedule, reinforcement is given after each sixth response. The classic example of fixed-ratio schedules is piecework, in which workers are paid on the basis of how many items they produce. Fixed-ratio schedules produce a constant, high level of response, with a slight dip in responses occurring after each reinforcement (see Figure 5.10). On a fixed-ratio schedule, the faster people work, the more items they produce and the more money they earn. However, quality may suffer if quantity alone determines how reinforcements are dispensed.

CONCEPT 5.21
There are four types of partial-reinforcement schedules: fixed-ratio, variable-ratio, fixed-interval, and variable-interval schedules.

Variable-Ratio (VR) Schedule

In a variable-ratio (VR) schedule, the number of correct responses needed before reinforcement is given varies around an average value. For example, a "VR-20" schedule means that reinforcement is administered after an average of every 20 responses. In some cases, reinforcement may be delivered after two, five, or 10 responses; at other times, 30 or 40 responses may be required.

© Yulia Ivanova, 2009/Shutterstock.com

Salespeople who make "cold calls" to potential customers are reinforced on a variable ratio schedule. They may average 20 or 30 calls to make a sale, but they don't know how many calls it will take to make a sale on any given day. Gambling is also reinforced on a variable-ratio schedule, as you never know how many bets it will take to produce a winner. When playing a slot machine, for example, a win (reinforcement) may occur after one, two, 10, or even 50 or more tries. (No wonder it's called a one-armed bandit.)

Variable-ratio schedules typically produce high and steady rates of response (see Figure 5.10). They are also more resistant to extinction than fixed-ratio schedules because we never know when a given response will be rewarded. This may explain why so many people routinely buy weekly lottery tickets, even though they may win only piddling amounts every now and then. As an advertisement for one state lottery puts it, "Hey, you never know."

Fixed-Interval (FI) Schedule

In a fixed-interval (FI) schedule, reinforcement is given only for a correct response made after a fixed amount of time has elapsed since the last reinforcement. On an "FI-30" schedule, for example, an animal in a Skinner box receives a food pellet if it makes the required response after an interval of 30 seconds has elapsed since the last food pellet was delivered, regardless of the number of responses it made during the 30-second interval. Workers who receive a regular paycheck at the end of every week or two are reinforced on a fixed-interval schedule.

Fixed-interval schedules tend to produce a "scalloped" response pattern in which the rate of response tends to dips just after reinforcement is given and then increases as the end of the interval approaches (see Figure 5.10). An example of this scalloping effect occurs when workers who receive monthly performance reviews show more productive behaviors in the days leading up to their evaluations than immediately afterward.

Variable-Interval (VI) Schedule

In a variable-interval (VI) schedule, the amount of time that must elapse before a reinforcement is given for a correct response varies rather than remaining fixed. In laboratory studies, a "VI-60" schedule means that the period of time that must elapse before reinforcement is given varies around an average of 60 seconds. On any given occasion, the interval could be as short as one second or as long as 120 seconds, but the average across occasions remains 60 seconds. Trying to hail a cab on a city street is a real-life example; it may take only a minute or two on some occasions, but much (much) longer on other occasions.

Teachers who spring pop quizzes in class are using a variable-ratio schedule of reinforcement to encourage regular studying. Because students never know the actual days that quizzes are given, they are more likely to be reinforced by receiving better grades if they prepare for each class by studying regularly. With scheduled tests, reinforcement is based on a fixed-interval schedule; that is, rewards for studying become available only at the regular times the tests are given. In this case, we expect a scalloped rate of response that is typical of fixed-interval reinforcement—an increased rate of studying, perhaps cramming, just before the test and a drop in studying immediately afterward. Radio stations try to get you to tune in regularly by periodically offering prizes on a variable schedule of reinforcement. You never know when they might announce, "Be the fifth caller and you'll receive free tickets to. . . ."

Variable-interval schedules tend to produce a slow but steady rate of response. They also tend to be more resistant to extinction than fixed-interval schedules, because one never knows when reinforcement may occur.

Escape Learning and Avoidance Learning

escape learning The learning of behaviors that allow an organism to escape from an aversive stimulus.

avoidance learning The learning of behaviors that allow an organism to avoid an aversive stimulus.

In **escape learning**, an organism learns to *escape* an aversive stimulus by performing an operant response. The escape behavior is negatively reinforced by the removal of the aversive or painful stimulus. A rat may be taught to press a bar to turn off an electric shock. We may learn to escape from the heat of a summer day by turning on a fan or air conditioner.

In **avoidance learning**, the organism learns to perform a response that *avoids* an aversive stimulus. The rat in a Skinner box may receive a signal (e.g., a tone) that a shock is about to be delivered. The animal learns to avoid the shock by performing the correct response, such as pressing a bar. You open an umbrella before stepping out in the rain to avoid the unpleasant experience of being drenched.

CONCEPT 5.22

In escape learning, organisms learn responses that allow them to escape aversive or painful stimuli; in avoidance learning, they learn responses that allow them to avoid these stimuli.

Like other forms of learning, escape learning and avoidance learning may be adaptive in some circumstances but not in others. We learn to apply sunscreen to avoid sunburn, which is adaptive. But skipping regular dental visits to avoid unpleasant or painful dental procedures is not, as it can lead to more serious dental problems or even to tooth loss. People may turn to alcohol or other drugs to escape from their problems or troubling emotions. But the escape is short lived, and problems resulting from drug or alcohol abuse can quickly compound the person's initial difficulties.

You may at this point wish to review the key concepts in operant conditioning outlined in Concept Chart 5.2.

CONCEPT CHART 5.2 Key Concepts in Operant Conditioning

Concept	Description	Example
Nature of operant conditioning	A form of learning in which responses are strengthened by the effects they have in the environment	If students receive answers to their questions only when they raise their hands before asking them, hand-raising behavior is strengthened
Discriminative stimulus	A stimulus that indicates that reinforcement will be available if the correct response is made	A child learns to answer the phone when it rings and to wait for a dial tone before dialing 
Positive reinforcer	A stimulus or event that makes the response it follows more likely to occur again	Praising children for picking up their clothes increases the likelihood that they will repeat the behavior
Negative reinforcer	An aversive stimulus whose removal strengthens the preceding behavior and increases the probability that the behavior will be repeated 	The annoying sound of a buzzer on an alarm clock increases the likelihood that we will get out of bed to turn it off
Primary reinforcer	A stimulus that is innately reinforcing because it satisfies basic biological needs or drives	Food, water, and sexual stimulation are primary reinforcers
Secondary reinforcer	A stimulus whose reinforcement value derives from its association with primary reinforcers	Money, which can be exchanged for food and clothing, is a secondary reinforcer
Shaping	A process of learning that involves the reinforcement of increasingly closer approximations to the desired response	A boy learns to dress himself when the parent reinforces him for accomplishing each small step in the process
Extinction	The gradual weakening and elimination of an operant response when it is not reinforced	A girl stops calling out in class without first raising her hand when the teacher fails to respond to her
Schedule of continuous reinforcement	A schedule for delivering reinforcement every time a correct response is produced	A girl receives praise each time she puts her clothes away
Schedule of partial reinforcement (fixed-ratio, variable-ratio, fixed-interval, or variable-interval schedule)	A schedule of delivering reinforcement in which only a portion of responses is reinforced	A boy receives praise for putting his clothes away every third time he does it (fixed-ratio schedule)
Escape learning	Learning responses that result in escape from an aversive stimulus	A motorist learns a detour to escape from congested traffic
Avoidance learning	Learning responses that result in avoidance of an aversive stimulus	A person leaves for work an hour early to avoid heavy traffic
Punishment	Imposing an unpleasant or aversive consequence (i.e., positive punishment), or withdrawing a desirable stimulus (i.e., negative punishment), in response to an undesirable behavior	The government imposes a late penalty when a taxpayer fails to file tax returns on time (positive punishment) A teen loses driving privileges for coming home after curfew (negative punishment)

© Ruslan Anatolevich Kuzmenkov/Shutterstock.com
© iStockphoto.com/Rouzes

Punishment

punishment The introduction of an aversive stimulus or the removal of a reinforcing stimulus after a response occurs, which leads to the weakening or suppression of the response.

CONCEPT 5.23
Though punishment may suppress or weaken behavior, psychologists generally advise parents not to rely on punishment as a means of disciplining their children.

© Tony Freeman/Photo Edit

Psychologists advocate the use of positive reinforcement rather than punishment when disciplining children. Scolding, a form of punishment, may temporarily suppress an undesirable behavior, but it does not help the child acquire more adaptive behaviors in its place.

Punishment is the flip side of reinforcement: It weakens the behavior it follows, whereas reinforcement strengthens the preceding behavior. Just as there are positive and negative forms of reinforcement, there are also positive and negative forms of punishment. In *positive punishment,* an aversive or unpleasant stimulus is imposed as a consequence of an undesirable behavior, which over time tends to reduce the frequency of the undesirable behavior. Examples include a parent who scolds or spanks a child who "talks back," or the imposition of penalties in the form of monetary fines for speeding or illegal parking.

In *negative punishment,* a reinforcing stimulus is removed as a consequence of an undesirable behavior, which over time tends to reduce the frequency of the undesirable behavior. Examples include turning off the TV when a child misbehaves, taking away privileges (e.g., grounding teenagers), or removing the misbehaving child from a reinforcing environment ("a time-out"). The use of punishment, whether positive or negative, tends to reduce the frequency of the behavior it follows.

Let's clarify the difference between two terms which mean very different things but are frequently confused, *negative reinforcement* and *punishment.* Behavior that leads to the *removal* of an unpleasant or aversive stimulus is negatively reinforced and becomes stronger as a result, such as fastening the seat belt in the car to turn off that annoying dinging sound. Behavior that leads to the *imposition* of an unpleasant stimulus (or *removal* of a desirable stimulus) is punished and becomes weaker as a result, such as driving over the speed limit after receiving a moving violation (or two) (see ■ Figure 5.11).

Psychologists and pediatricians encourage parents not to rely on punishment as a means of disciplining their children; instead, they recommend reinforcing desirable behaviors (American Academy of Pediatrics, 1998; Gershoff, 2002a, 2002b). Punishment, especially physical punishment, has many drawbacks, including the following:

- *Punishment may suppress undesirable behavior, but it doesn't eliminate it.* The punished behavior often returns when the punishing stimulus is withdrawn. For example, the child who is punished for misbehavior may perform the undesirable behavior when the parents aren't looking.
- *Punishment does not teach new behaviors.* Punishment may suppress an undesirable behavior, but it does not help the child acquire a more appropriate behavior in its place.

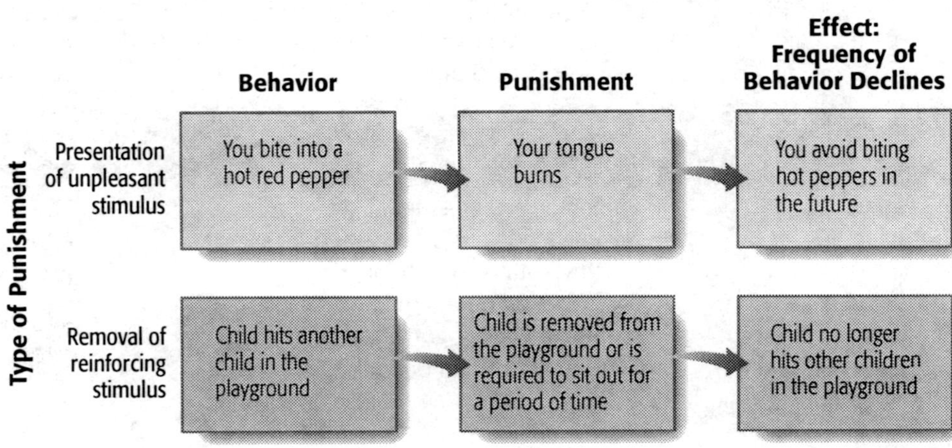

FIGURE 5.11 Types of Punishment
Punishment involves the introduction of an aversive stimulus or the removal of a reinforcing stimulus to weaken or suppress a behavior.

- *Punishment can have undesirable consequences.* Punishment, especially physical punishment, can lead to strong negative emotions in children, such as anger, hostility, and fear directed toward the parent or other punishing agent. Fear may also generalize. Children repeatedly punished for poor performance in school may lose confidence in themselves or develop a fear of failure that handicaps their academic performance. They may cut classes, withdraw from challenging courses, or even drop out of school.
- *Punishment may become abusive.* Stopping a child's undesirable behavior, at least temporarily, may reinforce the parents for using spankings or other forms of physical punishment. This may lead to more frequent physical punishment that crosses the line between discipline and abuse (Gershoff, 2002a, 2002b). Another type of abusive situation occurs when parents turn to ever-harsher forms of punishment when milder punishments fail. Abused children may harbor intense rage or resentment toward the punisher, which they may vent by responding aggressively against that person or other, less physically imposing targets, such as peers or siblings.
- *Punishment may represent a form of inappropriate modeling.* When children observe their parents resorting to physical punishment to enforce compliance with their demands, the lesson they learn is that using force is an acceptable way of resolving interpersonal problems.

Do the drawbacks of punishment mean that it should never be used? There may be some occasions when punishment is appropriate. Parents may need to use punishment to stop children from harming themselves or others (e.g., by running into the street or hitting other children in the playground). But parents should avoid using harsh physical punishment. Examples of milder punishments include (1) *verbal reprimand* ("No, Johnny, don't do that. You can get hurt that way."); (2) *removal of a reinforcer,* such as grounding teenagers or taking away a certain number of points or tokens that children receive each week that are exchangeable for tangible reinforcers (e.g., toys, special activities); and (3) *time-out,* or temporary removal of a child from a reinforcing environment following misbehavior.

Parents who use punishment should help the child understand why he or she is being punished. Children may think they are being punished because they are "bad." They may think negatively of themselves or fear that Mommy and Daddy no longer love them. Parents need to make clear exactly what behavior is being punished and what the child can do differently in the future. In this way, parents can help children learn more desirable behaviors. Punishment is also more effective when it is combined with positive reinforcement for desirable alternative behaviors.

Before going further, you may wish to review Table 5.1, which compares reinforcement and punishment.

Why It Matters: Applications of Operant Conditioning

In many ways, the world is like a huge Skinner box. From the time we are small children, reinforcements and punishments mold our behavior. We quickly learn which behaviors earn approval and which incur disapproval. How many thousands upon thousands of reinforcements have shaped your behavior over the years? Would you be taking

TABLE 5.1 Comparing Reinforcement and Punishment

Technique	What Happens?	When Does This Occur?	Example	Consequence on Behavior
Positive reinforcement	A positive event or stimulus is introduced	After a response	Your instructor smiles at you (a positive stimulus) when you answer a question correctly	You become more likely to answer questions in class
Negative reinforcement	An aversive stimulus is removed	After a response	Buckling the seat belt turns off the annoying buzzer	You become more likely to buckle your seat belt before starting the engine
Positive punishment (application of aversive stimulus)	An aversive stimulus is applied	After a response	A parent scolds a child for slamming a door	The child becomes less likely to slam doors
Negative punishment (removal of a reinforcing stimulus)	A reinforcing stimulus is removed	After a response	A child loses TV privileges for hitting a sibling	The child becomes less likely to engage in hitting

CONCEPT 5.24
Principles of operant conditioning are used in biofeedback training, behavior modification, and programmed instruction.

college courses today were it not for the positive reinforcement you received from an early age for paying attention in class, doing your homework, studying for exams, and getting good grades? Who were the major reinforcing agents in your life? Your mother or father? A favorite uncle or aunt? Your teachers or coaches? Yourself?

Psychologists have developed a number of applications of operant conditioning, including biofeedback training, behavior modification, and programmed instruction.

Biofeedback Training: Using Your Body's Signals as Reinforcers

Chapter 3 introduced the topic of biofeedback training, a technique for learning to change certain bodily responses, including brain wave patterns and heart rate. Biofeedback training relies on operant conditioning principles. Physiological monitoring devices record changes in bodily responses and transmit the information to the user, typically in the form of auditory signals that provide feedback regarding desirable changes in these responses. The feedback reinforces behaviors (e.g., thinking calming thoughts) that bring about these desirable changes.

Behavior Modification: Putting Learning Principles into Practice

behavior modification (B-mod) The systematic application of learning principles to strengthen adaptive behavior and weaken maladaptive behavior.

token economy program A form of behavior modification in which tokens earned for performing desired behaviors can be exchanged for positive reinforcers.

Behavior modification (B-mod) is the systematic application of learning principles to strengthen adaptive behavior and weaken maladaptive behavior. For example, Skinner and his colleagues applied operant conditioning principles in a real-world setting by establishing the first **token economy program** in a mental hospital. In a token economy program, patients receive tokens, such as plastic chips, for performing desired behaviors, such as dressing and grooming themselves, making their beds, or socializing with others. The tokens are exchangeable for positive reinforcers, such as extra privileges.

Behavior modification programs are also applied in the classroom, where they have produced measurable benefits in academic performance and social interactions, and reductions in aggressive and disruptive behaviors and truancy. Teachers may use tokens or gold stars to reward students for appropriate classroom behavior and academic achievement. Children can use the tokens or gold stars at a later time to "purchase" small prizes or special privileges, such as more recess time.

© optimarc/Shutterstock.com

Parent training programs bring behavior modification into the home. After training in using B-mod techniques, parents reward children's appropriate behaviors and punish noncompliant and aggressive behaviors with time-outs and suspension of privileges and rewards.

Programmed Instruction

Skinner applied operant conditioning to education in the form of **programmed instruction**. In programmed instruction, the learning of complex material is broken down into a series of small steps. The learner proceeds to master each step at his or her own pace. Skinner even designed a "teaching machine" that guided students through a series of questions of increasing difficulty. After the student responded to each question, the correct response would immediately appear. This provided immediate reinforcement for correct responses and allowed students to correct any mistakes they had made. Since questions were designed to build upon each other in small steps, students would generally produce a high rate of correct responses and thus receive a steady stream of reinforcement. Teaching machines have since given way to computerized forms of programmed instruction, called **computer-assisted instruction**, in which the computer guides the student through an inventory of increasingly more challenging questions.

programmed instruction A learning method in which complex material is broken down into a series of small steps that learners master at their own pace.

computer-assisted instruction A form of programmed instruction in which a computer is used to guide a student through a series of increasingly difficult questions.

5.2 MODULE REVIEW Operant Conditioning: Learning Through Consequences

Recite It

What is Thorndike's Law of Effect?

- Edward Thorndike's Law of Effect holds that responses that have satisfying effects will be strengthened, whereas those that lead to discomfort will be weakened.

What is operant conditioning?

- Operant conditioning is a form of learning in which the consequences of behavior influence the strength or likelihood that the behavior will occur.

What are the different types of reinforcers?

- Positive reinforcers are stimuli or events whose introduction following a response strengthens the response.
- Negative reinforcers are aversive stimuli whose removal following a response strengthens the response.
- Primary reinforcers, such as food and water, are naturally reinforcing stimuli because they satisfy basic biological needs.
- Secondary reinforcers, such as money and social approval, acquire reinforcing value because of their association with primary reinforcers.

What are the different schedules of reinforcement, and how are they related to learning?

- Schedules of reinforcement are predetermined plans for timing the delivery of reinforcement. In a schedule of continuous reinforcement, reinforcement is given after every correct response. In a partial-reinforcement schedule, only a portion of correct responses is reinforced.

- Partial reinforcement is administered under ratio or interval schedules.
- In a fixed-ratio schedule, reinforcement follows a specified number of correct responses.
- In a variable-ratio schedule, the number of correct responses needed before reinforcement is delivered varies around some average number.
- In a fixed-interval schedule, a specified period of time must pass before a correct response can be reinforced.
- In a variable-interval schedule, the period of time that must elapse before a response can be reinforced varies around some average interval.
- A schedule of continuous reinforcement produces the most rapid learning but also the most rapid extinction of a response when reinforcement is withheld.
- Response rates in partial-reinforcement schedules vary, as does the resistance of responses to extinction.

What are escape learning and avoidance learning?

- Through escape learning, organisms learn responses that allow them to escape from aversive stimuli, such as pain, whereas through avoidance learning, organisms learn to avoid these types of stimuli. Escape and avoidance learning may be adaptive in some situations but not in others.

What is punishment, and why are psychologists concerned about its use?

- Punishment is the introduction of a painful or aversive stimulus (or removal of a rewarding stimulus) following a response, which weakens or suppresses the response. The reasons psychologists are concerned about using punishment to discipline children include the following: Punishment may only suppress behavior, not eliminate it; it doesn't teach new and more appropriate behaviors; it can have undesirable emotional and behavioral consequences; it may cross the line into abuse; and it can model inappropriate ways of resolving conflicts.

What are some applications of operant conditioning?

- Principles of operant conditioning are used in biofeedback training, behavior modification, and programmed instruction.

Recall It

1. In operant conditioning, learning results from the association of a behavior with
   a. its consequences.
   b. conditioned stimuli.
   c. cognitions.
   d. unconditioned stimuli.
2. B. F. Skinner's belief that all behavior is determined by environmental and genetic influences, and that free will is an illusion or myth, is called ______.
3. Skinner demonstrated that superstitious behavior can be acquired through the coincidental pairing of a(n) ______ with a(n) ______.
4. In negative reinforcement, a behavior is strengthened by the
   a. introduction of a negative reinforcer.
   b. extinction of a positive stimulus.
   c. introduction of a positive reinforcer.
   d. removal of an aversive stimulus.
5. Operant responses are learned most rapidly under a schedule of ______ reinforcement; responses are most resistant to extinction under a schedule of ______ reinforcement.
   a. continuous; continuous
   b. partial; partial
   c. continuous; partial
   d. partial; continuous

Think About It

- B. F. Skinner believed that free will is but an illusion. Do you agree? Explain.
- The parents of a 13-year-old boy would like him to help out more around the house, including doing his share of the dishes. After a meal at which it is his turn to do the dishes, he first refuses, pleading that he has other things to do that are more important. Frustrated with his refusal, his parents start yelling at him and continue until he complies with their request. But as he washes the dishes, his mother notices that he is doing a very poor job, so she relieves him of his duty and finishes the job herself. What type of reinforcement did the parents use to gain the boy's compliance? What behaviors of the parents did the boy reinforce by complying with their request? What behavior did the mother inadvertently strengthen by relieving the boy of his chores? Based on your reading of the text, how would you suggest this family change these reinforcement patterns?

Cognitive Learning

- What is cognitive learning?
- What is insight learning?
- What is latent learning?
- What is observational learning?

MODULE 5.3

Let's say you wanted to learn the way to drive to your friend's new house. You could stumble around like Thorndike's laboratory animals until you happened upon the correct route by chance. Then again, you could ask for directions and form a mental image of the route ("Let's see, you make a left at the blue house on the corner, then a right turn at the stop sign, and then . . ."). Forming a mental road map allows you to perform new behaviors (e.g., driving to your friend's house) even before you have had the opportunity to be reinforced for it. Many psychologists believe that we need to go beyond classical and operant conditioning to explain this type of learning, which is called **cognitive learning**. Cognitive learning involves mental processes that cannot be directly observed—processes such as thinking, information processing, problem solving, and mental imaging. Psychologists who study cognitive learning maintain that humans and other animals are, at least to a certain extent, capable of new behaviors without actually having had the chance to perform them or being reinforced for them.

cognitive learning Learning that occurs without the opportunity of first performing the learned response or being reinforced for it.

In Chapter 7, we elaborate on cognitive processes involved in information processing, problem solving, and creativity. Here we focus on three types of cognitive learning: insight learning, latent learning, and observational learning.

Insight Learning

In an early experiment with a chimp named Sultan, German psychologist Wolfgang Köhler (1927) placed a bunch of bananas outside the animal's cage beyond its reach. Sultan, who was obviously hungry, needed to use a nearby object, a stick, as a tool to obtain the fruit. Before long, the chimp succeeded, using the stick to pull in the bananas. Köhler then moved the bananas farther away from Sultan, beyond the reach of the stick, but made a longer stick available to him. Sultan looked at the two sticks and held them in his hands. He tried reaching the bananas with one of the sticks and then the other, but to no avail. The bananas were too far away. He again held the two sticks, tinkered with them a bit, then attached one to the other to form a longer stick (the sticks were attachable), and *voilà*—the problem was solved. Sultan used the longer stick to pull the bananas into the cage. Unlike the animals in Thorndike's or Skinner's operant conditioning studies, Sultan did not gradually happen upon the reinforced response through an overt process of trial and error. Köhler believed Sultan had solved the problem on the basis of *insight*, the sudden flash of inspiration that reveals the solution to a problem.

Insight learning is the process of mentally working through a problem until the sudden realization of a solution occurs. We may call this moment of sudden insight the "Aha!" phenomenon (Topolinski & Reber, 2010). But insight learning may not depend on a flash of inspiration or arise "out of the blue." Insight may occur by restructuring or reorganizing a problem in your mind until you see how the various parts fit together to form a solution (Kounios & Jung-Beeman, 2009). As the nineteenth-century scientist Louis Pasteur

insight learning The process of mentally working through a problem until the sudden realization of a solution occurs.

CONCEPT 5.25
By reworking a problem in your mind, you may come to see how the various parts fit together to form a solution.

famously said, "Chance favors only the prepared mind." When it comes to insight learning, the prepared mind—the one that mulls over the problem from different angles—may be better able to arrive at that Aha! moment of apparently sudden inspiration.

In the behaviorist view, "insight" is neither sudden nor free of prior reinforcement. What you don't see, behaviorists claim, is the history of reinforced behavior leading to an apparently sudden flash of "insight." In this view, insight learning is nothing more than the chaining of previously reinforced responses. Perhaps there is room for compromise between these positions. Insight learning may arise from a *mental* process of trial and error—the working out in your mind of possible solutions to a problem based on responses that were reinforced in the past.

Latent Learning

CONCEPT 5.26
Latent learning occurs without apparent reinforcement and is not displayed until reinforcement is provided.

In an early study of the role of cognitive processes in learning, Edward Tolman and C. H. Honzik (1930) trained rats to run a maze. Some rats were rewarded with food placed in goal boxes at the end of the maze; others went unrewarded for their efforts. Each day for 10 days, the rats were put in the maze, and the experimenters counted the number of wrong turns they made. The rewarded rats quickly learned the maze, but the unrewarded rats did not. They seemed to wander aimlessly through the maze, making many wrong turns.

On the 11th day, food was placed in the goal boxes of some of the previously unrewarded rats. The next day, these rats ran the maze with even fewer errors than the rats that had been rewarded during the previous 10 days (see ■ Figure 5.12). The investigators argued that a single reinforced trial could not account for this dramatic improvement in performance. These rats must have learned the maze earlier, without reinforcement, but only demonstrated what they had learned when they were reinforced for doing so. This type of learning is called **latent learning**—a kind of "hidden" learning that occurs without apparent reinforcement and that is not revealed in performance at the time it occurs. The learned behavior is displayed only when it is reinforced. But what had the rats learned? The lead investigator, psychologist Edward Tolman (1886–1959), believed he had an answer. He argued that the rats had

latent learning Learning that occurs without apparent reinforcement and that is not displayed until reinforcement is provided.

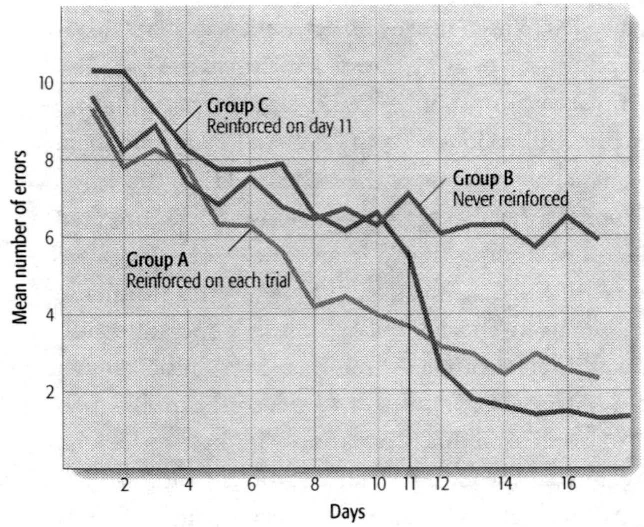

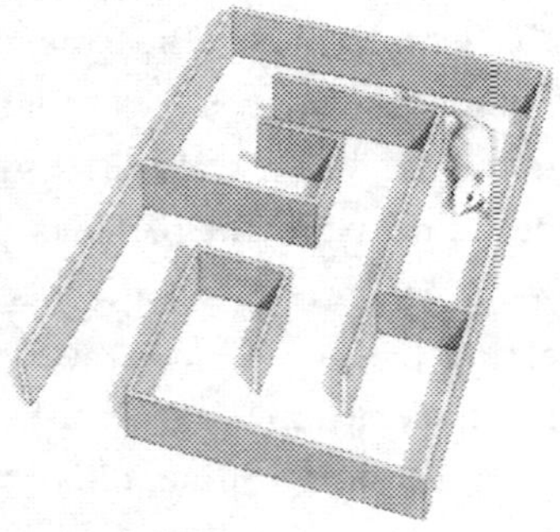

FIGURE 5.12 Tolman and Honzik's Study of Latent Learning
Notice the sharp reduction in errors that occurred among the rats that had not previously received reinforcement when on the 11th day they were reinforced for reaching the goal. Tolman argued that learning had occurred in these rats during the previous trials but that it had remained hidden until rewarded.

developed a **cognitive map**—a mental representation of the maze that allowed them to find their way to the goal box. Tolman's research laid a foundation for the view that humans and other animals create mental representations of the world around them.

cognitive map A mental representation of an area that helps an organism navigate its way from one point to another.

In a common example of latent learning, perhaps you've had the experience of learning lyrics to a song you've heard repeatedly on the radio, even though you never practice reciting them. Knowledge of the lyrics remains latent until someone prompts you to recite them at a party.

Observational Learning

In preschool, Jenny sees that the teacher praises Tina for picking up the blocks after playing with them. Tina's behavior provides Jenny with a cue to guide her own behavior. In **observational learning** (also called *vicarious learning* or *modeling*), we acquire new behaviors by imitating behaviors we observe in others. The person whose behavior is observed is called a *model.*

observational learning Learning by observing and imitating the behavior of others (also called *vicarious learning or modeling*).

Through observational learning, we become capable of behaviors even before we have had the chance to perform them ourselves. I have never fired a gun, but I expect I can do so because I've observed countless gun battles on television and in the movies. I expect I could even learn the basics of making a soufflé by watching a chef demonstrate each step in the process. Whether you'd want to eat it is another matter, which only goes to underscore a limitation of learning by observation—practice and aptitude also count in developing and refining skilled behavior.

CONCEPT 5.27
In observational learning, behaviors are acquired by observing and imitating the behaviors of others.

Social-cognitive theorists such as psychologist Albert Bandura (1986, 2008a, 2009) believe that children learn to imitate aggressive behavior they observe in the home, in the schoolyard, and on television. In a classic study, Bandura and his colleagues showed that children imitated the aggressive behavior of characters they observed on television, even cartoon characters (Bandura, Ross, & Ross, 1963). In a related study, children imitated an adult model who was shown striking a toy (the "Bobo doll") (see Figure 5.13). Other studies point to the same general conclusion: Exposure to violence on TV or in other mass media contributes to aggressive and violent behavior in children and adolescents (Uhlmann & Swanson, 2004). Childhood exposure to media violence is also linked to greater aggressiveness in adulthood (Huesmann et al., 2003).

Modeling effects are generally stronger when the model is similar to the learner and when positive reinforcement for performing the behavior is evident. In other words, we are more likely to imitate models with whom we can identify and who receive rewards for performing the observed behavior. Modeling influences a wide range of behavior, from learning what outfit to wear at a social occasion, to how to change a tire, to how to cook a soufflé (see *Try This Out*). People even express more positive opinions of a piece of music when they observe someone who shares their opinions on other matters express a favorable opinion of the music (Hilmert, Kulik, & Christenfeld, 2006).

People also develop styles of dealing with conflicts in intimate relationships based on their observations during childhood of how their mothers and fathers dealt with marital disagreements (Reese-Weber & Marchand, 2002). For example, young people may learn to imitate an attack style for handling disputes that they had observed in the relationship between their parents or between their parents and themselves (Reese-Weber, 2000).

© Getty Images/Creatas/Jupiter Images

We learn a wide range of skills by carefully observing and imitating behavior of others. But practice and aptitude also count in developing skilled behaviors

Does the idea of holding a rat make you squirm? Does the sight of a crab on the beach make you want to run in the other direction? How about

© Albert Bandura/Stanford University

© Albert Bandura/Stanford University

© Albert Bandura/Stanford University

FIGURE 5.13 Imitation of Aggressive Model
Research by psychologist Albert Bandura and his colleagues shows that children will display aggressive behavior after exposure to aggressive models. Here we see a boy and girl striking a toy "Bobo doll" after observing an adult model strike the doll.

TRY THIS OUT The Fine Art of Observing Others

How might you use modeling to expand your social skills? Here's an example. If you're at a loss to know what to say to someone you meet at a party, observe how others interact with each other, especially people you believe are socially skillful. What do you notice about their body language, facial expressions, and topics of conversation that could be helpful to you? Begin practicing these behaviors yourself. Note how other people respond to you. Polish your skills to produce a more favorable response. With some practice and fine-tuning, the behaviors are likely to become part of your regular behavioral repertoire.

touching an insect? Many of us fear various creatures even though we have never had any negative experience with them. These fears may be acquired by modeling—that is, by observing other people squirm or show fear when confronted with them (Merckelbach et al., 1996). In a study of 42 people with arachnophobia (a fear of spiders), modeling experiences were a greater contributor to the development of the phobia than were direct conditioning experiences (Merckelbach, Arntz, & de Jong, 1991).

Concept Chart 5.3 provides an overview of the three types of cognitive learning.

CONCEPT CHART 5.3 Types of Cognitive Learning

Type of Learning	Description	Example
Insight learning 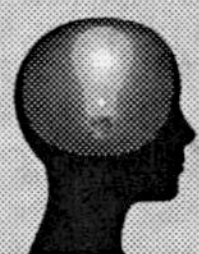 © Michael D Brown/Shutterstock.com	The process of mentally dissecting a problem until the pieces suddenly fit together to form a workable solution	A person arrives at a solution to a problem after thinking about it from a different angle
Latent learning  © Sebastian Crocker/Shutterstock.com	Learning that occurs but remains "hidden" until there is a reward for performing the learned behavior	A person learns the words of a song playing on the radio but doesn't sing them until friends at a party begin singing
Observational learning  © Monkey Business Images/Shutterstock.com	Learning by observing and imitating the behavior of others	Through observation, a child learns to imitate the gestures and habits of older siblings or characters on television

5.3 MODULE REVIEW Cognitive Learning

Recite It

What is cognitive learning?

➤ In cognitive learning, an organism learns a behavior before it can perform the behavior or be reinforced for it. Cognitive learning depends on mental processes such as thinking, problem solving, and mental imaging.

What is insight learning?

➤ Insight learning is a mental process in which the restructuring of a problem into its component parts leads to the sudden realization of a solution to the problem.

What is latent learning?

➤ Latent learning is a kind of "hidden" learning that occurs without apparent reinforcement and is not displayed until reinforcement is provided.

What is observational learning?

➤ In observational learning, behaviors are acquired by observing and imitating the behaviors of others.

Recall It

1. The type of learning that involves thinking, information processing, mental imaging, and problem solving is called ________.
2. The chimp named Sultan learned to reach bananas by attaching two sticks together. This type of learning is called
   a. insight learning.
   b. latent learning.
   c. observational learning.
   d. classical conditioning.
3. The type of learning that occurs without any apparent reinforcement and that is not displayed at the time it is acquired is called ________ learning.
4. Observational learning
   a. is also known as latent learning.
   b. involves imitating the behavior of others.
   c. may lead to the acquisition of useful new skills but not to fear responses.
   d. is based on the principles of operant conditioning.

Think About It

➤ Do you believe that learning can occur by insight alone? Why or why not?

➤ Who were the major modeling influences in your life? What behaviors, positive or negative, did you acquire by observing these models?

Putting Reinforcement into Practice

APPLICATION MODULE 5.4

When you smile at someone who compliments you or thank someone for doing you a favor, you are applying positive reinforcement, one of the principles of operant conditioning. Showing appreciation for desired behavior increases the likelihood that the behavior will be repeated.

To modify behavior through reinforcement, it is important to establish a clear *contingency*, or connection, between the desired behavior and the reinforcement. For example, parents can use a desired activity as a reinforcer (e.g., time playing video games) for completing daily homework assignments. *Contingency contracting*, which involves an exchange of desirable reinforcers, is a more formal way of establishing a contingency.

CONCEPT 5.28
To modify behavior through reinforcement, it is important to establish a clear connection, or contingency, between the desired behavior and the reinforcement.

In contingency contracting, two people in a relationship list the behaviors of the other that they would like changed. They then agree to reinforce each other for carrying out the desired behavioral changes by making a quid pro quo contract, as in this example between two college roommates:

Carmen: I agree to keep the stereo off after 8:00 P.M. every weekday evening if you agree to forbid your friends to smoke in the apartment.

Lukisha: I agree to replace the toilet paper when we run out if you, in return, clean your hair out of the bathroom sink.

Applying Reinforcement

As noted in our earlier discussion of behavior modification programs, teachers and parents apply reinforcement to help children develop more appropriate behaviors. Here are some guidelines for enhancing the effectiveness of reinforcement (adapted from Eberlein, 1997, and Samalin & Whitney, 1997):

1. *Be specific.* Identify the specific behavior you want to increase, such as having five-year-old Johnny put the blocks back on the shelf after playing with them.
2. *Use specific language.* Rather than saying "Johnny, I'd like you to clean your room when you finish playing," say "Johnny, when you finish with the blocks, you need to put them back on the shelf."
3. *Select a reinforcer.* Identify a reinforcer that the child values, such as access to TV or gold stars the child can accumulate and later redeem for small gifts. The reinforcer should be one that is readily available and that can be used repeatedly.
4. *Explain the contingency.* "Johnny, when you put back all of the blocks on the shelf, you'll get a gold star."
5. *Apply the reinforcer.* Reinforce the child immediately after each occurrence of the desired behavior. If the child cannot achieve the desired standard of behavior (e.g., a few blocks are left on the floor), demonstrate how to do so and give the child the opportunity to perform the behavior satisfactorily. Pair the reinforcer with praise: "Johnny, you did a great job putting those blocks away."
6. *Track the frequency of the desired behavior.* Keep a running record of how often the behavior occurs each day.
7. *Wean the child from the reinforcer.* After the desired response is well established, gradually eliminate the reinforcer but continue using social reinforcement (praise) to maintain the behavior: "Johnny, I think you did a good job in putting the blocks where they belong."

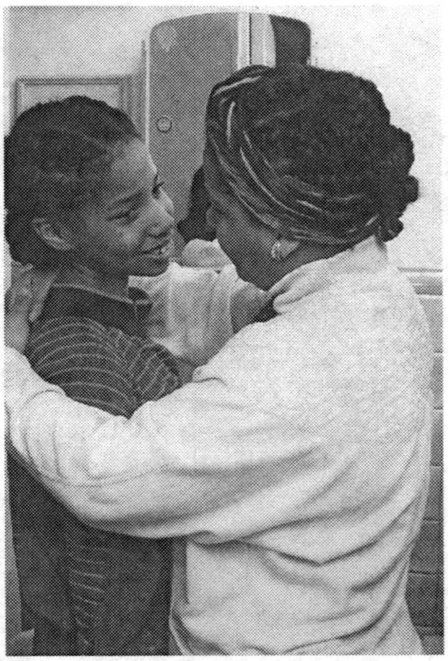

© Steve Skjold/Photo Edit

Hugs are a form of positive reinforcement when they follow desirable behavior.

Giving Praise

Praise can be a highly effective reinforcer in its own right. Here are some guidelines for using praise to strengthen desirable behavior in children:

- *Connect.* Make eye contact with the child and smile when giving praise.
- *Use hugs.* Combine physical contact with verbal praise.
- *Be specific.* Connect praise with the desired behavior (Belluck, 2000). Rather than offering vague praise—"You're a great older brother"—connect it with the

noteworthy effort or accomplishment. Say, for example, "Thanks for watching your little brother while I was on the phone. It was a big help."

- *Avoid empty flattery.* Children can see through empty flattery. Empty flattery may prompt them to think, why do people need to make up stuff about me? What is so wrong with me that people feel they need to cover up? (Henderlong & Lepper, 2002). Indiscriminant praise can also have the unfortunate effect of leading to an inflated sense of self-importance (Baumeister et al., 2003).
- *Reward the effort, not the outcome.* Instead of saying "I'm so proud of you for getting an A in class," say "I'm so proud of you for how well you prepared for the test." Praising the accomplishment, not the effort, may convey the message that the child will be prized only if he or she continues to get A's.
- *Avoid repeating yourself.* Avoid using the same words each time you praise the child. If you tell Timmy he's terrific each time you praise him, the praise will soon lose its appeal.
- *Don't end on a sour note.* Don't say "I'm proud of how you cleaned your room by yourself, but next time I think you can do it faster."

Thinking Critically About Psychology

Based on your reading of this chapter, answer the following questions. Then, to evaluate your progress in developing critical thinking skills, compare your answers to the sample answers found in Appendix A.

Recall the experiment described on p. 188 in which psychologist John Garcia and his colleagues left sheep carcasses on the open range that were laced with a poison that sickened coyotes when they ate the tainted meat. Apply your critical thinking skills to break down this study in classical conditioning terms.

1. What was the unconditioned stimulus in this example?
2. What was the conditioned stimulus?
3. What was the unconditioned response?
4. What was the conditioned response?

Log in to CengageBrain to access the resources your instructor requires. For this book, you can access:

CourseMate Psychology CourseMate brings course concepts to life with interactive learning, study, and exam preparation tools that support the printed textbook. A textbook-specific website, Psychology CourseMate includes an integrated interactive eBook and other interactive learning tools including quizzes, flashcards, videos, and more.

CENGAGENOW CengageNow is an easy-to-use online resource that helps you study in less time to get the grade you want—NOW. Take a pre-test for this chapter and receive a personalized study plan based on your results that will identify the topics you need to review and direct you to online resources to help you master those topics. Then take a post-test to help you determine the concepts you have mastered and what you will need to work on. If your textbook does not include an access code card, go to CengageBrain.com to gain access.

Visit www.cengagebrain.com to access your account and purchase materials.

VISUAL OVERVIEW Chapter 5 Learning

MODULE 5.1 Classical Conditioning

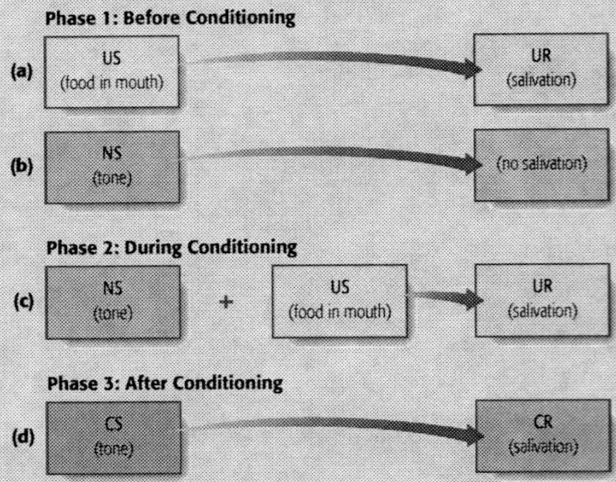

Key Concepts

- **How It Works:** Pairing an unconditioned stimulus (US) and a neutral stimulus (NS) results in acquisition of a conditioned response (CR) to the neutral stimulus, which is then called a conditioned stimulus (CS)
- **Extinction**: Weakening of a response following repeated exposure to the CS alone
- **Spontaneous Recovery**: The return of the CR after a lapse of time following extinction
- **Stimulus Generalization**: CR occurs in response to stimuli similar to the original CS
- **Stimulus Discrimination**: CR fails to occur to stimuli different from the original CS
- **Higher-Order Conditioning**: A neutral stimulus becomes a CS after it is paired with an already established CS

Examples of Classical Conditioning

- **Conditioned Emotional Reaction**: Conditioned emotional response, such as fear, to a particular object
- **Drug Cravings**: Cravings elicited by conditioned stimuli in the environment
- **Taste Aversions**: Conditioned aversions to foods and beverages
- **Immune-System Responses**: Immune-system responses may be influenced by conditioning

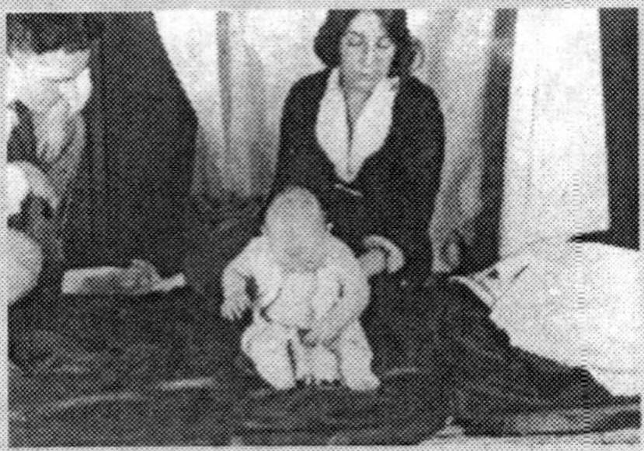

© Archives of the History of American Psychology—The University of Akron

John Watson and Rosalie Rayner with Little Albert

MODULE 5.2 Operant Conditioning

Key Concepts

- **Positive Reinforcement**: The strengthening of a response by presenting a rewarding stimulus after a response occurs
- **Negative Reinforcement**: The strengthening of a response by removing an unpleasant stimulus after a response occurs
- **Primary Reinforcers**: Stimuli that are naturally reinforcing
- **Secondary Reinforcers**: Stimuli that acquire reinforcement value through experience
- **Discriminative Stimuli**: Stimuli that signal the occasion for reinforcement
- **Shaping**: Rewarding gradual approximations to the desired behavior

- **Extinction**: Weakening of a response through withdrawal of reinforcement
- **Schedules of Reinforcement**: Systems for dispensing reinforcements, such as fixed-ratio, variable-ratio, fixed-interval, and variable-interval schedules
- **Punishment**: Introduction of an unpleasant stimulus or removal of a reinforcing stimulus after a response occurs, resulting in the weakening or suppression of the response

Applications of Operant Conditioning

- **Biofeedback Training**
- **Behavior Modification**
- **Programmed Instruction**

© Nina Leen/Time Life Pictures/Getty Images

B. F. Skinner with rat in Skinner Box

MODULE 5.3 Cognitive Learning

Types of Cognitive Learning

- **Insight Learning**: The "Aha!" phenomenon, or sudden realization of a solution to a problem
- **Latent Learning**: Learning not expressed outwardly in behavior until the response is reinforced
- **Observational Learning:** Learning by observing and imitating other people's behavior; also called vicarious learning or modeling

© Albert Bandura/Stanford University

© Albert Bandura/Stanford University

6 Memory

Now Try This . . .

Take a few minutes to see how many digits of *pi* you can recite from memory:

3.14159265358979323846264338327950 2 . . .

Where did you top off? Six digits? Ten? Twenty? Thirty? You probably fell well short of the world record set by a Japanese man, who was able to recite 40,000 digits of *pi* from memory (Takahashi et al., 2006). Like this man, we have other cases of people who could perform remarkable feats of memory.

SLICE OF LIFE Perhaps the most prodigious memory ever studied was that of a Russian man known only by his first initial, S. He could repeat 70 randomly selected numbers in the precise order in which he had just heard them (Luria, 1968). He could memorize lists of hundreds of meaningless syllables and recite them not only immediately after studying them but also when tested again some 15 years later. He memorized long mathematical formulas that were utterly meaningless to him except as an enormously long string of numbers and symbols. After but a single reading, he could recite stanza after stanza of Dante's *Divine Comedy* in Italian, even though he could not speak the language (Rupp, 1998).

Imagine what it would be like to have such an extraordinary memory—to be able to remember everything you read word for word or to recall lists of facts you learned years ago. Yet if S.'s life story is any indication, it may be just as well you don't possess such a prodigious memory. S.'s mind was so crammed with meaningless details that he had difficulty distinguishing between the trivial and the significant (Turkington, 1996). He had trouble holding conversations because individual words opened a floodgate of associations that distracted him from what the other person was saying. He couldn't shift gears when new information conflicted with fixed images he held in memory. For example, he had difficulty recognizing people who had changed small details of their appearance, such as by getting a haircut or wearing a new suit. Unfortunately, S.'s life didn't end well. He spent the last years of his life confined to a mental hospital. Most of us will probably never possess the memory of someone like S., nor

(*Continued on page 216*)

© Anthony Redpath/CORBIS

DID YOU KNOW THAT...

- A man was able to memorize lists of hundreds of meaningless syllables and recite them again 15 years later? (p. 214)
- When children lump together the letters "lmnop" in reciting the alphabet as though they were one word, they are using a memory skill that can stretch one's ability to remember a series of numbers or letters? (p. 223)
- A good way to retain information you've just learned is to sleep on it? (p. 233)
- Fewer than half of the people tested in a research study could pick out the correct drawing of a penny? (p. 235)
- If your hippocampus were removed, each new experience would come and go without any permanent trace left in your brain that the event ever happened? (p. 240)
- Scientists believe that when it comes to memory, cells that fire together, wire together? (p. 241)
- You are more likely to earn a good grade by spacing your study sessions than by cramming for a test? (p. 245)

Learning Objectives

By reading this chapter you will be able to . . .

1 **IDENTIFY** and **DESCRIBE** the basic processes and stages of memory.

2 **IDENTIFY** and **DESCRIBE** types of long-term memory.

3 **EXPLAIN** the roles of the semantic network model and levels-of-processing theory in memory.

4 **EXPLAIN** the difference between maintenance rehearsal and elaborative rehearsal.

5 **APPLY** constructionist theory to explain memory distortions.

6 **EVALUATE** the reliability of eyewitness testimony.

7 **EXPLAIN** why the concept of recovered memory is controversial.

8 **IDENTIFY** and **DESCRIBE** the major theories and factors in forgetting.

9 **IDENTIFY** and **DESCRIBE** methods of measuring memory.

10 **DESCRIBE** the two major types of amnesia.

11 **IDENTIFY** key brain structures involved in memory and explain the roles of neuronal networks and long-term potentiation.

12 **DESCRIBE** the genetic bases of memory.

13 **APPLY** knowledge of how memory works to powering up your memory.

© Y. Liu/Corbis

Preview

(*Continued from page 214*)

would we even want to. Yet learning how our memory works and what we can do to improve it can help us meet many of life's challenges, from performing better in school or on the job to remembering to water the plants before leaving the house.

Our study of memory begins with a discussion of the underlying processes that make memory possible. We then consider the loss of information that results from forgetting and discuss how the brain creates and stores memories. We end with some practical suggestions for improving your memory.

MODULE 6.1

Remembering

- What are the basic processes and stages of memory?
- What are the major types of long-term memory?
- What is the constructionist theory of memory?
- What are flashbulb memories?
- What factors influence the accuracy of eyewitness testimony?
- Are recovered memories of childhood sexual abuse credible?

memory The system that allows us to retain information and bring it to mind.

In Chapter 5, we defined learning as a relatively permanent change in behavior that occurs as the result of experience. But learning could not occur without memory. **Memory** is the system by which we retain information and bring it to mind. Without memory, experience would leave no mark on our behavior; we would be unable to retain the information and skills we acquire through experience. In this module, we focus on the factors that make memory possible.

Human Memory as an Information Processing System

CONCEPT 6.1
The three basic processes that make memory possible are encoding, storage, and retrieval.

Many psychologists conceptualize human memory as a type of information processing system that has three basic processes: *encoding, storage,* and *retrieval.* These processes allow us to take information from the world, encode it in a form that can be stored in memory, and later retrieve it when it is needed (see ■ Figure 6.1). As we shall see, these underlying processes work through a sequence of stages leading to the formation of enduring memories.

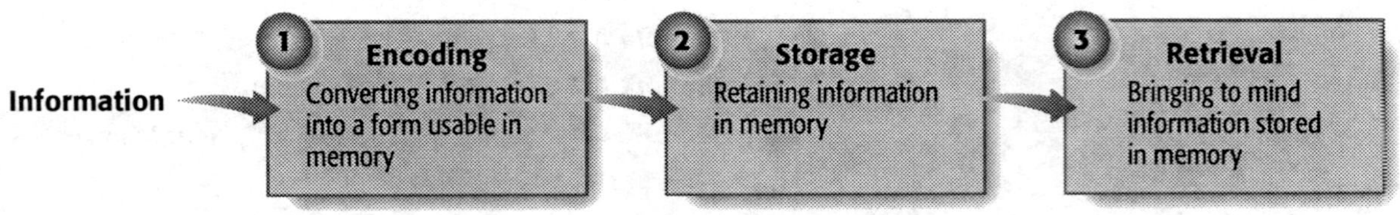

FIGURE 6.1 Three Basic Processes of Memory
Human memory can be represented as an information processing system consisting of three basic processes: encoding, storage, and retrieval of information.

Memory Encoding: Taking in Information

Information about the outside world comes to us through our senses. But for this information to enter memory, it must undergo a process of **memory encoding**, or conversion into a form we can store in memory. Encoding is akin to the process by which a computer converts keyed input into bits of information that can be stored in its memory (Payne & Kensinger, 2010).

memory encoding The process of converting information into a form that can be stored in memory.

We encode information in different ways, including *acoustically* (coded by sound), *visually* (coded by forming a mental picture), and *semantically* (coded by meaning). We encode information acoustically by converting auditory signals into strings of recognizable sounds. For example, you use acoustic coding when trying to keep a phone number in mind by repeating it to yourself. Or you might encode this information visually by picturing a mental image of the digits of the telephone number. But visual coding tends to fade more quickly than auditory coding, so it is generally less efficient for remembering strings of numbers. We tend to use visual coding to form lasting memories of people's faces. We use acoustic codes to retain familiar melodies and rhymes.

Encoding information semantically—by meaning—involves transforming sounds and visual images into words that express meaning. When talking with someone, you bring into memory the meaning of what the person is saying, not the sounds the person makes while speaking. Semantic encoding helps preserve information in memory. You're more likely to remember information when you make a conscious effort to understand what it means than when you simply rely on rote memorization (just repeating the information verbatim).

Memory Storage: Retaining Information in Memory

Memory storage is the process of retaining information in memory. Some memories—your first kiss or your wedding, for example—may last a lifetime. But not all information becomes an enduring or long-term memory. As we shall see when we discuss the stages of memory, some information is retained for only a fraction of a second.

memory storage The process of retaining information in memory.

Memory Retrieval: Accessing Stored Information

© Timothy Boomer, 2009/ Shutterstock.com

Memory retrieval is the process of accessing stored information to bring it to mind. Retrieving long-held information is one of the marvels of the human brain. At one moment, we can summon to mind the names of the first three presidents of the United States and, at the next moment, recall our Uncle Roger's birthday. But memory retrieval is far from perfect ("Now, when is Uncle Roger's birthday anyway?"). Though some memories seem to be retrieved effortlessly, others depend on using certain clues, called **retrieval cues**, to help jog them into awareness. Retrieval cues are stimuli associated with situations in which memories were originally formed. For example, you may jog your memory of what you learned in class yesterday by bringing to mind where you sat, what you were wearing, and so on. Police detectives take advantage of retrieval cues when they bring victims or witnesses back to the scene of the crime to help jog their memories.

The tendency for information to be better recalled in the context in which it was originally learned is called the **context-dependent memory effect**. Thus, students often perform better on examinations when they take them in the same classroom where they originally learned the material. Memories are linked to the context in which they were acquired because stimuli or cues associated with the setting may be encoded

memory retrieval The process of accessing and bringing into consciousness information stored in memory.

retrieval cues Cues associated with the original learning that facilitate the retrieval of memories.

context-dependent memory effect The tendency for information to be recalled better in the same context in which it was originally learned.

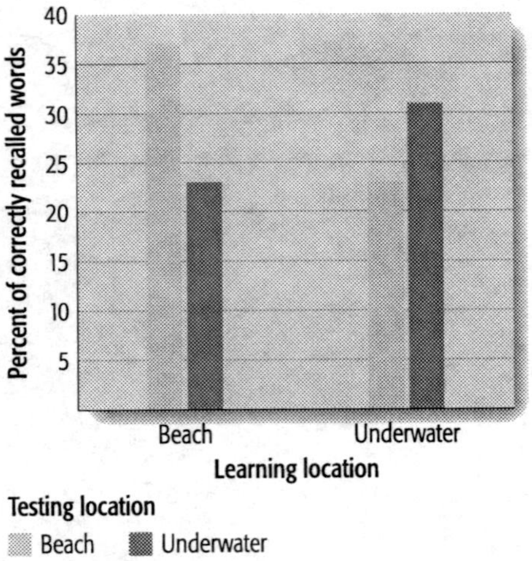

FIGURE 6.2 Context-Dependent Memory Effect
Students who originally learned material on the beach recalled the material better when they were tested on the beach. Similarly, students who originally learned material under water performed better on a recall test when they were again immersed in water.
Source: Adapted from Godden & Baddeley, 1975.

along with the material itself. These stimuli may then serve as retrieval cues to help bring the information more readily to mind. The context-dependent memory effect is explained by the **encoding specificity principle**, which holds that memory retrieval is more successful when cues available during recall are similar to those that were present when the information was first encoded.

Consider an experiment that literally went underwater to demonstrate a context-dependent memory effect. In a classic study, Duncan Godden and Alan Baddeley (1975) had members of two university swim clubs learn a list of words. Members of one club learned the words on the beach; those in the other club learned them while submerged in water. The "beach group" showed better recall when they were tested on the beach than when immersed in water. The other group also showed a context-dependent effect; their retention was better when they were again submerged in water (see ■ Figure 6.2).

Bodily or psychological states may also serve as retrieval cues. A **state dependent memory** effect occurs when people recall information better when they are in the same physical or psychological state as when they first learned the information. In a research example, Schramke and Bauer (1997) had participants either rest or exercise immediately before learning a list of 20 words. They later found that recall was better when participants were tested under the same condition as the original learning (rest or exercise). Similarly, people are generally better able to recall information when they are in the same mood (happy or sad) as when they first learned the information (Bower, 1992). We should caution, however, that context- and state-dependent memory effects do not occur in all situations and often are rather weak when they do occur.

CONCEPT 6.2
The three-stage model of memory proposes three stages of memory organized around the length of time that information is held in memory: sensory memory, short-term memory, and long-term memory.

Memory Stages

Some memories last but a few seconds, whereas others endure for a lifetime. The **three-stage model** of memory proposes three distinct stages that account for the length of time that information is held in memory: *sensory memory, short-term memory,* and *long-term memory* (Atkinson & Shiffrin, 1971).

Sensory Memory: Getting to Know What's Out There

Sensory memory is a memory system for storing sensory information for a very short period of time, ranging from a fraction of a second to as long as three or four seconds. Visual, auditory, and other sensory stimuli constantly strike your sensory receptors, forming impressions you briefly hold in sensory memory in a kind of temporary storage device called a **sensory register**. The sensory impression then disappears and is replaced by the next one. Visual stimuli encoded in the form of mental images enter a sensory register called **iconic memory**. Iconic memory is a type of photographic memory for holding a visual image of an object or a scene in mind for a mere fraction of a second. This visual image can be so clear that people may report exact details as though they were looking at a picture.

Some people can recall a visual image they have previously seen as accurately as if they are still looking at it. This form of visual memory is called **eidetic imagery**, or *photographic memory*. (The term *eidetic* is derived from the Greek word *eidos*, meaning "image.") Although eidetic images may be quite vivid, they are not perceived as clearly as actual photographs (Jahnke & Nowaczyk, 1998). Eidetic imagery is rare in adults, but it occurs in about 5 percent of young children (Haber, 1979). It typically disappears before the age of 10.

encoding specificity principle The belief that retrieval is more successful when cues available during recall are similar to those that were present when the information was brought into memory.

state-dependent memory effect The tendency for information to be better recalled when the person is in the same psychological or physiological state as when the information was first learned.

three-stage model A model of memory that posits three distinct stages of memory: sensory memory, short-term memory, and long-term memory.

sensory memory The storage system that holds memory of sensory impressions for a very short time.

sensory register A temporary storage device for holding sensory memories.

iconic memory A sensory store for holding a mental representation of a visual image for a fraction of a second.

Auditory stimuli encoded as mental representations of sounds are held in a sensory register called **echoic memory**. An auditory stimulus, such as the sound of a ambulance siren, creates an echolike impression in your mind for a few seconds after you hear it. Sounds held in echoic memory tend to last about two or three seconds longer than visual images. Although most sensory impressions fade quickly, some enter a longer storage system, called short-term memory.

eidetic imagery A lingering mental representation of a visual image (commonly called *photographic memory*).

echoic memory A sensory store for holding a mental representation of a sound for a few seconds after it registers in the ears.

Short-Term, or Working, Memory: The Mind's Blackboard

Many sensory impressions don't just fade away into oblivion. They are transferred into **short-term memory (STM)** for further processing. Short-term memory is a storage system for retaining and processing information for a maximum of about 30 seconds. It relies on both visual and acoustic coding, but mostly on acoustic coding. For example, you may try to remember directions by repeating them to yourself (turn right, then left, then right, then left again) just long enough to write them down.

short-term memory (STM) The memory subsystem that allows for retention and processing of newly acquired information for a maximum of about 30 seconds (also called *working memory*).

Many psychologists refer to short-term memory as working memory because it is the memory system we use to work on information we hold in mind for a brief period of time (Jonides, Lacey, & Nee, 2005; Unsworth, Spillers, & Brewer, 2010; Zhang & Luck, 2009). Think of working memory as a kind of mental blackboard or scratch pad of the mind. For example, we engage working memory when we form an image of a person's face and hold it in memory for the second or two it takes the brain to determine whether it is a familiar face. We also use working memory when we perform mental arithmetic (e.g., adding or subtracting in our head) or hold a conversation (Berg, 2008). When we converse with someone, we hold in our minds impressions of the sounds we hear the other person speak just long enough to convert them into recognizable words.

CONCEPT 6.3
People can normally retain a maximum of about seven items in short-term memory at any one time.

How much information can most people retain in short-term memory? Psychologist George Miller conducted landmark studies in the 1950s to determine the storage capacity of STM. He determined that people could retain about seven items, plus or minus two, in short-term memory (Cowan, Chen, & Rouder, 2004). Miller referred to the limit of seven as the "Magic 7."

The magic number seven appears in many forms in human experience, including the "seven ages of man" in Shakespeare's *As You Like It*, the Seven Wonders of the World, the Seven Deadly Sins, and even the seven dwarfs of Disney fame. People can normally repeat a maximum of six or seven single-syllable words they have just heard. Think about the "Magic 7" in the context of your daily experiences. Telephone numbers are seven-digit numbers, which means you can probably retain a telephone number in short-term memory just long enough to dial it.

People vary in their working memory capacities, with some people having somewhat greater capacity than others (Redick et al., 2011; Unsworth, Spillers, & Brewer, 2010). Before moving on, you can test your short-term memory by taking the challenge posed in the *Try This Out* feature, "Breaking Through the "Magic 7" Barrier."

Short-term memory holds only about seven pieces of information, such as the digits of a telephone number. However, a simple memory technique allows you to retain much longer sequences of letters or numbers. Take the challenge in the nearby *Try This Out* feature before reading further.

Were you better able to remember the 24 digits in Row 7 than the eight digits in Row 5 or the 10 in Row 6? If that was the case, you probably recognized that each set of four digits could be grouped together as individual years in a series of years that

TRY THIS OUT Breaking Through the "Magic 7" Barrier

At right are seven rows containing series of numbers. Read aloud the series in the first row. Then look away and repeat the numbers out loud in the order in which they appeared. Check whether your answer was correct or incorrect, and record it in the appropriate "yes" or "no" column. Repeat this procedure for each of the remaining rows.

How well did you do? Chances are you had little trouble with the first four series consisting of four to seven numbers. But you probably stumbled as you bumped up against the "Magic 7" barrier in the next two series, which have eight and ten digits. You may have had even more success with the last series, consisting of 24 digits. Why might you perform better with 24 digits than with eight or ten? An explanation is offered in the nearby section of the text.

		Get It Right?
Row 1:	6293	___ Yes ___ No
Row 2:	73932	___ Yes ___ No
Row 3:	835405	___ Yes ___ No
Row 4:	3820961	___ Yes ___ No
Row 5:	18294624	___ Yes ___ No
Row 6:	9284619384	___ Yes ___ No
Row 7:	202020252030203520402045	___ Yes ___ No

chunking The process of enhancing retention of a large amount of information by breaking it down into smaller, more easily recalled chunks.

maintenance rehearsal The process of extending retention of information held in short-term memory by consciously repeating the information.

phonological loop The speech-based part of working memory that allows for the verbal rehearsal of sounds or words.

visuospatial sketchpad The storage buffer for visual-spatial material held in short-term memory.

episodic buffer The workspace of working memory where information from visual, auditory, and other modalities are brought together.

increased each time by five (2020, 2025, 2030 . . .). The grouping of a larger number of bits of information into a smaller number to aid recall is called **chunking** (Chen & Cowan, 2005). Children typically learn the alphabet by chunking series of letters. That's why they often say the letters *lmnop* as if they were one word (Rupp, 1998).

Most information that passes through short-term memory fades away after about 30 seconds or is transferred to long-term memory. But you can extend short-term memory beyond 30 seconds by engaging in **maintenance rehearsal,** as when you try to remember a person's name by rehearsing it again and again in your mind. But when your rehearsal is interrupted, even for a few seconds, the contents of short-term memory quickly fade away. This is why it is difficult to keep a particular thought in mind and at the same time follow what someone is saying in conversation.

Memory theorists have developed a number of models to explain how working memory functions. One contemporary model conceptualizes working memory as a system consisting of four components: the *phonological loop,* the *visuospatial sketchpad,* *the episodic buffer,* and the *central executive* (see ■ Figure 6.3) (Baddeley, 2000, 2001). Let's break this down into its component parts:

1. The **phonological loop** is the speech-based, or verbal, part of working memory. Its job is to store auditory information. Think of it as a storage device for numbers and words we hold in mind when we are repeating them to ourselves or rehearsing them, such as telephone numbers, people's names, or plans for dinner.
2. The **visuospatial sketchpad** is like a drawing pad for storing visual information (Willingham, 2007). You use the visuospatial sketchpad whenever you picture in your mind an object, pattern, or image—the face of your beloved, the map of your home state, or the arrangement of the furniture in your living room.
3. The **episodic buffer,** the most recent addition to the model, is conceptualized as the workspace of working memory, a storage device for bringing together information from different modalities, such as visual, auditory, and possibly other modalities (Willingham, 2007). The episodic buffer allows you to work on both visual and auditory information at the same time, such as when you are holding a conversation with someone and trying to understand what the person is saying as well as "reading" the person's facial expressions.

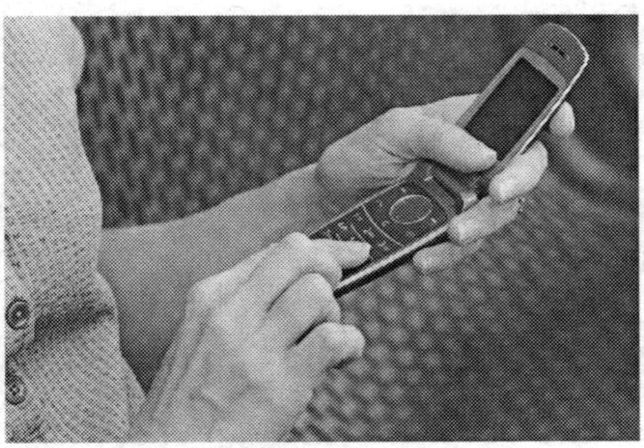

© Susan Law Cain, 2009/Shutterstock.com

Most of us can retain about seven bits of information in short-term memory, plus or minus two. You probably are able to retain in memory a seven-digit telephone number you get from an operator, at least for the few seconds it takes to dial it.

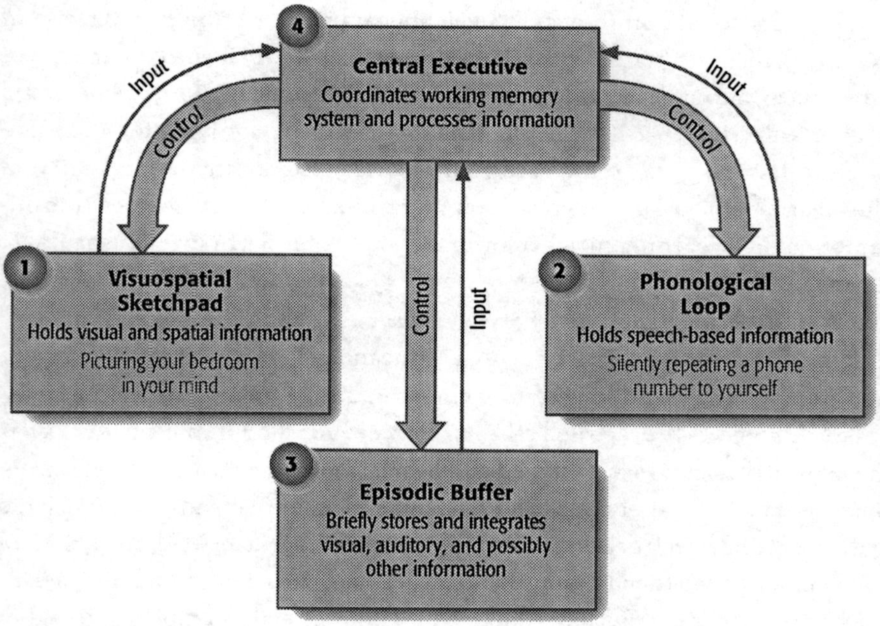

FIGURE 6.3 A Model of Working Memory
Working memory can be conceptualized in terms of four components or subsystems.

1. The visuospatial sketchpad stores visual/spatial material, such as a mental image of a room.
2. The phonological loop stores verbal or speech-based material, such as a telephone number we repeat to ourselves.
3. The episodic buffer allows us to briefly store and integrate different types of information.
4. Input from these subsystems are processed by the central executive component, which controls and coordinates the working memory system.

4. The **central executive** is the master control unit. It doesn't store information; rather, it receives input from the other components and coordinates the working memory system. It also receives and processes information from long-term memory and filters out distracting thoughts so we can focus our attention on information we hold in mind at any given moment. The other components—the phonological loop, visuospatial sketchpad, and episodic buffer—are "slave systems" because they do the bidding of the central executive (Willingham, 2007).

central executive The component of working memory responsible for coordinating the other subsystems, receiving and processing stored information, and filtering out distracting thought.

The "slaves" work independently, which means they can operate at the same time without interfering with one another. When you are driving, visual images of the road are temporarily stored in your visuospatial sketchpad. At the same time, your phonological loop allows you to carry on a conversation with a passenger or sing along with a song on the radio. The episodic buffer allows you to bring this information together. That said, as noted in Chapter 4, bear in mind the dangers associated with engaging in a complex conversation while driving.

As we also noted in Chapter 4, conflicts can arise when two or more simultaneous demands are placed on either component. It is difficult, indeed dangerous, to drive and read a roadmap at the same time. It is also difficult to hold two conversations at the same time.

THE BRAIN LOVES A PUZZLE

As you read ahead, use the information in the text to solve the following puzzle:

A young physicist was working on the problem of connecting the world's computers. After some false starts, he invented a model of a computer network based on how the brain performs memory tasks. What was this invention that changed the world? How was it based on the workings of the human brain?

Long-Term Memory: Preserving the Past

Long-term memory (LTM) is a storage system that allows you to retain information for periods of time beyond the capacity of short-term memory. Though some information may remain in long-term memory for only days or weeks, other information may remain for a lifetime. The storage capacity of short-term memory is limited, but long-term memory is virtually limitless in what it can hold. In all likelihood, we can always squeeze more facts and more experiences into long-term memory.

long-term memory (LTM) The memory subsystem responsible for long-term storage of information.

Consolidation is the process by which the brain converts unstable, fresh memories into stable, long-term memories. The first 24 hours after information is acquired

consolidation The process of converting short-term memories into long-term memories.

are critical for consolidation to occur. Sleep appears to play an important role in the process by which the brain consolidates or solidifies newly formed memories of daily experiences into more lasting remembrances (Ellenbogen, 2008; Fenn et al., 2009; Payne & Kensinger, 2010). This means that if you are studying for a test you have the next day and want to increase your chances of retaining the information you've just learned, make sure to get a good night's sleep. Sleep even helps consolidate memory of new learning in other animals, such as birds (Brawn, Nusbaum, & Margoliash, 2010).

Whereas short-term memory relies largely on acoustic coding, long-term memory depends more on semantic coding, or coding by meaning. One way of transferring information from short-term to long-term memory is through maintenance rehearsal, which, as we've noted, is the repeated rehearsal of words or sounds. But a better way is through **elaborative rehearsal**, a method of rehearsal in which you focus on the *meaning* of the material. A friend of mine has a telephone number that ends with the digits 1991, a year I remember well because it was the year my son Michael was born. I have no trouble remembering my friend's number because I associate it with something meaningful (my son's birth year). But I need to look up other friends' numbers that end in digits that have no personal significance for me.

elaborative rehearsal The process of transferring information from short-term to long-term memory by consciously focusing on the meaning of the information.

How do we manage to organize our long-term memory banks so we can retrieve what we want to know when we want to know it? Imagine being in a museum where bones, artifacts, and other holdings were strewn about without any organization. It would be difficult, perhaps impossible, to find the exhibit you were looking for. Now imagine how difficult it would be to retrieve specific memories if they were all scattered about in LTM without rhyme or reason. Fortunately, LTM is organized in ways that provide relatively quick access to specific memories.

semantic network model A representation of the organizational structure of long-term memory in terms of a network of associated concepts.

CONCEPT 6.4
According to the semantic network model, when you think of a particular concept, it causes a ripple effect to occur within the network of interlinking concepts, triggering memory of related concepts.

A leading conceptual model of how LTM is organized is the **semantic network model**, which holds that information is retained within networks of interlinking concepts (also called a *semantic hierarchy*) (Collins & Loftus, 1975). We understand the meaning of something by linking it to related information. For example, the concept of "animal" might be linked to concepts of "fish" and "bird," which in turn might be linked to associated concepts such as "salmon" and "robin," respectively (see ■ Figure 6.4) Thinking of a particular concept causes a ripple effect, called *spreading activation*, throughout the semantic network, triggering recall of related concepts (Willingham, 2007). In other words, you think the word "fish" and suddenly related concepts begin springing to mind, such as "salmon" or "cod," which in turn trigger other associations such as "pink," "tastes fishy," and so on.

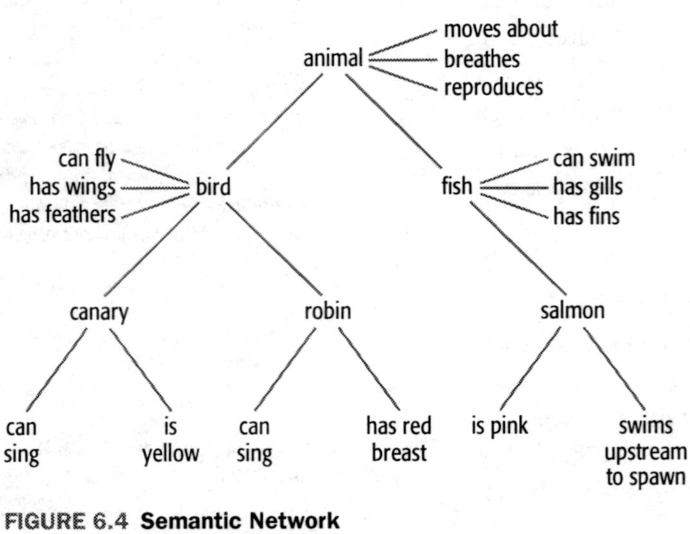

FIGURE 6.4 Semantic Network
The semantic network model posits that information in long-term memory is organized in networks of interlinking concepts.
Source: Adapted from A. M. Collins & Quillian, 1969.

The inventor of the World Wide Web, physicist Tim Berners-Lee, modeled his creation on the workings of the human brain. As he wrote in his memoir, "Suppose all the information stored on computers everywhere were linked, I thought. Suppose I could program my computer to create a space in which anything could be linked to anything. All the bits of information in every computer . . . on the planet . . . would be available to me and to anyone else . . ." (Berners-Lee, 1999). Today, whenever you surf the Web by clicking on one hyperlink after another, you are modeling what your brain does naturally—linking information in networks of interlinking concepts called semantic networks.

Why should elaborative rehearsal (rehearsal by meaning) result in better transfer of information from short-term to long-term memory than maintenance rehearsal (rehearsal by repetition)? One explanation, the **levels-of-processing theory**, holds that the level at which information is encoded or processed determines how well or how long information is stored in memory (Craik & Lockhart, 1972). In this view, information is better retained when it is processed more "deeply," or encoded on the basis of its meaning. By contrast, shallow processing is encoding by superficial characteristics, such as the rhyming of words (Willingham, 2007).

The levels-of-processing theory is correct that information is generally better retained when it is processed more deeply in terms of meaning. You're more likely to learn and retain knowledge of a concept, say "classical conditioning," by explaining what it means or by giving an example of how it applies in daily life, than by simply repeating the formal definition of the term. However, the model doesn't hold up as well for memory tasks pegged to shallow levels of processing, or rote memorization. For instance, you might be better able to remember the lines of a children's nursery rhyme by focusing on the sounds of the rhyming words than on their meaning. Simple repetition or rote memorization may also be effective for remembering simple number sequences that lack meaningful associations, like telephone numbers, or even names of people you meet for the first time.

We began our discussion of how memory works by recognizing that memory depends on underlying processes (encoding, storage, retrieval) that proceed through a series of stages (sensory memory, short-term memory, long-term memory). Concept Chart 6.1 summarizes these processes and stages; ■ Figure 6.5 shows the three stages in schematic form. Through these processes, we form long-term memories that we can recall at will or with some help (retrieval cues). Next we focus on the contents of long-term memory—those memories that enrich our lives.

© Andrew Brusso/Corbis

Do you know this man? He's Tim Berners-Lee, who modeled his creation, the World Wide Web, on the workings of the human brain in linking related concepts to each other within semantic networks.

levels-of-processing theory The belief that how well or how long information is remembered depends on the depth of encoding or processing.

CONCEPT 6.5
According to the levels-of-processing theory, information is better retained in memory when it is encoded or processed at a "deeper" level.

CONCEPT CHART 6.1 Stages and Processes of Memory

		Memory Process		
	Memory Stage	**Encoding**	**Storage**	**Retrieval**
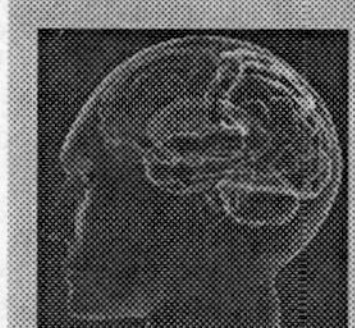 © Yakobchuk Vasyl, 2009/Shutterstock.com	Sensory memory	Iconic and echoic	Very brief—from a fraction of a second to 3 or 4 seconds	No retrieval; information is lost or transferred to short-term memory
 © Aleander Kalina, 2009/Shutterstock.com	Short-term memory	Acoustic and visual, but primarily acoustic	About 30 seconds at most. Maintenance or elaborative rehearsal may extend or convert it into long-term memory	No retrieval; information is lost or transferred to long-term memory
 © Andreja Donko, 2009/Shutterstock.com	Long-term memory	Acoustic, visual, and semantic, but primarily semantic	Long-term, possibly lifelong	Retrieval cues and activation of semantic networks boost retrieval

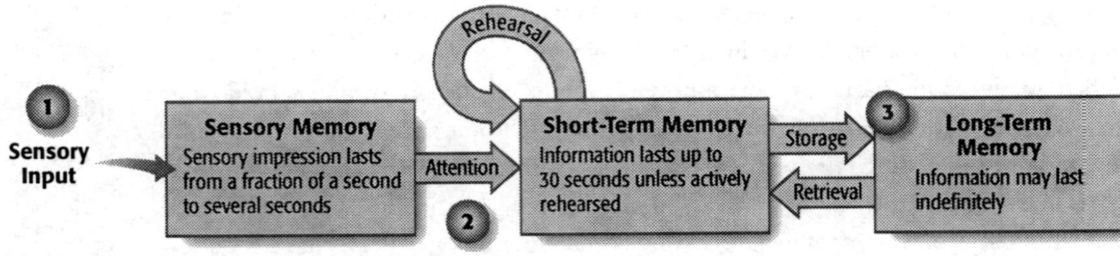

FIGURE 6.5 Three-Stage Model of Memory
The three-stage model of memory is a useful framework for understanding the relationships among the three memory systems. (1) Sensory input (visual images, sounds, etc.) creates impressions held briefly in sensory memory. (2) By directing attention to sensory information, we can bring this information into short-term memory, where we can keep it in mind for a brief period of time. We use two general types of rehearsal strategies (maintenance rehearsal and elaborative rehearsal) to transfer information held in short-term memory into long-term memory. (3) Once information is stored in long-term memory, it must be retrieved and brought back into short-term memory before it can be used.

What We Remember: The Contents of Long-Term Memory

What types of memories are stored in long-term memory? At the broadest level, we can distinguish between two general types of long-term memory: *declarative memory,* or "knowing that," and *procedural memory,* or "knowing how" (see ■ Figure 6.6) (Eichenbaum, 1997; Rupp, 1998; E. R. Smith, 1998).

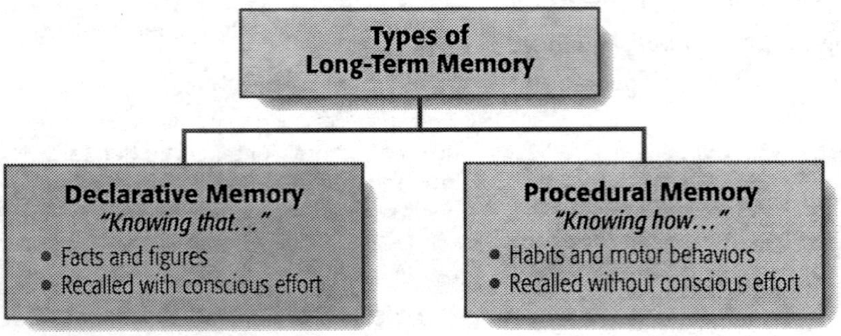

FIGURE 6.6 Types of Long-Term Memory
This organizational chart shows how long-term memory can be divided into two general types, declarative memory and procedural memory.

Declarative Memory: "Knowing That"

Declarative memory (also called *explicit memory*) is memory of facts and personal information that requires a conscious effort to bring to mind. Declarative memory allows us to know "what" and "that." We know that there are 50 states in the United States, that we live on such-and-such a street, and that water and oil don't mix. We know what elements are found in water and what colors are in the American and Canadian flags. We can group declarative memories into two general categories: (1) type of memory (*semantic* or *episodic memory*) and (2) time frame (*retrospective* or *prospective memory*) (see ■ Figure 6.7).

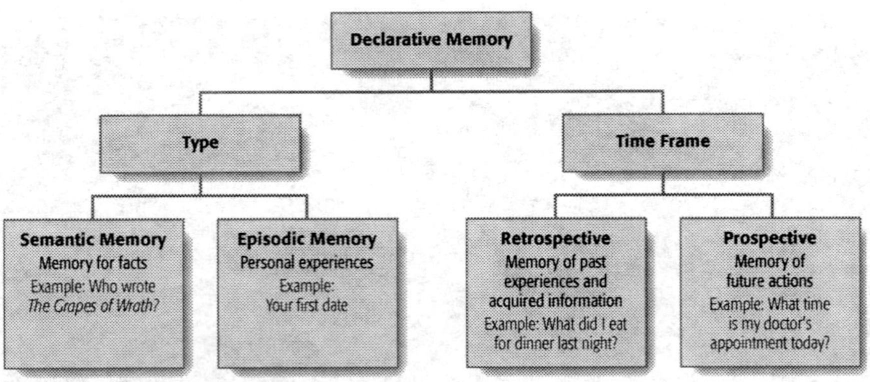

FIGURE 6.7 Declarative Memory
Here we see a diagram of the different types of declarative memory.

CONCEPT 6.6
The two major types of long-term memory are declarative memory ("knowing that") and procedural memory ("knowing how").

CONCEPT 6.7
Declarative memory consists of semantic memory (memory of facts) and episodic, or autobiographical, memory (memory of life events and experiences).

Semantic memory is memory of facts. We can liken semantic memory to a mental encyclopedia or storehouse of information we carry around in our heads. It allows us to remember who wrote *The Grapes of Wrath,* which film won the Academy Award for best picture last year, how to spell the word *encyclopedia,* and what day Japan attacked Pearl Harbor. Semantic memories are not indelibly imprinted in our brains, which is why you may no longer remember last year's Oscar winner or that John Steinbeck wrote *The Grapes of Wrath.* Semantic memories are better remembered when they are retrieved and rehearsed from time to time. So if you stumbled when it came to remembering the name of the author of

The Grapes of Wrath, reminding you of it today will probably help you remember it tomorrow.

Episodic memory (also called *autobiographical memory*) is memory of personal experiences that constitute the story of your life—everything from memories of what you had for dinner last night to the time you fell from a tree when you were 10 years old and needed 15 stitches. Episodic memory is a personal diary of things that have happened to you, whereas semantic memory comprises general knowledge of the world (Willingham, 2007). For example, remembering where you spent your summer vacation is an episodic memory. Remembering that Paris is the capital of France and that Google is an online search engine are semantic memories, or general facts about the world.

Retrospective memory is memory of your past experiences, such as where you went to school, as well as information you previously learned, including the knowledge you have acquired of the principles of psychology. **Prospective memory** is memory of things you need to do in the future. Think of it as memory of intentions (Kliegel, Mackinlay, & Jäger, 2008). You rely on prospective memory when remembering to take your medication, to pay your cell phone bill on time, or to call your mother on her birthday. It is remembering to remember. Some of our most embarrassing lapses of memory involve forgetting to do things. ("Sorry, I forgot to call the restaurant for reservations. It just slipped my mind.")

Procedural Memory: "Knowing How"

Procedural memory is memory of how to do things, such as how to ride a bicycle, climb stairs, tie shoelaces, perform mathematical operations, speak a particular language, or play a musical instrument. Whereas declarative memory is brought to mind by conscious effort, we draw upon procedural memory without making a conscious effort. Once you've acquired the skill of tying your shoelaces, you don't need to think about what your fingers are doing when tying the knot.

Declarative memory involves the recall of information we can verbalize ("Let's see, the definition of the word "precipice" is..."). But procedural memory involves motor or performance skills we perform without conscious thought and which are difficult, if not impossible to put into words. For example, try to describe in words how you move each of your muscles when riding a bicycle. We form and store declarative and procedural memories using different parts of the brain. Declarative memories are more prone to forgetting ("What was the name of my Spanish professor in college?"). By contrast, procedural memories are more enduring, which is why you may hear people say that once you learn to ride a bike, you never forget it.

Implicit memory—memory evoked without any deliberate effort to remember—is considered a form of procedural memory. Hearing a familiar song on the radio may evoke pleasant feelings associated with past experiences even though you made no conscious attempt to recall these experiences. In contrast, **explicit memory** requires a conscious or *explicit* effort to bring it to mind ("Hmm, what is the capital of Finland?").

One way of studying implicit or habit memory is through a *priming task*. This technique exposes individuals to a word or concept that sensitizes, or "primes," them to respond in a particular way to subsequent stimuli. Priming effects may occur even though subjects are unaware of having been exposed to the priming stimulus and make no conscious effort to recall it.

Let's break this down further by looking at an example. In a recent study, investigators showed how behavior could be subtly influenced by exposure to odors that lay outside of conscious awareness (Holland, Hendriks, & Aarts, 2005). Participants were unaware that they were exposed to a citrus-scented all-purpose cleaner. Later, when these participants

declarative memory Memory of facts and personal information that requires a conscious effort to bring to mind (also called *explicit memory*).

semantic memory Memory of facts and general information about the world.

episodic memory Memory of personal experiences.

CONCEPT 6.8
Prospective memory, or remembering to remember, has important applications in daily life, involving everything from remembering appointments to remembering to call people on their birthdays.

retrospective memory Memory of past experiences or events and previously acquired information.

prospective memory Memory of things one plans to do in the future.

procedural memory Memory of how to do things that require motor or performance skills.

CONCEPT 6.9
Implicit memory and explicit memory differ in terms of whether we make a conscious effort to bring information to mind.

implicit memory Memory accessed without conscious effort.

explicit memory Memory accessed through conscious effort.

Baseball manager Joe Torre once referred to the ability to throw a baseball accurately as "muscle memory." We rely on muscle memory, or procedural memory, whenever we perform complex motor skills such as riding a bike, dancing, typing, climbing stairs, hitting or throwing a baseball, or playing tennis.

were again exposed to the scent, they showed faster reaction times in a word-identification task in which they were challenged to identify cleaning-related words than did others in a control group who were exposed to the scent for the first time. The experimental group subjects also kept their immediate environment cleaner during an eating task than did the control group participants. In other words, exposure to the scent affected later behavior, even though individuals were unaware of having been exposed to it.

We are conscious beings, but we are not consciously aware of everything we do (Bargh & Williams, 2006). We often respond automatically by drawing upon implicit learning and memory processes that don't engage conscious thought. For example, we button our shirt and tie our shoelaces without thinking about the finger movements needed to perform these tasks.

Psychologists have extended the study of implicit processes to consumer research. In a recent study, investigators found that shoppers sometimes made better decisions about products they chose when they let their intuition guide them rather than careful deliberation (Dijksterhuis et al., 2006). The problem is we don't necessarily know when it is best to listen to our gut and when it is best to carefully examine our choices.

The Reliability of Long-Term Memory: Can We Trust Our Memories?

We might think our memories accurately reflect events we've witnessed or experienced. But personal memory may not be as reliable as we might think. Memory scientists reject the idea that memory works like a video camera that records exact copies of personal experiences. Rather, according to **constructionist theory**, personal memory is a representation or reconstruction of the past, not a verbatim copy (Aamodt & Wang, 2008). The brain stitches together bits and pieces of information in reconstructing memories of our past experiences. Reconstruction, however, can lead to distorted memories of events and experiences. The brain may invent details to weave a more coherent story of our past experiences.

constructionist theory A theory that holds that memory is not a replica of the past but a representation, or *reconstruction*, of the past.

CONCEPT 6.10
The constructionist theory holds that memory is a process of reconstructing past events and experiences, not of replaying them exactly as they occurred.

According to constructionist theory, memories are not carbon copies of reality. From this vantage point, it is not surprising that people who witness the same event or read the same material may have very different memories of the event or of the passage they read. Nor would it be surprising if recollections of your childhood are not verbatim records of what actually occurred but, rather, reconstructions based on pieces of information from many sources—from old photographs, from what your mother told you about the time you fell from the tree when you were 10, and so on.

Why It Matters

Why does it matter if memory is a process of reconstructing past experiences rather than recalling mental snapshots of experiences? One reason is that constructionist theory puts us on notice not to trust that our memories are verbatim accounts of past experiences. Some of our memories are flawed or distorted; others are completely false (Bernstein & Loftus, 2009). Memory distortions can range from simplifications, to omissions of details, to outright fabrications. Even so, we shouldn't presume that all memories are distorted. Some may be more or less accurate reflections of events. Others, perhaps most, can be likened better to impressionist paintings than mental snapshots.

The constructionist account of memory also provides an important perspective on how *negative stereotyping*—ascribing negative traits to people of certain groups—can influence perceptions and attitudes of people subjected to stereotyping. Investigators Cara Averhart and Rebecca Bigler (1997) examined the influence of racial stereotypes on memory in African American children of elementary school age. They used a memory test in which children recalled information embedded in stories in which light- and dark-complexioned African American characters were associated with either positive ("nice") or negative ("mean") attributes. The results showed that children had better memory for stories in which more favorable attributes were associated with light-complexioned characters and more negative characteristics were associated with dark-complexioned characters. The memory bias was even greater among children who rated themselves as having light skin tones. The results support a constructionist view that people are better able to recall information that is consistent with their existing concepts, or *schemas*, even when these schemas are grounded in prejudice.

© AP Photo/Marty Lederhandler

Emotionally charged experiences, such as the horrific attacks of September 11, 2001, can create "flashbulb memories" that seem permanently etched into our brains. Yet these memories may not be as accurate as we think they are.

A schema is an organized knowledge structure or set of beliefs about the world, such as the concepts in the study cited above that black/dark is associated with negative characteristics and white/light with positive characteristics. The schemas we develop reflect our experiences and expectancies. You can test for yourself whether your memory schemas lead to distorted memories by completing the exercise in the *Try This Out* feature, "What's in the Photograph?"

In the next sections, we take a look at two controversial issues that call into question the credibility of long-term memory: eyewitness testimony and recovery of repressed

TRY THIS OUT What's in the Photograph?

Look briefly at the photograph of a professor's office that appears in ■ Figure 6.8. Then continue with your reading of the chapter. After a few minutes, return here, and without looking at the photo again, list all the objects you saw in the office.

____

____

____

____

____

Now look again at the photo. Did you list any objects not actually present in the office but that may have fit your concept, or schema, of what a professor's office looks like, such as filing cabinets and bookshelves? Investigators who used this photograph in a similar experiment found that many subjects remembered seeing such objects, demonstrating that their memories were affected by their existing schemas (W. F. Brewer & Treyens, 1981).

© Courtesy of W.E. Brewer, from Brewer, W.E. and Treyens, J.C. (1981). "Role of Schemata in Memory of Places," Cognitive Psychology, 13, 207–230

FIGURE 6.8 Professor's Office

memories. These issues place memory research squarely in the public eye. First, however, we examine another type of long-term memory: flashbulb memories, which, regardless of their accuracy, seem indelibly etched in the brain.

Flashbulb Memories: What Were You Doing When . . . ?

flashbulb memories Enduring memories of emotionally charged events that seem permanently seared into the brain.

Extremely stressful or emotionally arousing personal or historical events may leave vivid, lasting, and highly detailed memories called **flashbulb memories** (Hirst et al., 2009). They are called flashbulb memories because they seem to have been permanently seared into the brain by the pop of the flashbulb on an old-fashioned camera. Many of us share a flashbulb memory of the World Trade Center disaster. We remember where we were and what we were doing at the time we heard of the attack, just as though it had happened yesterday. Many baby boomers share the flashbulb memory of the assassination of President John Kennedy in 1963.

CONCEPT 6.11
Emotionally arousing events may leave vivid, lasting impressions in memory, called flashbulb memories, that seem permanently etched into our brains.

→ Concept Link
People who develop posttraumatic stress disorder (PTSD) following emotionally traumatic events may re-experience the traumatic event in the form of intrusive memories or images of the trauma. See Module 12.1.

Some flashbulb memories are accurate, but others are prone to the kinds of distortion we see in other forms of long-term memory (Berntsen & Thomsen, 2005). A study of flashbulb memories of the terrorist attacks of September 11, 2001, for example, showed that they were not any more accurate than ordinary memories (Talarico & Rubin, 2003).

Eyewitness Testimony: "What Did You See on the Day in Question?"

CONCEPT 6.12
Memory reports of eyewitnesses may be flawed, even when eyewitnesses are convinced of the accuracy of their recollections.

In reaching a verdict, juries give considerable weight to eyewitness testimony. Yet memory researchers find that eyewitness testimony can be as flawed and strewn with error as other forms of memory. Psychologist Elizabeth Loftus (2004), a leading expert on eyewitness testimony, points out that a shockingly high number of people are wrongly convicted of crimes each year because of faulty eyewitness testimony.

Imagine your brother or sister told you about a childhood incident in which you fell off a swing. If he or she insisted that it really did happen, you might start to believe it. Similarly, people can be led to believe events occurred in their past that never actually happened. Investigators find they can induce false memories in many people's memories of events that never actually occurred (Brainerd, Reyna, & Ceci, 2008; Pezdek & Lam, 2007).

misinformation effect A form of memory distortion that affects eyewitness testimony and that is caused by misinformation provided during the retention interval.

Our memory of events can be altered by later exposure to misleading information about these events (Chan, Thomas, & Bulevich, 2009; Frenda, Nichols, & Loftus, 2011). Loftus described this phenomenon as a **misinformation effect**. In a landmark study, she and her colleagues had subjects view a film of a car accident that occurred at an intersection with a stop sign (Loftus, Miller, & Burns, 1978). Some subjects were then given misleading information telling them that the traffic sign was a yield sign. When subjects were later asked what traffic sign they saw at the intersection, those given the false information tended to report seeing the yield sign (see ■ Figure 6.9). Subjects who were not given the false information were much more likely to recall the correct traffic sign. This research calls into question the credibility of eyewitness testimony—especially when witnesses are subjected to leading or suggestive questioning that might "plant" ideas in their heads.

© Jeff Siner/The Charlotte Observer
Memory researcher Elizabeth Loftus

False memories of events that never took place can also be induced experimentally (Loftus, 2003). Imagination, too, can play tricks on your memory. Simply imagining a past experience can induce a false memory that the event actually occurred (Mazzoni & Memom, 2003).

FIGURE 6.9 Misinformation Effect
If you were one of the participants in this study, do you think your memory would be based on what you had actually seen (the stop sign) or on what you were later told you had seen (a yield sign)?

Since eyewitness testimony may be flawed, should we eliminate it from court proceedings? Loftus (1993) argues that if we dispensed with eyewitness testimony, many criminals would go free. As an alternative, we can attempt to increase the accuracy of eyewitness testimony. One way of doing so is to find corroborating evidence or independent witnesses who can back up each other's testimony. The accuracy of eyewitness testimony also involves the following factors:

1. *Ease of recall.* People who take longer to answer questions in giving testimony are less likely to be accurate in their recall than those who respond without hesitation (Sauerland & Sporer, 2009). Similarly, eyewitnesses who more quickly identify a perpetrator from a lineup tend to be more accurate than those who take longer (Dunning & Perretta, 2002; G. L. Wells & Olson, 2003).
2. *Degree of confidence.* Highly confident witnesses ("Yes, that's the guy. Definitely.") are generally more accurate than those with less confidence in their memories ("I think it's the guy, but I'm not really sure.") (Brewer & Wells, 2011). Yet even highly confident witnesses are sometimes wrong.
3. *General knowledge about a subject.* People who are more knowledgeable about a subject are more likely to be reliable witnesses than are less knowledgeable people. For example, when asked by a police officer to identify a motor vehicle involved in a crime, a person familiar with the various makes and models of automobiles may be better equipped to give a reliable answer than one who knows little or nothing of the subject.
4. *Racial identification.* People are generally better able to recognize faces of people of their own race than the faces of people of other races (Hehman, Mania, & Gaertner, 2010). Consequently, eyewitnesses may be more prone to make mistakes when identifying members of other races.
5. *Types of questions.* Leading or suggestive questions by investigators can result in the misidentification of perpetrators, whereas open-ended questions—for example, "What did you see?"—tend to increase the accuracy of eyewitness testimony (Fruzzetti et al., 1992; Loftus, 1997). On the other hand, open-ended questions tend to elicit fewer details from witnesses.
6. *Facial characteristics.* Faces with distinctive features are much more likely to be accurately recognized than nondistinctive faces (G. L. Wells & Olson, 2003). Also, highly attractive or highly unattractive faces are more likely to be accurately identified than are those of average attractiveness.

© Photos12/Alamy

"Me at Disneyland? What's up with that, Doc?" About one in three people who were shown a phony ad featuring a picture of Bugs Bunny just outside the Magic Kingdom at Disneyland later said they believed or remembered that they had once met Bugs at Disneyland (Loftus, 2004). But such meetings could never have occurred because the character of Bugs is owned by the Disney rival Time Warner. These findings suggest how easy it can be to create false memories in the minds of some people.

© Scott Adams/Dist. by United Features Syndicate, Inc.

In sum, we shouldn't think of the brain as a kind of mental camera that stores snapshots of events as they actually happened. Memory is more of a reconstructive process in which bits of information are pieced together in ways that can sometimes lead to distorted recollections of events, even if the person is convinced the memory is accurate.

Recovery of Repressed Memories

CONCEPT 6.13
Research showing that false memories may seem as real as actual events calls into question the credibility of recovered memories of childhood abuse.

→ Concept Link
Though we may question the validity of recovered memories of childhood abuse, sexual or physical abuse in childhood does play an important role in many psychological disorders, including dissociative identity disorder. See Module 15.3.

CONCEPT 6.14
Though some recovered memories of childhood abuse may be genuine, we lack the tools to determine which are true.

Controversy has swirled around the credibility of memories that suddenly surface in adulthood. In most cases, such memories come to light during hypnosis or psychotherapy. On the basis of recovered memories of sexual trauma in childhood, authorities have brought charges of sexual abuse against hundreds of people. A number of these cases have resulted in convictions and long jail sentences, even in the absence of corroborating evidence. But should recovered memories be taken at face value?

It is unusual, even rare, for someone to completely forget childhood traumas (Goodman et al., 2003; McNally & Geraerts, 2009). Techniques used in therapy to recover memories of sexual abuse, such as hypnosis and dream interpretation, may actually foster false memories of these events (Geraerts et al., 2009). Events that never happened can enter a subject's memory and seem just as real and accurate as memories of events that did occur. In all likelihood, some recovered memories are genuine, whereas others are undoubtedly false (Erdleyi, 2010). The problem is that we lack tools to reliably differentiate true memories from false ones (McNally & Geraerts, 2009). From a constructionist standpoint, we should not be surprised that memories may be distorted, even when the person believes them to be true.

6.1 MODULE REVIEW Remembering

Recite It

What are the basic processes and stages of memory?

- The three basic memory processes are encoding (converting stimuli into a form that can be stored in memory), storage (retaining information in memory), and retrieval (accessing stored information).
- We encode information by means of acoustic codes (coding by sounds), visual codes (coding by mental imaging), and semantic codes (coding by meaning).
- The three stages of memory are sensory memory (momentary storage of sensory impressions), short-term memory (working memory of information held in awareness for up to about 30 seconds), and long-term memory (long-term or permanent storage of information).
- The semantic network model posits that information is held in long-term memory in networks of interlinking concepts. Through a process of spreading activation, thinking of one concept brings related concepts within that semantic network to mind.

What are the major types of long-term memory?

➤ The two major types of long-term memory are declarative memory ("knowing what or that") and procedural memory ("knowing how").

➤ Declarative memory is brought to mind by conscious effort, whereas procedural memory is engaged without conscious effort.

What is the constructionist theory of memory?

➤ Constructionist theory holds that memory is a representation, or reconstruction, of past events or experiences.

What are flashbulb memories?

➤ Flashbulb memories are vivid, highly detailed, longlasting memories of emotionally charged personal or historical events.

What factors influence the accuracy of eyewitness testimony?

➤ Factors affecting the accuracy of eyewitness testimony include ease of recall, confidence in memory, general knowledge about the subject, same-race identification, and leading or suggestive questioning.

Are recovered memories of childhood sexual abuse credible?

➤ Some recovered memories may be credible, but others are not. We presently lack the tools to determine which are accurate and which are not.

Recall It

1. The type of memory that corresponds to "knowing how" is called ______ memory.
2. Which of the following is *not* correct? Constructionist theory suggests that
   a. memory recall may not be accurate.
   b. information is best recalled when it is consistent with a person's memory schemas.
   c. eyewitness testimony may be influenced by misinformation.
   d. flashbulb memories are immune to distortion.
3. Match the concepts on the left with their descriptions on the right:

i. sensory memory	a. process by which short-term memory is converted to long-term memory
ii. short-term memory	b. also known as "working" memory
iii. consolidation	c. process that uses semantic coding to transfer short-term memory to long-term memory
iv. elaborative rehearsal	d. storage system for fleeting iconic and echoic memories

Think About It

➤ Why is it incorrect to say that memory works like a mental camera?

➤ What factors influence the accuracy of eyewitness testimony?

Forgetting

MODULE 6.2

- What is decay theory?
- What is interference theory?
- What is retrieval theory?
- What is motivated forgetting?
- How is recall related to the methods used to measure it?
- What is amnesia, and what causes it?

Everyone is forgetful. Some of us are more forgetful than others. But why do we forget? Is it simply a matter of memories fading over time? Or do other factors account for forgetfulness? Degenerative brain diseases, such as Alzheimer's disease, are one cause of forgetfulness; another is amnesia, a memory disorder we discuss at the end of this module. Our main focus here, however, is on normal processes of forgetting. We recount

CONCEPT 6.15
The oldest theory of forgetting, decay theory, may explain memory loss that occurs due to the passage of time, but it fails to account for why some memories are more enduring.

several leading theories of forgetting and highlight the factors that make it easier or harder to remember information. We begin with decay theory.

decay theory A theory of forgetting that posits that memories consist of traces laid down in the brain that gradually deteriorate and fade away over time (also called *trace theory*).

savings method A method of testing memory retention by comparing the numbers of trials needed to learn material with the number of trials needed to relearn the material at a later time.

massed versus spaced practice effect The tendency for retention of learned material to be greater with spaced practice than with massed practice.

Decay Theory: Fading Impressions

The belief that memories consist of traces laid down in the brain that gradually deteriorate and fade away over time dates back to the writings of the Greek philosopher Plato some 2,500 years ago (Willingham, 2007). This theory of forgetting, known today as **decay theory** (also called *trace theory*), was bolstered by early experimental studies conducted by one of the founders of experimental psychology, Hermann Ebbinghaus (1850–1909).

SLICE OF LIFE With no teacher to guide him, no university affiliation, no laboratory, and no professional appointment, he painstakingly pursued the scientific study of memory processes entirely on his own and with himself as his only subject (Erdelyi, 2010). To study memory and forgetting, Ebbinghaus knew he had to eliminate any earlier associations he had to the material to be remembered. He devised a method for testing his memory that used nonsense syllables (combinations of letters that don't spell out anything), such as *nuz* and *lef* (Ebbinghaus, 1885). He presented these lists of syllables to himself and determined the number of trials it took for him to recall them perfectly. He then tested himself again at different intervals to see how much he would forget over time. The results showed a decline in memory that has since become known as the *Ebbinghaus forgetting curve* (see ■ Figure 6.10). Forgetting occurred rapidly in the first few hours after learning and then declined more gradually. It seemed as though memories simply faded over time. By the end of the first day, 66 percent of the information had been lost; after a month, nearly 80 percent was gone (Rupp, 1998).

Ebbinghaus also employed a **savings method** to test his memory retention. He first counted the number of times needed to rehearse a list of nonsense syllables in order to commit it to memory. Then he counted the number of times it took to relearn the list after a period of time had elapsed. If it took 10 repetitions to learn the list the first time and five the second, the savings would be 50 percent.

Memory researchers recognize that when people attempt to memorize information, they generally retain more information when they space their study sessions than when they cram them together within a single day (Cepeda et al., 2006). One reason for this effect, called the **massed versus spaced practice effect**, is that massed, or crammed, practice causes mental fatigue that interferes with learning and retention. A practical implication of this effect should be obvious: When studying for exams, don't cram. Rather, space out your study sessions. You'll learn more and remember more of what you learn. Also, spaced practice produces the same learning benefits for other animals, which is useful to keep in mind when trying to train your dog (Aamodt & Wang, 2008).

Decay theory helps account for memory loss due to the passage of time. However, a major weakness of the theory is that it fails to account for the unevenness with which memory decays over time. Some memories remain well preserved over time, whereas others quickly fade. One reason for this unevenness is that more distinctive or unusual information tends to be remembered better over time (Hunt & Worthen, 2006; Unsworth, Heitz, & Parks, 2008). You're likely to remember your first date better than your 14th. You're also more likely to later recall the name of a man you were introduced to at a party if the man's name was Oscar than if it had been Bob or John.

© Archives of the History of American Psychology, The Center for the History of Psychology—The University of Akron

Hermann Ebbinghaus

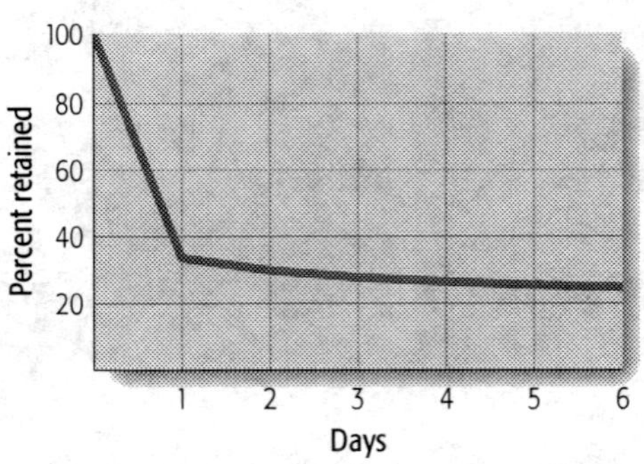

FIGURE 6.10 Ebbinghaus Forgetting Curve
Ebbinghaus showed that forgetting occurs most rapidly shortly after learning and then gradually declines over time.

Ebbinghaus studied retention of meaningless syllables. When we examine recall of more meaningful information, such as poetry or prose, we find a more gradual loss of memory over time. Then again, little if any forgetting may occur for important life events and knowledge we acquire about our work or career. Another factor that helps explain forgetting is interference (Wixted, 2005).

Interference Theory: When Learning More Leads to Remembering Less

Chances are you have forgotten what you ate for dinner a week ago Wednesday. The reason for your forgetfulness, according to **interference theory**, is interference from memories of dinners that preceded and followed that particular dinner. On the other hand, you are unlikely to forget your wedding day because it is so unlike any other day in your life (except for those, perhaps, who have taken many walks down the aisle). Interference theory helps explain why some events may be easily forgotten while others remain vivid for a lifetime. The greater the similarity between events, the greater the risk of interference. There are two general kinds of interference, *retroactive interference* and *proactive interference*.

interference theory The belief that forgetting is the result of the interference of memories with each other.

retroactive interference A form of interference in which newly acquired information interferes with retention of material learned earlier.

CONCEPT 6.16
Interference theory posits that memories held in short-term or long-term memory may be pushed aside by other memories.

Interference occurring after material is learned but before it is recalled is called **retroactive interference**. Perhaps you have found that material you learned in your 9:00 a.m. class, which seemed so clear when you left the classroom, quickly began to fade once you started soaking in information in the next class. In effect, new memories retroactively interfere with unstable earlier memories that are still undergoing the process of memory consolidation (Wixted, 2004).

Proactive interference is caused by the influence of previously learned material. Because of proactive interference, you may have difficulty remembering a new area code (you keep dialing the old one by mistake). Or you may forget to advance the year when writing checks early in a new year. ■ Figure 6.11 illustrates retroactive and proactive interference.

proactive interference A form of interference in which material learned earlier interferes with retention of newly acquired information.

overlearning Practice repeated beyond the point necessary to reproduce material without error.

Though some interference is unavoidable, we can take steps to minimize its disruptive effects:

- *Sleep on it.* Want to improve your recall of newly learned material? Sleep on it. Investigators believe that sleep enhances learning and memory by helping to convert fragile new memories into lasting ones (Gómez, Bootzin, & Nadel, 2006).
- *Rehearse fresh memories.* New long-term memories are fragile. Practicing or rehearsing fresh memories aloud or silently can strengthen them, making them more resistant to the effects of interference. Repeated practice beyond the point necessary to reproduce material without error is called **overlearning**. Apply the principle of overlearning to reviewing the material in this text, such as by rehearsing your knowledge of the key concepts in each chapter two or more times after you can demonstrate your knowledge without any errors.

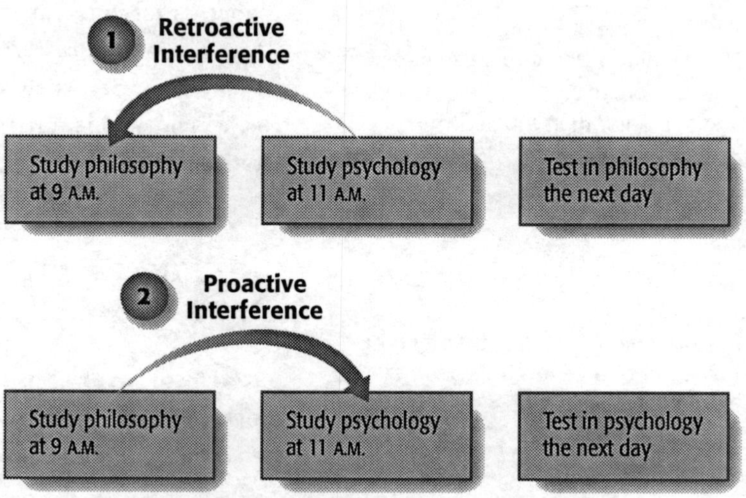

FIGURE 6.11 Retroactive and Proactive Interference
In 1 retroactive interference, new learning (psychology in the first example) interferes with recall of previously learned material (philosophy). In 2 proactive interference, previously learned material (philosophy in the second example) interferes with recall of new material (psychology).

© Hill Street Studios/Blend Images/Getty Images

This man remembered the broccoli his wife asked him to pick up at the store, but not the tuna. Based on your knowledge of the serial position effect, why do you suppose he remembered the broccoli and not the tuna?

- *Give yourself a break.* Try not to schedule one class directly after another. Give your recent memories time to consolidate in your brain.
- *Avoid sequential study of similar material.* Try not to study material that is similar in content in back-to-back fashion—for example, avoid scheduling a French class right after a Spanish one.

© John Kwan, 2009/Shutterstock.com

Interference may help explain the **serial position effect**, the tendency to recall the first and last items in a list, such as a shopping list, better than those in the middle of the list. The unfortunate items in the middle are often forgotten. In a study in which people were asked to name the last seven U.S. presidents in order, they were more likely to make mistakes in the middle of the list than at either the beginning or the end (Storandt, Kaskie, & Von Dras, 1998). Serial position effects influence both short-term and long-term memory.

Interference is the likely culprit in serial position effects. Items compete with one another in memory, and interference is greatest in the middle of a list than at either end of the list. For example, in a list of seven items, the fourth item may interfere with the item that it follows and the item that it precedes. But interference is least for the first and last items in the list—the first, because no other item precedes it; the last, because no other item follows it. The tendency to recall items better when they are learned first is called the **primacy effect.** The tendency to recall items better when they are learned last is called the **recency effect**. As the delay between a study period and a test period increases, primacy effects become stronger whereas recency effects become weaker (Knoedler, Hellwig, & Neath, 1999). This recency-primacy shift means that as time passes after you have committed a list to memory, it becomes easier to remember the early items but more difficult to remember the later-appearing items.

serial position effect The tendency to recall items at the start or end of a list better than items in the middle of a list.

primacy effect The tendency to recall items better when they are learned first.

recency effect The tendency to recall items better when they are learned last.

In sum, evidence shows that both the passage of time and interference contribute to forgetting. But neither decay theory nor interference theory can determine whether forgotten material becomes lost to memory or just more difficult to retrieve. Some forgotten material can be recovered if subjects are given retrieval cues to jog their memories, such as exposure to stimuli associated with the original situations in which the memories were formed. This brings us to a third model of forgetting, retrieval theory.

CONCEPT 6.17
The serial position effect explains why we are more likely to forget the middle items in a list than those at the beginning or end.

Retrieval Theory: Forgetting as a Breakdown in Retrieval

Retrieval theory posits that forgetting is the result of failing to access stored memories. Let us consider two principal ways in which the retrieval process can break down, *encoding failure* and *lack of retrieval* cues.

retrieval theory The belief that forgetting is the result of a failure to access stored memories.

Encoding Failure: What Image Is on the Back Side of a Nickel?

Memories cannot be retrieved if they were never encoded in the first place. The failure to encode information may explain why people often cannot recall details about

TRY THIS OUT What Does a Penny Look Like?

How well do you remember the features of a penny, the most commonplace of coins? Researchers Raymond Nickerson and Marilyn Jager Adams (1979) decided to find out. They showed subjects an array of drawings of a penny, only one of which was correct. Fewer than half of their subjects were able to pick out the correct one. Without looking at the coins in your pocket, can you tell which drawing of a penny in ■ Figure 6.12 is the correct one? The answer appears on p. 247.

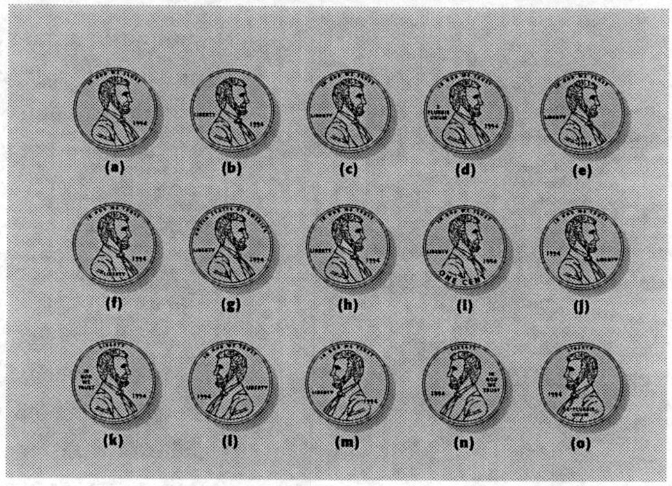

FIGURE 6.12 What Image Appears on the Front of a Penny?

common objects they use every day. For example, do you know what image appears on the back of a nickel? Before you rummage through your pockets, let me tell you it is an image of Monticello, the home of Thomas Jefferson, whose image is on the front of the coin. You may have glanced at this image of Monticello countless times but never brought it into memory because you failed to encode it. We tend to encode only as much information as we need to know (Rupp, 1998). Since we don't need to encode more specific details of a coin to recognize one or use it correctly, such information may not be encoded and thus cannot be retrieved (see also *Try This Out*).

Events that stand out tend to be better remembered. You are also more likely to remember events that occur irregularly (e.g., visits to a doctor because of an injury) than regularly occurring events (e.g., routine medical checkups). Events that are similar are generally encoded in terms of their common features rather than their distinctive characteristics (Conrad & Brown, 1996). Because similar events tend to be encoded in similar ways, it becomes more difficult to retrieve memories of the specific events.

CONCEPT 6.18
Memory retrieval may be impaired by a failure to encode information and by a lack of retrieval cues to access stored memories.

Lack of Retrieval Cues: What's His Name?

Information may be encoded in memory but remain inaccessible because of a lack of appropriate retrieval cues. A common and often embarrassing difficulty with memory retrieval is recalling proper names. Proper names have no built-in associations, no convenient retrieval cues or "handles" that can be used to distinguish among the many Jennifers, Marys, Davids, and Johns of the world. A lack of retrieval cues may account for a common experience called the **tip-of-the-tongue (TOT) phenomenon**, in which the information seems to be at the tip of one's tongue but just outside one's reach. If you've ever felt frustrated trying to recall something you're certain you know but just can't seem to bring to mind, you've experienced the TOT phenomenon. People who experience TOTs (and that includes most of us) may have partial recall of the information they are trying to retrieve, which is why they feel so sure the information is stored somewhere in their memory (Farrell & Abrams, 2011). They may recall the first few letters or sounds of the word or name ("I know it starts with a B"), or perhaps a similar-sounding word comes to mind. TOTs may result not only from a lack of available retrieval cues but also from more general difficulties with word retrieval. They tend to increase in later life, when word retrieval typically becomes more difficult (Branan, 2008).

tip-of-the-tongue (TOT) phenomenon An experience in which people are sure they know something but can't seem to bring it to mind.

CONCEPT 6.19
A common problem with memory retrieval involves the tip-of-the-tongue phenomenon–the experience of sensing you know something but just can't seem to bring it to mind.

Motivated Forgetting: Memories Hidden from Awareness

repression In Freudian theory, a type of defense mechanism involving motivated forgetting of anxiety-evoking material.

CONCEPT 6.20
In Freudian theory, the psychological defense mechanism of repression, or motivated forgetting, involves banishing threatening material from consciousness.

Sigmund Freud believed that certain memories are not forgotten but are kept hidden from awareness by **repression**, or motivated forgetting. In Freud's view, repression is a psychological defense mechanism that protects the self from awareness of threatening material, such as unacceptable sexual or aggressive wishes or impulses. Were it not for repression, Freud believed, we would be flooded with overwhelming anxiety whenever such threatening material entered consciousness. Repression is not simple forgetting; the repressed contents do not disappear but remain in the unconscious mind, hidden from awareness.

Freud's concept of repression does not account for ordinary forgetting—the kind that occurs when you try to retain information you read in your psychology textbook. Another problem with this concept is that people who are traumatized by rape, combat, or natural disasters, such as earthquakes or floods, tend to retain vivid if somewhat fragmented memories of these experiences. They often find it difficult to put such anxiety-evoking events out of their minds, which is the opposite of what we might expect from Freud's concept of repression. Moreover, since repression operates unconsciously, we may lack direct means of testing it scientifically. Nonetheless, many memory researchers, including a panel of experts appointed by the American Psychological Association, believe that repression can occur (Alpert, Brown, & Courtois, 1998; Willingham, 2007).

Measuring Memory: How It Is Measured May Determine How Much Is Recalled

CONCEPT 6.21
The methods used to measure memory, such as recall tasks and recognition tasks, affect how much we are able to recall.

Students who are given the choice generally prefer multiple-choice questions to questions that require a written essay. Why? The answer has to do with the different ways in which memory is measured.

free recall A type of recall task in which individuals are asked to recall as many stored items as possible in any order.

The methods used to measure memory can have an important bearing on how well you are able to retrieve information stored in memory. In a *recall task*, such as an essay question, you are asked to reproduce information you have committed to memory. There are three basic types of recall task. In **free recall**, you are asked to recall as much information as you can in any order you wish (e.g., randomly naming starting players on your college's basketball team). In a *serial recall* task, you are asked to recall a series of items or numbers in a particular order (e.g., reciting a telephone number). In *paired-associates recall*, you are first asked to memorize pairs of items, such as pairs of unrelated words such as *shoe–crayon* and *cat–phone*. You are then presented with one item in each pair, such as the word *shoe*, and asked to recall the item with which it was paired (*crayon*). If you've ever taken a foreign language exam in which you were presented with a word in English and asked to produce the foreign word for it, you know what a paired-associates recall task is.

recognition task A method of measuring memory retention that assesses the ability to select the correct answer from among a range of alternative answers.

In a **recognition task**, you are asked to pick out the correct answer from among a range of alternative answers. Tests of recognition memory, such as multiple-choice tests, generally produce much better retrieval than those of recall memory, largely because recognition tests provide retrieval cues. You're more likely to remember the name of the author of *Moby Dick* if you see the author's name among a group of multiple-choice responses than if you are asked to complete a recall task, such as a fill-in-the-blank item in which you are required to insert the author's name (Herman Melville).

Amnesia: Of Memories Lost or Never Gained

SLICE OF LIFE A medical student is brought by ambulance to the hospital after falling from his motorcycle and suffering a blow to his head. His parents rush to his side, keeping a vigil until he regains consciousness. Fortunately, he is not unconscious for long. As his parents are explaining what has happened to him, his wife suddenly bursts into the hospital room, throwing her arms around him and expressing her great relief that he wasn't seriously injured or killed. When his wife, whom he had married only a few weeks earlier, leaves the room, the medical student turns to his mother and asks, "Who is she?" (cited in Freemon, 1981).

CONCEPT 6.22
There are two general types of amnesia, retrograde amnesia (loss of memory of past events) and anterograde amnesia (loss or impairment of the ability to form or store new memories).

How can we explain this severe loss of memory? The medical student suffered from a type of **amnesia**, or memory loss. The term *amnesia* is derived from the Greek roots a ("not") and *mnasthai* ("to remember").

amnesia Loss of memory.

Types of Amnesia

The medical student suffered from **retrograde amnesia**, or loss of memory of past events (Riccio, Millin, & Gisquet-Verrier, 2003). A football player knocked unconscious by a blow to the head during a game may remember nothing beyond suiting up in the locker room. A boxer knocked cold in the ring may not remember the fight. A blow to the head can interfere with *memory consolidation*—which, as we noted in Module 6.1, is the process of converting unstable, short-term memories into stable and enduring ones. When this process is disrupted, memories of events occurring around the time of the disruption may be lost permanently. Some cases go beyond problems with memory consolidation. The medical student's memory loss extended beyond the time of his head injury to before he had met his wife. In such cases, whole chunks of memory are lost. Nonetheless, recent memories are generally more susceptible to retrograde amnesia than remote events (James & MacKay, 2001). In another form of amnesia, **anterograde amnesia**, people cannot form or store new memories or have difficulty doing so.

retrograde amnesia Loss of memory of past events.

anterograde amnesia Loss or impairment of the ability to form or store new memories.

childhood amnesia The normal occurrence of amnesia for events occurring during infancy and early childhood.

Amnesia typically involves impairment of episodic memory (memory of personal experiences). Amnesic patients generally retain procedural memory, the automatic form of memory we call upon when performing mechanical tasks such as tying our shoes or frying an egg. The retention of procedural memory in the face of loss of episodic memory in amnesic patients leads us to think that different memory systems in the brain may be responsible for these two types of memory.

Let's pose a more personal question. Do you remember your second birthday party—the balloons, the cake, your mom or dad snapping pictures? You may think you remember, but your memory is in all likelihood playing tricks on you. Adults have few if any memories before the age of three-and-a-half years (Bauer, 2007; Bauer et al., 2007; Tustin & Hayne, 2010). This form of amnesia, called **childhood amnesia**, is a perfectly normal process of development. Numerous theories have been proposed to explain childhood amnesia. One contemporary view suggests that preverbal memories—memories formed before language develops—are not well organized in the brain. They are thus difficult to retrieve through the word-based, or verbal, memory system that typically develops between ages two and three. Another possibility is that brain structures needed to form lasting memories do not mature until a child is about two or three years of age.

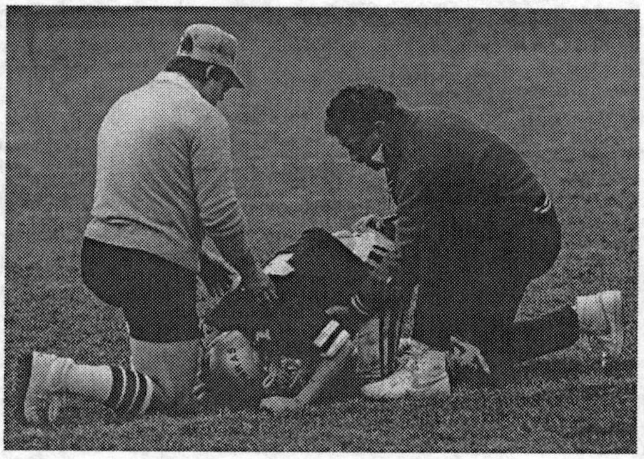

© Jeff Persons/Stock Boston

Amnesia is often caused by a traumatic injury to the brain, such as a blow to the head. This football player was knocked unconscious and may not remember anything about the play in which he was injured or events preceding the play.

Causes of Amnesia

Amnesia may be caused by physical or psychological factors. Physical causes include blows to the head, degenerative brain diseases (such as Alzheimer's disease; see Module 10.3), blockage of blood vessels to the brain, infectious diseases, and chronic alcoholism. Amnesias in some cases may be reversed if the underlying physical problem is successfully treated.

dissociative amnesia A psychologically based form of amnesia involving the "splitting off" from memory of traumatic or troubling experiences.

Amnesia resulting from psychological causes is called **dissociative amnesia**. *Dissociation* means "splitting off." Memories of a traumatic experience may become "dissociated" (split off) from consciousness, producing a form of amnesia for events occurring during a specific time. These events may be too emotionally troubling—provoking too much anxiety or guilt—to be consciously experienced. A soldier may have at best a dim memory of the horror he experienced on the battlefield and remember nothing of his buddy's being killed; yet his memory of other past events remains intact. Rarely is dissociative amnesia of the type that fuels many a daytime soap opera, the type in which people forget their entire lives—who they are, where they live, and so on.

Concept Chart 6.2 provides an overview of the key concepts of forgetting.

CONCEPT CHART 6.2 Forgetting: Key Concepts

© Image Source/Jupiter Images

	Concept	Description	Example
Theories of Forgetting	Decay theory	Gradual fading of memory traces as a function of time	Facts learned in school gradually fade out of memory over time
	Interference theory	Disruption of memory caused by interference of previously learned material or newly learned material	After a biology lecture, forgetting the information learned in chemistry class the hour before
	Retrieval theory	Failure to access material stored in memory because of encoding failure or lack of retrieval cues	Difficulty remembering something stored in memory
	Motivated forgetting	Repression of anxiety-provoking material	Failure to remember a traumatic childhood experience
Measuring Methods	Recall task	Test of the ability to reproduce information held in memory	Able to recite a phone number, the capitals of U.S. states or the provinces of Canada
	Recognition task	Test of the ability to recognize material held in memory	Able to recognize the correct answer in a multiple-choice question
Types of Amnesia	Retrograde amnesia	Loss of memory of past events	Unable to remember details of a car accident after suffering a blow to the head
	Anterograde amnesia	Loss or impairment of the ability to form or store new memories	Brain injury causes difficulty retaining new information

6.2 MODULE REVIEW Forgetting

Recite It

What is decay theory?

➤ Decay theory holds that forgetting results from the gradual deterioration of memory traces in the brain.

What is interference theory?

➤ Interference theory is the belief that forgetting results from the interference of memories with each other.

What is retrieval theory?

➤ Retrieval theory holds that forgetting is the result of a failure to access stored memories.

What is motivated forgetting?

➤ Motivated forgetting, or repression, is the Freudian belief that people banish anxiety-provoking material from conscious awareness.

How is recall related to the methods used to measure it?

➤ Recognition tasks (such as multiple-choice questions) generally produce better memory retrieval than recall tests (free recall, serial recall, or paired-associates recall) because they provide more retrieval cues that help jog memory.

What is amnesia, and what causes it?

➤ Amnesia, or memory loss, may be caused by psychological factors or by physical factors such as degenerative brain diseases and brain trauma. There are two general types of amnesia: retrograde amnesia and anterograde amnesia.

Recall It

1. The type of interference that accounts for why you may forget to advance the year when writing checks early in a new year is called ______ interference.
2. Which of the following is *not* a helpful way to reduce the effects of interference on memory?
   a. Avoid overlearning.
   b. Study material just before going to bed.
   c. Rehearse or practice material repeatedly.
   d. Avoid studying similar content simultaneously.
3. When it comes to remembering what you've learned, ______ practice is preferable to ______ practice.
4. Memory loss in which earlier life events are forgotten is known as
   a. dissociative amnesia.
   b. retrograde amnesia.
   c. retroactive amnesia.
   d. anterograde amnesia.

Think About It

➤ Have you had any tip-of-the-tongue experiences? Were you eventually able to retrieve the memory you were searching for? If so, how were you able to retrieve it?

➤ Why is it not a good idea to apply the principle of "massed practice" when preparing for exams? What study techniques are likely to be more effective?

The Biology of Memory

MODULE 6.3

- Where are memories stored in the brain?
- What is the role of the hippocampus in memory?
- What is LTP, and what role do scientists believe it plays in memory formation?
- What have scientists learned about the genetic basis of memory?

How are memories formed in the brain? Where are they stored? Breakthrough research is beginning to answer these and other questions that probe the biological underpinnings of memory. In this module, we examine what is presently known about those underpinnings.

Brain Structures in Memory: Where Do Memories Reside?

engram Lashley's term for the physical trace or etching of a memory in the brain.

Psychologist Karl Lashley (1890–1958) spent much of his career attempting to track down the elusive **engram**, the term he used to describe a physical trace or etching in the brain where he believed a memory is stored. A rat that learns to run a maze, for example, should have an engram somewhere in its brain containing a memory trace of the correct route leading to the exit or goal box.

Lashley spent years training rats to run mazes, then surgically removing parts of their cerebral cortexes, and testing the rats again to see if their memories for mazes remained intact. He reasoned that if removal of a part of the cortex wiped away a given memory, that part must be where the particular memory was stored. Despite years of painstaking research, he found that rats continued to run mazes they had learned previously regardless of the parts of the cortex he removed. The rats simply did not forget. He concluded that memories are not housed in any specific brain structure but must be scattered about the brain.

CONCEPT 6.23
Memories are stored in complex networks of interconnected brain cells called neuronal networks.

Neuronal Networks: The Circuitry of Memory

neuronal networks Memory circuits in the brain that consist of complicated networks of nerve cells.

Researchers believe that memories are not etched into particular brain cells but are stored within the intricate circuitry of constellations of neurons in the brain called **neuronal networks** (also called *neural networks*) (K. Matsumoto, Suzuki, & Tanaka, 2003; Ojemann, Schoenfield-McNeill, & Corina, 2002). Memory circuits exist in many parts of the brain, especially in the cerebral cortex. Memory scientists think of a memory as the form in which information is encoded, stored, and retrieved in neural circuits. In simplest terms, the circuit that is activated, or laid down, when information is first learned becomes the memory and then is fired again whenever the memory is either accessed or recalled (R. R. Thompson, 2005).

The Hippocampus: A Storage Bin for Memory

The hippocampus, a seahorse-shaped structure in the forebrain, is essential to forming new memories of facts and general information (semantic memory) and life experiences (episodic memory) (Dragoi & Tonegawa, 2011; Grove, 2008). But the hippocampus doesn't appear to play a role in procedural memory, the kind of memory we draw upon when riding a bicycle. Nor is the hippocampus believed to be the final destination for new memories (Stickgold & Wehrwein, 2009). Rather, the hippocampus may be a temporary storage bin for holding new memories, perhaps for weeks or months, before they are moved and filed away in the cerebral cortex and other parts of the brain for long-term storage (Wang & Aarnodt, 2008).

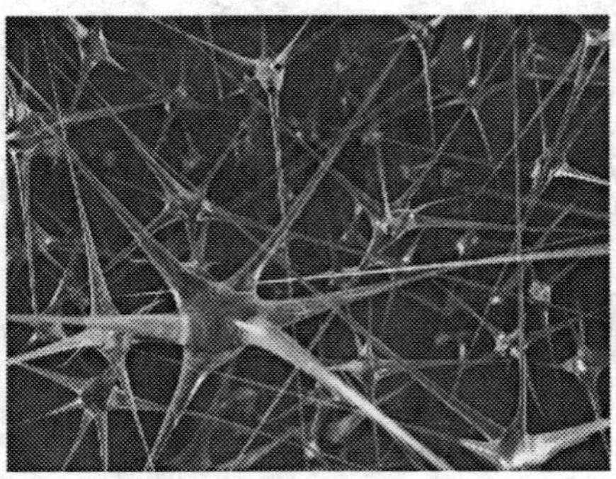
© iStockphoto.com/Simfo
Memory scientists believe that memories are embedded in dense neuronal networks in the brain.

If you unfortunately suffered extensive damage to your hippocampus, you might develop anterograde amnesia and be unable to form new memories (Thompson, 2005). Depending on the extent of the damage, you might retain earlier memories, but each new experience would fail to leave any mark in your memory (Dingfelder, 2004).

Memory also depends on many brain structures, including the thalamus and the amygdala. We know, for example, that damage to the thalamus can result in amnesia. The amygdala plays an important part in encoding emotional experiences, such as those involving fear or anger or other strong emotions. Scientists believe the amygdala and hippocampus become especially active during emotionally charged experiences, which serves to strengthen and preserve memories of these personally meaningful events (Adelson, 2004; Hassert, Miyashita, & Williams, 2004).

CONCEPT 6.24
Damage to the hippocampus could prevent you from forming new memories, so that you might be unable to remember someone you've just met.

→ Concept Link
The hippocampus plays a role in remembering the context in which the person experienced fear. See Module 8.3.

Strengthening Connections Between Neurons: The Key to Forming Memories

Locating neuronal networks corresponding to particular memories makes finding the proverbial needle in the haystack seem like child's play. The human brain contains many billions of neurons and perhaps trillions of synapses among them. Individual neurons in the brain can have thousands of synaptic connections with other neurons. In the hope of tracking down specific networks of cells where memories are formed, researchers have turned to a relatively simple animal: a large sea snail (*Aplysia*) that possesses a mere 20,000 neurons.

The landmark research that Eric Kandel, a molecular biologist and Nobel Prize winner, performed on *Aplysia* represented a major step forward in unraveling the biological bases of memory (Kandel, 1995; Kandel & Hawkins, 1993). Since learning results in the formation of new memories, Kandel needed to demonstrate that these animals were capable of learning new responses. To accomplish this, he and his colleagues first desensitized the snails to receiving a mild squirt of water. After a number of trials, the animals became habituated to the water squirt so that it no longer caused them to budge. In the second phase of the experiment, the researchers paired the squirt with a mild electric shock. The animals showed they could learn a simple conditioned response—reflexively withdrawing their gills (their breathing apparatus) when squirted with water alone. This self-defensive maneuver is the equivalent of the snails' "battening down the hatches" in anticipation of impending shock (Rupp, 1998).

© Eric Kandel

Nobel Prize winner Erik Kandel holding an aplysia, the sea snail he used to study the biological bases of memory.

Kandel observed that the amount of neurotransmitters released into synapses between the nerve cells that control the withdrawal reflex increased as the animals learned the conditioned response. The added neurotransmitter kicked the reflex into overdrive, making it more likely to fire. In effect, these synapses became stronger—that is, more capable of transmitting neural messages. Kandel had shown that memory formation involves biochemical changes occurring at the synaptic level.

"Cells That Fire Together, Wire Together"

The synaptic connections between neurons can be strengthened by repeated electrical stimulation. In effect, "cells that fire together, wire together" (Begley, 2011). This longlasting increase in the strength of synaptic connections is called **long-term potentiation (LTP)**. Potentiation simply means "strengthening." When synaptic connections become stronger, they can communicate better with each other, making the transmission of information between them more efficient (Griffiths et al., 2008; Murakoshi, Wang, & Yasuda, 2011).

long-term potentiation (LTP) The long-term strengthening of neural connections as the result of repeated stimulation.

CONCEPT 6.25
The key to forming memories may lie in strengthening the interconnections between the neurons that form neuronal networks in the brain.

LTP appears to play a key role in converting short-term memory into long-term memory (Griffiths et al., 2008; Hutchison, Chidiac, & Leung, 2009). The process

CONCEPT 6.26
Scientists suspect that long-term potentiation (LTP) may be needed for long-term memory to occur.

of forming long-term memories appears to depend on strengthening synaptic connections between neurons within the complex neural networks in the brain in which memories are encoded. But just how are these synaptic connections strengthened? One way may be to repeatedly practice or rehearse the information you want to remember (studying, anyone?). However, mere repeated practice or rote memorization may not be sufficient to remember complex material, such as the principles of memory discussed in this chapter. We may need to strengthen newly formed memories by elaborating on the meaning of the material—for example, by thinking of examples of the concepts discussed in this chapter or by relating them to your own personal experiences.

Genetic Bases of Memory

CONCEPT 6.27
Scientists have begun to unravel the genetic bases of memory, which may lead to the development of safe drugs that can help preserve or restore memory functioning.

Promising research with genetic engineering is offering new insights into how memory works. The transformation of short-term memory into long-term memory depends on the production of certain proteins, a process regulated by certain genes. Scientists have found that manipulation of a particular gene in fruit flies can enhance learning and memory ability, producing a kind of "smart fly" (S. S. Hall, 1998). Perhaps a similar gene might one day be found in humans.

Scientists hope that knowledge gained about the role of brain proteins in memory and the genes that help regulate their production may eventually lead to the development of drugs to treat or even cure Alzheimer's disease and other memory disorders. Perhaps we'll even have drugs that boost the memory functioning of normal individuals. In the meantime, think critically if you encounter claims about so-called memory-enhancing drugs. We have no compelling scientific evidence that any drug or supplement available today enhances memory in normal individuals (Begley, 2011).

Concept Chart 6.3 summarizes some of the key concepts relating to the biology of memory.

CONCEPT CHART 6.3 Biology of Memory: Key Concepts

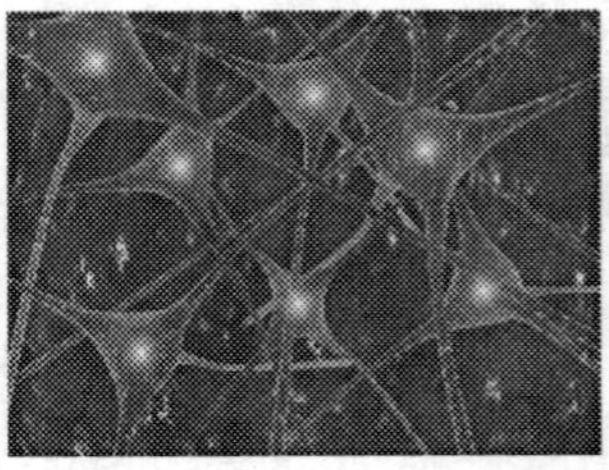
© Jurgen Ziewe/Shutterstock.com

Concept	Description
Lashley's engram	Karl Lashley failed to find evidence of the engram, his term for a physical trace or etching in the brain where he believed a memory is stored
Neuronal networks	Memory scientists believe that memories may "reside" in complex networks of neurons distributed across different parts of the brain
Biological underpinnings of memory	The hippocampus plays a key role in forming new semantic and episodic memories; conversion of short-term to long-term memory may depend on the process of long-term potentiation, the strengthening of synaptic connections between neurons
Genetic factors in memory	Long-term memory depends on genetic regulation of the production of brain proteins; advances in genetic engineering have demonstrated enhanced learning and memory in nonhuman organisms by means of genetic manipulation

6.3 MODULE REVIEW The Biology of Memory

Recite It

Where are memories stored in the brain?

➤ Memories are stored within the circuitry of constellations of nerve cells in the brain called neuronal networks.

What is the role of the hippocampus in memory?

➤ The hippocampus appears to play a key role in the formation and temporary storage of declarative memory, such as memory of events and daily experiences.

What is LTP, and what role do scientists believe it plays in memory formation?

➤ LTP (long-term potentiation) is the biochemical process by which repeated stimulation strengthens the synaptic connections between nerve cells.

➤ Scientists suspect that the conversion of short-term memory into long-term memory may depend on the production of LTP.

What have scientists learned about the genetic basis of memory?

➤ Genes regulate production of proteins involved in transforming short-term memory into long-term memory.

Recall It

1. Researchers today believe that memories are stored in constellations of brain cells known as ______.
2. Which of the following does not seem to be a function of the hippocampus?
   a. forming new memories of life experiences.
   b. forming procedural memories.
   c. creating long-term memories of facts (semantic memory) and life experiences (episodic memory).
   d. serving as a temporary storage area for new memories.
3. The strengthening of synaptic connections that may underlie the conversion of short-term memory into long-term memory is called ______.
4. Researchers are finding genetic influences in memory. How do genes appear to influence memory functioning?
   a. Genes regulate the production of certain proteins that are critical to long-term memory.
   b. A memory gene leads to the production of specialized neurotransmitters involved in learning and memory.
   c. Genes regulate the production of a memory molecule that allows new memories to form.
   d. Memories are directly encoded in genes, which are then passed from one generation to the next.

Think About It

➤ Why did Lashley's search for engrams prove elusive?

➤ Suppose memory boosters are found that would allow you to preserve perfect memories of everything you read and experience. Though memory pills might help you around exam time, would you really want to retain crystal-clear memories of every personal experience, including disappointments, personal tragedies, and traumatic experiences? What do you think?

Powering Up Your Memory

APPLICATION MODULE 6.4

Even if you never compete in a memory championship, you can learn to boost your memory power. Techniques specifically aimed at enhancing memory are called *mnemonics*, some of which have been practiced since the time of the ancient Greeks. Yet perhaps the most important ways to power up your memory are to take care of your health and to adopt more effective methods of studying, such as the SQ3R+ system (see "A Message to Students" in the Preface to this textbook).

CONCEPT 6.28
You can boost your memory power in many ways, such as by using mnemonics, focusing your attention, practicing repeatedly, taking care of your health, and adopting effective study habits.

mnemonic A device for improving memory.

acronym A word composed of the first letters of a series of words.

acrostic A verse or saying in which the first or last letter of each word stands for something else.

Using Mnemonics to Improve Memory

A **mnemonic** is a device for improving memory. The word *mnemonic* is derived from the name of the Greek goddess of memory, Mnemosyne, and is pronounced neh-MAHN-ik (the first *m* is silent). Here are some of the most widely used mnemonic devices.

Acronyms and Acrostics

The method of acronyms (also called the *first-letter system*) is among the easiest and most widely used mnemonic devices. An **acronym** is a word composed of the first letters of a series of words. The acronym HOMES can help you remember the names of the Great Lakes (Huron, Ontario, Michigan, Erie, and Superior). In Chapter 3, you learned the acronym Roy G. Biv, which spells out the first letters of the colors of the spectrum. You might try devising some acronyms to help you retain information you learned in class.

An **acrostic** is a verse or saying in which a letter of each word, typically the first letter, stands for something else. Generations of musicians have learned the lines of the treble clef staff (E, G, B, D, and F) by committing to memory the acrostic "*Every Good Boy Does Fine.*"

Popular Sayings and Rhymes

Popular sayings and poems help us remember a variety of things, including when to turn the clock forward or back ("Fall back, spring forward"). Rhymes can be used as a mnemonic for remembering specific information. A common example is the rhyme for remembering the number of days in each month: "Thirty days hath September, April, June, and November . . ."

Visual Cues and Visual Imagery

Visual cues can help us remember to remember. When you need to remember to do something, pin a reminder note where you will be most likely to notice it, such as on your shoes, the front door, or the steering wheel of your car.

Visual imagery can help us remember new words, names, and word combinations. For example, to remember the word *hippocampus,* think of an associated image, such as the image of a hippopotamus. To remember the name Bill Smith, picture a blacksmith who has a mouth shaped like a duck's bill (Turkington, 1996). The well-known memory expert Harry Lorayne (2002) recommended linking imagery to tasks that need to be remembered. For example, if you want to remember to mail a letter, picture the letter on the handle of the front door. Seeing the front door handle may cue you to take the letter to the mailbox.

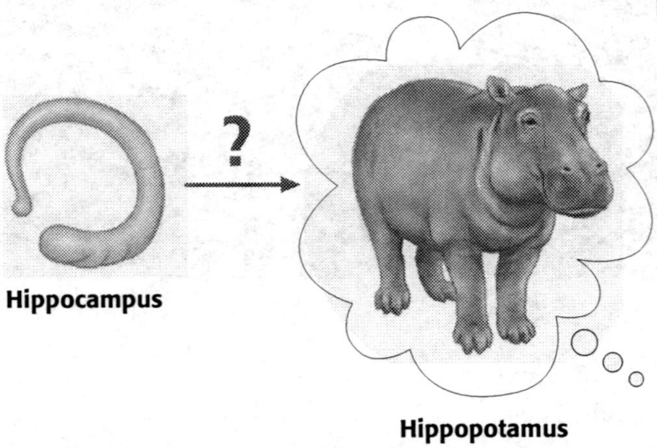

Funny, it doesn't look like a hippopotamus.
You may remember the word hippocampus better if you link it to a visual image of a hippopotamus.

Chunking

Chunking, which we discussed in Module 6.1, is one of the easiest ways to remember a series of numbers. To use it, break down a number series into more easily remembered bits. For example, the number 7362928739 may be difficult to remember as one long series. The task becomes easier when the digits are chunked like a telephone number into three bits: 736-292-8739. Learning the zip code 10024 becomes easier when it is chunked into 100-24.

General Suggestions for Improving Memory

Though mnemonic devices can help you remember bits and pieces of information, they are of little use when it comes to remembering more complex material, such as the content of your college courses. But following the guidelines offered below and adopting good study habits will help you keep your learning and memory processes as sharp as possible (Herrmann & Palmisano, 1992; Turkington, 1996).

Pay Attention

One of the best ways to boost your learning or memory ability is to pay close attention. Paying attention not only means focusing more closely on the material at hand; it also means placing yourself in a quiet area that is conducive to studying and free of distractions (no TV, radio, phone, etc.).

Practice, Practice, Practice

You may have heard the old saw that the way to get to Carnegie Hall is to practice. Well, a good way to retain information is to rehearse it, and then rehearse it some more. Repeating information out loud or silently can help convert it from a short-term memory into an enduring long-term memory. Make it a practice to "overlearn" material by repeating it two or more times beyond the point necessary for minimal proficiency.

You can also use elaborative rehearsal to strengthen retention of material you want to remember. One way of doing this is to relate the material to your personal experiences. Find examples in your own life of the concepts discussed in this chapter, such as declarative memory, procedural memory, implicit memory, and the tip-of-the-tongue phenomenon.

Spaced practice is more effective than massed practice at boosting retention. Spacing study sessions throughout the semester is a better strategy for preparing for exams than cramming at the end. Moreover, don't try to retain all the material in a chapter at one time. Break it down by sections or parts and rehearse your knowledge of each part. Then rehearse how the parts relate to each other as a whole.

Use External Memory Aids

Our daily lives are so packed with bits and pieces of information to be remembered that it makes sense to use whatever resources we can. Yes, you could use a mnemonic device to remember to tell your roommate that her mother called. But writing a reminder note to yourself will allow you to expend your mental efforts more profitably on something else. Class notes and Post-It notes are other tools that you can use to retain more information. External memory aids, such as electronic calendars

© Ilya Genkin, 2099/Shutterstock.com

and organizers and computerized to-do lists, may also be helpful. You might even try putting objects, such as your key ring, in conspicuous places (thereby reducing occurrences of the common cry, "Now, where did I leave those keys?").

Link Time-Based Tasks to External Cues

Linking time-based tasks to external cues or activities can help boost prospective memory (R. L. Marsh, Hicks, & Cook, 2005). For example, if you need to take medication in the early evening, link it with having dinner. Even the time-honored tradition of tying a string around your finger may be helpful.

Mentally Rehearse What You Intend to Do

Rehearsing what you plan to do may increase the likelihood of performing the intended action (Chasteen, Park, & Schwarz, 2001). Before leaving the house in the morning, practice saying to yourself the intended action—for example, "I intend to pick up my clothes from the dry cleaners today." Or form a mental image of yourself performing the intended action.

Control Stress

Though we may need some level of stress to remain active and alert, prolonged or intense stress can interfere with the transfer of new learning into long-term memory. The stress management techniques discussed in Chapter 12 can help you keep stress at a manageable level.

Adopt Healthy Habits

Adopting a healthier lifestyle, such as by following a healthy diet, maintaining a regular sleep schedule, and exercising regularly, may help enhance your memory. You should also avoid eating a large meal before cracking open your textbook, since consumption of large amounts of food puts your body in a restful mood that facilitates digestion, not mental alertness. On the other hand, avoid studying on an empty stomach, as hunger pangs make it more difficult to concentrate and retain new information. Remember, too, that using alcohol and other drugs does not mix with the mental alertness needed to learn and retain information. Finally, make sure to get enough sleep. Skipping sleep to cram for exams may make it more difficult to retain the information you've learned.

Thinking Critically About Psychology

Based on your reading of this chapter, answer the following questions. Then, to evaluate your progress in developing critical thinking skills, compare your answers to the sample answers found in Appendix A.

1. Two men observe an accident in which a car hits a pedestrian and speeds away without stopping. They both are alert enough to glance at the car's license plate before it disappears around the corner. Later, when interviewed by the police, the first man says, "I only got a glimpse of it but tried to picture it in my mind. I think it began with the letters QW." The second man chimes in, "Yes, but the whole plate number was QW37XT." Why do you think the second man was able to remember more details of the license plate than the first man?

2. An English-speaking singer gives a concert in Italy and includes a popular Italian folk song in her repertoire. Her rendition is so moving that an Italian woman from the audience later comes backstage to congratulate the singer, telling her, "That song was one of my favorites as a little girl. I've never heard it sung so beautifully. But when did you learn to speak Italian so well?" The singer thanks her for the compliment but tells her she doesn't speak a word of Italian. Drawing on your knowledge of memory processes, explain how the woman was able to learn a song in a language she couldn't speak.

Answer to Try This Out (p. 235)

Drawing (h) shows the correct image of a penny in Figure 6.12.

Log in to CengageBrain to access the resources your instructor requires. For this book, you can access:

CourseMate

Psychology CourseMate brings course concepts to life with interactive learning, study, and exam preparation tools that support the printed textbook. A textbook-specific website, Psychology CourseMate includes an integrated interactive eBook and other interactive learning tools including quizzes, flashcards, videos, and more.

CENGAGENOW

CengageNow is an easy-to-use online resource that helps you study in less time to get the grade you want—NOW. Take a pre-test for this chapter and receive a personalized study plan based on your results that will identify the topics you need to review and direct you to online resources to help you master those topics. Then take a post-test to help you determine the concepts you have mastered and what you will need to work on. If your textbook does not include an access code card, go to CengageBrain.com to gain access.

Visit www.cengagebrain.com to access your account and purchase materials.

VISUAL OVERVIEW Chapter 6 Memory

MODULE 6.1 Remembering

Memory Processes

- **Encoding**: Bringing information into memory
- **Storage**: Maintaining information in memory
- **Retrieval**: Accessing stored information

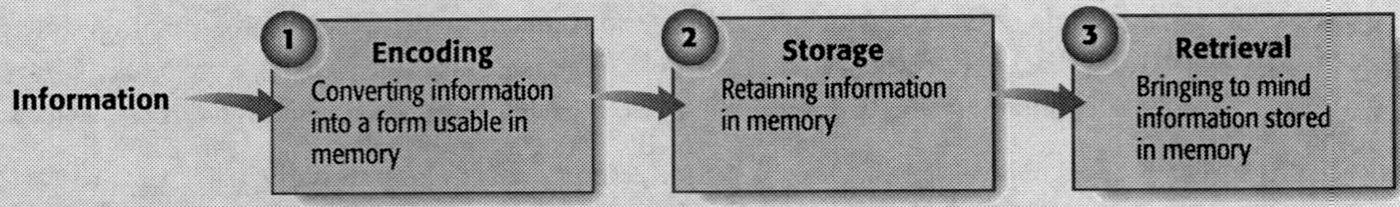

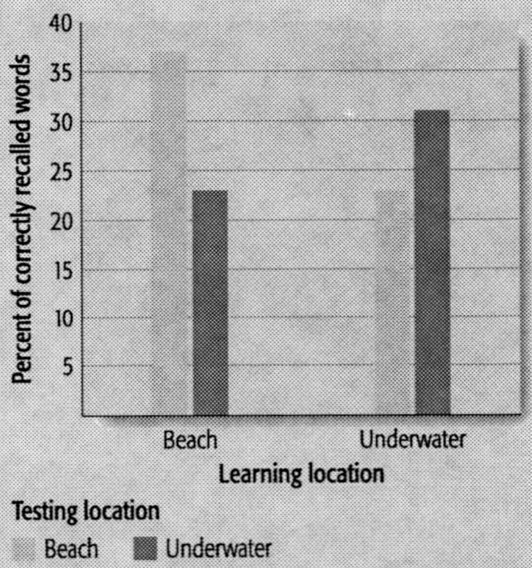

Stages of Memory

- **Sensory Memory**: Storage bin for fleeting sensory impressions
- **Short-Term Memory**: Holding in mind and working on information for upward of 30 seconds
- **Long-Term Memory**: Consolidating fresh memories into lasting ones

Types of Long-Term Memory

- **Declarative Memory**: "Knowing that"
- **Type**: Semantic memory versus episodic memory
- **Time frame**: Retrospective versus prospective
- **Procedural memory**: "Knowing how"

Techniques for Strengthening New Memories

- **Maintenance Rehearsal**: Repeated rehearsal or rote memorization
- **Elaborative Rehearsal**: Elaborating meaningful connections

Issues in Memory Research

- **Reliability of Long-Term Memory**: Memory as a construction of experience, not a copy
- **Repressed Memory**: Suddenly recovered memories, but may not be accurate
- **Flashbulb Memory**: Events frozen in time, but still prone to biases
- **Eyewitness Testimony**: Many factors affect reliability
- **Misinformation Effect**: Creating false memories

MODULE 6.2 Forgetting

Theories of Forgetting

- **Decay Theory**: Memories fading gradually over time
- **Interference Theory**: Two types, retroactive and proactive interference
- **Retrieval Theory**: Difficulty accessing stored memories; lack of retrieval cues
- **Motivated Forgetting**: Memories hidden from awareness

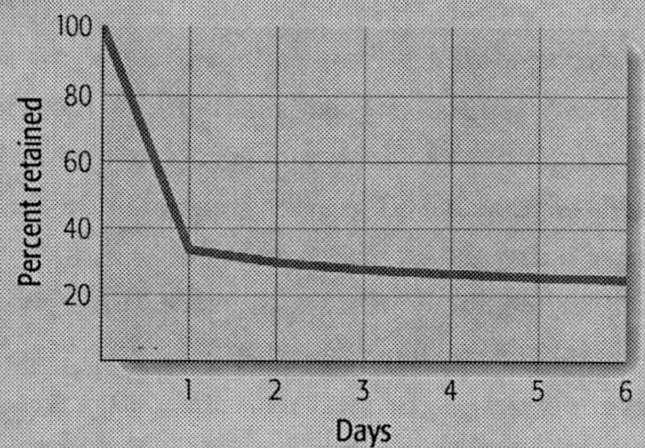

Ebbinghaus Forgetting Curve

Measuring Memory

- **Recall Tasks**: Includes three types (free recall, serial recall, paired-associates recall)
- **Recognition Tasks**: Recognizing correct answers, as in multiple-choice tests

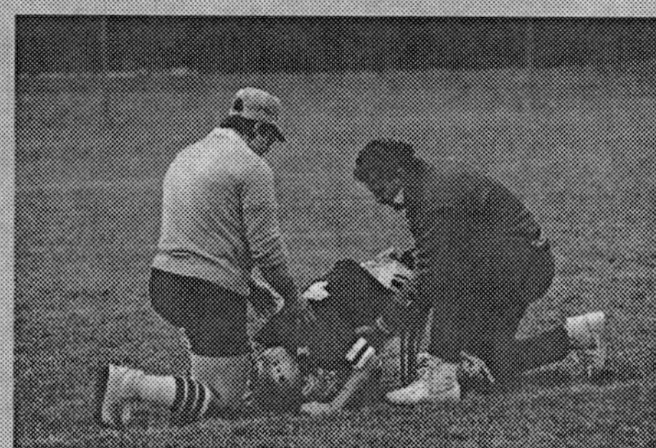

© Jeff Persons/Stock Boston

Types of Amnesia

- **Retrograde Amnesia**: Gaps in memory for past events
- **Anterograde Amnesia**: Difficulty forming new memories

MODULE 6.3 Biology of Memory

Key Concepts

- **Lashley's Engram**: Elusive search for memory traces in the brain
- **Neuronal Networks**: Complex assemblages of neurons in which memories are stored
- **Long-Term Potentiation (LTP)**: Memories strengthened at the synaptic level through repeated stimulation
- **Brain Structures**: Many brain structures involved, including the hippocampus and the cerebral cortex
- **Genetic Factors**: Genes codes for particular proteins needed to convert short-term memory into long-term memory

7 Thinking, Language, and Intelligence

Two Sticky Inventions

SLICE OF LIFE While working on adhesives, Arthur Fry, a chemist for the 3M company, came upon an unusual compound: an adhesive that could be used to stick paper to other objects. It was not nearly as strong as other adhesives then available, such as Scotch tape (Bellis, 2001), and 3M did not see any commercial use for it. Nothing more might have been made of the new compound had Fry not had a continuing problem finding his place in his church hymnal. The slips of paper he used as bookmarks often fell to the floor, leaving him scrambling to find his place. Then it dawned on him that the unusual compound he had developed in the lab might be of help in keeping bookmarks in place. What product that many people now use in their daily lives is based on Fry's adhesive?

Here's another story about a sticky invention (Bellis, 2001). A man in Switzerland took his dog out for a nature walk. Both returned covered with burrs, the plant seed sacs that stick to clothing and animal fur. The man decided to inspect the burrs under a microscope to determine what made them so sticky. It turned out they contained tiny hooks that grabbed hold of small loops in the fabric of his clothing. The man, George de Mestral, looked up from the microscope and a smile crossed his face. He knew in a flash what he must do. What widely used product today resulted from this discovery?

You may never have heard of Fry or de Mestral. But chances are you make use of their discoveries in your daily life. Fry's sticky compound is the adhesive in Post-it Notes. de Mestral's discovery led him to develop the fastening fabric we now call Velcro.

These sticky insights are examples of the creative mind at work. Creative thought is not limited to a few creative geniuses. It is a form of thinking that we are all capable of developing. This chapter focuses on creativity and other aspects of thinking, including concept formation, problem solving, and decision making.

We start out by looking at various forms of thinking, including ways we represent information in our minds. Then we examine language development and how language affects our thinking. We then explore the nature and measurement of intelligence—the mental ability or abilities used to solve problems, learn from our experiences, and adapt to the demands of the environment. We end by focusing on skills you can use to become a more creative problem solver.

DID YOU KNOW THAT...

- Albert Einstein used mental imagery in developing his theory of relativity? (p. 252)
- A commonly used rule of thumb could lead you to make the wrong decision about which movie to see or even which college to attend? (p. 259)
- Alexander Graham Bell used an analogy based on the human ear to develop the design for the first telephone? (p. 257)
- Children learn to speak in grammatically correct sentences long before they learn the rules of grammar in school? (p. 264)
- Humans may have learned to talk with their hands before they learned to speak with their mouths? (p. 267)
- A leading psychological theory of intelligence proposes not one but many different intelligences? (p. 274)

© Kuzma/Shutterstock.com

Learning Objectives

By reading this chapter you will be able to . . .

1 **DEFINE** thinking.

2 **DESCRIBE** the roles of mental imagery, concept formation, problem solving, and creativity in thinking.

3 **EXPLAIN** the difference between logical and natural concepts.

4 **DESCRIBE** mental strategies we can use to solve problems more effectively.

5 **APPLY** your knowledge of mental roadblocks and cognitive biases to how these factors affect problem solving and decision making.

6 **DESCRIBE** the basic processes of creative thinking and **EXPLAIN** the difference between divergent and convergent thinking.

7 **IDENTIFY** the basic components of language and the milestones in language development.

8 **EXPLAIN** the factors involved in language development.

9 **EVALUATE** whether language is unique to humans.

10 **EVALUATE** the linguistic relativity hypothesis in light of evidence.

11 **DEFINE** intelligence and **IDENTIFY** the major figures in the development of intelligence tests.

12 **DESCRIBE** different tests of intelligence and **EVALUATE** the characteristics of a good test of intelligence.

13 **DESCRIBE** the characteristics of the two extremes of intelligence.

14 **DESCRIBE** the major theories of intelligence and **IDENTIFY** the major theorists.

15 **EVALUATE** the roles of heredity and environment in intelligence.

16 **APPLY** skills of problem solving to become a creative problem solver.

Preview

Module 7.1 Thinking

Module 7.2 Language

Module 7.3 Intelligence

Module 7.4 Application: Becoming a Creative Problem Solver

MODULE 7.1

Thinking

- What is thinking?
- What are mental images?
- What are the major types of concepts people use, and how are they applied?
- What can we do to solve problems more efficiently?
- How do cognitive biases influence decision making?
- What cognitive processes underlie creative thinking?

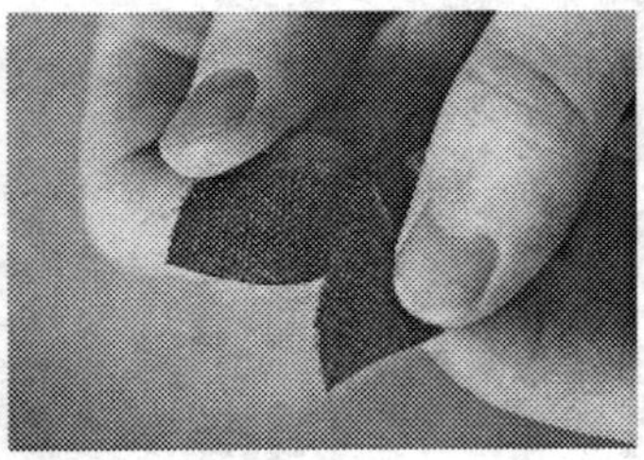
© iStockphoto.com/stocksnapper

Thanks to the creative insight of George de Mestral, an ordinary nature walk led to the development of a fastening device used by millions of people today.

Thinking, or *cognition*, is a major focus of study in **cognitive psychology**, the branch of psychology that explores how we acquire knowledge about the world. Cognitive psychologists investigate how we think, process information, use language, and solve problems.

Psychologists generally define **thinking** as the mental representation and manipulation of information. We can represent information in our minds in the form of images, words, and concepts (such as truth and beauty). We manipulate information in our minds when we solve problems, make decisions, and engage in creative pursuits. Let us first examine the ways in which we mentally represent and act upon information.

cognitive psychology The branch of psychology that focuses on such mental processes as thinking, problem solving, decision making, and use of language.

thinking The process of mentally representing and manipulating information.

mental image A mental picture or representation of an object or event.

CONCEPT 7.1
When we think, we represent information in our minds in the form of images, words, and concepts, and we manipulate that information to solve problems, make decisions, and produce creative works.

CONCEPT 7.2
Mental images help us perform cognitive functions, such as remembering directions and finding creative solutions to problems.

→ Concept Link
Behavior therapists use mental imagery in treating phobic individuals by having them engage in exercises in which they imagine confronting a series of fear-inducing stimuli. See Module 16.2.

Mental Images: In Your Mind's Eye

When we think, we represent information in our minds in the form of images, words, or concepts. A **mental image** is a mental picture or representation of an object or event. People form mental images of many different objects—faces of familiar people, the layout of the furniture in their homes, the letters of the alphabet, a graduation or religious ceremony. A mental image is not an actual or photographic representation. Rather, it is a reconstruction of the object or event from memory.

The ability to hold and manipulate mental images helps us perform many cognitive tasks, including remembering directions. You could use verbal descriptions ("Let's see, that was two lefts and a right, right?"). But forming a mental image—for example, picturing the church where you make a left turn and the gas station where you make a right—may work better.

Mental imaging can also lead to creative solutions to puzzling problems. Many of Albert Einstein's creative insights arose from personal thought experiments. His creative journey in developing his landmark theory of relativity began at age 16 when he pictured in his mind what it would be like to ride a light beam at the speed of light (Isaacson, 2007). He was later to say that words did not play any role in his creative thought. Words came only after he was able to create mental images of new ideas he had formulated in his thought experiments.

The parts of the visual cortex we use in forming mental images are very similar to those we use when actually observing objects. Yet there is an important difference between an image imagined and an image seen: The former can be manipulated, but the latter cannot. For example, we can manipulate imagined images in our minds by

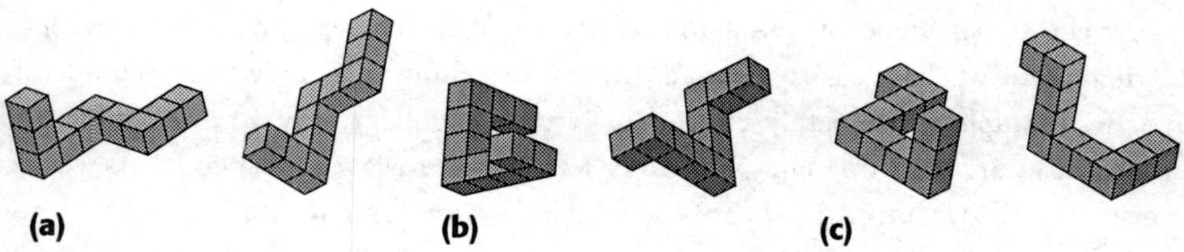

FIGURE 7.1 Mental Rotation
Are the objects in each pair the same or different? Answering this question depends on your ability to rotate objects in your mind's eye.*

*Answer: The objects in pairs *a* and *b* are the same; those in pair *c* are different.

rotating them or perusing them from different angles. ■ Figure 7.1 provides an opportunity to test your ability to manipulate mental images.

Investigators find gender differences in mental imagery. For example, women tend to outperform men in remembering the spatial location of objects (Aamodt & Wang, 2008). Perhaps that's why husbands seem so often to ask their wives where they have put their keys or their glasses. Women may be better at recalling where things are placed because of their greater skill in visually scanning an image of a particular location in their minds.

Mental imagery is not limited to visual images. Most people can experience mental images of other sensory experiences, such as "hearing" in their minds the rousing first chords of Beethoven's Fifth Symphony or recalling the taste of a fresh strawberry or the feel of cotton brushing lightly against the cheek. Yet people generally have an easier time forming visual images than images of other sensory experiences.

Some information is better represented by words and concepts than by images. Abstractions like justice, honor, liberty, and respect fall into this category. After all, we may describe in words what we mean by the term *justice*, but what sort of mental image would represent what justice might look like?

THE BRAIN LOVES A PUZZLE

As you read ahead, use the information in the text to solve the following puzzle:

We use many concepts in everyday speech without really knowing what they mean. Here's a puzzlement you can chew on: What makes a fruit a fruit?

CONCEPT 7.3
Forming concepts or mental categories for grouping objects, events, and ideas helps bring a sense of order and predictability to the world.

Concepts: What Makes a Bird a Bird?

You see objects moving along a road and mentally represent them in your mind in terms of categories such as "trucks" and "cars." Trucks and cars are examples of **concepts**, the mental categories we use to group objects, events, and ideas according to their common features. Forming concepts helps us to make sense of the world and prepares us to anticipate or predict future events more successfully. For example, classifying a slithering creature in the woods as a snake prompts us to keep a respectful distance—a response that could be a lifesaver. Think how differently you'd react to an approaching animal if you classified it as a skunk rather than a rabbit. Any species that failed to differentiate between something poisonous and something nutritious, or between a harmless creature and a predator, would quickly become extinct (Ashby & Maddox, 2005).

concepts Mental categories for classifying events, objects, and ideas on the basis of their common features or properties.

Imagine, too, what it would be like if you were unable to form concepts. Each time you encountered a four-legged furry creature that went "woof," you wouldn't know whether to pet it or to run from it. Nor would you know whether a spherical object placed before you is one to be eaten (a meatball) or played with (a baseball).

Concepts also help us respond more quickly to events by reducing the need for new learning each time we encounter a familiar object or event. Having acquired the concept *ambulance*, we immediately know how to respond when we see one pulling up behind us on the road.

© Tom Brakefield/The Image Works

Is a penguin a bird? Although a penguin doesn't fly, it is classified as a bird. Yet people may not recognize it as a bird if it does not closely resemble the model of a bird they have in mind, such as a robin.

CONCEPT 7.4
Cognitive psychologists classify concepts in two general categories, logical concepts and natural concepts.

logical concepts Concepts with clearly defined rules for membership.

natural concepts Concepts with poorly defined or fuzzy rules for membership.

We can classify concepts into two major types, *logical concepts* and *natural concepts*. **Logical concepts** have clearly defined rules for determining membership. Schoolchildren, for example, learn that the concept of a triangle applies to any three-sided form or figure. If a figure has three sides, it must be a triangle. However, most concepts we use in everyday life are **natural concepts**, in which the rules for determining how they are applied are poorly defined or fuzzy.

Abstract concepts such as justice, honor, and freedom are classified as natural concepts because people typically use them without applying a strict set of rules to determine how they are to be applied. Objects such as mammals and fruits may be used as either logical or natural concepts. For example, most people use a natural concept of "fruit" because they lack a precise idea about what makes a fruit a "fruit." They might readily agree that an apple is a fruit, but be unsure whether an avocado, a pumpkin, or an olive is a fruit. A botanist, however, is likely to use fruit as a logical concept by applying it only to objects that meet a specified botanical criterion (e.g., the ripened reproductive parts of seed plants). But what makes a fruit a fruit in the way most people typically use the concept? Typically, people base their judgment on taste (fruits are typically sweet, whereas vegetables are generally savory) rather than a botanical criterion.

© Myotis/shutterstock.com

How do we determine whether a particular animal—say, an ostrich or a penguin—is a bird? One commonly used basis for categorization involves judgments of probability—judging the likelihood that a particular object belongs to a particular category (Willingham, 2007). In forming these judgments, people perform a mental operation of comparing an object's characteristics with those of a model or example of a category member to determine whether the object is a good fit to the category. For example, they might think of a robin as a model or "best example" of a bird. They then classify a sparrow as a bird more readily than they would an ostrich or a penguin because the sparrow has more robin-like features (sparrows fly; ostriches and penguins don't).

CONCEPT 7.5
People determine whether objects belong to particular categories by comparing objects with models or examples of category members.

CONCEPT 7.6
We organize the concepts we use within hierarchies ranging from broader to narrower categories.

Hierarchies of Concepts

We typically organize concepts we use within hierarchies that range from broader to narrower categories. For example, one widely used model is based on a three-level hierarchy consisting of **superordinate concepts**, basic-level concepts, and subordinate concepts (Rosch et al., 1976). Superordinate concepts are broad categories, such as vehicle, animal, and furniture. Within these categories are narrower **basic-level concepts**, such as car, dog, and chair, and within these categories are yet narrower **subordinate concepts**, such as sedan, standard poodle, and rocking chair.

superordinate concepts The broadest concepts in a three-level hierarchy of concepts.

basic-level concepts The middle level of concepts in a three-level hierarchy of concepts, corresponding to the categories we most often use in grouping objects and events.

We tend to use basic-level concepts when describing objects, rather than superordinate or subordinate ones (e.g., calling an object a "car" rather than a "vehicle" or a "sedan") (Rosch et al., 1976). Children also more readily acquire words representing these basic-level concepts than those representing superordinate or subordinate concepts.

subordinate concepts The narrowest level of concepts in a three-level hierarchy of concepts.

Why do people gravitate toward basic-level concepts? One reason may be that basic-level concepts provide the most useful information about objects we encounter. Categorizing an object as a piece of furniture (a superordinate concept) tells us little about its specific features. (Is it something to sit on? To lie on? To eat on?) The features associated with a basic-level concept like "chair" give us more useful information. Subordinate concepts, like "rocking chair," are more specific and limited in range. They may be useful in certain situations, but they may also give us more information than we need.

Children learn to narrow and refine their concepts through exposure to both **positive instances** and **negative instances** of concepts. A positive instance exemplifies the concept, whereas a negative instance is one that doesn't fit the concept. A parent of a toddler identifies dogs in the street as "bow-wows," a positive instance. At first, the child may overextend the concept of "dog" (or bow-wow), calling all animals "bow-wows," even cats. But after repeated experience with positive and negative instances of "dogs," "cats," and the like, children learn to fine-tune their concepts. They identify features that distinguish different concepts and begin calling dogs *dogs* and cats *cats*. On the other hand, logical concepts are usually acquired by learning formal definitions rather than through direct experience. We might say to a child each time we see a square figure, "Hey, look at the square here. And, look, there's another one over there." But the child will acquire the concept more rapidly by learning the rule that any four-sided figure with sides of equal length is classified as a square.

positive instance An object that fits a particular concept (e.g., a terrier is a positive instance of dog).

negative instance An object that does not fit a particular concept (e.g., a calico kitten is a negative instance of dog but a positive instance of cat).

Let's now consider how we act on the information we represent in our minds, beginning with problem solving. Before going any further, try answering the following questions, which are intended to probe the way you think through problems. The answers are provided in various places throughout the chapter.

1. Do you perceive two interlocking squares in ■ Figure 7.2? Or might this figure represent something else?
2. Jane and Sue played six games of chess, and each of them won four. There were no ties. How was that possible? (Adapted from Willingham, 2007.)
3. An airliner from France crashes just off the coast of New Jersey within the territorial waters of the United States. Although all of the passengers and crew were French citizens, none of the survivors was returned to France for burial. Why not?
4. A man used a key that allowed him to enter but could not be used to open any locks. What kind of key was it?
5. ■ Figure 7.3 shows a classic problem called the nine-dot problem. Your task is to draw no more than four lines that connect all the dots without lifting your pen or pencil from the paper.

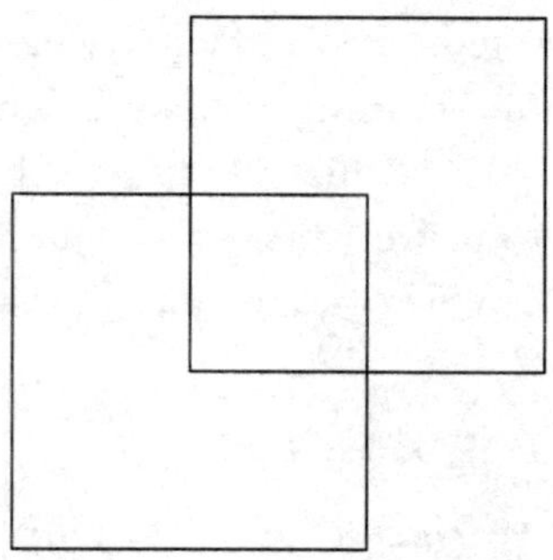

FIGURE 7.2 Two Interlocking Squares?
Source: Adapted from de Bono, 1970.

FIGURE 7.3 The Nine-Dot Problem

Problem Solving: Applying Mental Strategies to Solving Problems

Problem solving is a cognitive process in which we employ mental strategies to solve problems. As you may recall from Chapter 5, psychologist Edward Thorndike observed that animals placed in his puzzle box used trial and error to solve the problem of escaping from the enclosed compartment. The animals would try one response after another until they stumbled on the action that activated the escape mechanism. Solving a problem by trial and error is a "hit-or-miss" approach in which we try one solution after another until we find the correct one.

problem solving A form of thinking focused on finding a solution to a particular problem.

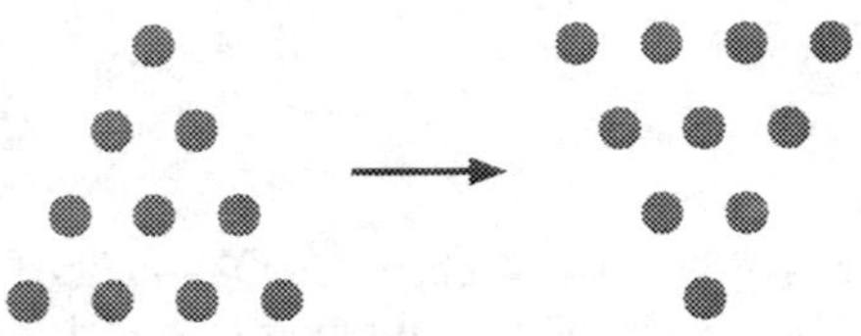

FIGURE 7.4 An Insight Problem
Your task here is to move only three of the dots to make a downward-facing triangle. You can try it using a stack of poker chips. If you get stuck, see Figure 7.5 on p. 258 for the answer.
Source: Metcalfe, 1986.

Some people solve problems by trial and error, whereas others report "Eureka!"-type experiences in which solutions just seem to suddenly "pop" into their minds. You'll recall from Chapter 5 that the Gestalt psychologist Wolfgang Köhler referred to this sudden awareness of a solution to a problem as *insight*. Cognitive psychologists believe that insight results from restructuring a problem so that its elements fit together to render a solution. Restructuring may occur when the person sees the problem from a different perspective, notices new information, or recognizes connections between elements of the problem that were previously overlooked. Recall the question of how Jane and Sue could each win four games of chess if they played six games and there were no ties. The answer is that Jane and Sue did not play against each other. The solution comes from restructuring the problem so that it does not depend on their playing each other. ■ Figure 7.4 shows another type of insight problem.

Want to jar a sudden flash of insight to solve a problem that's been plaguing you? How about getting a jolt to the brain? Recently, neuroscientists found that when people who were struggling to solve a difficult problem received a mild electrical current applied to a particular part of the head, they were more likely to generate a novel, workable solution than were those in a control group (Chi & Snyder, 2011). The electrical jolt may have disrupted brain networks involved in generating familiar but unworkable solutions, while triggering other brain networks to generate more creative solutions. Neuroscientists envision a possible future when people might don an "electric thinking cap" to trigger fresh insights when faced with a difficult problem ("Electric Thinking Cap?" 2011).

We may sometimes arrive at a correct solution through trial and error or by sudden insight, but these problem-solving approaches have certain drawbacks. Trial and error is tedious. You must try one solution after another until you happen on the right one. And mulling over a problem while waiting for a sudden flash of insight to occur may require quite a long wait. How might we approach problem solving more efficiently? Here we consider two problem-solving strategies that may prove helpful. We also explore common pitfalls that can impede our problem-solving efforts.

Algorithms

algorithm A step-by-step set of rules that will always lead to a correct solution to a problem.

An **algorithm** is a step-by-step set of rules for solving a problem. You probably first became acquainted with algorithms when you learned the basic rules (algorithms) of arithmetic, such as carrying the number to the next column when adding columns of numbers. As long as you applied the rules precisely to an arithmetic problem, you were guaranteed to get the right answer. But the major drawback to using algorithms in solving life problems is finding one that precisely fits the particular problem. Even if you lack a precise algorithm, you might still boost your chances of solving a problem by using an imprecise or *working algorithm*, which is a general set of guidelines for solving a particular problem. For example, a working algorithm for achieving a good grade in introductory psychology would be to set aside a certain number of hours to study the text and other readings each week, attend class regularly, and participate in a study group. Will this guarantee success? Perhaps not. But the odds are in your favor.

CONCEPT 7.7
Algorithms, heuristics, analogies, and incubation periods are problem-solving strategies that can help you solve problems more efficiently.

Heuristics

heuristic A rule of thumb for solving problems or making judgments or decisions.

A rule of thumb or mental shortcut used to solve problems or make judgments or decisions is called a **heuristic** (Wray, 2010). Heuristics do not guarantee a solution, but they may help you arrive at one more quickly (Schwab, 2009). One example is the *means-end* *heuristic*, by which we evaluate our current situation and compare it to the end result we want to achieve. We then develop a plan to reduce the distance between the two in a step-by-step approach. In using a *backward-working* heuristic, we start with a possible solution and then work backward to see if the data support the solution. For example, a psychologist seeking the causes of schizophrenia might start by proposing a model (schizophrenia as a genetic disease) and then gather evidence to test whether the available data fit the model.

In using another heuristic, *creating subgoals*, we start by breaking down a larger problem down into smaller, more manageable problems. Scientists use this strategy when they assign different teams to work on different parts of a problem, called subgoals. In AIDS research, for example, one team might work on how HIV penetrates the cell, another on how it reproduces, and so on. Solving the riddle of HIV may depend on knowledge gained from achieving each subgoal.

Analogies

When we use an **analogy** to solve a problem, we apply knowledge gained from solving similar problems in the past. However, we may fail to recognize how solutions to one problem can be modified or adapted to solve new problems. Analogies are most useful when similarities exist between old problems and new ones. Consider the analogy used by Alexander Graham Bell, the inventor of the telephone. By studying the human ear, he observed how sounds are transmitted when the eardrum, which is a type of membrane, vibrates. He applied this idea of a vibrating membrane used to transmit sounds in designing the first working telephone (M. Levine, 1994).

© CORBIS

Can you hear me now? The inventor Alexander Graham Bell used the workings of the human ear as an analogy in his design of the first telephone. Have you ever drawn upon an analogy to develop a creative solution to a problem?

Incubation Periods

It often helps to take a break from a problem, especially when you reach an impasse. This type of respite is called an **incubation period** because it is assumed that the passage of time helps the person develop a fresh perspective on the problem, which may lead to a sudden realization of the solution. The person may also better understand which pieces of information are relevant to solving the problem and which are not.

Mental Roadblocks to Problem Solving

SLICE OF LIFE Chris is sitting in the front passenger seat of a car waiting for the driver to return when the car suddenly begins to roll backward down a hill. In panic, he tries to climb over the gearshift lever, clumsily reaching with his foot for the brake pedal to stop the car. Unfortunately, he can't reach the brake pedal in time to prevent the car from slamming into a pole. What could he have done differently in this situation? Why do you think he responded the way he did? (Adapted from M. Levine, 1994.)

Perhaps Chris should have realized that a much simpler solution was available: pulling the emergency brake. Yet Chris was locked into a preconceived way of solving the problem: depressing the brake pedal. This solution works well if you're sitting in the driver's seat but may not be effective if you need to climb over from the passenger side. The tendency to rely on strategies that worked well in similar situations in the past is called a **mental set**.

analogy In problem-solving, a strategy based on using similarities between the properties of two things or applying solutions to past problem to the problem at hand.

incubation period A respite from active problem-solving efforts, which may facilitate finding a solution.

mental set The tendency to rely on strategies that worked in similar situations in the past but that may not be appropriate to the present situation.

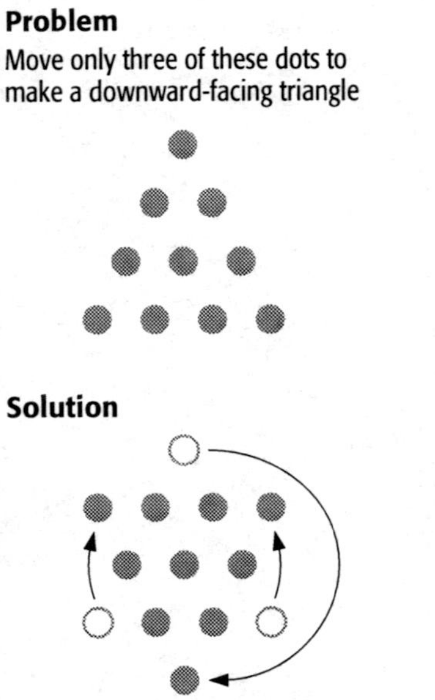

FIGURE 7.5 Solution to the Insight Problem in Figure 7.4
Assuming you solved the problem, did you rely on the trial-and-error method—moving the dots (or chips) around until you chanced on the correct solution? Or did you mull the problem over in your mind until a moment of illumination, or insight, arrived? If so, what do you think accounted for this sudden awareness?

functional fixedness The tendency to perceive objects as limited to the customary functions they serve.

In some instances, as when a new problem is similar to an old one, a mental set may help you reach an appropriate solution more quickly. But a mental set can be an impediment to problem solving if a new problem requires a solution different from an old one, as the example of Chris illustrates.

Another impediment to problem solving is **functional fixedness**, the inability to see how familiar objects can be used in new ways (German & Barrett, 2005). Suppose you're working at your desk and a gust of wind blows in from an open window, scattering your papers about (M. Levine, 1994). Would functional fixedness prevent you from recognizing new uses for familiar objects? Or would you reach for objects that don't ordinarily serve as paperweights, such as your eyeglasses or wallet, and use them to hold down your papers long enough for you to get up and close the window? The box-candle problem and the two-string problem are classic examples of functional fixedness (see ■ Figures 7.6 and 7.7).

Yet another impediment to problem solving is the tendency to allow irrelevant information to distract one's attention from the relevant information needed to solve the problem. Recall the problem on p. 255 which stated that none of the survivors of the crash of the French airliner were buried in France. Did the geographical details distract you so that you overlooked the statement that no *survivors* were returned for burial?

Why It Matters: Mental Roadblocks in Decision Making

We constantly make decisions, ranging from everyday ones ("What should I wear?" "What should I have for dinner?") to important life decisions ("What should I major in?" "Should I get married?" "Should I take this job or stay in college?"). **Decision making** is a form of problem solving in which we must select a course of action from among the available alternatives.

We may think we approach decision making logically, but researchers find that people often rely on biased ways of thinking, called *cognitive biases*, that hamper their ability to make rational or sound choices (Kahneman & Frederick, 2005). One example is the **confirmation bias**—the tendency to stick to an initial hypothesis even in the face of strong contrary evidence (Cook & Smallman, 2008). The confirmation bias leads us

CONCEPT 7.8
Mental set and functional fixedness are examples of cognitive tendencies that can impede problem solving.

decision making A form of problem solving in which we must select a course of action from among the available alternatives.

confirmation bias The tendency to maintain allegiance to an initial hypothesis despite strong evidence to the contrary.

FIGURE 7.6 The Two-String Problem
Two strings hang from the ceiling but are too far apart to be touched at the same time. The task is to tie them together. Except for the string and the pliers on the table, the room is empty. How would you tie the strings together? The solution is shown in Figure 7.8 on p. 260.

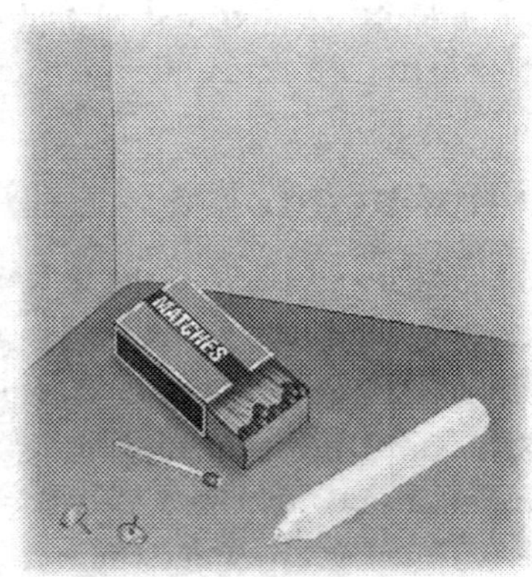

FIGURE 7.7 The Box-Candle Problem
Using only the material you see on the table, figure out a way to mount a candle on the wall so that it doesn't drip wax on the floor when it burns. The answer is shown in Figure 7.9 on p. 260.
Source: Adapted from Duncker, 1945.

to place greater weight on information that confirms our prior beliefs and expectations than on information that disputes it. Consider a juror who decides whether a defendant is guilty based on the preliminary evidence and then fails to reconsider that decision even when strong contradictory evidence is presented at trial.

Though heuristics may help us solve problems, they sometimes become mental traps that lead us make bad decisions (Wray, 2010). For example, the **representativeness heuristic** may lead us to make more of something than we should (Kahneman & Frederick, 2005). We apply this heuristic when we assume that a given sample is representative of a larger population. Thus, we might base a decision about seeing a certain movie on the opinion of someone we happen to overhear talking about it, as though that person's opinion is representative of moviegoers in general. We might then end up attending a bad movie or passing up a good one—an unhappy consequence but a relatively benign one. But the representativeness heuristic can have more profound consequences. For example, it can lead us to select a college that turns out to be subpar because we were impressed with the one or two students we happened to meet on a campus tour. One young woman was on her way to the admissions office for a college tour but turned around and headed home after noticing that one particular student was wearing what she felt were unfashionable shoes (R. Gardner, 2006).

We see the representativeness heuristic at work in forming first impressions. A positive (or negative) interaction with someone is but a small sliver of behavior that may not be representative of the person's behavior in general, but is often enough to create a lasting impression. We might decide not to pursue any further contact with someone based on a brief conversation or even on how the person dressed on a particular occasion. The next two *Try This Out* features offer examples of how the representativeness heuristic may bias your thinking.

The **availability heuristic** is the tendency to base decisions on examples we most easily recall or bring to mind. For example, we might buy a particular brand because we recall having seen it advertised on TV. The availability heuristic also comes into play in the judgments we make about risks we face in our daily lives (Paulos, 2009). Consider the many uncertainties we face in life. Driving to work, flying on an airplane, eating a fat-filled dessert—all entail some degree of risk. Even getting out of bed in the morning incurs some degree of risk (you could fall). The availability heuristic can lead to errors in judging relative risks. For example, the vivid images of a plane crash we see on a television news program may stick in our minds, leading us to overestimate the risk we face flying on a commercial airliner.

How a problem is described can also affect the decisions we make. Suppose you suffered from a chronic disease that could be treated with one of two drugs. You're then told that Drug A has a 35% cure rate, as compared to 25% cure rate with Drug B. You'd choose Drug A, right? Let's say you were also told that both drugs carry a low risk of a serious medical complication—hypertension. Drug A carries a 3% risk, as compared to 2% risk with Drug B. Which drug would you choose if you were offered a choice? Perhaps you'd think, "Okay, I'll take Drug A, the one with the higher cure rate, since the risk of hypertension is only 1% higher."

Now let's reframe the problem. Suppose you were told about the drug risks in the following way: "Although both drugs carry a low risk of hypertension, you should know that Drug A has a 50% greater risk of causing hypertension than Drug B." Now, would you be just less as willing to select Drug A? Why or why not?

representativeness heuristic A rule of thumb for making a judgment that assumes a given sample is representative of the larger population from which it is drawn.

CONCEPT 7.9
We may think we approach decision making in a logical way, but underlying biases in our thinking often hamper our ability to make rational decisions.

CONCEPT 7.10
The confirmation bias, the representativeness heuristic, the availability heuristic, and framing are examples of biases in thinking that can lead us to make bad decisions.

TRY THIS OUT
A Farmer or a Librarian?

You can see the representativeness heuristic in action by first looking at the man in the photograph. Do you think he is more likely to be a farmer or a librarian? If you said librarian, as many people do, your judgment was probably influenced by the representativeness heuristic: that is, you assumed that a thin man with glasses is more representative of the population of librarians than of the population of farmers.

© David Cordner/Photodisc/Jupiter Images

availability heuristic The tendency to judge events as more likely to occur when information pertaining to them comes readily to mind.

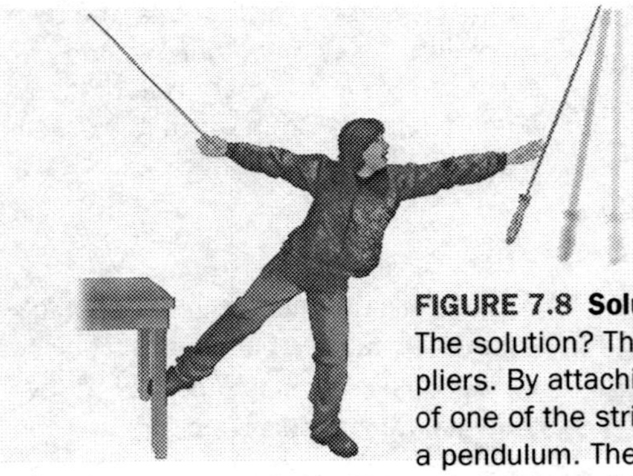

FIGURE 7.8 Solution to the Two-String Problem The solution? Think of an alternate use for the pliers. By attaching them as a weight to the end of one of the strings, you can swing the string as a pendulum. Then move to the other string and wait for the swinging string to come close enough to catch it so that you can tie the two strings together.

Source: Adapted from Maier, 1931.

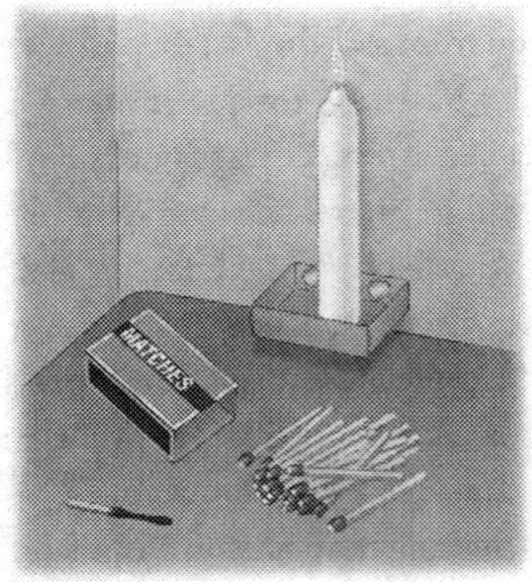

FIGURE 7.9 Solution to the Box-Candle Problem

TRY THIS OUT
The Coin Toss

A quarter is tossed six times. It lands heads up three times and tails up three times.Which of these sequences is most likely to have occurred?

1. HHHTTT
2. HTHTHT
3. TTTHHH
4. HTTHHT

The tendency for decisions to be influenced by how potential outcomes are phrased is called **framing**. In the example, the drug risk in both scenarios is exactly the same. But when the risks are framed in terms of a much greater chance (50% greater in the example) of serious side-effects than when phrased in terms of a 1% difference, fewer people are likely to choose the riskier drug, even though it has a higher cure rate. Rationally, decisions should not change if the facts remain the same. But framing can lead us to make a decision that is not based on a purely rational appraisal of the facts.

Did you select the last sequence? Many people do. The representativeness heuristic leads people to judge the irregular sequence in the last item to be more representative of a random order than the others. Yet the laws of probability teach us that each of these sequences is equally likely to have occurred.

framing The tendency for decisions to be influenced by how potential outcomes are phrased.

Creativity: Not Just for the Few

Creativity is thinking that leads to original, practical, and meaningful solutions to problems or that generates new ideas or artistic expressions. Thinking of a new product or a clever way of doing something are examples of creative thought when they lead to practical applications.

Creativity is not limited to a few geniuses in the arts or sciences. Psychologists recognize that virtually all of us have the ability to be creative in our daily lives. A parent who invents a new playtime activity for a four-year-old, a chef who combines ingredients in innovative ways, a worker who improves on a production method—all demonstrate creativity.

creativity Originality of thought associated with the development of new, workable products or solutions to problems.

Creativity is distinct from general intelligence (K. H. Kim, 2005; Nettelbeck & Wilson, 2005). Although most creative people have at least average intelligence, people at the higher echelons of intelligence are not necessarily any more creative than those of average intelligence. As psychologist Robert Sternberg (2001) notes, highly intelligent people may perform efficiently and productively, though not necessarily creatively.

Creativity is measured in different ways but most commonly through tests that tap *divergent thinking*. **Divergent thinking** is the wellspring of invention; it is the ability to conceive of new ways of viewing situations and new uses for familiar objects. By contrast, **convergent thinking** is the attempt to find the one correct answer to a problem. Refer to Figure 7.2 on p. 255. The answer (two interlocking squares) seems

divergent thinking The ability to conceive of new ways of viewing situations and new uses for familiar objects.

convergent thinking The attempt to narrow down a range of alternatives to converge on the one correct answer to a problem.

so obvious we may not think of any alternatives. Yet by thinking divergently we can find other answers: three squares (note the one in the area of intersection), two L-shaped pieces separated by a square (see ■ Figure 7.10), and a rectangle divided into two pieces that have been pushed askew.

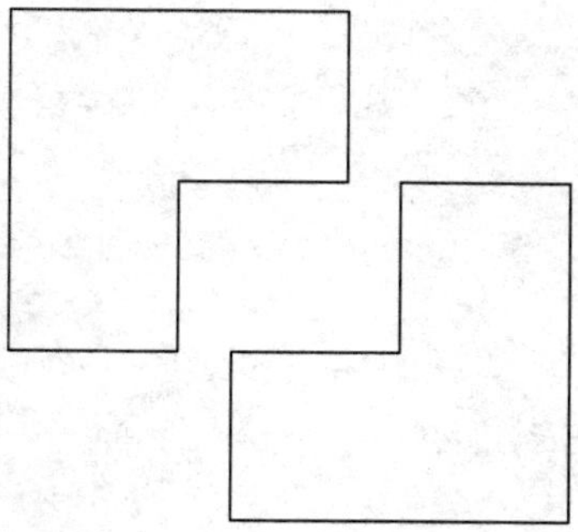

FIGURE 7.10 Divergent Thinking
Compare Figure 7.2 on p. 255 with the cutout shown here. Now imagine these two L-shaped figures pushed together so that they are separated by a square.

Tests that tap divergent thinking were originated by psychologist J. P. Guilford and his colleagues. One widely used measure, the Alternate Uses Test, instructs subjects to list as many possible uses as they can for a common object, such as a newspaper (Guilford et al., 1978). The person's score is based on the number of acceptable responses the person is able to generate. ■ Figure 7.11 shows another way of measuring creative thinking, which is based on judging the creativity of a person's drawings.

CONCEPT 7.11
Creativity is a cognitive ability found in varying degrees in most people.

CONCEPT 7.12
Creativity involves using cognitive processes to manipulate or act on stored knowledge.

When we think creatively, we use cognitive processes to manipulate or act on stored knowledge. Investigators identify a number of cognitive processes that underlie creative thinking, including the use of *metaphor* and *analogy, conceptual combination*, and *conceptual expansion* (Ward, 2004, 2007; Ward, Smith, & Vaid, 1997/2001).

1. *Metaphor and analogy.* Metaphor and analogy are creative products in their own right; they are also devices we use to generate creative solutions to puzzling problems. A metaphor is a figure of speech for likening one object or concept to another. Applying a metaphor involves a creative process of thinking of one thing as if it were another. For example, we might describe love as a candle burning brightly.

   An *analogy* is a comparison between two things based on their similar features or properties—for example, likening the actions of the heart to those of a pump. As we noted, Alexander Graham Bell showed creative use of analogy in his invention of the telephone.
2. *Conceptual combination.* Combining two or more concepts into one can result in novel ideas or applications that reflect more than the sum of the parts (Costello & Keane, 2001). Examples of **conceptual combinations** include "cell phone," "veggie burger," and "home page." Can you think of other ways in which concepts can be creatively combined?
3. *Conceptual expansion.* One way of developing novel ideas is to expand familiar concepts. Examples of **conceptual expansion** include an architect's adaptation of an existing building to a new use, a writer's creation of new scenes using familiar characters, and a chef's variation on a traditional dish that results in a new culinary sensation.

"Never, ever, think outside the box."

© The New Yorker Collection 1998 Leo Cullum from cartoonbank.com. All Rights Reserved.

conceptual combinations Combinations of two or more concepts into one concept, resulting in the creation of a novel idea or application.

conceptual expansion Expanding familiar concepts by applying them to new uses.

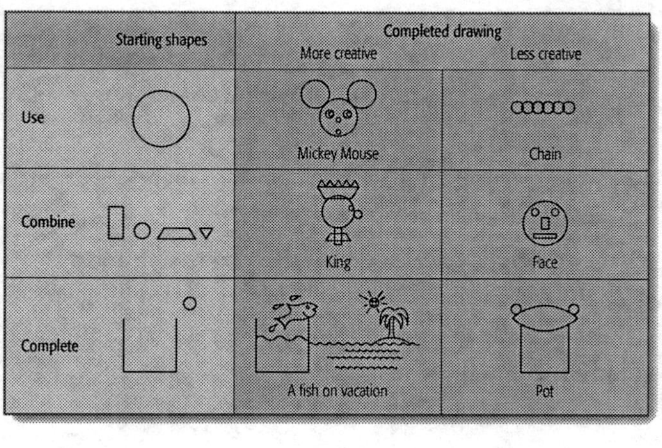

FIGURE 7.11 Torrance Test of Creative Thinking
People are given starting shapes (left column) and instructed to create a new drawing by using them (top row), combining them (middle row), or completing them (bottom row). Evaluators then judge the creativity of the completed drawings.
Source: Courtesy of Gehirn & Geist/Siganim, 2004.

CONCEPT CHART 7.1 Cognitive Processes in Thinking

Cognitive Process	Definition	Description
Mental imaging	Forming mental representations of objects or events	Images can be formed based on various sensory experiences, including vision, hearing, taste, and touch. Mental images can be manipulated to help us solve certain kinds of problems.
Concept formation	Grouping objects, events, and ideas on the basis of their common features	Most concepts are natural concepts, which have fuzzy or imprecise rules for membership. Logical concepts are those that have strict rules for membership. People tend to use basic-level concepts more often than superordinate (more general) or subordinate (more specific) concepts.
Problem solving	The process of arriving at a solution to a given problem	Strategies include algorithms, heuristics, analogies, and incubation periods. Pitfalls include mental set and functional fixedness.
Decision making	The process of deciding which of two or more courses of action to take	Decision making is often influenced by errors in thinking associated with the confirmation bias, the representativeness heuristic, the availability heuristic, and framing.
Creativity	The generation of novel, workable products or ideas	Creativity applies cognitive processes that act on or manipulate stored knowledge. These processes include the use of metaphor and analogy, conceptual combination, and conceptual expansion.

CONCEPT 7.13
When people approach creative tasks, they tend to expand on what is familiar to them.

Creativity typically springs from the expansion or modification of familiar categories or concepts. The ability to take what we know and modify and expand on it is one of the basic processes of creative thinking.

Before going further, you may wish to review the cognitive processes involved in thinking, which are outlined in Concept Chart 7.1.

7.1 MODULE REVIEW Thinking

Recite It

What is thinking?

- Thinking is the creation of mental representations of the external world through mental images, concepts, and words, and the mental manipulation of these representations.

What are mental images?

- Mental images are visual or other sensory representations of information in our minds.

What are the major types of concepts people use, and how are they applied?

- The major types of concepts are logical concepts, which have clearly defined rules for membership, and natural concepts, in which the rules for determining how the concepts are applied are poorly defined.

What can we do to solve problems more efficiently?

- Rather than relying on trial and error or a sudden insight, we can use such problem-solving strategies as algorithms, heuristics, analogies, and incubation periods.
- We can also remove impediments to problem solving, such as mental sets and functional fixedness.

How do cognitive biases influence decision making?

- The confirmation bias leads people to discount evidence that contradicts their prior beliefs and expectations.
- The representativeness heuristic leads people to make more of a given sample than they should.
- The availability heuristic leads people to make snap decisions based on whatever information comes most readily to mind.
- Framing leads people to base decisions on how a problem is phrased rather than on the facts at hand.

What cognitive processes underlie creative thinking?

- Cognitive processes involved in creative thinking include the use of metaphor and analogy, conceptual combination, and conceptual expansion.

Recall It

1. When we think, we form mental representations of information in the form of images, words, and ________.
2. A category with clearly defined rules for membership is called a ________ concept, whereas a category with poorly defined rules for membership is a ________ concept.
3. One mental roadblock to problem solving is the inability to see how a familiar object can be used in new ways. This impediment is known as
   a. mental set.
   b. functional fixedness.
   c. incubation period.
   d. confirmation bias.
4. Merging two or more concepts to produce novel ideas or applications is called
   a. conceptual expansion.
   b. creative combination.
   c. divergent thinking.
   d. conceptual combination.

Think About It

➤ Have you ever used mental imagery to find a creative solution to a problem? Might you use it in the future? Why or why not?

➤ How might you apply the concepts of analogy, conceptual combination, and conceptual expansion to develop a novel idea, application, or service?

Language

MODULE 7.2

- What are the major components of language?
- How does language develop?
- What is the linguistic relativity hypothesis?
- Can species other than humans use language?

The term **language** refers to a system of communication consisting of symbols—words or hand signs (as in the case of American Sign Language)—arranged according to a set of rules, called a **grammar**, to express meaning (Gertner, Fisher, & Eisengart, 2006). The ability to use language is a remarkable cognitive ability so tightly woven into the human experience, says prominent linguist Steven Pinker (1994), that "it is scarcely possible to imagine life without it. Chances are that if you find two or more people together anywhere on earth they will soon be exchanging words. When there is no one to talk with, people talk to themselves, to their dogs, even to their plants."

language A system of communication composed of symbols (words, hand signs, etc.) that are arranged according to a set of rules (grammar) to form meaningful expressions.

grammar The set of rules governing how symbols in a given language are used to form meaningful expressions.

In this module, we examine the remarkable capacity of humans to communicate through language. We consider the basic components of language, developmental milestones in language acquisition, and leading theories of language acquisition. We also consider the question of whether language is a uniquely human characteristic.

Components of Language

The basic units of sound in a spoken language are called **phonemes**. English has about 40 phonemes to sound out the 500,000 or so words found in modern unabridged English dictionaries. The word *dog* consists of three phonemes: "d," "au," and "g." Phonemes in English correspond both to individual letters and to letter combinations, including the "au" in *dog* and the sounds "th" and "sh." The same letter can make different sounds in different words. The "o" in the word *two* is a different phoneme from the "o" in the word *one*. Changing one phoneme in a word can change the meaning of the word. Changing the "r" sound in *reach* to the "t" sound makes it *teach*. Different languages

phonemes The basic units of sound in a language.

CONCEPT 7.14
Language consists of four basic components: phonemes, morphemes, syntax, and semantics.

morphemes The smallest units of meaning in a language.

syntax The rules of grammar that determine how words are ordered within sentences or phrases to form meaningful expressions.

semantics The set of rules governing the meaning of words.

have different phonemes. In some African languages, various clicking sounds are phonemes. Hebrew has a guttural "chhh" phoneme, as in the expression *l'chaim* ("to life").

Phonemes are combined to form **morphemes,** the smallest units of meaning in a language. Simple words such as *car, ball,* and *time* are morphemes, but so are other linguistic units that convey meaning, such as prefixes and suffixes. The prefix "un," for example, means "not." The suffix "ed" following a verb means that the action expressed by the verb occurred in the past. More complex words are composed of several morphemes. The word *pretested* consists of three morphemes: "pre," "test," and "ed."

Language requires more than phonemes and morphemes. It also requires **syntax,** the rules of grammar that determine how words are ordered within sentences and phrases to form meaningful expressions, and **semantics,** the set of rules governing the meaning of words. The sentence "buy milk I" sounds odd to us because it violates a basic rule of English syntax—that the subject ("I") must precede the verb ("buy"). We follow rules of syntax in everyday speech even if we are not aware of them or cannot verbalize them. But even when our speech follows proper syntax, it may still lack meaning. The famed linguist Noam Chomsky, to whose work we will return shortly, illustrated this point with the example "Colorless green ideas sleep furiously." The sentence may sound correct to our ears since it follows the rules of English syntax, but it doesn't convey any meaning. The same word may convey very different meanings depending on the context in which it is used. "Don't *trip* going down the stairs" means something very different from "Have a good *trip.*"

CONCEPT 7.15
Young children pass through a series of milestones of language acquisition, from crying and cooing to babbling, to one- and two-word phrases, and then to more complex speech.

language acquisition device Chomsky's concept of an innate, prewired mechanism in the brain that allows children to acquire language naturally.

Language Development

Children the world over develop language in basically the same stages, which unfold at basically the same ages. Until about six months of age, infants are limited to nonlinguistic forms of communication—crying and cooing. At around that time, the first sounds resembling human speech appear in the form of babbling. The child then progresses through stages of one- and two-word phrases, and between the ages of two and three begins developing more complex speech patterns (see Concept Chart 7.2). By around 30 months of age, children are speaking in full sentences and have a vocabulary of about 550 words (Golinkoff & Hirsh-Pasek, 2006).

The similar course of language development across cultures and the ease with which children naturally acquire language suggest that language depends on an innate mechanism that may be hard-wired in the human brain. Noam Chomsky (1965) called this mechanism the **language acquisition device**. We acquire the ability to speak, much as we do the ability to walk and jump, because we have an inborn propensity to develop it. As Steven Pinker (1994) has put it, "We don't teach our children to sit, stand, and walk, and they do it anyway." Children learn to use the rules of grammar without any formal instruction. In English-speaking cultures, they begin placing the subject before the verb long before they learn what the terms *subject* and *verb* mean. According to Chomsky and Pinker, children are able to learn grammatical structures as rapidly and easily as they do because the human brain contains the basic "blueprints," or neural circuitry, for using grammar.

Critics point out that Chomsky's language acquisition device is not an actual physical structure in the brain but a hypothesis—an abstract concept of how language centers in the brain work—and that it does

© Paolo Aguilar/EFE/Corbis

Noam Chomsky

CONCEPT CHART 7.2 Milestones in Language Acquisition

Age (Approximate)	Vocal Activity	Description
Birth	Crying	Crying expresses distress
2 months	Cooing	Infant begins making cooing sounds (e.g., "aah" and "oooh")
6 to 12 months	Babbling	Phonemes, the basic units of sound, appear
12 months	One-word phrases	Baby imitates sounds and can understand some words; begins to say single words
18 to 24 months	Two-word phrases or sentences	Vocabulary grows to about 50 words; baby emits two-word phrases or sentences
24 to 36 months	Complex speech	Sentences become longer and more complex and include plurals and past tense; speech shows elements of proper syntax

© iStockphoto.com/Kevin Visel

not explain the mechanisms by which language is produced. In fairness to Chomsky, we should point out that brain mechanisms responsible for language are extremely complex, consisting of complicated circuits in many areas of the brain that link together to produce language in ways we don't yet understand. However, the pieces of the puzzle may be starting to fall into place. Scientists are beginning to locate genes involved in the development of brain mechanisms responsible for speech and language (Lichtenbelt et al., 2005; Vargha-Khadem et al., 2005).

Regardless of the exact mechanisms involved in language production, both nature and nurture are necessary for language to develop. Our ability to use language depends not only on having a biological capacity for language production but also on experience with the sounds, meanings, and structures of human speech (Berko Gleason & Ratner, 2009). Children naturally acquire language by listening to the speech of others, well before they learn rules of formal grammar in school (Pancsofar & Vernon-Feagans, 2006; Sakai, 2005). They also enlarge their vocabularies by imitating the words others use to refer to particular objects. Parents can help children develop language skills by talking and reading to them frequently. They can also use principles of operant conditioning and observational learning (discussed in Chapter 5) by modeling proper language use and rewarding children for imitating it.

However language develops, it is clear that language and thinking are closely intertwined. As discussed in the next section, some theorists even propose that language determines how we think.

CONCEPT 7.16
Language development depends on both a biological capacity for language production and experience with the sounds, meanings, and structures of human speech.

CONCEPT 7.17
The belief that the language we speak determines how we think and perceive the world is a controversial viewpoint that has not been supported by research evidence.

TRY THIS OUT From the Mouths of Babes

If you have the opportunity to observe an infant over time, keep a running record of the infant's verbalizations, jotting down the types produced at different ages. Compare the chronology of these verbalizations with the one presented in Concept Chart 7.2: neonatal crying that progresses to cooing at about two months and is followed by babbling (starting at about six months), one-word speech (starting at around 12 months), two-word speech (starting at around 18 months), and more complex speech (between 24 and 36 months). Keep track of the infant's vocabulary, noting the rapid increase beginning at around 18 months.

Eleanor Rosch's research findings ran contrary to the Whorfian hypothesis. Members of a New Guinea tribe, even though they used only two words to distinguish among different colors, were just as able as English-speaking subjects to identify different colors.

Culture and Language: Does the Language We Use Determine How We Think?

Does the language we speak affect how we think? Might French Canadians, Chinese, and Africans see the world differently because of the vocabulary and syntax of their native languages? According to the **linguistic relativity hypothesis**, the answer is yes. This hypothesis—also called the *Whorfian hypothesis* after Benjamin Whorf, the amateur linguist who developed it—holds that the language we use determines how we think and how we perceive reality. Whorf (1956) pointed out that some cultures have many different words for colors, whereas others have only a few. English has 11 words for basic colors: black, white, red, green, yellow, blue, brown, purple, pink, orange, and gray (Adelson, 2005). At the other end of the spectrum is the Navajo language, which has no separate words for blue and green.

linguistic relativity hypothesis The proposition that the language we use determines how we think and how we perceive the world (also called the *Whorfian hypothesis*).

If we had only a few words to describe colors, would we be able to identity the many different colors in the spectrum? The answer is yes, based on landmark research conducted by Eleanor Rosch (Rosch, 1975; Rosch-Heider & Olivier, 1972). Rosch and her colleagues showed that members of a preliterate tribe in New Guinea, whose language contained but two color names, were just as capable of recognizing many different colors as English-speaking subjects. This finding suggests that people have the capacity to recognize colors regardless of differences in the words they use to describe them.

CONCEPT 7.18

Though research findings have not supported the original form of the linguistic relativity hypothesis, a weaker version which holds that culture and language influence thinking has merit.

→ **Concept Link**

People from Eastern and Western cultures tend to perceive the same visual scenes in different ways, as we examined in Chapter 3. See Module 3.5.

Overall, research evidence fails to support the strict version of the Whorfian hypothesis that holds that the language we use determines how we think and perceive the world (Pinker, 2003). But a weaker version of the theory does have merit, a version that proposes that our culture and the language we speak influences how we think and how we perceive the world (Fiedler, 2008; Boroditsky, 2011). This view is consistent with the experiences of many bilingual and multilingual people who say they think differently when using each of their languages (Tohidian & Tabatabaie, 2010).

Language influences thinking in other ways. Consider this sentence: "A person should always be respectful of *his* parents." If the very concept of personhood embodies maleness, where does that leave females? As *non*persons? If Sally sees that *he* is used when referring to professionals like doctors, engineers, or scientists, might she get the idea that such careers are not as available to her as they are to her brother?

Policeman or police officer? Language influences thinking in many ways. Traditional gender constructions of occupational titles that embody maleness, such as policeman and fireman, may lead young women to think that such careers are not available to them.

Is Language Unique to Humans?

Do animals other than humans use language? Consider the case of Koko, a gorilla trained to use American Sign Language (ASL). Apes lack the vocal apparatus needed to form human sounds, so researchers have turned to nonverbal means of expression, such as sign language used by people with impaired hearing, to communicate with them. One day Koko flashed the ASL sign for pain and pointed to her mouth ("Koko the Gorilla," 2004). Dentists were summoned and soon discovered that Koko had a decayed tooth. They removed the tooth to relieve the pain.

Koko was able to communicate with humans, but was she using language? In the 1960s, investigators Beatrice and Allen Gardner trained a chimpanzee named Washoe to use about 160 signs, including signs for "apple," "tickle," "flower," and "more" (R. A. Gardner & Gardner, 1969, 1978). Washoe learned to combine signs into simple

CONCEPT 7.19

Whether humans are unique in possessing the ability to communicate through language remains a controversial question.

FIGURE 7.12 Examples of Materials Used in Premack's Study

phrases, such as "more fruit" and "gimme flower." She even displayed a basic grammar by changing the position of the subject and object in her signing to reflect a change in meaning. For example, when she wanted her trainer to tickle her, she would sign, "You tickle Washoe." But when she wanted to do the tickling, she would sign, "Washoe tickle you" (Gardner & Gardner, 1978).

David Premack developed an artificial language in which plastic chips of different sizes, colors, and shapes symbolize different words (see ■ Figure 7.12). Using shaping and reinforcement techniques, he trained a chimp named Sarah to communicate by placing the chips on a magnetic board. Sarah learned to form simple sentences. For example, she would request food by putting together a sequence of chips that signaled "Mary give apple Sarah" (Premack, 1971).

Perhaps the most remarkable demonstration of simian communication involved Kanzi, a male pygmy chimpanzee (Savage-Rumbaugh, Shanker, & Taylor, 1998; Shanker & Savage-Rumbaugh, 1999). Kanzi's mother had been trained to communicate by pushing geometric symbols into a keyboard, but Kanzi had received no special training himself. He apparently had learned the keyboard system by observing his mother's training sessions. At age two, Kanzi stunned his trainers when he suddenly began manipulating symbols on the keyboard to ask for a specific fruit. By age six, he was using some 200 symbols to communicate.

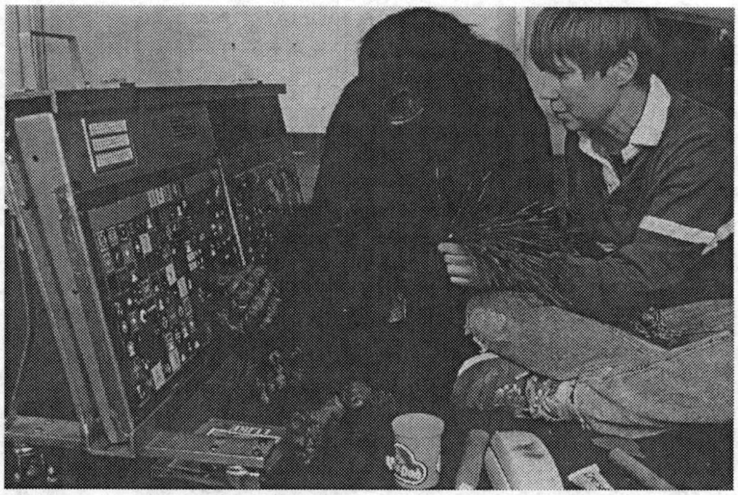

© Courtesy of Sue Rumbaugh

Questions remain about whether an ape's ability to manipulate symbols on a keyboard, as Kanzi is demonstrating here, is tantamount to human language.

So, can apes acquire and use language? Critics claim that Washoe, Sarah, and others merely learned to imitate gestures and other responses for which they were reinforced, rather than learning the complex syntax and morphemes of a true human language like ASL (Pinker, 1994; Terrace, 2005). A chimp signing "me cookie" is no different, critics say, than a pigeon learning to perform a series of responses to obtain a food pellet. Perhaps the question of whether apes can use language depends on how broadly we define language. If our definition includes communicating through the use of symbols, then apes as well as other nonhuman species may indeed be able to use language. But if our definition hinges on the use of complex syntax and grammatical structures, then the ability to use language may be unique to humans. The language abilities of Kanzi and other chimps may involve a kind of primitive grammar that is similar to that used by human infants or toddlers, not the complex forms of language that children naturally acquire as they mature (Seyfarth & Cheney, 2003).

Even so, scientists believe that ape communication may hold clues to the origins of human language (Pollick & de Waal, 2007). Apes frequently gesture with their hands, which scientists suspect may have represented a starting point in the development of human language (Tierney, 2007; Wade, 2007). Humans may have learned to talk with their hands before they learned to speak with their mouths (Wargo, 2008). People continue to use their hands for emphasis when they speak.

© namatae/Shutterstock.com

Scientists suspect that gesturing, a common form of communication in apes, may have been a starting point for the development of language in early humans.

7.2 MODULE REVIEW Language

Recite It

What are the major components of language?

➤ The major components of language are phonemes (basic units of sounds), morphemes (basic units of meaning), syntax (the rules of grammar that determine how words are ordered in sentences and phrases to express meaning), and semantics (the set of rules governing the meaning of words).

How does language develop?

➤ According to Noam Chomsky, language development depends on an innate mechanism that is "prewired" in the human brain.

➤ Language development also depends on exposure to the speech of others. Thus, both nature and nurture are necessary.

What is the linguistic relativity hypothesis?

➤ In its original form, this hypothesis (also called the Whorfian hypothesis) holds that language determines how we think and how we perceive the world. Research findings fail to support this version of the hypothesis, but a weaker version, which maintains that culture and language influence thinking, has some merit.

Can species other than humans use language?

➤ Research with chimps and gorillas has shown that these primates are capable of learning elementary forms of communication—for example, manipulating symbols to request food—but questions remain about whether these communication skills are equivalent to human language.

Recall It

1. The set of rules governing the proper use of words, phrases, and sentences is called
a. language.
b. grammar.
c. cultural determinism.
d. syntax.

2. The basic units of sounds in a language are called
a. phonemes.
b. morphemes.
c. semantics.
d. syntax.

3. The belief that language determines how we think and perceive reality is called the linguistic ________ hypothesis.

4. Apes have been taught American Sign Language (ASL) because
a. researchers have agreed to use this universal language.
b. sign language is easier to acquire than spoken language.
c. they lack the vocal apparatus needed to form human sounds.
d. sign language is more effective than spoken language in communicating basic needs.

Think About It

➤ In what ways are sexist biases reflected in the language we use in ordinary speech?

➤ Do you believe that chimps that learn to use signs are capable of communicating through language? Why or why not?

MODULE 7.3 Intelligence

- What is intelligence, and how is it measured?
- What constitutes a good intelligence test?
- What are some examples of the misuse of intelligence tests?
- What are some of the major theories of intelligence?
- Is intelligence determined by heredity or environment?

Perhaps no subject in psychology has sparked as much controversy as intelligence. Psychologists have long argued about how to define it, how to measure it, what factors govern it, whether different racial and ethnic groups have more or less of it, and, if so, what accounts for these differences. These debates are still very much at the forefront of contemporary psychology.

What Is Intelligence?

Just what is **intelligence**? Is it the ability to acquire knowledge from books or formal schooling? Or might it be "street smarts"—practical intelligence of the kind we see in people who survive by their wits rather than by knowledge acquired in school? Is it the ability to solve problems? Or is it the ability to adapt to the demands of the environment? Psychologists believe intelligence may be all these things and more. Though definitions of intelligence vary, a central belief of each is that intelligence is the ability to adapt to the environment. Perhaps the most widely used definition of intelligence is the one offered by psychologist David Wechsler (1975): "Intelligence is the global capacity of the individual to act purposefully, to think rationally, and to deal effectively with the environment."

Some theorists believe there are many different forms of intelligence, perhaps even multiple intelligences. Before we explore theories of intelligence, let us consider the history and nature of intelligence testing in modern times, as well as extremes of intelligence.

intelligence The capacity to think and reason clearly and to act purposefully and effectively in adapting to the environment and pursuing one's goals.

CONCEPT 7.20
Though theorists define intelligence in different ways, one widely used definition holds that intelligence is the capacity to act purposefully, think rationally, and deal effectively with the environment.

→ Concept Link
Some theorists believe that the ability to recognize and manage emotions is a form of intelligent behavior, called emotional intelligence. See Module 8.4.

© Bettmann/CORBIS

Alfred Binet

How Is Intelligence Measured?

In 1904, school officials in Paris commissioned Alfred Binet to develop methods of identifying children who were unable to cope with the demands of regular classroom instruction and required special classes to meet their needs. Today, we might describe such children as having learning disabilities or mild mental retardation.

To measure mental abilities, Binet and a colleague, Theodore Simon, developed an intelligence test consisting of memory tasks and other short tasks representing the kinds of everyday problems children might encounter, such as counting coins. By 1908, Binet and Simon decided to scale the tasks according to the age at which a child should be able to perform them successfully. A child began the testing with tasks scaled at the lowest age and then progressed to more difficult tasks, stopping at the point at which he or she could no longer perform them. The age at which the child's performance topped off was considered the child's **mental age**.

Binet and Simon calculated intelligence by subtracting the child's mental age from his or her chronological (actual) age. Children whose mental ages sufficiently lagged behind their chronological ages were considered in need of special education. In 1912, a German psychologist, William Stern, suggested a different way of computing intelligence, which Binet and Simon adopted. Stern divided mental age by chronological age, yielding a "mental quotient." It soon was labeled the **intelligence quotient (IQ)**. IQ is expressed by the following formula, in which MA is mental age and CA is chronological age:

$$IQ = \frac{MA}{CA} \times 100$$

Thus, if a child has a mental age of 10 and a chronological age of 8, the child's IQ would be 125 ($10 \div 8 = 1.25 \times 100 = 125$). A child with a mental age of 10 who is 12 years of age would have an IQ of 83 ($10 \div 12 = .8333 \times 100 = 83$).

Researchers following in Binet's footsteps developed intelligence tests that could be used with groups other than French schoolchildren. Henry Goddard (1865–1957),

mental age A representation of a person's intelligence based on the age of people who are capable of performing at the same level of ability.

CONCEPT 7.21
Alfred Binet and Theodore Simon developed the type of intelligence test in use today. Their work led to the concept of an intelligence quotient.

intelligence quotient (IQ) A measure of intelligence based on performance on tests of mental abilities, expressed as a ratio between one's mental age and chronological age, or derived from the deviation of one's scores from the norms for those of one's age group.

a research director at a school for children with mental retardation, brought the Binet-Simon test to the United States and translated it into English for use with American children. Early in his career, Goddard taught at the University of Southern California (USC), where he also briefly served as the school's first head football coach and remains to this day the only undefeated head coach in USC football history (Benjamin, 2009). (His 1888 team had a record of two wins and no losses against a local athletic club team).

During World War I, the U.S. Army developed group-administered intelligence tests used to screen millions of recruits. At about the same time, Stanford University psychologist Lewis Terman (1877–1956) adapted the Binet-Simon test for American use, adding many items of his own and establishing criteria, or **norms**, for comparing an individual's scores with those of the general population. The revised test, known as the Stanford-Binet Intelligence Scale (SBIS), was first published in 1916.

norms The standards used to compare an individual's performance on a test with the performance of others.

The Stanford-Binet Intelligence Scale is still commonly used to measure intelligence in children and young adults. However, tests developed by David Wechsler (1896–1981) are today the most widely used intelligence tests in the United States and Canada. Wechsler, a psychologist at Bellevue Hospital in New York, developed tests of intelligence for preschool children, school-age children, and adults (the Wechsler Adult Intelligence Scale, now in a fourth edition, WAIS-IV; see ■ Figure 7.13). The Wechsler scales introduced the concept of the *deviation IQ*—an IQ score based on the deviation, or difference, of a person's test score from the norms for the person's age group, rather than on the ratio of mental age to chronological age. The Wechsler scales are standardized in such a way that an average score is set at 100. The contemporary version of the Stanford-Binet Intelligence Scale also uses the deviation method to compute IQ.

CONCEPT 7.22
The Stanford-Binet Intelligence Scale and the Wechsler scales of intelligence are the major tests of intelligence in use today.

Sample Subtests

Comprehension
Why do people need to obey traffic laws? What does the saying, "The early bird catches the worm," mean?

Vocabulary
What does *capricious* mean?

Arithmetic
John wanted to buy a shirt that cost $31.50, but only had 17 dollars. How much more money would he need to buy the shirt?

Similarities
How are a stapler and a paper clip alike?

Picture Completion
What's missing from this picture?

Digit Span
Listen to this series of numbers and repeat them back to me in the same order:
6 4 5 2 7 3

Listen to this series of numbers and then repeat them backward:
9 4 2 5 8 7

Letter-Number Sequencing
Listen to this series of numbers and letters and repeat them back, first saying the numbers from least to most, and then saying the letters in alphabetical order:
S-2-C-1

Block Design
Using these blocks, match the design shown.

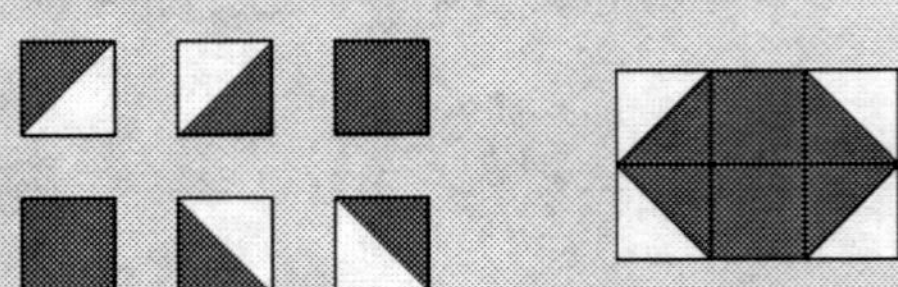

FIGURE 7.13 Examples of Items Similar to Those on the Wechsler Adult Intelligence Scale

What Are the Characteristics of a Good Test of Intelligence?

Like all psychological tests, tests of intelligence must be standardized, reliable, and valid. If they do not meet these criteria, we cannot be confident of the results.

CONCEPT 7.23
Like all psychological tests, intelligence tests must be standardized, reliable, and valid if we are to be confident of the results.

Standardization

Standardization is the process of establishing norms for a test by administering it to a large number of people that make up a *standardization sample.* The standardization sample must be representative of the population for whom the test is intended. As noted earlier, norms are the criteria, or standards, used to compare a person's performance with the performance of others. You can determine how well you do on an intelligence test by comparing your scores with the norms for people in your age group in the standardization sample.

standardization The process of establishing norms for a test by administering the test to large numbers of people who constitute a standardization sample.

As noted above, IQ scores are based on the deviation of a person's score from norms for others of the same age, and the mean (average) score is set at 100. IQ scores are distributed around the mean in such a way that about two-thirds of the scores in the general population fall within an "average" range of 85 to 115. In ■ Figure 7.14 we can see that distribution (spread) of IQ scores follows the form of a bell-shaped curve. Relatively few people score at either the very high or very low end of the curve, with most bunching up in the middle of the distribution.

Standardization has another meaning in test administration. It also refers to uniform procedures that must be followed to ensure that the test is used correctly.

Reliability

Reliability refers to the consistency of test scores over time. You wouldn't trust a bathroom scale that gave you different readings each time you used it. Nor would you trust an IQ test that gave you a score of 135 one day, 75 the next, and 105 the day after that. A reliable test is one that produces similar results over time. One way of assessing reliability is the *test-retest method,* where the subject takes the same test again after a short interval. Because familiarity with the test questions can result in consistent performance,

reliability The stability of test scores over time.

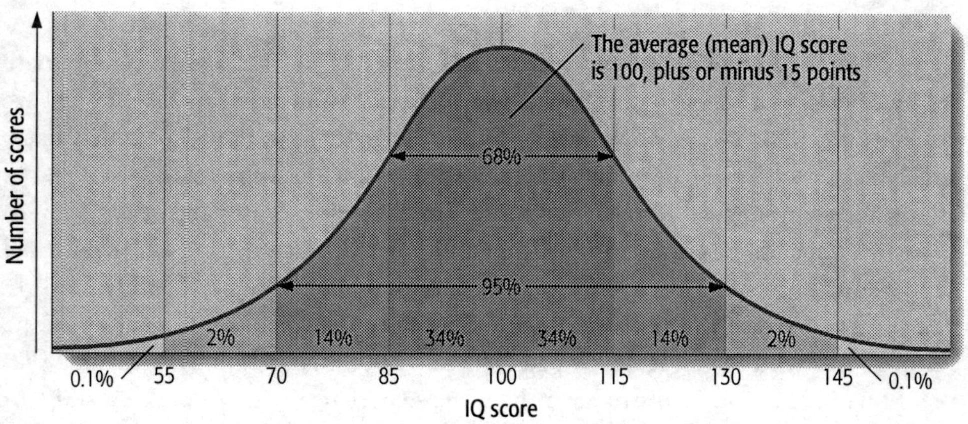

FIGURE 7.14 Normal Distribution of IQ Scores
The average (mean) IQ score is 100, plus or minus 15 points. The percentages shown are rounded off.

validity The degree to which a test measures what it purports to measure.

psychologists sometimes use the *alternate-forms method.* When this method is used, subjects are given a parallel form of the test.

© Archives of the History of American Psychology—University of Akron

Henry Goddard, the early psychologist who brought the Binet-Simon intelligence test to the United States, also held another important distinction. He briefly coached the USC football team and remains to this day the only undefeated head coach in USC history.

Validity

Validity is the degree to which a test measures what it purports to measure. A test may be reliable—producing consistent scores over time—but not valid. For example, a test that measures head size may be reliable, yielding consistent results over time, but invalid as a measure of intelligence.

There are several types of validity. One type is *predictive validity,* the degree to which test scores accurately predict future behavior or performance. IQ tests are good predictors of academic achievement and performance on general aptitude tests, such as the Scholastic Aptitude Test (SAT) and the Graduate Record Examination (GRE) (Neisser et al., 1996; Wadsworth et al., 1995). But that's not all. It turns out that IQ also predicts long-term health and longevity, perhaps because people who tend to do well on IQ tests have the kinds of problem-solving and learning skills needed to acquire and practice healthier behaviors (Gottfredson & Deary, 2004).

Misuses of Intelligence Tests

Even Binet, the father of the modern IQ test, was concerned that intelligence tests may be misused if teachers or parents lose interest or hope in children with low IQ scores and set low expectations for them. Low expectations can in turn become self-fulfilling prophecies, as children who are labeled as "dumb" may give up on themselves and become underachievers.

CONCEPT 7.24

Intelligence tests are misused when children with low scores are labeled as innately incapable or inferior, when too much emphasis is placed on IQ scores, and when cultural biases in the tests put children at a disadvantage.

Misuse also occurs when too much emphasis is placed on IQ scores. Though intelligence tests do predict future academic performance, they are far from perfect predictors and should not be used as the only basis for placing children in special education programs. Some children who test poorly may be able to benefit from regular classroom instruction. Placement decisions should be based on a comprehensive assessment that takes into account not only the child's performance on intelligence tests but also his or her cultural and linguistic background and ability to adapt to the academic environment.

culture-fair tests Tests designed to eliminate cultural biases.

Intelligence tests may be biased against children who are not part of the majority culture. Children from different cultural backgrounds may not have had any exposure to the types of information assessed by standard IQ tests, such as knowledge of famous individuals. Several **culture-fair tests**—tests designed to eliminate cultural biases—have been developed. They consist of nonverbal tasks that measure visual-spatial abilities and reasoning skills. However, these tests are not widely used, largely because they don't predict academic performance as well as standard IQ tests. This is not surprising, since academic success in the United States and other Western countries depends heavily on linguistic and knowledge-acquisition skills reflected in standard IQ tests. Moreover, it may be impossible to develop a purely culture-free IQ test because the skills that define intelligence depend on the values of the culture in which the test is developed (Benson, 2003). Nor should we assume that all people in the same culture have the same experience with test-taking skills or familiarity with the types of materials used on the tests. At best we may only be able to develop *culture-reduced tests,* not tests which are entirely culture-fair (Sternberg & Grigorenko, 2008).

Extremes of Intelligence: Mental Retardation and Giftedness

Low IQ scores alone are not sufficient to determine **mental retardation**, a psychological disorder in which there is a general delay in the development of intellectual and social skills. In addition to having an IQ score of approximately 70 or below, the person must have difficulty coping with the tasks appropriate to his or her age and life situation. The educational and support services needed by children with mental retardation depend to a large extent on the severity of the retardation.

mental retardation A generalized deficit or impairment in intellectual and social skills.

CONCEPT 7.25
Most people with mental retardation are able to acquire basic reading and arithmetic skills and can learn to function relatively independently and perform productive work.

Table 7.1 shows the capabilities of school-age children according to levels of mental retardation. Most individuals with mental retardation fall in a mild range of severity and are capable of meeting basic educational challenges, such as reading and solving arithmetic problems. Many children with mild retardation are placed in regular classrooms, a practice called **mainstreaming**. Those with severe intellectual deficits require more supportive programs, which may include institutional placement, at least until the person can function in less restrictive settings in the community.

mainstreaming The practice of placing children with special needs in a regular classroom environment.

The causes of mental retardation involve biological and environmental factors (Canfield et al., 2003). Biological causes include genetic or chromosomal disorders, brain damage, and exposure to lead. The most common environmental cause is a deprived family environment, one lacking in verbal interactions between the child and the parents, and also lacking in intellectually stimulating play activities.

People at the upper end of the IQ spectrum (typically about 130 or higher) are generally classified as intellectually gifted. As children, they may benefit from enriched educational programs that allow them to progress at a faster pace than standard programs. Today, the concept of giftedness includes not only children with high IQ scores but also those with special talents, such as musical or artistic ability—skills not typically assessed by standard IQ tests. Gifted children may play musical instruments as well as highly trained adults or solve algebra problems at an age when their peers have not yet learned to carry numbers in addition.

The systematic study of intellectually gifted children began with the work of Lewis Terman, the developer of the Stanford-Binet Intelligence Scale. Many of the

TABLE 7.1 Levels of Mental Retardation and Capabilities of School-Age Children

Level of Mental Retardation (IQ Range)	Percentage of Cases	Capabilities of School-Age Children
Mild (50–70)	85%	Able to acquire reading and arithmetic skills to about a sixth-grade level and can later function relatively independently and engage in productive work
Moderate (35–49)	10%	Able to learn simple communication and manual skills, but have difficulty acquiring reading and arithmetic skills
Severe (20–34)	3–4%	Capable of basic speech and may be able to learn repetitive tasks in supervised settings
Profound (below 20)	1–2%	Severe delays in all areas of development, but some may learn simple tasks in supervised settings

Source: Adapted from American Psychiatric Association, 2000.

intellectually gifted children he studied—the "little geniuses," as they were originally called—became successful executives and professionals and are credited with authoring 90 books and holding more than 100 patents (Feldhusen, 2004). But others in the group worked in occupations that failed to measure up to their intellectual potential. The high achievers were more likely than the low achievers to have personality traits such as persistence in pursuing goals and a desire to excel. The lesson we can draw from this is that while intelligence may contribute to success, other factors enter the equation.

Theories of Intelligence

CONCEPT 7.26
Psychologists have been debating the nature of intelligence ever since intelligence tests were first introduced.

Does intelligence consist of one general ability or a cluster of different abilities? Might there be different forms of intelligence, or even different intelligences? Throughout the history of modern psychology, theorists have attempted to explain intelligence. There are perhaps as many theories about it as there are theoreticians. Here we consider several major theories.

Spearman's "g": In Search of General Cognitive Ability

British psychologist Charles Spearman (1863–1945) observed that people who scored well on one test of mental ability tended to score well on other tests (Spearman, 1927). He reasoned there must be an underlying general factor of intelligence that allows people to do well on mental tests, a factor he labeled "g" for general intelligence. However, he also believed that intelligence includes specific abilities that, along with "g," contribute to performance on individual tests. For example, a person's performance on an arithmetic test might be determined by both general intelligence and specific mathematical ability. Intelligence tests, such as the SBIS and the Wechsler scales, were developed to measure Spearman's concept of general intelligence, or "g," which is expressed as an IQ score.

Thurstone's Primary Mental Abilities: Not Two Factors, but Seven

primary mental abilities Seven basic mental abilities that Thurstone believed constitute intelligence.

CONCEPT 7.27
Though IQ tests were developed to measure Spearman's concept of general intelligence, or "g," theorists like Thurstone believed that intelligence consists of a range of mental abilities that cannot be measured by one general IQ score.

Psychologist Louis L. Thurstone (1887–1955) did not believe that any one large, dominating factor like "g" could account for intelligence. Rather, his studies pointed to a set of seven **primary mental abilities**: verbal comprehension, numerical ability, memory, inductive reasoning, perceptual speed, verbal fluency, and spatial relations (Thurstone & Thurstone, 1941). Although Thurstone did not deny the existence of "g," he argued that a single IQ score does not hold much value in assessing intelligence. He and his wife, Thelma Thurstone, developed the *Primary Mental Abilities Test* to measure the seven primary abilities they believed constitute intelligence.

Gardner's Model of Multiple Intelligences

multiple intelligences Gardner's term for the distinct types of intelligence that characterize different forms of intelligent behavior.

Psychologist Howard Gardner (b. 1943) rejects the view that there is a single entity called "intelligence." Rather, he believes there exist different types of intelligence, called **multiple intelligences**, that vary from person to person. Gardner identifies eight different intelligences: linguistic, logical-mathematical, musical, spatial, bodily-kinesthetic, interpersonal, intrapersonal, and naturalist (H. Gardner, 1993, 1998) (see Table 7.2 and ■ Figure 7.15). These separate intelligences are believed to be independent

TABLE 7.2 Gardner's Multiple Intelligences

Types of Intelligence	Description	Groups with High Levels of the Intelligence
Linguistic	Ability to understand and use words	Writers, poets, effective public speakers
Logical-mathematical	Ability to perform mathematical, computational, or logical operations	Scientists, engineers, computer programmers
Musical	Ability to analyze, compose, or perform music	Musicians, singers, composers
Spatial	Ability to perceive spatial relationships and arrange objects in space	Painters, architects, sculptors
Bodily-kinesthetic	Ability to control bodily movements and manipulate objects effectively	Dancers, athletes, race car drivers, mechanics
Interpersonal	Ability to relate effectively to others and to understand others' moods and motives	Industrial and political leaders, effective supervisors
Intrapersonal	Ability to understand one's own feelings and behavior (self-perception)	Psychologically well-adjusted people
Naturalist	Ability to recognize objects and patterns in nature, such as flora and fauna	Botanists, biologists, naturalists

of one another. Thus, a person could be high in some intelligences but low in others. For example, you might have a high level of linguistic, or verbal, intelligence but a lower level of intelligence in mathematics, music, or spatial relationships. Some individuals have good "people skills" (interpersonal intelligence) but may not be highly skilled at mathematical and logical tasks.

CONCEPT 7.28
According to Gardner's model of multiple intelligences, we possess separate intelligences that we rely on to perform different types of tasks.

Gardner's model has had enormous influence, especially in educational settings. Many schools today seek to cultivate specific intelligences that go beyond verbal and mathematical abilities. However, a frequent criticism of the model is that its fails to account for how multiple intelligences interact with each other. Most cognitive activities involve the interaction of multiple abilities, not just one isolated type of intelligence. For example, the ability to relate effectively to others (interpersonal intelligence) depends in part on the linguistic skills needed to express oneself clearly (linguistic intelligence).

We also need to consider why we need to specify eight separate intelligences. Might there be more or fewer? Why musical intelligence but not, say, culinary intelligence or practical intelligence (i.e., common sense or "street smarts")? Presently, evidence suggests that some forms of intelligence (e.g., bodily-kinesthetic) stand on their own as distinctive abilities, but others show closer relationships (e.g., linguistic and logical/mathematical) than the model of multiple intelligences might suggest (Visser, Ashton, & Vernon, 2006). We should also recognize that people who have a high level of intelligence in one area—verbal skills, for instance—may also excel at mathematical and logical skills.

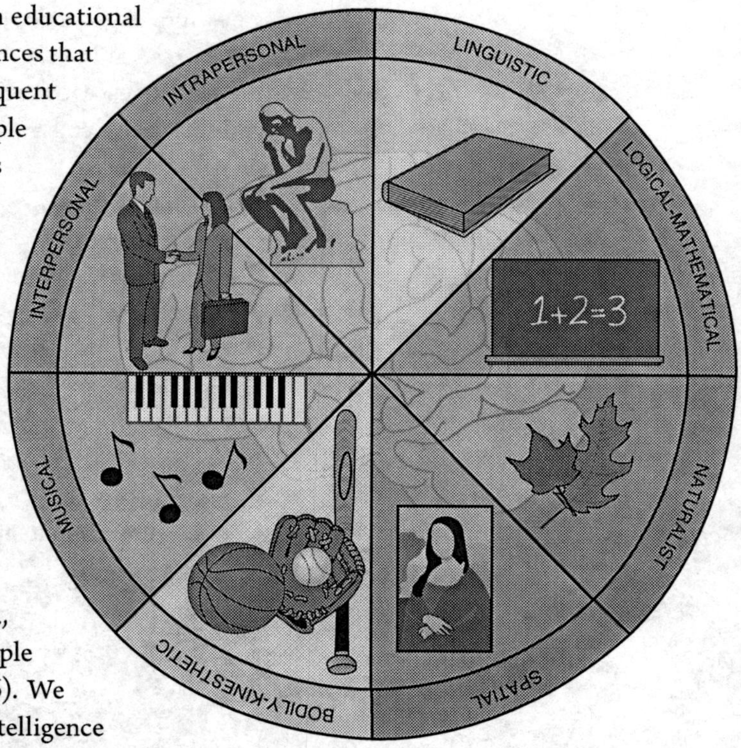

FIGURE 7.15 Gardner's Model of Multiple Intelligences

CONCEPT 7.29
Sternberg's triarchic theory of intelligence focuses on how we bring together the analytic, creative, and practical aspects of our intelligence to solve the range of problems we face in everyday situations.

triarchic theory of intelligence Sternberg's theory of intelligence that posits three aspects of intelligence: analytic, creative, and practical.

Sternberg's Triarchic Theory of Intelligence

Whereas Gardner focuses on different types of intelligence, psychologist Robert Sternberg (b. 1949) emphasizes how we bring together different aspects of our intelligence to meet the demands we face in our daily lives. Sternberg (1997b) proposes a **triarchic theory of intelligence**, which holds that intelligence has three aspects: analytic, creative, and practical (see ■ Figure 7.16).

Sternberg believes that people with high levels of intelligence are better able to integrate or organize these three aspects of intelligence in their daily lives. *Analytic intelligence* is the kind of intelligence measured by traditional intelligence tests. It comes into play when you analyze and evaluate familiar problems, break them down into their component parts, and develop strategies to solve them. *Creative intelligence* allows us to invent new ways of solving unfamiliar problems. *Practical intelligence* is the ability to apply what we know to everyday life—the common sense, or "street smarts," that traditional intelligence tests fail to measure. Sternberg argues that we need all three types of intelligence to succeed in life. He also believes we need to supplement standard intelligence tests with measures of creative intelligence and practical intelligence.

Overview of Theories of Intelligence

Scientists continue to debate just how much importance to place on the general factor of intelligence, or "g," in explaining mental abilities (see Gottfredson, 2004; W. Johnson et al., 2007; W. Johnson, Nijenhuis, & Bouchard, 2008). Evidence shows "g" is not merely a good predictor of school performance in children, but it is also a good predictor of job performance in adulthood (Greer, 2004a; Kuncel, Hezlett, & Ones, 2004).

Gardner's and Sternberg's models of intelligence take us in a different direction from a measure of general intelligence, or "g." They raise our awareness that traditional intelligence tests fail to capture important dimensions of intelligence, such as how people use their intelligence to meet the challenges and demands they face in everyday contexts. Presently, we lack a consensus in the field to support the existence of separate types of intelligence, such as Gardner's multiple intelligences or Sternberg's practical intelligence. Though Gardner's and Sternberg's theories are prompting renewed interest in the nature of intelligence, they have yet to be thoroughly evaluated through scientific tests (Gottfredson, 2003a, 2003b).

What can we conclude about these various theories of intelligence? First, it is clear that human intelligence consists of multiple abilities, perhaps even multiple intelligences. Second, we need to take into account cultural contexts in which intelligent behavior occurs. The abilities a society values determine how intelligence is defined and measured. Our society places a high value on verbal, mathematical, and spatial skills, so it is not surprising that conventional IQ tests measure these abilities and little else. Perhaps, as Sternberg argues, we need to think about measuring intelligence more broadly to assess the wider range of abilities that may constitute human intelligence. Concept Chart 7.3 offers an overview of the major theories of intelligence.

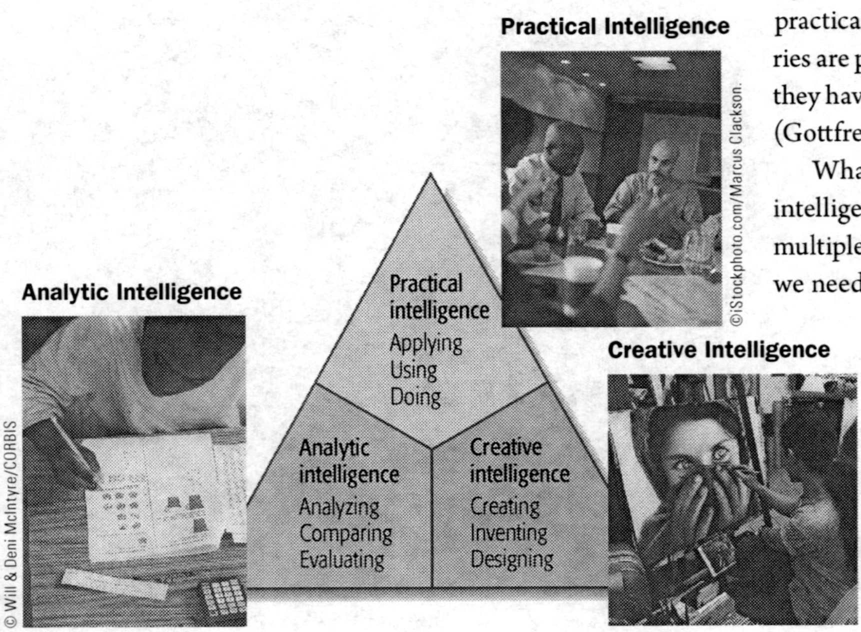

FIGURE 7.16 Sternberg's Triarchic Model of Intelligence

CONCEPT CHART 7.3 Theories of Intelligence

Theorist	Major Concepts	Comments
Spearman	Intelligence involves general cognitive ability, or "g."	Traditional intelligence tests are designed to measure "g" in the form of an IQ score.
Thurstone	Intelligence consists of seven primary mental abilities.	Thurstone argued that a single IQ score cannot capture the broad range of mental abilities that constitutes intelligence.
Gardner	Multiple intelligences are needed to account for the range of mental abilities.	Gardner's theory has popular appeal but does not account for the interrelationships among the different intelligences. It also does not draw the line in determining how many separate intelligences are needed to account for the full range of mental abilities.
Sternberg	Sternberg's triarchic theory proposes three aspects of intelligence: analytic, creative, and practical.	The triarchic theory is important because it provides a much-needed focus on how people use their intelligence in everyday life.

© iStockphoto.com/jpa1999

Intelligence and the Nature-Nurture Question

Scientists have long sought to answer the question of whether intelligence is primarily the result of nature (genetics) or nurture (environment). A focus of the heated nature-nurture debate is whether genetic factors or environmental ones are responsible for racial differences in IQ scores.

Separating the Effects of Nature and Nurture

A large body of evidence supports the view that intelligence has a strong genetic component (e.g., Deary, Johnson, & Houlihan, 2009; Haworth et al., 2009; Plomin & Haworth, 2009). The closer the genetic relationship between two people, the closer their IQ scores tend to be.

Figure 7.17 is based on over 100 kinship studies of more than 100,000 pairs of relatives (Plomin & Petrill, 1997). Notice how the statistical association (correlation) between IQs of twins raised together is greater among monozygotic (MZ), or identical, twins than among dizygotic (DZ), or fraternal, twins. Since MZ twins share 100 percent of their genes and DZ twins, like other siblings, have only a 50 percent genetic overlap, this finding suggests that heredity makes an important contribution to intelligence.

Another compelling piece of evidence supporting the role of genetics, also shown in ■ Figure 7.17, is that the IQ scores of MZ

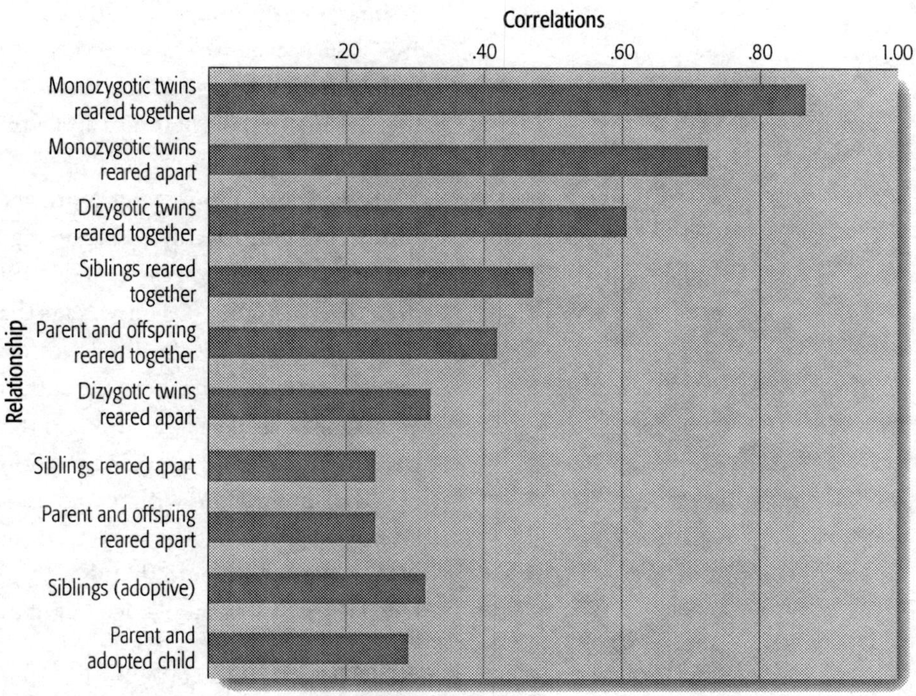

FIGURE 7.17 Similarity and Intelligence
Here we see the average correlations of IQ scores of people in different family relationships. The closer the genetic and environmental similarity between family members, the closer their IQ scores tend to be.
Source: Adapted from Plomin & Petrill, 1997.

twins who are raised in separate households are more similar than the IQ scores of DZ twins who are raised together.

Adoptee studies provide yet more evidence of the role of genetics in determining IQ. Studies have consistently shown that the IQ scores of adopted children are closer to those of their biological parents than to those of their adoptive parents (Bishop et al., 2003).

Heredity doesn't tell the whole story, however. Environmental influences are also important factors in intellectual development. A home environment that emphasizes verbal interactions, reading, and exploration fosters children's intellectual development. Refer again to Figure 7.17. Notice that the correlation for the IQ scores of MZ twins raised together is greater than the correlation for the IQ scores of MZ twins raised apart. Since MZ twins share the same genes, the difference in these correlations is evidence that the environment also plays a role in determining IQ. .

CONCEPT 7.30
Evidence indicates that genetic and environmental factors interact in complex ways in shaping intelligence.

The accumulated evidence makes a compelling case that both genetic and environmental factors interact in complex ways in determining intelligence (Posthuma & de Geus, 2006; Sternberg & Grigorenko, 2008). Recent evidence underscores the *genetic by environment* interaction. Investigators find that genetics plays a much larger role in accounting for mental abilities of two year olds who are raised in socially advantaged higher income families (who may provide more intellectually stimulating activities) than it does in more disadvantaged, lower income families (Tucker-Drob et al., 2011).

heritability The degree to which heredity accounts for variations on a given trait within a population.

How much of intelligence may be explained by genetic factors and how much by environmental factors? The **heritability** of a trait is the degree to which genetic factors explain the variability or differences among people on the particular trait. For example, a heritability estimate of 50 percent for intelligence would mean that genetics explains 50 percent of the differences (variations) among people in IQ scores. The remaining 50 percent would be explained by nongenetic factors, such as environment influences.

Genetics comes through as an important influence on intelligence, as heritability estimates vary from about 50 percent to about 75 percent (Begley, 2001; Gottesman, 1997). However, we cannot say whether 50 to 75 percent of a given person's IQ results from genetic factors and the rest from environmental or other influences. Understand that estimates of heritability apply to the population in general, not to any given individual in the population.

Speaking of family environments, investigators recently stirred the pot of a long-simmering controversy by reporting that firstborn children have an advantage in IQ scores. A large-scale Norwegian study of nearly 250,000 men showed firstborn children to have higher IQs on average than their younger siblings (Kristensen & Bjerkedal 2007; Sulloway, 2007). The investigators controlled for factors that might affect IQ scores, such as the mother's age at the child's birth and the educational levels of the parents. One possible explanation for the IQ advantage of firstborns is that for a time they have their parents' undivided attention, which may translate into spending more time in verbal interactions with their parents. Since IQ scores are not related to sex, the investigators suspect that the same birth-order differences may also apply to women (Carey, 2007). We should note that the IQ advantage for first borns is small, averaging only a few points. Still, a small edge might make a difference in educational achievement.

Racial Differences in IQ

White Americans of European background typically score higher on IQ tests than African Americans—about 15 points higher, on the average (Fagan & Holland, 2002). This racial gap in IQ scores exists even when differences in income levels are taken into account.

Are racial differences in IQ genetic or environmental in origin? Although the debate over the question continues, increasing evidence points to the importance of environmental factors in explaining racial differences. For one thing, minority children from disadvantaged backgrounds may lack exposure to the types of information and reasoning skills tested on traditional IQ tests (Fagan & Holland, 2007). For another, measurable gains in IQ scores are obtained among minority children from low-income families who participate in formal educational enrichment programs, such as the Head Start program for preschoolers (Zigler & Styfco, 1994).

Another factor arguing against genetic explanations is that racial differences in IQ scores have narrowed in recent years (Dickens & Flynn, 2006a, 2006b). IQ scores in the United States and in many other countries have been rising steadily for several generations—a trend not easily explained by genetic factors (C. Blair et al., 2005; J. R. Flynn, 2006; Pietschnig, Voraceka, & Formann, 2011). Even though the rise in IQ may have stopped or even reversed in recent years in some countries (Lynn & Harvey, 2008; Teasdale & Owen, 2008), genetic explanations are unlikely to account for these upward or downward changes in IQ scores during such a short period of time, or for the narrowing of the IQ gap between ethnicities. We need to look to environmental factors to explain these changes, such as increased educational opportunities leading to a narrowing of the racial gap in IQ (C. Blair et al., 2005).

CONCEPT 7.31
A gap between the IQ scores of African Americans and Euro-Americans has provoked a heated debate over the origins of these differences.

Perhaps the most telling evidence of environmental influences comes from a classic study of African American and interracial children who were adopted and raised by upper-middle-class white American families. The IQ scores of these adopted children were about 15 points higher on the average than would be expected of the average African American child from a socially disadvantaged background (Waldman, Weinberg, & Scarr, 1994). The investigators attributed the better performance of the African American adoptees to the social and cultural effects of being raised in an environment that places a strong value on educational achievement—effects that basically canceled out the oft-cited 15-point gap in IQ between these groups.

We still have much to learn about the role of genetics in intelligence. As psychologist Robert Sternberg and his colleagues argue, present evidence does not allow us to determine the role that genetic factors may play in determining racial or ethnic differences in intelligence (Sternberg, Grigorenko, & Kidd, 2005). Whatever the role of heredity might be, environmental factors certainly make a contribution to explaining ethnic or racial gaps in IQ. "Changing the environment," says Michael Rutter, a leading researcher in the field, "can make an enormous difference" in a child's intelligence (cited in Kirp, 2006). Affluent families "can provide the mental stimulation needed for genes to build the brain circuitry for intelligence," says another leading researcher, Erik Turkheimer (cited in Kirp, 2006). Unfortunately, children living in deprived or chaotic family circumstances may fail to reach their genetic potentials.

Let us also note that group differences in IQ tell us nothing about individual potential. Any group, no matter what its average IQ scores may be, can produce its share of intellectually gifted people. We also need to recognize that children from groups such as African Americans that place a strong value on creative expression may not give the obvious answers to questions on IQ tests. Psychologist Janet Helms (1992) points out that the use of different reasoning or test-taking strategies is not evidence of lack of intelligence.

© Michael Newman/Photo Edit

Parental emphasis on education can have an important bearing on a child's intellectual development.

7.3 MODULE REVIEW Intelligence

Recite It

What is intelligence, and how is it measured?

- One widely used definition holds that intelligence is the capacity to act purposefully, think rationally, and deal effectively with the environment.
- Standardized intelligence tests, such as the Stanford-Binet Intelligence Scale and the Wechsler scales of intelligence, are generally used to measure intelligence.

What constitutes a good intelligence test?

- The basic requirements of a good intelligence test are standardization (generation of norms based on samples representative of the population), reliability (stability of test scores over time), and validity (the test's ability to measure what it purports to measure).

What are some examples of the misuse of intelligence tests?

- Intelligence tests are misused when children with low scores are labeled as innately incapable or inferior, when too much emphasis is placed on IQ scores, and when cultural biases in the tests put children from diverse cultural backgrounds at a disadvantage.
- Mental retardation is defined as an IQ score of usually 70 or below and delayed or impaired social skills. Giftedness is usually associated with IQ scores of about 130 or above or with evidence of special talents.

What are some of the major theories of intelligence?

- Major theories of intelligence include Spearman's concept of general intelligence, or "g," Thurstone's theory of primary mental abilities, Gardner's model of multiple intelligences, and Sternberg's triarchic theory. Some theorists favor the view that intelligence consists of a general cognitive ability, whereas others favor a model based on multiple abilities or even multiple intelligences.

Is intelligence determined by heredity or environment?

- Most authorities believe that intelligence is based on a complex interaction of nature (genetic influences) and nurture (environmental influences).

Recall It

1. Match the terms on the left with the definitions on the right:

i. standardization	**a.** a test's ability to measure what it is designed to measure
ii. validity	**b.** the practice of placing children with mild mental retardation in regular classrooms
iii. mainstreaming	**c.** an underlying general factor of intelligence
iv. Spearman's "g"	**d.** the generation of test norms based on representative samples of the population

2. Problems with intelligence tests include potential ________ biases in test content.
3. Sternberg's theory of intelligence that emphasizes how we integrate various aspects of intelligence in meeting the challenges and demands of everyday life is called the ________ theory.
4. In recent years, IQ scores have been
   a. falling in many countries, but rising in the United States.
   b. rising in many countries, but falling in the United States.
   c. falling in the United States and many other countries.
   d. rising in the United States and many other countries.

Think About It

- Do you believe that conventional intelligence tests are culturally biased? Why or why not?
- In what ways are intelligence tests useful? In what ways might they be misused?

APPLICATION MODULE 7.4 Becoming a Creative Problem Solver

The range of problems we face in our personal lives is virtually limitless. Consider some common examples: getting to school or work on time; helping a friend with a personal problem; resolving disputes; juggling school, work, and family responsibilities. Creative problem solvers challenge preconceptions and consider as many alternative solutions to a problem as possible. Were you stumped by the problem on p. 255 about the key that opened no locks but allowed the man to enter? Perhaps it was because you approached the problem from only one vantage point—that the key was a door key. Solving the problem requires that you consider an alternative that may not have seemed obvious at first—that the key was an enter key on a keyboard. Speaking of keys, here are some key steps toward becoming a creative problem solver.

CONCEPT 7.32
Creative problem solvers challenge preconceptions and consider as many alternative solutions to a problem as possible.

Adopt a Questioning Attitude

Finding creative solutions to problems begins with adopting a questioning attitude. The creative problem solver asks, "What alternatives are available? What has worked in the past? What hasn't worked? What can I do differently?"

Gather Information

Creative problem solvers acquire the information and resources they need to explore possible solutions. People today have access to a wider range of information resources than ever before, including newspapers and magazines, college courses, and, of course, the Internet. Want to know more about combating a common problem like insomnia? Why not search the Internet to see what information is available? However, think critically about the information you find.

Avoid Getting Stuck in Mental Sets

Here's a question for you: "If there were three apples and you took two away, how many would you have?" If you answered one, chances are you had a mental set to respond to this type of problem as a subtraction problem. But the question did not ask how many apples were left. The answer is that you would have two apples—the two you took away.

To avoid slipping into a mental set that impairs problem-solving efforts, think through each question carefully. Ask yourself: What am I required to do? What type of problem is this? What problem-solving strategy would work best for this type of problem?

Put these skills into practice by responding to a few brainteasers (the answers are given on p. 283) ("Brainteaser Quizzes," 2001):

1. How many two-cent stamps are there in a dozen?
2. You are holding two U.S. coins that total 55 cents. One of the coins is not a nickel. What are the coins you are holding?
3. A farmer has 18 cows and all but 11 of them died. How many were left?

Generate Alternatives

Creative problem solvers generate as many alternative solutions to a problem as possible. They don't rely on their first gut reaction. Consider this puzzle: *A bat and a ball cost $1.10 together, and the bat costs one dollar more than ball. How much does the ball cost?*

Most people immediately jump to the wrong answer based on the first thought that comes to mind: 10 cents. (The correct answer is 5 cents. Do the math.) If you got it wrong, don't feel badly. About half of the undergraduates in some of the nation's best colleges (e.g., MIT, Princeton, Harvard) get it wrong (Kahneman & Klein, 2009). It's a normal tendency to go with your gut feelings, not only with puzzles, but with many decisions you face. By

© Michael Fein/Bloomberg via Getty Images

Nearly half the students tested at top universities got a simple arithmetic problem wrong, not because they were dumb, but because people tend to respond without thinking through problems.

contrast, creative problem solvers carefully think through problems and generate as many solutions as possible. They may decide upon their original solution, or they may decide that one of the alternatives works best. Here are a few suggestions for generating alternatives:

brainstorming A method of promoting divergent thinking by encouraging people to propose as many solutions to a problem as possible without fear of being judged negatively by others, no matter how far-fetched their proposals may be.

1. *Personal brainstorming.* Alex Osborne (1963) introduced the concept of brainstorming to help business executives and engineers solve problems more creatively. The basic idea is to encourage divergent thinking. **Brainstorming** encourages people to propose as many solutions to a problem as possible without fear of being judged negatively by others, no matter how far-fetched their proposals may seem. There are three general rules for brainstorming:
   - *Rule 1: Write down as many solutions to the problem as you can think of.* Quantity counts more than quality.
   - *Rule 2: Suspend judgment.* Don't evaluate any of the possible solutions or strike them off your list.
   - *Rule 3: Seek unusual, remote, or even weird ideas.* Today's strange or oddball idea may turn into tomorrow's brilliant solution.
2. *After generating your list, put it aside for a few days.* When you return to it, ask yourself which solutions are worth pursuing. Take into account the resources or additional information you will need to put these solutions into practice.
3. *Find analogies.* Finding a situation analogous to the present problem can lead to a creative solution. Ask yourself how the present problem is similar to problems you've encountered before. What strategies worked in the past? How can they be modified to fit the present problem? This is constructive use of mental sets—using past solutions as a guide, not an impediment, to problem solving.
4. *Think outside the box.* Recall the nine-dot problem in Figure 7.3 (p. 255). People have difficulty with this problem because of a tendency to limit the ways they think about it. If you didn't solve the nine-dot problem, you're in good company. In a laboratory test, none of the research participants who were given several minutes to solve the problem were able to do so (MacGregor, Ormerod, & Chronicle, 2001). The problem is solvable only if you think "outside the box"—literally, as shown to the left. Creative problem solvers make an effort to conceptualize problems from different perspectives, steering their problem-solving efforts toward finding new solutions (Ormerod, MacGregor, & Chronicle, 2002).

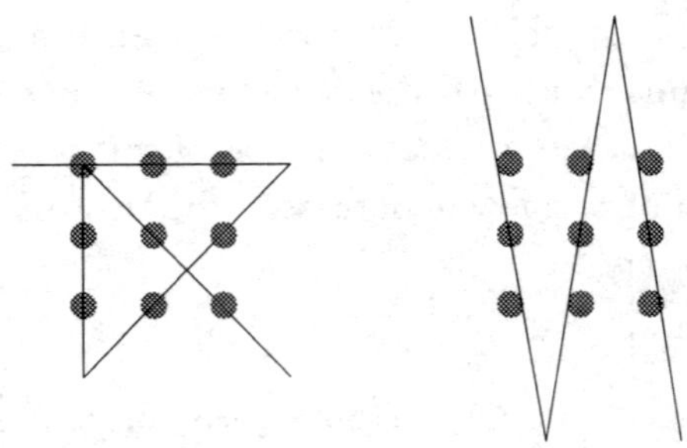

Sleep On It

People facing difficult problems may benefit from the age-old wisdom of "sleeping on it" Learning new information and then sleeping on it may help you retain more of what you learn. Investigators find that sleep enhances insight and creative thinking of research subjects challenged with solving difficult math problems (Wagner et al., 2004). Indeed, the cognitive benefits of getting a good night's sleep may account for the experiences of many famous scientists and artists whose inspired ideas occurred shortly following awakening from a deep sleep (Komaroff, 2004).

Test It Out

Try out possible solutions to see how they work. Gather information that will help you evaluate what you need to do differently to achieve a better solution. If you get stuck, take time away from the problem. Allow the problem to "incubate" in your mind. When you return to it, you may have a fresh perspective that will help you discover a workable solution.

Thinking Critically About Psychology

Based on your reading of this chapter, answer the following questions. Then, to evaluate your progress in developing critical thinking skills, compare your answers to the sample answers found in Appendix A.

1. An ambulance is heading toward the hospital on a country road, carrying an injured man who needs emergency surgery. When the ambulance comes around a bend, the driver notices a large flock of sheep blocking the road. The driver starts pounding on the horn and sounding the siren to part the sheep, but to no effect. A medical technician jumps out of the ambulance and tries to shove the rearmost sheep out of the way, hoping the others will follow. The driver starts screaming at the shepherd, imploring him to clear the road. The shepherd also starts screaming, but the sheep just keep on bleating. Suddenly, the shepherd raises his hand to signal the ambulance to stop. He then succeeds in clearing a path for the ambulance, but not by parting the sheep or by guiding the ambulance past them. (Adapted from M. Levine, 1994.)

a. How did the shepherd clear the road for the ambulance?

b. What impediment to problem solving does the behavior of the medical technician represent?

2. John receives an inheritance, which he decides to invest in the stock market. Like many other investors, he decides to open an online trading account. At first, he does well. Then he begins to trade more actively, buying and selling stocks almost daily. His losses soon begin to mount. Concerned, he consults a financial adviser, who asks him about his trading strategy. John recounts that he buys stocks in companies he hears positive things about and sells stocks in companies whenever he notices negative news items.

a. What cognitive error(s) in decision making might explain John's losses in the stock market?

b. How would you advise him to avoid such errors in the future?

Answers to Brainteasers (p. 281)

1. There are 12 two-cent stamps, since a dozen of anything is 12.

2. You are holding a 50-cent piece and a nickel. One of the two coins (the 50-cent piece) is not a nickel.

3. There are 11 cows left. All but 11 died.

Log in to CengageBrain to access the resources your instructor requires. For this book, you can access:

CourseMate — Psychology CourseMate brings course concepts to life with interactive learning, study, and exam preparation tools that support the printed textbook. A textbook-specific website, Psychology CourseMate includes an integrated interactive eBook and other interactive learning tools including quizzes, flashcards, videos, and more.

CENGAGENOW — CengageNow is an easy-to-use online resource that helps you study in less time to get the grade you want—NOW. Take a pre-test for this chapter and receive a personalized study plan based on your results that will identify the topics you need to review and direct you to online resources to help you master those topics. Then take a post-test to help you determine the concepts you have mastered and what you will need to work on. If your textbook does not include an access code card, go to CengageBrain.com to gain access.

Visit www.cengagebrain.com to access your account and purchase materials.

VISUAL OVERVIEW Chapter 7 Thinking, Language, and Intelligence

MODULE 7.1 Thinking

"Never, ever, think outside the box."

© The New Yorker Collection 1998 Leo Cullum from cartoonbank.com. All Rights Reserved.

What Is Thinking?

- Thinking is the mental representation and manipulation of information
- We can represent information in the form of images, words, and concepts used to categorize objects and events
- Thinking takes many forms, including problem solving, decision making, and creativity

Examples of Problem-Solving Strategies

- **Heuristics**: Rules of thumb for solving problems and making decisions
- **Algorithms**: Step-by-step recipes for solving problems
- **Incubation Period**: Taking a pause to allow ideas to gel
- **Analogies**: This problem is similar to ______.

Mental Roadblocks to Problem Solving and Decision Making

- **Mental Sets**: Using what's worked before, but may not work now
- **Functional Fixedness**: Failing to see new uses for familiar objects
- **Confirmation Bias**: Filtering evidence to confirm prior beliefs
- **Representativeness Heuristic**: Basing decisions on a limited sample
- **Availability Heuristic**: Basing decisions on what most easily comes to mind
- **Framing**: Decisions based on how the problem is framed or posed

The Nine-Dot Problem

Processes in Creative Thought

- **Divergent Thinking**: Conceiving new ideas and uses for familiar objects
- **Metaphor and Analogy**: Using metaphor and analogy for creative expression or problem solving
- **Conceptual Combination**: Putting together two or more different concepts to create new ideas or applications
- **Conceptual Expansion**: Taking existing concepts and expanding them to new uses

MODULE 7.2 Language

Parts of Language

- **Phonemes**: Basic units of sound in a language
- **Morphemes**: Basic units of meaning in a language
- **Semantics**: Rules governing meaning of words
- **Syntax**: Rules of grammar for ordering words

Factors in Language Development

- **Biological Capacity for Speech**: The brain is prewired for speech
- **Experience with Human Speech**: Development of language depends on hearing human speech

MODULE 7.3 Intelligence

Defining Intelligence

- Thinking Rationally
- Acting Purposefully
- Dealing Effectively with Environmental Demands

Standardized Tests of Intelligence

- **Widely Used Tests**: Stanford-Binet Intelligence Scale, Wechsler Scales of Intelligence
- **Standards of Good Intelligence Tests**: Reliability, validity, and norming (standardization)

Theories of Intelligence

- **Spearman's "g:"** General ability
- **Thurstone's Primary Mental Abilities**: Seven primary abilities
- **Gardner's Multiple Intelligences**: Multiple forms of intelligence, not just one
- **Sternberg's Triarchic Theory**: Analytic intelligence, creative intelligence, practical intelligence

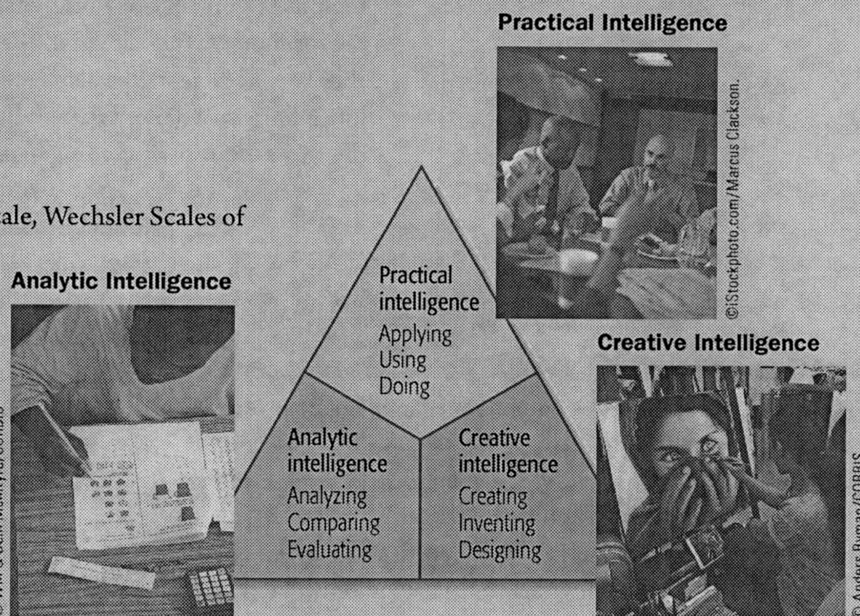

Sternberg's Triarchic Model of Intelligence

Extremes of Intelligence

- **Mental Retardation**: Low IQ and general delay in development of intellectual and social skills
- **Giftedness**: High IQ or special talents not measured by IQ tests

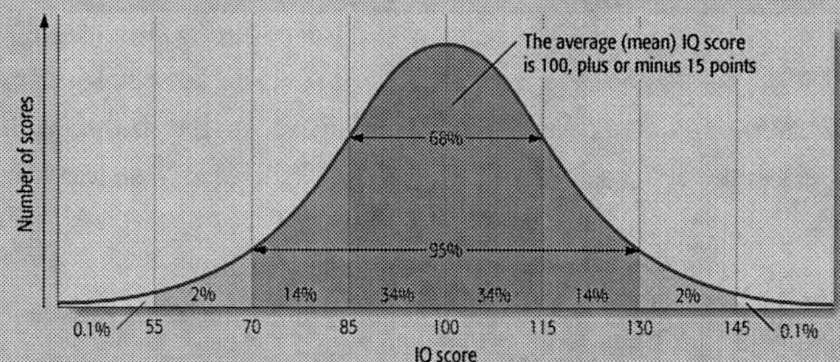

Normal Distribution of IQ Scores

8 Motivation and Emotion

The Woman Who Shows No Fear

SLICE OF LIFE Imagine what it would be like to be unable to experience fear—to be mildly amused when others at a 3D horror movie are jumping out of their seats or to remain calm even in the face of a threat to your life. A 44-year-old woman referred to in a medical journal as S.M. is a person who shows no fear (Feinstein et al., 2010; "The Fearless SM," 2010).

A team of researchers tried as they might to shake her up, exposing her to situations that would scare most people. They exposed her to snakes and spiders and even took her to one of the world's scariest haunted houses. They had her watch a series of horror movies. But across all these tests and measures, one thing remained constant: she showed no fear. She also recounted an experience in which she had been held-up at knife-point in a dark park, but didn't feel any fear. She did, however, experience a range of other emotions, including happiness and sadness.

The case study of S.M. illustrates the close connections between brain and behavior. The researchers who studied S.M. believe her fearlessness was due to the lack of an *amygdala*, a small structure in the brain's limbic system that plays a pivotal role in triggering fear. The amygdala in S.M.'s case had failed to develop because of a rare genetic condition.

Emotions are strong motivators of behavior. The word emotion shares a common Latin root, *movere* (meaning "to move") with the word motive. Both motives and emotions move us to act or to prepare for action. For example, hunger is a powerful motive that moves us toward finding and consuming food. Fear, perhaps our most basic emotion, motivates us to avoid threatening objects or situations, whereas love, the emotion that "makes the world go round," moves us toward approaching objects of our desire. Anger prompts us to respond aggressively to provocation. In this chapter we explore the motivating factors in our lives—our motives and our emotions.

We begin by considering sources of motivation that prompt our behavior and keep it going. We then focus on one of our most basic motives, hunger, and examine the problems of obesity and eating disorders. Finally, we explore human emotions, the felt experiences that infuse our lives with color.

DID YOU KNOW THAT...

- The founding father of American psychology believed there is a human instinct for cleanliness? (p. 289)
- People tend to eat more food when it is served in larger portion sizes or on larger plates? (p. 299)
- Among children, Ronald McDonald is the second most recognized personality figure, after Santa Claus? (p. 300)
- One in seven college women is embarrassed to buy a chocolate bar in a store? (p. 303)
- People in different cultures smile differently? (p. 307)
- Married people tend to be happier than single people? (p. 309)
- Money does not breed happiness? (p. 309)
- Practicing smiling can lift your mood? (p. 311)
- Responding without thinking can be a lifesaver in some situations? (p. 315)

Learning Objectives

By reading this chapter you will be able to . . .

1 **IDENTIFY** and **DESCRIBE** biological and psychological sources of motivation.

2. **DEFINE** cognitive dissonance and **EXPLAIN** how it can be reduced.

3. **IDENTIFY** and **DESCRIBE** the levels in Maslow's hierarchy of needs.

4. **EXPLAIN** how hunger and appetite are regulated.

5. **IDENTIFY** factors contributing to obesity.

6. **IDENTIFY** and **DESCRIBE** the types of eating disorders and **EXPLAIN** causal factors involved in these disorders.

7. **IDENTIFY** the basic components of emotions and the six basic emotional expressions.

8. **DESCRIBE** the roles of gender and cultural factors in emotions.

9. **EVALUATE** factors involved in human happiness.

10. **DESCRIBE** the three components of the triangular model of love and **APPLY** these components to different types of loving relationships based on these components.

11. **EXPLAIN** how the brain processes emotions.

12. **DESCRIBE** the major theories of emotions.

13. **DEFINE** emotional intelligence and **DESCRIBE** its features.

14. **APPLY** techniques of anger management to controlling anger.

© iStockphoto.com/Bob Thomas

Preview

MODULE 8.1

Motivation: The "Whys" of Behavior

- What is motivation?
- What is instinct theory?
- What is drive theory?
- How does arousal theory account for differences in motivational states?
- How does incentive theory differ from drive theory?
- What are psychosocial needs?
- What is cognitive dissonance theory?
- What is Maslow's hierarchy of needs?

motivation Factors that activate, direct, and sustain goal-directed behavior.

CONCEPT 8.1
Motivation refers to the "whys" of behavior—factors that activate, direct, and sustain goal-directed behavior.

motives Needs or wants that drive goal-directed behavior.

The term **motivation** refers to factors that *activate, direct,* and *sustain* goal-directed behavior. If, after a few hours of not eating, you get up from your chair and go to the kitchen to fix yourself a snack, we might infer that the *motive* for your behavior is hunger. The hunger motive activates your behavior (causing you to stand), directs it (moving you toward the kitchen), and sustains it (as you make yourself a snack and consume it) until you've achieved your goal (satisfying your hunger).

Motives are the "whys" of behavior—the needs or wants that drive behavior and explain why we do what we do. We don't actually observe a motive; rather, we infer that one exists based on the behavior we observe.

In this module, we focus on the biological and psychological sources of motivation and the various theories psychologists have constructed to explain motivated behavior. None of these theories offers a complete explanation of motivated behavior, but each contributes something to our understanding of the "whys" of behavior.

Biological Sources of Motivation

We need oxygen to breathe, food for energy, water to drink, and protection from the elements. These basic biological needs motivate much of our behavior. Biological needs are inborn. We don't learn to breathe or to become hungry or thirsty. Nonetheless, learning and experience influence how we satisfy our biological needs, especially our need for food. Eating tamales or mutton stew might satisfy our hunger, but our cultural backgrounds and learning experiences influence our choice of food and the ways in which we prepare and consume it.

Instincts: Behavior Programmed by Nature

instinctive behaviors Genetically programmed, innate patterns of response that are specific to members of a particular species.

instinct theory The belief that behavior is motivated by instinct.

Birds build nests, and salmon return upstream to their birthplaces to spawn. They do not acquire these behaviors through experience or by attending nest-building or spawning schools. These are **instinctive behaviors**—fixed, inborn patterns of response that are specific to members of a particular species. **Instinct theory** holds that behavior is motivated by instincts.

Does instinct theory explain the motives for human behavior? One theorist who thought so was Sigmund Freud, who believed that human behavior is motivated primarily by sexual and aggressive instincts (see Chapter 13). Another was William James (1890/1970), the father of American psychology, who compiled a list of 37 instincts that he believed could explain much of human behavior. His list included physical instincts, such as sucking, and mental instincts, such as curiosity, jealousy, and even cleanliness. Other early psychologists, notably William McDougall (1908), expanded on James's list. The list kept growing and growing, so much so that by the 1920s, it had ballooned to some 10,000 instincts covering a wide range of human behavior (Bernard, 1924).

The instinct theory of human motivation has long been out of favor. One reason for its decline is that the list of instincts simply grew too large to be useful. Another is that explaining behavior on the basis of instincts is merely a way of describing it, not explaining it (Gaulin & McBurney, 2001). For example, saying a person is lazy because of a laziness instinct or stingy because of a stinginess instinct doesn't really explain the person's behavior. It merely attaches a label to it. Perhaps most important, psychologists recognized that human behavior is much more variable and flexible than would be the case if it were determined by instinct. Moreover, instinct theory fails to account for the important roles of culture and learning in determining human behavior. Though instincts may account for some stereotypical behavior in other animals, most psychologists reject the view that instincts motivate complex human behavior.

CONCEPT 8.2
Instinct theorists believe that humans and other animals are motivated by instincts—fixed, inborn patterns of response that are specific to members of a particular species.

drive theory The belief that behavior is motivated by drives that arise from biological needs that demand satisfaction.

need A state of deprivation or deficiency.

drive A state of bodily tension, such as hunger or thirst, that arises from an unmet need.

drive reduction Satisfaction of a drive.

Needs and Drives: Maintaining a Steady Internal State

By the early 1950s, **drive theory** had replaced instinct theory as the major model of human motivation. Its foremost proponent, psychologist Clark Hull (1943, 1952), believed we have biological needs that demand satisfaction, such as the needs for food, water, and sleep. A **need** is a state of deprivation or deficiency. A **drive** is a state of bodily tension, such as hunger or thirst, arising from an unmet need. The satisfaction of a drive is called **drive reduction**.

CONCEPT 8.3
Drive theorists maintain that we are motivated by drives that arise from biological needs that demand satisfaction.

Drive theory is based on the principles of *homeostasis*, the tendency of the body to maintain a steady internal state (see Chapter 2). Homeostatic mechanisms in the body monitor temperature, oxygen, and blood sugar, and maintain them at steady levels. According to drive theory, whenever homeostasis is disturbed, drives activate the behavior needed to restore a steady balance. For example, when our blood sugar level drops because we haven't eaten in a while, we become hungry. Hunger is the drive that motivates us to seek nourishment, which restores homeostasis. Although drive theory focuses on biological needs, some needs, such as the needs for comfort and safety, have a psychological basis.

Though needs and drives are related, they are distinct from each other. We may have a bodily need for a certain vitamin but not become aware of it until we develop a vitamin deficiency disorder. In other words, the need may exist in the absence of a corresponding drive. Moreover, the strength of a need and the drive to satisfy it may differ. People who fast for religious or other reasons may find they are less hungry on the second or third day of a fast than on the first, even though their need for food is even greater.

© Jacek Chabraszewski, 2009/Shutterstock.com

primary drives Innate drives, such as hunger, thirst, and sexual desire, that arise from basic biological needs.

secondary drives Drives that are learned or acquired through experience, such as the drive to achieve monetary wealth.

CONCEPT 8.4
Stimulus motives prod organisms to explore their environments and manipulate objects.

stimulus motives Internal states that prompt inquisitive, stimulation-seeking, and exploratory behavior.

CONCEPT 8.5
Arousal theory postulates a biologically based need to maintain stimulation at an optimal level.

→ Concept Link
People with antisocial personalities may become quickly bored with routine activities because of a biological predisposition that leads them to crave higher levels of stimulation to maintain their optimum level of arousal. See Module 15.6.

arousal theory The belief that whenever the level of stimulation dips below an organism's optimal level, the organism seeks ways of increasing it.

Unlike instinct theory, drive theory posits an important role for learning, especially operant conditioning (discussed in Chapter 5). We learn responses (such as ordering a pizza when we're hungry) that are reinforced by drive reduction. A behavior that results in drive reduction is more likely to be repeated the next time the need arises. Drives may also be acquired through experience. Biological drives, such as hunger, thirst, and sexual desire, are called **primary drives** because they are considered inborn; drives that are the result of experience are called **secondary drives**. For example, a drive to achieve monetary wealth is not something we are born with; we acquire it as a secondary drive because we learn that money can be used to satisfy many primary and other secondary drives.

Optimal Level of Arousal: What's Optimal for You?

Drive theory focuses on drives that satisfy survival needs, such as needs for food and water. But classic experiments by psychologist Harry Harlow and his colleagues challenged the notion that all drives satisfy basic survival needs. When they placed a mechanical puzzle in a monkey's cage, they found that the monkey began manipulating it and taking it apart, even though the animal didn't receive any food or other obvious reinforcement for its efforts (Harlow, Harlow, & Meyer, 1950). Human babies, too, manipulate objects placed before them. They shake rattles, turn knobs, push buttons on activity toys, and mouth new objects, even though none of these behaviors is connected with satisfaction of their basic survival needs.

The work of Harlow and others suggests that humans and many other animals may have innate, biologically based needs for exploration and activity. These needs, which prod organisms to explore their environments and manipulate objects—especially unusual or novel objects—are called **stimulus motives**. Stimulus motives don't disappear as we get older. Adults seek to touch and manipulate interesting objects, as attested to by the many grown-ups who try their hand at the latest gizmos displayed at stores like Brookstone.

Other basic drives like hunger motivate behaviors that lead to reduced states of bodily arousal. For example, when we are hungry, the brain creates a state of heightened arousal that lasts until we satisfy our hunger; after eating, we may feel tranquil or sleepy. However, stimulus motives instigate behaviors that lead to increased, not decreased, arousal. In other words, even when our basic needs for food and water are met, we are motivated to seek out stimulation that heightens our level of arousal.

© Germanskydiver/Shutterstock.com

Are you motivated to seek adventure and excitement? If so, you may be a sensation-seeker and were born with a taste for thrills.

Stimulus motives represent a biologically based need, according to some theorists, to maintain an *optimal* level of arousal (Hebb, 1955; Zuckerman, 1980). **Arousal theory** holds that whenever the level of stimulation dips below an organism's optimal level, the organism seeks ways of increasing it. When stimulation exceeds an optimal level, the organism seeks ways of toning it down.

The optimal level of arousal varies from person to person. Some people require a steady diet of highly stimulating activities, such as mountain climbing, snowboarding, bungee jumping, or parasailing. Others are satisfied to spend quiet evenings at home, curled up with a good book or relaxing by watching TV.

People with a high need for arousal see life as an adventure. To maintain their optimal level of stimulation, they seek exciting experiences and thrills. Psychologist Marvin Zuckerman

TRY THIS OUT Are You a Sensation Seeker?

Do you pursue thrills and adventure? Or do you prefer quiet evenings at home? To evaluate whether you fit the profile of a sensation seeker, circle the number on each line that best describes you.

Interpreting your responses. Responses above 5 indicate a high level of sensation seeking; those 5 or below indicate a low level. On which side of the continuum do your responses lie? Draw a line connecting your responses. The further to the right the line falls, the stronger your personality fits the profile of a sensation seeker.

Prefer a job in one location	1	2	3	4	5	6	7	8	9	10	Prefer a job with lots of travel
Prefer staying out of the cold	1	2	3	4	5	6	7	8	9	10	Enjoy a brisk walk on a cold day
Prefer being with familiar people	1	2	3	4	5	6	7	8	9	10	Prefer meeting new people
Like to play it safe	1	2	3	4	5	6	7	8	9	10	Like living "on the edge"
Would prefer not to try hypnosis	1	2	3	4	5	6	7	8	9	10	Would like to try hypnosis
Would prefer not to try parachute jumping	1	2	3	4	5	6	7	8	9	10	Would like to try parachute jumping
Prefer quiet evenings at home	1	2	3	4	5	6	7	8	9	10	Prefer going out dancing at night
Prefer a safe and secure life	1	2	3	4	5	6	7	8	9	10	Prefer experiencing as much as possible
Prefer calm and controlled people	1	2	3	4	5	6	7	8	9	10	Prefer people who are a bit wild
Like to sleep in a comfortable room with a good bed	1	2	3	4	5	6	7	8	9	10	Enjoy camping out
Prefer avoiding risky activities	1	2	3	4	5	6	7	8	9	10	Like to do things that are a little dangerous

Source: Adapted from Zuckerman, 1980.

(2004) calls such people *sensation seekers.* Sensation seekers tend to get bored easily and may have difficulty restraining their impulses. They may limit their sensation seeking to reasonably safe activities, but the desire for stimulation leads some to engage in risky behaviors, or develop problems with alcohol or drugs, or engage in illegal activities (Day-Cameron et al., 2009; Joseph et al., 2009; McAdams & Donnellan, 2008). It's no surprise that surfers in a recent study scored higher on sensation seeking, on the average, than did golfers (Diehm & Armatas, 2004). Sensation seeking appears to have a strong genetic component—the taste for thrills may be something we are born with (Derringer et al., 2010).

Psychological Sources of Motivation

If motivation were simply a matter of maintaining homeostasis in our bodies, we would rest quietly until prompted again by hunger, thirst, or some other biological drive. But we don't sit idly by when our bellies are full and our other biological needs are met. We are also motivated by psychological needs, such as the need for friendship or achievement. We perceive certain goals as desirable or rewarding even though attaining them will not satisfy any biological needs. Clearly, such motivated behaviors are best addressed by considering the role of such psychological factors as incentives, cognitive dissonance, and psychosocial needs.

Incentives: The "Pull" Side of Motivation

incentive theory The belief that our attraction to particular goals or objects motivates much of our behavior.

incentives Rewards or other stimuli that motivate us to act.

According to **incentive theory**, our attraction to particular goals or objects motivates much of our behavior. **Incentives** are rewards or other stimuli that motivate us to act. The attraction, or "pull," exerted by an incentive stems from our perception that it can satisfy a need or is in itself desirable.

CONCEPT 8.6

Incentives motivate us by exerting a pull on our behavior; their strength varies in relation to the value we place on them.

In contrast to drive theory, which explains how unmet biological needs push us in the direction of satisfying them, incentive theory holds that incentives motivate us by pulling us toward them. Incentive theory thus focuses on the lure, or "pull," of incentives in motivating behavior, rather than the "push" of internal need states or drives. You may crave a scrumptious-looking dessert even though you've just eaten a full meal and no longer feel "pushed" by the drive of hunger. You may feel drawn to buy the latest fashions or technological gizmos even though obtaining these objects will not satisfy any biological need.

incentive value The strength of the "pull" of a goal or reward.

The strength of the "pull" that a goal or reward exerts on our behavior is its **incentive value**. Incentive values are influenced by many factors, including an individual's learning experiences and expectancies. We place more value on a goal if we have learned from past experience to associate it with pleasure and expect it will be rewarding when we obtain it. Many employers seek to boost employee productivity by offering them incentives such as bonuses, merit pay increases, stock options, and awards. Marketers manipulate the incentive value of the products they want us to buy. They try to persuade us that to be cool, healthy, sexy, or successful, we need to use their products.

Cultural influences play a large part in determining incentive values. Some cultures place great value on individual achievement and accumulation of wealth. Others place a premium on meeting obligations to one's family, religious group, employer, or community.

What incentives motivate your behavior—a college diploma, wealth, the man or woman of your dreams, status, or respect of your family or community? Which incentives have the strongest "pull" on your behavior?

Cognitive Dissonance: Maintaining Consistency Between Attitudes and Behaviors

Psychologists recognize that people are motivated to maintain consistency between their attitudes and their behavior. In a classic study, Leon Festinger and J. Merrill Carlsmith (1959) had two groups of college students complete an extremely boring task. They then paid one group $1 and the other group $20 to persuade other students that the task was exciting and interesting. Afterward, the subjects were asked to express their attitude toward the task—how much they liked it or disliked it. Curiously, those who received the lower payment expressed greater enthusiasm for the task than those in the higher-paid group. Why?

cognitive dissonance A state of internal tension brought about by conflicting attitudes and behavior.

Both groups had engaged in behavior (telling others the task was exciting) that was presumably incompatible with their underlying attitude (disliking the task because it was boring). Festinger and Carlsmith theorized that when attitudes are inconsistent with behavior, people are likely to experience an unpleasant state of tension called **cognitive dissonance**. They reasoned that this uncomfortable state motivates efforts to bring attitudes and behavior in line with each other. Subjects in the higher-paid group apparently were able to resolve their dissonance by telling themselves they had been paid handsomely for telling an untruth. Those in the lower-paid group could not use this justification, so they presumably had to resolve their dissonance by changing how they felt about the task.

cognitive dissonance theory The belief that people are motivated to resolve discrepancies between their behavior and their attitudes or beliefs.

Cognitive dissonance theory holds that people are motivated to resolve discrepancies between their behavior and their attitudes or beliefs by making them

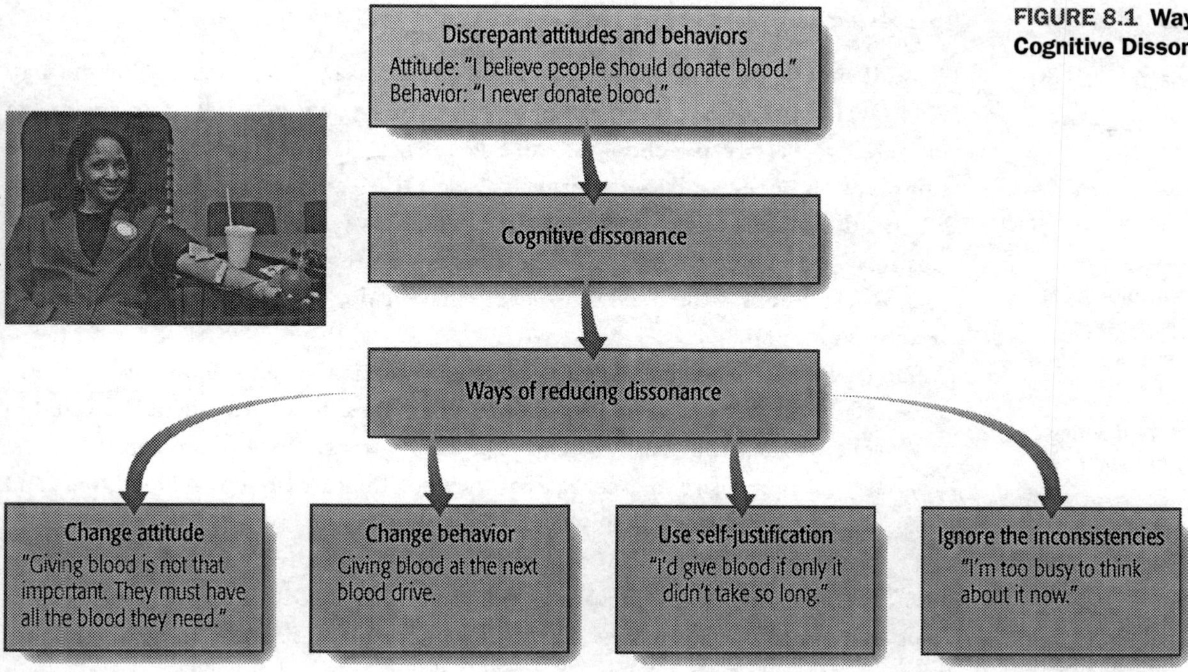

© iStockphoto.com/David H. Lewis

FIGURE 8.1 Ways of Reducing Cognitive Dissonance

more compatible. There are several ways to reduce cognitive dissonance (Matz & Wood, 2005). People can change their behavior to fit their attitudes or beliefs, change their attitudes or beliefs to fit their behavior, attempt to explain away any inconsistencies between their behavior and their attitudes or beliefs, or simply ignore any discrepancies. For example, smokers who believe that smoking causes cancer but continue to smoke may reduce cognitive dissonance by altering their behavior (quitting smoking), altering their belief (adopting the belief that smoking isn't really all that harmful), or using a form of rationalization to explain away the inconsistency ("Cancer doesn't run in my family"). Yet the most common way to reduce dissonance may be to ignore or overlook inconsistencies between behavior and attitudes for the time being ("I'll worry about my smoking when I get older") or to engage in distracting tasks that take one's mind off of the inconsistencies (Gosling, Denizeau, & Oberlé, 2006). ■ Figure 8.1 illustrates some ways of reducing cognitive dissonance.

Another way of reducing cognitive dissonance is **effort justification**, the tendency to justify the effort expended in attaining a difficult goal (Zentall, 2010). Thus, we tend to place greater value on rewards that are more difficult to obtain. The harder we have to work for a particular goal or object, the more highly we tend to value it as a way of justifying our effort. In other words, if we have to work more to get an A in a harder course than the same grade in an easier course, we tend to justify the greater effort by putting more value on the hard-earned A.

By and large, research evidence supports cognitive dissonance theory. Inconsistencies between attitudes and behavior tend to create emotional distress, whereas changing beliefs or attitudes to bring them more in line with each other reduces or eliminates this discomfort (Aronson, Wilson, & Akert, 2004; Jones, 1998). As we'll see in Chapter 14, salespersons, advertisers, fundraisers, and others who try to influence us often use strategies that take advantage of our need for consistency in behavior and belief.

CONCEPT 8.7

Cognitive dissonance theory holds that people are motivated to reconcile discrepancies between their behavior and their cognitions.

effort justification The tendency to place greater value on goals that are difficult to achieve in order to justify the effort expended in attaining them.

© Spencer Grant/Photo Edit

Can you think of examples in which your behavior was inconsistent with your deeply held beliefs or attitudes? Did you experience cognitive dissonance when you became aware of the inconsistency? Were you motivated to reconcile these differences? Or did you simply ignore them?

psychosocial needs Needs that reflect interpersonal aspects of motivation, such as the need for friendship or achievement.

need for achievement The need to excel in one's endeavors.

CONCEPT 8.8

Many psychologists believe we are motivated to satisfy not only biological needs, but also psychosocial needs, such as the need for achievement.

Psychosocial Needs

The fulfillment of basic biological needs is necessary for survival, but human beings seek more out of life than mere survival. We are social creatures who are motivated to satisfy **psychosocial needs** (also called *interpersonal needs*). One example is the need to be with other people (also called the *need for affiliation*). This need motivates us to seek out social contacts with others, form social relationships, and belong to groups. Here we focus on the most widely studied of the psychosocial needs—the need to excel at what we do, which is known as the **need for achievement.**

Some people strive relentlessly to get ahead, to earn vast sums of money, to invent, to create—in short, to achieve. People with a high need for achievement are found in many walks of life, from business and professional sports to academia and the arts. They have a strong desire to excel at what they do. They are driven and ambitious and take pride in accomplishing their goals.

extrinsic motivation Motivation reflecting a desire for external rewards, such as wealth or the respect of others.

intrinsic motivation Motivation reflecting a desire for internal gratification, such as the self-satisfaction derived from accomplishing a particular goal.

achievement motivation The motive or desire to achieve success.

avoidance motivation The motive or desire to avoid failure.

People with a high need for achievement set challenging but realistic goals for themselves, according to Harvard psychologist David McClelland (1958, 1985). Goals that are too easily achieved are of no interest to them, nor are goals that are patently unobtainable. Such people may not always succeed, but they take failure in stride and keep pushing ahead. By contrast, people with a low need for achievement are motivated by a desire to avoid failure. They set goals either so low that anyone can achieve them or so unrealistically high that no one can achieve them. If the bar is set too high, who can blame them if they fail? When they meet with failure, they are more likely to quit than to persevere.

The need for achievement is driven by *extrinsic motivation, intrinsic motivation*, or both (Ryan & Deci, 2000; Story et al., 2009). **Extrinsic motivation** reflects a desire for external rewards, such as money or the respect of one's peers or family. **Intrinsic motivation** reflects a desire for internal gratification, such as the self-satisfaction or pleasure derived from accomplishing a particular goal or performing a certain task. In other words, extrinsic motivation is a "means to an end," whereas intrinsic motivation is an "end in itself" (Pittman, 1998).

© Jeff Greenberg/Photo Edit

How strong is your need for achievement—your need not just to succeed, but to excel?

In achievement situations, we may be pulled in opposite directions by two kinds of motives: **achievement motivation** (the desire to achieve success) and **avoidance motivation** (the desire to avoid failure). Achievement motivation leads us to undertake challenges that run the risk of failure but that may also lead to success. Avoidance motivation leads us to avoid taking chances that could result in failure; it prompts us to stick with the sure and safe path. Although avoidance motivation may reduce the chance of failure, it also reduces the likelihood of success. In one study, students with a lower level of avoidance motivation did better in their courses and showed higher levels of emotional well-being than those with a higher level of avoidance motivation (Elliot & Sheldon, 1997).

Achievement motivation develops early in life and is strongly influenced by parents. Children who develop high needs for achievement typically have parents who encourage independence and trying difficult tasks. The parents reward them for persistence at difficult tasks with praise and other reinforcements and encourage them to attempt even more challenging tasks (Dweck, 1997).

The Hierarchy of Needs: Ordering Needs from the Basement to the Attic of Human Experience

We have seen that both biological and psychological needs play important roles in human motivation. But how do these needs relate to each other? We now consider a model that bridges both sources of motivation—the **hierarchy of needs** developed by humanistic psychologist Abraham Maslow (1943, 1970) (see ■ Figure 8.2).

Maslow's hierarchy of needs consists of five levels: (1) *physiological needs*, such as hunger and thirst; (2) *safety needs*, such as the need for secure housing; (3) *love and belongingness needs*, such as the need for intimate relationships; (4) *esteem needs*, such as the need for the respect of one's peers; and (5) *the need for self-actualization*, which motivates people to fulfill their unique potentials and become all they are capable of being. In Maslow's view, our needs are ordered in such a way that we are motivated to meet basic needs before moving upward in the hierarchy. In other words, once we fill our bellies, we strive to meet higher-order needs, such as our needs for security, love, achievement, and **self-actualization.**

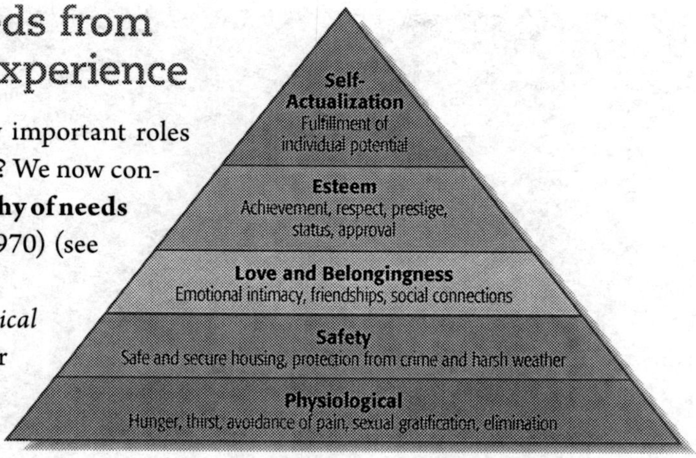

FIGURE 8.2 Maslow's Hierarchy of Needs

hierarchy of needs Maslow's concept that there is an order to human needs, which starts with basic biological needs and progresses to self-actualization.

self-actualization The motive that drives individuals to express their unique capabilities and fulfill their potentials.

Since no two people are perfectly alike, the drive for self-actualization leads people in different directions (Kenrick et al., 2010). For some, self-actualization may mean creating works of art; for others, striving on the playing field, in the classroom, or in the corporate setting. Not all of us climb to the top of the hierarchy; we don't all achieve self-actualization.

Maslow's hierarchical model of needs has intuitive appeal. We generally seek satisfaction of basic needs for food, drink, and shelter before concerning ourselves with psychologically based needs like belongingness. However, our needs may not be ordered in as fixed a manner as Maslow's hierarchy suggests. An artist might go for days with little if any nourishment in order to complete a new work. People may forgo seeking satisfaction of their need for intimate relationships to focus their energies on seeking status or prestige in their careers. Maslow might counter that eventually the emptiness of their emotional lives would motivate them to fill the gap.

CONCEPT 8.9

Maslow conceptualized human needs in the form of a hierarchy that ranges from biological needs at the base to the need for self-actualization at the top.

→ Concept Link

Maslow was a humanistic theorist who believed that the distinctly human drive toward self-actualization shapes our personality as well as our behavior. See Module 13.4.

Another problem with Maslow's model is that the same behavior may reflect multiple needs. Perhaps you are attending college to satisfy physiological and safety needs (to prepare for a career so that you can earn money to live comfortably and securely), love and belongingness needs (to form friendships and social ties), esteem needs (to achieve status or approval), and self-actualization needs (to fulfill your intellectual or creative potential). Despite its limitations, Maslow's model leads us to recognize that human behavior is motivated by higher pursuits as well as satisfaction of basic needs.

Maslow did not believe the need hierarchy captures all of human striving. Later in his career, he proposed other needs that motivate human behavior, including *cognitive needs* (needs to know, understand, and explore), *aesthetic needs* (needs for beauty, symmetry, and order), and *self-transcendence* (needs to connect to something beyond the self and help others realize their own potential) (Maslow, 1969, 1971, 1987). Whereas self-actualization is directed toward fulfilling one's own potential, self-transcendence represents a higher level need

What do these two people have in common? Maslow identified a number of historical figures, including Albert Einstein and Eleanor Roosevelt, whom he believed showed qualities of self-actualization. However, you needn't be a notable historical figure to become a self-actualizer. Maslow believed we all have the ability to follow our unique paths toward achieving self-actualization.

CONCEPT CHART 8.1 Sources of Motivation

© Dainis/Shutterstock.com

© photogl, 2009/Shutterstock.com

	Source	Description
Biological Sources	Instincts	Instincts are fixed, inborn response patterns that are specific to members of a particular species.
Biological Sources	Needs and drives	Unmet needs create internal drive states, which motivate behavior that leads to drive reduction.
Biological Sources	Stimulus motives and optimal level of arousal	Stimulus motives arise from biologically based needs to be curious and active and to explore the environment. Arousal theory holds that we are motivated to maintain a level of stimulation that is optimal for us.
Psychological Sources	Incentives	The value we place on goals or objects creates a lure, or "pull," to obtain them.
Psychological Sources	Cognitive dissonance	Inconsistency in attitudes and behavior induces cognitive dissonance, an unpleasant emotional state that motivates efforts to reconcile the inconsistency.
Psychological Sources	Psychosocial needs	These psychologically-based needs include needs for achievement and social relationships.

Note: According to Maslow, human needs are organized within a hierarchy that ranges from basic biological needs at the base to the need for self-actualization at the pinnacle.

expressed through commitment to ideals, purposes, or causes that go beyond the self (Koltko-Rivera, 2006). Although Maslow believed there is an interrelationship between his original needs and these additional needs, he did not specify how both sets of needs should be combined (Maslow, 1969; Ward & Lasen, 2009).

Before going forward, you may wish to review the sources of motivation outlined in Concept Chart 8.1.

8.1 MODULE REVIEW Motivation: The "Whys" of Behavior

Recite It

What is motivation?

➢ Motivation consists of the factors or internal processes that activate, direct, and sustain behavior toward the satisfaction of a need or the attainment of a goal.

What is instinct theory?

➢ Instinct theory proposes that behavior is motivated by genetically programmed, species-specific, fixed patterns of responses called instincts. Though this model may have value in explaining some forms of animal behavior, human behavior is too complex to be explained by instincts.

What is drive theory?

➢ Drive theory asserts that animals are driven to satisfy unmet biological needs, such as hunger and thirst. The theory is limited, in part because it fails to account for motives involving the desire to increase states of arousal.

How does arousal theory account for differences in motivational states?

➢ According to arousal theory, the optimal level of arousal varies from person to person. To maintain arousal at an optimal level, some people seek exciting, even potentially dangerous, activities, while others seek more tranquil ones.

How does incentive theory differ from drive theory?

➢ Incentive theory focuses on the "pull," or lure, of goals or objects that we perceive as attractive, whereas drive theory focuses on the "push" of unmet biological needs.

What is cognitive dissonance theory?

➢ Cognitive dissonance theory holds that inconsistencies between our behavior and our attitudes, beliefs, or perceptions produce a state of psychological tension (dissonance) that motivates efforts to reconcile these inconsistencies.

What are psychosocial needs?

- Psychosocial needs are distinctly human needs that are based on psychological rather than biological factors. They include the need for social relationships and the need for achievement.
- People with a high need for achievement are hard-driving and ambitious. They set challenging but realistic goals for themselves. They accomplish more than people with similar abilities and opportunities but a lower need for achievement.

What is Maslow's hierarchy of needs?

- Maslow believed we are motivated to meet basic biological needs, such as hunger and thirst, before fulfilling our psychological needs. His hierarchy has five levels, ranging from physiological needs at the base to self-actualization at the top.

Recall It

1. Factors that activate, direct, and sustain goal-directed behavior are referred to as ____________.
2. Match the terms on the left with the definitions on the right:

i. primary drive	**a.** a drive acquired through experience
ii. secondary drive	**b.** the tendency to maintain a steady internal state
iii. need	**c.** a state of deprivation or deficiency
iv. homeostasis	**d.** an innate biological drive

3. Sources of motivation that prompt us to explore our environment and manipulate objects, especially novel or unusual objects, are called ______.
4. The strength of the "pull" that a goal or reward exerts on our behavior is called its ______.
5. Discrepancies between behavior and attitudes may produce an unpleasant state of tension called ______.
6. At the top of Maslow's hierarchy of needs is the need that motivates people to fulfill their unique potentials and become all they are capable of being. This is known as the need for
   a. esteem.
   b. achievement.
   c. love and belongingness.
   d. self-actualization.

Think About It

- Do you believe that human behavior is motivated by instinct? Why or why not?
- Are you a self-actualizer? Upon what evidence do you base your judgment? What steps could you take to become a self-actualizer?

Hunger and Eating

MODULE 8.2

- What makes us hungry?
- What causes obesity?
- What is anorexia nervosa?
- What is bulimia nervosa?
- What are the causes of eating disorders?

Hunger, one of the most basic drives and one of the most difficult to ignore, motivates us to eat. But what makes us hungry? If your stomach is growling at this moment, you are unlikely to pay close attention to what you are reading. But there's a lot more to hunger than a grumbling stomach.

THE BRAIN LOVES A PUZZLE

As you read ahead, use the information in the text to solve the following puzzle:

Recent evidence suggests that obesity may be catching. How is that possible?

What Makes Us Hungry?

It may seem that pangs of hunger arise from the grumblings of an empty stomach, but it is the brain, not the stomach, that controls hunger. It works like this: When we haven't eaten for a while, our blood sugar levels drop. When this happens, fat is released from *fat cells*—body cells that store fat—to provide fuel that cells use until we are able to eat again. The *hypothalamus*, a small structure in the forebrain that helps regulate hunger and many other bodily processes (discussed in Chapter 2), detects these changes and triggers a cascading series of events, leading to feelings of hunger that motivate eating

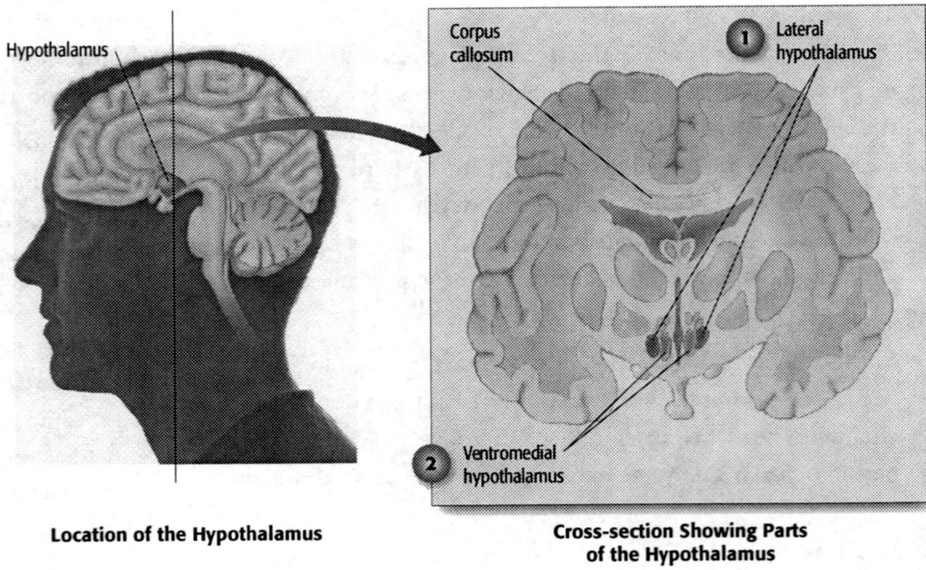

© iStockphoto.com/Kenneth C. Zirkel

FIGURE 8.3 Parts of the Hypothalamus Involved in Hunger and Eating
The hypothalamus plays a key role in regulating hunger and eating behavior. 1 The lateral hypothalamus stimulates appetite and eating behavior. 2 The ventromedial hypothalamus signals satiety and works like an off switch for eating.

CONCEPT 8.10
The hypothalamus detects decreases in blood sugar levels and depletion of fat from fat cells, which leads to the feelings of hunger that motivate eating.

lateral hypothalamus A part of the hypothalamus involved in initiating, or "turning on," eating.

ventromedial hypothalamus A part of the hypothalamus involved in regulating feelings of satiety.

behaviors. Eating restores an internally balanced state, or homeostasis, by bringing blood sugar levels back into balance and replenishing fat cells.

Different parts of the hypothalamus play different roles in regulating hunger and eating (see ■ Figure 8.3). Stimulating the **lateral hypothalamus** causes a laboratory animal to start eating even if it has just consumed a full meal. If the lateral hypothalamus is surgically destroyed, the animal will stop eating and eventually starve to death. Thus, we know that the lateral hypothalamus is involved in initiating, or "turning on," eating.

Another part of the hypothalamus, the **ventromedial hypothalamus**, acts as an off switch that signals when it is time to stop eating. When this area is destroyed, animals will overeat and eventually become severely obese.

A mixture of brain chemicals, including neurotransmitters and hormones, are involved in regulating hunger and appetite (Perello et al., 2009). One of these chemicals, the neurotransmitter *neuropeptide Y* (NPY), works on the hypothalamus to stimulate appetite and eating. When we haven't eaten in a while, the brain releases more NPY. The stomach also plays a role: When it is empty, it releases the hunger-inducing hormone *grhelin*, which sends hunger signals to the brain (Engel et al., 2008). Another hormone, *leptin* (from the Greek word *leptos*, meaning "thin"), is released by fat cells in the body and acts to curb hunger when we've had enough to eat (Baicy et al., 2007). One way leptin works is by reducing the brain's production of NPY. Other brain chemicals are also involved in curbing appetite and eating behavior when we've had enough to eat (Blüher & Mantzoros, 2009).

Feelings of pleasure we experience from eating a satisfying meal are regulated by the neurotransmitters dopamine and endorphins, which stimulate the brain's reward or pleasure circuits. Another neurotransmitter, serotonin, is involved in regulating the feeling of satiety when we've had enough to eat.

Why It Matters

The full story of the biological underpinnings of hunger and appetite is still being written. By learning more about the brain chemicals involved in hunger and appetite, and the brain structures they act upon, we may be able to develop better ways of helping people with problems of overweight and obesity. For example, research along these lines may lead to the development of effective antiobesity drugs that work directly on brain mechanisms that control hunger and appetite.

CONCEPT 8.11
Neurotransmitters and hormones play important roles in regulating appetite.

Obesity: A National Epidemic

Many of us consume more calories in food than we burn in maintaining bodily processes and engaging in physical activity. An imbalance between calories consumed ("energy in") and calories burned ("energy out") leads to the accumulation of body weight, which over time can lead to obesity.

More Americans are overweight than ever before. About two-thirds of U.S. adults today are overweight, and about one in three are obese (CDC, 2010b; Flegal et al., 2010) (see ■ Figure 8.4). About one in seven adults in the United States are severely obese (Ryan & Kushner, 2010). The obesity epidemic is worldwide, as global obesity rates have doubled since 1980 (Danaei et al., 2011; Farzadfar et al., 2011; Finucane et al., 2011).

Why should it matter if we weigh too much? It matters because obesity is a major health risk factor for many serious and life-threatening health problems, including cardiovascular disease (heart and artery disease), respiratory illnesses, diabetes, gallbladder disease, and some types of cancer (e.g., CDC, 2009; Snowden, 2009; Yan et al., 2006). Not surprisingly, being overweight or obese is associated with an increased risk of premature death (Berrington de Gonzalez et al., 2010). All told, obesity accounts for more than 100,000 excess deaths annually in the United States and shaves some six to seven years off the average person's life expectancy (Flegal et al., 2005; Fontaine et al., 2003).

Health experts fear that obesity may cut the life expectancy of today's children by as much as two to five years as compared to their parents' generation (Olshansky et al., 2005). People who are overweight but not obese also face an increased risk of premature death (Jee et al., 2006; NCI, 2006).

Why are problems of overweight and obesity on the rise? Health experts cite two main factors: too many calories consumed and too little exercise. Many of us have become "couch potatoes" and "cyberslugs" who sit around too much, exercise too little, and eat way too much high-fat, high-calorie food.

Portion sizes in restaurants are also up—way up. Portion size is telling. In a recent study, investigators found that people tended to select more food, as measured by weight, when food was offered in a larger portion or unit size or on larger plates (Geier, Rozin, & Doros, 2006). Another factor working against winning the battle of the bulge is the increasing dependence on the automobile rather than foot power to get from place to place, especially for those of us living in sprawling suburban areas.

Are you obese? Scientists use a yardstick called the **body mass index (BMI)** (see *Try This Out*). The BMI takes height into account in determining whether body weight falls within a healthy or obese range. According to the standards of the National Institutes of Health, people with a BMI of 30 or more are classified as obese. Those with a BMI of 25 to 29.9 are considered overweight.

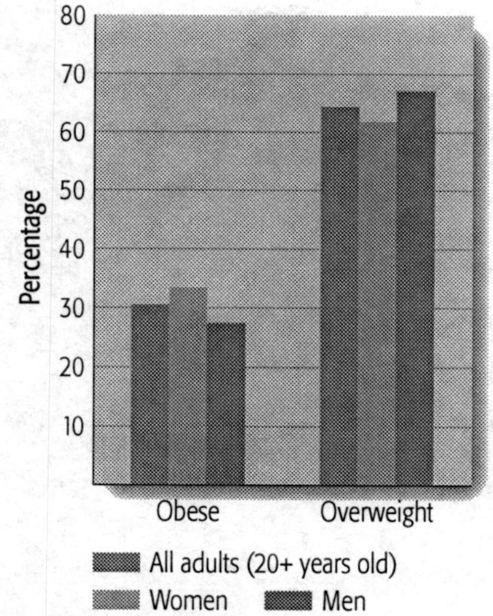

FIGURE 8.4 America's Vast Waistland
Nearly two-thirds of American adults are overweight, and nearly one in three is obese. What are the health risks associated with excess weight?
Source: WIN Weight Control Information Network, National Institute of Diabetes and Digestive and Kidney Diseases, National Institutes of Health.

body mass index (BMI) A standard measure of obesity based on body weight adjusted for height.

Causes of Obesity

Obesity results from taking in more food energy in the form of calories consumed ("energy in") than energy expended ("energy out") in meeting the body's needs (Levine et al., 2005) (see ■ Figure 8.5). Excess calories are converted into body fat, adding both weight and girth. But what leads to an imbalance between calories consumed and calories expended?

Genetics is one of the many factors that contributes to obesity (Loos et al., 2008). There is no one "obesity gene," but rather many genes that serve to predispose people to more easily gain weight (Freedman, 2011). Body weight is influenced by the person's *basal metabolic rate* (also called *basal metabolism*), the rate at which the body burns calories

FIGURE 8.5 Body Weight is a Balancing Act
Body weight is determined by the balance between calories consumed in food and calories expended by the body in meeting its needs for energy. Excess calories are converted into body fat.
Source: Physical Activity and Weight Control, National Institutes of Diabetes and Digestive and Kidney Diseases (NIDDK).

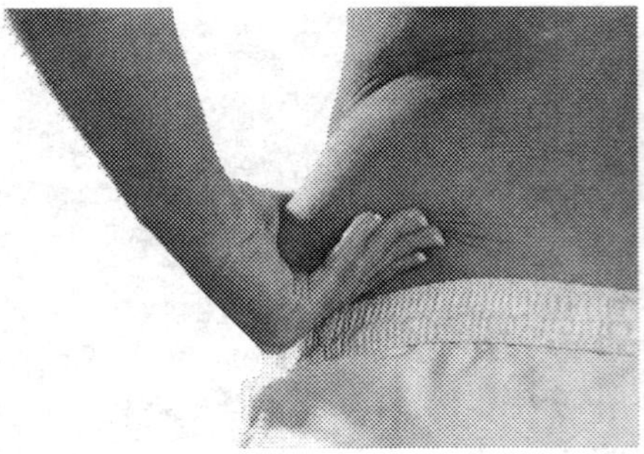
© iStockphoto.com/Steven Frame

while at rest. The slower the body's metabolic rate, the more likely the person is to gain weight easily. Genetics may explain why some people have slower metabolic rates than others.

According to **set point theory**, the brain regulates body weight around a genetically predetermined level or "set point." The theory proposes that when we gain or lose weight, the brain adjusts the basal metabolic rate to keep our weight around a set point (Major et al., 2007). If we lose weight, the brain slows the body's metabolic rate, and as this rate slows, the body conserves stores of fat. This may explain why dieters often find it hard to continue losing more weight or even maintain the weight they've lost. The body's ability to adjust its metabolic rate downward when caloric intake falls off may be a bane to many dieters today, but it may have helped ancestral humans survive times of famine.

set point theory The belief that brain mechanisms regulate body weight around a genetically predetermined "set point."

The number of fat cells in one's body is another factor in obesity. Obese people typically have far more fat cells than do people of normal weight. Severely obese people may have 200 billion or more fat cells, as compared with the 25 billion or 30 billion fat cells in normal-weight people. When we haven't eaten in a while, the body draws stored energy in the form of fat from its fat cells. The depletion of fat cells is an important trigger for hunger, which in turn motivates eating to restore the balance of stored fat. Because obese people typically have a great many more fat cells than normal-weight individuals, they may feel hungry sooner after eating than do normal-weight people. Consequently, they may be more strongly motivated to consume excess quantities of food. Unfortunately, we don't shed fat cells even when we lose weight (Hopkin, 2008).

Behavioral factors also play a role in obesity, such as eating habits—eating too fast, eating larger portions, and eating until feeling stuffed (Maruyama et al., 2008). Environmental factors also contribute to obesity. We live in a food-saturated environment in which we are constantly bombarded by food cues—TV commercials showing tempting foods, aromas permeating the air as we walk by the bakery, and on and on. Consider that, among children, Ronald McDonald is the second most widely recognized figure, after Santa Claus (Parloff, 2003). Laboratory research shows that exposure to food advertisements increases food consumption in both children and adults (J. L. Harris, Bargh, & Brownell, 2009).

TRY THIS OUT
What's Your BMI?

The BMI (body mass index) is the most widely used measure of overweight and obesity. Your BMI is given by the formula, BMI = kg/m^2. To compute your BMI, take your weight (in kilograms), and divide by your height (in meters) squared. You can find many BMI calculators on the Internet that will do the math for you, such as the one on this site: http://www.nhlbisupport.com/bmi/. All you need to know is your height (in inches) and weight (in pounds).

Emotional states, such as anger, fear, and depression, can also prompt excessive eating. Many of us overeat in anger, or when we're feeling lonely, bored, or depressed. Have you ever tried to quell anxiety over an upcoming examination by finishing off a carton of ice cream? We may find we can soothe our negative feelings, at least temporarily, by treating ourselves to food.

Might obesity even be catching? Recent evidence shows that obesity tends to be shared among people in social networks comprising friends, neighbors, spouses, and family members (Christakis & Fowler, 2007). These findings suggest that the people with whom we socialize influence what we eat, how much we eat, and judgments we make about the acceptability of obesity. The effects of social networks may be an even stronger determinant of obesity than genetics (Barabási, 2007). But just as social networks may encourage unhealthy eating, friends who make healthy eating choices may serve as positive role models.

CONCEPT 8.12

Obesity is a complex health problem in which behavioral patterns, genetics, and environmental and emotional factors all play a role.

→ Concept Link

Obesity is a major risk factor in coronary heart disease, the leading killer of Americans. See Module 12.2.

What's the bottom line (or curve) on the causes of obesity? Behavioral patterns, genetics, environmental factors, and emotional cues all play a role. Yet even people whose genes predispose them to weight problems can achieve and maintain a healthy body weight by eating sensibly and exercising regularly. Regular physical activity not only burns calories, but it also increases the metabolic rate because it builds muscles, and muscle tissue burns more calories than fatty tissue. Thus, regular exercise combined

TABLE 8.1 Suggestions for Maintaining a Healthy Weight

Watch your fat intake.	Limit your total daily fat intake to less than 30 percent of calories consumed, and keep your intake of saturated fat to less than 10 percent. This means that if you consume 2,000 calories a day on the average, limit your fat intake to 66 grams of fat and saturated fat to 22 grams. (Note that 1 gram of fat contains 9 calories.)
Control portion size.	To maintain a healthy weight, you need to strike a balance between calories consumed and calories expended. Controlling portion size will help you maintain this caloric balance.
Slow down your eating.	It takes about 15 minutes for your brain to register that your stomach feels full. Give it a chance to catch up to your stomach. Put the fork down between bites to slow the pace of eating.
Beware of hidden calories.	Check product labels for calories. Fruit drinks, for instance, are loaded with hidden calories. Try diluting fruit drinks with water, or substitute the actual fruit itself. Also, many processed foods, especially baked goods, are loaded with calories as the result of high sugar and fat content.
Make physical activity a part of your lifestyle.	Health experts recommend at least thirty minutes a day of moderate physical activity—activity equivalent in strenuousness to walking three to four miles per hour. This doesn't mean you need to work out in a gym or jog around a park every day. Taking a brisk walk from your car to your office or school, climbing stairs, or doing vigorous work around the house can help you meet your daily exercise needs. But additional aerobic exercise—like running, swimming, or using equipment specially designed for aerobic exercise—may help even more. Before starting any exercise program, discuss your health needs and concerns with a health care provider.

© Monkey Business Images/Shutterstock.com

with gradual weight reduction can help offset the reduction in the body's metabolic rate that may occur when we begin losing weight.

Health experts recognize that "quickie" diets are not the answer to long-term weight management. The great majority of people eventually regain any weight they lose on a diet. Diet or weight-loss drugs offer at best only a temporary benefit and may carry a risk of serious side effects. Long-term success in losing excess weight and keeping it off requires a lifelong commitment to following a sensible, healthy diet combined with regular exercise (Lamberg, 2006; Wadden et al., 2005).

We also need to become calorie conscious. For example, we need to recognize that "low-fat" does not necessarily mean "low-calorie." (Check the nutritional labels.) Even if obesity is not a current concern in your life, adopting healthy eating and exercise habits can help you avoid weight problems in the future. Table 8.1 offers suggestions for maintaining a healthy weight.

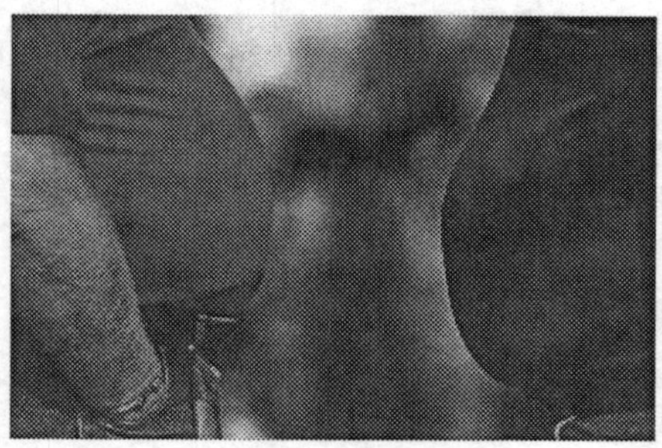

© Tom Raymond Stone/Getty Images

Obesity is an epidemic in our society and poses a significant health risk, cutting life expectancy by an average of six to seven years.

CONCEPT 8.13

Effective weight management requires a lifelong commitment to healthy eating and exercise habits that balance caloric intake with energy output.

Eating Disorders

Karen, the 22-year-old daughter of a famed English professor, felt her weight was "just about right" (Boskind-White & White, 1983). But at 78 pounds on a 5-foot frame, she looked more like a prepubescent 11-year-old than a young adult. Her parents tried to

CONCEPT 8.14
Eating disorders, such as anorexia nervosa and bulimia nervosa, disproportionately affect young women, in large part because of a cultural obsession to achieve unrealistic standards of thinness.

persuade her to seek help with her eating behavior, but she continually denied she had a problem. Ultimately, however, after she lost yet another pound, her parents convinced her to enter a residential treatment program where her eating could be closely monitored. Nicole, 19, wakes up each morning hoping this will be the day she begins living normally—that today she'll avoid gorging herself and inducing herself to vomit. But she doesn't feel confident that her eating behavior and purging are under her control. The disordered eating behavior of Karen and Nicole are characteristic of the two major types of eating disorders: *anorexia nervosa* and *bulimia nervosa.*

Anorexia Nervosa

Anorexia nervosa involves self-starvation, resulting in an unhealthy and potentially dangerous low body weight. It is characterized by both an intense fear of becoming fat and a distorted body image. Anorexia is found predominantly in young women. The anorectic woman may be convinced she is too fat, even though others see her as little more than "skin and bones."

Anorexia is a dangerous medical condition and poses serious risks, including cardiovascular problems, such as irregular heartbeat and low blood pressure; gastrointestinal problems, such as chronic constipation and abdominal pain; loss of menstruation; and even deaths due to suicide or to medical complications associated with severe weight loss.

In a typical case, the young woman begins to notice some weight gain in adolescence. She becomes overly concerned about getting fat. She resorts to extreme dieting and perhaps excessive exercise to reduce her weight to a prepubescent level. She denies that she is too thin or losing too much weight, despite the concerns of others. In her mind's eye, she is heavier than she actually is.

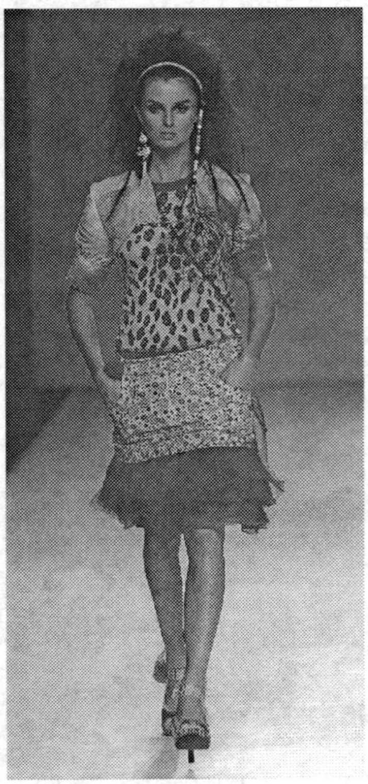
©AP Photo/Eugenio Savio

Brazilian fashion model Ana Carolina Reston was just 21 when she died in 2006 from medical complications due to anorexia. At the time of her death, the 5-foot, 7-inch young woman weighed but 88 pounds. Unfortunately, the problem of anorexia and other eating disorders among fashion models is widespread, as it is in other situations in which pressure is imposed to attain unrealistic standards of thinness.

Bulimia Nervosa

Bulimia nervosa is characterized by a repetitive pattern of binge eating followed by purging. Purging usually involves self-induced vomiting but may take other forms, such as excessive use of laxatives. Some people with bulimia purge regularly after meals, not just after binges. Some engage in excessive, even compulsive, exercise regimens to try to control their weight. Like those with anorexia, people with bulimia are obsessed with their weight and unhappy with their bodies. But unlike those with anorexia, they typically maintain a relatively normal weight.

Bulimia usually begins in late adolescence following a period of rigid dieting to lose weight. Bingeing may alternate with strict dieting. The binge itself usually occurs in secret. During the binge, the person consumes enormous amounts of foods that are sweet and high in fat. Bulimia can lead to many medical complications, including potentially dangerous potassium deficiencies and decay of tooth enamel from frequent vomiting, and severe constipation from overuse of laxatives.

What Motivates Disturbed Eating Behaviors?

What underlies the development of unhealthy eating habits associated with anorexia and bulimia? A principal factor is the pressure many young women feel to achieve an unrealistic standard of thinness (Chernyak & Lowe, 2010). The constant barrage of media images of ultrathin models conveys powerful messages to girls and young women, affecting how they view their own bodies and leading to feelings of body dissatisfaction and disordered eating behaviors (Hamilton et al., 2010; Rodgers, Salès, & Chabrol, 2010; Tiggemann & Miller, 2010). Even girls as young as three have begun internalizing a thinness ideal (Harriger et al., 2010).

Social pressure to achieve and maintain a slender figure falls most heavily on women in our society, especially young women. Concerns about weight can be expressed in different ways, such as feelings of guilt or shame associated with eating treats or even purchasing them. About one in seven college women surveyed by a team of investigators said they would be embarrassed to buy a chocolate bar in a store (Rozin, Bauer, & Catanese, 2003). Survey evidence shows that more female than male college students believe they are overweight, whereas more college men see themselves as underweight (see ■ Figure 8.6) (American College Health Association, 2005).

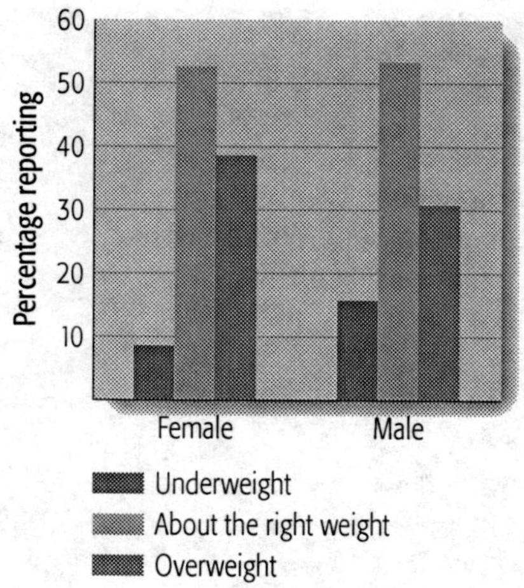

FIGURE 8.6 Students' Self-Reported Descriptions of Weight
Self-perceptions of overweight are more common among college women, whereas self-perceptions of underweight are more common among college men.
Source: Data from American College Health Association, 2005.

Anorexia affects about 0.9 percent of women in our society (about 9 in 1,000), according to the most recent population-based survey (Hudson et al., 2006). Estimates are that about 1 to 3 percent of women are affected by bulimia at some point in their lives (American Psychiatric Association, 2000). Eating disorders disproportionately affect young women, with prevalence rates among men estimated to be about 0.3 percent (3 in 1,000) for anorexia and 0.3 percent or less for bulimia (American Psychiatric Association, 2000; Hudson et al., 2006).

Many men with eating disorders participate in wrestling or other sports in which they face pressures to maintain body weight within a narrow range. Body dissatisfaction in men is linked to the desire to achieve an idealized standard of leanness or muscularity (Jung et al., 2010; Ricciardelli et al., 2007). Investigators also find that exposure to media images of heavily muscled men can damage the body perceptions of boys and men (Hargreaves & Tiggemann, 2009; Hobza & Rochlen, 2009).

© Jill Greenberg

If a slender woman like the one on the left had the same proportions as a Barbie doll, she would look like the woman on the right. To achieve this, she would need to grow nearly a foot in height, increase her bust size by 4 inches, and reduce her waist by 5 inches. What message do you think the Barbie doll sends to the average young woman?

Negative emotions such as depression and anxiety can trigger binge eating (Reas & Grilo, 2007). Many young women with eating disorders have issues relating to perfectionism and control. They may place unreasonable pressures on themselves to achieve a "perfect body" or feel that the only part of their lives they can control is their dieting. Eating disorders also frequently develop in young women with histories of childhood sexual or physical abuse or whose families are wracked by conflict (Jacobi et al., 2004). Some theorists speculate that anorexia may arise from an unconscious wish in female adolescents to remain little girls.

Eating disorders are much less common in other parts of the world that lack our cultural emphasis on thinness. They also appear to be less common among women of color for whom body image is not as closely tied to a slender form as it is among Euro-American women (Overstreet, Quinn, & Agocha, 2010; A. Roberts et al., 2006). Identification with African American culture may serve as kind of protective factor against disturbed eating behaviors (Henrickson, Crowther, & Harrington, 2010). That said, women of color may also develop body dissatisfaction as the result of exposure to a "thin is in" feminine ideal (Grabe & Hyde, 2006).

© Ruel Tafalla/Shutterstock.com

Is this normal? Body dissatisfaction is not limited to young women. The body image of young men may be adversely affected by exposure to overly masculinized male images in the media.

Biological factors, such as genetics and disturbances in brain mechanisms that control hunger and satiety, are also implicated in eating disorders (Kaye, 2009). Irregularities in activity of the neurotransmitter serotonin, which plays a key role in regulating feelings of satiation after eating, may underlie tendencies to binge in people with bulimia (Hildebrandt et al., 2010). Antidepressant drugs that boost the availability of serotonin in the brain may help reduce binges (Walsh et al., 2004).

CONCEPT CHART 8.2 Hunger, Obesity, and Eating Disorders: Key Concepts

Hunger and Appetite	Obesity	Eating Disorders
The hypothalamus detects low blood sugar levels and depletion of fat in fat cells, leading to feelings of hunger that motivate eating. Hormones and neurotransmitters work on the hypothalamus to influence appetite and eating behavior. 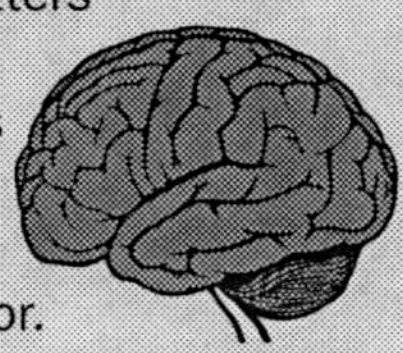 © takito, 2009/ Shutterstock.com	Causes of obesity involve genetic, psychological, and environmental factors, including differences in metabolic rates, number of fat cells in the body, behavioral patterns (unhealthy diet and lack of exercise), and emotional and environmental cues that prompt overeating.  © Shira Raz, 2009/ Shutterstock.com	Cultural pressure imposed on young women to achieve an unrealistic standard of thinness is a major underlying factor in anorexia (self- starvation) and bulimia (binge eating followed by purging). Psychological factors underlying eating disorders include issues of control and perfectionism, sexual or physical abuse during childhood, family conflicts, and, for anorexia, underlying fears of adulthood and sexual maturity. Biological factors implicated in eating disorders include genetics, abnormalities in brain mechanisms that control feelings of hunger and satiation, and irregularities in serotonin activity. 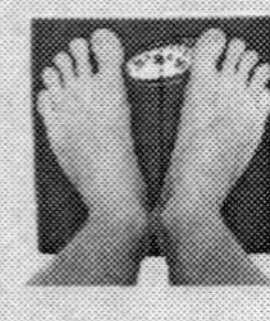 © saiko3p, 2009/ Shutterstock.com

Although we see have promising results in treating eating disorders with psychological and drug therapies, recovery is typically a long-term process that is often punctuated by relapses and continuing symptoms (Agency for Healthcare Research and Quality, 2006; Kaye, 2009). Concept Chart 8.2 presents an overview of our discussion of hunger, obesity, and eating disorders.

8.2 MODULE REVIEW Hunger and Eating

Recite It

What makes us hungry?

➢ Homeostatic processes in the brain regulate hunger and appetite. The hypothalamus plays a pivotal role. It senses changes in blood sugar levels and depletion of fat from fat cells, which leads to the feelings of hunger that motivate eating. Neurotransmitters and hormones also play important roles in regulating hunger and appetite.

What causes obesity?

➢ Obesity is a complex problem that has multiple causes, including behavioral patterns, genetics, metabolic factors, and environmental and emotional factors. Genetics may affect basal metabolic rate and the number of fat cells in the body.

What is anorexia nervosa?

➢ Anorexia nervosa is an eating disorder in which people starve themselves because of exaggerated concerns about weight gain.

What is bulimia nervosa?

➢ Bulimia nervosa is an eating disorder characterized by episodes of binge eating followed by purging. Purging is accomplished through self-induced vomiting or other means, such as excessive use of laxatives.

What are the causes of eating disorders?

➢ Many factors are implicated in eating disorders. They include cultural pressure on young women to achieve unrealistic standards of thinness, issues of control and perfectionism, childhood abuse, family conflicts, and possible disturbances in brain mechanisms that control hunger and satiety.

Recall It

1. Which of the following does *not* describe what happens physiologically after a person has not eaten for a while?
   a. Blood sugar level drops.
   b. Fat is released from fat cells.
   c. The ventromedial hypothalamus signals that it is time to start eating.
   d. The brain releases more neuropeptide Y.

2. If the lateral hypothalamus in a laboratory animal is stimulated, the animal
   a. stops eating.
   b. starves to death.
   c. begins to eat even if it has just consumed a full meal.
   d. becomes obese.
3. Match the terms on the left with the definitions on the right:

i. lateral hypothalamus	a. the rate at which the body at rest burns calories
ii. ventromedial hypothalamus	b. works like an on switch for eating
iii. basal metabolic rate	c. a genetically predetermined range for weight
iv. set point	d. works likes an off switch to signal when to stop eating

4. Irregularities in the regulation of the neurotransmitter _____ may be involved in prompting bulimic binges.

Think About It

➤ What would you say to someone who claims that people become obese because they lack willpower?

➤ How much should you weigh? Has your answer to this question changed as a result of our discussion of obesity? Are you aware of your daily caloric intake? If not, should you be? Do you have any unhealthy eating habits you would like to change? If so, how might you change them?

Emotions

MODULE 8.3

- What are the three components of emotions?
- Are facial expressions of emotion universal?
- What factors are associated with personal happiness?
- What are the three components of love in Sternberg's model of love?
- What role do brain structures play in emotions?
- What are the major theories of emotions?
- What is emotional intelligence?
- What is the polygraph? Does it work?

From the joy we feel at graduating from college or landing a desirable job, to the sadness we feel at the loss of a loved one, to the ups and downs we experience in everyday life, our lives are filled with emotions. **Emotions** are complex feeling states that infuse our lives with color. We commonly say we are "red" with anger, "green" with envy, and "blue" with sadness. Imagine how colorless life would be without emotions. But what are emotions? Are particular emotional expressions recognized universally or only by members of the same culture? What is the physiological basis of emotions?

emotions Feeling states that psychologists view as having physiological, cognitive, and behavioral components.

What Are Emotions?

Most people think of emotions simply as feelings, such as joy or anger. But psychologists view emotions as more complex feeling states that have three basic components: *bodily arousal* (nervous system activation), *cognitions* (subjective, or conscious, experience of the feeling, as well as the thoughts or judgments we have about people or situations that evoke the feeling), and *expressed behaviors* (outward expression of the emotion, such as approaching a loved object or avoiding a feared one).

CONCEPT 8.15
To psychologists, emotions are more than just feelings; they have physiological, cognitive, and behavioral components.

The physiological component of fear is bodily arousal. There is a degree of truth to the belief that we feel with our hearts. Strong emotions, such as fear and anger, are accompanied by activation of the sympathetic branch of the autonomic nervous system (ANS). As we noted in Chapter 2, activation of the sympathetic nervous system prompts the adrenal glands to release the hormones epinephrine and norepinephrine, which raise the body's level of arousal.

The cognitive component of fear includes the subjective experience of feeling afraid, as well as a judgment that the situation is threatening. (If someone tosses a rubber snake at your feet, it may startle you, but it will not evoke fear when you appraise it as a fake.) The cognitive component of anger includes the judgment (cognitive appraisal) that events or the actions of others are unjust.

The behavioral expression of emotions generally takes two forms. We tend to approach objects or situations associated with pleasant emotions, such as joy or love, and avoid situations associated with fear, loathing, or disgust. When afraid, we approach the feared object in the hope of fighting it off, or we try to flee from it. Similarly, when angry, we tend to attack (approach) the object of our anger or to withdraw from it (i.e., keep it at a distance). The behavioral component of emotions also encompasses ways in which we express emotions through facial features and other outward behaviors, such as gestures, tone of voice, and bodily posture.

Emotional Expression: Read Any Good Faces Lately?

Charles Darwin (1872) believed that emotions evolved because they have an adaptive purpose in helping species survive and flourish. Fear mobilizes animals to defend themselves in the face of a threatening predator; anger can be adaptive in provoking aggression that helps secure territory, resources, or mating partners. Darwin also recognized that the expression of emotions has communication value. For example, an animal displaying fear through its bodily posture or facial expression may signal others of its kind that danger lurks nearby. Darwin was the first to link specific facial expressions to particular emotions.

CONCEPT 8.16
Though we may say that people wear their hearts on their sleeves, it is more accurate to say that they wear their emotions on their faces.

We can see the evolutionary roots of emotional expression in the similarity of the facial expressions of humans and nonhuman primates, such as gorillas. You don't need instructions to interpret the emotion expressed by the bared teeth of the ape and human shown in ■ Figure 8.7. This cross-species similarity in facial expression supports Darwin's view that human modes of emotional expression evolved from nonhuman primate ancestors (Chevalier-Skolnikoff, 1973).

FIGURE 8.7 Cross-Species Similarity in Facial Expression
The bared teeth of both ape and man signal readiness to defend or to attack.

Facial Expressions of Emotion: Are They Universal?

Evidence supports the view that six basic emotions are universally recognized on the basis of facial expressions: anger, fear, disgust, sadness, happiness, and surprise (Ekman, 2003; Matsumoto, 2004) (see the *Try This Out* feature). Facial analysis tools developed by psychologist Paul Ekman, a leading authority on facial expressions of emotions, are now being used by airport screeners to detect telltale signs of emotions in people's faces in the effort to spot terrorists (Lipton, 2006).

A recent study suggests that facial expressions of emotion are hardwired into the brain, rather than learned as the result of visual experience (Matsumoto & Willingham, 2009). Investigators analyzed facial expressions of sighted and blind judo athletes based on photographs taken at the Olympic and Paralympic Games. Both sets of athletes used the same facial muscles in their emotional expressions, even though the blind athletes could not have acquired these responses through observation.

Cultural and Gender Differences in Emotions

Though people the world over may recognize the same basic facial expressions of emotions, subtle differences exist across cultures in the appearance of these expressions (Marsh, Elfenbein, & Ambady, 2003). We can think of cultural differences in facial expressions as akin to nonverbal accents.

CONCEPT 8.17
Evidence supports the view that facial expressions of at least six basic emotions are recognized universally.

Psychologist Dacher Keltner of University of California at Berkeley calls attention to a particular type of nonverbal accent he describes as a national style of smiling. He notes that Americans tend to draw the corners of their lips up, showing their upper teeth, whereas the British tend to draw their lips back as well as up, displaying their lower teeth (Max, 2005). The British smile may come across as a kind of suppressed grimace. See if you can tell the difference between the distinctive smiles of American actor Tom Cruise and British royal Prince Charles, in the nearby photos.

Research has also uncovered cultural differences in how accurately emotions are recognized and how they are experienced and displayed. For example, people are generally more accurate when recognizing facial expressions of emotions in people of their own national, ethnic, and regional groups (Elfenbein & Ambady, 2002a, 2002b). In addition, certain emotions are more common in some cultures or even unique to a particular culture (Niiya, Ellsworth, & Yamaguchi, 2006). For example, Japanese commonly report feeling such emotions as *fureai* (feeling closely linked to others) and *oime* (an unpleasant feeling of indebtedness to others, similar to our feeling of being "beholden"). Though not unknown in the United States, these emotions are not as central to our lives as they are in Japan, where there is a greater cultural emphasis on communal values and mutual obligations.

CONCEPT 8.18
Each culture has display rules that determine how emotions are expressed and how much emotion it is appropriate to express.

Cultures also differ in how, or even whether, emotions are displayed. The term **display rules** refers to customs and social norms used to regulate the expression or display of emotion in a given culture (Fok et al., 2008; Matsumoto et al., 2005; Matsumoto et al., 2008). Display rules are learned as part of the socialization process and become so ingrained that they occur automatically among members of the same culture. Chinese and other East Asian cultures tend to frown on public displays of emotion, whereas emotions are expressed more openly in many other cultures, including Mexican culture (Soto, Levenson, & Ebling, 2005). In East Asian cultures, people are expected to suppress their feelings in public; a failure to keep their feelings to themselves reflects poorly on their upbringing. The Japanese tend to hide negative emotions through smiling, which is one reason they tend to judge emotions in others based more on their tone of voice than their facial expressions (Tanaka et al., 2010). They tend to listen for emotional cues rather than read faces.

display rules Cultural customs and norms that govern the display of emotional expressions.

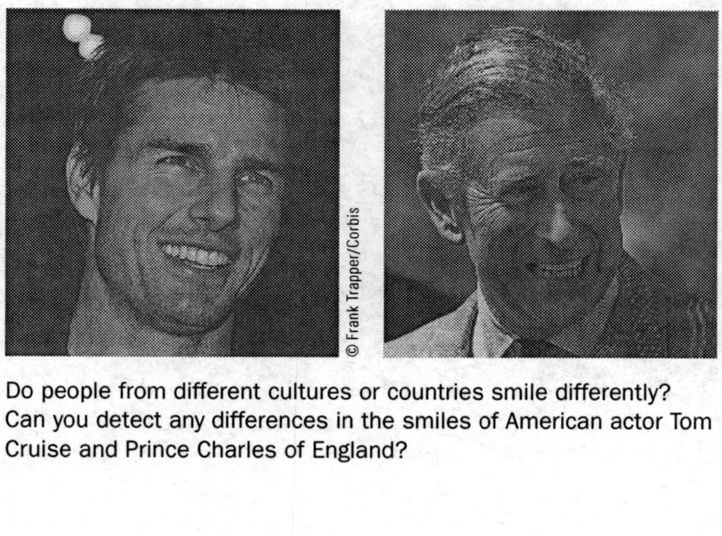

© Frank Trapper/Corbis

© Photo by POOL/Tim Graham Picture Library/Getty Images

Do people from different cultures or countries smile differently? Can you detect any differences in the smiles of American actor Tom Cruise and Prince Charles of England?

Cultures also have display rules governing the appropriate expression of emotions by men and women. In many cultures, women are given greater latitude than men in expressing

TRY THIS OUT Reading Emotions in Facial Expressions

The same emotional expressions found in the streets of Chicago are found in the distant corners of the world. The photographs accompanying this exercise show a man from a remote area of New Guinea. You'll probably have little difficulty recognizing the emotions he is portraying. Before reading further, match the following emotions to the numbers on the photos: (a) disgust, (b) sadness, (c) happiness, and (d) anger.

The man was asked to make faces as he was told stories involving the following: "Your friend has come and you are happy"; "Your child has died"; "You are angry and about to fight"; and "You see a dead pig that has been lying there a long time." The correct answers are 1 (c), 2 (b), 3 (d), and 4 (a).

© Paul Ekman, Ph.D./Paul Ekman Group, LLC

1. ________________

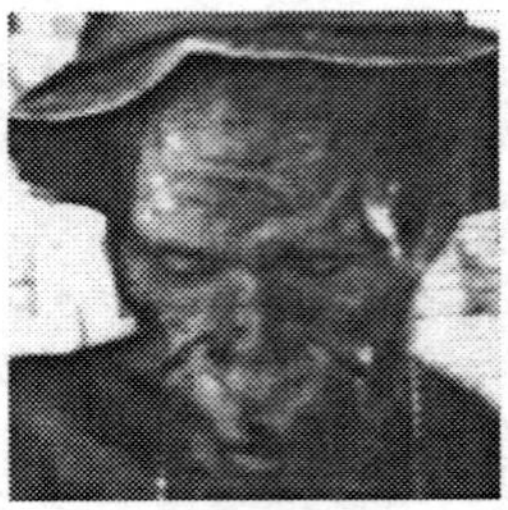
© Paul Ekman, Ph.D./Paul Ekman Group, LLC

2. ________________

© Paul Ekman, Ph.D./Paul Ekman Group, LLC

3. ________________

© Paul Ekman, Ph.D./Paul Ekman Group, LLC

4. ________________

certain emotions, such as joy, love, fear, and sadness, whereas men are permitted more direct displays of anger (Dittmann, 2003a). Evidence shows that women do tend to experience certain emotional states (joy, love, fear, sadness) more often than men (Brebner, 2003; Fischer et al., 2004). Yet the scientific jury is still out on whether there are gender differences in the experience of anger (Evers et al., 2005).

Women are generally better at expressing their feelings through words and facial expressions and recognizing feelings in others (DePaulo & Friedman, 1998; Ripley, 2005). Investigators suspect that women's brains may be wired differently, allowing them to better perceive and recall emotional cues (Canli et al., 2002). However, gender differences in expressing emotions may be more complex than first thought. Recent evidence showed that women were better at recognizing happy or sad faces, but men held the advantage in discerning angry faces (Bakalar, 2006b; M. A. Williams & Mattingley, 2006).

© erwinova/Shutterstock.com

Will she give him her number? The answer may depend on what song is playing in the background.

In Western cultures, men aren't supposed to cry or show their emotions, or even to smile very much. Not surprisingly, evidence shows that women tend to smile more than men (LaFrance, Hecht, & Paluck, 2003). However, the ideal of the stoic unemotional male epitomized by Hollywood action heroes may be giving way to a new ideal: the "sensitive" male character.

Listening to music can also affect our emotional states. Did you ever notice how certain songs or melodies make you feel happier, whereas other music leaves you feeling sad or sorrowful? Exposure to romantic music may even make people more receptive to dating overtures. Recently, French researchers played songs with romantic lyrics in the background while young female participants waited to participate in a marketing study (Guéguen, Jacob, & Lamy, 2010). The female participants then interacted with a male confederate of the experimenter during the study, who—during a break—asked for their phone numbers to call them for a date. Guess what happened? Nearly double the number of women (52%) who had been exposed to romantic songs complied with the request for their phone numbers than those who had been exposed to neutral songs (28%) ("Love Ballad," 2010).

Happiness: What Makes You Happy?

Happiness may be a primary human emotion, but it has long been neglected by psychologists, who have focused mostly on understanding negative emotions such as fear, anger, and sadness. However, promoting human happiness is a key goal of *positive psychology*, a growing movement within psychology (see Chapter 1). The architects of the positive psychology movement believe that psychology should focus more on promoting human happiness and building human strengths and assets, such as the capacity to love and be loved, rather than just repairing negative emotions such as anxiety and depression (e.g., Seligman et al., 2005; Snyder & Lopez, 2007).

What makes people happy? Is wealth the key? People may think they'd be a lot happier if they were wealthier, but evidence shows the link between money and happiness is largely an illusion (Kahneman et al., 2006). Wealth, and even good health, make only minor contributions to levels of happiness and life satisfaction (Boyce, Brown, & Moore, 2010; Diener, 2005; Hsee, Hastie, & Chen, 2008). It is the case that higher incomes are linked to greater happiness at lower levels of the income scale, but greater income beyond that needed to meet a family's basic needs (about $75,000 in annual income) translates into only small increases in personal happiness (Kahneman & Deaton, 2010; Munsey, 2010). As Harvard University psychologist Daniel Gilbert puts it, "Once you get basic human needs met, a lot more money doesn't make a lot more happiness" (cited in Futrelle, 2006). Happiness tends to level off at higher income levels (see ■ Figure 8.8). Even members of the vaunted Forbes 400, a listing of the nation's wealthiest individuals, are only modestly happier than other people (Kesebir & Diener, 2008). Consider too that while lottery winners often get an emotional boost from their winnings, their reported happiness tends to return to their earlier levels within about a year (Corliss, 2003).

If not money, might marriage be the key to happiness? Generally speaking, married people are happier than single folks (Gallup Organization, 2005; Munsey, 2010). But cause and effect may be muddled, as happier people might be more likely to get married or stay married (J. Stein, 2005; Wallis, 2005). This latter view is supported by evidence from a survey of more than 24,000 newly married people (Lucas et al., 2003). The results showed that the bounce in happiness felt by many newlyweds tended to be short-lived.

So, what does determine happiness? Although we lack a final answer, the available evidence points to two important factors: friends (a big plus) and religion (Kesebir & Diener, 2008; Paul, 2005). Having close friendships is an important ingredient in personal happiness. In recent research, investigators found clusters of happy and unhappy people within social networks of friends and family members, lending support to the view that a person's happiness or unhappiness spreads through networks of friends and other social contacts like a social contagion (J. H. Fowler & Christakis, 2008; Roy-Byrne, 2009; Steptoe & Diez Roux, 2008). In effect, a person's happiness may at least partly depend on the happiness of their close friends and family members.

With respect to religion, we don't know whether it is the sense of purpose and meaning associated with religious belief, the social participation in communal aspects of religion, or a combination of factors relating to religious commitment that contributes to happiness. But perhaps the greatest contribution to happiness is our inborn genetic potential.

Genetic factors appear to play an important role in determining happiness (Weiss,

© Monkey Business Images, 2009/Shutterstock.com

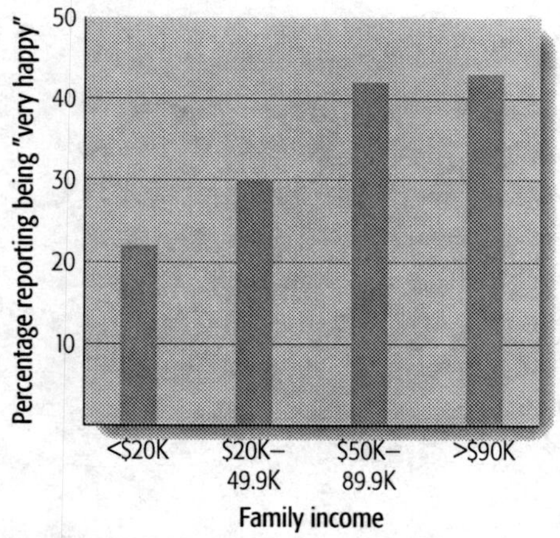

FIGURE 8.8 Happiness in Relation to Family Income
Personal happiness increases in relation to family income at lower income levels, but levels off as family income increases.
Source: Kahneman et al., 2006.

CONCEPT 8.19
People seem to have a particular "set point" for happiness, a level that remains fairly constant despite the ups and downs of life.

Bates, & Luciano, 2008). People may have a genetically determined "set point" for happiness, a level around which their level of happiness tends to settle, despite the ups and downs of their daily lives (Wallis, 2005). Still, researchers believe that people can move either above or below their genetic set points (Inglehart et al., 2008). Levels of happiness or well-being can change, and often do change, over the course of a lifetime (Fujita & Diener, 2005). The lesson here is that happiness is not genetically fixed. It is possible to enrich our lives in ways that will boost our personal happiness, as we'll see next.

Why It Matters: Applying Positive Psychology to Become Happier

Positive psychology founder Martin Seligman (2003) suggests that psychologists should help guide people toward the good life—the happy and meaningful life. He speaks of three kinds of human happiness: (1) *pleasure* of doing things, (2) *gratification* (being absorbed and engaged in life activities), and (3) *meaning* (finding personal fulfillment in life activities). Seligman offers advice people can use in their daily lives to increase personal happiness. Here are a few of these suggestions (adapted from Seligman, 2003; Seligman et al., 2005):

- *Gratitude visit.* Seligman believes that expressing gratitude is a key component of personal happiness. Close your eyes and visualize someone who has had a huge positive effect on your life—someone you never really thanked. Spend time during the next week writing a testimony of thanks to this person. Then schedule a visit to the person. When you arrive, read the testimonial and discuss with that person what he or she has meant to you. Gratitude visits can be infectious in a positive way. The recipients of the visit begin to think about the people *they* haven't thanked. They then make their own pilgrimage of thanks, which in turn leads to a kind of daisy chain of gratitude and contentment (Pink, 2003).
- *Three blessings.* Every night, before going to bed, think of three things that went well during the day. Write them down and reflect on them.
- *One door closes, another opens.* Think about the times in your life that a door closed because of a death or a loss. Then think of a later experience in which a door opened. Come to appreciate the ebbs and flows of your experiences.
- *Savorings.* Plan a perfect day. But be sure to share it with another person.

All in all, happiness is not so much a function of what you've got as what you make of it. Happiness is most likely to be found in meaningful work, investment in family and community life, and development of strong spiritual or personal values.

The Facial-Feedback Hypothesis: Putting on a Happy Face

facial-feedback hypothesis The belief that mimicking facial movements associated with a particular emotion will produce the corresponding emotional state.

Can practicing smiling lift your mood? According to the **facial-feedback hypothesis**, mimicking facial movements associated with an emotion induces the corresponding feelings. Evidence shows that practicing smiling can induce more positive feelings, whereas frowning can bring your mood down (J. I. Davis, Senghas, & Ochsner, 2009; Soussignan, 2002).

CONCEPT 8.20
Practicing or mimicking facial movements associated with particular emotions can produce corresponding emotional states.

SLICE OF LIFE Practicing smiling several times a day may lift your spirits, at least temporarily, perhaps because it prompts you to recall pleasant experiences (see *Try This Out*). This point was brought home, literally speaking, by Professor Diane Urban of Manhattan College, who recalled that while her mother had no knowledge of the facial-feedback hypothesis, she was nonetheless right about many things and always emphasized the importance of putting on a happy face. As Professor Urban notes, "When you

TRY THIS OUT The Facial-Feedback Effect

Hold a pencil between your teeth for about a minute. Notice any change in your mood? Now hold the pencil between your lips. Notice any change in your mood now?

Holding a pencil between your teeth engages facial muscles used for smiling, whereas holding a pencil between your lips activates muscles used in frowning. According to the facial-feedback hypothesis, you should find your mood cheerier after holding the pencil between your teeth than after holding it between your lips.

© Eduard Titov/Shutterstock.com

smile for no apparent reason, you start to feel silly, so you look for a reason to smile by recalling happy experiences and the next thing you know, you feel better. Also, when you smile, people respond positively to you, which is a form of positive reinforcement that makes it more likely you'll smile again."

The facial-feedback hypothesis has its limitations. A "put-on" smile is not the equivalent of a real one. Putting on a smile may induce more positive feelings, but it is not accompanied by the feeling of enjoyment that produces a genuine smile. In addition, the two types of smiles flex different facial muscles (Waller et al., 2006). A genuine smile is called a **Duchenne smile**, named after Guillaume Duchenne de Boulogne (1806–1875), the French physician who discovered the facial muscles used to produce a genuine smile. You can see the difference between a genuine smile and a phony one in the photographs of emotions researcher Paul Ekman in ■ Figure 8.9. Whereas smiling may induce a more positive emotion, you can apply the facial-feedback effect to induce other emotions, such as sadness (see *Try This Out*).

Duchenne smile A genuine smile that involves contraction of a particular set of facial muscles.

Then there's the most enigmatic smile of all, that of the *Mona Lisa*. Recently, computer programmers created emotion-recognition software that could analyze facial features for telltale signs of emotions (Bohrn, Carbon, & Hutzler, 2010). By analyzing facial features such as the curvature of the lips and the crinkles around the eyes, researchers decoded the emotions expressed in the *Mona Lisa* portrait as composed of 83 percent happiness, 9 percent disgust, 6 percent fear, and 2 percent anger. No wonder Da Vinci's *Mona Lisa* has such an enigmatic smile.

© Gianni Dagli Orti/CORBIS

Ah, her enigmatic smile. What is she really feeling? Researchers believe they may have an answer.

Love: The Deepest Emotion

Notions about love have long intrigued and puzzled poets and philosophers. Only recently, however, have psychologists applied the scientific method to the study of love (Sternberg & Weis, 2006). Psychologists consider love to be both a motive (a need or want that drives us) and an emotion (or feeling state).

The ancient Greeks taught that there are several kinds of love, including love between parents and children and love between close friends. But it is **romantic love** that is idealized in countless songs, poems, and books, not to mention daytime soap operas. Nor is the worship of romantic love limited to Western culture. The great majority of cultures studied by anthropologists, even many preliterate societies, have a concept of romantic love (Jankowiak & Fischer, 1992).

romantic love A form of love characterized by strong erotic attraction and desire for intimacy.

FIGURE 8.9 In Which Photo Is Paul Really Smiling?
As you probably guessed, the photo on the right shows a genuine smile; the smile in the photo on the left is simulated. One way to tell the difference is to look for crow's feet around the eyes, a characteristic associated with genuine smiles.

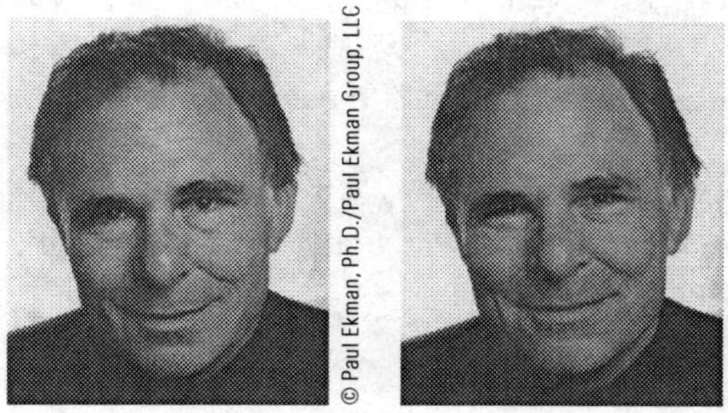

© Paul Ekman, Ph.D./Paul Ekman Group, LLC

© Paul Ekman, Ph.D./Paul Ekman Group, LLC

TRY THIS OUT Putting on a Sad Face

This exercise may be useful if you are involved in acting and need to project a particular emotion, such as sadness, to an audience (Ekman, 2003). Try imitating the facial features of sadness identified below. Then examine how you felt. It may help to use a mirror to check that you are practicing the facial movements correctly.

- Drop your mouth open.
- Pull the corners of your lips down.
- While holding your lip corners down, try to raise your cheeks, as if you are squinting. This pulls against the lip corners.
- Maintain this tension between the raised cheeks and the lip corners pulling down.
- Let your eyes look downward and your upper eyelids droop.

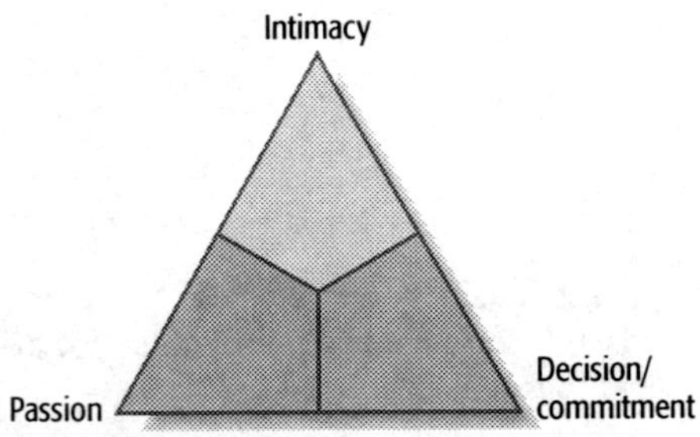

FIGURE 8.10 Sternberg's Triangular Model of Love
Sternberg conceptualizes love as a triangle with three components: intimacy, passion, and decision/commitment.

triangular model of love Sternberg's concept of love as a triangle with three components: intimacy, passion, and decision/commitment.

Psychologist Robert Sternberg's (1988) **triangular model of love** conceptualizes love in terms of three basic components (see ■ Figure 8.10):

1. *Intimacy,* the close bond and feeling of attachment between two people, including their desire to share their innermost thoughts and feelings
2. *Passion,* an intense sexual desire for the other person
3. *Decision/commitment,* the recognition that one loves the other person (decisional component) and is committed to maintaining the relationship through good times and bad (commitment component).Decision and commitment need not go hand in hand. A person may acknowledge being in love but not be ready or willing to make a lasting commitment.

Sternberg believes that different combinations of these three basic components characterize different types of loving relationships (see Table 8.2). In his view, *romantic love* combines intimacy and passion but is lacking in decision/commitment. Romantic love tends to burn brightly for a time but soon flickers out. On the other hand, it may develop into a more abiding form of love called *consummate love,* which combines all three components: intimacy, passion, and decision/commitment. Consummate love may be more of an ideal for many couples than an enduring reality. In *companionate love,*

TABLE 8.2 Types of Love According to Sternberg's Triangular Model

Nonlove	A relationship in which all three components of love are absent. Most of our personal relationships are of this type—casual acquaintanceships that do not involve any elements of love.
Liking	Friendship in which intimacy is present but passion and decision/commitment are not.
Infatuation	A kind of "love at first sight," in which one experiences passionate desire for another person but in which there is neither intimacy nor decision/commitment.
Fatuous (foolish) love	The type of love associated with whirlwind romances and "quickie marriages," in which both passion and decision/commitment are present but intimacy is not.
Empty love	Love characterized by a commitment to maintain the relationship but lacking passion and intimacy. Stagnant relationships that no longer have the intimacy or physical attraction that once characterized them are of this type.
Romantic love	Love characterized by the combination of passion and intimacy but that lacks decision/commitment.
Consummate love	The complete measure of love, which combines passion, intimacy, and decision/commitment. Many of us strive to attain this type of love in our romantic relationships. Maintaining it is often harder than achieving it.
Companionate love	A kind of love that combines intimacy with decision/commitment. This kind of love often occurs in marriages in which passionate attraction between the partners has died down and been replaced by a kind of committed friendship.

Source: Adapted from Sternberg, 1988.

the type of love found in many long-term marriages, intimacy and commitment remain strong even though passion has ebbed. Companionate love also occurs in other types of relationships, such as between siblings and between close friends (Reis & Aron, 2008).

Sternberg proposes that relationships are balanced when the love triangles of both partners are well matched or closely overlapping. But relationships may fizzle, rather than sizzle, when partners differ in these components. For example, one partner may want to make a lasting commitment to the relationship, while the other's idea of making a commitment is deciding to stay the night.

CONCEPT 8.21
Though we generally think of love in terms of romantic love, it has been recognized since the time of the ancient Greeks that there are different kinds of love.

CONCEPT 8.22
Sternberg's triangular model of love proposes that different types of loving relationships can be characterized by different combinations of three basic components of love: intimacy, passion, and decision/commitment.

How Your Brain Does Emotions

There is no one emotional center in the brain. Rather, emotional responses are regulated by complex brain networks located primarily in the limbic system and cerebral cortex (Etkin et al., 2006). Recall from Chapter 2 that the limbic system includes the amygdala and hippocampus. The almond-shaped amygdala is a kind of emotional computer that triggers fear responses to threatening objects or stimuli (Coelho & Purkis, 2009; Forgas, 2008; Herry et al., 2008). A microcircuit in the amygdala controls or "gates" the fear response, leading to behaviors associated with fear, such as freezing in place ("Delicate Balance," 2010; Haubensak et al., 2010). ■ Figure 8.11 shows an example of activation of the amygdala in response to viewing a fearful face.

The hippocampus processes information relating to the context in which fear responses have been experienced. The hippocampus is involved in helping us remember place information or context and circumstances in which fear occurs, such as the bend in the road where we suddenly lost control of the car we were driving (Aamodt & Wang, 2008). The amygdala also plays an important role in processing stimuli that elicit other emotional states, including grief and despair (L. Wang et al., 2005).

© iStockphoto.com/mocker_bat

In Sternberg's model, consummate love combines intimacy, passion, and decision/commitment. Consummate love may not be as enduring as companionate love, which combines intimacy and decision/commitment but lacks passion. But even couples for whom the flames of passion have ebbed may occasionally stir the embers.

The cerebral cortex—the brain's "thinking center"—is connected to the limbic system and plays several key roles in processing emotions. It evaluates the meaning of emotionally arousing stimuli and plans and directs how to respond to them. It determines whether we should approach a stimulus (as in the case of a love interest or a pleasurable situation) or avoid one (as in the case of a threat). The cerebral cortex also processes the subjective or felt experience of emotions, as well as controlling the facial expression of emotion.

We are learning that there are differences in how the right and left cerebral hemispheres process emotions. It turns out that positive emotions, such as happiness, are associated with increased activity in the prefrontal cortex of the left cerebral hemisphere, whereas negative emotions, such as disgust, are associated with increased activity in the right prefrontal cortex (Davidson et al., 2002; Herrington et al., 2005). As noted in Chapter 2, the prefrontal cortex is the part of the frontal lobe that lies in front of the motor cortex. We're not sure why the hemispheres differ in this way, but studying these differences may yield important clues to the biological bases of emotional disorders like depression.

CONCEPT 8.23
The cerebral cortex and brain structures in the limbic system play key roles in regulating our emotional responses.

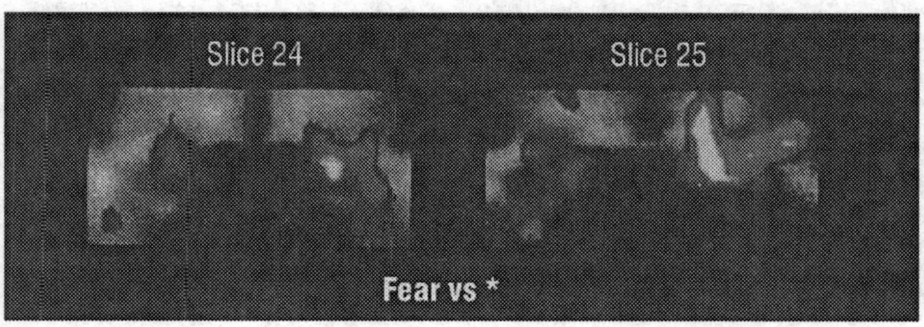

© National Institute of Mental Health

FIGURE 8.11 Activation of Amygdala in Response to a Fearful Face
Here we see functional MRI images of the amygdala in response to viewing a fearful face. More intense colors show greater activation in relation to a visual fixation point (control). Slice 24 shows the forward part of the amygdala, whereas Slice 25 shows the back part. The image is viewed as though the person were looking out from the page.
Source: National Institute of Mental Health (NIMH), 2001.

Theories of Emotion: Which Comes First: Feelings or Bodily Responses?

SLICE OF LIFE One night while I was driving home, my car hit an icy patch in the road and went out of control. The car spun completely around twice and wound up facing oncoming traffic. At that instant, I felt the way a deer must feel when it is caught in the headlights of a car bearing down on it—terrified and helpless. Fortunately, the cars coming toward me stopped in time, and I was able to regain control of my car. I arrived home safely but still shaking in fear. At the time, I didn't stop to consider the question pondered by many psychologists: Did my awareness of my fear precede or follow my bodily response (shaking, sweating, heart pounding)? The *commonsense* view of emotion is that we first perceive a stimulus (the car spinning out of control), then feel an emotion (fear), and only then become physiologically aroused (heart pounding) and perform a behavioral response (tightly gripping the steering wheel). Yet one of the more enduring debates in psychology concerns which comes first—the feeling state (anger, fear, etc.) or our physiological or behavioral responses.

James-Lange Theory

James-Lange theory The belief that emotions occur after people become aware of their physiological responses to the triggering stimuli.

William James (1890/1970) argued that bodily reactions or sensations precede emotions. Because Carl Georg Lange, a Danish physiologist, proposed similar ideas independently, this view is called the **James-Lange theory**. James used the now-classic example of confronting a bear in the woods. James asked the question, "Do we run from the bear because we are afraid, or do we become afraid because we run?" He answered this question by proposing that the response of running comes first. We see the bear. We run. Then we become afraid. We become afraid because we sense the particular pattern of bodily arousal associated with running, such as a pounding heart, rapid breathing, and muscular contractions (B. H. Friedman, 2010). Thus, emotions *follow* bodily reactions. In this view, we experience fear because we tremble; we experience the emotion of sadness because we cry. If this theory is correct, then my body would have reacted first when my car spun out of control. Only when I sensed my body's reaction would I have become consciously aware of fear.

CONCEPT 8.24
The James-Lange theory proposes that emotions follow bodily reactions to triggering stimuli.

James argued that distinct bodily changes are associated with each emotion. This is why fear feels different from other emotions, such as anger or love.

Cannon-Bard Theory

Cannon-Bard theory The belief that emotional and physiological reactions to triggering stimuli occur almost simultaneously.

In the 1920s, physiologist Walter Cannon (1927) proposed a second major theory of emotions. He based his theory on research conducted by his laboratory assistant, Philip Bard. This theory, called the **Cannon-Bard theory**, challenged the James-Lange theory. It holds that the same bodily changes that result from the activation of the sympathetic nervous system accompany different emotions. Sympathetic activation makes our hearts race, our breathing quicken, and our muscles contract whether we are experiencing anger, fear, or sexual arousal. How could these common responses in the body evoke different emotions, as the James-Lange theory suggests? The Cannon-Bard theory proposes that the subjective experience of an emotion and the bodily reactions associated with it occur virtually simultaneously. In other words, our emotions accompany our bodily responses but are not caused by them. In simplest terms, the Cannon-Bard theory postulates that we see the bear, we experience fear and a pounding heart, and then we run.

Two-Factor Model

The **two-factor model**, which was developed in the 1960s, held that emotions depend on two factors: (1) a state of general arousal and (2) a cognitive interpretation, or *labeling* (Schachter, 1971; Schachter & Singer, 1962). According to this model, when we experience bodily arousal, we look for cues in the environment to explain why we feel aroused or excited. Your heart may race when you see a monster jump onto the movie screen in the latest horror movie; it may also race when your car spins out of control. Your arousal in the safe confines of the movie theater is likely to be labeled and experienced as "pleasurable excitement." But the same pattern of arousal experienced in the spinning car will probably be labeled and experienced as "sheer terror."

The two-factor model continues to generate interest, but it fails to account for the distinctive physiological features associated with different emotions. Anger may feel different from fear not merely because of how we label our arousal but also because it is associated with different bodily responses.

Experimental evidence also casts doubt on whether we must label the state of arousal in order to experience an emotion. Psychologist Robert Zajonc (1980, 1984) exposed subjects to brief presentations of Japanese ideographs (written symbols). Later, he found that subjects preferred particular characters they had seen, even if they had no recall of ever having seen these stimuli. Zajonc believed that some emotional responses, such as liking and disliking, may not involve any cognitive appraisal—that they may occur through mere exposure to a stimulus.

CONCEPT 8.25
The Cannon-Bard theory proposes that the subjective experience of an emotion and the bodily reactions associated with it occur virtually simultaneously.

two-factor model The theory that emotions involve two factors: a state of general arousal and a cognitive interpretation (or labeling) of the causes of the arousal.

CONCEPT 8.26
The two-factor model proposes that the combination of physiological arousal and cognitive appraisal (labeling) of the source of the arousal produces the specific emotional state.

Dual-Pathway Model of Fear

According to the **dual-pathway model of fear** formulated by psychologist Joseph LeDoux (2000, 2003, 2008), the brain uses two pathways to process fear messages. An environmental stimulus (e.g., seeing a car barreling down on you) is first processed by the thalamus. From there the information branches off, with one pathway (the "high road") leading to the cerebral cortex, where it can be processed more carefully. Another pathway (the "low road") leads directly to the amygdala in a few thousandths of a second, allowing for a more immediate response to danger cues than if the signal were to first pass through the cortex (Winerman, 2005) (see ■ Figure 8.12). The "low road" thus allows a faster response to danger cues.

Suppose you are walking in the woods and see a curved object in the bush. This visual image is first processed by the thalamus, which makes a rough appraisal of the object as potentially dangerous (possibly a snake). The thalamus transmits this information directly to the amygdala via the "low road," which prompts an immediate bodily response. Heart rate and blood pressure jump, and muscles throughout the body contract as the body prepares to respond quickly to a possible threat. The cortex, slower to respond, processes the information further. ("No, that's not a snake. It's just a stick.") From the standpoint of survival, it is better to act quickly on the assumption that the suspicious object is a snake and to ask questions later. Responding without thinking can be a lifesaver. As LeDoux puts it, "The time saved by the amygdala in acting on the thalamic information, rather than waiting for the cortical input, may be the difference between life and death. It is better to have treated a stick as a snake than not to have responded to a possible snake" (1994). Whether the cortex interprets the object as a snake or a stick determines whether a fear response continues or is quickly quelled. The cortex is also responsible for producing the subjective or felt experience of fear.

dual-pathway model of fear LeDoux's theory that the brain uses two pathways (a "high road" and a "low road") to process fear messages.

CONCEPT 8.27
The dual-pathway model suggests two pathways for processing fear stimuli in the brain: a "high road" leading to the cerebral cortex, and a "low road" leading to the amygdala.

© Oshchepkov Dmitry/Shutterstock.com

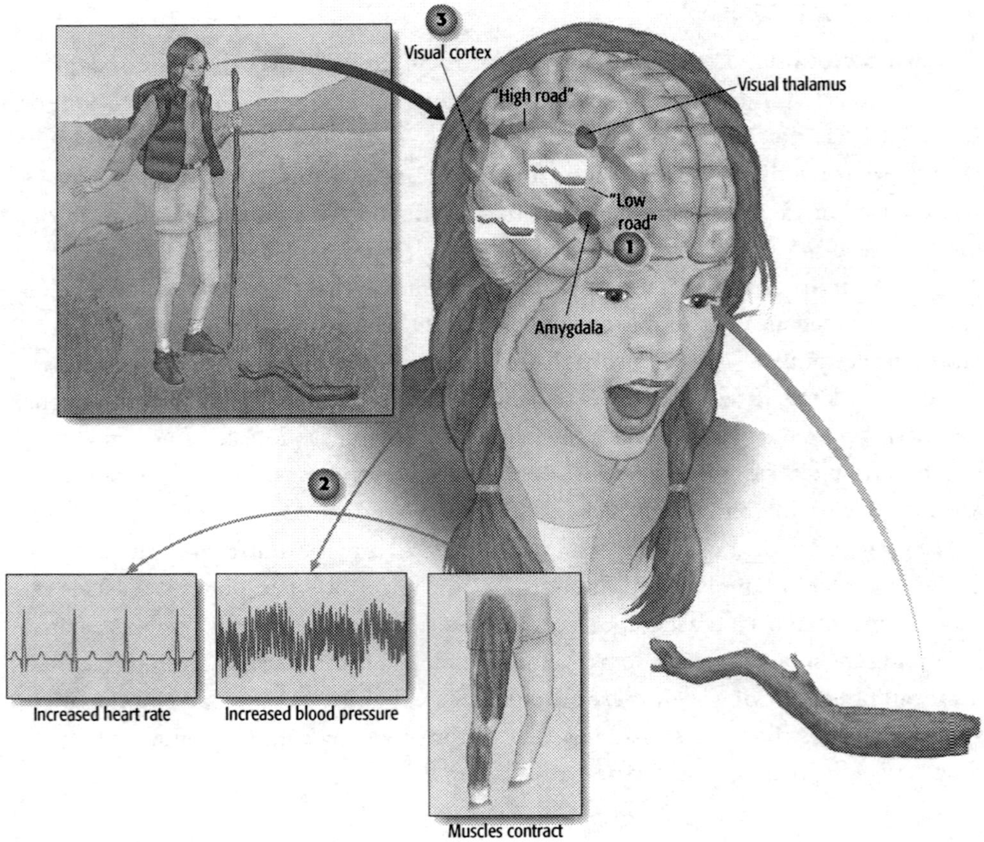

FIGURE 8.12 LeDoux's Dual-Pathway Model of Fear
LeDoux posits that fear messages are first processed in the thalamus and then branch off along two different pathways. (1) One pathway, a "low road," goes directly to the amygdala, bypassing the higher thinking centers of the brain. (2) The amygdala triggers a fear response that has multiple components. (3) A "high road" leads to the cerebral cortex, where the message is interpreted more carefully. ("Relax. It's only a stick, not a snake.")
Source: Adapted from LeDoux, 1996.

What Does All This Mean?

Where do these various theories of emotions, as represented in ■ Figure 8.13, leave us? The James-Lange theory implies that distinctive bodily responses are associated with each emotion, whereas the Cannon-Bard theory postulates that a similar pattern of bodily responses accompanies different emotions. Both views may be at least partially correct. There certainly are common physiological responses associated with such emotions as fear, anger, and love, as the Cannon-Bard theory proposes. We feel our hearts beating faster when we are in the presence of a new love and when we are faced with an intruder in the night. Yet, as the James-Lange theory proposes, evidence shows there are also distinctive bodily reactions associated with different emotions (B. H. Friedman, 2010). For example, we may have the sensation of "cold feet" when we are afraid but not when we are angry because blood flow is reduced to our extremities in fear reactions but not in anger reactions. Anger is associated with a sharp rise in skin temperature, which may explain why we often describe people who are angry as "hot under the collar."

Different emotions are also connected with different facial expressions. Blushing, for instance, is a primary characteristic of embarrassment. James considered facial expressions to be among the bodily responses that distinguish one emotion from another. Evidence favoring the facial-feedback hypothesis also provides some support for the James-Lange theory in showing that contractions of particular facial muscles (e.g., smiling or frowning) can influence corresponding emotional states (J. I. Davis, Senghas, & Ochsner, 2009).

Emotions may precede cognitions under some conditions, as suggested by Zajonc's studies and by the dual-pathway model proposed by LeDoux. That emotions may occur before cognitions does not dismiss the important role that cognitions play in emotions. Whether you are angered when an instructor springs an unexpected assignment on you or frightened

TRY THIS OUT
Tracking Your Emotions

Keep track of your emotions for a day or two by using a notebook to record situations in which you experience emotion. Include brief descriptions of your emotional state (joy, fear, anger, etc.), your bodily reactions (e.g., rapid heartbeat, rapid breathing, sweating, tingling sensation, jumpiness, shakiness), and the thoughts that passed through your mind at the time. Afterward, examine the relationships among your emotions, your bodily reactions, and your thought patterns. Compare your bodily reactions in different emotional states. Also compare the thoughts you had while in different emotional states. What does this exercise teach you about the connections between your emotional states and your bodily reactions and thought patterns?

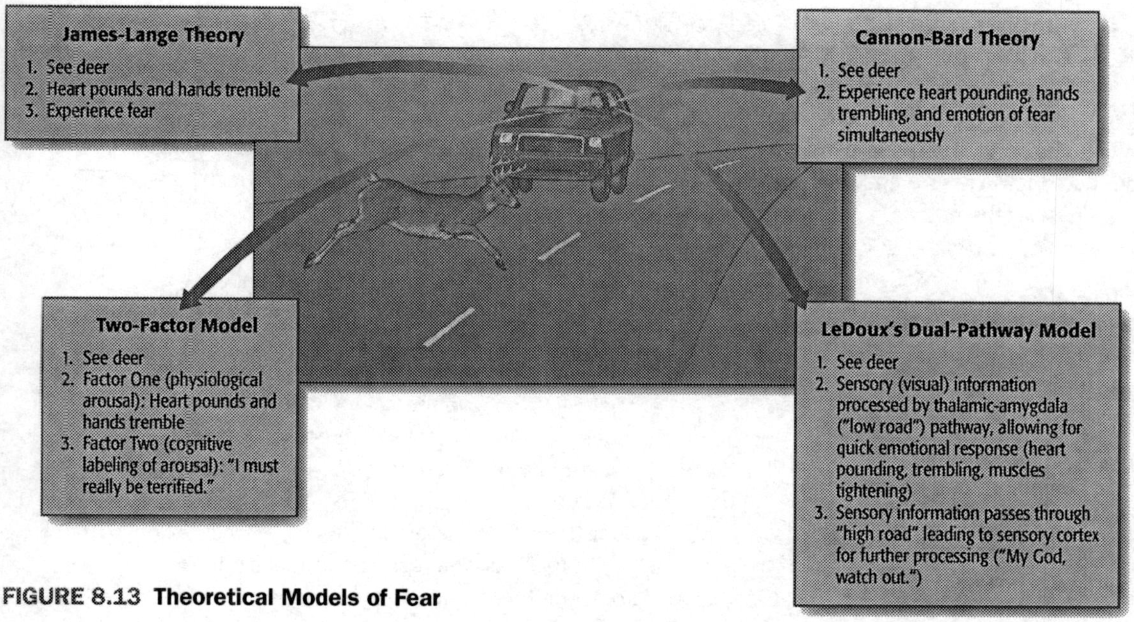

FIGURE 8.13 Theoretical Models of Fear

when a doctor points to a spot on your X-ray depends on the appraisal of the situation made in the cerebral cortex, not on automatic processing of stimuli by lower brain structures.

How we appraise events also depends on what the events mean to us personally (Lazarus, 1995, 2000). The same event, such as a pregnancy or a change of jobs, can lead to feelings of joy, fear, or even anger depending on the meaning the event has for the individual and its perceived importance. The *Try This Out* feature offers an exercise in tracking your emotions.

The final chapter in the debate about how emotions are processed in the brain is still to be written. Yet the belief that distinctive bodily changes are associated with different emotions has had at least one practical implication: It is the basis of a method of lie detection, which is discussed later in this module.

© Zsolt Nyulaszi, 2009/Shutterstock.com

What's your emotional IQ? Are you emotionally clued-in or clueless? How is emotional intelligence linked to positive outcomes?

Emotional Intelligence: How Well Do You Manage Your Emotions?

Some theorists believe that a person's ability to recognize and manage emotions represents a form of intelligent behavior, called **emotional intelligence**, or EI (Mayer, Salovey, & Caruso, 2008). Emotional intelligence is difficult to define precisely, but it can be generally described in terms of five main characteristics:

1. *Knowing your emotions.* Self-awareness, or knowing your true feelings, is a core feature of emotional intelligence.
2. *Managing your emotions.* Emotionally intelligent people are able to handle their emotions in appropriate ways. They can soothe themselves in difficult times, and they bounce back quickly from disappointments and setbacks.
3. *Motivating yourself.* People with a high level of emotional intelligence can marshal their emotions to pursue their goals. They approach challenges with enthusiasm, zeal, and confidence, which makes them better equipped to attain high levels of achievement and productivity. They also are able to delay gratification and constrain their impulses as they pursue long-term goals.

emotional intelligence The ability to recognize emotions in yourself and others and to manage your own emotions effectively.

CONCEPT 8.28

The ability to recognize emotions in yourself and others, and to regulate emotions effectively, may represent a form of intelligent behavior called emotional intelligence.

TRY THIS OUT Taking Stock of Your Emotional Intelligence

Though we lack a validated self-report scale of emotional intelligence, the following questions should give you some insight into how you measure up on the construct. Your answers are not for public consumption, so answer them as honestly as you can in terms of your real self, not your imagined or ideal self.

1. Would you say (honestly now) that
   a. you generally go through the day without paying attention to your emotions, OR
   b. you are generally attuned to your feelings?
2. Would you say that
   a. your emotions tend to get all lumped together, OR
   b. you are able to clearly discriminate one emotion from another?
3. Would you say that
   a. you seldom if ever experience negative emotions, such as anger or fear, OR
   b. you are able to recognize these emotions when you experience them?
4. Would you say that
   a. you deny feeling strong positive emotions, such as love or joy, OR
   b. you recognize these feelings when they occur?
5. Would you say that
   a. you are able to recognize emotions in others, OR
   b. you have a hard time reading emotions in other people?
6. Would you say that
   a. you try to understand what people are feeling, OR
   b. you would rather not deal with that mushy stuff?
7. Would you say that
   a. you tend to focus on what people say, not what they must be feeling, OR
   b. you tend to focus on both what people say and what they must be feeling?
8. If someone starts crying or gets angry, do you
   a. just want to leave the scene, OR
   b. seek to calm or comfort the person?
9. If you get into an argument with your partner or a family member, do you
   a. just try to stop the argument by becoming silent, OR
   b. try to focus on the issues and resolve them?
10. If someone has a gripe with you, do you
    a. immediately jump to defend yourself, OR
    b. try to understand the situation from the other person's perspective?

Did you detect a pattern? These items are scaled such that (b) responses are keyed to be reflective of emotional intelligence. How did you do? Would you consider yourself to be emotionally intelligent or emotionally challenged? Do you think you can change how you deal with your own emotions and how you respond to emotions in others? How would you go about it?

Source: Adapted from Nevid & Rathus, 2007. Reprinted with permission of John Wiley & Sons, Inc.

4. *Recognizing emotions in others.* Empathy, the ability to perceive emotions in others, is an important "people skill." It not only helps build strong relationships but also contributes to success in teaching, sales, management, and the helping professions.
5. *Helping others handle their emotions.* The ability to help others deal with their feelings is an important factor in maintaining meaningful relationships.

Emotional intelligence may be a more important contributor to success in life than IQ. Perhaps you know people who are intellectually brilliant but have no clue about their own or other people's emotions. Evidence links emotional intelligence to many positive outcomes, including higher levels of emotional well-being and life satisfaction, better health, happier marriages, higher GPAs in college, and better job performance (e.g., Gannon & Ranzijn, 2005; Gignac, 2006; Martins, Ramalho, & Morin, 2010; O'Boyle et al., 2010; Parker, et al., 2005). However, we await further research to determine whether EI predicts successful outcomes beyond what we can predict using measures of general intelligence and personality. The *Try This Out* feature offers an opportunity to evaluate your own level of emotional intelligence.

Lie Detection: In Search of Pinocchio's Nose

Let us end this module by commenting on the use of the polygraph, a device used to detect lying by comparing a person's responses to control (neutral) and test questions. It is based on the assumption that when people lie, they reveal telltale signs in breathing patterns, heart rates, and the electrical reactivity of the skin as the result of sweating. The polygraph measures patterns of bodily arousal, not lying per se. Many leading scientists, along with distinguished scientific groups such as the National Academy of Sciences, say the polygraph cannot accurately distinguish lying from the emotional reactions of honest people put in pressure situations (e.g., Kluger & Masters, 2006). Another problem is that many seasoned liars lie without any telltale physiological reactions. Unfortunately, the false findings of polygraphs have damaged the lives of many innocent people. Though the polygraph may occasionally catch a person in a lie, it is not reliable enough to pass scientific muster.

© iStockphoto.com/evaserrabassa

We have yet to find anything akin to the nose of the fictional character Pinocchio for reliably detecting when people are lying.

More sophisticated methods of detecting lying are in the experimental stage, such as measurement of subtle facial movements that may reveal deception (Warren, Schertler, & Bull, 2009). Some companies are using the fMRI to look for patterns of brain activation associated with lying. If this technique proves out, it may be especially useful to law enforcement, intelligence agencies, and transportation security officials. There may come a day when you will need to have your brain scanned when applying for a sensitive position in government or industry. But that day is not yet here, as we lack any reliable indicator of lying, let alone anything akin to Pinocchio's nose, which grew each time the fictional character told a lie (Vrij, Granhag, & Porter, 2010).

CONCEPT 8.29
Polygraphs are widely used, even though scientists remain skeptical of their ability to detect lying.

Concept Chart 8.3 provides an overview of the major concepts of emotion discussed in this module.

CONCEPT CHART 8.3 Major Concepts of Emotion

© AVAVA, 2009/ Shutterstock.com

© ARENA Creative, 2009/ Shutterstock.com

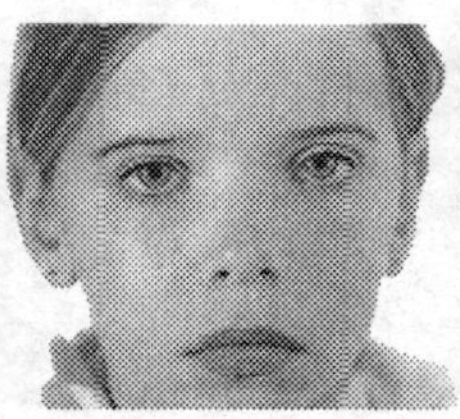

© Sergei Chumakov, 2009/ Shutterstock.com

© CREATISTA, 2009/ Shutterstock.com

Concept	Description
Facial expressions of emotion	Evidence from cross-cultural studies supports universal recognition of the facial expressions of six basic emotions: anger, fear, disgust, sadness, happiness, and surprise.
Facial-feedback hypothesis	Mimicking facial movements associated with an emotion can produce the corresponding emotional state.
Factors determining happiness	Friendships and having a religious commitment are linked to happiness; genetic factors may create a fairly stable level or set point for personal happiness.
Triangular model of love	Sternberg's conception of love as comprised of three components: intimacy, passion, and decision/commitment.
Physiological bases of emotions	Emotions are accompanied by activation of the sympathetic branch of the autonomic nervous system. Emotions are processed by the structures of the limbic system (the amygdala and hippocampus) and by the cerebral cortex.
James-Lange theory of emotions	Emotions follow our bodily reactions to triggering stimuli—we become afraid because we run; we feel sad because we cry.
Cannon-Bard theory of emotions	Emotions accompany bodily responses to triggering stimuli but are not caused by them.
Two-factor model of emotions	The combination of physiological arousal and cognitive appraisal (labeling) of the source of the arousal produces the emotional state.
LeDoux's dual-pathway model of fear	One pathway leads from the thalamus to the amygdala, which produces the initial fear response (bodily arousal), while a second pathway leads to the cortex, which further processes the fear stimulus and produces the conscious awareness of fear.
Emotional intelligence	According to this concept, the ability to manage emotions effectively is a form of intelligent behavior.
Polygraph	A device used to detect lying based on analysis of psychological responses to questions.

8.3 MODULE REVIEW Emotions

Recite It

What are the three components of emotions?

- Psychologists conceptualize emotions as having a physiological component (heightened bodily arousal), a cognitive component (a feeling state, as well as thoughts and judgments about experiences linked to the feeling state), and a behavioral component (approach or avoidance behaviors).

Are facial expressions of emotion universal?

- Evidence from cross-cultural studies supports the view that facial expressions of six basic emotions—anger, fear, disgust, sadness, happiness, and surprise—are universal.
- Cultural differences, as well as some similarities, exist in how emotions are experienced. Each culture has display rules, that determine how emotions are expressed and how much emotion is appropriate to express. Gender differences in emotional expression may reflect cultural expectations.

What factors are associated with personal happiness?

- Factors associated with personal happiness include the availability of friendships and religious commitment. On the other hand, wealth has but a modest relationship with personal happiness and life satisfaction. Happiness may also vary around a genetically influenced set point.

What are the three components of love in Sternberg's model of love?

- According to Sternberg's triangular model, the components of love are intimacy (emotional closeness and sharing), passion (romantic interest and sexual arousal), and decision/commitment (degree of commitment in the relationship).

What role do brain structures play in emotions?

- Parts of the limbic system, including the amygdala and the hippocampus, play key roles in emotional processing.
- The cerebral cortex interprets stimuli and plans strategies for either approaching or avoiding stimuli, depending on whether they are perceived as "friend" or "foe." The cortex also controls facial expression of emotions and is responsible for processing the felt experience of emotions.

What are the major theories of emotions?

- The major theories of emotions are the James-Lange theory (emotions occur after people become aware of their body's responses to triggering stimuli), the Cannon-Bard theory (emotional and physiological reactions to triggering stimuli occur almost simultaneously), the two-factor model (emotions depend on an arousal state and a labeling of the causes of the arousal), and LeDoux's dual-pathway model of fear (the amygdala responds to fear stimuli before the cerebral cortex gets involved).

What is emotional intelligence?

- Emotional intelligence refers to the ability to recognize emotions in oneself and others and to manage emotions effectively. Emotional intelligence may have an important bearing on our success in life and ability to maintain intimate relationships.

What is the polygraph? Does it work?

- The polygraph is a device used to detect physiological response patterns believed to indicate when a person is lying. However, we lack compelling scientific evidence that the polygraph can reliably detect lying.

Recall It

1. All of the following are basic components of emotion *except*
   a. bodily arousal.
   b. production of neuropeptide Y.
   c. cognition.
   d. expressed behavior.
2. Facial expressions of six basic emotions are recognized universally. What are these six emotions?
3. The belief that the subjective experience of an emotion and the bodily response that accompanies it occur at virtually the same time is the
   a. James-Lange theory.
   b. two-factor model.
   c. Cannon-Bard theory.
   d. dual-pathway model of fear.
4. Which of the following statements is *not* correct?
   a. Women are generally better able than men to express emotions in words.
   b. Women are generally better able than men to express emotions through facial expressions.
   c. In many cultures, men are given greater latitude in displaying anger.
   d. Evidence shows that men tend to smile more often than women.

Think About It

- How is emotional intelligence different from general intelligence? In what ways might it become more important for success in life than general intelligence?

Managing Anger

APPLICATION MODULE 8.4

Do you know people who have problems controlling their temper? Do you yourself do things in anger that you later regret? Anger can be a catalyst for physical or verbal aggression. Even if you never express your anger through aggression, anger and hostility can take a toll on your health, putting you at increased risk of developing coronary heart disease (Chida & Steptoe, 2009) (see Chapter 12). Anger floods the body with stress hormones that may eventually damage your heart and arteries.

Cognitive theorists recognize that anger is prompted by a person's reactions to frustrating or provocative situations, not by the situations themselves. Though people often blame the "other guy" for making them angry, people make themselves angry by thinking angering thoughts or making anger-inducing statements to themselves. To gain better control over their anger, people need to identify and correct such thoughts and statements. By doing so, they can learn to avoid hostile confrontations and perhaps save wear and tear on their cardiovascular systems. Here are some suggestions psychologists offer for identifying and controlling anger:

CONCEPT 8.30
By identifying and correcting anger-inducing thoughts, people can gain better control over their anger and develop more effective ways of handling conflicts.

→ Concept Link
Chronic anger is not only a problem when it comes to controlling your temper; it can also increase your risk of developing coronary heart disease. See Module 12.2.

- *Become aware of your emotional reactions in anger-provoking situations.* When you notice yourself getting "hot under the collar," take this as a cue to calm yourself down and think through the situation. Learn to replace anger-arousing thoughts with calming alternatives.
- *Review the evidence.* Might you be overreacting to the situation by taking it too personally? Might you be jumping to the conclusion that the other person means you ill? Are there other ways of viewing the person's behavior?
- *Practice more adaptive thinking.* For example, say to yourself, "I can handle this situation without getting upset. I'll just calm down and think through what I want to say."
- *Practice competing responses.* You can disrupt an angry response by conjuring up soothing mental images, by taking a walk, or by practicing self-relaxation. The time-honored practice of counting to 10 when you begin to feel angry may also help defuse an emotional response. If it doesn't, you can follow Mark Twain's advice and count to 100 instead. While counting, try to think calming thoughts.
- *Don't get steamed.* Others may do dumb or hurtful things, but you make yourself angry by dwelling on them. Take charge of your emotional responses by not allowing yourself to get steamed.
- *Oppose anger with empathy.* Try to understand what the other person is feeling. Rather than saying to yourself, "He's a miserable so-and-so who deserves to be punished," say, "He must really have difficulties at home to act like this. But that's his problem. I won't take it personally."

- *Congratulate yourself for responding assertively rather than aggressively.* Give yourself a mental pat on the back when you handle stressful situations with equanimity rather than with anger.
- *Scale back your expectations of others.* Perceptions of unfairness may result from the expectation that others "should" or "must" fulfill your needs or expectations. By scaling back your expectations, you're less likely to get angry with others when they disappoint you.
- *Modulate verbal responses.* Avoid raising your voice or cursing. Stay cool, even when others do not.
- *Learn to express positive feelings.* Expressing positive feelings can help diffuse negative emotions. Tell others you love them and care about them. They are likely to reciprocate in kind.

Think about situations in which you have felt angry or have acted in anger. How might you handle these situations differently in the future? What coping responses can you use to help you keep your cool? Table 8.3 offers some calming alternatives to thoughts that trigger anger.

TABLE 8.3 Anger Management: Replacing Anger-Inducing Thoughts with Calming Alternatives

Situation	Anger-Inducing Thoughts	Calming Alternatives
A provocateur says, "So what are you going to do about it?"	"That jerk. Who does he think he is? I'll teach him a lesson he won't forget!"	"He must really have a problem to act the way he does. But that's his problem. I don't have to respond at his level."
You get caught in a monster traffic jam.	"Why does this always happen to me? I can't stand this."	"This may be inconvenient, but it's not the end of the world. Don't blow it out of proportion. Everyone gets caught in traffic now and then. Just relax and listen to some music."
You're in a checkout line at the supermarket, and the woman in front of you is cashing a check. It seems as if it's taking hours.	"She has some nerve holding up the line. It's so unfair for someone to make other people wait. I'd like to tell her off!"	"It will take only a few minutes. People have a right to cash their checks in the market. Just relax and read a magazine while you wait."
You're looking for a parking spot when suddenly another car cuts you off and seizes a vacant space.	"No one should be allowed to treat me like this. I'd like to punch him out."	"Don't expect people always to be considerate of your interests. Stop personalizing things." Or "Relax, there's no sense going to war over this."
Your spouse or partner comes home several hours later than expected, without calling to let you know he or she would be late.	"It's so unfair. I can't let him (her) treat me like this."	Explain how you feel without putting your spouse or partner down.
You're watching a movie in a theater, and the people sitting next to you are talking and making a lot of noise.	"Don't they have any regard for others? I'm so angry with these people I could tear their heads off."	"Even if they're inconsiderate, it doesn't mean I have to get angry about it or ruin my enjoyment of the movie. If they don't quiet down when I ask them, I'll just change my seat or call the manager."

Source: Adapted from Nevid & Rathus, 2010.

Thinking Critically About Psychology

Based on your reading of this chapter, answer the following questions. Then, to evaluate your progress in developing critical thinking skills, compare your answers to the sample answers found in Appendix A.

People often think of thinking and feeling as opposite mental states. Is it correct to think of them as opposites? Why or why not?

Log in to CengageBrain to access the resources your instructor requires. For this book, you can access:

CourseMate

Psychology CourseMate brings course concepts to life with interactive learning, study, and exam preparation tools that support the printed textbook. A textbook-specific website, Psychology CourseMate includes an integrated interactive eBook and other interactive learning tools including quizzes, flashcards, videos, and more.

CENGAGENOW

CengageNow is an easy-to-use online resource that helps you study in less time to get the grade you want—NOW. Take a pre-test for this chapter and receive a personalized study plan based on your results that will identify the topics you need to review and direct you to online resources to help you master those topics. Then take a post-test to help you determine the concepts you have mastered and what you will need to work on. If your textbook does not include an access code card, go to CengageBrain.com to gain access.

Visit www.cengagebrain.com to access your account and purchase materials.

VISUAL OVERVIEW Chapter 8 Motivation and Emotion

MODULE 8.1 Motivation: The "Whys" of Behavior

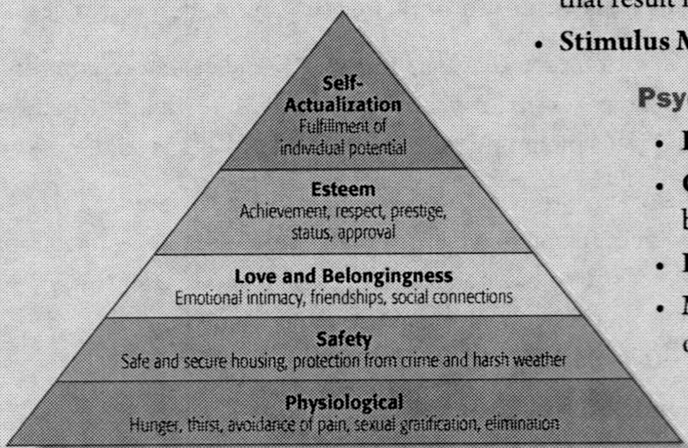

Biological Sources of Motivation

- **Instincts**: Inborn, species-specific responses as motives
- **Needs and Drives**: States of deficiency (needs) create drives that motivate behavior that result in drive reduction
- **Stimulus Motives**: Needs for exploration and optimal stimulation

Psychological Sources of Motivation

- **Incentives**: Rewards or goals that "pull" behavior
- **Cognitive Dissonance**: Discomfort arising from discrepancies between beliefs or attitudes and behavior
- **Psychosocial Needs**: Needs for friendship and achievement
- **Maslow's Hierarchy of Needs**: Biological and psychosocial needs ordered in a hierarchy

MODULE 8.2 Hunger and Eating

- **Control of Hunger and Appetite**: Hypothalamus (brain's appetite regulator); brain chemicals act on hypothalamus to stimulate or curb appetite
- **Obesity**: Many factors are involved including genetics, eating patterns, environmental influences, and emotions
- **Types of Eating Disorders**: Anorexia nervosa (self-starvation and distorted body image) and bulimia (cycles of binge eating and purging)
- **Causes of Eating Disorders**: Include social pressure to conform to ultrathin ideal, needs for perfectionism and control, genetic factors, irregularities in neurotransmitter functioning

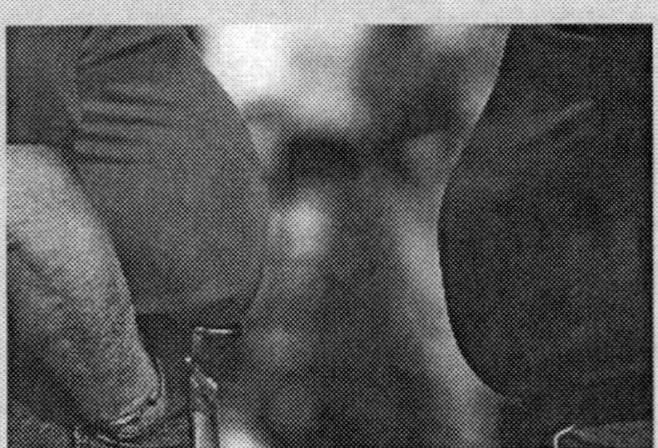

© Tom Raymond Stone/Getty Images

MODULE 8.3 **Emotions**

- **Components of Emotions**: Bodily arousal, cognitions, approach or avoidance behaviors
- **Universally Recognized Emotions**: Anger, fear, disgust, sadness, happiness, surprise

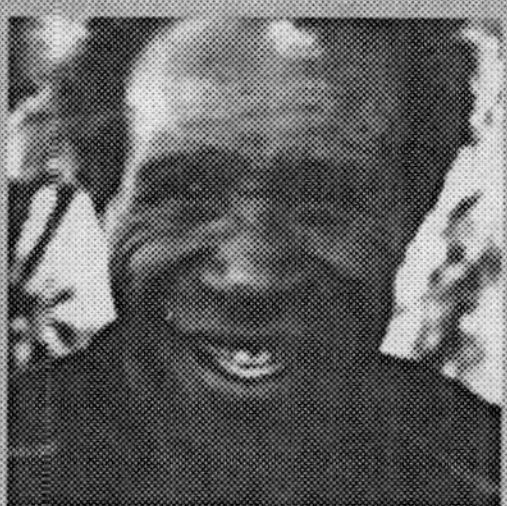
© Paul Ekman, Ph.D./Paul Ekman Group, LLC

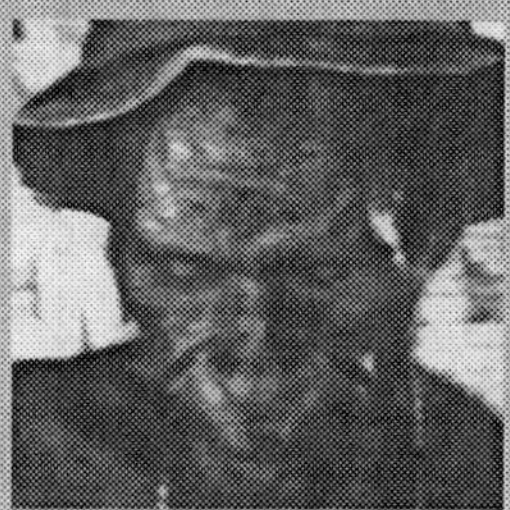
© Paul Ekman, Ph.D./Paul Ekman Group, LLC

© Paul Ekman, Ph.D./Paul Ekman Group, LLC

© Paul Ekman, Ph.D./Paul Ekman Group, LLC

What is this man feeling?

Major Theories of Emotions

- **Major Theories of Emotions**: James-Lange theory (see bear→run→feel afraid); Cannon-Bard theory (see bear→run and feel afraid); two-factor model (bodily arousal→labeling source of arousal→emotional state); dual-pathway model (the "low road" to the amygdala, the "high road" to the cerebral cortex)

Key Brain Structures in Regulating Emotions

- **Amygdala**: Fear-triggering center
- **Hippocampus**: Remembering the context of the emotion
- **Thalamus**: Initial processing center for fear-related messages
- **Cerebral Cortex**: Evaluating the threat

© National Institute of Mental Health

Activation of Amygdala in Response to a Fearful Face

9 Child Development

Keeping Peace at the Dinner Table

SLICE OF LIFE One thing parents learn when they have a second child is the everyday meaning of the concept of equality. They learn that whatever they give to one child they must give to the other in equal measure. This lesson in parenting was driven home for me one day when we sat down at the dinner table to share a pizza. Everything was fine until we divided the last two slices between Daniella, then age 5, and Michael, who was then 11. I noticed Daniella's eyes beginning to well up with tears. I asked her what was wrong. She pointed to Michael's slice and said that his was bigger. Michael had already begun eating his slice, so it was clear that pulling a last-minute switch wouldn't ease her concern, let alone be fair to Michael. It was then that the heavy hammer of equality came down squarely on my head.

To resolve the situation, I drew upon a concept you'll read about in this chapter: the principle of *conservation*. This principle holds that the amount or size of a substance does not change merely as the result of a superficial change in its outward appearance. You don't increase the amount of clay by merely flattening or stretching it out. Neither do you increase the amount of a liquid by pouring it from a wider container into a narrower one, even though the liquid rises to a higher level in the narrower container. Although the principle of conservation may seem self-evident to an adult or older child, the typical five-year-old has not yet mastered this concept. Knowing this, I quickly took a pizza slicer and divided Daniella's slice into two. "There," I said, "now you have twice as many slices as Michael." Michael gave me a quizzical look, as though he were wondering who would ever fall for such an obvious trick. Daniella, on the other hand, looked at the two slices and quite happily starting eating them, the tears quickly receding. Peace at the Nevid dining table was restored, at least for the moment.

The pizza incident illustrates a theme that carries through our study of human development. It's not about applying principles of child psychology to keep peace at the dinner table. Rather, it's about understanding that the world of the child is very different from that of the adolescent or adult. Children's cognitive abilities and ways of understanding the world change dramatically as they mature. Adolescents also see themselves and the world around them quite differently than do their parents and other adults. Even in adulthood, 20-somethings and 30-somethings perceive themselves and their place in the world quite differently than do others of more advanced years.

In this chapter we trace the remarkable journey that is human development. Our story would be incomplete without first considering the important events that occur well before a child takes its first breath.

DID YOU KNOW THAT...

- A fertilized egg cell is not yet attached to the mother's body during the first week or so after conception? (p. 334)
- By one year of age, infants have already mastered the most difficult balancing problem they will ever face in life? (p. 341)
- Baby geese followed a famous scientist around as if he was their mother? (p. 346)
- According to theorist Erik Erikson, the development of a sense of trust begins before the infant speaks its first word? (p. 354)
- It is normal for a four-year-old to believe the moon has feelings? (p. 359)
- Among third graders, those who had a TV set in their bedrooms did more poorly on standardized tests in school than did those without their own TV? (p. 365)

© Jiri Vaclavek/Shutterstock.com

Learning Objectives

By reading this chapter you will be able to . . .

1 **IDENTIFY** four major questions underlying the study of human development.

2 **IDENTIFY** and **DESCRIBE** two major methods psychologists use to study developmental changes and **EVALUATE** their strengths and weaknesses.

3 **IDENTIFY** and **DESCRIBE** the stages of prenatal development.

4 **APPLY** knowledge of teratogens to the threats faced during prenatal development.

5 **IDENTIFY** the major reflexes present at birth.

6 **DESCRIBE** how the infant's motor skills change through the first year of life.

7 **DESCRIBE** the infant's sensory, perceptual, and learning abilities.

8 **IDENTIFY** and **DESCRIBE** the major types of temperament and attachment styles.

9 **IDENTIFY** and **DESCRIBE** the major styles of parenting and **APPLY** this knowledge to outcomes associated with these types.

10 **IDENTIFY** Erikson's stages of psychosocial development in childhood and **DESCRIBE** the central challenge of each stage.

11 **DESCRIBE** the characteristics of each stage in Piaget's theory of cognitive development and **EVALUATE** his legacy.

12 **DESCRIBE** Vygotsky's psychosocial theory of cognitive development.

13 **EVALUATE** the effects of television viewing on children's behavior and cognitive development.

14 **APPLY** knowledge of responsible television viewing to steps parents can take to foster this behavior in their children.

© Tina Manley/Alamy

Preview

MODULE 9.1

Studying Human Development: Key Questions and Methods of Study

- What are the major questions that underlie the study of human development?
- How do developmental psychologists study age-related changes?

CONCEPT 9.1
The study of human development has been shaped by four major questions: nature versus nurture, continuity versus discontinuity, universality, and stability.

developmental psychology The branch of psychology that explores physical, emotional, cognitive, and social aspects of development.

We can think of development progressing chronologically in terms of the stages shown in ■ Figure 9.1. The branch of psychology that studies the systematic changes that occur during the life span is called **developmental psychology**. Developmental psychologists gather data on the kinds of changes that occur during development. But they also use this information to help answer larger questions about human development. In this section, we first consider four of these major questions: the nature versus nurture question, the continuity versus discontinuity question, the universality question, and the stability question. Then we examine the major methods developmental psychologists use in their studies.

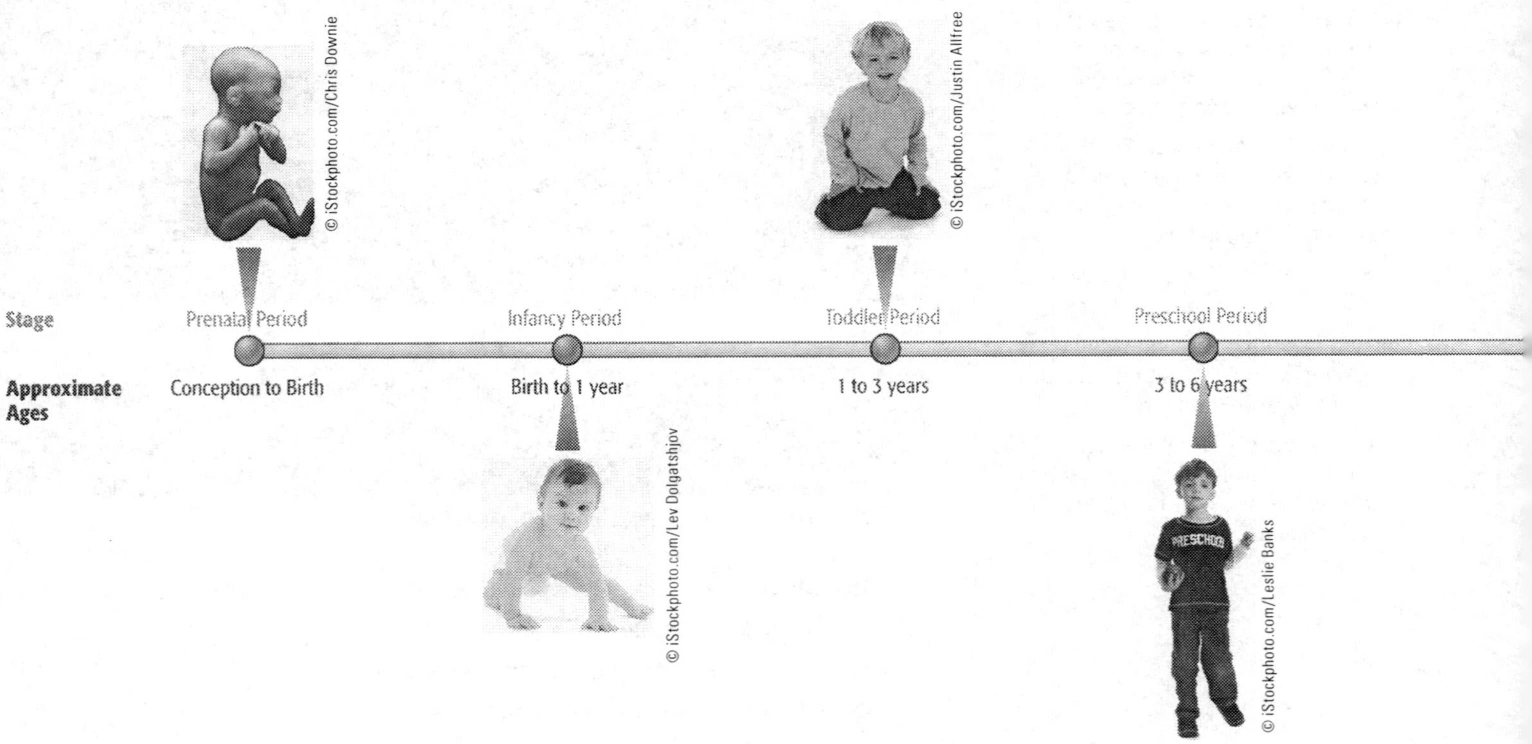

Figure 9.1 Stages of Development Through the Life Span

The Nature Versus Nurture Question

One of the oldest controversies in psychology is the **nature-nurture debate**. Is our behavior governed by nature (genetics) or nurture (environment and culture)? In the early twentieth century, the debate between opposing sides was more clearly drawn. Behaviorists such as John Watson maintained that behavior is determined by learning and experience. As explained in Chapter 1, Watson even boasted that he could take healthy, "well-formed" infants and, by controlling their environment, turn them into doctors, lawyers, or even beggars or thieves. Another early theorist, psychologist Arnold Gesell (1880–1961), emphasized the role of biological processes in human development. Gesell was heavily influenced by Darwin's theory of evolution and believed that child development proceeds through a series of genetically determined changes that unfold according to nature's plan.

nature-nurture debate The debate in psychology over the relative influences of genetics (nature) and environment (nurture) in determining behavior.

Though the nature-nurture debate continues, psychologists recognize that human behavior is influenced by a combination of genes and the environment. The contemporary version of the nature-nurture debate is more about the relative contributions of nature *and* nurture to particular behaviors than it is about nature *or* nurture (Bouchard, 2004). In other words, scientists recognize that biology and experience work together to enhance the organism's ability to adapt successfully to its environment (Gottesman & Hanson, 2005).

Developmental psychologists seek to determine how much of development can be attributed to nature, or genes, and how much to nurture, or the environment. For

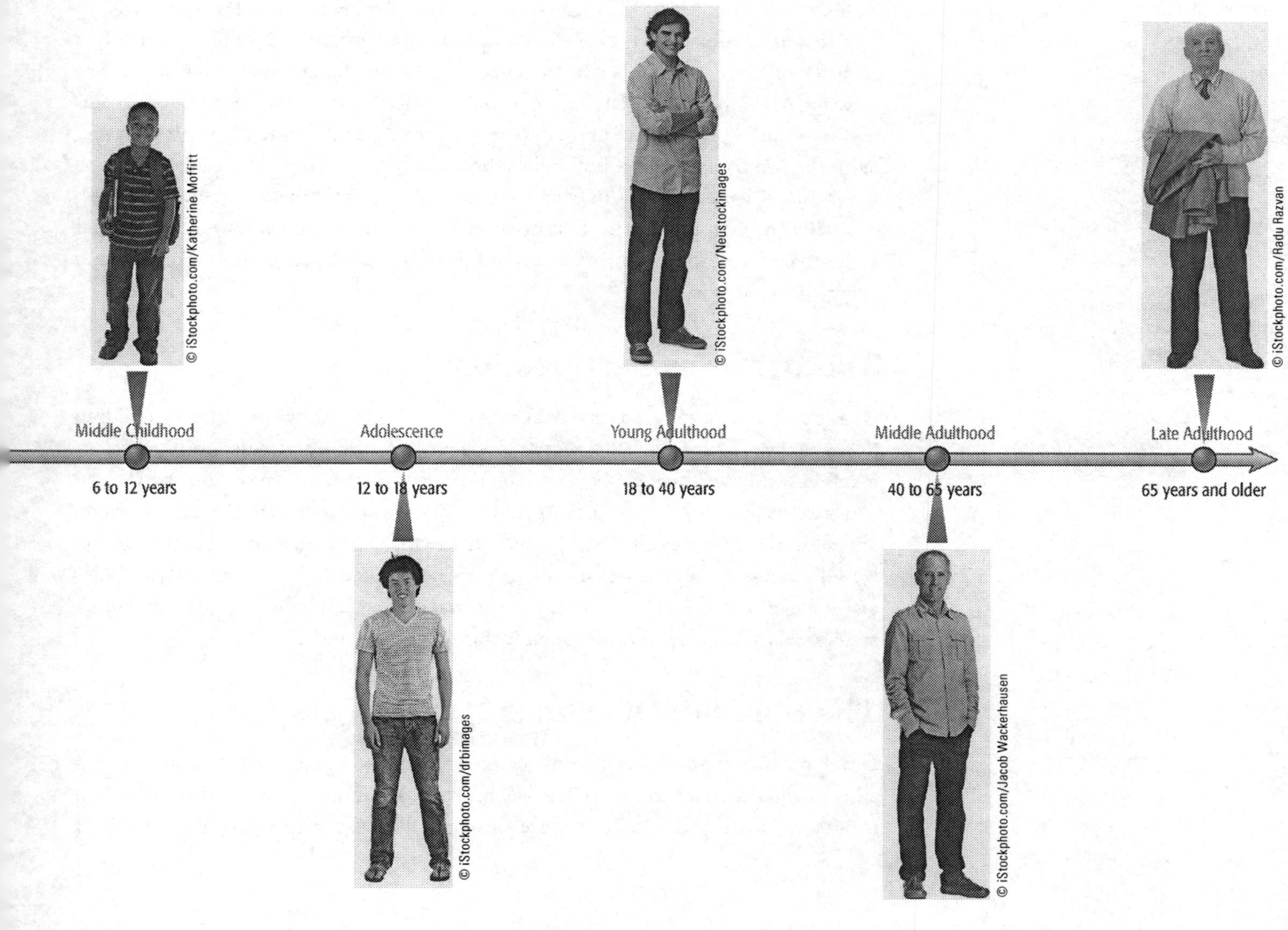

example, we've learned that genes account for about half of the variability in personality traits among people (Bouchard, 2004). The emergence of these genetically influenced traits depends largely on the cultural and family environment in which the child is reared (Li, 2003). Some physical traits, such as hair color, are determined by a single gene, but complex behavioral traits are influenced by multiple genes interacting with environmental factors (Plomin & McGuffin, 2003). Human development is best understood as a continuous interplay of biology and experience (Leve et al., 2010; Meaney, 2010). As discussed in Chapter 2, researchers use kinship studies (familial association studies, twin studies, and adoptee studies) to help determine the relative contributions of nature and nurture to particular traits.

The Continuity Versus Discontinuity Question

continuity model The model proposing that development involves quantitative changes that occur in small steps over time.

discontinuity model The model proposing that development progresses in discrete stages that involve abrupt, qualitative changes in cognitive ability and ways of interacting with the world.

Another question generating debate among developmentalists is whether development progresses continuously in a series of small changes or discontinuously in abrupt steps. According to the **continuity model**, the changes children undergo at various ages are *quantitative* in nature: they occur in small steps rather than in major leaps. Stage theorists, most notably the Swiss developmentalist Jean Piaget, subscribe to a **discontinuity model**—the view that development progresses in stages that are *qualitative* in nature. Development occurs as sudden transformations or abrupt leaps in the child's abilities and ways of interacting with the world. These theorists believe that development remains relatively stable within each stage but then suddenly jumps to the next stage.

Most developmentalists take a middle position: they believe development involves both quantitative and qualitative changes. On the one hand, no amount of practice crawling or "taking steps" will lead to walking until the infant reaches a stage of readiness in terms of physical maturation. Nor will coaxing an infant to speak produce recognizable words until the child reaches the stage at which language use first appears. On the other hand, many skills, such as vocabulary and arithmetical abilities, develop gradually through practice and experience. Even for these skills, however, we could argue that the child must reach a stage of developmental readiness for training and experience to matter.

The Universality Question

Does development follow a universal course that is essentially the same for children the world over, or does development depend more on culture and experience? Developmental psychologists generally take a compromise position. As we will see, strong evidence exists that children progress through a series of stages of cognitive development. Yet cultural differences also exist in the ages at which children reach certain stages, as we will discuss in the later section on cognitive development. Developmental psychologists take into account many social and cultural influences on development, including factors such as ethnicity, socioeconomic status, lifestyle, and diet.

The Stability Question

Developmental psychologists are also interested in the degree to which temperament and personality traits are stable over the life span. Do traits or temperament observed in infancy or early childhood endure throughout life, or might people change over time? Some theorists, such as Sigmund Freud, have argued that our personalities are generally fixed in early childhood, typically by age six or so. Today Freud's position is considered too limiting; even some of his own followers, such as the theorist Erik Erikson, recognized that our personality continues to develop as we age and face new life challenges. Even so, we will see that researchers find certain consistencies in behavior across time, especially in temperament.

Methods of Studying Human Development

Developmental psychologists employ a range of research strategies to study developmental changes. The two methods used most frequently are the *longitudinal method* and the *cross-sectional method.*

CONCEPT 9.2
Developmental psychologists use different research strategies to study age-related differences, most commonly longitudinal studies and cross-sectional studies.

→ Concept Link
A famous example of a longitudinal study was Terman's study of intellectually gifted children. See Module 7.3.

Longitudinal Method

A **longitudinal study** observes the same people repeatedly over time. Longitudinal studies may last years or decades. Investigators conduct longitudinal studies to examine how personality and behavior change over time (Warner et al., 2004). These studies may address such questions as "Do shy children become shy adults?" or "Is temperament stable or does it change over time?" In Chapter 7 we discussed results from the first and longest-running longitudinal study—Terman's study of the "little geniuses." Begun in 1921 by psychologist Louis Terman, the study tracked the life course of a group of intellectually gifted children from middle childhood into old age.

longitudinal study Study that compares the same individuals at periodic intervals over an extended period of time.

The major strength of longitudinal research is that it allows investigators to examine developmental processes by observing changes in the same individuals over time. However, the method has some major limitations. It is time-consuming and may require a continuing commitment of resources that only the best-funded research programs can afford. Moreover, research participants may drop out of the study for various reasons, such as death, disability, or relocation. In addition, the study sample may not be representative of the larger population, which limits the ability to generalize the results beyond the study group.

Cross-Sectional Method

Because of the limitations of the longitudinal method, developmental psychologists more often use an alternative approach, called the cross-sectional method, to study developmental changes. A **cross-sectional study** observes people of different ages at the same point in time. Thus, researchers can compare groups of people who are similar in background characteristics (income level, ethnicity, etc.) but differ in age. Differences among the groups on the variables of interest, such as shyness or temperament, will then presumably reflect age-related developmental processes.

cross-sectional study Study that compares individuals of different ages or developmental levels at the same point in time.

The cross-sectional method has several advantages. Compared to the longitudinal method, it is much less expensive and time-consuming, since participants need to be tested at only one point in time. However, it too has drawbacks. For one thing, investigators cannot be certain that the groups are comparable with respect to every important characteristic except age. For another, it is possible that some unrecognized variable other than age per se caused the observed differences among the groups.

CONCEPT CHART 9.1 Major Methods of Studying Human Development

	Longitudinal Method	Cross-Sectional Method
Method	The same individuals studied over time to track developmental changes	Individuals from different age groups or developmental stages are compared at the same time
Study Plan	The same group of individuals studied at 20 years of age, at 40 years, and at 60 years	Study three groups of participants at the same time: a group of 20-year-olds, a second group of 40-year-olds, and a third group of 60-year-olds
Strengths and Weaknesses	▪ Permits study of the same individuals over time. ▪ Costly, time-consuming, and limited in the generalizability of the findings	Less costly and more efficient than longitudinal studies, but subject to unrecognized factors that may distinguish the groups (other than age) and cohort effects (differences between groups reflecting historical rather than developmental factors)

cohort effect Differences between age groups as a function of historical or social influences affecting those groups rather than age per se.

Another problem with the cross-sectional method is the possibility of a **cohort effect** a limitation that results from research participants being members of a particular generation or being raised at a certain period in history. The term *cohort* describes a group of people who were born about the same time and so may share many historical and social background characteristics. Thus, differences among groups of people of different ages may be generationally or historically related rather than age related. A child born today may have different experiences than children from prior generations and therefore may see the world through different eyes. Children today may have no concept of the world earlier generations knew—a world without computers, microwave ovens, cell phones, or even TVs. Access to video and computer games and to the Internet may also give contemporary children an advantage in developing certain visual-spatial skills compared with earlier cohorts of children. Longitudinal studies, which track the same individuals over time, help disentangle such historical effects from age-related effects. Concept Chart 9.1 compares the longitudinal and cross-sectional methods.

9.1 MODULE REVIEW Key Questions and Methods of Study

Recite It

What are the major questions that underlie the study of human development?

- The nature versus nurture question refers to the relative contributions of heredity and environment to development.
- The continuity versus discontinuity question refers to the debate about whether development progresses continuously in a series of small changes or discontinuously in abrupt steps.
- The universality question deals with whether developmental changes are universal or variable across cultures.
- The stability question refers to whether traits and behaviors are consistent over time or change across the life span.

How do developmental psychologists study age-related changes?

- The longitudinal approach involves studying the same groups of individuals repeatedly over time.
- The cross-sectional approach involves comparing people of different ages at the same point in time.

Recall It

1. If we believe that development progresses in abrupt steps, leading to qualitatively different changes, our view holds to the ______ model of development.
   a. continuity.
   b. discontinuity.
   c. disparity.
   d. variability.
2. What does the universality question address?
3. In cross-sectional research,
   a. the same group of individuals are studied for many years, even decades.
   b. people of the same age are studied repeatedly over time.
   c. there may be problems with cohort effects.
   d. conducting it is typically more expensive and time-consuming than longitudinal studies.

Think About It

- How do present investigators reframe the traditional "nature-nurture" question?
- An investigator compared groups of older adults and younger adults on a memory task to study developmental changes in memory functioning. What type of study method (longitudinal or cross-sectional) did the investigator use?
- What are the advantages and disadvantages of the longitudinal and the cross-sectional methods of studying human development?

Prenatal Development: A Case of Nature and Nurture

MODULE 9.2

- What are the major stages of prenatal development?
- What are some major threats to prenatal development?
- What types of tests are used to detect chromosomal and genetic defects?

Prenatal development brings into focus the long-debated issue of how much of our development is due to nature (genes) and how much to nurture (the environment). Most psychologists today recognize that heredity and environment are closely intertwined. Though some physical traits, such as hair color, are determined by a single gene, complex behavioral traits such as intelligence and personality are influenced by multiple genes interacting with environmental factors (e.g., Diamond, 2009; Gottesman & Hanson, 2005; W. Johnson et al., 2009). **Maturation**, the biological unfolding of an organism according to its underlying genetic blueprint, largely determines how organisms, including ourselves, grow and develop physically. It explains why children of tall parents tend to be tall themselves and those with curly-haired parents tend to have curly hair. Yet development also depends on environmental factors, such as nutrition. The influences of nature and nurture begin to shape development even in the womb.

maturation The biological unfolding of the organism according to the underlying genetic code.

Stages of Prenatal Development

To begin literally at the beginning, the male of the species carries a combination of X and Y sex chromosomes, whereas the female carries two X chromosomes. Each reproductive cell or germ cell—the **sperm** in males and the **ovum** (egg cell)

sperm The male reproductive cell.

ovum An egg cell (pl: ova).

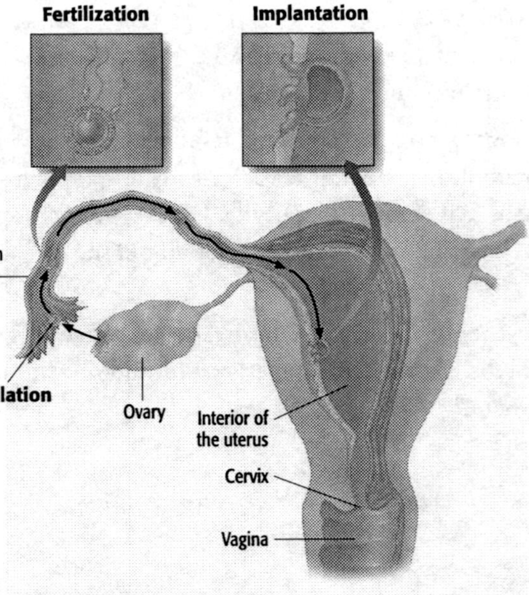

Figure 9.2 The Journey Begins
A mature egg cell (ovum) is released during ovulation by either the left or right ovary. It slowly travels to the opening of a fallopian tube and then inches down the tube. Fertilization, the union of sperm and ovum, usually takes place in a fallopian tube. The fertilized ovum, or zygote, makes its way to the uterus, where it becomes implanted within the uterine wall.

ovulation The release of an ovum from an ovary.

ovaries The female gonads, which secrete the female sex hormones estrogen and progesterone and produce mature egg cells.

fallopian tube A strawlike tube between an ovary and the uterus through which an ovum passes after ovulation.

fertilization The union of a sperm with an ovum during sexual reproduction.

zygote A fertilized egg cell.

germinal stage The stage of prenatal development that spans the period from fertilization through implantation.

uterus The female reproductive organ in which the fertilized ovum becomes implanted and develops to term.

embryonic stage The stage of prenatal development from implantation through about the eighth week of pregnancy during which the major organ systems begin to form.

embryo The developing organism at an early stage of prenatal development.

neural tube The area in the embryo from which the nervous system develops.

amniotic sac The uterine sac that contains the fetus.

in females—contains only one sex chromosome: A sperm cell carries either one X or one Y sex chromosome, whereas an ovum carries only one X. (All other body cells have two sex chromosomes.) When a sperm cell fertilizes an ovum during the process of conception, the resulting combination (XX for females or XY for males) determines the baby's sex.

During **ovulation**, an ovum is released from one of the **ovaries** and then begins a slow journey through a **fallopian tube** (see ■ Figure 9.2) If **fertilization** occurs (the uniting of a sperm and an ovum), the resulting combination (XX or XY) of the sex chromosomes in the fertilized ovum determines the baby's sex. The single cell, called a **zygote**, that forms from the uniting of sperm and ovum soon undergoes cell division. First, it divides into two cells; then each of these two cells divides, forming four cells; each of these four cells divides, resulting in eight cells; and so on. In the months that follow, organ systems form as the developing organism increasingly takes on the form and structure of a human being.

A typical nine-month pregnancy is commonly divided into three trimesters, or three-month periods. From the standpoint of prenatal development, we can also identify three major prenatal stages or periods: the germinal stage, which roughly corresponds to the first two weeks after conception; the embryonic stage, which spans the period of about two weeks to about eight weeks after conception; and the fetal stage, which continues until birth (see ■ Figure 9.3).

The **germinal stage** spans the time from fertilization to implantation in the wall of the **uterus**. For the first three or four days following conception, the mass of dividing cells moves about the uterus before implantation. The process of implantation is not completed for perhaps another week or so.

The **embryonic stage** spans the period from implantation to about the eighth week of pregnancy. The major organ systems begin to take shape in the developing organism, which we now call the **embryo**. About three weeks into pregnancy, two ridges fold together to form the **neural tube**, from which the nervous system will develop. The head and blood vessels also begin to form at this time. By the fourth week, a primitive heart takes shape and begins beating. It will normally (and hopefully) continue beating without a break for at least the next 80 or 90 years.

© David M. Phillips/Photo Researchers, Inc.

The dance of life. In this remarkable photograph, a single sperm is attempting to penetrate the egg covering. If it succeeds, the genetic material from both parents will combine into a single cell that marks the beginning of a new life.

The embryo is suspended in a protective environment within the mother's uterus called the **amniotic sac** (see ■ Figure 9.4). Surrounding the embryo is amniotic fluid, which acts as a kind of shock absorber to cushion the embryo and later the fetus from damage that could result from the mother's movements. Nutrients and waste materials are exchanged between the mother and the embryo (and fetus) through the **placenta**. The embryo, and later the fetus, are connected to the placenta by the umbilical cord. The placenta

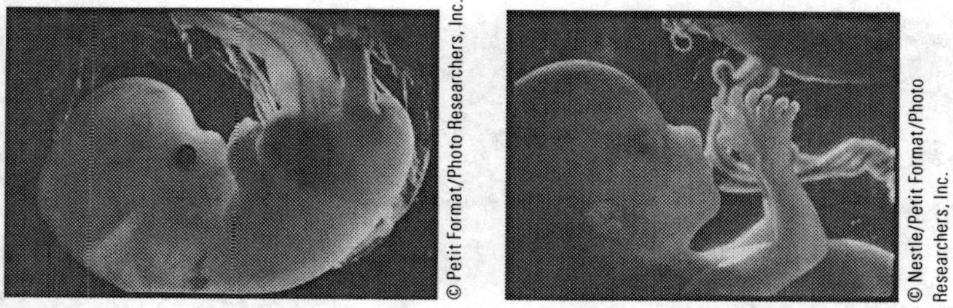

Figure 9.3 Prenatal Development
Dramatic changes in shape and form occur during prenatal development. Compare the embryo (a) at about six to seven weeks of development with the fetus (b) at approximately 16 weeks. The fetus has already taken on a clearly recognizable human form.

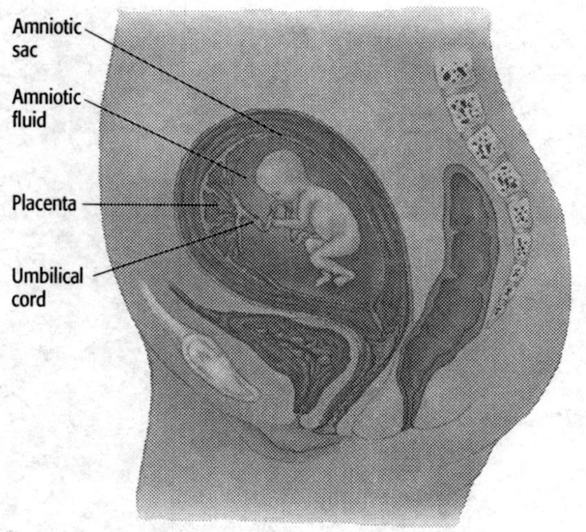

Figure 9.4 Structures in the Womb
During prenatal development, the embryo lies in a protective enclosure within the uterus called the amniotic sac. Nutrients and waste materials are exchanged between mother and embryo/fetus through the placenta. The umbilical cord connects the embryo and fetus to the placenta.

allows nutrients and oxygen to pass from mother to fetus. Their blood streams do not mix.

The **fetal stage**, or stage of the **fetus**, begins around the ninth week of pregnancy and continues until the birth of the child. All of the major organ systems, as well as the fingers and toes, are formed by about the 12th week of prenatal development, which roughly corresponds to the end of the first trimester. They continue to develop through the course of the pregnancy. The fetus increases more than 30-fold in weight during the second trimester of pregnancy, from about one ounce to about two pounds. It grows from about four inches in length to about 14 inches. Typically the mother will feel the first fetal movements around the middle of the fourth month. By the end of the second trimester, the fetus approaches the *age of viability,* the point at which it becomes capable of sustaining life on its own. However, fewer than half of infants born at the end of the second trimester that weigh less than two pounds will survive on their own, even with the most intense medical treatment.

placenta The organ that provides for the exchange of nutrients and waste materials between mother and fetus.

fetal stage The stage of prenatal development in which the fetus develops, beginning around the ninth week of pregnancy and lasting until the birth of the child.

fetus The developing organism in the later stages of prenatal development.

CONCEPT 9.3
The developing fetus faces many risks, including maternal malnutrition and teratogens.

Threats to Prenatal Development

A pregnant woman requires adequate nutrition for the health of the fetus as well as for her own. Maternal malnutrition is associated with a greater risk of premature birth (birth prior to 37 weeks of gestation) and low birth weight (less than five pounds, or about 2,500 grams). Preterm and low birth weight babies face a higher risk of infant mortality and later developmental problems, including cognitive deficits and attention difficulties (e.g., Lemons et al., 2001).

Women may receive prescriptions from their obstetricians for multivitamin pills to promote optimal fetal development. The federal government recommends that all women of childbearing age take 400 micrograms daily of the B vitamin *folic acid,* and that pregnant women take 800 micrograms. Folic acid greatly reduces the risk of neural tube defects such as **spina bifida**, but only if it is taken early in pregnancy (U.S. Preventive Services Task Force, 2009; Wolff et al., 2009).

spina bifida A neural tube defect in which the child is born with a hole in the tube surrounding the spinal cord.

teratogen An environmental influence or agent that may harm the developing embryo or fetus.

The word **teratogen** is derived from the Greek root *teras,* meaning "monster." Teratogens include certain drugs taken by the mother, X-rays, environmental contaminants such as lead and mercury, and infectious organisms capable of passing through the placenta to the embryo or fetus. The risks posed by teratogens are greatest during

CONCEPT 9.4
Certain environmental influences or agents, called teratogens, may harm the developing embryo or fetus.

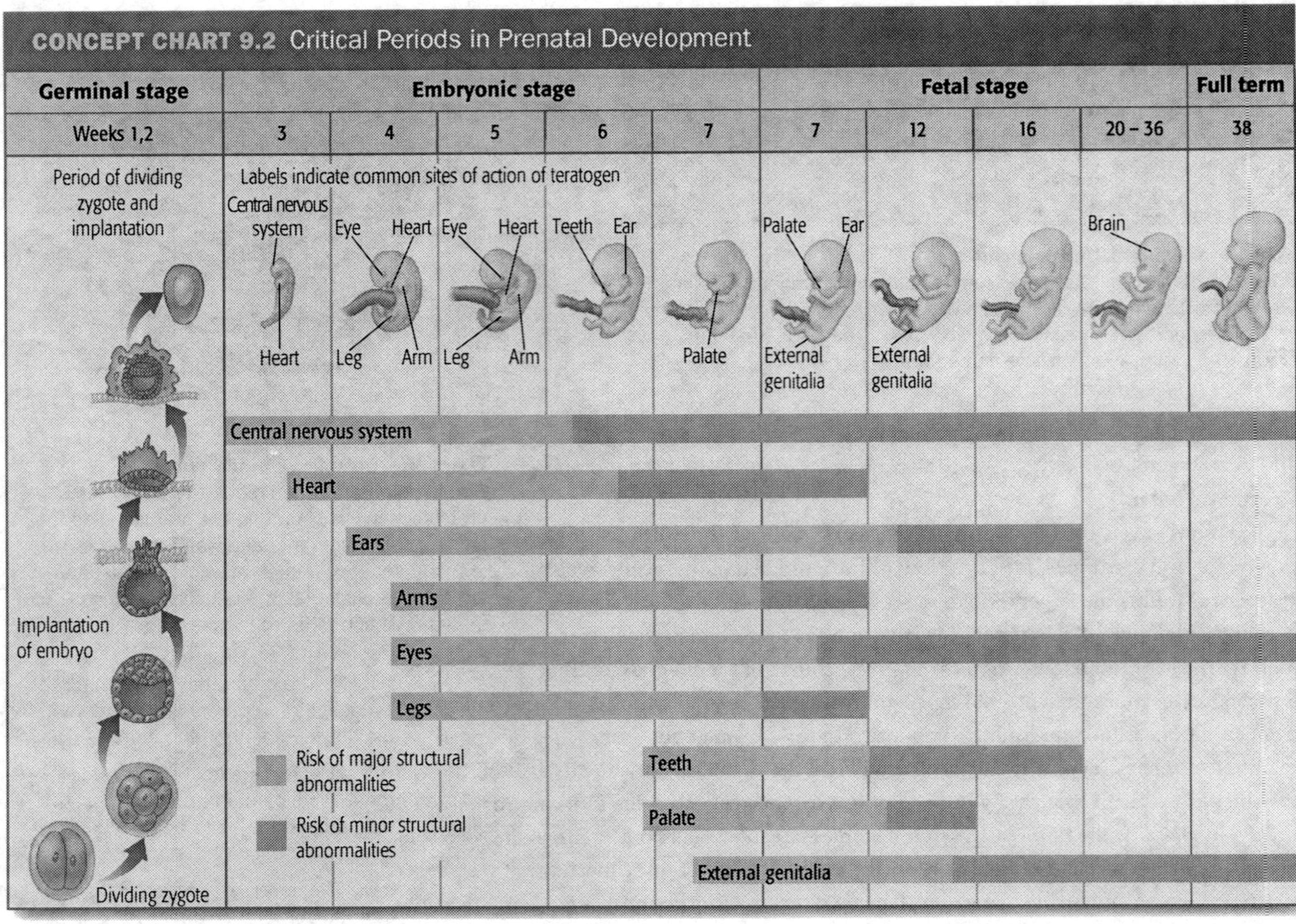

Source: Adapted from Berger & Thompson, 1995

certain critical periods of development. For example, teratogens that may damage the arms and legs are most likely to have an effect during the fourth through eighth weeks of development (see Concept Chart 9.2).

Let us now consider several of the most dangerous teratogens.

Infectious Diseases

rubella A common childhood disease that can lead to serious birth defects if contracted by the mother during pregnancy (also called German measles).

Rubella (also called *German measles*) is a common childhood disease that can lead to serious birth defects, including heart disease, deafness, and mental retardation, if contracted during pregnancy. Women exposed to rubella in childhood acquire immunity to the disease. Those who lack immunity may be vaccinated before becoming pregnant to protect their future offspring.

Some sexually transmitted infections, such as HIV/AIDS and syphilis, may be transmitted from mother to child during pregnancy. Fortunately, aggressive treatment of HIV-infected mothers with the antiviral drug AZT greatly reduces the risk of maternal transmission of the virus to the fetus. Children born with congenital syphilis may suffer liver damage, impaired hearing and vision, and deformities in their teeth and bones. The risk of transmission can be reduced if the infected mother is treated effectively with antibiotics prior to the fourth month of pregnancy.

Smoking

Maternal smoking can lead to miscarriage (spontaneous abortion), premature birth, low birth weight, and increased risk of infant mortality (I. M. Bernstein et al., 2005; Heilbronner & Berlin, 2005). The more the mother smokes, the greater the risks. Maternal smoking during pregnancy is also linked to increased risks of **sudden infant death syndrome (SIDS)** and lung problems, including childhood asthma, as well as developmental problems such as reduced attention span, learning problems, and behavioral problems (Goodwin et al., 2009; Oncken & Kranzler, 2003; Sasaki et al., 2008).

sudden infant death syndrome (SIDS) The sudden and unexplained death of infants that usually occurs when they are asleep in their cribs.

fetal alcohol syndrome (FAS) A syndrome caused by maternal use of alcohol during pregnancy in which the child shows developmental delays and facial deformities.

Alcohol and Drugs

Fetal alcohol syndrome (FAS), which results from the mother's use of alcohol during pregnancy, is a leading cause of mental retardation (Floyd et al., 2005). It is also associated with facial characteristics such as a flattened nose, an underdeveloped upper jaw, and widely spaced eyes. Although FAS is more likely to occur with heavy maternal drinking, there is actually no established safe limit for alcohol use in pregnancy. FAS may occur in babies whose mothers drink as little as two ounces of alcohol a day during the first trimester. Any drug used during pregnancy, whether legal or illegal (illicit), or any medication, whether prescribed or bought over the counter, is potentially harmful to the fetus.

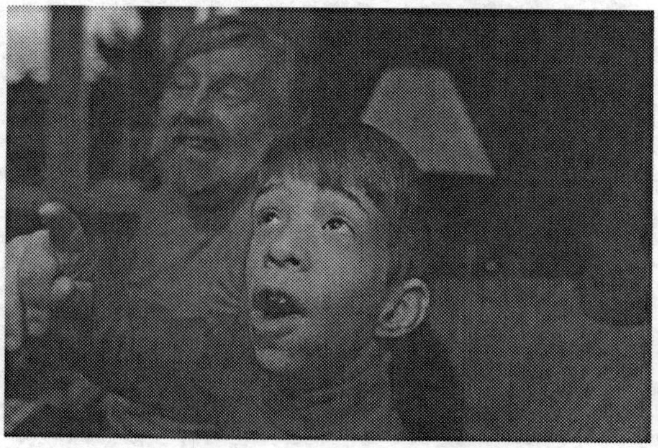
© David H. Wells

Fetal alcohol syndrome (FAS), a leading cause of mental retardation, is characterized by facial features such as an underdeveloped upper jaw, a flattened nose, and widely spaced eyes.

Prenatal Testing

Various methods are used to detect fetal abnormalities during prenatal development. In **amniocentesis**, generally performed between weeks 16 and 18 of pregnancy, a syringe is inserted into the amniotic sac and fluid containing fetal cells is extracted. The fetal cells are cultured and then analyzed for biochemical and chromosomal abnormalities. Another technique, **chorionic villus sampling (CVS)**, may be performed several weeks earlier than amniocentesis. A small amount of tissue from the **chorion**, the membrane that holds the amniotic sac and fetus, is analyzed. Both amniocentesis and CVS can detect a wide range of fetal abnormalities, including **Down syndrome**, a chromosomal disorder that results in mental retardation and physical abnormalities. This disorder, which occurs in about one in every 700 live births, occurs when three chromosomes are present on the 21st pair of chromosomes instead of the normal two (Nelson & Gibbs, 2004). The risk of Down syndrome increases with the mother's age (see Table 9.1).

amniocentesis A technique for diagnosing fetal abnormalities involving examination of extracted fetal cells.

chorionic villus sampling (CVS) A technique of detecting fetal abnormalities that involves examination of fetal material extracted from the chorion.

chorion The membrane that contains the amniotic sac and fetus.

Down syndrome A chromosomal disorder characterized by mental retardation and certain facial abnormalities.

TABLE 9.1 Risk of Giving Birth to an Infant with Down Syndrome

Age of Mother	Probability of Down Syndrome
30	1 in 885
35	1 in 365
40	1 in 109
45	1 in 32
49	1 in 11

ultrasound imaging A technique for using high-pitched sound waves to form an image of the fetus in the womb.

Ultrasound imaging is also used to detect fetal abnormalities. High-pitched sound waves are (harmlessly) bounced off the fetus, revealing an image of the fetus and amniotic sac that can be displayed on a monitor. In addition to using these tests, parents can have their blood tested to determine whether they are carriers of genetic disorders such as sickle cell anemia or Tay-Sachs disease. Still other tests examine fetal DNA to reveal other genetic disorders.

Perhaps in the future we will have the means to correct genetic defects to prevent them from being passed from generation to generation. At present, expectant couples facing this agonizing situation may rely upon genetic counselors, psychologists, and other health professionals for information and support.

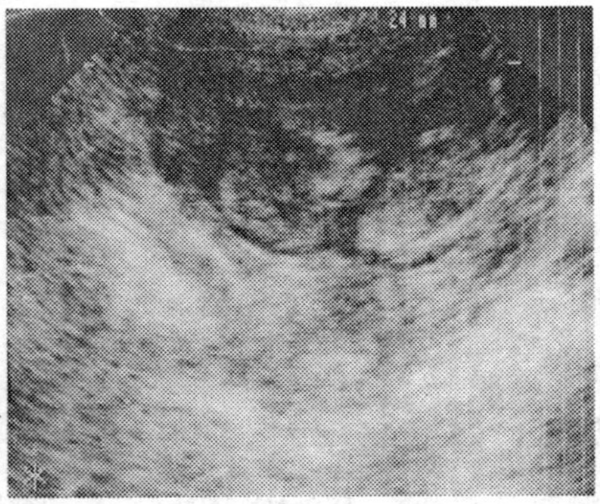

© Jeffrey Nevid

You may be able to make out the ultrasound image of the author's son Michael at 12 weeks of development. Michael's father notes that he was handsome even then!

9.2 MODULE REVIEW Prenatal Development: A Case of Nature and Nurture

Recite It

What are the major stages of prenatal development?

- The germinal stage is the period from conception to implantation.
- The embryonic stage begins with implantation and extends to about the eighth week of development; it is characterized by differentiation of the major organ systems.
- The fetal stage begins around the ninth week and continues until birth; it is characterized by continued maturation of the fetus's organ systems and dramatic increases in size.

What are some major threats to prenatal development?

- Threats include maternal diet, maternal diseases and disorders, and use of certain medications and drugs.
- Exposure to particular teratogens causes the greatest harm during critical periods of vulnerability.

What types of tests are used to detect chromosomal and genetic defects?

- Tests include amniocentesis, chorionic villus sampling (CVS), ultrasound imaging, and parental blood tests.

Recall It

1. The first stage of prenatal development, which ends with implantation in the uterine wall, is called the ______ stage.
2. Name two major risks to the developing embryo or fetus.
3. Match the following terms to their descriptions: (i) the first stage of pregnancy; (ii) a protective environment; (iii) the organ in which nutrients and wastes are exchanged within the uterus; (iv) a structure in the developing organism from which the nervous system develops.
   - **a.** neural tube.
   - **b.** amniotic sac.
   - **c.** placenta.
   - **d.** germinal stage.

Think About It

- Based on your reading of the text, what advice might you give someone about the risks posed by drinking alcohol or smoking during pregnancy?
- Would you want to know if you or your partner was at risk for carrying a genetic abnormality? Why or why not? How would such knowledge affect your decisions about having children?

Infant Development

- What reflexes do newborn babies show?
- How does the infant develop physically during the first year of life?
- What sensory, perceptual, and learning abilities do infants possess?
- How do the infant's motor abilities develop during the first year?

MODULE 9.3

It may seem that newborns do little more than sleep and eat, but, in fact, they come into the world with a wider range of responses than you might think. Even more remarkable are the changes that take place during development in the first two years of life. Let us enter the world of the infant and examine these remarkable changes.

Reflexes

A reflex is an unlearned, automatic response to a particular stimulus. Babies are born with a number of basic reflexes (see ■ Figure 9.5). For example, if you lightly touch a newborn's cheek, the baby will reflexively turn its head in the direction of the tactile (touch) stimulation. This is the **rooting reflex**, which, like many basic reflexes, has important survival value. It helps the baby obtain nourishment by orienting its head toward the breast or bottle. Another reflex that has survival value is the **eyeblink reflex**, the reflexive blinking of the eyes that protects the baby from bright light or foreign objects. Another is the **sucking reflex**, the rhythmic sucking action that enables the infant to obtain nourishment from breast or bottle. It is prompted whenever an object like a nipple or a finger is placed in the mouth.

Some reflexes appear to be remnants of our evolutionary heritage that may no longer serve any adaptive function. For example, if the infant is exposed to a loud noise, or if its head falls backward, the **Moro reflex** is elicited: The infant extends its arms, arches its back, and then brings its arms toward each other as if attempting to grab hold of someone. The **palmar grasp reflex**, or curling of the fingers around an object that touches the palm, is so strong that the infant can literally be lifted by its hands. In ancestral times, these reflexes may have had survival value by preventing infants from falling as their mothers carried them around all day. The **Babinski reflex** involves a fanning out and curling of the toes and inward twisting of the foot when the sole of the foot is stroked.

Most newborn reflexes disappear within the first six months of life. The presence and later disappearance of particular reflexes at expected periods of time are taken as signs of normal neurological development.

rooting reflex The reflexive turning of the newborn's head in the direction of a touch on its cheek.

eyeblink reflex The reflexive blinking of the eyes that protects the newborn from bright light and foreign objects.

sucking reflex Rhythmic sucking in response to stimulation of the tongue or mouth.

CONCEPT 9.5
Infants enter the world with some motor reflexes that may have had survival value among ancestral humans.

Moro reflex An inborn reflex, elicited by a sudden noise or loss of support, in which the infant extends its arms, arches its back, and brings its arms toward each other as though attempting to grab hold of someone.

palmar grasp reflex The reflexive curling of the infant's fingers around an object that touches its palm.

Babinski reflex The reflexive fanning out and curling of an infant's toes and inward twisting of its foot when the sole of the foot is stroked.

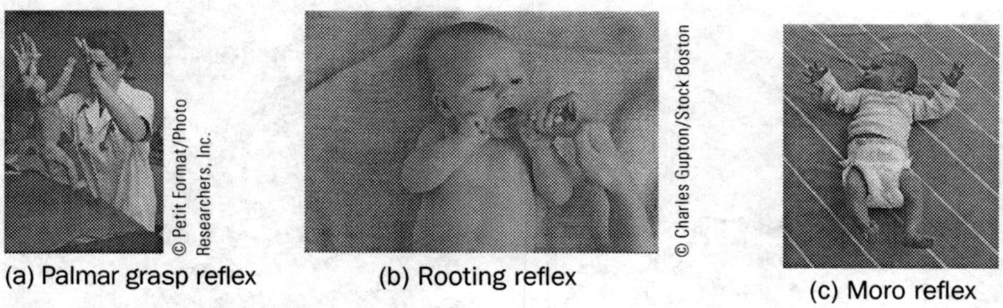

© Petit Format/Photo Researchers, Inc.

© Charles Gupton/Stock Boston

© Elizabeth Crews/The Image Works

(a) Palmar grasp reflex (b) Rooting reflex (c) Moro reflex

Figure 9.5 Infant Reflexes
The palmar grasp reflex (a) is so strong that the infant can literally be lifted by its hands. In the rooting reflex (b), the infant turns its head in the direction of a touch to its check. In the Moro reflex (c), when the infant is exposed to a noise or loss of support, it arches its back, extends its arms outward, and then brings the arms toward each other. What survival functions might these reflexes serve?

CONCEPT 9.6
Shortly after birth, the infant is able to discern many different stimuli, including its mother's odor, face, and voice, as well as different tastes.

During the first year of life, infants on average triple their birth weight from about seven pounds to about 21 or 22 pounds. They also grow in height from about 20 inches to around 30 inches. The interconnections or synapses between neurons in the brain grow denser in the first two years of life, enabling the infant to organize its movements and engage the world by manipulating objects and acquiring knowledge about its environment. Between birth and adulthood, the brain will increase four-fold in volume. But perhaps most remarkable is the rapid development of the infant's abilities to sense, perceive, learn, and direct its movements.

Sensory, Perceptual, and Learning Abilities in Infancy

Infants are capable of sensing a wide range of sensory stimuli and of learning simple responses and retaining them in memory.

Sensory and Perceptual Ability

Vision is the slowest of the senses to develop. Although the newborn's vision is blurry, its visual world is not a complete blur (see ■ Figure 9.6). For example, newborns show preferences for looking at facelike patterns over nonfacelike patterns, especially their mother's face (Gauthier & Curby, 2005; Turati, 2004). Not only can they recognize their mother's face, but they also show a preference for looking at her face over other faces.

By one month of age, an infant can follow a moving object; by two months, the infant has developed basic color vision. Depth perception develops by around six months. Using a *visual cliff apparatus* consisting of a glass panel that covers an apparent sudden drop-off, Eleanor Gibson and Richard Walk (1960) showed that most infants about six months or older will hesitate and then refuse to crawl across to the deep side, indicating that they have developed depth perception (see ■ Figure 9.7).

Newborns can hear many different types of sounds. They are particularly sensitive to sounds falling within the frequency of the human voice. In fact, they can discern

© 2003 PhotoDisc/Getty Images
© 2003 PhotoDisc/Getty Images

Figure 9.6 Newborn Vision and Face Recognition
To a newborn, mother's face may appear as blurry as the photograph on the left. But a newborn can still recognize its mother's face and shows a preference for her face over other faces.

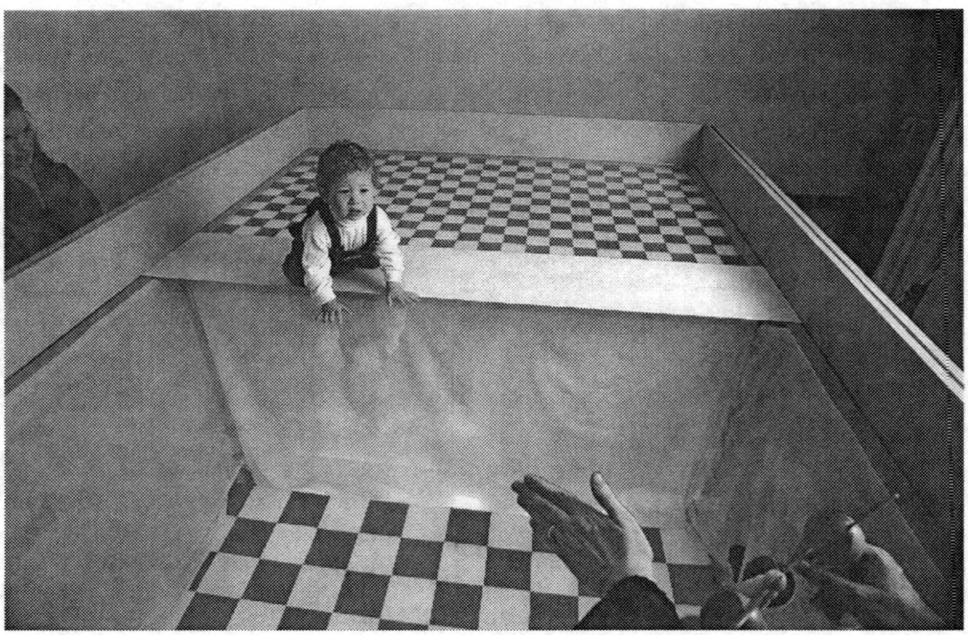

© Mark Richards/Photo Edit

Figure 9.7 The Visual Cliff
The visual cliff apparatus consists of a glass panel covering what appears to be a sudden drop-off. An infant who has developed depth perception will crawl toward a parent on the opposite end but will hesitate and refuse to venture into the "deep" end even if coaxed by the parent.

their mother's voice from other voices. Even fetuses respond more strongly (show elevated heart rates) to their mother's voice than to the voices of female strangers (Kisilevsky et al., 2003). By several months of age, infants can differentiate among various speech sounds, such as between "ba" and "ma." The ability to discriminate among speech sounds helps prepare them for the development of language.

At five to six days of age, infants can detect their mother's odor. They react with a frown to the smell of rotten eggs but show a smile when they get a whiff of chocolate or bananas. Newborns can also discriminate among different tastes and show preferences for sweetness (no surprise!) (Raymond, 2000). They will suck faster and longer if given sweetened liquids than if given bitter, salty, or plain water solutions.

The perceptual world of the infant is not a blooming, buzzing confusion of meaningless stimuli, as people once believed. Rather, infants begin making meaningful discriminations among stimuli shortly after birth. For example, newborns are extremely sensitive to a soothing voice and to the way in which they are held. They can also recognize a scrambled picture of their mother's face just as well as a properly arranged picture of her face (Wingert & Brant, 2005).

By the age of four to six months, babies can discriminate among happy, angry, and neutral facial expressions and show a preference for faces reflecting their own racial characteristics (Bar-Haim et al., 2006; Saxe, Carey, & Kanwisher, 2004). What we don't know is what, if anything, different facial expressions mean to infants. We might think "Mom looks mad," but what infants make of different facial expressions remains unclear.

CONCEPT 9.7
Infants may seem to do little more than eat and sleep, but a closer look reveals they are both active learners and active perceivers of their environment.

Learning Ability

Infants are capable of learning simple responses, which they can remember for days or even weeks. Infants as young as two to six months can learn and remember a kicking response that activates a crib mobile (see ■ Figure 9.8). Infants as young as six or seven months can retain memories for faces (Pascalis et al., 1998) and for sounds of particular words one day after hearing them (Houston & Jusczyk, 2003). Learning even occurs prenatally, which we know from evidence that newborns show preferences for their mother's voice and for sounds reflecting their native language (Moon, Cooper, & Fifer, 1993).

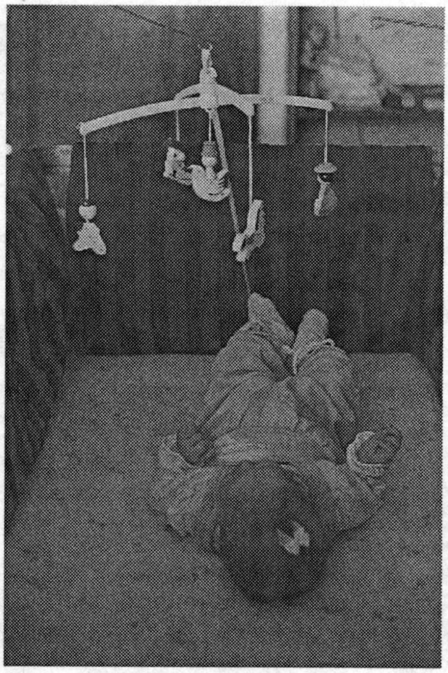
© Courtesy of Carolyn Rovee-Collier

Figure 9.8 Infant Learning
Infants as young as two months can learn and remember simple responses, such as performing a kicking response that activates the movement of a crib mobile.

Motor Development

Newborns' motor skills are not limited to simple reflexes. They can engage in some goal-directed behaviors, such as bringing their hands to their mouths to suck their thumbs, an ability that first appears prenatally during the third trimester. Minutes after birth, newborns can imitate their parents' facial expressions (Gopnik, 2000). Imitative behavior may be the basis for shared communication between the infant and others. The infant and caregiver begin imitating each other's facial expressions in a kind of nonmusical duet (Trevarthen, 1995) (see ■ Figure 9.9).

During the first three months, infants slowly begin replacing reflexive movements with voluntary, purposive movements. By the second or third month, they begin bringing objects to their mouths. By about six months, they can reliably grasp stationary objects and begin catching moving objects.

By two months of age, infants can lift their chins; by five months, they can roll over; and by nine months, they can sit without support. By the end of the first year, infants will master the most difficult balancing problem they'll ever face in life: standing without support. Why is standing alone so difficult? Because of its smaller size, a

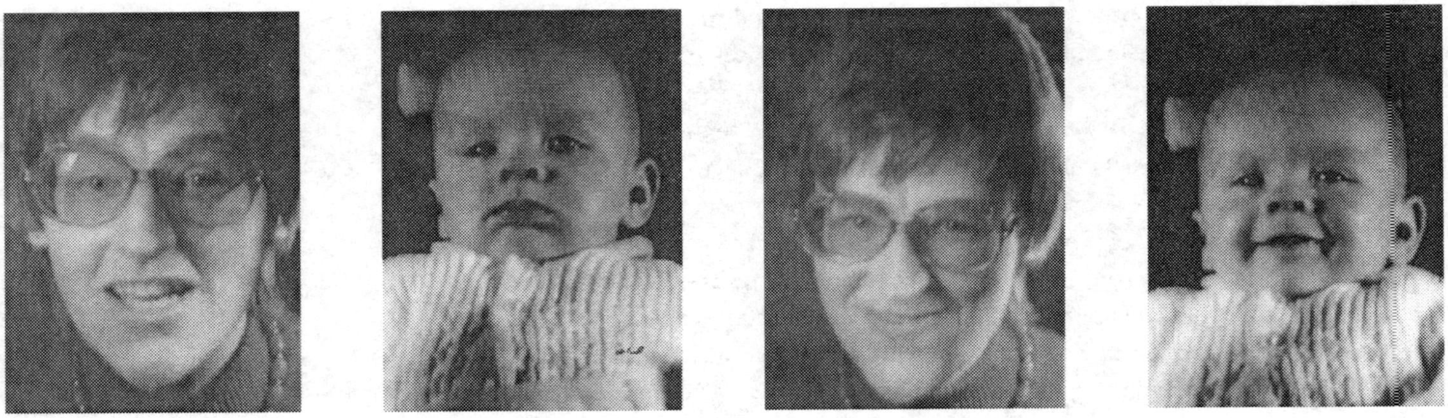

Figure 9.9 Infant Imitative Behavior
Two cameras are used to separately photograph the caregiver and infant. Notice how the infant and caregiver mirror each other's facial expressions.
Source: Murray, L. and Trevarthen, C. (1985). Emotional regulation of interactions between two month olds and their mothers. In, Field, T. and Fox, N. (Eds.). Social Perception in Infants. Norwood, N.J.: Ablex, 177 197.

CONCEPT 9.8
Motor development in infancy progresses rapidly through a series of steps from near immobility to coordinated running by around 18 months of age.

one-year-old will sway about 40 percent more while standing than will an adult and consequently will have less time to respond to balance disturbances to maintain itself in an upright position. To appreciate the challenge the one-year-old faces in attempting to stand, imagine trying to keep your balance while standing on a bridge that is constantly swaying. The development of motor skills, as outlined in Concept Chart 9.3, occurs in the same sequence among nearly all infants at about the same ages and in all cultures.

CONCEPT CHART 9.3 Milestones in Infant Development

Approximate Ages	Sensory Skills and Learning Abilities	Motor Skills
Birth to 1 month 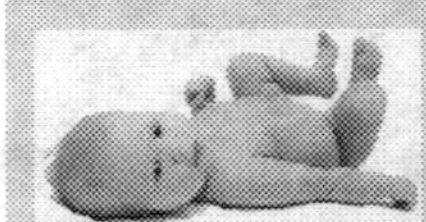 © iStockphoto.com/ Cindy Singleton	▪ Has blurry vision ▪ Visually tracks a moving object ▪ Sensitive to sounds within range of human voice ▪ Shows preference for mother's voice and native language sounds (develops prenatally) ▪ Detects mother's odor ▪ Discerns certain pleasant or unpleasant basic odors ▪ Shows taste preference for sweetness ▪ Responds to a soothing voice ▪ Discerns differences in how they are held ▪ Shows preferences for facelike stimuli and responds to certain facial features	▪ Demonstrates basic reflexes ▪ Sucks thumb ▪ Mimics facial movements
2–3 months  ©saiko3p/Shutterstock.com	▪ Discriminates direction of a moving object ▪ Has developed basic color vision ▪ Can discern differences in the tempo (beat) of a pattern of sounds ▪ Discriminates among faces of different people ▪ Learns simple responses and remembers them for several days (at 2 months) to several weeks (at 6 months)	▪ Lifts chin ▪ Brings objects to mouth

4–6 months  © iStockphoto.com/lostinbids	■ Develops depth perception ■ Discerns differences among certain facial expressions ■ Retains memory for certain faces	■ Grasps stationary objects ■ Catches moving objects ■ Brings objects into field of view ■ Able to roll over
7–9 months  © iStockphoto.com/by_nicholas	Further development of depth perception and visual acuity	■ Sits without support ■ Stands holding on
10–12 months  © Gelpi/Shutterstock.com	Develops nearly 20/20 vision	■ Walks holding on and without support

9.3 MODULE REVIEW Infant Development

Recite It

What reflexes do newborn babies show?

➤ Reflexes include the rooting, eyeblink, sucking, Moro, palmar grasp, and Babinski reflexes.

How does the infant develop physically during the first year of life?

➤ The weight of the average infant increases three-fold in the first year, from about seven pounds to about 21 or 22 pounds. Height increases by about 50 percent, from around 20 inches to about 30 inches. By adulthood, the brain will have quadrupled in volume.

What sensory, perceptual, and learning abilities do infants possess?

➤ The newborn can detect objects visually (though not with perfect acuity) and can discriminate among different sounds, odors, and tastes.

➤ The ability to respond to depth cues and discern facial expressions develops within the first six months.

➤ Infants are also capable of learning simple responses and retaining memories of those responses.

How do the infant's motor abilities develop during the first year?

➤ During the first year, the infant acquires the ability to move its body, sit without support, turn over, crawl, and begin to stand and walk on its own.

Recall It

1. Match the following reflexes to the appropriate description: (a) rooting reflex; (b) eyeblink reflex; (c) sucking reflex; (d) Moro reflex.
   - **i.** a rhythmic action that enables an infant to take in nourishment.
   - **ii.** a reflex action protecting one from bright lights and foreign objects.
   - **iii.** a grabbing movement, often in response to a loud noise.
   - **iv.** turning in response to a touch on the cheek; helps the baby find breast or bottle.
2. What evidence (based on the sense of hearing) do we have to support the belief that a fetus is capable of learning?
3. Motor abilities develop extremely rapidly in infants. Which of the following is *not* a motor ability of a baby during the first year of life?
   - **a.** imitation of parents' facial expressions.
   - **b.** development of voluntary, goal-directed movement.
   - **c.** balancing itself while sitting, without support.
   - **d.** speaking in complete sentences.

Think About It

➤ What is the adaptive value of certain basic infant reflexes?

➤ Why is it incorrect to say that the world of the infant is merely a jumble of disconnected stimuli?

MODULE 9.4

Emotional and Social Development

- What are the three basic types of infant temperament identified in the New York Longitudinal Study, and what are the major differences among them?
- What are the three types of attachment styles identified by Ainsworth?
- What are the three major styles of parenting in Baumrind's model, and how do they differ?
- What roles do peer relationships play in children's emotional and social development?
- What are the stages of psychosocial development during childhood according to Erikson?

Childhood is a period of wonderment, discovery, and, most of all, change. Here we examine the world of the growing child from the standpoint of its emotional and social development. Earlier we noted how infants the world over develop motor skills in the same sequence at about the same ages. But with emotional and social development, we see a wider range of expression of different behaviors, ways of relating to others, and emerging personalities in infants and young children. The influences on children's emotional and social development reflect roles for nature (genetics) and for nurture (environmental influences, including parents, peers, and the media).

In this section, we examine temperamental differences among infants, development of secure attachments, parenting styles, and peer relationships. We also introduce a key theory proposed by psychoanalyst Erik Erikson that represents a milestone in our understanding of psychosocial development. In the application section at the end of the chapter, we examine an area of concern to many parents: the influence of television viewing on children's development.

Temperament: The "How" of Behavior

CONCEPT 9.9
Many psychologists believe that children differ in their basic temperaments and that these differences are at least partially determined by genetic factors.

temperament A characteristic style of behavior or disposition.

SLICE OF LIFE Janet was talking about her two daughters, Tabitha (seven) and Alicia (two-and-a-half). "They're like day and night. Tabitha is the sensitive type. She's very tentative about taking chances or joining in with the other children. She can play by herself for hours. Just give her a book to read and she's in heaven. What can I say about Alicia? Where Tabitha will sit at the top of the slide and have to be coaxed to come down, Alicia goes down head first. Most kids her age stay in the part of the playground for the toddlers, but Alicia is off running to the big climbing equipment. She even thinks she's one of the older kids and tries to join them in their games. Can you picture that? Alicia is running after a baseball with the six- and seven-year-olds." Ask parents who have two or more children and you're likely to hear a similar refrain: "They're just different. I don't know why they're different, but they just are."

We may attempt to explain these differences in terms of the construct of **temperament** (Rothbart, 2007). A temperament is a characteristic style of behavior and emotional expression, or what we might call a disposition. We can think of temperament as the "how" of behavior—the characteristic way in which a child behaves and reacts to situations (Chess & Thomas, 1996). One child may be fearful or have a very limited attention span, whereas another shows a cheerful disposition or seeks out playful or exciting activities.

The most widely used classification of temperaments is based on a study of middle-class and upper-middle-class infants from the New York City area: the New York Longitudinal Study (NYLS) (Chess & Thomas, 1996). The investigators identified three general types of temperament that could be used to classify about two out of three of the children in the study group:

1. *Easy children.* These children are playful and respond positively to new stimuli. They adapt easily to changes; display a happy, engaging mood; and are quick to develop regular sleeping and feeding schedules. About 40 percent of the NYLS children were classified in this category.
2. *Difficult children.* These children react negatively to new situations or people, have irritable dispositions, and have difficulty establishing regular sleeping and feeding schedules. About 10 percent of the group fell into this category.
3. *Slow-to-warm-up children.* These children (sometimes called "inhibited children") have low activity levels; avoid novel stimuli; require more time to adjust to new situations than most children; and typically react to unfamiliar situations by becoming withdrawn, subdued, or mildly distressed. This category described about 15 percent of the group.

The remaining 35 percent of the children studied represented a mixed group who could not be easily classified.

The types of temperament we observe in infancy help predict later adjustment in life (Lahey et al., 2008; Rothbart, 2007; Volbrecht & Goldsmith, 2010). For example, the easy infant generally grows up to be a better adjusted adult than infants with other temperaments. Fussier infants tend to have more conduct problems in childhood, especially among boys. The slow-to-warm-up or inhibited infant is more likely to show signs of anxiety, shyness, and depression in childhood. The difficult infant is at higher risk for developing acting-out or other problem behaviors. However, they may also have positive qualities, such as being highly spirited and not being a "pushover."

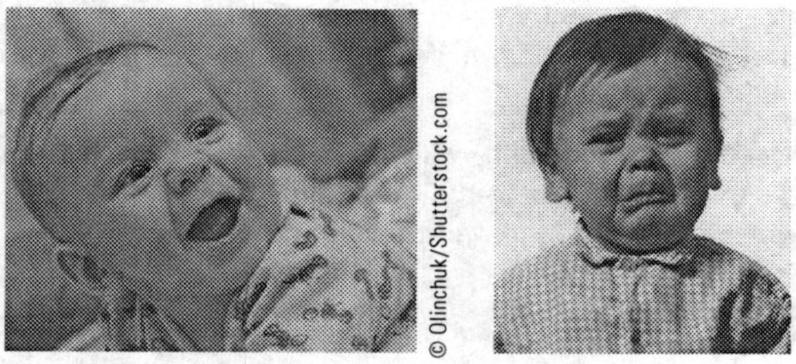
© Olinchuk/Shutterstock.com
© photobank.ch/Shutterstock.com

Psychologists find distinct differences in temperament among infants, with some infants showing easier and more agreeable behaviors and others showing more difficult and irritable behaviors. Differences in temperament predict later differences in adulthood and social development.

Why It Matters

Developmental psychologists believe temperament is shaped by nature and nurture—that is, by both genetic and environmental influences (Roisman & Fraley, 2008; van den Akker et al., 2010). However, the question of whether it is possible to change basic temperament remains unanswered. But even if basic temperament can't be changed, children adapt more successfully to their environment when parents, teachers, and other caregivers take their underlying temperaments into account. For example, the difficult or slow-to-warm-up child may need more time and gentle encouragement when adjusting to new situations such as beginning school, making friends, or joining in play activities with other children. Kagan (1997) found that mothers whose infants show signs of inhibited temperament but who relate to them in nurturing but not overly protective ways can help them overcome fearfulness of new experiences.

Let us also note that children with more adaptable or flexible temperaments tend to interact more effectively and cooperatively with peers than those with less adaptable temperaments (Mendez, Fantuzzo, & Cicchetti, 2002). On the other hand, toddlers with more difficult temperaments tend to show more aggressive and other undesirable behaviors as preschoolers (Rubin, Burgess, & Dwyer, 2003). Underscoring the importance of parenting behaviors, these differences were especially true of toddlers whose mothers were unresponsive toward them or punished them. Toddlers with difficult temperaments whose mothers were responsive and sensitive to their needs were not more aggressive as preschoolers. Complicating matters is that infants with more difficult temperaments tend to influence their parents to adopt harsher styles of parenting (Leve et al., 2010). We thus need to consider the mutual interactions between children and parents, as both influence each other.

CONCEPT 9.10
Attachment behaviors are found in a wide range of species, from ducks to humans.

© Jonathan Nourok/Photo Edit

Attachment behaviors are the ties that bind infants to their caregivers.

Attachment: Binding Ties

In human development, **attachment** is the enduring emotional bond that infants and older children form with their caregivers. This is not the same as **bonding**, which is the parent's tie to the infant that may form in the hours following birth. Rather, attachment develops over time during infancy. As attachment develops, infants may crawl to be near their caregivers, pull or grab at them to maintain contact, and cry and show other signs of emotional distress when separated from them, even if only momentarily.

attachment The enduring emotional bond that infants and older children form with their caregivers.

bonding The process by which parents develop strong ties to their newborns, which may form in the first few hours following birth.

imprinting The formation of a strong bond of the newborn animal to the first moving object seen after birth.

Attachment Behaviors in Other Animal Species

Many species exhibit attachment behaviors. Baby chimpanzees, tigers, and lions will cling for dear life to their mothers' fur. The famed scientist Konrad Lorenz (1903–1989) studied imprinting in geese and other species. **Imprinting** is the formation of a strong bond of attachment to the first moving object seen after birth. A gosling (baby goose) will instinctively follow its mother wherever she goes. But goslings hatched in incubators will imprint on objects that happen to be present at their birth, including humans (Lorenz was one) and even mechanical toys. The goslings that imprinted on Lorenz followed him everywhere, even to the point of ignoring adult female geese.

© De Agostini/World Illustrated/Photoshot

Goslings that had imprinted on scientist Konrad Lorenz, affectionately dubbed Dr. Goose, followed him everywhere.

©Nina Leen/Time Life Pictures/Getty Images

Harry Harlow showed that baby monkeys preferred contact with a "cloth mother," even though a "wire mother" fed them.

In landmark research, psychologists Harry and Marguerite Harlow showed that baby monkeys developed attachment behaviors to inanimate objects placed in their cages (Harlow & Harlow, 1966). Newborn rhesus monkeys were separated from their mothers within hours of birth and raised in experimental cages in which various objects served as surrogate (substitute) mothers. In one study, infant monkeys were raised in cages containing two types of surrogate mothers: a wire cylinder or a soft, terry-cloth-covered cylinder (Harlow & Zimmermann, 1959). The infants showed clear preferences for the cloth mother, even when they were fed by an apparatus containing a bottle attached to the wire mother. Contact comfort apparently was a stronger determinant of attachment than food.

© Courtesy of Robin Marvin

Mary Ainsworth

Attachment in Human Infants

Psychiatrist John Bowlby (1908–1990) was among the first theorists to focus on attachment in human infants (Bowlby, 1980). To Bowlby, people have an innate predisposition to attach themselves to caregivers. However, he believed the quality of the attachment an infant forms with its parent depends on the sensitivity and quality of care the parent provides during the infant's first year of life.

Psychologist Mary Ainsworth (1913–1999) shared with Bowlby the view that the parent-infant relationship is crucial to the development of secure attachments. She was first introduced to attachment theory in her graduate studies at the University of Toronto just prior to World War II. In her dissertation study, she expressed one of the core ideas of attachment theory: that infants and young children need to use their parents as a "secure base" to venture into unfamiliar situations (Bretherton, 1992).

CONCEPT 9.11
Using a laboratory method for measuring attachment behavior in infants, investigators can classify infants according to their basic attachment style.

Ainsworth developed a laboratory method for measuring attachment behavior, which she called the Strange Situation. In the **Strange Situation**, a child of about 12 months of age and its mother enter a playroom filled with attractive toys. The mother periodically leaves the room and returns shortly afterward. On some occasions, an unfamiliar adult is present in the room either with or without the mother. Trained observers rate the child's exploration of the room, its wariness of the stranger, and its response to the brief separations and reunions with the mother. These responses are used to determine the infant's style of attachment to its mother. The quality of the greeting the mother receives during reunions tells more about the infant's attachment than the child's behavior during separations. Using this method, Ainsworth and colleagues (Ainsworth, 1979; Ainsworth et al., 1978) noted three basic attachment styles, one characterized by secure attachments and the other two by insecure attachments:

Strange Situation Ainsworth's method for assessing infant attachment to the mother, based on a series of brief separations and reunions with the mother in a playroom situation.

1. *Secure type (Type B).* These infants used their mothers as a secure base for exploring the environment, periodically looking around to check on her whereabouts and limiting exploration when she was absent. They sometimes cried when the mother left but warmly greeted her and were easily soothed by her when she returned. Soon they began exploring again. About 65 to 70 percent of middle-class samples of infants were classified as having secure attachments (Seifert & Hoffnung, 2000; Thompson, 1997). Cross-cultural studies indicate that most infants show a secure pattern of attachment (Main, 1996).
2. *Insecure-avoidant type (Type A).* Insecure-avoidant infants paid little attention to the mother when she was in the room and separated easily from her to explore the environment. They showed little distress when the mother departed and ignored her when she returned. About 20 percent of the infants in the typical sample fit this type (Thompson, 1997).

3. *Insecure-resistant type (Type C)*. These infants clung to the mother and were reluctant to explore the environment despite the presence of desirable toys. They showed a high level of distress when the mother departed and continued to experience some distress despite her attempts to comfort them when she returned. They also showed ambivalence or resistance toward the mother, reaching out to her to be picked up one moment and rebuffing her the next by pushing her away or twisting their bodies to get free of her. About 10 percent of the infants showed this attachment pattern.

In later studies, researchers identified a fourth type of attachment style, labeled *Type D* for *disorganized/disoriented* attachment (Cassidy, 2003; Fish & Condon, 2005). These infants appeared to lack a consistent or organized strategy for responding to separations and reunions. They seemed confused and were unable to approach the mother directly for support even when they were very distressed.

The infant's development of secure attachments is influenced by the quality of maternal care. For example, infants are more likely to develop secure attachments when their mothers are high in *maternal sensitivity*, or ability to respond appropriately to the infant's needs and cues (Cummings et al., 2003; Thompson, Easterbooks, & Padilla-Walker, 2003). Mothers often recreate with their own children the kinds of attachment relationships they had with their mothers and caregivers during childhood (Kretchmar & Jacobvitz, 2002).

The Ainsworth method may not be appropriate for assessing attachment behaviors in children from cultures with different child-rearing practices. For example, Japanese cultural practices emphasize mother-infant closeness and interdependence, which may make it more difficult for these infants to manage brief separations from their mothers (Takahashi, 1990). More broadly, we need to recognize that substantial variations exist in attachment behavior across cultures. For example, Americans tend to place a greater emphasis on exploration and independence in young children than do the Japanese.

Attachment and Later Development

CONCEPT 9.12
Attachment patterns formed in infancy may set the stage for attachment styles in adolescence and adulthood.

Attachment behaviors do not end in infancy; they span the first love relationships in adolescence, marital and loving relationships and long-term friendships in adulthood, and bonds formed between friends in the retirement years (Holland & Roisman, 2010). A lack of solid attachments in adult life is linked to poorer physical and emotional health (Goodwin, 2003). Longitudinal studies generally find a correspondence between the attachment styles shown in infancy and those shown in later development (Main, 1996).

Bowlby believed that attachment patterns formed in infancy are carried forward into childhood and adult life in the form of generalized expectancies about how others are likely to respond in close relationships. These expectancies, called **internal working models**, become a guide for future relationships through childhood, adolescence, and adulthood. Children who form secure attachments in infancy will develop an internal working model of others as basically dependable and trustworthy and of themselves as deserving of love and capable of developing caring relationships. Those with insecure attachments may have difficulty trusting others in close relationships or expecting others to meet their needs.

internal working models Generalized expectations, developed in early childhood, about how others are likely to respond in close relationships.

CONCEPT 9.13
A more securely attached infant is likely to be better adjusted in childhood and adolescence than a less securely attached infant.

Attachment styles forged in early infancy may have lasting consequences for later development. The more securely attached infant is likely to be better adjusted in childhood and adolescence than the less securely attached infant, to have better relationships with their peers and teachers, higher self-esteem, and to exhibit fewer problems behaviors (e.g., Cassidy & Shaver, 2008; Fearon et al., 2010; Johnson, Dweck, & Chen, 2007;

CONCEPT CHART 9.4 Differences in Temperaments and Attachment Styles

	Major Types	General Characteristics
Temperaments  © Roman Rybaleov/ Shutterstock.com	Easy child	Playful; shows interest in new situations or novel stimuli; quickly develops regular sleeping and eating patterns
	Difficult child	Irritable; has difficulty adjusting to new situations or people and establishing regular sleeping and feeding schedules
	Slow-to-warm-up child	Shows low activity levels; becomes inhibited, withdrawn, or fretful when exposed to new situations
Attachment Styles  © niderlander/ Shutterstock.com	Secure type (Type B)	Uses mother as a secure base to explore the environment while frequently checking on her whereabouts; may cry when mother leaves, but quickly settles down and warms up to her when she returns and then begins exploring again
	Insecure-avoidant type (Type A)	Pays little attention to mother when she is present and shows little distress when she leaves
	Insecure-resistant type (Type C)	Clings to mother, avoiding venturing into unfamiliar situations; becomes very upset when mother leaves and fails to be comforted completely when she returns; shows some ambivalence or resistance toward mother
	Disorganized/disoriented type (Type D, from later research)	Lacks a consistent or organized strategy for responding to separations and reunions; seems confused and unable to approach mother directly for support even when very distressed

Kerns & Richardson, 2005). Before we move on, you may want to review the differences in infant temperaments and attachment styles as shown in Concept Chart 9.4.

Does Day Care Affect Attachment?

CONCEPT 9.14
Evidence shows that placing infants in day care does not prevent the development of secure attachments to their mothers.

Many working parents today rely on organized day-care centers to care for their young children. About six out of 10 mothers today work outside the home, which is nearly double the rate that existed in 1960 (Pew Social Trends Staff, 2010). But might infants placed in day-care centers become less attached to their mothers than those of stay-at-home moms? The answer, investigators inform us, is no. Studies find no harmful effects of day care on either the strength or security of infant-mother attachments (e.g., Sandlin-Sniffen, 2000).

Actually, research evidence shows that high-quality day care in organized day-care centers tends to have positive effects on the child's cognitive and social development with respect to fostering independence, cognitive development including language skills, and cooperative play (e.g., McCartney et al., 2007; Stein, 2010; Vandell et al., 2010). Not surprisingly, children show greater cognitive growth when day-care staff members are responsive and sensitive to their needs (Loeb et al., 2004).

Professionals recognize that the quality of day care makes a difference in the infant's emotional and cognitive development. Children placed in low-quality day-care settings tend to have somewhat more problem behaviors than do other children (McCartney et al, 2010; Vandell et al., 2010). Choosing a childcare center is no easy task. Since licensing regulations and standards vary widely, parents need to weigh alternatives carefully and ask many questions before making a commitment (see Table 9.2).

TABLE 9.2 Selecting a Day-Care Center: Asking the Right Questions

Placing an infant in day care is an important parenting decision. Here are some questions parents might ask when evaluating the quality of day-care centers:

© kaarsten/Shutterstock.com

- ***General Questions*** Is the center licensed? By whom? How long has it been providing care? Does it carry liability insurance? How does it handle emergencies? What is the ratio of childcare workers to children? Can the center provide a list of references? What is its illness policy? Are its fees reasonable for the area and services it provides? Are the hours suitable to your needs? Does the center encourage parents to stop by to visit at almost any time?
- ***Questions About the Facility*** Is the facility clean and cheerful? Is it safe for young children (covered outlets, no dangerous objects within reach, gates at the tops and bottoms of stairs, no furniture with sharp corners, window guards on all windows, secure outdoor facility, etc.)? Is there sufficient play space? Are the toys and equipment in good condition? Is the food nutritious and appealing? Are there separate cribs and sheets for each child? Are there ample supplies of diapers and other baby supplies? Are there toys, games, books, and structured activities that would engage your child's interest? Are children well supervised when using play equipment and walking up and down stairs? Does the schedule allow periods of active and quiet play? Is there a quiet area for napping?
- ***Questions About the Staff*** Are they warm and responsive to the child's needs? Do they avoid using harsh commands or reprimands? Do they interact verbally with the children? Do they encourage children toward exploration, creativity, and development of language skills? Do they engage the children in ways that are appropriate to their developmental levels? What is their training background and experience? Do they seem to enjoy their work?

Child-Rearing Influences

CONCEPT 9.15
The quality of parenting is an important influence on children's intellectual, emotional, and social development.

Many factors influence a child's intellectual, emotional, and social development, including genetics, peer influences, and quality of parenting.

Good parenting encompasses many behaviors, including spending time with children (plenty of time!), modeling appropriate behaviors, helping children acquire skills to develop healthy peer relationships, stating rules clearly, setting limits, being consistent in correcting inappropriate behavior and praising good behavior, and providing a warm, secure environment. Explaining to children how their actions affect others can also help them develop more appropriate social behaviors. Children whose parents use discipline inconsistently, rely on harsh punishment, and are highly critical are more likely than others to develop problem behaviors at home and school and are less likely to develop healthy peer relationships (Baumrind, Larzelere, & Cowan, 2002; Kilgore, Snyder, & Lentz, 2000).

Father's Influence

Although much of the research on parent–child relationships focuses on children and their mothers, we shouldn't lose sight of the importance of fathers in child development. Children whose fathers share meals with them, spend leisure time with them, and assist them with schoolwork tend to perform better academically than those with less engaged fathers (Cooksey & Fondell, 1996).

Children in two-parent, mother–father households tend to fare better academically and socially than those in households of mothers and nonmarried heterosexual partners and single-mother households, even after accounting for differences in income levels (Thomson, Hanson, & McLanahan, 1994). However, children of lesbian and gay parents tend to do as well in school and have as good relationships with their peers as children of heterosexual parents (Patterson, 2009; Rosenfeld, 2010).

Mothers and fathers tend to differ in their parenting behavior. Compared to mothers, fathers typically provide less basic care (changing, feeding, bathing, etc.) but engage in more physically active play with their children (Parke, 2004; Parke & Buriel, 1998). For example, a father might zoom the baby in the air ("play airplane"), whereas a mother might engage in more physically restrained games like peek-a-boo and patty-cake, and talk and sing soothingly to the infant (Berger, 2009a). However, greater physical play with fathers is not characteristic of all cultures. In Chinese, Malaysian, and Indian cultures, for example, fathers and mothers rarely engage in physical play with their children (Parke & Buriel, 1998).

© Tony Freeman/Photo Edit

What does research evidence teach us about the influence of fathers on children's development? How do mothers and fathers tend to differ in their parenting behavior?

Cultural Differences in Parenting

Cultural learning has a strong bearing on child rearing, leading to variations across cultures in the ways that children are raised. African American families, for example, tend to have strong kinship bonds and to involve grandmothers in more direct childcare responsibilities than may be typical of other groups (Nevid, Rathus, & Greene, 2008). In traditional Hispanic families, the father is expected to be the provider and protector of the female, and the mother assumes full responsibility for childcare (Javier, 2010). These traditional gender roles are changing, however, as more Hispanic women are entering the work force and pursuing advanced educational opportunities.

Asian cultures tend to emphasize respect for parental authority, especially the father's, and encourage warm maternal relationships (Berk, 2009; Nevid & Sta. Maria, 1999). All cultures help children move from a state of complete dependency in infancy toward assuming more responsibility for their own behavior. However, they vary in the degree to which they promote early independence in children and expect them to assume responsible roles within the family and community.

© Strauss/Curtis/CORBIS

In some cultures, children are expected to perform responsible roles needed to ensure the survival of the family and community.

Parenting Styles

CONCEPT 9.16
Diana Baumrind identified three different parenting styles: authoritative, authoritarian, and permissive.

An important investigation into parenting influences on children's development focuses on differences in parenting styles. Diana Baumrind, a leading researcher in this area, identified three basic parenting styles: authoritative, authoritarian, and permissive (Baumrind, 1971, 1991):

1. *Authoritative style.* Authoritative parents set reasonable limits for their children but are not overcontrolling. The parent is the authority figure, firm but understanding, willing to give advice, but also willing to listen to children's concerns. Parents explain the reasons for their decisions rather than just "laying down the law."
2. *Authoritarian style.* Authoritarian parents are rigid and overcontrolling. They expect and demand unquestioned obedience from their children. If children dare to ask why they are being told to do something, the answer is likely to be "Because I say so." Authoritarian parents are unresponsive to their children's needs and rely on harsh forms of discipline while allowing their children little control over their lives.
3. *Permissive style.* Permissive parents have an "anything goes" attitude toward raising their children. They may respond affectionately to children but are extremely lax in setting limits and imposing discipline.

TABLE 9.3 Keys to Becoming an Authoritative Parent

Authoritative parents set firm limits but take the time to explain their decisions and listen to their children's point of view. They also help children develop a sense of competence by setting reasonable demands for mature behavior. Here are some suggestions for becoming an authoritative parent.

© iStockphoto.com/skynesher

Rely on reason, not force.	Explain the rules, but keep explanations brief. If the child throws food against the wall, the parent may say, "We don't do that. That makes a mess, and I'll have to clean it up."
Show warmth.	Express feelings verbally by using praise and physically by hugs, kisses, and holding hands when walking together. Praise the child for accomplishing tasks, even small ones.
Listen to your child's opinions.	Encourage the child to express his or her opinions and feelings, but explain why it is important to follow the rules. When a child requires assistance, demonstrate how to perform the expected behavior, and give encouragement and feedback when the child attempts it independently.

Why It Matters

Baumrind believes that authoritative parenting is the most successful style of parenting and points to evidence showing that children of authoritative parents tend to show the most positive outcomes in childhood and adolescence (Baumrind, 1971, 1991). They tend to have high self-esteem and to be self-reliant, competent in tasks they undertake, and popular with their peers (Parke & Buriel, 1998). The flexible but firm child-rearing approach of authoritative parents encourages children to be independent and assertive but also respectful of the needs of others. Table 9.3 outlines some key steps in becoming an authoritative parent.

On the other hand, children of authoritarian parents tend to be inhibited, moody, withdrawn, fearful, and distrustful of others. The most negative outcomes in adolescence are typically found in boys with authoritarian parents. They often underperform in school; lack initiative and self-confidence; and tend to be conflicted, unhappy, and unfriendly toward peers. Children with permissive parents may develop problems with impulsivity and lack of self-control. Because they lack the experience of conforming to other people's demands, they have difficulty developing effective interpersonal skills (Parke & Buriel, 1998).

Table 9.4 summarizes these three parenting styles. However, we need to take sociocultural realities into account when applying Baumrind's parenting styles. It may

TABLE 9.4 Baumrind's Styles of Parenting

	Authoritative Style	Authoritarian Style	Permissive Style
Limit setting	High	High	Low
Style of discipline	Reasonable	Forceful	Low
Maturity expectations	High	High	Low
Communications with children	High	Low	Moderate
Warmth and support	High	Low	High

be unfair or misleading to apply the same categories in classifying parenting styles in other cultures that have different child-rearing traditions. For example, some cultures emphasize authoritarian styles of parenting more than others do. Within our own society, authoritarian styles in lower socioeconomic-status (SES) families may represent a type of adaptation to stresses that families in poorer, more dangerous neighborhoods might face, such as heightened risks of violence and drug abuse. In these circumstances, it may be an adaptive strategy for parents to enforce stricter obedience and to set stricter limits to protect children from outside threats (Parke, 2004). Parents in poorer families may also relate warmly to their children but become frustrated in the parenting role because they lack the psychological and economic resources needed to meet the many challenges they face (Weis, 2002).

We should also recognize that while parenting styles may affect children's adjustment, children's behaviors may influence how their parents relate to them. In other words, both parent-to-child and child-to-parent effects need to be considered (Kerr et al., 2003).

Peer Relationships

As children venture into the world, the relationships they form with peers affect many aspects of their development. Peer relationships provide the child with opportunities to develop socially competent behaviors in relating to others outside the family and as a member of a group. The acceptance and approval of peer group members help shape the child's developing self-esteem and sense of competence.

CONCEPT 9.17
Peer relationships provide opportunities for children to develop social competencies and establish feelings of closeness and loyalty that can serve as the basis for later relationships.

Friendships provide opportunities for children to learn prosocial behaviors such as sharing, cooperating, and resolving conflicts. Children with friends tend to have higher self-esteem and are perceived by others as more sensitive and caring (Vaughn et al., 2000). On the other hand, kindergartners who are rejected by peers tend to feel lonelier, more often want to avoid school, and don't perform as well on achievement measures as their more accepted peers (Buhs & Ladd, 2001). Older peer-rejected children tend to show higher levels of antisocial behavior, such as aggressiveness or social withdrawal (Rodkin et al., 2000). Having friends can also help protect children from physical or verbal abuse and bullying from other children.

Peer relationships can also have negative consequences (Monahan, Steinberg, & Cauffman, 2009). Children and adolescents have a strong need for peer acceptance and may be influenced by peers to engage in deviant activities they might never attempt on their own (Rubin, Bukowski, & Laursen, 2009).

Erikson's Stages of Psychosocial Development

CONCEPT 9.18
Erik Erikson described four stages of psychosocial development in childhood, each characterized by a particular life crisis or challenge: trust versus mistrust, autonomy versus shame and doubt, initiative versus guilt, and industry versus inferiority.

→ Concept Link
Erikson's stages of psychosocial development extend through adolescence and adulthood. See Modules 10.1, 10.2, and 10.3.

Erik Erikson (1902–1994), a prominent psychodynamic theorist, emphasized the importance of social relationships in human development (Erikson, 1963). In his view, psychosocial development progresses through a series of stages that begin in early childhood and continue through adulthood. He believed our personalities are shaped by how we deal with a series of psychosocial crises or challenges during these stages. In this section, we focus on the four stages of psychosocial development that occur during childhood.

Trust Versus Mistrust

The first psychosocial challenge the infant faces is the development of a sense of trust toward its social environment. When parents treat the infant warmly and are responsive to its needs, a sense of trust develops. But if the parents are seldom there when the infant needs them, or if they are detached or respond coldly, the infant develops a basic mistrust of others. The world may seem a cold and threatening place.

Autonomy Versus Shame and Doubt

Erikson believed that the central psychosocial challenge faced during the second and third years of life concerns autonomy. The child is now becoming mobile within the home and is "getting into everything." Parents may warmly encourage the child toward greater independence and nurture this newly developed sense of autonomy. However, if they demand too much too soon or make excessive demands that the child cannot meet (such as in the area of toilet training), the child may become riddled with feelings of self-doubt and shame that come to pervade later development, even into adulthood.

Initiative Versus Guilt

This stage, corresponding to the preschool years of three to six, is a time of climbing gyms and play dates, a time at which the child is challenged to initiate actions and carry them out. Children who largely succeed in their efforts and are praised for their accomplishments will come to develop a sense of initiative and competence. In contrast, children who frequently fail to accomplish tasks and can't seem to "get things right" may develop feelings of guilt and powerlessness, especially if they are ridiculed or harshly criticized for their awkwardness or missteps.

© iStockphoto.com/bonniej

Erikson believed that children of six to 12 years of age face the central challenge of developing industriousness and self-confidence. Performing competently in the classroom and the playing field enhances their self-confidence and willingness to apply themselves.

Industry Versus Inferiority

At this stage, which corresponds to the elementary school period of six to 12 years, the child faces the central challenge of developing industriousness and self-confidence. If children believe they perform competently in the classroom and on the playing field, they will likely become industrious by taking an active role in school and extracurricular activities. But if the pendulum swings too far in the other direction and failure outweighs success, feelings of inadequacy or inferiority may develop, causing the child to become withdrawn and unmotivated.

Table 9.5 provides an overview of Erikson's stages of psychosocial development in childhood. Though Erikson believed that childhood experiences can have lasting effects on the individual's psychological development, he emphasized that later experiences in life may counter these earlier influences and lead eventually to more successful resolutions of these life challenges.

TABLE 9.5 Erik Erikson's Stages of Psychosocial Development in Childhood

Approximate Ages	Life Crisis	Major Challenge in Psychosocial Development
Infancy (birth to 1 year)	Trust versus mistrust	Developing a basic sense of trust in the caregiver and the environment
Toddlerhood (1 to 3 years)	Autonomy versus shame and doubt	Building a sense of independence and self-control
Preschool period (3 to 6 years)	Initiative versus guilt	Learning to initiate actions and carry them out
Elementary school period (6 to 12 years)	Industry versus inferiority	Becoming productive and involved

Source: Adapted from Erikson, 1963.

9.4 MODULE REVIEW Emotional and Social Development

Recite It

What are the three basic types of infant temperament identified in the New York Longitudinal Study, and what are the major differences among them?

- The three types are the easy child, the difficult child, and the slow-to-warm-up child.
- Easy children have generally positive moods, react well to changes, and quickly develop regular feeding and sleep schedules.
- Difficult children have largely negative moods and have difficulty reacting to new situations and people and developing regular feeding and sleep schedules.
- Slow-to-warm-up children tend to become withdrawn when facing new situations and experience mild levels of distress.

What are the three types of attachment styles identified by Ainsworth?

- The secure type of infant attaches to the mother and uses her as a secure base to explore the environment.
- The insecure-avoidant type freely explores the environment but tends to ignore the mother.
- The insecure-resistant type clings excessively to the mother but shows ambivalence or resistance toward her.
- Securely attached infants tend to show better social and emotional adjustment in later development than insecurely attached infants.

What are the three major styles of parenting in Baumrind's model, and how do they differ?

- Authoritative parents expect mature behavior, use reasoning, and set firm limits.
- Authoritarian parents set firm limits but are overcontrolling and rely on harsh styles of discipline.
- Permissive parents have an "anything goes" style characterized by a lax approach to limit setting.
- Authoritative parenting is generally associated with better emotional and social adjustment in children than the other parenting styles.

What roles do peer relationships play in children's emotional and social development?

- Peers are important influences on children's psychosocial adjustment, especially on self-esteem and the development of social competencies.
- Peer relationships may also set the stage for deviant behavior.

What are the stages of psychosocial development during childhood according to Erikson?

- Erikson's stages are (1) trust versus mistrust (birth to one year), (2) autonomy versus shame and doubt (ages one to three), (3) initiative versus guilt (ages three to six), and (4) industry versus inferiority (ages six to 12).

Recall It

1. Researchers identify three basic infant temperament types: easy children, difficult children, and ________ - to-warm-up children.
2. Match the following types of attachment identified by Ainsworth and other researchers to the appropriate descriptions below: i. secure; ii. insecure-avoidant; iii. insecure-resistant; iv. disorganized/disoriented.
   a. child clings to mother, yet shows signs of ambivalence or negativity.
   b. mother is an important "base" for exploration; child is happy in mother's presence.
   c. child appears confused; seems unable to utilize mother for any support.
   d. child ignores mother when she is present and is unaffected by her departure or return.
3. Parenting style is an important influence on children's development. Which of the following terms describes a parent who is warm, supportive, and consistent; understands the child's point of view; and communicates well?
   a. permissive.
   b. authoritarian.
   c. authoritative.
   d. laissez-faire.
4. In which of the following stages in Erikson's theory of psychosocial development do children compare their abilities to those of their friends and classmates?
   a. trust versus mistrust.
   b. autonomy versus shame and doubt.
   c. initiative versus guilt.
   d. industry versus inferiority.

Think About It

- Based on your reading of Baumrind's work on parent-child relationships, what do you think you need to do to become a better parent now or in the future?
- Think of a child or young adult you know well. How do Erikson's stages of psychosocial development relate to this person's development in childhood? Which outcomes (trust versus mistrust, autonomy versus shame and doubt, initiative versus guilt, and industry versus inferiority) best describe the person's psychosocial development?

MODULE 9.5

Cognitive Development

- How do assimilation and accommodation differ?
- What are the major features associated with Piaget's stages of cognitive development?
- What is the basic theme in Vygotsky's theory of cognitive development?

THE BRAIN LOVES A PUZZLE

As you read ahead, use the information in the text to solve the following puzzle:

On a trip to the aquarium with his father, five-year-old Kamau sees a whale for the first time and says, "Wow, what a big fish!" His father points out that the whale is not a fish, but Kamau seems puzzled and continues to call it a fish. How would you explain Kamau's persistence in calling a whale a fish?

SLICE OF LIFE Seven-year-old Jason is upset with his younger brother Scott, age three. Scott just can't seem to get the basic idea of hide-and-go-seek. Every time Scott goes off to hide, he curls up in the corner of the room in plain sight of Jason. "You're supposed to hide where I can't see you," Jason complains. So Scott goes off and hides in the same spot, but now he covers his eyes. "Now you can't see me," he calls back to Jason. Though they live in the same home and share many family outings together, the world of a three-year-old like Scott is very different from that of a seven-year-old like Jason. Let's consider that difference by examining the changes in the way children think and reason as they progress through childhood. We begin with the work of the most influential theorist on cognitive development, Jean Piaget.

© cappi thompson/shutterstock.com

Piaget's Theory of Cognitive Development

Jean Piaget (1896–1980) is arguably the most important developmental theorist of all time—a "giant with a giant theory" (Hunt, 1993). Piaget began his studies of children by administering intelligence tests (Hogan, 2007). Always a keen observer, he noticed a pattern of errors in the children's thinking, such as confusing part-whole relationships and being unable to classify objects correctly. He believed these errors were not simply mistakes, but represented distinct ways of thinking in children.

Piaget was less concerned with whether children answered questions correctly than with the reasoning children used to arrive at their answers (Feldman, 2003). He believed the best way to understand how children think is to observe them closely as they interact with objects and solve problems. Much of his work was based on his observations of his own three children.

© Bettmann/CORBIS

Jean Piaget

To understand Piaget's theory of cognitive development, we must look at what he means by the term *schema*. To Piaget, a **schema** is an organized system of actions or a mental representation that people use to understand and interact with the world (Piaget, 1952). The child is born with simple schemas comprising basic reflexes such as sucking. This schema obviously has adaptive value, since the infant needs to obtain nourishment from its mother's breast or the bottle by sucking.

schema In Piaget's theory, a mental framework for understanding or acting on the environment.

SLICE OF LIFE Eventually the infant discovers that the schema works more effectively for some objects than for others. For my daughter Daniella, the sucking schema crashed the day we introduced her to an infant cup, commonly called a sippy cup. Her dad demonstrated how to tip the cup at an angle to draw the liquid into the mouth. Daniella was unimpressed and continued to hold the cup upright and suck on its lip, which unhappily failed to produce the desired result.

SLICE OF LIFE Eventually schemas change as the child adapts to new challenges and demands. According to Piaget, **adaptation** is a process by which people adapt or change to meet challenges in the environment more effectively. Through adaptation, we adjust our schemas to meet the changing demands the environment imposes on us. Adaptation, in turn, consists of two complementary processes: *assimilation* and *accommodation*.

SLICE OF LIFE **Assimilation** is the process of incorporating new objects or situations into existing schemas. For example, newborns will reflexively suck any object placed in their mouths, such as a finger or even a piece of cloth. Daniella applied her sucking schema to an infant cup by attempting to suck on its lip. Older children develop classification schemas, which consist of mental representations of particular classes of objects. When Daniella was a toddler, she applied her "dog schema" to any nonhuman animal, including cats, horses, sheep, and even fish. To her, all were "bow-wows."

Assimilation is adaptive when new objects fit existing schemas, as when the infant sucks on the nipple of a baby bottle for the first time rather than the mother's breast. But horses and fish are not dogs, and infant cups cannot be sucked to draw liquid into the mouth. **Accommodation** is the process of altering existing schemas or creating new ones to deal with objects or experiences that don't fit readily into existing schemas. Eventually Daniella developed a new "tipping schema" for using an infant cup: tipping it in her mouth so the contents would drip in.

CONCEPT 9.19
To Piaget, a schema is an action strategy or a mental representation that helps people understand and interact with the world.

→ Concept Link
People form mental images or representations called *social schemas* to make sense of their social environment, an example of which is the first impressions they form when meeting new people. See Module 14.1.

CONCEPT 9.20
In Piaget's view, adaptation to the environment consists of two complementary processes, assimilation and accommodation.

adaptation In Piaget's theory, the process of adjustment that enables people to function more effectively in meeting the demands they face in the environment.

assimilation In Piaget's theory, the process of incorporating new objects or situations into existing schemas.

accommodation In Piaget's theory, the process of creating new schemas or modifying existing ones to account for new objects or experiences.

Stages of Cognitive Development

In Piaget's view, the processes of assimilation and accommodation are ongoing throughout life. However, he held that the child's cognitive development progresses through a series of stages that occur in an ordered sequence at about the same ages in all children. Children at the different stages of cognitive development differ in how they view and interact with the world. Here we take a closer look at Piaget's four stages of cognitive development: the sensorimotor, preoperational, concrete operational, and formal operational stages.

CONCEPT 9.21
Piaget proposed that children progress at about the same ages through a series of four stages of cognitive development: the sensorimotor, preoperational, concrete operational, and formal operational stages.

Sensorimotor Stage: Birth to Two Years

The sensorimotor stage spans a period of momentous growth in the infant's cognitive development. During this stage, which actually consists of six substages, the child becomes increasingly capable of performing more complex behaviors and skills. Piaget used the term *sensorimotor* because the infant explores its world by using its senses and applying its developing motor skills (body movement and hand control). The infant's intelligence is expressed through action and purposeful manipulation of objects.

At birth through one month, the infant's behaviors are limited to inborn reflexes, such as grasping and sucking. From months one through eight, the infant gains increasing voluntary control over some of its movements, such as grasping objects placed above its crib. The infant is now beginning to act on the world and to repeat actions that have interesting effects, such as repeatedly squeezing a rubber duck to produce a squealing sound. By eight to 12 months, the infant's actions are intended to reach a particular goal. The child will perform purposeful actions such as crawling to the other side of the room to open the bottom drawers of cabinets where toys are kept.

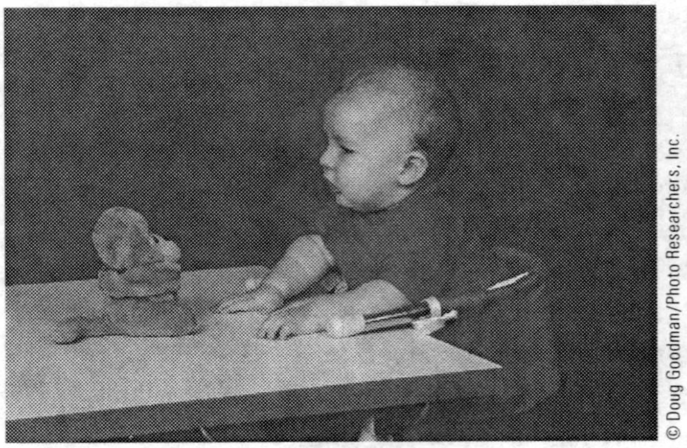

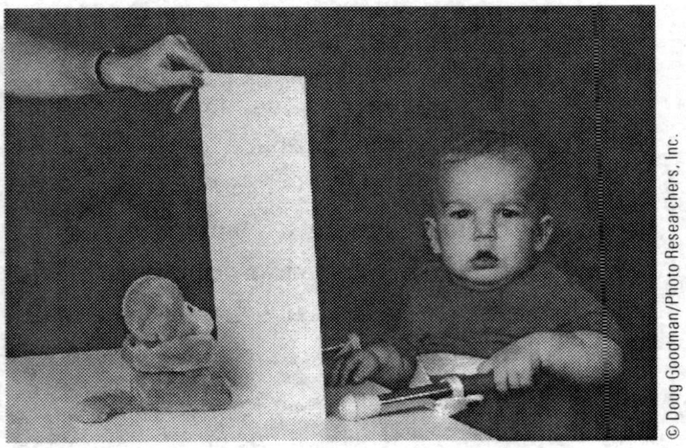

Infants who have not yet developed object permanence act as though objects that have disappeared from sight no longer exist.

Early in the sensorimotor stage, infants are aware of an object's existence only if it is physically present. Out of sight is, quite literally, out of mind. If you block a four-month-old's view of an object that he or she has been looking at, the child will immediately lose interest and begin looking at other objects. By about eight months, the child will begin looking for a hidden object. Now, if you place a pillow over a teddy bear, she or he will push the pillow out of the way to get the toy. By this age, the child has begun to develop a concept of **object permanence**, or the recognition that objects continue to exist even if they have disappeared from sight.

object permanence The recognition that objects continue to exist even if they have disappeared from sight.

Piaget believed that object permanence is not yet complete at this point. It reaches a mature level toward the end of the sensorimotor stage when the child begins to acquire the ability to form a mental representation of an object that is not visibly present. One sign that 22-month-old Daniella had acquired object permanence was that she began asking for her brother Michael upon awakening. She apparently was able to retain a mental representation of Michael. Her parents tried not to take it personally that she always asked for Michael first.

Which glass holds more water? Preoperational children fail to recognize that the quantity of an object remains the same when placed in a different-size container.

Preoperational Stage: 2 to 7 Years

Piaget used the term *preoperational* to describe the cognitive abilities of children roughly ages two to seven years because they lack the ability to perform basic logical operations—to apply basic principles of logic to their experiences. During this period, however, extraordinary growth occurs in the ability to form mental or **symbolic representations** of the world, especially with the use of language. Specifically, a child forms symbolic representations of objects and experiences by naming or describing them in words. Language makes the child's thinking processes far more expansive and efficient than was possible in the sensorimotor stage.

symbolic representations Symbols that stand for names and experiences; specifically, the words in a language.

Another form of representational thinking is make-believe or pretend play. In pretend play, children form mental representations that allow them to enact scenes with characters that are not physically present. Pretend play becomes increasingly complex as children progress through the preoperational stage. By age five or six, children are creating scenes with imagined characters or reenacting scenes they have seen on TV or in movies.

egocentrism In Piaget's theory, the tendency to see the world only from one's own perspective.

Though cognitive abilities expand dramatically during the preoperational stage, Piaget noted that the child's thinking processes are still quite limited. For example, the preoperational child demonstrates **egocentrism**, the tendency to view the world only from one's own point of view. Egocentric thinking doesn't mean the child is selfish or unconcerned about others; rather, the child at this stage lacks the cognitive ability to take another person's point of view or perspective. In the child's mind, he or she is the center of the universe. For example, five-year-old Michelle wants to play with Mommy but doesn't understand that Mommy is tired and needs to rest. When Michelle feels like playing, she thinks Mommy should feel like playing too. In our earlier example, three-year-old Scott is unable to take his brother's perspective when playing hide-and-go-seek. He doesn't realize that his hiding place is in plain view of his brother. He also assumes that since he can't see his brother when he covers his own eyes, his brother can't see him either.

SLICE OF LIFE Professor Jeff Stowell of Eastern Illinois University offers this example of egocentric thought from his son Spencer, who was four years old at the time: "While talking to me on the phone, Spencer said, 'Do you think my breath smells like M and M's?' I replied that I couldn't smell it from here. To which Spencer replied, 'Well, try again. Now can you?'"

Egocentrism leads to another type of thinking typical of the preoperational child: **animistic thinking**. The child believes that inanimate objects like the moon, the sun, and the clouds have living qualities such as wishes, thoughts, and feelings just as she or he does. A four-year-old, for instance, may think the moon is his friend and follows him as he walks home with his parents at night. Professor Stowell offers another example from his son Spencer at age three: "He cried when my wife did laundry and begged her to turn the washing machine off because 'The clothes will drown!'" (To get some first-hand experience with the thinking patterns of young children, see *Try This Out*).

animistic thinking In Piaget's theory, the child's belief that inanimate objects have living qualities.

irreversibility In Piaget's theory, the inability to reverse the direction of a sequence of events to their starting point.

centration In Piaget's theory, the tendency to focus on only one aspect of a situation at a time.

conservation In Piaget's theory, the ability to recognize that the quantity or amount of an object remains constant despite superficial changes in its outward appearance.

Two other limitations of the preoperational child's thinking are irreversibility and centration. **Irreversibility** is the inability to reverse the direction of a sequence of events to their starting point. **Centration** is the tendency to focus on only one aspect of a situation at a time to the exclusion of all other aspects.

Piaget illustrated these principles through his famous **conservation** tasks (see ■ Figure 9.10). (Conservation, the hallmark of the concrete operational stage, is discussed in the next section.) In a volume conservation task, the child is shown two

Type of Conservation	1 Initial Presentation	2 Transformation	Question	3 Preoperational Child's Answer
Liquids	Two equal glasses of liquid	Pour one into a taller, narrower glass	Which glass contains more?	The taller one
Number	Two equal lines of checkers	Increase spacing of checkers in one line	Which line has more checkers?	The longer one
Mass	Two equal balls of clay	Squeeze one ball into a long, thin shape	Which piece has more clay?	The long one
Length	Two sticks of equal length	Move one stick	Which stick is longer?	The one that is farther to the right

Figure 9.10 Piaget's Conservation Tasks

1. Children are presented with a substance of a certain quantity.
2. The substance is then transformed in some superficial way.
3. Children who have not yet developed the principle of conservation fail to recognize that the quantity of the substance remains the same.

Source: Adapted from Berger & Thompson, 1995.

identical glasses of water. Once the child agrees that the glasses contain the same amounts of water, the water in one glass is poured into a shorter, wider glass, which causes the water to come to rest at a lower level in the shorter glass than in the taller one. The preoperational child now insists that the taller, narrower glass contains more water. Because of centration, the child focuses on only one thing: the height of the column of water. Because of irreversibility, the child fails to recognize that the process can be reversed to its starting point—that pouring the water back into its original container would restore it to its original state.

TRY THIS OUT
Learning Through Observation

You may be able to acquire more direct knowledge of children's cognitive development by serving as a volunteer in a nursery or preschool setting. To what extent does the cognitive development of preschoolers correspond to Piaget's concepts of egocentrism, animistic thought, centration, and irreversibility?

Concrete Operational Stage: 7 to 11 Years

The stage of concrete operations is marked by the development of conservation. To Piaget, conservation is the ability to recognize that the amount or quantity of a substance does not change if its outward appearance is changed, so long as nothing is either added to it or subtracted from it. The kinds of conservation tasks that stymied the six-year-old become mere "child's play" to the average seven- or eight-year-old. The child at the concrete operational stage is able to mentally reverse the process in the conservation task and recognize that the amount of water doesn't change when poured into a container of a different shape. The child also becomes capable of decentered thinking, the ability to take into account more than one aspect of a situation at a time. The child now recognizes that a rise in the water level in the narrower container is offset by a change in the width of the column of water.

The child's thinking at this stage also becomes much less egocentric. The child recognizes that other people's thoughts and feelings may differ from his or her own. The child can also perform simple logical operations, but only when they are tied to concrete examples. Seven-year-old Timmy can understand that if he has more baseball cards than Sally and Sally has more than Sam, then he also has more than Sam. But Timmy would have great difficulty understanding the question if it were posed abstractly, such as "If A is greater than B and B is greater than C, is A greater than C?"

Formal Operational Stage (Puberty to Adulthood)

formal operations The level of full cognitive maturity in Piaget's theory, characterized by the ability to think in abstract terms.

The stage of **formal operations** is the final one in Piaget's theory—the stage of full cognitive maturity. In Western societies, formal operational thought tends to begin at around puberty, at about age 11 or 12. However, not all children enter this stage at this time, and some never do even as adults. Formal operations are characterized by the ability to think logically about abstract ideas, generate hypotheses, and think deductively. The person with formal operations can think through hypothetical situations, including the "A is greater than B" example earlier. He or she can follow arguments from their premises to their conclusions and back again. We will return to this stage of cognitive development when we consider the thinking processes of the adolescent.

Piaget's Shadow: Evaluating His Legacy

CONCEPT 9.22
Though Piaget continues to have an enormous impact on the field of developmental psychology, a number of challenges to his theory have surfaced.

Piaget, a luminous figure in the annals of psychology, left a rich legacy. Concepts such as schemas, assimilation and accommodation, egocentricity, conservation, and reversibility, among others, provide a strong basis for understanding cognitive processes in children and how they change during development. Piaget encouraged us to view children not as passive responders to stimuli but as natural scientists who seek to understand the world and to operate on it. However, although Piaget's theory of cognitive development offers many insights into the mental abilities of children, a number of criticisms of his theory have emerged.

Challenges to the Stage Model

Some theorists challenge Piaget's basic premise that cognitive development unfolds in stages. They believe a child's cognitive abilities develop through a more continuous process of gradual change over time (e.g., Bjorklund, 1995).

Underestimation of Children's Abilities

Critics also contend that Piaget underestimated the abilities of young children (e.g., Meltzoff & Gopnik, 1997). Infants clearly know more about the world and act on it in more meaningful ways than Piaget believed. We noted, for example, that even newborns can imitate facial expressions. Piaget believed this ability doesn't develop until late in the first year. Evidence suggests that children may begin to develop object permanence and ability to view events from other people's perspectives at earlier ages than Piaget's model would suppose (Aguiara & Baillargeon, 2002; Munakata et al., 1997).

Lack of Attention to Cultural Influences

Piaget believed the stages of cognitive development unfold naturally as the result of underlying maturational processes as long as the child has opportunities to interact with objects in the external world. However, critics claim he failed to account for cultural differences in the timing by which these stages unfold. In some respects, Piaget was right: cross-cultural studies shows that children do progress through the stages of cognitive development in the order he described (Dasen, 1994). But cross-cultural evidence also shows that the ages at which children pass through these stages do differ across cultures.

The anthropologist Pierre Dasen studied with Piaget and later tested Piaget's theory in different cultures. In one study, he tested aborigine children in Australia on the conservation-of-liquid task in which water is transferred from a shorter, wider glass to a taller, narrower glass. He found that aborigine children developed conservation between 10 and 13 years of age, or some three years or more later, on the average, than the Swiss children that Piaget had observed. Moreover, some adolescents and even some adults failed to demonstrate conservation on several different types of conservation tasks.

On the other hand, the aborigine children found spatial tasks easier to master than conservation tasks—just the opposite of what was found in Swiss children. In one spatial task, a landscape model is rotated by 180 degrees. The child is asked to find an object (such as a toy sheep) on one model and then locate it on the same spot on the rotated model. We shouldn't be surprised that aborigine children do well on spatial tasks. The ability to locate objects in the rugged landscape in which the aborigines live—to find fresh water and wild game—is crucial to their survival. The meat from the hunt is not divided evenly by weight but is allocated by pieces, with each particular part of the animal going to a designated person according to kinship relationships. The need for counting or comparing quantities, which are skills needed in conservation tasks, is minimal. In fact, the aborigine language contains words for numbers only through *five;* any quantity above that is simply "many." The message here is that the child's cultural experiences may affect both the rate of cognitive development and the eventual level of cognitive development.

Despite these challenges, Piaget's observations and teachings about how children develop have provided a guiding framework for researchers' study and exploration, and they will likely continue to do so for future generations.

Vygotsky's Sociocultural Theory of Cognitive Development

CONCEPT 9.23
Vygotsky's theory of cognitive development emphasizes the role of social and cultural factors.

The Russian psychologist Lev Vygotsky was born in the same year (1896) as Piaget, but he died of tuberculosis in 1934 at age 38. Whereas Piaget focused on children's understanding of their physical environment—the world of objects and things—Vygotsky (1978, 1986) was concerned primarily with how children come to understand their social world. He believed that cultural learning is acquired through a gradual process of social interactions between children and parents, teachers, and other members of the culture. These interactions provide the basis for acquiring the knowledge that children need to solve everyday challenges and to meet the demands the culture imposes on them. In Vygotsky's view, the adult is the expert and the child is the novice, and the relationship between them is one of tutor and student.

zone of proximal development (ZPD) In Vygotsky's theory, the range between children's present level of knowledge and their potential knowledge state if they receive proper guidance and instruction.

scaffolding In Vygotsky's theory, tailoring the degree and type of instruction to the child's current level of ability or knowledge.

Vygotsky developed a cognitive developmental theory that emphasizes the role of culture as the framework through which the child's understanding of the world develops. To Vygotsky, children are born as cultural blank slates (Zukow-Goldring, 1997). They must learn the skills, values, and behaviors valued by the given culture (Feldman, 2003). In American culture, this social knowledge includes such everyday behaviors as using the proper eating utensils, brushing teeth before bed, saying "excuse me" after sneezing, and waiting patiently in line.

Vygotsky emphasized that social learning occurs within a **zone of proximal development (ZPD)**, also called the *zone of potential development*. The ZPD refers to the range between the skills children can currently perform and those they could perform if they received proper guidance and instruction. Working "in the zone" means providing less experienced individuals, or novices, with the instruction they need to advance beyond the level they would be able to accomplish on their own (Holzman, 2009; Kleinspehn-Ammerlahn et al., 2011).

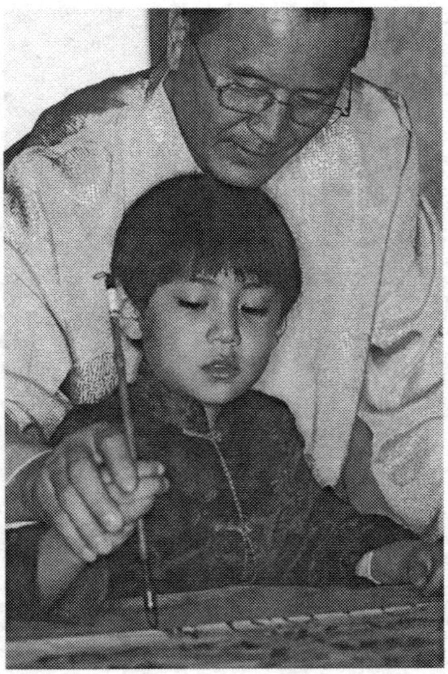

© Floresco Productions/Corbis

Vygotsky emphasized social interactions as the basis for children's acquisition of knowledge about the world.

Parents and educators who adopt Vygotksy's model use the technique of scaffolding to help children acquire new skills. In **scaffolding**, the parent or instructor scales the degree and type of instruction to the child's current level of ability or knowledge (see *Try This Out*). For example, in early picture book reading, the parent of a 12-month-old will read the book aloud and point to the figures in the pictures. With a 15- or 18-month-old, the parent may identify the subject in a picture by saying, "Is that a tiger?" or use "What's that?" types of questions. The parent of a two- or three-year-old may use a picture book as a platform for introducing other learning, perhaps by posing questions such as "What does a bee make?" (Zukow-Goldring, 1997). The scaffolding agent (parent or teacher) needs to be sensitive to signals from the novice (child) indicating the child's level of competence and readiness to progress to a higher level. Using such cues leads the agent to phase in or withdraw direct support as needed. As the child's competencies develop, less direct guidance and instruction become necessary. Vygotsky's work continues to have a major influence not only in developmental psychology but also in education. Concept Chart 9.5 provides an overview of the major theories of cognitive development reviewed in this module.

CONCEPT CHART 9.5 Theories of Cognitive Development

Theory	Overview	
Piaget's Theory of Cognitive Development	Piaget emphasized the role of adaptation in cognitive development, which he believed consists of two complementary processes: assimilation (incorporation of unfamiliar objects or situations into existing schemas) and accommodation (modification of existing schemas or creation of new ones to take into account new objects and situations).	
Piaget's Stages of Cognitive Development	The child progresses through a fixed sequence of stages involving qualitative leaps in ability and ways of understanding and interacting with the world.	
 © Flashon Studio/ Shutterstock.com	Sensorimotor stage (birth to 2 years)	The child uses its senses and developing motor skills to explore and act upon the world. The child begins to develop a concept of object permanence, which is the recognition that objects continue to exist even if they are not presently in sight.
 © maska/Shutterstock.com	Preoperational stage (2 to 7 years)	The child acquires the ability to use language to symbolize objects and actions in words. Yet the child's thinking is limited by egocentrism, animistic thought, centration, and irreversibility.
 © StockLite/ shutterstock.com	Concrete operational stage (7 to 11 years)	The child becomes capable of performing simple logical operations as long as they're tied to concrete problems. A key feature of this stage is the acquisition of the principle of conservation, or ability to recognize that the amount of a substance does not change if its shape or size is rearranged.
 © Yuri Arcurs/ Shutterstock.com	Formal operational stage (begins around puberty, age 11 or 12)	The child becomes capable of abstract thinking. Yet not all children, nor all adults, progress to this stage.
Critique of Piaget's Theory	Piaget's observations and teachings remain a guiding framework for understanding cognitive development, but his theory has been challenged on some grounds, including the ages at which he believed children acquire certain abilities and his lack of attention to cultural factors in development.	
Vygotsky's Sociocultural Theory	Vygotsky emphasizes the social interaction between children and adults as the basis for the child's acquisition of the skills, values, and behaviors needed to meet the demands imposed by the particular culture.	

TRY THIS OUT Using Scaffolding to Teach Skills

Apply the principle of scaffolding to help a child acquire a particular skill. Select a skill the child can potentially acquire with some instruction and practice. Begin by providing direct guidance and instruction, and gradually taper off the amount of direct support as the child achieves mastery. Afterward, review what you learned. Did you provide clear direction at a level the child could understand? Did you gradually withdraw support to allow the child to master the skill increasingly on his or her own? How might you do things differently in the future?

9.5 MODULE REVIEW Cognitive Development

Recite It

How do assimilation and accommodation differ?

- Assimilation is the process of incorporating new stimuli within existing schemas.
- Accommodation involves altering existing schemas or developing new ones to account for new stimuli that present schemas cannot handle effectively.

What are the major features associated with Piaget's stages of cognitive development?

- During the sensorimotor stage, from birth to about two years, children explore their world through their senses, motor responses, and purposeful manipulation of objects.
- During the preoperational stage, from about two to seven years of age, the child's thinking is more representational but is limited by centration, egocentricity, animistic thinking, and irreversibility.
- The concrete operational stage, beginning around age seven in Western cultures, is characterized by development of the principles of conservation and reversibility and the ability to draw logical relationships among concrete objects or events.
- The formal operational stage—the most advanced stage of cognitive development according to Piaget—is characterized by the ability to engage in deductive thinking, generate hypotheses, and engage in abstract thought.

What is the basic theme in Vygotsky's theory of cognitive development?

- Vygotsky focused on how children acquire knowledge of their social world. He believed this knowledge is achieved through the interaction of the child (novice) with the parent (expert) within a zone of proximal development that takes into account the child's present and potentially realizable knowledge structures.

Recall It

1. In which stage does Piaget suggest a child learns by interacting with the environment through using his or her senses and developing motor skills?
   a. sensorimotor.
   b. preoperational.
   c. concrete operational.
   d. formal operational.
2. Piaget believed that adaptation consists of two complementary cognitive processes, ______ and ______.
3. Anthropologist Pierre Dasen found that, unlike Swiss children, aborigine children in Australia were better able to master spatial skills than conservation skills. How might you explain this finding?
4. Russian psychologist Lev Vygotsky emphasized the role of ______ interactions and cultural learning in shaping the child's cognitive development.

Think About It

- Drawing upon Piaget's theory of cognitive development, how is the world of the child different from that of the adult?
- Think of examples of assimilation and accommodation in your own thinking. In which situations were you able to assimilate new information into existing schemas? In which situations did you need to alter your schemas or form new ones?

APPLICATION MODULE 9.6 TV and Kids

CONCEPT 9.24
Though violence on TV and in other media may foster aggressive behavior in children, there is evidence that viewing certain types of children's programs may improve the preacademic skills of preschoolers.

It's been called the *box*, the *tube*, even the *boob tube*. Is it a window to the world or, as one critic put it, a "vast wasteland"? Love it or hate it, it's here to stay—right smack in your living room or bedroom. It's your television.

The average American child today of age two to five watches 25 hours of TV a week—the highest figure on record (Mindlin, 2009). This figure is more than double the maximum amount of TV viewing recommended by the American Academy of

Pediatrics, which also recommends that TV viewing for young children be limited to one to two hours of high-quality programming and that TVs should be removed from children's bedrooms (Rosenberg et al., 2010).

We tend to blame TV for many problems kids have, from limited attention spans to overly aggressive behavior. It may surprise you to learn, then, that researchers believe that watching TV—at least some types of programs, such as *Sesame Street* and *Dinosaur Train!* —may actually have some benefits in fostering cognitive skills in preschoolers and even stimulating interest in science and technology at an early age in (Baydar et al., 2008; Rubenzahl, 2011). That said, most children's programs do not offer such intellectually enriching experiences.

Is watching TV, especially heavy viewing, harmful to a child's psychological and physical development? Many people certainly think so. Let's turn to the evidence to evaluate some widely touted claims about the negative effects of TV viewing.

Watching TV takes time away from important intellectual and leisure activities. Henry Shapiro of the American Academy of Pediatrics states the issue quite plainly: "Watching TV is far inferior to playing with toys, being read to or playing with adults or talking with parents" ("Kids' TV," 2003). Few authorities would argue Shapiro's point, but we should caution that there is little reason to assume that time not spent watching TV would be spent in imaginative play and other meaningful activities. For many children, TV viewing is a kind of default activity that fills time when there are few structured opportunities for other activities. The lesson for parents is to structure the child's time in more meaningful ways—through reading, physical activities, imaginative play, and adventure trips—and not to use the TV as a default activity or electronic babysitter.

© Franco Vogt/CORBIS

What's Billy learning? Evidence shows that exposure to violent programming on television and in other media contributes to aggressive behavior in children.

TV viewing is linked to poorer cognitive abilities in children. Watching more TV in early childhood is linked to poorer academic performance and greater attentional problems among children in the lower grades and even among adolescents (Christakis, 2009; Levine & Waite, 2000; Landhuis et al., 2007; Pagani et al., 2010). Third graders who have TV sets in their bedrooms also performed more poorly on standardized tests of math, reading, and language skills than did children without their own TV (Borzekowski & Robinson, 2005). But children who had a computer in their rooms actually did better on these tasks than did other children. In other words, when it comes to predicting academic skills, the mouse wins over the remote.

TV viewing fosters violent or aggressive behavior. TV is permeated with violent content, and not just during prime-time viewing hours. TV characters in hero roles commit much of the violence, particularly in cartoons pitched at young boys. The hero typically prevails against the "bad guys" through violence but always comes out unscathed. The resulting message is that violence on the side of right is not only acceptable but also heroic and carries minimal risk to the self.

A large and growing body of evidence ties exposure to violent media to increased aggressive behavior in both children and adolescents (Feshbach & Tangney, 2008; Huesmann, 2010; Rosenkoetter, Rosenkoetter, & Acock, 2009). Although not every child exposed to violent programming behaves aggressively, many psychologists argue that we should seek to protect children from exposure to media violence by limiting as much as possible their access to this type of programming. We also have learned that playing violent video games is associated with increased aggressive behavior in children, especially in more aggressive youth (Anderson et al., 2010; Fischer, Kastenmüller, & Greitemeyer, 2009; Ferguson, 2010; Huesmann, 2010; Markey & Markey, 2010).

Exposure to violent media may foster aggressive behavior in a number of ways, including the following:

1. It *models* aggressive ways of resolving conflicts that children learn to imitate.
2. It *kindles* or primes aggressive thoughts.
3. It *lessens inhibitions* against violence by showing that characters who use violence not only get away with it but are often rewarded for it.

When children are regularly exposed to TV violence, they come to believe violence is an effective way to resolve conflicts. Repeated exposure to televised violence may also desensitize young people to real-world violence, in effect numbing them to the plight of victims (Strenziok et al., 2010). That said, exposure to violence on television is not nearly as strong a predictor of aggressive behavior as violence observed in the home, in the schools, or in the community (Gunter & McAleer, 1990).

Heavy TV viewing fosters childhood obesity. TV viewing may also affect children's physical development. A strong link exists between heavy TV viewing and poorer dietary habits in children, including greater consumption of snack foods and less consumption of fruits and vegetables (Coon et al., 2001; Etheridge, 2001). Not surprisingly, children who watch more TV and those who have a TV in their rooms stand a greater risk of becoming obese (Dennison, Erb, & Jenkins, 2002). Time spent in front of the TV limits opportunities to burn off excess calories through physical activity. Moreover, children who are glued to the TV are likely to add unneeded calories by munching on the high-calorie snacks and treats so heavily advertised during children's programs.

Responsible Television Viewing: What Parents Can Do

Short of pulling the plug, parents can use a number of strategies to encourage more responsible television viewing in their children (Huston & Wright, 1996; Rosenkoetter, Rosenkoetter, & Acock, 2009):

1. *Screen violent or sexually provocative programming.* Television programs are rated by the TV industry for violence and sexual content. Parents can use the ratings to weed out shows they believe are inappropriate for their children. TV sets also come equipped with a V-chip to block out shows containing unwanted programming. Parents can explain differences between violence in the media and real-world violence. They can point out that actors on TV shows are able to wipe away fake blood and go home to their families unharmed, unlike the victims of actual violence.
2. *Watch TV with your kids.* Sharing the viewing experience with your children, or *coviewing,* can help them better understand what they are watching. Parents of young children can use shows such as *Sesame Street* as a kind of moving picture book by labeling and pointing out the characters on the screen. For older children, coviewing allows parents to help diffuse fears or anxiety children may have when watching disturbing material. Parents can also help children not to identify with superheroes on TV by distinguishing between fantasy and reality.
3. *Don't use television as a babysitter.* Planting a child in front of a TV screen is no substitute for actively engaging the child in stimulating activities.
4. *Set limits.* Parents should establish clear limits for TV viewing, such as an hour or two a day, and stick to the rules themselves to model appropriate behavior. Parents

may also limit the kinds of shows children watch and steer them away from violent programming and toward more educational programs.

5. *Encourage children to regulate their own television viewing.* Children can be taught to regulate their own viewing behavior. They can learn to identify and select only those shows that are appropriate for them. Younger children can be taught what to do when scary scenes are shown, such as covering their eyes and ears, quickly changing the channel, or turning the set off. Older children (age eight or older) can be helped to distinguish between fiction and reality so they understand that not everything they see on TV is real.
6. *Monitor the news.* Some of the most disturbing content on TV today is found on the evening news, especially local news shows that seem to follow the motto "If it bleeds, it leads." Parents of younger children can control their children's exposure to news programs and reality-based "cop shows." With older children, parents can explain that television news gives an unbalanced view of society by emphasizing the most sensationalistic crimes.
7. *Limit snacking while watching TV.* Restrict—or, better, avoid—snacking or having family meals in front of the TV.
8. *Encourage children to develop other interests.* Get children to participate in other activities besides watching TV, such as reading, sports, play-dates with friends (minus TV), and outdoor play.

There is little doubt that TV and other media can influence children and that the effects are neither all good nor all bad. By becoming more involved in their children's television viewing, parents can help shape how their children use and react to TV.

Thinking Critically About Psychology

Based on your reading of the chapter, answer the following question. Then, to evaluate your progress in developing critical thinking skills, compare your answer with the sample answer found in Appendix A.

SLICE OF LIFE One evening after the sun sets, Nick asks his three-year-old son Trevor, "Where did the sun go?" Trevor responds, "It went to sleep." Nick then asks, "Why did it go to sleep?" Trevor answers, "Because it was sleepy."

1. Based on your understanding of Piaget's theory of cognitive development, explain why Trevor believes that the sun went to sleep because it was sleepy.

Log in to CengageBrain to access the resources your instructor requires. For this book, you can access:

CourseMate

Psychology CourseMate brings course concepts to life with interactive learning, study, and exam preparation tools that support the printed textbook. A textbook-specific website, Psychology CourseMate includes an integrated interactive eBook and other interactive learning tools including quizzes, flashcards, videos, and more.

CENGAGENOW

CengageNow is an easy-to-use online resource that helps you study in less time to get the grade you want—NOW. Take a pre-test for this chapter and receive a personalized study plan based on your results that will identify the topics you need to review and direct you to online resources to help you master those topics. Then take a post-test to help you determine the concepts you have mastered and what you will need to work on. If your textbook does not include an access code card, go to CengageBrain.com to gain access.

Visit www.cengagebrain.com to access your account and purchase materials.

VISUAL OVERVIEW Chapter 9 Child Development

MODULE 9.1 Key Questions and Methods of Study

Key Questions

- **Nature vs. Nurture**: Genes or environment?
- **Continuity vs. Discontinuity**: Small steps or giant leaps?
- **Universality**: Here, there, and everywhere?
- **Stability**: Once and always?

Methods of Study

- **Longitudinal Approach**: Tracking changes in the same people over time
- **Cross-Sectional Approach**: Comparing people of different ages at the same point in time

MODULE 9.2 Prenatal Development

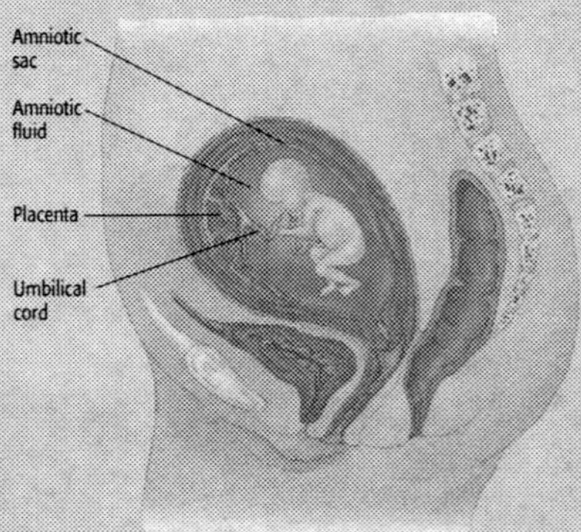

The Stages of Prenatal Development

- **Germinal Stage**: First two weeks after conception
- **Embryonic Stage**: From about two weeks to about eight weeks after conception
- **Fetal Stage**: From about eight weeks until birth

Threats to Prenatal Development

- **Teratogens**: Environmental agents that endanger fetal health
- **Maternal Malnutrition**: Risk of premature birth and low birth weight

MODULE 9.3 Infant Development

© Mark Richards/Photo Edit

- **Reflexes**: Rooting, eye blink, sucking, Moro, palmar grasp, and Babinski reflexes; some have survival value
- **Sensory and Perceptual Abilities**: Not a buzzing confusion, infants are capable of discerning a wide range of sensory stimuli
- **Learning Ability**: Can learn and remember simple responses
- **Development of Motor Skills**: Occurs in same sequence and about same ages in all cultures

MODULE 9.4 Emotional and Social Development

- **Individual Differences in Temperaments**: Three major types (easy children, difficult children, slow-to-warm-up children)
- **Attachment Styles**: Four identified types (secure type or Type B; insecure-avoidant type or Type A; insecure-resistant type or Type C; disorganized/disoriented type or Type D)
- **Child-Rearing Influences**: Genetics, peer-group influences, parenting behaviors, parenting styles (authoritative, authoritarian, permissive types)
- **Erikson's Stages of Psychosocial Development**: Stages of trust versus mistrust, autonomy versus shame and doubt, initiative versus guilt, and industry versus inferiority

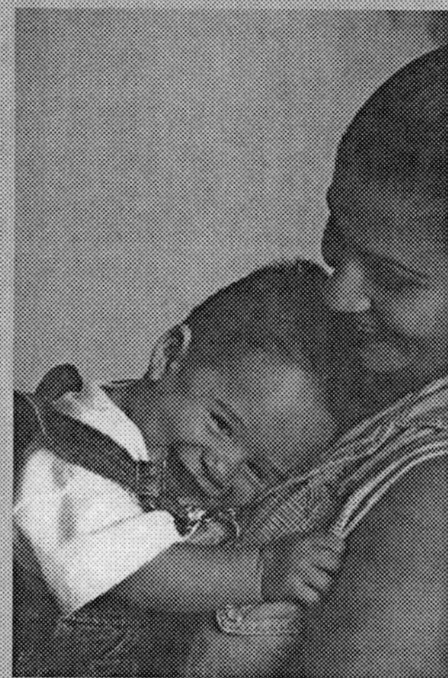

© Jonathan Nourok/Photo Edit

MODULE 9.5 Cognitive Development

Piaget's Stages of Cognitive Development:

- **Sensorimotor Stage** (ages birth to two): Engaging world through sensory and motor processes
- **Preoperational Stage** (ages two-seven): Forming symbolic representations in words
- **Concrete Operational Stage** (ages seven to eleven): Able to perform logical operations involving concrete objects
- **Formal Operational Stage** (puberty to adulthood): Able to engage in abstract reasoning

© Tony Freeman/Photo Edit

Vygotsky's Sociocultural Theory:

- **Zone of Proximal Development (ZPD) and Scaffolding**: emphasizes the role of cultural learning and social interactions

10 Adolescence and Adult Development

Why the Two Cents?

SLICE OF LIFE There's a story told about a retired electrical engineer who lived in the outskirts of a small town in Connecticut (adapted from Kanin, 1981). One day the town lost its electrical power, lights and all. None of the town officials or engineers could figure out how to get the power back. After a few days of rising frustrations, the town officials decided to pay a visit to the retired engineer, as he had been the one responsible for installing the town's electrical system. The old engineer was more than willing to help. Grabbing his toolbox, he made his way to a particular junction box off one of the main roads in town. After a few minutes of studying the situation, he tapped the box with his mallet in the way he had done many times before, and threw the switch. The power instantly returned to the town. The town officials were delighted, but were surprised a few days later when they opened the bill he had sent them for his services. The bill was for $1,000.02. Why the two cents, they wondered? The old engineer explained that the two cents was for tapping his mallet. The thousand dollars was for knowing where and how to tap. Wisdom does not come cheap.

As we will see in this chapter, development does not end with childhood. Physical, cognitive, and emotional and social changes are hallmarks of development throughout the life span. In this chapter we proceed through the major periods of development during adolescence and adulthood, focusing on the changes that occur in each stage of life. We begin with adolescence, which is a time of momentous developmental changes, both physical and psychological. But as we touch upon the changes we can expect as we age, it's good to keep in mind the story of the retired engineer. As we age, we may not be able to solve problems as quickly or run as fast as we could in our youth, but our ability to draw upon our accumulated knowledge or wisdom may be virtually timeless.

DID YOU KNOW THAT...

- Though we all go through puberty, the timing of puberty affects the psychological adjustment of boys and girls differently? (p. 373)
- Many adolescents see themselves as being continually on stage? (p. 374)
- People in the United States are getting married later than ever before? (p. 389)
- Since like generally marries like, stories like Cinderella remain by and large fairly tales? (p. 389)
- Dementia is not a normal consequence of aging? (p. 396)
- Older people usually lead better lives when they do more rather than less? (p. 399)
- The next best thing to a Fountain of Youth may be your neighborhood gym? (p. 403)

Learning Objectives

By reading this chapter you will be able to . . .

1 **DESCRIBE** the physical and psychological changes that occur during puberty and **EVALUATE** the effects of pubertal timing on boys and girls.

2 **DESCRIBE** changes in cognitive and psychosocial development during adolescence.

3 **IDENTIFY** and **DESCRIBE** Kohlberg's stages of moral reasoning and **EVALUATE** his theoretical model.

4 **DESCRIBE** changes in physical, cognitive, psychosocial, and emotional development from early to late adulthood.

5 **IDENTIFY** and **DESCRIBE** Erikson's stages of psychosexual development through adolescence and adulthood and **APPLY** this knowledge to our understanding of the major psychosocial challenges we face through the lifespan.

6 **DESCRIBE** the major variations in adult lifestyles today.

7 **EXPLAIN** differences between fluid intelligence and crystallized intelligence.

8 **IDENTIFY** qualities associated with successful aging.

9 **IDENTIFY** and **DESCRIBE** the stages of dying in Kübler-Ross's model.

10 **APPLY** research findings to living longer and healthier lives.

© Curtis Bridge / Alamy

Preview

MODULE 10.1

Adolescence

- What is puberty?
- What changes in cognitive development occur during adolescence?
- What are Kohlberg's levels of moral reasoning?
- Why did Gilligan criticize Kohlberg's theory?
- What did Erikson believe is the major developmental challenge of adolescence?

adolescence The period of life beginning at puberty and ending with early adulthood.

Adolescence is the link in the life chain between childhood and adulthood (Richter, 2006). The young person's body may seem to be sprouting in all directions at once. Adolescents may wonder what they will look like next year or even next month—who and what they will be. Intellectually, adolescents may suddenly feel like grownups. Expectations for adolescents are high: school subjects are more demanding and adults want them to seriously think about what lies ahead after high school. Yet their parents and teachers may continue to treat them as children—children masquerading in adult bodies who often must be restrained for their own good. Adolescents may find themselves in constant conflict with their parents over issues such as dating, using the family car, spending money, and ________________ (you fill in the blank). At a time when young people are stretching their wings and preparing to fly on their own, they remain financially, and often emotionally, dependent on their parents. No wonder the early psychologist and founder of the American Psychological Association, G. Stanley Hall, characterized adolescence as a time of *sturm und drang,* or "storm and stress." Contemporary research bears out the belief that many, though certainly not all, young people experience adolescence as a turbulent, pressure-ridden period. Let us now consider the physical, cognitive, social, and emotional changes that occur during the years when many young people feel they are betwixt and between—no longer children but not quite adults.

CONCEPT 10.1
The major event in physical development in adolescence is puberty, the period of physical growth and sexual maturation during which we attain full sexual maturity.

Physical Development

The growth spurt of adolescence lasts two to three years, during which time adolescents may shoot up eight inches to one foot. Compare this growth spurt with the two to three inches and four to six pounds typical children gain after infancy. Girls typically experience their growth spurt earlier than boys, so they may be taller than their male age mates for a while. But boys, on the average, eventually surpass girls in height and body weight. Boys also develop greater upper-body musculature.

puberty The stage of development at which individuals become physiologically capable of reproducing.

secondary sex characteristics Physical characteristics that differentiate males and females but are not directly involved in reproduction.

primary sex characteristics Physical characteristics, such as the gonads, that differentiate males and females and play a direct role in reproduction.

The major landmark of physical development during adolescence is **puberty**, the period of life during which young people reach full sexual maturity (see ■ Figure 10.1). Puberty is not a single event, but a process that unfolds over time (Jay, 2006). It begins with the appearance of **secondary sex characteristics**, physical characteristics that differentiate men and women but are not directly involved in reproduction, such as pubic hair, breast development, and deepening of the voice. **Primary sex characteristics**

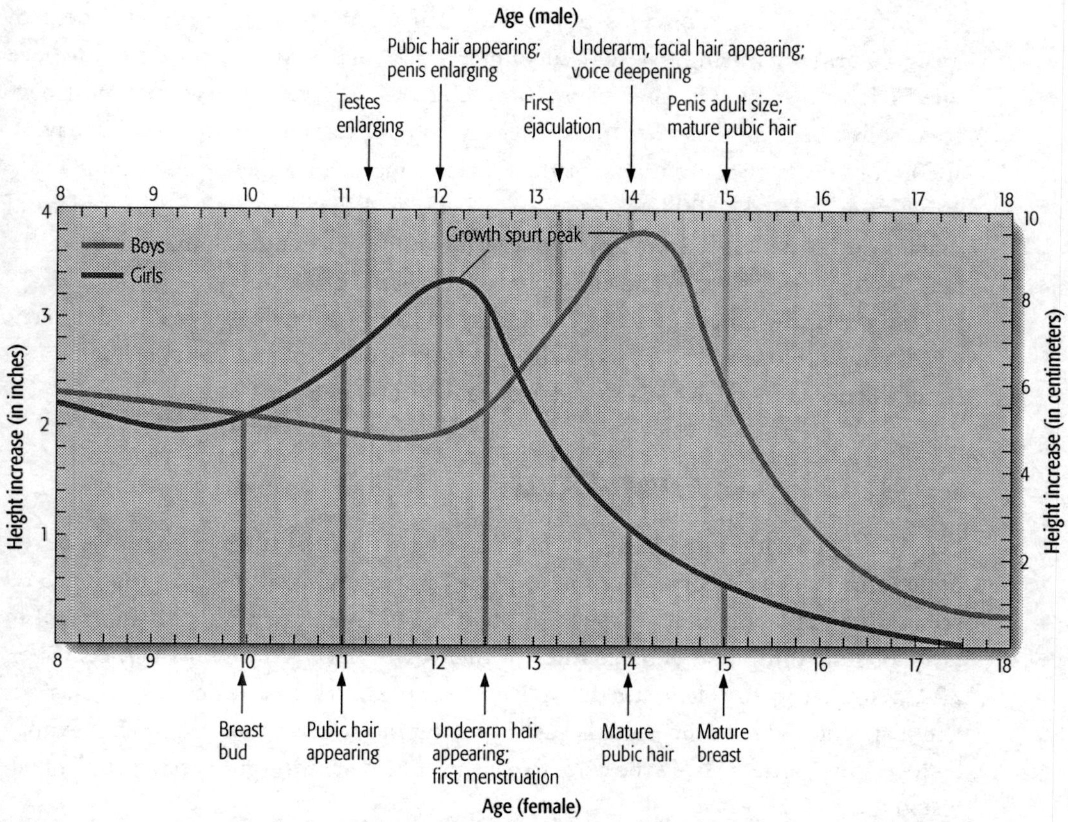

FIGURE 10.1 Physical Changes Occurring During Puberty
This graph illustrates a number of changes occurring during puberty in boys and girls. Note how the growth spurt begins sooner in girls than in boys. Note too that the graph represents the average ages at which these changes occur and that growth patterns in individuals often vary from these averages.
Source: Adapted from Seifert, Hoffnung, & Hoffnung, 2000.

also emerge; these are changes in sex organs directly involved in reproduction, such as enlargement of the testes and penis in boys and of the uterus in girls. Puberty lasts three to four years, by the end of which time adolescents become physically capable of reproduction.

Girls typically experience **menarche**, the beginning of menstruation, between ages 10 and 18, or at an average age between 12 and 13 (Irwin, 2005; Sun et al., 2002). Girls today enter puberty and experience menarche at much earlier ages than did girls in previous generations. The average European American girl today shows breast development and other signs of puberty by age 10, as compared to age 15 at the beginning of the twentieth century (Kantrowitz & Wingert, 1999). The average African American girl today begins showing signs of puberty and experiences menarche at a somewhat earlier age (S. E. Anderson, Dallal, & Must, 2003).

menarche The first menstruation.

The timing of puberty may have different consequences for boys and girls. For earlier-maturing boys, their greater size and strength give them an advantage in athletics and contribute to a more positive self-image. Later-maturing boys tend to be less popular than earlier-maturing boys and may be subject to ridicule or become socially ostracized (Berger, 2009b). Although early-maturing boys are more likely to engage in deviant social behavior such as drinking, smoking, or breaking the law, overall they generally have more positive outcomes than later-maturing boys.

For girls, the most obvious physical sign of maturation is the development of breasts. Earlier-maturing girls may encounter unwelcome sexual attention and believe they no longer "fit in" with their peers. They tend to have lower self-esteem, a more negative body image, more symptoms of anxiety and depression, earlier sexual behavior, and more substance abuse problems than do later-maturing girls (e.g., Copeland et al., 2010; Ge & Natsuaki, 2009; Reardon, Leen-Feldner, & Hayward, 2009). Bear in mind that how other people react to a girl's physical maturation, not the changes themselves, may best explain the social and emotional effects of pubertal timing.

The physical changes of adolescence may be the most obvious signs of adolescent development. However, major changes in cognitive abilities and social behavior also occur during adolescence. We consider these developments next.

Cognitive Development

CONCEPT 10.2
Adolescents who develop formal operational thinking become capable of solving abstract problems.

CONCEPT 10.3
Adolescents often show a form of egocentric thinking in which they believe their concerns and needs should be as important to others as they are to themselves.

People who develop formal operational thinking—the final stage of cognitive development in Piaget's theory—become capable of creating hypothetical situations and scenarios and playing them through in their minds. They can mount an argument in favor of something that runs counter to their own views (Flavell, Miller, & Miller, 2003). They are also able to use deductive reasoning in which one derives conclusions about specific cases or individuals based on a set of premises. For example, they may deduce "who-done-it" from the clues to a crime long before the guilty party in the television drama is revealed.

Not all adolescents, nor even all adults, reach the stage of formal operational thinking. Their thinking remains tied to concrete examples and relationships among objects rather than between ideas and abstract concepts. Whether or not formal operational thinking develops, many adolescents show certain forms of egocentric thinking. As Piaget noted, preschoolers show egocentrism with respect to their difficulty seeing things from other people's points of view. Psychologist David Elkind (1985) believes that adolescent egocentrism typically reveals itself in two ways: through the imaginary audience and the personal fable.

imaginary audience The common belief among adolescents that they are the center of other people's attention.

personal fable The common belief among adolescents that their feelings and experiences cannot possibly be understood by others and that they are personally invulnerable to harm.

The **imaginary audience** describes the adolescent's belief that other people are as keenly interested in his or her concerns and needs as the adolescent is. Adolescents may feel as though they are always on stage, as though all eyes are continually scrutinizing how they look, what they wear, and how they act. They view themselves as the center of attention and feel extremely self-conscious and overly concerned about the slightest flaw in their appearance ("How could they not notice this blemish? Everybody will notice!").

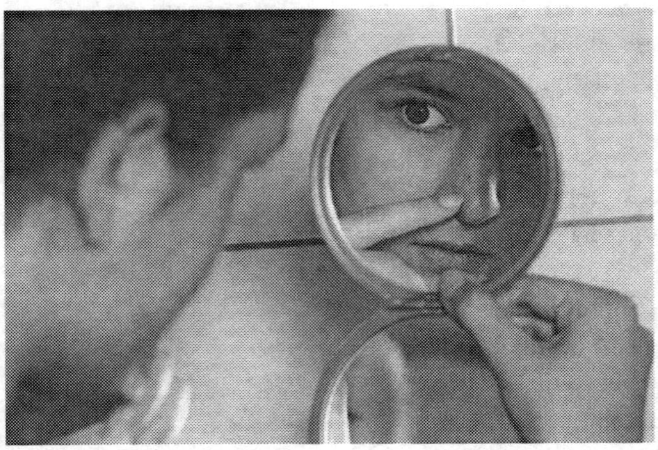
© Ronald Sumners/Shutterstock.com

"How could they not notice?" Adolescents may constantly scrutinize their appearance and become overly concerned about the slightest flaw.

The **personal fable** is an exaggerated sense of one's uniqueness and invulnerability. Adolescents may believe their life experiences or personal feelings are so unique that no one could possibly understand them, let alone have experienced them. When parents try to relate to what their adolescent is experiencing, they may be summarily rebuffed: "You can't possibly understand what I'm going through!"

Another aspect of the personal fable is the belief that "bad things can't happen to me." This sense of personal invulnerability may contribute to risk-taking behavior by adolescents, such as reckless driving, unsafe sex, and getting drunk (Curry & Youngblade, 2006).

Even if adolescents realize they are vulnerable to undesirable consequences of their behavior, they may decide that taking certain calculated risks is "worth it" (Reyna & Farley, 2006). Other factors associated with adolescent risk-taking include poor school performance, family problems, having close friends who take risks, impulsivity, and risk-taking opportunities (Boyer & Byrnes, 2008; Cooper et al., 2003).

We should also note that parts of the adolescent brain are still maturing, including the prefrontal cortex, the part of the brain responsible for judgment, reasoning, and putting the brakes on risky or impulsive behavior (Bell & McBride, 2010; Steinberg, 2007). Adolescents may be able to think logically and rationally, but, as psychiatrist David Fassler says, they "...are more likely to act impulsively, on instinct, without fully understanding or analyzing the consequences of their actions" ("Teens' Brains," 2007).

The developing cognitive abilities of adolescents change the way they see the world, including themselves, family and friends, and broad social and moral issues. These changes influence the ways people form judgments about questions of right and wrong, as we will see next.

Kohlberg's Stages of Moral Reasoning

Psychologist Lawrence Kohlberg (1927–1987) studied how individuals make moral judgments about conflict-laden issues. He was interested in the process by which people arrive at moral choices—what makes something right or wrong—rather than in the particular choices they make. He developed a methodology in which he presented subjects with hypothetical situations involving conflicting moral values, or moral dilemmas. Let's look at his most famous example (adapted from Kohlberg, 1969):

> *In Europe, a woman lies near death from a certain type of cancer. Only one drug that might save her is available, from a druggist in the same town who is charging 10 times what it costs him to make it. Lacking this sum, the woman's husband, Heinz, attempts to borrow money from everyone he knows but can raise only about half the amount. Heinz tells the druggist his wife is dying and pleads with him to sell it for less so he can buy it now, or allow him to pay for it later. The druggist refuses. Desperate, Heinz breaks into the druggist's store and steals the drug to give to his wife.*

Now Kohlberg poses the questions: "Should Heinz have stolen the drug? Why or why not?" Here we have the making of a moral dilemma, a situation that pits two opposing moral values against each other—in this case, the moral injunction against stealing versus the human value of attempting to save the life of a loved one. Kohlberg believed that one's level of moral development is reflected in the way one reasons about the moral dilemma, not in whether one believes the behavior in question was right or wrong.

Based on his studies of responses to these types of hypothetical situations, Kohlberg determined that moral development progresses through a sequence of six stages organized into three levels of moral reasoning: the preconventional level, the conventional level, and the postconventional level.

Preconventional Level Children at the *preconventional level* base their moral judgments on the perceived consequences of behavior. Kohlberg divided preconventional moral reasoning into two stages. Stage 1 is characterized by an *obedience and punishment orientation:* Good behavior is defined simply as behavior that avoids punishment by an external authority. In our example, we might reason that Heinz should take the drug because if he does not, he may be blamed for his wife's death; or he shouldn't take the drug because he could get caught and sent to jail. Stage 2 represents an *instrumental purpose orientation:* A behavior is judged good when it serves the person's needs or interests. Thus, we might reason that Heinz should have taken the drug because, by saving his wife, he would ensure that she'd be available to meet his needs for companionship, love, and support; or Heinz shouldn't have taken the drug because if he were caught and sent to jail, he would have done neither himself nor his wife any good.

CONCEPT 10.4
Psychologist Lawrence Kohlberg explored how individuals make moral judgments; his theory of moral development consists of a sequence of six stages organized in terms of three levels of moral reasoning.

Conventional Level At the *conventional level,* moral reasoning is based on conformity with conventional rules of right and wrong. Individuals at this level recognize that the purpose of social rules is to preserve the social order and ensure harmonious relationships among people.

Stage 3 is characterized by a *"good boy-good girl" orientation:* Individuals believe that conformity with rules and regulations is important because of the need to be perceived by others as a "good boy" or a "good girl." They value the need to do the "right thing" in the eyes of others. Thus, Heinz should steal the drug because others would be displeased with him for failing to help save his wife's life; or Heinz should not steal the drug because if he is caught, he will bring dishonor on himself and his family.

Stage 4 has an *authority or law-and-order orientation.* Moral reasoning now goes beyond the need to gain approval from others: Rules must be obeyed and applied evenhandedly because they are needed for the orderly functioning of society. Each of us has a duty to uphold the law, simply because it is the law. Heinz should steal the drug because it is a husband's duty to protect his wife's life, but he must repay the druggist as soon as he is able and accept responsibility and punishment for breaking the law. Or Heinz should not steal the drug because although we may sympathize with his wish to save his wife's life, people cannot be permitted to break the law even when they face such dire circumstances.

Postconventional Level Individuals generally reach the *postconventional level* of moral reasoning during adolescence, if they reach it at all. Postconventional reasoning involves applying one's own moral standards or abstract principles rather than relying on authority figures or blindly adhering to social rules or conventions (Haidt, 2008). The postconventional thinker believes that when laws are unjust, a moral person is bound to disobey them. In Kohlberg's (1969) studies, only about one in four people had reached the postconventional level by age 16. Even in adulthood, most people remain at the level of conventional moral reasoning.

Kohlberg identified two stages of postconventional moral reasoning. Stage 5, the *social contract orientation,* involves the belief that laws are based on mutual agreement among members of a society, but they are not infallible. They should be open to question rather than followed blindly out of respect for authority. Stage 5 reasoners weigh the rights of the individual against the rights of society. They might argue that although laws should be obeyed, protection of a life is a more important value than protection of property, and so an exception should be made in Heinz's case. Or they might reason that individuals must obey the law because the common good takes precedence over the individual good and that the ends, no matter how noble they may be, do not justify the means.

Stage 6 thinking involves adoption of *universal ethical principles,* an underlying set of self-chosen, abstract ethical principles that serve as a guiding framework for moral judgments. Beliefs in the sanctity of human life or in the "Golden Rule" exemplify such

CONCEPT CHART 10.1 Kohlberg's Levels and Stages of Moral Development

Level	Stage of Moral Reasoning	Heinz Should Steal the Drug Because:	Heinz Should Not Steal the Drug Because:
LEVEL I Preconventional Level	Stage 1: Obedience and punishment orientation; behavior is good if it avoids punishment	He would be blamed if his wife dies.	He would be punished for stealing if he were caught.
	Stage 2: Instrumental purpose orientation; behavior is judged good when it serves personal needs or interests	He needs his wife and she might die without it.	He would likely be sent to prison, and his wife would probably die before he gets out.
LEVEL II Conventional Level	Stage 3: "Good boy-good girl" orientation; conform with rules to impress others	He would lose people's respect if he didn't try to save his wife by stealing the drug.	Others will see him as a criminal, and that would bring shame and dishonor to his family.
	Stage 4: Authority or law-and-order orientation; obey rules and laws because they are needed to maintain social order	He has a duty to protect his wife even if punished for it.	People should not be permitted to break the law under any circumstances. The law must be respected.
LEVEL III Postconventional Level	Stage 5: Social contract orientation; view rules and laws as based on mutual agreement in the service of the common good	Obey laws to maintain order in society, but a law should not take precedence over protecting a human life.	He reasons that respect for the law outweighs individual needs no matter what the circumstances.
	Stage 6: Universal ethical principle orientation; adopt an internal moral code based on universal values that takes precedence over social rules and laws	Not stealing the drug would violate his belief in the absolute value of a human life.	Sometimes doing what we believe is right requires personal sacrifice. If he truly believes that stealing is worse than letting his wife die, he must not steal the drug.

Source: Adapted from Kohlberg, 1981.

universal ethical principles. People at this stage are guided by their own internal moral compass, regardless of the dictates of society's laws or the opinions of others. They may believe that if laws devalue the sanctity of human life, it becomes *immoral* to obey them. Hence it would be immoral for Heinz to obey laws that would ultimately devalue the sanctity of his wife's life. Kohlberg believed that very few people, even those within the postconventional level, reach Stage 6.

Concept Chart 10.1 summarizes the six stages of moral reasoning in Kohlberg's model.

Kohlberg's model of moral development continues to foster an understanding of how we develop our sense of right and wrong. But does moral reasoning dictate how we act in particular situations involving moral or ethical issues? Do people actually practice what they preach? The answer is complicated. On the one hand, there appears to be some overlap between our moral beliefs on the one hand and how we act in particular situations involving ethical or moral issues on the other. But on the other hand, we need to account for environmental demands in particular situations to better understand whether we act in ways that are consistent with our moral beliefs. (Hill & Roberts, 2010).

Evaluation of Kohlberg's Model

Kohlberg's central belief that children and adolescents progress through stages of moral development has been supported in later research (e.g., Boom, Wouters, & Keller, 2007). However, critics question whether Kohlberg's developmental perspective captures the ways in which people actually make morally laden decisions in their everyday lives (Krebs & Denton, 2005). Whether a stage-based developmental model like Kohlberg's should be replaced or refined remains an ongoing debate in the field. Critics also question whether Kohlberg's concept of postconventional thinking is more a reflection of his own personal ideals than a universal stage of moral development (Helwig, 2006). All in all, Kohlberg's classic studies set the stage for further research on moral reasoning that has continued to the present day (Hill & Roberts, 2010).

CONCEPT 10.5
Though evidence generally supports Kohlberg's stage model of moral reasoning, critics contend that his model may contain cultural and gender biases.

Another debate is whether Kohlberg's model is biased on cultural or gender grounds. Kohlberg's model emphasizes ideals found primarily in Western cultures, such as individual rights and social justice. A study of people in the United States and India showed cultural differences in the priorities people placed on justice and interpersonal factors (J. G. Miller & Bersoff, 1992). Americans placed greater value on a justice orientation in determining morally correct choices—believing that what is just or fair governs what is right. Indians placed a greater weight on interpersonal responsibilities, such as upholding one's obligations to others and being responsive to other people's needs.

Harvard psychologist Carol Gilligan raised the issue of gender bias in Kohlberg's work. She pointed out that Kohlberg's studies were based entirely on research with men. The voices of girls and women, Gilligan argued, had not been heard.

Prior to her own work, researchers applying Kohlberg's model found that men often achieved higher levels of moral reasoning than did women. Gilligan rejected the view that women are less capable of developing moral reasoning. By listening to women's voices, she argued that they tend to apply a different moral standard than men, one defined by a *care orientation* rather than a *justice orientation,* as is adopted by men (Gilligan, 1982). Men would argue, based on abstract principles of justice and fairness, that Heinz should steal the drug because the value of life supersedes that of property. Young women, however, sought solutions that responded both to the druggist's need to protect his property and to Heinz's need to save his wife—solutions that expressed a caring attitude and the need to preserve the relationship between them. Gilligan argued that the moral standards of men and women represent two different ways of thinking about moral behavior, with neither one standing on higher moral ground than the other. However, because young women are less willing to apply abstract moral principles when facing ethical situations like that of Heinz, they may be classified at lower levels in Kohlberg's system.

THE BRAIN LOVES A PUZZLE

As you read ahead, use the information in the text to solve the following puzzle:

It's a puzzlement that anything called a "crisis" could be a good thing, but psychologists believe that not only is an identity crisis a good thing, but it is also a normal part of adolescent development. How is that possible?

Research evidence bears out the belief that women tend to place greater emphasis on a care orientation, whereas men tend to place somewhat greater emphasis on a justice orientation (e.g., Jaffee & Hyde, 2000; Jorgensen, 2006). However, moral reasoning does not follow gender lines as strictly as Gilligan originally proposed. Men and women apply both a justice orientation and a care orientation when forming moral judgments. Nonetheless, Gilligan's work remains influential, partly because it encourages investigators to listen to female voices and partly because it encourages young women to find and develop their own voices.

Psychosocial Development

In this section we examine the psychosocial development of adolescents as they negotiate the transition from childhood to young adulthood. Throughout we focus on their relationships with parents and peers and the challenges they face in establishing a clear psychological identity of their own. We also consider an aspect of psychosocial development that often takes center stage during adolescence: sexuality.

© Elena Zidkova/shutterstock.com

Who am I? Where am I headed in life? Theorist Erik Erikson emphasized the process of coming to terms with one's personal identity as the major psychosocial challenge facing adolescents.

Adolescent–Parent Relationships

Adolescent yearnings for independence often lead to some withdrawal from family members and to arguments with parents over issues of autonomy and decision making. Some distancing from parents may be healthy during adolescence, as young people form meaningful relationships outside the family and develop a sense of independence and social competence. As it turns out, despite the common belief to the contrary, most adolescents and their parents say they love and respect one another and agree on many of the principal issues in life (Arnett, 2004; Collins & Laursen, 2006). Though disagreements with parents are common, serious conflict is neither normal nor helpful for adolescents (Smetana, Campione-Barr, & Metzger, 2006). Parents also influence their adolescents in more subtle ways, and not always for the better. For example, adolescents tend to mimic their parents' health-related behaviors, which may include negative behaviors such as smoking (Kodl & Mermelstein, 2004).

By psychologically separating from their parents, adolescents may begin to grapple with the major psychosocial challenge they face: developing a clear sense of themselves and of their future direction in life. As we will see next, the theorist Erik Erikson believed that the process of coming to terms with the question "Who am I?" represents the major life challenge of adolescence.

CONCEPT 10.6
Issues relating to independence come to the fore in the adolescent's social and personality development, but these issues often bring adolescents into conflict with their parents.

Identity Versus Role Diffusion: Who Am I?

Earlier we saw that Erik Erikson believed children progress through a series of four stages of psychosocial development. Erikson's fifth stage of psychosocial development occurs during adolescence: the stage of *identity versus role diffusion.*

Issues of identity come to prominence during adolescent development, as young people grapple with questions of "Who am I?," "What am I good at?," and "Where am I headed?" (Kuhn, 2006). The development of ethnic identity, of a connectedness with one's ethnic and cultural heritage, is an important part of the process of identity formation during adolescence, especially for adolescents of color (French et al., 2006; Fuligni, Witkow, & Garcia, 2005).

© David Burden/ shutterstock.com

CONCEPT 10.7
To Erik Erikson, the major life challenge adolescents face is the development of a sense of ego identity, a coming to terms with the fundamental question, "Who am I?"

Ego identity is the attainment of a firm sense of self—who one is, where one is headed in life, and what one believes in. People who achieve ego identity clearly understand their personal needs, values, and life goals. Erikson coined the term **identity crisis** to describe the stressful period of soul-searching and serious self-examination that many adolescents experience when struggling to develop a set of personal values and direction in life. Although Erikson believed that an identity crisis is a normal part of the development of the healthy personality, some contemporary scholars use the term *exploration* rather than *crisis* to avoid implying that the process of examining one's different possibilities in life is inherently fraught with anguish and struggle (Arnett, 2004).

ego identity In Erikson's theory, the attainment of a psychological sense of knowing oneself and one's direction in life.

identity crisis In Erikson's theory, a stressful period of serious soul-searching and self-examination of issues relating to personal values and one's direction in life.

© Goodshoot/Jupiter Images

Though conflicts between adolescents and parents are common, most adolescents say they have good relationships with their parents.

Adolescents who successfully weather an identity crisis emerge as their own persons, as people who have achieved a state of ego identity. Ego identity, however, continues to develop throughout life. Our occupational goals and our political, moral, and religious beliefs often change over time. Therefore, we may weather many identity crises in life.

Many adolescents or adults never grapple with an identity crisis. They may develop a firm sense of ego identity by modeling themselves after others, especially parents, without undergoing an identity crisis. Or they may fail to develop a clear sense of ego identity, remaining at sea, as it were, aimlessly taking each day as it comes. These individuals remain in a state of **role diffusion**, a confused and drifting state in which they lack a clear set of values and direction in life. They may be especially vulnerable to negative peer influences such as drug use.

role diffusion In Erikson's model, a lack of direction or aimlessness with respect to one's role in life or public identity.

Peer Relationships

As adolescents experiment with greater independence, peer relationships become increasingly important influences in their psychosocial development. "Fitting in" or belonging comes to play an even greater role in determining their self-esteem and emotional adjustment.

Parents are often concerned that their teenagers may "run with the wrong crowd." They also tend to believe their teens are subject to more peer pressure to engage in undesirable behaviors such as stealing or alcohol or drug use than their teens believe they are (see Table 10.1). Evidence bears out at least some parental concerns, as peer pressure is a major factor in teenagers initiating sexual intercourse as well as their use of tobacco, alcohol, and marijuana (Curran, Stice, & Chassin, 1997; S. Thompson, 1995; Wills & Cleary, 1999). A strong parent–teen connection and close communication also has a protective effect against negative outcomes such as emotional and behavioral problems and use of alcohol and other drugs (Brody et al., 2010; Taylor, 2010; Wagner et al., 2010).

Adolescent Sexuality

CONCEPT 10.8
Peer pressure is an important influence in the social and emotional development of adolescents.

Adolescents may be more than just "hormones with feet," as one observer put it, but sexual thoughts and interests often do take center stage during this period. Average age of first intercourse decreased during the second half of the twentieth century, and teen attitudes toward premarital sex became more permissive (B. E. Wells & Twenge, 2005). Today, nearly 50% of teens in the 15- to 19-year-old age range report having engaged in sexual intercourse, and nearly 500,000 teens give birth each year in the United States (Centers for Disease Control and Prevention, 2009e).

CONCEPT 10.9
Sexual maturation occurring during puberty leads to reproductive capability, whether or not youngsters are psychologically prepared for it.

The teen birth rate has declined from its peak in the early 1990s through the early years of the new millennium. However, the rate has since leveled off, which underscores the need for more targeted efforts to further reduce the numbers of teen births (Brownstein, 2010; E. Hamilton, Martin, & Ventura, 2009). The teenage pregnancy rate in the United States remains higher than in any other developed nation (D. E. Judge, 2007). Moreover, several million teens contract sexually transmitted diseases or infections each year. We should also note that patterns of sexual activity are changing, as more teens today than before are experimenting with alternatives to vaginal intercourse, including oral and anal sex.

Although some teen mothers become pregnant to fill an emotional void or to rebel against their families, most teenage pregnancies result from failure to use contraceptives reliably. Many sexually active teenagers get caught up in their own personal fables that lead them to believe pregnancy is something that could not happen to them.

TABLE 10.1 Teens and Peer Pressure

"How much peer pressure from friends do you feel (does your teen feel) today to do the following?"

Those Responding "a lot"	Teens	Parents
Have sex	10%	20%
Grow up too fast	16	34
Steal or shoplift	4	18
Use drugs or abuse alcohol	10	10
Defy parents or teachers	9	16
Be mean to kids who are different	11	12

© iStockphoto.com/Chris Schmidt

Source: Newsweek poll, based on a national sample of teens 13 to 19 years of age and 509 parents of these teens. Results reported in *Newsweek*, May 8, 2000, p. 56.

Unwed teenage mothers face serious obstacles to their educational and social development. They are more likely than other girls to live below the poverty level, to quit school, and to depend on public assistance (Arnett, 2004). Although the father (usually a teenager himself) is equally responsible for the pregnancy, he is usually absent or incapable of contributing to the child's support.

Why do some teens become sexually active whereas others abstain? For one thing, peer pressure, whether real or imagined, can promote or restrain sexual activity. Moral reasons, on the other hand, are often a basis for restraint. Teens who abstain may also be concerned about getting caught, becoming pregnant, or contracting a sexually transmitted disease. Other factors linked to sexual restraint among teens include the following (Aspy et al., 2008; J. D. Brown et al., 2006; Hardy & Raffaelli, 2003; McBride, Paikoff, & Holmbeck, 2003):

- Living in an intact family
- Having a family with low levels of conflict
- Having at least one parent who graduated from college
- Placing importance on religion and attending religious services frequently
- Having less exposure to sexual content in music, movies, television, and magazines

Many gay adolescents face the challenge of coming to terms with their sexuality against the backdrop of social condemnation and discrimination against gays in the broader culture (I. H. Meyer, 2003). Their struggle for self-acceptance often requires stripping away layers of denial about their sexuality. Some gay men and lesbians fail to achieve a "coming out" to themselves—that is, a personal acceptance of their sexual orientation—until young or middle adulthood. The process of achieving self-acceptance can be so difficult that many gay adolescents have suicidal thoughts or attempt suicide. Though some families are more accepting of a gay family member, many gay adolescents are reluctant to disclose their sexual orientation to their family and friends.

Before we leave our discussion of adolescence, it's important to note that most adolescents are generally happy and optimistic about their futures (Arnett, 2004). Though adolescents may have wider and more frequent changes in moods than adults, most of their mood swings fall within a mild range.

"We've been thinking a lot about what we want to do with your life."

© The New Yorker Collection 2002 David Sipress from cartoonbank.com. All Rights Reserved.

10.1 MODULE REVIEW Adolescence

Recite It

What is puberty?

- Puberty spans the period of physical development that begins with the appearance of secondary sex characteristics and ends with the attainment of full sexual maturity.

What changes in cognitive development occur during adolescence?

- Adolescents may progress to the stage of formal operations, which, according to Piaget, is denoted by the ability to engage in abstract thinking and reasoning.
- Egocentricity in adolescence involves concepts of the imaginary audience (believing everyone else is as concerned about us as we are ourselves) and the personal fable (an exaggerated sense of uniqueness and perceptions of personal invulnerability).

What are Kohlberg's levels of moral reasoning?

- At the preconventional level, moral judgments are based on the perceived consequences of behavior. Behaviors that avoid punishment are good; those that incur punishment from an external authority are bad.
- At the conventional level, conformity with conventional rules of right and wrong are valued because of the need to do what others expect or because one has an obligation to obey the law.
- At the postconventional level, moral judgments are based on the value systems the individual develops through personal reflection, such as valuing the importance of human life and the concept of justice above that of the law. Postconventional thinking does not develop until adolescence, if ever.

Why did Gilligan criticize Kohlberg's theory?

- Gilligan pointed out that Kohlberg's model was based only on the responses of males and did not take female voices into account.
- Through her own research, Gilligan concluded that females tend to adopt a care orientation, whereas males tend to adopt a justice orientation. Other researchers have found that differences in moral reasoning between men and women are less clear-cut, although women have a greater tendency to adopt a care orientation.

What did Erikson believe is the major developmental challenge of adolescence?

- Erikson believed the achievement of a sense of who one is and what one stands for (ego identity) is the major developmental challenge of adolescence.
- Erikson coined the term *identity crisis* to describe a period of serious soul-searching in which adolescents attempt to come to terms with their underlying beliefs and future direction in life.

Recall It

1. The physical growth period during which young people mature sexually and reach their full reproductive capacity is known as ________.
   a. adolescence.
   b. menarche.
   c. formal operations.
   d. puberty.
2. The beginning of menstruation is called ________.
3. What are two ways in which egocentric thinking becomes expressed during adolescence?
4. Lawrence Kohlberg posed moral dilemmas to children and then classified their responses. Children whose responses indicated that they based their moral judgments on the perceived consequences of actions were classified at the ________ level of moral reasoning.
   a. preconventional.
   b. conventional.
   c. concrete operational.
   d. postconventional.
5. Cite two types of biases for which Kohlberg's theory has been criticized.
6. According to Erikson, what is the major psychosocial challenge facing adolescents?
   a. trust versus mistrust
   b. initiative versus guilt
   c. identity versus role diffusion
   d. intimacy versus inferiority

Think About It

- Was your adolescence a period of *sturm und drang* (storm and stress) or was it relatively peaceful? Why do you suppose some teenagers move through adolescence with relative ease, whereas others find it a difficult period? What made adolescence easy or difficult for you?

Early and Middle Adulthood

- What physical and cognitive changes take place as people age?
- How do theorists conceptualize social and personality development during early and middle adulthood?
- What are the major variations in adult lifestyles today?

MODULE 10.2

Development doesn't stop with the end of puberty. Physical and psychological development is a continuing process that lasts a lifetime. When does adolescence end and adulthood—in the psychological, not the legal sense—begin? As we'll see in this module, we can think of the transition from adolescence to adulthood as a process that occurs over a period of years from the late teens through the middle twenties. It is not any particular date, like your 18th birthday, that you can mark on a calendar.

When does middle adulthood or *middle age* begin? When does it end? The most common conception of middle age is that it begins at age 40 and ends at age 60 or 65 with the beginning of late adulthood or old age. But for many people, age is more a state of mind than a matter of years. What do you think? When does a person cross the line between young and middle adulthood? Many baby boomers, now in their sixties, act younger than their parents did at the same age, or at least believe they do. The middle years can be a time to reflect upon what we have done (or haven't done) and determine what remains to be done.

In this module, we continue our journey through human development by examining the changes in our physical and psychological development that occur as we progress from early adulthood through middle age.

© FABRICE COFFRINI/AFP/Getty Images

Who's old? Veteran rock stars like the Rolling Stones and Madonna have led to a blurring of generational lines.

Physical and Cognitive Development

In many respects, physical and cognitive development peak in early adulthood. During their twenties, most people are at their height in terms of memory functioning, ability to learn new skills, sensory acuteness, muscle strength, reaction time, and cardiovascular condition.

People tend to reach their peak on standardized intelligence tests during early adulthood. Some decline in mental functioning is expected as people age during middle and late adulthood. The greatest declines occur in **fluid intelligence**, or mental flexibility—the type of intelligence needed to think quickly in solving problems, to engage in abstract reasoning, to identify patterns and relationships, to solve puzzles, and to remember names just heard or information just read (Bopp & Verhaeghen, 2009; Jacoby & Rhode, 2006; Sweatt, 2010). Fluid intelligence relies on working memory, the type of memory that enables us to hold and manipulate information in our mind, such as when performing mental arithmetic or juggling two or more ideas or concepts in our heads at the same time (National Science Foundation, 2008) (see Chapter 6).

CONCEPT 10.10
Though many cognitive abilities reach a peak in early adulthood, declines in memory functioning that normally occur with age may not interfere with occupational or social functioning.

fluid intelligence A form of intelligence associated with the ability to think abstractly and flexibly in solving problems.

FIGURE 10.2 Age-Related Changes in Intellectual Ability
Crystallized intelligence, which includes abilities such as verbal ability (vocabulary, comprehension) and numerical skills, remains relatively stable or may even improve as we age. The sharpest declines occur with fluid intelligence, the kind of intelligence needed for abstract reasoning skills, such as inductive reasoning and spatial orientation.

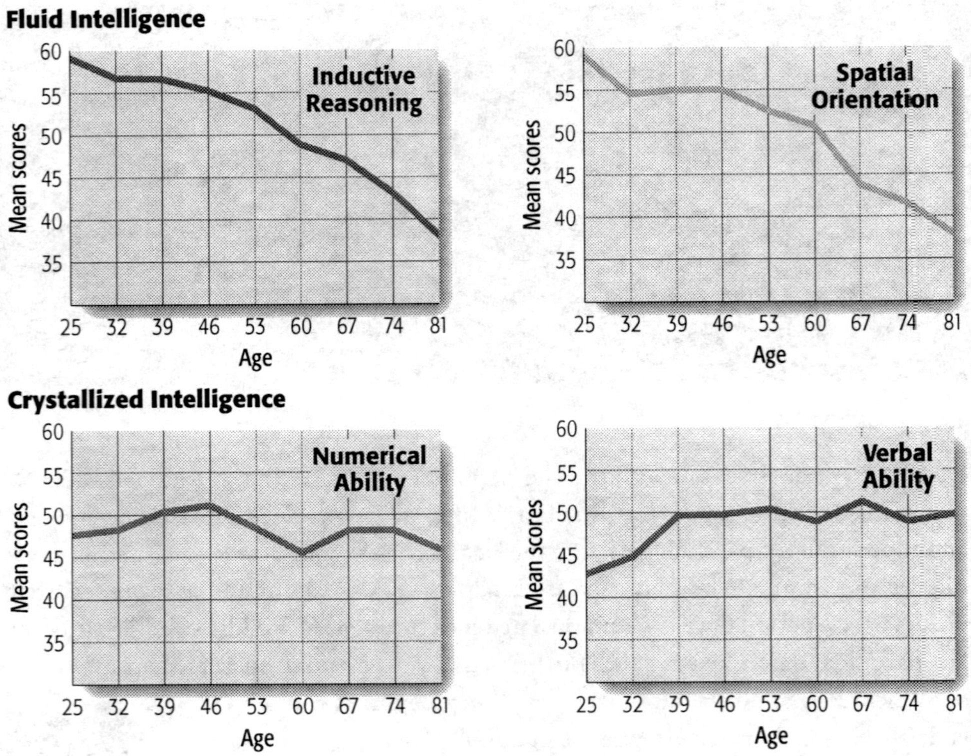

crystallized intelligence A form of intelligence associated with the ability to use accumulated knowledge.

Another form of intelligence, **crystallized intelligence**, involves the ability to use knowledge and skills accumulated through our lifetime, including vocabulary skills, technical know-how, and numerical ability. Crystallized intelligence remains relatively stable as we age and may even improve in certain ways, such as through a continuing expansion of vocabulary (Carstensen & Mikels, 2005; Verhaeghen, 2003) (see ■ Figure 10.2).

Apart from the occasional social embarrassment of fumbling over people's names, cognitive declines in midlife usually occur gradually and may not be noticeable or interfere with social or occupational functioning. These declines may also be offset by increased knowledge and experience.

CONCEPT 10.11
Menopause is a major life event for most women and may symbolize other issues they may face in middle adulthood, including changes in appearance, health, and sexuality.

Beginning in their late twenties, people start losing lean body tissue, especially muscle. With each passing decade, they tend to lose about seven pounds of lean body mass as more and more lean tissue turns to fat. From ages 20 to 70, people are likely to lose as much as 30 percent of their muscle cells. Even so, most physical changes in middle adulthood occur gradually, and the rates at which changes occur vary among individuals. Loss of muscle tissue leads to a gradual loss of muscle strength. A person can help offset this loss, however, by following a regular weight-bearing exercise program. Regular exercise, in combination with a proper diet, can also help prevent significant gains in weight. Major weight gains are neither a normal nor an inevitable consequence of aging.

menopause The time of life when menstruation ends.

CONCEPT 10.12
Men experience a gradual decline in production of the male sex hormone testosterone as they age, but unlike women they may maintain reproductive capability well into late adulthood.

The most dramatic physical change during middle age is the cessation of menstruation and reproductive capability in women. This biological event, called **menopause**, typically occurs in a woman's late forties or early fifties. With menopause, the ovaries no longer ripen egg cells or produce the sex hormones estrogen and progesterone.

A persistent stereotype about menopause is that it signals the end of the woman's sexual appetite or drive (see Table 10.2 for other myths about menopause). In fact,

TABLE 10.2 Myths Versus Facts About Menopause

Myth	Fact
A woman's body no longer produces estrogen after menopause.	Estrogen production decreases, but some estrogen is still produced by the adrenal glands and fatty tissue.
Women normally become depressed or anxious during menopause as a result of hormonal changes.	Most women do not experience serious depression or major mood change during, or around, the time of menopause (Bromberger et al., 2007; Wingert & Kantrowitz, 2007a, 2007b).
Menopause is a physical event, not a psychological event.	Physical changes occur in the woman's body during menopause, but the meaning she applies to these changes has a determining effect on her emotional response. If she views menopause as the beginning of the end of her life, she may develop a sense of hopelessness that can lead to depression. Investigators also have linked psychological factors such as marital dissatisfaction to greater menopausal symptoms (Kurpius, Nicpon, & Maresh, 2001).
Women can expect to experience severe hot flashes during menopause.	Many women experience mild flashes or none at all (Wingert & Kantrowitz, 2007a, 2007b).
Women lose all desire for sexual activity after menopause.	Not true. Sexual interest and responsiveness can be maintained throughout the woman's life span. Some women say sex actually becomes better around menopause, in part because children may be out of the house and they find they have more time to foster their intimate relationships (Wingert & Kantrowitz, 2007a, 2007b).

Source: Adapted from Nevid & Rathus, 2007a, and other sources.

a woman's sex drive is fueled by the small amounts of male sex hormones (androgens) produced by her adrenal glands, not by estrogen. Still, the meaning that menopause holds for the individual woman can have a strong bearing on her adjustment. Women who were raised to connect menopause with a loss of femininity may lose sexual interest or feel less sexually desirable. Others may actually feel liberated by the cutting of ties between sex and reproduction.

Unlike women, men can maintain fertility well into later adulthood. Men do experience a gradual decline in testosterone as they age, in contrast to the sharp decline in estrogen production that occurs in women during menopause. Although older adults may need to adjust to age-related changes in sexual response, such as allowing more time to become sexually aroused, most report continued sexual interest and satisfying sexual relationships (Hillman, 2008; Laumann et al., 2006).

Psychosocial Development

Sorting out adult roles and relationships are major challenges faced by young adults. Psychologist Jeffrey Arnett coined the term **emerging adulthood** to describe the gradual transition from adolescence to adulthood that occurs from the late teens through at least the mid-20s (Arnett, 2004, 2010). The concept of emerging adulthood recognizes that many young people today assume the typical roles of full-fledged adulthood in terms of marriage, holding a steady job, and parenthood later than their counterparts did in earlier generations. Yet for many young adults today, the twenties may be an extended adolescence, with age 30 becoming the threshold of full-fledged adulthood (Grigoriadis, 2003).

emerging adulthood The period of psychosocial development, roughly spanning the ages of 18 to 25, during which the person makes the transition from adolescence to adulthood.

We can distinguish emerging adulthood from other periods of life on the basis of five key characteristics (Arnett, 2004):

1. *The age of identity exploration.* Emerging adulthood is a period of examining our beliefs and determining where we are headed in life. It is also a time for exploration of romantic relationships and career alternatives in preparation for making lasting choices and commitments.
2. *The age of instability.* Exploring different possibilities in love and work entails a good deal of instability. The young person may switch majors or career objectives and move from one relationship to another or from one residence to another.
3. *The self-focused age.* Emerging adults become focused on themselves in terms of developing the skills, knowledge, and self-understanding that will help prepare them for meeting the responsibilities of adult life.
4. *The age of feeling in between.* We noted earlier how adolescents feel betwixt and between the worlds of children and adults. But emerging adults also have feelings of being in between, not quite adolescents but not quite fullly independent adults. As you can see in ■ Figure 10.3, it isn't until the late twenties or early thirties that most people say they feel they have reached full adulthood.
5. *The age of possibilities.* Emerging adulthood is a period of possibilities, not certainties, a time when one holds great hopes and expectations for a future life that hasn't yet been realized.

CONCEPT 10.13

Arnett's concept of emerging adulthood recognizes that in some cultures the transition from adolescence to adulthood involves a distinct period of development between the late teens and the early to mid-twenties.

Emerging adulthood is not found in all cultures. Arnett believes that it exists only in those cultures that allow a gradual transition from adolescence to adulthood (Arnett, 2004). In many cultures, young people are expected to assume the roles of full adulthood, such as marriage and parenthood, at earlier ages than is true of contemporary Western society. Cultural factors also come into play in our own society in determining when young adults set out on their own. For example, the sense of duty to family is especially strong among Filipino and Latino young adults, which may explain their tendency to continue to live with their families and contribute financially to them (Fuligni & Pedersen, 2002).

Arnett follows in the tradition of other theorists, most notably Erik Erikson (1963), in emphasizing the importance of identity formation in development. Erikson characterized the major identity challenge (crisis) of young adulthood as one of *intimacy versus isolation,* of forming intimate relationships versus remaining lonely and isolated.

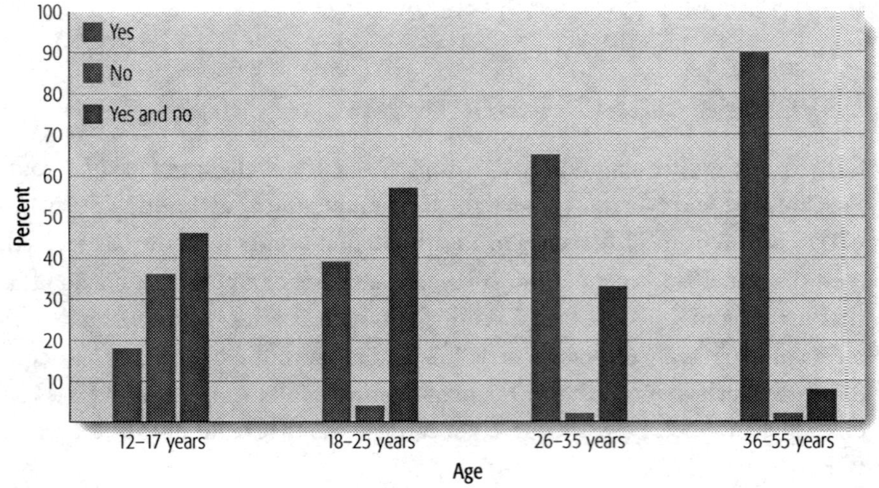

Figure 10.3 Are You an Adult?
Respondents were asked, "Do you feel that you have reached adulthood?" A majority of respondents did not perceive themselves to be adults until their late twenties or early thirties.
Source: From Arnett, J. J., *Adolescence and Emerging Adulthood: A Cultural* Approach (2nd ed.). Copyright © 2004 Pearson/ Prentice Hall. Reprinted by permission.

In Erikson's view, earlier difficulties navigating life challenges can affect the resolution of later-occurring challenges. For example, young adults who forge a strong ego identity or a commitment to a stable life role during adolescence may be prepared in early adulthood to form intimate attachments, to "fuse" their identities with others in marriage and in lasting friendships. Those who fail to establish intimate relationships may retreat into isolation and loneliness. People who did not learn a basic sense of trust early in life may also have a greater fear of intimacy in adulthood and so may experience more loneliness and difficulties establishing close relationships.

CONCEPT 10.14
Psychosocial development in early adulthood often centers on establishing intimate relationships and finding a place in the world.

In Erikson's view, the key psychosocial challenge adults face in midlife pits *generativity versus stagnation*. By generativity, he meant efforts directed at shaping the new generation or generations to come. Shaping may include efforts at raising one's own children or helping to make the world a better place for other children or future generations of children. A failure to achieve generativity leads to stagnation, a kind of self-absorption in which people indulge themselves as though they themselves were "their one and only child" (Erikson, 1980). Evidence supports Erikson's view that generativity is primarily a challenge of midlife and is perhaps a path toward life satisfaction (Peterson & Duncan, 2007; Zucker, Ostrove, & Stewart, 2002).

CONCEPT 10.15
Erikson characterized the challenge faced by people in midlife as one of generativity versus stagnation.

To Erikson, each stage of adult life presents unique challenges that can either strengthen and enrich us or weaken and diminish us. Other theorists focus less on stages of adult development and more on how people cope with the tasks and transitions they face during the course of their lives. For example, Robert Havighurst (1972) outlined a number of developmental tasks people face in their later years, including adjusting to physical changes and to retirement, coping with the loss of friends and loved ones, and establishing new relationships with aging peers. Daniel Levinson and his colleagues (1978) focused on life transitions, such as the midlife transition that may occur around age 40. To Levinson, the midlife transition is a time of reckoning when we assess our lives in terms of whether we have reached the dreams we held in our youth. We may feel life is starting to slip away and realize we are now a full generation older than the youngest of the young adults. We may start to wonder whether we have more to look back on than forward to. Many middle-age adults compare their accomplishments to their earlier dreams and may despair if they find they have fallen short.

This midlife transition can trigger a **midlife crisis**: a sense of entrapment from the closing down of future options, of feeling that life is open-ended no more, of a loss of purpose or a sense of failure from not having fulfilled one's youthful ambitions or aspirations. Some people may respond to the midlife crisis by attempting to recover their lost youth. Such behavior may include an extramarital affair to prove that one is still sexually desirable to others, increased risk taking, or perhaps the purchase of a two-seater sports car (red, of course).

midlife crisis A state of psychological crisis, often occurring during middle adulthood, in which people grapple with the loss of their youth.

Yet a midlife crisis is not inevitable and may in fact be more the exception than the rule (Lachman, 2004). Most people navigate through middle adulthood without a significant midlife crisis. In actuality, many people in middle adulthood today are focusing on what they believe will be another three to four decades of promise rather than decline. On this assumption, they are switching careers and aspiring to new dreams and goals. They feel that perhaps now they will make their greatest contributions to the next generation. This concept resonates with Erikson's concept of generativity.

CONCEPT 10.16
Although some people experience a midlife crisis, most appear to weather the changes in their middle years without a period of personal upheaval or crisis.

Another commonly held belief is that people in their forties and fifties, especially women, are likely to experience depression and loss of purpose and direction when their children leave home. The **empty nest syndrome**, or tendency for parents, especially mothers, to become depressed and feel a lack of purpose when their children

empty nest syndrome A cluster of negative emotions, involving a loss of purpose and direction that can occur when children have grown and left home.

CONCEPT CHART 10.2 Development in Young and Middle Adulthood

Physical Development	■ Physical and mental development typically peaks in early adulthood. ■ Declines in lean body tissue and muscle mass begin in the twenties. ■ Women experience menopause, the cessation of menstruation, and a sharp drop in estrogen production in middle age. ■ Men experience a more gradual reduction in testosterone as they age.
Cognitive Development	■ Fluid intelligence declines during middle and late adulthood, but crystallized intelligence shows little, if any, decline and may actually improve in some respects. ■ Memory skills may show age-related declines but social and occupational functioning is not significantly impacted.
Psychosocial Development	■ Emerging adulthood (18 to 25 years) is a period of gradually assuming more independent roles associated with full adulthood. ■ Erikson proposed two stages of psychosocial development in young and middle adulthood, respectively: *intimacy versus isolation* and *generativity versus stagnation*. ■ Levinson and colleagues focused on important transitions that occur during adulthood. One of these, the *midlife crisis*, is not as common as most people believe.

set off on their own, may have been fairly common in the days when a woman's identity centered on child-rearing. However, evidence shows that most men and women today experience the transition to an empty nest as a time of reconnecting with each other and pursuing their own interests (Clay, 2003; Gorchoff, John, & Helson, 2008). That said, many empty nests these days are refilling as increasing numbers of adult children are returning home (or deciding not to leave in the first place) because of a tough job market and high housing costs. Concept Chart 10.2 provides an overview of development during young and middle adulthood.

Marriage, American Style

Marriage is a universal societal institution found in every human culture, from industrialized societies of North America and Europe to preliterate societies in the farthest reaches of Micronesia. Most people in all human societies—in some cases, nearly all—marry at least once. More than 95 percent of Americans eventually marry by age 60. But only about half of adults in the United States today are currently married, as compared to nearly 70 percent some 50 years earlier (Luscombe, 2010; Pew Social TrendsStaff, 2010). For the first time in memory, a slight majority of adult women (51 percent) in the United States are living without a spouse (Roberts, 2007). Among adult men, a bare majority (55 percent) are married and living with their partners (Zernike, 2007).

© Cartoon by Steve Kelley, published January 17, 2007, in the Times Picayune.

Why the decline in the number of married adults? We can cite many factors, including the increased rate (and acceptability) of divorce, tendencies toward marrying later, increased numbers of women postponing marriage to pursue professional careers, more accepting attitudes toward having sex without the need to be married, and longer life spans, which often means one spouse outliving the other. The disparity between men and women living with their spouses is largely explained by the fact that women tend to live longer than men, which makes them more likely to become widowed.

Why People Marry

CONCEPT 10.17
Despite the wider range of lifestyles available to adults today, marriage remains the most common lifestyle in the United States.

Marriage is popular worldwide because it meets many personal and social needs. It legitimizes and provides opportunities for regular sexual relations and offers a family structure to raise children within a stable home environment. It is an institution in which children are supported and socialized into adopting the values of the family and of the culture at large. Marriage also permits the orderly transmission of wealth from one family to another and from one generation to the next.

Most people today become sexually active long before they march down the wedding aisle. Since marriage is no longer the point of entry for sexual relations for most couples, its continuing appeal primarily reflects other factors, such as providing a sense of security, offering opportunities for raising children within a family unit, providing opportunities for companionship and intimacy, and fulfilling a desire to travel with a partner down life's road.

Who We Marry

People today generally say they marry for love, but it wasn't always so. As late as the seventeenth and eighteenth centuries, most European marriages were arranged by parents to enhance the family's financial stability. Though parents in Western societies may no longer arrange marriages, they may still encourage their children to date the wonderful sons and daughters of those solid churchgoing couples who live down the block. The principle of **homogamy**, or "like marrying like," continues to hold true. People in our society tend to marry others from the same geographical area, race, educational level, religion, and social class. Stories like Cinderella's– a poor girl marrying a rich prince—by and large remain fairy tales. That being said, interracial marriages in the United States have been rising steadily and now constitute one in seven new marriages (Saulny, 2011). Investigators report similar levels of marital satisfaction in marriages between Mexican Americans and European Americans as compared to those between European Americans (Negy & Snyder, 2000).

homogamy The tendency for people to marry others who are similar to themselves.

Generally speaking, people also marry others who are similar to themselves in physical and psychological characteristics—in height, weight, personality traits, intelligence, and even use of tobacco and alcohol (Lamanna & Riedmann, 2005; Reynolds, Barlow, & Pedersen, 2006).

Singlehood

CONCEPT 10.18
Though marriage remains our most popular lifestyle overall, singlehood is the most common lifestyle among people in their early twenties.

Marriages may be made in heaven, but many people are saying heaven can wait. Many young adults are busy building their careers and pursuing their interests, not simply biding their time waiting for the arrival of Mr. or Ms. Right.

The average age of first marriage has risen to its highest level ever, to 28 for men and 26 for women (U.S. Census Bureau, 2010). Among today's young adults in the 20- to 24-year-old age range, more than four in five men and about three in four women are unmarried—percentages that have more than doubled since 1970. As we'll see shortly, more couples are also choosing to live together—to *cohabit*—without getting married.

No one specific pattern fits all singles. Many single adults are not sexually active, either by choice or through lack of opportunity. Some choose to remain celibate to focus more energy on their careers or interests. Many others practice *serial monogamy*, becoming involved in a series of exclusive relationships rather than having simultaneous sexual relationships. Some, but certainly not most, fit the stereotype of the "swinging single" in pursuing a series of casual sexual encounters or "one-night stands." Similar variations exist in the lifestyles of both gay and heterosexual singles and couples.

Singles often face a form of negative bias or discrimination that goes unrecognized. When asked to think about people who are married or single, college students in one study were more likely to describe singles as immature, unstable, and self-centered (Morris, Sinclair, & DePaulo, 2006). In another study, rental agents who read descriptions of potential tenants were much more likely to select a married couple over an unmarried cohabiting couple or a pair of friends (Morris, Sinclair, & DePaulo, 2006). It appears that changes in social attitudes have failed to keep up with the rapidly changing place of singles in our society (Byrne & Carr, 2005).

We should also recognize that singlehood is not limited to the young. Many older people are widowed or divorced. Because they tend to live longer than men, women are five times more likely than men to be widowed. The psychological adjustment of widows and widowers depends on many factors, such as physical and emotional health, financial security, and social support.

Cohabitation: Trial Marriage or Marriage Alternative?

CONCEPT 10.19
For many couples, cohabitation is an alternative both to living alone and to marriage.

SLICE OF LIFE Mark and Nancy live together with their seven-year-old daughter, Janet. Why are they not married? Mark says, "We feel we are not primarily a couple but rather primarily individuals who happen to be *in* a couple. It allows me to be a little more at arm's length. Men don't like committing, so maybe this is just some sort of excuse" (cited in Steinhauer, 1995).

A generation or two ago, people living together out of wedlock were branded as "shacking up" or "living in sin." Today we are more likely to use more descriptive terms—such as "living together" or the more official-sounding "cohabiting" rather than terms carrying a social stigma. Today, fewer than half of American adults think that cohabitation is a bad idea (Luscombe, 2010). Mirroring these changes in attitudes, the numbers of cohabiting male-female couples has risen sharply, increasing 12-fold since 1960 and nearly doubling since 1990 (Gregoire, 2010; Pew Social Trends Staff, 2010; Wilcox, 2010). About one in four unmarried women in the 25- to 39-year-old age range today are living with their male partners. Another striking statistic is that more than half of adults in the 30- to 49-year-old age range say they have cohabited at some point in their lives (Pew Social Trends Staff, 2010). Children are also a common part of the family mix, with about 40 percent of cohabiting couples today living with children in their households.

© Ambrophoto/Shutterstock.com

For Mark, as for many other adults, cohabitation is an alternative both to living alone and to marriage. Some partners have deep feelings for each other but are not ready to get married. Some prefer cohabitation because of its relative lack of legal and economic entanglements. Some view cohabitation as a type of trial marriage, an opportunity to give living together a trial run before deciding to "tie the knot." For many couples, cohabitation is a transitional stage leading to marriage. The most recent government statistics show that about half of cohabiting couples "tie the knot" within three years, and about two of three marry within five years (Lewin, 2010).

Cohabitation is not limited to heterosexual couples. In a recent research sample, adult gay men and lesbians in cohabiting couples expressed as much overall satisfaction with their relationships as unmarried, cohabiting heterosexual couples (Means-Christensen, Snyder, & Negy, 2003).

Many cohabiting couples believe that cohabitation is a trial marriage that will strengthen their eventual marriage. Living together, they say, helps them iron out the kinks in their relationship. But the evidence suggests otherwise. It turns out that cohabiting couples who later marry are more likely to divorce or to report lower marital satisfaction than couples who did not cohabit before marriage (Cohan & Kleinbaum, 2002; Rhoades, Stanley, & Markman, 2009). We should be cautious about making causal inferences, however. People who cohabit prior to marriage may be less committed to traditional values associated with the institution of marriage, such as the commitment to "sticking it out through thick and thin." Differences in attitudes or values, rather than cohabitation per se, may account for the higher rates of divorce among people who had cohabited before marriage.

Divorce

About four in 10 first marriages today (and about 65 percent of second marriages) in the United States end in divorce. The divorce rate doubled from 1960 to 1990 but has since leveled off. The increased acceptability of divorce as an alternative to a troubled marriage, the loosening of divorce laws, and the increased economic independence of women are among the contributors to the higher divorce rate today.

© Gladskikh Tatiana/Shutterstock.com

CONCEPT 10.20
Factors contributing to the rising divorce rates in recent years include changing attitudes toward the acceptability of divorce, the loosening of divorce laws, and the increased economic independence of women.

Marital separation and divorce are associated with financial and emotional problems and even with increased risk of earlier death (Donald et al., 2006; Lorenz et al., 2006; Sbarra & Nietert, 2008). The splitting up of a household's resources often leaves both partners with a lower standard of living. The financial burdens are not evenly distributed, however. More women contend with lower income levels after divorce than do men.

Couples coping with divorce often experience emotional difficulties such as depression, loneliness, and lingering fears about what the future may bring. They may feel a sense of personal failure as a spouse and parent. However, for those leaving failed marriages, divorce may offer opportunities for a new, more rewarding life.

The children of divorce also tend to suffer (Lansford, 2009). Children's adjustment to divorce depends on many factors, including family circumstances, age, and gender. Though many children of divorce fare well, evidence shows that, on average, they tend to have more emotional and behavioral problems, including substance abuse problems (Amato, 2006; Lansford, 2009). Some children in families of divorce appear to be well adjusted in childhood but experience problems in later development. For example, as adults they may have difficulty trusting that lovers or spouses will remain committed to them.

Divorce is difficult for children in the best of circumstances and is made worse when marital problems and conflicts spill over into parent-child relationships (Hetherington, 2006; Lansford, 2009). Conflict between ex-spouses can easily lead to a decline in the quality of parenting. Children of divorce fare better when their parents do the following:

- Try, in spite of their differences, to agree on how to handle the children
- Help each other maintain important roles in the children's lives
- Refrain from disparaging or criticizing each other in front of the children

Most divorced people eventually remarry. You might expect divorced people to be seasoned by their earlier experience to "get it right" this time, but later marriages are more likely than first marriages to end in divorce. One reason may be that people who divorce from their first spouses are less likely than others to stick it out when they encounter marital problems the second time around. Another may be the toll on the marital relationship resulting from conflicts over stepchildren, such as favoring one's own biological children, or the financial strain of supporting children from two (or more) marriages.

10.2 MODULE REVIEW Early and Middle Adulthood

Recite It

What physical and cognitive changes take place as people age?

- Beginning in their twenties, people start to experience a gradual decline in lean body mass and muscle tissue.
- Fluid intelligence—including rapid problem-solving ability and memory for lists of words, names, or text—tends to decline with increasing age during middle and late adulthood
- Crystallized intelligence remains relatively intact and may actually improve in some respects.
- Menopause, the cessation of menstruation, is the major physical marker of middle adulthood in women. Menopause is associated with a dramatic decline in estrogen production.
- Testosterone production in men also declines with age, but more gradually.

How do theorists conceptualize social and personality development during early and middle adulthood?

- Arnett defined a stage called emerging adulthood (ages 18 to 25) in some cultures that is a transition between adolescence and adulthood.
- Erikson focused on the stages of psychosocial development: intimacy versus isolation (forming intimate, stable relationships versus remaining emotionally detached) during early adulthood and generativity versus stagnation (making meaningful contributions to the future generation or generations versus becoming stagnant and self-absorbed) during middle adulthood.
- Other theorists, such as Havighurst and Levinson, focus on the developmental tasks and transitions that older adults are likely to face.

What are the major variations in adult lifestyles today?

- Though marriage remains the most common lifestyle, the proportion of single people has risen sharply during the past 20 years or so.
- The divorce rate, after rising dramatically from 1960 to 1990, has since leveled off. Eventually, most divorced people remarry.

Recall It

1. In general, people perform best on standardized tests of intelligence
   a. in middle childhood.
   b. in adolescence.
   c. in early adulthood.
   d. in middle adulthood.
2. Evidence supports the linkage between menopause and depression. True or false?
3. The transition from adolescence to adulthood can be described as a period of ________ adulthood.
4. The major psychosocial challenge of early adulthood, according to Erikson, is that of
   a. role identity versus confusion.
   b. intimacy versus isolation.
   c. generativity versus stagnation.
   d. ego integrity versus despair.
5. Tao-ran, a single man in his thirties, has been involved in a series of exclusive relationships with women. This relationship pattern is called ________.
   a. homogamy.
   b. cohabitation.
   c. serial monogamy.
   d. emerging adulthood.

Think About It

- What is your current "stage" of psychosocial development? Does your life reflect the issues and challenges framed by Erikson, Havighurst, and Levinson? If so, in what respects?
- The principle of homogamy suggests that "like marries like." How well does this principle apply to people you know, including yourself if you happen to be married or engaged?
- Do you believe cohabitation is an acceptable lifestyle choice? Do your views differ from those of your parents or friends? If so, what do you suppose may account for these differences?

Late Adulthood

MODULE 10.3

- What are some of the physical and cognitive changes that occur in late adulthood?
- What is Alzheimer's disease?
- How do theorists characterize the psychosocial challenges of late adulthood?
- How do our emotions change as we age?
- What qualities are associated with successful aging?
- What are the stages of dying as identified by Kübler-Ross?

If you are fortunate enough, you may one day join the ranks of the fastest-growing segment of the population: people age 65 and older. We are in the midst of a "graying of America," an aging of the population that has already begun to have profound effects on our society (see ■ Figure 10.4). About one in eight Americans (12.5 percent) is age 65 or older, a percentage that is expected to climb to 20 percent by the year 2030 (Vitiello, 2009). Life expectancy has been rising steadily and is expected to keep climbing through at least the middle of the twenty-first century ("In the Year 2040," 2009). The average baby born today can expect to live 80 years (for females) or 75 years (for males) (Arias, 2010; Centers for Disease Control, 2009b). The average 65-year-old man or woman today in good health has a 50 percent chance of living to at least age 85 (for men) or 88 (for women) (see Table 10.3).

One major reason for increased life expectancy is that many infectious diseases that took the lives of millions of people in the early twentieth century, especially children, have been largely controlled or even eliminated through the introduction of vaccinations, the development of antibiotics, and the creation of public health efforts to

CONCEPT 10.21
On average, Americans are living longer than ever before.

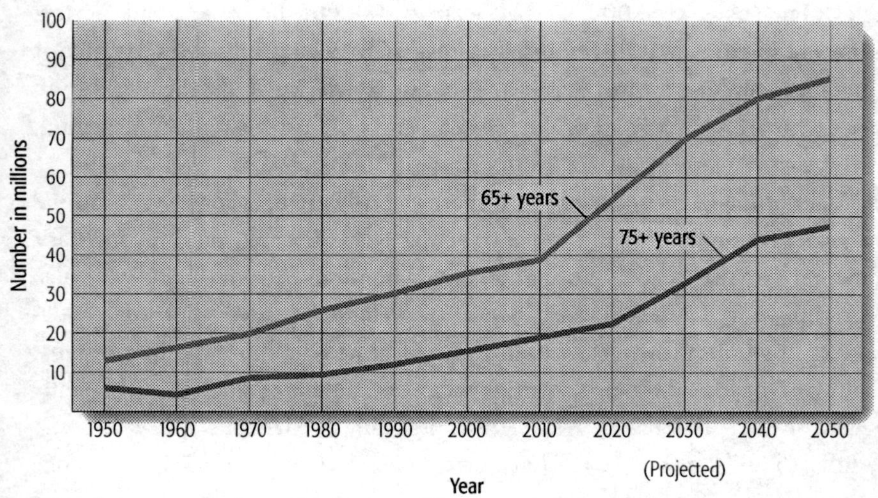

FIGURE 10.4 The Aging of America
The numbers of Americans over the age of 65 has been rising steadily and is projected to rise further through at least the first half of the twenty-first century.
Source: Centers for Disease Control and Prevention, National Center for Health Statistics, Health, United States, 2007, Figure 1. Data from the U.S. Census Bureau.

"Good news, honey—seventy is the new fifty."

© The New Yorker Collection 2000 Victoria Roberts from cartoonbank.com. All Rights Reserved.

TABLE 10.3 Good Health, Long Life

	50% Chance of Living to	25% Chance of Living to
65-year-old male in good health	Age 85	Age 92
65-year-old female in good health	Age 88	Age 94

Source: Carnahan, 2005.

ensure safer water supplies. Other factors contributing to increased longevity are improvements in health care and reductions in the number of Americans who smoke (see Chapter 12).

Physical and Cognitive Development

As we age, we experience a general decline in sensory and motor abilities. We continue to lose bone density as well as muscle mass, and our senses become less acute, especially our sense of smell (Rawson, 2006). The skin loses elasticity, and wrinkles and folds appear. Night vision fades and joints stiffen. Reaction times slow, so older drivers require more time to respond to traffic signals and changes in traffic conditions (Der & Deary, 2006; Tun & Lachman, 2008). Declines in the functioning of the immune system, the body's system of defense against disease-causing agents, makes older people more susceptible to illness, including life-threatening illnesses such as cancer.

The brain gradually shrinks as we age, in both volume and weight (von Hippel, 2007). The loss of brain tissue is especially prominent in the frontal lobes, the brain's executive center, which controls such functions as restraining inappropriate or impulsive behavior. The shrinkage of the frontal lobes may explain why older folks may blurt out inappropriate or embarrassing comments or have difficulty inhibiting prejudiced thoughts (von Hippel, 2007).

As noted in Module 10.2, the ability to perform tasks requiring fluid intelligence tends to decline as people age. For example, older people typically require more time to solve problems and perform mental calculations, and they tend to have greater difficulty with challenging tasks involving pattern recognition, such as piecing together jigsaw puzzles (Jenkins et al., 2000; Peters et al., 2007). On the other hand, performance on tasks requiring crystallized intelligence, such as vocabulary tests, remains relatively intact as people age. Moreover, our general knowledge about the world typically increases through virtually all of the life span and only begins to decline around the advanced age of 90 (Park et al., 2002; Singer et al., 2003).

Memory functioning tends to decline with age, especially memory for newly acquired information, such as remembering the names of people we've just met. Working memory, the type of memory we use to hold information briefly in mind while mulling it over, also tends to declines as we age (Bopp & Verhaeghen, 2009; Peters et al., 2007). Fortunately, declines in memory functioning do not significantly interfere with daily functioning for most people as they age. Nor should we mistake minor changes in memory, such as occasionally forgetting where one put one's glasses, with signs of dementia or Alzheimer's disease.

© iStockphoto.com/Catherine Yeulet

Remaining open to new experiences and challenges can help keep the mind sharp in later life.

Older adults should not be alarmed at normal, age-related memory lapses, since everyone has them. Still, older adults may need more time or repeated exposure to new material to commit information to memory and to later recall it. Older people who participate in stimulating mental activities and are open to new experiences are generally better able to preserve more of their intellectual ability in later life (Schaie, 1996).

Creativity, too, is not time-limited. The great architect Frank Lloyd Wright worked on the famed Guggenheim Museum until his death at the age of 91 (Springen &

TRY THIS OUT Examining Your Attitudes Toward Aging

What are your assumptions about growing old? Do you see older people as fundamentally different from younger people in their behavior and outlook, or just as more mature? To evaluate the accuracy of your attitudes toward aging, mark each of the following items true (T) or false (F). Then turn to the answer key at the end of the chapter.

True	False	
______	______	1. By age 60, most couples have lost their capacity for satisfying sexual relations.
______	______	2. Older people cannot wait to retire.
______	______	3. As individuals age, they become less able to adapt satisfactorily to a changing environment.
______	______	4. General satisfaction with life tends to decrease as people become older.
______	______	5. Most older people are depressed much of the time.
______	______	6. Church attendance increases with age.
______	______	7. The occupational performance of the older worker is typically less effective than that of the younger adult.
______	______	8. Most older people are unable to learn new skills.
______	______	9. Compared to younger adults, older people tend to think more about the past than the present or the future.
______	______	10. Most people in later life are unable to live independently and reside in nursing home-like institutions.

Source: Adapted from Nevid & Rathus, 2007a.

Seibert, 2005). Benjamin Franklin invented bifocals at the age of 78 to help with his own poor vision, and Michelangelo was still painting frescoes well into his seventies. The *Try This Out* exercise helps you evaluate your own attitudes toward aging.

Alzheimer's Disease: The Long Goodbye

Most people retain the bulk of their mental abilities throughout their lives and can compensate for gradual losses in memory and mental processing speed by applying acquired knowledge and skills to whatever demands they face in life (Freund & Riediger, 2003). However, some people develop **dementia** (commonly called senility) in late adulthood. Dementia is characterized by a sharp decline in mental abilities, especially in memory functioning and reasoning ability. Dementia is *not* a consequence of normal aging (Gatz, 2007). It involves a diseased condition of the brain that affects higher mental functions, resulting in more severe memory loss than ordinary forgetfulness and difficulty performing routine activities. Let's put it this way: It is normal as we age to fumble when trying to remember someone's name or occasionally forgetting where we put our glasses. But forgetting that you even wear glasses may well indicate the development of dementia (Aamodt & Wang, 2008).

Dementia has many causes, including brain infections, tumors, Parkinson's disease, brain injuries, strokes, and chronic alcoholism. But the most common cause is Alzheimer's disease (Coyle, 2003).

Alzheimer's disease, or AD, which affects more than 5 million Americans, is an irreversible brain disease of unknown origin that leads to a slow but steady deterioration of mental functioning (Querfurth & LaFerla, 2010). The disease is associated with the death of brain tissue in many parts of the brain and gradually strips the mind of memory and the ability to reason and think clearly. As the disease progresses, people require help selecting clothes, driving, recalling names and addresses, and maintaining personal hygiene. They may start wandering and no longer be able to recognize family and friends or speak coherently.

CONCEPT 10.22
In older adults, declines in cognitive and memory performance are typically not significant enough to impair daily functioning and are largely offset by use of acquired knowledge and skills.

dementia A condition involving a major deterioration or loss of mental abilities involved in memory, reasoning, judgment, and ability to carry out purposeful behavior.

CONCEPT 10.23
Alzheimer's disease is a degenerative brain disease and is not a consequence of normal aging.

Alzheimer's disease An irreversible brain disease with a progressive course of deterioration of mental functioning.

© RON T. ENNIS/MCT /Landov

A 2009 survey by the NFL showed that former professional football players were much more likely to report being diagnosed with Alzheimer's disease or other memory-related diseases than the national average. Suffering many blows to the head during their playing days may lead to the later development of dementia or other forms of cognitive impairment.

We presently lack a clear-cut diagnostic test for AD, although recent progress has been made in identifying certain markers based on brain scans and analysis of spinal fluid that may assist in the early diagnosis of the disease (De Meyer et al., 2010). Although we also lack a cure or effective treatment for AD, drugs that are presently available provide some modest benefits in boosting memory functioning (Kolata, 2010). One widely used drug, *donepezil* (brand name Aricept), increases the neurotransmitter *acetylcholine* in the brain. Acetylcholine levels are lower in AD patients, possibly because of the death of brain cells in parts of the brain that produce the chemical. The next *Try This Out* feature focuses on getting involved in helping people suffering from this debilitating disease.

Alzheimer's disease is associated with progressive death of brain cells in many parts of the brain. The risk of developing AD increases dramatically with advancing age. Alzheimer's affects an estimated one in eight people age 65 or older and more than one in three people over the age of 85 (Gross, 2007; Querfurth & LaFerla, 2010). All told, about 5 million Americans suffer from AD, a number that is expected to jump to more than 15 million by the year 2050 (Belluck, 2010; Wang, 2011). The disease can also affect younger people, but it is rare in people under age 65. The causes of AD remain unknown, but evidence points to roles for both genetic factors and as yet unspecified environmental factors (Bookheimer & Burggren, 2009; Lane et al., 2010; Potkin et al., 2009; Seshadri et al., 2010). Different genes may be involved in different forms of the disease. Scientists are trying to understand the possible significance of steel-wool-like plaques (clumps of degenerative brain tissue) found in the brains of AD patients (Lambracht-Washington et al., 2009). We don't yet know whether these plaques, which are composed of a fibrous material called *beta-amyloid*, play a causal role in AD or are merely a symptom of the disease ("Alzheimer's Disease," 2011; Herrup, 2010). Recently, scientists probing more deeply at the molecular level believe AD may result from destruction of synapses in the brain (Hongpaisan, Sun, & Alkon, 2011; "New Therapies," 2011). Hopefully, as this research advances, it will lead to new forms of treatment of this terrible disease.

© Laura Dwight/Photo Edit

Do you know my name? The man shown here can sometimes recall the names of his loved ones when he is prompted by viewing old photographs.

TRY THIS OUT
Getting Involved

You can acquire firsthand knowledge about the devastating effects of memory loss and help those suffering with Alzheimer's disease and related conditions by serving as a volunteer. Many communities have Alzheimer's support groups you can contact to offer assistance. Ask your family physician or college health office for help if you have trouble locating local support groups.

Gender and Ethnic Differences in Life Expectancy

While longevity has been rising across the board, not every group has benefited equally. The gender gap in longevity in the United States has narrowed in recent years, but women still outlive men by an average of about five years—75.1 years for men versus 80.2 years for women (Arias, 2010). One reason for the gender difference is that women are protected from heart disease by estrogen to some degree, so their risk of heart disease does not begin to approach men's until after menopause, when estrogen production falls off sharply. Men also are more likely than women to die from crimes of violence, accidents, cirrhosis of the liver (related to alcoholism), AIDS, suicide, and most forms of cancer.

Women may outlive men, but older men tend to live *better.* Older women are more likely than their male counterparts to be widowed and to live alone. They are also more likely to live in poverty and have chronic health problems.

White (non-Hispanic) Americans tend to live longer than African Americans, Asian Americans, Hispanic Americans, and Native Americans. ■ Figure 10.5 shows the changes in life expectancies for blacks and whites in the United States since 1950. One reason for ethnic differences in life expectancy is socioeconomic level (Siegler, Bosworth, & Poon, 2003). Members of ethnic minority groups are more likely to live below the poverty line, and people living in poverty tend to have shorter life spans than those of more affluent people (Nevid & Rathus, 2010). Several lifestyle factors associated with lower socioeconomic level may be responsible for the gap in life expectancy between rich and poor. Poor people are more likely to smoke and have high-fat diets, are less likely to exercise regularly, and are less likely to have access to regular health care. Genetic differences may also play a role in ethnic differences in longevity.

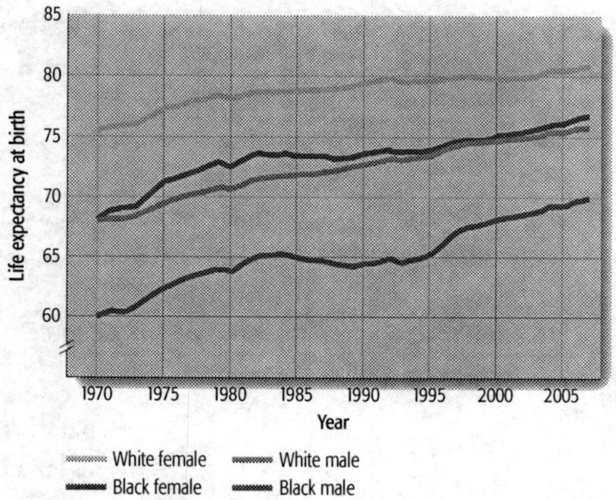

Figure 10.5 Life Expectancy
Life expectancy has been increasing for African Americans and whites, but whites still tend to live longer than African Americans of the same gender.
Source: Centers for Disease Control and Prevention, National Center for Health Statistics, National Vital Statistics Reports, Vol. 58, No. 19, May 20, 2010.

Psychosocial Development

A major determinant of psychological adjustment in later life is physical health status. For older adults in good health, reaching age 65 is experienced more as an extension of middle age than of entry into old age, particularly if they continue to work. In this section, we chronicle how theorists conceptualize the social and personal challenges often encountered in later adulthood. We also examine an emotional problem many older adults face: depression.

Psychosocial Theories of Adjustment in Late Adulthood

CONCEPT 10.24
Gender and ethnic factors play important roles in determining which Americans live longest and how well they live.

CONCEPT 10.25
Erikson believed the major psychosocial challenge of late adulthood involves maintaining a sense of ego integrity or meaningfulness even as one approaches the end of life.

Erik Erikson characterized the central challenge of psychosocial development in late adulthood as one of *ego integrity versus despair.* He believed that the basic psychological challenge of later adulthood is the struggle to maintain a sense of meaning and satisfaction in life rather than drifting into a state of despair and bitterness. People who achieve a state of ego integrity are able to come to terms with their lives: to accept the joys and sorrows, and the successes and failures, that make up the totality of their life experiences.

Erikson lived and worked productively into his nineties and was basically an optimist, believing we can remain fulfilled and maintain a sense of purpose at any stage of life and avoid falling into despair. Though Erikson is recognized for being among the first theorists to develop a model of lifelong development, his theory has been criticized for relying too much on the life experiences of highly educated males and failing to consider differences that may exist in the developmental trajectories of women and people from non-Western cultures (Bertrand & Lachman, 2003). Table 10.4 offers an overview of Erikson's stages of psychosocial development from adolescence through late adulthood.

Other theorists, such as Daniel Levinson, also recognize that late adulthood is characterized by increasing awareness of the psychological and physical changes that accompany aging and the need to come to terms with death. He points out that one of the important life tasks older adults face is to rediscover the self—to understand who one is and find meaningful activities that continue to fill life with meaning and purpose—as well as to maintain connections with families and friends. Lacking connections to others and engagement in meaningful activities that imbue life with purpose can set the stage for a common problem in later life—depression (Hinrichsen, 2008). Also note that suicide rates are much higher among older adults, especially older white males (Fiske, Wetherell, & Gatz, 2009). Although effective psychological and drug treatments for depression in older adults are available, the disorder often goes untreated,

TABLE 10.4 Erikson's Stages of Psychosocial Development During Adolescence and Adulthood

Life Period	Life Crisis	Major Challenge in Psychosocial Development
Adolescence	Identity versus role diffusion	To develop an occupational choice or public role and a set of firmly held beliefs
Early adulthood	Intimacy versus isolation	To develop intimate relationships and abiding friendships
Middle adulthood	Generativity versus stagnation	To contribute to the development and well-being of future generations
Late adulthood	Integrity versus despair	To maintain one's sense of dignity and psychological integrity

Source: Adapted from Erikson, 1963.

partly because health care providers may focus more on the physical complaints of older adults than on their emotional concerns.

Aging and Sexuality

ageism Prejudice and discrimination directed at older persons.

The stereotype that older adults with sexual interests are abnormal ("dirty old men") is a form of **ageism**, or prejudice against older people. Many older people themselves buy into the myth and believe they should withdraw from sexual activity as they surpass middle age. However, many older adults continue to be sexually active, although the frequency of sexual activity tends to decline as people age (Hyde et al., 2010; Reese et al., 2010; Schick et al., 2010). Not surprisingly, the availability of a partner and overall good health are associated with a greater likelihood of continued sexual activity in late adulthood. It is also the case that people need to adjust to physical changes as they age. Men may take longer to achieve erections, and their erections may not be as firm as when they were young. Women may experience reduced vaginal lubrication, or dryness, as estrogen production falls off after menopause. The muscle contractions of orgasm may be less intense for both men and women, and sexual interest may decline to some extent. Despite these age-related changes, sexual intimacy can remain satisfying and important at any age. Let us also note that changes in sexual responsiveness may be offset by the years of sexual experience older adults can bring to their intimate relationships.

CONCEPT 10.26
Though there are age-related changes in sexuality, social stereotypes underlie perceptions that older adults who maintain an active sexual life are somehow abnormal or deviant.

© iStockphoto.com/Kai Chiang

People who enjoy reasonably good physical health can expect to remain sexually active throughout their lives

Emotional Development in Late Adulthood

Despite the many challenges of late adulthood, including the aches and pains many people face as they age, aspects of psychological adjustment, such as life satisfaction and the sense of well-being, are as high in older adults as in younger adults, if not higher (Rettner, 2010; Soto et al., 2010; Stone et al., 2010; Urry & Gross, 2010). Self-esteem, another important component of psychological adjustment, tends to rise through much of adulthood before beginning to decline toward the end of life (Orth et al., 2010; Shaw, Liang, & Krause, 2010). Negative emotions such as anxiety and depression also tend to decline as people age, at least until they reach advanced old age when they begin to edge upwards (Byers et al., 2010; Teachman, 2006). Evidence also shows that older adults tend to worry less than younger adults (Gould & Edelstein, 2010). We have also learned that personal happiness and positive emotions are not only good for our psychological adjustment, but also boost our chances of living a healthier and longer life (Diener & Chan, 2011; Frey, 2011; Ong, 2010).

To be sure, not all older adults feel satisfied with their lives. Factors such as lack of social support and stress imposed by financial adversity play a role in determining one's personal happiness. Many older adults, perhaps as many as 20 percent, experience some symptoms of depression and between 1% and 5% experience a diagnosable depressive disorder

(Fiske, Wetherell, & Gatz, 2009; Luijendijk et al., 2008). Unfortunately, depression often goes untreated. Signs of depression are often overlooked by medical caregivers who are so absorbed with older people's physical problems that they ignore their emotional difficulties. Downplaying depression in elderly people comes at a significant risk, since the prevalence of suicide is higher in later adulthood, especially in older white males.

CONCEPT 10.27
Depression affects many older adults, though medical caregivers often overlook it.

→ Concept Link
Depression can occur at any stage in life and is classified as a type of mood disorder. See Module 15.4.

Older adults may become vulnerable to depression because of the particular stressors they face, such as loss of lifelong friends and loved ones; disability or infirmity; placement in a nursing care facility; and the burdens of caring for spouses in declining health. Retirement, whether voluntary or forced, may sap the sense of meaning and purpose in life and lead to a loss of role identity that can foster depression. Older adults who live alone and who lack social support stand a higher risk of depression. Support from others helps buffer the effects of stress that older adults encounter and thus may help reduce the risk of health problems as well as depression.

The deaths of close friends and relatives may deal a double blow, not only by removing important sources of social support but also by reminding the bereaved of their own advancing age. The older adult may also have a difficult time forming new friends or finding new life goals to give the later years a sense of meaning and purpose. Yet we should bear in mind that depression only affects a minority of older adults. Fortunately, those affected can benefit from available treatments for depression that work with younger adults, including antidepressant medication and psychotherapy (C. F. Reynolds et al., 2006; Unützer, 2007; Serfaty et al., 2009).

© Mark Richards / PhotoEdit

Depression is a common emotional problem in late adulthood. What factors contribute to depression among older adults?

Successful Aging: Will You Become a Successful Ager?

There is much we can do to preserve our emotional well-being as we age, such as engaging in meaningful activities and regular exercise, and coping with loss of companions and loved ones by connecting with friends and seeking out new friendships and social interactions. As Cornell University psychologist Anthony Ong puts it, "We all age. It is how we age, however, that determines the quality of our lives" (*Medical News Today*, 2011). Developmental psychologists highlight the importance of several key characteristics associated with successful aging:

CONCEPT 10.28
Developmental psychologists have identified certain behavior patterns associated with successful aging, including selective optimization and compensation, optimism, and self-challenge.

1. *Selective optimization and compensation.* Successful aging is associated with the ability to optimize one's time and use available resources to compensate for shortcomings in physical energy, memory, or fluid intelligence (Freund, 2006). Rather than compete on the athletic field or in the business arena, where younger people may have the advantage, older people may optimize their time by focusing on things that are both meaningful and important, such as visiting with family and friends more often—activities that allow them to pursue emotional goals that afford satisfaction. They may compensate for declining functioning by writing notes to jog their memories; giving themselves more time to learn; and using mechanical devices, such as hearing aids or canes, to compensate for any loss of sensory or motor ability.
2. *Optimism.* Maintaining an optimistic frame of mind is linked to higher levels of life satisfaction as well as lower levels of depressive symptoms in later life (Chang & Sanna, 2001). Moreover, people who hold more positive views about aging tend to live longer—an average of about 7.5 years longer—than those with more negative attitudes (Levy et al., 2002).

CONCEPT CHART 10.3 Development in Late Adulthood

© bikeriderlondon/shutterstock.com

Physical Development	Sensory acuity declines; muscles and bones lose mass; skin loses elasticity, causing wrinkles; reaction times increase; immune functioning declines; and sexual responsiveness is reduced, though not necessarily sexual satisfaction.
Cognitive Development	Learning and memory decline, especially recall of word lists or names, and in fluid intelligence. Crystallized intelligence—general verbal ability and accumulated knowledge—tends to remain stable or even improve in certain respects as we age. Dementias such as Alzheimer's disease are not normal aspects of aging but result from brain diseases or abnormalities.
Psychosocial Development	To Erikson, adults in later life face the psychosocial crisis of ego integrity versus despair. Havighurst and Levinson focused on tasks that accompany advancing age, such as maintaining meaningful connections to families and pursuing activities that continue to imbue life with meaning. Depression may be a concern for many older adults.

3. *Self-challenge.* Seeking new challenges is a primary feature of successful adjustment at any age. The key challenge for older people—as for younger people—is not to do less, but to do more of the things that matter.

Concept Chart 10.3 summarizes developmental changes in late adulthood.

© Ken Ross Photography

Elisabeth Kübler-Ross

Death and Dying: The Final Chapter

Now let us turn to a topic many of us would rather not think about: life's final transition, the one leading to death. When young, we may feel immortal. Our bodies may be strong and flexible, and our senses and minds sharp. We parcel thoughts about death and dying into a mental file cabinet to be opened much later in life, along with items like retirement, social security, and varicose veins. But death can occur at any age—by accident, violence, or illness. Death can also affect us deeply at any stage of life through the loss of loved ones. The issue of death raises questions well worth thinking about at any age, such as: Should I be an organ donor? How can I best leave my assets to those I care about? Shall I be buried or cremated? Shall I donate my body to science? Should I prepare a living will so that doctors will not need to use heroic measures to prolong my life when things are beyond hope?

Psychiatrist Elisabeth Kübler-Ross (1969) focused on how people cope with impending death. Based on her interviews with terminally ill people, she observed some common themes and identified five stages of dying through which many people pass:

CONCEPT 10.29
Elisabeth Kübler-Ross described the psychological experience of dying in terms of five identifiable stages: denial, anger, bargaining, depression, and final acceptance.

1. *Denial.* At first, the person thinks, "It can't be me. I'm not really dying. The doctors made a mistake."
2. *Anger.* Once the reality of impending death is recognized, feelings of anger and resentment take center stage. Anger may be directed at younger or healthier people or toward physicians who cannot save the person.
3. *Bargaining.* By the next stage, the person attempts to make a deal with God, such as promising to do good deeds in exchange for a few more months or years.
4. *Depression.* Depression reflects the growing sense of loss over leaving behind loved ones and losing life itself. A sense of utter hopelessness may ensue.

5. *Final acceptance.* As the person works through the earlier stages, he or she eventually achieves some degree of inner peace and acceptance. The person may still fear death, but comes to accept it with a kind of quiet dignity.

Kübler-Ross believed that family members and health professionals can help dying people by understanding the stages through which they are passing and helping them attain a state of final acceptance. Many dying people have experiences similar to those Kübler-Ross observed, but not necessarily all of them and not always in the order she proposed. Some dying people do not deny the inevitable but arrive at a rapid though painful acceptance of death. Some become hopelessly depressed; others experience mainly fear; still others have rapidly shifting feelings.

The death of a close friend or family member is often a traumatic experience leading to a state of **bereavement**, which is characterized by feelings of grief and a sense of loss. **Mourning** is the term used to describe the culturally determined manner of displaying grief. Various cultures prescribe different periods of mourning and different rituals for expressing grief. Religious and cultural traditions prescribe methods of mourning to help people express their grief and receive social support. For example, it is customary for Jewish families to "sit *shivah*" for seven days after the funeral. In sitting *shivah,* mourners customarily remain at home and receive a stream of visitors. Rituals include sitting on the floor or on wooden crates, covering mirrors, and wearing a shred of fabric from the deceased's clothing.

bereavement A psychological state of deprivation involving feelings of grief and loss resulting from the death of a loved one or close friend.

mourning The expression of sorrow or grief in accordance with a set of customs, such as wearing black clothing.

People grieve in different ways. Some people show stages of grief that parallel the stages of coping with impending death identified by Kübler-Ross. They may experience denial, anger, and depression, although not necessarily in the stages in the Kübler-Ross model. The bereaved may feel numbness and shock and find it difficult to accept the reality of the loss and feel dazed or detached from their surroundings. They may need others to take responsibility for making burial arrangements and attending to other necessities. They may become preoccupied with thoughts about the deceased person and consumed with feelings of grief. Fortunately, grief normally resolves for most people with the passage of time and return to their usual level of functioning.

10.3 MODULE REVIEW Late Adulthood

Recite It

What are some of the physical and cognitive changes that occur in late adulthood?

- In late adulthood, skin wrinkles, hair grays, and senses become less acute. Reaction time increases, and lean body mass, bone density, and strength decline. Other physical processes, including immune system functioning, decline.
- People generally experience a decline in some aspects of learning and memory, especially ability to learn or recall lists of words or names, and in fluid intelligence.
- Crystallized intelligence remains relatively stable and may even increase in some respects with age.

What is Alzheimer's disease?

- Alzheimer's disease (AD) is a form of dementia (loss of mental abilities) that is progressive and irreversible. It is characterized by a progressive loss of mental functioning. Though no one knows what causes AD, genetic factors are believed to be involved.

How do theorists characterize the psychosocial challenges of late adulthood?

- To Erikson, late adulthood is characterized by the psychosocial crisis of ego integrity versus despair (remaining meaningfully engaged in life while coming to terms with one's life versus despairing over the approaching finality of life).
- Other theorists, such as Havighurst and Levinson, focus on the developmental tasks and challenges that older adults are likely to face.

How do our emotions change as we age?

- Negative emotions tend to decline, whereas positive emotions tend to hold fairly steady. Still, many older adults suffer from emotional problems, especially depression.

What qualities are associated with successful aging?

➤ Successful aging is associated with the ability to concentrate on what is important and meaningful, to maintain a positive outlook, and to continue to challenge oneself.

What are the stages of dying as identified by Kübler-Ross?

➤ Kübler-Ross proposed that terminally ill people experience five stages of dying: denial, anger, bargaining, depression, and final acceptance. However, not all dying people experience these stages, and those who do may experience them in a different order.

Recall It

1. Which of the following cognitive skills is *not* likely to show a substantial decline as people age?
   a. rapid problem solving.
   b. memory for new information.
   c. speed at pattern recognition.
   d. ability to apply acquired knowledge.
2. Esperanza, a 78-year-old woman, suffers from the leading cause of dementia. What is the cause of her dementia?
   a. chronic alcoholism.
   b. Parkinson's disease.
   c. multiple strokes.
   d. Alzheimer's disease.
3. Which of the following is closest in meaning to Erikson's term *ego integrity*?
   a. focusing attention on oneself.
   b. achieving a sense of meaningfulness and satisfaction with one's life.
   c. the development of generativity, or the ability to give of oneself to the next generation.
   d. living an honest life.
4. According to Kübler-Ross's model, which stage of dying directly precedes final acceptance?
   a. depression.
   b. bargaining.
   c. anger.
   d. denial.

Think About It

➤ What key features of successful aging are highlighted in the text? How might you put this information to use in your own life?

➤ What changes in your current behavior can you make to improve your chances of living a longer and healthier life?

➤ Examine your own attitudes toward aging. How are your attitudes toward older adults affected by stereotypical perceptions?

APPLICATION MODULE 10.4 Living Longer, Healthier Lives

CONCEPT 10.31

Longevity is partly determined by genetic inheritance and partly by factors people can directly control, such as a healthy diet, regular exercise, avoidance of harmful substances, and an active, involved lifestyle.

→ Concept Link

Taking care of your body by eating right, avoiding harmful substances, getting adequate sleep, and exercising regularly can help you cope more effectively with stress. See Module 12.3.

Our longevity is partly determined by our genes, a factor that lies presently beyond our control. Although we may one day be able to alter our genes to extend our life span, perhaps even 50 or more years, for now we need to focus on what we can control—how we live our lives. As we'll see, our behaviors and lifestyles are important determinants of living longer and healthier lives.

Lifestyle factors such as exercise and dietary habits contribute not only to longevity but also to the quality of life as we age, improving our vitality. Young people who believe aging is a concern only for older people should note that the earlier they establish healthier habits, the greater their chances of living a longer and healthier life. In this section, we look at some guidelines for acquiring healthier behaviors.

Developing Healthy Exercise and Nutrition Habits

Ponce de León, the Spanish explorer who searched for the mythical "Fountain of Youth," might have been more successful had he just stayed home and built a gym. Exercise at any age is healthful, but especially as we age. Evidence points to the role of physical exercise in slowing the effects of aging such as loss of lean body mass, bone, and muscle strength (O'Neil, 2003). Regular exercise is also associated with a lower risk of certain cancers, such as cancer of the colon, and with other major killers such as heart disease, stroke, and diabetes, as well as the potentially disabling bone disorder **osteoporosis**. Weight-bearing exercise that requires working against gravity helps build bone density and keeps bones and muscles strong.

osteoporosis A bone disease characterized by a loss of bone density in which the bones become porous, brittle, and more prone to fracture.

People who engage in regular exercise and physical activity tend to be healthier and live longer than those who are physically unfit and sedentary (S. N. Blair & Haskell, 2006; Manini et al., 2006). Regular physical activity and vigorous exercise helps keep the body strong, as well as keeping the mind sharp and may even combat late-life depression and reduce the risk of Alzheimer's disease (Begley, 2011; Harris, Cronkite, & Moos, 2006; Scarmeas et al., 2009; van Praag, 2008). People of any age can benefit from physical exercise, especially muscle-strengthening exercise (working out with weights), stretching, and aerobic exercise such as brisk walking, swimming, bicycling, or jogging. Unfortunately, people tend to grow more sedentary as they age.

Regular exercise also helps us keep our weight at a healthy level. In Chapter 8 we noted that obesity is a major risk factor in several life-threatening and life-shortening diseases, such as coronary heart disease, diabetes, and some forms of cancer. Since metabolism tends to slow with age, we may need to curtail the calories we consume and keep exercising regularly to maintain a healthy weight. People planning to begin an exercise program, especially middle-age and older people, should first consult with a physician to ensure that they choose an exercise routine that is healthy for them. The exercise program should also be phased in gradually to allow the body to adjust to the increased demands placed on it.

Following a healthy, balanced diet is also a key factor in promoting health and longevity (Anderson et al., 2011). Adopting a low-fat diet rich in fruits, vegetables, and whole grains can reduce the risks of potentially life-shortening diseases, such as coronary heart disease.

Developing healthy habits also extends to avoiding the use of harmful substances. Tobacco use, illicit drug use, and excessive use of alcohol can lead to physical health problems that can cut life expectancy significantly. Many lives, young and old, have been lost to drug overdoses.

Exercise is not just for the young. Regular exercise in late adulthood can enhance longevity and physical health, as well as maintain mental sharpness.

Staying Involved and Lending a Hand

Staying actively involved in meaningful activities and personal projects can preserve not only mental sharpness but also emotional well-being. Research evidence gives credence to the familiar adage that it is better to give than to receive. A study of older adults showed that giving support to others was associated with a higher survival rate and was more strongly linked to extending longevity than was receiving support (Brown et al., 2003).

Thinking Positively About Aging

Think positively—you just might live longer if you do. As mentioned earlier, investigators find that people with more positive attitudes about aging lived about 7.5 years longer, on the average, than did those with less positive attitudes (Levy et al., 2002).

According to the lead researcher in the study, Beca Levy of Yale University, how a person feels about aging is a more powerful predictor of longevity than having either low blood pressure or cholesterol ("Think Positive," 2002). In a similar vein, older adults in a Dutch sample were less likely to die within a nine-year span of the study if they held more optimistic attitudes in general (Giltay et al., 2006).

Managing Stress

In Chapter 12, we'll see how stress impairs physical health and emotional well-being. Prolonged or intense stress can impair the immune system, the body's line of defense against disease-causing organisms and damaged cells. In turn, a weakened immune system makes people more likely to develop infectious diseases and less able to protect themselves from chronic diseases associated with aging, such as hypertension, cancer, and heart disease. The stress management techniques described in Chapter 12 can help take the distress out of stress and hopefully reduce the risk of developing stress-related disorders.

Exercising the Mind, Not Just the Body

© David Young-Wolff/Photo Edit

The mind, not just the body, needs to be continually stimulated to remain sharp.

Though the evidence is far from conclusive, studies suggest that participating in intellectually stimulating activities helps preserve cognitive functioning and memory in middle and late adulthood (e.g., Kramer & Willis, 2002; Schooler, 2007). Intellectual activities that may help maintain mental sharpness include mentally challenging games (such as chess), crossword or jigsaw puzzles, reading, writing, painting, and sculpting, to name but a few. We also have also have intriguing but tentative evidence linking high levels of challenging mental activity to lowered risks of developing Alzheimer's disease (e.g., Rabin, 2008; Wilson & Bennett, 2003).

Do Healthy Habits Pay Off?

People who adopt healthy habits (avoiding smoking, remaining physically and socially active, following a healthy diet, controlling excess body weight, and avoiding excessive drinking) and who maintain favorable levels of blood cholesterol and blood pressure are more likely to live longer and healthier lives than those with unhealthier habits (Hu et al., 2000; B. J. Willcox et al., 2006). The results of a large-scale study in the United Kingdom showed that persons adopting four healthy behaviors (nonsmoking, regular exercise, moderate alcohol consumption, eating five servings of fruits and vegetables daily) lived an average of 14 years longer than others who adopted none of these four behaviors (Khaw et al., 2008).

Critical thinkers recognize that we cannot draw a cause-and-effect relationship between healthy habits and longevity based simply on a statistical relationship. Since longevity researchers may not be able to control whether people adopt healthier habits, they are generally limited to studying differences in outcomes between those who do and those who do not. Still, correlational relationships can point to possible causal relationships, and it stands to reason that adoption of healthier habits may help extend life.

All in all, it is wise to take stock of your health habits sooner rather than later. It is like salting away money for your later years: Developing healthy habits now and maintaining them throughout life will likely boost your chances of living a longer and healthier life.

Thinking Critically About Psychology

Based on your reading of the chapter, answer the following questions. Then, to evaluate your progress in developing critical thinking skills, compare your answer with the sample answer found in Appendix A.

Erikson believed that an identity crisis is a normal part of the development of a healthy personality. To Erikson, an identity crisis is a time of serious self-examination of who we are, what we believe, and where we are headed in life. Many college students are in the process of creating their ego identities. But creation takes time, and the process need not be completed by graduation. Psychologist James Marcia (Marcia, 1980; Marcia et al., 1993) identified four identity statuses to describe where people stand in their ego identities at any given time:

Identity achievement describes people who have emerged from an identity crisis (a period of serious self-reflection) with a commitment to a relatively stable set of personal beliefs and to a course of action, such as following a major course of study in pursuing a particular career.

Foreclosure describes people who have adopted a set of beliefs or a course of action without undergoing any identity crisis, or period of serious self-exploration. They may adopt a set of beliefs and occupational plans based on what others, especially parents, have instilled in them.

Moratorium is a current state of identity crisis in which the person is actively grappling with questions of ego identity, such as struggling to determine which career course to pursue.

Identity diffusion describes people who are not yet committed to a set of personal beliefs or career choices and show no serious concern about these issues at the present time.

1. What evidence would you use to determine your identity status concerning your occupational choice and your adoption of a set of guiding political, religious, and moral beliefs? Bear in mind that you may have a different identity status in each of these areas.
2. Now apply these criteria to yourself to determine your ego identity status at this point in time in the areas of career choice and personal (moral, religious, and political) beliefs.

ANSWERS TO TRY THIS OUT (p. 395)

1. **False.** Most healthy couples continue to engage in satisfying sexual activities into their seventies and eighties.
2. **False.** This statement is too general. Those who find their work satisfying are less willing to retire.
3. **False.** Adaptability remains reasonably stable throughout adulthood.
4. **False.** Age itself is not linked to noticeable declines in life satisfaction. Of course, we may respond negatively to disease and losses, such as the death of a spouse.
5. **False.** Only a minority are depressed.
6. **False.** Actually, church attendance declines, but not verbally expressed religious beliefs.
7. **False.** Although reaction time may decrease and general learning ability may undergo a slight decline, older adults usually have little or no difficulty at familiar work tasks. In most jobs, experience and motivation are more important than age.
8. **False.** Learning may just take a bit longer.
9. **False.** Older adults do not direct a higher proportion of thoughts toward the past than do younger people. Regardless of our age, we may spend more time daydreaming if we have more time on our hands.
10. **False.** Fewer than 10 percent of older adults require some form of institutional care.

Log in to CengageBrain to access the resources your instructor requires. For this book, you can access:

CourseMate

Psychology CourseMate brings course concepts to life with interactive learning, study, and exam preparation tools that support the printed textbook. A textbook-specific website, Psychology CourseMate includes an integrated interactive eBook and other interactive learning tools including quizzes, flashcards, videos, and more.

CENGAGENOW

CengageNow is an easy-to-use online resource that helps you study in less time to get the grade you want—NOW. Take a pre-test for this chapter and receive a personalized study plan based on your results that will identify the topics you need to review and direct you to online resources to help you master those topics. Then take a post-test to help you determine the concepts you have mastered and what you will need to work on. If your textbook does not include an access code card, go to CengageBrain.com to gain access.

Visit www.cengagebrain.com to access your account and purchase materials.

VISUAL OVERVIEW Chapter 10 Adolescence and Adult Development

MODULE 10.1 Adolescence

PHYSICAL DEVELOPMENT

- **Physical Changes During Puberty**: Attainment of full sexual maturity
- **Timing of Puberty**: Early puberty may involve different consequences for boys and girls

PSYCHOSOCIAL DEVELOPMENT

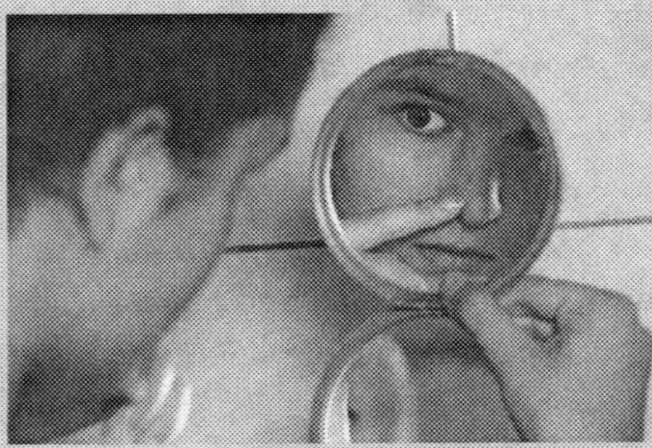

© Ronald Summers/Shutterstock.com

- **Adolescent-Parent Relationships**: Possibly stormy, but generally healthy
- **Development of Ego Identity**: To Erikson, the most important psychosocial challenge of adolescence
- **Peer Relationships**: Can be positive or negative influences
- **Emerging Sexuality**: Often takes center stage during adolescence

COGNITIVE DEVELOPMENT

- **Formal Operationalism**: Piaget's final stage of cognitive development in which abstract reasoning develops
- **Adolescent Egocentricity**:

  Imaginary Audience: Feeling like the world is watching

  Personal Fable: Risky if it leads to perceptions of personal invulnerability

KOHLBERG'S STAGES OF MORAL REASONING

- **Preconventional Level**: Moral judgments based on perceived consequences of behavior
- **Conventional Level**: Moral judgments based on conventional rules of right and wrong
- **Postconventional Level**: Moral judgments based on internalized value systems

"We've been thinking a lot about what we want to do with your life."

© The New Yorker Collection 2000 Victoria Roberts from cartoonbank.com. All Rights Reserved.

MODULE 10.2 Early and Middle Adulthood

PHYSICAL AND COGNITIVE DEVELOPMENT

- **Attainment of Physical Maturity:** Peaks in early twenties
- **Erikson's Stages Theory of Psychosocial Development:** Intimacy vs. isolation (young adulthood), generativity vs. stagnation (middle adulthood)
- **Life Transitions:** Midlife crisis not inevitable
- **Adult Lifestyles:** More varied lifestyles today, but marriage remains predominant lifestyle

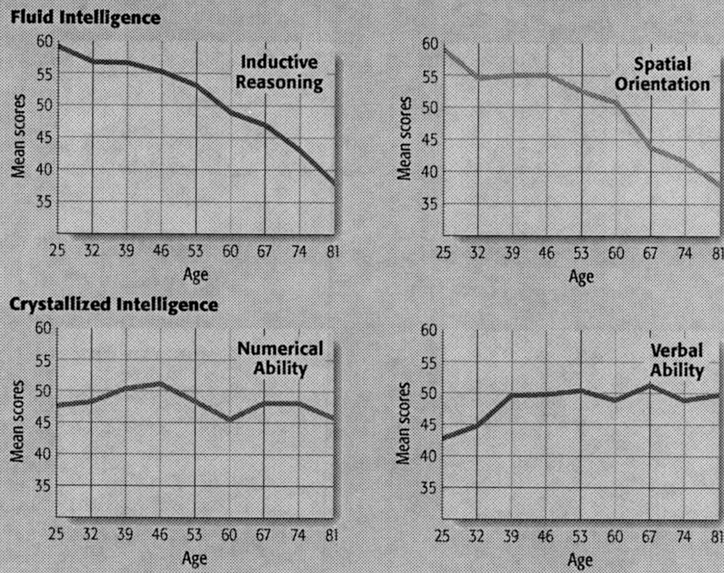

MODULE 10.3 Late Adulthood

PHYSICAL AND COGNITIVE DEVELOPMENT

- **Changes in Sensory and Motor Development:** Many effects on sensory, motor, and cognitive functioning
- **Changes in Cognitive Functioning:** Fluid intelligence and memory functioning affected most by aging
- **Differences in Life Expectancy:** Americans living longer, but women typically outlive men
- **Alzheimer's Disease:** A brain disease leading to progressive decline in mental abilities

© iStockphoto.com/Catherine Yeulet

PSYCHOSOCIAL DEVELOPMENT

- **Erikson's Stage Theory of Psychosocial Development:** Challenge of ego integrity vs. despair
- **Coping with Age-Related Physical and Mental Changes:** Successful aging associated with behavior patterns of selective optimization and compensation, optimism, and self-challenge; maintaining a sense of purpose and connection to others
- **Death and Dying:** Five stages in Kübler-Ross model (denial, anger, bargaining, depression, and final acceptance)

11 Gender and Sexuality

Our Sexuality

SLICE OF LIFE Sonya, 19, faces a dilemma. Raised in a traditional household, she has been taught to preserve her virginity until marriage. Yet she sees most of her friends at college having intimate relationships and wonders whether she is too old-fashioned.

Chanya and Janet have lived a secret life for six years, maintaining a pretense of being just "roommates"—just two 30-something career women splitting the rent in the big city. Although they move the twin beds apart every time their parents visit, maintaining the illusion that they are not lovers is becoming more difficult.

"It's kind of funny," Stewart said, "not 'ha-ha' funny but ironic, really. The last thing I expected at my age [27] was to have trouble getting erections." Since his divorce two years earlier, he has been unable to perform sexually. Failing to achieve erections has been so humiliating that he has given up trying. He makes excuses for avoiding sexual intimacy in new relationships, but his explanations have begun to sound hollow.

The concerns expressed by these young people touch upon a number of issues about human sexuality addressed in this chapter, such as sexual values, sexual orientation, and problems with sexual response. Sex is important biologically, psychologically, and socially. It is nature's way of ensuring we perpetuate our species, it shapes our behavior and our motives, and it influences our personality—the qualities that make us unique. Our sexuality encompasses not only our sexual response and behavior, but the many ways we experience ourselves as sexual beings. For example, our *gender identity* (sense of maleness or femaleness) and our *sexual orientation* (direction of sexual attraction) are essential parts of our self-identity. Our sexual behavior is shaped by family influences and the society in which we live. We learn social rules and customs that govern how we are permitted to express our sexuality. Each society not only imposes rules for governing sexual conduct but also imposes a set of cultural expectations, or *gender roles*, that designate behaviors it deems appropriate for men and women. In this chapter we explore these many facets of our sexuality, beginning with gender identity.

DID YOU KNOW THAT...

- Some people feel trapped in the body of the opposite gender by a mistake of nature? (p. 410)
- The traditional gender gap in math skills has shrunk to virtually nil? (p. 416)
- Women tend to be better at remembering where things are placed? ("Now, where are those car keys?") (p. 416)
- Gay males and lesbians have the same levels of sex hormones circulating in their bodies as heterosexual men and women? (p. 427)
- The major cause of cervical cancer is a sexually transmitted virus? (p.430)
- The male sex hormone testosterone activates sexual drives in both women and men? (p.435)
- Obesity is linked to erectile dysfunction? (p. 436)
- College women are much more likely to be raped by someone they know than by a stranger? (p. 441)

© iStockphoto.com/Fernando Kuster

Learning Objectives

By reading this chapter you will be able to . . .

1 **DEFINE** the terms gender identity and gender roles and **EXPLAIN** how they differ.

2 **DEFINE** transsexualism and **EVALUATE** current understandings of its development.

3 **IDENTIFY** gender differences in cognitive abilities, personality traits, and leadership styles.

4 **EXPLAIN** the development of gender role behavior in terms of psychological, biological, and sociocultural theories.

5 **DESCRIBE** the changes that take place in the body during sexual arousal.

6 **EVALUATE** evidence concerning the origins of sexual orientation.

7 **DESCRIBE** cultural differences in attitudes toward homosexuality

8 **IDENTIFY** different types of paraphilia and **DESCRIBE** the features of each type.

9 **IDENTIFY** different types of sexual dysfunctions and **APPLY** this knowledge to different kinds of sexual problems people may encounter.

10 **EVALUATE** the causes of sexual dysfunctions.

11 **DESCRIBE** current treatments for sexual dysfunctions.

12 **DEFINE** the terms rape and sexual harassment and **IDENTIFY** different types of rape.

13 **EVALUATE** factors contributing to rape and sexual harassment.

14 **APPLY** knowledge of factors underlying rape and sexual harassment to efforts we can take to combat them.

Preview

MODULE 11.1

Gender Identity, Gender Roles, and Gender Differences

- What is gender identity, and how does it differ from gender roles?
- What accounts for gender identity?
- What are the major theories of gender-role behavior?
- Are there gender differences in cognitive abilities?
- Are there gender differences in personality traits and leadership style?

This module examines gender identity and gender roles and how they develop. We will consider the biological and psychosocial influences that lead us to develop our sense of ourselves as male or female and the roles we play in society.

Gender Identity: Our Sense of Maleness or Femaleness

CONCEPT 11.1
Children early in life develop a firm gender identity, or psychological sense of being male or female.

→ Concept Link
Though the development of gender identity occurs in early childhood, the development of ego identity—the firm sense of one's basic beliefs and direction in life—doesn't usually take shape until adolescence, if not later. See Module 10.1.

CONCEPT 11.2
When exploring the underpinnings of gender identity, researchers consider both biological (prenatal) influences and environmental (rearing) influences.

Before moving forward, let's define some terms. In this text, *sex* refers to the biological division between males and females. So, when we identify anatomical differences between men and women, we use the term sexual organs. **Gender** is a psychosocial concept that distinguishes masculinity from femininity. Thus, we use the term **gender roles** to refer to the set of behaviors that a particular culture deems acceptable for men or women. The psychological experience of being male or female is called **gender identity**.

By the age of three, most children have acquired a firm sense of their gender identity, of being either male or female. But what determines gender identity? The answer is not yet clear. Some research points to biological influences. Investigators suspect that prenatal hormones sculpt the developing brain in ways that influence the later development of gender identity (Reiner & Gearhart, 2004). But research suggests that gender identity is not fully stamped in at birth. In this research, children who were born with ambiguous genitalia because of congenital birth defects developed a gender identity that was consistent with the gender to which they were assigned and raised accordingly, even when the assigned gender conflicted with their chromosomal (XY or XX) sex (Slijper, Drop, & Molenaar, 1998). All in all, most scientists believe that gender identity arises from a complex interaction of nature (biology) and nurture (rearing influences) (Berenbaum & Bailey, 2003).

gender The state of maleness or femaleness.

gender roles The cultural expectations imposed on men and women to behave in ways deemed appropriate for their gender.

gender identity The psychological sense of maleness or femaleness.

Whatever the determinants of gender identity may be, it is almost always consistent with one's chromosomal sex. But for a few individuals, gender identity and chromosomal sex are mismatched (Heath, 2006). These individuals have the gender identity of one gender but the chromosomal sex and sexual organs of the other.

Transsexualism: A Mismatch of Identity and Biology

transsexualism A mismatch in which one's gender identity is inconsistent with one's chromosomal and anatomic sex.

People with **transsexualism** feel trapped in the body of the opposite gender by a mistake of nature. A transsexual man is anatomically a male but has the gender identity of a woman. A transsexual woman is anatomically a female but possesses the gender identity of a man. Transsexuals (also called *transgender persons*) typically report feeling that they have belonged to the other gender for as long as they can remember (Zucker,

TABLE 11.1 Myths vs. Facts About Transsexualism (Transgender Identity)

Myth	Fact
Only people who have sex-change operations are transsexuals.	Many transsexual men and women do not have gender reassignment surgery because they want to avoid postsurgical pain and complications or because the costs are prohibitive.
Men who wear women's clothes are transsexuals.	Some are. But others cross-dress to become sexually aroused, not because they are transsexual. Also, some gay males known as "drag queens" dress in women's clothing but are not transsexual.
Transsexualism is just a form of homosexuality.	People with a gay male or lesbian sexual orientation have a gender identity consistent with their anatomic sex. They are sexually attracted to members or their own gender, but do not feel trapped in the body of the opposite gender.

2005a, 2005b). Myths around transsexualism or transgender identity abound, such as those found in Table 11.1.

Transgender people may be repulsed by the sight of their own genitals. To correct what they see as nature's mistake, many undergo gender reassignment surgery to surgically alter their genitals (Bockting & Fung, 2006). Gender reassignment surgery transforms the genitalia to a workable likeness of those of the opposite gender. But since surgeons cannot transplant internal reproductive organs that produce germ cells—the testes in the man and the ovaries in the woman—reproduction is impossible. Thus, surgery does not change a man into a woman or a woman into a man, if what it means to be a man or a woman depends on having the internal reproductive organs of their respective sex. Nonetheless, gender reassignment surgery generally permits the individual to perform sexual intercourse. Hormonal replacement therapy is used to foster growth of the beard and body hair in female-to-male cases and of the breasts in male-to-female cases.

CONCEPT 11.3
People with a transgender identity feel at odds with their anatomic sex and often undergo gender reassignment surgery to correct what they perceive to be a mistake of nature.

The causes of transgender identity remain unclear. Scientists suspect that a combination of sex hormones and other factors, such as genetic influences, act on the architecture of the developing brain during prenatal development (Dennis, 2004; Heath, 2006). The result may be a mismatch of mind and body in which the brain becomes sexually differentiated in one direction during prenatal development even as the genitals become sculpted in the other.

CONCEPT 11.4
Each society defines masculinity and femininity by imposing a set of gender-based expectations about behavior and personality.

Gender Roles and Stereotypes: How Society Defines Masculinity and Femininity

The cultural expectations imposed on men and women to behave in ways deemed appropriate for their gender are called *gender roles.* Fixed, conventional views of "masculine" and "feminine" behavior are called *gender-role stereotypes.* In our culture, the stereotypical female is perceived as nurturing, gentle, dependent, warm, emotional, kind, helpful, patient, and submissive. The stereotypical male, personified by the ruggedly masculine characters in countless movies, is tough, self-reliant, and independent, but also dominant and protective.

© Frank Edwards/Fotos International/Getty Images

© Gary Salter/Corbis

As a small child, Chastity Bono appeared on the television variety show hosted by her famous parents, Cher and Sonny Bono. But Chastity, now Chaz, always felt that he was a male. Chaz (right) recently underwent female-to-male gender reassignment surgery, and now says of his life, "I feel like I'm living in my body for the first time, and it feels really good."

CONCEPT 11.5
Though gender roles in our society have changed and are changing still, housekeeping and childcare roles still fall disproportionately on women.

Yet gender roles have changed and are changing still. Most women today work outside the home, and many are pursuing careers in traditionally male domains like law, medicine, and engineering. Some command naval vessels or pilot military helicopters. Household and childcare responsibilities still fall more heavily on women, even on those who work in full-time jobs outside the home.

But what accounts for the acquisition of gender roles? In other words, why do boys and girls act like, well, boys and girls? Is it simply a matter of cultural learning—imparting to children how men and women are expected to act and the roles they are expected to play? Or might there be biological origins for these behaviors? Here we consider several major theories that seek to account for the acquisition of gender-typed behaviors.

CONCEPT 11.6
Social-cognitive theorists emphasize the roles of observational learning and reinforcement in the development of gender-typed behavior.

→ Concept Link
Observational learning is a type of cognitive learning, as discussed in Chapter 5. See Module 5.3.

Social-Cognitive Theory: Learning What Others Expect of You

Social-cognitive theorists, such as Albert Bandura (1986) and Walter Mischel (1970), emphasize the roles of observational learning and reinforcement in the development of gender-role behaviors. Children are natural observers—taking in what they observe in other people's behavior and what they see on television and in the movies. Parents and older children are important modeling influences (Bronstein, 2006). If children see dad and mom and sister and brother dressing differently and performing different roles in the family, they begin to learn what is expected of males and females and to conduct themselves accordingly.

Parents use rewards and punishments (praise and criticism) to shape children's gender-role behavior. During infancy, parents may talk more to girls and engage in more physical or rough-housing play with boys. Later they may encourage sons to play tough on the athletic field and to hold back tears when they get hurt or feel upset. They may praise girls when they engage in cooperative play or help out in the kitchen. They may also punish or ignore gender-inappropriate behavior.

The toys that parents give their children also mirror the gender-role expectations of the society in which they live. Girls are given dolls and encouraged to practice caretaking behaviors in pretend play that prepares them for traditional feminine roles. Boys receive "action figures" (a euphemism for male dolls), which they use in pretend play to enact aggressive scripts that are characteristic of the traditional male role.

The popular media—TV, movies, books, magazines, video games, and the Internet—may reinforce traditional gender roles, with men portrayed in more aggressive and leadership roles and women playing subordinate roles. Although gender roles are becoming more balanced in popular media, TV and movies continue to portray men and women in traditional roles.

Gender-role expectations are changing as broader social changes occur in society. Daughters today are more likely than not to have a mother who works outside the home. Young girls today are encouraged to develop interests in competitive sports and to follow career paths in whatever fields they chose, even those traditionally reserved for men. Yet changes are slow (relatively few stockbrokers or computer programmers are women, for instance).

© Gary Salter/Corbis

Modeling is an important influence in the development of gender-typed behavior.

© Lisa F. Young/Shutterstock.com

In what ways have traditional gender roles changed in our society?

Gender-Schema Theory: What Does It Mean to Be a Girl (or Boy)?

gender-schema theory The belief that children form mental representations or schemas of masculinity and femininity, which they then use as a basis for organizing their behavior and evaluating their self-worth.

Gender-schema theory emphasizes the importance of cognitive factors in the development of gender-role behavior. The theory holds that children form mental categories or *schemas* for masculinity and femininity (Bem, 1993; Martin & Ruble, 2004). A schema is a way of organizing knowledge, a kind of lens through which one sees the world. Gender schemas incorporate the dress, toys, behaviors, and social roles considered appropriate for boys and men and for girls and women. By age three, children typically have developed a gender schema for toys such that they recognize that trucks are boys' toys and dolls are girls' toys. Gender schemas influence what children are likely to recall, such as remembering gender-linked objects and activities. An important early study showed that boys were better able to recall cars and trucks they had been shown earlier, whereas girls were better at recalling dolls previously seen (Bradbard& Endsley, 1983).

Once children acquire gender-role schemas, they begin using them as ways of organizing their behavior and as frames of reference for evaluating their self-worth. They begin acting in ways that reflect their concepts of how boys or girls are expected to act. They also begin judging themselves positively when they feel they measure up to the traits they deem important to their gender. Young boys may hitch their self-esteem to how well they compare to other boys in masculine traits such as body strength and aggressiveness. Young girls may judge themselves according to whether they perceive themselves as beautiful or their physical skills as graceful. Evidence shows that, among preadolescents, perceiving oneself as being typical of one's gender is associated with better psychological adjustment (Yunger, Carver, & Perry, 2004).

CONCEPT 11.7
Gender-schema theory holds that children form mental representations, or schemas, of the attributes and behaviors associated with masculinity and femininity, and then begin acting in ways that are consistent with these schemas.

Evolutionary Theory: It's Nature's Way

In the context of evolutionary theory, the existence of stereotypical gender roles—men as breadwinners and women as homemakers—merely reflects the natural order of things. Evolutionary psychologists argue that modern gender roles are merely modern adaptations of the traditional roles of men as hunters and warriors and women as gatherers of edible fruits and vegetables and nurturers of children (Buss & Kenrick, 1998). In this view, men's greater upper-body strength makes them more likely than women to succeed as hunters and warriors. Their physical attributes enable them to spear fleeing game and overpower adversaries. Men, on average, also possess better visual-spatial skills, such as mental rotation of objects and tracking movement through three-dimensional space (Cook & Saucier, 2010; Halpern et al., 2007). These skills may give men certain advantages in hunting or warfare, such as the ability to accurately shoot an arrow or to find their way home from the hunt. By contrast, women may be genetically predisposed to develop empathic and nurturing traits that allow them to sense the needs of infants before they can speak. These traits may have increased the chances that children of ancestral humans would survive and carry forward their genetic legacy. Evolutionary psychologists speculate that gender-linked traits that proved adaptive in the struggle of ancestral humans to survive may have been passed down genetically through the generations to modern humans.

CONCEPT 11.8
According to evolutionary psychologists, men and women may be genetically predisposed to develop gender-typed traits, such as aggressiveness and nurturance, respectively.

© Ellen Senisi/ImageWorks

Are all forms of aggression more common in boys than in girls?

Evolutionary psychologists buttress their claims by pointing to evidence that boys and men, by most any gauge, are more physically aggressive than girls and women (Archer, 2006; Feder, Levant, & Dean, 2007; Kimura, 2002). Boys engage in more rough-and-tumble play and play-fighting. Recently, we learned that even among children as young as 17 months of age, boys tend to show more physical aggression than girls (Baillargeon et al., 2007). Our prisons are largely populated by men who have committed violent crimes.

We should be careful not to overgeneralize, however. Evidence shows that both males and females engage in aggressive behavior, but the form it takes may differ along gender lines. Boys tend to be more physically aggressive than girls, but girls tend to show higher levels of *relational aggression* in which relationships are used as a means of hurting others (Godleski & Ostrov, 2010; Shoulberg, Sijtsema, & Murray-Close, 2011; Tackett, Waldman, & Lahey, 2009). Relational aggression includes excluding others from a friendship circle or "group" and starting or spreading rumors that damage another's social standing.

But the question remains: Are men more physically aggressive and women gentler and more cooperative by *nature*? Perhaps testosterone plays a role. Although much higher levels of the male sex hormone are produced in men than in women, evidence links higher testosterone levels in both men and women to more aggressive behavior (Ellis, Das, & Buker, 2007; Giotakos et al., 2005). That said, connections between testosterone and aggressive behaviors are complex. Testosterone is not an "on-off switch" for aggression.

Cultural influences also play important roles in accounting for male-female differences in aggression. For example, young boys are exposed to male action heroes who routinely use their fists or weapons to kill, dismember, and overpower their opponents. And physically aggressive play among boys and men in sporting events is encouraged by coaches and richly rewarded in the professional ranks.

Sociocultural Theory: Gender Roles as Cultural Adaptations

Margaret Mead (1935), the famed anthropologist, emphasized the importance of cultural influences in gender-role behaviors. In one New Guinea culture she studied, both men and women shared childcare responsibilities. In another, stereotypical gender roles were reversed: women were reared to be hunters and food gatherers, while men stayed close to home and tended the children. Mead's evidence suggests that gender roles may have more to do with how societies adapt to the environmental demands they face than with biology.

CONCEPT 11.9
According to sociocultural theorists, gender roles may be cultural adaptations that have helped societies adapt to the demands of their environments.

What can we conclude about the determinants of gender-typed behavior? Many investigators believe that biological and social-environmental factors interact in determining a child's gender-specific behavior (Bryant & Check, 2000; Wood & Eagly, 2002). Biological influences may create behavioral dispositions toward stereotypical gender-role behaviors, such as greater preferences among young boys for rough-and-tumble play and aggressive behavior. Yet biology is not destiny. Gender-role behaviors are neither universal nor fixed by nature. *How* children are socialized into particular gender roles is an important influence in itself (Bryant & Check, 2000).

Masculinity and Femininity: Opposite Poles or Different Dimensions?

CONCEPT 11.10
According to psychologist Sandra Bem, people can be psychologically androgynous, which means they have high levels of both masculine and feminine traits.

Conventionally we tend to think of masculinity and femininity as opposite poles of a single continuum. The more masculine traits you hold, the fewer feminine traits you're likely to possess. But must we assume that masculinity and femininity represent mutually exclusive categories? Why couldn't you have masculine traits such as independence and assertiveness *and* feminine traits such as nurturance and empathy? Psychologist Sandra Bem believes you could (Bem, 1993). Using a gender-role inventory she developed that includes separate measures of masculinity and femininity, she found that men and women could be either high or low in masculine traits or feminine traits. The category of psychological **androgyny** was used to type people who had high levels of both masculine and feminine traits (see ■ Figure 11.1). Others who were low on both dimensions were classified as "undifferentiated." The androgynous person may have the best of both worlds—able to draw upon "masculine" assertiveness or independence in business dealings and upon "feminine" nurturance and sensitivity when interacting with a child or baby animal.

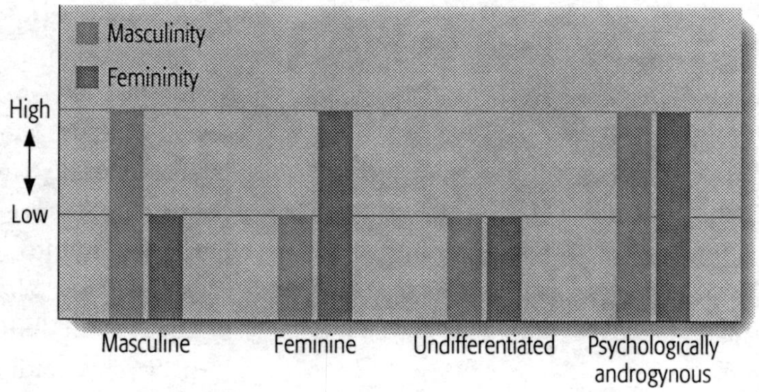

Figure 11.1 Gender-Role Identification
How would you classify yourself in terms of gender-role identification—as masculine, feminine, undifferentiated, or psychologically androgynous?

The concept of androgyny has been criticized, especially by feminists, on the grounds that it perpetuates a belief that masculinity and femininity are attributes of people rather than reflections of society's differential treatment of men and women. Shouldn't people be treated as individuals, not as exemplars of gender stereotypes? Even Bem (1993) recognizes that the concept of androgyny diverts attention away from examining gender inequalities in society. But many scholars, including Bem, believe that androgyny remains a useful construct for describing people who combine "masculine" and "feminine" traits in their personalities and behavior and cannot be easily classified on the basis of traditional gender roles (Arnett, 2004).

androgyny A type of gender-role identification that characterizes people who possess high levels of both masculine and feminine traits.

Investigators find that androgyny is useful in predicting a range of behaviors. For example, androgynous people tend to be more creative than people with a masculine or feminine gender-role orientation (Norlander, Erixon, & Archer, 2000). Other researchers find that men and women prefer androgynous partners as dates and as mates (Green & Kenrick, 1994). Basically, they prefer partners who are both *expressive* (a feminine trait) and *instrumental* (capable of acting effectively in the world, a masculine trait). Before going further, you may wish to review Concept Chart 11.1, which provides an overview of gender identity and gender roles.

Gender Differences: How Different Are We?

CONCEPT 11.11
Researchers find that, on average, girls outperform boys on some verbal skills, whereas boys typically do better on some visual-spatial tasks.

We have already examined gender differences in aggressiveness. Let us now consider gender differences in other areas: cognitive abilities, personality, and leadership style.

CONCEPT CHART 11.1 Gender Identity and Gender Roles

© Maxx-Studio/Shutterstock.com

Concept	Description	Additional Comments
Gender identity	The psychological sense of being male or female	Both biological influences (prenatal shaping of the brain along gender-specific lines) and environmental influences (being raised as a boy or girl) may be involved.
Gender roles	Cultural expectations of the behaviors and social roles deemed appropriate for men and women	Theoretical views on the acquisition of gender roles include social-cognitive theory (observational learning and reinforcement), gender-schema theory (gender schemas as ways of organizing behavior and as frameworks for self-evaluation), evolutionary theory (gender roles representing genetic predispositions), and sociocultural theory (gender roles as cultural adaptations).

Gender Differences in Cognitive Abilities

Who's smarter—men or women? Before you jump to defend your gender, note that research evidence shows that men and women perform similarly on tests of both general intelligence (IQ) and problem-solving ability. As former APA president Diane Halpern points out, "There is no evidence that one sex is smarter than the other" (Halpern, 2004). However, girls do hold an edge in verbal skills such as reading, writing, and spelling. Boys are more likely to have problems in reading that range from reading below grade level to more severe disabilities such as **dyslexia** (American Psychiatric Association, 2000).

dyslexia A learning disorder characterized by impaired ability to read.

Boys have traditionally held an advantage in math skills. However, the gender gap in math has narrowed so much in recent years that there is today essentially no difference in the math performance of boys and girls (Hyde et al., 2008; Lindberg et al., 2010). However, evidence based on worldwide study across 69 countries showed that girls tend to have less confidence in their math skills, even though they are no less skillful (Else-Quest, Hyde, & Linn, 2010). An important lesson from this study, said the lead researcher, psychologist Nicole Else-Quest, is that "... girls are likely to perform as well as boys when they are encouraged to succeed" (cited in "Few Gender Differences," 2010).

CONCEPT 11.12
Researchers find that, on average, girls outperform boys on some verbal skills, whereas boys typically do better on some visual-spatial tasks.

On average, males continue to outperform females in some visual-spatial skills, such as map reading and mental rotation of three-dimensional figures, like the ones in ■ Figure 11.2 (Halpern & LaMay, 2000; Valla & Ceci, 2011). The male advantage in mental rotation is even observed in infants (Moore & Johnson, 2008; Quinn & Liben, 2008). The ability to perceive relationships among three-dimensional objects may explain why boys and men tend to excel in certain skills, such as playing chess, solving geometry problems, and finding embedded shapes within geometric figures.

Women, again on average, are better skilled at remembering where objects are located—which may explain why women are often better at finding lost keys. But notice the qualifying term "on average": individuals do exhibit abilities in which the opposite gender tends to excel. Many women excel in math and science, and many men shine in writing and verbal skills. In fact, greater variations in cognitive abilities exist within genders than between genders. Thus it is important to avoid using traditional stereotypes to limit the interests and vocations that boys and girls may pursue.

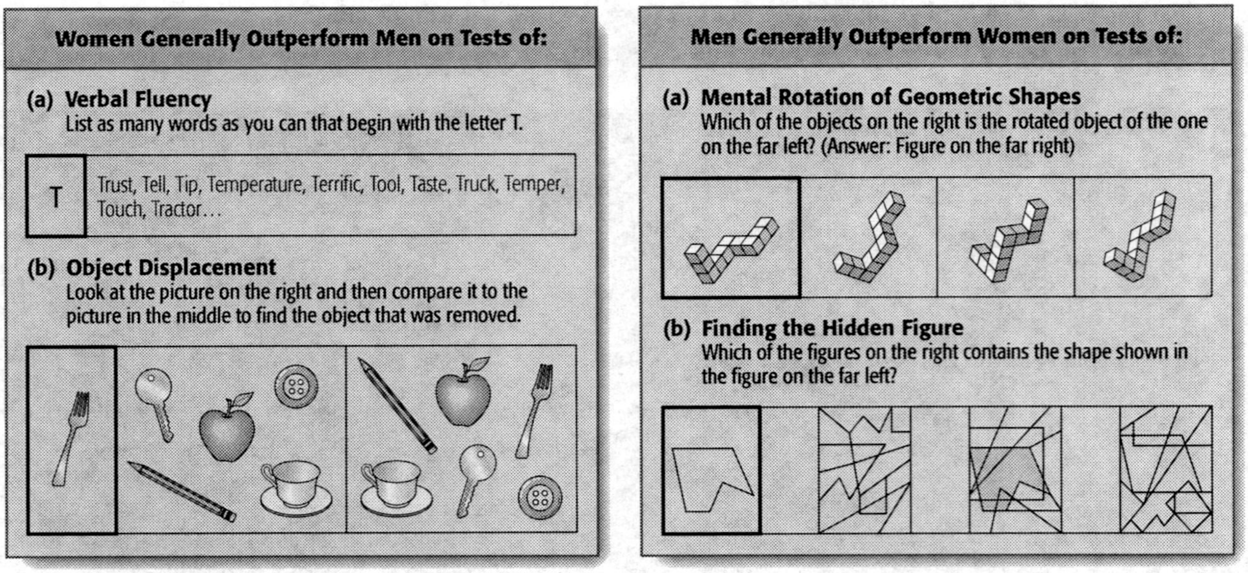

Figure 11.2 Gender Differences in Abilities
Source: Kimura, 1992.

What accounts for gender differences in cognitive ability? One possibility is that the brains of males may be more highly specialized for certain kinds of visual-spatial skills. Male fetuses are exposed to higher levels of testosterone, which may enhance development of brain circuitry involved in performing certain types of spatial tasks (Cohen-Bendahan et al., 2005). Psychological and social factors may also play a role, such as differences in expectations parents hold of their sons and daughters regarding math and science abilities—expectations that may influence whether children apply themselves in developing these skills.

Before going further, we need to interpret gender differences in cognitive abilities in light of several limiting factors:

- *Gender differences are typically small.* Gender differences in verbal and math abilities are typically small, and greater differences exist among males and among females than between males and females (Hyde, 2007). Thus it is important to avoid using traditional stereotypes that limit the interests and vocations that boys and girls may want to pursue.
- *Gender differences are group differences.* Gender differences relate to average differences between groups of males and females. They do not tell us about the particular abilities of any given Bill or Suzy. As noted, many women excel in math and science, and many men shine in writing and verbal skills.
- *Gender differences in math are narrowing.* The gender gap in math performance has shrunk considerably in recent years, so much so that today the average scores of boys and girls on standardized math tests, such as the SAT, are quite close (Halpern et al., 2007; Ripley, 2005).

Why It Matters

Parents who hold stereotypical views that "girls are not good at math and science" may not encourage their daughters to develop math skills or take science courses. Girls themselves may internalize these negative stereotypes and thus doubt their abilities in math or science and become discouraged from pursuing interests in these areas (Kiefer & Sekaquaptewa, 2007). Our culture appears to train women to perform a simple deduction based on a faulty premise that math is "masculine" (Nosek, Banaji, & Greenwald, 2003):

Math = Male
Me = Female
Therefore Math ≠ Me

The widely held stereotype that girls are not good at math is not supported by evidence. On average, boys and girls today obtain similar scores on standardized math tests.

© Ocean/Corbis

Yes, math is me. What messages do we communicate to young women about their abilities in math and science? How might cultural expectations keep young women from developing interests in these areas?

© PhotoDisc/Getty

Who's smarter—men or women? Let's call this age-old battle a draw, since evidence shows that men and women perform similarly on tests of general intelligence and problem-solving ability. However, gender differences do emerge on some specific cognitive abilities.

Training and experience also matter. A recent study showed that the male advantage in certain spatial skills was reduced when women were given 10 hours of training in playing action video games (Feng, Spence, & Pratt, 2007). Since spatial skills are so important in fields such as mathematics, engineering, and science, providing specific training in these skills may help redress the traditional imbalance between men and women in these fields.

Gender Differences in Personality and Leadership Style

CONCEPT 11.13
Gender differences in personality traits are borne out by evidence that men are generally more aggressive and have higher self-esteem, while women tend to be more nurturing and emotionally expressive.

Evidence points to some differences in personality traits between men and women. In general, men show higher levels of self-esteem and aggressiveness, whereas women tend to show more extraversion, warmth, openness to feelings, and emotional expression (Costa, Terracciano, & McCrae, 2002; Feingold, 1994; Ripley, 2005).

What about the stereotype that women are more talkative than men? This question may not be settled by any one scientific study, but researchers recorded conversations by several hundred male and female university students over the course of several days through the use of tiny microphones (Mehl et al., 2007). The investigators then estimated the numbers of words uttered by both men and women. The results? A virtual tie, with both men and women emitting about 16,000 words. The take-away message from this study and other related research is that the stereotype that women are gabbier than men just doesn't square with scientific evidence (Leaper & Ayres, 2007).

© CREATISTA/Shutterstock.com

Who chats more during the course of a day—*gabby Gabe* or *gabby Gabriella*? Contrary to the stereotype, investigators in a recent study found no significant difference in the number of words emitted by men and women.

Despite another common stereotype—that men make better leaders—experimental studies show that women are at least the equal of men in managerial and leadership ability (Eagly, Karau, & Makhijani, 1995). Yet because of prevailing sexist attitudes, effective leadership behavior may be evaluated more negatively in women than in men (Eagly & Karau, 2002). There are also differences between men and women in leadership styles. Women leaders tend to be more democratic—more inclined to seek opinions of subordinates when making decisions. Their male counterparts tend to adopt a more autocratic or domineering style, leading more by command than by consensus building (Eagly & Johnson, 1990). Table 11.2 summarizes the key findings on gender differences in cognitive abilities, personality, and leadership ability.

TABLE 11.2 Gender Differences

Skill or Trait	Research Findings	Additional Comments
Cognitive abilities	Girls generally perform better than boys in certain verbal skills, while boys generally perform better in specific visual-spatial skills and in math skills.	Differences within genders are greater than those between genders. Gender differences in abilities may reflect both biological and psychosocial factors.
Personality	Males are generally higher in aggressiveness and self-esteem. Females tend to be higher in extraversion, trust, nurturance, and emotional expressiveness.	Personality traits, cognitive abilities, and play behaviors are closely linked to gender-role expectations, so it may be impossible to separate the effects of culture from biological differences.
Leadership ability	Women and men are equally effective as leaders, but leadership styles typically vary in relation to gender.	Women leaders tend to focus more on seeking cooperation, whereas male leaders are more likely to lead by command or direction.

11.1 MODULE REVIEW Gender Identity, Gender Roles, and Gender Differences

Recite It

What is gender identity, and how does it differ from gender roles?

- Gender identity is the psychological sense we have of our maleness or femaleness, whereas gender roles are culturally imposed expectations of roles and behaviors deemed acceptable for each gender.

What accounts for gender identity?

- Gender identity may arise from a complex interaction of biological (genetic) and environmental (rearing) influences.

Though the brain becomes sexually differentiated before birth, our gender identity continues to be shaped by experiences during early childhood.

- In transsexualism a person's gender identity is inconsistent with his or her chromosomal sex and sexual organs.

What are the major theories of gender-role behavior?

- Biological models based on evolutionary theory propose that the acquisition of gender-role behaviors is a product of our genetic heritage, whereas psychosocial and cultural models (social-cognitive theory, gender-schema theory, sociocultural theory) focus on such factors as socialization, gender schemas, and cultural adaptation.

Are there gender differences in cognitive abilities?

- Girls tend to outperform boys on some verbal skills, such as reading, writing, and spelling. Boys hold an edge in some visual-spatial tasks and in math skills, though the gap in math abilities is narrowing. However, boys and girls perform similarly on tests of general intelligence and problem-solving skills.

Are there gender differences in personality traits and leadership style?

- Males tend to be more aggressive and have higher self-esteem, while females are generally higher in extraversion, trust, and nurturance.
- Female leaders tend to be more democratic in their leadership style, while male leaders tend to adopt a more autocratic or domineering style.

Recall It

1. Our sense of maleness or femaleness is our
   a. sexual orientation. **c.** gender identity.
   b. gender role. **d.** androgyny.
2. Hector, who feels he is a woman trapped in a man's body, would be described as ________.
   a. having a homosexual orientation. **c.** a transsexual.
   b. a transvestite. **d.** androgynous.
3. Which hormone have scientists linked to aggression in *both* males and females?
4. According to social-cognitive theory, gender-typed behavior is acquired through all of the following *except*
   a. observational learning and reinforcement.
   b. modeling of television and magazine content and adults' behavior.
   c. praise given for gender-appropriate behavior.
   d. genetically transmitted gender-based traits.
5. Boys have the upper hand in certain ________-spatial skills, such as mental ________ of objects in three-dimensional space.

Think About It

- Do you believe that gender-typed behavior is a product of our evolutionary history? Why or why not?
- Who, or what, were the major influences on your development of gender-specific behaviors? On your concepts of what it means to be a man or a woman?

Sexual Response and Behavior

MODULE 11.2

- What are the phases of the sexual response cycle?
- What are the origins of sexual orientation?
- How do attitudes toward homosexuality vary across cultures?
- What are paraphilias?

Our sexuality is a natural or biological function—indeed, a necessary function to perpetuate the species. Yet our sexual behavior is influenced by many factors, not simply by biological drives. These include cultural learning, individual experiences, and perhaps most importantly, personal values.

Why do people have sex? Yes, there are the obvious reasons—procreation, pleasure, and expressing love for the person (Peres, 2007). But there are also less obvious reasons, according to investigators who asked more than 1,500 college students at the University of Texas at Austin why they have sex (Meston & Buss, 2007; Tierney, 2007. These include celebrating a special occasion, returning a favor, burning calories, helping one fall asleep, feeling closer to God, and even getting rid of a headache. *Who knew?* Table 11.3 lists the top 10 reasons students gave for having sex in the Texas sample.

Though sexuality is a natural function, there is great variability in how people express themselves sexually. Each society establishes rules or codes of behavior that govern sexual conduct. We may not always follow the rules we were taught, but we learn from an early age what is acceptable behavior and what is not. Our values are shaped by our parents, teachers, religious leaders, and also—for better or worse—our peer groups.

A recent large-scale, nationally representative survey of sexual behaviors among American adults shows more variety in sexual practices than existed a generation earlier (Healy, 2010; Herbenick et al., 2010; Reece et al., 2010). Although vaginal intercourse remains the most common sexual activity, other sexual behaviors such as masturbation, either performed by oneself or one's partner, as well as oral sex and experimentation with same-gender sex are more common today than was the case some twenty years earlier, the last time a major sex survey in the United States was conducted. Today, a majority of adults in the 18- to 49-year-old age range report engaging in oral sex. More than 20 percent of men in the 25- to 49- year-old age range and women in the 20- to 39-year-old age range reported engaging in anal sex in the past year. A majority of men (63 to 69 percent) in the 20- to 39-year-old age range report masturbating at least once during the past month, as do 39 to 44 percent of women (NSSHB, 2010). An intriguing finding pointing to possible miscommunication in America's bedrooms was that about two of three (64 percent) women said they had achieved orgasm during their last sexual encounter, whereas a much higher proportion of men—85 percent—claimed their partners had achieved orgasm (Gardner, 2010).

TABLE 11.3 Why People Have Sex

A sample of college students were given a list of more than 200 reasons for having sex and were asked how often these reasons led them to have sex in the past. These are the top 10 reasons given by women and men in the sample.

	Reasons for Sex Endorsed by Women	Reasons for Sex Endorsed by Men
1.	I was attracted to the person.	I was attracted to the person.
2.	I wanted to experience the physical pleasure.	It feels good.
3.	It feels good.	I wanted to experience the physical pleasure.
4.	I wanted to show my affection to the person.	It's fun.
5.	I wanted to express my love for the person.	I wanted to show my affection to the person.
6.	I was sexually aroused and wanted the release.	I was sexually aroused and wanted the release.
7.	I was "horny."	I was "horny."
8.	It's fun.	I wanted to achieve an orgasm.
9.	I realized I was in love.	I wanted to express my love for the person.
10.	I was "in the heat of the moment."	I wanted to please my partner.

Source: Adapted from Meston & Buss, 2007.

It is important to note that variability in sexual practices is the norm. Couples vary in what sexual behaviors they perform and how often they engage in sexual relations. On the average, married couples report having intercourse slightly more than once a week (Deveny, 2003).

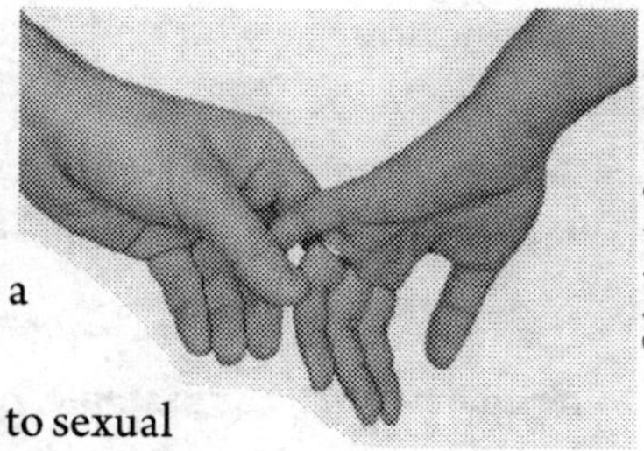
© Agnieszka Guzowska/ Shutterstock.com

In this module we examine how our bodies respond to sexual stimulation and explore the variations in sexual behavior with respect to sexual orientation and atypical forms of sexual arousal. First, however, let us examine cultural and gender differences in sexuality.

Cultural and Gender Differences

CONCEPT 11.14
The human body is sensitive to many forms of sexual stimulation, but how we express ourselves sexually has more to do with our cultural learning and personal values than does the capacity of our bodies for sexual pleasure.

Cultures vary widely in sexual values and practices. Some cultures are more permissive with respect to oral sex, anal sex, and masturbation, whereas others are more restrictive. Even in our culture, we gain a clearer understanding of variations in sexual values and behavior when we take into account cultural and gender differences. Hispanic Americans, for example, tend to hold conservative sexual values. But a recent study of Hispanic college students in a southern Texas university revealed that men expressed more permissive attitudes toward some sexual practices, such as oral sex and masturbation, and more disapproving attitudes toward homosexuality, than did female students (Dantzker & Eisenman, 2003).

From the perspective of evolutionary psychology, tendencies for men to have roving eyes and for women to be less interested in having a variety of sexual partners have evolutionary roots. Women are limited biologically to having a few potential offspring in their lifetimes, but men can sire a great many children, even thousands in the case of some tribal chieftains. Thus, women need to be careful about safeguarding their limited reproductive opportunities by seeking partners who would be most likely to support their offspring and help ensure their survival. They cannot afford to waste their precious reproductive opportunities on whatever prospective partner happens along. On the other hand, men may be more reproductively successful—that is, able to spread their seed as widely as possible—if they seek multiple partners. The question of whether these differences are based in our genes or in the messages ingrained in young people about acceptable sexual behavior for men and women remains a point of controversy in the field.

Psychologist Letitia Peplau (2003) reviewed scientific evidence on gender differences in sexual behavior. Here are her major conclusions:

- *Men show greater sexual desire than women.* Several lines of evidence support the view that men show greater interest in sex than women (also see Lippa, 2009). Men tend to want to have sex more frequently than women. They are also more likely to engage in masturbation and to masturbate more often. Men also tend to fantasize more often about sex and to have more frequent sexual desires.
- *Women place greater emphasis on commitment as a context for sexual intimacy.* Women are more likely to limit sexual intimacy to committed relationships. Men tend to have more permissive attitudes toward casual sex and extramarital sex than do women (also see Bradshaw, Kahn, & Saville, 2010). They also tend to report having more sexual partners. Males in the 30- to 44-year-oldage range report an average of six to eight female sexual

© Jack Hollingsworth/Corbis

Intimacy is more than skin deep. Sexual activity provides a way of sharing emotional, not just physical, intimacy.

partners in their lifetime, as compared to an average of four partners reported by women in the same age range (Mosher, Chandra, & Jones, 2005).

- *Sexual aggression is more strongly linked to sexuality in men.* Men are more likely to use physical force to compel someone to engage in a sexual act.

In drawing attention to gender differences in sexual behavior, we should be careful not to overgeneralize. For example, not all men hold permissive attitudes toward premarital sex. Nor do all women seek to limit sexual activity to committed relationships. There is a range of variation in sexual interest, desire, and activity both within and across genders.

The Sexual Response Cycle: How Your Body Gets Turned On

CONCEPT 11.15
Landmark research by Masters and Johnson showed that the body's response to sexual stimulation can be characterized in terms of a sexual response cycle consisting of four phases: excitement, plateau, orgasm, and resolution.

sexual response cycle The term used by Masters and Johnson to refer to the characteristic stages of physiological response to sexual stimulation.

What happens within your body when you are sexually aroused? Some of the changes may be obvious—penile erection in the male and vaginal lubrication in the female, for example. But are the bodily responses of men and women as different as they may seem? Or might there be some similarities in how our bodies respond sexually?

Much of what we've learned about the physical response of the body to sexual stimulation comes from the pioneering research of William Masters and Virginia Johnson. They demonstrated that the body responds to sexual stimulation with a characteristic pattern of changes, which they called the **sexual response cycle**. They divided the sexual response cycle into four phases: *excitement, plateau, orgasm,* and *resolution* (Masters & Johnson, 1966). ■ Figure 11.3 shows the levels of sexual arousal during the phases of the sexual response cycle in men and women, respectively. Below, we consider the changes in the body that occur during these phases according to Masters and Johnson's research. These changes are summarized in Table 11.4.

Excitement Phase

There are obvious gender differences in how our bodies respond to sexual stimulation. The penis in males becomes erect; the vagina in women becomes moist through a process called vaginal lubrication. Yet both of these markers of sexual excitement

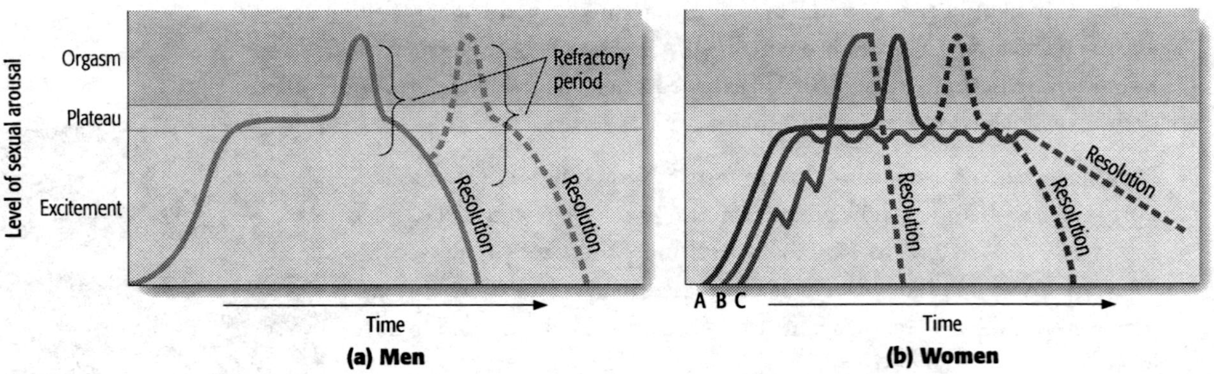

Figure 11.3 The Sexual Response Cycle
Here we see the level of sexual arousal across the four phases of the cycle. 1. Men enter a refractory period after orgasm in which they become unresponsive to sexual stimulation. But, as indicated by the broken line, men may become aroused again to the point of orgasm once the refractory period is past. 2. Women do not enter a refractory period. Pattern A shows a woman's cycle with multiple orgasms, as indicated by the dotted line. Pattern B shows a response cycle in which the woman reaches the plateau stage but does not achieve orgasm. Pattern C shows a pattern leading to orgasm in which the woman quickly passes through the plateau phase.

TABLE 11.4 Sexual Response Cycle: How Our Bodies Respond to Sexual Stimulation

Phase of Sexual Response	In Males	In Females	In Both Genders
Excitement Phase	Vasocongestion results in erection. The testes begin to elevate. Skin on the scrotum tenses and thickens.	Vasocongestion swells the vaginal tissue, the clitoris, and the area surrounding the opening of the vagina. Vaginal lubrication appears. The inner two-thirds of the vagina expand, and the vaginal walls thicken and turn a deeper color.	Vasocongestion of the genital tissues occurs. Heart rate, muscle tension (*myotonia*), and blood pressure increase. Nipples may become erect.
Plateau Phase	The tip of the penis turns a deep reddish-purple. The testes become completely elevated. Droplets of semen may be released from the penile opening before ejaculation.	The inner two-thirds of the vagina expands fully. The outer third of the vagina thickens. The clitoris retracts behind its hood, and the uterus elevates and increases in size.	Vasocongestion increases. Myotonia, heart rate, and blood pressure continue to increase.
Orgasm Phase	Sensations of impending ejaculation lasting 2 to 3 seconds precede the ejaculatory reflex. Orgasmic contractions propel semen through the penis and out of the body.	Contractions of the pelvic muscles surrounding the vagina occur.	Orgasmic release of sexual tension occurs, producing intense feelings of pleasure. Muscle spasms occur throughout the body; blood pressure, heart rate, and breathing rate reach a peak.
Resolution Phase	Men become physiologically incapable of achieving another orgasm or ejaculation for a period of time called the refractory period.	Multiple orgasms may occur if the woman desires it and sexual stimulation continues.	Lacking continued sexual stimulation, myotonia and vasocongestion lessen and the body gradually returns to its prearoused state.

reflect the same underlying biological process: **vasocongestion**, or pooling of blood in bodily tissues. When we are sexually stimulated, blood rushes to our genitals. In males, the pooling of blood in the penis causes it to swell, producing an erection. The penis consists of spongy tissue, not bone. These spongy masses soak up blood when the man becomes sexually aroused and thus become enlarged and stiff.

vasocongestion Swelling of tissues with blood, a process that accounts for penile erection and vaginal lubrication during sexual arousal.

In females, vasocongestion causes the walls of the vagina to swell, which forces moisture through the lining of the vagina, creating vaginal lubrication. The testes in men expand, as do the earlobes in both genders and the breasts in women. The testes and scrotum begin to elevate and the skin covering the scrotum tenses and thickens.

Vasocongestion causes the vaginal walls to thicken and the inner two-thirds of the vagina to expand. The uterus becomes elevated. The nipples may become erect in both men and women, especially if they are directly stimulated. Both men and women experience increased muscle tension throughout the body, as well as increased heart rate and blood pressure.

The **clitoris** in the female, composed of tissue that is similar to the penis in males, also enlarges and becomes erect in response to vasocongestion. The clitoris is a unique organ, the only organ in either sex devoted exclusively to sexual pleasure. (The penis

clitoris A sex organ in the female that is highly sensitive to sexual stimulation.

serves multiple functions—not just sexual pleasure but also passage of urine and sperm.) The clitoris is tightly packed with nerve endings and so is extremely sensitive to touch. It is the woman's most erotically sensitive organ, which explains why women typically masturbate through clitoral stimulation rather than vaginal penetration. Although the vagina also contains nerve endings that are sensitive to sexual stimulation, most of the sensory input that triggers orgasm in the woman comes from stimulation of the clitoris, even during intercourse (Mah & Binik, 2001). The thrusting of the penis during intercourse tugs on the clitoris, providing a source of indirect pleasurable stimulation.

Plateau Phase

The *plateau phase* precedes orgasm. Sexual arousal "plateaus" at a fairly high but stable level (see Figure 11.3). The tip of the penis turns a purplish hue, a sign of increasing vasocongestion. The testes become further elevated in preparation for ejaculation. Droplets of sperm-carrying seminal fluid are secreted and accumulate at the tip of the penis. This is why women may become pregnant even if the man doesn't fully ejaculate.

Vasocongestion in women leads to greater swelling of the tissues in the outer vagina and around the vaginal opening. The inner part of the vagina expands fully. The uterus reaches its full elevation and increases in size. The clitoris withdraws beneath a flap of tissue called the *clitoral hood*.

myotonia A state of muscle tension or rigidity.

Increased **myotonia** (muscle tension) may cause the face to grimace and muscles in the hands and feet to contract in spasms. Heart rate and breathing rate increase further in both genders, as does blood pressure.

Orgasmic Phase

Orgasm, like erection and lubrication, is a reflex. In the orgasm reflex, rhythmic contractions of the pelvic muscles occur, resulting in a release of sexual tension and feelings of intense pleasure. In both genders, orgasm is accompanied by muscle spasms throughout the body. Blood pressure and heart rate reach their peaks. The heart beats up to 180 times a minute. In the female, the pelvic muscles around the vagina contract rhythmically. Women typically experience between three and 15 contractions in total.

In the male, orgasm occurs in two stages of muscular contractions. In the first stage, pelvic contractions cause seminal fluid to collect in a small tube at the base of the penis. Muscles close off the urinary bladder to prevent urine from mixing with semen. This pooling of semen produces the feeling that nothing will stop the ejaculate from "coming"—a sensation, called *ejaculatory inevitability,* lasting perhaps two to three seconds. In the second stage, contractions of pelvic muscles propel the ejaculate through the penis and out of the body. Sensations of pleasure are typically associated with the strength of the contractions and the amount of semen. The first few contractions are most intense.

Resolution Phase

The resolution phase follows orgasm. The body now returns to its prearoused state. Following ejaculation, the man loses his erection. The testes and scrotum return to normal size. The scrotum regains its wrinkled appearance.

In women, blood is released from engorged areas. The nipples return to normal size. The clitoris, vagina, and surrounding tissue shrink to their prearoused sizes. Most muscle tension disappears within five minutes after orgasm in both men and women. Blood pressure, heart rate, and respiration return to normal within a few minutes. Both men and women may feel relaxed and satisfied.

Despite these similarities, the resolution phase is characterized by an important gender difference. Unlike women, men enter a *refractory period*. During this period, they cannot experience another orgasm or ejaculation. The refractory period of adolescent males may last only minutes. In men aged 50 and above, it may last from several minutes to a day. Women do not experience a refractory period. With continued stimulation they are capable of becoming quickly rearoused to the point of repeated (multiple) orgasms.

Now that we've examined how the body responds to sexual stimulation, let us consider the variations that exist in the directionality of sexual attraction.

© NBCU Photo Bank via AP Images

Pioneering sex researchers William Masters and Virginia Johnson, featured here in *Time* magazine.

Sexual Orientation

Sexual orientation refers to the direction of one's erotic attraction and romantic interests—whether one is attracted to members of one's own sex, the opposite sex, or both sexes. Heterosexuals are sexually attracted to members of the opposite sex. Gay males and lesbians are attracted to members of their own sex. And bisexuals are attracted to members of both sexes. Yet the boundaries between these different sexual orientations may not be as clearly drawn as you might think.

CONCEPT 11.16
Sexual orientation refers to the direction of one's erotic and romantic attraction: toward members of one's own gender, the opposite gender, or both genders.

sexual orientation The directionality of one's erotic interests.

In the 1930s and 1940s, the famed sex researcher Alfred Kinsey (1894–1956) and his associates challenged the widely held assumption that homosexuality and heterosexuality are mutually exclusive categories—that a person is either homosexual or heterosexual and never anything in between. Kinsey and his colleagues conducted the first large-scale survey of sexual practices by interviewing nearly 12,000 people in the United States about their sexual behaviors, including homosexual behavior.

Kinsey was a controversial figure—a quiet man who ignited a storm of controversy. Though trained as a zoologist, Kinsey decided to study intimate sexual behavior in humans. He and his associates conducted the first large-scale survey of sexual behavior in the United States—who was doing what with whom. At the time, America was rather close-lipped about sexuality, and even many scientists did not consider it a topic fit for scientific study. Kinsey believed that any topic, especially one as important to people as their sexuality, was open to scientific exploration. Kinsey and his research team conducted detailed interviews, asking people the kinds of questions no one had ever asked before—questions about how many sexual partners they had before marriage, whether they masturbated, whether they had extramarital affairs, and so on.

CONCEPT 11.17
Sexual orientation is generally conceptualized as a continuum ranging from exclusive homosexuality on one end to exclusive heterosexuality on the other end.

In Kinsey's research, most people said they were exclusively heterosexual or homosexual, but many reported sexual attraction to both sexes or felt they were primarily but not exclusively homosexual or heterosexual. "The world," Kinsey and his colleagues wrote, "is not to be divided into sheep and goats. . . . Only the human mind invents categories and tries to force facts into separated pigeonholes. The living world is a continuum in each and every one of its aspects" (Kinsey, Pomeroy, & Martin, 1948). Kinsey represented sexual orientation on a continuum extending from exclusive heterosexuality on one end to exclusive homosexuality on the other. Like Kinsey, many investigators today conceptualize sexual orientation as a continuum with many gradations, much like the colors in the spectrum of a rainbow.

How many people identify themselves as gay? Although survey results vary, a recent national survey reported that among men aged 18 to 44, 2.3 percent identified themselves as homosexual and 1.8 percent as bisexual (Mosher, Chandra, & Jones, 2005). Among women in that same age range, 1.3 percent considered themselves homosexual and 2.8 percent bisexual. Same-sex sexual practices are more commonly reported. Anal

© Michael Haegele/Corbis

© Anton Gvozdikov/Shutterstock.com

Kinsey proposed that sexual orientation varies along a continuum from exclusive heterosexuality to exclusive homosexuality.

receptive sex (penile penetration) during the past year is reported by about 4 to 5 percent of men, according to most recent national survey of sexual behaviors in the U.S. (NSSHB, 2010). About 9 percent of women aged 20 to 24 report giving oral sex to another woman in the past year, but the percentages decline to 4 percent or less for older women. Among men, between 5 and 8 percent of men under the age of 60 report giving oral sex to another man during the past year.

Psychological Theories of Sexual Orientation

What are the origins of sexual orientation? How would you explain your own sexual orientation? Though the causes of sexual orientation remain under study, one thing is clear: People don't consciously choose to be gay or straight. We don't make a conscious decision to adopt a particular sexual orientation, as we might select a college major or a life partner. Theories of the origins of sexual orientation abound, but none yet offers a full picture.

In an early attempt to explain sexual orientation, Freud (1922/1959) claimed that heterosexuality develops from a "normal" process of identification with the parent of the same sex. In contrast, he believed that homosexuality results from an *overidentification* with the parent of the opposite sex—boys with their mothers, girls with their fathers. Evidence, however, challenges this view. Investigators find such great variation among families of gay males, lesbians, and heterosexuals that no one pattern applies in all cases (Isay, 1990). Many gay males had close relationships with their fathers, whereas many heterosexual males had close relationships with their mothers.

As compared with people with a heterosexual orientation, gay males and lesbians generally recall having engaged in more cross-gender behaviors in childhood, such as preferring the clothes, games, and toys typically associated with the opposite sex—a finding that squares with Freud's expectations of gender role reversals (Lippa, 2008; Rieger, Linsenmeier, & Bailey, 2009). But does this evidence confirm Freud's views? Not necessarily. It is possible that underlying biological factors, such as genetic influences, are at play in determining gender nonconforming behaviors in childhood (Knafo, Iervolino, & Plomin, 2005). We should also note some limitations to these findings. Many gay males and lesbians had interest patterns in childhood that were typical of their own gender. Recognize, too, that gay males are found among the ranks of the most "macho" football and hockey players.

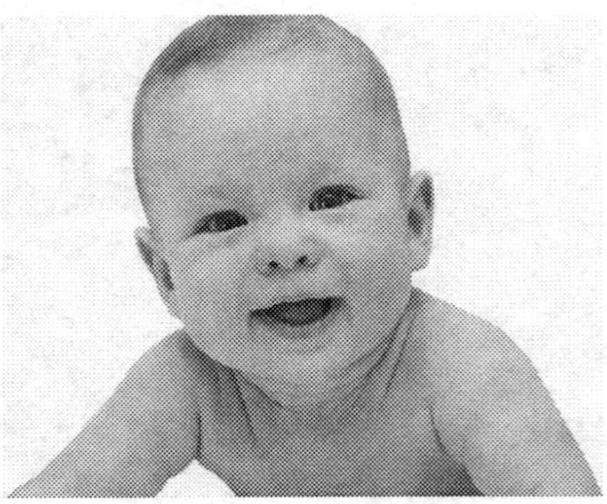

© Irina Rogova/Shutterstock.com

Was this baby born gay or heterosexual? Though evidence points to roles for genetic factors, we still have much to learn about the origins of sexual orientation.

Many gay males report childhood recollections of feeling and acting "different" than their peers at a very young age—often as early as three or four(Isay, 1990). Gay men are more likely than heterosexual comparison groups to recall being more sensitive than other boys and having fewer male buddies (Bailey & Zucker, 1995). Perhaps, as these boys mature, feelings of differentness become transformed into erotic attractions. As psychologist Darryl Bem (1996) put it, what was exotic now becomes erotic. A similar process may occur in girls who develop a lesbian sexual orientation.

Biological Theories of Sexual Orientation

Identical (MZ) twins are more likely to have the same sexual orientation than fraternal (DZ) twins, a finding that supports a genetic contribution to sexual orientation

(Bailey, 2003; Hyde, 2005). This pattern is found even among twins who were separated shortly after birth and raised in different families. But the fact that one identical twin is gay or heterosexual doesn't necessarily mean that the other will follow suit. Life experiences and environmental factors also influence the development of sexual orientation (Kendler et al., 2000; Långström et al., 2008, 2010). Moreover, genetic factors appear to play a larger role in determining homosexuality in men than in women (LeVay, 2003).

CONCEPT 11.18
While the underlying causes of sexual orientation continue to be debated, contemporary theorists focus on the interplay of biological and environmental factors.

What about the role of sex hormones? Most studies fail to find any differences in circulating sex hormones in adult gay males and lesbians in comparison with their heterosexual counterparts (LeVay, 2003). However, scientists speculate that the male sex hormone testosterone may play a role in shaping the developing brain during prenatal development in ways that later affect sexual orientation (LeVay, 2003).

In sum, research on the origins of sexual orientation remains inconclusive. Most experts believe that sexual orientation is explained not by any single factor but, rather, by a combination of genes, hormones, and the environment interacting throughout the life span (Bailey, Dunne, & Martin, 2000; Långström et al., 2010). As it is possible to arrive at the same destination via different routes, we should allow for the possibility that multiple pathways are involved in explaining the development of sexual orientation (Garnets, 2002). Table 11.5 explores some of the common myths about sexual orientation.

Cultural Differences in Attitudes Toward Homosexuality

Attitudes toward homosexuality vary widely across cultures. Some condemn it; others accept it. In some tribal societies, male homosexuality is practiced as a rite of passage for males into adulthood. In others, homosexual men are accorded an acceptable social role in which they are permitted to dress like women, perform women's tasks, and take the receptive (female) sexual role in sexual contacts with other men (Ford & Beach, 1951).

CONCEPT 11.19
In some cultures, an accepted social role is accorded to men who adopt female social and sexual roles.

We know little about lesbianism in non-Western cultures. The available evidence indicates that lesbianism is less common, or at least less commonly reported, than male homosexuality (Ford & Beach, 1951). This cross-cultural evidence is consistent with

TABLE 11.5 Myths vs. Facts About Sexual Orientation

Myth	Fact
A person's sexual orientation is a matter of choice.	Sexual orientation is not a matter of personal choice. One does not choose to be homosexual any more than one chooses to be heterosexual.
Children raised by gay or lesbian parents will turn out to be maladjusted or become gay themselves.	Children raised by gay or lesbian couples turn out to be as well adjusted as other children (Allen & Burrell, 1996; Victor& Fish, 1995). Nor is there any evidence that children raised by gay parents are more likely than other children to become gay.
You are either completely homosexual or completely heterosexual.	Since the time of Kinsey, investigators have classified sexual orientation on the basis of a continuum between exclusive homosexuality and exclusive heterosexuality.
Rates of homosexuality have increased sharply in recent years.	Though homosexuality is more openly discussed today, there is no evidence that underlying rates of homosexuality have changed in a significant way.
Gay males are responsible for most cases of sexual abuse of young boys.	Not true. The great majority of molesters of young boys and young girls are heterosexual men.
Gay males and lesbians really would prefer to be members of the opposite sex.	Not true. Gay males and lesbians have a gender identity that is consistent with their anatomic gender.
Homosexuality is mostly about sex.	Not so. Homosexuality, like heterosexuality, is about patterns of sexual attraction, not how often—or even if—one engages in sexual relationships.

findings from our own culture indicating that homosexual interest and activity are generally less common among women.

Perhaps the answer has to do with the need to either limit or expand the population. Anthropologists find intolerance toward homosexuality to be more common in cultures in which there is a perceived need to increase the size of the population (Ember, Ember, & Peregrine, 2007). On the other hand, cultures that experience periodic famines appear to be more tolerant of homosexuality, since it may help limit population growth.

Why It Matters

CONCEPT 11.20

Some forms of paraphilia are illegal and for good reason—they are associated with acts that cause harm to others.

homophobia Unreasoning fear and loathing of people with a homosexual sexual orientation.

Negative attitudes toward gay males and lesbians are widespread in our culture. **Homophobia** is a persistent, irrational fear of gay males or lesbians. Many people with homophobic attitudes feel justified in treating gay men and lesbians rudely, discriminating against them, or even acting violently toward them. Homophobic individuals may have rigid personalities and attitudes and cannot tolerate any deviation from their views of what is normal or appropriate behavior. The harm that homophobia can cause—ranging from insults directed toward gay men and lesbians to discrimination to outright physical attacks ("gay bashing")—highlights the importance of understanding the roots of the problem and developing ways of increasing tolerance (Nevid, Rathus, & Greene, 2008).

Atypical Sexual Variations: The Case of Paraphilias

paraphilia A psychological disorder involving atypical or deviant patterns of sexual attraction.

fetishism A type of paraphilia involving use of objects as sources of sexual arousal.

transvestism A type of paraphilia involving cross-dressing for purposes of sexual arousal.

voyeurism A type of paraphilia that involves watching unsuspecting others as they disrobe or engage in sexual activities.

exhibitionism A type of paraphilia characterized by exposing one's genitals to unsuspecting others for purposes of sexual arousal.

pedophilia A type of paraphilia involving sexual attraction to children.

sexual sadism A type of paraphilia involving the infliction of physical suffering or humiliation on another person for purposes of sexual gratification.

sexual masochism A type of paraphilia involving the receipt of painful or humiliating experiences as part of a sexual act.

The word **paraphilia** is derived from the Greek roots *para,* meaning "to the side of," and *philia,* meaning "love." People with paraphilias are sexually attracted to stimuli or situations that are "to the side of" the normal range of sexual variation (see Table 11.6). They may be sexually excited by caressing objects such as women's shoes, as in **fetishism**; wearing clothing of the opposite sex, as in **transvestism**; watching unsuspecting others disrobe or engage in sexual activities, as in **voyeurism**; or displaying their genitals to shock strangers, as in **exhibitionism**.

Some paraphilic behaviors are illegal and for good reason: They cause harm to others. For example, acts of exhibitionism and voyeurism violate the rights of others and can have damaging psychological effects on victims. **Pedophilia**, in which adults are sexually attracted to children, can cause severe psychological and physical harm when these urges are expressed in the form of child molestation. In **sexual sadism**, a person desires to inflict pain or humiliation on others for purposes of sexual gratification. On the other hand, some forms of paraphilic behavior, such as fetishism and transvestism, may not violate other people's rights.

Paraphilias are believed to occur almost exclusively among men, with one exception: **sexual masochism**, in which the person desires to experience pain or humiliation during sexual contacts. Even sexual masochism predominantly involves men. Not all cases of paraphilia involve overt acts. In some cases, people have paraphilic urges but do not act upon them.

People develop paraphilias for different reasons. Some exhibitionists may be shy and have difficulty relating to women or establishing meaningful sexual relationships (Leue et al., 2004). Flashing their genitals may be a substitute for the adult relationships they find too frightening or threatening to develop. A response of shock or surprise from their victims may reinforce their flagging sense of masculinity. Men with pedophilia may feel secure only in sexual relationships with children whom they can easily master. Or they may have been abused themselves as children and feel compelled to reverse the situation, with themselves in the aggressor's role.

TABLE 11.6 Paraphilias: Examples of Atypical Patterns of Sexual Attraction

Paraphilia	Related Behavior	Associated Features
Fetishism	Manipulating or caressing objects for sexual gratification	The person may masturbate while rubbing or fondling the object or smelling it. Women's undergarments, leather boots, high-heeled shoes, and other articles made of rubber, leather, silk, or furs are commonly used as fetishistic objects.
Transvestism	Cross-dressing for sexual arousal and gratification	Transvestism represents a type of fetishism in which the fetishistic object is worn rather than handled. Transvestites are almost always heterosexual men. They may cross-dress in private while masturbating and imagining themselves as women whom they are stroking. Some frequent transvestite clubs or become involved in a transvestic subculture.
Exhibitionism ("flashing")	Exposing one's genitals to unsuspecting strangers for sexual gratification	Exhibitionists seek to elicit a reaction of surprise or shock from their victims, perhaps to buttress their flagging sense of masculinity.
Voyeurism	"Peeping" at unsuspecting persons who are nude, disrobing, or engaging in sexual activity	Voyeurs may masturbate while peeping but typically do not seek any direct contact with their victims.
Sexual masochism and sexual sadism	Acts in which the individual is subject to pain or humiliation (masochism) or inflicts pain or humiliation on others (sadism) for purposes of sexual gratification	Sexual masochists and sadists may engage in mutually gratifying, consensual interactions—called *sadomasochism* (S & M)—to satisfy each other's sexual needs. The pain involved is usually mild or simulated (as when felt whips are used) and is incorporated within elaborate sexual rituals. In a few cases, sexual sadists commit sexual assaults on nonconsenting victims.
Pedophilia	Sexual contact with children	Most people with pedophilia do not fit the stereotype of a man in a trenchcoat lurking around the playground or schoolyard. Rather, most are otherwise law-abiding men, often married with children of their own. In most cases, they are either friends or relatives of the victim or victim's family.

Learning theorists believe that conditioning may account for paraphilic behavior. For example, people with rubber fetishes (sexual interest in touching or fondling rubber clothing) may have had experiences dating back to infancy in which erections were associated with contact with rubber pants or diapers (Reinisch, 1990). Such experiences might then have led to a conditioned response (sexual arousal) connected with touching the object.

Biological factors may also play a role. For example, investigators find different patterns of brain wave activity between men with paraphilias and other men in response to deviant images (fetishistic and sadomasochistic) and control images (nude women, genital intercourse) (Waismann et al., 2003). Although the meaning of these differences is not yet clear, they suggest that the brains of men with paraphilias may respond differently to sexual stimuli than those of other men.

Concept Chart 11.2 reviews key concepts relating to sexual response and behavior.

© Jutta Klee/CORBIS

Exhibitionists gain sexual satisfaction by provoking a shocked expression in their unsuspecting victims.

AIDS and Other STDs: Is Your Behavior Putting You at Risk?

AIDS (acquired immune deficiency syndrome) has become one of history's worst epidemics. More than 40 million people worldwide are living with HIV, the virus that causes AIDS. HIV/AIDS has claimed more than 430,000 lives in the United States, and

CONCEPT CHART 11.2 Sexual Response and Behavior

© macka/Shutterstock.com

Concept	Description	Additional Comments
Sexual response cycle	The characteristic pattern of bodily responses to sexual stimulation	According to Masters and Johnson, the sexual response cycle consists of four phases: excitement, plateau, orgasm, and resolution.
Sexual orientation	The direction of sexual attraction toward one's own gender, toward the opposite gender, or toward both genders	The roots of sexual orientation remain obscure, but interest among investigators and theorists has focused on biological factors (genetics, prenatal sex hormones) and psychosocial factors (self-perceptions in childhood of differentness, relationship patterns with parents).
Sexual behavior	Includes masturbation, sexual intercourse, oral sex, and anal sex	Though the human body can respond to many forms of sexual stimulation, sexual behavior is strongly influenced by cultural learning, personal values, and individual experiences, not simply by biological drives or capacities for sexual response.
Paraphilias	Atypical or deviant patterns of sexual attraction	Some forms of paraphilia are associated with behaviors that are illegal because of the harm these behaviors cause to others.

some 24 million lives worldwide, since the start of the epidemic (Bongaarts, Pelletier, & Gerland, 2010a, 2010b; H. I. Hall et al., 2008). Approximately 56,000 people in the United States contract HIV annually (CDC, 2011).

HIV is transmitted by contact with infected bodily fluids, generally through intimate sexual contact or needle-sharing. HIV attacks and disables the body's immune system, making the person vulnerable to other infections the body is normally able to fend off.

sexually transmitted disease (STD) A disease caused by an infectious agent that is spread by sexual contact.

HIV/AIDS is the most threatening **sexually transmitted disease (STD)** (also called a *sexually transmitted infection* or STI), but it is far from the most common. Approximately one million people in the United States are living with HIV or AIDS, but genital herpes affects at least 45 million Americans over the age of 12 (National Women's Health Information Center, 2009). More than 1 million new cases of chlamydia, the most common bacterial STD, are reported annually in the United States (CDC, 2010c). Some 20 million Americans are infected with *human papilloma viruses (HPVs)*, the group of viruses that cause genital warts. Most sexually active people can expect to contract HPV at some point in their lives (CDC, 2010d).

Many STDs, not just HIV/AIDS, pose serious threats to our health. HPV, for example, is the major cause of cervical cancer, accounting for at least 70 percent of cases (Drucker, 2010; National Cancer Institute, 2009b). Fortunately, an effective vaccine is now available that protects women from strains of HPV that cause most forms of cervical cancer (Barnack, Reddy, & Swain, 2010; CDC, 2010e). However, the vaccine does not protect women who have already been infected with the virus or against some less common types of HPV not covered by the vaccine.

CONCEPT 11.21
Many STDs, not just HIV/AIDS, pose serious threats to our health.

Untreated gonorrhea and chlamydia can lead to infertility in women, and untreated gonorrhea in men can lead to a serious infection of the internal reproductive system, which can cause fertility problems. Another bacterial disease, syphilis, can lead to serious damage to the heart and brain if left untreated. Genital herpes can cause serious complications, especially in women, including increased risks of miscarriage and cervical cancer.

Prevention and Treatment

CONCEPT 11.22
Many STDs, not just HIV/AIDS, pose serious threats to our health.

Though antibiotics can cure bacterial forms of STD, they are of no use against viral STDs. Antiviral drugs may help control viral STDs, such as HIV/AIDS and genital herpes, but they cannot eliminate the infectious organisms from the body. The use of antiviral drugs has significantly extended the lives of AIDS patients and raises hopes that HIV/AIDS may become a chronic but manageable disease. The lack of a cure for viral STDs, including HIV/AIDS, as well as awareness of the risks posed by untreated bacterial STDs, underscores the importance of prevention and early treatment.

Arming yourself with information about how these diseases are transmitted, early signs of infection, and available treatments (see Table 11.7) is an important step in protecting yourself from STDs. But information alone does not reduce the risks of transmitting STDs: It must be put into practice through changes in behavior. The following section lists suggestions for safer sexual practices and medical screening.

Protecting Yourself and Your Partners from STDs

CONCEPT 11.23
Modifiable behaviors such as unprotected sex and needle-sharing are major risk factors for transmission of sexually transmitted diseases, including HIV/AIDS.

The only sure way to prevent the sexual transmission of STDs is to practice lifelong abstinence or maintain a monogamous relationship with an uninfected partner who is also monogamous. Short of that, you can reduce the risk from sexual contact rather than eliminate it entirely; that is, you can practice *safer* sex rather than *safe* sex. Here are some guidelines that can lower the risk of contracting an STD or suffering the consequences of an untreated STD (adapted from Nevid, Rathus, & Greene, 2008).

1. *Be careful in your choice of sex partners.* Get to know the person's sexual background before engaging in sexual activity. (Even so, getting to know someone is no guarantee that the person is not carrying HIV or some other infectious agent.)
2. *Avoid multiple partners, especially partners who themselves may have multiple partners.*
3. *Communicate your concerns.* Be assertive with your partner. Openly state your concerns about the risks of AIDS and other STDs and the need to practice safer sex.
4. *Avoid engaging in sexual contact with anyone with a sore or blister around the genitals.* Inspect your partner's sex organs before any sexual contact. Rashes, blisters, chancres, discharges, warts, disagreeable odors, and so on should be treated as warning signs of a possible infection. But be aware that some STDs, including HIV infection, do not have any obvious signs.
5. *Avoid unprotected sexual contact.* Latex condoms (not "natural" condoms, which are more porous) offer the most reliable protection against the spread of HIV during sexual contact. Spermicides should be used along with latex condoms, not as a substitute for them. Although latex condoms may not prevent the transmission of genital herpes between an infected and uninfected partner, they can reduce the risk of transmission (Gupta, Warren, & Wald, 2007).
6. *Obtain a medical evaluation if you suspect that you may have been exposed to a sexually transmitted disease.*
7. *Get regular medical checkups to detect and treat disorders you may not be aware you have.*
8. *When in doubt, don't.* Abstain from intimate sexual contact if you have any doubts about whether it is potentially harmful. Your safety and that of your partner should be your top priority.

TABLE 11.7 Major Types of STDs

	Mode of Transmission	Symptoms	Treatment
Bacterial STDs			
Gonorrhea	Sexual contact (vaginal, oral, or anal intercourse); from mother to newborn during childbirth	Men may have a yellowish, thick penile discharge and burning urination; though most women do not show early symptoms, some have increased vaginal discharge, burning urination, and irregular menstrual bleeding.	Antibiotics
Syphilis	Sexual contact; by touching an infectious chancre (sore)	A round, painless, but hard chancre develops at the site of infection within two to four weeks; symptoms progress through additional stages if left untreated.	Antibiotics
Chlamydia in women, or nongonococcal urethritis (NGU) in men	Sexual contact; touching an eye after contact with genitals of an infected partner; from infected mother to newborn during childbirth	Most women are symptom-free, but some have frequent and painful urination, lower abdominal pain and inflammation, and vaginal discharge. Men, too, are generally symptom-free but may have gonorrhea-like symptoms.	Antibiotics
Viral STDs			
HIV/AIDS	Sexual contact; needle sharing; receiving contaminated blood; from mother to fetus during pregnancy or from mother to child during childbirth or breastfeeding	Infected persons may be initially symptom-free or have mild flu-like symptoms, but may progress to develop full-blown AIDS.	Antiviral drugs may help control the virus but do not cure the disease.
Genital herpes	Sexual contact	Painful, reddish bumps appear around the genitals, thighs, buttocks, or in the vagina or on the cervix in women. The bumps may develop into blisters or sores that fill with pus and break open before healing over.	Antiviral drugs can help control outbreaks but do not rid the body of the virus.
Viral hepatitis	Sexual contact, especially anal contact in the case of hepatitis A; contact with infected fecal matter; transfusion of contaminated blood (especially for hepatitis B and C)	Symptoms range from absence of symptoms to mild flu-like symptoms to more severe symptoms, such as fever, abdominal pain, vomiting, and "jaundiced" (yellowish) skin and eyes.	Bed rest and possible use of the drug alpha interferon in cases of hepatitis C
Genital warts	Sexual contact; contact with infected towels or clothing	Painless warts resembling cauliflowers may develop on the genitals, the internal reproductive organs, around the anus, or in the rectum.	Warts may be removed, but the virus (HPV) remains in the body.

11.2 MODULE REVIEW Sexual Response and Behavior

Recite It

What are the phases of the sexual response cycle?

- The excitement phase is characterized by erection in the male and vaginal lubrication in the female.
- The plateau phase is an advanced state of arousal that precedes orgasm.

- The orgasmic phase is characterized by orgasmic contractions of the pelvic musculature.
- During the resolution phase, the body returns to its prearoused state.

What are the origins of sexual orientation?

- The origins remain unknown. Psychological theories attempt to explain sexual orientation in terms of patterns of child rearing and early childhood experiences. Biological theories note possible roles for genetics and prenatal sex hormones.

How do attitudes toward homosexuality vary across cultures?

- Variations in cultural attitudes range from condemnation in some cultures to legitimization of a homosexual social role in others.

What are paraphilias?

- Paraphilias are atypical or deviant patterns of sexual attraction or arousal, such as fetishism (sexual arousal connected with inanimate objects such as shoes) and exhibitionism (sexual arousal from exposing one's genitals to unsuspecting strangers).

Recall It

1. Regarding the human sexual response cycle, match the following terms with their descriptions: i. excitement phase; ii. plateau phase; iii. orgasmic phase; iv. resolution phase
   a. sexual release, intense pleasure.
   b. body returns to prearoused state.
   c. increased myotonia and further increases in vasocongestion.
   d. initial response to sexual stimulation.
2. All of the following are sexual orientations *except*
   a. transsexuality. c. homosexuality.
   b. bisexuality. d. heterosexuality.
3. Cliff seeks sexual gratification by dressing in women's clothing. He has a paraphilia called ________.
   a. transsexualism. c. transvestism.
   b. fetishism. d. exhibitionism.
4. Bacterial forms of STDs include
   a. HIV/AIDS. c. genital herpes.
   b. HPV. d. chlamydia.

Think About It

- How do your sexual practices reflect your personal values?
- Are you struggling with issues concerning your sexual orientation? Do you know someone who is? Are there resources on your campus or in your community that provide counseling services to people with these types of questions? How can you find out more about these services?
- What are you doing to protect yourself from STDs? What—if anything—might you do differently?

Sexual Dysfunctions

MODULE 11.3

- What are sexual dysfunctions?
- What are the causes of sexual dysfunctions?
- What are the aims of sex therapy?

Although our bodies are capable of responding to many types of sexual stimulation, problems do occasionally arise. Some people experience a lack of sexual desire or interest; others have difficulties becoming aroused or reaching orgasm. Occasional problems with sexual interest or response are quite common and may affect virtually everyone at one time or another. Men may occasionally have difficulty achieving erections or may ejaculate sooner than they desire. Women may occasionally have difficulty becoming sexually aroused or reaching orgasm. When these types of problems become persistent and cause distress, they are classified as psychological disorders called **sexual dysfunctions**.

sexual dysfunctions Persistent or recurrent problems with sexual interest, arousal, or response.

As you can see in Concept Chart 11.3, sexual dysfunctions are quite common. Women are more likely to experience problems related to low sexual drive and difficulty or inability to achieve orgasm. Men more often experience difficulties achieving or maintaining erections or suffer from premature ejaculation.

CONCEPT CHART 11.3 Major Types of Sexual Dysfunctions

	Disorder	What It Is/Prevalence Rate (%)	Associated Features/Treatments
Sexual Desire Disorders	Hypoactive sexual desire disorder	Abnormally low level of sexual interest or drive; 32% women, 15% men	May occur in response to hormone deficiencies, relationship problems, depression, or other causes
	Sexual aversion disorder	Revulsion or strong aversion to genital contact; unknown prevalence	Typically represents a fear of sexual contact that may develop in the aftermath of sexual trauma
Sexual Arousal Disorders	Male erectile disorder	Persistent difficulty achieving or maintaining erections; 10–22%	May be due to psychological causes (e.g., self-doubt, performance-related anxiety), physical causes (e.g., diabetes, neurological problems), or a combination of causes
	Female sexual arousal disorder	Failure to become adequately sexually aroused in response to sexual stimulation; 21%*	May be caused by underlying health problems, a sexually repressive cultural or family background, or relationship problems
Orgasmic Disorders	Female orgasmic disorder	Difficulty achieving orgasm in response to adequate levels of sexual stimulation; 26%	Treatment techniques focus on helping women learn more about their sexual responsiveness (through directed masturbation) and transferring this learning to their relationship with their partners
	Male orgasmic disorder	Delay or inability to ejaculate; 8%	Relatively uncommon, but may stem from excessive anxiety, neurological problems, sexual guilt, or hostility toward the partner
	Premature ejaculation	Ejaculation occurring with a minimum of sexual stimulation and before the man desires it; 30%**	Affects men who have difficulty keeping the level of stimulation from rising to the point that the ejaculatory reflex is triggered

Sources: Laumann, Paik, & Rosen, 1999; Rosen & Laumann, 2003; Rosen et al., 2004.

Note: Prevalence rates reflect percentages of adults reporting problems and may not correspond to clinical diagnosis of sexual dysfunctions. Reports of climaxing too early were based on individuals who were sexually active during the past 12-month period. Also, note that the incidence of sexual problems tends to increase with age.

*having trouble lubricating

**climaxing too early

THE BRAIN LOVES A PUZZLE

As you read ahead, use the information in the text to solve the following puzzle:

A doctor tells his patient, a man with erectile dysfunction, that he should try to lose weight along with following other recommended treatments. What do you suppose weight has to do with a man's sexual response?

Although sexual dysfunctions are widespread, relatively few people with sexual problems seek professional help (Nicolosi et al., 2006). People with sexual dysfunctions may not know where to obtain help, or they may avoid seeking help because of the unfortunate but persistent stigma associated with admitting to sexual difficulties. In the following sections we discuss the major types of sexual dysfunctions and methods of therapy available to help people overcome them.

Types of Sexual Dysfunctions

Many different types of sexual problems are classified as sexual dysfunctions. Here we focus on three major classes of sexual dysfunctions: sexual desire disorders, sexual arousal disorders, and orgasmic disorders.

Sexual Desire Disorders

hypoactive sexual desire disorder A type of sexual desire disorder characterized by an absence or lack of sexual interest or desire.

Individuals with these disorders experience a lack of sexual desire or an aversion to genital sexual contact. People with **hypoactive sexual desire disorder**, which is among the most frequently diagnosed sexual dysfunctions, have little or no sexual interest or desire (I. Goldstein et al., 2006; Leiblum et al., 2006). The disorder affects more women than men, but the belief that all men are eager and willing to engage in sex is a myth. People with **sexual aversion disorder** have a strong aversion to genital sexual contact. They may enjoy other forms of affectionate contact, so long as it does not involve the genitals. Sexual aversion disorder often involves a fear of sexual contact that arises in individuals who have suffered some form of sexual trauma, such as childhood sexual abuse or rape.

CONCEPT 11.24

Though occasional problems with sexual interest or response may affect virtually everyone, people with sexual dysfunctions have persistent difficulties with sexual interest, arousal, or response.

sexual aversion disorder A type of sexual desire disorder involving repulsion or strong aversion to genital sexual contact.

male erectile disorder A type of sexual arousal disorder in men characterized by difficulty achieving or maintaining erections sufficient to engage in sexual intercourse.

female sexual arousal disorder A type of sexual arousal disorder in women involving difficulties in becoming sexually aroused.

female orgasmic disorder A type of orgasmic disorder in women characterized by a lack of orgasm, or persistent difficulties in achieving orgasm, following a normal phase of sexual excitement.

male orgasmic disorder A type of orgasmic disorder in men characterized by a lack of orgasm, or persistent difficulties in achieving orgasm, following a normal phase of sexual excitement.

premature ejaculation (PE) A type of orgasmic disorder in men characterized by rapid ejaculation following sexual stimulation.

Sexual Arousal Disorders

These disorders include **male erectile disorder** (also known as *erectile dysfunction*, or *ED*) and **female sexual arousal disorder**. Men with erectile disorder encounter persistent problems achieving or maintaining erections sufficient to engage in sexual intercourse. Women with sexual arousal disorder have persistent difficulty becoming sexually aroused or adequately lubricated.

Orgasmic Disorders

Women with **female orgasmic disorder** and men with **male orgasmic disorder** have problems reaching orgasm or cannot reach orgasm at all. In cases where the individual can achieve orgasm through masturbation but not through sexual relations with a partner, a clinician needs to determine whether there is adequate stimulation during sexual relations for orgasm to occur. However, experts continue to debate how to define sexual dysfunctions, especially in women (McCarthy et al., 2006). For example, do women have a sexual dysfunction if they can achieve orgasm reliably through masturbation but not with their partners? Might their difficulty result from a lack of effective stimulation (especially clitoral stimulation) from their partners rather than an orgasmic disorder?

Premature ejaculation (PE), the most common type of sexual dysfunction in males, is characterized by rapid ejaculation with minimal stimulation. Upwards of one in three men suffer PE at some point in their lives (Laumann et al., 1994).

Causes of Sexual Dysfunctions

There are many causes of sexual dysfunctions, including biological and psychosocial factors.

Biological Causes

Many biological factors can influence sexual interest, arousal, or response, leading to sexual dysfunctions (Rees, Fowler, & Maas, 2007). These conditions include diabetes, multiple sclerosis, spinal-cord injuries, epilepsy, complications from surgery (such as prostate surgery in men), side effects of certain medications, and hormonal problems. Psychoactive drugs, such as cocaine, alcohol, and narcotics, may dampen sexual interest or impair sexual responsiveness.

Testosterone energizes sexual drives in both men and women, and deficiencies of the hormone can dampen sexual desire in both sexes (S. R. Davis, Davison, et al., 2005; S. R. Davis, Moreau, et al., 2008). Although testosterone is a male sex hormone produced in the man's testes, it is also produced in smaller amounts in women's ovaries and in the adrenal glands of both men and women. That being said, most men and women with sexual dysfunctions have normal sex hormone levels. However, women whose adrenal glands and ovaries are surgically removed due to disease, and thus no longer produce testosterone, often report reduced sexual desire (Nappi, Wawra, & Schmitt, 2006; Traish et al., 2006).

Many, perhaps most, cases of erectile disorder can be traced to biological factors, with circulatory problems topping the list (McVary, 2007; Thompson et al., 2005). For example, diabetes can damage the blood vessels and nerves that service the penis,

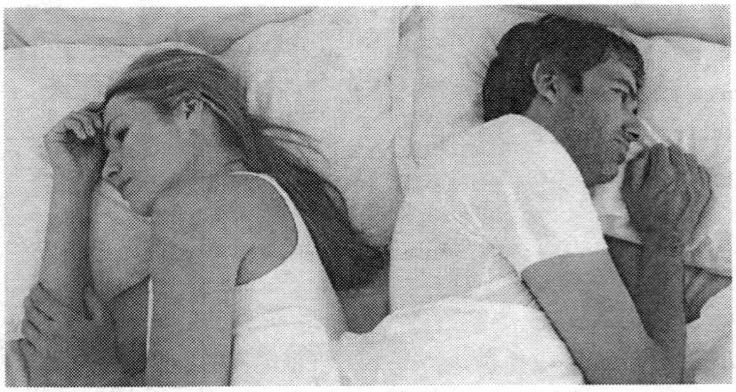
© Sean Prior/Shutterstock.com

Sexually dysfunctional couples often have difficulty communicating their sexual needs and interests.

leading to erectile problems. You probably knew that obesity is a major risk factor for many serious, chronic diseases, including heart disease and diabetes. But did you know that obesity also increases the risk of erectile dysfunction (Bajos et al., 2010)? The good news is that health interventions that focus on helping obese men lose weight and increase activity levels can lead to improved erectile functioning (Esposito et al., 2004).

Psychosocial Causes

Sexual dysfunctions are often rooted in psychological or cultural factors, such as relationship problems, performance-related anxiety, or repressive attitudes in the family toward sexuality. Children reared in sexually repressive cultures or families where negative attitudes toward sexuality prevail may struggle with feelings of anxiety, guilt, or shame when they become sexually active, rather than sexual arousal and pleasure. This is especially true of young women who have been exposed to sexually repressive cultural attitudes and to a sexual double-standard which permits greater sexual expression in men than in women. These women may learn that sex is a marital duty to be performed for reproduction purposes or to satisfy their husband's sexual cravings, not for their own sexual pleasure—a cultural framework that discourages them from learning about their sexual responsiveness or inhibits them from asserting their sexual needs with their partners.

CONCEPT 11.25
The underlying causes of sexual dysfunctions include biological factors, such as neurological or circulatory problems, and psychosocial factors, such as performance anxiety.

→ Concept Link
Maladaptive forms of anxiety are key features of the class of psychological disorders called *anxiety disorders*. See Module 15.2.

performance anxiety Anxiety experienced in performance situations (including sexual acts) stemming from a fear of negative evaluation of one's ability to perform.

Some couples fall into a sexual routine, perhaps even a rut. Couples who fail to communicate their sexual preferences or to regularly invigorate their lovemaking routines may find themselves losing interest. Relationship problems can also affect a couple's sexual responsiveness, especially when conflicts and long-simmering resentments are carried into bed (Moore & Heiman, 2006).

Survivors of rape and other sexual traumas, such as childhood sexual abuse, often develop deep feelings of disgust or revulsion toward sex, which can lead to a sexual aversion disorder (Firestone, Firestone, & Catlett, 2006). Not surprisingly, they often have difficulty responding sexually, even with loving partners. Other emotional factors—especially anxiety, depression, and anger—can also lessen sexual interest or arousal.

Anxiety, especially **performance anxiety**, may make it impossible for a man to achieve or sustain an erection or for a woman to become adequately lubricated or achieve orgasm (Bancroft et al., 2005; McCabe, 2005). Failure to perform then fuels further self-doubts and fears of repeated failure, which in turn heightens anxiety on subsequent occasions, causing yet more failure experiences, and the process repeats itself in the form of a vicious cycle.

Premature ejaculation may arise from a failure to keep the level of stimulation below the man's ejaculatory threshold, or "point of no return." Though ejaculation is a reflex, men need to learn (usually through a trial-and-error procedure) to gauge their level of stimulation so that it does not exceed their ejaculatory threshold. They need to signal their partners to stop stimulation before this point so that their sensations can subside before resuming again.

SLICE OF LIFE Performance anxiety leads people to become spectators of their own performance. Rather than immersing themselves in the sexual act, they mentally scrutinize how their bodies are responding. It is little wonder they have difficulty responding sexually. A man with erectile dysfunction said that on dates leading up to sexual relations he kept picturing his partner's face and how disappointed she'd be if he failed to perform. He went on to say, "By the time we did go to bed, I was paralyzed with anxiety" (cited in Nevid, Rathus, & Greene, 2011). In our culture there is such a deep-rooted connection between the man's ability to perform sexually and his sense of manhood that repeated failure experiences might lead him to feel he is no longer a man. He may consequently suffer a severe loss of self-esteem or become depressed. Performance anxiety may also contribute to male orgasmic disorder, especially in cases where men have difficulty achieving orgasm with a partner. Male orgasmic disorder may also arise from underlying neurological problems, sexual guilt, or hostility toward the partner. Although performance anxiety primarily affects men, women, too, may be burdened with performance anxiety about achieving orgasm.

Sex Therapy

CONCEPT 11.26
Sex therapy is a problem-focused form of therapy that aims to reduce performance anxiety and foster sexual skills and competencies.

The good news is that most cases of sexual dysfunctions can be treated successfully through either biological or psychological approaches, or a combination approach. Sex therapy, a relatively brief form of psychological treatment, was pioneered by William Masters and Virginia Johnson (1970). In sex therapy, the individual, but more commonly the couple, meet with a therapist or a pair of male and female therapists who use behavioral techniques to help them overcome their sexual difficulties. Sex therapy attempts to eliminate performance anxiety by removing pressures to perform.

Masters and Johnson treated couples in an intensive, two-week program that consisted of daily treatment sessions and nightly sexual homework assignments. An important part of their treatment method was **sensate-focus exercises,** in which partners massaged each other in nongenital areas of the body while relaxing in the nude. These exercises provided a source of pleasurable stimulation without the performance demands associated with sexual intercourse. Indeed, couples were instructed to postpone having intercourse until their confidence levels were restored. They were also helped to open channels of communication about the types of stimulation they found arousing and to gently guide or direct one another in providing effective stimulation.

sensate-focus exercises A technique used in sex therapy that consists of nongenital massage to lessen the anxiety associated with sexual interactions.

A number of specific techniques are used in sex therapy. For example, therapists may use a program of directed masturbation to help women who have never been able to achieve an orgasm by themselves or with their partners. Reported success rates from such programs are in the 70 to 90 percent range. The treatment itself typically consists of a therapist directing the woman to practice a series of masturbation exercises in the privacy of her own home. The purpose is to help the woman explore her body's sexual response and learn the skills needed to bring about an orgasm. Women are then guided to transfer this learning to their relationships with their partners. Another example is the *stop-start method,* the most common treatment for premature ejaculation. In this method, a couple practice suspending sexual stimulation before the man reaches the level at which his ejaculation reflex is triggered. The two partners then resume stimulation once his sensations subside, continuing to practice these start-stop cycles until the man gains better control. Overall, most people with sexual dysfunctions benefit from some form of sex therapy.

Biological therapies are also available to help people with sexual dysfunctions (Montorsi et al., 2010). Testosterone may help boost sexual interest or desire, but safety concerns about potential health risks of using the hormone need to be considered (Basaria et al., 2010; Davis et al., 2008). Viagra and other similar drugs are widely used to help men with erectile dysfunction achieve more reliable erections (Qaseem et al., 2009). These types of drugs work by relaxing blood vessels in the penis, allowing them to expand and carry more blood, which is needed to induce and sustain an erection. Although research is ongoing, we still lack safe and effective pharmacological treatments for female sexual dysfunction.

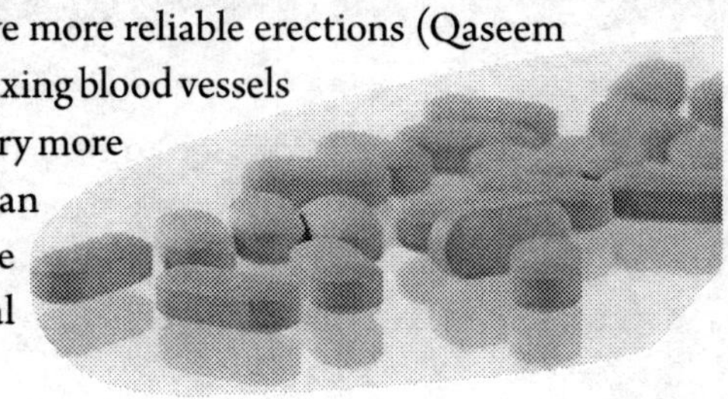
© iStockphoto.com/intst

Some drugs commonly used to treat depression, including the antidepressants Zoloft and Paxil, are also used to treat premature ejaculation. Delayed ejaculation is a common side effect of these drugs, which may be a benefit to men suffering from premature ejaculation.

11.3 MODULE REVIEW Sexual Dysfunctions

Recite It

What are sexual dysfunctions?

➤ Sexual dysfunctions are persistent and distressing problems in sexual interest, arousal, or response. They include sexual desire disorders, sexual arousal disorders, and orgasmic disorders.

What are the causes of sexual dysfunctions?

➤ Sexual dysfunctions can have biological causes, such as declining hormone levels or health problems, and psychosocial causes, such as sex-negative attitudes, communication problems, sexually traumatic experiences, and performance anxiety.

What are the aims of sex therapy?

➤ The general aims of sex therapy are to reduce performance anxiety, foster sexual skills or competencies, and improve communication between sexual partners.

Recall It

1. The term *sexual dysfunction* refers to problems with
   a. sexual response only.
   b. sexual interest or response only.
   c. sexual arousal or response only.
   d. sexual interest, arousal, or response.
2. Match the following sexual dysfunction terms with the appropriate descriptions: i. sexual desire disorders; ii. sexual arousal disorders; iii. orgasmic disorders; iv. premature ejaculation
   a. may include aversion to genital sexual contact.
   b. may occur in response to only minimal stimulation.
   c. difficulty experiencing sexual climax.
   d. includes erectile dysfunction (males) and insufficient lubrication (females).
3. Timothy has virtually no interest in sexual activity. Only rarely does he experience sexual fantasies or desires. Though he doesn't have any problems achieving erections, he wonders why so many people seem so interested in sex. Which type of sexual dysfunction would most probably apply in his case?
   a. sexual aversion disorder
   b. male sexual interest disorder.
   c. male orgasmic disorder.
   d. hypoactive sexual desire disorder.
4. List several *psychosocial* causes of sexual dysfunctions.

Think About It

➤ How are sexual dysfunctions in men and women similar? How are they different?

➤ Have you experienced a problem with sexual arousal or performance? How did it affect you? What did you do about it? Did the information in this chapter raise your awareness about factors that may have contributed to your problem or about ways of dealing with it?

APPLICATION MODULE 11.4 Combating Rape and Sexual Harassment

rape The use or threat of force to compel a person into having sexual intercourse.

statutory rape Sexual intercourse with a person who is under the legal age of consent, even if the person is a willing participant.

We use the term sexual coercion to refer to a continuum of behaviors that range from sexual taunts and insults to outright sexual assault and rape. Rape and sexual harassment are two major forms of sexual coercion. **Rape** is the use or threat of force to compel a person into having sexual intercourse. In cases of **statutory rape**, sexual intercourse occurs

TABLE 11.8 Types of Sexual Harassment

Type of Harassment	Description	Examples
Gender harassment	Making statements or displaying behaviors that are insulting or degrading to women in general	Sexual insults, obscene jokes or humor, offensive graffiti
Seductive behavior	Making unwelcome, inappropriate, and offensive sexual advances	Making repeated, unwanted sexual overtures or requests for dates; sending repeated letters or making repeated phone calls to offer sexual invitations
Sexual bribery	Soliciting sexual activity by promising rewards	Offering to advance someone's career for sexual favors
Sexual coercion	Coercing someone into sexual activity by threat of punishment	Threatening negative job evaluations, job termination, or withholding of promotions for failure to comply with sexual requests
Sexual imposition	Unwelcome sexual contact	Any form of unwelcome touching, including grabbing or fondling, or outright sexual assault

Note: The key feature of sexual harassment is that it is unwanted. Gender harassment is far and away the most common form of sexual harassment, followed by seductive behavior. Sexual bribery and coercion are relatively uncommon, but sexual imposition occurs more often than many people believe.

Source: Adapted from *Sexual Harassment: Myths and Realities*, American Psychological Association, Office of Public Affairs, 1996.

with a person who is under the legal age of consent, even if the person willingly cooperates. **Sexual harassment** is any act in which a person subjects someone else to unwanted sexual remarks, gestures, touching, overtures, or demands for sexual favors in exchange for favored treatment or as a condition of employment or advancement (see Table 11.8).

sexual harassment A form of sexual coercion involving unwelcome sexual comments, jokes, overtures, demands for sexual favors, or outright physical contact.

How Common Are Rape and Sexual Harassment?

Unfortunately, rape and sexual harassment are far too common in our society. The federal government estimates that some 90,000 forcible rapes are reported annually in the United States (U.S. Department of Justice, 2009). The actual numbers are undoubtedly far greater because the great majority of rapes and attempted rapes go unreported (Fisher et al., 2003).

The lifetime risk of rape is shockingly high. The best available estimates indicate that about one woman in four is raped at some point in their lives (Campbell & Wasco, 2005). Approximately 3 percent of college women suffer a rape or attempted rape each year (Fisher et al., 2003). Many married women—as many as 10 to 14 percent—are raped by their husbands (Martin, Taft, & Resick, 2007).

Though the majority of rapes are committed against young women in the 16- to 24-year-old age range, women of all ages, as well as all races and economic classes, are at risk of being raped (Burgess & Morgenbesser, 2005). The incidence of rape is much higher in the United States than in other industrialized societies such as Canada, Great Britain, and Japan.

Men, too, may be raped, although legally the act may be classified as sexual assault because it involves forced anal intercourse or anal penetration by objects, rather than vaginal intercourse. Most but certainly not all of these attacks occur in prison settings. An estimated one in 10 survivors of rape are men (U.S. Department of Justice, 2006). Contrary to the commonly held belief that men who rape other men are gay, most

© iStockphoto.com/Sean Locke

Are they flirting? Or are they just being friendly? Who makes more errors interpreting nonverbal social cues—men or women? What does the evidence show?

assailants are heterosexual men who commit rape as a form of retaliation, humiliation, or domination and control.

The prevalence of sexual harassment is difficult to pin down, because, as with rape, the great majority of women who experience sexual harassment do not file formal complaints. What is clear is that sexual harassment occurs everywhere, from high school to college campuses, from the workplace to the military, and even the Internet (Barak, 2005; Chaiyavej & Morash, 2009; Sullivan, 2006). Survey evidence shows that between 25 and 30 percent of female college students report experiencing at least one incident of sexual harassment during college (Menard et al., 2003). Another recent survey of working women showed that 41 percent reported experiencing sexual harassment in the workplace (Das, 2009).

Although men and women may suffer sexual harassment, women are much more likely to be harassed and men are much more likely to be harassers (Mansnerus & Kocieniewski, 2004; Stockdale et al., 2004; Street et al., 2007). Women in traditionally male-dominated work settings, such as construction sites or firehouses, and those with more stereotypically masculine personality traits (assertive, dominant, and independent) face an increased risk of sexual harassment on the job than do other women (Berdahl, 2007). Women of color also stand a higher risk than white women of being sexually harassed in the workplace (Berdahl & Moore, 2006).

Women tend to judge a wider range of behaviors as forms of sexual harassment than men do, especially behaviors that involve derogatory remarks, dating pressures, and direct sexual contact such as kissing or fondling (Rotundo, Nguyen, & Sackett, 2001). Men and women agree more strongly on whether more extreme behaviors such as rape, requests for sexual involvement as a condition of employment or promotion, and unwanted pressure or requests for sexual involvement constitute harassment.

Men and women also tend to read social cues differently. A recent study of college students showed that men more often misinterpreted a woman's friendly overtures, such as a subtle smile or gesture, as signs of sexual interest (Farris et al., 2008). Interestingly, the researchers found that men also made more mistakes than women in misinterpreting overtly sexual cues as signs of friendliness. When it comes to reading nonverbal cues, whether they are intended to be friendly or provocative, it appears that men generally have blurrier social perception than do women. As lead researcher Coreen Farris of Indiana University put it, "Young men just find it difficult to tell the difference between women who are being friendly and women who are interested in something more" (cited in Bryner, 2008).

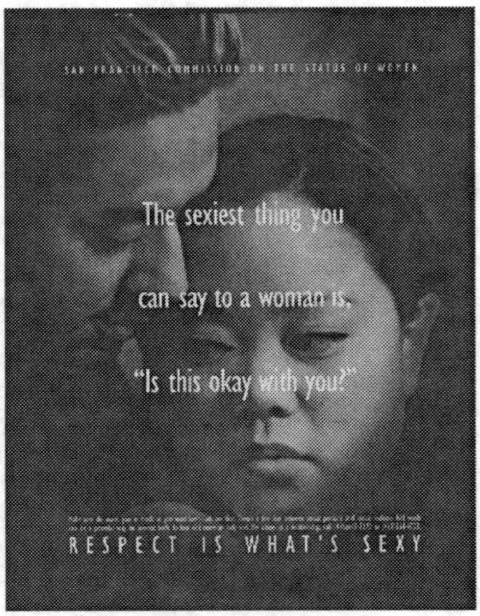

© Courtesy Department on the Status of Women, City and County of San Francisco

"Respect Is Sexy." This message emphasizes the importance of respect and communication in combating date rape.

Acquaintance Rape: The Most Common Type

Women are much more likely to be raped or sexually assaulted by men they know than by strangers. According to the U.S. Department of Justice (2006), more than four out of five rapes (83 percent) are committed by acquaintances. In the most recent population-based survey of American women, 14.3 percent reported a history of sexual assault or rape by a man they knew, such as a date, spouse, family member, or friend of the family, compared with 5.6 percent reporting sexual assault or rape by a stranger (Moracco et al., 2007).

Men, especially sexually aggressive men, tend to misjudge women's sexual intent by perceiving greater sexual interest in their behavior than women do (Farris et al., 2008). Date rapists may misinterpret a woman's friendly interest as willingness to engage in sexual intercourse, believing that even if she says "no," she is merely being coy.

Sexually aggressive men may erroneously believe that women who accompany them home or who frequent singles bars or attend parties are "just asking for it" (Bletzer & Koss, 2006). Sexually aggressive men often endorse myths about rape, such as the belief that women secretly desire to be raped or overpowered. In their minds they may not believe they are actually committing rape, but they are. To set the record straight, when a woman refuses to consent, or she says "no," she means "no."

What Motivates Rape and Sexual Harassment?

CONCEPT 11.27
Though sexual motivation is involved in rape, the primary motives involve issues of power, anger, revenge, and intentional cruelty.

Though rape is a sexual act, make no mistake: It is fundamentally a crime of sexual violence. Complex motives underlie rape, including power, anger, revenge, and intentional cruelty, intermingled with sexual desire. For some rapists, it is a means of controlling and dominating women; for others, it is a way of exacting revenge against women because of a history of perceived mistreatment and humiliation by them. Similarly, sexual harassment is a means by which the harasser seeks to dominate and control someone who holds a subordinate position (Huerta et al., 2006). In traditional male bastions, it also becomes a tactic of social control, of keeping "women in their place" by treating them as sexual objects or by making them feel uncomfortable and unwelcome. Many harassers trivialize their own behavior, sometimes claiming they were only "kidding around" when accused of a pattern of sexual taunts, gestures, or unwelcome overtures. Efforts must be made to raise people's awareness of the types of behaviors that may be experienced by recipients as harassment.

What Are We Teaching Our Sons?

Though some rapists have antisocial personalities, many others appear perfectly normal except for their sexual violence (Lalumière et al., 2005). A rapist may be just like the boy next door; in fact, he may be the boy next door. Though not every young man becomes a rapist, a surprising number of college men engage in sexual assaults. About one in 13 college men in a large-scale college survey reported committing rape or attempted rape (Koss et al., 1987). The sheer ordinariness of the great majority of rapists surely prompts the question "What are we teaching our sons?"

The answer may lie in the stereotypical messages conveyed by the media and the community that have the effect of socializing young men into sexually aggressive roles (Malamuth, Huppin, & Paul, 2005). Young men may come to label their sexually aggressive behavior as appropriate behavior in the context of dating relationships (Loh et al., 2007). Moreover, men who were reinforced for aggressive and competitive behavior on the playing fields from an early age may come to believe the cultural stereotype that a masculine man should be sexually assertive and be able to overcome a woman's resistance. Adding alcohol to the mix further increases the potential for acts of sexual aggression, including date rape (Cole, 2006; Scribner et al., 2010). Treating women as sexual objects in films and other media such as video games further encourages men to objectify women.

For some men, the dating situation is not a chance to get to know their partners but, rather, an opportunity for sexual conquest in which the object is to overcome a woman's resistance—to "score"—by whatever means it may take. Drinking alcohol only increases the likelihood that this underlying attitude will become expressed in sexually aggressive behavior. As noted in Chapter 4, alcohol has the effect of *disinhibiting* (releasing) impulsive behavior as well as clouding one's judgment and making it more difficult to weigh the consequences of one's behavior. Moreover, consuming alcohol leads men to be more likely to believe that ambiguous cues from a woman signal sexual interest rather than mere friendliness (Farris, Treat, & Viken, 2010).

Preventing Rape and Sexual Harassment

© iStockphoto.com/Richard Bowden

Is this sexual harassment? Do men and women perceive behaviors that constitute sexual harassment in the same way? What does the research teach us?

Education programs that expose young men to feminist and multicultural viewpoints may help promote more respectful attitudes toward women. So, too, might rape-prevention workshops, many of which have sprung up on college campuses and are sometimes incorporated into the college orientation process. Generally speaking, these programs help change student attitudes toward rape, but questions remain about whether they reduce the incidence of sexual assault (Breitenbecher, 2000). On a broader level, we need to adopt a public policy that sends a clear and consistent message that sexual coercion of any kind will not be tolerated.

Women are not responsible for preventing rape. Rape is a violent sexual crime, and the assailant bears the responsibility for the act. Yet we may take steps, such as those listed below, to reduce the risks of sexual victimization (Boston Women's Health Book Collective, 1992; Powell, 1991; Rathus, Nevid, & Fichner-Rathus, 2011). These suggestions do not prevent rape, but they may help reduce the chances of sexual victimization. Importantly, focusing on ways of protecting ourselves does not mean that responsibility for rape and other acts of sexual coercion falls on the victim.

- *Have your keys handy when opening the car, or, if possible, equip your car with a keyless entry system.*
- *Secure your front door with dead-bolt locks and lock all windows.* Secure first-floor windows with iron gates.
- *List your first name by its initial on your mailbox and in the phone directory.*
- *Keep hallways and entrances around doorways well lit and avoid walking alone at night or walking in deserted areas.*
- *Meet first dates in a common place.* Avoid getting into a car with a new date.
- *Stay sober and expect your date to do the same.* Many date rapes occur when alcohol or other drugs are used.
- *Check the credentials of any service people who request to enter your home.* Ask to call their dispatcher or supervisor to ensure that they are legitimate.
- *Drive with your doors locked and your windows up.* Make sure no one is lurking in the back seat of the car upon entering. Don't pick up any hitchhikers.
- *Carry a loud alarm that can be sounded in the event of attack.*
- *Take rape-prevention courses or workshops offered by your college or community organizations.*
- *Establish clear limits in dating situations.* Tell your date what you are willing to do and not willing to do.
- *Be firm in establishing boundaries.* The more clearly you state where the sexual boundaries are, the less likely a date will misinterpret your wishes. If your date doesn't seem to take "no" for an answer, consider it a signal to end the relationship.
- *Trust your feelings.* Acquaintance rapes, by far the most common form of rape, are committed by men known to the women they assault. If you have a strange feeling about your date or acquaintance, pay attention to it. Don't assume you're merely imagining things.

Let us also note that there is no one correct way to respond to sexual harassment. People respond in different ways. However, the following suggestions may be helpful in the event you or someone close to you is subjected to sexual harassment:

- *Adopt a professional attitude.* Conveying a businesslike but courteous attitude may stop harassment dead in its tracks.
- *Avoid meeting with the harasser behind closed doors.* If you need to interact with the person, make sure others are present or insist on meeting in a public place or leaving the office door open so that others can see you.
- *Keep a journal.* If you are being harassed, keep a journal, noting what happened in each incident, where and when it occurred, and the names of any witnesses who were present.
- *Put the harasser on notice.* Let the harasser know that you find his or her behavior unwelcome and will not tolerate it. Provide the harasser with a copy of your journal record of the harassing behavior. If you feel uncomfortable approaching the harasser directly, ask a friend to accompany you or write the harasser a letter detailing your complaints.
- *Speak to your supervisor or to the company or school official responsible for handling sexual harassment complaints.* Inquire about the company grievance procedure and protection of confidentiality. Most college campuses have designated individuals for handling sexual harassment complaints; ask your adviser or college dean for their names.
- *Consider legal actions.* Sexual harassment is legally actionable. Consult an attorney familiar with the law in this area, or contact the Equal Employment Opportunity Commission (listed in the government section of your phonebook).

Thinking Critically About Psychology

Based on your reading of the chapter, answer the following questions. Then, to evaluate your progress in developing critical thinking skills, compare your answers to the sample answers found in Appendix A.

1. How is homosexuality different from transsexualism?
2. John, a 29-year-old information technology manager, has been dating Jessica, a 25-year-old biology graduate student, for the past few months. They recently began having sexual relations, but John has been unable to achieve an erection each time. On each sexual occasion, he has tried to free his mind of other concerns and to focus all of his attention on achieving an erection. But it doesn't seem to be working. What do you think he might be doing wrong?

Log in to CengageBrain to access the resources your instructor requires. For this book, you can access:

CourseMate

Psychology CourseMate brings course concepts to life with interactive learning, study, and exam preparation tools that support the printed textbook. A textbook-specific website, Psychology CourseMate includes an integrated interactive eBook and other interactive learning tools including quizzes, flashcards, videos, and more.

CENGAGENOW

CengageNow is an easy-to-use online resource that helps you study in less time to get the grade you want—NOW. Take a pre-test for this chapter and receive a personalized study plan based on your results that will identify the topics you need to review and direct you to online resources to help you master those topics. Then take a post-test to help you determine the concepts you have mastered and what you will need to work on. If your textbook does not include an access code card, go to CengageBrain.com to gain access.

Visit www.cengagebrain.com to access your account and purchase materials.

VISUAL OVERVIEW Chapter 11 Gender and Sexuality

MODULE 11.1 Gender Identity, Gender Roles, and Gender Differences

© Gary Salter/Corbis

Gender Identity and Gender Roles

- **Gender Identity**: Psychological sense of maleness and femaleness
- **Gender Roles**: Cultural expectations of gender appropriate roles and behaviors
- **Theories of Gender-Role Behavior**: Social-cognitive theory, gender-schema theory, evolutionary theory, sociocultural theory

Gender Differences

- **Gender Difference in Cognitive Abilities**: Males have edge in some visual-spatial skills and math or quantitative skills, but gender differences in math performance are shrinking. Females have the edge in verbal abilities, especially writing skills, and remembering where objects are located
- **Gender Differences in Personality**: Women tend to be higher in extraversion, warmth, openness, and emotional expression; men tend to be higher in self-esteem and aggressiveness
- **Gender Differences in Leadership Styles**: Women tend to show a more democratic, consensus-building style versus a more autocratic, command style among men

MODULE 11.2 Sexual Response and Behavior

- **Sexual Response Cycle**: Comprising four phases

1. Excitement: initial arousal
2. Plateau: increasing arousal to a plateau level
3. Orgasm: muscular contractions release sexual tension; accompanied by ejaculation in males
4. Resolution: return to prearoused state

- **Sexual Orientation**

Directionality of sexual attraction along a continuum ranging from exclusively heterosexual to exclusively homosexual

Origins remain under study but probably involve biological and psychosocial influences

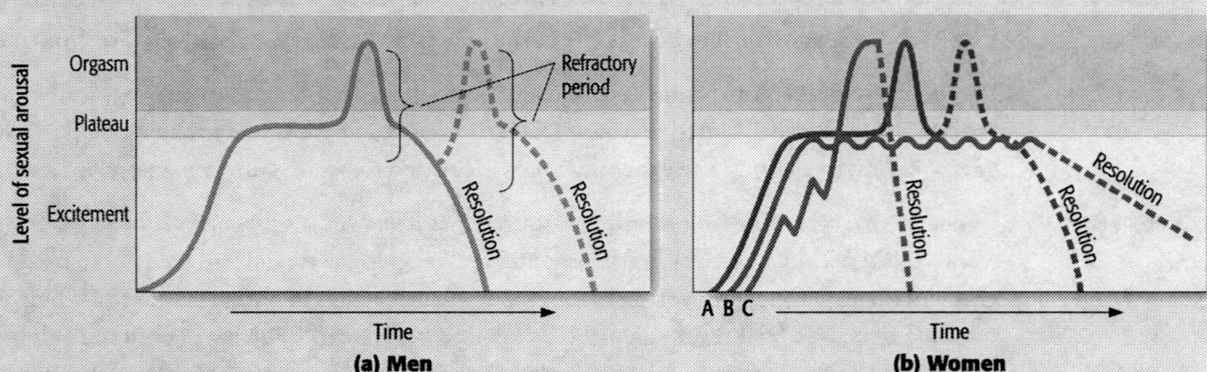

The Sexual Response Cycle

- **Types of Paraphilias**: A typical sexual variations
- **Protecting Yourself and Your Partners from STDs**: Practicing safer sexual behaviors and getting regular medical checkups

MODULE 11.3 Sexual Dysfunctions

Types of Sexual Dysfunctions

- **Sexual Desire Disorders** (problems with sexual interest or drive): Hypoactive sexual desire disorder, sexual aversion disorder
- **Sexual Arousal Disorders** (problems with sexual excitement or arousal): Male erectile disorder, female sexual arousal disorder
- **Orgasmic Disorders** (problems with orgasmic response): Female orgasmic disorder, male orgasmic disorder, premature ejaculation

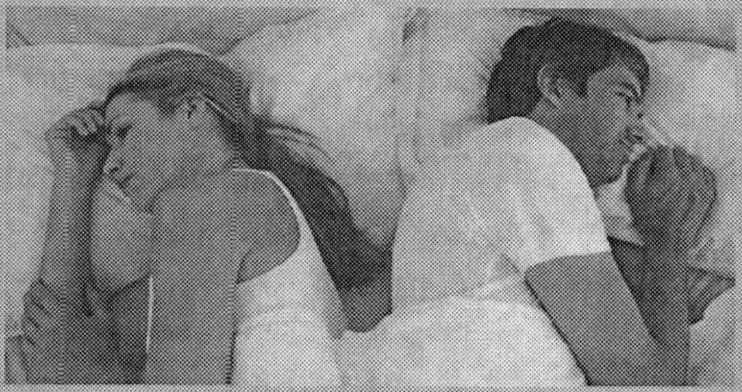

© Sean Prior/Shutterstock.com

Causes of Sexual Dysfunctions

- **Biological Causes**: Physical diseases such as diabetes and multiple sclerosis, effects of drugs or medications, hormonal problems
- **Psychosocial Causes**: Relationship problems, performance anxiety, culturally repressive sexual attitudes

Treatment of Sexual Dysfunctions

- **Sex Therapy**: Brief, behaviorally oriented therapy
- **Biomedical Therapies**: Erectile dysfunction drugs, testosterone therapy, antidepressants

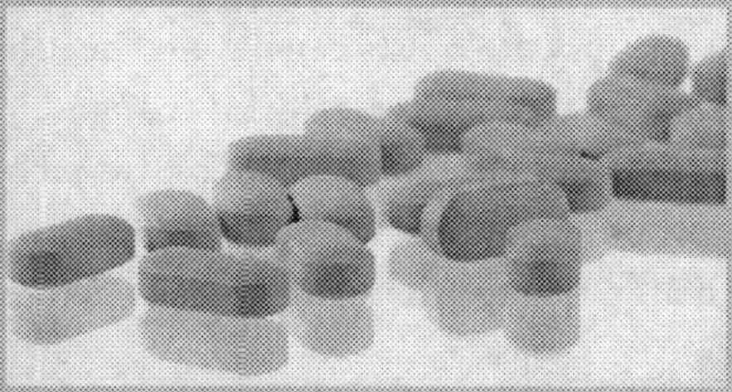

© iStockphoto.com/intst

12 Psychology and Health

The Philosopher in the Morgue

SLICE OF LIFE The Paris morgue is a strange place for a famous philosopher to be rummaging about. But there among the corpses in seventeenth-century Paris was the philosopher René Descartes (1596–1650) (Searle, 1996). You probably know Descartes for his famous statement "I think, therefore I am." Descartes believed that the mind and body are two fundamentally different entities. But if the mind and body are separate, there must be some connection between them. For example, if you decide to raise your arm and a fraction of a second later your arm moves up, the mind must have had an effect on the body. By examining corpses, Descartes hoped to find the part of the brain where the mind connected to the body. Despite his efforts to find the point of intersection of mind and body, modern science teaches that the mind and the body—the psychological and the physical—are much more closely intertwined than Descartes would ever have imagined. We will see in this chapter, for example, how our psychological health and physical health are closely interconnected. Sorry, René, but the mind and body do not intersect at any one point; they are inextricably connected in many ways.

In previous chapters we focused on how the workings of the body, especially the brain, affect mental experiences such as sensations, perceptions, emotions, and thinking. Here we look at the other side of the coin by considering how the mind affects the body—how psychological factors, especially stress, affect our health and well-being.

In this chapter we examine the role of stress in our physical and mental health and look at the psychological factors that moderate the impact of stress. We then examine how psychological factors influence such major health problems as heart disease and cancer, the two leading killers of Americans. We will see that unhealthy behaviors and lifestyles, such as smoking and consumption of a high-fat diet, are linked to the risk of developing these life-threatening diseases. By better understanding the psychological links to physical illness, psychologists can develop health promotion programs to help people make healthful changes in their behaviors and lifestyles. Finally, we consider how each of us can apply psychological techniques and principles to better manage the stress we face in our daily lives.

DID YOU KNOW THAT...

- Happy or joyous events can be a source of stress? (p. 449)
- The emotional stress of divorce or even college examinations may damage your health? (p. 460)
- Skimping on sleep may make you more vulnerable to the common cold? (p. 460).
- Writing about traumatic experiences may boost the body's immune system? (p. 460)
- Chronic anger may be harmful to your heart? (p. 466)
- Two modifiable behaviors, smoking and diet, account for nearly two of three cancer deaths in the United States? (p. 468)
- Regular exercise can increase your resilience to stress? (p. 473)

© Alexey1976/BigStockPhoto.com

Learning Objectives

By reading this chapter you will be able to . . .

1 **DEFINE** stress in psychological terms.

2 **DESCRIBE** the effects of stress on the body.

3 **IDENTIFY** and **DESCRIBE** the major sources of stress.

4 **IDENTIFY** and **DESCRIBE** different types of psychological conflicts and **APPLY** this knowledge to examples of these types of conflicts.

5 **IDENTIFY** the stages of the general adaptation syndrome and **APPLY** this knowledge to changes that occur in the body during each stage.

6 **IDENTIFY** and **DESCRIBE** psychological factors that buffer the effects of stress.

7 **IDENTIFY** psychological factors linked to coronary heart disease and **APPLY** this knowledge to steps we can take to reduce the risk of heart disease.

8 **EVALUATE** the relationship between emotions and the heart.

9 **IDENTIFY** psychological factors linked to cancer and **APPLY** this knowledge to steps we can take to reduce the risk of cancer.

10 **IDENTIFY** psychological factors linked to other physical disorders such as asthma, headaches, and peptic ulcers.

11 **APPLY** stress management techniques to daily life.

© Harald Eisenberger/LOOK/Getty Images

Preview

MODULE 12.1

Stress: What It Is and What It Does to the Body

- What is stress?
- What are the major sources of stress?
- How does the body respond to stress?
- How does stress affect the immune system?
- What psychological factors buffer the effects of stress?

health psychology The specialty in psychology that focuses on the interrelationships between psychological factors and physical health.

CONCEPT 12.1
When the level of stress in our lives taxes our ability to cope, we may experience states of distress in the form of psychological or physical health problems.

stress Pressure or demand placed on an organism to adjust or adapt.

distress A state of emotional or physical suffering, discomfort, or pain.

The study of interrelationships between psychology and physical health is called **health psychology**. Health psychologists work in universities, hospitals, and government agencies conducting research and using the knowledge they gain to develop health promotion and disease prevention programs.

Health psychologists are especially concerned with the effects of stress on physical health. But what is stress, and how does it affect our health?

Psychologists use the term **stress** to describe pressures or demands placed upon an organism to adjust or adapt to its environment. Stress is a fact of life. We may even need a certain amount of stress to remain active, alert, and energized. We can characterize these healthy forms of stress as good stress. But when stress increases to a point that it taxes our ability to cope, we may experience **distress**, which is an internal state of physical or mental pain or suffering.

Distress may be expressed in psychological problems, especially anxiety, depression, anger, and irritability; and in physical health problems such as headache, fatigue, upset stomach, and such serious medical conditions as cardiovascular disorders (see ■ Figure 12.1).

Many Americans say that stress is on the rise. According to recent surveys by the American Psychological Association, one-third of Americans say they are facing extreme levels of stress in their lives, and nearly half (43 percent) report adverse health effects from stress (American Psychological Association, 2006, 2007). Nearly half of Americans (48 percent) say that stress in their lives has increased over the past five years.

Stress is taking a toll on the emotional health of college students today. A 2010 national survey of first-year college students showed that student ratings of their emotional health declined to record low levels (Higher Education Research Institute, 2011; Lewin, 2011). Increasing financial concerns are adding to academic and adjustment problems as sources of stress many students are facing.

© Digital Vision/Jupiter Images

© Digital Vision.

What are the stressors in your life?

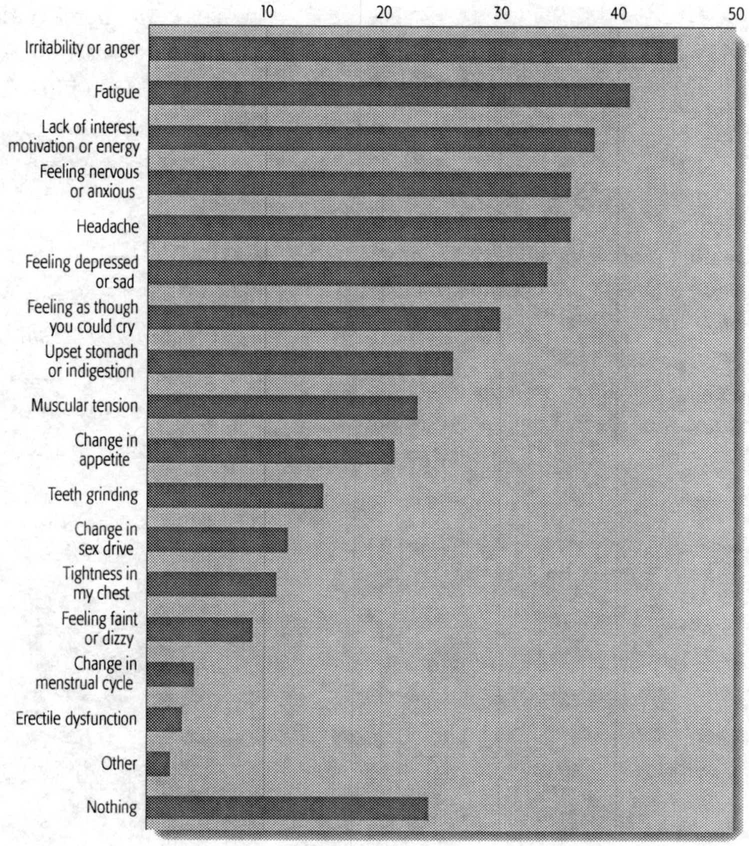

Figure 12.1 Physical and Psychological Symptoms Resulting from Stress
Here we see that percentages of Americans surveyed by the American Psychological Association who reported various psychological and physical symptoms resulting from stress during the past month.
Source: From *Physical Symptoms of Stress: American Psychological Association, Stress In America Findings*. Copyright © 2010 American Psychological Association. Reprinted by permission.

Sources of Stress

What stresses you out? School and work demands, relationship problems, traffic jams, or maybe the kinds of daily stress from needing to prepare meals, shop, or doing household chores? The American Psychological Association asked people to report on the major causes of stress in their lives. Concerns about money, work, and the economy topped the list in 2010 (see ■ Figure 12.2).

Sources of stress are called **stressors**. In this section we examine a number of stressors that many people face—daily hassles, life events or life changes, frustration, conflict, trauma, Type A behavior pattern, and pressures on immigrant groups trying to adjust to life in a new country.

Positive as well as negative experiences can be sources of stress. Happy or joyous events, such as having a baby, getting married, or graduating from college, are stressors because they impose demands on us to adjust or adapt. Positive changes in our lives, like negative ones, can tax our ability to cope, as any new parent will attest. How well we are able to cope with stress plays a key part in determining our mental and physical well-being.

stressors Sources of stress.

hassles Annoyances of daily life that impose a stressful burden.

Hassles

Hassles are annoyances we commonly experience in our daily lives. Examples include traffic jams, household chores, coping with inclement weather, and balancing job demands and social relationships. Few, if any, of us are immune from daily hassles.

We may experience some hassles on a daily basis, such as hunting for a parking spot in overcrowded parking lots. Others occur irregularly or unexpectedly, such as getting caught in a downpour without an umbrella. A single hassle may not amount to much in itself. But the accumulation of daily

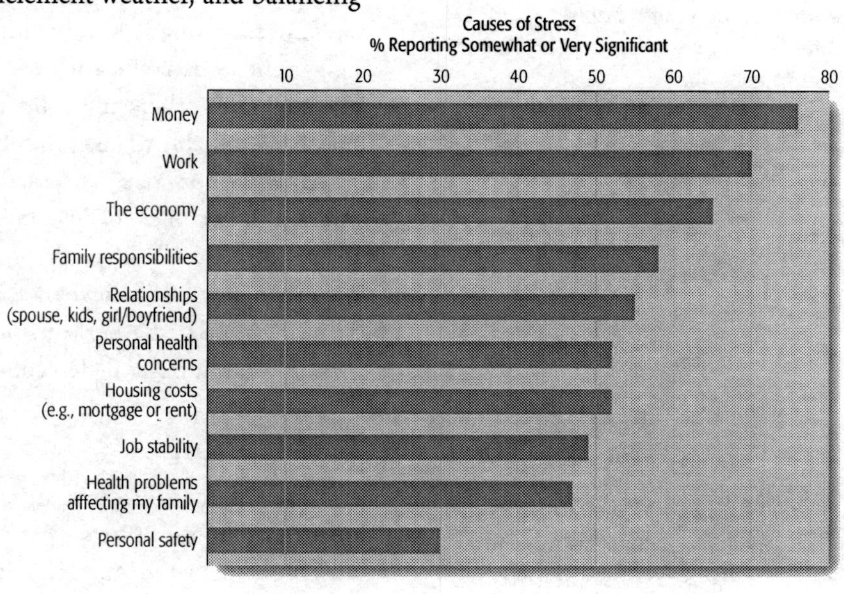

FIGURE 12.2 Causes of Stress
Here are some things people say cause stress in their lives. How significant are these causes of stress in your life?
Source: From *Physical Symptoms of Stress: American Psychological Association, Stress In America Findings*. Copyright © 2010 American Psychological Association. Reprinted by permission.

CONCEPT 12.2
Stressors are sources of stress, such as hassles, life changes, frustration, and conflict.

CONCEPT 12.3
Sources of chronic stress in our lives include hassles, financial problems, job-related problems, relationship problems, and persistent pain or other medical problems.

→ Concept Link
Psychological factors may affect the severity of chronic pain and how people are able to cope with it. See Module 3.6.

chronic stress Continuing or lingering stress.

hassles contributes to the general level of **chronic stress** in our lives. Chronic stress is a state of persistent tension or pressure that can lead us to feel exhausted, irritable, and depressed. In addition to daily hassles, sources of chronic stress include ongoing financial problems, job-related problems, marital or relationship conflicts, and persistent or recurrent pain or other chronic medical conditions.

Life Events

Stress can also result from major changes in life circumstances, which psychologists call *life events* or *life changes*. These may be negative events, such as the loss of a loved one or a job termination, or positive events, such as getting married, receiving a promotion, or having a baby. In other words, changes for better or for worse can impose stressful burdens that require adjustment. Unlike daily hassles, life events occur irregularly and sometimes unexpectedly. To determine how much stress is in your life, see the *Try This Out* section.

© woraput/Shutterstock.com

People who experience more life changes are at higher risk of suffering from psychological and physical health problems (Dohrenwend, 2006). We need to observe some caution when interpreting these data, however. Relationships between life changes and psychological and physical problems are typically small, and the links are correlational. As you may recall from Chapter 1, a correlation is a statistical association between two variables (in this case, level of stress and poor health) and, as such, does not necessarily reflect a causal linkage. It is possible that exposure to life events causes or aggravates mental or physical problems. But it is also possible that such problems disrupt people's lives, leading them to encounter more life change events, such as job relocations or conflicts with family members. In the final analysis, relationships between life events and our physical health likely cut both ways.

CONCEPT 12.4
People experiencing more life changes are at increased risk of psychological and physical health problems, but questions of cause and effect remain open to debate.

Although everyone experiences hassles and life changes, some people are less vulnerable than others to these types of stressors. They may have higher thresholds for coping with daily annoyances and are not as rattled by them. Or they may have the skills needed to adjust to changes in life circumstances, such as the ability to make new friends when relocating to a new community. Then too, some hold more optimistic attitudes than others and believe they can control the future course of their lives. They may be better able to meet the challenges posed by various stressors.

How we appraise or evaluate a life event also has an important bearing on how stressful it becomes for us. The same event may hold different meanings for different people. A life event like a pregnancy is probably less stressful to people who welcome the pregnancy and believe they can cope with the changes that the birth of a child will bring. Similarly, whether you find work demands to be stressful may depend on whether you like your job and feel in control of how and when you do your work.

Frustration

frustration A negative emotional state experienced when one's efforts to pursue one's goals are thwarted.

Another major source of stress is **frustration**, the negative emotional state that occurs when our efforts to pursue our goals are blocked or thwarted. Adolescents may feel frustrated when they want to drive, date, or drink alcoholic beverages but are told they are too young. People desiring higher education may be frustrated when they lack the financial resources to attend the college of their choice. We may frustrate ourselves when we set unrealistically high goals that we are unable to achieve.

CONCEPT 12.5
In a state of psychological conflict, a person may vacillate between two or more competing goals.

→ Concept Link
Incentive theory focuses on the "pull" or lure of goals and desired objects as an important source of motivation. See Module 8.1.

Conflict

Conflict is a state of tension resulting from the presence of two or more competing goals that demand resolution. People in conflict often vacillate, or shift back and forth, between competing goals. The longer they remain in conflict, the more stressed and frustrated they feel. Psychologists identify four major types of conflicts. Let us consider each in turn.

conflict A state of tension brought about by opposing motives operating simultaneously.

CONCEPT 12.6
The four major types of psychological conflict are approach-approach, avoidance-avoidance, approach-avoidance, and multiple approach-avoidance conflict.

Approach-Approach Conflict In an approach-approach conflict (see ■ Figure 12.3), you feel drawn toward two positive but mutually exclusive goals at the same time. You may need to decide between taking a vacation in the mountains or at the beach, or dating Taylor or Alex this weekend, or choosing between two attractive job offers. Though you may initially vacillate between the two goals, an approach-approach conflict is generally resolved by deciding on one course of action or another. The approach-approach conflict is generally considered the least stressful type of conflict.

Avoidance-Avoidance Conflict In avoidance-avoidance conflicts, you face two opposing goals, both of which are unpleasant. Moreover, avoiding one of these undesirable goals requires approaching the other. You may want to avoid a painful dental procedure, but you also want to prevent tooth loss. You may avoid taking a less demanding major because of your strong tendency to avoid failure, but you also want to avoid settling for a lesser job or career. If there is no obvious resolution, you may put off dealing with the conflict, at least for a period of time. In cases where the conflict is highly stressful, you could become virtually immobilized and unable to attend to your usual responsibilities.

Approach-Avoidance Conflict In approach-avoidance conflicts, you face a goal that has both positive and negative qualities. You may want to ask someone for a date, but feel panic-stricken by fears of rejection. You may want to attend graduate school, but fear incurring heavy loans. Resolution of the conflict seems possible if you compare the relative pluses and minuses and then decide to commit yourself to either pursuing the goal or abandoning it. But like a piece of metal within proximity of a magnet's two opposing poles, you may at first feel pulled toward the goal by its desirable qualities, only to be repelled by its unattractive qualities as you get closer to it.

Multiple Approach-Avoidance Conflict The most complex type of conflict, this one involves two or more goals, each with compelling positive and negative characteristics. You may want to pursue further training after graduation because it will expand your career options,

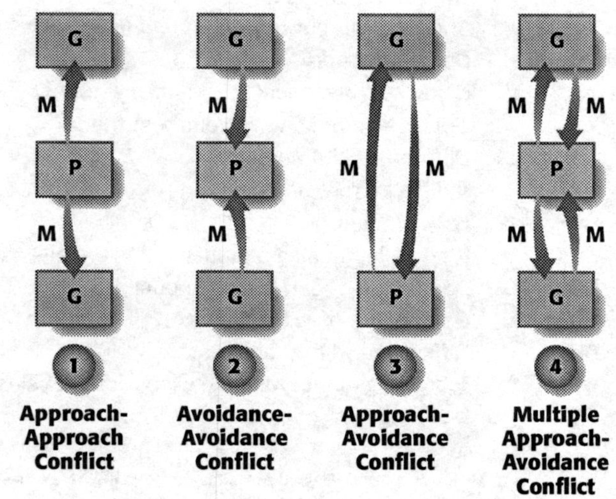

FIGURE 12.3 Types of Conflicts
1 In an approach-approach conflict, the person (P) is motivated (M) to pursue two goals (G) but cannot pursue both of them at the same time. 2 In an avoidance-avoidance conflict, the person is motivated to avoid each of two undesirable goals. 3 In an approach-avoidance conflict, the same goal has both positive and negative qualities. 4 In a multiple approach-avoidance conflict, the person faces two or more goals, each with positive and negative features.

TRY THIS OUT How Stressful Is Your Life?

The College Life Stress Inventory was designed to measure the amount of life stress experienced by college students. Circle the items in the inventory that you have experienced during the past year. Then compute your stress level by adding the stress ratings of the circled items. Use the scoring key to help you interpret your score.

© GeoM/Shutterstock.com

Stress Rating	Event
100	Being raped
100	Finding out that you are HIV-positive
98	Being accused of rape
97	Death of a close friend
96	Death of a close family member
94	Contracting a sexually transmitted disease (other than AIDS)
91	Concerns about being pregnant
90	Finals week
90	Concerns about your partner being pregnant
89	Oversleeping for an exam
89	Flunking a class
85	Having a boyfriend or girlfriend cheat on you
85	Ending a steady dating relationship
85	Serious illness in a close friend or family member
84	Financial difficulties
83	Writing a major term paper
83	Being caught cheating on a test
82	Drunk driving
82	Sense of overload in school or work
80	Two exams in one day
77	Cheating on your boyfriend or girlfriend
76	Getting married
75	Negative consequences of drinking or drug use
73	Depression or crisis in your best friend
73	Difficulties with parents
72	Talking in front of a class
69	Lack of sleep
69	Change in housing situation (hassles, moves)
69	Competing or performing in public
66	Getting in a physical fight
66	Difficulties with a roommate
65	Job changes (applying, new job, work hassles)
65	Declaring a major or concerns about future plans

Stress Rating	Event
62	A class you hate
61	Drinking or use of drugs
60	Confrontations with professors
58	Starting a new semester
57	Going on a first date
55	Registration
55	Maintaining a steady dating relationship
54	Commuting to campus or work, or both
53	Peer pressures
53	Being away from home for the first time
52	Getting sick
52	Concerns about your appearance
51	Getting straight A's
48	A difficult class that you love
47	Making new friends; getting along with friends
47	Fraternity or sorority rush
40	Falling asleep in class
20	Attending an athletic event (e.g., football game)

Scoring Key: You can gauge your overall level of stress by comparing your total score with the scores obtained by the developers of the scale based on a sample of 257 introductory psychology students. The average (mean) score was 1,247, and approximately two out of three students obtained scores ranging from 806 to 1,688. Though your total score may give you insight into your level of stress, it does not reveal how much stress may be affecting you. Some people thrive on higher levels of stress than do others. They may possess the coping skills and social support that they need to handle stress more effectively. But anyone can become overstressed as pressures and life changes continue to pile up. If you are facing a high level of stress in your life, perhaps you can reduce some sources of stress. You might also benefit by learning effective ways of handling stressors you can't avoid. Module 12.3 offers some helpful guidelines for managing stress.

Source: From M. J. Renner and R. Scott Mackin, "College Life Stress Inventory," *Teaching of Psychology*, 25 (1), p. 47. Copyright © 1998 Michael J. Renner and R. Scott Mackin, West Chester University of Pennsylvania. Reprinted by permission.

© CWB/shutterstock.com

but you are put off by the expense and additional time commitments involved. On the other hand, you may have a job opportunity that will get you started in a career now, but worry that you'll come to regret not having gone further with your education. Such conflicts can sometimes be resolved by combining both goals (getting started at the new job while taking night courses). At other times, the resolution comes from making a commitment to a course of action, even though it may entail nagging concerns about "the road not taken."

Conflicts are most easily resolved and least stressful when one goal is decidedly more attractive than another or when the positive qualities of a goal outweigh the negative. But when two goals pull you in opposite directions, or when the same goal both strongly attracts and repels you, you may experience high levels of stress and confusion about which course of action to pursue.

CONCEPT 12.7
Traumatic events can be sources of intense stress that, in turn, can have profound, enduring effects on our psychological adjustment.

posttraumatic stress disorder (PTSD) A psychological disorder involving a maladaptive reaction to traumatic stress.

Traumatic Stressors

Traumatic stressors are potentially life-threatening events. Included in this category are natural or technological disasters (hurricanes, tornadoes, floods, nuclear accidents, etc.); combat experiences; serious accidents; physical or sexual assaults; a diagnosis of cancer, AIDS, or other life-threatening illness; and terrorist attacks, such as the horrific attacks on September 11, 2001.

People who experience traumatic events may develop a type of psychological disorder called **posttraumatic stress disorder (PTSD)**. People with PTSD encounter lingering problems in adjustment, such as those listed below, often for years after the traumatic event has passed.

© EPA/KIMIMASA MAYAMA /LANDOV

Exposure to traumatic events, such as natural disasters and violent crimes, can lead to the development of PTSD, a psychological disorder characterized by lingering problems in adjustment and psychological functioning.

- *Avoidance of cues associated with the trauma.* People with PTSD may avoid situations or cues that may be reminders of the traumatic experience. The rape survivor may avoid traveling in the same part of town in which she was attacked. The combat veteran may avoid viewing war movies or socializing with service buddies.
- *Reexperiencing the traumatic event.* Such people may experience intrusive memories, images, or dreams of the traumatic experience. They may even have flashbacks of the traumatic experience, as with combat veterans who momentarily have the feeling of being back on the battlefield.
- *Impaired functioning.* They may experience depression or anxiety that interferes with the ability to meet ordinary responsibilities as workers, students, parents, or family members.
- *Heightened arousal.* They may be unusually tense or keyed-up, find it difficult to relax or fall asleep, or have a heightened heart rate. They may also appear to be constantly on guard and show an exaggerated startle response to sudden noises.
- *Emotional numbing.* They may experience a numbing of emotional responses and find it difficult to feel love or other strong emotions.

Many trauma survivors suffer from PTSD, although their symptoms may not develop until months or years after the traumatic stressor. But recent evidence shows that the majority of people who experience trauma recover on their own without developing significant psychological problems such as PTSD (Bonanno et al., 2010).

Type A Behavior Pattern

Type A behavior pattern (TABP) A behavior pattern characterized by impatience, time urgency, competitiveness, and hostility.

Do others describe you as hard-driving, competitive, impatient, and ambitious? Do you seem to take life at a faster pace than others? Does the idea of waiting in line or being stuck in traffic make you want to pull out your hair or pound your fists? If these characteristics ring true, your personality style probably fits the **Type A behavior pattern (TABP)**.

People with the Type A behavior pattern are impatient, competitive, and aggressive. They are constantly in a rush and have a strong sense of time urgency. They feel pressured to get the maximum amount done in the shortest possible amount of time.

TRY THIS OUT Are You Type A?

Check the appropriate column to indicate whether or not the item is generally true of you. Then consult the scoring key below to determine whether you fit the Type A profile.

Yes	No	Do you . . .
☐	☐	1. Walk briskly from place to place or from meeting to meeting?
☐	☐	2. Strongly emphasize important words in your ordinary speech?
☐	☐	3. Think that life is by nature dog-eat-dog?
☐	☐	4. Get fidgety when you see someone complete a job slowly?
☐	☐	5. Urge others to complete what they're trying to express?
☐	☐	6. Find it exceptionally annoying to get stuck in line?
☐	☐	7. Envision all the things you have to do even when someone is talking to you?
☐	☐	8. Eat while you're getting dressed, or jot down notes while you're driving?
☐	☐	9. Catch up on work during vacations?
☐	☐	10. Direct the conversation to things that interest you?
☐	☐	11. Feel as if things are going to pot because you're relaxing for a few minutes?
☐	☐	12. Get so wrapped up in your work that you fail to notice beautiful scenery passing by?
☐	☐	13. Get so wrapped up in money, promotions, and awards that you neglect expressing your creativity?

Yes	No	Do you . . .
☐	☐	14. Schedule appointments and meetings back to back?
☐	☐	15. Arrive early for appointments and meetings?
☐	☐	16. Make fists or clench your jaw to drive home your views?
☐	☐	17. Think that you've achieved what you have because of your ability to work fast?
☐	☐	18. Have the feeling that uncompleted work must be done now and fast?
☐	☐	19. Try to find more efficient ways to get things done?
☐	☐	20. Struggle always to win games instead of having fun?
☐	☐	21. Interrupt people who are talking?
☐	☐	22. Lose patience with people who are late for appointments and meetings?
☐	☐	23. Get back to work right after lunch?
☐	☐	24. Find that there's never enough time?
☐	☐	25. Believe that you're getting too little done, even when other people tell you that you're doing fine?

Scoring Key: "Yes" answers suggest a Type A behavior pattern—and the more items to which you answered "yes," the stronger your TABP. You should have little difficulty determining whether you are strongly or moderately inclined toward this behavior pattern—that is, if you are honest with yourself.

Source: From Jeffrey S. Nevid, Spencer A. Rathus, and Beverly Greene, *Abnormal Psychology in a Changing World*. Copyright © 2003 by Prentice-Hall, Inc. Reproduced by permission of Pearson Education, Inc.

They tend to do everything fast; they talk fast, walk fast, even eat fast. They quickly lose patience with others, especially those who move or work more slowly than they would like. They may become hostile and prone to anger when others fail to meet their expectations. They are intense even at play. While others are content to bat the ball around on the tennis court, people with the Type A behavior pattern play to win at all costs. By contrast, those with the opposite personality style, sometimes called the Type B behavior pattern, take a slower, more relaxed pace in life. The *Try This Out* section can help you determine whether you fit the Type A profile.

Why It Matters

CONCEPT 12.8
Chronic hostility is the component of the Type A behavior pattern most strongly linked to increased risk of heart disease.

Is there a connection between personality patterns and the risk of coronary heart disease? Although early research linked the Type A personality to an increased risk of coronary heart disease (CHD), later evidence casts doubt on this relationship (Geipert, 2007). However, evidence points to a strong link between CHD and a component of the Type A profile, hostility (Chida & Steptoe, 2009; Denollet & Pedersen, 2009). Hostile people tend to have "short fuses" and are prone to get angry easily and often. People

Frank and Ernest

© 2007 Thaves. Reprinted with permission.
© Bob Thaves

who often experience strong negative emotions, such as anger and hostility, stand an increased risk of developing coronary heart disease and other significant health problems (Kiecolt-Glaser et al., 2002; Steptoe, Wardle, & Marmot, 2005). Their bodies also respond more strongly to stress, which, over time, can take a toll on their physical health. On the other hand, a study of Mexican American elders showed that those reporting more frequent positive emotions tended to have healthier blood pressures (Ostir et al., 2006). Other evidence links positive emotions to living a longer and healthier life (Ostir et al., 2006; J. Xu & Roberts, 2010). The lesson for us here is that our emotions are associated not only with our psychological well-being, but also with our physical health and longevity.

Before moving on, we should note that the question of whether the "hurry-up" features of the Type A behavior pattern contributes to health problems remains open to further study. Nonetheless, this behavior pattern is a modifiable source of stress. If you are seeking to reduce the level of stress in your life, a good place to start might be with modifying Type A behavior. Module 12.3 contains helpful suggestions for reducing Type A behavior.

CONCEPT 12.9
Acculturative stress is a source of stress faced by immigrants struggling to meet the demands of adjusting to a new culture.

→ Concept Link
Acculturation plays an important role in explaining drug use and abuse. See Module 4.4.

acculturative stress Demands faced by immigrants in adjusting to a host culture.

Acculturative Stress

For immigrants, the demands of adjusting to a new culture can be a significant source of stress (Ayers et al., 2009; Schwartz et al., 2010). Establishing a new life in one's adopted country can be a difficult adjustment, especially when there are differences in language and culture and few available job or training opportunities. One significant source of stress is pressure to become *acculturated*—to adapt to the values, linguistic preferences, and customs of the host or dominant culture. How does **acculturative stress**, which results from this pressure, affect psychological health and adjustment?

Adjusting to a new society depends on a number of factors. For example, stress associated with economic hardship is a major contributor to adjustment problems in immigrant groups, as it is for members of the host culture. Less well acculturated immigrants often have difficulty gaining an economic foothold in the host country, which can lead to anxiety and depression. Exposure to racism or discrimination are other sources of stress that can take a toll on the physical and psychological health of immigrant groups (Delgado et al., 2010; Smart Richman et al., 2010; Woods-Giscombé & Lobel, 2008). But acculturation, as it turns out, can be a double-edged sword. It can erode traditional family networks and values, leaving people more vulnerable to psychological problems in the face of stress and fostering undesirable behaviors such as substance abuse (Ortega et al., 2000). Erosion of traditional cultural values may also help explain the

© Ronnie Kaufman/CORBIS

Acculturative stress is faced by immigrants struggling to meet the demands of adjusting to a new culture.

CONCEPT CHART 12.1 Sources of Stress

Source	Description	Key Points
Hassles	Common annoyances of everyday life	An accumulation may contribute to chronic stress, which can lead to impaired psychological and physical well-being.
Life events	Positive or negative changes in life circumstances that place demands on us to adapt	A high level of life change is associated with poorer psychological and physical health outcomes.
Frustration	A state of negative arousal resulting from the thwarted efforts to attain personal goals	Occurs when obstacles prevent us from achieving our goals.
Conflict	Tension occurring when we feel torn between two opposing goals	Conflicts are most stressful when opposing goals are equally strong and no clear resolution is apparent.
Traumatic stressors	Sudden, life-threatening events	Traumatic events can tax our coping abilities to the limit. Trauma survivors may develop psychological disorders, such as PTSD.
Type A behavior pattern (TABP)	A behavior pattern characterized by impatience, competitiveness, aggressiveness, and time urgency	Hostility, a component of the TABP, is linked to a higher risk of coronary heart disease.
Acculturative stress	Pressures imposed on immigrant people to adapt to the cultural and linguistic demands of the host country	Adjustment of immigrant groups depends on many factors, including economic opportunity, language proficiency, ethnic identification, and a supportive social network.

© Ghislain & Marie David De Lossy/The Image Bank/Getty images

A strong sense of ethnic identity may help buffer stress, including acculturative stress.

greater likelihood of engaging in premarital intercourse among more acculturated Hispanic teens (Adam et al., 2005).

To understand connections between acculturation and psychological health, we need to take many factors into account, including economic opportunities, language proficiency in the language of the larger culture, connections to a social network of people with whom one can identify and seek support, as well as ethnic identity (Ayers et al., 2009; B. S. K. Kim et al., 2003; Tran & Lee, 2010). Withdrawal from the larger culture may prevent the individual from making the necessary adjustments to function effectively in a multicultural society. For many groups, making a successful transition to life in America is a process of balancing their participation in the mainstream culture while maintaining their ethnic identity or cultural heritage. Overall, evidence supports the view that adjusting to the demands of the larger culture while maintaining one's own ethnic identity is associated with better psychological adjustment (LaFromboise, Albright, & Harris, 2010; Oyserman, 2008; Rodriguez et al., 2009; C. O. Smith et al., 2009).

Before reading further you may wish to review the sources of stress outlined in Concept Chart 12.1.

THE BRAIN LOVES A PUZZLE

As you read ahead, use the information in the text to solve the following puzzle:

How the body responds to stress can be a lifesaver in some situations yet pose a health risk in others. How is that possible?

The Body's Response to Stress

Much of what we know about the body's response to stress is the result of pioneering research by Hans Selye (1907–1982), the famed stress researcher known affectionately as "Dr. Stress."

The General Adaptation Syndrome

Selye recognized that specific stressors, such as an invading virus, do elicit specific reactions in the body. But layered over these specific responses is a more general response to stress, which he called the **general adaptation syndrome (GAS)** (also called the *stress response*). The body responds in a similar manner to various stressors—cold, noise, infectious agents, pressures on the job, or mental stress in the form of worry or anxiety. Investigating this syndrome led him to believe that the way the body responds to persistent stress is much like a car alarm that does not shut off until the car battery becomes depleted. The general adaptation syndrome consists of three stages, each of which we consider below.

Courtesy of Philatelia Hungarica LLC.

Hungarian postage stamp honoring native son Hans Selye for his contributions to medical science.

general adaptation syndrome (GAS) Selye's term for the three-stage response of the body to persistent or intense stress.

alarm stage The first stage of the general adaptation syndrome, involving mobilization of the body's resources to cope with an immediate stressor.

fight-or-flight response The body's built-in alarm system that allows it to quickly mobilize its resources to either fight or flee when faced with a threatening stressor.

Alarm Stage The **alarm stage** is the body's first stage of response to a stressor, during which it prepares its defenses for action. Suppose a car ahead of you on the road suddenly veers out of control. This is an immediate stressful event. Your heart starts pounding faster, speeding the flow of blood to your extremities and providing muscles with the oxygen and fuel they need to take swift action, such as performing an emergency maneuver to avoid a collision. The body's response during the alarm stage is called the **fight-or-flight response** because it is characterized by biological changes that prepare the body to deal with a threat by either fighting it off or fleeing from it.

The alarm stage is accompanied by strong physiological and psychological arousal. Our hearts pound, our breathing quickens, sweat pours down our foreheads, and we are flooded with strong emotions such as terror, fright, anxiety, rage, or anger.

Different stressful events may trigger the alarm stage of the GAS. The threat may be physical, as in an attack by an assailant, or psychological, as in an event that induces fear of failure (e.g., a professor handing out an examination). In some people, the alarm is triggered whenever they meet a new person at a social gathering; they find themselves sweating heavily and feeling anxious, and they may become tongue-tied. In others, the body alarm system is activated whenever they visit the dentist. Whether the perceived threat is physical or psychological, the body's response is the same.

The alarm stage is like a "call to arms" that is prewired into the nervous system. This wiring is a legacy inherited from our earliest ancestors, who faced many potential threats in their daily lives. A glimpse of a suspicious-looking object or a rustling sound in the bush might have cued them to the presence of a predator, triggering the fight-or-flight response, which helped prepare them to defend against a threat. But the fight-or-flight response didn't last long: If people survived the immediate threat, their bodies returned to the normal state; if they failed, they perished.

CONCEPT 12.10
The general adaptation syndrome (GAS) is a three-stage process by which the body responds to different types of stressors.

CONCEPT 12.11
The three stages in the general adaptation syndrome (GAS) are the alarm stage, the resistance stage, and the exhaustion stage.

CONCEPT 12.12
During the alarm stage of the GAS, the body mobilizes its resources in the face of stress, preparing to fend off a threat by either fighting or fleeing.

CONCEPT 12.13
During the resistance stage of the GAS, the body conserves its resources to adapt to the effects of enduring stress.

© 2006 Universal Press Syndicate

Resistance Stage Death may occur within the first few hours or days of exposure to a stressor that is so damaging (such as extreme cold) that its persistence is incompatible with life. But if survival is possible and the stressor continues, the body attempts to adapt to it as best it can. Selye called this part of the GAS

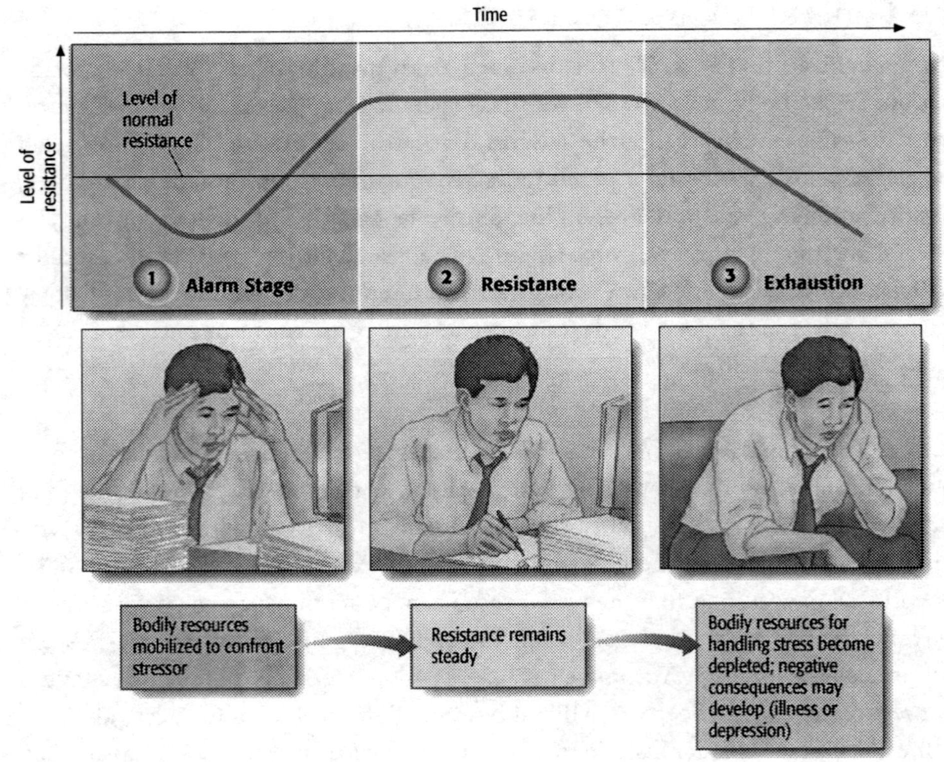

FIGURE 12.4 Level of Resistance During the Stages of the General Adaptation Syndrome
The body's resistance to stress first dips during the 1 *alarm stage*, as the impact of the stressor takes a toll, but then increases as the body mobilizes its resources. Resistance remains steady through the 2 *resistance stage* as the body attempts to cope with the stressor. But if the stressor persists, 3 *exhaustion* eventually sets in as bodily reserves needed to resist stress become dangerously depleted.

resistance stage The second stage of the general adaptation syndrome, characterized by the body's attempt to adjust or adapt to persistent stress.

exhaustion stage The third stage of the general adaptation syndrome, characterized by depletion of bodily resources and a lowered resistance to stress-related disorders or conditions.

the **resistance stage** (also called *adaptation stage*). During this stage, the body attempts to return to a normal biological state by restoring spent energy and repairing damage. Arousal remains high, though not as high as during the alarm reaction. This prolonged bodily arousal may be accompanied by such emotional reactions as anger, fatigue, and irritability.

Exhaustion Stage If the stressor persists, the body may enter the final stage of the GAS—the **exhaustion stage**. Heart rate and respiration now *decrease* to conserve bodily resources. Yet with continued exposure to stress, the body's resources may become seriously depleted and the individual may develop what Selye called "diseases of adaptation"—stress-related disorders such as kidney disease, heart disease, allergic conditions, digestive disorders, and depression. Some people are hardier than others, but relentless, intense stress can eventually exhaust anyone. ■ Figure 12.4 shows the changes that occur in the body's level of resistance across the three stages of the GAS.

CONCEPT 12.14
During the exhaustion stage of the GAS, continuing stress can lead to severe depletion of bodily resources and development of stress-related diseases.

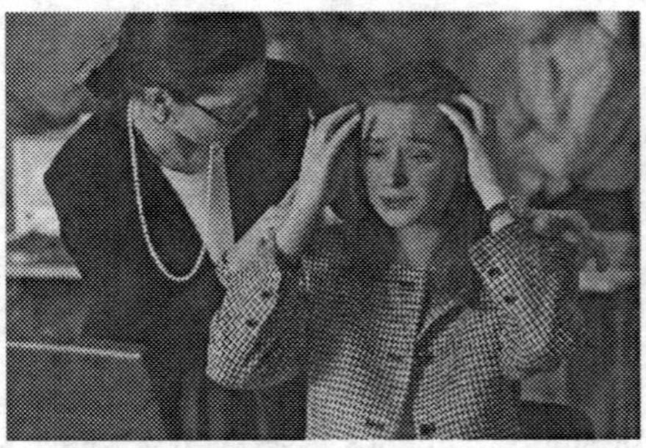

© Ghislain & Marie David De Lossy

Fight or flight? Or friend or befriend? Women tend to adopt a "tend and befriend" approach to dealing with stress, engaging in nurturing behaviors that may reflect the role of female reproductive hormones.

The body's stress response may have helped our ancient ancestors survive many of the physical threats they faced. Yet the alarm reaction in response to a threatening stressor was designed to be brief. Our ancestors either escaped a predator or fought it off; within seconds, minutes perhaps, the threat was over and their bodies returned to their normal, prearoused state. The types of stress we face in contemporary life are more persistent. Our ancestors didn't need to juggle school and jobs, fight daily traffic jams, or face the daily grind of working a double shift to make ends meet. The reality for many of us is that the stressful demands of ordinary life may repeatedly activate our alarm reaction day after day, year after year. Over time, persistent stress may overtax the body's resources, making us more susceptible to stress-related disorders (Kemeny, 2003).

Psychologists have found behavioral differences in how men and women respond to stress. Women tend to engage in more nurturing behaviors during times of stress than do men, such as comforting and soothing infants and children, and befriending others who might help protect them and their children from threats. UCLA Psychologist Shelley Taylor describes women's stress-related behavior in terms of a "tend and befriend" pattern (S. E. Taylor, 2007; S. E. Taylor et al., 2000). By contrast, men react more typically to stressful experiences with aggressive or hostile responses in which the male hormone testosterone may play a pivotal role. Women's attachment and caregiving behaviors may be influenced by female reproductive and maternal hormones.

CONCEPT 12.15
The endocrine system plays a key role in the body's response to stress.

Stress and the Endocrine System

The endocrine system is a system of ductless glands throughout the body that release secretions, called *hormones,* directly into the bloodstream (see Chapter 2). The hypothalamus, a small endocrine gland located in the midbrain, coordinates the endocrine system's response to stress. Like a series of falling dominoes, the chain reaction it sets off prompts other glands to release their hormones (Ellis, Jackson, & Boyce, 2006).

Let's look closer at the falling dominoes. The body's stress regulatory process involves coordinated action within a group of endocrine organs labeled the **hypothalamus pituitary adrenal (HPA) axis** (G. E. Miller, Chen, & Zhou, 2007). Here's how it works: Under stress, the hypothalamus secretes **corticotrophin-releasing hormone (CRH)**, which in turn stimulates the pituitary gland to secrete **adrenocorticotrophic hormone (ACTH)**. ACTH travels through the bloodstream to the **adrenal glands,** the pair of small endocrine glands located just above the kidneys. ACTH stimulates the **adrenal cortex**, the outer layer of the adrenal glands, to release stress hormones called **corticosteroids** (or *cortical steroids*). These hormones reduce inflammation and help the body resist stress by making stored nutrients more available to meet the demands for energy that may be required to cope with a stressful event (Ditzen et al., 2008). (A synthetic version of cortisol is hydrocortisone, a drug used to treat allergies and inflammation.).

The sympathetic branch of the autonomic nervous system triggers the **adrenal medulla,** the inner layer of each adrenal gland, to secrete the stress hormones *epinephrine* and *norepinephrine.* These hormones make the heart pump faster, allowing more oxygen and nutrient-rich blood to reach the muscles, where it is needed to allow the organism to either flee from a threatening stressor or fight it. The "racing heart" we experience during times of stress is the result of this surge of stress hormones. The body's response to stress is depicted in ■ Figure 12.5.

hypothalamus pituitary adrenal (HPA) axis The integrated system of endocrine glands involved in the body's response to stress.

corticotrophin-releasing hormone (CRH) A hormone released by the hypothalamus that induces the pituitary gland to release adrenocorticotrophic hormone.

adrenocorticotrophic hormone (ACTH) A pituitary hormone that activates the adrenal cortex to release corticosteroids (cortical steroids).

adrenal glands A pair of endocrine glands located just above the kidneys that produce various stress-related hormones.

adrenal cortex The outer layer of the adrenal glands that secretes corticosteroids (cortical steroids).

corticosteroids Adrenal hormones that increase the body's resistance to stress by increasing the availability of stored nutrients to meet the increased energy demands of coping with stressful events. Also called *cortical steroids.*

adrenal medulla The inner part of the adrenal glands that secretes the stress hormones epinephrine (adrenaline) and norepinephrine (noradrenaline).

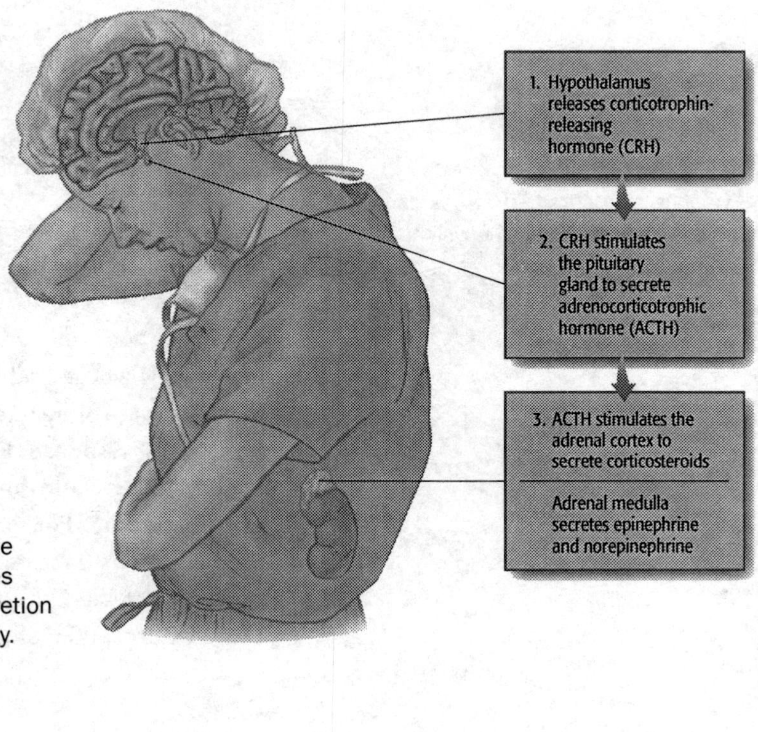

FIGURE 12.5 The Body's Response to Stress
Under stress, the body responds by releasing stress hormones (epinephrine and norepinephrine) from the adrenal medulla and corticosteroids from the adrenal cortex. These substances help the body prepare to cope with an immediate stressor. Stress hormones increase heart rate, respiration, and blood pressure, whereas secretion of corticosteroids leads to the release of stored reserves of energy.

Stress and the Immune System

The *immune system* is the body's primary system of defense against infectious diseases and worn-out or diseased cells. The immune system fights disease in several ways (Jiang & Chess, 2006). It dispatches billions of specialized white blood cells called **lymphocytes**. Lymphocytes constantly circulate throughout the body and remain on alert to the presence of foreign agents or **antigens** (literally *anti*body *gen*erators). An antigen is any substance recognized as foreign to the body, such as a bacterium, virus, foreign protein, or a body cell that has turned cancerous. As the term's literal meaning suggests, antigens activate the immune system to produce **antibodies**, specialized protein molecules that fit the invading antigen like a key fitting a lock. When antibodies lock into position on an antigen, they mark it for destruction by specialized "killer" lymphocytes that act like commandos on a search-and-destroy mission (Greenwood, 2006; Kay, 2006).

lymphocytes White blood cells that protect the body against disease-causing organisms.

antigens Substances, such as bacteria and viruses, that are recognized by the immune system as foreign to the body and that induce it to produce antibodies to defend against them.

antibodies Protein molecules produced by the immune system that serve to mark antigens for destruction by specialized lymphocytes.

Some lymphocytes hold a "memory" of specific antigens to which the body has been exposed, allowing the immune system to render a quick blow the next time the invader appears. Thus we may develop immunity or resistance to many disease-causing antigens—which is why we do not contract certain illnesses, such as chicken pox, more than once. We may also acquire immunity through **vaccination** (also called *immunization*). A vaccination involves the administration of dead or weakened infectious agents that will not cause an infection themselves but are capable of stimulating the body's natural production of antibodies to the particular antigen.

vaccination A method of acquiring immunity by means of injecting a weakened or partial form of an infectious agent that can induce production of antibodies but does not produce a full-blown infection.

Why It Matters

Can stress make you sick? Perhaps not directly, but prolonged or intense exposure to stress can reduce your body's ability to defend itself against disease-causing organisms, which in turn can increase your vulnerability to illness. Occasional stress may not be harmful, but chronic stress can weaken the immune system, making us more vulnerable to disease (Fan et al., 2009; Gorman, 2007). Stressors linked to health problems include divorce; chronic illness; prolonged unemployment; persistent lack of sleep; loss of loved ones; exposure to trauma such as hurricanes, other natural or technological disasters, or acts of violence; and college examination periods. Perhaps you've noticed that you become more vulnerable to "catching a cold" during times of stress, such as around final exams.

Stress and physical illness are also linked through the actions of the stress hormones called *corticosteroids*. These adrenal hormones are released as part of the body's reaction to stress. While they initially help the body cope with stress, their continued secretion dampens the ability of immune-system cells to respond to invading microbes (E. M. Sternberg, 2000). (Immune functioning also can be impaired by the use of synthetic steroids, such as those taken by some body builders and wrestlers.)

CONCEPT 12.16
Evidence suggests that stress can increase vulnerability to physical illness by impairing the functioning of the body's immune system.

Stress hormones may even affect our relationship health. Evidence shows that newlyweds whose bodies pumped out more stress hormones during the first year of marriage were more likely to get divorced within 10 years than were newlyweds with a lower stress response (Kiecolt-Glaser, Bane, et al., 2003).

Psychological techniques can help combat stress and may improve immunological functioning. For example, research participants who were instructed to express their emotions through writing about traumatic or stressful experiences showed fewer psychological and physical symptoms than did control participants (Low, Stanton, & Danoff-Burg, 2006; Sloan & Marx, 2004; Smyth & Pennebaker, 2001).

FIGURE 12.6 Psychological Moderators of Stress
Social support, self-efficacy, perceptions of control and predictability, psychological hardiness, and optimism are psychological moderators that help us better withstand the effects of stress.

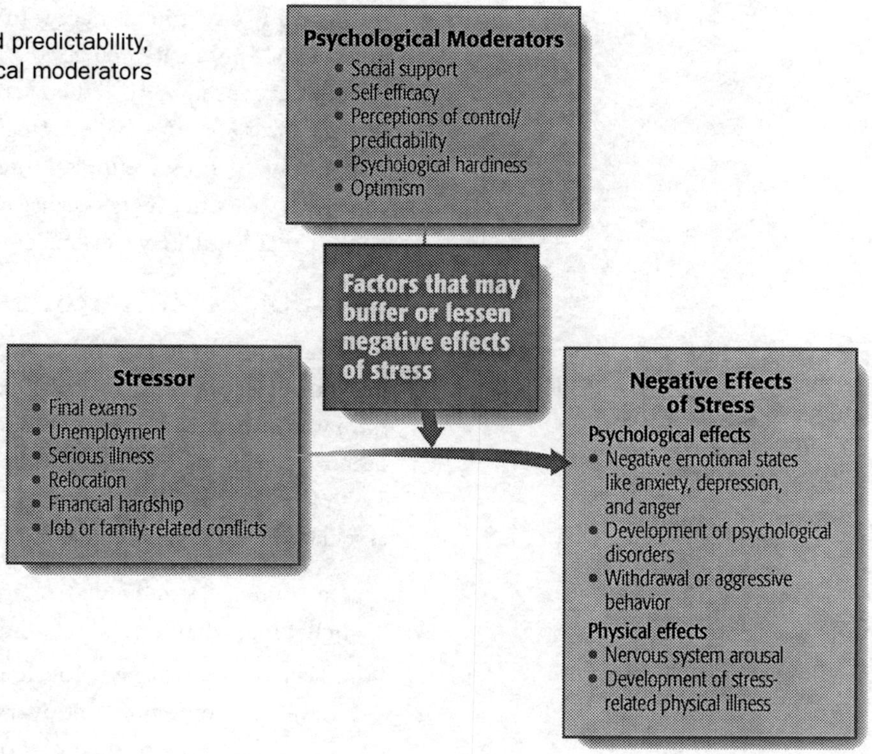

Psychological Moderators of Stress

Here we examine psychological moderators that may lessen the impact of stress, including social support, self-efficacy, perceptions of control and predictability, psychological hardiness, and optimism (see ■ Figure 12.6).

Social Support

Social support is a major factor in determining how well people cope with stress. A mounting body of evidence points to links between loneliness and social isolation and significant health problems, including cardiovascular and immune-related problems (Miller, 2011). Having friends, especially close friends, may help us cope better with stress and protect the body from stress-related disorders. Landmark research along these lines showed that more sociable people and those with larger social networks were more resistant to developing the common cold after they voluntarily received injections of a cold virus than were others who were less socially connected (S. Cohen et al., 1997, 2003). The lesson is that loneliness and lack of social support may be dangerous to our physical as well as emotional health.

CONCEPT 12.17
Social support, self-efficacy, perceptions of control and predictability, psychological hardiness, and optimism are psychological factors that moderate or buffer the effects of stress.

Self-Efficacy

Self-efficacy is the belief that we are capable of accomplishing what we set out to do. High levels of self-efficacy are linked to an increased ability to withstand stress (Montpetit & Bergeman, 2007). People with high levels of self-efficacy tend to view stressful situations as challenges to be met rather than obstacles to be overcome. Self-confidence in their abilities leads them to tackle stressors head-on and persevere when they confront barriers in their path.

Predictability and Controllability

The impact of particular stressors varies with how predictable and controllable they seem (Koolhaas, de Boer, & Buwalda, 2006). Stressful events that seem more predictable and controllable, such as school assignments, have less impact on us than other events, such as hurricanes and fluctuations in the stock market, which seem to lie beyond our ability to predict or control.

© Tyler Olson/shutterstock.com

People also vary in the degree to which they perceive themselves as capable of controlling events. Those with an *internal locus of control* believe that rewards or reinforcements are a direct consequence of their actions (Wallston, 2001; see Chapter 13). Those with an *external locus of control* believe that their fate is determined by external factors or blind luck, not by their own efforts. "Internals" may be better able to marshal their efforts to cope with stressful events because of their belief that they can control them. "Externals," on the other hand, may feel helpless and overwhelmed in the face of stressful events.

Psychological Hardiness

psychological hardiness A cluster of traits (commitment, openness to challenge, internal locus of control) that may buffer the effects of stress.

An internal locus of control is also a defining characteristic of **psychological hardiness**, a cluster of personality traits associated with an increased resilience to stress. This term was introduced by psychologist Suzanne Kobasa based on her studies of business executives who maintained good physical health despite high levels of stress (Kobasa, 1979; Kobasa, Maddi, & Kahn, 1982). She and her colleagues identified three key traits associated with psychological hardiness:

- *Commitment.* The hardy executives had a strong commitment to their work and a belief that what they were doing was important.
- *Openness to challenge.* The hardy executives viewed the stressors they faced as challenges to be met, not overwhelming obstacles. They believed that change is a normal part of life, not something to be dreaded.
- *Internal locus of control.* The hardy executives believed that they could control the future direction of their lives, for better or worse.

© iStockphoto.com/Ben Blakenburg

In short, people with psychological hardiness accept stress as a normal challenge of life. They feel in control of the stress they encounter and believe that the challenges they face make life more interesting. They seek to solve problems, not to avoid them. They show "stick-to-itiveness." Investigators find links between psychological hardiness and positive outcomes such as the ability to handle stress and achieving higher grades in college (e.g., Ouellette & DiPlacido, 2001; Pengilly & Dowd, 2000; Sheard & Golby, 2007).

Optimism

Another buffer to stress is optimism. Holding a more optimistic attitude is associated with better ability to handle stress and the tendency to tackle stressful problems or difficulties directly rather than avoid them (Carver, Scheier, & Segerstrom, 2010). Researchers find links between optimism and many positive health outcomes, such as the following (Bjerklie, 2005; Carver, Scheier, & Segerstrom, 2010; Tindle et al., 2009; Trunzo & Pinto, 2003):

- More optimistic women show lower rates of heart disease and have lower death rates overall.
- Among heart disease patients, optimistic attitudes are associated with less emotional distress.
- Among cancer patients, optimism is linked to less emotional distress, better psychological adjustment, and lower levels of reported pain.
- Among pregnant women, optimism is associated with better birth outcomes, such as higher infant birth weights.

TRY THIS OUT Are You an Optimist or a Pessimist?

Do you tend to look on the bright side of things? Or do you usually expect the worst? The following scale, a revised version of the Life Orientation Test, can help raise your awareness about whether you are the type of person who tends to see the proverbial glass as half full or half empty.

Directions: Using numbers from 0 to 4, indicate your responses to the following items in the spaces provided. Then check the scoring key.

4 = strongly agree
3 = agree
2 = neutral
1 = disagree
0 = strongly disagree

______ 1. In uncertain times, I usually expect the best.
______ 2. It's easy for me to relax.
______ 3. If something can go wrong for me, it will.
______ 4. I'm always optimistic about my future.
______ 5. I enjoy my friends a lot.
______ 6. It's important for me to keep busy.
______ 7. I hardly ever expect things to go my way.
______ 8. I don't get upset too easily.
______ 9. I rarely count on good things happening to me.
______ 10. Overall, I expect more good things to happen to me than bad.

Scoring Key: The first step is to reverse the scoring for items 3, 7, and 9. In other words, change 4 to 0, 3 to 1, 1 to 3, and 0 to 4. A 2 remains a 2. Next, add your scores for items 1, 3, 4, 7, 9, and 10 to obtain an overall score. (Do not score items 2, 5, 6, and 8. These items are considered "fillers" and are not scored as part of the test.) Total scores can range from 0 to 24.

Now you can compare your score to those of a sample of 2,055 college students. Higher scores indicate greater optimism, whereas lower scores indicate greater pessimism. The average (mean) score in the college sample was 14.33 (standard deviation = 4.28). About two-thirds of the sample scored from 10 to 19. Scores greater than 14 reflect relatively higher levels of optimism. Psychologists believe that people can change their attitudes—that optimism can be learned. If you scored low on optimism, it might make sense to talk to a counselor or psychologist about your attitudes and ways of changing them.

Source: From M. F. Scheier, C. S. Carver and M. W. Bridges, 1994, "Distinguishing Optimism from Neuroticism (and Trait Anxiety, Self-Mastery, and Self-Esteem): A Re-Evaluation of the Life Orientation Test," *Journal of Personality and Social Psychology*, 67, pp. 1063–1078. Copyright © 1994 by the American Psychological Association. Reprinted with permission.

Evidence tying optimism to better health outcomes is correlational, so we should be careful not to draw a causal link. Still, doesn't it make sense to take an optimistic approach toward the stressors you face, seeing the glass as half full rather than half empty?

Let's turn the discussion around to you. What about your own outlook on life? Do you tend to be an optimist or a pessimist? The *Try This Out* section allows you to evaluate your outlook on life.

12.1 MODULE REVIEW Stress: What It Is and What It Does to the Body

Recite It

What is stress?

➤ The term *stress* refers to pressures and demands to adjust or adapt.

What are the major sources of stress?

➤ The major sources of stress include daily hassles, life changes, frustration, conflict, Type A behavior pattern, traumatic events, and pressures of acculturation faced by immigrant groups.

How does the body respond to stress?

➤ Stress activates a general pattern of physiological responses, described by Selye as the general adaptation syndrome, or GAS. GAS consists of three stages: the alarm stage, the resistance stage, and the exhaustion stage.

How does stress affect the immune system?

➤ Persistent or severe stress can impair the functioning of the immune system, leaving us more susceptible to many illnesses, including the common cold.

What psychological factors buffer the effects of stress?

➤ Psychological buffers against stress include social support, self-efficacy, perceptions of controllability and predictability, psychological hardiness, and optimism.

Recall It

1. (a) Provide a psychological definition of stress. (b) At what point does stress lead to distress?
2. Match the following types of stressors with the appropriate descriptions: (a) hassles; (b) life events; (c) conflict; (d) traumatic stressors.
   - **i.** two or more competing goals where a choice must be made.
   - **ii.** common annoyances such as traffic jams and balancing work and social demands.
   - **iii.** major changes in life circumstances.
   - **iv.** potentially life-threatening events.
3. The stage of the GAS characterized by the fight-or-flight response is the ________ stage.
4. List some psychological moderators of stress.
5. Which of the following are characteristics of the Type A behavior pattern?
   - **a.** impatient, competitive, hard-driving behavior.
   - **b.** experiencing flashbacks, heightened arousal, and emotional numbness.
   - **c.** approach-avoidance conflicts or multiple approach-avoidance conflicts.
   - **d.** experiencing chronic stress or frustration.
6. The body's general response to different kinds of stressors is called the ________ ________ syndrome.

Think About It

➤ What is the role of the nervous system in the general adaptation syndrome? What is the role of the endocrine system?

➤ Agree or disagree and support your answer: Stress can be healthy or unhealthy.

MODULE 12.2

Psychological Factors in Physical Illness

- How are psychological factors linked to the health of our heart and circulatory system?
- What roles do psychological factors play in the development of cancer?

Here's a shocker: Eventually we all die. But to what extent are our health and longevity a function of our behavioral patterns and lifestyles? What behaviors contribute to living healthier lives? What behaviors put our health at risk?

Our health and our longevity are affected by what we eat, whether we use tobacco and alcohol, and whether we exercise regularly. The leading causes of death are not microbial agents like bacteria and viruses but, rather, unhealthy behaviors such as smoking (which contributes to cancer and heart disease), poor diet and inactivity (which contribute to obesity and heart disease), and excessive use of alcohol (which contributes to cancer and diseases of the liver). All told, unhealthy behaviors account for an estimated 40 percent of premature deaths in the United States (Schroeder, 2007). In ■ Figure 12.7, we see the numbers of deaths annually in the United States that are linked to behavioral causes, about one million in total. Let's take a closer look at the unhealthy behaviors and lifestyles that contribute to the nation's two leading killer diseases: heart disease and cancer.

Coronary Heart Disease

The heart is composed of muscle tissue, which, like other body tissue, requires oxygen and nutrients carried through blood vessels called **arteries**. **Coronary heart disease (CHD)** is a disorder in which the flow of blood to the heart becomes insufficient to meet its needs. In most cases, the underlying cause is **atherosclerosis**, the narrowing of arteries resulting from a buildup of fatty deposits called **plaque** along artery walls. Atherosclerosis impairs circulation of blood to the heart. It is the major form of **arteriosclerosis**, or "hardening of the arteries," a condition in which artery walls become thicker, harder, and less elastic.

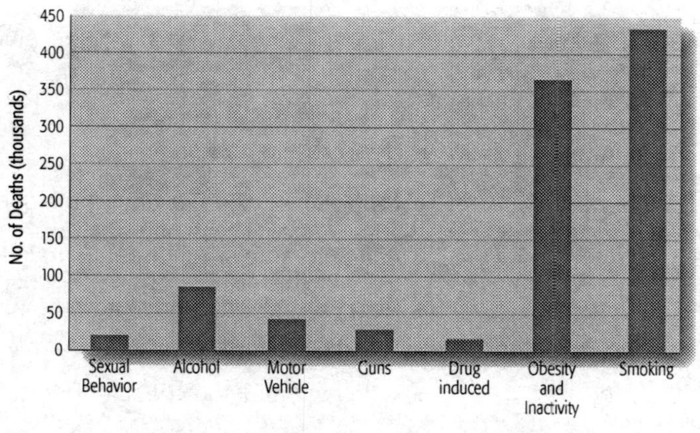

Figure 12.7 Numbers of Deaths in U.S. Due to Behavioral Causes
Source: From Schroeder, S. A. "We Can Do Better—Improving the Health of the American People". *New England Journal of Medicine*, 357, pp. 1221–1228. Copyright © Massachusetts Medical Society. All rights reserved.

Blood clots are more likely to become lodged in arteries narrowed by atherosclerosis. If a blood clot forms in a coronary artery (an artery that brings oxygen and nutrients to the heart), it may nearly or fully block the flow of blood to a part of the heart, causing a **heart attack** or *myocardial infarction (MI)*. During a heart attack, heart tissue literally dies from lack of oxygenated blood. Whether or not one survives a heart attack depends on the extent of damage to heart tissue and to the electrical system of the body that controls the heart rhythm.

CHD is the nation's leading killer of both men and women. It accounts for one out of every five deaths, nearly 500,000 in total, with most of these deaths resulting from heart attacks (American Heart Association, 2009). CHD accounts for more deaths in women than breast cancer. The good news, as we shall see, is that we can take steps to greatly reduce our risks of developing this killer disease.

arteries Blood vessels that carry oxygen-rich blood from the heart through the circulatory system.

coronary heart disease (CHD) The most common form of heart disease, caused by blockages in coronary arteries, the vessels that supply the heart with blood.

atherosclerosis A form of arteriosclerosis involving the narrowing of artery walls resulting from the buildup of fatty deposits or plaque.

plaque In the circulatory system, fatty deposits that accumulate along artery walls.

arteriosclerosis A condition in which artery walls become thicker and lose elasticity. Commonly called *hardening of the arteries*.

heart attack A potentially life-threatening event involving the death of heart tissue due to a lack of blood flow to the heart. Also called *myocardial infarction*.

Risk Factors for CHD

A person's risk of developing CHD varies with a number of factors such as age (CHD increases with age after about age 40), gender (men are at greater risk until about age 65), family history (heredity), hypertension (high blood pressure), smoking, obesity, diabetes, lack of physical activity, and high cholesterol levels (American Heart Association, 2009).

Why It Matters

Some risk factors cannot be controlled: You can't choose your parents or your gender or stop aging. Other factors, such as hypertension, smoking, obesity, diabetes, and cholesterol level, can be controlled through either behavioral changes (diet and exercise) or medical treatment. Adoption of healthy behaviors is associated with a lower risk of hypertension and heart disease—behaviors such as exercising regularly, avoiding smoking and excessive alcohol use, adopting a healthy diet and making efforts to keep body weight at a healthy level (Djoussé, Driver, & Gaziano, 2009; Forman, Stampfer, & Curhan, 2009; Roger, 2009).

Looking closer at these behavioral factors, we see that a sedentary lifestyle doubles the risk of coronary heart disease (Manson et al., 2004). The good news is that by becoming more active, even seasoned couch potatoes can reduce their risk of cardiovascular disease (Alford, 2010; Borjesson & Dahlof, 2005).

Smoking doubles the risk of heart attacks and is linked to more than one in five deaths from CHD and about one in three deaths due to cancer. Many Americans

CONCEPT 12.18
Health-related behaviors, such as diet, exercise, and smoking, affect a person's risk of developing many physical disorders, including coronary heart disease.

→ Concept Link
Smoking is the leading cause of premature death in the United States and worldwide. See Module 4.4.

CONCEPT 12.19
Risk factors for coronary heart disease include some factors you can't control, such as heredity, and some you can, such as hypertension, physical activity, and tobacco use.

→ Concept Link
Adopting healthy behaviors can help us lead longer and healthier lives. See Module 12.4.

TABLE 12.1 Health Benefits of Quitting Smoking

After You Quit Smoking . . .	
20 minutes	▪ Heart rate drops
12 hours	▪ Carbon monoxide level in the blood drops to normal
2 days	▪ Ability to smell and taste improve
2 to 3 weeks	▪ Heart attack risk begins to drop and lung function improves; walking becomes easier
1 month	▪ Coughing and shortness of breath decrease
1 year	▪ Risk of heart disease is cut in half
5 years	▪ Risk of stroke is reduced to that of a nonsmoker
10 years	▪ Risk of dying from lung cancer is about half that of a continuing smoker
15 years	▪ Risk of coronary heart disease returns to the level of people who have never smoked

© sagasan/shutterstock.com

Source: NYC Department of Health and Mental Hygiene, 2010

have heeded the health warnings and quit smoking or never started in the first place. The percentage of smokers in the United States has dropped by more than half during the past 50 years, but there still remain some 45 million Americans, or about 20% of the adult population, who continue to smoke (Benowitz, 2010; CDC, 2009a). The message is clear: If you don't smoke, don't start; if you do smoke, quit. Smokers begin accruing benefits from quitting smoking within hours, and the benefits accumulate the longer they remain free of smoking (see Table 12.1). (Some suggestions for quitting smoking are provided in the next *Try This Out* section.)

Heart disease is not an equal opportunity destroyer. Black (non-Hispanic) Americans have a much higher death rate due to coronary heart disease than do whites and other racial or ethnic groups in the United States (Freeman & Payne, 2000). One reason for this racial gap is that African Americans are much more likely to have obesity and hypertension, two of the major risk factors for heart disease, as well as stroke and diabetes (M. J. Brown, 2006; Ferdinand & Ferdinand, 2009). Another reason is that African American heart patients and heart attack victims typically receive less aggressive treatments than do whites (J. Chen et al., 2001; Stolberg, 2001b). This dual standard of care may reflect unequal access to quality health care and discrimination by health care providers.

Emotions and Your Heart

As noted earlier, hostility is the component of the Type A behavior profile most strongly linked to an increased risk of coronary heart disease. Hostile people are angry much of the time, and chronic anger increases the risk of hypertension and CHD (Chida & Steptoe, 2009; Denollet & Pedersen, 2009; Pressman & Cohen, 2005).

Persistent emotional arousal may damage the cardiovascular system due to the effects of the stress hormones epinephrine (adrenaline) and norepinephrine (noradrenaline). These hormones are released during the emotional states of anger and anxiety. They accelerate the heart rate, raise blood pressure, and increase the strength of heart contractions, resulting in a greater burden on the heart and circulatory system. These

TRY THIS OUT Suggestions for Quitting Smoking

© iStockphoto.com/Gary Woodard

Deciding to quit smoking is the first step in quitting. Many smokers quit on their own. Others seek help from health professionals or organizations that offer smoking cessation programs either free of charge or at modest cost. Some suggestions if you decide to quit, either on your own or with help from others:

- *Set a quit date*. Tell your friends and family about your plan to quit smoking by that date. Announcing your intentions will increase the likelihood that you'll stick to your plan of action.
- *Taper off*. Reduce the number of cigarettes you smoke daily in anticipation of your quitting date. A typical schedule to follow is cutting back the number of cigarettes you smoke daily by 25 percent each week for three weeks before quitting completely during the fourth week. Lengthen the interval between cigarettes to keep your smoking rate down to your daily limit.
- *Limit exposure to smoking environments*. Limit where you smoke to one particular room in or outside your house. Do not smoke while watching TV or on the phone.
- *Increase exposure to nonsmoking environments*. Spend more time in settings where smoking isn't permitted or customary, such as the library. Socialize more with nonsmokers and, to the extent possible, avoid socializing with friends who smoke.
- *Limit the availability of cigarettes*. Carry only as many cigarettes as you need to meet your daily limit. Never buy more than a pack at a time.
- *Practice competing responses when tempted to smoke*. Before and after your quit date, substitute responses that are incompatible with smoking whenever you feel the urge to smoke. Delay reaching for a cigarette. Practice relaxation exercises. Exercise instead of smoking until the urge passes. Take a bath or a walk around the block (without your cigarettes). Use sugar-free mints or gum as substitutes whenever you feel the urge to smoke.
- *Mentally rehearse the benefits of not smoking*. Imagine yourself living a longer, healthier, noncoughing life.
- *Learn to cope, not smoke*. Learn healthy ways of coping with negative feelings, such as anxiety, sadness, and anger, rather than reaching for a cigarette.

Once you have quit smoking completely, remove all smoking-related paraphernalia from your house, including ashtrays and lighters. Establish a nonsmoking rule in your house and request friends and family members to respect it. Ask others not to smoke in your presence (explain that you have recently quit and would appreciate their cooperation). If you should lapse, don't despair. Make a commitment then and there not to have another cigarette. Many people succeed completely after a few near misses.

increased demands may eventually compromise the cardiovascular system, especially in vulnerable people. Stress hormones (primarily epinephrine) also increase the stickiness of blood-clotting factors, which in turn may heighten the risk of potentially dangerous blood clots that can lead to heart attacks or strokes.

Persistent emotional distress in the form of strong negative emotions such as anger, depression, and anxiety may take a toll on the cardiovascular system (Chida & Steptoe, 2009; Denollet & Pedersen, 2009; Glassman, Bigger, & Gaffney, 2009). Psychologists are developing ways of helping chronically angry or anxious people learn to control their emotional responses to reduce their risks of CHD and other serious health problems.

CONCEPT 12.20
Negative emotions, such as anger, anxiety, and depression, may have damaging effects on the cardiovascular system.

Cancer

The word *cancer* may strike more fear in people's hearts than any other word in the English language. The fear is understandable. Nearly one out of every five deaths in the United States is caused by cancer. About 1.5 million Americans receive the dreaded diagnosis of cancer each year, and more than a half a million die from the disease (Heron, 2010; National Cancer Institute, 2010a). The good news is that the cancer death rate began to decline steadily in the early 1990s and has continued to decline through the early part of the new millennium.

Cancer is a disease in which body cells exhibit uncontrolled growth. The body normally manufactures new cells only when they are needed. The genes in our cells direct them to replicate in orderly ways. But in cancer, cells lose the ability to regulate their growth. They multiply even when they are not needed, leading to the formation of masses of excess body tissue called **malignant tumors**. Malignant or cancerous tumors may spread to other parts of the body, where they invade healthy tissue. Cancerous tumors damage vital body organs and systems, leading to death in many cases. Cancers can form in any body tissue or organ.

malignant tumors Uncontrolled growths of body cells that invade surrounding tissue and spread to other parts of the body.

There are many causes of cancer, including heredity, exposure to cancer-causing chemicals, and even exposure to some viruses (Chen, Odenike, & Rowley, 2010; Samuels et al., 2004; T. Walsh et al., 2006). Nearly two of three cancer deaths in this country are attributable to two modifiable behaviors: smoking and an unhealthy diet. Other modifiable behaviors, such as alcohol consumption and excess sun exposure, also contribute to the development of cancer (Snowden, 2009). The good news is that these behaviors can be controlled.

CONCEPT 12.21
Nearly two of three cancer deaths in the United States are accounted for by two modifiable behaviors: smoking and diet.

© David Harry Stewart/Stone/Getty Images

Psychological support groups can help cancer patients cope with the disease.

Risk Factors for Cancer

Some risk factors, like family history and age (older people are at greater risk), are unavoidable. Others, including the factors we now review, can be controlled through lifestyle changes. If everyone practiced these cancer-preventive behaviors, hundreds of thousands of lives would be saved each year (see Table 12.2).

Smoking You probably know that smoking causes lung cancer, which is the leading cancer killer of men and women. Nearly 90 percent of lung cancer deaths are directly attributable to smoking. But smoking is linked to many other cancers, including colorectal (colon or rectal) cancer. As noted earlier, smoking accounts for about one-third of all cancer deaths in the United States.

CONCEPT 12.22
If everyone practiced cancer-preventative behaviors, hundreds of thousands of lives would be saved each year.

Diet and Alcohol Consumption High levels of consumption of saturated fat, the type of fat found in meat and dairy products, is linked to two leading cancer killers: prostate cancer in men and colorectal cancer. All told, dietary factors account for about 30 percent of cancer deaths. Obesity, which is linked to a high-fat diet, is also associated with an increased risk of some types of cancer (D. Li et al., 2009; Stolzenberg-Solomon et al, 2008).

Smoking and diet are not the only forms of behavior associated with higher risks of cancer. Heavy alcohol consumption raises the risk of several cancers, including those of the mouth, pharynx, and esophagus.

TABLE 12.2 Behaviors That Can Help Prevent Cancer

■ Avoid tobacco use.
■ If you use alcohol, limit consumption to one drink per day for women or two drinks per day for men.
■ Maintain a physically active lifestyle.
■ Follow a healthy diet and limit intake of saturated fat.
■ Maintain a healthy weight.
■ Avoid unprotected exposure to the sun.
■ Get regular medical examinations and follow recommended cancer screening procedures (ask your health care provider).

© ragsac/BigStockPhoto.com

© iStockphoto.com/ Evgeny Kuklev

Sun Exposure Prolonged sun exposure can lead to **basal cell carcinoma**, the most common type of skin cancer but also the least dangerous. This form of cancer, which accounts for 75 percent of skin cancers, typically appears on the head, neck, and hands—areas of the body frequently exposed to the sun. It is readily curable as long as it is detected at an early stage and removed surgically. Severe sunburns early in life increase the risk of developing the least common but most deadly form of skin cancer, **melanoma**, which accounts for fewer than 10 percent of skin cancers but claims about 8,700 lives in the United States annually (NCI, 2010b, 2010c). To protect ourselves from skin cancer, we need to limit our exposure to the sun and use a sunscreen whenever exposure exceeds a few minutes.

basal cell carcinoma A form of skin cancer that is easily curable if detected and removed early.

melanoma The most deadly form of skin cancer.

Stress Is the risk of developing cancer related to stress? Unfortunately, we don't yet have a clear answer (S. Cohen, Janicki-Deverts, & Miller, 2007). Recently, a large-scale study of women's health showed no relationship between stressful life events and breast cancer risk (Michael et al., 2009). We also lack compelling evidence that psychological techniques help cancer patients live longer or that adoption of any particular coping style, such as a "fighting spirit," boosts the odds of surviving cancer (Coyne et al., 2009; Kissane et al., 2007). That said, many cancer patients benefit psychologically from counseling to help them cope with the devastating emotional effects of cancer, especially feelings of depression, anxiety, and hopelessness (Foley et al., 2010; Hopko et al., 2007; Manne et al., 2010).

Stress and Other Physical Disorders

Stress is implicated in many physical disorders, including asthma, headaches, and possibly peptic ulcers.

CONCEPT 12.23
Stress plays a role in many physical disorders, including asthma, headaches, and possibly peptic ulcers.

Asthma **Asthma** is a chronic lung disease in which the tubes in the lungs needed for breathing—the bronchial airways, or *bronchi*—become obstructed or blocked. This blockage makes breathing difficult during acute attacks and can be life-threatening in some cases. Nearly one in 10 adults and nearly one in seven children in the United States suffer from asthma (Akinbami, 2010). Asthma has many causes, including underlying allergic reactions, respiratory infections (such as bronchitis or pneumonia), exposure to environmental pollutants (such as soot and cigarette smoke), and genetic and immunological factors. Psychological factors such as stress, depression, and anxiety do not directly cause asthma, but they can increase susceptibility to asthmatic attacks (Lehrer et al., 2002).

asthma A chronic lung disease characterized by temporary obstruction of the breathing tubes, leading to attacks of wheezing and difficulty breathing.

Headaches Does your head ache or throb when you are under stress? Millions of people suffer from stress-related headaches. When we are under stress, the muscles in our scalp, face, neck, and shoulders may tense up, leading to a muscle-tension headache, the most common type of headache. Muscle-tension headaches typically involve dull, steady pain experienced on both sides of the head, along with feelings of pressure or tightness.

Stress plays a role in another type of headache that affects about one in 10 Americans, the **migraine headache.** A migraine is a severe type of headache that can last for hours or even days and involves piercing or throbbing sensations (usually on one side

migraine headache An intense, prolonged headache brought on by changes in blood flow in the brain's blood vessels.

CONCEPT CHART 12.2 Psychological Risk Factors in Physical Disorders

Health Problem	Psychological or Behavioral Risk Factors	Healthier Habits
Coronary heart disease 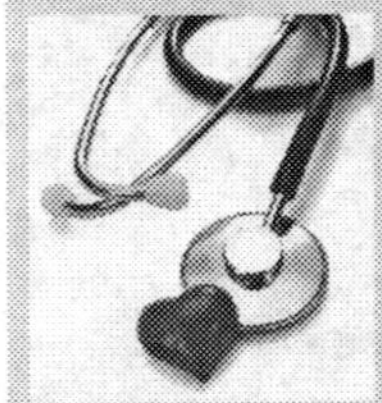 © Picsfive/shutterstock.com	Smoking, unhealthy diet, lack of physical activity, persistent negative emotions	Avoid tobacco use, get regular exercise, control negative emotions, limit dietary fat, reduce excess weight, practice stress-management techniques
Cancer 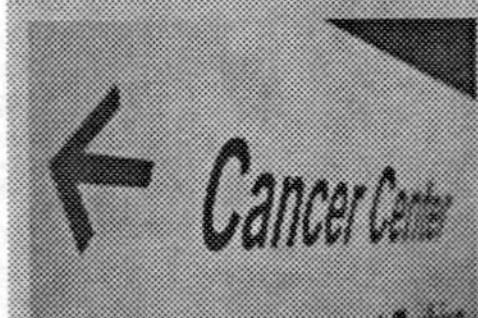 © iStockphoto.com/ Braden Gunem	Smoking, high-fat diet, heavy alcohol consumption, unsafe sun exposure, inactivity, possibly stress	Avoid tobacco use and excessive alcohol consumption, regular exercise, use sunscreens, reduce excess weight, practice stress-management techniques
Asthma 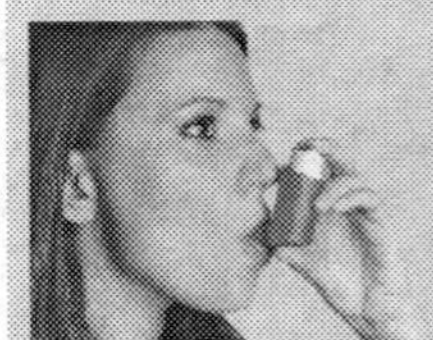 © keeweeboy/ BigStockPhoto.com	Stress may trigger asthma attacks in vulnerable individuals	Practice stress-management and relaxation techniques
Headaches  © PaulMaguire/ BigStockPhoto.com	Stress may contribute to muscle-tension headaches and migraines	Practice relaxation techniques or biofeedback
Peptic Ulcers  © iStockphoto.com/ Robert Kneschke	Stress may increase susceptibility to *H. pylori* or exacerbate the condition	Keep stress at tolerable levels to reduce risk

of the head) that may become so intense they seem intolerable. It results from changes in blood flow to the brain, which may be caused by imbalances in the neurotransmitter serotonin. Serotonin plays a role in many bodily processes, including the regulation of the size of blood vessels in the brain, which in turn affects the amount of blood flow. Differences in the amount of blood flowing to different parts of the brain may account for the throbbing, piercing sensations associated with migraine attacks.

Genetic factors also play a role in susceptibility to migraines (Estevez & Gardner, 2004). Migraines can be triggered by many factors such as hormonal fluctuations, fatigue, use of certain drugs or chemicals, foods such as ripened cheese or chocolate, and even exposure to glaring lights or changes in barometric pressure.

Pain relievers such as aspirin and ibuprofen (including the brand-names Advil, Nuprin, and Motrin) are widely used in treating headache pain. Other drugs work on regulating serotonin levels in the brain, which may benefit migraine sufferers. Psychological treatment, including stress-reduction techniques such as relaxation training and biofeedback, can also help reduce pain associated with muscle-tension and migraine headaches (Gatchel, 2001; Holroyd, 2002).

Peptic Ulcers About one in 10 people in the United States suffers from **peptic ulcers,** which are sores that form on the lining of the stomach or small intestine. The great majority of cases are caused by a bacterium, *H. pylori.* The bacterium damages the protective lining of the stomach or intestines, leading to ulcers. Peptic ulcers can be cured in many cases with antibiotics that directly attack *H. pylori.* Still, it is puzzling that only about 10 to 20 percent of people who harbor *H. pylori* in their stomachs develop ulcers. Psychological factors, such as stress and behaviors such as smoking and alcohol abuse, may increase susceptibility. One possibility is that stress may increase the release of stomach acid, which together with *H. pylori* may cause ulcers to form on the linings of the stomach or small intestine.

peptic ulcers Sores that form on the lining of the stomach or small intestine.

In the following module we will examine ways of handling stress so that it does not lead to distress. But first you may want to review Concept Chart 12.2, which highlights some key points about psychological risk factors in physical disorders.

12.2 MODULE REVIEW Psychological Factors in Physical Illness

Recite It

How are psychological factors linked to the health of our heart and circulatory system?

- Behaviors such as smoking, inactivity, and adopting an unhealthy diet as well as psychological traits such as hostility are associated with an increased risk of heart disease.

What roles do psychological factors play in the development of cancer?

- Unhealthy behaviors, such as smoking and consumption of a high-fat diet, are linked to an increased risk of various forms of cancer.

Recall It

1. Match the following terms with the appropriate descriptions: (a) arteriosclerosis; (b) myocardial infarction (MI); (c) plaque; (d) atherosclerosis.
   - **i.** narrowing of vessels carrying blood to the heart.
   - **ii.** fatty deposits on artery walls.
   - **iii.** a heart attack (blood clot blocks blood flow in a coronary artery).
   - **iv.** thicker, harder, and less elastic artery walls.
2. (a) List some of the major risk factors for coronary heart disease. (b) Which of these are we able to control?
3. Smoking ________ the risk of suffering a heart attack.
   - **a.** doubles.
   - **b.** triples.
   - **c.** quadruples.
   - **d.** has no effect on.
4. ________ of cancer deaths are associated with two lifestyle factors: ________ and ________.

Think About It

- What risk factors do you have for cardiovascular disease that you can control? What steps do you need to take to control these factors?
- What steps are you taking to protect yourself from the risk of cancer? What steps are you taking to ensure early detection of cancer?

APPLICATION MODULE 12.3

Taking the Distress Out of Stress

We may not be able to eliminate all stress from our lives—indeed, a certain amount of stress might be good for us. But we can learn to cope more effectively so that stress doesn't lead to distress. Here, we summarize some basic skills needed to manage stress more effectively (adapted from Nevid and Rathus, 2010).

Maintain Stress at a Tolerable Level

CONCEPT 12.24
Though stress may be an unavoidable part of life, how we cope with stress lies within our control.

Examine your daily life. Are you constantly running from place to place just to keep pace with all the demands on your time? Is it difficult to find time just to relax? Following are some suggestions for keeping stress within a manageable level:

1. *Reduce daily hassles.* What can you do to reduce the stressful burdens of daily hassles? Might you rearrange your school or work schedule to avoid morning traffic jams? How about joining a car pool? You might still be stuck in traffic, but you can use that time to catch up on your reading rather than fighting traffic.
2. *Know your limits.* Don't bite off more than you can chew. Avoid taking on more tasks than you can reasonably accomplish. Whenever possible, delegate responsibilities to others.
3. *Follow a reasonable schedule.* Learn to schedule tasks so they don't pile up. In this way, you break down stressful tasks into more manageable doses. If stressful demands become too taxing, try to extend some deadlines to give yourself added time to finish your work.
4. *Take frequent breaks.* When working on an assignment, take frequent breaks to refresh your mind and body.
5. *Develop more effective time-management skills.* Use a monthly calendar to organize your activities and tasks. Schedule as many of your activities as you can in advance to ensure that you have enough time to accomplish your goals. But don't over-schedule yourself. Allow yourself some free, unstructured time.
6. *Learn to prioritize.* Use a monthly calendar to list the tasks you must accomplish each day. Prioritize your daily goals. Assign the number 1 to tasks you must accomplish, the number 2 to those you'd like to accomplish but are less essential, and the number 3 to tasks you'd like to accomplish if time permits. Then arrange your daily schedule to progress through your list.

Learn Relaxation Skills

Tone down your body's response to stress by learning to relax. Some people find that listening to music helps them unwind at the end of the day. Some like to curl up with a book (not a textbook—not even this one). Others use more formal relaxation techniques, such as biofeedback training (see Chapter 3), meditation (see Chapter 4), and deep breathing exercises. To practice deep breathing, breathe only through your nose. Take about the same amount of time breathing in as breathing out, and pace yourself by silently repeating a resonant word like "relax" on each out breath. Elongating the "x" sound can help you lengthen each breath to ensure that you breathe deeply and evenly. Many colleges offer seminars or workshops in stress-management techniques where students can learn to develop relaxation skills. Why not check them out?

© MICHAEL BUSH/UPI/Newscom

Humor can help relieve stresses of everyday life. Treating yourself to a comedy tonight may help relieve stressful burdens at least temporarily.

Take Care of Your Body

Prepare your body to cope more effectively with stress by getting enough sleep, following a nutritionally balanced diet, exercising regularly, obtaining regular medical checkups, and avoiding harmful substances such as drugs. Evidence indicates that regular exercise increases resilience to stress and lessens the emotional consequences of stress, such as anxiety and depression (Harris, Cronkite, & Moos, 2006; Salmon, 2001). That said, fewer than half (43 percent) of American adults exercise at least three times a week, according to a recent national survey (D. E. King et al., 2009).

Gather Information

People facing a serious illness may cope more effectively if they obtain information about their underlying condition rather than keeping themselves in the dark. Whether you are facing an illness or the stress of adjusting to life in a new town or city, gather the information you need to adjust more effectively.

Expand Your Social Network

Social support helps people cope better during times of stress. You can expand your social network by forming relationships with others through participation in clubs and organizations sponsored at your college. The office of student life or counseling services at your college should be able to advise you about the availability of these resources.

Take in a Comedy Tonight

Humor can be an antidote to stress. A dose of humor not only makes us laugh, but it also provides at least temporary relief from stressful concerns of daily life. The idea that humor can be good medicine is hardly new, as we see in this biblical maxim: "A merry heart doeth good like a medicine" (Proverbs 17:22).

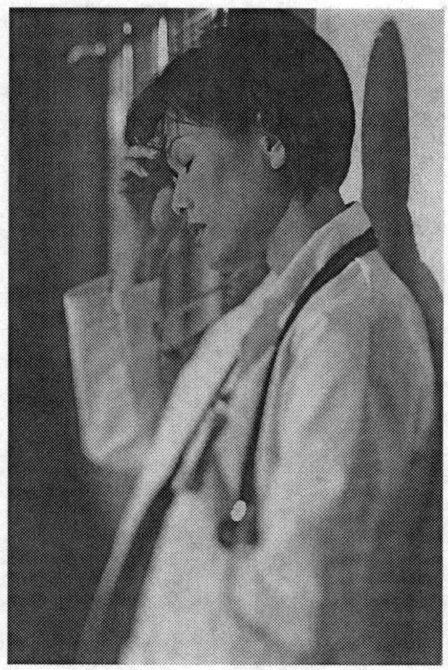

© Rubberball/ Jupiter Images

Are you at risk of burnout? What steps can you take to relieve excessive stress due to work or other commitments?

Prevent Burnout

Burnout is a state of physical and emotional exhaustion and reduced effectiveness resulting from excessive job demands, caregiving responsibilities, and other stress-laden commitments (Maslach & Leiter, 2008). Evidence links burnout to a higher risk of cardiovascular disease and other significant health problems (Melamed et al., 2006). You can take steps to prevent burnout, such as setting reasonable goals and limits for yourself. Establish personal goals that are attainable, and don't push yourself beyond your limits. Learn to say "no" when people make excessive demands on you. Start delegating responsibilities, and learn to cut back on low-priority tasks when commitments begin piling up.

Replace Stress-Inducing Thoughts with Stress-Busting Thoughts

What you say to yourself under your breath about stressful events can influence your adjustment to them. Do you react to disappointing events by blowing them out of proportion—treating them as utter disasters rather than as mere setbacks? Do you see events only in all-or-nothing, black-and-white terms—as either total successes or total failures? Do you place unrealistic expectations on yourself and then hold yourself accountable for failing to measure up? If you have thought patterns like these, you may benefit from replacing them with rational alternatives. Examples include: "This is a problem, not a catastrophe. I am a good problem-solver. I can find a solution to this problem."

We are better able to withstand stressful demands when we believe we are capable of handling them. If your self-confidence has been shaky, try to boost it by setting achievable goals for yourself and taking steps to accomplish them. Remind yourself to respond to disappointments as opportunities to learn from your mistakes, not as signs of inevitable failure.

Don't Keep Upsetting Feelings Bottled Up

Keeping disturbing thoughts and feelings under wraps may place stressful demands on your autonomic nervous system, which in turn may weaken your immune system and make you more vulnerable to physical illness. Expressing your feelings about stressful or traumatic events may have positive effects on your emotional and physical health. In particular, consider writing down your feelings in a journal or sharing them with a trusted person or a helping professional.

Control Type A Behavior

© Getty Images/jupiter images

What can you do to reduce Type A behavior?

People with the Type A behavior pattern place additional stressful demands on themselves by attempting to accomplish as much as possible in as little time as possible. Though it may not be feasible (or even desirable) to turn "hares" into "tortoises," researchers find that such people can learn to modify their Type A behavior, such as by reducing their sense of time urgency (M. Friedman & Ulmer, 1984). These behavioral changes may prove helpful, even to people who are not bona fide Type A's:

- *Take things slower.* Slow down your walking pace. Enjoy looking at your surroundings rather than rushing past them. Bear in mind that posted speed limits are the maximum speeds you are permitted to drive, not the minimum.
- *Read books for enjoyment.* Spend time reading enjoyable books—perhaps that latest techno-thriller or a romance novel, but not a book designed to help you climb the corporate ladder.
- *Leave your computer at home.* Don't bring a laptop or other work-related gadgets with you on vacation or when visiting friends.
- *Avoid rushing through your meals.* Don't wolf down your food. Take time to talk to your family members or dining companions.
- *Engage in enjoyable activities.* Go to the movies, visit art galleries and museums, or attend the theater or concerts. Give yourself a break from the stressful demands of daily life.

- *Develop relaxing interests.* Daily stress is more manageable when you make it a practice to engage in some pleasant events every day. Choose activities you truly enjoy, not simply those that are preferred by others. Take up a hobby or pursue an interest that can help you unwind.
- *Set realistic daily goals.* Don't overschedule your activities or impose unrealistic demands on yourself. Lighten up.

Hostility, a component of the Type A behavior profile, is associated with quickness to anger. Suggestions for controlling anger are discussed in Chapter 8.

In sum, stress is an inescapable part of life. But handling stress more effectively can help you keep it at a manageable level and tone down your body's alarm reaction. Stress may be a fact of life, but it is a fact you can learn to live with.

Thinking Critically About Psychology

Based on your reading of this chapter, answer the following questions. Then, to evaluate your progress in developing critical thinking skills, compare your answers to the sample answers found in Appendix A.

Every now and then we hear claims touting some miracle drug, vitamin, hormone, or alternative therapy that promises to enhance health and vitality, cure or prevent disease, or even reverse the effects of aging. Some of these claims are outright hoaxes. Others take promising scientific leads and exaggerate or distort the evidence. Still others tout psychological therapies as cures for medical conditions on the basis of unsupported testimonials. Although the federal watchdog agency, the Food and Drug Administration (FDA), regulates health claims for drugs and medications, many of the substances found in your health-food store or neighborhood supermarket purporting to have disease-preventive or anti-aging effects are classified as foods and are not regulated as drugs. It's basically a case of "buyer beware."

Critical thinkers do not take health claims at face value. They recognize that alternative therapies and health care products may not work as promised and could even be harmful. Another concern is that people advocating particular therapies may have a vested interest in getting consumers to try their services or use their products, and may play fast and loose with the truth.

Use your critical thinking skills to read between the lines in evaluating health claims. What do you think these claims for products found in your neighborhood health store actually mean?

- Designed to enhance vitality and well-being.
- Promotes muscle growth.
- Recommended by leading physicians.
- Backed by advanced research.
- Super-charge your metabolism!

Log in to CengageBrain to access the resources your instructor requires. For this book, you can access:

CourseMate

Psychology CourseMate brings course concepts to life with interactive learning, study, and exam preparation tools that support the printed textbook. A textbook-specific website, Psychology CourseMate includes an integrated interactive eBook and other interactive learning tools including quizzes, flashcards, videos, and more.

CENGAGENOW

CengageNow is an easy-to-use online resource that helps you study in less time to get the grade you want—NOW. Take a pre-test for this chapter and receive a personalized study plan based on your results that will identify the topics you need to review and direct you to online resources to help you master those topics. Then take a post-test to help you determine the concepts you have mastered and what you will need to work on. If your textbook does not include an access code card, go to CengageBrain.com to gain access.

Visit www.cengagebrain.com to access your account and purchase materials.

VISUAL OVERVIEW Chapter 12 Psychology and Health

MODULE 12.1 Stress: What It Is and What It Does to the Body

What Is Stress?

- Pressure to adjust or cope with environmental demands or challenges

Sources of Stress

- Hassles
- Life Events
- Frustration
- Conflict
- Traumatic Stressors
- Type A Behavior Pattern
- Acculturation

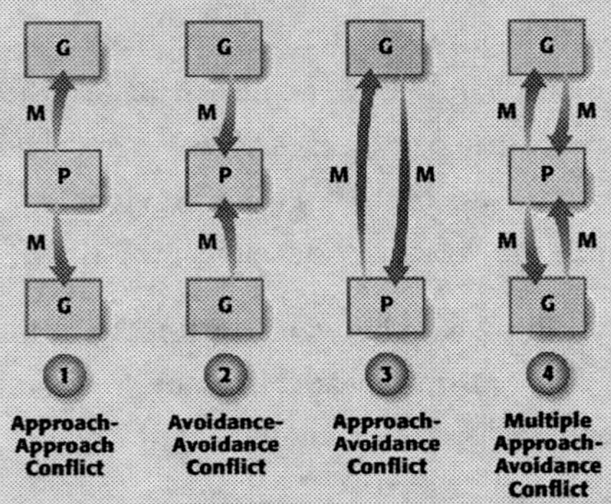

Types of Conflicts

Types of Conflicts

- Approach-Approach
- Avoidance-Avoidance
- Approach-Avoidance
- Multiple Approach-Avoidance

The Body's Response to Stress

- **General Adaptation Syndrome**: Comprises three stages: Alarm Stage→Resistance Stage→Exhaustion Stage
- **Stress and the Endocrine System**: Coordinated endocrine response within HPA axis
- **Stress and the Immune System**: Chronic stress can weaken immune system responses

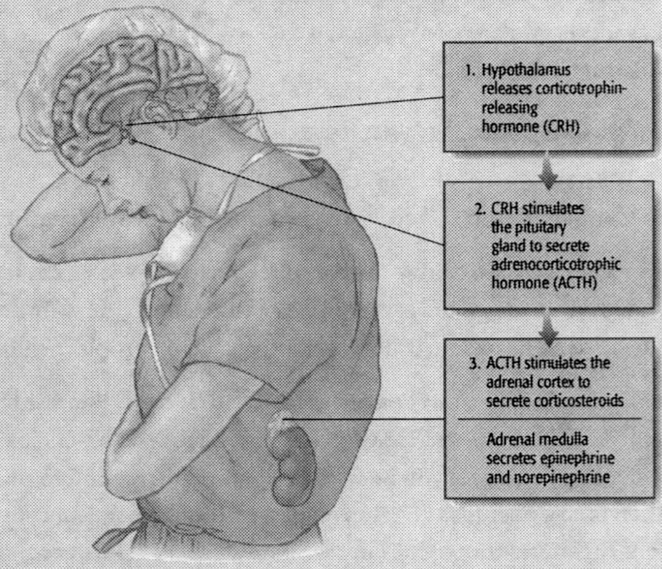

The Body's Response to Stress

Psychological Moderators of Stress

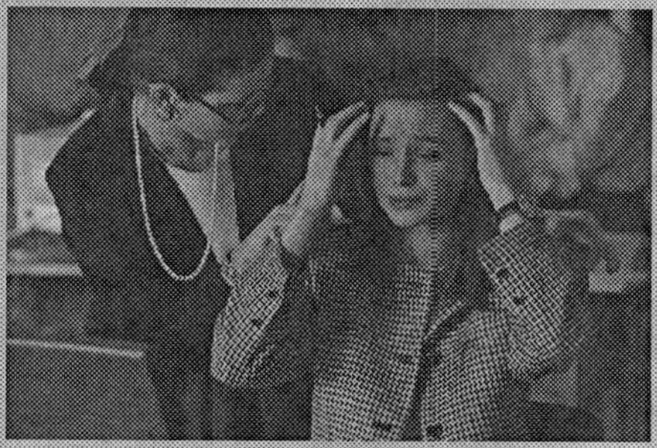
© Ghislain & Marie David De Lossy

- **Social Support**: A helping hand in times of stress
- **Self-Efficacy**: Confidence in handling stressful challenges
- **Predictability and Controllability**: Stress is more manageable when it is predictable and controllable
- **Psychological Hardiness**: Commitment, challenge, and control
- **Optimism**: Believing the proverbial glass is half full

Managing Stress

- Maintain stress at a tolerable level
- Develop relaxation skills
- Take care of your body
- Gather information
- Expand your social network
- Prevent burnout
- Replace stress-inducing thoughts with stress-busting thoughts
- Control Type A behavior

MODULE 12.2 Psychological Factors in Physical Illness

Behavioral Risk Factors

- **Coronary Heart Disease**: Smoking, unhealthy diet, inactivity, hostility, and chronic negative emotions
- **Cancer**: Smoking, high-fat diet, excessive sun exposure
- **Stress Implicated in Other Health Conditions**: Asthma, ulcers, headaches

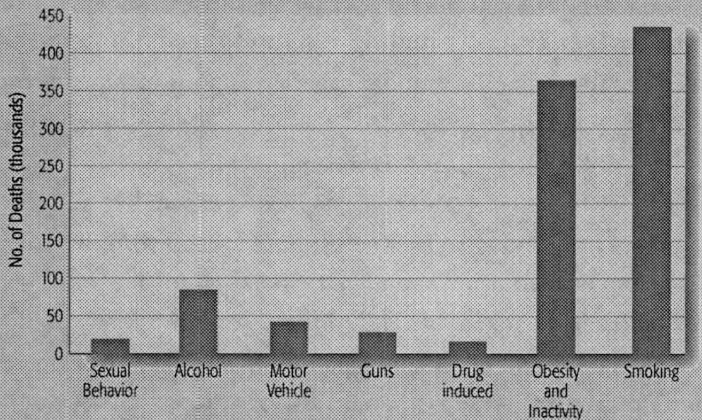

Numbers of Deaths in U.S. Due to Behavioral Causes

13 Personality

Three Blind Men and the Elephant

There is an ancient parable about three blind men who encounter an elephant for the first time. They each touch a different part of the elephant and try to relate to the others what the animal is like. Each claims that he alone knows the true nature of the beast. One grabs the legs and announces to the others that here is an animal built like a tree—strong and upright. The second man strokes the animal's trunk and exclaims that the first man is mistaken; the animal is long, narrow, and squirmy, like a snake. Not so, claims the third man, who touches the tail and claims the animal is like a rope. Each of the blind men believed they were correct in their views, but each was limited by their own perspective. They didn't realize there is more than one way of looking at something, and that one can gain a more complete understanding by seeing things from different perspectives.

In this chapter, the "elephant" we describe is *personality*, the relatively stable set of psychological characteristics and behavior patterns that make individuals unique and account for the consistency of their behavior over time. The human personality is a composite of the ways in which we relate to others and adapt to demands placed upon us in our environment. We will see there are different perspectives on the nature of personality, and that each perspective contributes to a fuller understanding.

In this chapter we consider the views of several leading personality theorists. Each brings a different perspective to bear on the study of personality. Some, including Sigmund Freud, the originator of psychoanalytic theory, emphasize unconscious influences on personality. They believe our personalities are shaped by a struggle between opposing forces within the mind.

Other theorists, called trait theorists, view personality as composed of a set of underlying traits that account for the consistencies in behavior from one situation to another. Social-cognitive theorists view personality in terms of the individual's learning history and ways of thinking. To humanistic psychologists, such as Carl Rogers and Abraham Maslow, our personalities are expressed through our efforts to actualize our unique potential as human beings. We explore these different perspectives and examine what each has to say about personality, beginning with the views of Freud and his followers.

DID YOU KNOW THAT...

- According to the originator of psychodynamic theory, Sigmund Freud, slips of the tongue may reveal hidden motives and wishes of which we are unaware? (p. 483)
- According to Carl Gustav Jung, another psychodynamic theorist, we inherit a shared unconscious mind containing archetypal images that can be traced back to ancestral times? (p. 486)
- The "Big Five" is not the name of a new NCAA basketball conference but the label used to describe the leading trait theory of personality today? (p. 492)
- Getting good grades in college may depend in part on your personality traits? (p. 492)
- A leading humanistic theorist, Carl Rogers, believed that children should receive love and approval unconditionally from their parents regardless of their behavior at any particular point in time? (p. 501)
- According to a widely held view in the nineteenth century, you can learn about a person's character by examining the bumps on the person's head? (p. 506)

Learning Objectives

By reading this chapter you will be able to . . .

1 **DEFINE** the concept of personality.

2 **IDENTIFY** and **DESCRIBE** three levels of consciousness and three mental structures in Freud's psychoanalytic theory.

3 **DESCRIBE** the different types of defense mechanisms and **APPLY** this knowledge to examples.

4 **IDENTIFY** the stages of psychosexual development in Freud's theory and **DESCRIBE** the features of each stage.

5 **DESCRIBE** the personality theories of Jung, Adler, and Horney.

6 **DESCRIBE** the trait theories of Allport, Cattell, Eysenck, and the Big Five model and **APPLY** this knowledge to examples of various traits.

7 **EVALUATE** the genetic basis of personality traits.

8 **DESCRIBE** the social-cognitive theories of Rotter, Bandura, and Mischel.

9 **DESCRIBE** the humanistic theories of Carl Rogers and Abraham Maslow.

10 **EXPLAIN** the roles of collectivism and individualism in self-identity.

11 **IDENTIFY** different types of personality tests and **DESCRIBE** their features.

12 **EVALUATE** self-report (MMPI) and projective personality tests (Rorschach, TAT).

13 **APPLY** behavioral principles to building self-esteem.

© Noel Hendrickson/Jupiter Images

Preview

MODULE 13.1

The Psychodynamic Perspective

- What are the three levels of consciousness in Freud's theory of the mind?
- What are the structures of personality in Freud's theory?
- What are psychological defense mechanisms?
- What are the five stages of psychosexual development in Freud's theory?
- What are some of the major contributions of other psychodynamic theorists?

personality The relatively stable constellation of psychological characteristics and behavioral patterns that account for our individuality and consistency over time.

psychoanalytic theory Freud's theory of personality that holds that personality and behavior are shaped by unconscious forces and conflicts.

Sigmund Freud was the architect of the first major theory of **personality**, called **psychoanalytic theory**. The central idea underlying his theory of personality is the belief that a dynamic struggle takes place within the human psyche (mind) between unconscious forces. For this reason, Freud's views and those of his followers are often called psychodynamic theory. In this module, we first discuss Freud's ideas and then describe the contributions of other theorists in the psychodynamic tradition who followed in Freud's footsteps.

Sigmund Freud: Psychoanalytic Theory

CONCEPT 13.1
The study of personality involves efforts to understand our uniqueness as individuals and the characteristics that account for consistencies in our behavior over time.

CONCEPT 13.2
Freud developed the first psychodynamic theory of personality, the belief that personality is shaped by underlying conflicts between opposing forces within the mind.

In the tradition of Darwin, Freud recognized that we share with nonhuman animals certain common processes that have *survival* as their aim. We need to breathe, eat, and eliminate bodily wastes. And to survive as a species, we need to reproduce. Freud believed we are endowed with a sexual instinct that has as its purpose the preservation of the species. He later would add an aggressive instinct to explain human aggression. Yet Freud believed that giving free rein to these instincts might tear apart the very fabric of society and of the family unit itself. To live in an ordered society, Freud maintained, humans need to control their primitive sexual and aggressive impulses. In other words, humans need to channel their sexual and aggressive instincts in socially appropriate ways so as to live harmoniously with one another. They need to learn that aggression or sexual touching is unacceptable except in socially acceptable contexts, such as the football field (aggressive impulses) and the marital bed (sexual impulses).

Freud developed psychoanalytic theory to account for how the mind accomplishes the task of balancing these conflicting demands of instinct and social acceptability. Freud's theory of personality is complex, but it can be represented in terms of four major concepts: levels of consciousness, structure of personality, defense mechanisms, and stages of psychosexual development.

© Time & Life Pictures/Getty Images

Sigmund Freud

Levels of Consciousness: The Conscious, the Preconscious, and the Unconscious

We can liken Freud's model of the human mind to a giant iceberg. Like an iceberg, which has much of its mass hidden below the surface of the water, most of the mind lies below the surface of conscious awareness (see ■ Figure 13.1). Freud represented

FIGURE 13.1 Levels of Consciousness in Freud's Theory
The human mind in Freudian theory can be likened to an iceberg in which only the tip rises above the level of conscious awareness. Though information held in the preconscious can be brought into the conscious mind at any time, much of the contents of the mind—including many of our deepest wishes, ideas, and urges—remain mired in the dark recesses of the unconscious.
Source: Adapted from Nevid et al., 2006.

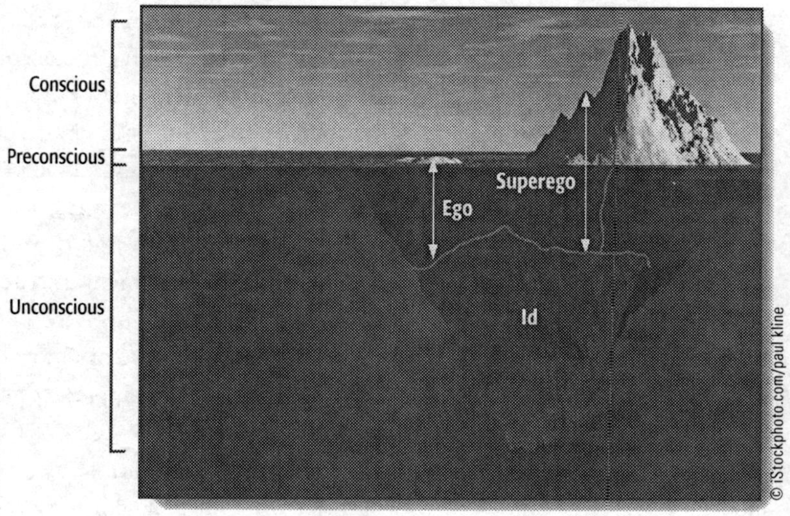

the mind as consisting of three levels of consciousness: the **conscious,** the **preconscious,** and the **unconscious.** The conscious is the tip of the iceberg. It is the level of consciousness that corresponds to our present awareness—what we are thinking or feeling at any given moment in time. The preconscious holds information we've stored from previous life experience or prior learning. This information can be retrieved from memory and brought into awareness at any time. Your telephone number, for example, is information stored in the preconscious that you can bring into awareness when needed.

The unconscious is like the large mass of the iceberg lying under the surface of the water. It contains primitive sexual and aggressive impulses as well as memories of troubling emotional experiences (e.g., traumatizing events) and unacceptable sexual or aggressive wishes or ideas. The contents of the unconscious cannot be brought directly into consciousness simply by focusing on them; they are brought into consciousness only with great difficulty, if at all. With so much of the contents of the mind mired in the unconscious, we remain unaware of our deepest wishes, ideas, and urges.

conscious To Freud, the part of the mind corresponding to the state of present awareness.

preconscious To Freud, the part of the mind whose contents can be brought into awareness through focused attention.

unconscious To Freud, the part of the mind that lies outside the range of ordinary awareness and that holds troubling or unacceptable urges, impulses, memories, and ideas.

The Structure of Personality: Id, Ego, and Superego

Freud proposed that personality consists of three mental entities called **id**, **ego**, and **superego**. The balance and interactions of these three parts of the personality largely determine our behavior and our ability to function effectively in meeting the life challenges we face. Freud did not consider these mental entities to be actual structures we could locate in the brain. Rather, he conceived of them as hypothetical concepts that represent the opposing forces within the personality.

As Figure 13.1 shows, the id (literally, "it") operates only in the unconscious. The id contains our baser animal drives and instinctual impulses, including hunger, thirst, elimination, sex, and aggression. The id stirs us to action to ensure that our basic biological needs are met. It is the only psychic structure present at birth and follows what Freud called the **pleasure principle**, the demand for instant gratification without regard to social rules or customs. In essence, the id wants what it wants when it wants it. Think of the infant. When a need arises, such as hunger or elimination, the infant demands immediate satisfaction of that need. It doesn't wait patiently until an appropriate time comes to feed or to move its bowels. According to Freud, when the desired object is not available (mother's nipple, for example), the id achieves partial gratification by forming a mental image of the desired object.

The infant soon finds that not every demand is instantly gratified. It also learns that conjuring a mental image of the desired object is a poor substitute for the real thing. It finds it must cope with frustration and learn to delay gratification. So a second part of the mind forms during the first year of life that is responsible for organizing ways to handle delays of gratification. Freud called this entity ego. The ego represents "reason and good sense" (Freud, 1964).

CONCEPT 13.3
Freud believed that the mind consists of three levels of consciousness: the conscious, the preconscious, and the unconscious.

CONCEPT 13.4
Freud believed that personality consists of three mental entities: the id, the ego, and the superego.

id Freud's term for the psychic structure existing in the unconscious that contains our baser animal drives and instinctual impulses.

ego Freud's term for the psychic structure that attempts to balance the instinctual demands of the id with social realities and expectations.

superego Freud's term for the psychic structure that corresponds to an internal moral guardian or conscience.

pleasure principle In Freudian theory, a governing principle of the id that is based on demand for instant gratification without regard to social rules or customs.

reality principle In Freudian theory, the governing principle of the ego that takes into account what is practical and acceptable in satisfying basic needs.

The ego operates according to the **reality principle**, the basis for operating in the world by taking into account what is practical and acceptable. The ego seeks ways to satisfy the demands of the id without incurring social disapproval. The id may motivate you to rise from your chair and seek nourishment when you are hungry. But the ego enables you to make a sandwich and keeps you from grabbing food from someone else's plate.

The superego is our internal moral guardian or conscience. It develops by around ages three to five through a process in which it splits off from the ego to form an internalized mental structure comprising the moral teachings of one's parents or other significant figures. Part of the superego may be available to consciousness, the part that corresponds to our moral convictions—our personal beliefs about right and wrong. But much of the superego operates in the unconscious, standing in judgment of whether the actions of the ego are morally right or wrong. When they are not, the superego can impose self-punishment in the form of guilt or shame.

CONCEPT 13.5

Freud believed that the ego uses defense mechanisms as a means of preventing anxiety that would result from conscious awareness of disturbing impulses, wishes, or ideas arising from the id.

Our behavior is a product of the dynamic struggles among the id, the ego, and the superego. These conflicts take place outside of conscious awareness, on the stage of the unconscious mind. The ego is the great compromiser. It stands between the superego and the id. It seeks to satisfy the demands of the id without offending the moral standards of the superego. Part of the ego rises to the level of consciousness, such as when we consciously seek to fix ourselves a sandwich in response to hunger pangs. But much of the ego operates below the surface of consciousness, where it employs strategies called *defense mechanisms* to prevent awareness of unacceptable sexual or aggressive impulses or wishes.

defense mechanisms In Freudian theory, the reality-distorting strategies of the ego to prevent awareness of anxiety-evoking or troubling ideas or impulses.

repression In Freudian theory, a type of defense mechanism involving motivated forgetting of anxiety-evoking material.

denial In Freudian theory, a defense mechanism involving the failure to recognize a threatening impulse or urge.

reaction formation In Freudian theory, a defense mechanism involving behavior that stands in opposition to one's true motives and desires so as to prevent conscious awareness of them.

rationalization In Freudian theory, a defense mechanism involving the use of self-justification to explain away unacceptable behavior, impulses, or ideas.

projection In Freudian theory, a defense mechanism involving the projection of one's own unacceptable impulses, wishes, or urges onto another person.

sublimation In Freudian theory, a defense mechanism involving the channeling of unacceptable impulses into socially sanctioned behaviors or interests.

regression In Freudian theory, a defense mechanism in which an individual, usually under high levels of stress, reverts to a behavior characteristic of an earlier stage of development.

displacement In Freudian theory, a defense mechanism in which an unacceptable sexual or aggressive impulse is transferred to an object or person that is safer or less threatening than the original object of the impulse.

Defense Mechanisms

In Freud's view, the ego uses **defense mechanisms** to prevent the anxiety that would result if troubling desires and memories residing in the unconscious were fully realized in conscious awareness (Murray, Kilgour, & Wasylkiw, 2000). The major defense mechanism—**repression**, or motivated forgetting—involves the banishment to the unconscious of unacceptable wishes, fantasies, urges, and impulses (Boag, 2006). Other defense mechanisms identified by Freud include **denial, reaction formation, rationalization, projection, sublimation, regression**, and **displacement** (see Table 13.1).

Repression permits people to remain outwardly calm and controlled even though they harbor hateful or lustful urges under the surface of awareness. Yet repressed desires or wishes may be revealed in disguised forms, such as in dream symbols and in slips of the tongue (so-called *Freudian slips*) (Freud, 1938). From a Freudian perspective, saying to a friend "I hate what you're saying" when you intended to say, "I know what you're saying," may reveal underlying hateful impulses you may harbor toward that person (Nevid, Rathus, & Greene, 2011).

SLICE OF LIFE Slips of the tongue are open to many interpretations. Some may simply represent memories kindled by similarities in wording. Professor Fred Nesbit of Sauk Valley Community College recalls that one day during class he intended to say that psychologists receive "extensive" training in psychopharmacology, but what he actually said was that they receive "expensive" training, which may reflect a memory of his own training experiences.

Defense mechanisms may be a normal process by which the ego adapts to the unreasonable demands of the id, but they can also give rise to abnormal or maladaptive forms of behavior. For example, a man who sexually assaults a woman may rationalize to himself that "she had it coming" rather than directly confronting his aggressive

TABLE 13.1 Major Defense Mechanisms in Psychodynamic Theory

Type of Defense Mechanism	Description	Example
Repression	Expulsion from awareness of unacceptable ideas or motives	A person remains unaware of harboring hateful or destructive impulses toward others.
Regression	Emergence of behavior typical of earlier stages of development	Stressed college student starts biting his nails or becomes totally dependent on others.
Displacement	The transfer of unacceptable impulses away from their original objects onto safer or less threatening objects	A worker slams a door after his boss chews him out.
Denial	Refusal to recognize a threatening impulse or desire	A person who nearly chokes someone to death acts afterward like it was "no big deal."
Reaction formation	Behaving in a way that is the opposite of one's true wishes or desires in order to keep these repressed	A sexually frustrated person goes on a personal crusade to stamp out pornography.
Rationalization	The use of self-justifications to explain away unacceptable behavior	When asked why she continues to smoke, a woman says, "Cancer doesn't run in my family."
Projection	Imposing one's own impulses or wishes onto another person	A sexually inhibited person misinterprets other people's friendly approaches as sexual advances.
Sublimation	The channeling of unacceptable impulses into socially constructive pursuits	A person channels aggressive impulses into competitive sports.

urges. A person who regresses to a dependent infantile-like state during times of extreme stress may be shielded from the anxiety of facing the stressful situation but be unable to function effectively.

Stages of Personality Development

In Freud's view, personality develops through five psychosexual stages of development. He considered these stages to be psychosexual in nature because they involve changes in how the child seeks physical pleasure from sexually sensitive parts of the body, called **erogenous zones**. He further believed that physical activities connected to basic life functions, such as feeding, elimination, and reproduction, are basically "sexual" because they are inherently pleasurable. So the infant sucking at the mother's breast or eliminating bodily wastes is performing acts that are sexual in Freud's view. And why are these activities pleasurable? The answer, Freud believed, is clear: They are essential to survival. The infant needs to suck to obtain nourishment. If sucking weren't pleasurable, the infant wouldn't do it and would likely die. As the child progresses through the stages of psychosexual development, the primary erogenous zone shifts from one part of the body to another.

erogenous zones Parts of the body that are especially sensitive to sexual or pleasurable stimulation.

Psychological conflicts may emerge during each psychosexual stage of development. These conflicts, which often arise from receiving too much or too little gratification, can lead to the development of **fixations**—personality traits or behavior patterns characteristic of the particular stage. It's as though one's personality gets "stuck" at an early level of development. Let us briefly consider these five stages and the conflicts that may emerge during each one.

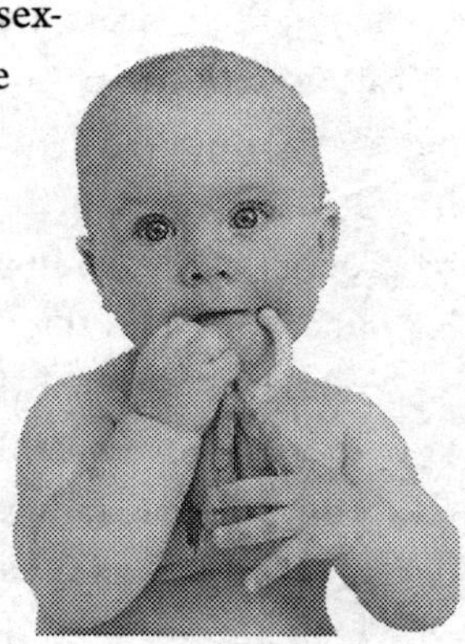
© Dmitry Naumov/shutterstock.com

fixations Constellations of personality traits characteristic of a particular stage of psychosexual development, resulting from either excessive or inadequate gratification at that stage.

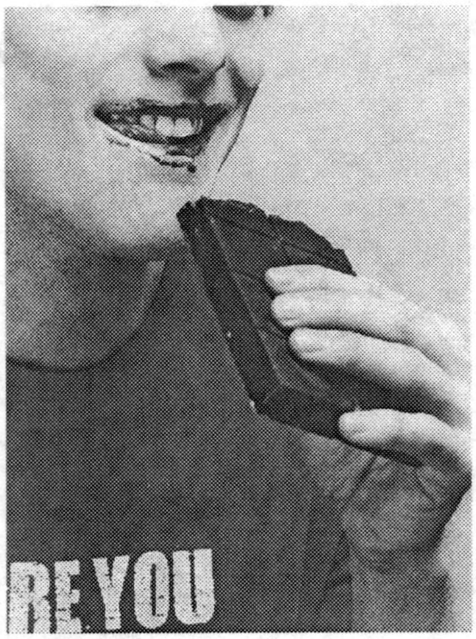

© Oliver Eltinger/Corbis

An oral fixation? Freud believed that insufficient or excessive gratification in the oral stage can lead to an oral fixation that becomes a stable part of the individual's personality.

oral stage In Freudian theory, the first stage of psychosexual development, during which the infant seeks sexual gratification through oral stimulation (sucking, mouthing, and biting).

anal stage In Freudian theory, the second stage of psychosexual development, during which sexual gratification is centered on processes of elimination (retention and release of bowel contents).

anal-retentive personality In Freudian theory, a personality type characterized by perfectionism and excessive needs for self-control as expressed through extreme neatness and punctuality.

anal-expulsive personality In Freudian theory, a personality type characterized by messiness, lack of self-discipline, and carelessness.

phallic stage In Freudian theory, the third stage of psychosexual development, marked by erotic attention on the phallic region (penis in boys, clitoris in girls) and the development of the Oedipus complex.

Oedipus complex In Freudian theory, the psychological complex in which the young boy or girl develops incestuous feelings toward the parent of the opposite gender and perceives the parent of the same gender as a rival.

Electra complex The term given by some psychodynamic theorists to the form of the Oedipus complex in young girls.

Oral Stage The **oral stage** spans the period of birth through about 12 to 18 months of age. During this stage the primary erogenous zone is the mouth. The infant seeks sexual pleasure through sucking at its mother's breast and mouthing (taking objects into the mouth) or, later, biting objects that happen to be nearby, including the parents' fingers. Whatever fits into the mouth goes into the mouth. Too much gratification in the oral stage may lead to oral fixations in adulthood such as smoking, nail biting, alcohol abuse, and overeating. Too little gratification, perhaps from early weaning, may lead to the development of traits that suggest a failure to have needs met for nurturance and care during infancy, such as passivity, clinging dependence, and a pessimistic outlook.

Anal Stage By about the age of 18 months, the child has entered the **anal stage**. The anal cavity becomes the primary erogenous zone as the child develops the ability to control elimination by contracting and releasing the sphincter muscles at will. Yet this stage, which lasts until about age three, is set for conflict between the parents and the child around the issue of toilet training. To earn the parents' approval and avoid their disapproval, the child must learn to "go potty" at the appropriate time and to delay immediate gratification of the need to eliminate whenever the urge is felt.

In Freud's view, anal fixations reflect either too harsh or too lenient toilet training. Training that is too harsh may lead to traits associated with the so-called **anal-retentive personality**, such as perfectionism and extreme needs for self-control, orderliness, cleanliness, and neatness. Extremely lax training may lead to an opposite array of traits associated with the **anal-expulsive personality**, such as messiness, lack of self-discipline, and carelessness.

Phallic Stage During the phallic stage, which roughly spans the ages of three to six, the erogenous zone shifts to the phallic region—the penis in males and the clitoris in females. Conflicts with parents over masturbation (self-stimulation of the phallic area) may emerge at this time. But the core conflict of the **phallic stage** is the **Oedipus complex**, which involves the development of incestuous desires for the parent of the opposite sex leading to rivalry with the parent of the same sex. Freud named the Oedipus complex after the ancient Greek myth of Oedipus the King—the tragic story of Oedipus who unwittingly slew his father and married his mother. He believed that this ancient tale revealed a fundamental human truth about psychosexual development. Some of Freud's followers dubbed the female version of the Oedipus complex the **Electra complex**, after another figure in ancient Greek tragedy, Electra, who avenged her father's death by killing his murderers—her own mother and her mother's lover.

In Freud's view, boys normally resolve the conflict by forsaking their incestuous wishes for their mother and identifying with their rival—their father. Girls normally surrender their incestuous desires for their father and identify with their mother. Identification with the parent of the same sex leads to the development of gender-based behaviors. Boys develop aggressive and independent traits associated with masculinity. Girls develop nurturant and demure traits associated with femininity. Another by-product of the Oedipus complex is the development of the superego—the internalization of parental values in the form of a moral conscience.

Freud believed that the failure to successfully resolve Oedipal conflicts may cause boys to become resentful of strong masculine figures, especially authority figures. For either boys or girls, failure to identify with the parent of the same gender may lead to the development of traits associated with the opposite gender and perhaps homosexuality.

Freud also believed that young boys develop **castration anxiety**, the fear that their father will punish them for their sexual desires for their mother by castrating them. An unconscious fear of castration motivates boys to forsake their incestuous desires for their mother and to identify with their father. In Freud's view, girls experience **penis envy**, or jealousy of boys for having a penis. Penis envy leads girls to feel inferior or inadequate in relation to boys and to unconsciously blame their mother for bringing them into the world so "ill-equipped." But fears of losing their mother's love and protection over their incestuous desires for their fathers prompts girls to forsake these incestuous desires and to identify with their mother. As the girl becomes sexually mature, she forsakes her wish to have a penis of her own (to "be a man") for a desire to have a baby—that is, as a kind of penis substitute. Bear in mind that Freud believed the Oedipus complex, with its incestuous desires, rivalries, and castration anxiety and penis envy, largely occurs at an unconscious level. On the surface, all may seem quiet, masking the turmoil occurring within.

Latency Stage The turbulent psychic crisis of the phallic period gives way to a period of relative tranquility—the **latency stage**, spanning the years between about six and 12. The latency stage is so named because of the belief that sexual impulses remain latent (dormant) during this time.

Genital Stage The child enters the **genital stage** at about the time of puberty. The forsaken incestuous desires for the parent of the opposite sex give rise to yearnings for more appropriate sexual partners of the opposite gender. Girls may be attracted to boys who resemble "dear old Dad," while boys may seek "the kind of girl who married dear old Dad." Sexual energies seek expression through mature (genital) sexuality in the form of sexual intercourse in marriage and the bearing of children.

See Table 13.2 for a summary of Freud's psychosexual stages of development.

Other Psychodynamic Approaches

Freud attracted a host of followers, many of whom are recognized as important personality theorists in their own right. These followers held views that differed from Freud's in some key respects, but they retained certain central tenets of psychodynamic theory, especially the belief that behavior is influenced by unconscious conflicts within the personality. Yet, as a group, the theorists who followed in Freud's footsteps (often

CONCEPT 13.6

Freud believed that personality develops through five stages of psychosexual development: the oral, anal, phallic, latency, and genital stages.

→ Concept Link

In contrast to Freud, the psychodynamic theorist Erik Erikson posited stages of psychosocial development that begin in early childhood and continue through adulthood (discussed in Chapters 9 and 10).

castration anxiety In Freudian theory, unconscious fear of removal of the penis as punishment for having unacceptable sexual impulses.

penis envy In Freudian theory, jealousy of boys for having a penis.

latency stage In Freudian theory, the fourth stage of psychosexual development, during which sexual impulses remain latent or dormant.

genital stage In Freudian theory, the fifth and final stage of psychosexual development, which begins around puberty and corresponds to the development of mature sexuality and emphasis on procreation.

TABLE 13.2 Freud's Psychosexual Stages of Development

Psychosexual Age	Approximate Zone	Erogenous Zone	Source of Sexual Pleasure	Source of Conflict	Adult Characteristics Associated with Conflicts at This Stage
Oral	Birth to 12 to 18 months	Oral cavity	Sucking, biting, and mouthing	Weaning	Oral behaviors such as smoking, alcohol use, nail biting; dependency; passivity; pessimism
Anal	18 months to 3 years	Anal region	Retention and release of bodily waste	Toilet training	Anal-retentive vs. anal-expulsive traits
Phallic	3 to 6 years	Penis in boys; clitoris in girls	Masturbation	Masturbation; Oedipus complex	Homosexuality; resentment of authority figures in men; unresolved penis envy in women
Latency	6 years to puberty	None	None (focus on play and school activities)	None	None
Genital	Puberty to adulthood	Genitals (penis in men; vagina in women)	Return of sexual interests expressed in mature sexual relationships	None	None

CONCEPT 13.7

As a group, neo-Freudians placed a lesser emphasis on sexuality than did Freud and a greater emphasis on the roles of conscious choice, self-direction, creativity, and ways of relating to others.

personal unconscious Jung's term for an unconscious region of the mind comprising a reservoir of the individual's repressed memories and impulses.

collective unconscious In Jung's theory, a part of the mind containing ideas and archetypal images shared among humankind that have been transmitted genetically from ancestral humans.

archetypes Jung's term for the primitive images contained in the collective unconscious that reflect ancestral or universal experiences of human beings.

individual psychology Adler's theory of personality, which emphasizes the unique potential of each individual.

creative self In Adler's theory, the self-aware part of personality that organizes goal-seeking efforts.

called *neo-Freudians*) placed a lesser emphasis on sexual and aggressive motivations and a greater emphasis on social relationships and the workings of the ego, especially the development of a concept of the self. Here we discuss the major ideas of several of the leading neo-Freudians: Carl Jung, Alfred Adler, and Karen Horney. The contributions of another neo-Freudian, Erik Erikson, are discussed in Chapter 9.

Carl Jung: Analytical Psychology

Carl Gustav Jung (1875–1961) was once part of Freud's inner circle, but he broke with Freud as he developed his own distinctive views of personality. Jung shared with Freud the beliefs that unconscious conflicts influence human behavior and that defense mechanisms distort or disguise people's underlying motives. However, he placed greater emphasis on the present than on infantile or childhood experience, as well as greater emphasis on conscious processes, such as self-awareness and pursuit of self-directed goals (Boynton, 2004; I. Kirsch, 1996).

Jung believed that people possess both a **personal unconscious**, which consists of repressed memories and impulses, and a **collective unconscious**, or repository of ideas and images in the unconscious mind that is shared among all humans and passed down genetically through the generations. Jung believed that the collective unconscious holds primitive images called **archetypes** that reflect ancestral or universal human experiences, including images of an omniscient and all-powerful God, a young hero, and a fertile and nurturing mother figure. Jung believed that while these images remain unconscious, they influence our dreams and waking thoughts and emotions. It is the collective unconscious, Jung maintained, that explains similarities among cultures in dream images, religious symbols, and artistic expressions (such as movie heroes and heroines).

© NEW LINE CINEMA / THE KOBAL COLLECTION

The young hero is a Jungian archetype, as is the wise old man and the mother figure. Jung believed that these symbols of universal human experiences are embedded in a part of the mind he called the collective unconscious.

Alfred Adler: Individual Psychology

Alfred Adler (1870–1937) was another member of Freud's inner circle who broke away to develop his own theory of personality. Adler called his theory **individual psychology** because of its emphasis on the unique potential of each individual. He believed that conscious experience plays a greater role in our personalities than Freud had believed. The **creative self** is what he called the part of the personality that is aware of itself and organizes goal-seeking behavior. As such, our creative self strives toward overcoming obstacles that lie in the path of pursuing our potentials, of becoming all that we seek to become.

Adler is perhaps best known for his concept of the **inferiority complex**. He believed that because of their small size and limited abilities, all children harbor feelings of inferiority to some degree. How they compensate for these feelings influences their emerging personalities. Feelings of inferiority lead to a desire to compensate, which Adler called the **drive for superiority** or *will-to-power*. The drive for superiority may motivate us to try harder and achieve worthwhile goals, such as professional accomplishments and positions of prominence. Or it may lead us to be domineering or callous toward others, to perhaps step on or over people as we make our way up the professional or social ladder.

Karen Horney: An Early Voice in Feminine Psychology

One of the staunchest critics of Freud's views on personality development of women was one of his own followers, Karen Horney (1885–1952) (pronounced *HORN-eye*), a German physician and early psychoanalyst who became a prominent theorist in her own right. Horney accepted Freud's belief that unconscious conflicts shape personality, but she focused less on sexual and aggressive drives and more on the roles of social and cultural forces. She also emphasized the importance of parent–child relationships. When parents are harsh or uncaring, children may develop a deep-seated form of anxiety she called **basic anxiety**, which is associated with the feeling of "being isolated and helpless in a potentially hostile world" (cited in S. Quinn, 1987). Children may also develop a deep form of resentment toward their parents, which she labeled **basic hostility**. Horney believed, as did Freud, that children repress their hostility toward their parents out of fear of losing them or suffering their reprisals. Yet repressed hostility generates more anxiety and insecurity.

Horney accepted the general concept of penis envy in girls, but she believed that the development of young women must be understood within a social context as well. For example, she rejected Freud's belief that a female's sense of inferiority derives from penis envy. She argued that if women feel inferior, it is because they envy men their social power and authority, not their penises (Stewart & McDermott, 2004). Horney even raised the possibility that men may experience "womb envy" over the obvious "physiological superiority" of women with respect to their biological capacity for creating and bringing life into the world.

© Bettmann/CORBIS

Karen Horney

inferiority complex In Adler's theory, a concept involving the influence that feelings of inadequacy or inferiority in young children have on their developing personalities and desires to compensate.

drive for superiority Adler's term for the motivation to compensate for feelings of inferiority. Also called the *will-to-power*.

basic anxiety In Horney's theory, a deep-seated form of anxiety in children that is associated with feelings of being isolated and helpless in a world perceived as potentially threatening and hostile.

basic hostility In Horney's theory, deep feelings of resentment that children may harbor toward their parents

Evaluating the Psychodynamic Perspective

Psychodynamic theory remains the most detailed and comprehensive theory of personality yet developed. Many of the terms Freud introduced—such as ego, superego, repression, fixation, and defense mechanisms—are used today in everyday language, although perhaps not precisely in the ways that Freud defined them.

Perhaps the major contribution of Freud and later psychodynamic thinkers was to put the study of the unconscious mind on the map (Lothane, 2006). To know oneself, Freud believed, means to plumb the depths of our unconscious mind, to ferret out the unconscious motives that underlie our behavior. As we shall see in Chapter 16, Freud developed a method of psychotherapy, called *psychoanalysis*, that focuses on helping people gain insight into the unconscious motives and conflicts that he believed were at the root of their problems.

Psychodynamic theory has had its critics, however. Many, including some of Freud's own followers, believe Freud placed too much importance on sexual and aggressive drives and too little emphasis on the role of social relationships in the development of personality. Other psychodynamic thinkers, including Horney, place greater emphasis on social influences in personality development. Another challenge to Freud is the lack of evidence to support many of the principles on which his theory is based, including his beliefs in castration anxiety, penis envy, and the universality of the Oedipus complex. Some critics question whether the Oedipus complex even exists at all (see Kupfersmid, 1995).

CONCEPT 13.8
Although the psychodynamic perspective has had a major impact on psychology and beyond, critics contend that it lacks support from rigorous scientific studies for many of its key concepts.

Other critics challenged the progression and timing of Freud's psychosexual stages of development. Still others challenged psychodynamic theory itself as resting almost entirely on evidence gathered from a relatively few case studies. Case studies may be open to varied interpretations. Moreover, the few individuals who are subjects of case studies may not be representative of people in general.

Perhaps the greatest limitation of the psychodynamic approach is the difficulty in scientifically testing many of its key concepts, especially those involving the unconscious mind. The scientific method requires that theories lend themselves to testable hypotheses. By their nature, unconscious processes are not open to direct observation or scientific measurement, which makes them difficult—some would say impossible—to study scientifically. Still, we find today a number of investigators attempting to objectively test certain aspects of psychodynamic theory, including Freud's beliefs about repression. A growing body of evidence from different areas of research in psychology supports the existence of psychological functioning outside of awareness, including defense mechanisms (Cramer, 2000; Westen & Gabbard, 2002).

Concept Chart 13.1 provides an overview of the psychodynamic perspective on personality. In subsequent modules, we will consider other leading perspectives on personality—namely, the trait, social-cognitive, and humanistic approaches.

CONCEPT CHART 13.1 Major Concepts in Psychodynamic Theory

	Concept	Description	Summary
Freud's Psychoanalytic Theory	Levels of consciousness	The mind consists of three levels of consciousness: the conscious, the preconscious, and the unconscious.	Only a small part of the mind is fully conscious. The unconscious mind is the largest part of the mind and contains baser drives and impulses.
Freud's Psychoanalytic Theory	Structure of personality	Id, ego, and superego	Existing in the unconscious, the id is a repository of instinctual impulses. The ego seeks to satisfy demands of the id through socially acceptable ways without offending the superego, the moral guardian of the self.
Freud's Psychoanalytic Theory	Governing principles	Pleasure principle and reality principle	The id follows the pleasure principle, the demand for instant gratification regardless of social necessities. The ego follows the reality principle, by which gratification of impulses is weighed in terms of social acceptability and practicality.
Freud's Psychoanalytic Theory	Defense mechanisms	The ego uses defense mechanisms to conceal or distort unacceptable impulses, thus preventing them from rising into consciousness.	Defense mechanisms include repression, regression, projection, rationalization, denial, reaction formation, sublimation, and displacement.
Freud's Psychoanalytic Theory	Stages of psychosexual development	Sexual motivation is expressed through stimulation of different body parts or erogenous zones as the child matures.	The five stages of psychosexual development are oral, anal, phallic, latency, and genital. Overgratification or undergratification can lead to personality features or fixations characteristic of that stage.
Other Theories	Key points	Greater emphasis on the ego and social relationships than was the case with Freud, and lesser emphasis on sexual and aggressive motivation	▪ Jung's analytical psychology introduced concepts of the personal unconscious, archetypes, and the collective unconscious. ▪ Adler's individual psychology emphasized self-awareness, goal-striving, and ways people compensate for underlying feelings of inadequacy or inferiority. ▪ Karen Horney focused on interpersonal relationships, especially parent–child relationships.

13.1 MODULE REVIEW The Psychodynamic Perspective

Recite It

What are the three levels of consciousness in Freud's theory of the mind?

- According to Freud, the three levels of consciousness are the conscious, the preconscious, and the unconscious.
- The conscious represents your present awareness; the preconscious represents the region of the mind that contains information you can readily retrieve from memory; and the unconscious represents a darkened region of the mind that contains primitive urges, wishes, and troubling memories that cannot be directly summoned to consciousness.

What are the structures of personality in Freud's theory?

- Freud represented personality as composed of three mental structures: the id, the ego, and the superego.
- The ego attempts to satisfy the sexual and aggressive urges of the id in ways that avoid social disapproval or condemnation from the superego, the internal moral guardian or conscience.

What are psychological defense mechanisms?

- Psychological defense mechanisms are strategies used by the ego, such as repression, displacement, and projection, to prevent awareness of troubling desires and memories.

What are the five stages of psychosexual development in Freud's theory?

- Freud believed that psychological development is influenced by changes in the sexually sensitive areas of the body, or erogenous zones, during early childhood.
- The stages of psychosexual development parallel these changes in erogenous zones and are ordered as follows: oral, anal, phallic, latency, and genital.

What are some of the major contributions of other psychodynamic theorists?

- Jung believed in both a personal unconscious and a shared unconscious he called the collective unconscious.
- Adler developed the concept of the "inferiority complex," the tendency to compensate for feelings of inferiority by developing a drive to excel ("drive for superiority").
- Horney challenged Freud's ideas about female psychology and focused on the emotional effects in children of impaired relationships with their parents.

Recall It

1. Psychoanalytic theory attempts to explain how humans balance
   a. sexual instincts and social standards.
   b. demands for productivity with demands for leisure.
   c. desire for wealth with desires for sexual reproduction.
   d. basic biological needs with self-actualization needs.
2. To Freud, the part of the mind that organizes efforts to satisfy basic impulses in ways that avoid social condemnation is the
   a. id.
   b. superego.
   c. ego.
   d. preconscious.
3. To Freud, the psychosexual developmental stage during which a young boy experiences the Oedipus complex is the
   a. oral stage.
   b. anal stage.
   c. phallic stage.
   d. genital stage.
4. Match the following terms with their descriptions: (a) defense mechanisms; (b) repression; (c) Freudian slip; (d) projection.
   i. motivated forgetting.
   ii. accidentally revealing underlying thoughts.
   iii. aimed at shielding the self from anxiety.
   iv. imposing one's own impulses or desires on others.
5. Which of the following psychodynamic theorists supported the view that humans share a collective unconscious?
   a. Carl Jung.
   b. Karen Horney.
   c. Erik Erikson.
   d. Alfred Adler.

Think About It

- Underlying the psychodynamic perspective is the belief that we are not aware of the deeper motives and impulses that drive our behavior. Do you agree? Why or why not?
- Can you identify any of your behaviors that might be examples of defense mechanisms? How would you even know?

MODULE 13.2

The Trait Perspective

- What are the three types of traits in Allport's trait model?
- What was Cattell's view on the organization of traits?
- What three traits are represented in Eysenck's model of personality?
- What is the "Big Five" trait model of personality?
- What role do genes play in personality?

THE BRAIN LOVES A PUZZLE

As you read ahead, use the information in the text to solve the following puzzle:

How might your personality traits contribute to living a longer and healthier life?

traits Relatively enduring personal characteristics.

cardinal traits Allport's term for the more pervasive dimensions that define an individual's general personality.

central traits Allport's term for personality characteristics that have a widespread influence on the individual's behavior across situations.

secondary traits Allport's term for specific traits that influence behavior in relatively few situations.

CONCEPT 13.9
Allport believed that personality traits are ordered in a hierarchy of importance from cardinal traits at the highest level through central traits and secondary traits at the lower levels.

CONCEPT 13.10
Raymond Cattell believed that the structure of personality consists of two levels of traits: surface traits that correspond to ordinary descriptions of personality, and a deeper level of more general traits, called source traits, that give rise to these surface traits.

Like psychodynamic theorists, trait theorists look within the personality to explain behavior. But the structures of personality they bring into focus are not opposing mental states or entities. Rather, they believe that personality consists of a distinctive set of relatively stable or enduring characteristics or dispositions called **traits**. They use personality traits to predict how people are likely to behave in different situations. For example, they may describe Rosa as having personality traits such as cheerfulness and outgoingness. Based on these traits, they might predict that she is likely to be involved in many social activities and to be the kind of person people describe as always having a smile on her face. We might describe Derek, however, as having traits such as suspiciousness and introversion. Based on these traits, they might expect Derek to shun social interactions and to feel that people are always taking advantage of him.

Trait theorists are interested in learning how people differ in their underlying traits. They are also interested in measuring traits and understanding how traits are organized or structured within the personality. Some trait theorists believe that traits are largely innate or inborn; others argue that traits are largely acquired through experience. In this module, we focus on the contributions of several prominent trait theorists, beginning with an early contributor to the trait perspective, Gordon Allport.

Gordon Allport: A Hierarchy of Traits

To Gordon Allport (1897–1967), personality traits are inherited characteristics that are influenced by experience. He claimed that traits could be ranked within a hierarchy in relation to the degree to which they influence behavior (Allport, 1961). **Cardinal traits** are at the highest level. They are pervasive characteristics that influence a person's behavior in most situations. For example, we might describe the cardinal trait in Martin Luther King's personality as the commitment to social justice. Yet Allport believed that relatively few people possess such dominant traits. More common but less wide-reaching traits are **central traits**, the basic building blocks of personality that influence behavior in many situations. Examples of central traits are characteristics such as competitiveness, generosity, independence, arrogance, and fearfulness—the kinds of traits you would generally use when describing the general characteristics of other people's behavior. At a more superficial level are **secondary traits**, such as preferences for particular styles of clothing or types of music, which affect behavior in fewer situations.

TRY THIS OUT Sizing Up Your Personality

You can use the personality traits found in Cattell's 16PF to compare your personality with those of the occupational groups shown in Figure 13.2. Place a mark at the point on each dimension that you feel best describes your personality. Connect the points using a black pen. Then examine your responses in relation to those of the other groups. Which of these groups most closely matches your perceptions of your own personality? Were you surprised by the results? Did you learn anything about yourself by completing this exercise?

Raymond Cattell: Mapping the Personality

Trait theorist Raymond Cattell (1905–1998) believed that there are two basic levels of traits (Cattell, 1950, 1965). **Surface traits** lie on the "surface" of personality. They are characteristics of personality that can be inferred from observations of behavior. Surface traits are associated with adjectives commonly used to describe personality, such as friendliness, stubbornness, emotionality, and carelessness—types of traits we infer from observing behavior of others. Cattell observed that surface traits often occur together. A person who is perceived as stubborn also tends to be perceived as rigid and foul tempered. These linkages suggested that there is a deeper level of personality consisting of more general, underlying traits that are not directly observable in behavior but give rise to surface traits. To explore this deeper level, Cattell used statistical techniques to map the structure of personality by analyzing the relationships among surface traits (Horn, 2001). Through this work, he derived a set of more general factors of personality, which he called **source traits.** Cattell went on to construct a paper-and-pencil personality scale to measure 16 source traits, which he called the Sixteen Personality Factor Questionnaire, or 16PF. Each trait on the 16PF is represented on a continuum, such as "reserved versus outgoing." ■ Figure 13.2 compares the scores of groups of writers, airline pilots, and creative artists on the 16PF. To compare your personality with those in Figure 13.2, see *Try This Out*.

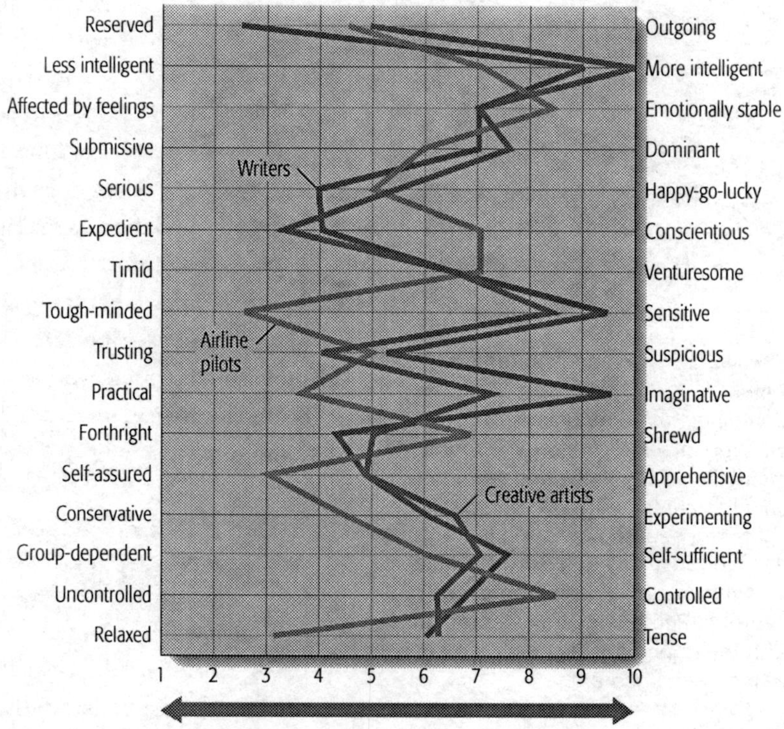

FIGURE 13.2 Cattell's 16PF
The 16PF is a personality test that compares individuals on 16 source traits or key dimensions of personality, each of which is represented on a continuum ranging from one polar extreme to the other. Here we see the average scores of samples composed of three occupational groups: creative artists, airline pilots, and writers. Notice the differences in the personalities in these groups. For example, compared to the other groups, airline pilots tend to be more controlled, self-assured, and relaxed—traits that should help put airline passengers at ease.
Source: Adapted from Cattell, Eber, & Tatsuoka, 1970.

Hans Eysenck: A Simpler Trait Model

In contrast to Cattell's model, which organized personality traits into a complex hierarchy, Hans Eysenck (1916–1997) constructed a simpler model of personality. This model describes personality using three major traits (Eysenck, 1981):

1. **Introversion-extraversion** People who are introverted are solitary, reserved, and unsociable, whereas those who are extraverted are outgoing, friendly, and people oriented.
2. **Neuroticism** People who are high on neuroticism, or emotional instability, tend to be tense, anxious, worrisome, restless, and moody. Those who are low on neuroticism tend to be relaxed, calm, stable, and even tempered.

surface traits Cattell's term for personality traits at the surface level that can be gleaned from observations of behavior.

source traits Cattell's term for traits at a deep level of personality that are not apparent in observed behavior but must be inferred based on underlying relationships among surface traits.

introversion-extraversion Tendencies toward being solitary and reserved on the one end or outgoing and sociable on the other end.

neuroticism Tendencies toward emotional instability, anxiety, and worry.

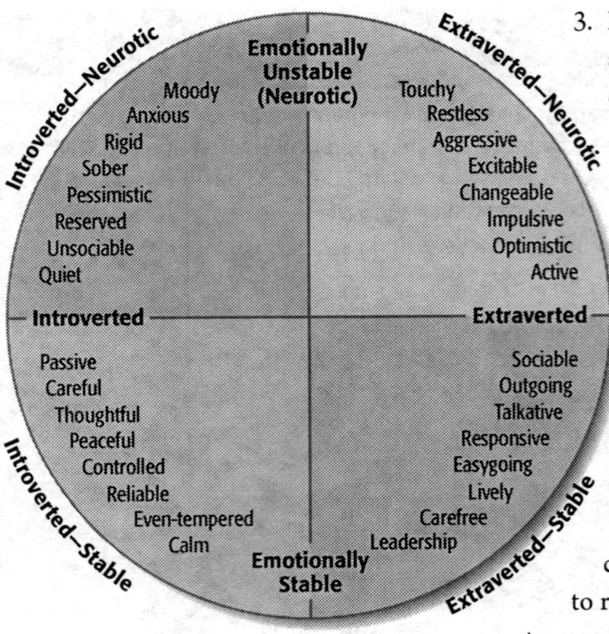

FIGURE 13.3 Eysenck's Personality Types
Combining the dimensions of introversion-extraversion and emotional instability in Eysenck's model of personality yields four basic personality types represented by four quadrants: extraverted-neurotic, extraverted-stable, introverted-stable, and introverted-neurotic. Personality traits associated with these personality types are shown within each quadrant.
Source: From Eyesenck, *Personality, Genetics & Behavior*. Copyright © 1982. Reproduced with permission of ABC-CLIO, LLC.

3. **Psychoticism** People who are high on psychoticism are perceived as cold, antisocial, hostile, and insensitive. Those who are low on psychoticism are described as warm, sensitive, and concerned about others.

Eysenck classified people according to four basic personality types based on the combinations of these traits: extraverted-neurotic, extraverted-stable, introverted-stable, and introverted-neurotic (Eysenck, 1982). ■ Figure 13.3 shows these four types, as represented by the four quadrants of the chart, along with the observed characteristics identified with each type.

Eysenck believed that biological differences are responsible for variations in personality traits from person to person. He argued that introverts inherit a nervous system that operates at a higher level of arousal than does that of extraverts. Consequently, introverts require less stimulation to maintain an optimal level of arousal. An introvert would be most comfortable enjoying quiet activities. Extraverts may require more stimulation to raise their arousal to optimal levels, which could explain why they are drawn to more exciting activities. It would come as no surprise to Eysenck that a group of mountain climbers who were attempting to scale Mount Everest, the world's tallest peak, scored high on extraversion (Egan & Stelmack, 2003). They were also low on neuroticism (emotional instability)—a good thing if you happen to be climbing the face of a mountain.

CONCEPT 13.11
Eysenck believed that the combinations of three general traits of introversion-extraversion, neuroticism, and psychoticism could be used to classify basic personality types.

The Five-Factor Model of Personality: The "Big Five"

The most widely adopted trait model of personality today is the **five-factor model (FFM)**, or "Big Five" model (McCrae, 2004). This model captures the five broad factors that are found most consistently in research on personality traits in many different cultures (Hofstee, 2003; McCrae & Terracciano, 2005; Widiger, 2005). The Big Five isn't so much a new set of personality traits as a consolidation and integration of traits previously identified by Cattell, Eysenck, and other trait theorists. In fact, the first two traits, *neuroticism* and *extraversion*, parallel those in Eysenck's model. The three other factors making up the Big Five are *openness*, *agreeableness*, and *conscientiousness* (see Table 13.3). Researchers believe that the Big Five factors have a substantial genetic component (Jang et al., 2006).

Why It Matters

Why does it matter where people stand on particular personality traits, including the Big Five? It matters because personality traits are useful in predicting many types of behavior, including how well students do in college (Chamorro-Premuzic & Ahmetoglou, 2008; Kaufman, Agars, & Lopez-Wagner, 2008; Noftle & Robins, 2007). Neuroticism is linked to lower grades, whereas conscientiousness is associated with both higher grades and stronger performance motivation (setting goals and pursuing them) (Cheng & Ickes, 2009; Judge & Ilies, 2002; Kappe & van der Flier, 2010; Poropat, 2009). In college freshmen, higher neuroticism tracks to a greater likelihood of experiencing depression in dealing with stressful demands of college life (Hutchinson & Williams, 2007). Moreover, extraverts tend to be happier than introverts, and more agreeable people tend to be more giving and cooperative with others, report greater satisfaction in their relationships, and drive more safely (less aggressively) than less agreeable people (Cellar, Nelson, & Yorke, 2000; Fleeson, Malanos, & Achille, 2008; Graziano & Tobin, 2009;

psychoticism Tendencies to be perceived as cold and antisocial.

five-factor model (FFM) The dominant contemporary trait model of personality, consisting of five broad personality factors: neuroticism, extraversion, openness, agreeableness, and conscientiousness.

TABLE 13.3 The Big Five Trait Model

Personality Factor	Description
Neuroticism	Prone to anxiety, worry, guilt, emotional instability vs. relaxed, calm, secure, emotionally stable
Extraversion	Outgoing, friendly, enthusiastic, fun loving vs. solitary, shy, serious, reserved
Openness	Imaginative, curious, intellectual, open to nontraditional values vs. conforming, practical, conventional
Agreeableness	Sensitive, warm, tolerant, easy to get along with, concerned with other's feelings and needs vs. cold, suspicious, hostile, callous
Conscientiousness	Reliable, responsible, self-disciplined, ethical, hard working, ambitious vs. disorganized, unreliable, lax, impulsive, careless

Sources: Adapted from Costa & McCrae, 1992a, 1992b; Goldberg, 1993; McCrae & Costa, 1986, 1996.

J. K. White, Hendrick, & Hendrick, 2004). Conscientiousness tends to increase in early and middle adulthood, the time of life when people tend to take on more career and family responsibilities (Caspi, Roberts, & Shiner, 2005; Donnellan & Lucas, 2008).

Big Five traits also relate to behavior on social networking sites. Among Facebook users on an Israeli college campus, more extraverted students tended to have more Facebook friends, whereas those who scored high on openness to new experiences tended to use more of the different features on Facebook's personal information section (Amichai-Hamburger & Vinitzky, 2010).

© iStockphoto.com/ SamBurt

Conscientiousness is also linked to living longer and healthier lives, perhaps because it is associated with lower rates of reckless behavior, such as unsafe driving, and with healthier eating patterns, lower body weight, and less use of alcohol and drugs (Brummett et al., 2006; Deary et al., 2008; Kern & Friedman, 2008; B. W. Roberts et al., 2009).

Is the Big Five the final word on describing the structure of personality? Perhaps not. For one thing, the Big Five factors may not be as independent of each other as many investigators believe (Blackburn et al., 2004). Or perhaps more factors (a Big Seven?) may provide a better approximation of how people describe personalities (Simms, 2007). Then again, many psychologists continue to question whether any model that reduces personality to only a few broadly defined categories can capture the richness and uniqueness of personality or account for an individual's behavior in specific contexts.

CONCEPT 13.12
The five-factor model of personality—the "Big Five"—identifies the five most common personality factors derived from research on personality.

In Concept Chart 13.2, you'll find a review of the major trait models of personality.

CONCEPT CHART 13.2 Trait Models of Personality

Trait Theorist/Model	Traits	Summary
Gordon Allport	Cardinal traits, central traits, and secondary traits	Traits are ranked in a hierarchy according to how much they influence behavior. Few people possess cardinal traits, the more encompassing traits that determine behavior across most situations.
Raymond Cattell	Surface traits and source traits	Traits corresponding to clusters of observed behaviors are surface traits. Source traits account for relationships among surface traits.
Hans Eysenck	Three major traits: introversion-extraversion, neuroticism, and psychoticism	Biological factors influence the development of these traits.
Five-Factor Model (FFM): The "Big Five"	Neuroticism, extraversion, openness, agreeableness, and conscientiousness	The FFM is based on five general traits that most consistently emerge in research on personality. Critics contend that such broad factors cannot explain the richness or uniqueness of personality.

© iStockphoto.com/Jacob Wackerhausen

Conscientiousness is one of the five major traits that make up the Big Five model of personality. People who are conscientious are reliable, hard working, and self-disciplined. Where do you think you stand on each of the Big Five traits?

© Joe Seer/Shutterstock.com

Where do you think Mike ("The Situation") Sorrentino from the TV show, *Jersey Shore*, would stand on a scale of extraversion? How about conscientiousness?

The Genetic Basis of Traits: Moving Beyond the Nature-Nurture Debate

How much of our personality is inherited? Evolutionary psychologists (see Chapter 1) have brought genetic contributions to personality into sharper focus, and increasing evidence points to the important role that heredity plays in shaping our personalities (see Bouchard, 2004). Evidence supports the role of genetics in many personality traits, including the Big Five traits, as well as shyness, aggressiveness, and interest in seeking novel experiences (e.g., DeYoung, Quilty, & Peterson, 2007; Derringer et al., 2010; Harro et al., 2009; Lahey, 2009; Wray et al., 2008).

Researchers today are moving beyond the old nature-nurture debate. They recognize that genes create a predisposition or likelihood for certain personality traits to develop, not a certainty. Whether these traits actually do emerge depends on the interaction of genetic factors with environmental and social influences, including learning experiences. Early life experiences can affect how the brain develops, which in turn influences later personality development. Teasing out the relative influences and interactions of genes and environment remains a major challenge to researchers in the field (e.g., Loehlin, 2010).

CONCEPT 13.13
Psychologists are moving beyond the nature-nurture debate to examine how heredity and environment interact in the development of personality.

→ Concept Link
The interaction of genetic and environmental factors is implicated in the development of many psychological disorders, such as schizophrenia. See Module 15.5.

Evaluating the Trait Perspective

The trait perspective has intuitive appeal. People commonly use trait terms when describing their own and other people's personalities. We might describe Samantha as cold or callous, but think of Li Ming as kind and compassionate. Thus, trait theories are useful to the extent that they provide convenient categories or groupings of traits that people commonly use. Trait theories have also proved to be useful in the development of many personality tests, including Cattell's 16PF and the Eysenck Personality Inventory. Psychologists use these tests to compare how people score on different traits.

Personality traits tend to be relatively stable over time (e.g., Costa & McCrae, 2006; B. W. Roberts, Walton, & Viechtbauer, 2006a, 2006b; Trzesniewski, Donnellan, & Robins, 2003). That said, we should not think of personality as fixed early in life. Personality traits are not "set like plaster" by the time we enter adulthood; rather, they continue to change over time, although at a somewhat slower pace as the person ages (L. A. Clark, 2009). For example, people tend to become more agreeable (friendlier) and more conscientious (reliable and dependable) as they age (Lucas & Donnellan, 2009). These changes suggest that people become better adapted to their environment as they get older.

CONCEPT 13.14
Though trait theories provide convenient ways of describing personality features, they have been criticized on grounds of circular reasoning and failure to account for differences in behavior across situations.

Trait theories do have their drawbacks, however. Perhaps the major criticism is that trait theories merely attach a label to behavior rather than explaining it. Consider the following example:

1. You can always count on Mary. She's very reliable.
2. Why is Mary reliable? Because she is a conscientious person.
3. How do you know she is a conscientious person? Because she's reliable.

This is *circular reasoning*—explaining Mary's behavior in terms of a trait ("conscientiousness") whose existence is based on observing the very same behavior. Traits may represent nothing more than shorthand descriptions of the apparent behaviors of people, with little to offer in terms of explaining the underlying causes of the behaviors.

Even as descriptions, trait theories are based on broadly defined traits, such as the Big Five, that may not fully capture the unique characteristics of individuals.

Another argument against trait theories is that behavior may not be as stable across time and situations as trait theorists suppose. How you act with your boss, for example, may be different from how you act around the house. How you relate to people today may be very different from how you related to people in the past. Learning theorists argue that we need to take into account environmental or situational factors, such as stimulus cues and reinforcements, in order to more accurately predict behavior (Sherman, Nave, & Funder, 2010).

A developing consensus in the field is emerging around the concept of *interactionism*—the belief that behavior reflects an interaction between traits and situational factors (Fleeson & Noftle, 2009; Griffo & Colvin, 2009; Pincus et al., 2009; Webster, 2009). Situational factors clearly affect behavior in that people tend to act differently in different situations depending upon the particular demands they face (Funder, 2009). But we also need to account for the fact that people have typical ways of acting that cut across various situations (Fleeson, 2004).

Measurement of personality traits in humans is well established, but can we assess personality traits in other animals, such as dogs? When people are asked to judge the personality traits of dogs, their ratings show about as much agreement as they do when they make personality judgments of humans (Gosling, Kwan, & John, 2003). Big Five factors have also been applied to orangutans (Stambor, 2006b; Weiss, King, & Perkins, 2006). People who rated these primates higher on personality traits of extraversion, neuroticism, and agreeableness also tended to give them higher ratings on general well-being—findings that dovetail with prior work with both chimpanzees and humans. Yet the question remains, do dogs or other animals have personality traits? What do you think?

Many dog owners and cat owners believe their pets have distinct personalities. Recent evidence indicates that judgments of personality traits in dogs achieve as much agreement among raters as judgments of traits in humans. Do other animals have personalities? What do you think?

13.2 MODULE REVIEW The Trait Perspective

Recite It

What are the three types of traits in Allport's trait model?

- The three types of traits are cardinal traits (pervasive characteristics that govern behavior), central traits (more commonly found general characteristics around which behavior is organized), and secondary traits (interests or dispositions that influence behavior in specific situations).

What was Cattell's view on the organization of traits?

- Cattell believed that traits are organized in terms of surface traits (consistencies in a person's observed behavior) and source traits (general, underlying traits that account for relationships among surface traits).

What three traits are represented in Eysenck's model of personality?

- Eysenck believed that variations in personality could generally be explained in terms of three major traits: introversion-extraversion, neuroticism, and psychoticism.

What is the "Big Five" trait model of personality?

- The Big Five (neuroticism, extraversion, openness, agreeableness, conscientiousness) are five broad dimensions or traits that have consistently emerged in personality research.

What role do genes play in personality?

- Genetic influences are implicated in many personality traits, including neuroticism, shyness, aggressiveness, and novelty seeking. Scientists today are exploring how genes interact with environmental influences in the development of personality.

Recall It

1. In the field of personality, relatively stable or enduring characteristics or dispositions are called ________.
2. In Gordon Allport's view, the most common characteristics that form the basic building blocks of personality are
   a. cardinal traits.
   b. central traits.
   c. secondary traits.
   d. universal traits.

3. The 16PF Questionnaire, developed by Raymond Cattell, is designed to measure
   a. source traits.
   b. surface traits.
   c. introversion-extraversion.
   d. psychoticism traits.
4. Among the personality psychologists discussed in this module, who described personality on the basis of three major traits?
5. The personality dimensions of neuroticism, extraversion, openness, agreeableness, and conscientiousness together constitute
   a. the Eysenck Personality Inventory.
   b. the 16PF.
   c. the Big Five model of personality.
   d. the MMPI.
6. Name some of the personality characteristics for which a genetic link has been supported.

Think About It

- What psychological traits would you use to describe your personality? What traits do you believe others might use to describe you? How do you account for any differences?
- Do you believe that your personality traits are fixed or unchangeable? Or might your personality be open to adjustment here and there? What would you like to change about yourself and how you relate to others?

MODULE 13.3 The Social-Cognitive Perspective

- What are expectancies and subjective values?
- What is reciprocal determinism?
- What are situation and person variables?

CONCEPT 13.15
To behaviorists, the concept of personality refers to the sum total of an individual's learned behavior.

CONCEPT 13.16
Social-cognitive theorists expanded traditional learning theory by focusing on the cognitive and social-learning aspects of behavior.

social-cognitive theory A learning-based model of personality that emphasizes both cognitive factors and environmental influences in determining behavior.

Some psychologists developed models of personality that were quite different from those of Freud and the trait theorists. Behaviorists such as John Watson and B. F. Skinner believed that personality is shaped by environmental influences (rewards and punishments), not by unconscious influences, as in Freud's theory, or by underlying traits, as the trait theorists believed. The behaviorists believed that personality consists of the sum total of an individual's learned behavior. Consider your own personality as a behaviorist might view it. Others may see you as friendly and outgoing; but to a behaviorist, terms like *friendly* and *outgoing* are merely labels describing a set of behaviors, such as showing an interest in others and participating in a wide range of social activities.

Behaviorists believe that behavior is learned on the basis of classical and operant conditioning. Rather than probe the depths of your unconscious to understand the roots of your behavior, behaviorists might explore how you were reinforced in the past for displaying friendly and outgoing behaviors. People with different histories of rewards and punishments develop different patterns of behavior. If Maisha is respectful and conscientious in her work habits, it is because she has been rewarded for this kind of behavior in the past. If Tyler spends more time socializing than studying, it is likely he has been reinforced more for social interactions than for academic performance.

Many learning theorists today adopt a broader view of learning than did the traditional behaviorists, such as Watson and Skinner. This contemporary model, called **social-cognitive theory**, maintains that to explain behavior we need to take into account cognitive and social aspects of behavior, not just the rewards and punishments to which we are exposed in the environment. These social and cognitive variables include expectancies we hold about the outcomes of our behavior, the values we place on rewards, and the learning that occurs through imitating the behavior of others we observe interacting in social situations. To social-cognitive theorists, personality comprises not only learned behavior but also the ways individuals think about themselves and the world around them. They believe that people act upon the environment in pursuing their goals, not just react to it (Bandura, 2006). The three primary contributors to social-cognitive theory are the psychologists Julian Rotter, Albert Bandura, and Walter Mischel.

CONCEPT 13.17
Social-cognitive theorists believe that personality consists of individuals' repertoires of behavior and ways of thinking about themselves and the world.

expectancies In social-cognitive theory, personal predictions about the outcomes of behavior.

subjective value In social-cognitive theory, the importance individuals place on desired outcomes.

locus of control In Rotter's theory, one's general expectancies about whether one's efforts can bring about desired outcomes or reinforcements.

Julian Rotter: The Locus of Control

To Julian Rotter (1990), explaining and predicting behavior involves knowing an individual's reinforcement history as well as the person's expectancies and subjective values. **Expectancies** are your personal predictions of the outcomes of your behavior. For example, students who hold a positive expectancy about schoolwork believe that studying will improve their chances of getting good grades. **Subjective value** is the worth you place on desired outcomes. A dedicated student will place a high subjective value on getting good grades. In this instance, a student with high positive expectancy and high subjective value would be more likely to study for a forthcoming exam than someone who does not link studying with grades or who does not care about grades.

Rotter also believed that people acquire general expectancies about their ability to obtain reinforcements in their lives. Some, for example, have an internal **locus of control** (*locus* is the Latin word for "place"). They believe they can obtain reinforcements through work and effort. Others feel that reinforcements are largely controlled by external forces beyond their control, such as luck or fate. They have an external locus of control. Locus of control is linked to various outcomes. For example, people with an internal locus of control tend to more satisfied with their lives, and are more likely to succeed in school and make healthy changes in their diet and exercise patterns (Holt, Clark, & Kreuter, 2001; Kalechstein & Nowicki, 1997; Wang, Bowling, & Eschleman, 2010).

CONCEPT 13.18
Rotter believed that our ability to explain and predict behavior depends on knowing an individual's reinforcement history as well as the person's expectancies, subjective values, and perceptions of control.

→ Concept Link
Perceptions of control and predictability are important factors in determining a person's ability to cope with stressful life events. See Module 12.1.

reciprocal determinism Bandura's model in which cognitions, behaviors, and environmental factors influence and are influenced by each other.

Albert Bandura: Reciprocal Determinism and the Role of Expectancies

Albert Bandura sees people as active agents in directing their lives (Bandura, 2006, 2008b, 2010). As he recently wrote, "They [people] are not simply onlookers of their behavior. They are contributors to their life circumstances, not just products of them" (Bandura, 2006, p. 164). His model of **reciprocal determinism** holds that cognitions, behaviors, and environmental factors influence each other (see ■ Figure 13.4). Bandura focuses on the interaction between what we do (our behavior) and what we think (our cognitions). For example, suppose a motorist is cut off by another motorist on the road. The first motorist may think angering thoughts, such as "I'm going to teach that guy a lesson." These thoughts or cognitions increase the likelihood of aggressive behavior (e.g., cutting in front of the other motorist). The aggressive behavior, in turn, affects the social environment (the other motorist responds aggressively). The other motorist's actions then lead the first to have even more angering thoughts ("I can't let him get away with that!"), which, in turn, lead to more aggressive behavior. This vicious cycle of escalating aggressive behavior and angering thoughts may result in an incident of *road rage*, which can have tragic consequences.

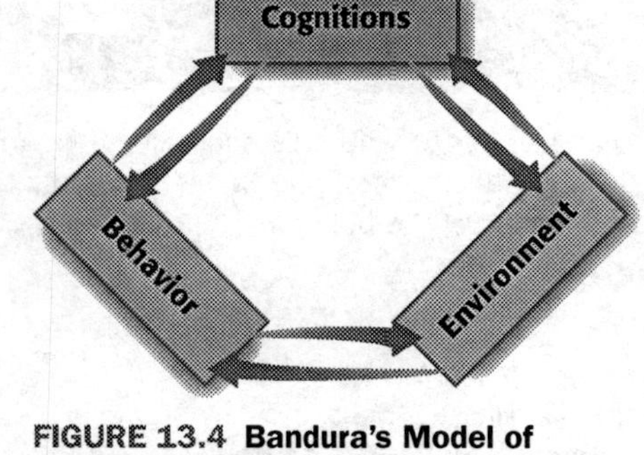

FIGURE 13.4 Bandura's Model of Reciprocal Determinism
Bandura believes that cognitions, behaviors, and environmental factors are reciprocally determined, which means that they mutually influence each other.
Source: Adapted from Bandura, 1986.

CONCEPT 13.19
Bandura's model of reciprocal determinism holds that cognitions, behaviors, and environmental factors mutually influence each other.

outcome expectations Bandura's term for our personal predictions about the outcomes of our behavior.

efficacy expectations Bandura's term for the expectancies we have regarding our ability to perform behaviors we set out to accomplish.

Bandura (1986, 1997) also emphasized the role of observational learning, or learning by observing and imitating the behavior of others in social contexts. He also emphasized the importance of two cognitive variables: outcome expectations and efficacy expectations.

Outcome expectations are predictions of the outcomes of behavior. You are more likely to drink alcohol in a social situation if you believe it will be a pleasant experience and perhaps increase your self-confidence than if you think it will make you sick or act silly.

Efficacy expectations are predictions you hold about your ability to perform tasks or behaviors you set out to accomplish. People with high self-efficacy stay the course when confronting difficult challenges. They are likely to undertake challenges and persevere in the face of adversity because they believe they can surmount obstacles placed in their path. By contrast, people with low self-efficacy tend to quickly give up trying when they confront obstacles in their path (Bandura, 2006) . Success also boosts efficacy expectations. This is one reason that success experiences are important to children and adults alike.

"*I can do this.*" Bandura's social-cognitive model of personality emphasizes the importance of cognitive factors such as self-efficacy—the belief in our ability to accomplish tasks we set out to do.

Why It Matters

Self-efficacy is linked to success in a number of ways. For example, people with higher levels of self-efficacy are less likely to relapse after quitting smoking and more likely to maintain regular physical activity (Gwaltney et al., 2009; Motl et al., 2002). They also tend to do better mending their lives following calamitous events, such as natural disasters and terrorist attacks (Benight & Bandura, 2004). We've also learned that self-efficacy is associated with better academic performance and greater persistence in academic pursuits (S. M. Harris & Halpin, 2002).

Walter Mischel: Situation Versus Person Variables

situation variables Mischel's term for environmental influences on behavior, such as rewards and punishments.

person variables Mischel's term for internal personal factors that influence behavior, including competencies, expectancies, and subjective values.

Walter Mischel's (1973) theoretical model overlaps to a large extent with Rotter's and Bandura's. Mischel argues that behavior is influenced by both **situation variables**, which are environmental factors such as rewards and punishments, and **person variables**, or internal personal factors. Two of these person variables, *expectancies* and *subjective values*, have the same meaning as in Rotter's model. But Mischel adds other person variables, including (1) *competencies*, or the knowledge and skills we possess, such as the ability to play an instrument or to speak a foreign language; (2) *encoding strategies*, or personal perceptions of events, such as whether we see a sudden gift of a basket of flowers as a gesture of love or as a way of making amends; and (3) *self-regulatory systems and plans*, or the ability to plan courses of action to achieve our goals and to reward ourselves for accomplishing them. In Mischel's view, as in Bandura's, environmental and personal factors interact to produce behavior. In predicting a specific person's behavior, we need to take into account what we know about the person as well as the situation at hand.

In his more recent work, Mischel focuses on the interactions of emotions (affects) and cognitions (e.g., Mischel, 2009). One example is how negative feeling states such as depression cast a dim outlook on the ways that people encode experiences and form expectancies about future outcomes. But Mischel also recognizes that emotional reactions, in turn, depend on how we interpret and label experiences, a point to which we shall return when we consider cognitive theories of depression in Chapter 15.

CONCEPT 13.20
Mischel proposed that behavior is influenced both by environmental factors, called situation variables, and by internal personal factors, called person variables.

Evaluating the Social-Cognitive Perspective

Learning theorists have increased our understanding of how behavior is influenced by environmental factors, such as a history of rewards and punishments. Reinforcement principles are now applied in a wide range of programs, including those designed to help parents learn better parenting skills and to help children learn more effectively in the classroom. Learning theory has also given rise to a major contemporary model of psychotherapy, *behavior therapy*, in which learning principles are applied to help people deal with emotional and behavioral problems (see Chapter 16).

CONCEPT 13.21
Though social-cognitive theory broadened traditional learning theory, critics claim that it doesn't account for unconscious processes and genetic factors in personality.

Social-cognitive theorists broadened the scope of learning theory to include cognitive influences on learning and the recognition that much of what we learn occurs by observing others in social contexts. Today, many behavior therapists subscribe to a broader treatment model, called *cognitive-behavioral therapy*, or *CBT* (see Chapter 16), which incorporates cognitive as well as behavioral approaches to therapy and mirrors the teachings of the social-cognitive theorists. But perhaps the most important influence of the social-cognitive theorists is that they have presented us with a view of people as active seekers and interpreters of information, not just responders to environmental influences. Indeed, many psychologists have come to believe that behavior is best explained by the reciprocal interactions between the person and the environment.

To some of its critics, social-cognitive theory presents a limited view of personality because it fails to account for the roles of unconscious influences and heredity. To others, specifically trait theorists, social-cognitive theorists fail to take personality traits into account when attempting to explain underlying consistencies in behavior across situations. Social-cognitive theorists counter that traits don't explain behavior but merely attach labels to behavior—and, moreover, behavior is not as consistent across situations as trait theorists may suppose. Finally, social-cognitive theory is criticized by those who believe that it focuses too little on subjective experience, such as self-awareness and the flow of consciousness. Social-cognitive theorists may believe the emphasis they place on cognitive factors, such as expectancies and subjective values, addresses these concerns. As you'll see next, subjective experience takes center stage in another perspective on personality, the humanistic approach. But first you may want to review Concept Chart 13.3, which summarizes the major concepts associated with the behavioral and social-cognitive perspectives on personality.

CONCEPT CHART 13.3 Behavioral and Social-Cognitive Perspectives on Personality

© Noel Hendrickson/Jupiter Images

Traditional Behaviorism	Social-Cognitive Theory
Personality is the sum total of an individual's learned behavior; distinctive patterns of behavior are determined by differences in learning experiences.	Personality consists of both learned behaviors and ways of thinking. We need to understand the roles of cognitions, observational learning, and environmental influences, such as rewards and punishments, in order to explain and predict behavior.

13.3 MODULE REVIEW The Social-Cognitive Perspective

Recite It

What are expectancies and subjective values?

- Rotter believed that to explain and predict behavior we need to take into account a person's expectancies (personal predictions about the outcomes of events) and subjective values (worth placed on particular goals).

What is reciprocal determinism?

- Reciprocal determinism refers to Bandura's belief that cognitions, behaviors, and environmental factors mutually influence each other.

What are situation and person variables?

- Mischel proposed that both situation variables (environmental influences such as rewards and punishments) and person variables (factors relating to the person such as competencies, expectancies, encoding strategies, subjective values, and self-regulatory systems and plans) are needed to explain and predict behavior.

Recall It

1. Unlike Freudian and trait theorists, behaviorists believe that personality is due to
   a. deep, underlying, unconscious conflicts.
   b. the sum total of a person's history of reinforcements and punishments.
   c. ways we think about ourselves and the world.
   d. ways we think about others in the world.
2. According to Julian Rotter, the individual who expects a good outcome due to hard work and effort has a(n) __________ locus of control.
   a. internal.
   b. positive.
   c. external.
   d. negative.
3. Describe Albert Bandura's concept of *reciprocal determinism*.
4. Match the following terms with the appropriate descriptions: (a) self-efficacy; (b) situation variables; (c) competencies; (d) encoding strategies.
   i. personal perceptions of events.
   ii. belief in personal effectiveness.
   iii. personal knowledge and skills.
   iv. environmental influences.

Think About It

- How does social-cognitive theory represent a shift in learning-based theories of personality?
- Do you believe the roots of personality lie more in the environment or in the person? Explain.
- How is your behavior influenced by outcome and efficacy expectations? By subjective values?

MODULE 13.4 The Humanistic Perspective

- What is self-theory?
- How do collectivistic and individualistic cultures view the concept of self?

Humanistic psychology departed from the psychodynamic and behaviorist schools in proposing that conscious choice and personal freedom are central features of what it means to be a human being (Bargh & Chartrand, 1999). To humanistic psychologists, we are not puppets whose movements are controlled by strings pulled by the unconscious mind or the environment; rather, we are endowed with the ability to make free choices that give meaning and personal direction to our lives. Two of the major contributors to humanistic thought were the American psychologists Carl Rogers (1902–1987) and Abraham Maslow (1908–1970).

CONCEPT 13.22
Rogers's theory of personality emphasizes the importance of the self, the sense of the "I" or "me" that organizes how you relate to the world.

→ Concept Link
The importance of the self is emphasized in the model of therapy Rogers developed, called client-centered therapy. See Module 16.2.

Carl Rogers: The Importance of Self

Rogers (1961, 1980) believed that each of us possesses an inner drive that leads us to strive toward *self-actualization*—toward realizing our own unique potentials. The roadway toward self-actualization is an unfolding process of self-discovery and self-awareness, of tapping into our true feelings and needs, accepting them as our own, and acting in ways that genuinely reflect them.

Rogers believed that the self is the center of the human experience. Thus it is no surprise that he referred to his theory of personality as **self-theory**. To Rogers, the self is the executive part of your personality that organizes how you relate to the world. It is the sense of being "I" or "me"—the person who looks back at you in the mirror, the sense of being a distinct individual with your own likes, dislikes, needs, and values. The self also includes the impressions you have of yourself, impressions that constitute your *self-concept*. The theory of personality Rogers developed reflects the importance of coming to know yourself and being true to yourself, regardless of what others might think or say.

self-theory Rogers's model of personality, which focuses on the importance of the self.

One of the primary functions of the self, as Rogers viewed it, is to develop self-esteem, or a degree of liking for ourselves. Rogers noted that self-esteem at first mirrors how other people value us, or fail to value us. For this reason, he believed it is crucial for parents to bestow on their children **unconditional positive regard**, or acceptance of a person's basic worth regardless of whether their behavior pleases or suits us. In other words, Rogers believed that parents should prize their children regardless of their behavior at any particular moment in time. In this way, children learn to value themselves as having intrinsic worth, rather than judging themselves as either good or bad depending on whether they measure up to other people's expectations or demands. Rogers didn't mean that parents should turn a blind eye toward undesirable behavior. Parents do not need to accept all of their children's behavior; they can correct their children's poor behavior without damaging their self-esteem. Parents need to clarify that it is the *behavior* that is undesirable, not the child.

unconditional positive regard Valuing another person as having intrinsic worth, regardless of the person's behavior at the particular time.

conditional positive regard Valuing a person only when the person's behavior meets certain expectations or standards.

self-ideals Rogers's term for the idealized sense of how or what we should be.

Unfortunately, many parents show **conditional positive regard** toward their children. They bestow approval only when the children behave "properly." Children given conditional positive regard may learn to think of themselves as being worthwhile only when they are behaving in socially approved ways. Their self-esteem may become shaky, as it comes to depend on what other people think of them at a particular moment in time. To maintain self-esteem, they may need to deny their genuine feelings, interests, and desires. They learn to wear masks or to don social facades to please others. Their sense of themselves, or self-concept, may become so distorted that they feel like strangers to themselves. They may come to question who they really are.

Our self-esteem is ultimately a function of how close we come to meeting our **self-ideals**—our idealized sense of who or what we should be. When these ideals are shaped by what others expect of us, we may have a hard time measuring up to them. Our self-esteem may plummet. The model of therapy Rogers developed, called *client-centered therapy* (discussed in Chapter 16), helps people get in touch with their true feelings and come to value and prize themselves.

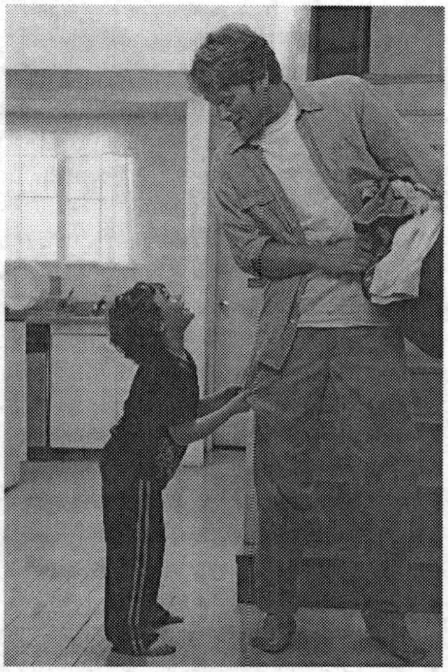

© Bruce Laurance/Getty Images

The makings of unconditional positive regard?

Rogers was an optimist who believed in the essential worth and goodness of human nature. He believed that people become hurtful toward each other only when their own pathways toward self-actualization are blocked or stymied by obstacles. Parents can help their children in this personal voyage of discovery by bestowing on them unconditional approval, even if the children's developing interests and values differ from their own.

Ethnic identity is a strong predictor of self-esteem, especially among people of color (Pierre & Mahalik, 2005; Umaña-Taylor, 2004). Overall, African American children, adolescents, and young adults actually show higher levels of self-esteem, on average, than do their white counterparts (Gray-Little & Hafdahl, 2000; Hafdahl & Gray-Little, 2002). One explanation of the self-esteem advantage among young African Americans is that they tend to have a stronger sense of ethnic identity than young whites. The application module at the end of the chapter focuses on ways of enhancing self-esteem.

The next *Try This Out* feature gives you the opportunity to evaluate how well your self-concept measures up with your self-ideal. If your self-esteem is lagging, don't give up hope.

TRY THIS OUT **Examining Your Self-Concept**

What do you *really* think of yourself? Are you pleased with the person you see in the mirror? Or do you put yourself down at every opportunity?

One way to measure your self-concept is to evaluate yourself on the dimensions listed below. Add other dimensions that are important to you. Circle the number that corresponds to your concept of yourself along each dimension.

Now consider your self-ratings. Did you rate yourself toward the positive or negative end of these dimensions? People with higher self-esteem tend to rate themselves more positively than do those with lower self-esteem. Some dimensions, such as "wise-foolish," may have a greater bearing on your self-esteem than other dimensions. The general pattern of your ratings should give you insight into your overall self-concept and how it affects your self-esteem.

Next, repeat the exercise with a marker of a different color. But this time indicate where you think you *ought* to be according to each dimension by marking the space above the corresponding number. Ignore your original ratings during this step. (Ratings for some dimensions might overlap, indicating a match between your self-concept and your self-ideal.)

Now consider the *differences* between your ratings of your present self and your ideal self on each dimension. Pay particular attention to dimensions you consider most important. The higher the *differences* between your actual self and your ideal self, the *lower* your self-esteem is likely to be. The *closer* your self-perceptions are to your ideal self, the *higher* your self-esteem is likely to be.

What aspects of your personality show the greatest discrepancies? Which, if any, of these characteristics would you like to change in yourself? Do you think it is possible to move closer to your desired self? How would you do it? What would you need to change about yourself and how you relate to others?

	Extremely	Mostly	Somewhat	In between	Somewhat	Mostly	Extremely	
Fair	1	2	3	4	5	6	7	Unfair
Independent	1	2	3	4	5	6	7	Dependent
Creative	1	2	3	4	5	6	7	Uncreative
Unselfish	1	2	3	4	5	6	7	Selfish
Self-Confident	1	2	3	4	5	6	7	Lacking Confidence
Competent	1	2	3	4	5	6	7	Incompetent
Important	1	2	3	4	5	6	7	Unimportant
Attractive	1	2	3	4	5	6	7	Unattractive
Educated	1	2	3	4	5	6	7	Uneducated
Sociable	1	2	3	4	5	6	7	Unsociable
Kind	1	2	3	4	5	6	7	Cruel
Wise	1	2	3	4	5	6	7	Foolish
Graceful	1	2	3	4	5	6	7	Awkward
Intelligent	1	2	3	4	5	6	7	Unintelligent
Artistic	1	2	3	4	5	6	7	Unartistic

Add other traits of importance to you:

______	1	2	3	4	5	6	7	______
______	1	2	3	4	5	6	7	______
______	1	2	3	4	5	6	7	______

Source: Adapted from Nevid & Rathus, 2010.

Abraham Maslow: Scaling the Heights of Self-Actualization

Like Rogers, Maslow believed in an innate human drive toward self-actualization—toward becoming all that we are capable of being (Maslow, 1970, 1971). To Maslow, this drive toward self-actualization shapes our personality by motivating us to develop our unique potentials as human beings. He believed that if people were given the opportunity, they would strive toward self-actualization. Yet he recognized that few of us become fully self-actualized. In the humanistic view, personality is perhaps best thought of as a continuing process of personal growth and realization—more a road to be followed than a final destination.

Humanistic psychologists, following the principles established by Maslow and Rogers, note that each of us has unique feelings, desires, and needs. Therefore, we cannot completely abide by the wishes of others and still be true to ourselves. The path to psychological health is paved with full awareness and acceptance of ourselves—warts and all.

Let's not leave our discussion of humanistic concepts of the self without discussing the important role that culture plays in the development of our self-concept.

© B2M Productions

Do you like yourself? Why or why not?

Culture and Self-Identity

How you define yourself may depend on the culture in which you were raised. If you were raised in a **collectivistic culture**, you might define yourself in terms of the social roles you assume or the groups to which you belong (Markus & Kitayama, 1991; Triandis & Suh, 2002). You might say, "I am a Korean American" or "I am Jonathan's father." By contrast, if you were raised in an **individualistic culture**, you are likely to define yourself in terms of your unique individuality (the characteristics that distinguish you from others) and your personal accomplishments. You might say, "I am a systems analyst" or "I am a caring person." Differences also exist among individuals within cultures in how they define their self-identity.

collectivistic culture A culture that emphasizes people's social roles and obligations.

individualistic culture A culture that emphasizes individual identity and personal accomplishments.

Many cultures in Asia, Africa, and Central and South America are considered collectivistic, whereas those of the United States, Canada, and many Western European countries are characterized as individualistic. Collectivistic cultures value the group's goals over the individual's. They emphasize communal values such as harmony, respect for authority and for one's elders, conformity, cooperation, interdependence, and conflict avoidance. For example, traditional Filipino culture emphasizes deference to elders at any cost (Nevid & Sta. Maria, 1999). Filipino children are taught to never disrespect their older siblings, no matter how slight the age difference and, in many cases, regardless of who is "right."

Individualistic cultures, by contrast, emphasize values relating to independence and self-sufficiency. They idealize rugged individualism as personified in tales of the nineteenth-century American West. Despite differences between individualistic and collectivistic cultures, we possess the ability to think both individualistically and collectivistically depending on the circumstances (Oyserman, Coon, & Kemmelmeier, 2002).

Differences in cultural values also affect how people attain status. In individualistic cultures, status is associated with individual accomplishment or the accrual of wealth: how much money you earn, the kind of house you own, the car you drive, the awards you receive, and the individual goals you've achieved or failed to achieve. In collectivistic cultures, status is achieved by placing the needs of the group above your own and being willing to sacrifice your needs for the welfare of the group or society.

CONCEPT 13.23
Whereas Freud was primarily concerned with our baser instincts, Maslow focused on the highest reaches of human endeavor, the process of realizing our unique potentials.

CONCEPT 13.24
Whether we define ourselves in terms of our individuality or the social roles that we perform is influenced by the values of the culture in which we are raised.

CONCEPT 13.25
The humanistic perspective focuses on the need to understand conscious experience and one's sense of self, but difficulties exist in studying private, subjective experiences and in measuring such core concepts as self-actualization.

SLICE OF LIFE One aspect of collectivism is the value placed on acting honorably in meeting one's social obligations, even to the extent of turning in cash someone dropped on a sidewalk (Onishi, 2004). In Japan, for example, there is a strong tradition of turning in lost money found by passersby in the street so that it can be returned to its rightful owners. In one example, a 24-year-old woman, Hitomi Sasaki, found $250 lying next to a plant outside the restaurant where she worked, and she promptly turned it in. Probably not many New Yorkers would follow Ms. Sasaki's lead if they happened upon a wad of cash lying in the street. *Would you?*

Extremes of either individualism or collectivism can have undesirable outcomes. Excessive collectivism may stifle creativity, innovation, and personal initiative, whereas excessive individualism may lead to unmitigated greed and exploitation.

Evaluating the Humanistic Perspective

The humanistic perspective provided much of the impetus for the broad social movement of the 1960s and 1970s in which many people searched inward to find direction and meaning in their lives. It renewed the age-old debate about free will and determinism and focused attention on the need to understand the subjective or conscious experiences of individuals. Rogers's method of therapy, *client-centered therapy*, remains highly influential. And perhaps most important of all, humanistic theorists helped restore to psychology the concept of self—that center of our conscious experience of being in the world.

Yet the very strength of the humanistic viewpoint, its focus on conscious experience, is also its greatest weakness when approached as a scientific endeavor. Ultimately your conscious experience is known or knowable only to an audience of one—you. As scientists, how can humanistic psychologists ever be certain that they are measuring with any precision the private, subjective experience of another person? Humanistic psychologists might answer that we should do our best to study conscious experience scientifically, for to do less is to ignore the very subject matter—human experience—we endeavor to know. Indeed, they have been joined by cognitive psychologists in developing methods to study conscious experience, including rating scales and thought diaries that allow people to make public their private experiences—to report their thoughts, feelings, and attitudes in systematic ways that can be measured reliably.

Critics also contend that the humanistic approach's emphasis on self-fulfillment may lead some people to become self-indulgent and so absorbed with themselves that they develop a lack of concern for others. Even the concept of self-actualization poses challenges. For one thing, humanistic psychologists consider self-actualization to be a drive that motivates behavior toward higher purposes. Yet how do we know that this drive exists? If self-actualization means different things to different people—one person may become self-actualized by pursuing an interest in botany, another by becoming a skilled artisan—how can we ever measure self-actualization in a standardized way? To this, humanistic psychologists might respond that because people are unique, we should not expect to apply the same standard to different people.

© Alex Kosev/shutterstock.com

Concept Chart 13.4 provides a summary of the major concepts in the humanistic perspective on personality.

CONCEPT CHART 13.4 The Humanistic Perspective: Key Points

	Concept	Summary	Key Principle
 © iofoto/ shutterstock.com	Rogers's self-theory	The self is the executive or organizing center of the personality—the "I" that determines how we relate to the world and pursue our goals.	People who are not encouraged in their upbringing to develop their individuality and uniqueness—but instead are valued only when they meet other people's expectations—tend to develop distorted self-concepts.
 © Carlos Neto/ shutterstock.com	Maslow's concept of self-actualization	Self-actualization is a key element of personality and human motivation.	If given the chance, people will strive toward achieving self-actualization, a goal that is better thought of as a continuing journey than as a final destination.
 © Christopher Futcher/ shutterstock.com	Culture and self-identity	Self-identity may be influenced by collectivistic or individualistic cultural values.	Collectivistic cultures foster communal or interdependent concepts of the self; individualistic cultures encourage individuality and uniqueness.

13.4 MODULE REVIEW The Humanistic Perspective

Recite It

What is self-theory?

- In Rogers's view, the self is the organized center of our experience. The self naturally moves toward self-actualization, or development of its unique potential.
- Movement toward self-actualization is assisted when the person receives unconditional positive regard (noncontingent approval) from others. By contrast, when approval is contingent on "proper" behavior, the person may develop a distorted self-concept and become detached from his or her genuine feelings and needs.

How do collectivistic and individualistic cultures view the concept of self?

- Collectivistic cultures view the self in terms of the role or place of the individual within the larger group or society.
- Individualistic cultures emphasize the uniqueness or individuality of the self.

Recall It

1. Which statement best describes the humanistic belief about our freedom to make personal choices in our lives?
   a. The ability to make conscious choices is true only of people who were raised in cultures that encouraged them to think freely.
   b. Free will is but an illusion.
   c. The choices we make are largely determined by the social influences we encounter.
   d. Our free will is a basic feature of our humanity.
2. Self-actualization involves
   a. self-awareness and self-discovery.
   b. tapping into one's true feelings and needs.
   c. acknowledging and acting upon one's individual characteristics.
   d. all of the above.
3. What did Rogers believe was the center of our experience of being human?
4. Defining oneself in terms of the roles one plays within the group or society is most likely to occur in
   a. collectivist culture.
   b. an individualistic culture.
   c. Western European cultures.
   d. traditional U.S. culture.

Think About It

- How has your cultural background affected your goals and ambitions? Your values? Your self-identity? Your relationships with others? Do you think you would have developed a different personality had you been raised in another culture? Why or why not?
- Do you consider yourself more of an individualist or a collectivist? How are your views of yourself connected with your cultural background?

MODULE 13.5

Personality Tests

- What are self-report personality inventories?
- What are projective tests of personality?

Let us now move from attempts to describe or explain personality to ways of measuring it. Attempts to measure personality actually have a long history. In the eighteenth and nineteenth centuries, many well-respected scientists believed one could make reasonable judgments about a person's character and mental abilities by examining the bumps on the person's head, or even the shape of the person's nose. According to **phrenology**, a popular view at the time, you could judge people's character and mental abilities based on the pattern of bumps on their heads. Such views have long been debunked. We no longer believe you can assess people's personality traits by their superficial biological characteristics.

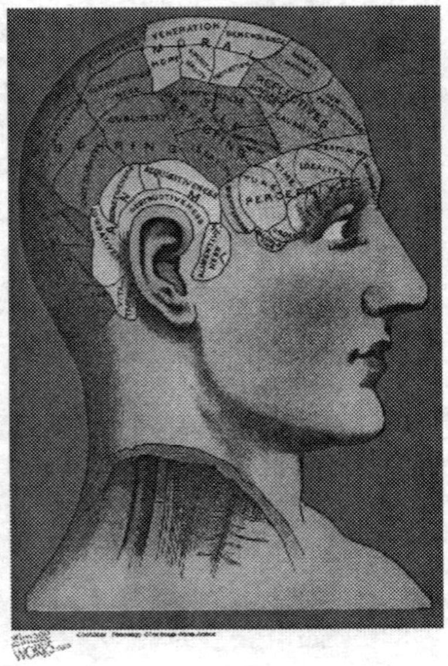

© The Image Works Archive

Phrenology is based on a misconception that one can determine mental abilities and personality traits by examining the bumps or indentations on a person's skull.

phrenology The now-discredited view that one can judge a person's character and mental abilities by measuring the bumps on his or her head.

personality tests Structured psychological tests that use formal methods of assessing personality.

self-report personality inventories Structured psychological tests in which individuals are given a limited range of response options to answer a set of questions about themselves.

objective tests Tests of personality that can be scored objectively and are based on a research foundation.

The methods used by psychologists today to assess personality include case studies, interviews, observational techniques, and experimental studies (see Chapter 1). But the most widely used method for learning about personality is based on the use of formal **personality tests**. The two major types of personality tests are self-report personality inventories and projective tests.

Self-Report Personality Inventories

CONCEPT 13.26
Self-report personality inventories are widely used measures of personality in which a person's response options are limited so as to make scoring them objective.

Self-report personality inventories are structured psychological tests in which individuals are given a set of questions to answer about themselves in the form of "yes–no" or "true–false" or "agree–disagree" types of response formats. Self-report personality inventories are also called **objective tests**. They are not objective in the same sense that your bathroom scale is an objective measure of your weight. Unlike scales of weight, they rely on people's opinions or judgments as to whether they agree or disagree with particular statements. The tests are objective in the sense that they can be scored objectively because the responses they require are limited to a few choices, such as true or false. They are also considered objective because they were constructed from evidence gathered from research studies. Some self-report personality tests measure single dimensions of personality, such as assertiveness or hostility. Others attempt to capture multiple dimensions of personality. A leading example of a multidimensional personality test is the Minnesota Multiphasic Personality Inventory (MMPI), the most widely used self-report personality inventory in the world (Camara, Nathan, & Puente, 2000).

TABLE 13.4 Clinical Scales of the MMPI

Scale Number and Label	Items Similar to Those Found on MMPI Scale	Sample Traits of High Scorers
1. Hypochondriasis	I am frequently bothered by an upset stomach. At times, my body seems to ache all over.	Many physical complaints, cynical defeatist attitudes, often perceived as whiny, demanding.
2. Depression	Nothing seems to interest me anymore. My sleep is often disturbed by worrisome thoughts.	Depressed mood; pessimistic, worrisome, despondent, lethargic.
3. Hysteria	I sometimes become flushed for no apparent reason. I tend to take people at their word when they're trying to be nice to me.	Naive, egocentric, little insight into problems, immature; develops physical complaints in response to stress.
4. Psychopathic deviate	My parents often disliked my friends. My behavior sometimes got me into trouble at school.	Difficulties incorporating values of society; rebellious, impulsive, antisocial tendencies; strained family relationships; poor work and school history.
5. Masculinity–femininity*	I like reading about electronics. (M) I would like the work of an interior decorator. (F)	Males endorsing feminine attributes: cultural and artistic interests, effeminate, sensitive, passive. Females endorsing male interests: aggressive, masculine, self-confident, active, assertive, vigorous.
6. Paranoia	I would have been more successful in life but people didn't give me a fair break. It's not safe to trust anyone these days.	Suspicious, guarded, blames others, resentful, aloof, may have paranoid delusions.
7. Psychasthenia	I'm one of those people who have to have something to worry about. I seem to have more fears than most people I know.	Anxious, fearful, tense, worried, insecure, difficulties concentrating, obsessional, self-doubting.
8. Schizophrenia	Things seem unreal to me at times. I sometimes hear things that other people can't hear.	Confused and illogical thinking, feels alienated and misunderstood, socially isolated or withdrawn, may have blatant psychotic symptoms such as hallucinations or delusional beliefs, or may lead a detached lifestyle.
9. Hypomania	I sometimes take on more tasks than I can possibly get done. People have noticed that my speech is sometimes pressured or rushed.	Energetic, possibly manic, impulsive, optimistic, sociable, active, flighty, irritable, may have overly inflated or grandiose self-image or unrealistic plans.
10. Social introversion*	I don't like loud parties. I was not very active in school activities.	Shy, inhibited, withdrawn, introverted, lacks self-confidence, reserved, anxious in social situations.

*The construction of these scales was based on nonclinical comparison groups.
Source: Adapted from Nevid, Rathus, & Greene, 20011

Minnesota Multiphasic Personality Inventory (MMPI)

Do you like fashion magazines? Are you frequently troubled by feelings of anxiety or nervousness? Do you feel that others "have it in for you"? What might your answers to questions such as these tell us about your underlying personality or mental health?

These questions model the items found in the MMPI, now in a revised edition called the MMPI-2. The MMPI-2 consists of 567 true–false items that yield scores on 10 clinical scales (see Table 13.4) and additional scales measuring other personality dimensions and response tendencies.

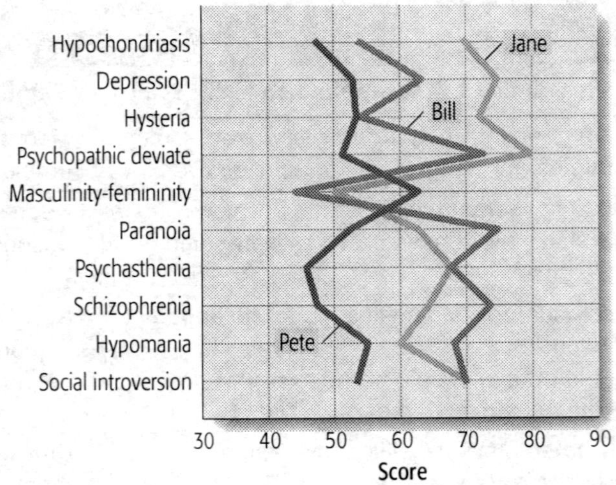

FIGURE 13.5 Sample MMPI-2 Profiles (a) Jane is a 21-year-old woman who was admitted to a psychiatric facility following a suicide attempt; (b) Bill is a 34-year-old schizophrenia patient; and (c) Pete is a well-adjusted, 25-year-old editor.
Note: Scores of 50 are average. Scores on masculinity–femininity are keyed here in the masculine direction for females and in the feminine direction for males.

The MMPI was constructed to help clinicians diagnose mental disorders. Items are grouped on particular scales if they tend to be answered differently by particular diagnostic groups than by normal reference groups. For example, an item such as "I feel moody at times" would be placed on the depression scale if it tended to be endorsed more often by people in a depressed group than by normal controls. The more items a person endorses in the same direction as the diagnostic group, the higher the score the person receives on the scale.

standard scores Scores that represent an individual's relative deviation from the mean of the standardization sample.

When scoring the MMPI, one converts raw scores (number of items scored in the same direction as the diagnostic group) into **standard scores**, which are then plotted on a graph similar to the one shown in ■ Figure 13.5. Scores of 65 or higher on the clinical scales are considered clinically elevated or abnormally high. Examiners take into account the elevations on individual scales and the pattern of relationships among the scale scores to form impressions of individuals' personality characteristics and their possible psychological problems. For another use of personality tests, see *Try This Out.*

Evaluation of Self-Report Personality Tests

A large body of evidence supports the validity of self-report personality inventories such as the MMPI (e.g., Graham, 2006; Sellbom, Graham, & Schenk, 2006; Veltri et al., 2009). The MMPI provides a wealth of information about a person's interests, areas of concern, needs, and ways of relating to others, and assists therapists in making diagnoses of psychological or mental disorders. However, it should not be used by itself to make a diagnosis. A high score on the depression scale does not necessarily mean that a person has a depressive disorder, for example. Yet the person may share certain personality traits or complaints in common with people who do, which may be important for treatment providers to know.

Self-report personality inventories have several strengths. They are relatively inexpensive to administer and score—in fact, many can be machine scored and interpreted by computer. People may also be more willing to disclose personal information on paper-and-pencil tests than when facing an interviewer. Most important, the results of these tests may be used to predict a wide range of behaviors, including the ability to relate effectively to others and to achieve positions of leadership or dominance in work settings (see the next *Try This Out*).

Reliance on self-report data in personality tests such as the MMPI can introduce potential biases, however. Some responses may be outright lies. Others may be prone to more subtle distortions, such as tendencies to respond in a socially desirable direction—in other words, to put one's best foot forward. The more sophisticated

TRY THIS OUT What Should I Become?

Many college counseling centers use personality tests to help students make more informed career decisions. These instruments allow people to compare their own personality profiles and interest patterns to those of people in different occupational groups. If you think you might benefit from a vocational evaluation, see if your college counseling center offers such services.

self-report scales, including the MMPI, have validity scales that help identify response biases. Yet even these scales may not eliminate all sources of bias (McGovern & Nevid, 1986; Nicholson et al., 1997).

Projective Tests

In **projective tests**, people are presented with a set of unstructured or ambiguous stimuli, such as inkblots, that can be interpreted in various ways. Projective tests are based on the belief in psychodynamic theory that people transfer, or "project," their unconscious needs, drives, and motives onto their responses to unstructured or vague stimuli. Unlike objective tests, projective tests have a response format that is not restricted to "yes–no" or multiple-choice answers or other limited response options. Accordingly, an examiner must interpret the subject's responses, thus bringing more subjectivity to the procedure. Here we focus on the two most widely used projective tests, the Rorschach test and the TAT (Camara, Nathan, & Puente, 2000).

CONCEPT 13.27
Projective tests are based on the belief that the ways in which people respond to ambiguous stimuli are determined by their underlying needs and personalities.

projective tests Personality tests in which ambiguous or vague test materials are used to elicit responses that are believed to reveal a person's unconscious needs, drives, and motives.

Rorschach Test

As a child growing up in Switzerland, Hermann Rorschach (1884–1922) amused himself by playing a game of dripping ink and folding the paper to make symmetrical inkblot figures. He noticed that people would perceive the same blots in different ways and came to believe that their responses revealed something about their personalities. His fascination with inkblots earned him the nickname *Klex,* meaning "inkblot" in German. Rorschach, who went on to become a psychiatrist, turned his childhood pastime into the psychological test that bears his name. Unfortunately, Rorschach did not live to see how popular and influential his inkblot test would become. He died at the age of 37 from complications following a ruptured appendix, only months after the publication of his test (Exner, 2002).

The Rorschach test consists of 10 cards similar to those in ■ Figure 13.6. Five have splashes of color, and the others are in black and white and shades of gray. Subjects are asked what each blot

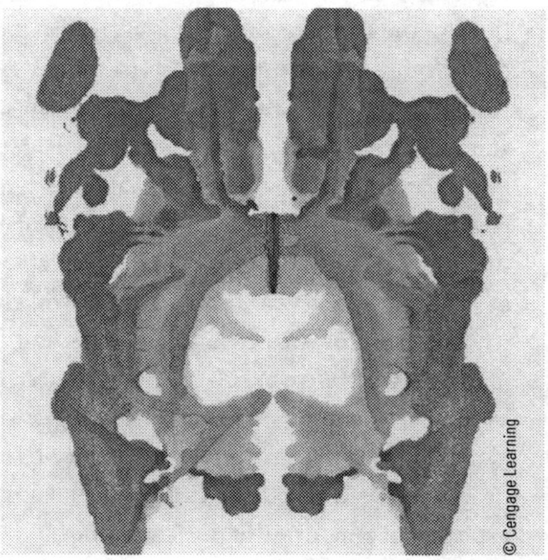

© Cengage Learning

FIGURE 13.6 What Does This Look Like to You?
The Rorschach test is based on the assumption that people project aspects of their own personalities onto their responses to ambiguous figures, such as inkblots.

looks like. After the responses to each card are obtained, the examiner conducts a follow-up inquiry to probe more deeply into the person's responses.

Scoring Rorschach responses is a complex task. The scoring is based on such features as content (what the blot looked like—a "bat," for example) and form level (consistency of the response with the actual shape of the blot). Poor form level may indicate problems with perceiving reality clearly or perhaps an overly fertile imagination. Those who see formless figures dominated by color—who see reddened areas as "blood," for instance—may have difficulties controlling their emotions. The content of the response may indicate underlying conflicts with others. For example, someone who sees only animal figures and no human forms may have difficulties relating to other people.

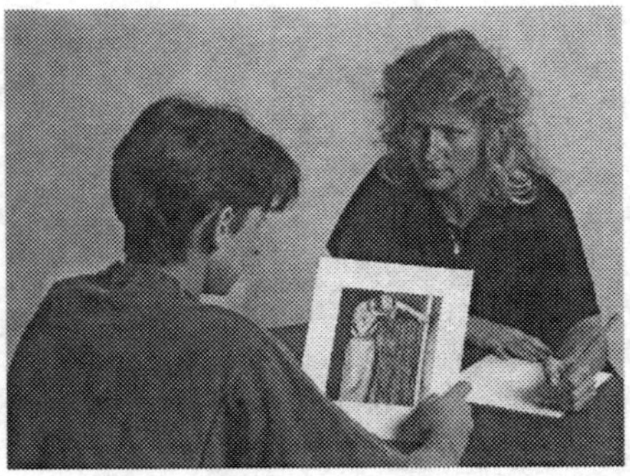

© Lewis J. Merrim/Photo Researchers, Inc.

In the TAT, the person is asked to tell a story about each picture in a set of picture cards depicting ambiguous scenes. What is happening in this one? What led up to this scene and what will happen next? What might a person's responses reveal about his or her own personality?

Thematic Apperception Test (TAT)

Harvard psychologist Henry Murray developed the Thematic Apperception Test (TAT) in the 1930s (H. A. Murray, 1938). The test consists of a set of pictures depicting ambiguous scenes that may be interpreted differently. The subject is asked to tell a story about the scene, what led up to these events, and what the eventual outcome will be. Murray believed that the stories people tell reveal aspects of their own personalities, or projections of their own psychological needs and conflicts into the events they describe. For example, people whose stories consistently touch upon themes of parental rejection may be saying something about their own underlying psychological issues.

Evaluation of Projective Tests

CONCEPT 13.28

Though projective tests are widely used by psychologists, controversy over their validity and clinical utility persists.

One drawback of projective tests is that the scoring of test responses is largely based on the examiner's subjective impressions. Two examiners may disagree on the scoring of the form level of a particular Rorschach response, for example. Although more structured scoring systems have been developed (e.g., Exner, 1993), questions remains about whether interpretations of Rorschach responses are valid or useful.

One problem with projective tests is *stimulus pull.* Despite efforts to make stimuli ambiguous, they often contain cues, such as sad-looking faces in the TAT, that may elicit (pull for) certain types of responses. In such cases, responses may involve reactions to the stimulus properties of the test materials themselves rather than projections of one's underlying personality (Murstein & Mathes, 1996).

Although the value of the Rorschach continues to be debated, recent evidence supports the validity of at least some Rorschach interpretations (Meyer et al., 2001; Perry, 2003). Researchers find that Rorschach responses can be predict success in psychotherapy (G. J. Meyer, 2000), distinguish between certain types of psychological disorders (Dao & Prevatt, 2006), and detect underlying needs for dependency (Garb et al., 2005). However, critics of the Rorschach claim it lacks sufficient overall validity and usefulness to be used as a method of personality or clinical assessment (e.g., Garb, Klein, & Grove, 2002; Hamel, Shafer, & Erdberg, 2003; Wood et al., 2010). However, proponents of projective tests argue that, in skilled hands, these tests can yield valuable information about personality that cannot be gleaned from self-report tests or interviews (Stricker & Gold, 1999). Concept Chart 13.5 compares the methods of assessment and forms of therapy associated with each of the major perspectives on personality covered in this chapter.

CONCEPT CHART 13.5 Overview of Theoretical Perspectives on Personality

Theoretical Model	Key Theorists	Major Concepts	Assessment Techniques	Associated Therapy
Psychoanalytic	Freud	An unconscious struggle among the id, the ego, and the superego influences personality development.	Interviews, projective techniques	Psychoanalysis (discussed in Chapter 16)
Psychodynamic (neo-Freudians)	Adler, Jung, Horney, Erikson	Social factors and development of the self influence personality more than sexual motivation.	Interviews, projective techniques	Psychodynamic therapy (discussed in Chapter 16)
Trait	Allport, Cattell, Eysenck	Personality consists of traits that account for the characteristic ways people act in different situations.	Self-report personality inventories, such as Cattell's 16PF	None
Behaviorism	Watson, Skinner	Personality comprises the sum total of learned behavior.	Behavioral observation	Behavior therapy (discussed in Chapter 16)
Social-cognitive	Rotter, Bandura, Mischel	Personality comprises learned behavior and ways of thinking about the world.	Behavioral observation, interviewing, self-report measures, thought checklists	Cognitive-behavioral therapy (discussed in Chapter 16)
Humanistic	Rogers, Maslow	Personality represents the experience of being in the world, organized around a concept of the self.	Interviews, self-concept measures	Rogers's client-centered therapy (discussed in Chapter 16)

13.5 MODULE REVIEW Personality Tests

Recite It

What are self-report personality inventories?

➤ Self-report personality tests are psychological tests that consist of sets of questions that people answer about themselves by using limited response options. They are classified as objective tests because they use objective methods of scoring and are based on a research foundation.

What are projective tests of personality?

➤ Projective tests are based on the use of ambiguous test materials that are answered in ways believed to reflect projections of the person's unconscious needs, drives, and motives.

Recall It

1. What are two major types of personality tests?
2. Which of the following is *not* correct with regard to the Minnesota Multiphasic Personality Inventory?
   a. It was originally designed to detect mental disorders.
   b. Scales are composed of items that differentiate responses of people from particular diagnostic groups from those of people in a normal reference group.
   c. It is the most widely used self-report personality inventory in the world.
   d. Test responses to self-report personality inventories are free of response biases.

3. A test score that represents the relative deviation of a person's score from the mean of the standardization sample is called a ________ score.

4. Which of the following statements about projective tests is true?
   a. Projective tests rely upon limited response options, such as "yes–no" type questions.
   b. Projective tests are based on the Freudian defense mechanism of regression.
   c. Projective tests are most closely associated with the behaviorist perspective.
   d. Projective tests were developed to help reveal unconscious desires and motives.

Think About It

- Have you ever taken a personality test? What, if anything, do you believe you learned about your personality?
- Consider the debate over the validity of projective tests. Do you believe that people reveal underlying aspects of their personality in their responses to unstructured stimuli, such as inkblots? Why or why not?

APPLICATION MODULE 13.6 Building Self-Esteem

The humanistic psychologists Carl Rogers and Abraham Maslow recognized the importance of self-esteem in developing a healthy personality. When our self-esteem is low, it is usually because we see ourselves as falling short of some ideal. Yet our self-esteem is not a fixed quality; it goes through ups and downs throughout the course of life. Enhancing self-esteem is important, as evidence links higher self-esteem in adolescence to better emotional and physical health, lower levels of criminal behavior, and greater financial success in adulthood (Trzesniewski et al., 2006). We can boost self-esteem by developing our competencies—skills and abilities that enable us to achieve our goals and that enhance our sense of self-worth. But to build self-esteem, we must also challenge perfectionistic expectations and learn to accept ourselves when we inevitably fall short of our ideals.

Acquire Competencies: Become Good at Something

CONCEPT 13.29
Self-esteem, rather than being a fixed quality, can be enhanced by developing competencies and adopting more realistic goals and expectations.

Social-cognitive theorists recognize that our self-esteem is related to the skills or competencies we can marshal to meet the challenges we face. Competencies include academic skills such as reading, writing, and math; artistic skills such as drawing and playing the piano; athletic skills such as walking a balance beam and throwing a football; social skills such as knowing how to start conversations; and job or occupational skills. The more competencies we possess, especially in areas that matter most to us, the better we feel about ourselves.

Competencies can be acquired through training and practice. You may not be able to throw a baseball at 90 miles per hour unless you have certain genetic advantages in arm strength and coordination. However, most skills can be developed within a normal range of genetic variation. Most people can learn to play the piano well, although only a few can become concert pianists. Indeed, a majority of the skills valued in our society are achievable by most people.

Set Realistic, Achievable Goals

Part of boosting self-esteem is setting realistic goals. This does not mean that you should not strive to be the best that you can be. It does mean that you may find it helpful to evaluate your goals in light of your true needs and capabilities.

Enhance Self-Efficacy Expectations

Success breeds success. You can enhance your self-efficacy expectations by choosing tasks that are consistent with your interests and abilities and working at them. Start with small, clearly achievable goals. Meeting these challenges will boost your self-confidence and encourage you to move toward more challenging goals. Regard the disappointments that life inevitably has in store as opportunities to learn from your mistakes, not as signs of ultimate failure.

Create a Sense of Meaningfulness in Your Life

To psychologically healthy individuals, life is not just a matter of muddling through each day. Rather, each day provides opportunities to pursue higher purposes. There are many different kinds of meaning in life, many different purposes. Some people find meaning in connecting themselves spiritually to something larger—whether it be a specific religion or the cosmos. Other people find meaning in community, among those who share a common ethnic identity and cultural heritage. Still others find meaning in love and family. Their spouses and their children provide them with a sense of fulfillment. People may also find meaning in their work.

Challenge Perfectionistic Expectations

Many of us withdraw from life challenges because of unreasonable demands we impose on ourselves to be perfect in everything we attempt. If you place perfectionistic demands on yourself, consider an attitude shift. Try lightening up on yourself and adopting more realistic expectations based on a fair-minded appraisal of your strengths and weaknesses. You may not measure up to an idealized image of perfection, but chances are you already have some abilities and talents you can cultivate, thus bolstering your self-esteem.

Challenge the Need for Constant Approval

Psychologist Albert Ellis believed that an excessive need for social approval is a sure-fire recipe for low self-esteem (Ellis, 1977; Ellis & Dryden, 1987). He recognized that incurring disapproval from others, even significant others, is an inevitable part of life. Ellis challenges us to consider whether experiencing disapproval is truly as awful or intolerable as we might have thought. He encourages us to replace irrational needs for approval with more rational expectations that can help bolster our self-esteem, especially when we run into people who fail to appreciate our finer points.

© VILevi/shutterstock.com

Thinking Critically About Psychology

Based on your reading of this chapter, answer the following questions. Then, to evaluate your progress in developing critical thinking skills, compare your answers to the sample answers found in Appendix A.

Personality and astrology: Is your personality all in the stars? What's in store for you? Let's see what the stars say about Gemini and Scorpio:

> ***Gemini (May 21–June 20):*** *It is now time to focus on meeting your personal needs. Your energy level is high, and you can make the best use of your personal resources. There are many creative opportunities available to you, but you will need to apply yourself to take full advantage of them. You are the type of person who can go beyond what others expect of you. You are facing an important financial decision that can have a great impact on your future. But allow others to counsel you in reaching the best decision. All in all, now is the time to fully enjoy the many blessings in your life.*
>
> ***Scorpio (October 23–November 21):*** *Your best-laid plans may need to be altered because of an unforeseen development. This can cause stress with others, but you will be able to use your sense of humor to ease the situation. You are a caring person whose concern for others shines through. Even though the next month or two may be unsettled, it is best to stay calm. Pursue what it is that is important to you and take advantage of the romantic opportunities you may find or discover. Above all, maintain that sense of humor through trying times and don't accept more responsibilities than you can handle.*

Believers in astrology hold that our personalities and destinies are fixed at the time of our birth by the positions of the sun, the moon, and the planets in the zodiac. Do you believe your personality was determined by the alignment of the heavens at the time of your birth? Do you read the astrology charts in your local newspaper? Do you believe them?

Astrology can be traced back thousands of years and still attracts many adherents, even among people with advanced education. More than 30 percent of college students polled in a recent survey expressed beliefs in astrology (Duncan, Donnelly, & Nicholson, 1992).

A recent study examined scores on the Eysenck Personality Inventory (EPI) in relation to the birth positions of the sun and moon. The results failed to confirm beliefs that such personality factors as extraversion and neuroticism conform to astrological predictions (Clarke, Gabriels, & Barnes, 1996). Other research points to the same conclusion—namely, that there is no scientific basis for astrology (Crowe, 1990; Dean, Mather, & Kelly, 1996). Given the absence of scientific evidence supporting astrology, why does it remain so popular?

One reason may be the *Barnum effect*—the tendency to believe overgeneralized descriptions of personality as accurate descriptions of oneself. The "Barnum" after whom the effect is named was the famous nineteenth-century circus showman P. T. Barnum, who once said "There's a sucker born every minute." The next time you glance at an astrology forecast in your local paper, notice how often the statements are phrased in general terms that can apply to just about anyone (e.g., "Now is the time to focus on your personal needs . . .," "Even though the next month or two may be unsettled . . ."). Look again at the astrological readings for Gemini and Scorpio. Chances are that you will identify with characteristics found in both descriptions, regardless of your particular date of birth.

The Barnum effect may also explain the continued popularity of other pseudosciences, such as psychic reading and fortune-telling. The special "insights" into our futures that psychics and fortune-tellers claim they have are based on general characteristics that fit just about everyone ("You are likely to encounter some financial difficulty . . ."). In addition, they tend to be good observers who notice subtle cues in their clients' attire, gestures, or responses to leading questions that they can use to personalize their predictions.

Another contributor to beliefs in astrology and other pseudosciences is the tendency for people to filter information about themselves in terms of how it reflects upon them. For instance, we tend to give greater credence to information that confirms a positive image of ourselves than to information that casts us in a negative light. Notice that the astrology readings shown above contain many positive attributes (e.g., "caring person," "sense of humor"). The tendency to place greater emphasis on information that bolsters a positive self-image is called the *self-serving bias*—a bias that also accounts for the tendency of people to take credit for their successes and to explain away their failures or disappointments (see Chapter 14).

Now it's your turn to try a little critical thinking. Explain how another type of cognitive bias, the *confirmation bias* (see Chapter 7), contributes to beliefs in astrology.

Log in to CengageBrain to access the resources your instructor requires. For this book, you can access:

CourseMate

Psychology CourseMate brings course concepts to life with interactive learning, study, and exam preparation tools that support the printed textbook. A textbook-specific website, Psychology CourseMate includes an integrated interactive eBook and other interactive learning tools including quizzes, flashcards, videos, and more.

CENGAGENOW

CengageNow is an easy-to-use online resource that helps you study in less time to get the grade you want—NOW. Take a pre-test for this chapter and receive a personalized study plan based on your results that will identify the topics you need to review and direct you to online resources to help you master those topics. Then take a post-test to help you determine the concepts you have mastered and what you will need to work on. If your textbook does not include an access code card, go to CengageBrain.com to gain access. Visit www.cengagebrain.com to access your account and purchase materials.

VISUAL OVERVIEW Chapter 13 Personality

MODULE 13.1 The Psychodynamic Perspective

Sigmund Freud

Freud's Psychoanalytic Theory

- **Three Levels of Consciousness**: Conscious, preconscious, unconscious
- **Three Structures of Personality**: Id (primitive drives), ego ("reason and good sense"), superego (moral conscience)
- **Defense Mechanisms**: Shielding the self from awareness of troubling impulses and memories; examples include repression, displacement, and projection
- **Stages of Psychosexual Development**: Oral stage (birth to two years), anal stage (18 months to three years), phallic stage (three to six years), latency stage (six to puberty), genital stage (puberty to adulthood)

Other Psychodynamic Theorists

- **Carl Jung's Analytical Psychology**: Personal conscious, collective unconscious, archetypes
- **Alfred Adler's Individual Psychology**: Creative self, inferiority complex, drive for superiority
- **Karen Horney**: Basic anxiety and basic hostility; criticized Freud over theory of female development

MODULE 13.2 The Trait Perspective

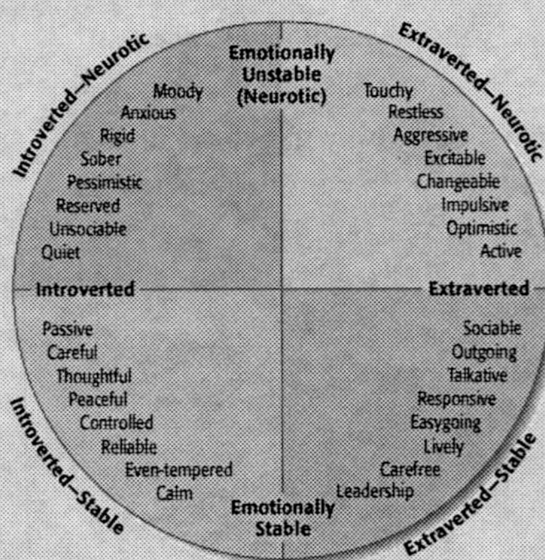

Eysenck's Personality Types

Major Trait Theorists

- **Gordon Allport**: Three levels of traits (cardinal, central, specific)
- **Raymond Cattell**: Two levels of traits (surface traits apparent in behavior vs. deeper source traits reflecting underlying structure of personality)
- **Hans Eysenck**: three trait model (extraversion, neuroticism, psychoticism)

Contemporary Trait Theories

- **Big Five Model**: Consolidation of earlier trait models, comprising five broad traits (extraversion, neuroticism, openness, agreeableness, conscientiousness)
- **Trait-Situational Interactionism**: Behavior involves interaction of traits and situational factors
- **Genetic Bases of Traits**: Personality traits derive from combination of genetic factors and life experiences

MODULE 13.3 Social-Cognitive Perspective

Social Cognitive Theorists

- **Julian Rotter**: Expectancies, subjective values, locus of control
- **Albert Bandura**: Reciprocal determinism, outcome and efficacy expectations
- **Walter Mischel**: Person variables and situation variables

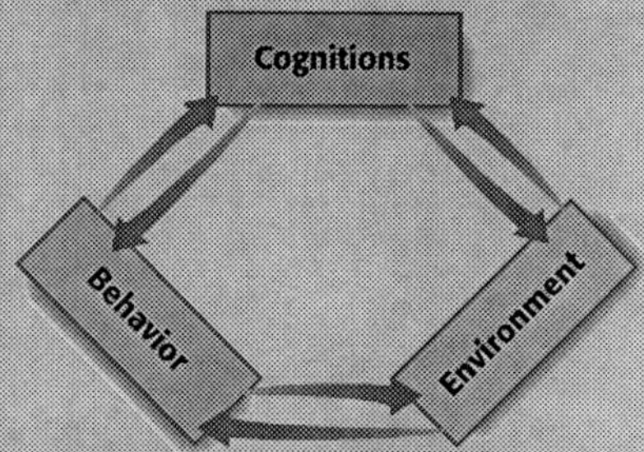

Bandura's Model of Reciprocal Determinism

MODULE 13.4 The Humanistic Perspective

- **Carl Rogers**: Emphasis on the self; importance of self-understanding and self-acceptance
- **Abraham Maslow**: Emphasis on self-actualization
- **Culture and Self-Identity**: Collectivistic versus individualistic cultures

MODULE 13.5 Personality Tests

- **Self-Report Personality Inventories**: Inventories of likes and dislikes, emotional problems, and attitudes. The person's responses are compared to those of normal and clinical samples (e.g., MMPI-2)

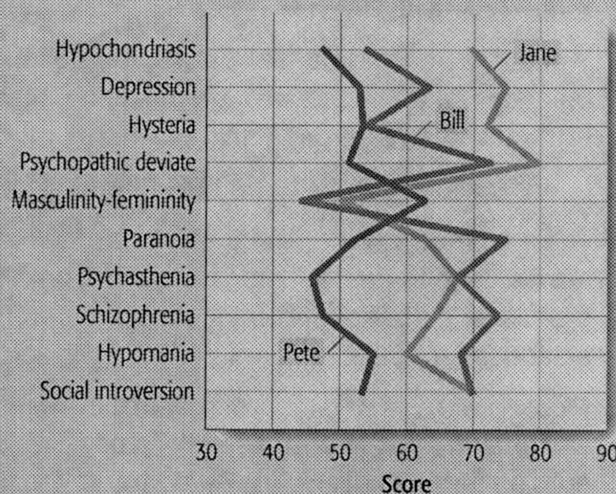

Sample MMPI-2 Profiles

- **Projective Tests**: Projecting underlying needs and conflicts in responses to ambiguous stimuli (e.g., Rorschach Inkblot Test and TAT)

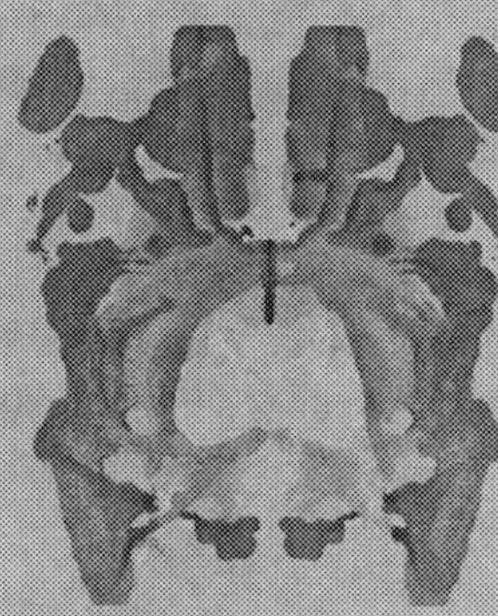
© Cengage Learning

What Does This Look Like to You

14 Social Psychology

The Psychology of Us

A stranger faints on a crowded street as you pass by. Several people gather about the fallen person. Do you offer assistance or continue on your way?

You participate in a psychology experiment in which you and other members of a group are asked to determine which of two lines is longer. One person after another chooses the line that looks shorter to you. Now comes your turn. Do you go along with the crowd or stand your ground and select the line you think is longer?

A man and a woman are standing on a street corner speaking privately in Italian. The man hands the woman an envelope, which she puts in her handbag. What do you make of this interaction? Do you suppose it was a lover's note that was passed between them? Do you think it was an exchange related to Mafia business?

You volunteer for a psychology experiment on the effects of electric shock on learning. You are instructed to administer to another participant what you are told are painful shocks each time the other participant gives a wrong answer. At first you refuse. But the experimenter insists you continue and tells you the shocks will cause no serious harm to the other participant. You would still refuse such an unreasonable demand, wouldn't you?

These questions fall within the domain of *social psychology*, the branch of psychology that deals with how our thoughts, feelings, and behaviors are influenced by our social interactions with others and the culture in which we live. In this chapter we touch upon these questions and others as we explore how we perceive others in our social environment, how we relate to them, and how we are influenced by them. We consider what social psychologists have learned about these social processes, beginning with how we perceive others and how our perceptions of others influence our behavior.

© iStockphoto.com/Amanda Rohde

DID YOU KNOW THAT...

- The Japanese are more likely than Americans to attribute their successes to luck or fate than to themselves? (p. 523)
- When it comes to casual sexual relationships, both men and women place a premium on the physical attractiveness of prospective partners? (p. 529)
- In our society, it pays to be tall—literally? (p. 530)
- The common stereotype that "girls can't do math" may discourage young women from pursuing promising career opportunities in engineering and the sciences? (p. 536)
- Most people who participated in a famous but controversial study administered what they believed to be painful and dangerous electric shocks to other people when instructed to do so by the experimenter? (p. 547)
- Studying in the presence of others who are hitting the books is likely to influence how hard you study? (p. 549)
- A month before taking office as president, Barack Obama commented on the dangers posed by the psychological phenomenon of groupthink? (p. 552)

Learning Objectives

By reading this chapter you will be able to . . .

1 **IDENTIFY** the major influences on first impressions and **EXPLAIN** why first impressions often become lasting impressions.

2 **IDENTIFY** two major types of causal attributions and **APPLY** this knowledge to examples.

3 **EXPLAIN** how causal attributions are affected by cognitive biases.

4 **DESCRIBE** the components and sources of attitudes.

5 **EVALUATE** pathways and factors involved in persuasion.

6 **IDENTIFY** and **DESCRIBE** factors that influence attraction.

7 **IDENTIFY** and **DESCRIBE** factors linked to helping behavior and **APPLY** this knowledge to examples.

8 **EXPLAIN** how prejudice develops and how it may be reduced.

9 **IDENTIFY** and **EXPLAIN** factors that contribute to human aggression.

10 **EXPLAIN** differences between social identity and personal identity.

11 **DESCRIBE** the results of the classic Asch study and **IDENTIFY** factors that influence conformity.

12 **APPLY** knowledge of factors involved in compliance to resisting persuasive sales techniques.

13 **EVALUATE** the findings and significance of Milgram's experiments.

14 **DEFINE** social facilitation and social loafing and **EXPLAIN** how they affect performance.

15 **DEFINE** groupthink and **EXPLAIN** how it can lead to wrong decisions.

16 **DESCRIBE** factors involved in job satisfaction and ways in which the workplace is changing.

© Yuri Arcurs/Shutterstock.com

Preview

MODULE 14.1

Perceiving Others

- What are the major influences on first impressions, and why do first impressions often become lasting impressions?
- What role do cognitive biases play in the judgments we make about the causes of behavior?
- What are attitudes, and how are they acquired?
- How are attitudes related to behavior?
- How do persuasive appeals lead to attitude change?

© AP Photo/Chiaki Tsukumo

People from East Asian cultures are typically more reserved about disclosing personal information when meeting new people.

In Chapter 3 we explored the ways in which we perceive the physical world of objects and shapes. As we turn to the study of **social psychology**, we focus on the ways in which we perceive the social world, composed of the people whom we see and with whom we interact in our daily lives. **Social perception** is the process by which we come to form an understanding of our social environment based on observations of others, personal experiences, and information we receive. In this section we examine three major aspects of social perception: forming impressions of others, making sense of the causes of our own and other people's behaviors, and developing attitudes that incline us to respond to people, issues, and objects in positive or negative ways.

Impression Formation: Why First Impressions Count So Much

Impression formation is the process by which we form an opinion or impression of another person. We form first impressions quickly. Just how quickly? Researchers find that people begin forming impressions of others in a fraction of a second or mere blink of an eye when they first see them (Willis & Todorov, 2006).

What does this mean for the rest of us? Think about the fact that the moment you meet a blind date or a job interviewer, that person may well be sizing you up before you even utter a word (Wargo, 2006). Although impressions may change as people get to know you better, you never get a second chance to make a first impression. It's best to make that first impression count in your favor.

First impressions count so much because they tend to be long-lasting and difficult to change, even in the face of discrepant information (Gawronski et al., 2010). Let us examine factors that influence impressions we form of others, including personal disclosure, social schemas, stereotyping, and the role of self-fulfilling prophecies.

Personal Disclosure: Going Beyond Name, Rank, and Serial Number

We generally form more favorable impressions of people who are willing to disclose personal information about themselves. But revealing too much too soon can lead to a negative impression. People who disclose too much about themselves in the first stages of a social relationship tend to be perceived as less secure, less mature, and more poorly adjusted than

social psychology The subfield in psychology that deals with how our thoughts, feelings, and behaviors are influenced by our social interactions with others.

social perception The processes by which we form impressions, make judgments, and develop attitudes about the people and events that constitute our social world.

impression formation The process of developing an opinion or impression of another person.

those who are more restrained regarding what they say about themselves. Cultural differences also come into play in determining how much disclosure is deemed acceptable. People in East Asian societies, such as China and Japan, tend to disclose less about themselves than do people in the West (H. S. Kim & Sherman, 2007; Nevid & Sta. Maria, 1999).

CONCEPT 14.1
Our preconceived ideas influence the impressions we form of people even before we meet them.

CONCEPT 14.2
The amount of personal information we disclose affects the impressions that other people form of us.

CONCEPT 14.3
By filtering information through existing social schemas, first impressions become lasting impressions.

Impressions as Social Schemas: Why Early Impressions Are Hard to Budge

An impression is a type of **social schema** or mental representation we form about people in our social environment. One reason that first impressions tend to endure is that we filter new information about people through the earlier impressions or social schemas we formed about them (Hamilton & Sherman, 1994). Say we form a favorable impression (schema) of someone we recently met. If that person should then do something that annoys or upsets us, we're more likely to look for extenuating factors to explain the person's behavior ("He must be having a bad day") than we are to alter our existing impression. On the other hand, when we form a negative impression of someone, we're more likely to ignore or explain away positive information we later receive about that person.

social schema A mental image or representation that we use to understand our social environment.

Stereotyping: Judging Groups, Not Individuals

We all have preconceived ideas about groups of people, called **stereotypes**, that influence our first impressions (Aronson, Wilson, & Akert, 2004). Stereotypes are sets of beliefs about the characteristics, attributes, and behaviors of members of a particular group or category. For example, we might stereotype fraternity members as big drinkers or people who wear glasses as intelligent.

stereotypes The tendency to characterize all members of a particular group as having certain characteristics in common.

Stereotypes influence first impressions. Recall the couple speaking in Italian on the street corner. Did you think they were engaged in a romantic exchange or in illegal, Mafia-related activities? Both interpretations are based on stereotypes of Italians as romantic or crooks (Lepore & Brown, 1997). As the example suggests, stereotypes may include positive attributes (romantic in this case) or negative attributes (criminal). However, stereotypes about members of other social or ethnic groups are usually more negative than those about members of one's own group.

Social psychologists believe that stereotyping is a normal cognitive tendency, a kind of cognitive shorthand that simplifies the process of making social judgments (T. D. Nelson, 2002). Upon meeting someone for the first time, we may automatically classify the person as belonging to a particular group or category. Stereotypes allow us to more efficiently use stored information about other groups instead of expending cognitive resources to evaluate each individual member of the groups we encounter (Hilton & von Hippel, 1996). Efficient, perhaps—but not necessarily accurate.

Why It Matters

Stereotyping on the basis of race, ethnicity, gender, age, disability, body weight, or sexual orientation can lead us to make inferences about people that prove unfounded when we get to know them as individuals. Although there may be a "kernel of truth" in some stereotypes (e.g., that Mexicans enjoy spicy food) (McCrae & Terracciano, 2006), stereotypes are nonetheless exaggerated and overgeneralized concepts that fail to take individual differences into account. Moreover, once stereotypes are formed, they tend to stick and become resistant to change even in the face of contrary information.

Stereotyping can damage group relations and be used to justify social inequities. For example, beliefs that blacks lacked the ability to govern themselves were long used as a justification for colonial rule in Africa by the European powers. Stereotypes of obese people as lazy and undisciplined may lead employers to unfairly pass them over for jobs or promotions.

Self-Fulfilling Prophecies: What Goes Around Comes Around

self-fulfilling prophecy An expectation that helps bring about the outcome that is expected.

When you form an initial impression of someone, you may act toward the person in a way that mirrors your impression. Let's say you form an impression of someone as unfriendly. This belief can become a type of **self-fulfilling prophecy** if it leads you to be somewhat standoffish when interacting with the person and he or she responds in kind. Self-fulfilling prophecies may also lead to underperformance in school. Teachers who expect students to do poorly may convey their lower expectations to their students. Expecting less of themselves, the students may apply less than their best efforts, leading them to underperform (Jussim & Eccles, 1992).

Attributions: Why the Pizza Guy Is Late

CONCEPT 14.4
We tend to explain events by attributing them to either dispositional or situational causes—that is, to factors within either the individual or the environment.

The pizza guy delivers your pizza 30 minutes late. Do you believe the guy was loafing on the job or that some external influence (e.g., traffic, orders backing up) caused the delay? What about the times *you* arrive late? Are you likely to reach the same judgments about your own behavior as you do when explaining the behavior of others?

attribution An assumption about the causes of behavior or events.

dispositional causes Causes relating to the internal characteristics or traits of individuals.

situational causes Causes relating to external or environmental events.

An **attribution** is a personal explanation of the causes of behavior or events we observe. When interpreting our social world, we act like personal scientists who seek to understand underlying causes. We tend to explain events by attributing them to either dispositional causes or situational causes. **Dispositional causes** are internal factors, such as the internal traits, needs, or personal choices of the person involved (the "actor"). **Situational causes** are external or environmental factors, such as the pressures or demands imposed upon the actor. Saying that the pizza guy is late because he is a loafer invokes a dispositional cause. Saying he is late because he had to wait on several other pies in the oven invokes a situational cause. Social psychologists have found that attributions can be affected by certain cognitive biases, such as the *fundamental attribution error*, the *actor-observer effect*, and the *self-serving bias*.

Fundamental Attribution Error

fundamental attribution error The tendency to attribute behavior to internal causes without regard to situational influences.

Social psychologist Fritz Heider (1958) proposed that people tend to focus more on the behavior of others than on the circumstances in which the behavior occurs. Consequently, they tend to overlook situational influences when explaining other people's behavior. The **fundamental attribution error** is a term that social psychologists use to describe the tendency to attribute behavior to internal causes, such as traits like intelligence or laziness, without regard to the situational influences that come to bear on people.

CONCEPT 14.5
People tend to overemphasize internal causes and to overlook situational influences when explaining other people's behavior.

Note a cross-cultural difference: People in individualistic cultures such as the United States and Canada are more likely to commit fundamental attribution errors than those in collectivist cultures such as China and Japan (Kitayama et al., 2003). Collectivist cultures tend to emphasize external causes of behavior that stem from the social environment, such as obligations imposed on people (Choi et al., 2003). Individualistic cultures, by contrast, emphasize individuality and autonomy of the self. People from these cultures are quicker to assume that behavior results from internal factors, such as traits, attitudes, or motives.

The Actor-Observer Effect

When people commit the fundamental attribution error, they ignore the external circumstances that influence the behavior of others. But do we commit the same error when explaining our own behavior? Apparently not. Social psychologists have identified another type of cognitive bias that comes into play, called the **actor-observer effect**—the tendency to attribute the causes of one's own behavior to external factors, such as situational demands, while attributing other people's behavior to internal causes or dispositions. If you do poorly on an exam, you're likely to attribute your poor performance to external causes—the exam wasn't fair, you didn't have time to study, the material you studied wasn't on the exam, and so on. But when someone else does poorly, you're likely to think the person lacked the ability to do well or was too lazy to study.

actor-observer effect The tendency to attribute the causes of one's own behavior to situational factors while attributing the causes of other people's behavior to internal factors or dispositions.

Heider (1958) attributed the actor-observer effect to differences in perspective. As an actor, you look outward to the environment, so the situation engulfs your view. But your perspective as an observer is engulfed by your view of the actor within the situation. Recent research indicates that actor-observer effect may be weaker that many people had believed (Malle, 2006; Malle, Knobe, & Nelson, 2007).

CONCEPT 14.6
The actor-observer effect leads us to attribute the behavior of others to dispositional internal causes but to explain our own behavior in terms of the situational demands we face in the environment.

Self-Serving Bias

A specific type of attributional bias in performance situations is the **self-serving bias**—the tendency to attribute personal successes to internal or dispositional causes and personal failures to external or situational causes. In other words, people tend to take credit for their successes but disclaim responsibility for their failures. If you get a good grade on an exam, you are likely to attribute it to your ability or talent—an internal attribution ("I got an A"). Yet you are likely to attribute a poor grade to an external cause beyond your control—an external attribution ("I didn't have enough time to study" or "The questions were unfair").

self-serving bias The tendency to take credit for our accomplishments and to explain away our failures or disappointments.

The self-serving bias—letting failures flow off our backs while taking success to heart—helps bolster self-esteem. Members of sports teams show a similar bias. They make more internal attributions about the success of their teams after victories ("We played well as a team") than defeats ("They were just lucky") (Sherman, Kim, & Heejung, 2005).

The self-serving bias is widespread in Western cultures such as the United States and Canada, but it is much less common in East Asian cultures such as Japan, China, and Taiwan (DeAngelis, 2003; Heine et al., 2001). Unlike Americans, the Japanese tend to attribute their successes to luck and their failures to lack of ability or talent. The self-serving bias may be embedded within a cultural ethic in the United States and other individualistic Western cultures that place a premium on self-esteem (Markus & Kitayama, 1991). The opposite tendency (valuing self-criticism and humility) is associated with collectivist cultures, such as in China or Japan (Oyserman, Coon, & Kemmelmeier, 2002). In these cultures, people are more attuned to their responsibilities to the group than to expressing their individuality or seeking to enhance their own self-esteem. When they experience a personal disappointment or failure, they are more inclined to accept responsibility and focus on working harder to improve their performance in the future than to look for someone else to blame.

CONCEPT 14.7
Another type of cognitive bias, the self-serving bias, comes into play in accounting for the tendency of people to take credit for their successes but explain away their failures.

→ Concept Link
As discussed in Chapter 7, cognitive biases can impair our ability to make rational or sound decisions. See Module 7.1.

Research in the developing field of social neuroscience is uncovering differences between people from Eastern and Western cultures in how the brain processes social cues. In a fMRI study, Japanese and American participants viewed silhouettes of bodies shown in either a slumped posture with head and arms hanging down, which was suggestive of submissiveness, or a dominant posture with the head held high and the arms crossed (Freeman et al., 2009). The brain scans showed greater activation in the reward circuitry in the brain's limbic system in Japanese participants in response to a "submissive" silhouette than to a "dominant" silhouette. The opposite pattern—more activation of reward circuitry in response to dominant than submissive silhouettes—was observed among American participants. It appears that the greater

CONCEPT 14.8
The self-serving bias is widespread in Western cultures but virtually absent in some Eastern cultures.

cultural value placed on submissiveness in Eastern cultures and on dominance in Western cultures is reflected in how the brain processes signals relating to dominance and submissiveness.

Attitudes: How Do You Feel About . . . ?

attitude A positive or negative evaluation of persons, objects, or issues.

What are your attitudes toward gun control laws, sport utility vehicles (SUVs), and vegetarian diets? An **attitude** is an evaluation or judgment of either liking or disliking a person, object, or social issue. Social psychologists conceptualize attitudes as consisting of three components: (1) *cognitions* (sets of beliefs), (2) *emotions* (feelings of liking or disliking), and (3) *behaviors* (inclinations to act positively or negatively) (Olson & Maio, 2003). For example, you may hold favorable or unfavorable views about SUVs, feel positively or negatively toward them, and be either inclined or disinclined to purchase one if you are shopping for a vehicle (see ■ Figure 14.1).

CONCEPT 14.9
To social psychologists, attitudes are judgments of liking or disliking that can be conceptualized in terms of three components: cognitions, emotions, and behaviors.

→ Concept Link
You'll recall from Chapter 8 that emotions also include three basic components: bodily arousal, cognitions, and expressed behaviors. See Module 8.4.

The importance we ascribe to attitudes is a function of their personal relevance. Our attitudes toward sport utility vehicles (love them, hate them) will be more important to us if we happen to be considering buying one. But the more often we express a particular attitude, the more important it is likely to become to us.

Source of Attitudes

Our attitudes are acquired from many sources in our social environment—our parents, teachers, peers, personal experiences, and media sources such as newspapers, television, and movies. Not surprisingly, people from similar backgrounds tend to hold similar attitudes. Yet evidence also points to a possible genetic contribution (Kruglanski & Stroebe, 2005). Studies of twins reared apart show a surprising degree of shared attitudes on a range of issues that cannot be explained by a common environmental influence. People do not inherit a gene or genes for a particular attitude, such as liking or disliking SUVs. Rather, heredity works indirectly by influencing intelligence, temperament, or personality traits that make people more or less likely to develop certain attitudes (Petty, Wegener, & Fabrigar, 1997). However, genetic factors appear to be less important determinants of attitudes than are environmental influences (DeAngelis, 2004).

CONCEPT 14.10
Our social environments shape the attitudes we develop, but research points to possible genetic influences as well.

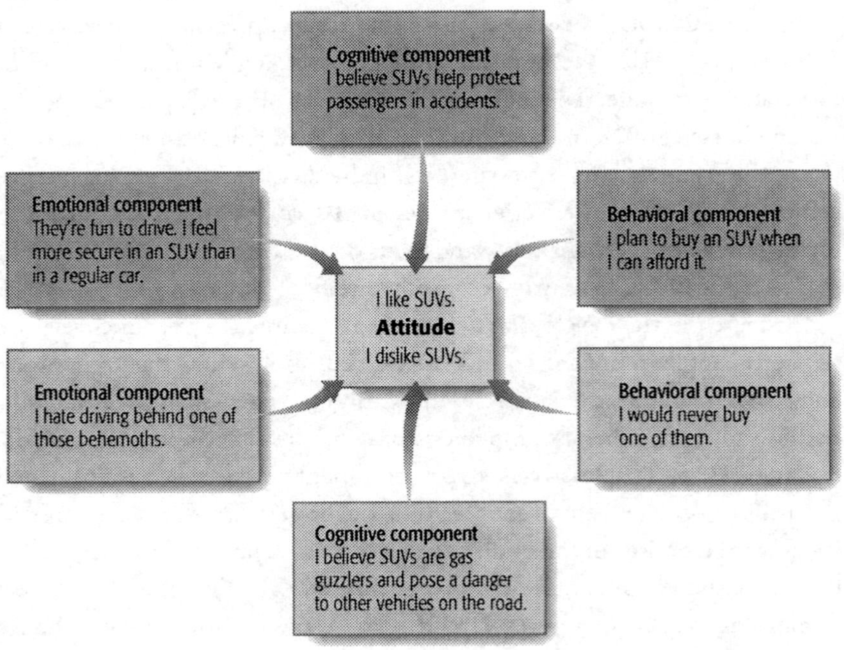

FIGURE 14.1 Attitudes
The attitudes we hold consist of cognitive, emotional, and behavioral components.

Attitudes and Behavior: Not as Strong a Link as You Might Expect

Attitudes may not carry over into behavior (Polinko & Popovich, 2001; Wallace et al., 2005). The lack of consistency between attitudes and behavior reflects many factors, especially situational constraints. We may have an inclination to act in a certain way but be unable to carry out the action because of the particular demands we face in that particular situation. For example, you may hold a positive attitude toward a specific charity but be unable to make a contribution to the latest fund drive because you are running short of cash or need the money for another important purpose. Under other conditions, however, attitudes are more strongly linked to behavior—such as when the attitudes are more stable, are held with greater confidence or certainty, when they relate specifically to the behavior at hand, when the person is free to perform or not perform the behavior, and when the attitude can be more readily recalled from memory (e.g., Glasman & Albarracín, 2006; Olson & Maio, 2003).

CONCEPT 14.11
Though attitudes predispose us to act in certain ways, they are not very strong predictors of behavior.

Persuasion: The Fine Art of Changing People's Minds

We are constantly bombarded with messages attempting to persuade us to change our beliefs and attitudes. Commercials on radio and TV, and advertisements in newspapers and magazines, attempt to persuade us to adopt more favorable attitudes toward advertised products and to purchase them. Political candidates and political action groups seek to sway us to support their candidacies and causes. Doctors, religious leaders, teachers, friends, and family members regularly urge us to change our behaviors, beliefs, and attitudes in ways they believe would be beneficial to us.

Short of secluding ourselves in an isolated cabin in the woods, we can hardly avoid persuasive appeals. But how do such appeals lead to attitude change? And what factors are likely to increase their effectiveness?

CONCEPT 14.12
According to the elaboration likelihood model, attitude change occurs through either a central processing route or a peripheral processing route.

elaboration likelihood model (ELM) A theoretical model that posits two channels by which persuasive appeals lead to attitude change: a central route and a peripheral route.

The Elaboration Likelihood Model: Two Pathways to Persuasion

A leading model of attitude change is the **elaboration likelihood model (ELM)** (Petty & Briñol, 2008). According to this model, people are more likely to carefully evaluate ("elaborate") a persuasive message when their motivational state is high (i.e., when they are willing to exert the mental effort needed to evaluate the message) and when they possess the skills or knowledge needed to evaluate the information (see ■ Figure 14.2).

When evaluation likelihood is high, attitude change occurs via a *central route* of processing information, whereby people carefully evaluate the content of the message. When elaboration likelihood is low, attitude change occurs through a *peripheral route* of cognitive processing, whereby people focus on cues not centrally related to the content of the message. Let us use the example of a televised political debate. Assume that viewers are alert, well informed about the issues, and interested in the views held by the candidates.

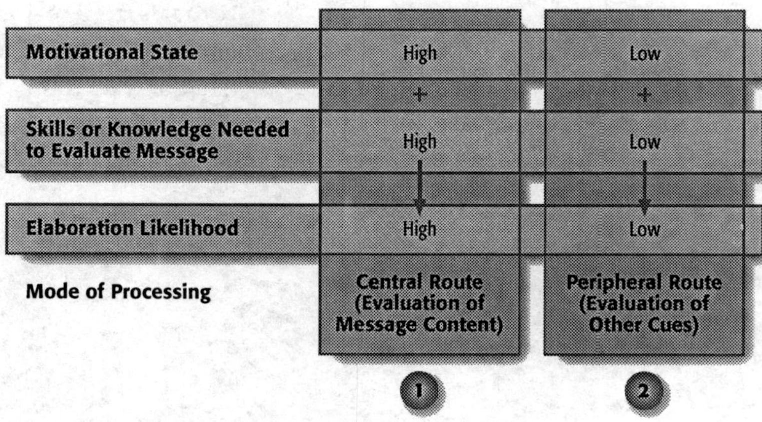

FIGURE 14.2 Elaboration Likelihood Model
According to the elaboration likelihood model, attitude change occurs through one of two routes of cognitive processing—(1) a central route or (2) a peripheral route. When elaboration likelihood is high, we attend more carefully to the content of the message itself. When it is low, as when we are distracted or disinterested, we attend to peripheral cues unrelated to the content of the message.

Under these conditions, elaboration likelihood is high and attitude change is likely to occur through a central processing route by which the viewers carefully evaluate the arguments made by the respective candidates. Conversely, if the viewers are distracted, fatigued, or uninterested in the issues, they are not likely to carefully evaluate each candidate's message. Attitude change occurring under these conditions is likely to be based on peripheral cues that are not directly related to the content of the candidate's message, such as the physical attractiveness of the candidate. In other words, the viewers may be persuaded to endorse candidates on the basis of how they look in the debate rather than how they stand on the issues.

Advertisers often take advantage of the peripheral route of attitude change by using leading sports stars as commercial spokespersons. Celebrity endorsers needn't even mention the distinctive qualities of the product. Just using the product or wearing it may be sufficient to convey the message that the advertiser wants to get across.

Variables Influencing Persuasion

CONCEPT 14.13
The effectiveness of persuasive appeals is influenced by variables relating to the source, the message itself, and the recipient.

Some persuasive appeals are more effective than others. Persuasion is influenced by many variables, as shown in ■ Figure 14.3, including those relating to the source, the message, and the recipient (Littlejohn, 2002; J. Park & Banaji, 2000; Visser & Cooper, 2003).

- *Source variables.* Source variables are features of the communicator who presents the message. Communicators are generally more persuasive when they are perceived as *credible* (knowledgeable and trustworthy), *likable* (attractive and personable), and *similar* to the receiver in key respects (e.g., a former substance abuser may be more successful in persuading current substance abusers to accept treatment than a person who has never abused drugs).
- *Message variables.* Messages that contain emotional appeals are often persuasive. Political candidates, for example, frequently appeal to voters' fears when they characterize their opponents as "soft" on national security issues. Presenting both sides of an argument is generally more effective than presenting only one side, as long as the communicator refutes the other side. Messages that run counter to the perceived interests of the communicator tend to be perceived as more credible. Not surprisingly, people paid great attention a few years ago when a member of the R. J. Reynolds family of tobacco growers spoke out on the dangers of smoking. Third, the more often we are exposed to a message, the more favorably we are likely to evaluate it, but only up to a point. When the message is repeated often enough, people may come to believe it, whether or not it is true. But with further repetition, irritation and tedium begin to set in and acceptance of the message begins to decline.
- *Recipient variables.* Though nobody is immune to persuasive appeals, some people are easier to persuade than others. Those of low intelligence or low self-confidence are generally more susceptible to persuasive appeals. People also tend to be more receptive to persuasive messages when they are in a positive rather than a negative mood. A good mood may motivate people to see things in a more positive light.

The major influences on social perception are reviewed in Concept Chart 14.1.

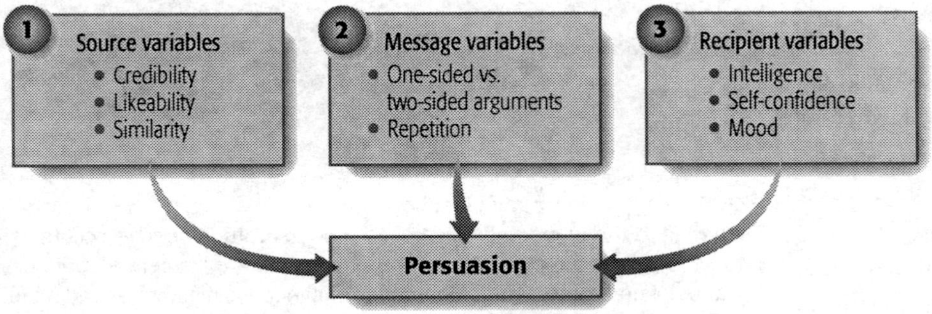

FIGURE 14.3 Getting Your Message Across: Factors in Persuasive Appeals
The effectiveness of persuasive appeals depends upon (1) characteristics of the source of the message, (2) the message itself, and (3) the recipient of the message.

CONCEPT CHART 14.1 Perceiving Others

Topic	What It Is	Influences on Social Perception
Initial impressions	Initial evaluation (liking or disliking) of others	Physical appearance, attire, stereotypes, and degree of personal disclosure influence first impressions. They are difficult to dislodge because we tend to filter new information through them and because they may become self-fulfilling prophecies.
Attributions	Personal explanations of the causes of behavior	Attributional biases affecting social perception include the fundamental attribution error, the actor-observer effect, and the self-serving bias.
Attitudes	Judgments of liking or disliking persons, objects, and issues	The social environment and possible genetic factors influence attitudes. According to the elaboration likelihood model, attitude change occurs through either a central or peripheral route of processing, depending on the degree to which the message is elaborated. The effectiveness of persuasive appeals depends on source variables, recipient variables, and message variables.

14.1 MODULE REVIEW Perceiving Others

Recite It

What are the major influences on first impressions, and why do first impressions often become lasting impressions?

- First impressions are influenced by surface characteristics, such as physical appearance and attire, and by stereotypes and personal disclosures.
- A modest amount of self-disclosure is associated with a more favorable impression. However, self-disclosure is generally looked upon more favorably in Western cultures than in Eastern cultures.
- First impressions may become lasting impressions when people reconcile discrepant information with their existing impressions, or social schemas. Impressions may also become self-fulfilling prophecies.

What role do cognitive biases play in the judgments we make about the causes of behavior?

- The fundamental attribution error is an overemphasis on internal or dispositional causes of behavior to the exclusion of situational factors.
- The actor-observer effect is the tendency to explain our own behavior in terms of the demands of the situation while explaining the behavior of others in terms of internal or dispositional causes.
- The self-serving bias bolsters self-esteem in that it involves attributing personal success to one's talents or abilities while explaining personal failure in terms of external causes.

What are attitudes, and how are they acquired?

- Attitudes are evaluations or judgments of liking or disliking people, objects, or issues. Psychologists conceptualize attitudes as having three components: cognitions, emotions, and behaviors.
- The social environment, which encompasses our relationships and experiences with others as well as our exposure to mass media, is the learning ground for the acquisition of attitudes. Genetic factors may also play a role.

How are attitudes related to behavior?

- Attitudes are related to behavior modestly at best. Our behavior is influenced by many factors, not just our attitudes.

How do persuasive appeals lead to attitude change?

- According to the elaboration likelihood model, attitudes may be altered by persuasive messages that are processed through either a central route (careful evaluation of the content of the message) or a peripheral route (focusing on cues that are peripheral to the content of the message).

Recall It

1. A mental image or representation we use to understand our social environment is called a social ________.
2. When we interpret a behavior or an event, we usually see it as due to either ________ or ________ causes.
3. The fundamental attribution error refers to an (underestimation or overestimation?) of internal factors.
4. Give a social-psychological definition of the term *attitude*.

5. Match the following terms with the appropriate descriptions: (a) peripheral processing route; (b) source variable(s); (c) message variable(s); (d) recipient variable(s).
   i. the tendency for repetition to lead to more favorable evaluations.
   ii. applies when people are not likely to carefully evaluate message contents.
   iii. the relationship between low self-confidence and greater susceptibility to persuasion.
   iv. credibility, likability, and similarity.

Think About It

- Why do first impressions tend to become lasting impressions?
- Do you have a tendency to take credit for your successes and explain away your failures? How might the self-serving bias prevent you from learning from your mistakes and taking appropriate steps to prevent them in the future?

MODULE 14.2

Relating to Others

- What are the major determinants of attraction?
- What factors are linked to helping behavior?
- What is prejudice, and how does it develop?
- What can be done to reduce prejudice?
- What factors contribute to human aggression?

THE BRAIN LOVES A PUZZLE

As you read ahead, use the information in the text to solve the following puzzle:

If you were to collapse on a city street and needed immediate help from a passerby, why would you be less likely to receive help if the street was crowded with people than if there were only a few people around?

Social psychologists are interested in how individuals relate to each other in their social environments. We may categorize ways of relating to others in terms of positive and negative interactions. Attraction, love, and helping are positive interactions. Negative ways of relating include prejudiced behavior and aggression. In this module we examine what psychologists have learned about these positive and negative ways of relating to others.

Attraction: Getting to Like (or Love) You

In nature, attraction is the tendency for two objects or bodies to be drawn toward each other, like the opposite poles of a magnet. In psychology, **attraction** describes feelings of liking others as well as having positive thoughts about them and inclinations to act positively toward them. Attraction is not limited to romantic or sexual attraction. Social psychologists use the term more broadly to include other kinds of attraction as well, such as feelings of liking toward friends. Here we consider key determinants of attraction as well as that special type of attraction.

attraction Feelings of liking for others, together with having positive thoughts about them and inclinations to act toward them in positive ways.

Determinants of Attraction

Psychologists have identified several key determinants of attraction, including similarity, physical attractiveness, proximity, and reciprocity.

Similarity Like birds of a feather, we are generally attracted to people who share similar values and attitudes (Buston & Emlen, 2003; Rushton & Bons, 2005). We also tend to like people who are similar to us in characteristics such as physical appearance, social class, race, height, musical tastes, and intelligence. People tend to select mates who are similar to themselves on attitudes, religious views, and values (Luo & Klohnen, 2005). People are even more likely to marry others whose first or last names resemble their own (J. T. Jones et al., 2004).

Why are people attracted to similar others? The mostly widely held view is that similarity is gratifying because each person in the relationship serves to validate, reinforce, and enhance the other's self-concept. If you echo my sentiments about movies, politics, and the like, I might feel better about myself.

CONCEPT 14.14
Attraction is influenced by similarity, physical attractiveness, proximity, and reciprocity.

Does this mean that relationships are doomed to fail if two people (roommates, friends, or lovers) differ in their attitudes, interests, or tastes? Not necessarily. For one thing, no two people are identical in all respects (fortunately so!). At least some common ground is necessary to anchor a relationship, but every successful relationship still requires compromise and accommodation to keep it afloat. Not surprisingly, the attitudes of dating partners tend to become more closely aligned over time (J. L. Davis & Rusbult, 2001).

Physical Attractiveness We might think we are attracted romantically to people because of their inner qualities. However, evidence shows that the major determinant of initial attraction is the outer packaging, not the inner soul (Berscheid & Reis, 1998; Berscheid & Regan, 2005). Note some gender differences, however. Men typically place greater emphasis than do women on the physical attractiveness of potential mates (Buss, 1994; Furnham, 2009). But when it comes to casual sexual relationships, both men and women tend to place a premium on the physical attractiveness of prospective partners (N. P. Li & Kenrick, 2006; Nevid, 1984; Stambor, 2006a).

Our physical appearance affects how others perceive us. Not only are people attracted to pretty packages, but they tend to adopt a "what is beautiful is good" stereotype. That is, people tend to judge attractive people not simply as more attractive but as psychologically better adjusted and more intelligent, competent, and socially skillful than less attractive people (e.g., Little, Burt, & Perret, 2006; Lorenzo, Biesanz, & Human, 2010). Yet there are exceptions to the "beautiful is good" stereotype: Attractive people are typically judged as more vain and less modest than their less attractive peers (Feingold, 1992).

People tend to date and to marry others who are similar to themselves in level of attractiveness (Lee et al., 2008). When we do find a mismatch, the less attractive partner usually compensates by having greater wealth or social position than the more attractive partner (Berscheid & Reis, 1998).

In our society, it also pays to be tall—literally. Evidence shows that height is associated with higher incomes (Dittmann, 2004). The reason, investigators suspect, is that taller workers tend to be favored for sales and executive positions (T. A. Judge & Cable, 2004). Even standing tall by adopting a power pose has strong effects on feeling more powerful, thinking and acting more powerful, taking more risks, and even boosting levels in both men and women of testosterone (Carney et al., 2010; Huang et al., 2011; "Standing Tall," 2011).

Beauty may be in the eye of the beholder, but beholders tend to view beauty in highly similar ways. We tend to agree on whom we find attractive or not attractive. Faces with symmetrical features and a clear complexion are universally perceived as more attractive (Fink & Penton-Voak, 2002; Fink et al., 2006).

© Panorama Productions Inc./Alamy

Evidence suggests that it pays to be tall—literally. Researchers find that taller people typically earn more than shorter workers. How might you explain this finding?

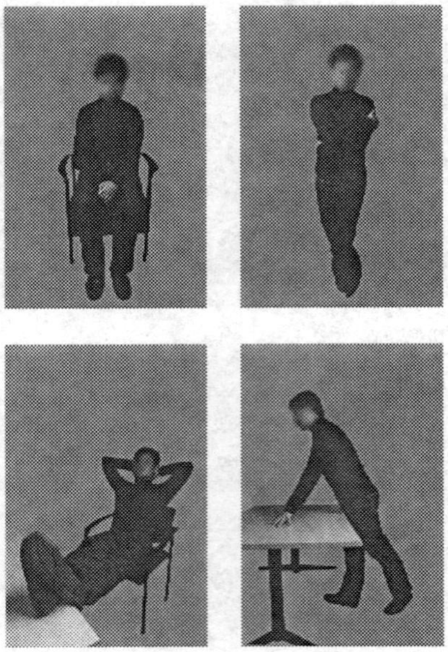

Source: Carney, D. R., Cuddy, A. J. C., & Yap, A. J. Psychological Science, 21, pp. 1363-1368, © 2010 by SAGE Publications. Reprinted by Permission of SAGE Publications.

Psychologists study how our physical behavior affects our social behavior and mental processes. For example, adopting more open or powerful poses, such as those shown on the bottom, leads people to feel, think, and act more powerfully, as well as boosting levels of testosterone in both men and women, as compared to adopting closed or constricted poses, such as those on the top.

What features comprise a beautiful face? Investigators asked white, Euro-American students and recently emigrated Asian and Hispanic students to judge the attractiveness of photographs of Asian, Hispanic, black, and white women (Cunningham et al., 1995). Judgments of physical beauty were generally consistent for photographs of members of the different groups. Faces rated as more attractive typically had features such as high cheekbones and eyebrows, widely spaced eyes, a small nose, thin cheeks, a large smile, a full lower lip, a small chin, and a fuller hairstyle. Both male and female raters tended to judge the same faces as attractive; they also tended to agree that faces of women with more feminine features were more attractive than those with more masculine features (Angier, 1998). Yet, and this might surprise you, both men and women generally rated male faces with *more feminine features* as more attractive than those with more masculinized features—findings consistent with other research as well (e.g., DeBruine et al., 2010). The more refined or delicate features of a youthful Leonardo DiCaprio, for example, tend to be preferred over the more squared-jawed, masculinized features of the young Arnold Schwarzenegger.

Although some features of physical beauty appear to be universal, cultural differences certainly do exist (Swami & Furnham, 2008). In certain African cultures, for example, feminine beauty is associated with such physical features as long necks and round, disk-like lips. Female plumpness is valued in some societies, whereas in others, including our own, the female ideal is associated with an unrealistic standard of thinness (see Chapter 8). Women themselves tend to associate curvaceousness with female attractiveness, but only so long as the curvaceous figure is lean and does not have large hips (Forestell, Humphrey, & Stewart, 2004). Slenderness in men is also valued in Western society, but social pressures to be thin are placed disproportionately on women.

matching hypothesis The belief that people tend to pair off with others who are similar to themselves in physical attractiveness and other characteristics.

One explanation for why people who fall short of a physical ideal are likely to be saved from a lifetime of dinners-for-one is the **matching hypothesis**, the prediction that people will seek partners who are similar to themselves in physical attractiveness. When mismatches occur, it is generally the less attractive partner that compensates by possessing some other valued attribute, such as having greater wealth or social position. The matching hypothesis applies to other characteristics as well. We tend to be attracted to mates who are similar to ourselves in personality, attitudes, and even body weight (Angier, 2003; Schafer & Keith, 1990).

© Frank Trapper

© Vince Bucci/Stringer/Getty Images

Sorry, Arnold. When rating male faces, both men and women tend to rate those having more feminine features, such as the refined and delicate features of a Johnny Depp or Leonardo DiCaprio, as more attractive than those with more masculinized features, such as those of the young Arnold Schwarzenegger.

Proximity Friendship patterns are strongly influenced by physical **proximity**. If you live in a college dormitory, your friends are more likely to live down the hall than across campus. Your earliest friends were probably children who lived next door or down the block from you.

proximity Nearness or propinquity.

Proximity increases the chances of interacting with others and getting to know them better, thus providing a basis for developing feelings of attraction toward them. Another explanation for the positive effects of proximity on attraction is the tendency for people to have more in common with people who live nearby or attend the same classes. Similarity in attitudes and background can increase feelings of liking. Proximity can also increase negative attraction, or dislike. Repeated contact with someone you dislike may intensify negative feelings.

Reciprocity **Reciprocity** is the tendency to like others who like us back. We typically respond in kind to people who compliment us, do us favors, or tell us how much they like us (Baron, Branscombe, & Byrne, 2009). Reciprocal interactions build upon themselves, leading to feelings of liking. Yet we may be wary of people who compliment us too quickly or seem to like us too much before they get to know us. We may suspect that they want something from us or are not very discriminating.

reciprocity The principle that people tend to like others who like them back.

The principle of reciprocity comes into play in many aspects of social behavior, including, researchers find, tipping behavior (Cialdini & Goldstein, 2004). Investigators found that when waitresses wrote helpful messages on the back of the customers' checks, or when they gave customers a small piece of chocolate along with their checks, patrons tended to reciprocate by leaving larger tips (Rind & Strohmetz, 1999; Strohmetz et al., 2002).

When it comes to romantic attraction, playing hard to get by holding back whether you are attracted to someone may make you hard to forget. Recently, investigators told female college students that a group of college men had rated them and a number of other women on desirability based on their Facebook profiles (Whitchurch, Wilson, & Gilbert, 2011). Some women were told the men liked them the best, whereas other women were told men gave them only average ratings. Other women were left to wonder, being told only that the men's ratings wouldn't be revealed to them and that the men might have liked them best or might have rated them as average. Now it was the women's turn to rate the guys based on their Facebook profiles. In reality, but unbeknownst to the women, the male students were actually a fiction, a concoction the experimenter used to manipulate liking. Which group of women do you think gave the men the highest ratings? It turned out the reciprocity principle was supported, as women who were told the men had rated them highest returned the favor, rating the men higher than did women in the average-liking condition. But women in the uncertainty condition (*Did he like me best or not?*) gave the men the highest ratings of all, supporting the view that keeping people guessing about how much you like them might just pique their interest in wanting to get to know you better.

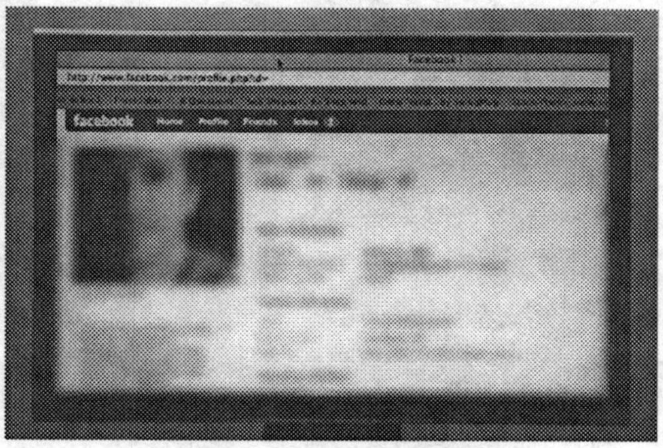

© Eric Carr / Alamy

Like him, or like him not? The answer may depend on whether he keeps his feelings toward you under wraps.

Next we turn to another positive way of relating to others—helping others in time of need. We begin with a tragic story of nonhelping in which a young woman was brutally attacked and many people who heard her agonizing screams did nothing to help her.

Helping Behavior: Lending a Hand to Others in Need

SLICE OF LIFE Even now, nearly 50 years after the 1964 murder of 28-year-old Kitty Genovese on a quiet street in Queens, New York, the shock remains. Kitty screamed for help as she was viciously and repeatedly attacked by an assailant who stabbed her until

CONCEPT 14.15
Helping may be motivated by both altruistic and self-centered motives.

prosocial behavior Behavior that benefits others.

bystander intervention Helping a stranger in distress.

CONCEPT 14.16
According to the decision-making model, bystander intervention depends on a series of decisions leading to intervention.

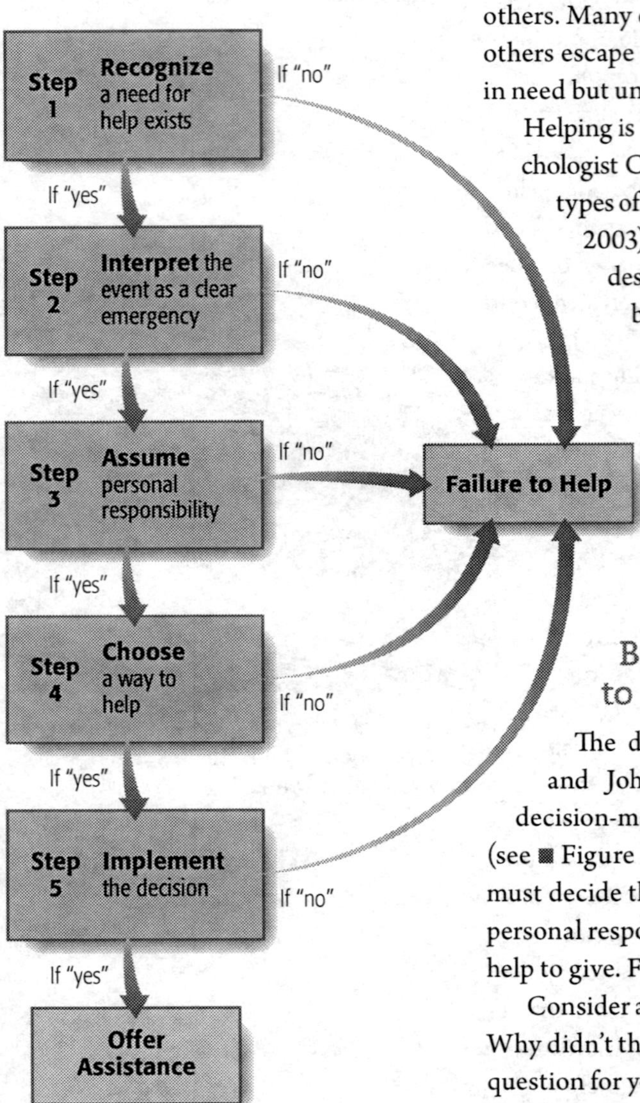

FIGURE 14.4 A Decision-Making Model of Bystander Intervention
The decision-making model of bystander intervention identifies five decision-making steps that precede either helping or failing to offer help.
Source: From D. A. Schroeder et al., *The Psychology of Helping and Altruism*. Copyright © 1995. Reprinted with permission of the author.

she lay dying from her wounds. From their nearby apartment windows, a number of witnesses (the exact number is unclear) heard Kitty's screams or saw the attack. None rushed to her aid, although at least one person reportedly called the police, but not until after the first attack (Manning, Levine, & Collins, 2007). This tragic case prompted serious scientific inquiry into factors that determine helping behavior. Why do some bystanders help a stranger in need while others just pass by?

Is there something so callous in human nature that we would turn our backs on someone in desperate need of assistance? If so, how are we to explain the countless acts of simple kindness of people who selflessly help people in need, let alone the heroic acts of people who risk their lives in emergency situations to save others? Consider the heroic efforts of the firefighters and police officers who responded to the terrorist attack at the World Trade Center, many of whom lost their lives in a valiant attempt to save others. Many civilians at this site of tragedy also lost their lives as they stopped to help others escape the inferno. Clearly, the question is not whether people will help others in need but under what conditions they will help.

Helping is a form of **prosocial behavior**, or behavior that is beneficial to others. Psychologist C. Daniel Batson, a leading authority on helping, distinguishes between two types of motives that underlie helping behavior (Batson et al., 2002; Batson & Powell, 2003). One type of helping arises from *altruistic* motives—the pure, unselfish desire to help others without expecting anything in return. But another type is based on self-centered motives, such as the desire to help someone in order to make oneself look good in the eyes of others or to avoid feeling guilty from failing to help. Batson believes that altruistic helping results from the helper's identification with the plight of the victim. By putting ourselves in the victim's shoes, so to speak, we are able to empathize with the person's suffering, which prompts us to take action. Batson's belief in pure altruism is not universally accepted, as some social psychologists believe that all forms of helping benefit the helper to a certain extent.

Bystander Intervention: Deciding to Get Involved—Or Not

The decision-making model of helping behavior proposed by Bibb Latané and John Darley (1970) explains **bystander intervention** in terms of a decision-making process that can be broken down into a series of five decisions (see ■ Figure 14.4). First, people must decide that a need for help exists. Second, they must decide that the situation is a clear emergency. Third, they must decide to assume personal responsibility for providing assistance. Fourth, they must decide what kind of help to give. Fifth, they must decide to implement this course of action.

Consider again the people who witnessed Kitty Genovese's murder but did nothing. Why didn't they help? The critical thinking exercise at the end of the chapter poses this question for you to answer. For now, however, let us examine what social psychologists have learned about the factors that affect helping behavior. Some of these factors may shed light on the inaction of those witnesses.

Influences on Helping

Many factors influence people's willingness to help, including the ambiguity of the situation, perceived cost, diffusion of responsibility, similarity, empathy, facial features, mood and gender, attributions of the cause of need, and social norms.

- *Situational ambiguity.* In ambiguous situations, as Latané and Darley would predict, people are much less likely to offer assistance than in situations involving a clear-cut emergency (Baron, Branscombe, & Byrne, 2009). They are also less likely to help in unfamiliar environments than in familiar ones (e.g., when they are in strange cities rather than in their hometowns).
- *Perceived cost.* The likelihood of helping increases as the perceived cost to ourselves declines (Simmons, 1991). We are more likely to lend our class notes to someone we believe will return them than to a person who doesn't appear trustworthy.
- *Diffusion of responsibility.* The presence of others may diffuse the sense of individual responsibility. It follows that if you suddenly felt faint and were about to pass out on the street, you would be more likely to receive help if there were only a few passers-by present than if the street were crowded with pedestrians. With fewer people present, it becomes more difficult to point to the "other guy" as the one responsible for taking action. If everyone believes the other guy will act, then no one acts.
- *Similarity.* People are more willing to help others whom they perceive to be similar to themselves—people who share a common background and beliefs. They are even more likely to help others who dress the way they do than those in different attire (Cialdini, 2007). People also tend to be more willing to help relatives than unrelated people (Gaulin & McBurney, 2001).
- *Empathy.* Another factor influencing altruistic helping is the helper's identification or empathy with the victim (Batson et al., 2009; Penner et al., 2005).
- *Facial features.* People with babyfaced features are more likely to elicit help than people with more mature facial features (Keating et al., 2003).
- *Mood and gender.* People are generally more willing to help others when they are in a good mood (Baron, Branscombe, & Byrne, 2009). Despite changes in traditional gender roles, it remains the case that women in need are more likely to get help from strangers than are men in need.
- *Attributions of the cause of need.* People are much more likely to help others they judge to be innocent victims than those they believe have brought their problems on themselves (Batson, 1998). Thus, they may fail to lend assistance to homeless people and drug addicts whom they feel "deserve what they get."
- *Social norms.* **Social norms** prescribe behaviors that are expected of people in social situations. The social norm of "doing your part" in helping a worthy cause places a demand on people to help, especially in situations where their behavior is observed by others (Gaulin & McBurney, 2001). For example, people are more likely to make a charitable donation when they are asked to do so by a coworker in full view of others than when they receive an appeal in the mail in the privacy of their own homes.

CONCEPT 14.17
Helping behavior is influenced by situational and individual factors and by social norms.

© baranq/shutterstock.com

Would you help this man? What influences the decision to help a person in need?

social norms Standards that define what is socially acceptable in a given situation.

Let us now explore negative ways of relating to others, including prejudice and discrimination as well as human aggression.

Prejudice: Attitudes That Harm

Prejudice is a preconceived attitude, usually unfavorable, that is formed without critical thought or evaluation of the facts. Some prejudices reflect positive biases, such as when we prejudge members of our own ethnic or religious group more favorably than members of other groups. But most prejudices reflect negative biases against other

prejudice A preconceived opinion or attitude about an issue, person, or group.

CONCEPT 14.18

Social psychologists conceptualize prejudice, as they do other types of attitudes, as consisting of cognitive, emotional, and behavioral components.

discrimination Unfair or biased treatment of people based on their membership in a particular group or category.

racism Negative bias toward others based on their ethnicity or racial identification.

groups or categories on the basis of race, ethnicity, social class, gender, age, and occupational, disability, or social status.

Prejudice, like other attitudes, consists of cognitive, emotional, and behavioral components. The cognitive component is the set of biased beliefs and stereotypes that a person holds about other groups. The emotional component consists of feelings of dislike that the person has toward members of these groups. And the behavioral component is the person's inclination to discriminate against them. **Discrimination** is unfair or biased treatment of people based on group membership. Examples of discrimination include denial of housing or job opportunities, exclusion from social clubs, and increased scrutiny by police officers or security guards. Exposure to **racism** and discrimination can have damaging effects on the psychological and physical health of targeted groups (Mays, Cochran, & Barnes, 2007).

Note the disparities between what people say about their racial attitudes and how they respond to racial cues. For example, people who think of themselves as unprejudiced might nonetheless clutch their pocketbooks or briefcases more tightly when a person from a negatively stereotyped group boards an elevator with them or sits down next to them on a train or bus.

Stereotypes and prejudices are generally resistant to change. Social psychologists find that whites who hold stereotypical views of blacks may perceive them as "lazy" even when they perform in exactly the same way as the whites (Hilton & von Hippel, 1996).

Social scientists have long observed that prejudice and discrimination typically increase during times of social upheaval and increased competition among groups. Competition over jobs and scarce economic opportunities can strain intergroup relationships. It comes as no surprise, then, that acts of racial hatred tend to increase during economic downturns, when unemployment is high. Members of ethnic or racial minority groups may become convenient scapegoats when the economic security of the majority is threatened.

How Does Prejudice Develop?

CONCEPT 14.19

Prejudice develops as an outgrowth of negative stereotypes and is acquired in the same way that other attitudes are learned.

Prejudice arises as an outgrowth of negative stereotypes of other groups as lazy, dishonest, violent, dumb, and so on. These stereotypes are learned or acquired. Children may begin forming negative attitudes toward other groups by imitating the prejudiced attitudes they see modeled by parents, teachers, and peers. Prejudices may also be acquired through repeated exposure to negative, stereotypical depictions of other groups, especially racial minorities, in the media. We are repeatedly exposed to television and movie depictions of racial minorities in negative roles—as criminals, gang members, abusers, drug pushers, and so on.

Prejudice may also be acquired through direct experience. If a person has a few experiences with members of a particular group who are cold or nasty, he or she may overgeneralize and develop a stereotyped belief that all members of the particular group share these characteristics.

Though we may differ in the prejudices we acquire, we all harbor some prejudices. The universality of prejudice points to a basic cognitive tendency we have to parse our social environment into two general categories: people who belong to the same groups as we do and those who do not belong. Social psychologists describe these social categories as **in-groups** (one's own social, religious, ethnic, racial, and national groups) and **out-groups** (all other groups) (Hewstone, Rubin, & Willis, 2002).

in-groups Social, religious, ethnic, racial, or national groups with which one identifies.

out-groups Groups other than those with which one identifies.

Prejudice develops when our thinking becomes biased in such a way that we attribute more negative characteristics to members of out-groups and more positive characteristics to members of in-groups. These two biased ways of thinking are called **out-group negativism** (also called *out-group prejudice*) and **in-group favoritism** (or *in-group bias*), respectively (Gaertner et al., 2006; M. A. Olson, Crawford, & Devlin, 2009). Negative stereotypes of out-groups—beliefs that "we" are better than "they"—bolster the self-esteem of in-group members. Labeling other groups as dumb, lazy, dishonest, and so on makes us feel good in comparison.

out-group negativism A cognitive bias involving the predisposition to attribute more negative characteristics to members of out-groups than to those of in-groups.

in-group favoritism A cognitive bias involving the predisposition to attribute more positive characteristics to members of in-groups than to those of out-groups.

out-group homogeneity A cognitive bias describing the tendency to perceive members of out-groups as more alike than members of in-groups.

Another type of biased thinking associated with prejudice is **out-group homogeneity.** This is the tendency to perceive members of other racial or ethnic groups as being alike or *homogeneous* while perceiving members of one's own group as being "different as snowflakes" (Nelson, 2002). An extension of this bias is the tendency to think that people of other groups all "look alike" (Ackerman et al., 2006). One prominent explanation of out-group homogeneity is the *exemplar model* (Linville & Fischer, 1993). It holds that people are likely to know more in-group members than out-group members and so can more easily recall differences among people within their own groups.

The cognitive bases of prejudice may have evolved over thousands of generations. As social psychologist Martin Fishbein (1996) argues, ancestral humans organized themselves into tribal groups that shared a common language and culture, and they needed to keep their guard up against threats posed by outsiders—people from other groups who might harm them or kill them. Stereotyping other groups as "dangerous" or "evil" may have served an adaptive function to these early humans, who had good reason to fear outsiders. In today's multicultural society of, however, we face very different adaptive demands. We need to learn to get along with people of diverse backgrounds and to avoid branding people who are different from ourselves with unwarranted stereotypes.

CONCEPT 14.20
The cognitive bases of prejudice reflect tendencies to separate people into two basic categories, in-groups and out-groups, and to attribute more negative characteristics to out-group members and more positive characteristics to in-group members.

→ Concept Link
We use mental categories or concepts to group objects, events, and ideas according to their common features. See Module 7.1.

Why Are Some People More Prejudiced Than Others?

Learning experiences play a key role in explaining individual differences in prejudice. Children exposed to the teachings of less prejudiced parents are likely to develop less prejudiced attitudes than are children of more intolerant parents. Low-prejudiced individuals also tend to differ in their cognitive style. They tend to look more at similarities among people than at differences, a cognitive framework that psychologists call a *universalist orientation* (Phillips & Ziller, 1997). By contrast, people with more prejudiced attitudes emphasize differences among people and use ethnicity as a basis for judging people.

CONCEPT 14.21
Individual differences in prejudice may be explained by learning experiences, personality traits, and the tendency to emphasize either similarities or differences between people.

The presence of an underlying personality type called the **authoritarian personality** may also contribute to the development of highly prejudiced attitudes (Johnson et al., 2011; Mavor et al., 2009). Theodore Adorno and his colleagues (1950) coined this term to describe a cluster of personality traits that include rigidity and excessive concern with obedience and respect for authority. People with authoritarian personalities are prone to hate people who are different from themselves and those they perceive as weak or downtrodden.

authoritarian personality A personality type characterized by rigidity, prejudice, and excessive concerns with obedience and respect for authority.

Why It Matters: Effects of Racism and Stereotyping on Stereotyped Groups

Racism is unfortunately a part of the everyday experience of many minority-group members in our society who are targets of stereotyping. As noted in Chapter 13, exposure to racism and discrimination can have damaging effects on the psychological and physical health of stereotyped groups.

CONCEPT 14.22
As a result of being subjected to stereotyping and prejudice, stereotyped groups may internalize the negative stereotypes and set lower expectations for themselves.

Stereotyping has yet more subtle effects. Members of stereotyped and stigmatized groups may be "on guard" for cues or signals associated with stereotypes like "Girls can't do math" or "Blacks don't do well on IQ tests" (Kaiser, Vick, & Major, 2006; Steele & Ambady, 2006). This "on-guard" phenomenon, labeled **stereotype threat**, hangs like a "threat in the air." It can trigger negative expectations in members of stereotyped groups, leading them to underperform in test situations in which the stereotypes are evoked (Grimm et al., 2009; Muzzatti & Agnoli, 2007; Nguyen & Ryan, 2008). For instance, the stereotypical belief that "Girls can't do math" may discourage young women from pursuing promising career opportunities in engineering and the sciences. Drawing attention to this stereotype in a testing situation (or simply even mentioning gender in a testing situation) can impair women's math performance by diverting their attention to worrying about their abilities (Kiefer & Sekaquaptewa, 2007; Krendl et al., 2008; Rydell, Rydell, & Boucher, 2010). Negative stereotypes may also become internalized by members of stereotyped groups, leading them to perceive themselves as inadequate or inferior. Becoming aware of negative stereotypes may undermine how children from stereotyped groups perform in school, sap their motivation to succeed, and lower their self-esteem (McKown & Strambler, 2009). In effect, the negative stereotype becomes a type of self-fulfilling prophecy, as underperformance serves to confirm the stereotype.

stereotype threat A sense of threat evoked in people from stereotyped groups when they believe they may be judged or treated stereotypically.

CONCEPT 14.23
Stereotyping and prejudice negatively affect stereotyped groups in a number of ways, producing lowered expectations and internalization of negative stereotypes.

But how does stereotype threat affect performance? In one instructive study, Stanford psychologist Claude Steele and his colleague Joshua Aronson had black and white Stanford University students take a test consisting of the most difficult items from the verbal section of the SAT (Steele & Aronson, 1995). Some of the students were informed beforehand that the test measured intellectual ability. Others were told it was a laboratory problem-solving task unrelated to intellectual ability. Black students underperformed white students of equal aptitude when the task was defined as a measure of intelligence but equaled them in the laboratory problem-solving condition.

Steele believes that identifying the test as a measure of intellectual ability activated stereotype threat in the black students, which in turn impaired their performance. In another study, white students underperformed in a golf task under a condition in which they were told the task tapped "natural athletic ability," whereas black students underperformed when they were led to believe the golf task measured "sports intelligence" (Stone et al., 1999). Steele believes that the damaging effects of stereotype threat has broader effects on members of stereotyped groups, such as sapping their motivation to attain higher educational goals. For example, exposure to stereotypical depictions of women and ethnic minorities in the media may lead young women with good math ability to opt out of science and math courses, or influence blacks to drop out of college.

TRY THIS OUT
Examining Prejudice

Interview two or three friends or acquaintances from different ethnic or religious backgrounds. Ask them to describe any experiences they may have had in which they encountered prejudice or discrimination. How did these experiences affect them? How did they affect their perceptions of their social environment? Of themselves? How did they cope with these experiences? Based on your reading of the text, how might you counter your own tendencies to think in stereotyped or prejudiced ways?

What can be done to counter effects of stereotype threat? Steele suggests that stereotype threat may be lessened if teachers hold genuinely optimistic beliefs about the potentials of all their students. Encouraging minority students to positively affirm their competence and abilities may also lessen the effects of negative stereotyping (Cohen et al., 2006).

What can be done to counter stereotypes and prejudices? Social psychologists suggest some possible remedies (also see *Try This Out*).

What Can We Do to Reduce Prejudice?

Albert Einstein said that "It is harder to crack a prejudice than an atom." Despite the challenge, psychologists have developed models for reducing prejudice. Perhaps the best known model is the **contact hypothesis** formulated in 1954 by psychologist Gordon Allport. He proposed that the best way to reduce prejudice and intergroup tension was to

contact hypothesis Allport's belief that under certain conditions, increased intergroup contact helps reduce prejudice and intergroup tension.

bring groups into closer contact with each other. But he recognized that intergroup contact alone was not sufficient. Under some conditions, intergroup contact may increase negative attitudes by making differences between groups more apparent. Allport posited four conditions, as specified below, that must be met for intergroup contact to have a desirable effect on reducing prejudice and intergroup tension. Before describing these conditions, note that an important question remains as to whether they represent more of an ideal than an achievable reality in today's world (Dixon et al., 2005, 2010).

CONCEPT 14.24
According to Allport, intergroup contact can help reduce prejudice, but only under conditions of social and institutional support, acquaintance potential, equal status, and intergroup cooperation.

- *Social and institutional support.* People in positions of authority must be clearly behind the effort to bring groups closer together.
- *Acquaintance potential.* Opportunities must exist for members of different groups to become better acquainted with each other. With opportunities for more face-to-face interaction, members of different groups have a better chance of finding common ground. They may also discover evidence that refutes negative stereotypes they hold about each other. Even knowing that a member of one's own group has a close relationship with a member of another group can promote more positive attitudes toward the other group (S. C. Wright et al., 1997).
- *Equal status.* Increased opportunities for contact with members of other groups who occupy subordinate roles may actually reinforce existing stereotypes and prejudices. When opportunities exist for members of different groups to meet on an equal footing, it becomes more difficult to maintain prejudiced beliefs.
- *Intergroup cooperation.* Working cooperatively to achieve a common goal can help reduce intergroup bias by bringing members of different groups closer together (Pettigrew & Tropp, 2006). Whether it involves a baseball team, a project team in the office, or citizens banding together to fight a common cause, cooperation can foster feelings of friendliness and mutual understanding.

© Cory Smith/shutterstock.com

Combating prejudice and discrimination begins with the lessons we teach our children in the home and at school (Sleek, 1997). Teaching empathy may be one way to reduce prejudice. *Empathy* is the ability to take the perspective of other people and understand their feelings. Popular movies that allow us to share emotional experiences of members of stigmatized groups—films such as *Rain Man*, *Schindler's List*, and *The Color Purple*—may be useful in promoting more accepting and tolerant attitudes. Enforcing laws against discrimination and encouraging tolerance are societal measures that help combat prejudice and discrimination.

We as individuals can also take steps to counter prejudiced thinking. Simply telling ourselves not to think in stereotypical terms may actually strengthen these beliefs by bringing them more readily to mind (J. W. Sherman et al., 1997). Though stereotypical and biased attitudes may occur automatically or unconsciously, investigators find that it is possible to change these attitudes (Ashburn-Nardo, Voils, & Monteith, 2001; Dasgupta & Greenwald, 2001). Social psychologists offer a number of suggestions that may help reduce prejudiced and stereotypical thinking, including repeated practice rejecting these thoughts when they occur, rehearsing more positive mental images of out-group members, taking part in cooperative projects in which we get to interact with people of different backgrounds, and participating in diversity education, such as workshops or seminars on prejudice and intergroup conflict (e.g., I. V. Blair, Ma, & Lenton, 2001; Nelson, 2002; Rudman, Ashmore, & Gary, 2001).

Human Aggression: Behavior That Harms

Far too often in human history negative attitudes toward members of other groups have set the stage for killing and warfare. But are human beings inherently aggressive? Or is aggression a form of learned behavior that can be modified by experience? There are many opinions among psychologists and other scientists about the nature of human aggression. Let us consider what the major perspectives in psychology might teach us about our capacity to harm one another.

Is Human Aggression Instinctual?

Some theorists believe that aggression in humans and other species is based on instinct. For example, the famed ethologist Konrad Lorenz (1966) believed that the fighting instinct is a basic survival mechanism in many animal species. Predators need to survive by instinctively attacking their prey. The more fortunate animals on which they prey survive by either instinctively fleeing from these attacks or fighting them off. In Lorenz's view, aggression can be an adaptive response that increases the chances of survival of predator and prey. But what of human aggression? Might it also be explained by instinct?

© Getty Images

These empty shoes of gunshot victims in the United States provide a poignant reminder of the consequences of violent behavior.

Contemporary theorists believe that human aggression is far too complex to be based on instinct. Human aggression takes many forms, from organized warfare and acts of terrorism to interpersonal forms of violent behavior such as muggings, spousal abuse, and sexual assaults. These different forms of aggression reflect a variety of political, cultural, and psychological motives. Moreover, instinct theories fail to account for the important roles that learning and culture play in shaping behavior, nor do they explain the diversity that exists in human aggression. Violence is unusual in some cultures but all too common in others—unfortunately including our own.

Theorists today believe that human aggression cannot be explained by any one cause. Accordingly, we next consider the multiple factors that contemporary theorists believe contribute to human aggression, including biological influences, learning influences, sociocultural influences, use of alcohol, emotional states, and environmental influences (Anderson & Bushman, 2003).

Biological Influences

CONCEPT 14.25
Like other forms of human behavior, aggression is too complex to be reduced to the level of instinct.

We are making progress toward a better understanding of the biological underpinnings of aggression. For example, investigators recently identified genes linked to violent or impulsive behavior (Meyer-Lindenberg et al., 2006). Research also points to abnormalities in neural circuitry in the brain that regulate anger in aggressive people (Davidson, Putnam, & Larson, 2000). Another focus of study is the neurotransmitter serotonin, which is involved in brain circuits responsible for curbing impulsive behavior (Carver, Johnson, & Joormann, 2008). Serotonin works as a kind of "behavioral seat belt" or "emergency brake" for restraining aggressive impulses (Raine, 2008). That said, we need further evidence that directly ties deficiencies in serotonin, or perhaps irregularities in how serotonin is used in the brain, to aggressive behavior.

CONCEPT 14.26
The biological underpinnings of aggression reflect genetic, hormonal, and neurotransmitter influences.

The male sex hormone testosterone is linked to aggressive behavior (Bennett, Farrington, & Huesmann, 2005; Klinesmith, Kasser, & McAndrew, 2006). Men have higher levels of testosterone than women, and evidence from cross-cultural studies shows that men are more likely to engage in aggressive and violent behavior than women. Men with higher levels of testosterone levels also tend to show higher levels of aggression than men with lower levels. However, not all aggressive or violent men have high testosterone levels, nor do all—or even most—men with high testosterone levels engage in violent behavior. Clearly, the factors involved in aggression are more complex.

Evolutionary psychologists speculate that among ancestral humans, aggression may have benefited men in their primary role as hunters. Ancestral women, so far as we know, primarily engaged in food gathering and child care roles in which aggressiveness may have been counterproductive. Perhaps the greater aggressiveness we find in males today is explained in part by inherited tendencies passed down through generations from ancestral times.

"You've been charged with driving under the influence of testosterone."

© William Haefeli

Learning Influences

The social-cognitive theorist Albert Bandura (2008a) highlights the role of observational learning in the development of aggressive behavior. He notes that children learn to imitate aggressive behavior that they observe in the home, in school, and in the media, especially television (see Module 5.3). For example, by observing their peers or watching male characters on television, young boys may learn that conflicts are settled with fists or weapons, not with words.

Aggressive or violent children often come from homes in which aggression was modeled by parents and other family members. Reinforcement also contributes to the learning of aggressive behavior. If children are rewarded for aggressive behavior, such as by receiving approval or respect from peers, or by getting their way, they are more likely to repeat the same behavior. Indeed, people in general are more likely to resort to aggressive behavior if they have failed to learn alternative ways of resolving conflicts. Violent behavior may be perpetuated from generation to generation as children who are exposed to violence in the home learn that violent behavior is an acceptable way to settle disagreements.

CONCEPT 14.27

Social-cognitive theorists view aggression as learned behavior that is acquired through observational learning and reinforcement.

Sociocultural Influences

Sociocultural theorists encourage us to consider the broader social contexts in which aggression takes place. Interpersonal violence often occurs against a backdrop of social stressors such as poverty, prolonged unemployment, lack of opportunity, child abuse and neglect, family breakdown, and exposure to violence in the family and community. Children who are abused or neglected by their parents may fail to develop the secure loving attachments to their parents that would otherwise provide the basis for acquiring empathy and concern for others. Not surprisingly, abused or neglected children often display violent behavior in childhood and adulthood (Dodge, Pettit, & Bates, 1997; Kotch et al., 2008).

Social psychologists recognize that violence may also be used as a social influence tactic—a means of coercion by which individuals seek to compel others to comply with their wishes. We need only consider such examples as the "mob enforcer" who uses strong-arm tactics to obtain compliance, or the abusive husband who uses physical force or threat of force to get his wife to accede to his demands.

CONCEPT 14.28

Sociocultural theorists explore the social stressors that contribute to aggressive behavior, including poverty, child abuse and neglect, family breakdown, and exposure to violence.

CONCEPT 14.29
Alcohol is linked to aggressive behavior through its effects on loosening inhibitions, impairing the ability to weigh the consequences of behavior and interpret social cues, and reducing sensitivity to punishment-related cues.

→ Concept Link
As discussed in Chapter 4, alcohol use is linked to many crimes of violence. See Module 4.4.

Alcohol Use

Investigators find strong links between alcohol use and violent behaviors, including domestic violence, homicide, and rape (Boles & Miottoa, 2003; Fals-Stewart, 2003). Alcohol loosens inhibitions or restraints on impulsive behavior, including acts of impulsive violence. It also impairs our ability to weigh the consequences of our actions, reduces our sensitivity to cues that signal the threat of punishment, and leads us to misperceive other people's motives as malevolent. Not everyone who drinks becomes aggressive, of course. Relationships between alcohol use and aggression may be influenced by the user's biological sensitivity to alcohol as well as by the social demands of the situation in which provocation occurs, such as a bar versus at home.

Emotional States

Psychologists have long recognized that certain negative emotions, especially frustration and anger, may trigger aggression. As we learned in Chapter 12, frustration is a negative emotional state that is induced when our efforts to reach a goal are thwarted or blocked. Though frustration often leads to aggression, other outcomes are possible. You may feel frustrated when someone behind you in a movie theater talks throughout the picture, prompting a *state of readiness* to respond aggressively either verbally or physically. But whether you actually respond aggressively may depend on your expectation that an aggressive response will yield a positive outcome and your history of aggressive behavior, among other factors. Questions remain about whether aggression is necessarily preceded by frustration. The cool, premeditated aggression of a mob "hit man" does not fit the pattern of frustration-induced aggression.

CONCEPT 14.30
Frustration and anger are negative emotions that may serve as triggers for aggression.

Anger is another negative emotion that can induce aggressive responses in some individuals. We might think of the husband who strikes out violently at his wife when she says something that angers him or the child abuser who lashes out angrily when a child is slow to comply with a demand. People who think angering thoughts ("I can't let him/her get away with this . . .") or who blow minor provocations out of proportion are more likely to respond aggressively in conflict situations than those who think calmer thoughts.

Environmental Influences

CONCEPT 14.31
High temperatures are linked to aggressive behavior, perhaps because they induce angry, hostile thoughts and feelings that become expressed in aggressive behavior.

People may get hot under the collar as the outdoor temperature rises, but are they more likely to become aggressive? Indeed they are. Environmental psychologists find that aggressive and violent behavior increases with rising temperatures, although they continue to explore whether it then declines at very high temperatures (Bushman, Wang, & Anderson, 2005; Cohn & Rotton, 2005).

From the perspective of social-cognitive theory, hot temperatures incite aggression by inducing angry, hostile thoughts and feelings, which in turn increase the readiness to respond aggressively to social provocations. Links between rising temperature and aggression raise some interesting questions that might be pursued through more formal study: Might the use of air conditioning in prisons reduce the problems of inmate violence? Might air conditioning have a similar effect in reducing aggression in the workplace or in schools?

Before reading further, you may want to review the positive (helping) and negative ways of relating to others outlined in Concept Chart 14.2.

CONCEPT CHART 14.2 Relating to Others

	Concept	Description	More About It
Determinants of Helping	**Decision-making processes**	The Latané and Darley model: (1) recognize a need for help, (2) interpret the situation as an emergency, (3) assume personal responsibility for helping, (4) determine the type of help needed, and (5) decide to act	Helping is based on a decision-making process involving the appraisal of the situation at hand as well as one's personal responsibility and resources to address it
	Influences on helping	Includes factors such as situational ambiguity, perceived cost, diffusion of responsibility, similarity, empathy, facial features, mood and gender effects, attributions of the cause of need, and social norms	Helping depends on a combination of personal and situational factors
Negative Ways of Relating	**Prejudice**	Negative beliefs, feelings, and behavioral tendencies toward members of other groups	Efforts to reduce prejudice can be directed at increasing intergroup contacts under conditions of social and institutional support, acquaintanceship potential, equal status, and cooperativeness, practicing nonstereotyped ways of thinking; instilling nonprejudiced attitudes in children by setting an example of tolerance
	Aggression	Takes many forms, from organized warfare to interpersonal violence, such as assaults, rapes, and partner abuse	Biological, learning, sociocultural, emotional, and environmental influences, and alcohol use are implicated in aggression

14.2 MODULE REVIEW Relating to Others

Recite It

What are the major determinants of attraction?

- The major determinants of attraction include similarity, physical attractiveness, proximity, and reciprocity.

What factors are linked to helping behavior?

- The decision-making model holds that bystander intervention is based on a series of decisions that must be made before helping occurs.
- Factors that influence helping behavior include the ambiguity of the situation, perceived cost, diffusion of responsibility, similarity, empathy, facial features, mood and gender, attributions of the cause of need, and social norms.

What is prejudice, and how does it develop?

- Prejudice is a preconceived attitude or bias, usually unfavorable, that is formed without critical thought or evaluation.
- Prejudice derives from negative group stereotypes to which people are exposed in their social environment. The development of prejudice may also reflect basic cognitive processes that evolved over thousands of generations.
- Individual differences in prejudice may be explained by differences in learning experiences, authoritarian personality traits, and the adoption of a universalist orientation.

What can be done to reduce prejudice?

- Prejudice may be reduced by creating opportunities for intergroup contact that have strong social and institutional support, are based on equal status relationships, allow acquaintanceships to develop, and emphasize cooperation rather than competition.

What factors contribute to human aggression?

- Contemporary theorists attempt to explain human aggression on the basis of biological influences, learning influences, sociocultural influences, alcohol use, emotional states, and environmental influences.

Recall It

1. Name several key factors that determine attraction.
2. Regarding physical attractiveness, which of the following statements is incorrect?
   a. Men tend to place greater emphasis on the physical attractiveness of their partners than do women.
   b. Standards for physical attractiveness cross cultural boundaries.
   c. Attractive people tend to be more favorably judged on many personality traits.
   d. People tend to rate male and female faces as more attractive when they have more masculine characteristics.
3. What is the proper order of the steps involved in determining whether bystanders will become involved in helping someone in need?
   a. Assume personal responsibility for helping.
   b. Determine that the situation is a true emergency.
   c. Implement the chosen course of action.
   d. Determine that a true need for help exists.
   e. Choose what kind of help to provide.
4. Prejudice, like other attitudes, consists of (a) cognitive, (b) emotional, and (c) behavioral components. Describe the major features of each component as they relate to prejudice.
5. What are the four conditions that Allport said must be met in order for intergroup contact to reduce prejudice?

Think About It

- To what extent was your attraction to your friends and romantic partners a function of similarity of attitudes, backgrounds, physical attractiveness, proximity, and reciprocity?
- Do you believe that people can be completely altruistic or selfless? Or might there be underlying self-serving motives even in acts of kindness and self-sacrifice? Explain.
- Suppose you were asked to develop a proposal to improve intergroup relations among students of different ethnic groups on campus by bringing them together. What factors do you think would determine whether your efforts are successful?

MODULE 14.3

Group Influences on Individual Behavior

- What is social identity?
- What was the significance of the Asch study on conformity?
- Why were Milgram's findings so disturbing, and why were his methods so controversial?
- How does the presence of others affect individual performance?
- What is deindividuation?
- What is group polarization and groupthink?

The view that humans are social creatures was expressed perhaps most clearly by the fourteenth-century English poet John Donne, who wrote "no man is an island, sufficient unto himself." We influence others and are influenced in turn by them. In this module we consider ways in which others influence our behavior and even our self-concepts. We examine the tendency to conform our behavior to social pressure, even when we consider such demands unreasonable or immoral. We examine situations where the presence of others may enhance our performance and those where it may not. Finally, we explore the phenomenon of *groupthink* and see how group influences can sometimes lead to bad decisions.

personal identity The part of our psychological identity that involves our sense of ourselves as unique individuals.

social identity The part of our psychological identity that involves our sense of ourselves as members of particular groups. Also called *group identity*.

Our Social Selves: "Who Are We?"

Many social psychologists separate psychological identity or self-concept into two parts: **personal identity** (individual identity) and **social identity** (group identity) (Ellemers, Spears, & Doosje, 2002; Verkuyten, 2005). Your personal identity ("Who am I?") is the

TRY THIS OUT Sign on the Dotted Line

Sign your name on the line below:

____

Sign your name again, but now imagine that you are signing as the president of the United States:

____

Were your signatures the same size? Psychologist Richard Zweigenhaft (1970) found that students penned larger signatures when they were signing as president. Zweigenhaft also found that signatures of college professors were larger than those of blue-collar university employees. The social roles we play, as student, employee, husband or wife, or even president, are part of our social identity. Holding a high-status position bolsters our self-image, which may be reflected in the size of our signatures.

part of your psychological makeup that distinguishes you as a unique individual. You might think of yourself as a caring, creative person who likes pepperoni pizza, jazz, and sci-fi movies. Your social identity ("Who are we?") is your sense of yourself as a member of the various family, kinship, religious, national, and social groups to which you belong. You might refer to this part of your identity by saying, "I am a Catholic... I am a software developer... I am a Mexican American... I am Jonathan's dad." Our social identity converts the "I" to the "we." Social or ethnic identity is for many people the core aspect of who they are.

CONCEPT 14.32
Our social or group identity is an important part of our psychological identity or self-concept.

Social psychologists believe we have a fundamental need to be members of groups—in other words, to belong. Our social identity tends to rub off on our self-esteem. (see *Try This Out*). We are likely to feel better about ourselves when someone of the same ethnicity, religion, or even locality accomplishes something special.

Social identity is generally a more prominent part of one's psychological identity in collectivist cultures, such as those in the Far East, than it is in individualistic societies in the West. In collectivist cultures, individuals have a stronger desire to fulfill their social obligations to the group, whereas Western societies emphasize a more individualistic or autonomous sense of self. People in Western cultures tend to define themselves less by what they share in common with others and more in terms of their unique abilities, interests, and attributes. They expect to stand out from the crowd—being themselves means becoming unique individuals. Yet there are variations within Western cultures. Women tend to place a greater emphasis on an interdependent sense of self—defining themselves more in terms of their roles as mothers, wives, daughters, and so on, whereas men tend to have a more independent sense of self (Cross & Madson, 1997).

© interactimages/shutterstock.com

Conformity: Bending the "I" to Fit the "We"

You would not get arrested if you arrived at work in your pajamas, but you probably would hear some snickering comments or be asked to go home and change. Then again, pajama wearing might become something of a new fashion statement. You might actually be thought of as a trendsetter. Well, perhaps not. In any event, we are expected to conform our behavior to prevailing social standards or norms. Though social norms don't carry the force of law, violation of these standards can incur social disapproval. If we deviate too far from social standards, we might even lose our friends or jobs or alienate our family members.

Conformity affects many aspects of our daily behavior, from the clothes we wear for specific occasions, to the custom of covering our mouths and saying "excuse me" when we sneeze, to choosing a college to attend ("You're going to State, like your brother,

conformity The tendency to adjust one's behavior to actual or perceived social pressures.

CONCEPT 14.33
When we conform, we behave in ways that adhere to social norms.

right?"). Conformity pressures may also lead us to date or even marry the kinds of persons whom others deem acceptable.

We conform not only to general social norms but also to group or peer norms. Young people who color their hair purple may not be conforming to the standards of mainstream society, but they are conforming to those of their peer group—just as their parents are to their own.

We might consider ourselves to be free thinkers who can resist pressures to conform when we don't see eye to eye with others. But the results of a classic study by psychologist Solomon Asch (1956) lead us to recognize that we may conform more than we think. Asch set out to study independence, not conformity. He believed that if participants in the study were faced with a unanimous group judgment that was obviously false, they would stick to their guns, resist pressures to conform, and report the correct information. He was wrong.

CONCEPT 14.34
People are more likely to conform than they might think, even to the extent of claiming that something is true when they know it to be false.

Asch placed individuals in a group consisting of people who were actually in league with the experimenter. The group was presented with the task of choosing the one line among a group of three that was the same length as a test line (see ■ Figure 14.5). But the twist was that the other group members—all confederates of the experimenter—unanimously made the wrong choice. Now it was the individual's turn. Would the person go along with the group and make an obviously incorrect choice? Asch was surprised by the results. Bowing under the pressure to conform, three out of four of the college students who participated in the study gave at least one incorrect answer in a series of trials.

Why were people so willing to conform in the Asch experiment, even to the extent of claiming that something was true when it was obviously false? Later research has established at least three reasons: (1) People assume the majority must be correct; (2) they are so concerned about being accepted by the group that they don't care whether their judgments were correct; (3) they feel it is easier to go along with the group than to disagree (Cialdini & Trost, 1998; E. E. Jones, 1998). Even so, some groups are more susceptible to pressures to conform than others (Baron, Vandello, & Brunsman, 1996; Cialdini & Trost, 1998). Women, by a small margin, are more likely to conform than men. People from collectivist cultures such as China tend to conform more than people from individualistic cultures such as the United States, Canada, and Great Britain. And conformity tends to be greater among people with low self-esteem, social shyness, and a

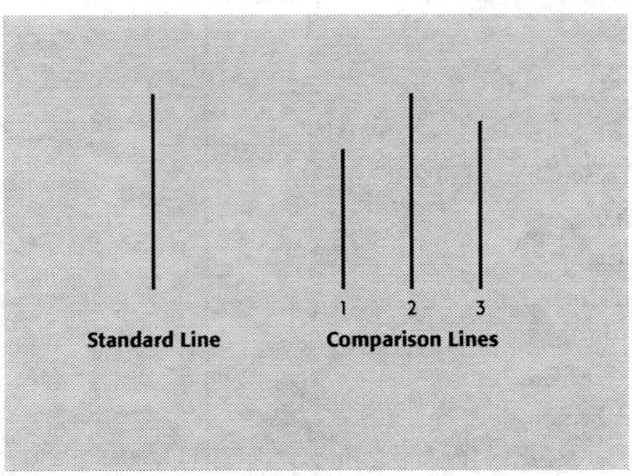

FIGURE 14.5 Stimuli Similar to Those Used in the Asch Conformity Studies

© Reprinted with permission. Copyright © 1955 Scientific American, a division of Nature America, Inc. All rights reserved.

The person third from the right in the photograph was an actual participant in the classic Asch studies. The others are confederates of the experimenter. The participant is asked to indicate which of three lines matches a standard line after the others in the room have unanimously given the wrong response.

strong desire to be liked by the group. More generally, conformity tends to decline with age from childhood through older adulthood (Pasupathi, 1999).

Conformity is also influenced by situational factors. In the Asch paradigm, people were more likely to conform when they were required to disclose their responses publicly rather than privately, when the size of the group increased to about four or five people (beyond that number, conformity leveled off with increasing group size), and when more ambiguous stimuli were used (Cialdini & Trost, 1998). Yet just one dissenting voice in the group—one fellow traveler down the road of defection—can override group influence, regardless of the size of the group (Morris, Miller, & Spangenberg, 1977).

Asch believed that conformity can stifle individuality and independence. Yet some degree of conformity may help groups to function more smoothly. After all, sneezing on someone might be taken as a social affront; covering our noses and mouths and saying "excuse me" afterward shows consideration for others.

CONCEPT 14.35
Many factors influence conformity, including personal and situational characteristics.

Compliance: Doing What Others Want You to Do

Compliance is the process of acceding to the requests or demands of others (Cialdini & Goldstein, 2004). One factor influencing compliance is authority. Appeals from a recognized authority figure are often extremely influential. You may be more willing to follow your doctor's advice about making changes in your diet than advice from your next-door neighbor. Another factor is *social validation.* We tend to use the actions of others as a standard or social norm for judging the appropriateness of our own behavior (Cialdini & Goldstein, 2004). Thus, we are more likely to donate to a charity appeal if we find out that other people in the office are giving than if they are not. Marketers often get us to comply with sales pitches by first softening us up with snowball questions (*How are you today?*) before landing the sales punch (Fennis, Janssen, & Vohs, 2009).

compliance The process of acceding to the requests or demands of others.

CONCEPT 14.36
Need for consistency, social validation, reciprocity, and perceptions of authority are important determinants of compliance.

The desire for consistency is yet another important determinant of compliance (Cialdini & Goldstein, 2004; Petrova, Cialdini, & Sills, 2006). Salespeople, advertisers, fundraisers, and others try to get us to comply with their appeals by using consistency to their advantage. Several market-honed techniques succeed because they first obtain a person's commitment to a particular course of action that is consistent with a later requested action. Here are three examples:

© Bob Daemmrich/The Image Works

Are you being low-balled? What are some common types of manipulative sales tactics? What psychological principles underlie these tactics? What would you do if you were low-balled?

1. *Low-ball technique.* Say a car salesperson offers you an attractive price, only to pull the offer minutes later, claiming the sales manager couldn't approve it or the allowance offered for your trade-in came in lower than expected. You are then offered a higher price, which the salesperson swears is the best possible price. This is the **low-ball technique** at work.

   Committing yourself to the prior action of accepting a lower price may make you more likely to follow through on the subsequent, more costly action.
2. *Bait-and-switch technique.* In the **bait-and-switch technique**, a marketer advertises merchandise at an unusually low price. When people come to buy the merchandise, they learn that it is actually of inferior quality or is sold out or back-ordered. Then comes the switch, as they are shown more expensive merchandise for sale. Here again the person making the pitch capitalizes on the desire for consistency. Prospective buyers who expressed an initial interest in the merchandise are often more receptive to buying more expensive merchandise than they would be otherwise.
3. *Foot-in-the-door technique.* In the **foot-in-the door technique**, the person making an appeal first asks for a small favor that will almost certainly be granted. After

low-ball technique A compliance technique based on obtaining a person's initial agreement to purchase an item at a lower price before revealing hidden costs that raise the ultimate price.

bait-and-switch technique A compliance technique based on "baiting" a person by making an unrealistically attractive offer and then replacing it with a less attractive offer.

foot-in-the-door technique A compliance technique based on securing compliance with a smaller request as a prelude to making a larger request.

TRY THIS OUT Why It Matters: Fending Off Manipulative Sales Tactics

You are in the market for a new car. The salesperson shows you a model you like, and after haggling for a while, you settle on a price that seems fair to you. The salesperson then says, "Let me get this approved by my manager and I'll be right back." What would you say to protect yourself against the types of influence tactics described in the text? For each of the following examples, write your response in the column provided below. Then compare your answers with some sample responses you'll find below.

Type of Tactic	What the Salesperson Says	What Do You Say Now?
Low-ball technique	"I'm sorry. He says we can't let it go for this amount. It has nothing to do with you, but he's getting more pressure from the boss. Maybe if we went back to him with another two or three hundred dollars, he'd accept it."	______
Bait-and-switch technique	"My manager tells me that we're having difficulty placing orders for that model. Something to do with a strike in Osaka. We can definitely get the LX version, however. It's got some great features."	______
Foot-in-the-door technique	"Okay, we can get you the car." After completing some paperwork, the salesman slips in the following comment: "You know, you really should think about this factory-installed security system. You can never be too safe these days."	______

obtaining initial compliance, the person raises the ante by asking for a larger, related favor. Evidence shows that people who agree to smaller requests are more likely to comply with larger ones, apparently due to the desire for consistency (Cialdini & Trost, 1998). In an early example, Patricia Pliner and her colleagues (1974) showed that people who agreed to wear a lapel pin promoting a local charity were subsequently more willing to make a monetary donation to the charity. Yet investigators find that only those people with a strong preference for consistency show evidence of the foot-in-the-door effect (Cialdini, Trost, & Newsom, 1995).

door-in-the-face technique A compliance technique in which refusal of a large, unreasonable request is followed by a smaller, more reasonable request.

Another sales strategy, the **door-in-the-face technique**, takes advantage of the psychological principle of *reciprocity* (Cialdini & Trost, 1998). First comes a large unreasonable request, which is rejected out of hand. Then the person making the request offers a lesser alternative in the form of a smaller request, which is actually what the person wanted in the first place. This smaller request is more likely to be accepted following rejection of the large unreasonable request than it would be had it been presented first. Why? Recall the concept of reciprocity. When requesters appear willing to compromise by withdrawing the original request in favor of a smaller one, people receiving the request may feel obliged to reciprocate by becoming more accommodating.

Now let's turn the discussion around to you. The *Try This Out* feature offers the opportunity to practice your skills at resisting persuasive sales tactics.

Obedience to Authority: When Does It Go Too Far?

obedience Compliance with commands or orders issued by others, usually persons in a position of authority.

The study of **obedience** to authority has implications that go far beyond psychology. The atrocities of the Nazi regime in Germany preceding and during World War II raised disturbing questions about the tendency of soldiers and even ordinary citizens to obey authority figures in the commission of horrific acts. Many individuals, including civilians, participated in the Holocaust—the systematic genocide of the Jewish population of Europe. When later called to account for their deeds, many Nazis claimed they were "only following orders" (Elms, 1995). Years afterward, American soldiers who participated in a massacre of civilians in the village of My Lai during the Vietnam War would offer a similar defense.

Yale University psychologist Stanley Milgram developed a unique and controversial research program to find out whether ordinary Americans would perform clearly immoral actions if they were instructed to do so. Milgram's decision to study obedience to immoral authority was rooted in his Jewish heritage and his determination to better understand the atrocities committed by ordinary German citizens during the Holocaust (Blass, 2009).

Participants in his studies were residents of New Haven, Connecticut, and surrounding areas who answered newspaper ads requesting participants for studies on learning and memory. They ranged in age from 20 to 50 and included teachers, engineers, salespeople, and laborers. Some were college graduates; others had not even completed elementary school. When they arrived at the lab, they were told that they would be participating in a study designed to test the effects of punishment on learning. They would play the role of a "teacher." Another person to whom they were introduced would be the "learner."

The learner was seated in one room, the teacher in an adjoining room. The teacher was placed in front of a console that was described as a device for administering electric shocks to the learner. The console consisted of a series of levers with labels ranging from "Slight Shock" to "Danger: Severe Shock." The learner was presented with a list of word pairs to memorize. Then one word in each pair was presented and the learner's task was to respond with the correct word with which it had been paired in the list. The teacher was instructed that following each incorrect response from the learner, he was to deliver an electric shock. With each additional error, the voltage of the shock was to increase by 15 volts.

Unbeknown to the teachers, the learners were confederates of the experimenter. It was all part of an elaborate ruse. The experiment was not intended to study learning; it actually tested the teacher's willingness to inflict pain on another person when instructed to do so. No actual shocks were given. The learner's incorrect responses were all predetermined. But to the teachers it was all too real.

Each teacher was informed that although the shocks might be extremely painful they would cause "no permanent tissue damage" to the learner. To provide teachers with a sense of what a mild shock felt like, they were administered an electric shock corresponding to 45 volts. As the number of errors mounted, the teacher was instructed to increase the voltage until it reached the "danger" level. Most teachers were visibly upset when given the order to raise the shock level to apparently hazardous levels. When they hesitated, the experimenter simply instructed them: "The experiment requires that you continue." If they still hesitated, the experimenter pressured them further, telling them: "It is absolutely essential that you continue. . . . You have no other choice. . . . You must go on." Now, would they comply and throw the switch? Would you?

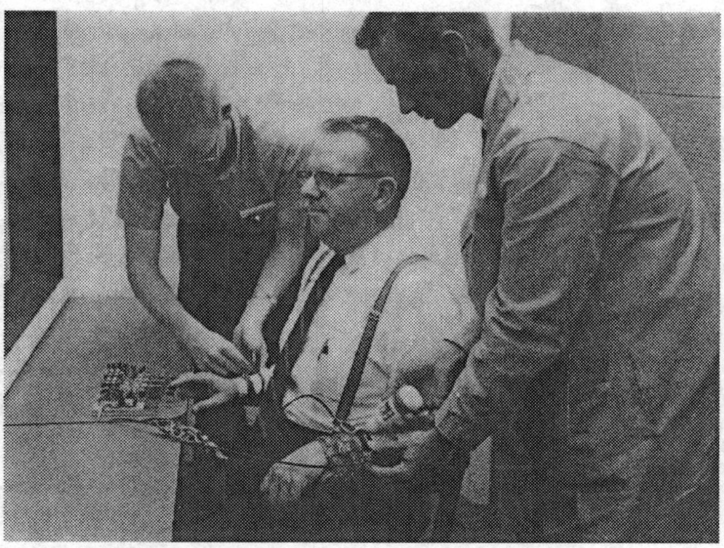

© Courtesy of Alexandra Milgram

The participant in Milgram studies was led to believe that the "learner," as shown here, would receive electric shocks following each wrong answer. If you were a participant, would you have obeyed the experimenter even as the learner cried out for help?

The results were disturbing (Milgram, 1963, 1974). Some participants disobeyed commands to inflict painful and potentially dangerous shocks on learners (Packer, 2008). Most initially protested but eventually relented to continuing pressure from the experimenter. Of the 40 original participants, 26 (65 percent) obeyed every order, including the one to deliver the highest voltage shock. In another experimental condition, the teachers could hear the learner screaming to be let go and pounding on the wall. Even so, 25 of the 40 participants administered the full series of shocks (Elms, 1995). In a variation in which participants themselves did not throw the switch activating the shock but instructed others (actually confederates) to do so, the rate of obedience rose to 92.5 percent (Meeus & Raaijmakers, 1995). Placing the learner in the same room as the participant reduced obedience, but 40 percent still obeyed. Milgram later obtained similar results with female participants and groups of college undergraduates (Milgram, 1974).

CONCEPT 14.37
In the classic Milgram studies of obedience, ordinary people were willing to obey the dictates of an external authority even to the extent of inflicting what they believed were serious and even dangerous shocks to other supposed participants.

The disturbing findings of the Milgram studies may help us better understand the behavior of ordinary people who participated in seemingly inexplicable and horrific events such as the behavior of German citizens in the Holocaust and mass suicides at the behest of cult leaders. Milgram's studies may teach us how good people can commit bad deeds in situations where they are led to blindly follow authority. Yet many critics have contended that laboratory-based experimental claims should not be generalized to the destructive obedience found in Nazi Germany or other real-life atrocities. One related argument is that participants may not have believed that anything terrible was happening to the learner—after all, this was a respected university and someone would have stopped them if it were truly dangerous. *Wouldn't they?* In fact, a majority of Milgram's participants believed that the learner was receiving significant levels of pain (Meeus & Raaijmakers, 1995). Even when Milgram moved his laboratory away from the hallowed halls of the university to a dingy storefront in a commercial district, nearly half of the participants (48 percent) complied (Milgram, 1974).

Are people today as likely as those in Milgram's time to comply with unreasonable and immoral demands? We don't have a definitive answer because ethical restrictions imposed since Milgram's time make a full replication of his experiment clearly out of bounds for contemporary investigators (Burger, 2009; Elms, 2009). However, a recent partial replication that administered the Milgram procedure but stopped well short of the highest level of shock (so as to avoid imposing undue stress on participants) showed similar rates of compliance to those in Milgram's original work (Burger, 2009). We should caution, however, that some psychologists have raised reservations about the partial replication procedure (e.g., Elms, 2009; A. G. Miller, 2009; Twenge, 2009).

Milgram's studies provoked controversy on other grounds as well, much of it concerning the ethics of deceiving participants in research studies and the emotional aftereffects of raising people's awareness that they were capable of such behavior. The ethical issues raised by the Milgram experiments informed the development of the set of ethical guidelines later adopted by the American Psychological Association to protect the welfare of participants in psychological research (Benjamin & Simpson, 2009). (See Chapter 1 for a discussion of ethical principles in psychology.)

Why Do People Obey Immoral Commands?

legitimization of authority The tendency to grant legitimacy to the orders or commands of persons in authority.

The **legitimization of authority** is one explanation of the behavior of participants in Milgram's studies. We are taught from an early age to obey authority figures such as parents and teachers and not to question or second-guess them. This early socialization prepares us to comply when directed to do so by a legitimate authority figure, be it a police officer, a government or military official, or a scientist. Another likely reason for obedience is **social validation** (also called *social comparison*). Participants in Milgram's studies may have lacked any basis for knowing what other people would do in a similar situation. The only basis for social comparison was the example set by the experimenter. For people in Nazi Germany, seeing respected others perform atrocities may have served to legitimize their activities not only as socially acceptable but, more disturbingly, as admirable. People are generally more willing to comply with more extreme requests once they have shown a willingness to comply with lesser requests. Once participants began to deliver shocks to learners, they may have found it increasingly difficult to stop—just as soldiers who have been trained to respond unstintingly to commands may not hesitate to follow orders, even immoral ones.

social validation The tendency to use other people's behavior as a standard for judging the appropriateness of one's own behavior.

CONCEPT 14.38
The willingness to obey immoral commands may arise from the legitimization of authority.

Evaluating Milgram's Legacy

The scientific jury is still out regarding the ultimate significance of Milgram's findings. Perhaps the ultimate significance of Milgram's studies is to remind us to look inward to our capacity for blind and destructive obedience. As some have observed, the Milgram studies may indicate that we do too good a job at socializing young people to be obedient to authority (Vecchio, 1997). Perhaps more emphasis should be placed on personal responsibility for one's actions, a teaching that might go a long way toward preventing destructive obedience.

Now we consider ways in which the presence of groups may influence individual performance—for better or worse.

Social Facilitation and Social Loafing: When Are You Most Likely to Do Your Best?

Do you perform better when you work in front of others? **Social facilitation** is the term social psychologists use to refer to the tendency for people to work better or harder when in the presence of others than when they work alone (Mendes, 2007).

social facilitation The tendency to work better or harder in the presence of others than when alone.

Social facilitation helps explain why you may study better when studying in a group or in the library than when studying alone. Having others around may present something of challenge or even a threat, which energizes your performance and brings out the best in you. When you are studying alone, you have no handy social comparison, as there's no one around to compare your behavior against. In the library, you may take your cues from others who have their heads buried in their books and measure your performance against theirs. An historical footnote: The first research example of social facilitation may be from 1898, when researchers reported that cyclists who "rode with others performed better" (Joyce & Baker, 2008).

On the other hand, the presence of others does not always *improve* performance. According to noted social psychologist Robert Zajonc (1965), the presence of others increases the performance of dominant responses. In the case of simple or well-learned tasks, the dominant response will usually be the correct response. However, for complex tasks in which the dominant response may be incorrect, the presence of others tends to impair performance. So, if you are a good typist, you may type faster when others are present than when you are alone. But if you need to solve complex math problems, having an audience would likely slow your performance.

CONCEPT 14.39
The presence of others may enhance individual performance on simple tasks but impair performance on more complex tasks.

Social loafing is the tendency for people to apply less effort when they work as members of a group than when they work on their own. Perhaps you have observed

social loafing The tendency to expend less effort when working as a member of a group than when working alone.

© Bob Krist

Does the presence of others help or hinder your ability to perform at your best? The presence of others may impair performance of complex tasks but strengthen performance of simple or well-learned tasks.

CONCEPT 14.40

In social loafing, people fail to pull their own weight because they believe others will pick up the slack.

CONCEPT 14.41

People who are caught up in a mob may engage in behavior they might not otherwise commit.

deindividuation The loss of self-awareness that may occur when one acts in concert with the actions of a crowd.

social loafing in work that you did as part of a team effort. Did one or more members of the team fail to apply themselves as much as they could?

Social loafing reflects the tendency for people to avoid making an effort when they expect other team members to pick up the slack. But social loafing is not inevitable. It is more likely to occur when individual performance is not evaluated. Social loafing may be reduced in a number or ways, such as by making individual performance more obvious, making tasks more interesting or appealing, and holding each member accountable for his or her own contributions.

Mob Behavior: The Dangers of Losing Yourself in a Crowd

Have you ever been so swept up in the actions of a crowd that you felt as though you'd momentarily lost your sense of individuality? This sense of losing self-awareness ("being lost in a crowd") is called **deindividuation**. Perhaps you experienced it while attending a football or baseball game and became part of a human "wave" that undulated through the spectators, or when everyone rose in unison when a football player on the home team made a diving catch in the end zone.

Deindividuation may be destructive when it loosens inhibitions that normally constrain deviant or reckless behavior and lead to mob behavior. We see the tragic results of mob behavior in race-related lynchings and looting during urban riots. Hate groups capitalize on deindividuation, even augmenting it by having members wear the same outfits or uniforms. The white sheets worn by members of the Ku Klux Klan promote a loss of individual identity and diffusion of responsibility that can foster unrestrained moblike behavior. Deindividuation appears to result from many factors, including *anonymity* (becoming part of a large, unstructured group), *shifting attention* from one's own thoughts and personal standards to the actions of the group, and *conforming* one's behavior to the social norms of the group or mob (Cialdini & Goldstein, 2004; Nowak, Vallacher, & Miller, 2003).

Role-playing is an important feature of deindividuation. A dramatic illustration of the power of role-playing is seen in a classic experiment by psychologist Phillip Zimbardo (Zimbardo, 1975; Zimbardo et al., 1973) in which student volunteers were paid to participate in a two-week simulation of a prison environment. Students were randomly assigned to play the roles of either guards or prisoners. The guards received uniforms, whistles, and night sticks and were instructed to enforce a set of rules. Prisoners were issued shapeless smocks to be worn as prison clothes and confined to small, barren cells under the control of prison guards. What happened in the next few days was so troubling that Zimbardo called a halt to the two-week study after only six days. Students took their roles much further than the investigators expected. Some guards became abusive and even sadistic in their treatment of the prisoners, verbally insulting them and subjecting them to degrading and humiliating tasks for the slightest disobedience, such as cleaning toilets with bare hands. Some prisoners broke down sobbing, fell into fits of rage, or developed other stress-related problems.

© Image Source / Alamy

Getting caught up in the behavior of a crowd may take the form of a pleasant diversion, such as the human wave, but can also lead to destructive behaviors when a crowd becomes a mob.

The prisoner simulation study raised important questions about the tendency of ordinary people (all the students were judged to be emotionally stable before the study) to become so absorbed playing their assigned roles that they begin to lose their moral compass and even their individuality. Scholars continue to debate whether the prisoner simulation study teaches us anything about brutality in real-life situations, such as the abusive and humiliating treatment of prisoners by young American soldiers in the Abu Ghraib military prison in Iraq in 2004. What do you think?

The larger question is, How can we resist destructive forms of deindividuation? Social psychologists point to several steps we can take, such as focusing on our internal standards when we are caught up in the actions of a crowd or become absorbed in roles we are expected to play, and maintaining our individuality by refusing to hide our personal identities behind a hood or a uniform.

Group Decision Making: Help or Hindrance?

CONCEPT 14.42
Group biases arising from group decision-making processes, such as group polarization and groupthink, may foster more extreme views among group members.

Are decisions made by groups such as committees, councils, and executive boards more level-headed than those made by individuals? Group members may build off the ideas of others by trying out different ideas on each other. This brainstorming process may energize creative thinking and enhance problem solving, especially for complex problems (Kohn, Paulus, & Choi, 2011; Laughlin et al., 2006) (see the next *Try This Out*). Group decision making may also avoid the pitfalls of relying on any one individual's judgment. However, groups may also reach poor decisions, in part because of the effects of two types of group biases, *group polarization* and *groupthink*.

Group Polarization: Going to Extremes

group polarization The tendency for members of decision-making groups to shift toward more extreme views in whatever direction they were initially leaning.

risky-shift phenomenon A type of group polarization effect in which group discussion leads to the adoption of a riskier course of action than the members would have endorsed initially.

Group polarization is the tendency for group members to adopt views that are more extreme but in the same direction as their original views. Members who were slightly in favor of a particular point of view become more strongly committed to their original views; those who originally opposed a particular course of action become more committed in their opposition. Depending on the group's original orientation, the adoption of more extreme views may lead to riskier actions, a tendency called the **risky-shift phenomenon**. Or it may lead to more staunchly conservative actions. In either case, initial opinions may be hardened and alternative points discouraged.

Why does group polarization occur? One common reason is *social validation.* Since groups are often composed of people holding similar views, interactions with like-minded people allow individuals to express attitudes or arguments that echo their own, thus strengthening their confidence in their attitudes. Another explanation is based on normative influences. Groups define the appropriate (or normative) level of strength that an attitude should have. When individuals discover that their own attitudes are less extreme than the group norm, they may strengthen their attitudes to conform to that norm.

Groupthink: How Can Smart People Make Dumb Decisions?

groupthink Janis's term for the tendency of members of a decision-making group to be more focused on reaching a consensus than on critically examining the issues at hand.

SLICE OF LIFE This was the question President John Kennedy asked his advisers in the aftermath of the disastrous invasion of Cuba at the Bay of Pigs in 1961, when Cuban forces easily defeated a brigade of U.S.-backed Cuban exiles. Yale psychologist Irving Janis believed that stupidity wasn't the explanation. To Janis, the fault lay in a flawed approach to group decision making he named **groupthink** (Janis, 1997).

Groupthink is the tendency for members of a group to become so concerned with reaching a consensus that they lose the ability to critically evaluate the problem before them. Groupthink can be likened to a kind of "tunnel vision" in which the group's perspective is limited to a single point of view (Nowak, Vallacher, & Miller, 2003).

CONCEPT 14.43
When groups tackle a problem, they may become so focused on reaching a consensus that they fail to critically examine the issues before them.

In groupthink, the pressure to conform to majority opinion squelches any serious debate. Janis believed that groupthink is more likely to occur (1) when members are strongly attached to the group, (2) when an external threat is present, and (3) when

© SIPA USA/SIPA/SIPA USA/SIPA/Newscom

"One of the dangers in the White House . . . is that you get wrapped up in groupthink, and everybody agrees with everything."

a strong-minded leader is directing the group. Group members may not want to "rock the boat" by expressing a dissenting opinion, or they may have a misplaced confidence that the leader and other group members must be right. Critics, however, point out that research evidence supporting the groupthink model is mixed (Kerr & Tindale, 2004).

Janis's recommendations for avoiding negative effects of groupthink are well worth considering at any level of decision making:

- Group members should be encouraged to consider all alternatives and carefully weigh the evidence on all sides of an issue.
- The group leader should avoid stating any preferences as the group begins its work.
- Outsiders should be called upon to offer their opinions and analyses.
- Group members or outsiders should be encouraged to play the role of "devil's advocate."
- The group should be subdivided into smaller groups to independently review the issues that are before the larger group.
- Several group meetings should be held to reassess the situation and evaluate any new information before final decisions are reached.

A month before taking office as President, Barack Obama reflected on the risks posed by groupthink:

> One of the dangers in a White House, based on my reading of history, is that you get wrapped up in groupthink, and everybody agrees with everything, and there's no discussion and there are no dissenting views. So, I'm going to be welcoming a vigorous debate inside the White House. But, I understand . . . as Harry Truman said, the buck will stop with me."
>
> —Barack Obama, December 2008

Concept Chart 14.3 summarizes the group influences on identity and behavior discussed in this module.

CONCEPT CHART 14.3 Group Influences on Identity and Behavior

Sources of Group Influence	Description
Conformity	Adherence to social standards or norms
Obedience	Adherence to the commands of external authority
Social facilitation	Improvement in performance occurring when we perform in front of others
Social loafing	Impaired performance occurring when our individual effort is obscured by a group effort
Deindividuation	Temporary loss of self-awareness in members of a crowd or mob
Group polarization	Tendency for group members to adopt more extreme versions of their original views
Groupthink	Tendency for groups to emphasize consensus building rather than thoughtful consideration of the issues

14.3 MODULE REVIEW Group Influences on Individual Behavior

Recite It

What is social identity?

- Social identity (also called group identity) is our social self—that part of our self-concept that relates to our family and social roles and the collective identities we share with members of our own religious, ethnic, fraternal, or national groups.
- Social identities play a stronger role in collectivist cultures than in individualistic cultures.

What was the significance of the Asch study on conformity?

- Asch showed that people often conform to group judgments, even when those judgments are obviously false.
- Factors that influence conformity include gender, cultural background, self-esteem, social shyness, desire to be liked by the group, age, and situational features such as public disclosure, group size, and stimulus ambiguity.

Why were Milgram's findings so disturbing, and why were his methods so controversial?

- Milgram found that people from various walks of life could be induced to obey unreasonable or even immoral commands given by an authority figure.
- The use of deception, as well as the potential emotional after effects of raising awareness of participants' capabilities for such behavior, led to controversy over Milgram's methods.

How does the presence of others affect individual performance?

- The presence of others may improve performance in simple, well-learned tasks but impair performance in complex tasks.
- People may also exert less than their best effort in a group task when they know others will pick up the slack and their performance will not be individually evaluated.

What is deindividuation?

- Deindividuation, the loss of self-awareness that occurs when one becomes swept up in a crowd, can lead to diffusion of responsibility and loss of individuality, resulting in a loosening of constraints on reckless or deviant behavior.

What are group polarization and groupthink?

- Group polarization and groupthink are sources of biases that affect group decision making. In group polarization, group members adopt more extreme versions of their original views. Groupthink is a type of group decision making that can lead to bad decisions. In groupthink, decisions derive from a desire for consensus rather than from a critical evaluation of the issues.

Recall It

1. Our _________ identity reflects the fundamental need to be part of a group.
2. Which of the following statements is *not* correct with regard to characteristics associated with greater levels of conformity?
   a. Individuals who conform assume that the majority must be correct.
   b. Individuals who conform exhibit greater independence and self-esteem.
   c. Individuals who conform find it difficult to disagree with group opinion.
   d. Public disclosure leads to more conformity than disclosing responses in private.
3. In Milgram's classic study, what percentage of original participants administered the full series of electric shocks (i.e., to the highest level)?
4. The presence of others is likely to lead to _________ performance on simpler, well-learned tasks and _________ performance on less familiar or more difficult tasks.
   a. enhanced, impaired
   b. impaired, enhanced.
   c. enhanced, enhanced.
   d. impaired, impaired.
5. The phenomenon of groupthink explains how.
   a. groups often make better-informed decisions than individuals.
   b. groups often make bad decisions because of the desire to maintain harmony within the group.
   c. group members tend to think in similar ways because of their similar backgrounds.
   d. groups often make good decisions because of the desire to reach a consensus.

Think About It

- Agree or disagree with this statement, and support your answer: "Had I been a participant in the Milgram study, I would have refused to comply with the experimenter's demands."

APPLICATION MODULE 14.4

Psychology Goes to Work

CONCEPT 14.44
Industrial/organizational (I/O) psychology is the branch of psychology that studies people at work and the organizational structures in which they work.

Many of us spend more time interacting with others in the workplace than we do with our families or friends. According to the latest government statistics, about 70 percent of men and about 60 percent of women work in gainful employment (Bureau of Labor Statistics, 2010a). The branch of psychology that studies people at work and the organizations in which they work is called *industrial/organizational (I/O) psychology.*

I/O psychologists perform many different functions in companies and organizations. They develop tests to find the most suitable workers for particular jobs, design equipment for optimum efficiency and safety, overcome obstacles to successful employment of workers with disabilities, and help companies develop management structures to maximize productivity and worker satisfaction. They also develop incentive programs (bonuses) to motivate workers to achieve productivity goals. In this module we examine two key areas of interest to I/O psychologists today: job satisfaction and adjustment to a changing workplace.

Understanding Job Satisfaction: It's Not Just About the Job

Job satisfaction—the degree to which workers have positive feelings toward their jobs—depends not only on the job itself but also on traits or characteristics of the workers themselves (Gerhart, 2005; Staw & Cohen-Charash, 2005). Some factors that predict job satisfaction have to do with the job itself, such as higher status, good pay and fringe benefits, opportunities for social interactions with co-workers, availability of childcare facilities, and opportunities for interesting and personally fulfilling work (e.g., Morgeson & Humphrey, 2006). But other factors have more to do with differences in personality traits. People with higher levels of self-esteem, stronger belief in themselves or self-efficacy, and better emotional stability tend to be more satisfied with their jobs than others with lower levels of these traits (Judge, Heller, & Mount, 2002; Zalewska, 2010). We've also learned that people with more cheerful dispositions tend to be happier with their jobs than those with more downcast moods (Thoresen et al., 2003). Given the importance of personal characteristics in job satisfaction, we shouldn't be surprised that people who are unhappy at one job tend to be unhappy at whatever job they hold (Bowling et al., 2005). Evidence also links genetic influences to job satisfaction and even the likelihood of becoming self-employed (Olson, Vernon, & Harris, 2001; Shane et al., 2010).

Job satisfaction may also depend on the fit between attributional style (a cognitive factor) and the amount of control people have at work. For many workers, the ability to have some control over the work they do reduces job-related stress and contributes to a more positive work experience. Having control over the job is also linked to better overall health and well-being (Spector, 2005).

However, it is important to think critically and avoid overgeneralizing. Recall our earlier discussion of the self-serving bias, which is the tendency of people to take credit for their successes and explain away their disappointments and failures. The self-serving bias protects self-esteem because disappointments are blamed on external factors rather than the self. Yet research on job satisfaction indicates that the self-serving bias isn't true of everyone. Some people have the opposite tendency, a negative attributional style in which they minimize their accomplishments and blame themselves for negative outcomes. In Chapter 15 we will see how a negative attributional style may predispose individuals to become depressed in the face of disappointing life experiences. On the job, people with a negative attributional style tend to fault themselves for missing a sales target or losing a customer, especially when they feel in control of the work they do. Investigators suspect that for these people, having control on the job may actually create unhealthy levels of stress (Schaubroeck, Jones, & Xie, 2001).

Research along these lines may have practical applications. For example, companies may find it useful to train workers for specific types of jobs on the basis of their attributional styles. In a broader context, research on job satisfaction links different areas of research in psychology, including studies of personality, emotional well-being, genetic influences on behavior, and attributional styles.

The Changing American Workplace

The workplace that young college graduates are entering is a very different place than the one their parents and grandparents found. The economy is transitioning from a smokestack-based industrial economy to one based more on technology and service-based commerce. For one thing, the workplace is less secure than it was in past generations. Workers today are less likely to be able to rely on lifetime employment with the same company as many of their parents and grandparents did. Rapid change in technology changes existing jobs and leads to the creation of new ones at dizzying speed. Advances in technology allow workers to interact electronically with their home offices through e-mail, video conferencing, and wireless networks.

Many work-related changes involve the way we work. Where is it written that people always perform best on a traditional nine-to-five schedule? Companies are increasingly restructuring the workday to allow more flextime (flexible work shifts) and increased off-site work, such as **telecommuting** (working at home at least for all or part of the workweek). Many companies provide satellite offices or telework centers where telecommuting workers can drop in to perform work they cannot complete at home. One work model provides temporary office space in a central office for workers only as needed—much as they would check into a hotel when traveling.

telecommuting A form of working at home in which people communicate with their home office and clients via computer or telecommunications.

The number of telecommuters is rising rapidly and is expected to continue to rise in the years ahead. According to recent surveys, an estimated 45 million workers in the United States are telecommuters ("Telecommuting," 2007). Telecommuting allows workers greater control over their work environment, so it is no surprise that it is linked to greater job satisfaction, better work performance, and lower worker turnover rates (Gajendran & Harrison, 2007).

I/O psychologists can assist companies in shaping their organizational culture in ways that help them adapt to the changing workplace. **Organizational culture** is the

organizational culture The system of shared values and norms within an organization.

system of shared values (what the organization deems important) and norms (rules and regulations for acceptable behavior) that exists within the organization. Relationships between organizational culture and company performance are complex, and I/O psychologists recognize that no one culture fits the needs of all organizations. Aware that companies must also adapt to the trend toward globalization and the need to interact with suppliers, manufacturers, and customers in many other cultures, I/O psychologists are helping companies develop a greater sensitivity to cultural differences and ways of working more effectively in today's global business environment.

© Fancy / Alamy

Advances in computer systems and telecommunications enable millions of American workers to work at home on one or more days a week (shoes not mandatory).

The Changing American Worker

In his bestselling book, *The World Is Flat*, *New York Times* columnist Thomas Friedman (2006) focused on changes in the workplace brought about increasing globalization. Factors such as outsourcing work and the rapid flow of information made possible by the Internet have led to a flatter global playing field for companies today. To remain competitive, Friedman argues, American workers need to keep updating their skills and develop the self-motivation needed to compete in a worldwide commercial marketplace.

Many workers move between jobs and even change their careers a number of times during their working lives. Younger "baby boomers" born between 1957 and 1964 held an average of 11 different jobs between the ages of 18 and 44 (Bureau of Labor Statistics, 2010b). Younger people first entering the workforce today need to be prepared for even greater job mobility in the years ahead.

Workers who succeed are likely to be those who take responsibility for retooling themselves and redirecting their careers to meet the demands of a changing world. Even workers who staff corporate offices and keep assembly lines humming will need continuing training to keep pace with changes in technology and job responsibilities. The twenty-first-century workplace is also emerging as a more entrepreneurial environment as well, and efforts to promote self-initiative and entrepreneurship are needed to keep workers and the economy overall competitive. Companies will also need to need to redesign jobs to allow more flexible work schedules. I/O psychologists can help companies identify individuals who can work best in this changing work environment; they can also redesign that environment to best suit the needs of workers and employers in the twenty-first century.

The U.S. Department of Labor offers the following tips to help people manage their careers (Bureau of Labor Statistics, 2010c). Whether you're planning a career or returning to school to retool for a new career, these suggestions can help you prepare for the changing American workplace:

- *Learn throughout your life.* Being a lifelong learner does not necessarily mean you have to be enrolled in a school or formal training program. It means that you are open to learning new skills, technology and ways of doing business. People who are willing to learn new things about their profession or company are more likely to have job stability and continued career success.
- *Find organizations and associations to help you stay up on new things in your profession.*
- *Find opportunities for professional development through short-term training or community education courses.*
- *Finding the right job is useless unless you know how to keep that job.* Knowing what employers expect of new employees will help with job retention.

TABLE 14.1 Finding Your Dream Job

Is your work personally fulfilling? Does it allow you to pursue your dreams? Industrial-organizational psychologist Nashá London-Vargas (2001) offers some self-study questions to help determine whether your present (or perhaps future) job meets your personal needs, not just your financial obligations:

- Is your work connected to your interests or passions in life?
- Is it a vehicle to pursue your dreams?
- Do you have a passion about your work?
- How did you get to this job at this point in your life? Did you seek it, or did it find you?
- Are you satisfied each day from a job well done, or does your job leave you feeling unfulfilled or depressed?

Finally, psychologist Nashá London-Vargas (2001) suggests that our career choices have the potential to help us fulfill our basic values and life goals. Connecting work with our interests, passions, personal fulfillment, and need for challenges can help add meaning and value to our lives and those of others (see Table 14.1).

Thinking Critically About Psychology

Based on your reading of this chapter, answer the following questions. Then, to evaluate your progress in developing critical thinking skills, compare your answers to the sample answers found in Appendix A.

Why didn't they help? Many people heard Kitty Genovese being viciously attacked but did nothing. Based on your reading of factors influencing helping behavior, speculate on the reasons why these bystanders failed to help.

Sample Responses to *Try This Out*, "What Do You Say Now?" (p. 546)

- Low-ball technique: You might say, "Sorry, that's my best offer. We agreed on a price and I expect you to stick to it."
- Bait-and-switch technique: You might say, "If I wanted the LX version I would have asked for it. If you're having difficulty getting the car I want, then it's your problem. Now, what are you going to do for me?"
- Foot-in-the-door technique: You might say, "If you want to lower the price of the car, we can talk about it. But the price I gave you is all I can afford to spend."

Log in to CengageBrain to access the resources your instructor requires. For this book, you can access:

CourseMate

Psychology CourseMate brings course concepts to life with interactive learning, study, and exam preparation tools that support the printed textbook. A textbook-specific website, Psychology CourseMate includes an integrated interactive eBook and other interactive learning tools including quizzes, flashcards, videos, and more.

CENGAGENOW

CengageNow is an easy-to-use online resource that helps you study in less time to get the grade you want—NOW. Take a pre-test for this chapter and receive a personalized study plan based on your results that will identify the topics you need to review and direct you to online resources to help you master those topics. Then take a post-test to help you determine the concepts you have mastered and what you will need to work on. If your textbook does not include an access code card, go to CengageBrain.com to gain access.

Visit www.cengagebrain.com to access your account and purchase materials.

VISUAL OVERVIEW Chapter 14 Social Psychology

MODULE 14.1 Perceiving Others

Factors in Impression Formation and Attributions

- Personal disclosure
- Social schemas
- Stereotyping
- Self-fulfilling prophecies
- Attributions
- Fundamental attribution error
- Actor-observer effect
- Self-serving bias

Attitudes

- **Components**: Cognitions, emotions, and behavior
- **Sources**: Parents, teachers, peers, personal experiences, media, and possible genetic influences
- **Elaboration Likelihood Model**: Persuasion works through either a central route (evaluation of the content of the message) or a peripheral route (focus on incidental cues)

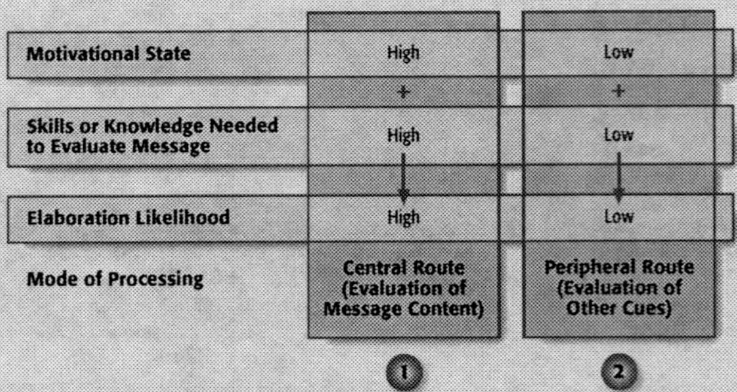

Elaboration Likelihood Model

MODULE 14.2 Relating to Others

Positive Ways of Relating

- **Factors Influencing Attraction**: Similarity, physical attractiveness, proximity, reciprocity
- **Decision-Making Model of Bystander Intervention**: Predicts likelihood of bystanders helping a person in need
- **Factors Influencing Helping**: Situational ambiguity, perceived cost, diffusion of responsibility, similarity, empathy, facial features, gender and mood effects, attributions of the cause of need, social norms

Negative Ways of Relating

- **Factors Relating to Prejudice and Discrimination**: Negative stereotyping, in-group favoritism and out-group negativism, out-group homogeneity, authoritarian personality, and stereotype threat
- **Influences on Aggression**: Biological, learning, sociocultural, and environmental factors; use of alcohol; emotional states

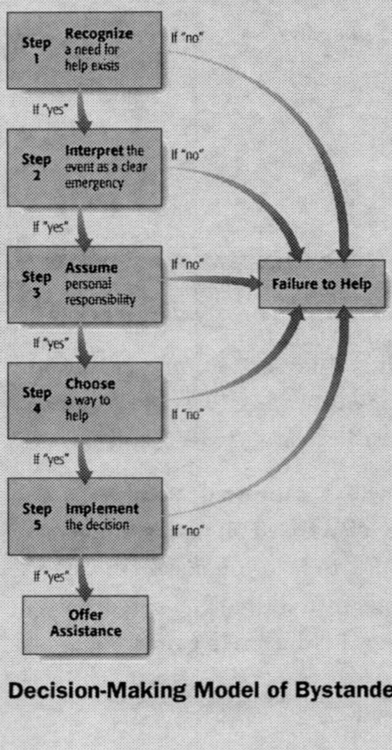

Decision-Making Model of Bystander Intervention

MODULE 14.3 Group Influences on Individual Behavior

Social vs. Personal Identity

- **Social identity**: Ethnic, group, and role identity
- **Personal identity**: Individual identity

Conformity

- **Asch Experiments**: Conforming to group judgments
- **Factors Influencing Conformity**: Individual differences and situational factors such as group size and stimulus ambiguity

Compliance

Acceding to requests or demands of others

- **Influenced By**: Authority and social validation
- **Consistency-Based Sales Tactics**: Foot-in-the-door techniques, bait-and-switch technique, low-ball technique
- **Reciprocity-Based Sales Tactic**: Door-in-the-face technique

Obedience to Authority

- **Milgram's Studies**: Obedience to unreasonable or immoral commands
- **Controversies**: Ethical issues, relevance of findings to real-life atrocities
- **Factors Influencing Obedience to Authority**: Legitimization of authority, social validation

© Bob Krist

Other Social Influences

- **Social Facilitation**: Performing better when others are present
- **Social Loafing**: Sloughing off in group work
- **Mob Behavior**: Losing one's individuality in a crowd
- **Factors in Group Decision Making**: Group polarization, risky-shift phenomenon, groupthink

15 Psychological Disorders

The "Garlic Lady"

SLICE OF LIFE It was about 2 a.m. when the police brought Claire to the emergency room. She seemed to be about 45; her hair was matted, her clothing was disheveled, and her face was fixed in a blank stare. She clutched a clove of garlic in her right hand. She did not respond to the interviewer's questions: "Do you know where you are? Can you tell me your name? Can you tell me if anything is bothering you?"

The police officers filled in the details. Claire had been found meandering through town along the painted line that divided the main street, apparently oblivious to the cars swerving around her. She was waving the clove of garlic in front of her. She said nothing to the officers when they arrived on the scene, but she offered no resistance.

Claire was admitted to the hospital and taken to the psychiatric ward. The next morning, she was brought before the day staff, still clutching the clove of garlic, and interviewed by the chief psychiatrist. She said little, but her intentions could be pieced together from mumbled fragments. Claire said something about "devils" who were trying to "rob" her mind. The garlic was meant to protect her. She had decided that the only way to rid the town of the "devils" that hounded her was to walk down the main street, waving the garlic in front of her. Claire would become well known to the hospital. This was but one of a series of such episodes.

"Pretty Grisly Stuff"

Phil was 42, a police photographer. It was his job to take pictures at crime scenes. "Pretty grisly stuff," he admitted, "corpses and all." Phil was married and had two teenage sons. He sought a psychological consultation because he was bothered by fears of being confined in enclosed spaces. Many situations evoked his fears. He was terrified of becoming trapped in an elevator and took the stairs whenever possible. He felt uncomfortable sitting in the back seat of a car. He had lately become fearful of flying, although in the past he had worked as a news cameraperson and would often fly to scenes of news events at a moment's notice—usually by helicopter.

"I guess I was younger then and more daring," he related. "Sometimes I would hang out of the helicopter to shoot pictures with no fear at all. But now, just thinking about flying makes my heart race. It's not that I'm afraid the plane will crash. I just start trembling when I think of them closing that door, trapping us inside. I can't tell you why."

In this chapter we examine the behavior of people like Claire and Phil—behavior that psychologists would consider abnormal. Let us begin by examining the criteria that psychologists use to determine

(*Continued on page 562*)

DID YOU KNOW THAT...

- Psychological disorders affect just about everyone in one way or another? (p. 567)
- Some people are so afraid of leaving the house that they literally are unable to go out to buy a quart of milk? (p. 571)
- Some people have lost all feeling in an arm or leg but remain strangely unconcerned about their ailments? (p. 577)
- Women are nearly twice as likely as men to develop major depression? (p. 580)
- Some people with schizophrenia sit motionless for hours, as though they were statues? (p. 589)
- People who are labeled as psychopaths are not psychotic? (p. 593)

Learning Objectives

By reading this chapter you will be able to . . .

1 **IDENTIFY** criteria used to distinguish normal behavior from abnormal behavior and **APPLY** this knowledge to examples.

2 **DESCRIBE** different conceptual models of abnormal behavior.

3 **EXPLAIN** how psychological disorders are classified in the DSM system.

4 **IDENTIFY** and **DESCRIBE** different types of anxiety disorders, dissociative and somatoform disorders, and mood disorders, and **APPLY** this knowledge to examples of these different disorders.

5 **EVALUATE** causal factors in these disorders.

6 **IDENTIFY** factors linked to risk of suicidal behavior.

7 **DESCRIBE** the major features or symptoms of schizophrenia and **EVALUATE** underlying causal factors.

8 **EXPLAIN** the diathesis-stress model of schizophrenia.

9 **DESCRIBE** the features of antisocial personality disorder and borderline personality disorder.

10 **EVALUATE** causal factors in antisocial personality disorder and borderline personality disorder.

11 **APPLY** knowledge of steps you can take to help a friend who may be suicidal.

© Sami Sarkis/Getty Images

Preview

(*Continued from page 560*)

when behavior crosses the line between normal and abnormal. Later we will explore different kinds of abnormal behavior patterns that psychologists and other professionals classify as psychological or mental disorders.

The descriptions in this chapter may raise your awareness about psychological problems of people you know, or perhaps even problems you've faced yourself. But it is not intended to make you a diagnostician. If the problems discussed in the chapter hit close to home, it makes sense to discuss your concerns with a qualified professional.

MODULE 15.1

What Is Abnormal Behavior?

- What criteria are used to determine whether behavior is abnormal?
- What are the major models of abnormal behavior?
- What are psychological disorders?

Determining whether behavior is abnormal is a more complex problem than it may seem at first blush. Most of us get anxious or depressed from time to time, but our behavior is not abnormal. The same behavior may be deemed normal under some circumstances but abnormal in others. For example, anxiety during a job interview is normal, but anxiety experienced whenever you board an elevator is not. Deep feelings of sadness are appropriate when you lose a loved one, but not when things are going well or following a mildly upsetting event that others take in stride.

Charting the Boundaries Between Normal and Abnormal Behavior

CONCEPT 15.1
Psychologists use multiple criteria in determining whether behavior is abnormal, including unusualness, social deviance, emotional distress, maladaptive behavior, dangerousness, and faulty perceptions or interpretations of reality.

Where, then, might we draw the line between normal and abnormal behavior? Psychologists typically identify abnormal behavior based on a combination of the following criteria (Nevid, Rathus, & Greene, 2011):

1. *Unusualness.* Behavior that is unusual, or experienced by only a few, may be abnormal—but not in all cases or situations. Surely it is unusual for people to report "hearing voices" or, like Claire, to walk through town warding off demons. Yet uncommonness, by itself, is not sufficient to be deemed abnormal. Exceptional behavior, such as the ability to hit a three-point jump shot with some regularity or to become a valedictorian, is also unusual, but it is not abnormal.
2. *Social deviance.* All societies establish standards or social norms that define socially acceptable behaviors. Deviation from these norms is often used as a criterion for labeling behavior as abnormal. The same behavior might be considered abnormal in some contexts but perfectly acceptable in others. For example, we might consider it abnormal to shout vulgarities at strangers in the street. Yet shouting vulgarities at an umpire or referee who misses an important call in a ballgame may fall within the range of acceptable social norms, however offensive it might be.

3. *Emotional distress.* States of emotional distress, such as anxiety or depression, are considered abnormal when inappropriate, excessive, or prolonged relative to the person's situation.
4. *Maladaptive behavior.* Behavior is maladaptive when it causes personal distress, is self-defeating, or is associated with significant health, social, or occupational problems. For example, abuse of alcohol or other drugs may threaten an individual's health and ability to function in meeting life's responsibilities.
5. *Dangerousness.* Violent or dangerous behavior is another criterion for which we need to examine the social context. For example, engaging in behavior that is dangerous to oneself or others may be an act of bravery in times of war, but not in peacetime. Hockey players and football players regularly engage in physically aggressive behavior that may be dangerous to themselves or their opponents, but their behavior in athletic competitions is often rewarded with lucrative contracts and endorsement deals. Apart from the sanctioned contexts of warfare and sports, however, violent behavior is likely to be considered abnormal.
6. *Faulty perceptions or interpretations of reality.* **Hallucinations** ("hearing voices" or seeing things that are not there) involve distorted perceptions of reality. Similarly, fixed but unfounded beliefs, called **delusions**, such as believing that FBI agents are listening in on your phone conversations, represent faulty interpretations of reality (unless of course the FBI really is tapping your phone).

© IMAGENFX/Shutterstock.com

hallucinations Perceptions ("hearing voices" or seeing things) that are experienced in the absence of external stimuli.

delusions Fixed but patently false beliefs, such as believing that one is being hounded by demons.

As we shall see next, the cultural context in which behavior occurs must also be evaluated when making judgments about whether behavior is abnormal.

Cultural Bases of Abnormal Behavior

Psychologists take the cultural context into account when making judgments about abnormal behavior. They realize that the same behavior can be normal in one culture but abnormal in another. For example, in the majority American culture, "hearing voices" is deemed abnormal. Yet among some Native American peoples, it is considered normal for individuals to hear the voices of their recently deceased relatives. They believe that the voices of the departed call out as their spirit ascends to the afterworld (Kleinman, 1987). Such behavior, because it falls within the normal spectrum of the culture in which it occurs, is not deemed abnormal—even if it may seem so to people from other cultures.

In addition, abnormal behavior patterns may be expressed differently in different cultures. For example, people in Western cultures may experience anxiety in the form of excessive worries about finances, health, or jobs. Among some native African peoples and Australian aboriginal peoples, anxiety may take the form of fear that witchcraft or sorcery is being directed against them (Kleinman, 1987). Among the Chinese, depression is associated more strongly with physical symptoms, such as headaches, fatigue, and weakness, than by feelings of sadness or guilt (Draguns & Tanaka-Matsumi, 2003; Parker, Gladstone, & Chee, 2001).

CONCEPT 15.2
Behavior that is deemed to be normal in some cultures may be considered abnormal in others.

Alternatively, the same behavior may be judged abnormal at some points in time but not at others. For example, although the American Psychiatric Association once classified homosexuality as a type of mental disorder, it no longer does so. Many professionals today consider homosexuality a variation of sexual behavior rather than an abnormal behavior pattern.

Applying the Criteria to Abnormal Behavior

Consider the examples of Claire and Phil, described at the start of this chapter. Was their behavior abnormal? Claire's behavior certainly met several of the criteria of abnormal behavior. It was clearly unusual as well as socially deviant, and it represented what most people would take to be a delusion—believing you are protecting the community from demons. It was also clearly maladaptive and dangerous, as it put at risk not only Claire herself but also the drivers who were forced to swerve out of the way to avoid hitting her.

Phil, on the other hand, had good contact with reality. He understood that his fears exceeded the dangers he faced. Yet his phobia was a source of considerable emotional distress and was maladaptive because it impaired his ability to carry out his occupational and family responsibilities. We might also employ a criterion of unusualness here. Relatively few people have such fears of confinement that they avoid flying or taking elevators. Yet, as we have noted, unusualness alone is not a sufficient criterion for abnormality.

Although the behaviors of these individuals invoke different criteria, they could each be considered abnormal. Overall, professionals apply multiple criteria when making judgments about abnormality.

© Igor Akimov/ITAR-TASS/Corbis

Is he abnormal? Abnormality must be judged in relation to cultural standards. Are heavy body tattooing and piercings a sign of abnormality or a fashion statement?

Models of Abnormal Behavior

Abnormal behavior has existed in all societies, even though the view of what is or is not abnormal varies from culture to culture and has changed over time. In some cases, these explanations have led to humane treatment of people with abnormal behavior, but more frequently, people deemed to be "mad" or mentally ill have been treated cruelly or harshly.

Early Beliefs

Throughout much of Western history, from ancient times through the Middle Ages, people thought that those displaying abnormal behavior were controlled by supernatural forces or possessed by demonic spirits. Beliefs in supernatural causes of abnormal behavior, especially the doctrine of demonic possession, held sway until the rise of scientific thinking in the seventeenth and eighteenth centuries. The treatment of choice for demonic possession—*exorcism*—was used to ferret out satanic forces or the Devil himself from the afflicted person's body. If that didn't work, there were even more forceful "remedies," such as the torture rack. Not surprisingly, many recipients of these "cures" attempted to the best of their ability to modify their behavior to meet social expectations.

CONCEPT 15.3
Throughout much of Western history, the prevailing view of abnormal behavior was based on a concept of demonic possession.

The Medical Model

The eighteenth and nineteenth centuries were times of rapid advances in medical science. Among the more notable advances were the development of a vaccine against the ancient scourge of smallpox, the discovery of the bacterial causes of diseases such as anthrax and leprosy, and the use of antiseptics in surgery to prevent infections. During this time of medical advancement, the first modern model of abnormal behavior was developed, the **medical model.** The medical model is based on the belief that abnormal behavior patterns represent *mental illnesses* that have a biological, not demonic, basis and can be classified by their particular characteristics, or symptoms.

medical model A framework for understanding abnormal behavior patterns as symptoms of underlying physical disorders or diseases.

Psychological Models

Even as the medical model was taking shape, theorists were actively developing psychological models of abnormal behavior. The first major psychological model of abnormal behavior was the psychodynamic model developed by Sigmund Freud, which posited that unconscious, unresolved conflicts from childhood are at the root of abnormal behavior. These conflicts result from the need to control instinctual sexual and aggressive impulses arising from the unconscious mind or to channel them into socially acceptable outlets. Psychological symptoms (e.g., a phobia) are merely outward expressions of this inner turmoil. The person may be aware of the symptom (the phobia) but not of the unconscious conflicts that gave rise to it. Contemporary psychodynamic theorists differ from Freud in some respects, but they retain the central belief that unconscious conflicts are at the root of abnormal behavior patterns.

CONCEPT 15.4
With the rise of scientific thought, attention began to shift from religious dogma to scientific or naturalistic explanations of human behavior.

CONCEPT 15.5
Psychodynamic, behavioral, humanistic, and cognitive models focus on the psychological roots of abnormal behavior.

→ Concept Link
These major psychological models give rise to different forms of psychotherapy. See Module 16.2.

At about the time that Freud was plumbing the depths of the unconscious, behaviorists were exploring the role of learning in the development of abnormal behavior. Pavlov's discovery of the conditioned response gave the early behaviorist movement a model for studying how maladaptive behaviors, such as phobias, could be learned or acquired through experience. The behavioral model is based on the belief that most forms of abnormal behavior are learned in the same ways that normal behavior is learned. Among the early demonstrations of the role of learning in the development of abnormal behavior was the experiment with "Little Albert" (discussed in Chapter 5). In this experiment, John B. Watson and his colleague Rosalie Rayner (1920) induced a fear of white rats in a young boy by presenting a noxious stimulus (a loud banging sound) whenever a rat was brought close to the child. The repeated pairing of the conditioned stimulus (rat) and unconditioned stimulus (loud banging) instilled a conditioned response (fear evoked by the rat itself).

© irin-k/Shutterstock.com

The humanistic model offers another psychological perspective on abnormal behavior. Humanistic theorists such as Carl Rogers and Abraham Maslow rejected the belief that human behavior is the product of either unconscious processes or simple conditioning. They argue that humans possess an intrinsic ability to make conscious choices and strive toward self-actualization. Abnormal behavior develops when people encounter roadblocks on the path toward personal growth or self-actualization. To satisfy the demands of others to think, feel, and act in certain ways, people may become detached from their true selves and develop a distorted self-image that can lead to emotional problems such as anxiety and depression. Humanistic theorists believe that people with psychological problems need to become more aware of their true feelings and accept themselves for who they truly are.

Cognitive theorists, such as Albert Ellis and Aaron Beck, believe that irrational or distorted thinking leads to emotional problems and maladaptive behavior. Examples of faulty styles of thinking include magnifying or exaggerating the consequences of negative events ("making mountains out of molehills") and interpreting events in an overly negative way, as though one were seeing things through blue-colored glasses.

The Sociocultural Model

The sociocultural model views the causes of abnormal behavior within the broader social and cultural contexts in which the behavior develops. Theorists in this tradition believe that abnormal behavior may have more to do with social ills or failures of society than with problems within the individual. They examine a range of social and cultural influences on behavior, including social class, poverty, ethnic and cultural background, and racial and gender discrimination. Sociocultural theorists believe that the stress of coping with poverty and social disadvantage can eventually take its toll on mental health. Consistent with this view, evidence shows that schizophrenia and depression occur proportionately more often among poor and socially disadvantaged groups (Ostler et al., 2001). Minority youth often face stressors such as acculturation, poverty, and discrimination, which may help explain findings that they have higher rates of anxiety and depression (Anderson & Mayes, 2010).

CONCEPT 15.6
The sociocultural model views abnormal behavior in terms of the social and cultural contexts in which it occurs.

CONCEPT 15.7
Today there is increasing convergence toward a biopsychosocial model of abnormal behavior, which focuses on the contributions and interactions of biological and psychosocial influences.

Sociocultural theorists also focus on the effects of labeling people as mentally ill. They recognize that because of social prejudices, people who are labeled mentally ill are often denied job or housing opportunities and become stigmatized or marginalized in society. These theorists join with other professionals in arguing for greater understanding and support for people with mental health problems.

The Biopsychosocial Model

Today we have many different models to explain abnormal behavior. Indeed, because there are different ways of looking at a given phenomenon, we can't conclude that one particular model is necessarily right and all the others wrong. Each of these models—medical, psychological, and sociocultural—has something unique to offer our understanding of abnormal behavior. None offers a complete view.

Abnormal behavior presents us with many puzzles as we attempt to unravel its causes. How are our mental functions affected by biology—by genes, brain structures, and neurotransmitter systems? What psychological factors, such as underlying motives or conflicts, personality traits, cognitions, and learned behaviors, are involved? And how is our behavior affected by society and culture?

biopsychosocial model An integrative model for explaining abnormal behavior patterns in terms of the interactions of biological, psychological, and sociocultural factors.

diathesis-stress model A type of biopsychosocial model that relates the development of disorders to the combination of a diathesis, or predisposition, usually genetic in origin, and exposure to stressful events or life circumstances.

diathesis A vulnerability or predisposition to developing a disorder.

Many psychologists today subscribe to the **biopsychosocial model**—the view that abnormal behavior is best explained by complex interactions of biological, psychological, and sociocultural factors (Levine & Schmelkin, 2006; Moffitt, Caspi, & Rutter, 2006). We are only beginning to put together the pieces of what has turned out to be a very complicated puzzle—the subtle and often complex patterns of underlying factors that give rise to abnormal behavior patterns.

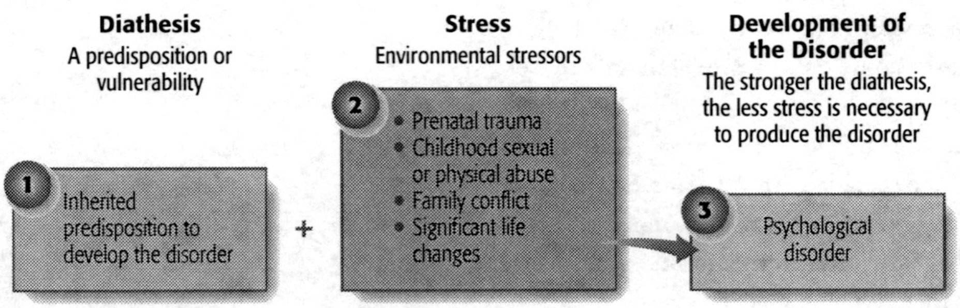

FIGURE 15.1 The Diathesis-Stress Model
The diathesis-stress model posits that the development of particular disorders involves an interaction of a (1) predisposition (diathesis), usually genetic in nature, and (2) exposure to life stress, which leads to (3) the development of psychological disorders.
Source: Nevid, Rathus, & Greene, 2008.

A prominent example of the biopsychosocial model is the **diathesis-stress model**. According to this model, certain people have a vulnerability or predisposition, called a **diathesis**, which increases their risk of developing a particular disorder. A diathesis is usually genetic in nature, but it can also involve psychological factors, such as maladaptive personality traits or dysfunctional thinking patterns. Whether the person possessing a diathesis develops the particular disorder depends on the level of stress in the person's life (see ■ Figure 15.1) (Pruessner et al., 2011). If the person encounters a low level of stress or has effective skills for handling stress, the disorder may never emerge even if a diathesis is present. In some cases, however, the diathesis is so strong that the disorder develops even under the most benign life circumstances.

CONCEPT 15.8
Psychological disorders are patterns of disturbed behavior, mood, thinking, or perception that cause personal distress or impaired functioning.

What Are Psychological Disorders?

Distinctive patterns of abnormal behavior are classified as **psychological disorders**—also known as *mental disorders* or *mental illnesses* within the medical model. Psychological disorders involve disturbances of mood, behavior, thought processes, or perception that result in significant personal distress or impaired functioning. Examples of psychological disorders include schizophrenia, anxiety disorders such as phobias and panic disorder, and mood disorders such as major depression.

psychological disorders Abnormal behavior patterns characterized by disturbances in behavior, thinking, perceptions, or emotions that are associated with significant personal distress or impaired functioning. Also called *mental disorders* or *mental illnesses*.

How Many Are Affected?

Chances are that someone you know, or perhaps you yourself, will be affected by a psychological disorder at one time or another. Nearly half of adult Americans develop a diagnosable psychological disorder at some point in their lifetimes (Kessler, Berglund, et al., 2005, USDHHS, 2010; see ■ Figure 15.2). About one in four adult Americans have a diagnosed psychological disorder in any given year. If we also take into account the economic costs of diagnosing and treating these disorders, and the lost productivity and wages that result from them, it is fair to say that virtually everyone is affected by psychological disorders.

How Are Psychological Disorders Classified?

One reference book found on the shelves of virtually all mental health professionals and probably dog-eared from repeated use is the *Diagnostic and Statistical Manual of Mental Disorders,* or DSM—currently in a fourth, revised edition, the DSM-IV-TR (American Psychiatric Association, 2000). The manual contains descriptions and diagnostic criteria for every recognized psychological disorder, which in the manual are called *mental disorders.*

CONCEPT 15.9
The DSM, the diagnostic system used most widely for classifying psychological or mental disorders, consists of five dimensions or axes of evaluation.

The DSM classifies mental disorders on the basis of their distinctive features or symptoms. But the DSM goes beyond merely classifying various disorders. It represents a multiaxial system consisting of multiple axes or dimensions that help the examiner conduct a comprehensive evaluation of a person's mental health (see Table 15.1). Axis I and Axis II comprise the various diagnostic categories. The DSM classifies mental disorders into several major groupings, including anxiety disorders, mood disorders, eating disorders, and personality disorders.

Axis III lists general medical conditions and diseases, such as cancer and AIDS, that may affect a person's mental health, whereas Axis IV allows the examiner to note any psychosocial and environmental problems that impair the person's ability to function, such as stressful life events, homelessness, and lack of social support. Axis V allows the examiner to make a global assessment of the person's overall level of functioning in meeting life responsibilities.

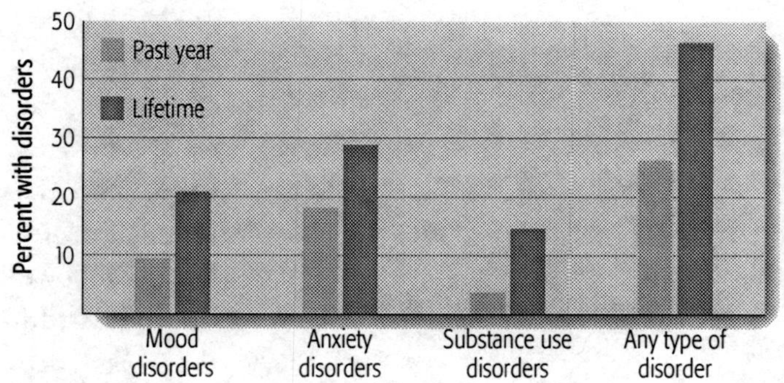

FIGURE 15.2 Prevalence of Psychological Disorders
Nearly half of adult Americans suffer from a diagnosable psychological disorder at some point in their lives. More than one in four are currently suffering from a psychological disorder or had a disorder during the past year.
Sources: Kessler, Berglund, et al., 2005; Kessler, Chiu, et al., 2005; based on data from National Comorbidity Survey Replication (NCS-R).

TABLE 15.1 The Multiaxial DSM System

Axis	Type of Information	Brief Description
Axis I	Clinical disorders	Mental disorders that impair functioning or cause distress, including anxiety disorders, mood disorders, dissociative and somatoform disorders, schizophrenia, eating disorders, sleep disorders, and disorders usually first diagnosed in infancy, childhood, or adolescence
	Other conditions that may be a focus of clinical attention	Problems that may warrant attention, but do not represent diagnosable mental disorders, such as academic, vocational, or social problems affecting daily functioning
Axis II	Personality disorders	A class of mental disorders characterized by excessively rigid, enduring, and maladaptive ways of relating to others and adjusting to external demands
	Mental retardation	A generalized delay or impairment in the development of intellectual and adaptive skills or abilities
Axis III	General medical conditions	Illnesses and other medical conditions that may be important to the understanding or treatment of the person's psychological disorder
Axis IV	Psychosocial and environmental problems	Problems in the person's social or physical environment that may affect the diagnosis, treatment, and outcome of mental disorders
Axis V	Global assessment of functioning	Overall judgment of the person's level of functioning in meeting the responsibilities of daily life

Source: Adapted from the DSM-IV-TR (American Psychiatric Association, 2000).

Though the DSM is the most widely used diagnostic system, questions remain about the reliability and validity of certain diagnostic classifications and the criteria used to make those diagnoses (e.g., L. A. Clark, 2007; D. Watson & Clark, 2006). Some mental health professionals challenge the system as based too heavily on the medical model, in which abnormal behaviors are assumed to be symptoms of underlying disorders or mental illnesses. Yet many clinicians find the system useful in providing specific criteria they can use to arrive at a diagnosis. Perhaps it is best to consider the DSM as a work in progress rather than a finished product. The development of the next revision of the DSM, the DSM-5, is presently underway and is expected to be published in 2013 (Holden, 2010).

The following modules describe the prominent symptoms or features of specific disorders within several of the major classes of psychological disorders, along with the rates of occurrence of these disorders and theories about their underlying causes. Before we turn to consider the individual disorders, let us note that comorbidity, or co-existence of two or more disorders at the same time, is a common occurrence among patients treated in mental health facilities. For example, people may suffer from both a depressive disorder and an anxiety disorder at the same time, or have an Axis II personality disorder together with an Axis I disorder.

See Concept Chart 15.1 for a listing of the major contemporary models of abnormal behavior.

CONCEPT CHART 15.1 Contemporary Models of Abnormal Behavior

	Model	Focus	Key Questions
Psychological Models	Medical model	Biological underpinnings of abnormal behavior	What roles do neurotransmitters, genetics, and brain abnormalities play in abnormal behavior?
	Psychodynamic model	Unconscious conflicts and motives underlying abnormal behavior	How do particular symptoms represent or symbolize unconscious conflicts? What are the childhood roots of a person's problem?
	Behavioral model	Learning experiences that shape the development of abnormal behavior	How are abnormal patterns of behavior learned? What role does the environment play in explaining abnormal behavior?
	Humanistic model	Roadblocks to self-awareness and self-acceptance	How do a person's emotional problems reflect a distorted self-image? What roadblocks did the person encounter in the path toward self-realization?
	Cognitive model	Faulty thinking underlying abnormal behavior	What styles of thinking characterize people with particular types of psychological disorders? What roles do personal beliefs, thoughts, and ways of interpreting events play in the development of abnormal behavior patterns?
	Sociocultural model	Social ills contributing to the development of abnormal behavior, such as poverty, racism, and prolonged unemployment; relationships between abnormal behavior and ethnicity, gender, culture, and socioeconomic level	What relationships exist between social class status and risks of psychological disorders? Are there gender or ethnic group differences in various disorders? How are these explained? What are the effects of stigmatization on people who are labeled mentally ill?
	Biopsychosocial model	Interactions of biological, psychological, and sociocultural factors in the development of abnormal behavior	How might genetic or other factors predispose individuals to psychological disorders in the face of life stress? How do biological, psychological, and sociocultural factors interact in the development of complex patterns of abnormal behavior?

15.1 MODULE REVIEW What Is Abnormal Behavior?

Recite It

What criteria are used to determine whether behavior is abnormal?

- There are several criteria, including unusualness, social deviance, emotional distress, maladaptive behavior, dangerousness, and faulty perceptions or interpretations of reality.

What are the major models of abnormal behavior?

- The major contemporary models are the medical model, the psychological model, the sociocultural model, and the biopsychosocial model.

What are psychological disorders?

- Varying in symptoms and severity, psychological disorders (also called *mental disorders*) are disturbances in behavior, thought processes, or emotions that are associated with significant personal distress or impaired functioning. About one person in two in the United States develops a diagnosable psychological disorder at some point in life.

- The DSM (*Diagnostic and Statistical Manual of Mental Disorders*) is the American Psychiatric Association's diagnostic manual for classifying mental disorders.

Recall It

1. List the six criteria for defining abnormal behavior discussed in the text.
2. _______ are distorted perceptions of reality; _______ are fixed but unfounded beliefs.
   a. Delusions; hallucinations.
   b. Dreams; fantasies.
   c. Fantasies; dreams.
   d. Hallucinations; delusions.
3. The explanation for abnormal behavior during much of the history of Western civilization was
   a. brain malfunction or chemical disorder.
   b. harsh and cruel treatment by close family members.
   c. possession by demons or supernatural forces.
   d. falsehoods or other retaliation spread by a sufferer's enemies.
4. Match the following psychological models for abnormal behavior with the appropriate descriptions: (a) psychodynamic; (b) behavioral; (c) humanistic; (d) cognitive.
   i. distorted self-image, loss of sense of true self.
   ii. faulty styles of thinking, exaggeration of negative aspects of events.
   iii. learned patterns of behavior.
   iv. unresolved unconscious conflicts dating from childhood.

Think About It

- Why is it important to consider the cultural context when determining abnormal behavior? Can you think of any examples of behaviors that are deemed acceptable in some cultures but not in others?

MODULE 15.2

Anxiety Disorders

- What are the major types of anxiety disorders?
- What causal factors are implicated in anxiety disorders?

Anxiety is a general emotional state of uneasiness or distress associated with worry or apprehension about future uncertainties. There is a lot to be anxious about—our health, our jobs, our families, climate change, the state of the nation and the world. Indeed, anxiety can be an adaptive response in some situations. It can motivate us to study before an exam and to seek regular medical checkups, for example. But when anxiety is excessive in a given situation or interferes with the ability to function, it can become abnormal. *Fear* is the term we use to describe anxiety experienced in specific situations, as when boarding an airplane or taking a final exam.

Types of Anxiety Disorders

CONCEPT 15.10
An anxiety disorder is a psychological disorder characterized by excessive or inappropriate anxiety reactions.

Anxiety disorders are among the most common psychological disorders, affecting about one in five adults—more than 40 million people—in the United States (Torpy, Burke, & Golub, 2011). Anxiety disorders, which in earlier conceptualizations were labeled *neuroses*, involve excessive or maladaptive forms of anxiety that interfere with a person's behavior or functioning. The four major types of anxiety disorders are phobias, panic disorder, generalized anxiety disorder, and obsessive-compulsive disorder. A fifth major type, posttraumatic stress disorder, is discussed in Chapter 12.

Phobias

Phobias are irrational or excessive fears of particular objects or situations. The DSM classifies three types of phobic disorders: *social phobia, specific phobia,* and *agoraphobia.* People with **social phobia** have intense fears of social interactions, such as meeting others, dating, or giving a speech or presentation in class. People with **specific phobias** have excessive fears of specific situations or objects, such as animals, insects, heights (**acrophobia**), or enclosed spaces (**claustrophobia**). People with **agoraphobia** fear venturing into open places or going out in public.

People with claustrophobia may refuse to use elevators despite the inconvenience of climbing many flights of stairs several times a day. Those with agoraphobia may become literally housebound, unable even to go to the local store to buy a quart of milk. Those with social phobia may have difficulty maintaining a normal social life. People with phobias usually recognize that their fears are irrational or excessive, but they still avoid the objects or situations they fear.

What do you fear? Where do we draw the line between ordinary fear and phobias?

phobias Irrational or excessive fears of particular objects or situations.

social phobia A type of anxiety disorder involving excessive fear of social situations.

specific phobia Phobic reactions involving specific situations or objects.

acrophobia Excessive fear of heights.

claustrophobia Excessive fear of enclosed spaces.

agoraphobia Excessive irrational fear of being in public places.

panic disorder A type of anxiety disorder involving repeated episodes of sheer terror called panic attacks.

Panic Disorder

People with **panic disorder** experience sudden episodes of sheer terror called *panic attacks.* Panic attacks are characterized by intense physical symptoms: profuse sweating, nausea, numbness or tingling, flushes or chills, trembling, chest pain, shortness of breath, and pounding of the heart. These symptoms may lead people to think they are having a heart attack, or "going crazy," or losing control. A specific attack can last anywhere from a few minutes to more than an hour. A young man who suffered a series of panic attacks recounted what it felt like: "All of a sudden, I felt a tremendous wave of fear for no reason at all. My heart was pounding, my chest hurt, and it was getting harder to breathe. I thought I was going to die."

Panic attacks initially seem to come "out of the blue." Yet they can later become connected with the situations in which they occur, such as shopping in a crowded department store or riding on a train. Agoraphobia, too, sometimes develops in people with panic disorder when they begin avoiding public places out of fear of having panic attacks while away from the security of their homes (Grant, Hasin, Stinson, et al., 2006; White et al., 2006).

CONCEPT 15.11

The major types of anxiety disorders are phobias, panic disorder, generalized anxiety disorder, obsessive-compulsive disorder, and posttraumatic stress disorder.

Generalized Anxiety Disorder

People with **generalized anxiety disorder (GAD)** experience persistent anxiety that is not tied to any particular object or situation. In such cases the anxiety has a "free-floating" quality, as it seems to travel with the person from place to place. A key feature of GAD is excessive worry (Newman & Llera, 2011). Recent advances in neuroscience show stronger connections between the brain's thinking center, the prefrontal cortex, and its fear-triggering center, the amygdala, in people with GAD (Etkin et al., 2009). This suggests that in people with GAD, the brain may be predisposed to respond to fear signals from the amygdala by generating cognitive coping responses that take the form of worrying.

generalized anxiety disorder (GAD) A type of anxiety disorder involving persistent and generalized anxiety and worry.

People with GAD tend to worry over just about everything. They are seldom if ever free of worry. Other characteristics of GAD include shakiness, inability to relax, fidgeting, and feelings of dread and foreboding.

Obsessive-Compulsive Disorder

obsessive-compulsive disorder (OCD) A type of anxiety disorder involving the repeated occurrence of obsessions and/or compulsions.

Have you ever had a thought you couldn't shake off? Have you ever felt compelled to repeat the same behavior again and again? People with **obsessive-compulsive disorder (OCD)** experience persistent obsessions and/or compulsions. Obsessions are nagging, intrusive thoughts the person feels unable to control. Compulsions are repetitive behaviors or rituals the person feels compelled to perform again and again. Some people with this disorder are obsessed with the thought that germs contaminate their skin, spending hours each day compulsively washing their hands or showering. Others repeatedly perform checking rituals upon leaving the house to ensure the doors and windows are securely locked and gas jets turned off.

Causes of Anxiety Disorders

Nearly everyone experiences anxiety from time to time, but only some people develop anxiety disorders. Although we don't know precisely why these disorders develop, we can identify biological and psychological factors that contribute to them and surmise that an interaction of these factors affects their development.

Biological Factors

Investigators are beginning to make headway in understanding the biological underpinnings of anxiety. Results of twin studies and adoptee studies point to an important role for genetic factors in many types of anxiety disorders (Kendler, 2005b; Leckman & Kim, 2006; Smoller et al., 2008; Taylor, Jang, & Asmundson, 2010).

Genetic factors may affect underlying brain circuitry involved in the body's response to threatening stimuli. Recent evidence indicates that the amygdala, the fear-generating part of the limbic system in the brain, may be overreactive in people with anxiety disorders, making them especially anxious or jumpy in response to threatening cues (Beesdo et al., 2009; Nitschke et al., 2009; Stein & Stein, 2008). In panic disorder, biochemical changes in the brain may trigger an internal alarm system that induces feelings of panic in susceptible people (Katon, 2006). In OCD, the brain may be continually sending messages that something is terribly wrong and requires immediate attention—a situation that may lead to obsessive worrisome thoughts. The compulsions we see in OCD may be linked to abnormalities or disturbances in brain circuits that ordinarily curb repetitive, ritualistic behaviors (Harrison et al., 2009; Monk et al., 2008).

CONCEPT 15.12
Both biological factors, such as disturbed neurotransmitter functioning, and psychological factors, such as learning experiences, are implicated as causal influences in anxiety disorders.

Psychological Factors

Some phobias may be learned through classical conditioning in which a previously neutral or benign stimulus becomes paired with an aversive stimulus (Field, 2006; J. J. Kim & Jung, 2006). A person bitten by a dog during childhood may come to develop a fear of dogs or other animals; a person trapped in an elevator for hours may acquire a fear of elevators or of confinement in other enclosed spaces. The previously neutral stimulus is the conditioned stimulus (CS), the aversive stimulus is the unconditioned stimulus (US), and the acquired fear response is the conditioned response (CR).

Operant conditioning may help account for avoidance behavior. Avoidance of the phobic object or situation (as when a person with an elevator phobia takes the stairs instead of the elevator) is negatively reinforced by relief from anxiety. However, though avoiding a fearful situation may offer short-term relief from anxiety, it doesn't help people overcome their fears. (The principle of negative reinforcement is discussed in Chapter 5.)

Negative reinforcement (relief from anxiety) may also contribute to obsessive-compulsive disorder. People with OCD often become trapped in a repetitive cycle of obsessive thinking and compulsive behavior. Obsessive thoughts ("My hands are covered with germs") trigger anxiety, which, in turn, is partially relieved through performance of a compulsive ritual (repetitive handwashing). In effect, the solution to obsessive thinking (performing the compulsive ritual) becomes the problem. However, since relief from the obsessive thoughts is at best incomplete or fleeting, the thoughts soon return, prompting yet more compulsive behavior—and so on in a continuing cycle.

The cognitive model of panic disorder focuses on the interrelationship between biological and psychological factors. In this view, panic disorder arises from the misinterpretation of relatively minor changes in bodily sensations (e.g., sudden light-headedness or dizziness) as signs of an imminent catastrophe, such as an impending heart attack or loss of control (Teachman, Marker & Clerkin, 2010). Misinterpretation of bodily sensations—a cognitive factor—leads to anxiety (e.g., sweating, racing heart), which, like a series of falling dominoes, leads to yet more catastrophic thinking and then to more anxiety symptoms, and so on in a vicious cycle that quickly can spiral into a full-blown panic attack (see ■ Figure 15.3). Internal cues (dizziness, heart palpitations) and external cues (boarding a crowded elevator) that were linked with previous panic attacks may become conditioned stimuli (CS's) that elicit anxiety or panicky symptoms when the person encounters them.

Cognitive factors come into play in other anxiety disorders as well. Social phobias, for example, can arise from excessive concerns about social embarrassment or being judged negatively by others (Schmidt et al., 2009). In sum, anxiety disorders involve a complex interplay of biological and psychological factors.

Before going further, you may wish to review the summary of anxiety disorders presented in Concept Chart 15.2.

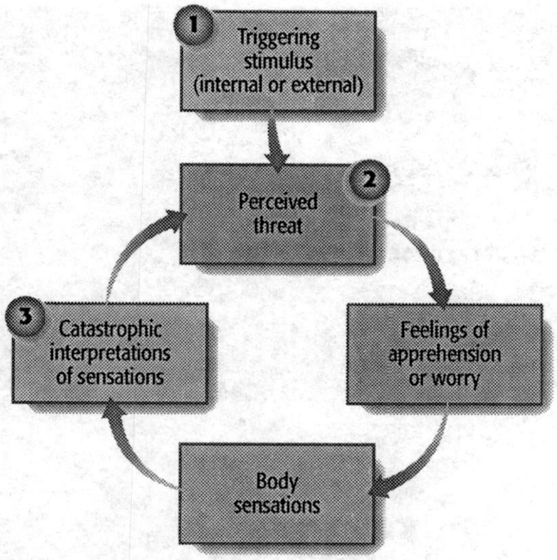

FIGURE 15.3 Cognitive Model of Panic Cognitive theorists conceptualize panic disorder in terms of a panic cycle that involves an interaction of physiological and cognitive factors. (1) A triggering stimulus or cue, such as sudden light-headedness or boarding a crowded train, sets the cycle in motion. (2) The stimulus is perceived as threatening, leading to feelings of apprehension (anxiety and worry), which in turn lead to bodily sensations associated with anxiety, such as a tightening feeling in the chest. (3) These sensations are misconstrued as signs of an impending catastrophe, such as a heart attack. Catastrophic misinterpretations reinforce perceptions of threat, leading to more anxiety and yet more catastrophic misinterpretations, resulting in a vicious cycle that can quickly spiral into a full-fledged panic attack.

Source: Adapted from D. M. Clark, 1986.

CONCEPT CHART 15.2 Anxiety Disorders

Type of Disorder	Lifetime Prevalence in Population (%) (approx.)	Symptoms	Associated Features
Agoraphobia	For panic disorder with agoraphobia: 1%. For agoraphobia without panic disorder: 0.17%	Fear and avoidance of public places	Generally develops secondarily to panic disorder, as the person attempts to avoid situations in which attacks have occurred or in which help might be unavailable in the event of an attack.
Panic disorder	5%	Repeated panic attacks accompanied by persistent concern about future attacks	Panic attacks have strong physiological symptoms; beginning attacks occur without warning; may be accompanied by agoraphobia.

(*Continued*)

CONCEPT CHART 15.2 (Continued)

Type of Disorder	Lifetime Prevalence in Population (%) (approx.)	Symptoms	Associated Features
Generalized anxiety disorder	4%	Persistent, excessive levels of anxiety and worry	Anxiety is "free-floating" and not tied to particular objects or situations.
Specific phobia	9%	Fear and avoidance of a specific object or situation	Avoidance of the phobic object or situation is negatively reinforced by relief from anxiety.
Social phobia	5%	Fear and avoidance of social situations or performance situations	Underlying fear of rejection, humiliation, or embarrassment in social situations.
Obsessive-compulsive disorder	2–3%	Recurrent obsessions and/or compulsions	A repetitive cycle may ensue in which obsessive thoughts engender anxiety that, in turn, is partially relieved (negatively reinforced) by performing the compulsive ritual.

Note: Another type of anxiety disorder, posttraumatic stress disorder, is discussed in Chapter 12.
Sources: American Psychiatric Association, 2000; Conway et al., 2006; Grant, Hasin, Blanco, et al., 2006; Grant, Hasin, Stinson, et al., 2006.

15.2 MODULE REVIEW Anxiety Disorders

Recite It

What are the major types of anxiety disorders?

- Anxiety disorders are characterized by excessive or inappropriate anxiety reactions. The major types are phobic disorders (phobias), panic disorder, generalized anxiety disorder, obsessive-compulsive disorder, and posttraumatic stress disorder.

What causal factors are implicated in anxiety disorders?

- These include psychological factors, such as prior learning experiences and thinking patterns, and biological factors, such as genetic influences and underlying brain abnormalities.

Recall It

1. The earlier diagnostic term for anxiety disorders was
   a. frenzy.
   b. phobias.
   c. neuroses.
   d. psychoses.
2. Acrophobia and claustrophobia are two examples of ______ phobia.
3. Match the following anxiety disorders with the appropriate descriptions: (a) phobic disorder; (b) panic disorder; (c) generalized anxiety disorder; (d) obsessive-compulsive disorder.
   i. sudden onset; intense fear and dread
   ii. excessive, persistent worry
   iii. irrational, extreme fear of a particular object or situation
   iv. repeated, uncontrollable thoughts or behaviors

Think About It

- Apply learning principles to explain the development of certain types of anxiety disorders, including specific fears and obsessive-compulsive disorder.
- Is anxiety normal? What might evolutionary psychologists say about the survival value of anxiety? When does a normal response become abnormal?
- Have you ever "panicked"? Do you think you suffered a true panic attack? Why or why not?

Dissociative and Somatoform Disorders

MODULE 15.3

- What are some types of dissociative disorders?
- What causal factors are implicated in dissociative disorders?
- What are some types of somatoform disorders?
- What causal factors are implicated in somatoform disorders?

Among the most puzzling psychological disorders are the **dissociative disorders** and **somatoform disorders**. People with dissociative disorders may show multiple personalities, have amnesia that cannot be explained by a physical cause, or even assume a completely new self-identity. The dissociative disorders are fodder for countless television melodramas and soap operas. In real life they are relatively uncommon, even rare. Indeed, there is controversy among professionals as to whether multiple personality (now called *dissociative identity disorder*) even exists.

dissociative disorders A class of psychological disorders involving changes in consciousness, memory, or self-identity.

somatoform disorders A class of psychological disorders involving physical ailments or complaints that cannot be explained by organic causes.

Although they have different symptoms or characteristics, dissociative disorders and somatoform disorders are often grouped together because of the classic view that they involve psychological defenses against anxiety. Here we examine several of these mystifying disorders, beginning with dissociative disorders.

Dissociative Disorders

Dissociative disorders involve problems with memory or changes in consciousness or self-identity that fracture the continuity or wholeness of an individual's personality. Normally we know who we are and where we've been. We may forget how we spent last weekend, but we don't suddenly lose the capacity to remember whole chunks of our lives or abruptly shift back and forth between very different personalities. Dissociative disorders, however, affect the ability to maintain a cohesive sense of self or unity of consciousness, resulting in unusual, even bizarre behavior. Here we consider two major types of dissociative disorders: dissociative identity disorder and dissociative amnesia.

Dissociative Identity Disorder

In **dissociative identity disorder (DID)**, commonly called *multiple personality* or *split personality*, two or more distinct personalities exist within the same individual. Each of these alternate personalities (also called *alter personalities*) has its own distinctive traits, manner of speech, and memories. In some cases, there is a core personality that is generally known to the outside world and hidden alternate personalities that reveal themselves at certain times or in certain situations. Sometimes the alternate personalities compete for control. The alter personalities may lack any memory of events experienced by other alter personalities or even any knowledge of the existence of alters (Huntjens et al., 2005). The alter personalities may represent different genders, ages, sexual orientations, or conflicting sexual urges. One personality may be morally

CONCEPT 15.13
In dissociative identity disorder, the personality is split into two or more distinct alternate personalities residing within the same individual.

dissociative identity disorder (DID) A type of dissociative disorder characterized by the appearance of multiple personalities in the same individual.

© Denver Police Department/MCT/Newscom

"Does anybody know me?" Diagnosed with a type of amnesia linked to severe stress, 40-year-old Jeffrey Ingram searched for his identity for more than a month, eventually winding up in Denver asking people there for help. Family members in Washington state recognized him when he appeared on a TV news program. When he returned home, he still had no memory, but reported that it felt like home to him. His mother reported he had had a similar incident in the past and had never fully regained his memory.

upright, another licentious; one heterosexual, another homosexual. The dominant personality may be unaware of the existence of these alternates, though it may vaguely recognize that something is wrong. Women with the disorder tend to have 15 or more identities, whereas men average about eight (American Psychiatric Association, 2000).

Dissociative Amnesia

People with *dissociative amnesia* (first discussed in Chapter 6) experience a loss of memory for information about themselves or their life experiences. The absence of any physical cause for their amnesia (a blow to the head, a neurological condition, or drug or alcohol abuse) suggests that the disorder is psychological in nature. The information lost to memory is usually a traumatic or stressful experience that the person may be motivated to forget. A soldier returning from the battlefield or a survivor of a serious accident may have no memory of the battle or the accident. These memories sometimes return, perhaps gradually in bits and pieces, or suddenly all at once. Much less common, except in the imaginations of soap opera writers, is *generalized amnesia* in which people forget their entire lives. They forget who they are, what they do for a living, and to whom they are married or related. More commonly, however, amnesia involves loss of memory for specific events or periods of time linked to traumatic experiences.

Causes of Dissociative Disorders

CONCEPT 15.14

In dissociative amnesia, people experience a loss of memory for personal information that cannot be explained by a blow to the head or some other physical cause.

CONCEPT 15.15

The formation of alternate personalities in dissociative identity disorder may represent a psychological defense against trauma or unbearable abuse.

Dissociative amnesia may represent an attempt to disconnect or dissociate one's conscious state from awareness of traumatic experiences or other sources of psychological pain or conflict. Dissociative symptoms may protect the self from anxiety that might occur if these memories and experiences became fully conscious. Similarly, individuals with dissociative identity disorder may split off parts of themselves from consciousness. Severe, repetitive physical or sexual abuse in childhood, usually beginning before the age of five, figures prominently in case histories of people with DID (Dale et al., 2009; Foote et al., 2005; Spiegel, 2006).

Many people with DID were highly imaginative as children, often creating games of make-believe. Perhaps in these early years, they used their fertile imaginations to split off parts of themselves in order to distance themselves psychologically from the abusive situations they faced. Over time, these parts may have become consolidated as distinct personalities. In adulthood, they may continue to use their alternate personalities to block out memories of childhood trauma and of the conflicting emotions that these experiences evoked. The alternate personalities themselves may represent a psychological means of expressing the deep-seated hatred and anger they are unable to integrate within their primary personalities.

Some psychologists believe that DID is a rare but genuine disorder that arises in a few individuals as a way of coping with terrible physical and sexual abuse occurring during childhood. But there are dissenting voices who doubt the existence of DID, ascribing the behavior to a form of attention-seeking role playing (Lilienfeld et al., 1999; Spanos, 1994). In this view, troubled individuals with a history of abuse might inadvertently be cued by their therapists to enact alternate personalities that help them make sense of the confusing and conflicting emotions they experience, eventually identifying so closely with the role they are performing that it becomes a reality to them. This description is not meant to suggest that people with DID are faking their alternate selves, any more than we would suggest that you are faking your behavior whenever you adopt the role of a student, spouse, or worker. Whatever the underlying process in

DID may be, authorities agree that people with the disorder need help dealing with the underlying traumas they have experienced and working through the often conflicting emotions and impulses these brutal experiences evoked.

Somatoform Disorders

People with somatoform disorders may have physical (somatic) symptoms or complaints that cannot be explained medically (De Gucht & Maes, 2006). Or they may believe they are gravely ill, despite reassurances from their doctors to the contrary. One type of somatoform disorder, **conversion disorder**, figured prominently in the history of psychology. It was conversion disorder—called *hysteria* or *hysterical neurosis* at the time—that attracted a young physician named Sigmund Freud to study the psychological bases of abnormal behavior.

conversion disorder A type of somatoform disorder characterized by a change in or loss of a physical function that cannot be explained by medical causes.

Conversion Disorder

In conversion disorder, a person suffers a loss of physical function, such as loss of movement in a limb (hysterical paralysis), loss of vision (hysterical blindness), or loss of feeling in a hand or arm (anesthesia). Yet there is no physical cause that can account for these symptoms. Conversion disorder or hysteria is uncommon, even rare, today, but appears to have been more frequent in Freud's day. In Freud's time, hysteria was considered a female problem; however, experience with male soldiers in combat who experience a loss of function (blindness or paralysis) that cannot be explained medically has taught us that the disorder can affect both men and women.

CONCEPT 15.16
People with conversion disorder experience a loss of a physical function that defies any medical explanation.

If you suddenly lost feeling in your hand, you would probably be quite upset. But curiously, some people with conversion symptoms appear indifferent to their situations—a phenomenon called *la belle indifférence* ("beautiful indifference") (Stone et al., 2006). This lack of concern suggests that the symptoms may be of psychological value to the individual, perhaps representing a way of avoiding anxiety associated with painful or stressful conflicts or situations. Let us note, however, that hysteria and conversion symptoms are sometimes incorrectly diagnosed in people who turn out to have bona fide medical conditions (Stone et al., 2006).

Hypochondriasis

People with **hypochondriasis** are preoccupied with the idea that something is terribly wrong with their health. They have physical complaints or symptoms that they take to be signs of underlying serious illness, such as cancer or heart disease (Abramowitz, Olatunji, & Deacon, 2008; Barsky & Ahern, 2004). Although they may receive assurances from their doctors that they are not gravely ill, they believe their doctors are wrong or may have missed something. They may not realize how their anxiety contributes to their physical complaints—for example, by leading to sweating, dizziness, rapid heartbeat, and other signs of sympathetic nervous system arousal.

hypochondriasis A somatoform disorder in which there is excessive concern that one's physical complaints are signs of underlying serious illness.

CONCEPT 15.17
People with hypochondriasis mistakenly believe that their minor physical complaints are signs of serious underlying illness.

Causes of Somatoform Disorders

To Freud, the hysterical symptom (loss of movement in a limb) is the outward sign of an unconscious dynamic struggle between opposing motives. On one side are sexual or aggressive impulses from the id seeking expression. On the other side are forces of restraint, marshaled by the ego. The ego seeks to protect the self from the flood of anxiety that would occur if these unacceptable impulses were to enter the conscious mind. It uses defense mechanisms, especially repression, to keep these impulses buried in the unconscious. But the leftover energy from these impulses becomes "strangulated," or cut off from its source, and converted into physical symptoms like paralysis or blindness. One problem with Freud's view, however, is that it doesn't explain how conversion occurs—that is, how leftover sexual or aggressive energy becomes channeled into particular physical symptoms.

Freud also believed that the symptom itself both symbolizes the underlying struggle and serves an underlying purpose. For instance, hysterical paralysis of the arm prevents the person from using the arm to act out an unacceptable sexual (e.g., masturbatory) or aggressive (e.g., murderous) impulse. The symptom has yet another function, called **secondary gain**. It can prevent the individual from having to confront stressful or conflict-laden situations. If Freud was correct in his belief that conversion symptoms serve hidden purposes, it may explain why many people with conversion appear strangely unconcerned or untroubled about their symptoms.

secondary gain Reward value of having a psychological or physical symptom, such as release from ordinary responsibilities.

Learning theorists, too, recognize that conversion symptoms may serve a secondary role of helping the individual avoid painful or anxiety-evoking situations. (The bomber pilot who develops night blindness may avoid the danger of night missions, for example.)

People with conversion disorders may be reinforced by others for adopting a "sick role," drawing sympathy and support from them and being relieved of ordinary work or household responsibilities. This is not meant to suggest that these individuals are consciously faking their symptoms. They may be deceiving themselves, but they do not appear to be deliberately attempting to deceive others.

Cognitive theorists focus on cognitive biases associated with somatoform disorders (e.g., Abramowitz & Braddock, 2008; Cororve & Gleaves, 2001). People with hypochondriasis, for example, may "make mountains out of molehills" by misinterpreting bodily sensations as signs of underlying catastrophic causes (cancer, heart disease, etc.). In this respect they may resemble people with panic disorder, who tend to misinterpret their bodily sensations as signs of an impending catastrophe.

CONCEPT 15.18
Though Freudian and learning theory explanations of somatoform disorders differ, they both focus on the anxiety-reducing role of somatoform symptoms.

Dissociative and somatoform disorders are summarized in Concept Chart 15.3.

CONCEPT CHART 15.3 Dissociative and Somatoform Disorders

	Type of Disorder	Lifetime Prevalence	Features	Comments
Dissociative Disorders	Dissociative identity disorder	Rare	An individual exhibits multiple personalities	May represent a type of psychological defense against trauma or unbearable abuse from childhood
	Dissociative amnesia	Rare	Memory loss that cannot be explained as the result of head trauma or other physical cause	Typically involves loss of memories associated with specific traumatic events
Somatoform Disorders	Conversion disorder	Rare	A loss or change of physical function that cannot be explained by a medical condition	May have been much more common in Freud's day than in our own
	Hypochondriasis	Unknown	Preoccupation with fear of having a serious illness	May have features similar to those of anxiety disorders

15.3 MODULE REVIEW Dissociative and Somatoform Disorders

Recite It

What are some types of dissociative disorders?

➤ Dissociative disorders involve disturbances in memory, consciousness, or identity that affect the ability to maintain an integrated sense of self. These disorders include dissociative identity disorder and dissociative amnesia.

What causal factors are implicated in dissociative disorders?

➤ Exposure to childhood abuse figures prominently in the backgrounds of people with dissociative identity disorder, leading theorists to believe that the disorder may represent a psychological defense that protects the self from troubling memories or feelings. Avoidance of painful or troubling memories is also implicated in dissociative amnesia.

What are some types of somatoform disorders?

➤ People with somatoform disorders either exaggerate the meaning of physical complaints or have physical complaints that cannot be accounted for by organic causes. Two major somatoform disorders are conversion disorder and hypochondriasis.

What causal factors are implicated in somatoform disorders?

➤ Freud believed that conversion disorder represents the transformation of inner psychological conflicts into physical symptoms. Learning theorists focus on the anxiety-reducing roles of somatoform symptoms, whereas cognitive theorists focus on underlying cognitive biases.

Recall It

1. In ________ identity disorder, a person exhibits multiple personalities.

2. Dissociative amnesia

a. involves a clear physical underlying cause.
b. does not seem to be related to a particular traumatic event.
c. involves extensive and permanent memory loss.
d. has no apparent neurological cause.

3. What are some common characteristics of individuals with dissociative identity disorder?

a. Their early childhood experiences included severe and prolonged abuse.
b. They tended to be highly imaginative as youngsters.
c. Their alternate personalities have very different and distinctive traits.
d. All of the above are correct.

4. Conversion disorder (is or is not?) caused by underlying physical problems.

Think About It

➤ Do you believe that dissociative identity disorder is a true disorder? Or do you think it is an exaggerated form of role playing? Explain your answer.

Mood Disorders

MODULE 15.4

- What are some types of mood disorders?
- What causal factors are implicated in mood disorders?
- Who is at risk for suicide?
- Why do people commit suicide?

Most people have occasional ups and downs, but those with **mood disorders** have more severe or persistent disturbances of mood. These mood disturbances limit their ability to function and may even sap their will to live. It is normal to feel sad when unfortunate events occur and to be uplifted when fortune shines on us. But people with mood disorders often feel down when things are going right. Or they remain down following a disappointing experience long after others would have snapped back. Some people with mood disorders have exaggerated mood swings. Their moods may alternate between dizzying heights and abysmal depths.

mood disorders A class of psychological disorders involving disturbances in mood states, such as major depression and bipolar disorder.

Types of Mood Disorders

CONCEPT 15.19
Two of the major types of mood disorders are major depressive disorder and bipolar disorder.

Here we focus on the two general types of mood disorders: depressive disorders and bipolar disorders.

Depressive Disorders

major depression The most common type of depressive disorder, characterized by periods of downcast mood, feelings of worthlessness, and loss of interest in pleasurable activities.

In **major depression** (also called *major depressive disorder*) people typically feel sad or "down in the dumps" and may experience feelings of worthlessness, changes in sleep or appetite, lethargy, and loss of interest in pleasurable activities. Major depression occurs in episodes that can last months or even a year or longer, especially when untreated, and has a high rate of recurrence (Reifler, 2006). Unfortunately, despite the availability of safe and effective treatments, about half of Americans suffering from major depression do not receive professional care (González et al., 2010). Latinos and African Americans are less likely than other ethnic groups to receive care.

CONCEPT 15.20
In major depression, there is a dampening of mood to the point that the person may become unmotivated, lose interest in pleasurable activities, develop feelings of worthlessness, or attempt suicide.

People with major depression may feel they cannot get out of bed to face the day. They may be unable to make decisions, even about small things, such as what to have for dinner. They may be unable to concentrate. They may feel helpless or say that they don't "care" anymore. They may have recurrent thoughts of suicide or attempt suicide.

About one in six adult Americans (about 16.5%) suffer from major depression at some point in their lives (Conway et al., 2006). This prevalence rate masks an underlying gender difference, as women are nearly twice as likely as men to develop major depression (about 12 percent for men vs. 21 percent for women) (Hyde, Mezulis, & Abramson, 2008). Hormonal or other biological differences between men and women may contribute to the gender gap in depression, but we also need to consider the greater stress burdens that many women carry. Women are more likely to encounter significant stressors such as physical and sexual abuse, poverty, single parenthood, and sexism. Even when both spouses work, women typically shoulder the bulk of household and childcare chores. Women also are more likely than men to provide support for aging family members or those coping with disabling medical conditions.

© Kzenon/Shutterstock.com

Many psychologists believe that the stressors faced by many women today contribute to their increased risk of depression.

Differences in how men and women cope with emotional distress also come into play. Psychologist Janet Nolen-Hoeksema suggests that men are more likely to distract themselves from their emotional problems, such as by going to a favorite hangout to get their mind off their problems, whereas women tend to ruminate or brood about them (Nolen-Hoeksema, 2008; Nolen-Hoeksema, Morrow, & Frederickson, 1993; Nolen-Hoeksema, Wisco, & Lyubomirsky, 2008). Distraction may temporarily blunt emotional responses, but ruminating or dwelling on one's problems can amplify emotional distress, setting the stage for depression (Koster et al., 2011; Loa, Ho, & Hollon, 2008). Then again, turning to alcohol to blunt negative feelings can lead to other problems, such as substance abuse. To raise your awareness of the signs of depression, see the next *Try This Out* section.

seasonal affective disorder (SAD) A type of major depressive disorder that involves a recurring pattern of winter depressions followed by elevations of mood in spring and summer.

dysthymic disorder A type of mood disorder characterized by mild, chronic depression.

Seasonal affective disorder (SAD) is a type of major depression in which people experience a repeated pattern of severe depression in the fall and winter, followed by elevated moods during the spring and summer. SAD has been treated successfully with exposure to bright artificial light as a kind of substitute for natural sunlight.

Dysthymic disorder (also called dysthymia) is a relatively mild but chronic form of depression. Although the symptoms of dysthymic disorder are less severe than those of major depressive disorder, people with dysthymia tend to be dispirited for long periods of time, typically for five years or longer. About 6 percent of people in the general population develop dysthymic disorder at some point in their lives (American Psychiatric Association, 2000). Like major depression, dysthymic disorder is more common in women.

Bipolar Disorders

People with **bipolar disorder** (formerly called *manic-depression*) experience mood swings that shift between periods of euphoric or elevated mood, or **manic episodes** (mania), and periods of depression. They may have intervening periods of normal moods. During a manic episode, people may feel unusually euphoric or become extremely restless, excited, talkative, and argumentative. They may spend lavishly, drive recklessly, destroy property, or become involved in sexual escapades that appear out of character with their usual personalities. Even those who care about such individuals may find them abrasive. Other symptoms include *pressured speech* (talking too rapidly), *flight of ideas* (jumping from topic to topic), and an inflated sense of self-worth (grandiosity). During manic episodes, people may become delusional (hold false beliefs) or undertake tasks well beyond their abilities, such as attempting to write a symphony or devising a plan to solve world hunger. They may show poor judgment, such as by giving away their life savings. They may have boundless energy and little need for sleep. Then, when their moods sink into depression, they feel a sense of hopelessness and despair. Some people with bipolar disorder commit suicide on the way down, apparently wanting to avoid the depths of depression they have come to expect. About 1 percent of the U.S. population develop bipolar disorder at some point in their lives (Frye, 2011; Merikangas & Pato, 2009).

bipolar disorder A type of mood disorder characterized by mood swings from extreme elation (mania) to severe depression.

manic episodes Periods of mania, or unusually elevated mood and extreme restlessness.

Cyclothymic disorder (the word cyclothymia is derived from the Greek roots *kyklos*, meaning "circle," and *thymos*, or "spirit") is a bipolar mood disorder with milder mood swings than those seen in bipolar disorder. Among the general population, an estimated four to 10 persons in 1,000 (0.4 to 1 percent) develop the disorder at some point in their lives. It usually develops during late adolescence or early adulthood and lasts for years (American Psychiatric Association, 2000). Unlike unipolar depression, which is more common in women, bipolar disorder and cyclothymic disorder affect about as many men as women.

cyclothymic disorder A mood disorder characterized by a recurring pattern of relatively mild mood swings.

Causes of Mood Disorders

Like anxiety disorders, mood disorders are believed to have both psychological and biological causes.

Psychological Factors

Several psychological models of depression have been proposed. The classic psychodynamic view espoused by Freud (1917/1957) and his followers held that depression involves anger turned inward against the self. By contrast, the behavioral model focuses on the role of reinforcement. In the behavioral view, depression results from a loss or shortfall in reinforcement, especially reinforcement one receives from others in the way of attention, approval, and emotional support. Loss of reinforcement may occur for many reasons. The death of a spouse or close friend removes that person as a potential source of reinforcement. A young person attending college away from home may feel cut off from high school friends and have difficulty forming new social networks that might provide opportunities for reinforcement. The more depressed people become,

CONCEPT 15.21
People with bipolar disorder experience mood swings between extreme elation and severe depression.

CONCEPT 15.22

Psychological causes implicated in mood disorders include changes in reinforcement levels, distorted ways of thinking, depressive attributional style, and stress.

→ Concept Link

Cognitive therapy is a form of psychotherapy that focuses on helping distressed individuals recognize and correct distorted or self-defeating ways of thinking. See Module 16.2.

the less motivated they may be to make the effort to find new sources of reinforcement. In some cases, reinforcement opportunities may abound, but the person lacks effective social skills to establish and maintain relationships that lead to reinforcing interactions.

Cognitive theorists believe that the ways in which people interpret events contributes to emotional disorders such as depression. One of the most influential cognitive theorists is the psychiatrist Aaron Beck, the developer of cognitive therapy (discussed in Chapter 16). Beck and his colleagues (A. T. Beck, Freeman, et al., 2003; A. T. Beck, Rush, et al., 1979) believe that people who have a negatively biased or distorted way of thinking are prone to depression when they encounter disappointing or unfortunate life events. Distorted, negative thinking becomes a kind of mental filter that puts a slant on how people interpret their life experiences, especially disappointments such as getting a bad grade or losing a job. A minor disappointment is blown out of proportion—experienced more as a crushing blow than as a mild setback. Beck and his colleagues have identified a number of these types of faulty thinking patterns, called *cognitive distortions*, that they believe increase vulnerability to depression following negative life events. The more these distorted thinking patterns come to dominate a person's thinking, the greater the person's vulnerability to depression is likely to be. Table 15.2 lists cognitive distortions most closely associated with depression.

TABLE 15.2 Cognitive Distortions Linked to Depression

Type of Cognitive Distortion	Description	Example
All-or-nothing thinking	Viewing events as either all good or all bad	Do you view a relationship that ended as a total failure, or are you able to see some benefits in the relationship? Do you consider any less-than-perfect performance as a total failure?
Misplaced blame	Blaming or criticizing yourself for disappointments or setbacks while ignoring external circumstances	Do you automatically assume when things don't go as planned that it's your fault?
Misfortune telling	Tendency to think that one disappointment will inevitably lead to another	If you get a rejection letter from a job you applied for, do you assume that all the other applications you sent will meet the same fate?
Negative focusing	Focusing your attention only on the negative aspects of your experiences	When you get a job evaluation, do you overlook the praise and focus only on the criticism?
Dismissing the positives	Snatching defeat from the jaws of victory by trivializing or denying your accomplishments; minimizing your strengths or assets	When someone compliments you, do you find some way of dismissing it by saying something like "It's no big deal" or "Anyone could have done it"?
Jumping to conclusions	Drawing a conclusion that is not supported by the facts at hand	Do you usually or always expect the worst to happen?
Catastrophizing	Exaggerating the importance of negative events or personal flaws (making mountains out of molehills)	Do you react to a disappointing grade on a particular examination as though your whole life is ruined?
Emotion-based reasoning	Reasoning based on your emotions rather than on a clear-headed evaluation of the available evidence	Do you think that things are really hopeless because it feels that way?

TABLE 15.2 Continued

Type of Cognitive Distortion	Description	Example
Shouldisms	Placing unrealistic demands on yourself that you *should* or *must* accomplish certain tasks or reach certain goals	Do you feel that you *should* be further along in your life than you are now? Do you feel you *must* ace this course or else? (Not that it wouldn't be desirable to ace the course, but is it really the case that you *must*?)
Name calling	Attaching negative labels to yourself or others as a way of explaining your own or others' behavior	Do you label yourself *lazy* or *stupid* when you fall short of reaching your goals?
Mistaken responsibility	Assuming that you are the cause of other people's problems	Do you automatically assume that your partner is depressed or upset because of something you said or did (or didn't say or do)?

Source: Adapted from Burns, 1980; Nevid & Rathus, 2007; Nevid, Rathus, & Greene, 2011.

Another psychological model of depression, the **learned helplessness model**, suggests that people become depressed when they come to believe that they are helpless to control the reinforcements in their lives. This concept, developed by psychologist Martin Seligman (1973, 1975), is based on experiments showing that laboratory animals who were exposed to inescapable shocks failed to learn to avoid the shocks when the conditions changed in such a way as to make escape possible. The animals seemed to give up trying, becoming lethargic and unmotivated—behaviors that resembled depression in people. Seligman

learned helplessness model The view that depression results from the perception of a lack of control over the reinforcements in one's life that may result from exposure to uncontrollable negative events.

TRY THIS OUT Self-Screening for Depression

Many people suffer depression in silence out of ignorance or shame. They believe that depression is not a real problem because it doesn't show up on an X-ray or CT scan. They think it's just all in their heads. Or they may feel that asking for help is an admission of weakness and that they should bear it on their own.

The following test is widely used to help people become more aware of the warning signs of depression. The test is not meant to provide a diagnosis of a depressive disorder; rather, its purpose is to raise awareness of problems that should be evaluated further by a mental health professional.

		YES	NO
1.	I feel downhearted, blue, and sad.	☐	☐
2.	I don't enjoy the things that I used to.	☐	☐
3.	I feel that others would be better off if I were dead.	☐	☐
4.	I feel that I am not useful or needed.	☐	☐
5.	I notice that I am losing weight.	☐	☐
6.	I have trouble sleeping through the night.	☐	☐
7.	I am restless and can't keep still.	☐	☐
8.	My mind isn't as clear as it used to be.	☐	☐
9.	I get tired for no reason.	☐	☐
10.	I feel hopeless about the future.	☐	☐

Source: Adapted from J. E. Brody, 1992.
Scoring key: If you answered "yes" to at least five of the statements, including either the first or second one, and if these complaints have persisted for at least 2 weeks, then professional help is strongly recommended. If you answered "yes" to the third statement, we suggest that you immediately consult a health professional. Contact your college or university counseling or health center, or talk to your instructor.

proposed that exposure to uncontrollable situations may induce a learned helplessness effect in humans, leading to depression. In essence, when repeated efforts prove futile, the person may eventually give up trying and sink into a state of depression.

Seligman and his colleagues later revised the helplessness model to include cognitive factors (Abramson, Seligman, & Teasdale, 1978). In particular, they borrowed from social psychology the concept of **attributional style**, which refers to the characteristic ways in which individuals explain the causes of events that happen to them. The reformulated helplessness model proposes that attributions vary along three dimensions: *internal versus external, global versus specific,* and *stable versus unstable.*

attributional style A person's characteristic way of explaining outcomes of events in his or her life.

Consider a negative event, such as receiving a poor grade on a math test. An internal attribution fixes blame on oneself ("I screwed up"), whereas an external attribution places responsibility on external factors ("The exam was too hard"). A global attribution treats the cause as reflecting generally on one's underlying personality or abilities ("I'm really not very good at math"), whereas a specific attribution knocks it down to size ("I tripped up on the equations"). A stable attribution treats the cause as more or less permanent ("I'll never be able to learn this stuff"), whereas an unstable attribution views it as changeable ("Next time I'll be better prepared"). People who tend to explain disappointments and failures by attributing them to *internal, global,* and *stable* causes have a **depressive attributional style** that predisposes them to depression when they face such negative events, according to Seligman and his colleagues.

depressive attributional style A characteristic way of explaining negative events in terms of internal, stable, and global causes.

Depressed people are often plagued by negative, distorted thinking, just as the cognitive theorists propose (e.g., Koster et al., 2011; Riso et al., 2003). But questions remain about whether negative, distorted thinking cause depression or are merely effects of depression. We don't yet have a final answer, but it is probable that the causal linkages work both ways—that thinking styles affect moods and moods affect thinking styles.

© Con Tanasiuk/Design Pics/Corbis

"Why do I always screw up?" Cognitive theorists believe that the way in which we interpret negative events has an important bearing on our proneness to depression in the face of disappointing life experiences

Stress also contributes to depression (Kendler & Gardner, 2010; Liu & Alloy, 2010). Stressful life events, which include the following, put people at increased risk of developing major depression: loss of a loved one, prolonged unemployment, serious physical illness, marital problems or separation, divorce, pressures at work, and financial hardship (e.g., Kõlves, Ide, & De Leo, 2010; Monroe & Reid, 2009; Muscatell et al., 2009).

Biological Factors

Depression is linked to irregularities in the activity of neurotransmitters in the brain (Carver, Johnson, & Joormann, 2008). Drugs that help relieve depression, called *antidepressants,* increase levels of neurotransmitters in the brain, especially *serotonin* and *norepinephrine* (Richardson-Jones et al., 2010). For example, the widely used antidepressants Prozac and Zoloft increase serotonin levels by interfering with reabsorption (reuptake) of this mood-regulating chemical by transmitting neurons in the brain.

Although depression appears to be linked to neurotransmitter activity, it cannot be explained simply by a deficiency of neurotransmitters. More complex processes are at work, perhaps involving an oversensitivity of receptors on receiving neurons where neurotransmitters dock or an imbalance in the numbers of these receptors (either too many or too few) (Cipriani et al., 2009; Oquendo et al., 2007). Antidepressants may help relieve depression by either altering the number of receptors or the sensitivity of receptors to particular neurotransmitters, a process that takes time to unfold. Not surprisingly, then, it usually takes several weeks before the therapeutic effects of antidepressants kick in. Other biological factors are likely involved in mood disorders, such as abnormalities in parts of the brain involved in regulating mood states (e.g., Ellison-Wright & Bullmore, 2010; Kieseppä et al., 2010; Lorenzetti, Allen, Whittle, & Yücel, 2010).

CONCEPT 15.23

Biological causes implicated in mood disorders include disturbances in neurotransmitter functioning in the brain and genetic influences.

→ Concept Link

Psychiatric drugs are chemicals used to normalize neurotransmitter functioning in the brain. See Module 16.3.

CONCEPT CHART 15.4 Mood Disorders

© Atalanta07/BigStockPhoto.com

Type of Disorder	Lifetime Prevalence (%) (approx.)	Symptoms	Associated Features
Major depression	12% in men, 21% in women, 16.5% overall	Downcast mood, feelings of hopelessness and worthlessness, changes in sleep patterns or appetite, loss of motivation, loss of pleasure in pleasant activities	Following a depressive episode, the person may return to his or her usual state of functioning, but recurrences are common.
Bipolar disorder (with manic episodes)	Approx. 1%	Periods of shifting moods between mania and depression, perhaps with intervening periods of normal mood	Manic episodes are characterized by pressured speech, flight of ideas, poor judgment, hyperactivity, and inflated mood and sense of self.

Sources: American Psychiatric Association, 2000; Conway et al., 2006; Frye, 2011.

Evidence from twin studies points to genetics playing an important role in mood disorders, especially bipolar disorder (e.g., Edvardsen et al., 2009; Hyman, 2011). Researchers are now zeroing in on genes that increase susceptibility to mood disorders, especially genes involved in regulating neurotransmitter functioning (Barnett & Smoller, 2009; Duric et al., 2010; Karg et al., 2011). However, biological causes of mood disorders do not entirely account for their development. Psychological or environmental factors also play a role. All things considered, mood disorders are complex phenomena involving a number of factors interacting in complex ways we are still trying to understand (see Concept Chart 15.4).

© Burstein Collection/Corbis

"Starry, Starry Night." The artist Vincent van Gogh suffered from terrible bouts of depression that eventually led to his suicide at the age of 37 from a self-inflicted gunshot wound. In this melancholy self-portrait, his eyes and facial countenance reveal the despair with which he struggled through much of his life.

Suicide

What would you say is the second leading cause of death among college students, after motor vehicle accidents? AIDS? Drugs? The answer is suicide (Rawe & Kingsbury, 2006). More than 1,000 college students end their own lives each year in the United States. Despite these tragic statistics, the rate of suicide is actually highest among older adults, especially older white males (Bruce et al., 2004; Joe et al., 2006). About one million adult Americans (about one in 200) made a suicide attempt during the previous year and more than 36,000 "succeeded" in taking their own lives (Centers for Disease Control and Prevention, 2011; USDHSS, 2010).

Who Is Most at Risk?

Suicide cuts across every stratum of our society. Yet certain factors are related to an increased risk:

- *Age.* Though much attention is focused on adolescent suicides, suicide rates are greater among older adults, especially white males age 75 and above (Joe et al., 2006; Szanto et al., 2003) (see ■ Figure 15.4).

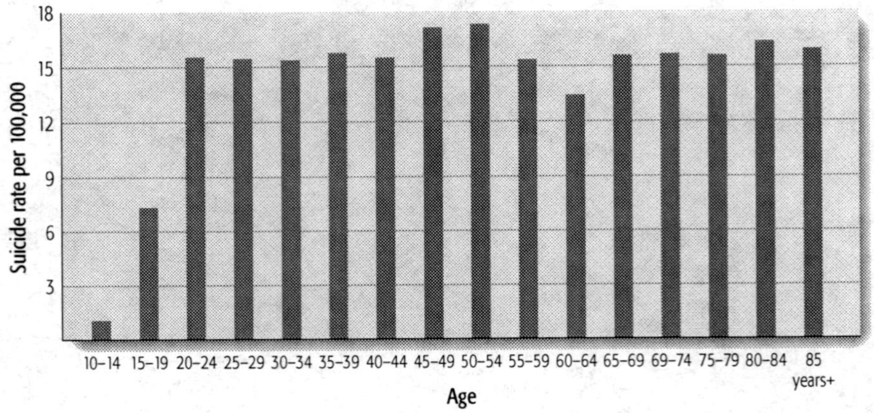

FIGURE 15.4 Suicide Rates in Relation to Age As you can see, suicide rates increase in middle and late adulthood.
Source: Centers for Disease Control and Prevention, 2009d.

- *Gender.* More women attempt suicide, but about four times as many men complete the act (Houry, 2004; M. Miller, Azrael, & Hemenway, 2004). The primary reason is that men typically use more lethal means, especially firearms. Women are more apt to use pills, poison, or other methods that may be less lethal.
- *Race/Ethnicity.* White (European) Americans and Native Americans are more likely to take their own lives than are African Americans and Hispanic Americans (Centers for Disease Control and Prevention, 2009e; Joe et al., 2006). The highest suicide rates in the United States are reported among Native American youth and young adults (Meyers, 2007). The widespread sense of hopelessness among Native Americans arising from lack of opportunities and segregation from the dominant culture helps set the stage for alcohol and drug abuse, which is often a prelude to depression and suicide.

Causal Factors in Suicide

Suicide is closely linked to major depression and bipolar disorder, and to the deep feelings of hopelessness and helplessness that often accompany these mood disorders (Holma et al., 2010; Johnson et al., 2011; Witte et al., 2009). Like depression, suicide is also linked to biochemical factors, including irregularities in how serotonin is used in neural networks in the brain, and to genetic factors, possibly involving genes involved in regulating serotonin functioning (Crowell et al., 2008; Must et al., 2009). Serotonin helps curb excess nervous system activity. Irregularities in the workings of serotonin in the brain may cause a **disinhibition effect**—the removal of inhibitions that might otherwise constrain impulsive behavior, including impulses to commit suicide.

disinhibition effect The removal of normal restraints or inhibitions that serve to keep impulsive behavior in check.

Drug and alcohol dependence is an important risk factor in suicide. Use of alcohol may lead people to act impulsively, with the result that suicidal thoughts are carried over into action. Other psychological disorders, such as schizophrenia and severe anxiety disorders, as well as prolonged unemployment and serious medical illness, also figure into many suicides (e.g., Ben-Ya'acov & Amir, 2004; McGirr et al., 2006; Oquendo et al., 2003).

Suicide expert Edwin Shneidman (1996) points to the lack of coping responses in people who attempt or commit suicide. They may see no other way of resolving their problems or ending unendurable emotional or physical pain. Suicide is also linked to *exit events,* or losses of supportive persons through death, divorce or separation, or family separations. Exit events leave vulnerable people feeling stripped of crucial sources of social support. Myths about suicide abound, as you can see in Table 15.3.

CONCEPT 15.24
Suicide is closely linked to depression and, especially, to feelings of utter hopelessness.

TABLE 15.3 Myths About Suicide

Myth	Fact
People who threaten suicide are only seeking attention.	People who commit suicide often give clear clues concerning their intentions, such as disposing of their possessions or suddenly making arrangements for a burial plot.
A person must be insane to attempt suicide.	Most people who attempt suicide may feel hopeless, but they are not insane (i.e., out of touch with reality).
Talking about suicide with a depressed person may prompt the person to attempt it.	An open discussion of suicide with a depressed person does not prompt the person to attempt it. In fact, extracting a promise that the person will not attempt suicide before calling or visiting a mental health worker may well *prevent* a suicide.
People who attempt suicide and fail aren't serious about killing themselves.	Most people who commit suicide have made previous unsuccessful attempts.
If someone threatens suicide, it is best to ignore it so as not to encourage repeated threats.	Though some people do manipulate others by making idle threats, it is prudent to treat every suicidal threat as genuine and to take appropriate action.

15.4 MODULE REVIEW Mood Disorders

Recite It

What are some types of mood disorders?

➤ Mood disorders are disturbances in mood that are unusually severe or prolonged. Two of the major types of mood disorders are major depression and bipolar disorder.

What causal factors are implicated in mood disorders?

➤ Suspected causes include genetic factors, heredity, biochemical imbalances in neurotransmitter activity in the brain, self-directed anger, changes in reinforcement patterns, and dysfunctional thinking.

Who is at risk for suicide?

➤ Groups at highest risk for suicide include older white men and Native Americans. Men are more likely than women to "succeed" at suicide attempts because they tend to use more lethal means.

Why do people commit suicide?

➤ Most suicides result from deep feelings of hopelessness and despair.

Recall It

1. The type of mood disorders characterized by severe mood swings is called ________.
2. Which factors may help explain the greater prevalence of depression in women than men? (Identify at least one factor.)
3. The widely used antidepressant Prozac boosts levels of the neurotransmitter _____ by interfering with the _____ of this chemical by the transmitting neuron.
4. In Seligman's early research on learned _____, animals who were earlier exposed to inescapable shock failed to try to escape shock when it became possible to do so.

Think About It

➤ Which, if any, of the errors in thinking and negative attributions described in the text describe how you typically explain disappointing events in your life? How do your thinking patterns affect your moods? Your motivation? Your feelings about yourself? How might you change your ways of thinking about negative experiences in the future?

➤ How do bipolar disorders differ from the ordinary "ups and downs" of everyday life?

MODULE 15.5

Schizophrenia

- What are some common symptoms of schizophrenia?
- What are three specific types of schizophrenia?
- What causal factors are implicated in schizophrenia?
- What is the diathesis-stress model of schizophrenia?

THE BRAIN LOVES A PUZZLE

As you read ahead, use the information in the text to solve the following puzzle:

Genetics plays an important role in schizophrenia, but why have scientists never been able to find any particular gene that causes schizophrenia and probably never will?

schizophrenia A severe and chronic psychological disorder characterized by disturbances in thinking, perception, emotions, and behavior.

CONCEPT 15.25
Schizophrenia is a puzzling and disabling disorder that fills the mind with distorted perceptions, false ideas, and loosely connected thoughts.

Schizophrenia is the disorder that most closely corresponds to popular concepts of insanity, madness, or lunacy. The word *schizophrenia* comes from Greek roots meaning "split brain." In cases of schizophrenia, the mind is stripped of the intimate connections among thoughts, perceptions, and feelings. Individuals with this disorder may giggle in the face of disaster, hear or see things that aren't physically present, or maintain beliefs that are firmly held but patently false.

Schizophrenia affects about one adult in 100, which amounts to more than 2 million people in the United States (Centers for Disease Control and Prevention, 2009d). Nearly 1 million people are treated for schizophrenia each year, with about one-third receiving hospitalized care.

Schizophrenia is characterized by bizarre, irrational behavior, as in the case of Claire, who was convinced she was protecting the populace from demons. The disorder is somewhat more common in men than in women (Tandon, Keshavan, & Nasrallah, 2008). Men also tend to develop schizophrenia somewhat earlier than women and to experience a more severe form of the disorder. Schizophrenia follows a lifelong course and typically develops in late adolescence or early adulthood, at about the time that people are beginning to make their way in the world (Tandon, Nasrallah, & Keshavan, 2009; Walker et al., 2010). It occurs about as frequently in other cultures as in our own, although the particular symptoms may vary from culture to culture.

A young woman who is battling schizophrenia speaks about the time the voices entered her head, uninvited. She was spending her last year at summer camp before her senior year in high school when the Voices came:

SLICE OF LIFE *"You must die!" Other Voices joined in. "You must die! You will die!"*

At first I didn't realize where I was. Was I at the lake? Was I asleep? Was I awake? Then I snapped back to the present. I was here at camp, alone... But as soon as I realized that I was in my bunk, and awake—and that my roommate was still sleeping peacefully—I knew I had to run. I had to get away from these terrible, evil Voices....

Since that time, I have never been completely free of those Voices. At the beginning of that summer, I felt well, a happy, healthy girl—I thought—with a normal head and heart. By summer's end, I was sick, without any clear idea of what was happening to me or why. And as the Voices evolved into a full-scale illness, one that I only later learned was called schizophrenia, it snatched from me my tranquility, sometimes my self-possession, and very nearly my life.

...During the years when my friends were marrying, having their babies and moving into the houses I once dreamed of living in, I have been behind locked doors, battling the Voices who took over my life without even asking my permission.

(From Schiller & Bennett, 1994)

Symptoms of Schizophrenia

Schizophrenia is a **psychotic disorder**—that is, a disorder in which an individual confuses reality with fantasy, seeing or hearing things that aren't there (hallucinations) or holding fixed but patently false beliefs (delusions). *Hallucinations* are perceptions that occur in the absence of external stimuli. They may affect different senses. Auditory hallucinations ("hearing voices") are most common. Visual hallucinations (seeing things that are not there) and other sensory hallucinations (sensing odors or having taste sensations without any physical stimulus) are much less common. *Delusions* may represent many different themes, but the most common are themes of persecution, such as the belief that demons or "the Devil" are trying to harm the person.

psychotic disorder A psychological disorder, such as schizophrenia, characterized by a "break" with reality.

People with schizophrenia may exhibit bizarre behavior, incoherent speech, and illogical thinking. They may not know the time of day, nor the day or the year. Or where they are. Or *who* they are. Note that not all of these symptoms must be present for a diagnosis of schizophrenia.

Many people with schizophrenia exhibit a **thought disorder**, a breakdown in the logical structure of thinking and speech characterized by *loose associations* between expressed ideas. Normally, our thoughts are tightly connected or associated; one thought follows another in a logical sequence. But in schizophrenia, there may be an absence of logical connections between thoughts. The ideas expressed are strung loosely together or jumbled in such a way that the listener is unable to follow the person's train of thought. In severe cases, speech becomes completely incoherent or incomprehensible. The person may begin to form meaningless words or mindless rhymes.

thought disorder A breakdown in the logical structure of thought and speech, revealed in the form of a loosening of associations.

The more flagrant signs of schizophrenia, such as hallucinations, delusions, bizarre behavior, and thought disorder, are behavioral excesses classified as **positive symptoms**. Yet people with schizophrenia may also have behavioral deficits or **negative symptoms**, such as extreme withdrawal or social isolation, apathy, and lack of emotional expressiveness. People with schizophrenia may feel strong emotions, but they tend to show less facial expression of emotions than other people (Kring & Caponigro, 2010). Although positive symptoms may fade after an acute episode, negative symptoms are typically more enduring, making it difficult for the person to meet the demands of daily life.

positive symptoms Symptoms of schizophrenia involving behavioral excesses, such as hallucinations and delusions.

negative symptoms Behavioral deficits associated with schizophrenia, such as withdrawal and apathy.

Types of Schizophrenia

Several types of schizophrenia have been identified on the basis of their distinctive symptoms or characteristics. Here we discuss the three major subtypes.

Disorganized Type

The **disorganized type** of schizophrenia is characterized by confused behavior, incoherent speech, vivid and frequent hallucinations, inappropriate emotions or lack of emotional expression, and disorganized delusions that often have religious or sexual themes. People with this form of schizophrenia may giggle inappropriately, act silly, or talk nonsensically. They tend to neglect their personal hygiene, may have difficulty controlling their bladders or bowels, and have significant problems relating to others.

disorganized type A subtype of schizophrenia characterized by confused behavior and disorganized delusions, among other features.

Catatonic Type

People with the **catatonic type** of schizophrenia show bizarre movements, postures, or grimaces. Some persist in a motionless or stuporous state for hours and then abruptly switch into a highly agitated state. Others display highly unusual body movements or

catatonic type A subtype of schizophrenia characterized by bizarre movements, postures, or grimaces.

waxy flexibility A feature of catatonic schizophrenia in which people rigidly maintain the body position or posture in which they were placed by others.

© Grunnitus Studio/Photo Researchers, Inc.

The body position of some persons with catatonic schizophrenia can be molded by others into unusual postures that they then hold for hours at a time.

paranoid type The most common subtype of schizophrenia, characterized by the appearance of delusional thinking accompanied by frequent auditory hallucinations.

CONCEPT 15.26

There are three distinct types of schizophrenia: the disorganized, catatonic, and paranoid types.

CONCEPT 15.27

Though the causes of schizophrenia remain a mystery, scientists suspect that stressful life experiences and a combination of biological factors, including heredity, biochemical imbalances, and structural abnormalities in the brain, contribute to its development.

positions, such as holding a fixed posture for hours. They may be mute or uncommunicative during these episodes, showing no evidence of responding to the environment. Later, however, they may report that they heard what others were saying at the time. Less commonly they may show **waxy flexibility**, a behavior pattern in which their body position can be molded by others (like wax) into unusual, even uncomfortable positions that they then hold for hours at a time. The catatonic type is a rare form of schizophrenia.

Paranoid Type

The most common form of schizophrenia, the **paranoid type**, is characterized by delusions that are accompanied by frequent auditory hallucinations. The delusions often have themes of grandeur (e.g., believing that one is Jesus or has superhuman abilities), persecution (e.g., believing that one is being persecuted by demons or by the Mafia), or jealousy (e.g., believing that one's spouse or lover is unfaithful despite an absence of evidence).

Causes of Schizophrenia

Schizophrenia remains a puzzling—indeed, mystifying—disorder. Though we have not solved the puzzle, researchers have made substantial progress in putting many of the pieces into place.

Genetic Factors

A large and growing body of evidence indicates that heredity plays an important role in schizophrenia (e.g., Bassett et al., 2010; Hyman, 2011; Moreno-De-Luca et al., 2010). The closer the genetic relationship a person shares with someone who has schizophrenia, the greater the likelihood the person will also have or develop schizophrenia. Consistent with a genetic contribution, monozygotic or identical twins are more likely to share the disorder in common (a concordance rate of about 45 to 50 percent) than are dizygotic or fraternal twins (about a 17 percent concordance rate).

We also know that adopted children whose biological parents had schizophrenia are more likely to develop schizophrenia themselves than are adopted children whose parents did not have the disorder (Tienari et al., 2003). All in all, investigators believe that multiple genes are responsible for creating a genetic predisposition or susceptibility to schizophrenia (e.g., International Schizophrenia Consortium et al., 2009; Walker et al., 2010). Scientists are presently trying to pinpoint these genes (e.g., Ohi et al., 2010; Wratten et al., 2009; Vacic et al., 2011).

Though heredity clearly plays an important role in schizophrenia, genes do not tell the whole story. Consider that only about 13 percent of people who have a parent with schizophrenia develop the disorder. Consider, too, that if one identical twin has schizophrenia, the other twin, though genetically identical, has a 45 to 50 percent chance of having the disorder as well. If only genetics were involved, we would expect 100 percent concordance among monozygotic twins. In short, genetic vulnerability is not genetic inevitability. People at high genetic risk for schizophrenia may only go on to develop the disorder if they experience significant life stressors (Tienari et al., 2004). Some stressors have a biological basis, such as early brain trauma. But others may be environmental or psychological in origin, such as child abuse or neglect or persistent and intense family conflict.

Biochemical Imbalances

Researchers suspect that overactivity or a kind of "overdrive" of dopamine transmission in the brain plays an important role in the development of schizophrenia (Grace et al., 2010). Dopamine is suspected because *antipsychotic drugs* that help control hallucinations and delusions reduce dopamine activity by blocking dopamine receptors in the brain (Abbott, 2010; Nasrallah et al., 2009). We still have much to learn about the complex biological underpinnings of schizophrenia. Although dopamine transmission is implicated in the disorder, the brains of schizophrenia patients do not appear to produce too much dopamine. Rather, they may have an excess number of dopamine receptors (E. Walker et al., 2004). Or perhaps their dopamine receptors are overly sensitive to the chemical. Hopefully, future research will clarify these underlying mechanisms.

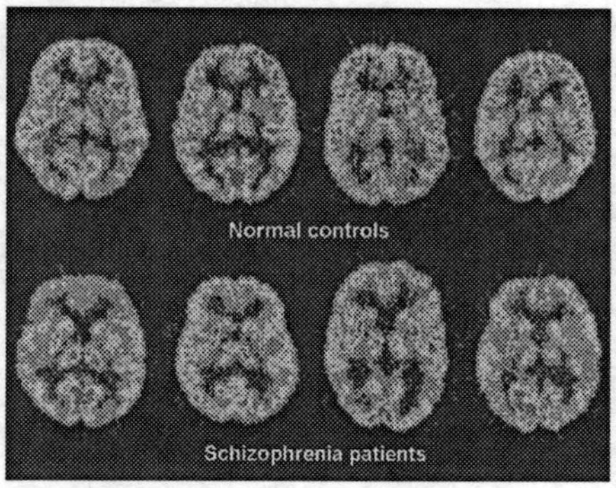

Courtesy of Monte S. Buchsbaum, M.D./Mount Sinai School of Medicine, New York, NY

FIGURE 15.5 Brain Images of Schizophrenia Patients Versus Normal Controls
Here we see PET scan images of metabolic activity in the brains of schizophrenia patients versus normal controls. Note the lower level of activity in the frontal lobes of the brains of schizophrenia patients (denoted by less yellow and red in the upper part of the brain images in the lower row). This evidence supports the belief that schizophrenia involves abnormalities in the frontal lobes of the brain, and more specifically, in the prefrontal cortex.

Brain Abnormalities

Brain-imaging studies show brain abnormalities in many schizophrenia patients (e.g., Karlsgodt, Sun, & Cannon, 2010; Moriya et al., 2010; Schultz et al., 2010) (see ■ Figure 15.5). For example, schizophrenia patients often show enlarged ventricles, which are hollow spaces in the brain associated with loss of brain tissue (Kempton et al., 2010). We don't yet know what causes this loss or shrinkage of brain tissue, but the process may begin during prenatal periods when brain structures are first forming or during early childhood when they are developing further (King, St-Hilaire, & Heidkamp, 2010; Walker et al., 2010).

The areas of the brain that seem to be most affected are the prefrontal cortex and the limbic system (e.g., Dobbs, 2010; Ellison-Wright & Bullmore, 2010; Minzenberg et al., 2009). The prefrontal cortex is the part of the brain responsible for keeping information in mind (i.e., working memory), organizing thoughts and behavior, and formulating and carrying out goals and plans—the very functions that are often disrupted in schizophrenia. The limbic system plays key roles in forming new memories and processing emotions—functions which are also found to be disturbed in schizophrenia patients.

CONCEPT 15.28
The diathesis-stress model holds that schizophrenia results from the interaction of a genetic predisposition and stressful life events or trauma.

Psychosocial Influences

Psychosocial influences, such as significant life stress, may interact with a genetic vulnerability in the development of schizophrenia (Byrne et al., 2003). The belief that schizophrenia results from an interaction of a *diathesis* (a vulnerability factor such as a genetic predisposition) and stressful life experiences is represented in the form of the *diathesis-stress model* (Zubin & Spring, 1977) (refer to Figure 15.1). Sources of stress

TRY THIS OUT Exploring the Human Side of Abnormal Behavior

SLICE OF LIFE During my college years I volunteered in a state psychiatric hospital. I had been interested in psychology and was eager to learn first-hand about the types of disorders I read about in textbooks. I spent several hours a week at a nearby state hospital just talking to a resident who seemed to enjoy talking to me. He was a man in his early thirties who had been diagnosed with schizophrenia and had lived in a locked, inpatient unit for about three years. We sometimes played cards or watched TV, but mostly we just talked. The most important lesson I learned is that the individuals I met were human beings with unique personalities, experiences, interests, and needs—not simply "cases" I had read about in a textbook. If you would like to explore the human side of abnormal behavior, a good place to start would be the volunteer office at a local psychiatric facility. Keep a journal of your experiences and evaluate how your experiences either confirm or disconfirm your prior expectations about people with psychological disorders.

CONCEPT CHART 15.5 Schizophrenia

© Tramper/Shutterstock.com

What It Is	Symptoms	Probable Causes
A chronic psychotic disorder affecting about 1 percent of the population	Delusions, hallucinations, bizarre behavior, incoherent or loosely connected speech, inappropriate emotions or lack of emotional expression, social withdrawal, and apathy	An interaction of a genetic predisposition and life stress; underlying brain abnormalities

may include biological factors, such as prenatal or early brain trauma; psychosocial factors, such as being raised in an abusive family environment or experiencing disturbed patterns of communication in the family; and negative life events, such as the loss of a loved one or failure in school. Though we lack a precise understanding of how these factors fit together, one possibility is that genetic and stressful influences combine to produce abnormalities in the brain that interfere with thinking, memory, and perceptual processes, leading eventually to the welter of confusing thoughts and perceptions that afflict people with schizophrenia.

The symptoms and suspected causes of schizophrenia are summarized in Concept Chart 15.5.

15.5 MODULE REVIEW Schizophrenia

Recite It

What are common symptoms of schizophrenia?

➤ Schizophrenia is a psychotic disorder, meaning that it is characterized by a break with reality. Gross confusion, delusions, and hallucinations are common symptoms in schizophrenia patients.

What are three specific types of schizophrenia?

➤ Three specific types of schizophrenia are the disorganized type, the catatonic type, and, most common, the paranoid type.

What causal factors are implicated in schizophrenia?

➤ Precise causes are unknown, but suspected causes include biological factors such as a genetic predisposition, disturbed neurotransmitter activity in the brain, brain abnormalities, and stress.

What is the diathesis-stress model of schizophrenia?

➤ The diathesis-stress model refers to the belief that schizophrenia arises from an interaction of a genetic predisposition and stressful life experiences.

Recall It

1. More (males or females?) are affected by schizophrenia.

2. The subtype of schizophrenia characterized by confused behavior and incoherent speech is ________.

3. About how many people will develop schizophrenia if they have an identical (MZ) twin with this disorder?

a. 10 to 15 percent

b. 20 to 25 percent

c. 45 to 50 percent

d. more than 50 percent

4. Scientists believe that abnormalities involving the neurotransmitter ________ are closely linked to the development of schizophrenia.

a. serotonin

b. dopamine

c. epinephrine

d. acetylcholine

Think About It

➤ In what sense does schizophrenia correspond to the Greek roots from which it derives its name?

➤ Have you known anyone who was diagnosed with schizophrenia? How did the disorder affect the person's behavior and ability to function? How is the person functioning today?

Personality Disorders

MODULE 15.6

- What are personality disorders?
- What characteristics are associated with antisocial personality disorder?
- What causal factors are implicated in antisocial personality disorder?
- What characteristics are associated with borderline personality disorder?
- What causal factors are implicated in borderline personality disorder?

People with **personality disorders** show excessively rigid and maladaptive patterns of behavior that make it difficult for them to adjust to the demands they face in their daily lives and to form long-term, satisfying relationships. These maladaptive behaviors reflect extreme variations on underlying personality traits, such as excessive emotionality, undue suspiciousness, and excessive dependency. Personality disorders become so deeply ingrained that they are often highly resistant to change.

There are many different types of personality disorders. Our focus here is on two of the most widely studied types, *antisocial personality disorder* and *borderline personality disorder* (see Concept Chart 15.6).

personality disorders A class of psychological disorders characterized by rigid personality traits that impair people's ability to adjust to the demands they face in the environment and that interfere with their relationships with others.

antisocial personality disorder (APD or ASPD) A type of personality disorder characterized by callous attitudes toward others and by antisocial and irresponsible behavior.

Antisocial Personality Disorder

Antisocial personality disorder (APD or ASPD) is characterized by a flagrant disregard for the rules of society and a lack of concern for the welfare of others. People with antisocial personalities (sometimes called *psychopaths* or *sociopaths*) tend to act on impulse—doing what they want when they want it (Swann et al., 2009). They are typically irresponsible, treat others callously, and take advantage of others for their own needs or personal gain. They may engage in criminal or other antisocial behaviors. They also tend to lack remorse for their misdeeds or mistreatment of others and appear to be untroubled by anxiety or undeterred from antisocial behavior by the threat of punishment or even by punishment itself (R. B. Goldstein et al., 2006; Kiehl et al., 2006). Some people with antisocial personality disorder engage in criminal behavior, but most are law abiding. They may display a high level of intelligence and a superficial charm that attracts others. The disorder is found more commonly in men (see Concept Chart 15.6).

© AP Photo/David J. Phillip

Serial killer Henry Lee Lucas, a career drifter, fit the stereotype of the psychopath. Not all psychopaths break the law; nor are they psychotic. They are typically irresponsible, callous in their treatment of others, and lacking remorse for their misdeeds.

CONCEPT CHART 15.6 Overview of Two Major Types of Personality Disorders

Disorder	Lifetime Prevalence in Population (approx.)	Symptoms	Associated Features
Antisocial personality disorder	3%–6% in men, 1% in women	A pattern of antisocial and irresponsible behavior; callous treatment of others; lack of remorse for wrongdoing	Lacks empathy for others and may take advantage of people or fail to meet their commitments
Borderline personality disorder	2%–6%	Unstable moods and stormy relationships with others; unstable self-image; lack of impulse control	May engage in self-destructive behaviors, such as cutting themselves

Sources: American Psychiatric Association, 2000; Gunderson, 2011; Kernberg & Michels, 2009; Kessler et al., 1994.

Causal Factors in Antisocial Personality Disorder

CONCEPT 15.29
People with personality disorders exhibit excessively rigid patterns of behavior that ultimately make it difficult for them to relate to others or meet the demands that are placed upon them.

Evidence points to a role for biological factors in the development of antisocial personality disorder, including genetic factors and brain abnormalities (Gabbard, 2005; Raine, 2008). Brain-imaging studies also link antisocial personality disorder to abnormalities in the prefrontal cortex, the part of the brain responsible for regulating emotions, controlling impulsive aggressive behavior, and weighing the consequences of one's actions (Kiehl et al., 2006; Raine, 2008). Still, we should note that we don't know how many people with antisocial personality disorder actually have underlying brain abnormalities.

People with antisocial personalities may have a genetic predisposition to crave higher levels of stimulation to maintain an optimum level of arousal. They may become quickly bored with routine activities and turn to more dangerous activities that provide immediate thrills, such as alcohol and drug use, racing cars or motorcycles, high-stakes gambling, or risky sexual encounters.

CONCEPT 15.30
Features of antisocial personality disorder include showing a blatant disregard for social rules and regulations, antisocial behavior, impulsivity, irresponsibility, lack of remorse for wrongdoing, and a tendency to take advantage of others.

What role does environment play? Many people with APD were raised in families characterized by lack of parental warmth and nurturing, as well as by parental neglect, abuse, rejection, and use of harsh punishment (J. G. Johnson et al., 2006; Lobbestael & Arntz, 2009). A history of emotional or physical abuse in childhood may lead to failure to internalize a sense of empathy or concern for the welfare of others and lead to a failure to develop a moral compass or sense of conscience. The lack of empathy about the feelings or needs of others may explain why people with APD act in a callous way toward others. In all likelihood, both genetic and environmental factors contribute to the development of APD, as is the case with many forms of abnormal behavior (Gabbard, 2005).

Borderline Personality Disorder

borderline personality disorder A type of personality disorder characterized by unstable emotions and self-image.

People with **borderline personality disorder** (BPD) tend to have stormy relationships with others, show dramatic mood swings, have difficulty controlling their emotions, and have an unstable self-image (Ferraz et al., 2009; Gratz et al., 2010; Gunderson, 2011; Kernberg & Michels, 2009; Selby & Joiner, 2009). Their turbulent moods can range from anger and irritability to depression and anxiety. They may feel a deep emptiness inside that reflects their unstable self-image and lack of a clear identity or direction in life. Fear of abandonment and difficulty being alone lead them to become excessively clinging or dependent on others, which may push away the very people on whom they depend. They have difficulty controlling their impulses and regulating their emotions, especially anger, and may act out by hurting or mutilating themselves, such as by cutting themselves. Impulsive behaviors may take the form of spending sprees, gambling and drug binges, unsafe sexual activity, reckless driving, binge eating, and shoplifting.

CONCEPT 15.31
People with borderline personality disorder have abrupt shifts in mood, lack a coherent sense of self, act impulsively, and often have stormy relationships with others.

People with BPD often have alternating feelings toward others, which shift abruptly from complete adulation when they feel others are meeting their needs to utter loathing when they feel rejected or frustrated. Psychoanalysts refer to this process as "splitting," which is the tendency to perceive people in either all good or all bad terms and to abruptly shift from one extreme to the other. Partners whom they adored and depended upon they treat with utter contempt when feeling their needs are not being met. Not surprisingly, people with BPD tend to have stormy, turbulent relationships.

Women are more often diagnosed with the disorder, but it is unclear whether women truly are more likely to be affected or simply more likely to be diagnosed with the disorder. Many historical figures have been thought to have features of borderline personality disorder, including Marilyn Monroe, Lawrence of Arabia, Adolf Hitler, and the philosopher Sören Kierkegaard.

Causal Factors in Borderline Personality Disorder

Causal factors in BPD continue to be studied, but histories of physical or sexual abuse or neglect in childhood figure prominently in many cases. Psychoanalytic theorists, such as Otto Kernberg (1975), believe that people with BPD were unable to develop a cohesive concept of themselves and others in early childhood, resulting in the difficulties they encounter in synthesizing the contradictory (good and bad) elements of themselves and others into complete, stable wholes. Rather than recognizing that people are sometimes loving and sometimes rejecting, they shift back and forth in their appraisal of others between pure idealization and utter hatred.

Brain-imaging studies show abnormalities in parts of the brain involved in regulating emotions and restraining impulsive behaviors, especially aggressive behaviors (Schmahl & Bremner, 2006; Siegle, 2008). An intriguing possibility requiring further study is that the prefrontal cortex fails to restrain impulsive behaviors at times of strong negative emotions (Silbersweig et al., 2008). Genetic factors also play a role, perhaps by influencing underlying brain structures and functions (Distel et al. 2008; Ni et al., 2006). BPD, like many other forms of abnormal behavior, may involve an interaction of genetics and life experiences (Gabbard, 2005; Gunderson, 2011).

CONCEPT 15.32
Evidence points to an interaction of environmental and biological factors in the development of personality disorders.

15.6 MODULE REVIEW Personality Disorders

Recite It

What are personality disorders?

- Personality disorders are deeply ingrained patterns of behavior that become maladaptive because they either cause personal distress or impair the person's ability to relate to others.

What characteristics are associated with antisocial personality disorder?

- The characteristics associated with antisocial personality disorder include impulsivity, irresponsibility, a callous disregard for the rights and feelings of others, and antisocial behavior.

What causal factors are implicated in antisocial personality disorder?

- A number of causal factors are implicated, including environmental factors, such as a family environment characterized by a lack of parental warmth, neglect, rejection, and use of harsh punishment, and biological factors, such as a genetic predisposition, abnormalities in higher brain centers that control impulsive behavior, and a greater need for arousing stimulation.

What characteristics are associated with borderline personality disorder?

- Borderline personality disorder is characterized by problems in forming a stable self-image, maintaining stable moods and relationships, and difficulty controlling impulses.

What causal factors are implicated in borderline personality disorder?

- Evidence points to such factors as a history of childhood abuse or neglect, genetic influences, and brain abnormalities involving mechanisms that regulate control of impulsive behaviors.

Recall It

1. What are personality disorders?
2. Investigators link antisocial personality disorder to abnormalities in what area of the brain?
3. Match the following characteristics to either (a) antisocial personality disorder or (b) borderline personality disorder:
   - **i.** turbulent relationships with others.
   - **ii.** lack of empathy.
   - **iii.** need for higher levels of stimulation.
   - **iv.** unstable self-image.

Think About It

- What are the differences between criminality and antisocial personality? Or are they one and the same? Explain.
- Have you known anyone with a personality disorder? What factors might have led to the development of these problem personality traits? How did these traits affect the person's relationships with others? With you?

APPLICATION MODULE 15.7

Suicide Prevention

"I don't believe it. I saw him just last week and he looked fine."

"She sat here just the other day, laughing with the rest of us. How were we to know what was going on inside her?"

"I knew he was depressed, but I never thought he'd do something like this. I didn't have a clue."

"Why didn't she just call me?" (Nevid, Rathus, & Greene, 2011)

We may respond to the news of a suicide of a friend or family member with shock or with guilt that we failed to pick up any warning signs. Yet even professionals have difficulty predicting whether someone is likely to commit suicide. But when signs are present, the time to take action is now. Encourage the person, calmly but firmly, to seek professional assistance. Offer to accompany the person to a helping professional—or make the first contact yourself.

Facing the Threat

CONCEPT 15.33
A suicide threat should be taken seriously, and the immediacy of the threat should be assessed; but above all, professional help should be sought at the first opportunity.

Suppose a friend confides in you that he or she is contemplating suicide. You know your friend has been going through a difficult time and has been depressed. You didn't think it would come to this, however. You want to help but are unsure about what to do. It's normal to feel frightened. Here are some suggestions to consider; since the situation at hand may call for specific responses, these are offered as general guidelines, not as direct instructions.

1. *Recognize the seriousness of the situation.* Don't fall for the myth of thinking that people who talk about suicide are not truly serious. Treat any talk of suicide as a clear warning sign.
2. *Take implied threats seriously.* Some suicidal people don't come right out and say they are planning to kill themselves. They might say something like "I just don't feel I can go on anymore."
3. *Express understanding.* Engage the person in conversation to allow his or her feelings to be expressed. Show that you understand how troubled the person is. Don't dismiss his or her concerns by saying something like "Everyone feels like this from time to time. It'll pass."
4. *Focus on alternatives.* Tell the person that other ways of dealing with his or her problems may be found, even if they are not apparent at the moment.
5. *Assess the immediate danger.* Ask the person whether he or she has made a specific plan to commit suicide. If the person plans to use guns or drugs kept at home, prevent the person from returning home alone.
6. *Enlist the person's agreement to seek help.* Insist that the person accompany you to a health professional or nearby hospital emergency room. If that's not immediately

possible, and call a health professional or suicide prevention hotline. Help is available by calling 1-800-SUICIDE or a local crisis center or health center.

7. *Accompany the person to seek help.* Above all, don't leave the person alone. If you do get separated for any reason, or if the person refuses help and leaves, call a mental health professional, suicide hotline service, or the police for assistance.

Thinking Critically About Psychology

Based on your reading of this chapter, answer the following questions. Then, to evaluate your progress in developing critical thinking skills, compare your answers to the sample answers found in Appendix A.

1. Ron, a 22-year-old stock clerk in an auto parts store, sought a consultation with a psychologist because he was feeling "down in the dumps." He explained that he was involved in a three-year-long relationship with Katie. The relationship followed a seesawing pattern of numerous breakups and brief reconciliations. Most of the breakups occurred after incidents in which Ron became angry when he felt Katie was becoming distant from him. On one occasion, he accused her of sitting too far away from him in the car. If she was in a bad mood, he assumed it was because she didn't really want to be with him. The relationship meant everything to him, he told the psychologist, saying further that "I don't know what I'd do if she left me, you know, for good. I've got to figure out how to make this relationship work" (adapted from Nevid, Rathus & Greene, 2006).

Review the characteristic errors in thinking associated with depression listed in Table 15.2. Give some examples of these cognitive errors in Ron's thinking.

2. Lonnie, a 38-year-old chemical engineer for a large pharmaceutical company, sought a consultation at the urging of his wife, Maria. He told the psychologist that Maria had grown exasperated over his "little behavioral quirks." It seems that Lonnie was a compulsive checker. Whenever the two of them would leave their apartment, he would insist on returning to check and recheck that the gas jets were turned off, the windows were shut, the door was securely locked, and the refrigerator door was tightly shut. Sometimes he'd get as far as the garage before the compulsion to return to the apartment would strike. He would apologize to Maria and leave her fuming. When retiring to bed at night, he performed an elaborate ritual of checking and rechecking to see that everything was secure. But even then, he would often bolt out of bed to check everything again, which would disturb Maria's sleep. Leaving for vacation was especially troublesome, as it required checking rituals that consumed the better part of the morning. Yet he would still be bothered by nagging doubts that would plague him throughout his trip. Lonnie recognized that his compulsive behavior was wrecking his marriage and causing him emotional distress. However, he feared that giving it up would leave him defenseless against the anxieties it helped to ease (adapted from Nevid, Rathus, & Greene, 2003).

Review the six criteria used to define abnormal behavior. Which of these criteria do you think would apply to Lonnie's case? Which wouldn't apply?

Log in to CengageBrain to access the resources your instructor requires. For this book, you can access:

CourseMate — Psychology CourseMate brings course concepts to life with interactive learning, study, and exam preparation tools that support the printed textbook. A textbook-specific website, Psychology CourseMate includes an integrated interactive eBook and other interactive learning tools including quizzes, flashcards, videos, and more.

CENGAGENOW — CengageNow is an easy-to-use online resource that helps you study in less time to get the grade you want—NOW. Take a pre-test for this chapter and receive a personalized study plan based on your results that will identify the topics you need to review and direct you to online resources to help you master those topics. Then take a post-test to help you determine the concepts you have mastered and what you will need to work on. If your textbook does not include an access code card, go to CengageBrain.com to gain access.

Visit www.cengagebrain.com to access your account and purchase materials.

VISUAL OVERVIEW Chapter 15 Psychological Disorders

MODULE 15.1 What Is Abnormal Behavior?

Criteria for Determining Abnormal Behavior

- Unusualness
- Social Deviance
- Emotional Distress
- Maladaptive Behavior
- Dangerousness
- Faulty Perceptions or Interpretations of Reality

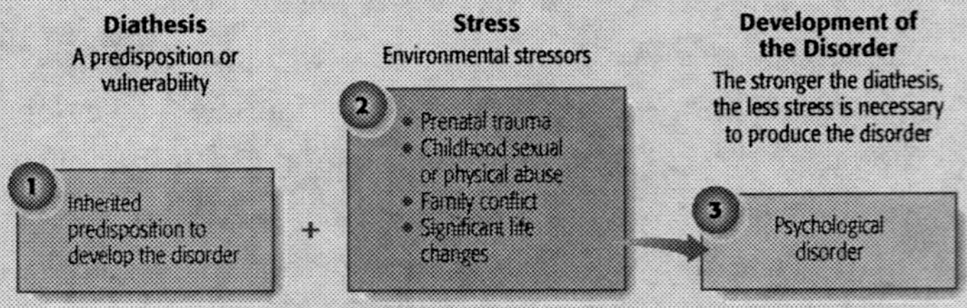

Diathesis-Stress Model

Models of Abnormal Behavior

- **Early Beliefs**: Dominated by beliefs in supernatural or demonic forces
- **Medical Model**: Abnormal behavior as medical illness
- **Psychological Models**: Psychodynamic, behavioral, humanistic, and cognitive models
- **Sociocultural Model**: Abnormal behavior rooted in social ills
- **Biopsychosocial Model**: Interaction of multiple factors, as represented by the diathesis-stress model

Psychological Disorders

- **Prevalence of Psychological Disorders**: Nearly one in two adults affected at some point in their lives
- **Classification of Psychological Disorders**: DSM diagnostic system comprising five axes or dimensions of evaluation of psychological functioning

MODULE 15.2 Anxiety Disorders

© Zurijeta/Shuttestock.com

- **Phobias**: Excessive or inappropriate fear reactions, such as specific phobia, social phobia, and agoraphobia
- **Panic Disorder**: Intense anxiety reactions called panic attacks
- **Generalized Anxiety Disorder**: Anxiety not limited to specific objects or situations
- **Obsessive-Compulsive Disorder**: Bothersome obsessive thoughts and compulsive rituals
- **PTSD**: Maladaptive reactions to traumatic stress (discussed in Chapter 12)

MODULE 15.3 Dissociative and Somatoform Disorders

Dissociative Disorders

- **Dissociative Identity Disorder**: Formerly called multiple personality, it involves a splitting of the self into alternate personalities
- **Dissociative Amnesia**: Memory loss resulting from psychological causes
- **Causal Factors**: Psychological defense against severe childhood abuse (dissociative identity disorder) or painful or troubling memories (dissociative amnesia)

Somatoform Disorders

- **Conversion Disorder:** A loss or major change in bodily function that cannot be explained medically
- **Hypochondriasis:** Mistakenly believing that physical symptoms are signs of underlying serious illness

MODULE 15.4 Mood Disorders

- **Major Depression:** Periods of significant downcast mood and loss of interest and pleasure
- **Dysthymic Disorder:** Lingering episodes of relatively mild depression
- **Bipolar Disorder:** Mood swings from extremely elevated moods to periods of deep depression
- **Cyclothymic Disorder:** Milder mood swings than those in bipolar disorder

© Burstein Collection/Corbis

Van Gogh Self-Portrait

MODULE 15.5 Schizophrenia

- **Key features:** Break with reality and severely impaired cognitive and social functioning
- **Three Major Subtypes:** Disorganized type, catatonic type, paranoid type

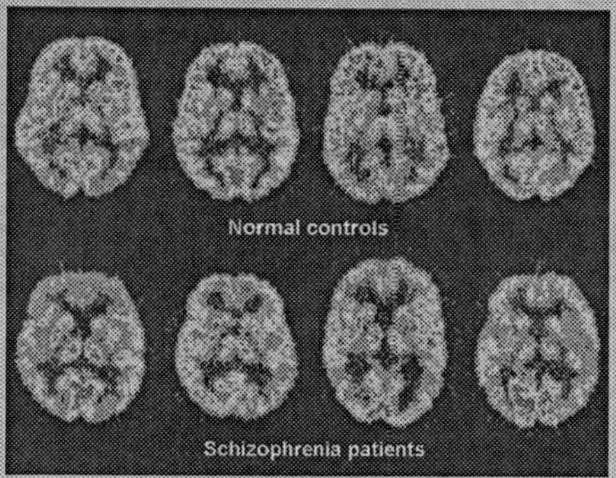

Courtesy of Monte S. Buchsbaum, M.D./Mount Sinai School of Medicine, New York, NY

Brain Images of Schizophrenia Patients Versus Normal Controls

MODULE 15.6 Personality Disorders

- **Key Features:** Rigid, maladaptive behavior patterns that interfere with interpersonal relationships and ability to meet life demands

Two Major Types

- **Antisocial Personality Disorder:** Callous treatment of others, disregard for rules of society, lack of remorse for misdeeds, irresponsible behavior, and antisocial behavior
- **Borderline Personality Disorder:** Unstable self-image, turbulent relationships, unstable moods, and lack of impulse control

16 Methods of Therapy

"The Beast Is Back"

SLICE OF LIFE My body aches intermittently, in waves, as if I had malaria. I eat with no appetite, simply because the taste of food is one of my dwindling number of pleasures. I am tired, so tired. Last night I lay like a pile of old clothes, and when David came to bed I did not stir. Sex is a foreign notion. At work today I am forgetful; I have trouble forming sentences, I lose track of them halfway through, and my words keep getting tangled. I look at my list of things to do today, and keep on looking at it; nothing seems to be happening. Things are sad to me. . . . I feel as if my brain were a lump of protoplasm with tiny circuits embedded in it, and some of the wires keep shorting out. There are tiny little electrical fires up there, leaving crispy sections of neurons smoking and ruined.

I don't even know when this current siege began—a week ago? A month ago? The onset is so gradual, and these things are hard to tell. All I know is, the Beast is back.

It is called depression, and my experiences with it have shaped my life—altered my personality, affected my most intimate relationships, changed the course of my career—in ways I will probably never be fully aware of.

Source: T. Thompson, 1995.

In this chapter, we discuss ways of helping people, like the woman in this case example, who suffer from psychological disorders. As we shall see in Modules 16.2 and 16.3, help takes many forms, including psychotherapy and biomedical therapies such as drug therapy and electroconvulsive therapy (ECT). We will then review the information that informed consumers need to know—and the questions they need to ask—when seeking the assistance of mental health professionals.

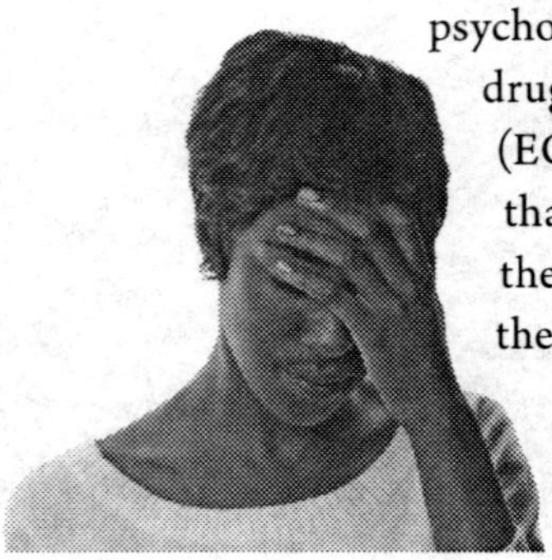

© iStockphoto.com/drbimages

DID YOU KNOW THAT...

- Sigmund Freud believed that clients bring into the therapeutic relationship the underlying conflicts they have had with important persons in their lives? (p. 611)
- Gestalt therapists have their clients talk to an empty chair? (p. 613)
- Behavior therapists have used virtual reality techniques to help people overcome a fear of heights? (p. 614)
- Cognitive therapists believe that emotional disorders arise from the ways in which we interpret our life experiences, not from the experiences themselves? (p. 626)
- Antidepressant drugs are used to treat many types of psychological disorders, not just depression? (p. 625)
- Stimulant drugs are used to help hyperactive children? (p. 626)
- Sending jolts of electricity through a person's head can help relieve severe depression? (p. 628)

Learning Objectives

By reading this chapter you will be able to . . .

1 **DESCRIBE** the development and decline of moral therapy.

2 **DESCRIBE** the community mental health movement and **EVALUATE** whether the policy of deinstitutionalization has succeeded.

3 **IDENTIFY** the major types of mental health professionals and **DESCRIBE** the training backgrounds and roles associated with each type.

4 **DEFINE** psychotherapy and **IDENTIFY** the major types of psychotherapy and the developers of these therapies.

5 **DESCRIBE** the techniques used in different types of psychotherapy.

6 **EVALUATE** evidence regarding the effectiveness of psychotherapy.

7 **EVALUATE** how cultural factors affect the practice of psychotherapy.

8 **IDENTIFY** different types of psychiatric drugs and **EVALUATE** their advantages and disadvantages.

9 **DESCRIBE** other biomedical therapies and **EXPLAIN** why they are controversial.

10 **APPLY** steps you can take to obtain help for a psychological problem.

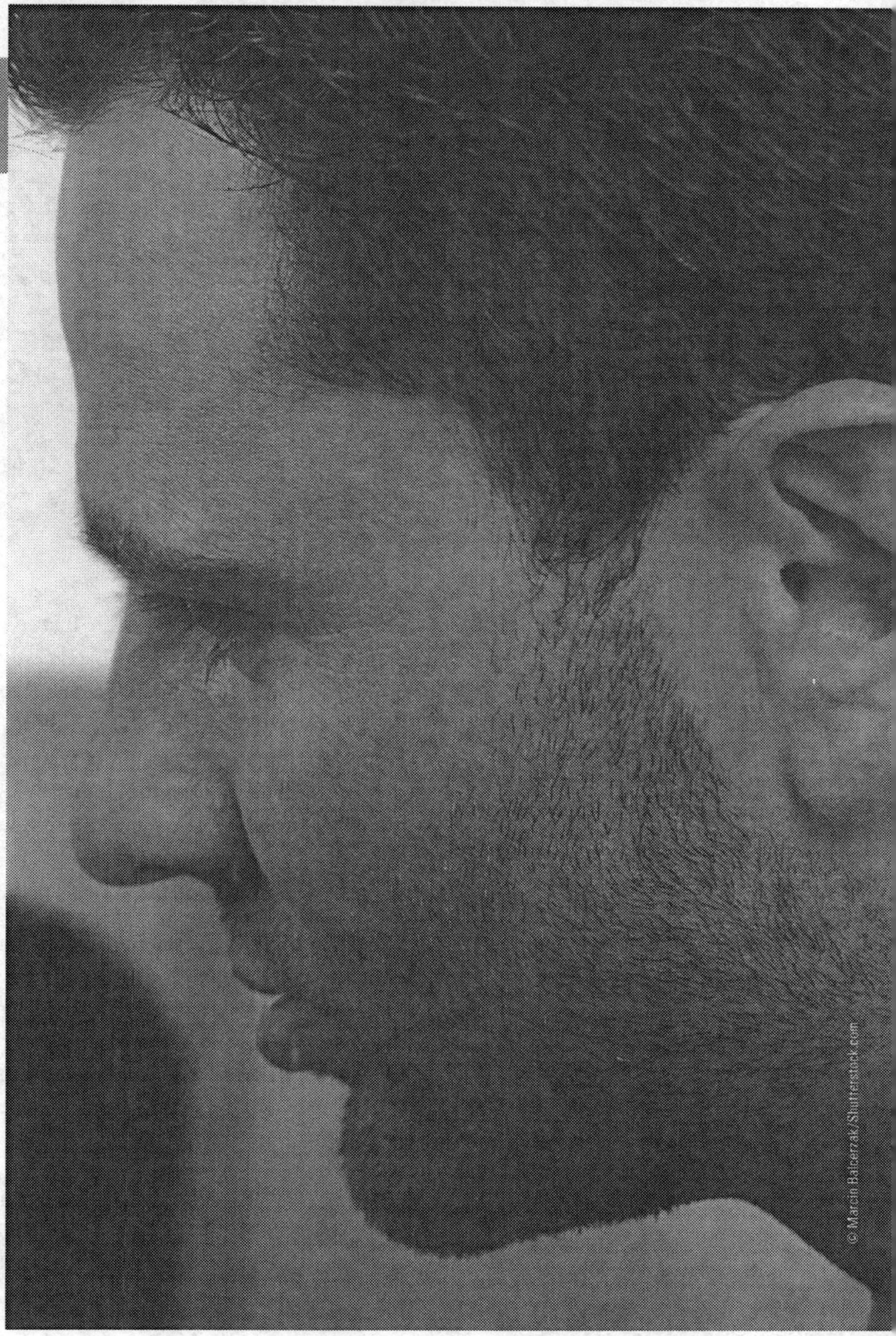

Preview

MODULE 16.1

Pathways to the Present: A Brief History of Therapy

- How has the treatment of people with disturbed behavior changed over time?
- What are community mental health centers?
- How successful is the policy of deinstitutionalization?

Throughout much of Western history, society's treatment of people with severe emotional or behavioral problems was characterized more by neglect and harsh remedies than by compassion and humane care. Even today, many people with serious and persistent mental health problems, such as schizophrenia, are essentially left to fend for themselves on city streets. In this module, we briefly explore the history of society's treatment of mentally disturbed people from the beginnings of more humane forms of treatment to the community mental health movement of today.

CONCEPT 16.1
The rise of moral therapy in the late eighteenth and early nineteenth centuries was a major step toward humanizing the treatment of mental patients.

The Rise of Moral Therapy

moral therapy A philosophy of treatment that emphasized treating mentally ill people with compassion and understanding, rather than shackling them in chains.

The philosophy of treatment called **moral therapy** emerged in large measure from the efforts of two eighteenth-century Frenchmen, Jean-Baptiste Pussin and Philippe Pinel. They believed that mentally disturbed people suffer from diseases and should be treated with compassion and humane care. Their views were unpopular at the time, because deranged people were widely viewed as threats to society, not as sick people who required treatment. Many mental patients were chained to prevent them from harming others.

In 1784, Pussin (1746–1811), though not a medical doctor, was placed in charge of a ward for the "incurably insane" at La Bicêtre, a large mental hospital in Paris. It was Pussin, not Pinel as many people believe, who first unchained mental patients in the hospital. He believed that if they were treated with kindness, they would not need to be chained. He also insisted that staff members treat inmates with respect and compassion.

© Bettmann/CORBIS

Pinel unchaining inmates at La Bicêtre.

Pinel (1745–1826) became the medical director of the ward at La Bicêtre in 1793 and continued Pussin's humane philosophy of treatment, including unchaining inmates. He eliminated harsh treatments, such as bleeding and purging, and had patients moved out of darkened dungeons into sunny, well-ventilated rooms. Based on the belief that humane treatment could help restore disturbed people to normal functioning, moral therapy led to similar reforms in mental health treatment in England and the United States.

A leading nineteenth-century proponent of moral therapy was Dorothea Dix (1802–1887), a Boston schoolteacher who brought attention to the plight of the mentally ill in the United States. She crusaded for kinder treatment of mentally disturbed people, who at the time were often housed under deplorable conditions. In Massachusetts, she found them locked away in jails or poorhouses, where they were ". . . chained, naked, beaten with rods and lashed into obedience!" (cited in Winerip, 1999). Dix found similarly dreadful conditions in her travels elsewhere in the country. Her efforts helped lead to the establishment of 32 mental hospitals throughout the United States.

Moral therapy fell out of favor in the latter half of the nineteenth century as it became clear that this technique failed to restore severely disturbed people to normalcy. In the absence of effective alternative treatments, the ensuing years were a period of apathy characterized by the "warehousing" of patients in the back wards of large state hospitals (Grob, 1996). Patients were largely neglected and left with little hope or expectation of returning to the community. Little if any "therapy" was offered long-term patients, and the majority of facilities were dreadful places.

Though more humane exceptions existed, conditions in state mental hospitals through the middle part of the twentieth century were often deplorable. Patients were typically crowded together in locked wards, some lacking even basic sanitation. At the time, social observers described many state-run mental hospitals as "human snakepits."

The Movement Toward Community-Based Care

© y_ntousiopoulos/Big stock.com

By the 1950s, the public outcry over deplorable conditions in mental hospitals led to a call for reform. The result was the community mental health system, which began to take shape in the 1960s. The hope was that community-based facilities would provide people suffering from schizophrenia or other severe and persistent psychological disorders with alternatives to long-term hospitalization. The advent of antipsychotic drugs, which helped control the flagrant symptoms of schizophrenia, was an additional impetus for the massive exodus of chronic mental patients from state institutions that began in earnest during the 1960s.

The social policy that redirected care of persons with severe mental disorders from state mental hospitals toward community-based treatment settings is called **deinstitutionalization**. As a result of this policy, the back wards of many mental hospitals were largely vacated. Many state mental hospitals were closed entirely and were replaced by community-based mental health centers and residential treatment facilities. The state hospital census in the United States dropped from about 550,000 in 1955 to fewer than 130,000 by the late 1980s.

deinstitutionalization A policy of reducing the population of mental hospitals by shifting care from inpatient facilities to community-based outpatient facilities.

CONCEPT 16.2

The community mental health movement offers the hope that mental patients can be reintegrated into society, but in far too many cases it remains a hope as yet unfulfilled.

Today, community-based mental health centers offer a variety of services, including outpatient care, day treatment programs, and crisis intervention. Supervised residential facilities, such as halfway houses, help formerly hospitalized patients make the transition to community life. The contemporary mental hospital now exists as a resource

© David Young-Wolff/Photo Edit

Meeting the multifaceted needs of the psychiatric homeless population challenges the mental health system and the broader society.

to provide patients with more structured treatment alternatives that may be needed during times of crisis and a protective living environment for long-term patients who are unable to manage the challenges of adjusting to life in the community.

Why It Matters

The objectives of deinstitutionalization are certainly laudable. But the question remains: Has it succeeded in its goal of reintegrating mental patients into their communities? Unfortunately, deinstitutionalization receives at best a mixed grade. Critics claim that mental hospitals today are like revolving doors, repeatedly admitting patients and then rapidly discharging them once they become stabilized. Far too many patients fail to receive the comprehensive range of psychological and support services they need to adapt successfully to community living (Frank & Glied, 2006). Some simply fall through the cracks of the mental health system and are left to fend for themselves (Folsom et al., 2005). Many homeless people seen wandering about or sleeping in bus terminals have serious mental health and substance-abuse problems but are not receiving the help they need.

The U.S. government estimates that about one out of three homeless adults in the United States suffers from a severe psychological disorder (National Institutes of Health, 2003). Understaffed and underfunded, community-based mental health facilities continue to struggle to meet the demands of a generation of people with severe mental health problems who have come of age during the era of deinstitutionalization.

More intensive outreach programs that match mental health and community services to the needs of people with severe and persistent mental health problems generally achieve better results (e.g., Coldwell & Bender, 2007). These outreach efforts are especially needed to reach the large numbers of psychiatric homeless people who fail to seek out mental health services on their own (Price, 2009c). All in all, we should think of deinstitutionalization as a work in progress rather than as a failed policy.

Concept Chart 16.1 reviews the history of therapy discussed in this module. See the next *Try This Out* feature to explore how you can get involved in providing help to people in crisis.

TRY THIS OUT "Hello, Can I Help You?"

Many campuses and local communities have telephone hotlines that people who are distressed or suicidal can call for immediate assistance, day or night. The volunteers who staff these call centers receive specialized training in crisis intervention services. The staffers field phone calls, provide emotional support to people in crisis, and make referrals to mental health agencies or counseling centers in the area. Serving as a volunteer for a hotline service can be a formative experience in helping you prepare for a career in the helping professions, including psychology, counseling, or social work. The work can be rewarding but also very challenging. Make sure the hotline is well supervised and provides the support and guidance you will need to handle the responsibilities of providing help to people in crisis. Keep a journal to document your experiences, noting how they shape your views of psychology and, more important, of yourself.

CONCEPT CHART 16.1 From Institutional Care to Community-Based Care

Type of Institution	Period of Time	Comments
State hospital system	19th century through mid-20th century	Large state institutions that provided little more than custodial care. Conditions in some institutions were so deplorable they were sometimes called "human snakepits."
Modern state hospitals	1955 to present	Significantly downsized institutions that provide more humane care than earlier institutions. Yet critics claim that some institutions function as little more than revolving doors for chronic patients who are repeatedly shuttled back and forth between the hospital and the community.
Community mental health centers	1960s to present	Comprehensive treatment facilities in the community that offer alternatives to hospitalization, including outpatient treatment, day hospital programs, and transitional treatment facilities such as halfway houses. However, many marginally functioning mental patients have been released to the community without access to adequate housing and other necessary support. Meanwhile, more intensive community-based programs are beginning to show better outcomes in helping patients adjust more successfully to community living.

16.1 MODULE REVIEW Pathways to the Present: A Brief History of Therapy

Recite It

How has the treatment of people with disturbed behavior changed over time?

- In the late eighteenth century, a more humane approach to the treatment of mental patients, called "moral therapy," began to gain prominence.
- As this movement declined, a state of apathy ensued and the focus shifted from therapy to custodial treatment in large, forbidding state mental institutions.
- Pressures to reform the mental health system in the United States led to the creation of a nationwide network of community mental health centers in the 1960s. The community mental health movement shifted the delivery of care from large inpatient facilities to community-based facilities.

What are community-based mental health centers?

- Community-based mental health centers are treatment facilities that provide a comprehensive range of mental health services and other supportive services to psychiatric patients in the communities in which they reside.

How successful is the policy of deinstitutionalization?

- The policy of deinstitutionalization remains a promise not yet fulfilled, as many patients fail to receive the services they need to adjust successfully to the community.

Recall It

1. The eighteenth-century Frenchmen Jean-Baptiste Pussin and Philippe Pinel adopted a more humane approach to the treatment of mental patients, called ________ therapy.
2. The nineteenth-century American reformer who campaigned for more compassionate care of the mentally ill was ________.
3. Why did moral therapy eventually fall out of favor?
4. The policy of ________ greatly reduced the census of state mental hospitals and shifted treatment of people with severe psychological disorders largely to community-based programs.

Think About It

- How has society's treatment of people with mental health problems changed over time? Are we more tolerant and understanding today? What do you think?
- What should be done about the problem of psychiatric homelessness?
- If you or someone you know needed mental health services, where would you turn? How might you find out what types of mental health services are available in your college and your community?

MODULE 16.2

Types of Psychotherapy

- What is psychotherapy?
- What are the major types of mental health professionals?
- What are the major types of psychotherapy?
- What is eclectic therapy?
- What are group, family, and couple therapy?
- Does psychotherapy work?
- What cultural factors do therapists need to consider when working with members of diverse groups?

psychotherapy A verbal form of therapy derived from a psychological framework that consists of one or more treatment sessions with a therapist.

CONCEPT 16.3
Psychotherapy consists of one or more verbal interactions between a therapist and a client and is used to help people understand and resolve their psychological problems.

CONCEPT 16.4
Mental health services are offered by different types of professionals who vary in their training backgrounds and areas of competence.

Psychotherapy is a psychologically based form of treatment used to help people better understand their emotional or behavioral problems and resolve them. It consists of a series of verbal interactions between a therapist and a client, which is why it is often referred to as "talk therapy." In some forms of psychotherapy, there is an ongoing back-and-forth dialogue between the therapist and client, whereas in others, especially in classical psychoanalysis, the client does most or virtually all of the talking. There are literally hundreds of types of psychotherapy, but the most widely used derive from the major psychological models of abnormal behavior discussed in Chapter 15: the psychodynamic, behavioral, humanistic, and cognitive models. Although most forms of psychotherapy focus on the individual, some therapists extend their model of treatment to couples, families, and groups of unrelated individuals.

Before we consider the major forms of psychotherapy, have a look at Table 16.1, which lists the major types of helping professionals who provide mental health services. Note the differences in their training backgrounds and areas of expertise.

CONCEPT 16.5
Psychodynamic therapy is based on the belief that insight into unresolved psychological conflicts originating in childhood can help people overcome psychological problems.

Psychodynamic Therapy

What comes to mind when you think of psychotherapy? If you picture a person lying on a couch and talking about the past, especially early childhood, you are probably thinking of **psychoanalysis**, the first form of *psychodynamic therapy* to be developed. Psychodynamic therapies share the belief that psychological problems are rooted in unconscious psychological conflicts dating from childhood. They also assume that gaining insight into these conflicts and working through them in the light of the individual's adult personality are the key steps toward restoring psychological health (Johansson et al., 2010).

psychoanalysis The method of psychotherapy developed by Freud that focuses on uncovering and working through the unconscious conflicts that he believed were at the root of psychological problems.

psychoanalysts Practitioners of psychoanalysis who are schooled in the Freudian tradition.

Traditional Psychoanalysis: Where Id Was, Ego Shall Be

Psychoanalysis, the form of psychotherapy developed by Sigmund Freud, is based on the belief that unconscious conflicts originating in childhood give rise to psychological problems. Practitioners of psychoanalysis are called **psychoanalysts**, or *analysts* for short. Recall from Chapter 13 that Freud believed that conflicts over primitive sexual or aggressive impulses cause the ego to employ *defense mechanisms*, especially *repression*, to keep unacceptable impulses out of conscious awareness. In some instances,

TABLE 16.1 Major Types of Mental Health Professionals

Clinical psychologists	Clinical psychologists have earned a doctoral degree in psychology (either a Ph.D., Doctor of Philosophy; Psy.D., Doctor of Psychology; or Ed.D., Doctor of Education) from an accredited college or university and have passed a licensing examination. Clinical psychologists specialize in administering psychological tests, diagnosing mental disorders, and practicing psychotherapy. Until a few years ago, they were not permitted to prescribe psychiatric drugs. However, as of this edition, two states (New Mexico and Louisiana) had enacted laws granting prescription privileges to psychologists who complete specialized training programs (Bradshaw, 2010). Whether other states will follow suit remains to be seen. Moreover, the granting of prescription privileges to psychologists remains a hotly contested issue between psychologists and psychiatrists and within the field of psychology itself (Brehm, 2008).
Counseling psychologists	Counseling psychologists hold doctoral degrees in psychology and have passed a licensing examination. They typically provide counseling to people with psychological problems falling within a milder range of severity than those treated by clinical psychologists, such as difficulties adjusting to college or uncertainties regarding career choices. Many counseling psychologists in college settings are also involved in providing appropriate services to students covered by the Americans with Disabilities Act (ADA).
Psychiatrists	Psychiatrists have earned a medical degree (M.D.) and completed residency training programs in psychiatry, which usually are three years in length. They are physicians who specialize in the diagnosis and treatment of psychological disorders. As licensed physicians, they can prescribe psychiatric drugs and may employ other medical techniques, such as electroconvulsive therapy (ECT). Many also practice psychotherapy based on training they receive during their residency programs or in specialized training institutes.
Clinical or psychiatric social workers	Clinical or psychiatric social workers have earned a master's degree in social work (M.S.W.) and use their knowledge of community agencies and organizations to help people with severe mental disorders receive the services they need. Many clinical social workers practice psychotherapy or specific forms of therapy, such as marital or family therapy.
Psychoanalysts	Psychoanalysts are typically either psychiatrists or psychologists who have completed extensive additional training in psychoanalysis. They are required to undergo psychoanalysis themselves as part of their training.
Counselors	Counselors have typically earned a master's degree and work in settings such as public schools, college testing and counseling centers, and hospitals and health clinics. Many specialize in vocational evaluation, marital or family counseling, or substance abuse counseling. Counselors may focus on providing psychological assistance to people with milder forms of disturbed behavior or those struggling with a chronic or debilitating illness or recovering from a traumatic experience.
Psychiatric nurses	Psychiatric nurses are typically R.N.'s who have completed a master's program in psychiatric nursing. They may work in a psychiatric facility or in a group medical practice where they treat people suffering from severe psychological disorders.

unconscious impulses threaten to leak into consciousness, resulting in anxiety. The person may experience anxiety or a vague sense of dread or foreboding but have no idea about its underlying cause. In other cases, energy attached to the impulse is channeled or converted into a physical symptom, as in hysterical blindness or paralysis. The symptom itself, say the inability to move an arm, serves a hidden purpose—preventing the person from using the arm to express an unacceptable impulse, such as an urge to attack others or to masturbate.

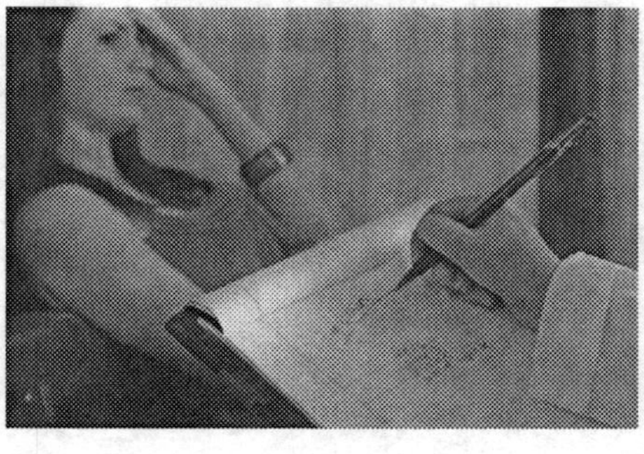
© Phase4Photography/Shutterstock.com

People with a fear of heights keep unconscious self-destructive impulses in check by avoiding height situations in which they might lose control over the impulse to jump.

"Strip down to your ego and the doctor will be in shortly."

© 2003 Mike Twohy

The task of therapy, Freud believed, was to help people gain insight into their unconscious conflicts and work them through—to shine the conscious light of the ego on the darkest reaches of the id. With self-insight, the ego would no longer need to maintain defensive behaviors or psychological symptoms that shield the self from inner conflicts or turmoil. The ego would then be free to focus its efforts on pursuing more constructive interests, such as work and relationships.

Freud used psychoanalysis to probe the unconscious mind for these inner conflicts, a lengthy process that typically would take years. He believed that unconscious conflicts are not easily brought into consciousness, so he devised several techniques to help clients gain awareness of them, including free association, dream analysis, and interpretation.

Free Association In **free association**, the client is instructed to say anything that crosses his or her mind, no matter how trivial or irrelevant it may seem. Freud believed the client's associations would eventually yield clues about deep-seated conflicts and wishes lurking in the unconscious mind. In classical psychoanalysis, the client lies on a couch with the analyst sitting off to the side, out of the client's direct view, saying little. By remaining detached, the analyst hopes to create an atmosphere that encourages the client to focus inwardly on his or her own thoughts.

CONCEPT 16.6
Freud devised a number of techniques, including free association, dream analysis, and interpretation, to help clients gain awareness of their unconscious conflicts.

→ Concept Link
Freud believed that dreams have both manifest (transparent) and latent (symbolic) content. See Module 4.2.

Dream Analysis In **dream analysis**, the analyst helps the client gain insight into the symbolic or *latent* content of dreams, as opposed to the overt or *manifest* content (see Chapter 4). Freud called dreams the "royal road to the unconscious." He encouraged clients to freely associate to the manifest content of their dreams, hoping that doing so would lead to a better understanding of the dreams' hidden meanings.

Interpretation **Interpretation** is an explanation of the connections between the client's behavior and verbal expressions—how the client acts and what the client says—and the client's unconscious motives and conflicts. By offering interpretations, the analyst helps the client gain **insight** into the unconscious origins of the problem.

Interpretation of the client's **resistance** plays an important role in psychoanalysis. Resistance is the blocking that occurs when therapy evokes anxiety-related thoughts and feelings that touch upon underlying conflicts or issues. The client may suddenly draw a blank when free associations touch upon sensitive areas, or "forget" to show up for an appointment when deeper issues are being discussed. Psychoanalysts interpret signs of resistance as clues to important underlying issues or concerns that need to be addressed in therapy.

The most important use of interpretation, in Freud's view, is analysis of the **transference relationship**. Freud believed that clients reenact troubled, conflicted relationships with others in the context of the relationship they develop with the analyst. A female client may respond to the analyst as a "father figure," perhaps transferring her ambivalent feelings of love and hate toward her own father onto the therapist. A young man may view the analyst as a competitor or rival, reenacting an unresolved Oedipal conflict from his childhood. By interpreting the transference relationship, the analyst raises the client's awareness about how earlier conflicted relationships intrude upon the client's present relationships. Freud believed that the client's ability to come to an understanding of the transference relationship is an essential ingredient in a successful analysis.

Transference is a two-way street. Freud himself recognized that he sometimes responded to clients in ways that carried over from his relationships with others. He

free association A technique in psychoanalysis in which the client is encouraged to say anything that comes to mind.

dream analysis A technique in psychoanalysis in which the therapist attempts to analyze the underlying or symbolic meaning of the client's dreams.

interpretation In psychoanalysis, the attempt by the therapist to explain the connections between the material the client discloses in therapy and his or her unconscious conflicts.

insight In Freud's theory, the awareness of underlying unconscious wishes and conflicts.

resistance In psychoanalysis, the blocking that occurs when therapy touches upon anxiety-evoking thoughts or feelings.

transference relationship In therapy, the tendency of clients to reenact earlier conflicted relationships in the relationship they develop with their therapists.

called this process **countertransference** and believed that it damaged the therapeutic relationship. A male therapist, for example, may react to a male client as a competitor or rival, or to a female client as a rejecting love interest.

CONCEPT 16.7
Freud believed that the ability to understand the transference relationship is essential to the client's success in psychoanalysis.

countertransference The tendency for therapists to relate to clients in ways that mirror their relationships with important figures in their own lives.

Modern Psychodynamic Approaches

Traditional psychoanalysis is a lengthy, intensive process. It may require three to five sessions a week for many years. Some contemporary psychoanalysts continue to practice in much the same way as Freud did. However, many psychodynamic therapists today focus less on sexual issues and the remote past and more on the client's present relationships (Knoblauch, 2009). Many modern analysts adopt a briefer treatment model than is the case with traditional psychoanalysis and consequently take a more direct approach in exploring how underlying defenses and transference issues cause problems in how clients relate to others—a process likened to "peeling an onion" (Gothold, 2009). One obvious difference is that many modern analysts prefer to have their clients sit facing them, rather than lying on a couch. There is also more dialogue between analyst and client, and clients typically come to only one or two sessions a week (Grossman, 2003).

© Zigy Kaluzny/Stone/Getty Images

Many contemporary psychoanalysts have replaced the traditional couch with more direct, face-to-face verbal interaction with clients.

Here we see an example of the give-and-take between a contemporary psychoanalyst and a young adult male patient. The analyst focuses on the client's competitiveness; in an analytic framework, his competitiveness represents the transference of the client's unresolved Oedipal rivalry with his own father:

Client: I continue to have success, but I have been feeling weak and tired. I saw my doctor yesterday and he said there's nothing organically wrong.

Analyst: Does anything come to mind in relation to weak and tired feelings?

Client: I'm thinking of the way you looked last year after you came out of the hospital. [The patient was referring to a hospitalization that, in fact, I had the previous year during which time our treatment sessions were suspended.]

Analyst: Do you recall how you felt when you saw me looking that way?

Client: It made me upset, even guilty.

Analyst: But why guilty?

Client: I'm not sure why I said that. There was nothing to feel guilty about.

Analyst: Perhaps you had some other feelings.

Client: Well, it's true that at one point I felt faintly pleased that I was young and vigorous and you seemed to be going downhill. . . .

Analyst: . . . Clearly you're not very comfortable when you contrast your state with mine—to your advantage.

Client: Well, you know, I've never felt comfortable when thinking of myself outdoing you in any way. . . .

Analyst: . . . Perhaps your weak and tired feelings represent an identification with me brought on by your feeling guilty about your successes, since that implies that you are outdoing me. . . . Your discomfort with feeling that in certain respects you're surpassing me is posing a problem for you.

Source: Silverman, 1984.

Humanistic Therapy

CONCEPT 16.8
Compared to traditional psychoanalysis, modern forms of psychodynamic therapy are briefer, allow for more interaction between therapist and client, and focus more on current relationships.

Humanistic therapists believe that human beings possess free will and can make conscious choices that enrich their lives. The methods of therapy developed within the humanistic tradition emphasize the client's subjective, conscious experiences.

Humanistic therapists focus on what the individual is experiencing at the particular moment in time, rather than on the distant past. It's not that they view the past as unimportant; they believe that past experiences do affect present behavior and feelings. But they emphasize that change must occur in the present, in the *here-and-now*. The two major forms of humanistic therapy are *client-centered therapy*, developed by Carl Rogers, and *gestalt therapy*, developed by Fritz Perls.

CONCEPT 16.9
Humanistic therapies emphasize subjective, conscious experience and development of one's unique potential.

→ Concept Link
Maslow believed the highest level of human motivation involves self-actualization, the drive to realize one's unique potential. See Module 8.1.

Client-Centered Therapy

Rogers (1951) believed that when children are valued only when they behave in ways that please others, they may become psychologically detached from parts of themselves that meet with disapproval or criticism. They may become so good at playing the "good boy" or "good girl" role that they develop a distorted self-concept—a view of themselves that does not reflect who they really are and what they truly feel. Well-adjusted people make choices that are consistent with their own unique selves, needs, and values. But people with a distorted self-concept remain largely strangers to themselves.

The form of therapy that Rogers developed, *client-centered therapy*, focuses on the exploration of the self (Raskin, Rogers, & Witty, 2008). Client-centered therapists seek to create a warm and accepting therapeutic environment in which clients feel safe to explore their innermost feelings and become more accepting of their true selves. The therapist takes a *nondirective* approach by allowing the client to take the lead and set the tone. The therapist's role is to reflect back the client's feelings in a supportive manner so as to encourage self-exploration and self-acceptance. Here, Rogers illustrates how a client-centered counselor uses reflection to help a client clarify and further explore her feelings:

Client: Now—one of the things that . . . had worried me was . . . living at the dorm, it's hard—not to just sort of fall in with a group of people . . . that aren't interesting, but just around. . . . So, now I find that I'm . . . getting away from that group a little bit . . . and being with a group of people . . . I really find I have more interests in common with.

Counselor: That is, you've really chosen to draw away from the group you're just thrown in with by chance, and you pick people whom you want more to associate with. Is that it?

Client: That's the idea. . . . They [my roommates] . . . had sort of pulled me in with a group of their friends that I wouldn't have picked myself, especially. And . . . so that I found that all my time was being taken up with these people, and now I'm beginning to seek out people that I prefer myself . . . rather than being drawn in with the bunch.

Counselor: You find it a little more possible, I gather, to express your real attitudes in a social situation . . . [to] make your own choice of friends. . . .

Client: . . . I tried to see if I was just withdrawing from this bunch of kids I'd been spending my time with. . . . It's not a withdrawal, but it's more of an assertion of my real interest.

Counselor: M-hm. In other words, you've tried to be self-critical in order to see if you're just running away from the situation, but you feel really, it's an expression of your positive attitudes.

Client: I—I think it is.

Source: Rogers, 1951.

Rogers believed that effective therapists display three qualities that are necessary to create an atmosphere of emotional support needed for clients to benefit from therapy:

1. *Unconditional positive regard.* The therapist is unconditionally accepting of the client as a person, even though he or she may not approve of all the client's choices or behaviors.
2. *Empathy.* The therapist demonstrates *empathy,* the ability to accurately mirror or reflect back the client's experiences and feelings—to see the world through the client's eyes or frames of reference. By entering the client's subjective world, the therapist encourages the client to do likewise—to get in touch with deeper feelings of which he or she may be only dimly aware.
3. *Genuineness.* The therapist is able to express genuine feelings and demonstrates that one's feelings and actions can be congruent or consistent. Even when the therapist is feeling bored or down, it is best to express these feelings, so as to encourage the client to do the same, rather than distorting true feelings or concealing them.

CONCEPT 16.10
Carl Rogers believed that for therapists to be effective, they must demonstrate empathy and unconditional positive regard for their clients, as well as genuineness in their expression of feelings.

Gestalt Therapy

Fritz Perls (1893–1970), the originator of gestalt therapy, was trained as a psychoanalyst but became dissatisfied with the lack of emphasis on the client's subjective experiences in the present. Perls was influenced by Gestalt psychology and believed that it was important to help clients blend the conflicting parts of their personalities into an integrated whole, or "gestalt." Unlike client-centered therapists, who attempt to create a warm and accepting atmosphere, gestalt therapists take a direct and even confrontational approach in helping clients get in touch with their underlying feelings. They repeatedly challenge clients to express how they are feeling at each moment in time—in the here-and-now. They don't let them off the hook by allowing them to slide into discussing events from their past or to ramble in general, abstract terms about their feelings or experiences.

CONCEPT 16.11
Fritz Perls, who developed gestalt therapy, believed that therapists should help clients blend the conflicting parts of their personalities into an integrated whole or "gestalt."

© Cheryl Casey/Shutterstock.com

Gestalt therapists use role-playing exercises to help clients integrate their inner feelings into their conscious experience. In the *empty chair* technique, therapists place an empty chair in front of the clients. The clients are told to imagine that someone with whom they have had a troubled relationship (mother, father, spouse, boss) is sitting in the chair and to express their feelings toward that person. In this way, clients feel they can safely express their innermost feelings and unmet needs without fear of criticism from the other person.

Perls also had clients role-play different parts of their own personalities. One part might bark a command, like "Take chances. Get involved." A more restrained part might bark back, "Play it safe. Don't risk it." By helping the individual become more aware of these opposing parts, gestalt therapists hope to bring about an integration of the client's personality that may take the form of a compromise between opposing parts.

CONCEPT 16.12
Behavior therapy involves the systematic application of learning principles to weaken undesirable behaviors and strengthen adaptive behaviors.

Behavior Therapy

In **behavior therapy** (also called *behavior modification*), therapists systematically apply principles of learning to help individuals make adaptive changes in their behavior. Behavior therapists believe that psychological problems are largely learned and thus can be unlearned. Like humanistic and cognitive therapies, behavior therapy addresses the client's present situation, not the distant past. But behavior therapy focuses directly

behavior therapy A form of therapy that involves the systematic application of the principles of learning to bring about desired changes in emotional states and behavior.

on changing problem behaviors, rather than on exploring the client's feelings. Behavior therapy is relatively brief, usually lasting weeks or months rather than years.

Methods of Fear Reduction

CONCEPT 16.13
To help people overcome phobic responses, behavior therapists use learning-based techniques such as systematic desensitization, gradual exposure, and modeling.

systematic desensitization A behavior therapy technique for treating phobias through the pairing of exposure in imagination to fear-inducing stimuli and states of deep relaxation.

fear hierarchy An ordered series of increasingly fearful objects or situations.

gradual exposure A behavior therapy technique for treating phobias based on direct exposure to a series of increasingly fearful stimuli. Also called *in-vivo ("real life") exposure*.

Behavior therapists use several techniques to treat phobias, including systematic desensitization, gradual exposure, and modeling. In **systematic desensitization**, the client is first trained in skills needed to deeply relax muscle groups in the body. The therapist and client then work together to construct a **fear hierarchy**, or ordered series of fearful stimuli scaled from the least to the most fearful. For example, a person with a spider phobia might create a hierarchy that might range from looking at a picture of a spider in book on the low end to having a harmless spider placed on the hand on the high end. The therapist then guides the client to induce deep relaxation. Once a state of deep relaxation is achieved, the client imagines confronting the least threatening stimulus in the fear hierarchy. If anxiety occurs, the client stops imagining the fearful stimulus and restores deep relaxation before trying the exercise again. When the client is able to remain deeply relaxed while imagining an encounter with the least threatening stimulus, he or she progresses to the next stimulus in the hierarchy. This procedure is repeated for each step in the hierarchy. The objective is to use relaxation as an incompatible response to fear, so as to weaken the bonds between the stimuli and the fear they evoke.

Behavior therapists also use **gradual exposure** (also called *in-vivo exposure*, meaning exposure in "real life") to help people overcome phobias. Clients progress at their own pace through a series of real-life encounters with increasingly fearful stimuli arranged in a hierarchy from least to most fearful. In this way, they learn to confront situations they had previously avoided. Exposure therapy is based on a learning model that proposes that fear should extinguish (lessen or disappear) as the person experiences repeated, uneventful encounters with fearful stimuli.

A sample hierarchy for a person with an elevator phobia might include the following steps:

1. Standing outside the elevator.
2. Standing in the elevator with the door open.
3. Standing in the elevator with the door closed.
4. Taking the elevator down one floor.
5. Taking the elevator up one floor.
6. Taking the elevator down two floors.
7. Taking the elevator up two floors.
8. Taking the elevator down two floors and then up two floors.
9. Taking the elevator down to the basement.
10. Taking the elevator up to the highest floor.
11. Taking the elevator all the way down and then all the way up.

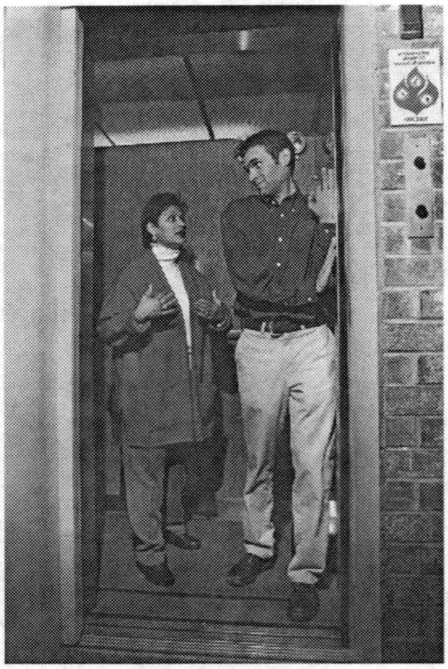
© Jim Whitmer Photography

Through gradual exposure, people with phobias learn to handle fearful situations more effectively, sometimes assisted by a therapist or supportive others.

Gradual exposure helps people overcome specific fears, such as fear of riding on trains or elevators, as well as social phobias, such as fear of meeting new people or speaking in public (Choy, Fyer, & Lipsitz, 2007; Hofmann, 2008; McEvoy, 2008). A person with a social phobia might be instructed to create a hierarchy of fearful social situations. The person would then learn relaxation skills and begin a series of exposure trials, beginning with the least stressful social situation and working upward in the hierarchy to the most stressful situation. Gradual exposure is also used to help people with posttraumatic stress disorder (PTSD) overcome anxiety by directly confronting cues and situations linked to the traumas they experienced (J. G. Beck et al., 2009; Ehlers et al., 2010; Henslee & Coffey, 2010). (See Chapter 12 for further discussion of PTSD.)

A form of observational learning called **modeling** may be used to help people overcome fears and acquire more adaptive behaviors. Modeling involves observing and imitating desirable behaviors in others. People who lack social skills, for example, may be asked to observe more socially skillful people interacting with others. Psychologist Albert Bandura pioneered the use of modeling in helping people overcome phobias, such as fears of snakes, dogs, and other small animals (Bandura, Blanchard, & Ritter, 1969).

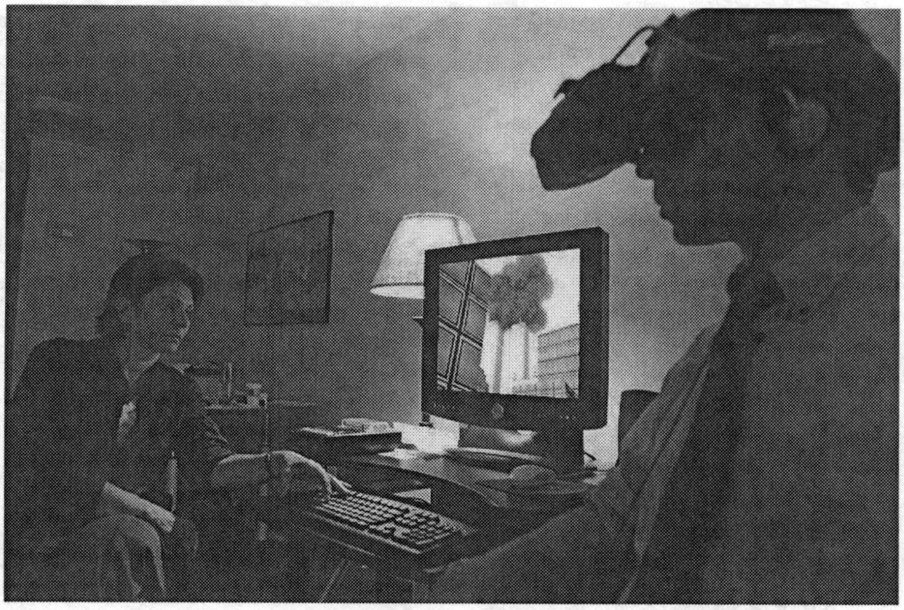

© AP Photo/Bebeto Matthews

Virtual therapy has been used to help people overcome a fear of heights by guiding them through a series of encounters with height situations in virtual reality.

Behavior therapists today have adapted the technology of *virtual reality* to create simulated environments in which phobic people can confront virtual representations of fearful stimuli. For example, using a specialized helmet and gloves connected to a computer, a phobic person with a fear of heights can simulate a ride in a glass-enclosed virtual elevator or peer out over a virtual balcony on the 33rd floor. With this form of exposure therapy, called **virtual reality therapy**, therapists can simulate real-life environments, including some that would be difficult to arrange in reality (e.g., simulated airplane takeoffs). Virtual therapy has been shown to be effective in treating a wide range of phobias, including fear of heights, fear of flying, and fear of spiders (Coelho et al., 2009; T. D. Parsons & Rizzo, 2008; Powers & Emmelkamp, 2008).

modeling A behavior therapy technique for overcoming phobias and acquiring more adaptive behaviors, based on observing and imitating models.

virtual reality therapy A form of exposure therapy in which virtual reality is used to simulate real-world environments.

We have "virtually" only scratched the surface that this new technology has to offer as a therapeutic tool. Today, therapists are expanding the application of VRT to include treatment of other phobias, including fear of public speaking and agoraphobia. Iraq war veterans suffering from posttraumatic stress disorder have been treated in hospital settings in which they are desensitized to emotionally charged memories of the war by repeatedly confronting war-related images in a virtual reality simulation called "Virtual Iraq" (Schaffer, 2007).

Therapists are also beginning to use other technologies (e.g., Carlbring et al., 2011; Ljótsson et al., 2011). In one example, researchers equipped patients with electronic devices that prompted them (like "tweets") several times a day to report about their symptoms, whether they had taken their medication, and whether they had used any drugs (Swendsen, Ben-Zeev, & Granholm, 2010). Next up may be smartphone apps that provide a means of tracking psychological symptoms of patients in the community, much like a Holter monitor is currently being used to provide ambulatory measures of heart functioning (Yager, 2011).

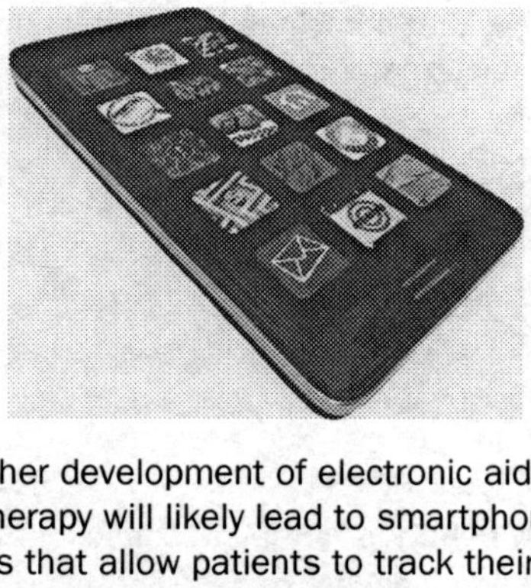

© iQoncept/Shutterstock.com

Further development of electronic aids in therapy will likely lead to smartphone apps that allow patients to track their symptoms, with information wirelessly transmitted to their therapists for evaluation in real-time.

Aversive Conditioning

In **aversive conditioning**, a form of classical conditioning, stimuli associated with an undesirable response are paired with aversive stimuli, such as an electric shock or a nausea-inducing drug. The idea is to make these stimuli elicit a negative response (fear or nausea) that would discourage the person from performing the undesirable behavior. For

aversive conditioning A form of behavior therapy in which stimuli associated with undesirable behavior are paired with aversive stimuli to create a negative response to these stimuli.

CONCEPT 16.14
Aversive conditioning applies principles of classical conditioning to create an unpleasant response to stimuli associated with undesirable behaviors.

→ Concept Link
Principles of classical conditioning can be used to explain a wide range of behaviors, from fear responses to drug cravings. See Module 5.1.

example, adults who are sexually attracted to children might receive a mild but painful electric shock when they view sexually provocative pictures of children. Or in alcoholism treatment, a nausea-inducing drug could be paired with sniffing or sipping an alcoholic beverage. In conditioning terms, the nausea-inducing drug is the unconditioned stimulus (US) and nausea is the unconditioned response (UR). The alcoholic beverage becomes a conditioned stimulus (CS) that elicits nausea (CR) when it is paired repeatedly with the US. Unfortunately, the effects of aversive conditioning are often temporary; outside the treatment setting, the aversive stimulus no longer accompanies the undesirable behavior. Partly for this reason, aversive conditioning is not in widespread use, although it may be useful as a component of a broader treatment program.

Operant Conditioning Methods

CONCEPT 16.15
Behavior therapists apply operant conditioning principles to strengthen desirable behavior and weaken or eliminate undesirable behavior.

Behavior therapists apply operant principles of reinforcement and punishment to help people strengthen desirable behaviors and weaken undesirable behaviors. For example, therapists may train parents to reward children for appropriate behavior and to withdraw attention (a social reinforcer) following problem behavior to weaken or eliminate it. Or they may train parents to use mild forms of punishment, such as a *time-out* procedure, in which children are removed from a rewarding environment when they misbehave and "sit out" for a prescribed period of time before resuming other activities.

In Chapter 5 you were introduced to another operant conditioning technique, the *token economy,* a behavior modification program used in mental hospitals and other settings such as schools. For example, residents of mental hospitals may receive tokens, or plastic chips, as positive reinforcers for performing certain desirable behaviors such as self-grooming, tidying their rooms, and socializing appropriately with others. Tokens can then be exchanged for tangible reinforcers such as extra privileges or candy. Token economy programs have been used successfully in mental hospitals, institutions and group homes for people with mental retardation, and residential treatment facilities for delinquents.

Cognitive-Behavioral Therapy

cognitive-behavioral therapy (CBT) A form of therapy that combines behavioral and cognitive treatment techniques.

Cognitive-behavioral therapy (CBT) combines behavioral techniques, such as gradual exposure, with cognitive techniques that focus on helping clients recognize and correct faulty beliefs and ways of thinking. Cognitive-behavioral therapists draw upon the principles and techniques of cognitive models of therapy, such as those pioneered by psychologist Albert Ellis and psychiatrist Aaron Beck, whose work we consider in the next section.

Cognitive Therapy

CONCEPT 16.16
Many behavior therapists subscribe to a broader concept of behavior therapy called cognitive-behavioral therapy, which focuses on changing maladaptive thoughts and beliefs as well as problem behaviors.

CONCEPT 16.17
Cognitive therapists help clients challenge maladaptive thoughts and beliefs and replace them with more adaptive ways of thinking.

Cognitive therapists focus on helping people change how they think. Their techniques are based on the view that distorted or faulty ways of thinking underlie emotional problems (e.g., anxiety disorders and depression) as well as self-defeating or maladaptive behavior. In short, they argue that emotional problems are not caused by negative events or life experiences but, rather, by ways in which people interpret their experiences. As Shakespeare penned in *Hamlet,* "there is nothing either good or bad, but thinking makes it so."

Shakespeare certainly didn't mean that misfortunes are painless or easy to cope with. Rather, he seems to imply that the ways in which we think about upsetting events can either heighten or diminish our discomfort and affect how we cope with life's misfortunes. Several hundred years later, cognitive therapists would adopt Shakespeare's simple but elegant expression as a kind of motto for their approach to therapy.

Cognitive therapies are relatively brief forms of treatment (involving months rather than years). Like practitioners of the humanistic approach, they focus more on what is happening in the present than on what happened in the distant past. Clients are given homework assignments to help them identify, evaluate, and challenge distorted thoughts as they occur and develop adaptive behaviors and rational ways of thinking. The two major cognitive therapies today are *rational emotive behavior therapy*, which was developed by Ellis, and *cognitive therapy*, which was developed by Beck.

© Dr. Debbie Joffe Ellis

Albert Ellis

Rational-Emotive Behavior Therapy: The Importance of Thinking Rationally

Albert Ellis (1913–2007) developed **rational emotive behavior therapy (REBT)** based on his view that irrational or illogical thinking is at the root of emotional problems (Ellis, 1977, 2001). To overcome these problems, the therapist must teach the client to recognize these irrational beliefs and replace them with logical, self-enhancing beliefs. Ellis viewed this process as a kind of "pounding-away" at the client's irrational beliefs until the client is persuaded to change these beliefs and replace them with more logical ways of thinking.

rational emotive behavior therapy (REBT) Developed by Albert Ellis, a form of therapy based on identifying and correcting irrational beliefs that are thought to underlie emotional and behavioral difficulties.

CONCEPT 16.18
Rational emotive behavior therapy is based on the view that irrational beliefs cause people to suffer emotional distress in the face of disappointing life experiences.

Ellis contends that irrational beliefs often take the form of *shoulds* and *musts*, such as the belief that we must have the approval of all of the important people in our lives all of the time. Ellis notes that although the desire for approval is understandable, it is irrational to believe we will always garner approval or that we couldn't possibly survive without it. REBT encourages clients to replace irrational beliefs (such as those listed in Table 16.2) with rational ones and learn more adaptive ways of dealing with their life situations. To Ellis, negative emotional reactions, such as anxiety and depression, are not the direct result of life experiences. Rather, they stem from the irrational beliefs we hold about these experiences. Irrational beliefs are illogical because they are based on a distorted, exaggerated appraisal of the situation, not on the facts at hand. Ellis uses an "ABC" approach to explain the causes of emotional distress. This model can be diagrammed as follows:

Activating event ⟶ *Beliefs* ⟶ *Consequences*

Consider a person who feels worthless and depressed after getting a poor grade on a college exam (see ■ Figure 16.1). The poor grade is the *activating event* (A). The *consequences* (C), or outcomes, are feelings of depression. But the activating event (A) does not lead directly to the emotional consequences (C). Rather, the event is filtered through the person's *beliefs* (B) ("I'm just a complete jerk. I'll never succeed."). People often have difficulty

TABLE 16.2 Examples of Irrational Beliefs According to Ellis

- You absolutely must have love and approval from virtually all the people who are important to you.
- You must be completely competent in all your activities in order to feel worthwhile.
- It is awful and catastrophic when life does not go the way you want it to go. Things are awful when you don't get your first choices.
- People must treat each other fairly, and it is horrible when they don't.
- It's awful and terrible when there is no clear or quick solution to life's problems.
- Your past must continue to affect you and determine your behavior.

Source: Adapted from Ellis, 1991.

cognitive therapy Developed by Aaron Beck, a form of therapy that helps clients recognize and correct distorted patterns of thinking associated with negative emotional states.

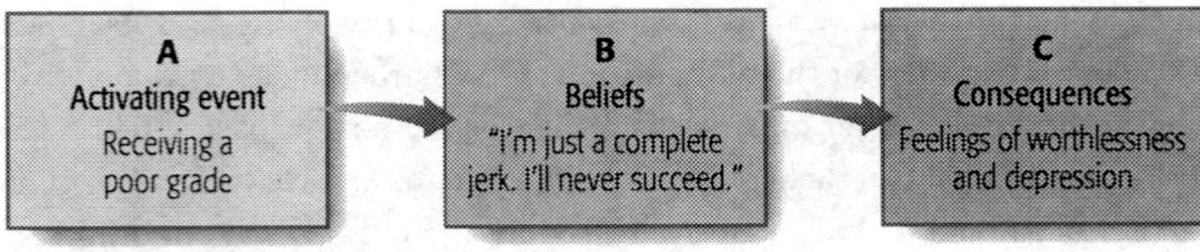

FIGURE 16.1 The Ellis "ABC" Model

© Courtesy of Aaron Beck

Aaron Beck

identifying their underlying beliefs (B)—in part, because they are generally more aware of their feelings than what they are thinking when responding to an event (A) and, in part, because the event (A) and emotional consequences (C) occur so closely together that the event seems to be the direct cause of the emotion. People may also have difficulty focusing inwardly on their thoughts to reflect on what they are telling themselves about their experiences. Ellis recognizes that disappointment is an understandable reaction in the face of upsetting or frustrating events. But when people exaggerate the consequences of negative events, they convert disappointment into depression and despair.

Ellis later added a "D" (dispute) to the ABC model by helping clients challenge or dispute their irrational beliefs. The accompanying cartoon, "Maria Managing Anxiety with ABC's," illustrates the ABCD model in relation to a common source of anxiety, public speaking. REBT also helps people develop more effective interpersonal behaviors to replace self-defeating or maladaptive behavior. Therapists give clients specific tasks or homework assignments, such as disagreeing with an overbearing relative or asking someone for a date. They also help clients practice or rehearse more adaptive behaviors.

Cognitive Therapy: Correcting Errors in Thinking

CONCEPT 16.19
Cognitive therapy focuses on helping clients identify and correct distorted thoughts and beliefs that have no basis in reality.

Cognitive therapy helps people identify and correct errors in thinking and replace them with rational alternatives (Beck, 2006; Beck & Alford, 2009; Beck et al., 1979). The developer of cognitive therapy, psychiatrist Aaron Beck (b. 1921), believes that faulty thinking about life experiences is at the root of negative emotional states, such

TRY THIS OUT Replacing Distorted Thoughts with Rational Alternatives

For each of the automatic thoughts listed below, fill in a rational alternative response. If necessary, refer again to Table 15.2 (p. 582) for a listing of the common types of cognitive distortions. Sample rational alternatives can be found in the key at the end of the chapter.

Automatic Thought	Type of Cognitive Distortion	Rational Alternative
1. This relationship is a disaster, a complete disaster.	All-or-nothing thinking	______
2. I'm falling apart. I can't handle this.	Catastrophizing	______
3. Things must really be awful for me to feel this way.	Emotion-based reasoning	______
4. I know I'm going to flunk this course.	Jumping to conclusions	______
5. ______'s problems are really my fault.	Mistaken responsibility	______
6. I'm just a loser.	Name calling	______
7. Someone my age should be further along than I am.	Shouldism	______
8. It would be awful if I don't get this job.	Catastrophizing	______
9. I know that if ______ got to know me, he/she would not like me.	Jumping to conclusions	______
10. All I can think about are the negatives.	Negative focusing	______

as depression. Distorted or faulty thoughts are like tinted glasses that darken a person's perceptions of life experiences (Smith, 2009).

Beck refers to errors in thinking as "cognitive distortions." For example, he believes that depressed people tend to magnify or exaggerate the consequences of negative events and blame themselves for their disappointments while ignoring the role of external circumstances. Cognitive therapists give clients homework assignments, such as recording the negative, distorted thoughts that pop into their head during the day and then substituting rational alternative thoughts in their place (see the *Try This Out* section).

Another type of homework assignment is *reality testing*, in which clients test their negative beliefs in the light of reality to determine whether they are true. For example, a depressed client who feels unwanted by everyone might be asked to call two or three friends on the phone to gather data about how friends actually respond to the calls. The therapist might then ask the client to report on the assignment: "Did they immediately hang up the phone? Or did they seem pleased that you called? Did they express any interest at all in talking to you again or getting together sometime? Does the evidence support the conclusion that *no one* has any interest in you?"

REBT and cognitive therapy are similar in many respects. Both focus primarily on helping people replace dysfunctional thoughts and beliefs with more adaptive, rational ones. The major difference may be one of therapeutic style: The REBT therapist typically adopts a more direct and sometimes confrontational approach in disputing the client's irrational beliefs, whereas the cognitive therapist usually takes a gentler, more collaborative approach to help clients identify and correct the distortions in their thinking.

Differences between specific psychotherapies are not as clear-cut as they may seem. For example, there is a blurring of lines between cognitive and behavioral therapies in the sense that we can classify the cognitive therapies of Ellis and Beck as forms of cognitive-behavioral therapy. Both rely on behavioral and cognitive techniques to help people develop more adaptive behaviors and change distorted thinking patterns. Other therapists identify themselves with an even broader eclectic approach, as we see next.

Eclectic Therapy

Therapists who practice **eclectic therapy** look beyond the theoretical barriers that divide one school of psychotherapy from another. They integrate principles and techniques representing different approaches in designing treatments they believe provide the maximum benefits for a particular client (Prochaska & Norcross, 2010). In a particular case, an eclectic therapist might use behavior therapy to help the client change problem behaviors and psychodynamic approaches to help the client develop insight into underlying conflicts.

Eclecticism is the most widely endorsed theoretical orientation among clinical psychologists today (see ■ Figure 16.2). Eclectic therapists may have learned through experience the value of drawing upon different points of view.

eclectic therapy A therapeutic approach that draws upon principles and techniques representing different schools of therapy.

CONCEPT 16.20
Many therapists identify with an eclectic orientation in which they adopt principles and techniques from different schools of therapy.

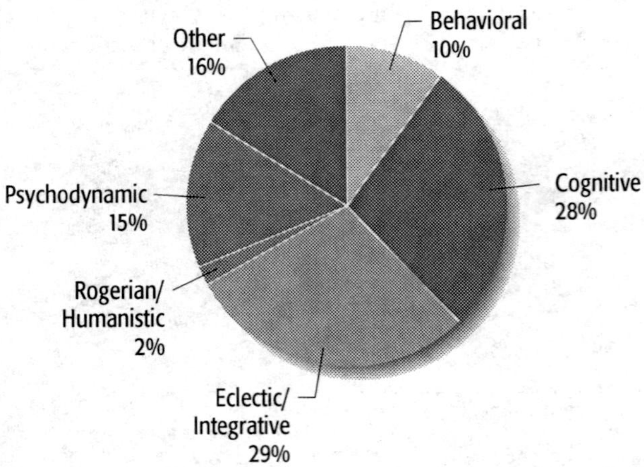

FIGURE 16.2 Clinical Psychologists Identifying with Each Therapeutic Orientation
The eclectic/integrative orientation emerged as the most popular orientation among clinical psychologists polled in a recent survey.
Source: Adapted from Norcross, Karpiak, & Santoro (2005).

Not all therapists subscribe to an eclectic approach. Many believe that the differences between schools of therapy are so compelling that therapeutic integration is neither desirable nor achievable. Trying to combine them, they argue, leads to a veritable hodgepodge of techniques that lack a cohesive conceptual framework. Nevertheless, the movement toward eclecticism continues to grow within the therapeutic community.

Group, Family, and Couple Therapy

group therapy A form of therapy in which clients are treated within a group format.

Group therapy brings people together in small groups to help them explore and resolve their problems (Donigian & Malnati, 2005). Compared to individual therapy, it offers several advantages. For one thing, because the therapist treats several people at a time, group therapy is generally less costly than individual therapy. For another, it may be particularly helpful for people experiencing interpersonal problems such as loneliness, shyness, and low self-esteem. These individuals often benefit from interacting with supportive others in a group treatment program. The give-and-take within the group may help improve a member's social skills. And clients in group therapy can learn how others in the group have coped with similar problems in their lives.

Group therapy may not be for everyone. Some clients prefer the individual attention of a therapist. They may feel that one-on-one therapy provides an opportunity for a deeper exploration of their emotions and experiences. They may also be reluctant to disclose their personal problems to other members of a group. Or they may feel too inhibited to relate comfortably to others in a group, even if they themselves are perhaps the ones for whom group interaction is most beneficial.

CONCEPT 16.21
Therapists often treat individuals in group settings, where the "group" may be a collection of unrelated persons, a family, or a couple.

Group therapists can offset some of these drawbacks by creating an atmosphere that promotes trust and self-exploration. In particular, they require that information disclosed by group members is kept in strict confidence, ensure that group members relate to each other in a supportive and nondestructive fashion, and prevent any single member from monopolizing their attention or dominating the group. In short, effective group therapists attempt to provide each member with the attention he or she needs.

family therapy Therapy for troubled families that focuses on changing disruptive patterns of communication and improving the ways in which family members relate to each other.

Family therapy helps troubled families learn to communicate better and resolve their differences. The family, not the individual, is the unit of treatment. Most family therapists view the family unit as a complex social system in which individuals play certain roles (Gehar, 2009). In many cases there is one family member whom the family brands as the source of the family's problems. Effective family therapists demonstrate how the problems of this individual are symptomatic of larger problems in the family involving a breakdown in the family system, not in the individual per se. They help dysfunctional families change how family members interact and relate to one another so that members can become more accepting and supportive of each other's needs and differences.

couple therapy Therapy that focuses on helping distressed couples resolve their conflicts and develop more effective communication skills.

In **couple therapy** (often called *marital therapy* when applied to married couples), the couple is the unit of the treatment. Couple therapy builds healthier relationships by helping couples learn to communicate better and work out solutions to their problems (Christensen et al., 2010). Couple therapists identify power struggles and lack of communication as among the typical problems faced by troubled couples seeking help. Their aim is to help open channels of communication between partners and encourage them to share personal feelings and needs in ways that do not put each other down.

© iStockphoto.com/clearstockconcepts

Group therapy brings together small groups of people to help them explore and work through their psychological problems.

Is Psychotherapy Effective?

Yes, psychotherapy works. A wealth of scientific findings supports the effectiveness of psychotherapy. Yet questions remain about whether some forms of therapy are more effective than others.

CONCEPT 16.22
A wealth of scientific findings supports the effectiveness of psychotherapy, but questions remain about whether some forms of therapy are more effective than others.

Measuring Effectiveness

The strongest body of evidence supporting the effectiveness of psychotherapy comes from controlled studies in which people who received psychotherapy are compared with those who were placed in waiting-list control groups. Investigators commonly use a statistical technique called **meta-analysis** to average the results across a large number of such studies.

meta-analysis A statistical technique for averaging results across a large number of studies.

An early but influential meta-analysis was conducted by Mary Lee Smith, Gene Glass, and Thomas Miller (1980). Based on an analysis of more than 400 controlled studies comparing particular types of therapy (psychodynamic, behavioral, humanistic, etc.) against control groups, they reported that the average person receiving psychotherapy achieved better outcomes than did 80 percent of people in waiting-list control groups (see ■ Figure 16.3). More recent meta-analyses also point to better outcomes for people treated with psychotherapy than for those in control groups (e.g., Lambert & Ogles, 2004; Shadish et al., 2000).

The greatest gains in therapy are typically achieved during the first few months of treatment. Fifty percent of people who participate in psychotherapy show significant improvement within the first 21 sessions (E. M. Anderson & Lambert, 2001; Lambert, Hansen, & Finch, 2001). Many other patients respond with additional treatment. But not everyone benefits from therapy, and some people even deteriorate. Then too, some people who receive other forms of treatment, such as drug therapy, also have negative outcomes.

Which Therapy Is Best?

To say that therapy overall is effective does not mean that all therapies are equally effective, or that one form of therapy is as good as any other for a particular problem.

We need to ask which therapy works best for which types of problems. Evidence showing the effectiveness of specific therapies for particular problems is mounting. For example, evidence shows that cognitive-behavioral therapy works well in treating a wide range of disorders, including panic disorder, phobia, posttraumatic stress disorder, obsessive-compulsive disorder, depression, and bulimia (e.g., Crow et al., 2009; Ehlers et al., 2010; Gunter & Whittal, 2010; Rapee, Gaston, & Abbott, 2009; Roy-Byrne et al., 2010; Shafran et al., 2009; Tolin, 2010). Evidence also supports the effectiveness of contemporary forms of psychodynamic therapy in treating

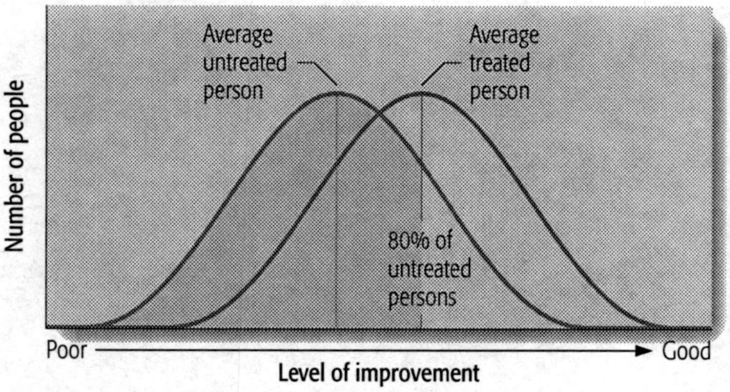

FIGURE 16.3 Effectiveness of Psychotherapy
A meta-analysis of more than 400 outcome studies showed that the average therapy client achieved greater improvement than 80 percent of untreated controls.
Source: Adapted from M. L. Smith, Glass, & Miller, 1980.

psychological disorders such as depression, borderline personality disorder, and bulimia (e.g., Bateman & Fonagy, 2009; DeRubeis et al., 2005; Driessen et al., 2010; Leichsenring & Rabung, 2008; Paris, 2008; Rieger et al., 2010; Shedler, 2010). Humanistic therapies may have their greatest benefits in helping individuals develop a more cohesive sense of self, connect with their innermost feelings, and mobilize their efforts toward self-actualization.

CONCEPT 16.23
Evidence points to both specific and nonspecific factors in accounting for the benefits of psychotherapy.

The Movement Toward Evidence-Based Treatments

A major development in recent years is the growing emphasis on evidence-based treatments (EBTs)—that is, treatments shown to be effective when measured against control groups in treating specific problems or disorders (APA Presidential Task Force on Evidence-Based Practice, 2006; McHugh & Barlow, 2010; Weisz, Jensen-Doss, & Hawley, 2006). A partial listing of these evidence-based therapies, which are also called *empirically supported treatments* (ESTs), is shown in Table 16.3. Other treatments may be added to the list as evidence supporting their effectiveness becomes available. The emphasis on evidence-based treatment mirrors the larger concern in the health community on the need for accountability—that is, basing practice on treatments that have been shown to work.

What Accounts for the Benefits of Therapy?

nonspecific factors General features of psychotherapy, such as attention from a therapist and mobilization of positive expectancies or hope.

Might the benefits of therapy have to do with the common characteristics shared by different therapies? These common characteristics are called **nonspecific factors** because they are not limited to any one therapy. They include a positive expectation of treatment success, as well as aspects of the interpersonal relationship between client and therapist, such as the *therapeutic alliance*—that is, the attachment the client feels

TABLE 16.3 Examples of Empirically Supported Treatments (ESTs)

Treatment	Effective in Treating
Cognitive therapy	Depression
Behavior therapy	Depression
	Persons with developmental disabilities
	Enuresis ("bed-wetting")
	Headache
	Agoraphobia and specific phobia
	Obsessive-compulsive disorder
Cognitive-behavioral therapy (CBT)	Panic disorder
	Generalized anxiety disorder
	Bulimia
	Smoking cessation
Interpersonal psychotherapy (a structured brief form of psychodynamic therapy)	Depression

toward the therapist and the therapy (Prochaska & Norcross, 2010; A. E. M. Smith, Msetfi, & Golding, 2010). The quality of the therapeutic alliance is strongly associated with better outcomes in therapy (e.g., Strauss et al., 2006; Zuroff & Blatt, 2006). Having a positive expectancy or sense of hopefulness that problems can be overcome can become a self-fulfilling prophecy by motivating clients to mobilize their efforts to resolve their problems. Responses to positive expectancies are called **placebo effects** or *expectancy effects*. In all likelihood, the benefits of psychotherapy involve a combination of specific factors, such as the particular techniques used, and nonspecific factors.

placebo effects Positive outcomes of a treatment resulting from positive expectations rather than from the effects of the treatment itself. Also called *expectancy effects*.

Multicultural Issues in Treatment

Therapists treat people from many different ethnic and racial groups. Members of ethnic and racial minorities may have different customs, beliefs, and philosophies than members of the dominant majority culture, and therapists must be aware of these differences to provide successful treatment. For example, with African American clients, therapists need to understand the long history of extreme racial discrimination and oppression to which African Americans have been exposed in our society. This history of negative treatment and cultural oppression may lead African Americans to develop a heightened sense of suspiciousness or reserve toward whites, including white therapists, as a type of coping skill—a defense against exploitation. They may thus be hesitant to disclose personal information in therapy, especially during the early stages. Therapists should not press for disclosure or confuse culturally laden suspiciousness with paranoid thinking.

The traditional value in Asian cultures of keeping one's feelings to oneself, especially negative emotions, may conflict with the emphasis in psychotherapy on open expression of emotions. Culturally competent therapists recognize that Asian clients who appear passive or emotionally restrained when judged by Western standards may be responding in ways that are culturally appropriate and should not be judged as shy, uncooperative, or avoidant (Hwang, 2006). Moreover, the emphasis on collective or group values in Asian cultures over those of the individual may conflict with the emphasis in Western psychotherapy on the importance of individuality and self-determination.

CONCEPT 16.24
Therapists are trained to be sensitive to cultural differences among the different groups of people they treat.

Value conflicts may also come into play in therapeutic situations involving Latinos from traditional Hispanic backgrounds. Traditional Hispanic cultures place a strong value on interdependency among family members—a value that may clash with the emphasis on independence and self-reliance in mainstream U.S. culture. Treatment providers need to be respectful of this difference and avoid imposing their own values on Latino clients. In working with Latinos, as well as other ethnic groups, therapists must also be sensitive to their linguistic preferences.

Culturally sensitive therapists also need to respect and understand the customs, cultures, and values of the people they treat (Stuart, 2004). In working with Native Americans, for example, therapists may find it helpful to bring elements of tribal culture into the therapy setting, such as healing ceremonies that are part of the client's cultural or religious traditions (Rabasca, 2000). Native American clients may expect therapists to do most of the talking, consistent with the traditional healer role within their culture.

Therapists also need to demonstrate that the treatment methods they use work effectively with the particular ethnic groups they treat (Horrell, 2008; Soa, Leung, &

TABLE 16.4 Disparities in Mental Health Care: Culture, Race, and Ethnicity

Disparities

- As compared to other groups, racial or ethnic minorities have less access to mental health care and receive lower quality care.

Causes

- Minority group members are more likely to lack health insurance.
- Minority group members lack access to treatment providers who are similar in ethnicity or who possess appropriate language skills.
- The lingering stigma about mental illness discourages minority group members from seeking help.
- There are few treatment providers in rural or isolated locations where minority group members, especially Native Americans, may reside.

Vision for the Future

- Expand the scientific base to better understand relationships between mental health and sociocultural factors such as acculturation, stigma, and racism.
- Improve access to treatment—for example, by improving language access and geographic availability of mental health services.
- Reduce barriers to mental health care, such as costs of services and the societal stigma toward mental illness.
- Improve quality of care—for example, by individualizing treatment to the person's age, gender, race, ethnicity, and culture.
- Increase minority representation among mental health treatment providers.
- Promote mental health by strengthening supportive families and working to eradicate contributors to mental health problems, such as poverty, community violence, racism, and discrimination.

Source: U.S. Department of Health and Human Services, 2001.

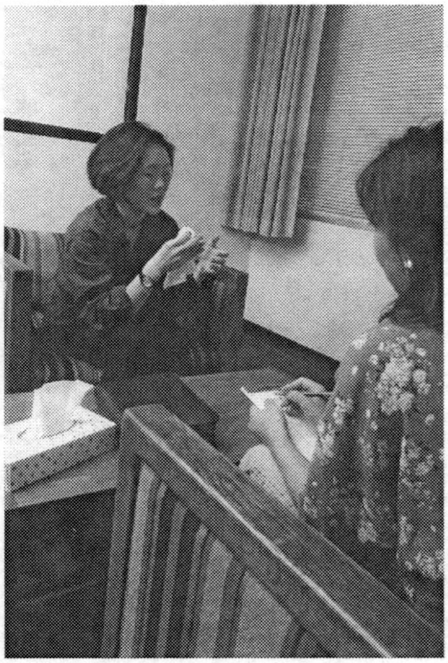
© Michael Newman/Photoedit

Culturally sensitive therapy is structured to create a more receptive therapeutic environment for people from varied cultural backgrounds.

Hung, 2008). In short, therapists need to adapt their treatment approaches to clients from diverse backgrounds (Hwang, 2006). Therapists also need to be aware of their own cultural biases to avoid stereotyping clients from other cultural groups. When a therapist's own cultural biases are left unexamined, they can quickly become destructive of the therapeutic relationship.

The mental health system also needs to do a better job of providing quality care to all groups. A 2001 report by the U.S. Surgeon General concluded that minority group members typically receive lower quality care and have less access to care than other Americans (U.S. Department of Health and Human Services, 2001; see Table 16.4). Consequently, minority group members typically shoulder a greater mental health burden because their mental disorders go undiagnosed and untreated (P. S. Wang et al., 2005; U.S. Department of Health and Human Services, 2001).

Concept Chart 16.2 summarizes the differences among the types of psychotherapy discussed in this module.

CONCEPT CHART 16.2 Major Types of Psychotherapy: How They Differ

© Marcin Balcerzak/Shutterstock.com

Type of Therapy	Focus	Length	Therapist's Role	Techniques
Classical psychoanalysis	Insight into unconscious causes of behavior	Long, at least several years	Passive, interpretive	Free association, dream analysis, interpretation
Modern psychodynamic approaches	Insight-oriented, but focus is more on current relationships than is the case in Freudian psychoanalysis	Briefer than traditional analysis	Probing; engaging client in back-and-forth discussion	More direct analysis of client's defenses and transference relationships; less use of free association
Humanistic, client-centered therapy	Promotes self-growth by helping clients become more aware of, and accepting of, their inner feelings, needs, and interests	Varies	Nondirective; allows client to lead, with therapist serving as an empathic listener	Demonstrating empathy, unconditional positive regard, and genuineness to create a warm and accepting therapeutic atmosphere
Humanistic, gestalt therapy	Helps clients develop a unified sense of self by bringing into present awareness their true feelings and conflicts with others	Brief, sometimes only a few sessions	Directive, engaging, even confrontational	Empty chair technique and other role-playing exercises
Behavior therapy	Changes problem behavior through use of learning-based techniques tailored to the specific problem	Brief, lasting perhaps 10 to 20 sessions	Direct, active problem solving	Systematic desensitization, exposure therapy, aversion therapy, operant conditioning techniques
Cognitive-behavioral therapy	Focuses on changing both maladaptive cognitions and overt behaviors	Brief, usually lasting 10 to 20 sessions	Direct, active problem solving	Combines cognitive and behavioral techniques
Rational-emotive behavior therapy	Helps clients replace irrational beliefs with more adaptive, logical alternatives	Brief, typically 10 to 20 sessions	Directive, challenging, sometimes confrontational	Identifying and disputing irrational beliefs, with behavioral homework assignments
Cognitive therapy	Helps clients identify and correct faulty styles of thinking	Brief, typically 10 to 20 sessions	Collaborative process of engaging client in an effort to logically examine beliefs and find evidence to support or refute them	Identifying and correcting distorted thoughts; specific homework assignments including thought recording and reality testing

16.2 MODULE REVIEW Types of Psychotherapy

Recite It

What is psychotherapy?

- Psychotherapy is a verbal form of therapy intended to help people overcome psychological or personal problems.

What are the major types of mental health professionals?

- The major types of professionals who provide mental health services are clinical and counseling psychologists, psychiatrists, clinical or psychiatric social workers, psychoanalysts, counselors, and nurses. They vary in their training backgrounds as well as in the services they provide.

What are the major types of psychotherapy?

- Psychodynamic therapy is an insight-oriented approach to therapy based on the Freudian model. The psychodynamic therapist helps clients uncover and work through the unconscious conflicts dating from childhood that are believed to be at the root of their problems.
- Humanistic therapy focuses primarily on the client's subjective, conscious experience in the here-and-now.
- Behavior therapy is the systematic application of learning principles to help people unlearn maladaptive behaviors and acquire more adaptive behaviors. The techniques of behavior therapy include systematic desensitization, gradual exposure, modeling, aversive conditioning, and methods based on operant conditioning.
- Cognitive-behavioral therapy is a broader form of behavior therapy that incorporates both behavioral and cognitive techniques in treatment. Cognitive therapies, such as rational emotive behavior therapy (REBT) and cognitive therapy, focus on modifying the individual's maladaptive thoughts and beliefs that are believed to underlie emotional problems, such as anxiety and depression, and self-defeating or maladaptive forms of behavior.

What is eclectic therapy?

- In eclectic therapy, the therapist adopts principles or techniques from different schools of therapy.

What are group, family, and couple therapy?

- Group therapy is a form of psychotherapy in which several individuals receive treatment at the same time in a group format.
- Family therapy helps conflicted families learn to resolve their differences, clarify communications, resolve role conflicts, and avoid tendencies toward blaming individual family members.
- Couple therapy is used to help distressed couples improve their communication skills and resolve their differences.

Does psychotherapy work?

- The answer is yes. Meta-analyses show that people who participate in psychotherapy are more likely to achieve a good outcome than those who remain untreated.
- There is a continuing debate about whether some forms of therapy are better than others.
- Evidence supports the effectiveness of particular forms of therapy for specific disorders.

What cultural factors do therapists need to consider when working with members of diverse groups?

- The cultural factors to be considered include differences in cultural beliefs, customs, values, and linguistic preferences, as well as the therapists' own cultural biases and stereotyping tendencies.

Recall It

1. Match the following concepts from psychodynamic therapy with the appropriate descriptions: (a) free association; (b) insight; (c) resistance; (d) transference relationship.
   - **i.** understanding the unconscious origins of a problem.
   - **ii.** responding to the analyst as a "father figure."
   - **iii.** blocking that occurs when emotionally sensitive topics arise.
   - **iv.** saying whatever comes to mind.
2. Name three important qualities shown by an effective client-centered therapist.
3. Jonathan's therapist trains him to use deep muscle relaxation and helps him construct a fear hierarchy. Which behavior therapy technique is this therapist likely to be using?
4. The form of therapy that holds that irrational beliefs underlie the development of psychological problems is ______.
5. List two advantages and two disadvantages of group therapy.

Think About It

- Which approach to therapy would you prefer if you were seeking help for a psychological problem? Why would you prefer this approach?
- What cultural factors should therapists take into account when providing services to members of diverse cultural or racial groups?

Biomedical Therapies

MODULE 16.3

- What are the major types of psychotropic or psychiatric drugs?
- What are the advantages and disadvantages of psychiatric drugs?
- What is ECT, and how is it used?
- What is psychosurgery?

Remarkable gains have been made in treating a wide range of psychological disorders with biomedical forms of treatment, which most often involve the use of **psychotropic drugs** (also called *psychiatric* or *psychotherapeutic drugs*). Despite their success, psychiatric drugs have limitations, including unwelcome side effects and potential for abuse. Other forms of biomedical treatment, such as electroconvulsive therapy (ECT) and psychosurgery, are more controversial.

THE BRAIN LOVES A PUZZLE

As you read ahead, use the information in the text to solve the following puzzle:

A man suffering from panic attacks seeks help from a psychiatrist. After a thorough evaluation, the psychiatrist prescribes an antidepressant. The man appears puzzled and says, "You must be mistaken. I'm not depressed." Did the psychiatrist make a mistake?

Drug Therapy

Neurotransmitters ferry nerve impulses from one neuron to another. But irregularities in the workings of neurotransmitters in the brain are implicated in a wide range of psychological disorders, including anxiety disorders, mood disorders, eating disorders, and schizophrenia. Scientists have developed drugs that work on neurotransmitters in the brain to help regulate moods and thinking processes. These drugs, called *psychotropic drugs* or *psychiatric drugs*, help relieve symptoms of psychological disorders ranging from panic disorder to depression to schizophrenia. However, they are not cures. There are three major groupings of psychotropic drugs: *antianxiety drugs, antidepressants,* and *antipsychotics.*

CONCEPT 16.25

Psychotropic drugs work on neurotransmitter systems in the brain to help regulate moods and thinking processes.

→ Concept Link

Neurotransmitters are chemicals that carry nerve messages from neuron to neuron. See Module 2.1.

Antianxiety Drugs

Antianxiety drugs (sometimes called *minor tranquilizers*) help quell anxiety, induce calmness, and reduce muscle tension. The most widely used antianxiety drugs are minor tranquilizers such as *diazepam* (Valium), *chlordiazepoxide* (Librium), and *alprazolam* (Xanax). They act on the neurotransmitter *gamma-aminobutyric acid*—or GABA for short (first discussed in Chapter 2). GABA is an inhibitory neurotransmitter, which means that it inhibits the flow of nerve impulses and thus prevents neurons in the brain from overly exciting their neighbors. The most widely used antianxiety drugs, including Valium, Librium, and Xanax, make GABA receptors more sensitive, which enhances the chemical's calming (inhibitory) effects.

psychotropic drugs Psychiatric drugs used in the treatment of psychological or mental disorders.

antianxiety drugs Drugs that combat anxiety.

Antidepressants

Antidepressants increase levels of the neurotransmitters norepinephrine and serotonin in brain synapses. There are three major types of antidepressants: **tricyclics, monoamine oxidase (MAO) inhibitors**, and **selective serotonin-reuptake inhibitors (SSRIs)**.

The tricyclics, which include *imipramine* (Tofranil) and *amitriptyline* (Elavil), raise levels of norepinephrine and serotonin by interfering with the reuptake process by which these chemical messengers are reabsorbed by the transmitting cells. MAO inhibitors, which include *phenelzine* (Nardil) and *tranylcypromine* (Parnate), inhibit the

antidepressants Drugs that combat depression by affecting the levels or activity of neurotransmitters.

tricyclics A class of antidepressant drugs that increase the availability of neurotransmitters in the brain by interfering with the reuptake of these chemicals by transmitting neurons.

CONCEPT 16.26
Three major classes of psychotropic drugs are antianxiety drugs, antidepressants, and antipsychotics.

→ Concept Link
Psychotropic drugs work as agonists or antagonists depending on their actions on particular neurotransmitter systems. See Module 2.1.

monoamine oxidase (MAO) inhibitors A class of antidepressant drugs that increase the availability of neurotransmitters in the brain by inhibiting an enzyme, monoamine oxidase, that breaks down or degrades them in the synapse.

selective serotonin-reuptake inhibitors (SSRIs) A class of antidepressant drugs that work specifically on increasing availability of the neurotransmitter serotonin by interfering with its reuptake.

antipsychotics Drugs used in the treatment of psychotic disorders that help alleviate hallucinations and delusional thinking.

action of the enzyme *monoamine oxidase*, which normally breaks down (degrades) these neurotransmitters in the synapse. The SSRIs, which include *fluoxetine* (Prozac) and *sertraline* (Zoloft), have more specific effects on raising levels of serotonin in the brain by interfering with its reuptake. Tricyclics and SSRIs work in a similar way by blocking the removal of key neurotransmitters in the synapse. Although these types of antidepressants are about equally effective, the SSRIs are generally preferred because they typically produce less severe side effects and are less dangerous in overdose situations (Gartlehner et al., 2008; Ksir, Hart, & Ray, 2008). Additional drugs, such as *aripiprazole* (Abilify), may be added to antidepressant medication to boost the treatment effect when antidepressants alone fail to produce an adequate treatment response (Blier & Blondeau, 2011).

Did you know that antidepressants are used in treating other psychological disorders besides depression? These drugs have therapeutic effects in treating other disorders such as bulimia, panic disorder, social phobia, posttraumatic stress disorder, generalized anxiety disorder, and obsessive-compulsive disorder (e.g., Davidson, 2009; Hudson et al., 2003; Katon, 2006; Pampaloni et al., 2009).Why do antidepressants have such broad-ranging effects? One reason is that neurotransmitters, especially serotonin, are involved in regulating emotional states such as anxiety and depression. Another, as noted in Chapter 8, is that serotonin plays a key role in regulating appetite. Antidepressants such as Zoloft that specifically target this neurotransmitter may help reduce episodes of binge eating associated with bulimia.

Antipsychotics

Antipsychotics (sometimes called *major tranquilizers*) are powerful drugs used to treat schizophrenia and other psychotic disorders. The first class of antipsychotic drugs were *phenothiazines*, which included the drugs Thorazine and Mellaril. The introduction of these drugs in the 1950s revolutionized the treatment of schizophrenia, making it possible to control the more flagrant symptoms of the disorder, such as hallucinations and delusions (Abbott, 2010). With their symptoms largely controlled on maintenance doses of these drugs, many schizophrenia patients were able to leave the confines of state hospitals and return to their families and communities.

© iStockphoto.com/Alex_Smith

Phenothiazines and a newer generation of antipsychotic drugs block the action of the neurotransmitter dopamine at receptor sites in the brain. Though the underlying causes of schizophrenia remain unknown, researchers suspect that the disorder arises from disturbances in neural pathways that utilize dopamine (see Chapter 15).

A newer generation of antipsychotics (e.g., *clozapine, risperidone*, and *olanzapine*) have about the same level of effectiveness as the earlier phenothiazines, but have largely replaced them because they may carry fewer neurological side effects (Alexander et al., 2011; Crespo-Facorro et al., 2011; Leucht et al., 2009). However, researchers are concerned about the risks of troubling side effects of these newer drugs, including substantial weight gain and serious metabolic problems (Foley & Morley, 2011; Morrato et al., 2010; The Lancet, 2011).

Other Psychiatric Drugs

Mood-stabilizing drugs, such as the powdered form of the metallic element *lithium*, help stabilize mood swings in people with bipolar disorder and reduce the risks of recurrent manic episodes (The BALANCE Investigators, 2010; Lichta, 2010). Other mood stabilizers are available to treat mania, including anticonvulsant drugs used in the treatment of epilepsy (Frye, 2011; Yatham, 2011).

Stimulant drugs, such as *methylphenidate* (Ritalin) and *pemoline* (Cylert), are widely used to improve attention spans and reduce disruptive behavior in hyperactive children (Van der Oord et al., 2008). These drugs appear to work by increasing activity of the neurotransmitter dopamine in the frontal lobes of the cerebral cortex, the parts of the brain that regulate attention and control impulsive or acting-out behavior (Devilbiss & Berridge, 2008).

Evaluating Psychotropic Drugs

Though therapeutic drugs can provide some degree of relief from troubling symptoms, they are not panaceas. None produces a cure, nor do all patients respond well to them. For example, nearly 40% of depressed patients treated with antidepressants fail to respond within 12 weeks of treatment (Qaseem et al., 2008). Another major limitation is that relapses are quite common when patients stop taking psychiatric drugs (Donovan et al., 2010). Relapses even occur among many patients who continue to take psychiatric drugs (Mulder et al., 2009). One reason why relapses are so common is that psychiatric drugs do not teach patients new skills they can use to solve their problems, handle stress, and cope with disappointments they may face in the future (Dobson et al., 2008).

CONCEPT 16.27
Psychotropic drugs help control symptoms of psychological disorders, but they do not cure the disorders.

Psychiatric drugs also carry risks of some troubling side effects, including drowsiness (from antianxiety drugs), dry mouth and problems with sexual response (from antidepressants), and muscular tremors, rigidity, and even severe movement disorders (from antipsychotic drugs). Drugs can also have adverse, sometimes even dangerous, effects. For example, use of antidepressants can increase the risk of suicidal behavior in children and adolescents (Roy-Byrne, 2010). The drug lithium needs to be closely monitored because of potential toxic effects. It can also produce mild impairments in memory.

Clozapine (Clozaril), one of a newer generation of antipsychotics, appears to be at least as effective as earlier antipsychotics in controlling symptoms of schizophrenia—but with fewer neurological side effects than the earlier antipsychotics (Correll & Shenk, 2009). However, other complications with these drugs have emerged, including significant weight gain and metabolic disorders associated with increased risk of sudden death from heart disease and stroke (Kuehn, 2009; Parsons et al., 2009).

Some psychiatric drugs, such as the antianxiety drug Valium, can lead to psychological and physical dependence (addiction) if used regularly over time. Valium can also be very dangerous, even deadly, in overdoses or if mixed with alcohol or other drugs. Some people come to depend on antianxiety drugs to cope with life's travails rather than confronting the sources of their anxiety or relationship problems.

Although antidepressants can help relieve depression, their effects are not as dramatic as we see represented in many drug commercials on TV (J. C. Nelson et al., 2010; Rief et al., 2009). Complete symptom relief occurs in 30 percent or fewer of patients treated with antidepressant medication (Menza, 2006). Moreover, although antidepressants provide substantial benefits in treating very severe depression as compared to placebos (inert drugs or "sugar pills"), recent evidence shows they offer little if any benefit over placebos in treating mild or moderate cases of depression (DeRubeis, Fournier, & Fawcett, 2010; Fournier et al., 2010).

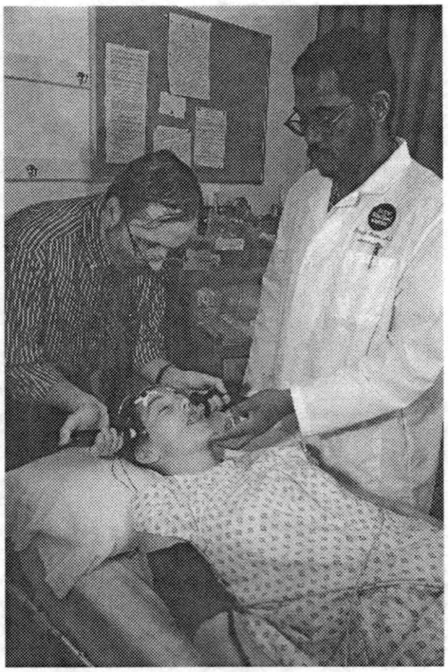

© Najlah Feeney/Stock Boston

In electroconvulsive therapy (ECT), an electric current is passed through the head while the patient is anesthetized. It often produces dramatic relief from severe depression, but relapses are common.

Critics also claim that the large number of children treated with psychiatric drugs such as Ritalin and antidepressants indicates that mental health professionals may be too eager to find a "quick fix" for complex problems. We know little about the long-term effects of Ritalin and other stimulant drugs on the developing brain (Geller, 2006). On the other hand, advocates of drug therapy point to benefits of using psychiatric drugs to control symptoms in children with serious psychological problems and to the risks of leaving these children untreated or undertreated (Kluger, 2003).

Are psychiatric drugs used to treat depression more effective than psychotherapy? Investigators find that when practiced by experienced therapists, cognitive therapy is at least as effective as antidepressants, even in cases of moderate to severe depression (DeRubeis et al., 2005). Behavioral treatment that aims to help depressed people increase the frequency of rewarding activities and goal-directed behaviors also show results that compare favorably with antidepressant medication (Dimidjian et al., 2006; Mazzucchelli, Kane, & Rees, 2009). That said, some patients with depression or anxiety disorders respond better to a combination of psychological and drug therapy than to either treatment alone (e.g., Blanco et al., 2010; Cuijpers, Muñoz, et al., 2009; Cuijpers, van Straten, et al., 2010).

Electroconvulsive Therapy

electroconvulsive therapy (ECT) A form of therapy for severe depression that involves the administration of an electrical shock to the head.

Electroconvulsive therapy (ECT) sounds barbaric. A jolt of electricity is passed through the patient's head strong enough to cause convulsions similar to those of a grand mal epileptic seizure. Yet it often produces dramatic relief from severe depression and can be a lifesaver for people who are suicidally depressed. The patient is anesthetized to prevent pain or discomfort, and muscle relaxants are used to prevent injuries that may result from convulsive jerking. The person awakens minutes later, with no memory of the procedure. ECT typically involves a series of six to 12 treatments over several weeks.

ECT is used almost exclusively in the treatment of severe depression, especially in cases that are unresponsive to other forms of treatment (Faedda et al., 2010; Kennedy et al., 2009). More than 100,000 people receive ECT annually in the United States (Wilson, 2011). We don't yet know precisely how ECT works in relieving depression. Most probably it alters levels of neurotransmitters in brain circuits that control moods. However, it is associated with a high rate of relapse in the weeks and months following a course of treatment (Prudic et al., 2004). ECT may also produce memory loss, especially for events occurring around the time of treatment. In light of these concerns, it is not surprising that many health professionals view ECT as a treatment of last resort.

CONCEPT 16.28
Many mental health professionals view electroconvulsive therapy as a treatment of last resort for severe depression in cases where less invasive treatments have failed.

Psychosurgery

psychosurgery Brain surgery used to control violent or deviant behavior.

prefrontal lobotomy A surgical procedure in which neural pathways in the brain are severed in order to control violent or aggressive behavior.

Psychosurgery is a procedure in which the brain is surgically altered to control deviant or violent behavior. The most widely practiced form of psychosurgery in the past was the **prefrontal lobotomy**, developed in the 1930s by Portuguese neurologist António Egas Moniz. In a prefrontal lobotomy, nerve pathways between the frontal lobe and lower brain centers are severed in order to control a patient's violent or aggressive behavior. More than 1,000 patients underwent the procedure before it was eliminated because of serious complications, including death in some cases. Meanwhile, the introduction of psychiatric drugs offered a less radical alternative to controlling aberrant behavior. A sad footnote to this story was that one of Moniz's own patients (for whom the treatment failed) later shot him, leaving his legs paralyzed.

More sophisticated psychosurgery techniques have been introduced in recent years, involving surgical alterations limited to smaller areas of the brain. These procedures are presently experimental and used rarely—and, again, only as a treatment of last resort—in some cases of severe obsessive-compulsive disorder, bipolar disorder, and major depression (Carey, 2009; Kopell, Machado, & Rezai, 2005). Concerns remain—understandably so—about both the safety and effectiveness of these experimental procedures (Carey, 2011; Lipsman, Neimat, & Lozano, 2007).

© Tetra Images/Tetra Images/Corbis

FIGURE 16.4 A Pacemaker for the Brain
Here we see locations for implantation of electrodes for deep brain stimulation. This remains a promising but still experimental procedure for patients with severe OCD.
Source: "Pacemaker for the Brain," 2008.

A less invasive but still experimental surgical technique is **deep brain stimulation (DBS)** (see ■ Figure 16.4). In one example, surgeons implant electrodes in specific areas of the brain in patients with severe obsessive-compulsive disorder (OCD). A pacemaker-like device is used to stimulate the electrodes to transmit electrical signals into surrounding brain tissue, which blocks brain circuitry believed to be overactive in severe forms of OCD (Carey et al., 2009; Denys et al., 2010). Deep brain stimulation is also being tested as a treatment for severe depression that has failed to respond to less invasive treatments (e.g., Blomsted et al., 2011). Other brain stimulation techniques for treating depression are also being studied, including magnetic stimulation of deep areas in the brain (Bewernick et al., 2010; Raya et al., 2011).

deep brain stimulation Use of electrical stimulation of deep parts of the brain in the treatment of psychological disorders such as severe forms of obsessive-compulsive disorder and depression.

Concept Chart 16.3 summarizes the major types and uses of the psychotropic drugs discussed in this module.

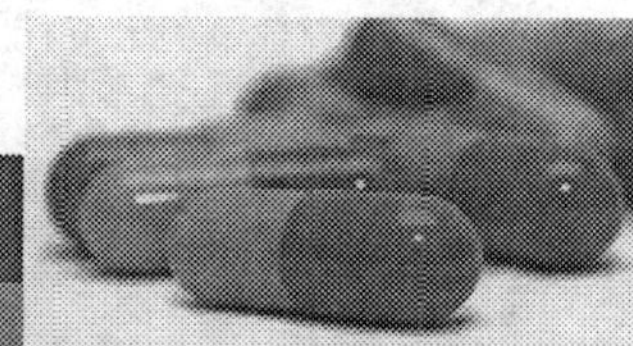

© iStockphoto.com/Alex_Smith

CONCEPT CHART 16.3 Major Types and Uses of Psychotropic Drugs

	Generic Name	Brand Name	Clinical Uses	Possible Side Effects or Complications
Antianxiety Drugs	Diazepam Chlordiazepoxide Lorazepam Alprazolam	Valium Librium Ativan Xanax	Treatment of anxiety and insomnia	Drowsiness, fatigue, impaired coordination, nausea
Antidepressant Drugs	**Tricyclics** Imipramine Amitriptyline Doxepin	 Tofranil Elavil Sinequan	Depression, bulimia, panic disorder	Changes in blood pressure, heart irregularities, dry mouth, confusion, skin rash
	MAO Inhibitors Phenelzine	 Nardil	Depression	Dizziness, headache, sleep disturbance, agitation, anxiety, fatigue
	Selective Serotonin-Reuptake Inhibitors Fluoxetine Sertraline Paroxetine Citalopram	 Prozac Zoloft Paxil Celexa	Depression, bulimia, panic disorder, obsessive-compulsive disorder, posttraumatic stress disorder (Zoloft)	Nausea, constipation, diarrhea, vomiting, anxiety, insomnia, sweating, dry mouth, sexual side effects, dizziness, drowsiness

(*Continued*)

CONCEPT CHART 16.3 *(Continued)*

	Generic Name	Brand Name	Clinical Uses	Possible Side Effects or Complications
	Other Antidepressant Drugs			
	Bupropion	Wellbutrin, Zyban	Depression, nicotine dependence	Dry mouth, insomnia, headaches, nausea, constipation, tremors
	Venlafaxine Duloxetine	Effexor Cymbalta	Depression	Nausea, constipation, dry mouth, drowsiness, insomnia, dizziness, anxiety
Antipsychotic Drugs	**Phenothiazines**		Schizophrenia and other psychotic disorders	
	Chlorpromazine	Thorazine		Movement disorders, drowsiness, restlessness, dry mouth, blurred vision, muscle rigidity
	Thioridazine	Mellaril		
	Atypical Antipsychotics		Schizophrenia and other psychotic disorders	
	Risperidone	Risperdal		Difficulty sitting still, constipation, dizziness, drowsiness, weight gain
	Clozapine	Clozaril		Potentially lethal blood disorder, seizures, fast heart rate, drowsiness, dizziness, nausea
	Olanzapine	Zyprexa		Drowsiness, low blood pressure, dizziness, heart palpitations, fatigue, constipation, weight gain
Antimanic Drugs	Lithium carbonate	Eskalith	Manic episodes and stabilization of mood swings associated with bipolar disorder	Tremors, thirst, diarrhea, drowsiness, weakness, lack of coordination
	Divalproex sodium	Depakote		Nausea, vomiting, dizziness, abdominal cramps, sleeplessness
Stimulant Drugs	Methylphenidate	Ritalin	Attention-deficit hyperactivity disorder (ADHD)	Nervousness, insomnia, nausea, dizziness, heart palpitations, headache; may temporarily retard growth

16.3 MODULE REVIEW Biomedical Therapies

Recite It

What are the major types of psychotropic or psychiatric drugs?

- The major classes of psychiatric drugs are antianxiety agents (e.g., Valium, Xanax), antidepressants (e.g., Elavil, Prozac), and antipsychotics (e.g., Thorazine, Clozaril).
- Other drugs, such as lithium and Ritalin, are used to treat specific disorders.

What are the advantages and disadvantages of psychiatric drugs?

- Psychiatric drugs can help relieve or control symptoms of many psychological disorders, including anxiety disorders, mood disorders, and schizophrenia.
- The major disadvantages of these drugs are the occurrence of troubling side effects, high relapse rates following discontinuance, and, in some cases, possible chemical dependence.

What is ECT, and how is it used?

- ECT (electroconvulsive therapy) involves the administration of brief pulses of electricity to the brain. It is used to treat severe depression, especially in cases that do not respond to other treatments.

What is psychosurgery?

➤ Psychosurgery is the use of surgical procedures on the brain to control deviant or violent behavior. It is rarely used today because of concerns about the safety and efficacy of these procedures.

Recall It

1. Psychiatric drugs are used to regulate ______ in the brain.
2. The drugs Valium and Xanax are examples of which class of psychiatric drugs?
3. A widely used treatment for childhood hyperactivity involves the use of
   a. extensive psychotherapy.
   b. a stimulant drug.
   c. lithium.
   d. gamma-aminobutyric acid.
4. Psychiatric drugs are widely used because they
   a. teach people how to better solve their problems.
   b. correct nutritional deficiencies that give rise to psychological disorders.
   c. help reduce and control symptoms of psychological disorders.
   d. cure most types of psychological disorders.
5. Electroconvulsive therapy (ECT) is used
   a. only after successful treatment with antidepressant drugs.
   b. in treating severe cases of schizophrenia as well as depression.
   c. in treating mild to moderate cases of depression.
   d. in treating cases of severe depression, especially when other approaches have proved unsuccessful.

Think About It

➤ Do you know children who have been treated with stimulant medication for hyperactivity and attentional problems? What were the outcomes? Do you believe that stimulant medication is used too often or not often enough?

➤ What are the advantages and disadvantages of psychotropic drugs? Would you consider using psychotropic drugs if you developed an anxiety disorder or a mood disorder? Why or why not?

Getting Help

APPLICATION MODULE 16.4

In most areas in the United States and Canada, there are pages upon pages of clinics and health professionals in telephone and Internet directories. Many people have no idea whom to call for help. If you don't know where to go or whom to see, there are a number of steps you can take to ensure that you receive appropriate care.

CONCEPT 16.29
Though consumers face a bewildering array of mental health services providers, there are a number of things they can do to ensure that they receive quality care.

1. *Seek recommendations from respected sources,* such as your family physician, course instructor, clergyperson, or college health service.
2. *Seek a referral from a local medical center or local community mental health center.* When making inquiries, ask about the services that are available or about opportunities for referral to qualified treatment providers in the area.
3. *Seek a consultation with your college counseling center or health services center.* Most colleges and universities offer psychological assistance to students, generally without charge.
4. *Contact professional organizations for recommendations.* Many local or national organizations maintain a referral list of qualified treatment providers in your area. If you would like to consult a psychologist, contact the American Psychological Association in Washington, DC (by telephone at 202-336-5650, or on the Internet

at www.apa.org), and ask for local referrals in your area. Alternatively, you can call your local or state psychology association in the United States, or your provincial or territorial psychological association in Canada.

5. *Be wary of direct advertisements for mental health services.* Online or telephone directory advertisements may contain exaggerated or misleading claims or outright falsehoods. Be especially wary of mental health care providers who claim to be experts in treating many different kinds of problems.
6. *Make sure the treatment provider is a licensed member of a recognized mental health profession, such as psychology, medicine, counseling, or social work.* In many states, anyone can set up practice as a "therapist," even as a "psychotherapist." These titles may not be limited by law to licensed practitioners. Licensed professionals clearly display their licenses and other credentials in their offices, usually in plain view. If you have any questions about the licensure status of a treatment provider, contact the licensing board in your state, province, or territory.
7. *Inquire about the type of therapy being provided (e.g., psychoanalysis, family therapy, behavior therapy).* Ask the treatment provider to explain how his or her particular type of therapy is appropriate to treating the problems you are having.
8. *Inquire about the treatment provider's professional background.* Ask about the person's educational background, supervised experience, and credentials. An ethical practitioner will not hesitate to provide this information.
9. *Inquire whether the treatment provider has had experience treating other people with similar problems.* Ask about their results and how they were measured.
10. *Once the treatment provider has had the opportunity to conduct a formal evaluation of your problem, discuss the diagnosis and treatment plan before making any commitments to undertake treatment.*
11. *Ask about costs and insurance coverage.* Ask about what types of insurance are accepted by the provider and whether copayments are required on your part. Ask whether the provider will adjust his or her fees on a sliding scale that takes your income and family situation into account. If you are eligible for Medicaid or Medicare, inquire whether the treatment provider accepts these types of coverage. College students may also be covered by their parents' health insurance plans or by student plans offered by their colleges. Find out if the treatment provider participates in any health maintenance organization to which you may belong.
12. *Find out about the treatment provider's policies regarding charges for missed or canceled sessions.*
13. *If medication is to be prescribed, find out how long a delay is expected before it starts working.* Also inquire about possible side effects, and about which side effects should prompt you to call with questions. Don't be afraid to seek a second opinion before undergoing any course of medication.
14. *If the treatment recommendations don't sound quite right to you, discuss your concerns openly.* An ethical professional will be willing to address your concerns rather than feeling insulted.
15. *If you still have any doubts, request a second opinion.* An ethical professional will support your efforts to seek a second opinion. Ask the treatment provider to recommend other professionals—or select your own.
16. *Be wary of online therapy services.* The use of online counseling and therapy services is growing rapidly, even as psychologists and other mental health professionals

raise the yellow flag of caution. Concerns arise because unqualified practitioners may be taking advantage of unwary consumers, as we lack a system for ensuring that online therapists have the appropriate credentials and licensure to practice. We also lack evidence that therapy can be effective when people interact with a therapist they never meet in person. Despite these concerns, many psychologists believe that online therapy services can have value when proper safeguards are established (e.g., Amstadter et al., 2009; Hustad et al., 2010; Ljótsson et al., 2010; Marks & Cavanagh, 2009).

Thinking Critically About Psychology

Based on your reading of this chapter, answer the following questions. Then, to evaluate your progress in developing critical thinking skills, compare your answers to the sample answers found in Appendix A.

Lauren has been depressed since the breakup of her relationship with her boyfriend two months ago. She is crying frequently, has difficulty getting out of bed in the morning, and has been losing weight. She claims she doesn't feel like eating. She tells the psychologist that she hasn't ever felt like hurting herself, but wavers when asked if she feels she might reach a point where she would consider ending her life. She says she feels like a failure and that no one will ever want her. Looking down at the floor, she tells the psychologist, "Everyone's always rejected me. Why should this be any different?"

Review the major approaches to therapy (psychodynamic, humanistic, behavioral, cognitive) and biomedical treatments discussed in this chapter. Then briefly describe how each might be used to help someone like Lauren.

KEY TO SAMPLE RATIONAL ALTERNATIVES IN TRY THIS OUT (P. 616)

1. We've got problems, but it's not a complete disaster. It's better to think of ways of making it better than to think the worst.
2. I sometimes feel overwhelmed, but I've handled things like this before. I need to take things a step at a time to get through this.
3. Just because it feels that way doesn't make it so.
4. Focus on getting through this course, not on jumping to conclusions.
5. Stop taking the blame for other people's problems. There are many reasons why _______ has these problems that have nothing to do with me.
6. Stop dumping on yourself. Focus on what you need to do.
7. It doesn't help to compare myself to others. All I can expect of myself is to do the best I can.
8. It would be upsetting, but it wouldn't be the end of the world. It's awful only if I make it so.
9. What evidence do I have for believing that? People who get to know me like me more often than not.
10. Putting everything in context, it's really not so bad.

Log in to CengageBrain to access the resources your instructor requires. For this book, you can access:

CourseMate

Psychology CourseMate brings course concepts to life with interactive learning, study, and exam preparation tools that support the printed textbook. A textbook-specific website, Psychology CourseMate includes an integrated interactive eBook and other interactive learning tools including quizzes, flashcards, videos, and more.

CENGAGENOW

CengageNow is an easy-to-use online resource that helps you study in less time to get the grade you want—NOW. Take a pre-test for this chapter and receive a personalized study plan based on your results that will identify the topics you need to review and direct you to online resources to help you master those topics. Then take a post-test to help you determine the concepts you have mastered and what you will need to work on. If your textbook does not include an access code card, go to CengageBrain.com to gain access.

Visit www.cengagebrain.com to access your account and purchase materials.

VISUAL OVERVIEW Chapter 16 Methods of Therapy

MODULE 16.1 Pathways to the Present: A Brief History of Therapy

- **Moral Therapy**: Compassion supplants harsh treatment
- **State Hospital System**: Institutional care characterized by neglect
- **Community-based Treatment**: Community care in the age of deinstitutionalization

© Bettmann/CORBIS

Pinel unchaining inmates at La Bicêtre

MODULE 16.2 Types of Psychotherapy

Psychodynamic Therapy

- **Traditional Psychoanalysis**: "Where Id is, Ego shall be"
- **Major Techniques**: Free association, dream analysis, interpretation, analysis of transference relationship
- **Modern Psychodynamic Approaches**: More direct "give and take" between therapist and client, greater focus on current relationships

© Jim Whitmer Photography

Behavior Therapy

- **Methods of Fear Reduction**: Gradual exposure, systematic desensitization, modeling
- **Aversive Conditioning**: Eliciting a negative response to undesirable stimuli
- **Operant Conditioning Techniques**: Applying principles of reinforcement to strengthen more adaptive behaviors
- **Cognitive-Behavioral Therapy**: Combining cognitive and behavioral techniques

Humanistic Therapy

- **Carl Rogers, Client-Centered Therapy**: Focuses on enhancing self-understanding and self-acceptance; nondirective approach; emphasizes unconditional positive regard, empathy, and genuineness in therapeutic relationship
- **Fritz Perls, Gestalt Therapy**: Integrating parts of the personality into a cohesive whole, or "gestalt"; uses role-playing exercises such as the "empty chair" technique

Cognitive Therapy

- **Beck's Cognitive Therapy**: Replacing distorted thoughts and beliefs with rational alternatives
- **Ellis's Rational-Emotive Behavior Therapy**: Uses the ABC model to help clients correct irrational beliefs

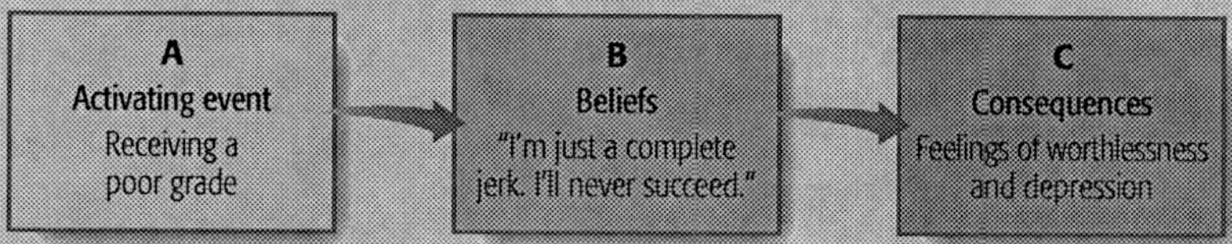

The Ellis "ABC" Model

Other Therapies

- **Eclectic Therapy**: Using different approaches tailored to particular cases
- **Group, Family, and Couple Therapy**: Expanding treatment beyond the individual client

Effectiveness of Psychotherapy

- **Meta-Analysis**: Average person receiving psychotherapy achieves a better outcome than 80 percent of untreated controls
- **Evidence-Based Therapies**: Specific types of therapy that demonstrate effectiveness in carefully controlled studies

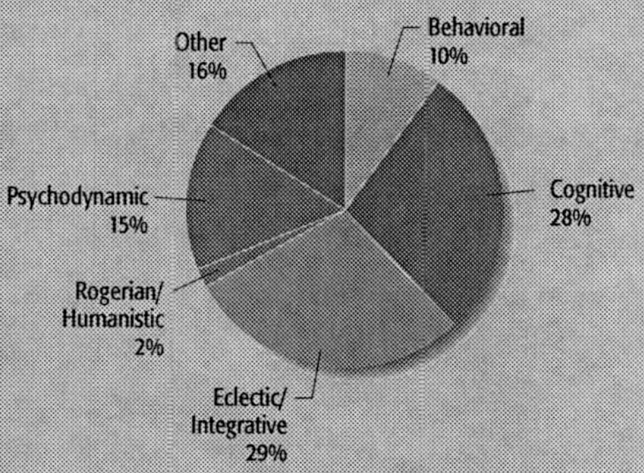

Clinical Psychologists Identifying with Each Therapeutic Orientation

MODULE 16.3 Biomedical Therapies

Drug Therapy

- **Antianxiety Drugs**: Valium, Librium, Xanax
- **Antidepressants**: Tricyclics, monoamine oxidase (MAO) inhibitors, and selective serotonin-reuptake inhibitors (SSRIs).
- **Antipsychotics**: Used to treat schizophrenia and other psychotic disorders
- **Other Psychiatric Drugs**: Mood stabilizers to treat bipolar disorder; Ritalin for childhood hyperactivity

Other Biomedical Therapies

- **Electroconvulsive Therapy (ECT)**: Used to treat severe depression, but can cause memory loss for recent past events
- **Psychosurgery**: Rarely used because of serious complications

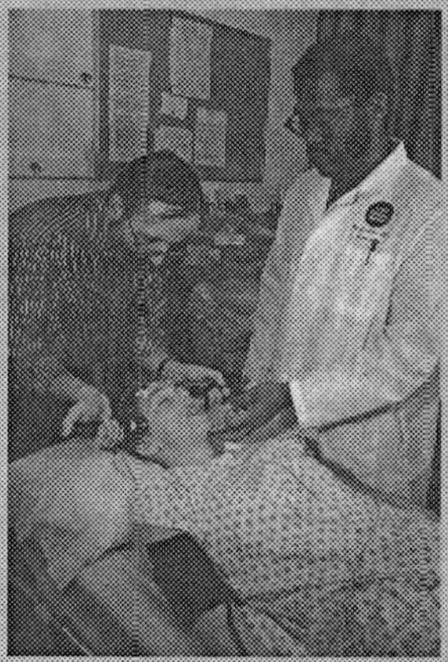

© Najlah Feanny/Stock Boston

Appendix A

Sample Answers to Thinking Critically About Psychology Questions

CHAPTER 1 The Science of Psychology

1. Unfortunately, a basic flaw in the research design casts serious doubt on the experimenter's conclusions. The experimenter did not use random assignment as the basis for assigning subjects to the experimental (sleep learning) or control (nonparticipating) groups. Rather, students who responded to the invitation to participate constituted the experimental group, and the control group was selected from nonparticipating students from the same class. Lacking random assignment, we have no way of knowing whether differences between the two groups were due to the independent variable (sleep learning) or to the characteristics of subjects comprising these groups.
2. In the absence of random assignment, it is conceivable that the more motivated and committed students opted to participate and that these students would have achieved higher test grades than the nonparticipating students, whether they had participated in the sleep learning study or not.
3. To provide a fairer test of the sleep learning method, the experimenter should have randomly assigned students to experimental and control groups. Experimenters use random assignment to equate groups on differences that may exist among individuals in level of ability or other subject characteristics.

CHAPTER 2 Biological Foundations of Behavior

1. Fortunately for Gage, the rod that penetrated his skull did not damage structures in the brainstem that control basic bodily processes, such as breathing and heart rate. However, the rod did damage the prefrontal cortex, the part of the brain responsible for personality and other higher mental functions.
2. The prefrontal cortex, which was damaged in the accident, helps us weigh the consequences of our actions and inhibit impulsive behaviors, including aggressive behaviors.

CHAPTER 3 Sensation and Perception

1. The woman located an area on the map where the missing man might be found. But her success at locating the missing man could be explained in a number of ways other than ESP. It could have been a lucky guess. Or perhaps the woman used the process of elimination to systematically narrow the possible search areas by ruling out those in which the police had already focused their efforts. Or perhaps she arrived at a possible location by identifying areas where a person would be likely to have wandered off. What other explanations can you generate that do not rely on positing the existence of ESP?
2. To evaluate whether the woman's predictions were likely to have been mere chance events, we would need to know how often her predictions turn out to be right. In other words, we'd need to know whether her success rate significantly exceeds chance expectations. But even if she turned out to be right more often than you would expect by chance alone, we still couldn't conclude that her success was attributable to ESP rather than to more conventional explanations.

CHAPTER 4 Consciousness

1. Evidence that ethnic or racial groups differ in rates of illicit drug use is not sufficient to establish that ethnicity accounts for these differences. We also need to demonstrate that ethnic or racial groups do not differ on other factors that may be related to drug use, such as differences between groups in education or income levels or characteristics of the neighborhoods in which people of different ethnic or racial groups may live.
2. Higher rates of illicit drug use in Group A than Group B may reflect higher rates of unemployment in Group A, as people who are unemployed tend to abuse drugs more often. Alternatively, people with Group A may be disproportionately represented in poorer, more socially distressed neighborhoods in which illicit drug use may be more prevalent. Can you think of other alternative explanations?

CHAPTER 5 Learning

1. the poison; **2.** the sheep meat; **3.** nauseating sickness; **4.** taste aversion to sheep meat

CHAPTER 6 Memory

1. It is likely that the second man rehearsed the information by repeating the license plate number to himself a number of times. Acoustic rehearsal is generally a more efficient method of holding information in short-term memory and transferring it to long-term memory than trying to retain a visual image of the stimulus in mind.

2. The woman apparently had memorized the song phonologically (by sound) rather than semantically (by meaning).

CHAPTER 7 Thinking, Language, and Intelligence

1a. The shepherd led the sheep to reverse direction and move back behind the ambulance, thus freeing the ambulance to move ahead without obstruction.

1b. The medical technician relied on a mental set for making one's way past a crowd.

2a. The availability heuristic and the representativeness heuristic may help explain John's poor investment decisions. The availability heuristic applies when we base our decisions on whatever happens to come most readily to mind—in John's case, the news reports of the day or comments he hears from others. When using the representativeness heuristic, we treat small samples of occurrences as though they were representative of occurrences in general. An individual news report about a company may be a poor indication of the company's overall financial health or future prospects. Comments from others may be even less trustworthy as a basis for making sound investment decisions.

2b. As John's investment adviser, you should probably recommend that he adopt a sound investment strategy and stick to it rather than basing his investment decisions on daily news reports or passing comments from others.

CHAPTER 8 Motivation and Emotion

People commonly think of thoughts and feelings as opposites. You may have heard people say how they feel with their hearts, but think with their heads. Though poets take license with the view that the human heart can "feel," critical thinkers question underlying assumptions, including the assumption that thoughts and feelings are independent of each other (let alone the assumption that the heart has feelings). Psychologists conceptualize emotions as complex feeling states that have important cognitive (thinking) components. They believe that our emotions reflect our cognitions (beliefs, judgments, appraisals, etc.) about our experiences. For example, anger reflects a judgment we make that we have been treated unfairly, whereas fear reflects an appraisal of a situation or object as threatening. In this view, thoughts are bridges to our emotions. To better understand emotions, we need to better understand the interconnections between thoughts and feelings.

CHAPTER 9 Child Development

1. Three-year-old children like Trevor show a type of thinking pattern that Piaget called animistic thinking—the tendency to attribute human qualities to inanimate objects, such as the sun and the clouds. To Trevor, the sun has feelings ("gets sleepy") and engages in behaviors ("goes to sleep"), just as people do.

CHAPTER 10 Adolescence and Adulthood

1. To determine your identity status, you first need to decide whether you have achieved a commitment in each area (i.e., occupational choice, and moral, religious, and political beliefs). A commitment represents either the adoption of a relatively firm set of beliefs or the pursuit of a course of action consistently over time. Critical thinkers weigh the validity of claims in terms of the evidence at hand—in this case, claims of achieving a commitment. What evidence would you seek to support these claims? Here are some examples of the types of criteria you may wish to apply:
   - Showing evidence in your actions and pronouncement to others of a relatively permanent or unswerving commitment to an occupational choice, set of religious beliefs, political philosophy, or set of moral values.
   - Being able to describe your beliefs or actions in an organized and meaningful way.
   - Pursuing a course of action consistent with your career choice and your religious, political, and moral beliefs or values.
2. Now you need to carefully evaluate whether you experienced an identity crisis to arrive at any of the commitments you have achieved. Bearing in mind, again, that critical thinkers weigh the evidence at hand, consider that evidence of an identity crisis might be based on meeting the following criteria:
   - Having undergone a serious examination of alternatives before arriving at a commitment (or are now undergoing this serious examination).
   - Having devoted a serious effort to arriving at a commitment (or are now devoting a serious effort).
   - Having gathered information (or are now gathering information) to seriously evaluate different points of view or courses of action.

   Classify yourself in the *identity achievement* status in a given area (career choice, and moral, religious, and political beliefs) if you have developed a commitment to a set of beliefs or a course of action and underwent an identity crisis to arrive at this commitment. Place yourself in the *moratorium* status if you are presently in a state of identity crisis and are making active efforts to arrive at a commitment. Place yourself in the *foreclosure* category if you arrived at a commitment without having experienced an identity crisis. Classify yourself in the *identity diffusion* category if you have neither achieved a commitment (i.e., currently lack a clear career course or a firmly held set of beliefs or values) nor are currently struggling to arrive at one.

CHAPTER 11 Gender and Sexuality

1. Homosexuality is a type of sexual orientation in which one's erotic attraction and choice of partners are directed toward members of one's own sex. It is not a statement about one's gender identity, or sense of maleness or femaleness. In transsexualism, by contrast, there is a mismatch between one's gender identity and one's anatomic sex. Gay males and lesbians prefer having partners of the same gender as themselves, but their gender identity is consistent with their anatomic sex.
2. Since an erection is an involuntary reflex, it cannot be forced or willed. Thus John may be making it more difficult to achieve an erection by focusing his attention on his penis rather than on his partner. As a result, he is likely to become less aroused and more anxious.

CHAPTER 12 Psychology and Health

The claims may mean the following:

- We may have designed our product to enhance vitality and well-being, but we can't claim that it actually accomplishes this purpose.
- Our product contains amino acids that the body uses to build muscle, but so do many other sources of protein, including meat and dairy products.
- We hired a few physicians with respectable credentials who said they would recommend our product, and we paid them for their endorsements.
- By *backed,* we mean that we conducted research on our product. We're not saying what our research actually found or whether the studies were well designed or carried out by impartial investigators. And when we say *advanced,* we're referring to research methods that went beyond just asking people if they liked our product.
- We're not really sure what we mean by *supercharge,* but it sounded good in the advertising copy.

CHAPTER 13 Personality

The confirmation bias leads us to give credence to information that confirms our preexisting beliefs and to ignore contrary evidence. Thus, for example, we are more likely to believe astrological readings when they conform to beliefs we already hold about ourselves than when they provide contrary information. Astrological readings typically contain general personality descriptions that apply to a wide range of people, so it's not surprising that many individuals believe these descriptions are true of themselves.

CHAPTER 14 Social Psychology

Why didn't they help? Though we will never know for certain, several hypotheses can be offered based on factors known to influence bystander behavior:

- *Situational ambiguity.* It was dark, and observers may not have had a direct view of the situation. Perhaps they were confused or uncertain about what was happening and whether it was a true emergency.
- *Diffusion of responsibility.* Even if they recognized the situation as an emergency, perhaps they weren't willing to assume personal responsibility for getting involved. Or perhaps they thought others would act, so they didn't need to. Or perhaps they thought it was "none of their business."
- *Perceived cost.* Perhaps they believed the costs of helping would be too great—including possible injury or loss of their own lives. But what about the minimal costs involved in calling the police? Perhaps they didn't want to accept a personal role in the incident and become involved in a lengthy court case.
- *Attributions of cause of need.* Perhaps they reasoned that the victim deserved what she got. Perhaps they figured the assailant was her boyfriend or husband and that she shouldn't have chosen such a partner.

What do you think is the likely explanation? What do you think *you* would do in a similar situation?

CHAPTER 15 Psychological Disorders

1. Ron's thought patterns illustrate several cognitive distortions or errors in thinking, including mistaken responsibility (assuming his girlfriend's bad moods were a response to him), catastrophizing (exaggerating the consequences of breaking off the relationship), and jumping to conclusions (assuming that when his girlfriend sat farther away from him in the car it meant she was trying to distance herself emotionally).
2. Lonnie's behavior appears to meet four of the six listed criteria: (1) unusualness (relatively few people are troubled by such obsessive concerns or compulsive rituals); (2) social deviance (repeated checking may be considered socially unacceptable behavior); (3) emotional distress (his compulsive behavior was a source of emotional distress), and (4) maladaptive behavior (his checking rituals were damaging his marital relationship). His behavior does

not meet the criterion of dangerousness, since it does not appear to have posed any danger to himself or others. Nor does he exhibit faulty perceptions or interpretations of reality, such as experiencing hallucinations or holding delusional beliefs.

CHAPTER 16 Methods of Therapy

A psychodynamic therapist might help Lauren explore how her present relationships and feelings of rejection are connected with disappointments she may have experienced in other relationships, including her early relationships with her parents. A humanistic therapist might help Lauren learn to accept and value herself for who she is, regardless of how others respond to her, and not to judge herself by other people's expectations. A behavioral therapist might help Lauren increase reinforcing or pleasurable activities in her life, whereas a cognitive therapist might help her identify and correct distorted thinking patterns ("Everyone's always rejected me. Why should this be any different?"). Biomedical treatment might involve antidepressant medication, or perhaps even electroconvulsive therapy if her depression deepens and fails to respond to other treatment approaches.

Appendix B

Answers to Recall It Questions

CHAPTER 1

Module 1.1: 1. Wundt; 2. c; 3. behaviorism; 4. b; 5. a; 6. psychodynamic. **Module 1.2:** 1. Basic, applied; 2. (a) iv, (b) i, (c) ii, (d) iii; 3. c; 4. b. **Module 1.3:** 1. c; 2. d; 3. experimental; 4. d; 5. b.

CHAPTER 2

Module 2.1: 1. b; 2. soma; 3. sensory neurons, motor neurons, and interneurons; 4. a; 5. b. **Module 2.2:** 1. central, peripheral; 2. central; 3. sympathetic nervous system; 4. A. **Module 2.3:** 1. d; 2. (a) iv, (b) i, (c) iii, (d) ii; 3. d; 4. temporal lobes. **Module 2.4:** 1. c; 2. b; 3. a; 4. a. **Module 2.5:** 1. c; 2. left, right; 3. c; 4. d; 5. b. **Module 2.6:** 1. endocrine; 2. b; 3. homeostasis; 4. pituitary. **Module 2.7:** 1.c; 2. c; 3. a; 4. familial association studies, twin studies, and adoptee studies; 5. b.

CHAPTER 3

Module 3.1: 1. c; 2. b; 3. sensory adaptation. **Module 3.2:** 1. d; 2. rods, cones; 3. occipital; 4. (a) iv; (b) vi; (c) i; (d) ii; (e) v; (f) iii. **Module 3.3:** 1. amplitude and frequency; 2. basilar; 3. (a) i; (b) v; (c) vi; (d) iv; (e) iii; (f) ii. **Module 3.4:** 1. b; 2. 10,000; 3. pheromones; 4. touch, pressure, warmth, cold, and pain; 5. a; 6. kinesthetic. **Module 3.5:** 1. perception; 2. b; 3. perceptual set; 4; connectedness; 5. interposition; 6. a; 7. b

CHAPTER 4

Module 4.1: 1. a; 2. selectivity; 3. d. **Module 4.2:** 1. circadian; 2. c; 3. restorative; 4. i. c, ii. b, iii. d, iv. a. **Module 4.3:** 1. transcendental meditation; 2. hypnotic analgesia; 3. neodissociation theory. **Module 4.4:** 1. psychoactive; 2. d; 3. depressants; 4. b; 5. tranquilizers; 6. dopamine.

CHAPTER 5

Module 5.1: 1. stimulus generalization; 2. d; 3. c; 4. b; 5. b. **Module 5.2:** 1. a; 2. radical behaviorism; 3. response, reinforcer; 4. d; 5. c. **Module 5.3:** 1. cognitive learning; 2. a; 3. latent learning; 4. b.

CHAPTER 6

Module 6.1: 1. procedural; 2. d, 3. i-d, ii-b, iii-a, iv-c. **Module 6.2:** 1. proactive; 2. a; 3. spaced, massed; 4. b. **Module 6.3:** 1. neuronal networks; 2. b; 3. long-term potentiation (LTP); 4. A.

CHAPTER 7

Module 7.1: 1. concepts; 2. logical, natural; 3. b; 4. d. **Module 7.2:** 1. b; 2. a; 3. relativity; 4. c. **Module 7.3:** 1. i (d); ii (a); iii (b); iv (c); 2. cultural; 3. triachic; 4. d.

CHAPTER 8

Module 8.1: 1. motivation; 2. i (d), ii (a), iii (c), iv (b); 3. stimulus motives; 4. incentive value; 5. cognitive dissonance; 6. d. **Module 8.2:** 1. c; 2. c; 3. i(b), ii (d), iii (a), iv (c); 4. serotonin. **Module 8.3:** 1. b; 2. anger, fear, disgust, sadness, happiness, and surprise; 3. c; 4. d.

CHAPTER 9

Module 9.1: 1. b; 2. the degree to which developmental changes occur universally across cultures; 3. c. **Module 9.2:** 1. germinal; 2. maternal malnutrition, teratogens; 3. i. (d), ii (b), iii (c), iv (a). **Module 9.3:** 1. i (c), ii (b), iii (d), iv (a); 2. newborns show preferences for their mothers' voices and sounds reflecting their native languages; 3. d. **Module 9.4:** 1. slow; 2. i. b, ii. d, iii. a, iv. c; 3. c; 4. d. **Module 9.5:** 1. a; 2. assimilation, accommodation; 3. the cultural experiences of aborigine children emphasize the importance of spatial skills rather than quantification skills; 4. social.

CHAPTER 10

Module 10.1: 1. d; 2. menarche; 3. imaginary audience, personal fable; 4. a; 5. cultural, gender; 6. c. **Module 10.2:** 1. c; 2. false; 3. emerging; 4. b; 5. c. **Module 10.3:** 1. d; 2. d; 3. b; 4. a.

CHAPTER 11

Module 11.1: 1. c; 2. c; 3. testosterone; 4. d; 5. visual, rotation. **Module 11.2:** 1. i (d), ii (c), iii (a), iv (b); 2. a; 3. c; 4. d. **Module 11.3:** 1. d; 2. i (a), ii (d), iii (c), iv (b); 3. d; 4. performance anxiety, guilt, exposure to sexually repressive cultural attitudes.

CHAPTER 12

Module 12.1: 1. (a) pressures or demands placed upon an organism to adjust or adapt to its environment, (b) when stress reaches a level that taxes our ability to cope effectively; 2. (a) ii, (b) iii, (c) i, (d) iv; 3. alarm stage; 4. social support, self-efficacy, perceptions of control and predictability, psychological hardiness, and optimism; 5. a; 6. general adaptation. **Module 12.2:** 1. (a) iv, (b) iii, (c) ii, (d) i; 2. (a) age, gender, heredity, lack of physical activity, obesity, high cholesterol, diabetes, high blood pressure, (b) all but the first three can potentially be controlled; 3. a; 4. Two-thirds, smoking and diet.

CHAPTER 13

Module 13.1: 1. a; 2. c; 3. c; 4. (a) iii, (b) i, (c) ii, (d) iv; 5. a. **Module 13.2:** 1. traits; 2. b; 3. a; 4. Hans Eysenck; 5. c; 6. shyness, aggressiveness, novelty-seeking. **Module 13.3:** 1. b; 2. a; 3. Thoughts, behaviors, and environmental factors mutually influence each other; 4. (a) ii, (b) iv, (c) iii, (d) i. **Module 13.4:** 1. d; 2. d; 3. the self; 4. a. **Module 13.5:** 1. self-report personality inventories and projective tests; 2. d; 3. standard; 4. d.

CHAPTER 14

Module 14.1: 1. schema; 2. dispositional, situational; 3. overestimation; 4. an evaluation or judgment of liking or disliking a person, object, or social issue; 5. (a) ii, (b) iv, (c) i, (d) iii. **Module 14.2:** 1. similarity, physical attractiveness, proximity, reciprocity; 2. d; 3. The correct order is (d), (b), (a), (e), (c); 4. (a) biased beliefs and stereotypes, (b) feelings of dislike toward target, (c) discrimination; 5. social and institutional support, acquaintance potential, equal status, intergroup. **Module 14.3:** 1. social; 2. b; 3. 65%; 4.a; 5. b.

CHAPTER 15

Module 15.1: 1. unusualness, social deviance, emotional distress, maladaptive behavior, dangerousness, faulty perceptions or interpretations of reality; 2. d; 3. c; 4. (a) iv, (b) iii, (c) i, (d) ii. **Module 15.2:** 1. c; 2. specific; 3. (a) iii, (b) i, (c) ii, (d) iv. **Module 15.3:** 1. dissociative; 2. d; 3. d; 4. is not. **Module 15.4:** 1. bipolar disorder; 2. Women appear to be exposed to greater stress and are more likely to ruminate or dwell on their problems; 3. serotonin, reabsorption or reuptake; 4. helplessness. **Module 15.5:** 1. males; 2. disorganized; 3. c; 4. b. **Module 15.6:** 1. excessively rigid patterns of behavior making it difficult to adjust to external demands and relate effectively to other people; 2. frontal lobes; 3. (i) b, ii (a), iii (a), iv (b).

CHAPTER 16

Module 16.1: 1. moral; 2. Dorothea Dix; 3. Compassionate care of severely disturbed people was not sufficient to restore them to normalcy; 4. deinstitutionalization. **Module 16.2:** 1. (a) iv, (b) i, (c) iii, (d) ii; 2. unconditional positive regard, empathy, genuineness; 3. systematic desensitization; 4. rational-emotive behavior therapy; 5. The advantages of group therapy include its lower cost and the fact that clients can gain experience relating to others and learn from others how to cope with problem situations; its disadvantages include a lower level of individual attention and clients' potential fear of revealing very personal matters to other members of the group. **Module 16.3:** neurotransmitters; 2. antianxiety drugs; 3. b; 4. c; 5. d.

Appendix C

Statistics in Psychology

Dennis Hinkle Towson University
Leping Liu Towson University

The word statistics means different things to different people. Weatherpersons report daily weather statistics, such as high and low temperatures, amount of rainfall, and the average temperatures recorded for this day in history. Sportscasters flood us with statistics that include players' batting averages, fielding percentages, and ratios of home runs to times at bat. And in televised football games, commentators give half-time statistics that include total yards rushing and total yards passing.

Psychologists, too, use statistics. But to them, statistics are procedures for analyzing and understanding the results of research studies. For example, research evidence shows that night-shift workers in sensitive positions tend to be sleepier and less alert than day-shift workers. Investigators in these studies used statistical techniques to determine whether the two groups of workers—night-shift and day-shift workers—differed from each other, on the average, on measures of sleepiness and alertness, among other variables. Psychologists also use statistics for describing the characteristics of particular groups of people, including themselves. In Chapter 1, for example, you learned about the characteristics of psychologists with respect to their ethnicities and places of employment.

Fundamental theories in modern psychology would not exist without the application of statistics in psychological research. Psychologists rely on statistics to explain the results of their research studies, as well as to provide empirical evidence to support or refute particular theories or beliefs. For example, investigators used statistical techniques to refute the original version of the *linguistic relativity hypothesis*, which was based on the theory that language determines how we think (see Chapter 7). In this case, statistical analysis of the research findings supported an alternative theory—that cultural factors influence how we think. We all need to understand statistics in order to become more knowledgeable consumers of psychological research. For example, we need to understand how the IQ scores of people in the general population are distributed in order to determine the relative standing of a particular score (again, see Chapter 7). And when seeking psychological assistance, we need to know which forms of therapy have been shown through methods of statistical analysis to be effective for which types of psychological problems (see the discussion in Chapter 16 about *empirically supported treatments*). Whatever the reason for using statistics, researchers and consumers alike should understand the information that statistics provide and the conclusions that can be drawn from them.

Populations and Samples

The terms *population* and *sample* are used frequently in psychological research involving statistical analysis. By definition, a *population* includes all members of a specified group, such as "all residents living in Washington, DC," "all patients in a psychiatric hospital at a specified time who are being treated for various psychological disorders," or "all students enrolled in an introductory psychology class in a particular university during the fall semester." In many research situations, however, it is not feasible to include all members of a given population. In such instances, a subset or segment of the population, called a *sample,* is selected to participate, and only the members of that sample are included in the research study.

Descriptive Statistics and Inferential Statistics

descriptive statistics Procedures used for classifying and summarizing information in numerical form—in short, for describing data.

inferential statistics Procedures for making generalizations about a population by studying the characteristics of samples drawn from the population.

The study of statistics can be divided into two broad categories: descriptive statistics and inferential statistics. Investigators use **descriptive statistics** to describe data (i.e., to classify and summarize information expressed in numerical form), and they use **inferential statistics** to make generalizations about a population by studying results based on a sample drawn from the population.

Descriptive and inferential statistics have three main purposes in scientific inquiry:

1. *To describe*
2. *To relate*
3. *To compare*

These approaches form a general framework for applying statistical procedures that allow researchers to interpret the results of a study, draw conclusions, make generalizations and inferences from samples to populations, and provide a focus for future studies. In the remainder of this appendix, we provide an overview of these three approaches to statistical analysis.

Using Statistics to Describe

The simplest application of statistics involves describing a distribution of scores collected from a group of individuals. Suppose, for example, that we have the final examination scores for 180 freshman psychology students, as shown in Table 1. In order to describe

TABLE 1 Final Examination Scores for Freshman Psychology Students

68	52	69	51	43	36	44	35	54	57	55	56
55	54	54	53	33	48	32	47	47	57	48	56
65	57	64	49	51	56	50	48	53	56	52	55
42	49	41	48	50	24	49	25	53	55	52	56
64	63	63	64	54	45	53	46	50	40	49	41
45	54	44	55	63	55	62	56	50	46	49	47
56	38	55	37	68	46	67	45	65	48	64	49
59	46	58	47	57	58	56	59	60	62	59	63
56	49	55	50	43	45	42	46	53	40	52	41
42	33	41	34	56	32	55	33	40	45	39	46
38	43	37	44	54	56	53	57	57	46	56	45
50	40	49	39	47	55	46	54	39	56	38	55
37	29	36	30	37	49	36	50	36	44	35	45
42	43	41	42	52	47	51	46	63	48	62	49
53	60	52	61	49	55	48	56	38	48	37	47

this distribution of scores, we must (1) identify the shape of the distribution, (2) compute the "average" score, and (3) determine the variability of the scores.

Frequency Distribution

The first step in describing a distribution of scores is to develop a **frequency distribution** for individual scores or categories of scores.

Table 2 shows a frequency distribution constructed by combining our 180 scores into categories, called *class intervals,* beginning with the category of scores 20–24 and ending with the category of scores 65–69. Note that the categories with the most scores are 45 to 49, which contains 42 scores, and 55–59, which contains 37 scores. We can depict this frequency distribution using a type of bar graph, called a histogram. As shown in ■ Figure 1, a **histogram** depicts the frequencies of class intervals of scores using bars of different lengths. Thus, for example, the class interval of 45–49 is represented by a bar with a value of 42.

Another way of graphing a frequency distribution is to use a **frequency polygon**, as shown in ■ Figure 2. Here, the frequencies of class intervals are plotted at the intervals' midpoints, which are then connected with straight lines.

TABLE 2 Frequency Distribution of Final Examination Scores Using Class Intervals

Class Interval	*f*
65–69	6
60–64	15
55–59	37
50–54	30
45–49	42
40–44	22
35–39	18
30–34	7
25–29	2
20–24	1

Measures of Central Tendency. The second step in describing a distribution of scores is to compute the **central tendency** of the scores. Central tendency is an indicator of the average score in a distribution of scores. Three different statistical measures of central tendency are available. The researcher can determine the **mode** (most frequent score), the **median** (middle score), or the **mean** (arithmetic average).

As an example, consider the following distribution: 2, 5, 9, 10, 12, 13, 13. The mode is 13, which is the score that occurs most often. The median is the score that slices the distribution of scores in half (half of the scores fall above the median and half fall below). The median is 10, since three scores fall above this value and three fall below.

The mean is the most often used measure of central tendency. To find the mean ($\overline{X}$), sum all the scores (X) and then divide the sum by the number of scores. Symbolically,

$$\overline{X} = \Sigma X / n$$

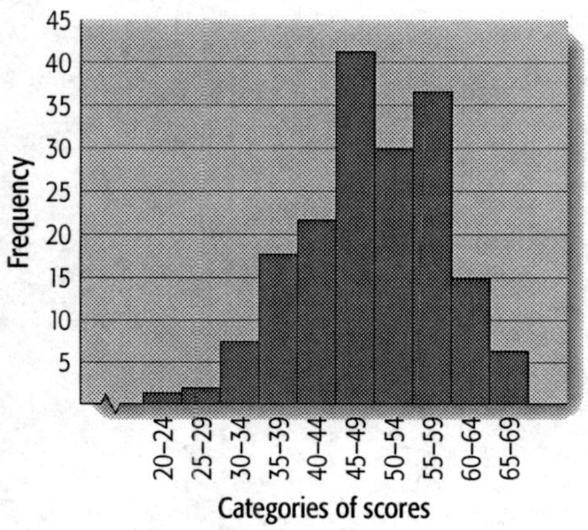

Figure 1 Histogram of Final Examination Scores

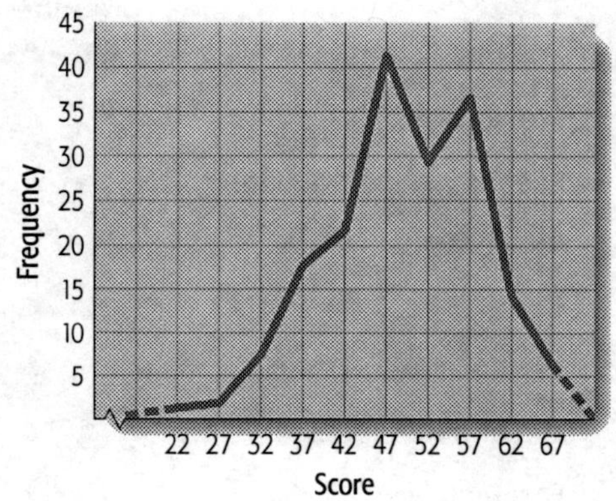

Figure 2 Frequency Polygon of Final Examination Scores

frequency distribution A tabulation that indicates the number of times a given score or group of scores occurs.

histogram A graph that depicts the frequencies of individual scores or categories of scores, using bars of different lengths.

frequency polygon A graph on which the frequencies of class intervals are at their midpoints, which are then connected with straight lines.

central tendency A central point on a scale of measurement around which scores are distributed.

mode The most frequent score in a distribution of scores.

median The middle score in a distribution, above and below which half of the scores fall.

mean The arithmetic average of the scores in a distribution.

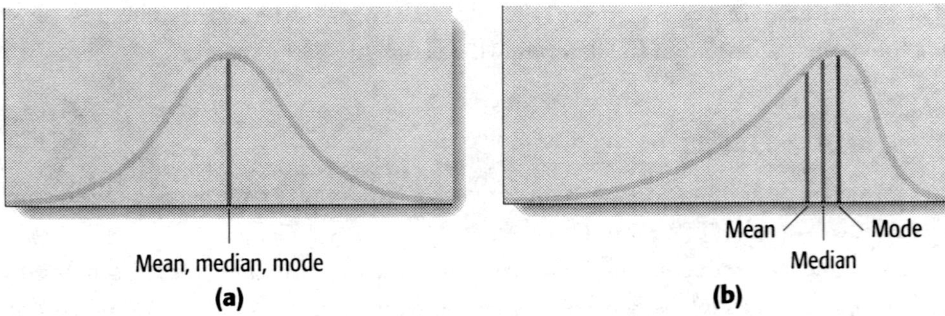

Figure 3 Comparisons of the Mode, Median, and Mean in Two Distributions

where ΣX is the sum of all the scores and n is the total number of scores. For the above distribution of scores, the mean would be computed as follows:

$$\overline{X} = 64/7 = 9.14$$

As you can see, the mode, median, and mean sometimes represent different values.

Similarly, for the final examination scores for the 180 freshman psychology students, the mean would be computed as follows:

$$\overline{X} = 8860/180 = 49.22$$

In other cases, such as the distribution shown in ■ Figure 3(a), the mean, median, and mode are represented by the same value. But when the distribution is skewed ("tilted" to the right or left), as in Figure 3(b), the mean, median, and mode do not coincide.

What is the best measure of central tendency? The answer depends on what we want to know. If we're interested in finding out what score has been received most often on an examination, we would use the mode. But the most frequently occurring score may not be the best representation of how the class performed on the average. For that determination, we could use the median, which indicates the middle score in the distribution—that is, the score below which half of the scores fall and above which half of the scores fall. By knowing the median, we could specify which score separates the top half of the class from the bottom half.

We could also use the mean, which provides us with the arithmetic average of the whole class. But one limitation of the mean is that it is greatly influenced by extreme scores. Consider the following example of the distribution of salaries for employees in a small manufacturing company:

Position	Number of Employees	Salary	Measure of Central Tendency
President/CEO	1	$350,000	
Executive vice president	1	120,000	
Vice presidents	2	95,000	
Controller	1	60,000	
Senior salespeople	3	58,000	Mean
Junior salespeople	4	40,000	
Foreman	1	36,000	Median
Machinists	12	30,000	Mode

In this example, the mean is greatly influenced by one very high score—the salary of the president/CEO. If you were the chairperson of the local machinists' union, which measure of central tendency would you use to negotiate a new wage agreement? Alternatively, which would you use if you represented management's position in the negotiations?

Another consideration in choosing the best measure concerns how it is to be used. If we wish to generalize from samples to populations, the mean has a distinct advantage. It can be manipulated mathematically in ways that are inappropriate for the median or the mode. But if the purpose is primarily descriptive, then the measure that best characterizes the data should be used. In general, reporting all three measures of central tendency provides the most accurate description of a given distribution.

Measures of Variability. The final step in describing a distribution of scores is to compute the **variability** of the scores. Variability is the spread of scores throughout the distribution of scores. One measure of variability is the **range** of scores, or the difference between the highest and lowest scores in the distribution. The final examination scores for the 180 freshman psychology students range from a low of 24 to a high of 69, so the range would be 69 − 24 = 45.

Another, more commonly used measure of variability is the **standard deviation (SD)**, conceptually defined as the average difference between each individual score and the mean of all scores in the data set. A large standard deviation suggests considerable variability (spread) of scores around the mean, whereas a small standard deviation indicates little variability. Table 3 illustrates the computations involved in calculating the standard deviation based on a hypothetical data set. (The standard deviation of the 180 final examination scores is 8.98.)

variability In statistics, the spread or dispersion of scores throughout the distribution.

range A measure of variability that is given by the difference in value between the highest and lowest scores in a distribution of scores.

standard deviation (SD) A measure of variability defined as the average difference between each individual score and the mean of all scores in the data set. More precisely, the square root of the average of the squared deviations of individual scores from the mean.

The Normal Distribution. The histogram for the 180 final examination scores in Figure 1 illustrates a commonly observed phenomenon in psychological data—namely, that the majority of scores tend to fall in the middle of the distribution, with fewer scores in the extreme categories. For many measures used in psychological research, score distributions have this general shape and are said to resemble a "bell-shaped curve," which

TABLE 3 Calculation of a Standard Deviation

Score	Deviation from Mean (D)	Deviation Squared (D^2)
3	3 − 9 = −6	36
5	5 − 9 = −4	16
6	6 − 9 = −3	9
9	9 − 9 = 0	0
12	12 − 9 = 3	9
13	13 − 9 = 4	16
15	15 − 9 = 6	36
$\overline{X} = 63/7 = 9$		$\Sigma D^2 = 122$

Standard Deviation $= \sqrt{\Sigma D^2/n} = \sqrt{122/7} = \sqrt{17.43} = 4.17$

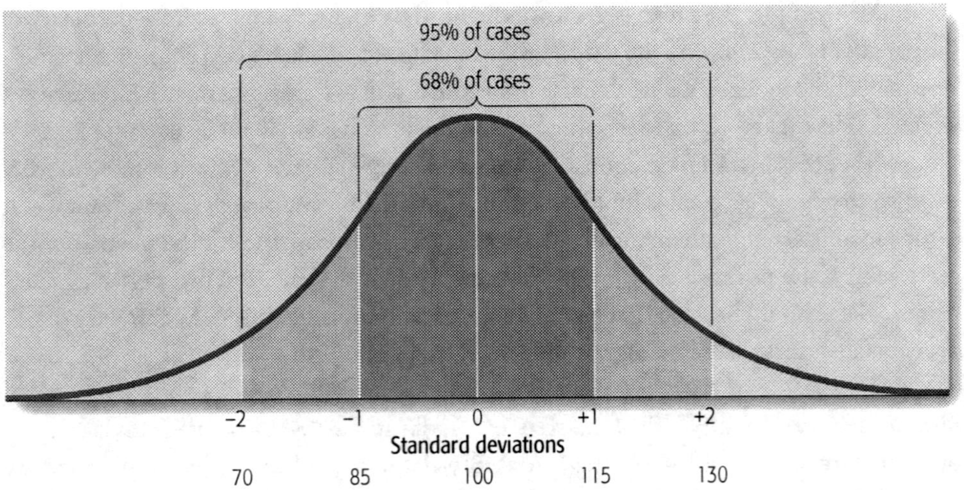

Figure 4 A Normal Distribution Showing the Approximate Percentages of Cases Falling Within One and Two Standard Deviations from the Mean

is otherwise known as a "normal curve" or "normal distribution." In statistics, the true normal distribution is a mathematical model. However, when the shape of a particular score distribution closely aligns with a normal distribution, we can use the general properties of the normal distribution to describe the distribution of actual scores under study. The normal distribution provides a good description of the distribution of many sets of data, such as measures of intelligence and achievement. Moreover, in a normal distribution, the mean, median, and mode all have the same value, so we can use the standard deviation to describe a particular score in the distribution relative to all scores in the distribution.

In a normal distribution, such as the one shown in ■ Figure 4, half of all cases fall above the mean and half fall below. Based on the properties of the normal distribution, we can determine the percentages of cases that fall within each segment of the distribution. For example, approximately 68 percent of cases fall within one standard deviation above and below the mean (between −1.0 and +1.0), and approximately 95 percent of cases fall within two standard deviations above and below the mean (between −2.0 and +2.0).

standard score A transformed score that indicates the number of standard deviations a corresponding raw score is above or below the mean. Also called a *z*-score.

The properties of the normal distribution can also be used to describe the distance between a score and the mean. Scores on most IQ tests, for example, are distributed with a mean of 100 and a standard deviation of 15. Thus, an IQ score of 115 would be about one standard deviation above the mean. We use the term **standard score** (also called a *z-score*) to refer to a transformed score that indicates how many standard deviations the actual (raw) score is above or below the mean. For example, the standard score corresponding to a raw score of 115, based on a mean of 100 and a standard deviation of 15, would be +1.0. Similarly, we could say that a score of 70 is two standard deviations below the mean; in this case, the standard score would be −2.0. These standard score properties of the normal distribution are critical in applying inferential statistical procedures in psychological research.

Using Statistics to Relate

A second application of statistics involves determining the relationship between two variables. As an example, let's say we want to determine the relationship between quantitative SAT scores and final examination scores, using the data for 15 introductory psychology students, as shown in Table 4.

TABLE 4 Quantitative SAT Scores and Final Examination Scores for 15 Introductory Psychology Students

Student	Quantitative SAT Score (X)	Final Examination Score (Y)
1	595	68
2	520	55
3	715	65
4	405	42
5	680	64
6	490	45
7	565	56
8	580	59
9	615	56
10	435	42
11	440	38
12	515	50
13	380	37
14	510	42
15	565	53
Σ	8,010	772
	$\overline{X} = 534.00$	$\overline{Y} = 51.47$
	$s_x = 96.53$	$s_y = 10.11$

scatterplot A graph in which pairs of scores are plotted for each research participant on two variables.

The Scatterplot: Plotting the Data. Our first step would be to enter these data in a **scatterplot**, a type of graph that represents the "scatter" of scores obtained by plotting each individual's scores on two variables. The two variables can be symbolized by the terms X and Y.

In ■ Figure 5, each point represents the paired measurements for each of the 15 students, three of whom—Students 1, 8, and 13—are labeled specifically. (For example, the point for Student 1 represents the paired scores "SAT = 595" and "Final Score = 68.") Notice that these points form a pattern that starts in the lower left corner and ends in the upper right corner of the scatterplot. This pattern occurs when there is a positive relationship, or *positive correlation*, between the two variables. A positive correlation between two variables means that higher scores on one variable are associated with higher scores on the other variable. The pattern shown in Figure 5 thus illustrates that students with higher SAT scores tend to have higher final examination scores, and vice versa.

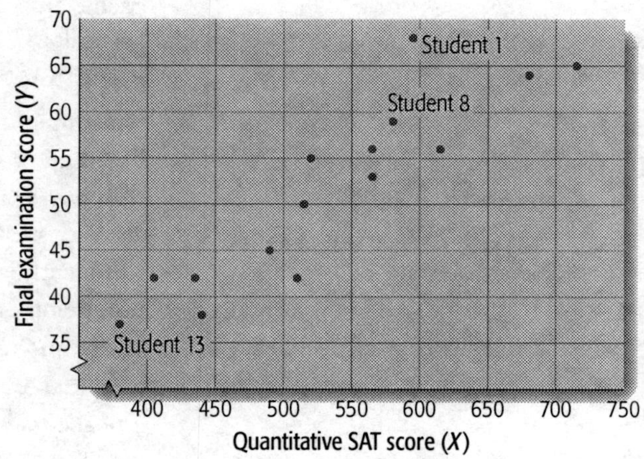

Figure 5 Scatterplot Illustrating the Relationship Between Final Examination (Y) and Quantitative SAT Scores (X)

Different scatterplot patterns emerge as a result of different types of relationships between two variables. Three of these patterns are illustrated in ■ Figure 6. Pattern A depicts a positive correlation between two variables. Pattern B

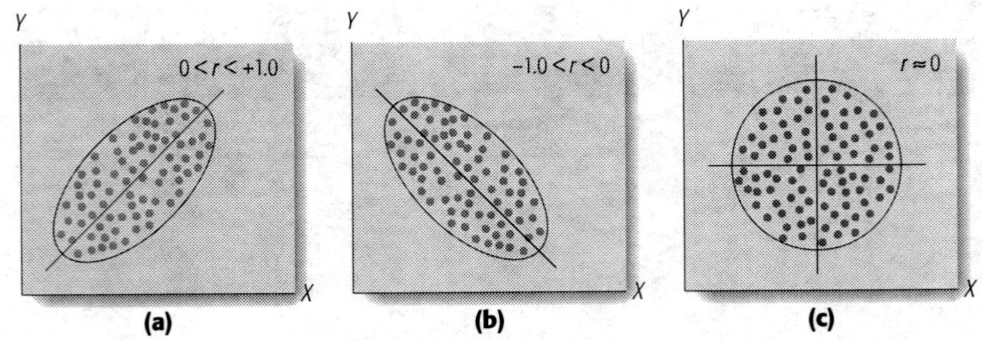

Figure 6 Scatterplots Illustrating Varying Degrees of Relationship Between *X* and *Y*

depicts a negative correlation—a relationship in which higher scores on one variable are associated with lower scores on the other variable. And Pattern C is a scatterplot in which the points have neither an upward nor a downward trend. This last pattern occurs in situations where there is a zero correlation (no relationship) between the two variables.

The Correlation Coefficient: Calculating the Relationship Between Two Variables. The scatterplot gives us a visual representation of the relationship between two variables. But researchers also use a statistical measure that provides a more precise indication of both the magnitude (strength) and direction (positive or negative) of the relationship. The statistical measure of the relationship between two variables is called the *correlation coefficient* (expressed by the letter r). The range of values for positive correlation coefficients is from 0 (minimum) to +1.0 (maximum); the range of values for negative correlation coefficients is from 0 (minimum) to −1.0 (maximum).

Table 5 shows a worked-out example of the computations involved in calculating a correlation coefficient based on the data presented in Table 4. The correlation coefficient is found to be +0.90, which represents a very high, positive relationship between SAT scores and final examination scores. In other words, as we saw earlier, freshmen with higher SAT scores tend to achieve higher scores in their psychology exams.

Table 6 provides some rules of thumb for interpreting the magnitude of a correlation coefficient.

Using One Variable to Predict Another. An important use of correlational statistics is prediction. If two variables are correlated, we can predict scores on one variable based upon scores on the other variable. For example, after determining the relationship between SAT scores and final examination scores for our 15 introductory psychology students, let's suppose that we want to predict the final examination scores of similar students based upon our knowledge of their SAT scores. The process of prediction involves developing a mathematical equation that incorporates the paired sets of scores on the two variables obtained in the study. This equation can then be used to predict final examination scores based on SAT scores for comparable groups of students. The accuracy of the prediction reflects the magnitude of the correlation between the variables: The higher the correlation, the better the prediction. If a strong relationship exists between the two variables, knowing how students score on the SAT would allow us to make fairly accurate predictions about how they will perform in their psychology courses.

TABLE 5 Calculation of Correlation Coefficient Between Quantitative SAT Scores and Final Examination Scores

Quantitative SAT Scores		Final Exam Scores		
X	X^2	Y	Y^2	XY
595	354,025	68	4,624	40,460
520	270,400	55	3,025	28,600
715	511,225	65	4,225	46,475
405	164,025	42	1,764	17,010
680	462,400	64	4,096	43,520
490	240,100	45	2,025	22,050
565	319,225	56	3,136	31,640
580	336,400	59	3,481	34,220
615	378,225	56	3,136	34,440
435	189,225	42	1,764	18,270
440	193,600	38	1,444	16,720
515	265,225	50	2,500	25,750
380	144,400	37	1,369	14,060
510	260,100	42	1,764	21,420
565	319,225	53	2,809	29,945
8,010	4,407,800	772	41,162	424,580

$$\text{Raw Score Formula} = \frac{n\Sigma X\Sigma Y}{\sqrt{n\Sigma X^2 - (\Sigma X)^2}\sqrt{n\Sigma Y^2 - (\Sigma Y)^2}}$$

$$= \frac{15(424{,}580) - (8{,}010)(772)}{\sqrt{12(4{,}407{,}800) - (8{,}010)^2}\sqrt{15(41{,}162) - (772)^2}}$$

$$= 0.90$$

TABLE 6 Rule of Thumb for Interpreting the Size of a Correlation Coefficient

Size of Correlation	Interpretation
.90 to 1.00 (−.90 to −1.00)	Very high positive (negative) correlation
.70 to .90 (−.70 to −.90)	High positive (negative) correlation
.50 to .70 (−.50 to −.70)	Moderate positive (negative) correlation
.30 to .50 (−.30 to −.50)	Low positive (negative) correlation
.00 to .30 (.00 to −.30)	Little if any correlation

Using Statistics to Compare

A third application of statistics involves comparing two or more groups. Let's say, for example, that an educational psychologist is interested in examining the effects of computerized instruction on the mathematics achievement of fourth-grade students. The psychologist's first step would be to assign participants to either an experimental group or a control group based on the technique of *random assignment* (discussed in Chapter 1). The experimental group would use a computer program that allows them to acquire mathematical concepts through interactive on-screen exercises, whereas the control group would receive standard classroom instruction. Then, at the conclusion of the study, both groups would be tested on a mathematics achievement test.

Let's further suppose that the results of the initial descriptive data analysis are as follows:

	Control Group	Experimental Group
Mean ($\overline{X}$)	62.4	77.6
Standard Deviation (SD)	15.8	16.3

Using these data, the educational psychologist would be able to describe the performance of the two groups by examining their means and standard deviations. Note, however, that for drawing conclusions and making generalizations from these data, inferential statistical procedures would also be needed.

Beyond Description: Using Inferential Statistics. Descriptive statistics allow us to summarize data, but the meaning of these statistical measures cannot be fully understood through descriptive statistics alone. In psychological research, it is important to determine whether the size of a correlation coefficient, or the difference between the means of two groups, is statistically significant. As discussed in Chapter 1 of the text, *statistical significance* indicates that the results obtained from a study are unlikely to have been due to chance or to the random fluctuations that would be expected to occur among scores in the general population.

Statistical significance can be determined only through the use of statistical techniques, called inferential statistics, that enable us to draw conclusions from our data and to make inferences and generalizations from samples to the populations from which they are drawn.

null hypothesis A prediction of no difference between groups or no relationship between variables.

Stating the Null Hypothesis. The first step in using inferential statistics is to state a **null hypothesis** for the study in question. Defined literally, the word null refers to something of no value or significance. By the same token, a null hypothesis is a prediction that a given finding has no value or significance. For the study of the relationship between SAT scores and final examination scores, we can state the following null hypothesis: "There is *no relationship* between the two variables." And for the study of the difference between experimental and control groups on the question of computerized versus standard instruction, we can offer this null hypothesis: "There is *no difference* between the two groups."

Testing the Null Hypothesis. The main purpose of inferential statistics is to test the null hypothesis. Using these techniques, scientific investigators can apply principles of probability to determine whether relationships between variables or differences between groups are large enough to be unlikely to be due to chance. In the process, they typically apply a criterion by which an outcome is judged to be significant when its likelihood of arising from chance is less than 5 percent. In other words, if the probability that an outcome would occur by chance alone is less than 5 percent, they would say that the finding is statistically significant. Depending on the nature of the research, researchers may set either more stringent or more liberal criteria for determining the threshold at which they would represent a given finding as statistically significant.

Let's return to our example of the 15 introductory psychology students. First, if the correlation coefficient between their SAT scores and final examination scores is high enough to reach a level of statistical significance, we would reject the null hypothesis of "no relationship." In other words, we would conclude that the correlation is significantly different from zero (which in itself means "no relationship"). Second, in applying inferential statistics to the prediction of scores on one variable from scores on another, we would say that the null hypothesis is that SAT scores do not predict final examination scores. But since there is a statistically significant relationship between these two variables, our conclusion (based on probability theory) would be that SAT scores are a significant predictor of final examination scores.

Inferential statistics are used in a similar way when investigating differences between two or more groups. These statistical techniques involve mathematical constructs based on probability theory for determining whether differences between sample means are large enough to reject the null hypothesis of "no difference." If the difference between the means of the computer instruction group and the classroom instruction group are large enough to meet the threshold of statistical significance, we would reject the null hypothesis and conclude that the difference between the groups is statistically significant. The underlying rationale is that when group differences between samples of research participants on measures of interest meet the threshold for statistical significance, they are unlikely to reflect chanceful variations that would be expected to occur on these measures in the population in general.

Summing Up

In this brief introduction to statistics, we have provided some basic terminology, identified several approaches to using statistics in psychological research, and discussed descriptive and inferential statistics as well as their general application in research studies. We have also offered a convenient way of categorizing the main purposes of statistics: (1) to describe, (2) to relate, and (3) to compare. An understanding of all these aspects of statistics is necessary not only for researchers in psychology but also for consumers of research results.

Glossary

absolute threshold The smallest amount of a given stimulus a person can sense.

accommodation In Piaget's theory, the process of creating new schemas or modifying existing ones to account for new objects or experiences.

accommodation The process by which the lens changes its shape to focus images more clearly on the retina.

acculturative stress Demands faced by immigrants in adjusting to a host culture.

achievement motivation The motive or desire to achieve success.

acronym A word composed of the first letters of a series of words.

acrophobia Excessive fear of heights.

acrostic A verse or saying in which the first or last letter of each word stands for something else.

action potential An abrupt change from a negative to a positive charge of a nerve cell; also called a neural impulse.

activation-synthesis hypothesis The proposition that dreams represent the brain's attempt to make sense of the random discharges of electrical activity that occur during REM sleep.

actor-observer effect The tendency to attribute the causes of one's own behavior to situational factors while attributing the causes of other people's behavior to internal factors or dispositions.

acupuncture An ancient Chinese practice of inserting and rotating thin needles in various parts of the body in order to release natural healing energy.

adaptation In Piaget's theory, the process of adjustment that enables people to function more effectively in meeting the demands they face in the environment.

adolescence The period of life beginning at puberty and ending with early adulthood.

adoptee studies Studies that examine whether adoptees are more similar to their biological or adoptive parents with respect to their psychological traits or to the disorders they develop.

adrenal cortex The outer layer of the adrenal glands that secretes corticosteroids (cortical steroids).

adrenal glands A pair of endocrine glands located just above the kidneys that produce various stress-related hormones.

adrenal medulla The inner part of the adrenal glands that secretes the stress hormones epinephrine (adrenaline) and norepinephrine (noradrenaline).

adrenocorticotrophic hormone (ACTH) A pituitary hormone that activates the adrenal cortex to release corticosteroids (cortical steroids).

afterimage The visual image of a stimulus that remains after the stimulus is removed.

ageism Prejudice and discrimination directed at older persons.

agonists Drugs that either increase the availability or effectiveness of neurotransmitters or mimic their actions.

agoraphobia Excessive irrational fear of being in public places.

alarm stage The first stage of the general adaptation syndrome, involving mobilization of the body's resources to cope with an immediate stressor.

alcoholism A chemical addiction characterized by impaired control over the use of alcohol and physiological dependence on it.

algorithm A step-by-step set of rules that will always lead to a correct solution to a problem.

all-or-none principle The principle by which neurons will fire only when a change in the level of excitation occurs that is sufficient to produce an action potential.

altered states of consciousness States of awareness during wakefulness that are different than the person's usual waking state.

Alzheimer's disease An irreversible brain disease with a progressive course of deterioration of mental functioning.

amnesia Loss of memory.

amniocentesis A technique for diagnosing fetal abnormalities involving examination of extracted fetal cells.

amniotic sac The uterine sac that contains the fetus.

amphetamines A class of synthetically derived stimulant drugs, such as methamphetamine, or "speed."

amygdala A set of almond-shaped structures in the limbic system believed to play an important role in aggression, rage, and fear.

anal stage In Freudian theory, the second stage of psychosexual development, during which sexual gratification is centered on processes of elimination (retention and release of bowel contents).

anal-expulsive personality In Freudian theory, a personality type characterized by messiness, lack of self-discipline, and carelessness.

analogy In problem-solving, a strategy based on using similarities between the properties of two things or applying solutions to past demands to the problem at hand.

anal-retentive personality In Freudian theory, a personality type characterized by perfectionism and excessive needs for self-control as expressed through extreme neatness and punctuality.

androgyny A type of gender-role identification that characterizes people who possess high levels of both masculine and feminine traits.

animistic thinking In Piaget's theory, the child's belief that inanimate objects have living qualities.

antagonists Drugs that block the actions of neurotransmitters by occupying the receptor sites in which the neurotransmitters dock.

anterograde amnesia Loss or impairment of the ability to form or store new memories.

antianxiety drugs Drugs that combat anxiety.

antibodies Protein molecules produced by the immune system that serve to mark antigens for destruction by specialized lymphocytes.

antidepressants Drugs that combat depression by affecting the levels or activity of neurotransmitters.

antigens Substances, such as bacteria and viruses, that are recognized by the immune system as foreign to the body and that induce it to produce antibodies to defend against them.

antipsychotics Drugs used in the treatment of psychotic disorders that help alleviate hallucinations and delusional thinking.

antisocial personality disorder (APD or ASPD) A type of personality disorder characterized by callous attitudes toward others and by antisocial and irresponsible behavior.

aphasia Loss or impairment of the ability to understand or express language.

applied research Research that attempts to find solutions to specific problems.

archetypes Jung's term for the primitive images contained in the collective unconscious that reflect ancestral or universal experiences of human beings.

arousal theory The belief that whenever the level of stimulation dips below an organism's optimal level, the organism seeks ways of increasing it.

arteries Blood vessels that carry oxygen-rich blood from the heart through the circulatory system.

arteriosclerosis A condition in which artery walls become thicker and lose elasticity. Commonly called *hardening of the arteries.*

assimilation In Piaget's theory, the process of incorporating new objects or situations into existing schemas.

association areas Areas of the cerebral cortex that piece together sensory information to form meaningful perceptions of the world and perform higher mental functions.

asthma A chronic lung disease characterized by temporary obstruction of the breathing tubes, leading to attacks of wheezing and difficulty breathing.

atherosclerosis A form of arteriosclerosis involving the narrowing of artery walls resulting from the buildup of fatty deposits or plaque.

attachment The enduring emotional bond that infants and older children form with their caregivers.

attitude A positive or negative evaluation of persons, objects, or issues.

attraction Feelings of liking for others, together with having positive thoughts about them and inclinations to act toward them in positive ways.

attribution An assumption about the causes of behavior or events.

attributional style A person's characteristic way of explaining outcomes of events in his or her life.

audition The sense of hearing.

auditory nerve The nerve that carries neural impulses from the ear to the brain, which gives rise to the experience of hearing.

authoritarian personality A personality type characterized by rigidity, prejudice, and excessive concerns with obedience and respect for authority.

autonomic nervous system The part of the peripheral nervous system that automatically regulates involuntary bodily processes, such as breathing, heart rate, and digestion.

availability heuristic The tendency to judge events as more likely to occur when information pertaining to them comes readily to mind.

aversive conditioning A form of behavior therapy in which stimuli associated with undesirable behavior are paired with aversive stimuli to create a negative response to these stimuli.

avoidance learning The learning of behaviors that allow an organism to avoid an aversive stimulus.

avoidance motivation The motive or desire to avoid failure.

axon The tubelike part of a neuron that carries messages away from the cell body toward other neurons.

Babinski reflex The reflexive fanning out and curling of an infant's toes and inward twisting of its foot when the sole of the foot is stroked.

bait-and-switch technique A compliance technique based on "baiting" a person by making an unrealistically attractive offer and then replacing it with a less attractive offer.

basal cell carcinoma A form of skin cancer that is easily curable if detected and removed early.

basal ganglia An assemblage of neurons lying in the forebrain that is important in controlling movement and coordination.

basic anxiety In Horney's theory, a deep-seated form of anxiety in children that is associated with feelings of being isolated and helpless in a world perceived as potentially threatening and hostile.

basic hostility In Horney's theory, deep feelings of resentment that children may harbor toward their parents.

basic research Research focused on acquiring knowledge, even if such knowledge has no direct practical application.

basic-level concepts The middle level of concepts in a three-level hierarchy of concepts, corresponding to the categories we most often use in grouping objects and events.

basilar membrane The membrane in the cochlea that is attached to the organ of Corti.

behavior modification (B-mod) The systematic application of learning principles to strengthen adaptive behavior and weaken maladaptive behavior.

behavior therapy A form of therapy that involves the systematic application of the principles of learning to bring about desired changes in emotional states and behavior.

behavioral perspective An approach to the study of psychology that focuses on the role of learning in explaining observable behavior.

behaviorism The school of psychology that holds that psychology should limit itself to the study of overt, observable behavior.

bereavement A psychological state of deprivation involving feelings of grief and loss resulting from the death of a loved one or close friend.

binocular cues Cues for depth that involve both eyes, such as retinal disparity and convergence.

biofeedback training (BFT) A method of learning to control certain bodily responses by using information from the body transmitted by physiological monitoring equipment.

biopsychosocial model An integrative model for explaining abnormal behavior patterns in terms of the interactions of biological, psychological, and sociocultural factors.

bipolar cells A layer of interconnecting cells in the eye that connect photoreceptors to ganglion cells.

bipolar disorder A type of mood disorder characterized by mood swings from extreme elation (mania) to severe depression.

blind spot The area in the retina where the optic nerve leaves the eye and that contains no photoreceptor cells.

body mass index (BMI) A standard measure of obesity based on body weight adjusted for height.

bonding The process by which parents develop strong ties to their newborns, which may form in the first few hours following birth.

borderline personality disorder A type of personality disorder characterized by unstable emotions and self-image.

bottom-up processing A mode of perceptual processing by which the brain recognizes meaningful patterns by piecing together bits and pieces of sensory information.

brain The mass of nerve tissue encased in the skull that controls virtually everything we are and everything we do.

brainstem The "stalk" in the lower part of the brain that connects the spinal cord to higher regions of the brain.

brainstorming A method of promoting divergent thinking by encouraging people to propose as many solutions to a problem as possible without fear of being judged negatively by others, no matter how far-fetched their proposals may be.

brightness constancy The tendency to perceive objects as retaining their brightness even when they are viewed in dim light.

Broca's area An area of the left frontal lobe involved in speech.

bystander intervention Helping a stranger in distress.

Cannon-Bard theory The belief that emotional and physiological reactions to triggering stimuli occur almost simultaneously.

cardinal traits Allport's term for the more pervasive dimensions that define an individual's general personality.

carpentered-world hypothesis An attempt to explain the Müller-Lyer illusion in terms of the cultural experience of living in a carpentered, right-angled world like our own.

case study method An in-depth study of one or more individuals.

castration anxiety In Freudian theory, unconscious fear of removal of the penis as punishment for having unacceptable sexual impulses.

catatonic type A subtype of schizophrenia characterized by bizarre movements, postures, or grimaces.

central executive The component of working memory responsible for coordinating the other subsystems, receiving and processing stored information, and filtering out distracting thought.

central nervous system The part of the nervous system that consists of the brain and spinal cord.

central traits Allport's term for personality characteristics that have a widespread influence on the individual's behavior across situations.

centration In Piaget's theory, the tendency to focus on only one aspect of a situation at a time.

cerebellum A structure in the hindbrain involved in controlling coordination and balance.

cerebral cortex The wrinkled, outer layer of gray matter that covers the cerebral hemispheres; controls higher mental functions, such as thought and language.

cerebral hemispheres The right and left masses of the cerebrum, which are joined by the corpus callosum.

cerebrum The largest mass of the forebrain, consisting of two cerebral hemispheres.

childhood amnesia The normal occurrence of amnesia for events occurring during infancy and early childhood.

chorion The membrane that contains the amniotic sac and fetus.

chorionic villus sampling (CVS) A technique of detecting fetal abnormalities that involves examination of fetal material extracted from the chorion.

chromosomes Rodlike structures in the cell nucleus that house the individual's genes.

chronic stress Continuing or lingering stress.

chunking The process of enhancing retention of a large amount of information by breaking it down into smaller, more easily recalled chunks.

circadian rhythm The pattern of fluctuations in bodily processes that occur regularly each day.

clairvoyance The ability to perceive objects and events without using the known senses.

classical conditioning The process of learning by which a previously neutral stimulus comes to elicit a response identical or similar to one that was originally elicited by another stimulus as the result of the pairing or association of the two stimuli.

claustrophobia Excessive fear of enclosed spaces.

clinical psychologists Psychologists who use psychological techniques to evaluate and treat individuals with mental or psychological disorders.

clitoris A sex organ in the female that is highly sensitive to sexual stimulation.

closure The perceptual principle that people tend to piece together disconnected bits of information to perceive whole forms.

cochlea The snail-shaped organ in the inner ear that contains sensory receptors for hearing.

cognitive dissonance A state of internal tension brought about by conflicting attitudes and behavior.

cognitive dissonance theory The belief that people are motivated to resolve discrepancies between their behavior and their attitudes or beliefs.

cognitive learning Learning that occurs without the opportunity of first performing the learned response or being reinforced for it.

cognitive map A mental representation of an area that helps an organism navigate its way from one point to another.

cognitive perspective An approach to the study of psychology that focuses on the processes by which we acquire knowledge.

cognitive psychology The branch of psychology that focuses on such mental processes as thinking, problem solving, decision making, and use of language.

cognitive therapy Developed by Aaron Beck, a form of therapy that helps clients recognize and correct distorted patterns of thinking associated with negative emotional states.

cognitive-behavioral therapy (CBT) A form of therapy that combines behavioral and cognitive treatment techniques.

cohort effect Differences between age groups as a function of historical or social influences affecting those groups rather than age per se.

collective unconscious In Jung's theory, a part of the mind containing ideas and archetypal images shared among humankind that have been transmitted genetically from ancestral humans.

collectivistic culture A culture that emphasizes people's social roles and obligations.

color constancy The tendency to perceive an object as having the same color despite changes in lighting conditions.

comparative psychologists Psychologists who study behavioral similarities and differences among animal species.

compliance The process of acceding to the requests or demands of others.

computer-assisted instruction A form of programmed instruction in which a computer is used to guide a student through a series of increasingly difficult questions.

concepts Mental categories for classifying events, objects, and ideas on the basis of their common features or properties.

conceptual combinations Combinations of two or more concepts into one concept, resulting in the creation of a novel idea or application.

conceptual expansion Expanding familiar concepts by applying them to new uses.

concordance rates In twin studies, the percentages of cases in which both members of twin pairs share the same trait or disorder.

concussion A jarring of the brain caused by a blow to the head.

conditional positive regard Valuing a person only when the person's behavior meets certain expectations or standards.

conditioned emotional reaction (CER) An emotional response to a particular stimulus acquired through classical conditioning.

conditioned response (CR) An acquired or learned response to a conditioned stimulus.

conditioned stimulus (CS) A previously neutral stimulus that comes to elicit a conditioned response after it has been paired with an unconditioned stimulus.

conditioned taste aversions Aversions to particular tastes acquired through classical conditioning.

conduction deafness A form of deafness, usually involving damage to the middle ear, in which there is a loss of conduction of sound vibrations through the ear.

cones Photoreceptors that are sensitive to color.

confirmation bias The tendency to maintain allegiance to an initial hypothesis despite strong evidence to the contrary.

conflict A state of tension brought about by opposing motives operating simultaneously.

conformity The tendency to adjust one's behavior to actual or perceived social pressures.

connectedness The principle that objects positioned together or moving together will be perceived as belonging to the same group.

conscious To Freud, the part of the mind corresponding to the state of present awareness.

consciousness A state of awareness of ourselves and of the world around us.

conservation In Piaget's theory, the ability to recognize that the quantity or amount of an object remains constant despite superficial changes in its outward appearance.

consolidation The process of converting short-term memories into long-term memories.

constructionist theory A theory that holds that memory is not a replica of the past but a representation, or *reconstruction*, of the past.

consumer psychologists Psychologists who study why people purchase particular products and brands.

contact hypothesis Allport's belief that under certain conditions, increased intergroup contact helps reduce prejudice and intergroup tension.

context-dependent memory effect The tendency for information to be recalled better in the same context in which it was originally learned.

continuity model The model proposing that development involves quantitative changes that occur in small steps over time.

continuity The principle that a series of stimuli will be perceived as representing a unified form.

control groups Groups of participants in a research experiment who do not receive the experimental treatment or intervention.

convergence A binocular cue for distance based on the degree of tension required to focus both eyes on the same object.

convergent thinking The attempt to narrow down a range of alternatives to converge on the one correct answer to a problem.

conversion disorder A type of somatoform disorder characterized by a change in or loss of a physical function that cannot be explained by medical causes.

cornea A transparent covering on the eye's surface through which light enters.

coronary heart disease (CHD) The most common form of heart disease, caused by blockages in coronary arteries, the vessels that supply the heart with blood.

corpus callosum The thick bundle of nerve fibers that connects the two cerebral hemispheres.

correlation coefficient A statistical measure of association between variables that can vary from −1.00 to +1.00.

correlational method A research method used to examine relationships between variables, which are expressed in the form of a statistical measure called a correlation coefficient.

corticosteroids Adrenal hormones that increase the body's resistance to stress by increasing the availability of stored nutrients to meet the increased energy demands of coping with stressful events. Also called *cortical steroids.*

corticotrophin-releasing hormone (CRH) A hormone released by the hypothalamus that induces the pituitary gland to release adrenocorticotrophic hormone.

counseling psychologists Psychologists who help people clarify their goals and make life decisions or find ways of overcoming problems in various areas of their lives.

countertransference The tendency for therapists to relate to clients in ways that mirror their relationships with important figures in their own lives.

couple therapy Therapy that focuses on helping distressed couples resolve their conflicts and develop more effective communication skills.

creative self In Adler's theory, the self-aware part of personality that organizes goal-seeking efforts.

creativity Originality of thought associated with the development of new, workable products or solutions to problems.

critical thinking The adoption of a skeptical, questioning attitude and careful scrutiny of claims or arguments.

cross-sectional study Study that compares individuals of different ages or developmental levels at the same point in time.

crystallized intelligence A form of intelligence associated with the ability to use accumulated knowledge.

CT (computed tomography) scan A computer-enhanced imaging technique in which an X-ray beam is passed through the body at different angles to generate a three-dimensional image of bodily structures (also called a CAT scan, short for *computerized axial tomography*).

culture-fair tests Tests designed to eliminate cultural biases.

cyclothymic disorder A mood disorder characterized by a recurring pattern of relatively mild mood swings.

daydreaming A form of consciousness during a waking state in which one's mind wanders to dreamy thoughts or fantasies.

decay theory A theory of forgetting that posits that memories consist of traces laid down in the brain that gradually deteriorate and fade away over time (also called *trace theory*).

decision making A form of problem solving in which we must select a course of action from among the available alternatives.

declarative memory Memory of facts and personal information that requires a conscious effort to bring to mind (also called *explicit memory*).

deep brain stimulation Use of electrical stimulation of deep parts of the brain in the treatment of psychological disorders such as severe forms of obsessive-compulsive disorder and depression.

defense mechanisms In Freudian theory, the reality-distorting strategies of the ego to prevent awareness of anxiety-evoking or troubling ideas or impulses.

deindividuation The loss of self-awareness that may occur when one acts in concert with the actions of a crowd.

deinstitutionalization A policy of reducing the population of mental hospitals by shifting care from inpatient facilities to community-based outpatient facilities.

delirium A mental state characterized by confusion, disorientation, difficulty in focusing attention, and excitable behavior.

delusions Fixed but patently false beliefs, such as believing that one is being hounded by demons.

dementia A condition involving a major deterioration or loss of mental abilities involved in memory, reasoning, judgment, and ability to carry out purposeful behavior.

dendrites Rootlike structures at the end of axons that receive neural impulses from neighboring neurons.

denial In Freudian theory, a defense mechanism involving the failure to recognize a threatening impulse or urge.

deoxyribonucleic acid (DNA) The basic chemical material in chromosomes that carries the individual's genetic code.

dependent variables The effects or outcomes of an experiment that are believed to be dependent on the values of the independent variables.

depolarization A positive shift in the electrical charge in the neuron's resting potential, making it less negatively charged.

depressants Drugs, such as alcohol and barbiturates, that dampen central nervous system activity.

depressive attributional style A characteristic way of explaining negative events in terms of internal, stable, and global causes.

detoxification A process of clearing drugs or toxins from the body.

developmental psychologists Psychologists who focus on processes involving physical, cognitive, social, and personality development.

developmental psychology The branch of psychology that explores physical, emotional, cognitive, and social aspects of development.

diathesis A vulnerability or predisposition to developing a disorder.

diathesis-stress model A type of biopsychosocial model that relates the development of disorders to the combination of a diathesis, or predisposition, usually genetic in origin, and exposure to stressful events or life circumstances.

dichromats People who can see some colors but not others.

difference threshold The minimal difference in the magnitude of energy needed for people to detect a difference between two stimuli.

discontinuity model The model proposing that development progresses in discrete stages that involve abrupt, qualitative changes in cognitive ability and ways of interacting with the world.

discrimination Unfair or biased treatment of people based on their membership in a particular group or category.

discriminative stimulus A cue that signals that reinforcement is available if the subject makes a particular response.

disinhibition effect The removal of normal restraints or inhibitions that serve to keep impulsive behavior in check.

disorganized type A subtype of schizophrenia characterized by confused behavior and disorganized delusions, among other features.

displacement In Freudian theory, a defense mechanism in which an unacceptable sexual or aggressive impulse is transferred to an object or person that is safer or less threatening than the original object of the impulse.

display rules Cultural customs and norms that govern the display of emotional expressions.

dispositional causes Causes relating to the internal characteristics or traits of individuals.

dissociative amnesia A psychologically based form of amnesia involving the "splitting off" from memory of traumatic or troubling experiences.

dissociative disorders A class of psychological disorders involving changes in consciousness, memory, or self-identity.

dissociative identity disorder (DID) A type of dissociative disorder characterized by the appearance of multiple personalities in the same individual.

distress A state of emotional or physical suffering, discomfort, or pain.

divergent thinking The ability to conceive of new ways of viewing situations and new uses for familiar objects.

divided consciousness A state of awareness characterized by divided attention to two or more tasks or activities performed at the same time.

door-in-the-face technique A compliance technique in which refusal of a large, unreasonable request is followed by a smaller, more reasonable request.

double-blind studies In drug research, studies in which both participants and experimenters are kept uninformed about which participants are receiving the active drug and which are receiving the placebo.

Down syndrome A chromosomal disorder characterized by mental retardation and certain facial abnormalities.

dream analysis A technique in psychoanalysis in which the therapist attempts to analyze the underlying or symbolic meaning of the client's dreams.

drifting consciousness A state of awareness characterized by drifting thoughts or mental imagery.

drive for superiority Adler's term for the motivation to compensate for feelings of inferiority. Also called the *will-to-power*.

drive reduction Satisfaction of a drive.

drive theory The belief that behavior is motivated by drives that arise from biological needs that demand satisfaction.

drive A state of bodily tension, such as hunger or thirst, that arises from an unmet need.

drug abuse Maladaptive or dangerous use of a chemical substance.

drug addiction Drug dependence accompanied by signs of physiological dependence, such as the development of a withdrawal syndrome.

drug dependence A severe drug-related problem characterized by impaired control over the use of the drug.

dual-pathway model of fear LeDoux's theory that the brain uses two pathways (a "high road" and a "low road") to process fear messages.

Duchenne smile A genuine smile that involves contraction of a particular set of facial muscles.

dyslexia A learning disorder characterized by impaired ability to read.

dysthymic disorder A type of mood disorder characterized by mild, chronic depression.

eardrum A sheet of connective tissue separating the outer ear from the middle ear that vibrates in response to auditory stimuli and transmits sound waves to the middle ear.

echoic memory A sensory store for holding a mental representation of a sound for a few seconds after it registers in the ears.

eclectic therapy A therapeutic approach that draws upon principles and techniques representing different schools of therapy.

educational psychologists Psychologists who study issues relating to the measurement of intelligence and the processes involved in educational or academic achievement.

EEG (electroencephalograph) A device that records electrical activity in the brain.

efficacy expectations Bandura's term for the expectancies we have regarding our ability to perform behaviors we set out to accomplish.

effort justification The tendency to place greater value on goals that are difficult to achieve in order to justify the effort expended in attaining them.

ego identity In Erickson's theory, the attainment of a psychological sense of knowing oneself and one's direction in life.

ego Freud's term for the psychic structure that attempts to balance the instinctual demands of the id with social realities and expectations.

egocentrism In Piaget's theory, the tendency to see the world only from one's own perspective.

eidetic imagery A lingering mental representation of a visual image (commonly called *photographic memory*).

elaboration likelihood model (ELM) A theoretical model that posits two channels by which persuasive appeals lead to attitude change: a central route and a peripheral route.

elaborative rehearsal The process of transferring information from short-term to long-term memory by consciously focusing on the meaning of the information.

Electra complex The term given by some psychodynamic theorists to the form of the Oedipus complex in young girls.

electrical recording As a method of investigating brain functioning, a process of recording the electrical changes that occur in a specific neuron or groups of neurons in the brain in relation to particular activities or behaviors.

electrical stimulation As a method of investigating brain functioning, a process of electrically stimulating particular parts of the brain to observe the effects on behavior.

electroconvulsive therapy (ECT) A form of therapy for severe depression that involves the administration of an electrical shock to the head.

electromyographic (EMG) biofeedback A form of BFT that involves feedback about changes in the level of muscle tension in the forehead or elsewhere in the body.

embryo The developing organism at an early stage of prenatal development.

embryonic stage The stage of prenatal development from implantation through about the eighth week of pregnancy during which the major organ systems begin to form.

emerging adulthood The period of psychosocial development, roughly spanning the ages of 18 to 25, during which the person makes the transition from adolescence to adulthood.

emotional intelligence The ability to recognize emotions in yourself and others and to manage your own emotions effectively.

emotions Feeling states that psychologists view as having physiological, cognitive, and behavioral components.

empirical approach A method of developing knowledge based on evaluating evidence gathered from experiments and careful observation.

empty nest syndrome A cluster of negative emotions, involving a loss of purpose and direction that can occur when children have grown and left home.

encoding specificity principle The belief that retrieval is more successful when cues available during recall are similar to those that were present when the information was brought into memory.

endocrine system The body's system of glands that release secretions, called hormones, directly into the bloodstream.

endorphins Natural chemicals released in the brain that have pain-killing and pleasure-inducing effects.

engram Lashley's term for the physical trace or etching of a memory in the brain.

environmental psychologists Psychologists who study relationships between the physical environment and behavior.

enzymes Organic substances that produce certain chemical changes in other organic substances through a catalytic action.

epilepsy A neurological disorder characterized by seizures that involve sudden, violent discharges of electrical activity in the brain.

episodic buffer The workspace of working memory where information from visual, auditory, and other modalities are brought together.

episodic memory Memory of personal experiences.

erogenous zones Parts of the body that are especially sensitive to sexual or pleasurable stimulation.

escape learning The learning of behaviors that allow an organism to escape from an aversive stimulus.

ethics review committees Committees that evaluate whether proposed studies meet ethical guidelines.

evolutionary psychology A branch of psychology that focuses on the role of evolutionary processes in shaping behavior.

exhaustion stage The third stage of the general adaptation syndrome, characterized by depletion of bodily resources and a lowered resistance to stress-related disorders or conditions.

exhibitionism A type of paraphilia characterized by exposing one's genitals to unsuspecting others for purposes of sexual arousal.

expectancies In social-cognitive theory, personal predictions about the outcomes of behavior.

experimental method A method of scientific investigation involving the manipulation of independent variables and observation or measurement of their effects on dependent variables under controlled conditions.

experimental psychologists Psychologists who apply experimental methods to the study of behavior and mental processes.

explicit memory Memory accessed through conscious effort.

extinction The gradual weakening and eventual disappearance of a conditioned response.

extrasensory perception (ESP) Perception that occurs without benefit of the known senses.

extrinsic motivation Motivation reflecting a desire for external rewards, such as wealth or the respect of others.

eyeblink reflex The reflexive blinking of the eyes that protects the newborn from bright light and foreign objects.

facial-feedback hypothesis The belief that mimicking facial movements associated with a particular emotion will produce the corresponding emotional state.

fallopian tube A strawlike tube between an ovary and the uterus through which an ovum passes after ovulation.

familial association studies Studies that examine the degree to which disorders or characteristics are shared among family members.

family therapy Therapy for troubled families that focuses on changing disruptive patterns of communication and improving the ways in which family members relate to each other.

fear hierarchy An ordered series of increasingly fearful objects or situations.

feature detectors Specialized neurons in the visual cortex that respond only to particular features of visual stimuli, such as horizontal or vertical lines.

female orgasmic disorder A type of orgasmic disorder in women characterized by a lack of orgasm, or persistent difficulties in achieving orgasm, following a normal phase of sexual excitement.

female sexual arousal disorder A type of sexual arousal disorder in women involving difficulties in becoming sexually aroused.

fertilization The union of a sperm with an ovum during sexual reproduction.

fetal alcohol syndrome (FAS) A syndrome caused by maternal use of alcohol during pregnancy in which the child shows developmental delays and facial deformities.

fetal stage The stage of prenatal development in which the fetus develops, beginning around the ninth week of pregnancy and lasting until the birth of the child.

fetishism A type of paraphilia involving use of objects as sources of sexual arousal.

fetus The developing organism in the later stages of prenatal development.

fight-or-flight response The body's built-in alarm system that allows it to quickly mobilize its resources to either fight or flee when faced with a threatening stressor.

five-factor model (FFM) The dominant contemporary trait model of personality, consisting of five broad personality factors: neuroticism, extraversion, openness, agreeableness, and conscientiousness.

fixations Constellations of personality traits characteristic of a particular stage of psychosexual development, resulting from either excessive or inadequate gratification at that stage.

flashbulb memories Enduring memories of emotionally charged events that seem permanently seared into the brain.

fluid intelligence A form of intelligence associated with the ability to think abstractly and flexibly in solving problems.

focused awareness A state of heightened alertness in which one is fully absorbed in the task at hand.

foot-in-the-door technique A compliance technique based on securing compliance with a smaller request as a prelude to making a larger request.

forebrain The largest and uppermost part of the brain; contains the thalamus, hypothalamus, limbic system, basal ganglia, and cerebral cortex.

forensic psychologists Psychologists involved in the application of psychology to the legal system.

formal operations The level of full cognitive maturity in Piaget's theory, characterized by the ability to think in abstract terms.

fovea The area near the center of the retina that contains only cones and that is the center of focus for clearest vision.

framing The tendency for decisions to be influenced by how potential outcomes are phrased.

fraternal twins Twins who developed from separate zygotes and so have 50 percent of their genes in common (also called *dizygotic*, or *DZ*, twins).

free association A technique in psychoanalysis in which the client is encouraged to say anything that comes to mind.

free recall A type of recall task in which individuals are asked to recall as many stored items as possible in any order.

frequency theory The belief that pitch depends on the frequency of vibration of the basilar membrane and the volley of neural impulses transmitted to the brain via the auditory nerve.

frontal lobes The parts of the cerebral cortex, located at the front of the cerebral hemispheres, that are considered the "executive center" of the brain because of their role in higher mental functions.

frustration A negative emotional state experienced when one's efforts to pursue one's goals are thwarted.

functional fixedness The tendency to perceive objects as limited to the customary functions they serve.

functionalism The school of psychology that focuses on the adaptive functions of behavior.

fundamental attribution error The tendency to attribute behavior to internal causes without regard to situational influences.

ganglion cells Nerve cells in the back of the eye that transmit neural impulses in response to light stimulation, the axons of which make up the optic nerve.

gender The state of maleness or femaleness.

gender identity The psychological sense of maleness or femaleness.

gender roles The cultural expectations imposed on men and women to behave in ways deemed appropriate for their gender.

gender-schema theory The belief that children form mental representations or schemas of masculinity and femininity, which they then use as a basis for organizing their behavior and evaluating their self-worth.

general adaptation syndrome (GAS) Selye's term for the three-stage response of the body to persistent or intense stress.

generalized anxiety disorder (GAD) A type of anxiety disorder involving persistent and generalized anxiety and worry.

genes Basic units of heredity that contain the individual's genetic code.

genital stage In Freudian theory, the fifth and final stage of psychosexual development, which begins around puberty and corresponds to the development of mature sexuality and emphasis on procreation.

genotype An organism's genetic code.

germ cells Sperm and egg cells from which new life develops.

germinal stage The stage of prenatal development that spans the period from fertilization through implantation.

geropsychologists Psychologists who focus on psychological processes involved in aging.

Gestalt psychology The school of psychology that holds that the brain structures our perceptions of the world in terms of meaningful patterns or wholes.

gestalt A German word meaning "unitary form" or "pattern."

glands Body organs or structures that produce secretions called hormones.

glial cells Small but numerous cells in the nervous system that support neurons and form the myelin sheath found on many axons.

gonads Sex glands (testes in men and ovaries in women) that produce sex hormones and germ cells (sperm in the male and egg cells in the female).

gradual exposure A behavior therapy technique for treating phobias based on direct exposure to a series of increasingly fearful stimuli. Also called *in-vivo ("real-life") exposure.*

grammar The set of rules governing how symbols in a given language are used to form meaningful expressions.

group polarization The tendency for members of decision-making groups to shift toward more extreme views in whatever direction they were initially leaning.

group therapy A form of therapy in which clients are treated within a group format.

groupthink Janis's term for the tendency of members of a decision-making group to be more focused on reaching a consensus than on critically examining the issues at hand.

hair cells The auditory receptors that transform vibrations caused by sound waves into neural impulses that are then transmitted to the brain via the auditory nerve.

hallucinations Perceptions ("hearing voices" or seeing things) that are experienced in the absence of external stimuli.

hallucinogens Drugs that alter sensory experiences and produce hallucinations.

hassles Annoyances of daily life that impose a stressful burden.

health psychologists Psychologists who focus on the relationship between psychological factors and physical health.

health psychology The specialty in psychology that focuses on the interrelationships between psychological factors and physical health.

heart attack A potentially life-threatening event involving the death of heart tissue due to a lack of blood flow to the heart. Also called *myocardial infarction.*

heritability The degree to which heredity accounts for variations on a given trait within a population.

heuristic A rule of thumb for solving problems or making judgments or decisions.

hidden observer Hilgard's term for a part of consciousness that remains detached from the hypnotic experience but aware of everything that happens during it.

hierarchy of needs Maslow's concept that there is an order to human needs, which starts with basic biological needs and progresses to self-actualization.

higher-order conditioning The process by which a new stimulus comes to elicit a conditioned response as a result of its being paired with a conditioned stimulus that already elicits the conditioned response.

hindbrain The lowest and, in evolutionary terms, oldest part of the brain; includes the medulla, pons, and cerebellum.

hippocampus A structure in the limbic system involved in memory formation.

homeostasis The tendency of systems to maintain a steady, internally balanced state.

homogamy The tendency for people to marry others who are similar to themselves.

homophobia Unreasoning fear and loathing of people with a homosexual sexual orientation.

hormones Secretions from endocrine glands that help regulate bodily processes.

humanistic perspective An approach to the study of psychology that applies the principles of humanistic psychology.

humanistic psychology The school of psychology that believes that free will and conscious choice are essential aspects of the human experience.

hypnosis An altered state of consciousness characterized by focused attention, deep relaxation, and heightened susceptibility to suggestion.

hypnotic age regression A hypnotically induced experience that involves re-experiencing past events in one's life.

hypnotic analgesia A loss of feeling or responsiveness to pain in certain parts of the body occurring during hypnosis.

hypoactive sexual desire disorder A type of sexual desire disorder characterized by an absence or lack of sexual interest or desire.

hypochondriasis A somatoform disorder in which there is excessive concern that one's physical complaints are signs of underlying serious illness.

hypothalamus pituitary adrenal (HPA) axis The integrated system of endocrine glands involved in the body's response to stress.

hypothalamus A pea-sized structure in the forebrain that helps regulate many vital bodily functions, including body temperature and reproduction, as well as emotional states, aggression, and responses to stress.

hypothesis A precise prediction about the outcomes of an experiment.

iconic memory A sensory store for holding a mental representation of a visual image for a fraction of a second.

id Freud's term for the psychic structure existing in the unconscious that contains our baser animal drives and instinctual impulses.

identical twins Twins who developed from the same zygote and so have identical genes (also called *monozygotic*, or *MZ*, twins).

identity crisis In Erikson's theory, a stressful period of serious soul-searching and self-examination of issues relating to personal values and one's direction in life.

imaginary audience The common belief among adolescents that they are the center of other people's attention.

immune system The body's system of defense against disease.

implicit memory Memory accessed without conscious effort.

impression formation The process of developing an opinion or impression of another person.

imprinting The formation of a strong bond of the newborn animal to the first moving object seen after birth.

incentive theory The belief that our attraction to particular goals or objects motivates much of our behavior.

incentive value The strength of the "pull" of a goal or reward.

incentives Rewards or other stimuli that motivate us to act.

incubation period A respite from active problem-solving efforts, which may facilitate finding a solution.

independent variables Factors that are manipulated in an experiment.

individual psychology Adler's theory of personality, which emphasizes the unique potential of each individual.

individualistic culture A culture that emphasizes individual identity and personal accomplishments.

industrial/organizational (I/O) psychologists Psychologists who study people's behavior at work.

inference A conclusion drawn from observations.

inferiority complex In Adler's theory, a concept involving the influence that feelings of inadequacy or inferiority in young children have on their developing personalities and desires to compensate.

informed consent Agreement to participate in a study following disclosure of information about the purposes and nature of the study and its potential risks and benefits.

in-group favoritism A cognitive bias involving the predisposition to attribute more positive characteristics to members of in-groups than to those of out-groups.

in-groups Social, religious, ethnic, racial, or national groups with which one identifies.

insight learning The process of mentally working through a problem until the sudden realization of a solution occurs.

insight In Freud's theory, the awareness of underlying unconscious wishes and conflicts.

insomnia Difficulty falling asleep, remaining asleep, or returning to sleep after nighttime awakenings.

instinct theory The belief that behavior is motivated by instinct.

instinctive behaviors Genetically programmed, innate patterns of response that are specific to members of a particular species.

intelligence quotient (IQ) A measure of intelligence based on performance on tests of mental abilities, expressed as a ratio between one's mental age and chronological age, or derived from the deviation of one's scores from the norms for those of one's age group.

intelligence The capacity to think and reason clearly and to act purposefully and effectively in adapting to the environment and pursuing one's goals.

interference theory The belief that forgetting is the result of the interference of memories with each other.

internal working models Generalized expectations, developed in early childhood, about how others are likely to respond in close relationships.

interneurons Nerve cells within the central nervous system that process information.

interpretation In psychoanalysis, the attempt by the therapist to explain the connections between the material the client discloses in therapy and his or her unconscious conflicts.

intoxicant A chemical substance that induces a state of drunkenness.

intrinsic motivation Motivation reflecting a desire for internal gratification, such as the self-satisfaction derived from accomplishing a particular goal.

introspection Inward focusing on mental experiences, such as sensations or feelings.

introversion-extraversion Tendencies toward being solitary and reserved on the one end or outgoing and sociable on the other end.

ions Electrically charged chemical particles.

iris The pigmented, circular muscle in the eye that regulates the size of the pupil to adjust to changes in the level of illumination.

irreversibility In Piaget's theory, the inability to reverse the direction of a sequence of events to their starting point.

James-Lange theory The belief that emotions occur after people become aware of their physiological responses to the triggering stimuli.

jet lag A disruption of sleep-wake cycles caused by the shifts in time zones that accompany long-distance air travel.

kinesthesia The body sense that keeps us informed about the movement of the parts of the body and their position in relation to each other.

laceration A type of brain trauma in which a foreign object, such as a bullet or a piece of shrapnel, pierces the skull and injures the brain.

language acquisition device Chomsky's concept of an innate, prewired mechanism in the brain that allows children to acquire language naturally.

language A system of communication composed of symbols (words, hand signs, etc.) that are arranged according to a set of rules (grammar) to form meaningful expressions.

latency stage In Freudian theory, the fourth stage of psychosexual development, during which sexual impulses remain latent or dormant.

latent learning Learning that occurs without apparent reinforcement and that is not displayed until reinforcement is provided.

lateral hypothalamus A part of the hypothalamus involved in initiating, or "turning on," eating.

lateralization The specialization of the right and left cerebral hemispheres for particular functions.

Law of Effect Thorndike's principle that responses that have satisfying effects are more likely to recur, whereas those that have unpleasant effects are less likely to recur.

laws of perceptual organization The principles identified by Gestalt psychologists that describe the ways in which the brain groups bits of sensory stimulation into meaningful wholes or patterns.

learned helplessness model The view that depression results from the perception of a lack of control over the reinforcements in one's life that may result from exposure to uncontrollable negative events.

learning A relatively permanent change in behavior acquired through experience.

legitimization of authority The tendency to grant legitimacy to the orders or commands of persons in authority.

lens The structure in the eye that focuses light rays on the retina.

lesioning In studies of brain functioning, the intentional destruction of brain tissue in order to observe the effects on behavior.

levels-of-processing theory The belief that how well or how long information is remembered depends on the depth of encoding or processing.

limbic system A formation of structures in the forebrain that includes the hippocampus, amygdala, and parts of the thalamus and hypothalamus.

linguistic relativity hypothesis The proposition that the language we use determines how we think and how we perceive the world (also called the *Whorfian hypothesis*).

locus of control In Rotter's theory, one's general expectancies about whether one's efforts can bring about desired outcomes or reinforcements.

logical concepts Concepts with clearly defined rules for membership.

longitudinal study Study that compares the same individuals at periodic intervals over an extended period of time.

long-term memory (LTM) The memory subsystem responsible for long-term storage of information.

long-term potentiation (LTP) The long-term strengthening of neural connections as the result of repeated stimulation.

low-ball technique A compliance technique based on obtaining a person's initial agreement to purchase an item at a lower price before revealing hidden costs that raise the ultimate price.

lucid dreams Dreams in which the dreamer is aware that he or she is dreaming.

lymphocytes White blood cells that protect the body against disease-causing organisms.

mainstreaming The practice of placing children with special needs in a regular classroom environment.

maintenance rehearsal The process of extending retention of information held in short-term memory by consciously repeating the information.

major depression The most common type of depressive disorder, characterized by periods of downcast mood, feelings of worthlessness, and loss of interest in pleasurable activities.

male erectile disorder A type of sexual arousal disorder in men characterized by difficulty achieving or maintaining erections sufficient to engage in sexual intercourse.

male orgasmic disorder A type of orgasmic disorder in men characterized by a lack of orgasm, or persistent difficulties in achieving orgasm, following a normal phase of sexual excitement.

malignant tumors Uncontrolled growths of body cells that invade surrounding tissue and spread to other parts of the body.

manic episodes Periods of mania, or unusually elevated mood and extreme restlessness.

mantra A sound or phrase chanted repeatedly during transcendental meditation.

massed versus spaced practice effect The tendency for retention of learned material to be greater with spaced practice than with massed practice.

matching hypothesis The belief that people tend to pair off with others who are similar to themselves in physical attractiveness and other characteristics.

maturation The biological unfolding of the organism according to the underlying genetic code.

medical model A framework for understanding abnormal behavior patterns as symptoms of underlying physical disorders or diseases.

meditation A process of focused attention that induces a relaxed, contemplative state.

medulla A structure in the hindbrain involved in regulating basic life functions, such as heartbeat and respiration.

melanoma The most deadly form of skin cancer.

memory encoding The process of converting information into a form that can be stored in memory.

memory retrieval The process of accessing and bringing into consciousness information stored in memory.

memory storage The process of retaining information in memory.

memory The system that allows us to retain information and bring it to mind.

menarche The first menstruation.

menopause The time of life when menstruation ends.

mental age A representation of a person's intelligence based on the age of people who are capable of performing at the same level of ability.

mental image A mental picture or representation of an object or event.

mental retardation A generalized deficit or impairment in intellectual and social skills.

mental set The tendency to rely on strategies that worked in similar situations in the past but that may not be appropriate to the present situation.

meta-analysis A statistical technique for averaging results across a large number of studies.

midbrain The part of the brain that lies on top of the hindbrain and below the forebrain.

midlife crisis A state of psychological crisis, often occurring during middle adulthood, in which people grapple with the loss of their youth.

migraine headache A prolonged, intense headache brought on by changes in blood flow in the brain's blood vessels.

mindfulness meditation A form of meditation in which one adopts a state of nonjudgmental attention to the unfolding of experience on a moment-to-moment basis.

mirror neurons Neurons that fire both when an action is performed and when the same action is merely observed.

misinformation effect A form of memory distortion that affects eyewitness testimony and that is caused by misinformation provided during the retention interval.

mnemonic A device for improving memory.

modeling A behavior therapy technique for overcoming phobias and acquiring more adaptive behaviors, based on observing and imitating models.

monoamine oxidase (MAO) inhibitors A class of antidepressant drugs that increase the availability of neurotransmitters in the brain by inhibiting an enzyme, monoamine oxidase, that breaks down or degrades them in the synapse.

monochromats People who have no color vision and can see only in black and white.

monocular cues Cues for depth that can be perceived by each eye alone, such as relative size and interposition.

mood disorders A class of psychological disorders involving disturbances in mood states, such as major depression and bipolar disorder.

moral therapy A philosophy of treatment that emphasized treating mentally ill people with compassion and understanding, rather than shackling them in chains.

Moro reflex An inborn reflex, elicited by a sudden noise or loss of support, in which the infant extends its arms, arches its back, and brings its arms toward each other as though attempting to grab hold of someone.

morphemes The smallest units of meaning in a language.

motivation Factors that activate, direct, and sustain goal-directed behavior.

motives Needs or wants that drive goal-directed behavior.

motor cortex A region of the frontal lobes involved in regulating body movement.

motor neurons Neurons that convey nerve impulses from the central nervous system to muscles and glands.

mourning The expression of sorrow or grief in accordance with a set of customs, such as wearing black clothing.

MRI (magnetic resonance imaging) A technique that uses a magnetic field to create a computerized image of internal bodily structures.

multiple intelligences Gardner's term for the distinct types of intelligence that characterize different forms of intelligent behavior.

multiple sclerosis (MS) A disease of the central nervous system in which the myelin sheath that insulates axons is damaged or destroyed.

myelin sheath A layer of protective insulation that covers the axons of certain neurons and helps speed transmission of nerve impulses.

myotonia A state of muscle tension or rigidity.

narcolepsy A disorder characterized by sudden unexplained "sleep attacks" during the day.

narcotics Addictive drugs that have pain-relieving and sleep-inducing properties.

natural concepts Concepts with poorly defined or fuzzy rules for membership.

naturalistic observation method A method of research based on careful observation of behavior in natural settings.

nature-nurture debate The debate in psychology over the relative influences of genetics (nature) and environment (nurture) in determining behavior.

need for achievement The need to excel in one's endeavors.

need A state of deprivation or deficiency.

negative instance An object that does not fit a particular concept (e.g., a calico kitten is a negative instance of dog but a positive instance of cat).

negative reinforcement The strengthening of a response through the removal of a stimulus after the response occurs.

negative symptoms Behavioral deficits associated with schizophrenia, such as withdrawal and apathy.

neodissociation theory A theory of hypnosis based on the belief that hypnosis represents a state of dissociated (divided) consciousness.

nerve deafness Deafness associated with nerve damage, usually involving damage to the hair cells or to the auditory nerve itself.

nerve A bundle of axons from different neurons that transmit nerve impulses.

nervous system The network of nerve cells and support cells for communicating and processing information from within and outside the body.

neural tube The area in the embryo from which the nervous system develops.

neuromarketing An emerging field of marketing that explores brain responses to advertisements and brand-related messages.

neuromodulators Chemicals released in the nervous system that influence the sensitivity of the receiving neuron to neurotransmitters.

neuronal networks Memory circuits in the brain that consist of complicated networks of nerve cells.

neurons Nerve cells.

neuropsychologists Psychologists who study relationships between the brain and behavior.

neuroticism Tendencies toward emotional instability, anxiety, and worry.

neurotransmitters Chemical messengers that transport nerve impulses from one nerve cell to another.

neutral stimulus (NS) A stimulus that before conditioning does not produce a particular response.

nightmare disorder A sleep disorder involving a pattern of frequent, disturbing nightmares.

nodes of Ranvier Gaps in the myelin sheath that create noninsulated areas along the axon.

nonspecific factors General features of psychotherapy, such as attention from a therapist and mobilization of positive expectancies or hope.

norms The standards used to compare an individual's performance on a test with the performance of others.

obedience Compliance with commands or orders issued by others, usually persons in a position of authority.

object permanence The recognition that objects continue to exist even if they have disappeared from sight.

objective tests Tests of personality that can be scored objectively and are based on a research foundation.

observational learning Learning by observing and imitating the behavior of others (also called *vicarious learning or modeling*).

obsessive-compulsive disorder (OCD) A type of anxiety disorder involving the repeated occurrence of obsessions and/or compulsions.

occipital lobes The parts of the cerebral cortex, located at the back of both cerebral hemispheres, that process visual stimuli.

Oedipus complex In Freudian theory, the psychological complex in which the young boy or girl develops incestuous feelings toward the parent of the opposite gender and perceives the parent of the same gender as a rival.

olfaction The sense of smell.

olfactory bulb The area in the front of the brain above the nostrils that receives sensory input from olfactory receptors in the nose.

olfactory nerve The nerve that carries impulses from olfactory receptors in the nose to the brain.

operant conditioning The process of learning in which the consequences of a response determine the probability that the response will be repeated.

operant response A response that operates on the environment to produce certain consequences.

operational definition A definition of a variable based on the procedures or operations used to measure it.

opponent-process theory Holds that the experience of color results from opposing processes involving two sets of color receptors, red-green receptors and blue-yellow receptors; another set of opposing receptors, black-white, detects differences in brightness.

optic nerve The nerve that carries neural impulses generated by light stimulation from the eye to the brain.

oral stage In Freudian theory, the first stage of psychosexual development, during which the infant seeks sexual gratification through oral stimulation (sucking, mouthing, and biting).

organ of Corti A gelatinous structure in the cochlea containing the hair cells that serve as auditory receptors.

organizational culture The system of shared values and norms within an organization.

ossicles Three tiny bones in the middle ear (the hammer, anvil, and stirrup) that vibrate in response to vibrations of the eardrum.

osteoporosis A bone disease characterized by a loss of bone density in which the bones become porous, brittle, and more prone to fracture.

outcome expectations Bandura's term for our personal predictions about the outcomes of our behavior.

out-group homogeneity A cognitive bias describing the tendency to perceive members of out-groups as more alike than members of in-groups.

out-group negativism A cognitive bias involving the predisposition to attribute more negative characteristics to members of out-groups than to those of in-groups.

out-groups Groups other than those with which one identifies.

oval window The membrane-covered opening that separates the middle ear from the inner ear.

ovaries The female gonads, which secrete the female sex hormones estrogen and progesterone and produce mature egg cells.

overlearning Practice repeated beyond the point necessary to reproduce material without error.

ovulation The release of an ovum from an ovary.

ovum An egg cell (pl: ova).

palmar grasp reflex The reflexive curling of the infant's fingers around an object that touches its palm.

pancreas An endocrine gland located near the stomach that produces the hormone insulin.

panic disorder A type of anxiety disorder involving repeated episodes of sheer terror called panic attacks.

paranoid type The most common subtype of schizophrenia, characterized by the appearance of delusional thinking accompanied by frequent auditory hallucinations.

paraphilia A psychological disorder involving atypical or deviant patterns of sexual attraction.

parapsychology The study of paranormal phenomena.

parasympathetic nervous system The branch of the autonomic nervous system that regulates bodily processes, such as digestion, that replenish stores of energy.

parietal lobes The parts of the cerebral cortex, located on the side of each cerebral hemisphere, that process bodily sensations.

Parkinson's disease A progressive brain disease involving destruction of dopamine-producing brain cells and characterized by muscle tremors, shakiness, rigidity, and difficulty in walking and controlling fine body movements.

pedophilia A type of paraphilia involving sexual attraction to children.

penis envy In Freudian theory, jealousy of boys for having a penis.

peptic ulcers Sores that form on the lining of the stomach or small intestine.

perception The process by which the brain integrates, organizes, and interprets sensory impressions to create representations of the world.

perceptual set The tendency for perceptions to be influenced by one's expectations or preconceptions.

performance anxiety Anxiety experienced in performance situations (including sexual acts) stemming from a fear of negative evaluation of one's ability to perform.

peripheral nervous system The part of the nervous system that connects the spinal cord and brain with the sensory organs, muscles, and glands.

person variables Mischel's term for internal personal factors that influence behavior, including competencies, expectancies, and subjective values.

personal fable The common belief among adolescents that their feelings and experiences cannot possibly be understood by others and that they are personally invulnerable to harm.

personal identity The part of our psychological identity that involves our sense of ourselves as unique individuals.

personal unconscious Jung's term for an unconscious region of mind comprising a reservoir of the individual's repressed memories and impulses.

personality disorders A class of psychological disorders characterized by rigid personality traits that impair people's ability to adjust to the demands they face in the environment and that interfere with their relationships with others.

personality psychologists Psychologists who study the psychological characteristics and behaviors that distinguish us as individuals and lead us to act consistently over time.

personality tests Structured psychological tests that use formal methods of assessing personality.

personality The relatively stable constellation of psychological characteristics and behavioral patterns that account for our individuality and consistency over time.

PET (positron emission tomography) scan An imaging technique in which a radioactive sugar tracer is injected into the bloodstream and used to measure levels of activity of various parts of the brain.

phallic stage In Freudian theory, the third stage of psychosexual development, marked by erotic attention on the phallic region (penis in boys, clitoris in girls) and the development of the Oedipus complex.

phenotype The observable physical and behavioral characteristics of an organism, representing the influences of the genotype and environment.

pheromones Chemical substances that are emitted by many species and that have various functions, including sexual attraction.

phobias Excessive fears of particular objects or situations.

phonemes The basic units of sound in a language.

phonological loop The speech-based part of working memory that allows for the verbal rehearsal of sounds or words.

photoreceptors Light-sensitive cells (rods and cones) in the eye upon which light registers.

phrenology The now-discredited view that one can judge a person's character and mental abilities by measuring the bumps on his or her head.

physiological dependence A state of physical dependence on a drug caused by repeated usage that changes body chemistry.

physiological perspective An approach to the study of psychology that focuses on the relationships between biological processes and behavior.

physiological psychologists Psychologists who focus on the biological underpinnings of behavior.

pineal gland A small endocrine gland in the brain that produces the hormone melatonin, which is involved in regulating sleep-wake cycles.

pitch The highness or lowness of a sound that corresponds to the frequency of the sound wave.

pituitary gland An endocrine gland in the brain that produces various hormones involved in growth, regulation of the menstrual cycle, and childbirth.

place theory The belief that pitch depends on the place along the basilar membrane that vibrates the most in response to a particular auditory stimulus.

placebo effects Positive outcomes of a treatment resulting from positive expectations rather than from the effects of the treatment itself. Also called *expectancy effects.*

placebo effects Positive outcomes of an experiment resulting from a participant's positive expectations about the treatment rather than from the treatment itself.

placebo An inert substance or experimental condition that resembles the active treatment.

placenta The organ that provides for the exchange of nutrients and waste materials between mother and fetus.

plaque In the circulatory system, fatty deposits that accumulate along artery walls.

plasticity The ability of the brain to adapt itself after trauma or surgical alteration.

pleasure principle In Freudian theory, a governing principle of the id that is based on demand for instant gratification without regard to social rules or customs.

polyabusers People who abuse more than one drug at a time.

polygenic traits Traits that are influenced by multiple genes interacting in complex ways.

pons A structure in the hindbrain involved in regulating states of wakefulness and sleep.

population All the individuals or organisms that constitute particular groups.

positive instance An object that fits a particular concept (e.g., a terrier is a positive instance of dog).

positive psychology A contemporary movement within psychology that emphasizes the study of human virtues and assets, rather than weaknesses and deficits.

positive reinforcement The strengthening of a response through the introduction of a stimulus after the response occurs.

positive symptoms Symptoms of schizophrenia involving behavioral excesses, such as hallucinations and delusions.

posthypnotic amnesia An inability to recall what happened during hypnosis.

posthypnotic suggestion A hypnotist's suggestion that the subject will respond in a particular way following hypnosis.

posttraumatic stress disorder (PTSD) A psychological disorder involving a maladaptive reaction to traumatic stress.

precognition The ability to foretell the future.

preconscious To Freud, the part of the mind whose contents can be brought into awareness through focused attention.

prefrontal cortex The area of the frontal lobe that lies in front of the motor cortex and is involved in higher mental functions, including thinking, planning, impulse control, and weighing the consequences of behavior.

prefrontal lobotomy A surgical procedure in which neural pathways in the brain are severed in order to control violent or aggressive behavior.

prejudice A preconceived opinion or attitude about an issue, person, or group.

premature ejaculation (PE) A type of orgasmic disorder in men characterized by rapid ejaculation following sexual stimulation.

premenstrual syndrome (PMS) A cluster of physical and psychological symptoms occurring in the days preceding the menstrual flow.

primacy effect The tendency to recall items better when they are learned first.

primary drives Innate drives, such as hunger, thirst, and sexual desire, that arise from basic biological needs.

primary mental abilities Seven basic mental abilities that Thurstone believed constitute intelligence.

primary reinforcers Reinforcers, such as food or sexual stimulation, that are naturally rewarding because they satisfy basic biological needs or drives.

primary sex characteristics Physical characteristics, such as the gonads, that differentiate males and females and play a direct role in reproduction.

proactive interference A form of interference in which material learned earlier interferes with retention of newly acquired information.

problem solving A form of thinking focused on finding a solution to a particular problem.

procedural memory Memory of how to do things that require motor or performance skills.

programmed instruction A learning method in which complex material is broken down into a series of small steps that learners master at their own pace.

projection In Freudian theory, a defense mechanism involving the projection of one's own unacceptable impulses, wishes, or urges onto another person.

projective tests Personality tests in which ambiguous or vague test materials are used to elicit responses that are believed to reveal a person's unconscious needs, drives, and motives.

prosocial behavior Behavior that benefits others.

prospective memory Memory of things one plans to do in the future.

proximity Nearness or propinquity.

proximity The principle that objects that are near each other will be perceived as belonging to a common set.

psychiatrists Medical doctors who specialize in the diagnosis and treatment of mental or psychological disorders.

psychoactive drugs Chemical substances that affect a person's mental or emotional state.

psychoanalysis Freud's method of psychotherapy; it focuses on uncovering and working through unconscious conflicts he believed were at the root of psychological problems.

psychoanalysis The method of psychotherapy developed by Freud that focuses on uncovering and working through the unconscious conflicts that he believed were at the root of psychological problems.

psychoanalysts Practitioners of psychoanalysis who are schooled in the Freudian tradition.

psychoanalytic theory Freud's theory of personality that holds that personality and behavior are shaped by unconscious forces and conflicts.

psychodynamic perspective The view that behavior is influenced by the struggle between unconscious sexual or aggressive impulses and opposing forces that try to keep this threatening material out of consciousness.

psychokinesis The ability to move objects by mental effort alone.

psychological dependence A pattern of compulsive or habitual use of a drug to satisfy a psychological need.

psychological disorders Abnormal behavior patterns characterized by disturbances in behavior, thinking, perceptions, or emotions that are associated with significant personal distress or impaired functioning. Also called *mental disorders* or *mental illnesses*.

psychological hardiness A cluster of traits (commitment, openness to challenge, internal locus of control) that may buffer the effects of stress.

psychology The science of behavior and mental processes.

psychophysics The study of the relationships between features of physical stimuli, such as their intensity, and the sensations we experience in response to them.

psychosocial needs Needs that reflect interpersonal aspects of motivation, such as the need for friendship or achievement.

psychosurgery Brain surgery used to control violent or deviant behavior.

psychotherapy A verbal form of therapy derived from a psychological framework that consists of one or more treatment sessions with a therapist.

psychotic disorder A psychological disorder, such as schizophrenia, characterized by a "break" with reality.

psychoticism Tendencies to be perceived as cold and antisocial.

psychotropic drugs Psychiatric drugs used in the treatment of psychological or mental disorders.

puberty The stage of development at which individuals become physiologically capable of reproducing.

punishment The introduction of an aversive stimulus or the removal of a reinforcing stimulus after a response occurs, which leads to the weakening or suppression of the response.

pupil The black opening inside the iris that allows light to enter the eye.

questionnaire A written set of questions or statements to which people reply by marking their responses on an answer form.

racism Negative bias toward others based on their ethnicity or racial identification.

random assignment A method of randomly assigning subjects to experimental or control groups.

random sampling A method of sampling in which each individual in the population has an equal chance of being selected.

rape The use or threat of force to compel a person into having sexual intercourse.

rapid-eye-movement (REM) sleep The stage of sleep that involves rapid eye movements and that is most closely associated with periods of dreaming.

rational emotive behavior therapy (REBT) Developed by Albert Ellis, a form of therapy based on identifying and correcting irrational beliefs that are thought to underlie emotional and behavioral difficulties.

rationalization In Freudian theory, a defense mechanism involving the use of self-justification to explain away unacceptable behavior, impulses, or ideas.

reaction formation In Freudian theory, a defense mechanism involving behavior that stands in opposition to one's true motives and desires so as to prevent conscious awareness of them.

reality principle In Freudian theory, the governing principle of the ego that takes into account what is practical and acceptable in satisfying basic needs.

recency effect The tendency to recall items better when they are learned last.

receptor site A site on the receiving neuron in which neurotransmitters dock.

reciprocal determinism Bandura's model in which cognitions, behaviors, and environmental factors influence and are influenced by each other.

reciprocity The principle that people tend to like others who like them back.

recognition task A method of measuring memory retention that assesses the ability to select the correct answer from among a range of alternative answers.

reconditioning The process of relearning a conditioned response following extinction.

reflex An automatic unlearned response to particular stimuli.

refractory period A temporary state in which a neuron is unable to fire in response to continued stimulation.

regression In Freudian theory, a defense mechanism in which an individual, usually under high levels of stress, reverts to a behavior characteristic of an earlier stage of development.

reinforcer A stimulus or event that increases the probability that the response it follows will be repeated.

reliability The stability of test scores over time.

replication The attempt to duplicate findings.

representativeness heuristic A rule of thumb for making a judgment that assumes a given sample is representative of the larger population from which it is drawn.

repression In Freudian theory, a type of defense mechanism involving motivated forgetting of anxiety-evoking material.

resistance stage The second stage of the general adaptation syndrome, characterized by the body's attempt to adjust or adapt to persistent stress.

resistance In psychoanalysis, the blocking that occurs when therapy touches upon anxiety-evoking thoughts or feelings.

resting potential The electrical potential across the cell membrane of a neuron in its resting state.

reticular formation A weblike formation of neurons involved in regulating states of attention, alertness, and arousal.

retina The light-sensitive layer of the inner surface of the eye that contains photoreceptor cells.

retinal disparity A binocular cue for distance based on the slight differences in the visual impressions formed in both eyes.

retrieval cues Cues associated with the original learning that facilitate the retrieval of memories.

retrieval theory The belief that forgetting is the result of a failure to access stored memories.

retroactive interference A form of interference in which newly acquired information interferes with retention of material learned earlier.

retrograde amnesia Loss of memory of past events.

retrospective memory Memory of past experiences or events and previously acquired information.

reuptake The process by which neurotransmitters are reabsorbed by the transmitting neuron.

risky-shift phenomenon A type of group polarization effect in which group discussion leads to the adoption of a riskier course of action than the members would have endorsed initially.

rods Photoreceptors that are sensitive only to the intensity of light (light and dark).

role diffusion In Erikson's model, a lack of direction or aimlessness with respect to one's role in life or public identity.

romantic love A form of love characterized by strong erotic attraction and desire for intimacy.

rooting reflex The reflexive turning of the newborn's head in the direction of a touch on its cheek.

rubella A common childhood disease that can lead to serious birth defects if contracted by the mother during pregnancy (also called German measles).

samples Subsets of a population.

savings method A method of testing memory retention by comparing the numbers of trials needed to learn material with the number of trials needed to relearn the material at a later time.

scaffolding In Vygotsky's theory, tailoring the degree and type of instruction to the child's current level of ability or knowledge.

schedule of continuous reinforcement A system of dispensing a reinforcement each time a response is produced.

schedule of partial reinforcement A system of reinforcement in which only a portion of responses is reinforced.

schedules of reinforcement Predetermined plans for timing the delivery of reinforcement.

schema In Piaget's theory, a mental framework for understanding or acting on the environment.

schizophrenia A severe and chronic psychological disorder characterized by disturbances in thinking, perception, emotions, and behavior.

school psychologists Psychologists who evaluate and assist children with learning problems or other special needs.

scientific method A method of inquiry involving careful observation and use of experimental methods.

seasonal affective disorder (SAD) A type of major depressive disorder that involves a recurring pattern of winter depressions followed by elevations of mood in spring and summer.

secondary drives Drives that are learned or acquired through experience, such as the drive to achieve monetary wealth.

secondary gain Reward value of having a psychological or physical symptom, such as release from ordinary responsibilities.

secondary reinforcers Learned reinforcers, such as money, that develop their reinforcing properties because of their association with primary reinforcers.

secondary sex characteristics Physical characteristics that differentiate males and females but are not directly involved in reproduction.

secondary traits Allport's term for specific traits that influence behavior in relatively few situations.

selective attention The process by which we attend to meaningful stimuli and filter out irrelevant or extraneous stimuli.

selective serotonin-reuptake inhibitors (SSRIs) A class of antidepressant drugs that work specifically on increasing availability of the neurotransmitter serotonin by interfering with its reuptake.

self-actualization The motive that drives individuals to express their unique capabilities and fulfill their potentials.

self-fulfilling prophecy An expectation that helps bring about the outcome that is expected.

self-ideals Rogers's term for the idealized sense of how or what we should be.

self-report personality inventories Structured psychological tests in which individuals are given a limited range of response options to answer a set of questions about themselves.

self-serving bias The tendency to take credit for our accomplishments and to explain away our failures or disappointments.

self-theory Rogers's model of personality, which focuses on the importance of the self.

semantic memory Memory of facts and general information about the world.

semantic network model A representation of the organizational structure of long-term memory in terms of a network of associated concepts.

semantics The set of rules governing the meaning of words.

semicircular canals Three curved, tubelike canals in the inner ear that are involved in sensing changes in the direction and movement of the head.

sensate-focus exercises A technique used in sex therapy that consists of nongenital massage to lessen the anxiety associated with sexual interactions.

sensation The process by which we receive, transform, and process stimuli from the outside world to create sensory experiences of vision, touch, hearing, taste, smell, and so on.

sensory adaptation The process by which sensory receptors adapt to constant stimuli by becoming less sensitive to them.

sensory memory The storage system that holds memory of sensory impressions for a very short time.

sensory neurons Neurons that transmit information from sensory organs, muscles, and inner organs to the spinal cord and brain.

sensory receptors Specialized cells that detect sensory stimuli and convert them into neural impulses.

sensory register A temporary storage device for holding sensory memories.

serial position effect The tendency to recall items at the start or end of a list better than items in the middle of a list.

set point theory The belief that brain mechanisms regulate body weight around a genetically predetermined "set point."

sexual aversion disorder A type of sexual desire disorder involving repulsion or strong aversion to genital sexual contact.

sexual dysfunctions Persistent or recurrent problems with sexual interest, arousal, or response.

sexual harassment A form of sexual coercion involving unwelcome sexual comments, jokes, overtures, demands for sexual favors, or outright physical contact.

sexual masochism A type of paraphilia involving the receipt of painful or humiliating experiences as part of a sexual act.

sexual orientation The directionality of one's erotic interests.

sexual response cycle The term used by Masters and Johnson to refer to the characteristic stages of physiological response to sexual stimulation.

sexual sadism A type of paraphilia involving the infliction of physical suffering or humiliation on another person for purposes of sexual gratification.

sexually transmitted disease (STD) A disease caused by an infectious agent that is spread by sexual contact.

shape constancy The tendency to perceive an object as having the same shape despite differences in the images it casts on the retina as the viewer's perspective changes.

shaping A process of learning that involves the reinforcement of increasingly closer approximations of the desired response.

short-term memory (STM) The memory subsystem that allows for retention and processing of newly acquired information for a maximum of about 30 seconds (also called *working memory*).

signal-detection theory The belief that the detection of a stimulus depends on factors involving the intensity of the stimulus, the level of background stimulation, and the biological and psychological characteristics of the perceiver.

similarity The principle that objects that are similar will be perceived as belonging to the same group.

single-blind studies In drug research, studies in which subjects are kept uninformed about whether they are receiving the experimental drug or a placebo.

situation variables Mischel's term for environmental influences on behavior, such as rewards and punishments.

situational causes Causes relating to external or environmental events.

size constancy The tendency to perceive an object as having the same size despite changes in the images it casts on the retina as the viewing distance changes.

skin senses The senses of touch, pressure, warmth, cold, and pain that involve stimulation of sensory receptors in the skin.

Skinner box An experimental apparatus developed by B. F. Skinner for studying relationships between reinforcement and behavior.

sleep apnea Temporary cessation of breathing during sleep.

sleep terror disorder A sleep disorder involving repeated episodes of intense fear during sleep, causing the person to awake abruptly in a terrified state.

sleepwalking disorder A sleep disorder characterized by repeated episodes of sleepwalking.

social desirability bias The tendency to respond to questions in a socially desirable manner.

social facilitation The tendency to work better or harder in the presence of others than when alone.

social identity The part of our psychological identity that involves our sense of ourselves as members of particular groups. Also called *group identity*.

social loafing The tendency to expend less effort when working as a member of a group than when working alone.

social norms Standards that define what is socially acceptable in a given situation.

social perception The processes by which we form impressions, make judgments, and develop attitudes about the people and events that constitute our social world.

social phobia A type of anxiety disorder involving excessive fear of social situations.

social psychologists Psychologists who study group or social influences on behavior and attitudes.

social psychology The subfield in psychology that deals with how our thoughts, feelings, and behaviors are influenced by our social interactions with others.

social schema A mental image or representation that we use to understand our social environment.

social validation The tendency to use other people's behavior as a standard for judging the appropriateness of one's own behavior.

social-cognitive theory A contemporary learning-based model that emphasizes the roles of cognitive and environmental factors in determining behavior.

social-cognitive theory A learning-based model of personality that emphasizes both cognitive factors and environmental influences in determining behavior.

sociocultural perspective An approach to the study of psychology that emphasizes the role of social and cultural influences on behavior.

soma The cell body of a neuron that contains the nucleus of the cell and carries out the cell's metabolic functions.

somatic nervous system The part of the peripheral nervous system that transmits information between the central nervous system and the sensory organs and muscles; also controls voluntary movements.

somatoform disorders A class of psychological disorders involving physical ailments or complaints that cannot be explained by organic causes.

somatosensory cortex The part of the parietal lobe that processes information about touch and pressure on the skin, as well as the position of our body parts as we move about.

source traits Cattell's term for traits at a deep level of personality that are not apparent in observed behavior but must be inferred based on underlying relationships among surface traits.

specific phobia Phobic reactions involving specific situations or objects.

sperm The male reproductive cell.

spina bifida A neural tube defect in which the child is born with a hole in the tube surrounding the spinal cord.

spinal cord The column of nerves that transmits information between the brain and the peripheral nervous system.

spinal reflex A reflex controlled at the level of the spinal cord that may involve as few as two neurons.

spine The protective bony column that houses the spinal cord.

split-brain patients Persons whose corpus callosum has been surgically severed.

spontaneous recovery The spontaneous return of a conditioned response following extinction.

sport psychologists Psychologists who apply psychology to understanding and improving athletic performance.

standard scores Scores that represent an individual's relative deviation from the mean of the standardization sample.

standardization The process of establishing norms for a test by administering the test to large numbers of people who constitute a standardization sample.

state-dependent memory effect The tendency for information to be better recalled when the person is in the same psychological or physiological state as when the information was first learned.

states of consciousness Levels of consciousness ranging from alert wakefulness to deep sleep.

statistics The branch of mathematics involving the tabulation, analysis, and interpretation of numerical data.

statutory rape Sexual intercourse with a person who is under the legal age of consent, even if the person is a willing participant.

stereotype threat A sense of threat evoked in people from stereotyped groups when they believe they may be judged or treated stereotypically.

stereotypes The tendency to characterize all members of a particular group as having certain characteristics in common.

stimulant A drug that activates the central nervous system, such as amphetamines and cocaine.

stimulants Drugs that activate the central nervous system.

stimulus discrimination The tendency to differentiate among stimuli so that stimuli that are related to the original conditioned stimulus, but not identical to it, fail to elicit a conditioned response.

stimulus generalization The tendency for stimuli that are similar to the conditioned stimulus to elicit a conditioned response.

stimulus motives Internal states that prompt inquisitive, stimulation-seeking, and exploratory behavior.

Strange Situation Ainsworth's method for assessing infant attachment to the mother, based on a series of brief separations and reunions with the mother in a playroom situation.

stress Pressure or demand placed on an organism to adjust or adapt.

stressors Sources of stress.

stroboscopic movement A type of apparent movement based on the rapid succession of still images, as in motion pictures.

structuralism The school of psychology that attempts to understand the structure of the mind by breaking it down into its component parts.

structured interview An interview in which a set of specific questions is asked in a particular order.

subjective value In social-cognitive theory, the importance individuals place on desired outcomes.

sublimation In Freudian theory, a defense mechanism involving the channeling of unacceptable impulses into socially sanctioned behaviors or interests.

subliminal perception Perception of stimuli that are presented below the threshold of conscious awareness.

subordinate concepts The narrowest level of concepts in a three-level hierarchy of concepts.

sucking reflex Rhythmic sucking in response to stimulation of the tongue or mouth.

sudden infant death syndrome (SIDS) The sudden and unexplained death of infants that usually occurs when they are asleep in their cribs.

superego Freud's term for the psychic structure that corresponds to an internal moral guardian or conscience.

superordinate concepts The broadest concepts in a three-level hierarchy of concepts.

superstitious behavior In Skinner's view, behavior acquired through coincidental association of a response and a reinforcement.

surface traits Cattell's term for personality traits at the surface level that can be gleaned from observations of behavior.

survey method A research method in which structured interviews or questionnaires are used to gather information about groups of people.

symbolic representations Symbols that stand for names and experiences; specifically, the words in a language.

sympathetic nervous system The branch of the autonomic nervous system that accelerates bodily processes and releases stores of energy needed to meet increased physical demands.

synapse The small fluid-filled gap between neurons through which neurotransmitters carry neural impulses.

syntax The rules of grammar that determine how words are ordered within sentences or phrases to form meaningful expressions.

systematic desensitization A behavior therapy technique for treating phobias through the pairing of exposure in imagination to fear-inducing stimuli and states of deep relaxation.

taste buds Pores or openings on the tongue containing taste cells.

taste cells Nerve cells that are sensitive to tastes.

telecommuting A form of working at home in which people communicate with their home office and clients via computer or telecommunications.

telepathy Communication of thoughts from one mind to another that occurs without using the known senses.

temperament A characteristic style of behavior or disposition.

temporal lobes The parts of the cerebral cortex lying beneath and somewhat behind the frontal lobes that are involved in processing auditory stimuli.

teratogen An environmental influence or agent that may harm the developing embryo or fetus.

terminal buttons Swellings at the tips of axons from which neurotransmitters are dispatched into the synapse.

testes The male gonads, which produce sperm and secrete the male sex hormone testosterone.

thalamus A structure in the forebrain that serves as a relay station for sensory information and plays a key role in regulating states of wakefulness and sleep.

theory A formulation that accounts for relationships among observed events or experimental findings in ways that make them more understandable and predictable.

thermal biofeedback A form of BFT that involves feedback about changes in temperature and blood flow in selected parts of the body; used in the treatment of migraine headaches.

thinking The process of mentally representing and manipulating information.

thought disorder A breakdown in the logical structure of thought and speech, revealed in the form of a loosening of associations.

three-stage model A model of memory that posits three distinct stages of memory: sensory memory, short-term memory, and long-term memory.

thyroid gland An endocrine gland in the neck that secretes the hormone thyroxin, which is involved in regulating metabolic functions and physical growth.

tip-of-the-tongue (TOT) phenomenon An experience in which people are sure they know something but can't seem to bring it to mind.

token economy program A form of behavior modification in which tokens earned for performing desired behaviors can be exchanged for positive reinforcers.

tolerance A form of physical habituation to a drug in which increased amounts are needed to achieve the same effect.

top-down processing A mode of perceptual processing by which the brain identifies patterns as meaningful wholes rather than as piecemeal constructions.

traits Relatively enduring personal characteristics.

transcendental meditation (TM) A form of meditation in which practitioners focus their attention by repeating a particular mantra.

transference relationship In therapy, the tendency of clients to reenact earlier conflicted relationships in the relationship they develop with their therapists.

transsexualism A mismatch in which one's gender identity is inconsistent with one's chromosomal and anatomic sex.

transvestism A type of paraphilia involving cross-dressing for purposes of sexual arousal.

triangular model of love Sternberg's concept of love as a triangle with three components: intimacy, passion, and decision/commitment.

triarchic theory of intelligence Sternberg's theory of intelligence that posits three aspects of intelligence: analytic, creative, and practical.

trichromatic theory A theory of color vision that posits that the ability to see different colors depends on the relative activity of three types of color receptors in the eye (red, green, and blue-violet).

trichromats People with normal color vision who can discern all the colors of the visual spectrum.

tricyclics A class of antidepressant drugs that increase the availability of neurotransmitters in the brain by interfering with the reuptake of these chemicals by transmitting neurons.

twin studies Studies that examine the degree to which concordance rates between twin pairs for particular disorders or characteristics vary in relation to whether the twins are identical or fraternal.

two-factor model The theory that emotions involve two factors: a state of general arousal and a cognitive interpretation (or labeling) of the causes of the arousal.

Type A behavior pattern (TABP) A behavior pattern characterized by impatience, time urgency, competitiveness, and hostility.

ultrasound imaging A technique for using high-pitched sound waves to form an image of the fetus in the womb.

unconditional positive regard Valuing another person as having intrinsic worth, regardless of the person's behavior at the particular time.

unconditioned response (UR) An unlearned response to a stimulus.

unconditioned stimulus (US) A stimulus that elicits an unlearned response.

unconscious To Freud, the part of the mind that lies outside the range of ordinary awareness and that holds troubling or unacceptable urges, impulses, memories, and ideas.

uterus The female reproductive organ in which the fertilized ovum becomes implanted and develops to term.

vaccination A method of acquiring immunity by means of injecting a weakened or partial form of an infectious agent that can induce production of antibodies but does not produce a full-blown infection.

validity The degree to which a test measures what it purports to measure.

variables Factors or measures that vary within an experiment or among individuals.

vasocongestion Swelling of tissues with blood, a process that accounts for penile erection and vaginal lubrication during sexual arousal.

ventromedial hypothalamus A part of the hypothalamus involved in regulating feelings of satiety.

vestibular sacs Organs in the inner ear that connect the semicircular canals.

vestibular sense The sense that keeps us informed about balance and the position of our body in space.

virtual reality therapy A form of exposure therapy in which virtual reality is used to simulate real-world environments.

visual illusions Misperceptions of visual stimuli.

visuospatial sketchpad The storage buffer for visual-spatial material held in short-term memory.

volley principle The principle that relates the experience of pitch to the alternating firing of groups of neurons along the basilar membrane.

volunteer bias The type of bias that arises when people who volunteer to participate in a survey or research study possess characteristics that make them unrepresentative of the population from which they were drawn.

voyeurism A type of paraphilia that involves watching unsuspecting others as they disrobe or engage in sexual activities.

waxy flexibility A feature of catatonic schizophrenia in which people rigidly maintain the body position or posture in which they were placed by others.

Weber's law The principle that the amount of change in a stimulus needed to detect a difference is given by a constant ratio or fraction, called a constant, of the original stimulus.

Wernicke's area An area of the left temporal lobe involved in processing written and spoken language.

withdrawal syndrome A cluster of symptoms associated with abrupt withdrawal from a drug.

zone of proximal development (ZPD) In Vygotsky's theory, the range between children's present level of knowledge and their potential knowledge state if they receive proper guidance and instruction.

zygote A fertilized egg cell.

References

Aamodt, S., & Wang, S. (2008). *Welcome to your brain: Why you lose your car keys but never forget how to drive and other puzzles of everyday life.* New York: Bloomsbury.

Abbott, A. (2010). Schizophrenia: The drug deadlock. *Nature, 468,* 158–159. doi:10.1038/468158a

Abraham, W. C. (2006). Memory maintenance: The changing nature of neural mechanisms. *Current Directions in Psychological Science, 15,* 5–8.

Abramowitz, J. S., & Braddock, A., E. (2008). *Psychological treatment of health anxiety and hypochondriasis: A biopsychosocial approach.* Toronto, CA: Hogrefe & Huber.

Abramowitz, J. S., Olatunji, B. O., & Deacon, B. J. (2008). Health anxiety, hypochondriasis, and the anxiety disorders. *Behavior Therapy, 38,* 86–94. doi:10.1016/j.beth.2006.05.001

Abramson, L. T., Seligman, M. E. P., & Teasdale, J. D. (1978). Learned helplessness in humans: Critique and reformulation. *Journal of Abnormal Psychology, 87,* 49–74.

Ackerman, J. M., Shapiro, J. R., Neuberg, S. L., Kenrick, D. T., Becker, D. V., Griskevicius, V., et al. (2006). They all look the same to me (unless they're angry): From out-group homogeneity to out-group heterogeneity. *Psychological Science, 17,* 836–840. doi: 10.1111/j.1467-9280

Adam, M. B., McGuire, J. K., Walsh, M., Basta, J., & LeCroy, C. (2005). Acculturation as a predictor of the onset of sexual intercourse among Hispanic and white teens. *Archives of Pediatrics and Adolescent Medicine, 159,* 261–265.

Adelson, R. (2004, April). Stimulating the vagus nerve: Memories are made of this. *Monitor on Psychology,* 35(4), 36–38.

Adelson, R. (2005, February). Hues and views. *Monitor on Psychology, 36*(2), 26–29.

Ader, R., & Cohen, N. (1982). Behaviorally conditioned immunosuppression and murine systemic lupus erythematosus. *Science, 215,* 1534–1536.

Adolescent cigarette smoking at lowest recorded levels. (2010). *NIDA Notes, 23*(1), 14.

Adorno, T. W., Frenkel-Brunswik, E., Levinson, D., & Sanford, R. N. (1950). *The authoritarian personality.* New York: Harper.

Afraz, A., Pashkam, M. V., & Cavanagh, P. (2010). Spatial heterogeneity in the perception of face and form attributes. *Current Biology, 20,* 2112–2116. doi: 10.1016/j.cub.2010.11.017

Agency for Healthcare Research and Quality. (2006). New report finds no effective medications for anorexia nervosa, but behavioral therapy may have a limited benefit. *DHHS Press Release.* Retrieved from http://www.ahrq.gov/news/press/pr2006/eatdispr.htm

Aguiara, A., & Baillargeon, R. (2002). Developments in young infants' reasoning about occluded objects. *Cognitive Psychology, 45,* 267–336.

Ainsworth, M. D. S. (1979). Infant-mother attachment. *American Psychologist, 34,* 932–937. doi: 10.1016/S0010-0285(02)00005-1

Ainsworth, M. D. S., Blehar, M. C., Waters, E., & Wall, S. (1978). *Patterns of attachment: A psychological study of the Strange Situation.* Hillsdale, NJ: Erlbaum.

Akinbami, L. (2010, April). *Asthma prevalence, health care use and mortality: United States, 2003–05.* Centers for Disease Control and Prevention. Retrieved from http://www.cdc.gov/nchs/data/hestat/asthma03-05/asthma03-05.htm.

Alexander, G. C., Gallagher, S. A., Mascola, A., Moloney, R. M., & Stafford, R. S. (2011). Increasing off-label use of antipsychotic medications in the United States, 1995–2008. *Pharmacoepidemiology and Drug Safety, 20,* 177–184. doi: 10.1002/pds.2082

Alford, L. (2010). What men should know about the impact of physical activity on their health. *International Journal of Clinical Practice, 64,* 173. doi:10.1111/j.1742-1241.2010.02478.x

Allen, M., & Burrell, N. (1996). Comparing the impact of homosexual and heterosexual parents on children: Meta-analysis of existing research. *Journal of Homosexuality, 32,* 19–35.

Allport, G. W. (1954). *The nature of prejudice.* Reading, MA: Addison-Wesley.

Allport, G. W. (1961). *Pattern and growth in personality.* New York: Holt, Rinehart & Winston.

Alterman, A. I., Cacciola, J. S., Mulvaney, F. D., Rutherford, M. J., & Langenbucher, J. (2002). Alcohol dependence and abuse in three groups at varying familial alcoholism risk. *Journal of Consulting and Clinical Psychology, 70,* 336–343.

Alzheimer's Disease: Are plaques and tangles a symptom, not the cause? (2011, January 11). *ScienceDaily.* Retrieved from http://www.sciencedaily.com/releases/2010/12/101214181932.htm.

Amato, P. R. (2006). Marital discord, divorce, and children's well-being: Results from a 20-year longitudinal study of two generations. In A. Clarke-Stewart & J. Dunn (Eds.), *Families count: Effects on child and adolescent development. The Jacobs Foundation series on adolescence* (pp. 179–202). Cambridge, UK: Cambridge University Press.

American Academy of Pediatrics, Committee on Psychosocial Aspects of Child and Family Health. (1998). Guidance for effective discipline. *Pediatrics, 101,* 723.

American College Health Association. (2005). National College Health Assessment (ACHA-NCHA), Spring 2003 Reference Group Report. *Journal of American College Health, 53,* 199–210.

American Heart Association (2009). Heart disease and stroke statistics, 2009 update. *Circulation, 119,* e21-e181. doi: 10.1161/CIRCULATIONAHA.108.191261

American Psychiatric Association. (2000). *DSM-IV-TR: Diagnostic and statistical manual of mental disorders* (4th ed., Text Revision). Washington, DC: Author.

American Psychological Association (2010). *Stress in America findings.* Retrieved from http://www.apa.org/news/press/releases/stress/national-report.pdf

American Psychological Association (APA) (2007, October 25). *Stress, a major health problem in the U.S., warns APA.* Retrieved from http://www.apa.org/releases/stressproblem.html.

American Psychological Association (APA). (2002). Ethical principles of psychologists and code of conduct. *American Psychologist, 57,* 1060–1073.

American Psychological Association. (2003, July). *Employment settings for PhD: 2001.* Washington, DC: APA Research Office.

American Psychological Association. (2004, April). *Current major fields of APA membership by membership status, 2002.* Washington, DC: APA Research Office.

American Psychological Association. (2006, March 4). *Americans engage in unhealthy behaviors to manage stress.* Retrieved from http://apahelpcenter.mediaroom.com/index.php?spress_releases&item23.

Amichai-Hamburger, Y. & Vinitzky, G. (2010). Social network use and personality. *Computers in Human Behavior, 26,* 1289–1295.

Amstadter, A. B., Broman-Fulks, J., Zinzowa, H., Ruggiero, K. J., & Cercone, J. (2009). Internet-based interventions for traumatic stress-related mental health problems: A review and suggestion for future research. *Clinical Psychology Review, 29,* 410–420. doi: 10.1016/j.cpr.2009.04.001

Anderson, A. L., Harris, T. B., Tylavsky, F. A., Perry, S. E., Houston, D. K., Hue, T. F., et al. (2011). Dietary patterns and survival of older adults. *Journal of the American Dietetic Association, 111,* 84–91. doi:10.1016/j.jada.2010.10.012

Anderson, C. A., & Bushman, B. J. (2003). Human aggression. *Annual Review of Psychology, 53,* 27–51. doi: 10.1146/annurev.psych.53.100901.135231

Anderson, C. A., Shibuya, A., Ihori, N., Swing, E. L., Bushman, B. J., Sakamoto, A., et al. (2010). Violent video game effects on aggression, empathy, and prosocial behavior in Eastern and Western countries: A meta-analytic review. *Psychological Bulletin, 136,* 151–173.

Anderson, E. M., & Lambert, M. J. (2001). A survival analysis of clincially significant change in outpatient psychotherapy. *Professional Psychology: Research and Practice, 57,* 875–888.

Anderson, E. R., & Mayes, L. C. (2010). Race/ethnicity and internalizing disorders in youth: A review. *Clinical Psychology Review, 30,* 338–348. doi:10.1016/j.cpr.2009.12.008

Anderson, J. W., Liu, C., & Kryscio, R. J. (2008). Blood pressure response to transcendental meditation: A meta-analysis. *American Journal of Hypertension* (online edition). Retrieved from http://www.nature.com/ajh/journal/v21/n3/abs/ajh200765a.html

Anderson, S. E., Dallal, G. E., & Must, A. (2003). Relative weight and race influence average age at menarche: Results from two nationally representative surveys of US girls studied 25 years apart. *Pediatrics, 111,* 844–850.

Andrews, J. A., Hampson, S. E., Barckley, M., Gerrard, M., & Gibbons, F. X. (2008). The effect of early cognitions on cigarette and alcohol use during adolescence. *Psychology of Addictive Behaviors, 22,* 96–106. doi: 2008-01797-010

Angier, N. (1998, September 1). Nothing becomes a man more than a woman's face. *The New York Times,* p. F3.

Angier, N. (2003, July 8). Opposites attract? Not in real life. *The New York Times,* pp. F1, F6.

Angier, N. (2009, October 27). A molecule of motivation, dopamine excels at its tasks. *The New York Times,* pp. D1, D3.

Anton, R. F. (2008). Naltrexone for the management of alcohol dependence. *New England Journal of Medicine, 359,* 715–721.

APA Presidential Task Force on Evidence-Based Practice. (2006). Evidence-based practice in psychology. *American Psychologist, 61,* 271–285.

Archer, J. (2006). Testosterone and human aggression: An evaluation of the challenge hypothesis. *Neuroscience & Biobehavioral Reviews, 30,* 319–345.

Arias, E. (2010). *United States Life Tables.* Centers for Disease Control and Prevention, National Center for Health Statistics, National Vital Statistics System, *National Vital Statistics Reports, 58,* No. 21.

Arnett, J. J. (2000). Emerging adulthood: A theory of development from the late teens through the twenties. *American Psychologist, 55,* 469–480.

Arnett, J. J. (2004). *Adolescence and emerging adulthood: A cultural approach* (2nd ed.). Upper Saddle River, NJ: Pearson/Prentice Hall.

Arnett, J. J. (2010). Oh, grow up! Generational grumbling and the new life stage of emerging adulthood—commentary on Trzesniewski & Donnellan (2010). *Perspectives on Psychological Science, 5,* 89–92. doi:10.1177/1745691609357016

Arnett, J. J. (2010). Oh, grow up! *Perspectives on Psychological Science, 5,* 89–92. doi: 10.1177/1745691609357016

Arnold, Carrie. (2011). Why sleep is good for you. *Scientific American, 304*(1), 26.

Aronson, E., Wilson, T. D., & Akert, R. M. (2004). *Social psychology: Media and research update* (5th ed.). Upper Saddle River, NJ: Prentice Hall.

Asch, S. E. (1956). Studies of independence and conformity: I. A minority of one against a unanimous majority. *Psychological Monographs, 70,* 70.

Ashburn-Nardo, L., Voils, C. I., &. Monteith, M. J. (2001). Implicit associations as the seeds of intergroup bias: How easily do they take root? *Journal of Personality and Social Psychology, 81,* 789–799.

Ashby, F. G., & Maddox, W. T. (2005). Human category learning. *Annual Review of Psychology, 56,* 149–178.

Aspy, C.B., Vesely, S.K., Oman, R.F., Rodine, S., Marshall, L., & McLeroy, K. (2008). Parental communication and youth sexual behavior. *Journal of Adolescence, 30,* 449–466. doi:10.1016/j.adolescence.2006.04.007

Atkinson, R. C., & Shiffrin, R. M. (1971). The control of short-term memory. *Scientific American, 225,* 82–90.

Averhart, C. J., & Bigler, R. S. (1997). Shades of meaning: Skin tone, racial attitudes, and constructive memory in African American children. *Journal of Experimental Child Psychology, 67,* 363–388.

Ayers, J. W., Hofstetter, C. R., Usita, P., Irvin, V. L., Kang, S., Hovell, M. F. (2009). Sorting out the competing effects of acculturation, immigrant stress, and social support on depression: A report on Korean Women in California. *The Journal of Nervous and Mental Disease, 197,* 742–747. doi: 10.1097/NMD.0b013e3181b96e9e

Azañón, E., Longo, M. R., Soto-Faraco, S., & Haggard, P. (2010). The posterior parietal cortex remaps touch into external space. *Current Biology, 20,* 1304–1309. doi: 10.1016/j.cub.2010.05.063

Azar, B. (1996, April). Musical studies provide clues to brain functions. *APA Monitor, 27*(4), 1, 4.

Azar, B. (2006, January). Wild findings on animal sleep. *Monitor on Psychology, 37*(1), 54–55.

Bäckström T., Andreen, L.,Birzniece, V., Björn, I., Johansson, I-M., Nordenstam-Haghjo, M., et al. (2003). The role of hormones and hormonal treatments in premenstrual syndrome. *CNS Drugs, 17,* 325–342.

Baddeley, A. D. (2000). The episodic buffer: A new component of working memory? *Trends in Cognitive Sciences, 4,* 417–423.

Baddeley, A. D. (2001). Levels of working memory. In M. Naveh-Benjamin, M. Moscovitch, & H. L. Roediger (Eds.), *Perspectives on human memory and cognitive aging: Essays in honor of Fergus Craik.* Hove, England: Psychology Press.

Bahrami, B., Lavie, N., & Rees, G. (2007). Attentional load modulates responses of human primary visual cortex to invisible stimuli. *Current Biology, 17,* 509–513.

Baicy, K., London, E. D., Monterosso, J., Wong, M.-L., Delibasi, T., Sharma, A., et al. (2007). Leptin replacement alters brain response to food cues in genetically leptin-deficient adults. *Proceedings of the National Academy of Sciences.* Retrieved from http://www.pnas.org/cgi/content/abstract/0706481104v1.

Bailar, J. C., III. (2001). The powerful placebo and the wizard of Oz. *New England Journal of Medicine, 344,* 1630–1632.

Bailey, J. M. (2003). *The man who would be queen: The science of gender-bending and stranssexualism.* Washington, D.C.: Joseph Henry Press.

Bailey, J. M., Dunne, M. P., & Martin, N. G. (2000). Genetic and environmental influences on sexual orientation and its correlates in an Australian twin sample. *Journal of Personality and Social Psychology, 78,* 524–536.

Bailey, J. M., & Zucker, K. J. (1995). Childhood sex-typed behavior and sexual orientation: A conceptual analysis and quantitative review. *Developmental Psychology, 31,* 43–55.

Baillargeon, R. H., Zoccolillo, M., Keenan, K., Côté, S., Pérusse, D., Wu, H.-Z., et al. (2007). Gender differences in physical aggression: A prospective population-based survey of children before and after 2 years of age. *Developmental Psychology, 43,* 13–26.

Baird, J. D., Wagner, M., & Fuld, K. (1990). A simple but powerful theory of the moon illusion. *Journal of Experimental Psychology: Human Perception and Performance, 16,* 675–677.

Bajos, N., Wellings, K., Laborde, C., & Moreau, C. (2010). Sexuality and obesity, a gender perspective: Results from French national random probability survey of sexual behaviours. *British Medical Journal, 340,* c2573. doi: 10.1136/bmj.c2573

Bakalar, N. (2006a, April 18). Research ties lack of sleep to risk for hypertension. *The New York Times,* p. F7.

Bakalar, N. (2006b, June 13). Men are better than women at ferreting out that angry face in a crowd. *The New York Times,* p. F5.

Bancroft, J., Carnes, L. Janssen, E., Goodrich, D., & Long, J. S. (2005). Erectile and ejaculatory problems in gay and heterosexual men. *Archives of Sexual Behavior, 34,* 285–297.

Bandler, R., Jr. (2006). Predatory aggression: Midbrain-pontine junction rather than hypothalamus as the critical structure? *Aggressive Behavior, 1,* 261–266.

Bandura, A. (1997). *Self-efficacy: The exercise of control.* New York: Freeman.

Bandura, A. (1986). *Social foundations of thought and action: A social-cognitive theory.* Englewood Cliffs, NJ: Prentice-Hall.

Bandura, A. (2006). Toward a psychology of human agency. *Perspectives on Psychological Science, 1,* 164–180.

Bandura, A. (2008a). Observational learning. In W. Donsbach, (Ed.) *International encyclopedia of communication* (Vol. 7, pp. 3359–3361). Oxford, UK: Blackwell.

Bandura, A. (2008b). An agentic perspective on positive psychology. In S. J. Lopez (Ed.), *Positive psychology: Exploring the best in people* (Vol. 1, pp. 167–196). Westport, CT: Greenwood Publishing Company.

Bandura, A. (2009). Vicarious learning. In D. Matsumoto (Ed.), *Cambridge dictionary of psychology.* Cambridge: Cambridge University Press.

Bandura, A. (2010). Agency. In D. Carr (Ed.), *Encyclopedia of life course and human development.* New York: Macmillan.

Bandura, A., Blanchard, E. B., & Ritter, B. (1969). The relative efficacy of desensitization and modeling approaches for inducing behavioral, affective, and cognitive changes. *Journal of Personality and Social Psychology, 13,* 173–199.

Bandura, A., Ross, S. A., & Ross, D. (1963). Imitation of film-mediated aggressive models. *Journal of Abnormal Psychology, 66,* 3–11.

Barabási, A.-L. (2007). Network medicine—from obesity to the "diseasome." *New England Journal of Medicine, 357,* 404–407.

Barak, A. (2005). Sexual harassment on the internet. *Social Science Computer Review, 23,* 77–92.

Baranzini, S. E., Mudge, J., van Velkinburgh, J C., Khankhanian, P., Khrebtukova, I., Miller, N. A., et al (2010). Genome, epigenome and RNA sequences of monozygotic twins discordant for multiple sclerosis. *Nature, 464,* 1351. doi:10.1038/nature08990

Barber, T. X. (1999). A comprehensive three-dimensional theory of hypnosis. In I. Kirsch et al. (Eds.), *Clinical hypnosis and self-regulation: Cognitive-behavioral perspectives* (pp. 21–48). Washington, DC: American Psychological Association.

Bargh, J. A., & Chartrand, T. L. (1999). The unbearable automaticity of being. *American Psychologist, 54,* 462–279.

Bargh, J. A., & Morsella, E. (2008). The unconscious mind. *Perspectives on Psychological Science, 3,* 73–79. doi: 10.1111/j.1745-6916.2008.00064.x

Bargh, J. A., & Williams, E. L. (2006). The automaticity of social life current. *Directions in Psychological Science, 15,* 1–48.

Bar-Haim, Y., Ziv, T., Lamy, D., & Hodes, R. M. (2006). Nature and nurture in own-race face processing. *Psychological Science, 17,* 159–163.

Barnack, J. L., Reddy, D. M., & Swain, C. (2010). Predictors of parents' willingness to vaccinate for human papillomavirus and physicians' intentions to recommend the vaccine. *Women's Health Issues, 20,* 28–34. doi:10.1016/j.whi.2009.08.007

Barnett, J. H., & Smoller, J. W. (2009). The genetics of bipolar disorder. *Neuroscience, 24, 164,* 331–343.

Baron, R. A., Branscombe, N. R., & Byrne, D. (2009). *Social psychology* (12th ed). Boston: Allyn and Bacon.

Baron, R. S., Vandello, J. A., & Brunsman, B. (1996). The forgotten variable in conformity research: Impact of task importance on social influence. *Journal of Personality and Social Psychology, 71,* 915–927.

Barrett, M. B. (1990). *Invisible lives: The truth about millions of women-loving women.* New York: Harper & Row.

Barsky, A. J., & Ahern, D. K. (2004). Cognitive behavior therapy for hypochondriasis: A randomized controlled trial. *Journal of the American Medical Association, 291,* 1464–1470.

Bartho, P., Hirase, H., Monconduit, L., Zugaro, M., Harris, K. D., & Buzsaki, G. (2004). Characterization of neocortical principal cells and interneurons by network interactions and extracellular features. *Journal of Neurophysiology, 92,* 600–608.

Bartholow, B. D., & Heinz, A. (2006). Alcohol and aggression without consumption: Alcohol cues, aggressive thoughts, and hostile perception bias. *Psychological Science, 17,* 30–37.

Bartoshuk, L. (2007, January). *Do you taste what I taste?Using genetic variation in taste to teach about taste, diet and health.* Paper presented at the National Institute for the Teaching of Psychology, St. Petersburg, FL.

Basaria, S., Coviello, A. D.,Travison, T. G., Storer, T. W., Wildon, R., Farwell, A., et al. (2010). Adverse events associated with testosterone administration *New England Journal of Medicine, 363,* 109–122.

Bassett, A. S., Scherer, S. W., & Brzustowicz, L. M. (2010). Copy number variations in schizophrenia: Critical review and new perspectives on concepts of genetics and disease. *American Journal of Psychiatry, 167,* 899–914. doi: 10.1176/appi.ajp.2009

Bateman, A., & Fonagy, P. (2009). Randomized controlled trial of outpatient mentalization-based treatment versus structured clinical management for borderline personality disorder. *American Journal of Psychiatry.* Retrieved from http://dx.doi.org/10.1176/appi.ajp.2009.09040539.

Batson, C. D. (1998). Altruism and prosocial behavior. In D. T. Gilbert, S. T. Fiske, & G. Lindzey (Eds.), *The handbook of social psychology* (4th ed., Vol. 2, pp. 282–316). Boston: McGraw-Hill.

Batson, C. D., Ahmad, N., Lishner, D. A., & Tsang, J. (2002). Empathy and altruism. In C. R. Snyder & S. J. Lopez (Eds.), *Handbook of positive psychology* (pp. 485–498). New York: Oxford University Press.

Batson, C., D, & Powell, A. A. (2003). Altruism and prosocial behavior. In T. Millon & M. J. Lerner (Eds.), *Handbook of psychology: Personality and social psychology* (Vol. 5, pp. 463–484). New York: Wiley.

Bauer, P. J., Burch, M. M., Scholin, S. E., & Güler, O. E. (2007). Using cue words to investigate the distribution of autobiographical memories in childhood. *Psychological Science, 18*, 910–916.

Bauer, P. J. (2007). *Remembering the times of our lives: Memory in infancy and beyond.* Mahwah, NJ: Erlbaum.

Baumeister, R. F., Campbell, J. D., Krueger, J. I., & Vohs, K. D. (2003). Does high self-esteem cause better performance, interpersonal success, happiness, or healthier lifestyle? *Psychological Science in the Public Interest, 4*, 1–44.

Baumrind, D. (1971). Current patterns of parental authority. *Developmental Psychology, 4*(1), Part 2, 1–103.

Baumrind, D. (1991). Parenting styles and adolescent development. In J. Brooks-Gunn, R. Lerner & A. C. Petersen (Eds.), *Encyclopedia of adolescence, II.* New York: Garland.

Baumrind, D., Larzelere, R. E., & Cowan, P. A. (2002). Ordinary physical punishment: Is it harmful? Comment on Gershoff (2002). *Psychological Bulletin, 128*, 580–589.

Baydar, N., Kağitçibaşi, C., Küntay, A. C., & Gökşen, F. (2008). Effects of an educational television program on preschoolers: Variability in benefits. *Journal of Applied Developmental Psychology, 29*, 349–360.

Beck, A. T. (2006). How an anomalous finding led to a new system of psychotherapy. *Nature Medicine, 12*, 1139–1141.

Beck, A. T., & Alford, B. A. (2009). *Depression: Causes and treatment* (2nd ed.). Baltimore, MD: University of Pennsylvania Press.

Beck, A. T., & Young, J. E. (1985). Depression. In D. H. Barlow (Ed.), *Clinical handbook of psychological disorders* (pp. 206–244). New York: Guilford Press.

Beck, A. T., Freeman, A., Davis, D. D., & Associates. (2003). *Cognitive therapy of personality disorders* (2nd ed.). New York: Guilford.

Beck, A. T., Rush, A. J., Shaw, B. F., & Emery, G. (1979). *Cognitive therapy of depression.* New York: Guilford Press.

Beck, H. P., Levinson, S, & Irons, G. (2009). Finding Little Albert: A journey to John B. Watson's infant laboratory. *American Psychologist, 64, 605–614.* doi: 10.1037/a0071234

Beck, J. G., Coffey, S. F., Foy, D. W., Keane, T. M., & Blanchard, E. B. (2009). Group cognitive behavior therapy for chronic posttraumatic stress disorder: An initial randomized pilot study. *Behavior Therapy, 40*, 82–92. doi:10.1016/j.beth.2008.01.003

Beck, M. (1992, December 7). The new middle age. *Newsweek*, pp. 50–56.

Beesdo, K., Lau, J. Y.F., Guyer, A. E., McClure-Tone, E. B., Monk, C. S., Nelson, E. E., et al. (2009). Common and distinct amygdala-function perturbations in depressed vs anxious adolescents. *Archives of General Psychiatry, 66*, 275–285.

Begley, S. (2001, April 23). Are we getting smarter? *Newsweek*, pp. 50–51.

Begley, S. (2011, January 10/17). Can you build a better brain? *Newsweek*, pp. 40–45.

Bell, C. C., & McBride, D. F. (2010). Affect regulation and prevention of risky behaviors. *Journal of the American Medical Association, 304*, 565–566. doi:10.1001/jama.2010.1058

Bellis, M. (2001, April 14). *Your about.com guide to inventors.* Retrieved from http://inventors.about.com/science/inventors/library/bl/bl12_ 2a_u.htm.

Belluck, P. (2000, October 18). New advice for parents: Saying "That's great!" may not be. *The New York Times*, p. A18.

Belluck, P. (2010, December 15). With Alzheimer's patients growing in number, Congress endorses a national plan. *The New York Times*, p. A2

Bem, D. J. (1996). Exotic becomes erotic: A developmental theory of sexual orientation. *Psychological Review, 103*, 320–335.

Bem, S. L. (1993). *The lenses of gender.* New Haven: Yale University Press.

Benjamin, L. T. (1988). *A history of psychology: Original source and contemporary research.* New York: McGraw-Hill.

Benjamin, L. T. (1997). The origin of psychological species: History of the beginnings of American Psychological Association Divisions. *American Psychologist, 51*, 725–732.

Benjamin, L. T. (2000). The psychology laboratory at the turn of the 20th century. *American Psychologist, 55*, 318–321.

Benjamin, L. T. Jr., & Simpson, J. A. (2009). The power of the situation: The impact of Milgram's obedience studies on personality and social psychology. *American Psychologist, 64*, 12–19. doi: 10.1037/a0014077

Benjamin, L. T., Jr. (2009, January). The birth of American intelligence testing. *Monitor on Psychology, 40*(1), 20–21.

Bennett, J. (2009). Gene therapy for color blindness. *New England Journal of Medicine, 361*, 2483–2484.

Bennett, S., Farrington, D. P., & Huesmann, L. R. (2005). Explaining gender differences in crime and violence: The importance of social cognitive skills. *Aggression and Violent Behavior, 10*, 263–288.

Benowitz, N. L. Nicotine addiction. (2010). *New England Journal of Medicine, 362*, 2295–2303.

Benson, E. (2003, February). Intelligence across cultures. *Monitor on Psychology, 34*(2), 56–58.

Benson, E. S. (2006, January). Psychology by design. *APS Observer, 19*(1), 20–25.

Ben-Ya'acov, Y., & Amir, M. (2004). Posttraumatic symptoms and suicide risk. *Personality and Individual Differences, 36*, 1257–1264.

Berdahl, J. L. & Moore, C. (2006). Workplace harassment: Double jeopardy for minority women. *Journal of Applied Psychology, 91*, 426–436.

Berdahl, J. L. (2007). The sexual harassment of uppity women. *Journal of Applied Psychology, 92*, 425–437.

Berenbaum, S. A., & Bailey, J. M. (2003). Effects on gender identity of prenatal androgens and genital appearance: Evidence from girls with congenital adrenal hyperplasia. *Journal of Clinical Endocrinology and Metabolism, 88*, 1102–1106.

Berg, D. H. (2008). Working memory and arithmetic calculation in children: The contributory roles of processing speed, short-term memory, and reading. *Journal of Experimental Child Psychology, 89*, 140–158. doi:10.1016/j.jecp.2004.07.001

Berger, K. S. (2009a). *The developing person through childhood.* (5th ed.). New York: Worth Publishers.

Berger, K. S., & Thompson, R. A. (1995). *The developing person through childhood and adolescence* (4th ed.). New York: Worth Publishers.

Berger, R. A. (2009b). *The developing person through childhood and adolescence* (8th ed.). New York: Worth Publishers.

Berk, L. E. (2009). *Child development* (8th ed.). Needham Heights, MA: Pearson Education.

Berko Gleason, J., & Ratner, N. (Eds.). (2009). *The development of language* (7th ed.). Boston: Allyn & Bacon.

Berland, G. K., Elliott, M. N., Morales, L. S., Algazy, J. I., Kravitz, R. L., Broder, M. S., et al. (2001). Information on the Internet: Accessibility, quality, and readability in English and Spanish. *Journal of the American Medical Association, 285*, 2612–2621.

Bernard, L. L. (1924). *Instinct.* New York: Holt, Rinehart & Winston.

Berners-Lee, R. (with Fischetti, M.). (1999, October 24). Weaving the Web: The original design and ultimate destiny of the World Wide Web by its inventor. In K. Hafner (Ed.), Putting the W's in www. *The New York Times Book Review*, 20.

Bernstein, D. M., & Loftus, E. F. (2009). The consequences of false memories for food preferences and choices. *Perspectives on Psychological Science, 4*, 135–139. doi: 10.1111/j.1745-6924.2009.01113.x

Bernstein, I. M., Mongeon, J. A., Badger, G. J., Solomon, L., Heil, S. H., & Higgins, S. T. (2005). Maternal smoking and its association with birth weight. *Obstetrics and Gynecology, 106*, 986–991.

Berntsen, D., & Thomsen, D. K. (2005). Personal memories for remote historical events: Accuracy and clarity of flashbulb memories related to World War II. *Journal of Experimental Psychology: General, 134*, 242–257.

Berrington de Gonzalez, B., Hartge, P., Cerhan, J. R., Flint, A. J., Hannan, L., MacInnis, R. J., et al. (2010). Body-mass index and mortality—prospective analysis of 1.46 million white adults. *New England Journal of Medicine, 363*, 2211–2219. doi: 10.1056/NEJMoa1000367

Berrocal, C., Moreno, M. A. R., Rando, M. A., Benvenuti, A., & Cassano, G. B. (2008). Borderline personality disorder and mood spectrum. *Psychiatry Research, 159*, 300–307.

Berscheid, E., & Regan, P. (2005). *The psychology of interpersonal relationships.* New York: Prentice-Hall.

Berscheid, E., & Reis, H. T. (1998). Attraction and close relationships. In D. T. Gilbert, S. T. Fiske, & G. Lindzey (Eds.), *The handbook of social psychology* (4th ed., Vol. 2, pp. 193–281). Boston: McGraw-Hill.

Bertrand, R. M., & Lachman, M. E. (2003). Personality development in adulthood and old age. In R. M. Lerner, M. A. Easterbrooks, & J. Mistry (Eds.), *Handbook of psychology: Developmental psychology* (Vol. 6, pp. 463–486). New York: John Wiley & Sons.

Bewernick, B. H., Hurlemanna, R., Matuscha, A., Kaysera, A., Gruberta, C., Hadrysiewicza, B., et al. (2010). Nucleus accumbens deep brain stimulation decreases ratings of depression and anxiety in treatment-resistant depression. *Biological Psychiatry, 67*, 110–116. doi:10.1016/j.biopsych.2009.09.013

Bishop, E. G., Cherny, S. S., Corleya, R., Plomin, R., DeFriesa, J. C., & Hewitt, J. K. (2003). Developmental genetic analysis of general cognitive ability from 1 to 12 years in a sample of adoptees, biological siblings, and twins. *Intelligence, 31*, 31–49.

Bjerklie, D. (2005, January 17). Can sunny thoughts halt cancer? *Time Magazine*, p. A14.

Bjorklund, D. F. (1995). *Children's thinking* (2nd ed.). Pacific Grove, CA: Brooks/ Cole.

Blackburn, R., Renwick, S. J. D., Donnelly, J. P., & Logana, C. (2004). Big five or big two? Superordinate factors in the NEO Five Factor Inventory and the Antisocial Personality Questionnaire. *Personality and Individual Differences, 37*, 957–970.

Blair, C., Gamson, D., Thorne, S., & Baker, D. (2005). Rising mean IQ: Cognitive demand of mathematics education for young children, population exposure to formal schooling, and the neurobiology of the prefrontal cortex. *Intelligence, 33*, 93–106.

Blair, I. V., Ma, J. E., & Lenton, A. P. (2001). Imagining stereotypes away: The moderation of implicit stereotypes through mental imagery. *Journal of Personality and Social Psychology, 81*, 828–841.

Blair, S. N., & Haskell, W. L. (2006). Objectively measured physical activity and mortality in older adults. *Journal of the American Medical Association, 296*, 216–218.

Blakeslee, S. (2005, November 22). This is your brain under hypnosis. *The New York Times*, pp. F1, F4.

Blanco, C., Heimberg, R. G., Schneier, F. R., Fresco, D. M., Chen, H., Turk, C. L., . . . Liebowitz, M. R. (2010). A placebo-controlled trial of phenelzine, cognitive behavioral group therapy, and their combination for social anxiety disorder. *Archives of General Psychiatry, 67,* 286–295.

Blascovich, J., Spencer, S. J., Quinn, D., & Steele, C. (2002). African Americans and high blood pressure: The role of stereotype threat. *Psychological Science, 12,* 225–229.

Blass, T. (2009). From New Haven to Santa Clara: A historical perspective on the Milgram obedience experiments. *American Psychologist, 64,* 37–45.

Bletzer, K. V., & Koss, M. P. (2006). After-rape among three populations in the Southwest: a time of mourning, a time for recovery. *Violence Against Women, 12,* 5–29.

Blier, P., & Blondeau, C. (2011). Neurobiological bases and clinical aspects of the use of aripiprazole in treatment-resistant major depressive disorder. Aripiprazole in the treatment of anxiety, major depressive disorder, and bipolar depression/disorder. *Journal of Affective Disorders, 128,* S3–S10. doi:10.1016/S0165-0327(11)70003-9 |

Blomeyer, D., Treutlein, J., Esser, G., Schmidt, M. H., Schumann, G., & Laucht, M. (2008). Interaction between *CRHR1* gene and stressful life events predicts adolescent heavy alcohol use. *Biological Psychiatry, 63,* 146.

Blomsted, P., Sjöberg, R. L., Hansson, M., Bodlund, O., & Hariz, M. I. (2011). Deep brain stimulation in the treatment of depression. *Acta Psychiatrica Scandinavica,* 123, 4–11. doi 10.1111/j.1600-0447.2010.01625.x

Blühler, S. & Mantzoros, C. S. (1009). Lepton in humans: Lessons from translational research. *American Journal of Clinical Nutrition, 89,* 991s–997s.

Blum, R. W., Beuhring, T., Shew, M. L., Bearinger, L. H., Sieving, R. E., & Resnick, M. D. (2000). The effects of race/ethnicity, income, and family structure on adolescent risk behaviors. *American Journal of Public Health, 90,* 1879–1884.

Boag, S. (2006). Freudian repression, the common view, and pathological science. *Review of General Psychology, 10,* 74–86.

Bockting, C. L. H., Schene, A. H., Spinhoven, P., Koeter, M. W. J., Wouters, L. F., Huyser, J., et al. (2005). Preventing relapse/recurrence in recurrent depression with cognitive therapy: A randomized controlled trial. *Journal of Consulting and Clinical Psychology, 73,* 647–657.

Boecker, H., Sprenger, T., Spilker, M.E., Henriksen, G., Koppenhoefer, M., Wagner, K. J., et al. (2008). The runner's high: opioidergic mechanisms in the human brain. *Cerebral Cortex, 18,* 2523–2531.

Bohrn, I., Carbon, C.-C., & Hutzler, F. (2010). Mona Lisa's smile—perception or deception? *Psychological Science, 21,* 378–380. doi: 10.1177/0956797610362192

Boles, S. M., & Miottoa, K. (2003). Substance abuse and violence: A review of the literature. *Aggression and Violent Behavior, 8,* 155–174.

Bolhuis, J. J., & Wynne, C. D. L. (2009). Can evolution explain how minds work? *Nature, 458,* 832–833.

Bonanno, G. A., Brewin, C. R., Kaniasty, K., & La Greca, A. M. (2010). Weighing the costs of disaster: Consequences, risks, and resilience in individuals, families, and communities. *Psychological Science in the Public Interest, 11,* 1–49. doi:10.1177/1529100610387086

Bongaarts, J., Pelletier, F., & Gerland, P. (2010a). How many more AIDS deaths? *The Lancet, 375,* 103–104. doi:10.1016/S0140-6736(09)61756-6

Bongaarts, J., Pelletier, F., & Gerland, P. (2010b). Global trends in AIDS mortality. In R. G. Rogers, & E. M. Crimmins (Eds.), *International handbook of adult mortality.* New York: Springer.

Bookheimer, S., and Burggren, A. (2009). APOE-4 genotype and neurophysiological vulnerability to alzheimer's and cognitive aging. *Annual Review of Clinical Psychology, 5,* 343–362.

Boom, J., Wouters, H., & Keller, M. A. (2007). A cross-cultural validation of stage development: A Rasch re-analysis of longitudinal socio-moral reasoning. *Cognitive Development, 22,* 213–229.

Bopp, K. L. & Verhaeghen, P. (2010). Working memory and aging: Separating the effects of content and context. *Psychology and Aging, 24,* 968–980. doi: 10.1037/a0017731.

Borgland, S. L., Taha, S. A., Sarti, F., Fields, H. L., & Boncil, A. (2006). Orexin A in the VTA is critical for the induction of synaptic plasticity and behavioral sensitization to cocaine. *Neuron, 49,* 589–601.

Borgs, L., Beukelaers, P., Vandenbosch, R., Belachew, S., Nguyen, L., & Malgrange, B. (2009). Cell "circadian" cycle: new role for mammalian core clock genes. *Cell Cycle, 8,* 832–837.

Borjesson, M., & Dahlof, B. (2005). Physical activity has a key role in hypertension therapy. *Lakartidningen, 102,* 123–124, 126, 128–129.

Boroditsky, L. (2011, February). How language shapes thought: the languages we speak affect our perceptions of the world. *Scientific American.* Retrieved from http://www.scientificamerican.com/sciammag/

Borzekowski, D. L., G., & Robinson, T. N. (2005). The remote, the mouse, and the No. 2 pencil. The household media environment and academic achievement among third-grade students. *Archives of Pediatrics & Adolescent Medicine, 159,* 607–613.

Boskind-White, M., & White, W. C. (1983). *Bulimarexia: The binge-purge cycle.* New York: W. W. Norton.

Bouchard, T. J., Jr. (2004). Genetic influence on human psychological traits. *Current Directions in Psychological Science, 13,* 148–151.

Boutron, I., Kaptchuk, T. J., Friedlander, E., Kelley, J. M., Sanchez, M. N., Kokkotou, E., . . . Lembo, A. J. (2010). Placebos without deception: a randomized controlled trial in irritable bowel syndrome. *PLoS ONE, 5*(12):, e15591. doi:10.1371/journal.pone.0015591

Bower, G. H. (1992). How might emotions affect learning? In S. A. Christianson (Ed.), *Handbook of emotions and memory* (pp. 3–31). Hillsdale, NJ: Erlbaum.

Bowlby, J. (1980). *Attachment and loss* (3rd ed.). New York: Basic Books.

Bowling, N. A., Beehr, T. A., Wagner, S. H., & Libkuman, T. M. (2005). Adaptation-level theory, opponent process theory, and dispositions: An integrated approach to the stability of job satisfaction. *Journal of Applied Psychology, 90,* 1044–1053.

Boyce, C. J., Brown, G. D. A., & Moore, S. C. (2010). Money and happiness: Rank of income, not income, affects life satisfaction. *Psychological Science, 21,* 471–475. doi: 10.1177/0956797610362671

Boyer, T. W., & Byrnes, J. P. (2008). Adolescent risk-taking: Integrating personal, cognitive, and social aspects of judgment. *Journal of Applied Developmental Psychology, 30,* 23–33. doi:10.1016/j.appdev.2008.10.009

Boynton, R. S. (2004, January 11). In the Jung archives. *The New York Times Book Review,* p. 8.

Bradbard, M. R., & Endsley, R. C. (1983). The effects of sex-typed labeling on preschool children's information-seeking and retention. *Sex Roles, 9,* 247–261.

Bradshaw, C., Kahn, A. S., & Saville, B. K. (2010). To hook up or date: Which gender benefits? *Sex Roles, 62,* 661–669. 10.1007/s11199-010-9765-7

Bradshaw, J. (2008, July/August). Consulting authority expanding for RxP psychologist. *The National Psychologist,* p. 7.

Bradshaw, J. (2010, May/June). Oregon governor vetoes RxP. *The National Psychologist,* p. 6.

Brainerd, C. J., Reyna, V. F., & Ceci, S. J. (2008). Developmental reversals in false memory: A review of data and theory. *Psychological Bulletin, 134,* 343–382. doi: 10.1037/0033-2909.134.3.343

Brainteaser quizzes. (2001). *National Institute of Environment Health Sciences, National Institutes of Health.* Retrieved from http://www. niehs.nih.gov/kids/questionstx.htm.

Branan, N. (2008, May). The brain region responsible for that word on the tip of your tongue: Wait, don't tell me . . . *Scientific American.* Retrieved from http://www.sciam.com/article.cfm?id=wait-dont-tell-me

Brawn, T. P., Nusbaum, H. C., & Margoliash, D. (2010). Sleep-dependent consolidation of auditory discrimination learning in adult starlings. *Journal of Neuroscience, 30,* 609–613. doi:10.1523/JNEUROSCI.4237-09.2010

Brebner, J. (2003). Gender and emotions. *Personality and Individual Differences, 34,* 387–394.

Brehm, S. S. (2008). Looking ahead: The future of psychology and APA. *American Psychologist, 63,* 337–344.

Breitenbecher, K. H. (2000). Sexual assault on college campuses: Is an ounce of prevention enough? *Applied and Preventive Psychology, 9,* 23–52.

Bretherton, I. (1992). The origins of attachment theory: John Bowlby and Mary Ainsworth. *Developmental Psychology, 28,* 759–775.

Brewer, N., & Wells, G. L. (2011). Eyewitness identification. *Current Directions in Psychological Science, 20,* 24–27. doi:10.1177/0963721410389169

Brewer, W. F., & Treyens, J. C. (1981). Role of schemata in memory for places. *Cognitive Psychology, 13,* 207–230.

Brien, S. E., Ronksley P. E., Turner, B. J., Mukamal, K. J., & Ghali, W. A. (2011). Effect of alcohol consumption on biological markers associated with risk of coronary heart disease: systematic review and meta-analysis of interventional studies. *British Medical Journal, 342,* d636. doi: 10.1136/bmj.d636

Brinkhaus, B., Witt, C. M., Jena, S., Linde, K., Streng, A., Wagenpfeil, S. et al. (2006). Acupuncture in patients with chronic low back pain: A randomized controlled trial. *Archives of Internal Medicine, 166,* 450–457.

Brody, G. H., Beach, S. R. H., Philibert, R. A., Chen, Y.-F., Lei, M.-K., McBride, M. V., & Brown, A. C. (2009). Parenting moderates a genetic vulnerability factor in longitudinal increases in youths' substance use. *Journal of Consulting and Clinical Psychology, 77,* 1–11. doi: 10.1037/a0012996

Brody, G. H., Chen, Y.-F., Kogan, S. M., Murry, V. M., & Brown, A. C. (2010). Long-term effects of the strong African American families program on youths' alcohol use. *Journal of Consulting and Clinical Psychology, 78,* 281–285. doi: 10.1037/a0018552

Brody, J. E. (1992, September 30). Myriad masks hide an epidemic of depression. *The New York Times,* p. C12.

Brody, J. E. (2006, April 18). A slight change in habits could lull you to sleep. *The New York Times,* p. F7.

Bromberger, J. T., Matthews, K. A., Schott, L. L., Brockwell, S., Avis, N. E., & Kravitz, H. M. (2007). Depressive symptoms during the menopausal transition: The Study of Women's Health Across the Nation (SWAN). *Journal of Affective Disorders, 103,* 267–272.

Bronstein, P. (2006). The family environment: Where gender role socialization begins. In J. Worrell, & C. D. Goodheart (Eds.), *Handbook of girls' and women's psychology health: gender and well-being across the lifespan* (pp. 262–271). New York: Oxford University Press.

Brown, J. D., L'Engle, K. L., Pardun, C. J., Guo, G., Kenneavy, K., & Jackson, C. (2006). Sexy media matter: Exposure to sexual content in music, movies, television, and magazines predicts Black and White adolescents' sexual behavior. *Pediatrics, 117*, 1018–1027.

Brown, M. J. (2006). Hypertension and ethnic group. *British Medical Journal, 332*, 833–836.

Brown, P. L., & Jenkins, H. M. (2009). On the law of effect. In D. Shanks (Ed.), *Psychology of learning*. Thousand Oaks, CA: Sage.

Brown, S. L., Nesse, R. M., Vinokur, A. D., & Smith, D. M. (2003). Providing social support may be more beneficial than receiving it: Results from a prospective study of mortality. *Psychological Science, 14*, 320–327.

Brownstein, J. (2010, October 20). Teen pregnancy rates dip, but vary widely by state. Retrieved from http://www.msnbc.msn.com/id/39761335/ns/health-kids_and_parenting/.

Bruce, M. L., Ten Have, T. R., Reynolds, C. F., III, Katz, I. I., Schulberg, H. C., Mulsant, B. et al. (2004). Reducing suicidal ideation and depressive symptoms in depressed older primary care patients: a randomized controlled trial. *Journal of the American Medical Association, 291*, 1081–1091.

Brummett, B. H., Babyak, M. A., Williams, R. B., Barefoot, J. C., Costa, P. T., & Siegler, I. C. (2006). NEO personality domains and gender predict levels and trends in body mass index over 14 years during midlife. *Journal of Research in Personality, 40*, 222–236.

Bruner, J. S., & Minturn, A. L. (1955). Perceptual identification and perceptual organization. *Journal of General Psychology, 53*, 21–28.

Bryant, A., & Check, E. (2000, Fall/Winter). How parents raise boys and girls: A sense of self. *Newsweek Special Issue*, pp. 64–65.

Bryant, R. A., & Mallard, D. (2002). Hypnotically induced emotional numbing: A real simulating analysis. *Journal of Abnormal Psychology, 111*, 203–207.

Bryner, J. (2008). *Clueless guys can't read women, study confirms*. Retrieved March 23, 2008 from http://www.msnbc.msn.com/id/23726891/

Bucheryt, R., Thomasius, R., Wilke, F., Petersen, K., Nebeling, B., Obrocki, J., et al. (2004). A voxel-based pet investigation of the long-term effects of "ecstasy" consumption on brain serotonin transporters. *American Journal of Psychiatry, 161*, 1181–1189.

Buddie, A. M., & Testa, M. (2005). Rates and predictors of sexual aggression among students and nonstudents. *Journal of Interpersonal Violence, 20*, 713–724.

Budney, A. J., Hughes, J. R., Moore, B. A., & Vandrey, R. (2004). Review of the validity and significance of cannabis withdrawal syndrome. *American Journal of Psychiatry, 161*, 1967–1977.

Bureau of Labor Statistics, U.S. Department of Labor (2010b, September 23). *National longitudinal surveys*. Retrieved from http://www.bls.gov/nls/nlsfaqs.htm#anch41.

Bureau of Labor Statistics, U.S. Department of Labor (2010c). *Career exploration*. Retrieved from http://www.acinet.org/explore/View.aspx?pageID=31.

Bureau of Labor Statistics, U.S. Department of Labor. (2010a, December 8). *Work experience of the population–2009*. Retrieved from http://www.bls.gov/news.release/work.nr0.htm.

Burgdorf, J., & Panksepp, J. (2006). The neurobiology of positive emotions. *Neuroscience and Biobehavioral Reviews, 30*, 173–187.

Burger, J. M. (2009). Replicating Milgram: Would people still obey today? *American Psychologist, 64*, 1–11.

Burgess, A. W., & Morgenbesser, L. I. (2005). Sexual violence and seniors. *Brief Treatment and Crisis Intervention, 5*, 193–202.

Burns, D. D. (1980). *Feeling good: The new mood therapy*. New York: Morris.

Buscemi, N., Vandermeer, B., Hooton, N., Pandya, R., Tjosvold, L., Vroha, S. et al. (2006). Efficacy and safety of exogenous melatonin for secondary sleep disorders and sleep disorders accompanying sleep restriction: Meta-analysis. *British Medical Journal, 332*, 385–393.

Bushman, B., Wang, M., & Anderson, C. (2005). Is the curve relating temperature to aggression linear or curvilinear? Assaults and temperature in Minneapolis reexamined. *Journal of Personality and Social Psychology, 89*, 62–66. doi:10.1037/0022-3514.89.1.62.

Buss, D. M. (1994). *The evolution of desire*. New York: Basic Books.

Buss, D. M. (2008). *Evolutionary psychology* (3rd ed). Boston: Allyn & Bacon.

Buss, D. M., & Kenrick, D. T. (1998). Evolutionary social psychology. In D. T. Gilbert, S. T. Fiske, & G. Lindzey (Eds.), *The handbook of social psychology* (4th ed., Vol. 2, pp. 982–1026). Boston: McGraw-Hill.

Buston, P. M., & Emlen, S. T. (2003). Cognitive processes underlying human mate choice: The relationship between self-perception and mate preference in Western society. *Proceedings of the National Academy of Sciences, 100*, 8805–8810.

Buysse, D. J., Germain, A., Moul, D. E., Franzen, P. L., Brar, L. K., Fletcher, M. E., Monk, T. H. (2011). Efficacy of brief behavioral treatment for chronic insomnia in older adults. *Archives of Internal Medicine*. Retrieved from http://dx.doi.org/10.1001/archinternmed.2010.535

Byers, A. L., Yaffe, K., Covinsky, K. E., Friedman, M. B., & Bruce, M. L. (2010). High occurrence of mood and anxiety disorders among older adults: The National Comorbidity Survey Replication. *Archives of General Psychiatry, 67*, 489–496.

Byers, E. S., & Grenier, G. (2003). Premature or rapid ejaculation: Heterosexual couples' perceptions of men's ejaculatory behavior. *Archives of Sexual Behavior, 32*(3), 261–270.

Byrne, A., & Carr, D. (2005). Caught in the cultural lag: The stigma of singlehood. *Psychological Inquiry, 16*, 84–91.

Byrne, M., Clafferty, B. A., Cosway, R., Grant, E., Hodges, A, Whalley, H. C., et al. (2003). Neuropsychology, genetic liability, and psychotic symptoms in those at high risk of schizophrenia. *Journal of Abnormal Psychology, 112*, 38–48.

Caetano, R. (1987). Acculturation and drinking patterns among U.S. Hispanics. *British Journal of Addiction, 82*, 789–799.

Calderon de Anda, F., Pollarolo, G., Santos Da Silva, J., Camoletto, P. G., Feiguin, F., & Dotti, C. G. (2005). Centrosome localization determines neuronal polarity. *Nature, 436*, 704–708.

Cale, E. M., & Lilienfeld, S. O. (2002). Sex differences in psychopathy and antisocial personality disorder. A review and integration. *Clinical Psychology Review, 22*, 1179–1207.

Camara, W. J., Nathan, J. S., & Puente, A. E. (2000). Psychological test usage: Implications in professional psychology. *Professional Psychology: Research and Practice, 31*, 141–154.

Campbell, R., & Wasco, S. M. (2005). Understanding rape and sexual assault: 20 years of progress and future directions. *Journal of Interpersonal Violence, 20*, 127–131.

Canfield, R. L., Henderson, C. R., Cory-Slechta, A. A., Cox, C., Jusko, T. A., & Lanphea, B. P. (2003). Intellectual impairment in children with blood lead concentrations below 10 μg per deciliter. *New England Journal of Medicine, 348*, 1517–1526.

Canli, T., Desmond, J. E., Zhao, Z., & Gabrieli, J. D. E. (2002). Sex differences in the neural basis of emotional memories. *Proceedings of the National Academy of Sciences, 99*(16), 10789–94.

Cannon, W. (1927). The James-Lange theory of emotions: A critical examination as an alternative theory. *American Journal of Psychology, 39*, 106–112.

Canter, D. V. (2011). Resolving the offender "profiling equations" and the emergence of an investigative psychology. *Current Directions in Psychological Science, 20*, 5–10. doi: 10.1177/0963721410396825

Carey, B. (2007, June 22). Research finds firstborns gain the higher I.Q. *The New York Times*, p. A1, A16.

Carey, B. (2009, November 26). Surgery for mental ills offers both hope and risk. *The New York Times Online*. Retrieved from http://www.nytimes.com.

Carey, B. (2009, November 26). Surgery for mental ills offers both hope and risk. *The New York Times Online*. Retrieved from http://www.nytimes.com/2009/11/27/health/research/27brain.html?_r=1&scp=1&sq=psychosurgery&st=cse

Carey, B. (2011). Wariness on surgery of the mind. *The New York Times, Science Times*, pp. D5, D6.

Carlbring, P., Maurin, L, Törngren, C., Linna, E., Eriksson, T., Sparthan, E., et al. (2011)., Individually tailored, Internet-based treatment for anxiety disorders: A randomized controlled trial. *Behaviour Research and Therapy, 49*, 18–24. doi:10.1016/j.brat.2010.10.002

Carmichael, M. (2004, March 8). How a brain heals. *Newsweek*, p. 49.

Carmody, T. P., Duncan, C., Simon, J., Solkowitz, S., Huggins, J., Lee, S., et al. (2008). Hypnosis for smoking cessation: A randomized trial. *Nicotine and Tobacco Research, 10*, 811–818.

Carnahan, I. (2005, June 6). Do-it-yourself retirement. *Forbes*, p. 93.

Carney, D. R., Cuddy, A. J. C., & Yap, A. J. (2010). Power posing: Brief nonverbal displays affect neuroendocrine levels and risk tolerance. *Psychological Science, 21*, 1363–1368. doi: 10.1177/0956797610383437

Carpenter, S. (2000, October). Biology and social environments jointly influence gender development. *Monitor on Psychology, 31*(9), 35.

Carroll, L. (2004, February 10). Parkinson's research focuses on links to genes and toxins. *New York Times*, p. F5.

Carroll, S. B. (2009, October 19). For fish in coral reefs, it's useful to be smart. *The New York Times*. Retrieved from www.nytimes.com

Carstensen, L. L., & Mikels, J. A. (2005). At the intersection of emotion and cognition aging and the positivity effect. *Current Directions in Psychological Science, 14*, 117–121.

Carver, C. S., Johnson, S. L., & Joormann, J. (2008). Serotonergic function, two-mode models of self-regulation, and vulnerability to depression: What depression has in common with impulsive aggression. *Psychological Bulletin, 134*, 912–943. doi: 10.1111/j.1467-8721.2009.01635

Carver, C. S., Johnson, S. L., & Joormann, J. (2009). Two-mode models of self-regulation as a tool for conceptualizing effects of the serotonin system in normal behavior and diverse disorders. *Current Directions in Psychological Science, 18*, 195–199.

Carver, C. S., Scheier, M. F., & Segerstrom, S. C. (2010). Optimism. *Clinical Psychology Review, 30*, 879–889. doi:10.1016/j.cpr.2010.01.006

Caspi A., Hariri A. R., Holmes A., Uher R., Moffitt T. E. (2010). Genetic sensitivity to the environment: The case of the serotonin transporter gene and its implications for studying complex diseases and traits. *American Journal of Psychiatry, 167,* 509–527. doi: 10.1176/appi.ajp.2010.09101452

Caspi, A., Roberts, B. W., & Shiner, R. L. (2005). Personality development: Stability and change. *Annual Review of Psychology, 56,* 453–484.

Cassidy, J. (2003). Continuity and change in the measurement of infant attachment: Comment on Fraley and Spieker (2003). *Developmental Psychology, 39,* 409–412.

Cassidy, J., & Shaver, P. R. (Eds.) (2008). *Handbook of attachment* (2nd ed.). New York: Guilford.

Cattell, R. B. (1950). *Personality: A systematic, theoretical, and factual study.* New York: McGraw-Hill.

Cattell, R. B. (1965). *The scientific analysis of personality.* Baltimore: Penguin.

Cattell, R. B., Eber, H. W., & Tatsuoka, M. M. (1970). *Handbook for the Sixteen Personality Factor Questionnaire (16PF).* Champaign, IL: Institute for Personality and Ability Testing.

Cellar, D. F., Nelson, Z. C., & Yorke, C. M. (2000). The five-factor model and driving behavior: Personality and involvement in vehicular accidents. *Psychological Reports, 86,* 454–456.

Centers for Disease Control and Prevention (CDC). (2007). *Suicide: Facts at a glance.* National Center for Injury Prevention and Control. Retrieved from www.cdc.gov/injury/wisqars/index.html

Centers for Disease Control and Prevention, National Center for Health Statistics (2008). *Sleep duration as a correlate of smoking, alcohol use, leisure-time physical inactivity, and obesity among adults: United States, 2004–2006.* Retrieved August 14, 2008, from http://www.cdc.gov/nchs/products/pubs/pubd/hestats/sleep04-06/sleep04-06.htm.

Centers for Disease Control and Prevention (CDC). (2009a). Cigarette smoking among adults and trends in smoking cessation: United States, 2008. *Morbidity and Mortality Weekly Report, 58*(44), 1227–1232.

Centers for Disease Control and Prevention (CDC). (2009b). *FastStats: How healthy are we?* Retrieved from http://www.cdc.gov/nchs/fastats/healthy.htm.

Centers for Disease Control and Prevention (CDC) (2009c). *Overweight and obesity: Health consequences.* Retrieved from http://www.cdc.gov/obesity/causes/health.html

Centers for Disease Control and Prevention (CDC). (2009d). Suicide rates among persons ages 10 years and older, by race/ethnicity and sex, United States, 2002–2006. Retrieved from http://www.cdc.gov/violenceprevention/suicide/statistics/rates02.html.

Centers for Disease Control and Prevention (CDC). (2009e) *Genital HPV Infection—Fact Sheet.* Retrieved from http://www.cdc.gov/std/HPV/STDFact-HPV.htm#common

Centers for Disease Control and Prevention. (CDC) (2010a). *Fast stats: illegal drug use.* Retrieved from http://www.cdc.gov/nchs/fastats.

Centers for Disease Control and Prevention. (2010b, June). *Obesity and overweight.* Retrieved from http://www.cdc.gov/nchs/fastats/overwt.htm.

Centers for Disease Control and Prevention (CDC). (2010c, December 17). Sexually transmitted diseases treatment guidelines, 2010. *Morbidity and Mortality Weekly Report, Vol. 5,* No. RR-12.

Centers for Disease Control and Prevention (CDC). (2010d). Sexually transmitted diseases treatment guidelines, 2010. *Morbidity and Mortality Weekly Report, Vol. 5,* No. RR-12

Centers for Disease Control and Prevention (CDC) (2010e). FDA licensure of bivalent human papillomavirus vaccine (HPV2, Cervarix) for use in females and updated HPV vaccination recommendations from the Advisory Committee on Immunization Practices (ACIP). *Morbidity and Mortality Weekly Report, 59,* 626.

Centers for Disease Control and Prevention (CDC). (2011). Vital signs: HIV testing and diagnosis among adults—United States, 2001–2009. *Morbidity and Mortality Weekly Report. Journal of the American Medical Association, 305,* 244–246.

Centers for Disease Control and Prevention (CDC). (2011, March 11.) *National Vital Statistics Report. Deaths: Preliminary Data 2009,* Vol. 59, No. 4. Retrieved from www.cdc.gov.

Cepeda, N. J., Pashler, H., Vul, E., Wixted, J. T., & Rohrer, D. (2006). Distributed practice in verbal recall tasks: A review and quantitative synthesis. *Psychological Bulletin, 132,* 354–380.

Chaiyavej, S., & Morash, M. (2009). Reasons for policewomen's assertive and passive reactions to sexual harassment. *Police Quarterly, 12,* 63–85.

Chaiyavej, S., and Morash, M. (2009). Reasons for policewomen's assertive and passive reactions to sexual harassment. *Police Quarterly,* 12 (2009), 63–85.

Chamorro-Premuzic, T., & Ahmetoglou, G. (2008). Little more than personality: Dispositional determinants of test anxiety (the Big Five, core self-evaluations, and self-assessed intelligence). *Learning and Individual Differences, 18,* 258–263.

Champagne, F. A., & Mashoodh, R. (2009). Genes in context: Gene–environment interplay and the origins of individual differences in behavior. *Current Directions in Psychological Science, 18,* 127–131. doi: 10.1111/j.1467-8721.2009.01622.x

Chan, D. (2005). Current directions in personnel selection research. *Current Directions in Psychological Science, 14,* 220–223.

Chance, P. (2009). *Learning and behavior* (6th ed.). Belmont, CA: Cengage.

Chang, E. C., & Sanna, L. J. (2001). Optimism, pessimism, and positive and negative affectivity in middle-aged adults: A test of a cognitive-affective model of psychological adjustment. *Psychology and Aging, 16,* 524–531.

Chen, J., Odenike, O., & Rowley, J. D. (2010). Leukaemogenesis: More than mutant genes. *Nature Reviews: Cancer, 10,* 23–36.

Chen, J., Rathore, S. S., Radford, M. J., Wang, Y., & Krumholz, H. M. (2001). Racial differences in the use of cardiac catheterization after acute myocardial infarction. *New England Journal of Medicine, 344,* 1443–1449.

Chen, X., Williamson, V. S., An, S.-S., Hettema, J. M., Aggen, S. H., Neale, M. C., et al. (2008). Cannabinoid receptor 1 gene association with nicotine dependence. *Archives of General Psychiatry, 65,* 743.

Chen, Z., & Cowan, N. (2005). Chunk limits and length limits in immediate recall: A reconciliation. *Journal of Experimental Psychology: Learning, Memory, and Cognition, 31,* 1235–1249.

Cheng, W., & Ickes, W. (2009). Conscientiousness and self-motivation as mutually compensatory predictors of university-level GPA. *Personality and Individual Differences, 47,* 817–822. doi:10.1016/j.paid.2009.06.029

Chernyak, Y., & Lowe, M. R. (2010). Motivations for dieting: Drive for thinness is different from drive for objective thinness. *Journal of Abnormal Psychology, 119,* 276–281. doi: 10.1037/a0018398

Chess, S., & Thomas, A. (1996). *Temperament: Theory and practice.* New York: Brunner/Mazel.

Chetrit, J. Ballion, B,. Laquitaine, S., Belujon, P., Morin, S., et al. (2009) Involvement of basal ganglia network in motor disabilities induced by typical antipsychotics. *PLoS ONE 4,* e6208. doi:10.1371/journal.pone.0006208

Chevalier-Skolnikoff, S. (1973). Facial expression of emotion in nonhuman primates. In P. Ekman (Ed.), *Darwin and facial expression: A century of research in review* (pp. 11–82). New York: Academic Press.

Chi, R. P., & Snyder, A. W. (2011). Facilitate insight by non-invasive brain stimulation. *PLoS, 6,* e16655. doi:10.1371/journal.pone.0016655

Chida, Y., & Steptoe, A. (2009). The association of anger and hostility with future coronary heart disease: A meta-analytic review of prospective evidence. *Journal of the American College of Cardiology, 53,* 936–946. doi:10.1016/j.jacc.2008.11.044

Choi, I., Dalal, R., Kim-Prieto, C., & Park, H. (2003). Culture and judgment of causal relevance *Journal of Personality and Social Psychology, 84,* 46–59.

Chomsky, N. (1965). Aspects of the theory of syntax. Cambridge, MA: MIT Press.

Choy, Y., Fyer, A. J., & Lipsitz, J. D. (2007). Treatment of specific phobia in adults. *Clinical Psychology Review, 27,* 266–286.

Christakis, D. A. (2009). The effects of infant media usage: what do we know and what should we learn? *Acta Pædiatrica, 98,* 8–16. doi: 10.1111/j.1651-2227.2008.01027.x

Christakis, N. A., & Fowler, J. H. (2007). The spread of obesity in a large social network over 32 years. *New England Journal of Medicine, 357,* 370–379.

Christensen, A., Atkins, D. C., & Baucom, B., & Yi, J. (2010). Marital status and satisfaction five years following a randomized clinical trial comparing traditional versus integrative behavioral couple therapy. *Journal of Consulting and Clinical Psychology, 78,* 225–235. doi: 10.1037/a0018132

Christensen, A., Atkins, D. C., & Baucom, B., & Yi, J. (2010). Marital status and satisfaction five years following a randomized clinical trial comparing traditional versus integrative behavioral couple therapy. *Journal of Consulting and Clinical Psychology, 78,* 225–235. doi: 10.1037/a0018132

Chua, H. F., Boland, J. E., & Nisbett, R. E. (2005). Cultural variation in eye movements during scene perception. *Proceedings of the National Academy of Sciences, 102,* 12629–12633.

Cialdini, R. B. (2007). *Influence:The psychology of persuasion.* New York: HarperCollins.

Cialdini, R. B., & Goldstein, N. J. (2004). Social influence: Compliance and conformity. *Annual Review of Psychology, 55,* 591–621.

Cialdini, R. B., & Trost, M. R. (1998). Social influence: Social norms, conformity, and compliance. In D. T. Gilbert, S. T. Fiske, & G. Lindzey (Eds.), *The handbook of social psychology* (4th ed., Vol. 2, pp. 151–192). Boston: McGraw-Hill.

Cialdini, R. B., Trost, M. R., & Newsom, J. T. (1995). Preference for consistency: The development of a valid measure and the discovery of surprising behavioral implications. *Journal of Personality and Social Psychology, 69,* 318–328.

Cipriani, A., La Ferla, T., Furukawa, T. A., Signoretti, A., Nakagawa, A., Churchill, R., et al. (2009). Sertraline versus other antidepressive agents for depression. *Cochrane Databse of Systematic Reviews, 2.* doi: 10.1002/14651858.CD006117.pub2

Clark, D. M. (1986). A cognitive approach to panic. *Behaviour Research and Therapy, 24,* 461–470.

Clark, K. B., & Clark, M. P. (1939). The development of self and the emergence of racial identification in Negro preschool children. *Journal of Social Psychology, 10,* 591–599.

Clark, L. A. (2007). Assessment and diagnosis of personality disorder: Perennial issues and an emerging reconceptualization. *Annual Review of Psychology, 58,* 227–257.

Clark, L. A. (2009). Stability and change in personality disorder. *Current Directions in Psychological Science, 18,* 27–31. doi: 10.1111/j.1467-8721.2009.01600.x

Clarke, D., Gabriels, T., & Barnes, J. (1996). Astrological signs as determinants of extroversion and emotionality: an empirical study. *Journal of Psychology, 130,* 131–140.

Clay, R. A. (2003, April). An empty nest can promote freedom, improved relationships. *Monitor on Psychology, 34*(4), 40–41.

Cloud, J. (2011, March 7). Beyond drugs: How alternative treatments can ease pain. *Time,* pp. 80–88.

Coelho, C. M., & Purkis, H. (2009). The origins of specific phobias: Influential theories and current perspectives. *Review of General Psychology, 13,* 335–348. doi:10.1037/a0017759

Coelho, C. M., Waters, A. M., Hine, T. J., & Wallis, G. (2009). The use of virtual reality in acrophobia research and treatment. *Journal of Anxiety Disorders, 23,* 563–574. doi:10.1016/j.janxdis.2009.01.014

Cohan, C. L., & Kleinbaum, S. (2002). Toward a greater understanding of the cohabitation effect: Premarital cohabitation and marital communication. *Journal of Marriage and the Family, 64,* 180–192.

Cohen, G. L., Garcia, J., Apfel, N., & Master, A. (2006). Reducing the racial achievement gap: A social-psychological intervention. *Science, 313,* 1307–1310.

Cohen, L. B., & Cashon, C. H. (2003). Infant perception and cognition. In R. M. Lerner, M.A. Easterbrooks, & J. Mistry (Eds.), *Handbook of psychology: Vol. 6. Developmental psychology* (pp. 65–90). New York: John Wiley & Sons.

Cohen, S., Doyle, W. J., Alper, C. M., Janicki-Deverts, D., & Turner, R. B. (2009). Sleep habits and susceptibility to the common cold. *Archives of Internal Medicine, 169,* 62–66.

Cohen, S., Doyle, W. J., Skoner, D. P., Rabin, B. S., Gwaltney, J. M., Jr., et al. (1997). Social ties and susceptibility to the common cold. *Journal of the American Medical Association, 277,* 1940–1944.

Cohen, S., Doyle, W. J., Turner, R., Alper, C. M., & Skoner, D. P. (2003). Sociability and susceptibility to the common cold. *Psychological Science, 14,* 389–395.

Cohen, S., Frank, E., Doyle, W. J., Skoner, D. P., Rabin, B. S., & Gwaltney, J. M., Jr. (1998). Types of stressors that increase susceptibility to the common cold in healthy adults. *Health Psychology, 17,* 214–223.

Cohen-Bendahan, C. C. C., van de Beek, C., & Berenbaum, S. A. (2005). Prenatal sex hormone effects on child and adult sex-typed behavior: Methods and findings. *Neuroscience & Biobehavioral Reviews, 29,* 353–384.

Cohn, E. G., & Rotton, J. (2005). The curve is still out there: a reply to Bushman, Wang, and Anderson's (2005) "Is the curve relating temperature to aggression linear or curvilinear?" *Journal of Personality and Social Psychology, 89,* 67–70.

Coldwell, C. M., & Bender, W. S. (2007). The effectiveness of assertive community treatment for homeless populations with severe mental illness: a meta-analysis. *American Journal of Psychiatry, 164,* 393–399.

Cole, S. W. (2009). Social regulation of human gene expression. *Current Directions in Psychological Science, 18,* 132–137. doi: 10.1111/j.1467-8721.2009.01623.x

Cole, T. B. (2006). Rape at US colleges often fueled by alcohol. *Journal of the American Medical Association, 296,* 504–505.

Collins, A. M., & Loftus, E. F. (1975). A spreading-activation theory of semantic processing. *Psychological Review, 82,* 407–428.

Collins, W. A., & Laursen, B. (2006). Parent-adolescent relationships. In P. Noller & J. A. Feeney (Eds.), *Close relationships: Functions, forms and processes* (pp. 111–125). Hove, England: Psychology Press/Taylor & Francis.

Combe, E., & Wexler, M. (2010). Observer movement and size constancy. *Psychological Science, 21,* 667–675. doi: *10.1177/0956797610367753*

Confer, J. C., Easton, J. A., Fleischman, D. S., Goetz, C. D., Lewis, D. M. G., Perilloux, C., & Buss, D. M. (2010). Evolutionary psychology: Controversies, questions, prospects, and limitations. *American Psychologist, 65,* 110–126. doi: 10.1037/a0018413

Conkle, A., & West, C. (2008, June/July). *APS Observer, 21*(6), pp. 18–23.

Conner, B. T. (2010). Genetic, personality, and environmental predictors of drug use in adolescents. *Journal of Substance Abuse Treatment, 38,* 178–190. doi:10.1016/j.jsat.2010.03.009

Connor, C. E. (2010). A new viewpoint on faces. *Science, 330,* pp. 764–765. doi: 10.1126/science.1198348

Conrad, F. G., & Brown, N. R. (1996). Estimating frequency: A multiple-strategy perspective. In D. Herrmann, C. McEvoy, C. Hertzog, P. Hertel, & M. K. Johnson (Eds.), *Basic and applied memory research: Practical applications* (Vol. 2., pp. 166–178). Mahwah, NJ: Lawrence Erlbaum Associates.

Conway, K. P., Compton, W., Stinson, F. S., & Grant, B. F. (2006). Lifetime comorbidity of DSM-IV mood and anxiety disorders and specific drug use disorders: Results from the National Epidemiologic Survey on Alcohol and Related Conditions. *Journal of Clinical Psychiatry, 67,* 247–257.

Cook, C. M., & Saucier, D. M. (2010) Mental rotation, targeting ability and Baron-Cohen's empathizing–systemizing theory of sex differences. *Personality and Individual Differences, 49,* 712–716. doi:10.1016/j.paid.2010.06.010 |

Cook, M. B., & Smallman, H. S. (2008). Human factors of the confirmation bias in intelligence analysis: Decision support from graphical evidence landscapes. *Human Factors: The Journal of the Human Factors and Ergonomics Society, 50,* 745–754. doi: 10.1518/001872008X354183

Cooksey, E. C., & Fondell, M. M. (1996). Spending time with his kids: Effects of family structure on fathers' and children's lives. *Journal of Marriage and the Family, 58,* 693–707.

Coon, K. A., Goldberg, J., Rogers, B. L., & Tucker, K. L. (2001). Relationships between use of television during meals and children's food consumption patterns. *Pediatrics, 107,* 7.

Cooper, M. L., Wood, P. K., Orcutt, H. K., & Albino, A. (2003). Personality and the predisposition to engage in risky or problem behaviors during adolescence. *Journal of Personality and Social Psychology, 84,* 390–410.

Copeland, W., Shanahan, L., Miller, S., Costello, E. J., Angold, A., & Maughan, B. (2010). Outcomes of early pubertal timing in young women: a prospective population-based study. *American Journal of Psychiatry,* 167, 1218–1225.

Corbett J., Saccone, N. L., Foroud, T., Goate, A., Edenberg, H., Nurnberger, J., et al. (2005). Sex adjusted and age adjusted genome screen for nested alcohol dependence diagnoses. *Psychiatric Genetics, 15,* 25–30.

Corliss, R. (2003, January 20). Is there a formula for joy? *Time Magazine,* pp. 44–46.

Cornelis, M. C., El-Sohemy, A., Kabagambe, E. K., & Campos, H. (2006). Coffee, CYP1A2 genotype, and risk of myocardial infarction. *Journal of the American Medical Association, 295,* 1135–1141.

Cororve, M. B., & Gleaves, D. H. (2001). Body dysmorphic disorder: A review of conceptualizations, assessment, and treatment strategies. *Clinical Psychology Review, 21,* 949–970.

Correll, C., & Shenk, E. (2009). Tardive dyskinesia and new antipsychotics. *Current Opinion in Psychiatry, 21,* 151–156. doi: 10.1097/YCO.0b013e3282f53132

Costa, P. T., & McCrae, R. R. (1992a). Four ways five factors are basic. *Personality and Individual Differences, 13,* 653–665.

Costa, P. T., & McCrae, R. R. (1992b). Normal personality assessment in clinical practice: The NEO Personality Inventory. *Psychological Assessment, 4,* 5–13.

Costa, P. T., & McCrae, R. R. (2006). Changes in personality and their origins: Comment on Roberts, Walton, and Viechtbauer (2006). *Psychological Bulletin, 132,* 26–28.

Costa, P., Jr., Terracciano, A., & McCrae, R. R. (2002). Gender differences in personality traits across cultures: Robust and surprising findings. *Journal of Personality and Social Psychology, 81,* 322–331.

Costello, F. J., & Keane, M. T. (2001). Testing two theories of conceptual combination: Alignment versus diagnosticity in the comprehension and production of combined concepts. *Journal of Experimental Psychology:Learning, Memory, and Cognition, 27,* 255–271.

Cowan, N., Chen, Z., & Rouder, J. N. (2004). Constant capacity in an immediate serial-recall task: A logical sequel to Miller (1956). *Psychological Science, 15,* 634–640.

Coyle, J. T. (2003). Use it or lose it—do effortful mental activities protect against dementia? *New England Journal of Medicine, 348,* 2489–2490.

Coyne, J. C., Thombs, B. D., Stefanek, M., & Palmer, S. C. (2009). Time to let go of the illusion that psychotherapy extends the survival of cancer patients: Reply to Kraemer, Kuchler, and Spiegel (2009). *Psychological Bulletin, 135,* 179–182.

Craik, F. I. M., & Lockhart, R. S. (1972). Levels of processing: A framework for memory research. *Journal of Verbal Learning and Verbal Behavior, 11,* 671–684.

Crain, C. (2004, October 3). Doctor Strangelove. *New York Times,* Section 2, pp. 1, 20.

Cramer, P. (2000). Defense mechanisms in psychology today: Further processes for adaptation. *American Psychologist, 55,* 637–646.

Crespo-Facorro, B., Pérez-Iglesias, R-O., Mata, I., Ramirez-Bonilla, M., Martínez-Garcia, O., Pardo-Garcia, G., et al. (2011). Effectiveness of haloperidol, risperidone and olanzapine in the treatment of first-episode non-affective psychosis: results of a randomized, flexible-dose, open-label 1-year follow-up comparison. *Journal of Psychopharmacology,* in press. doi: 10.1177/0269881110388332

Crick, N. R., Ostrov, J. M., & Werner, N. E. (2006). A longitudinal study of relational aggression, physical aggression and children's social-psychological adjustment. *Journal of Abnormal Child Psychology, 34,* 131–142.

Crockett, M. J. (2009). The neurochemistry of fairness: clarifying the link between serotonin and prosocial behavior. *Annals of the New York Academy of Sciences, 1167,* 76–86.

Cross, S. E., & Madson, L. (1997). Models of the self: Self-construals and gender. *Psychological Bulletin, 122,* 89–103.

Crow, S. J., Mitchell, J. E., Crosby, R. D., Swanson, S. A., Wonderlich, S., & Lancaster, K. (2009). The cost effectiveness of cognitive behavioral therapy for bulimia nervosa delivered via telemedicine versus face-to-face. *Behaviour Research and Therapy, 47,* 451–453. doi:10.1016/j.brat.2009.02.006

Crowe, R. A. (1990). Astrology and the scientific method. *Psychological Reports, 67,* 163–191.

Crowell, S. E., Beauchaine, T. P., McCauley, E., Smith, C. V., Vasilev, C. A., & Stevens, A. (2008). Parent-child interactions, peripheral serotonin, and self-inflicted injury in adolescents. *Journal of Consulting and Clinical Psychology, 76,* 15–21. 10.1037/0022-006X.76.1.15

Csernansky, J. G., & Cronenwett, W. J. (2008). Neural networks in schizophrenia. *American Journal of Psychiatry, 165,* 937–939. doi: 10.1176/appi.ajp.2008.08050700

Csicsvari, J., Henze, D. A., Jamieson, B., Harris, K. D., Sirota, A., Bartho, P., et al. (2003). Massively parallel recording of unit and local field potentials with silicon-based electrodes. *Journal of Neurophysiology, 90,* 1314–1323.

Cuijpers, P., Muñoz, R. F, Clarke, G.N. & Lewinsohn, P M. (2009). Psychoeducational treatment and prevention of depression: The "Coping with Depression" course thirty years later. *Clinical Psychology Review, 29*, 449–458. doi:10.1016/j.cpr.2009.04.005

Cuijpers, P., van Straten, A., Schuurmans, J., van Oppen, P., Hollon, S. D., & Andersson, G. (2010). Psychotherapy for chronic major depression and dysthymia: A meta-analysis. *Clinical Psychology Review, 30*, 51–62. doi:10.1016/j.cpr.2009.09.003

Cunningham, M. R., Roberts, A. R, Barbee, A. P., Druen, P. B., et al. (1995). "Their ideas of beauty are, on the whole, the same as ours." *Journal of Personality and Social Psychology, 68*, 261–279.

Curran, P. J., Stice, E., & Chassin, L. (1997). The relation between adolescent alcohol use and peer alcohol use: A longitudinal random coefficients model. *Journal of Consulting and Clinical Psychology, 65*, 130–140.

Curry, L. A., & Youngblade, L. M. (2006). Negative affect, risk perception, and adolescent risk behavior. *Journal of Applied Developmental Psychology, 27*, 468–485.

Cynkar, A. (2007, June). The changing gender composition of psychology. *Monitor on Psychology, 38*(6), 46–47.

Cyranoski, D. (2011). Neuroscience: Thought experiment. *Nature, 469*, 148–149. doi:10.1038/469148a

Dagher, A. & Robbins, T. W. (2009). Personality, addiction, dopamine: Insights from parkinson's disease. *Neuron, 61*, 502–510.

Dale, K. Y., Berg, R., Elden, A., Ødegård, A., & Holte A. (2009). Testing the diagnosis of dissociative identity disorder through measures of dissociation, absorption, hypnotizability and PTSD: A Norwegian pilot study. *Journal of Trauma and Dissociation, 10*, 102–112. doi: 10.1080/15299730802488478

Dalen, K., Ellertsen, B., Espelid, I., & Grønningsaeter, A. G. (2009). EMG feedback in the treatment of myofascial pain dysfunction syndrome. *Acta Odontologica Scandinavica, 44*, 279–284.

Danaei, G., Finucane, M. M., Lin, J. K., Singh, G. M., Paciorek, C. J., Cowan, M. J., Ezzati, M. (2011). National, regional, and global trends in systolic blood pressure since 1980. *The Lancet, 377*, 568–577. doi: 10.1016/S0140-6736(10)62036-3

Dantzker, M. L., & Eisenman, R. (2003). Sexual attitudes among Hispanic college students: Differences between males and females. *International Journal of Adolescence and Youth, 11*, 79–89.

Dao, T. K., & Prevatt, F. (2006). A psychometric evaluation of the Rorschach Comprehensive System's Perceptual Thinking Index. *Journal of Personality Assessment, 86*, 180–189.

Darwin, C. A. (1872). *The expression of the emotions in man and animals.* London: J. Murray.

Das, A. (2009). Sexual harassment at work in the United States. *Archives of Sexual Behavior, 38*, 909–921. doi: 10.1007/s10508-008-9354-9

Dasen, P. R. (1994). Culture and cognitive development from a Piagetian perspective. In W. J. Lonner & R. Malpass (Eds.), *Psychology and culture.* Boston: Allyn & Bacon.

Dasgupta, N., & Greenwald, A. G. (2001). On the malleability of automatic attitudes: Combating automatic prejudice with images of admired and disliked individuals. *Journal of Personality and Social Psychology, 81*, 800–814.

Dauvilliers, Y., Arnulf, I., & Mignot, E. (2007). Narcolepsy with cataplexy. *Lancet, 369*, 499–511.

Davidson, J. R. (2009). First-line pharmacotherapy approaches for generalized anxiety disorder. *Journal of Clinical Psychiatry, 70*, Suppl. 2, S25–S31.

Davidson, R. J., Pizzagalli, D., Nitschke, J. B., & Putnam, K. (2002). Depression: Perspectives from affective neuroscience. *Annual Review of Psychology, 53*, 545–574.

Davidson, R. J., Putnam, K. M., & Larson, C. L. (2000). Dysfunction in the neural circuitry of emotion regulation—A possible prelude to violence. *Science, 289*, 591–594.

Davis, J. I., Senghas, A., & Ochsner, K. N. (2009). How does facial feedback modulate emotional experience? *Journal of Research in Personality, 43*, 822–829. doi:10.1016/j.jrp.2009.06.005

Davis, J. L., & Rusbult, C. E. (2001). Attitude alignment in close relationships. *Journal of Personality and Social Psychology, 81*, 65–84.

Davis, J. M., Chen, N, & Glick, I. D. (2003). A meta-analysis of the efficacy of second-generation antipsychotics. *Archives of General Psychiatry, 60*, 553–564.

Davis, S., Papalia, M.-A., Norman, R. J., O'Neill, S., Redelman, M., Williamson, M., et al. (2008). Safety and efficacy of a testosterone metered-dose transdermal spray for treating decreased sexual satisfaction in premenopausal women: A randomized trial. *Annals of Internal Medicine, 148*, 569–577.

Davis, S. R., Davison, S. L., Donath, S., & Bell, R. J. (2005). Circulating androgen levels and self-reported sexual function in women. *Journal of the American Medical Association, 294*, 91–96.

Davis, S. R., Moreau, M., M.D., Kroll, R., Bouchard, C., Panay, N., Gass, M., et al. (2008). Testosterone for low libido in postmenopausal women not taking estrogen. *New England Journal of Medicine, 359*, 2005-2017.

Day, B. L., & Fitzpatrick, R. C. (2005). The vestibular system. *Current Biology, 15*, R583–R586.

Day-Cameron, J. M., Muse, L., Hauenstein, J., Simmons, L., & Correia, C. J. (2009). Alcohol use by undergraduate students on their 21st birthday: Predictors of actual consumption, anticipated consumption, and normative beliefs. *Psychology of Addictive Behaviors, 23*, 695–701.

de Bono, E. (1970). *Lateral thinking: Creativity step by step.* New York: Harper & Row.

De Gucht, V., & Maes, S. (2006). Explaining medically unexplained symptoms: Toward a multidimensional, theory-based approach to somatization. *Journal of Psychosomatic Research, 60*, 349–352.

De Meyer, G., Shapiro, F., Vanderstichele, H., Vanmechelen, E., Engelborghs, S., De Deyn, P. P., et al. (2010). Diagnosis-independent Alzheimer disease biomarker signature in cognitively normal elderly people. *Archives of Neurology, 67*, 949–956.

De Silva, P. (1993). Post-traumatic stress disorder: Cross-cultural aspects. *International Review of Psychiatry, 5*, 217–229.

Dean, G., Mather, A., & Kelly, I. W. (1996). Astrology. In G. Stein (Ed.), *The encyclopedia of the paranormal.* Buffalo, NY: Prometheus.

DeAngelis, T. (2003, February). Why we overestimate our competence. *Monitor on Psychology, 34*, 60–62.

DeAngelis, T. (2004, April). Are beliefs inherited? *Monitor on Psychology, 35*, pp. 50–51.

Deary, I. J., Batty, G. D., Pattie, A., & Gale, C. R. (2008). More intelligent, more dependable children live longer: A 55-year longitudinal study of a representative sample of the Scottish nation. *Psychological Science, 19*, 874–880. doi: 10.1111/j.1467-9280.2008.02171.x

Deary, I. J., Johnson, W., & Houlihan, L. M. (2009). Genetic foundations of human intelligence. *Human Genetics, 126*, 215–232. doi: 10.1007/s00439-009-0655-4

DeBruine, L. M., Jones, B.C., Smith, F., G., & Little, A. C. (2010). Are attractive men's faces masculine or feminine? The importance of controlling confounds in face stimuli. *Journal of Experimental Psychology: Human Perception and Performance, 36*, 751–758. doi:10.1037/a0016457

Decety, J., & Cacioppo, J. (2010). Frontiers in human neuroscience: The golden triangle and beyond. *Perspectives on Psychological Science, 5*, 767–771. doi:10.1177/1745691610388780

Delaney, P. F., Sahakyan, L., Kelley, C. M., &. Zimmerman, C. A. (2010). Remembering to forget: The amnesic effect of daydreaming. *Psychological Science, 21*, 1036–1042. doi: 10.1177/0956797610374739

Delgado, M. Y., Updegraff, K. A., Roosa, M. W., & Umaña-Taylor, A. J. (2010). Discrimination and Mexican-origin adolescents' adjustment: The moderating roles of adolescents', mothers', and fathers' cultural orientations and values. *Journal of Youth and Adolescence, 40*, 125–139. doi: 10.1007/s10964-009-9467-z

Delicate balance in the brain controls fear. (2010, November 10). *ScienceDaily*. Retrieved from http://www.sciencedaily.com/releases/2010/11/101110131210.htm.

Democrats smell a rat. (2000, September 13). Retrieved from http://abcnews.go.com/sections/politics/DailyNews/gopad0000912.html.

Dennis, C. (2004, January 29). Brain development: The most important sexual organ. *Nature, 427*, 390–392.

Dennison, B. A., Erb, T. A., & Jenkins, P. L. (2002). Television viewing and television in bedroom associated with overweight risk among low-income preschool children. *Pediatrics, 109*, 1028–1035.

Denollet, J., & Pedersen, S. S. (2009). Anger, depression, and anxiety in cardiac patients: the complexity of individual differences in psychological risk. *Journal of the American College of Cardiology, 53*, 947–949.

Denollet, J., & Pedersen, S. S. (2009). Anger, depression, and anxiety in cardiac patients: the complexity of individual differences in psychological risk. *Journal of the American College of Cardiology, 53*, 947–949. doi:10.1016/j.jacc.2008.12.006

Denys, D., Mantione, M., Figee, M., van den Munckhof, P., Koerselman, F., Westenberg, H., et al. (2010). Deep brain stimulation of the nucleus accumbens for treatment-refractory obsessive-compulsive disorder. *Archives of General Psychiatry, 67*, 1061–1068. doi:10.1001/archgenpsychiatry.2010.122

DePaulo, B. M., & Friedman, H. S. (1998). Nonverbal communication. In D. T. Gilbert, S. T. Fiske, & G. Lindzey (Eds.), *The handbook of social psychology* (4th ed., Vol. 2, pp. 3–40). Boston: McGraw-Hill.

Der, G., & Deary, I.J. (2009). Age and sex differences in reaction time in adulthood: Results from the United Kingdom Health and Lifestyle Survey: Correction. *Psychology and Aging, 24*, 229.

Der, G., & Deary, I. J. (2006). Age and sex differences in reaction time in adulthood: results from the United Kingdom Health and Lifestyle Survey. *Psychology and Aging, 21*, 62–73.

Dermitzakis, E. T. (2011). Genome literacy. *Science, 331*, 689–690. doi: 10.1126/science.1203237

Derringer, J., Krueger, R. F., Dick, D. M., Saccone, S., Grucza, R. A., Agrawal, A., et al. Gene Environment Association Studies (GENEVA) Consortium. (2010). Predicting sensation seeking from dopamine genes: A candidate-system approach. *Psychological Science, 9*, 1282–1290. doi: 10.1177/0956797610380699

Derrington, A. M. (2004). Visual mechanisms of motion analysis and motion perception. *Annual Review of Psychology, 55*, 181–205.

DeRubeis, R. J., Fournier, J. C., & Fawcett, J. (2010). Depression severity and effect of antidepressant medications—reply. *Journal of the American Medical Association, 303*, 1599. [Letter] doi: 10.1001/jama.2010.510

DeRubeis, R. J., Hollon, S. D., Amsterdam, J. D., Shelton, R. C., Young, P. R., Salomon, R. M. et al. (2005). Cognitive therapy vs medications in the treatment of moderate to severe depression. *Archives of General Psychiatry, 62*, 409–416.

Deveny, K. (2003, June 30). We're not in the mood. *Newsweek*, pp. 41–46.

Devilbiss, D. M., & Berridge, C. W. (2008). Cognition-enhancing doses of methylphenidate preferentially increase prefrontal cortical neuronal responsiveness. *Biological Psychiatry, 64*, 626–635. doi:10.1016/j.biopsych.2008.04.037

DeWeese, M., R., & Zador, A. (2006). Neurobiology: Efficiency measures. *Nature, 439*, 920–921.

Dewsbury, D. A. (2000). Issues in comparative psychology at the dawn of the 20th century. *American Psychologist, 55*, 750–753.

Di Castelnuovo, A., Costanzo, S., Bagnardi, V., Donati, M. B., Iacoviello, L., & de Gaetano, G. (2006). Alcohol dosing and total mortality in men and women: An updated meta-analysis of 34 prospective studies. *Archives of Internal Medicine, 166*, 2437–2445.

Diamond, A. (2009). The interplay of biology and the environment broadly defined. *Developmental Psychology, 45*, 1–8. doi: 10.1037/a0014601

Dickens, W. T., & Flynn, J. R. (2006a). Black Americans reduce the racial IQ gap: Evidence from standardization samples. *Psychological Science, 17*, 913–920.

Dickens, W. T., & Flynn, J. R. (2006b). Common ground and differences. *Psychological Science, 17*, 923–924.

Diehm, R., & Armatas, C. (2004). Surfing: An avenue for socially acceptable risk-taking, satisfying needs for sensation seeking and experience seeking. *Personality and Individual Differences, 36*, 663–677.

Diener, E. (2005, April). Income and happiness. *APS Observer, 18*, p. 35.

Diener, E., & Chan, M. Y. (2011). Happy people live longer: Subjective well-being contributes to health and longevity. Retrieved from http://papers.ssrn.com/sol3/papers.cfm?abstract_id=1701957.

Dijksterhuis, A., Bos, M. W., Nordgren, L. F., & van Baaren, R. B. (2006). On making the right choice: The deliberation-without-attention effect. *Science, 311*, 1005–1007.

Dimidjian, S., Hollon, S. D., Dobson, K. S., Schmaling, K. B., Kohlenberg, R. J., Addis, M. E., et al. (2006). Randomized trial of behavioral activation, cognitive therapy, and antidepressant medication in the acute treatment of adults with major depression. *Journal of Consulting and Clinical Psychology, 74*, 658–670.

Dingfelder, S. F. (2005, July/August). A two-front war on alcoholism. *Monitor on Psychology, 36*(7), 38–39.

Distein I., Thomas C., Behrmann M., & Heeger D. J. (2008). A mirror up to nature. *Current Biology, 18*, R13–R18.

Distel, M. A., Hottenga, J. J., Trull, T. J., & Boomsma, D. I. (2008). Chromosome 9: Linkage for borderline personality disorder features. *Psychiatric Genetics, 18*, 302–307.

Dittmann, M. (2003a, March). Anger across the gender divide. *Monitor on Psychology, 34*(3), 52–53.

Dittmann, M. (2004, July/August). Standing tall pays off, study finds. *Monitor on Psychology, 35*(7), 14.

Ditzen, B., Schmidt, S., Strauss, B., Nater, U. M., Ehlert, U., & Heinrichs, M. (2008). Adult attachment and social support interact to reduce psychological but not cortisol responses to stress. Cortisol response to stress use for mention. *Journal of Psychosomatic Research, 64*, 479–486.

Dixon, J., Durrheim, K., & Tredoux, C. (2005). Beyond the optimal contact strategy: A reality check for the contact hypothesis. *American Psychologist, 60*, 697–711.

Dixon, J., Tropp, L. R., Durrheim, K., & Tredoux, C. (2010). "Let them eat harmony": Prejudice-reduction strategies and attitudes of historically disadvantaged groups. *Current Directions in Psychological Science, 19*, 76–80. doi: 10.1177/0963721410363366

Djoussé, L., Driver, J. A., & Gaziano, J. M. (2009). MPH relation between modifiable lifestyle factors and lifetime risk of heart failure. *Journal of the American Medical Association, 302*, 394–400.

Dobbs, D. (2010). Schizophrenia appears during adolescence. But where does one begin and the other end? *Nature, 468*, 154–156. doi:10.1038/468154a

Dobson, K. S., & Dozois, D. J. A. (2001). Historical and philosophical bases of the cognitive-behavioral therapies. In K. S. Dobson (Ed.), *Handbook of cognitive-behavioral therapies* (2nd ed., pp. 3–40). New York: Guilford Press.

Dobson, K. S., Hollon, S. D., Dimidjian, S., Schmaling, K. B., Kohlenberg, R. J., Gallop, R. J.,.et al. (2008). Randomized trial of behavioral activation, cognitive therapy, and antidepressant medication in the prevention of relapse and recurrence in major depression. *Journal of Consulting and Clinical Psychology, 76*, 468–477. doi: 10.1037/0022-006X.76.3.468

Dodge, K. A., Pettit, G. S., & Bates, J. E. (1997). How the experience of early physical abuse leads children to become chronically aggressive. In D. Cicchetti & S. L. Toth (Eds.), *Developmental perspectives on trauma: Theory, research, and intervention*. Rochester, NY: Boydel.

Dohrenwend, B. P. (2006). Inventorying stressful life events as risk factors for psychopathology: Toward resolution of the problem of intracategory variability. *Psychological Bulletin, 132*, 477–495.

Dolan, D. C., Taylor, D. J., Bramoweth, A. D., & Rosenthal, L. D. (2010). Cognitive behavioral therapy of insomnia: A clinical case series study of patients with comorbid disorders and using hypnotic medications. *Behavior Research and Therapy, 48*, 321–327. doi:10.1016/j.brat.2009.12.004

Doll, R., Peto, R., Boreham, J., & Sutherland, I. (2004). Mortality in relation to smoking: 50 years' observations on male British doctors. *British Medical Journal, 328*, 1519–1529.

Domjan, M. (2005). Pavlovian conditioning: A functional perspective. *Annual Review of Psychology, 56*, 179–206.

Donald, M., Dower, J., Correa-Velez, I., & Jones, M. (2006). Risk and protective factors for medically serious suicide attempts: A comparison of hospital-based with population-based samples of young adults. *Australian and New Zealand Journal of Psychiatry, 40*, 87–96.

Donigian, J., & Malnati, R. (2005). *Systematic group therapy: A triadic model*. Belmont, CA: Cengage.

Donnellan, M. B., & Lucas, R. E. (2008). Age differences in the big five across the life span: Evidence from two national samples. *Psychology and Aging, 23*, 558–566. doi: 10.1037/a0012897

Donovan, M. R., Glue, P., Kolluri, S., & Emir, B. (2010). Comparative efficacy of antidepressants in preventing relapse in anxiety disorders—A meta-analysis. *Journal of Affective Disorders, 123*, 9–16. doi:10.1016/j.jad.2009.06.021

Dougherty, D. M., Mathias, C. W., Marsh, D. M., Moeller, F. G., & Swann, A. C. (2004). Suicidal behaviors and drug abuse: Impulsivity and its assessment. *Drug and Alcohol Dependence, 76*, S93–S105.

Dragoi, G., & Susumu Tonegawa, S. (2010). Preplay of future place cell sequences by hippocampal cellular assemblies. *Nature*, Published online December 22, 2010. doi: 10.1038/nature09633

Dragoi, G., & Tonegawa, S. (2011). Preplay of future place cell sequences by hippocampal cellular assemblies. *Nature, 469*, 397–401. doi: 10.1038/nature09633

Draguns, J. G., & Tanaka-Matsumi, J. (2003). Assessment of psychopathology across and within cultures: Issues and findings. *Behaviour Research and Therapy, 41*, 755–776.

Drews, F. A., Pasupathi, M., & Strayer, D. L. (2008). Passenger and cell phone conversations in simulated driving. *Journal of Experimental Psychology: Applied, 14*, 392–400. doi: 10.1037/a0013119

Drews, F. A., Yazdani, H., Godfrey, C. N., Cooper, J. M., & Strayer, D. L. (2009). Text messaging during simulated driving. *Human Factors: The Journal of the Human Factors and Ergonomics Society, 51*, 762–770. doi: 10.1177/0018720809353319

Driessen, E., Cuijpers, P., de Maat, S. C. M., Abbass, A. A., de Jonghe, F., & Dekker, J. J. M. (2010). The efficacy of short-term psychodynamic psychotherapy for depression: A meta-analysis. *Clinical Psychology Review, 30*, 25–36. doi:10.1016/j.cpr.2009.08.010

Drucker, R. (2010, June 23). Human papillomavirus vaccine updates. *Journal Watch Pediatrics and Adolescent Medicine*. Retrieved from http://pediatrics.jwatch.org/cgi/content/full/2010/623/2.

Duncan, D. F., Donnelly, J. W., & Nicholson, T. (1992). Belief in the paranormal and religious belief among American college students. *Psychological Reports, 70*, 15–18.

Duncker, K. (1945). On problem-solving. *Psychological Monographs, 58* (Whole No. 270).

Dunning, D., & Perretta, S. (2002). Automaticity and eyewitness accuracy: A 10- to 12-second rule for distinguishing accurate from inaccurate positive identifications. *Journal of Applied Psychology, 87*, 951–962.

Durham, P. L. (2004). CGRP-receptor antagonists—a fresh approach to migraine therapy? *New England Journal of Medicine, 350*, 1073–1075.

Duric, V., Banasr, M., Licznerski, P., Schmidt, H. D., Stockmeier, C. A., Simen, A. S., Newton, S. S., & Duman, R. S. (2010). A negative regulator of MAP kinase causes depressive behavior. *Nature Medicine, 16*, 1328–1332. doi:10.1038/nm.2219

Durrant, R. (2011). Evolutionary explanations in the social and behavioral sciences: Introduction and overview. *Aggression and Violent Behavior*, in press. doi:10.1016/j.avb.2011.02.

Dweck, C. (1997, June). Cited in B. Murray, Verbal praise may be the best motivator of all. *APA Monitor, 28*(6), 26.

Dying to eat: A graphical view of U.S. obesity. (2010, September 24). *Scientific American*. Retrieved from http://www.scientificamerican.com/article.cfm?id=dying-to-eat.

Eagly, A. H., & Karau, S. J. (2002). Role congruity theory of prejudice toward female leaders. *Psychological Review, 109*, 573–598.

Ebben, M. R., & Spielman, A. J. (2009). Non-pharmacological treatments for insomnia. *Journal of Behavioral Medicine, 32*, 244–254. doi: 10.1007/s10865-008-9198-8

Ebbinghaus, H. (1885). *Über das Gedachtnis*. Leipzig: Duncker & Humblot.

Eberlein, T. (1997). *Child magazine's guide to whining*. New York: Pocket Books.

Edenberg, H. J., Strother, W. N., McClintick, J. N., Tian, H., Stephens, M., Jerome, R. E., et al. (2005). Gene expression in the hippocampus of inbred alcohol-preferring and nonpreferring rats. *Genes, Brain and Behavior, 4*, 20–30.

Edvardsen, J., Torgersen, S., Røysamb, E., Lygren, S., Skre, I., Onstad, S., & Øien, P. A. (2009). Unipolar depressive disorders have a common genotype. *Journal of Affective Disorders, 117*, 30–41. doi:10.1016/j.jad.2008.12.004

Edwards, R., R., Campbell, C., Jamison, R. N., & Wiech, K. (2009). The neurobiological underpinnings of coping with pain. *Current Directions in Psychological Science, 18*, 237–241. doi: 10.1111/j.1467-8721.2009.01643.x

Egan, B. M. (2006). Sleep and hypertension: burning the candle at both ends really is hazardous to your health. *Hypertension, 47*, 816–817.

Egan, S., & Stelmack, R. M. (2003). A personality profile of Mount Everest climbers. *Personality and Individual Differences, 34,* 1491–1494.

Ehlers, A., Bisson, J., Clark, D., M., Creamer, M., Pilling, S., Richards, D., et al.(2010). Do all psychological treatments really work the same in posttraumatic stress disorder? *Clinical Psychology Review, 30,* 269–276. doi:10.1016/j.cpr.2009.12.001

Ehlers, C. L., & Wilhelmsen, K. C. (2005). Genomic scan for alcohol craving in mission Indians. *Psychiatric Genetics, 15,* 71–75.

Eichenbaum, H. (1997). How does the brain organize memories? *Science, 277,* 330–332.

Eisner, R. (2005, January). Study suggests cognitive deficits in MDMA-only drug abusers. *NIDA Notes, 19*(5). Retrieved from http:// www.nida.nih.gov/NIDA_notes/NNvol19N5/Study.html.

Ekman, P. (2003). *Emotions revealed: Recognizing faces and feeling to improve communication and emotional life.* New York: Times Books.

Electric thinking cap? Flash of fresh insight by electrical brain stimulation. (2011, February 3). *ScienceDaily.* Retrieved from http://www.sciencedaily.com/releases/2011/02/110202172300.htm

Elfenbein, H. A., & Ambady, N. (2002a). Is there an in-group advantage in emotion recognition? *Psychological Bulletin, 128,* 243–249.

Elfenbein, H. A., & Ambady, N. (2002b). On the universality and cultural specificity of emotion recognition: A meta-analysis. *Psychological Bulletin, 128,* 203–235.

Elkind, D. (1985). Egocentrism redux. *Developmental Review, 5,* 218–226.

Ellemers, N., Spears, R., & Doosje, B. (2002). Self and social identity. *Annual Review of Psychology, 53,* 161–186.

Ellenbogen, J. M. (2008). The sleeping brain's influence on memory. *Sleep, 31,* 163–1644.

Ellenbogen, J. M., Hulbert, J. C., Stickgold, R., Dinges, D. F., & Thompson-Schill, S. L. (2006). Interfering with theories of sleep and memory: sleep, declarative memory, and associative interference. *Current Biology, 16,* 1290–1294. doi:10.1016/j.cub.2006.05.024

Elliot, A. J., & Sheldon, K. M. (1997). Avoidance achievement motivation: A personal goals analysis. *Journal of Personality and Social Psychology, 73,* 171–185.

Elliot, A. J., Niesta Kayser, D.,Greitemeyer, T., Lichtenfeld, S., Gramzow, R. H., Maier, M. A., et al. (2010). Red, rank, and romance in women viewing men. *Journal of Experimental Psychology: General, 139,* 399–417. doi: 10.1037/a0019689

Ellis, A. (1977). The basic clinical theory of rational-emotive therapy. In A. Ellis & R. Grieger (Eds.), *Handbook of rational-emotive therapy.* New York: Springer.

Ellis, A. (1991). *Reason and emotion in psychotherapy.* New York: Carol Publishing.

Ellis, A. (2001, January). "Intellectual" and "emotional" insight revisited. *NYS Psychologist, 13,* 2–6.

Ellis, A., & Dryden, W. (1987). *The practice of rational emotional therapy.* New York: Springer Publishing Company.

Ellis, B. J., Jackson, J. J., & Boyce, W. T. (2006). The stress response systems: Universality and adaptive individual differences. *Developmental Review, 26,* 175–212.

Ellis, L., & Bonin, S. L. (2003). Genetics and occupation-related preferences. Evidence from adoptive and non-adoptive families. *Personality and Individual Differences, 35,* 929–937.

Ellis, L., Das, S., & Buker, H. (2008). Androgen-promoted physiological traits and criminality: A test of the evolutionary neuroandrogenic theory. *Personality and Individual Differences, 44,* 701–711.

Ellison-Wright, I., & Bullmore, E. (2010). Anatomy of bipolar disorder and schizophrenia: A meta-analysis. *Schizophrenia Research, 117,* 1–12. doi:10.1016/j.schres.2009.12.022

Elms, A. C. (1995). Obedience in retrospect. *Journal of Social Issues, 51,* 21–31.

Elms, A. C. (2009). Obedience lite. *American Psychologist, 64,* 32–36.

Else-Quest, N. M., Hyde, J. S., & Linn, M. C. (2010). Cross-national patterns of gender differences in mathematics: A meta-analysis. *Psychological Bulletin, 136,* 103–127. doi: 10.1037/a0018053

Ember, C. R., Ember, M., & Peregrine, P. N. (2007). *Anthropology* (12ed). Upper Saddle River, NJ: Prentice Hall.

Emotional signals are chemically encoded in tears, researchers find. (2011, January 6). *ScienceDaily.* http://www.sciencedaily.com/releases/2011/01/110106144741.htm

Engel, J., Landgren, S., Jerlhag, E., Zetterberg, H., Blennow, K., Gonzalez-Quintela, A. & Campos, J. (2008). Association of pro-ghrelin and GHS-R1A gene polymorphisms and haplotypes with heavy alcohol-use and body mass. *Alcoholism: Clinical & Experimental Research.* Retrieved from http://www.sciencedaily.com /releases/2008/09/080923164535.htm

Eny, K. M., Wolever, T. M. S., Fontaine-Bisson, B., & El-Sohemy, A. (2008). Genetic variant in the glucose transporter type 2 (GLUT 2) is associated with higher intakes of sugars in two distinct populations. *Physiological Genomics, 33,* 355–360. doi:10.1152/physiolgenomics.00148.2007

Erdelyi, M. H. (2010). The ups and downs of memory. *American Psychologist, 65, 623–633. doi: 10.1037/a0020440*

Erikson, E. H. (1963). *Childhood and society* (2nd ed.). New York: Norton.

Erikson, E. H. (1980). *Identity and the life cycle.* New York: Norton.

Erlacher, D., & Schredl, M. (2008). Cardiovascular responses to dreamed physical exercise during REM lucid dreaming. *Dreaming, 18,* 112–121. Doi: 10.1037/1053-0797.18.2.112

Espenshade, T. (1993, April 25). Cited in F. Barringer, "Polling on sexual issues has its drawbacks." *The New York Times,* p. A23.

Esposito, K., Giugliano, F., Di Palo, C., Giugliano, G., Marfella, R., D'Andrea, F., et al. (2004). Effect of lifestyle changes on erectile dysfunction in obese men: A randomized controlled trial. *Journal of the American Medical Association, 291,* 2978–2984.

Estevez, M., & Gardner, K. L. (2004). Update on the genetics of migraine. *Human Genetics, 114,* 225–235.

Etheridge, P. (2001, January 8). Kids' TV watching linked to unhealthy eating habits. Retrieved from http://www.cnn.com/2001/HEALTH/children/01/08/tv.eating/index.html.

Etkin, A., Egner, T., Peraza, D. M., Kandel, E. R., & Hirsch, J. (2006). Resolving emotional conflict: A role for the rostral anterior cingulate cortex in modulating activity in the amygdala. *Neuron, 51,* 871–882.

Etkin, A., Prater, K. E., Schatzberg, A. F., Menon, V., & Greicius, M. D. (2009). Disrupted amygdalar subregion functional connectivity and evidence of a compensatory network in generalized anxiety disorder. *Archives of General Psychiatry, 66,* 1361–1372.

Evers, C., Fischer, A. H., Mosquera, P. M. R., & Manstead, A. S. R. (2005). Anger and social appraisal: A "spicy" sex difference? *Emotion, 5,* 258–266.

Exner, J. E. (1993). *The Rorschach: A comprehensive system: Vol. 1. Basic foundations* (3rd ed.). New York: Wiley.

Exner, J. E., Jr. (2002). Early development of the Rorschach test. *Academy of Clinical Psychology Bulletin, 8,* 9–24.

Eysenck, H. J. (1982). *Personality, genetics, and behavior.* New York: Praeger.

Eysenck, H. J. (Ed.). (1981). *A model for personality.* New York: Springer.

Faedda, G. L., Becker, I., Baroni, A., Tondo, L., Aspland, E., & Koukopoulos, A. (2010). The origins of electroconvulsive therapy: Prof. Bini's first report on ECT. *Journal of Affective Disorders, 120,* 12–15. doi:10.1016/j.jad.2009.01.023

Fagan, J. F., & Holland, C. R. (2002). Equal opportunity and racial differences in IQ. *Intelligence, 30,* 361–387.

Fagan, J.F. & Holland, C.R. (2007). Racial equality in intelligence: Predictions from a theory of intelligence as processing. *Intelligence, 35,* 319–334.

Falk, E. B., Berkman, E. T., Mann, T., Harrison, B, & Lieberman, M. D. (2010). Predicting persuasion-induced behavior change from the brain. *Journal of Neuroscience, 30,* 8421–8424. doi:10.1523/JNEUROSCI.0063-10.2010

Fals-Stewart, W. (2003). The occurrence of partner physical aggression on days of alcohol consumption: A longitudinal diary study. *Journal of Consulting and Clinical Psychology, 71,* 41–52.

Fan, Y., Tang, Y., Lu, Q., Feng, S., Yu, Q., Sui, D., et al. (2009). Dynamic changes in salivary cortisol and secretory immunoglobulin A response to acute stress. *Stress and Health, 25,* 189–194. doi: 10.1002/smi.1239 10.1002/smi.1239

Farell, B. (2006). Orientation-specific computation in stereoscopic vision. *Journal of Neuroscience, 26,* 9098–9106.

Farrell, M. T., & Abrams, L. (2011). Tip-of-the-tongue states reveal age differences in the syllable frequency effect. *Journal of Experimental Psychology: Learning, Memory, and Cognition, 37,* 277–285. doi: 10.1037/a0021328

Farris, C., Treat, T. A., & Viken, R. J. (2010). Alcohol alters men's perceptual and decisional processing of women's sexual interest. *Journal of Abnormal Psychology, 119,* 427–432. doi: 10.1037/a0019343

Farris, C., Treat, T.A., Viken, R.J. & McFall, R.M. (2008). Perceptual mechanisms that characterize gender differences in decoding women's sexual intent. *Psychological Science, 19,* 348–354.

Farzadfar, F., Finucane, M., Danaei, G., Pelizzari, P. M., Cowan, M. J., Paciorek, C. J., Ezzati, M. (2011). National, regional, and global trends in serum total cholesterol since 1980. *The Lancet, 16,* 377 578–586. doi: 10.1016/S0140-6736(10)62038-7

Fearon, R. P., Bakermans-Kranenburg, M. J., van IJzendoorn, M. H., Lapsley, A.-M., & Roisman, G. I. (2010). The significance of insecure attachment and disorganization in the development of children's externalizing behavior: A meta-analytic study. *Child Development, 81,* 435–345.

Feder, J., Levant, R. F., & Dean, J. (2007). Boys and violence: A gender-informed analysis. Professional *Psychology: Research and Practice, 38,* 385–391.

Federal Bureau of Investigation (FBI) (2009). *Uniform Crime Reports: Crimes in the United States, 2009.* Retrieved from http://www2.fbi.gov/ucr/cius2009/index.html

Feingold, A. (1992). Good-looking people are not what we think. *Psychological Bulletin, 111,* 304–341.

Feingold, A. (1994). Gender differences in personality: A meta-analysis. *Psychological Bulletin, 116,* 429–456.

Feinstein, J.S., Adolphs, R., Damasio, A., & Trane, D. (2010). The human amygdala and the induction and experience of fear. *Current Biology, 21,* 34–38, 16 doi: 10.1016/j.cub.2010.11.04

Feldhusen, J. F. (2004). Can we be intelligent and creative simultaneously? *Contemporary Psychology: APA Review of Books, 49,* 616–617.

Feldman, D. H. (2003). Cognitive development in childhood. In R. M. Lerner, M.A. Easterbrooks, & J. Mistry (Eds.), *Handbook of psychology: Vol. 6. Developmental psychology* (pp. 195–210). New York: John Wiley & Sons.

Feng, J., Spence, I., & Pratt, J. (2007). Playing an action video game reduces gender differences in spatial cognition. *Psychological Science, 18*(10), 850–855.

Fenn, K. M., Gallo, D. A., Margoliash, D., Roediger, H. L, & Nusbaum, H. C. (2009). Reduced false memory after sleep. *Learning & Memory*. Retrieved from http://learnmem.cshlp.org/content/current. doi:10.1101/lm.1500808

Fennis, B. M., Janssen, L., & Vohs, K. D. (2009). Acts of benevolence: A limited-resource account of compliance with charitable requests. *Journal of Consumer Research, 35*, 906–924. doi: 10.1086/593291

Ferdinand, K. C., & Ferdinand, D. P. (2009). Cardiovascular disease disparities: Racial/ethnic factors and potential solutions. *Current Cardiovascular Risk Reports, 3*, 187–193. doi:10.1007/s12170-009-0030-y

Ferguson, C. J. (2010). Blazing angels or resident evil? Can violent video games be a force for good? *Review of General Psychology, 14*, 68–81. doi: 10.1037/a0018941

Ferguson, M. J., & Zayas, V. (2009). Automatic evaluation. *Current Directions in Psychological Science, 18*, 362–366. doi: 10.1111/j.1467-8721.2009.01668.x

Fernández-Ballesterosa, R. (2006). Geropsychology: An applied field for the 21st century. *European Psychologist, 11*, 312–323.

Ferraz, L., Vállez, M., Navarro, B., Gelabert, E., Martín-Santos, R., & Subirà, S. (2009). Dimensional assessment of personality and impulsiveness in borderline personality disorder. *Personality and Individual Differences, 46*, 140–146. doi:10.1016/j.paid.2008.09.017

Ferreira, G., Ferry, B, Meurisse, M., & Lévy, F. (2006). Forebrain structures specifically activated by conditioned taste aversion. *Behavioral Neuroscience, 120*, 952–962.

Ferri, M., Amato, L., & Davoli, M. (2006). Alcoholics Anonymous and other 12-step programmes for alcohol dependence. *The Cochrane Database of Systematic Reviews*, No. 3. Retrieved from http://dx.doi. org/10.1002/14651858.CD005032.pub2

Feshbach, S, & Tangney, J. (2008). Television viewing and aggression. *Perspectives on Psychological Science, 3*, 387–389. doi: 10.1111/j.1745-6924.2008.00086.x

Festinger, L., & Carlsmith, J. M. (1959). Cognitive consequences of forced compliance. *Journal of Abnormal and Social Psychology, 58*, 203–210.

Few gender differences in math abilities, worldwide study finds. (2010, January 10). *ScienceDaily*. Retrieved from http://www.sciencedaily.com/releases/2010/01/100105112303.htm.

Fiedler, K. (2008). Language: A toolbox for sharing and influencing social reality. *Perspectives on Psychological Science, 3*, 38–47. doi: 10.1111/j.1745-6916.2008.00060.x

Field, A. (2006). I don't like it because it eats sprouts: Conditioning preferences in children. *Behaviour Research and Therapy, 44*, 439–455.

Figueredo, A. J., Sefcek, J. A, & Jones, D. N. (2006). The ideal romantic partner: Absolute or relative preferences in personality? *Personality and Individual Differences, 41*, 431–441.

Fink, B., & Penton-Voak, I. (2002). Evolutionary psychology of facial attractiveness. *Current Directions in Psychological Science, 11*, 154–158.

Fink, B., Neave, N., Manning, J. T., & Grammer, K. (2006). Facial symmetry and judgements of attractiveness, health and personality. *Personality and Individual Differences, 41*, 491–499.

Finucane, M. M., Stevens, G. A., Cowan, M. J., Danaei G., Lin, J. K., Paciorek, C. J., Singh, G. M., Ezzati, M. (2011). National, regional, and global trends in body-mass index since 1980. *The Lancet, 377*, 557–567 doi: 10.1016/S0140-6736(10)62037-5

Firestone, R. W., Firestone, L. A., & Catlett, J. (2006). *Sex and love in intimate relationships*. Washington, DC: American Psychological Association.

Fischer, A. H., Mosquera, P. M. R., van Vianen, A. E. M., & Manstead, A. S. R. (2004). Gender and culture differences in emotion. *Emotion, 4*, 87–94.

Fischer, P., Kastenmüller, A., & Greitemeyer, T. (2009). Media violence and the self: The impact of personalized gaming characters in aggressive video games on aggressive behavior. *Journal of Experimental Social Psychology, 46*, 192–195. doi:10.1016/j.jesp.2009.06.010

Fish, B., & Condon, S. (2005). A discussion of current attachment research and its clinical applications. *Child and Adolescent Social Work Journal, 11*, 93–105.

Fishbein, M. D. (1996). *Peer prejudice and discrimination: Evolutionary, cultural, and developmental dynamics*. Boulder, CO: Westview Press.

Fisher, B. S., Daigle, L. E., Cullen, F. T., & Turner, M. G. (2003). Reporting sexual victimization to the police and others: Results from a national-level study of college women. *Criminal Justice and Behavior, 30*, 6–38.

Fisher, M. A. (2008). Protecting confidentiality rights: The need for an ethical practice model. *American Psychologist, 63*, 1–13. doi: 10.1037/0003-066X.63.7.624

Fiske, A. P., Kitayama, S., Markus, H. R., & Nisbett, R. E. (1998). The cultural matrix of social psychology. In D. T. Gilbert, S. T. Fiske, & G. Lindzey (Eds.), *The handbook of social psychology* (4th ed., Vol. 2, pp. 915–981). Boston: McGraw-Hill.

Fiske, A., Wetherell, J. L, & Gatz, M. (2009). Depression in older adults. *Annual Review of Clinical Psychology, 5*, 363–389. doi:10.1146/annurev.clinpsy.032408.153621

Fiske, A., Wetherell, J. L, & Gatz, M. (2009). Depression in older adults. *Annual Review of Clinical Psychology, 5*, 363–389. doi:10.1146/annurev.clinpsy.032408.153621

Fitzsimons, G., M., Chartrand, T. L., & Fitzsimons, G. J. (2008). Automatic effects of brand exposure on motivated behavior: How Apple makes you "think different." *Journal of Consumer Research, 35*, 21–35. Retrieved from http://www.journals.uchicago.edu/doi/pdf/10.1086/527269

Flagel, S. B., Clark, J. J., Robinson, T. E., Mayo, L., Czuj, A., Willuhn, I. et al. (2011). A selective role for dopamine in stimulus–reward learning. *Nature, 469*, 53–57. doi:10.1038/nature09588

Flavell, J. H., Miller, P. H., & Miller, S. A. (2002). *Cognitive development* (4th ed.). Upper Saddle River, NJ: Prentice Hall.

Fleeson, W. (2004). Moving personality beyond the person-situation debate: The challenge and the opportunity of within-person variability. *Current Directions in Psychological Science, 13*, 83–87.

Fleeson, W., & Noftle, E.E. (2009). In favor of the synthetic resolution to the person–situation debate. *Journal of Research in Personality, 43*, 150–154. doi: 10.1016/j.jrp.2009.02.008

Fleeson, W., Malanos, A. B., & Achille, N. M. (2008). An intraindividual process approach to the relationship between extraversion and positive affect: is acting extraverted as "good" as being extraverted? *Journal of Personality and Social Psychology, 83*, 1409–1422.

Flegal, K. M., Carroll, M. D.,Ogden, C. L., & Curtin, L. R. (2010). Prevalence and trends in obesity among US Adults, 1999–2008. *Journal of the American Medical Association, 303*, 235–241. doi:10.1001/jama.2009.2014

Flegal, K. M., Graubard, B. L., Williamson, D. F., & Gail, M. H. (2005). Excess deaths associated with underweight, overweight, and obesity. *Journal of the American Medical Association, 293*, 1861–1867.

Floyd, R. L., O'Connor, M. J., Sokol, R. J., Bertrand, J., & Cordero, F. F. (2005). Recognition and prevention of fetal alcohol syndrome. *Obstetrics & Gynecology, 106*, 1059–1064.

Flynn, J.R. (2006). The history of the American mind in the 20th century: A scenario to explain IQ gains over time and a case for the irrelevance of g. In P.C. Kyllonon, R.D. Roberts, & L. Stankov (Eds.), *Extending intelligence: Enhancement and new constructs*. Hillsdale, NJ: Erlbaum.

Fok, H. K., Hui, C. M., Bond, M. H., Matsumoto, D., & Yoo, S. H. (2008). Integrating personality, context, relationship, and emotion type into a model of display. *Journal of Research in Personality, 42*, 133–150. doi:10.1016/j.jrp.2007.04.005

Foley, D. L., & Morley, K. J. (2011). Systematic review of early cardiometabolic outcomes of the first treated episode of psychosis. *Archives of General Psychiatry*, Published online February 7, 2011. doi:10.1001/archgenpsychiatry.2011.2

Foley, E., Baillie, A., Huxter, M., Price, M., & Sinclair, E. (2010). Mindfulness-based cognitive therapy for individuals whose lives have been affected by cancer: A randomized controlled trial. *Journal of Consulting and Clinical Psychology, 78*, 72–79. doi: 10.1007/s10826-009-9272-z.

Folsom, D. P., Hawthorne, W., Lindamer, L., Gilmer, T., Bailey, A., Golshan, S., et al. (2005). Prevalence and risk factors for homelessness and utilization of mental health services among 10,340 patients with serious mental illness in a large public mental health system. *American Journal of Psychiatry, 162*, 370–376.

Fontaine, K. R., Redden, D. T., Wang, C., Westfall, A. O.,& Allison, D. B. (2003). Years of life lost due to obesity. *Journal of the American Medical Association, 289*, 187–193.

Foote, B., Smolin, Y., Kaplan, M., Legatt, M. E., & Lipschitz, D. (2005). Prevalence of dissociative disorders in psychiatric outpatients. *American Journal of Psychiatry, 163*, 623–629.

Ford, C. S., & Beach, F. A. (1951). *Patterns of sexual behavior*. New York: Harper & Row.

Forestell, C. A., Humphrey, T. M., & Stewart, S. H. (2004). Involvement of body weight and shape factors in ratings of attractiveness by women: A replication and extension of Tassinary and Hansen (1998). *Personality and Individual Differences, 36*, 295–305.

Forgas, J. P. (2008). Affect and cognition. *Perspectives on Psychological Science, 3*, 94–101. doi: 10.1111/j.1745-6916.2008.00067.x

Forman, J. P., Stampfer, M. J., & Curhan, G. C. (2009). Diet and lifestyle risk factors associated with incident hypertension in women. *Journal of the American Medical Association, 302*, 401–411.

Fountain, H. (2007, June 19). Cockroaches conditioned to salivate at a scent, not Pavlov's dinner bell. *The New York Times Science Section*. Retrieved from www.nytimes.com

Fournier, J. C., DeRubeis, R. J., Hollon, S. D., Dimidjian, S., Amsterdam, J. D., Shelton, R. C., et al. (2010). Antidepressant drug effects and depression severity: A patient-level meta-analysis. *Journal of the American Medical Association, 303*, 47–53.

Fournier, J. C., DeRubeis, R. J., Shelton, R. C., Hollon, S. D., Amsterdam, J. D., & Gallop, R. (2009). Prediction of response to medication and cognitive therapy in the treatment of moderate to severe depression. *Journal of Consulting and Clinical Psychology, 77*, 775–787. doi: 10.1037/a0015401

Fowler, J. H., & Christakis, N. A. (2008). Dynamic spread of happiness in a large social network: Longitudinal analysis over 20 years in the Framingham Heart Study. *British Medical Journal, 337*, 2338. doi: 10.1136/bmj.a2338

Frank, R. G., & Glied, S. A. (2006). *Better but not well: Mental health policy in the United States since 1950*. Baltimore, MD: Johns Hopkins University Press.

Freedman, D. H. (2011). How to fix the obesity crisis. *Scientific American* Retrieved from http://www.scientificamerican.com/article.cfm?id=how-to-fix-the-obesity-crisis

Freeman, H. P., & Payne, R. (2000). Racial injustice in health care. *New England Journal of Medicine, 342,* 1045–1047.

Freeman, J. B., Rule, N. O., Adams, R. B., & Ambady, N. (2009). Culture shapes a mesolimbic response to signals of dominance and subordination that associates with behavior. *NeuroImage, 47,* 353–359.

Freeman, M. S., Spence, M. J., & Oliphant, C. M. (1993, June). *Newborns prefer their mothers' low-pass filtered voices over other female filtered voices.* Paper presented at the annual meeting of the American Psychological Society, Chicago.

French, S. E., Seidman, E., Allen, L., & Aber, J. L. (2006). The development of ethnic identity during adolescence. *Developmental Psychology, 42,* 1–10.

Frenda, S. J., Nichols, R. M., & Loftus, E. F. (2011). Current issues and advances in misinformation research. *Current Directions in Psychological Science, 20,* 20–23. doi:10.1177/0963721410396620

Freud, S. (1900). The interpretation of dreams. In J. Strachey (Ed.), *The standard edition of the complete psychological works of Sigmund Freud: Vol. 8.* London: Hogarth Press.

Freud, S. (1917/1957). Mourning and melancholia. In J. Rickman (Ed.), *A general selection from the works of Sigmund Freud.* Garden City, NY: Doubleday.

Freud, S. (1922/1959). Analysis of a phobia in a 5-year-old boy. In A. J. Strachey (Ed. & Trans.), *Collected papers* (Vol. 3). New York: Basic Books. (Original work published 1909.)

Freud, S. (1938). *The psychopathology of everyday life.* Hammondsworth: Pelican Books.

Freud, S. (1964). New introductory lectures. In *Standard edition of the complete psychological works of Sigmund Freud* (Vol. 22). London: Hogarth. (Original work published 1933.)

Freund, A. A. (2006). Age-differential motivational consequences of optimization versus compensation focus in younger and older adults. *Psychology and Aging, 21,* 40–52.

Freund, A. M., & Riediger, M. (2003). Successful aging. In R. M. Lerner, M.A. Easterbrooks, & J. Mistry (Eds.), *Handbook of psychology: Vol. 6. Developmental psychology* (pp. 601–628). New York: John Wiley & Sons.

Frey, B. S. (2011). Happy people live longer. *Science, 331,* 542–543. doi: 10.1126/science.1201060

Friedman, B. H. (2010). Feelings and the body: The Jamesian perspective on autonomic specificity of emotion. *Biological Psychology, 84,* 383–393. doi:10.1016/j.biopsycho.2009.10.006

Friedman, M. (2008). *Sleep apnea and snoring: Surgical and non-surgical therapy.* Philadelphia: Saunders/Elsevier.

Friedman, M., & Ulmer, D. (1984). *Treating Type A behavior and your heart.* New York: Fawcett Crest.

Friedman, T. L. (2006). *The world is flat: Updated and expanded.* (2nd ed). New York: Farrar, Straus and Giroux.

Fruzzetti, A. E., Toland, K., Teller, S. A., & Loftus, E. F. (1992). Memory and eyewitness testimony. In M. M. Gruneberg & P. E. Morris (Eds.), *Aspects of memory: Vol. 1. The practical aspects* (2nd ed., pp. 18–50). Florence, KY: Taylor & Francis/Routledge.

Frye, M. A. (2011). Bipolar disorder—a focus on depression. *New England Journal of Medicine, 364,* 51–59.

Fujita, F., & Diener, E. (2005). Life satisfaction set point: Stability and change. *Journal of Personality and Social Psychology, 88,* 158–164.

Fuligni, A. J., Witkow, M., & Garcia, C. (2005). Ethnic identity and the academic adjustment of adolescents from Mexican, Chinese, and European backgrounds. *Developmental Psychology, 41,* 799–811.

Funder, D. C. (2009). Persons, behaviors and situations: An agenda for personality psychology in the postwar era. *Journal of Research in Personality, 43,* 120–126. doi:10.1016/j.jrp.2008.12.041

Furnham, A. (2009). Sex differences in mate selection preferences. *Personality and Individual Differences, 47,* 262–267.

Futrelle, D. (2006, August). Can money buy happiness? *Money,* pp. 127–131.

Gabbard, G. O. (2005). Mind, brain, and personality disorders. *American Journal of Psychiatry, 162,* 648–655.

Gaertner, L., Iuzzini, J., Witt, J. G., & Oriña, J. M. (2006). Us without them: Evidence for an intragroup origin of positive in-group regard. *Journal of Personality and Social Psychology, 90,* 426–439.

Gajendran, R. S., & Harrison, D. A. (2007). The good, the bad, and the unknown about telecommuting: Meta-analysis of psychological mediators and individual consequences. *Journal of Applied Psychology, 92*(6), 1524–1541.

Galanter, E. (1962). Contemporary psychophysics. In R. Brown, E. Galanter, H. Hess, & G. Mandler (Eds.), *New directions in psychology.* New York: Holt, Rinehart & Winston.

Gallego, M., Eide, E. J., Woolf, M. F., Virshup, D. M., & Forger, D. B. (2006). An opposite role for tau in circadian rhythms revealed by mathematical modeling. *Proceedings of the National Academy of Sciences,* published online July 3, 2006. Retrieved from http://www.pnas.org/cgi/content/abstract/0604511103v1.

Gallistel, C. R. (2006). Dopamine and reward: Comment on Hernandez et al. (2006). *Behavioral Neuroscience, 120,* 992–994.

Gallup Organization. (2005). *Americans' Personal Satisfaction, 2005.* Retrieved from http://www.gallup.com/poll/content/default.aspx?

Gallup, G. G, Jr., & Frederick, D. A. (2010). The science of sex appeal: An evolutionary perspective. *Review of General Psychology, 14,* 240–250. doi: 10.1037/a0020451

Gandevia, S. C., Smith, J. L., Crawford, M., Proske, U., & Taylor, J. L. (2006). Motor commands contribute to human position sense. *Journal of Physiology, 571,* 703–710.

Gannon, N., & Ranzijn, R. (2005). Does emotional intelligence predict unique variance in life satisfaction beyond IQ and personality? *Personality and Individual Differences, 38,* 1353–1364.

Garb, H. N., Wood, J. M., Lilienfeld, S. O., & Nezworski, M. T. (2005). Roots of the Rorschach controversy. *Clinical Psychology Review, 25,* 97–118.

Garcia, J., & Koelling, R. A. (1966). Relation of cue to consequence in avoidance learning. *Psychonomic Science, 4,* 123–124.

Garcia, J., & Koelling, R. A. (1971). The use of ionizing rays as a mammalian olfactory stimulus. In H. Autrum et al. (Eds.), *Handbook of sensory physiology: Vol. 4. Chemical senses* (Part 1). New York: Springer-Verlag.

Garcia, J., & Koelling, R. A. (2009). Specific hungers and poison avoidance as adaptive specialization of learning. In D. Shanks (Ed.), *Psychology of learning.* Thousand Oaks, CA: Sage.

Gardner, A. (2010, October 4). *Variety spices up Americans' sex lives, survey says.* Retrieved from http://www.businessweek.com/lifestyle/content/healthday/643856.html.

Gardner, H. (1993). Intelligence in seven phases. In H. Gardner (Ed.), *Multiple intelligences: The theory in practice* (pp. 213–230). New York: Basic Books.

Gardner, H. (1998). Are there additional intelligences? The case for naturalist, spiritual, and existential intelligences. In J. Kane (Ed.), *Education information, and transformation.* Upper Saddle River, NJ: Prentice-Hall.

Gardner, R. A., & Gardner, B. T. (1969). Teaching sign language to a chimpanzee. *Science, 165,* 664–672.

Gardner, R. A., & Gardner, B. T. (1978). Comparative psychology and language acquisition. *Annals of the New York Academy of Science, 309,* 37–76.

Gardner, R., Jr. (2006, October 8). The farewell tour. *The New York Times,* Section 9, pp. 1, 14.

Garnets, L. D. (2002). Sexual orientations in perspective. *Cultural Diversity and Ethnic Minority Psychology, 8,* 115–129.

Gartlehner, G., Gaynes, B. N., Hansen, R. A., Thieda, P., DeVeaugh-Geiss, A., Krebs, E. E., et al. (2008). Comparative benefits and harms of second-generation antidepressants: Background paper for the American College of Physicians. *Annals of Internal Medicine, 149,* 734–750. Retrieved from http://www.ncbi.nlm.nih.gov/pubmed/19017592.

Garwood, S. G., Cox, L., Kaplan, V., Wasserman, N., and Sulzer, J. (1980). Beauty is only "name deep": The effect of first name in ratings of physical attraction. *Journal of Applied Social Psychology, 10,* 431–435.

Gatchel, R. J. (2001). Biofeedback and self-regulation of physiological activity: A major adjunctive treatment modality in health psychology. In A. Baum, T. A. Revenson, & J. E. Singer (Eds.), *Handbook of health psychology* (pp. 95–104). Mahwah, NJ: Lawrence Erlbaum Associates.

Gatz, M. (2007) Genetics, dementia, and the elderly. *Current Directions in Psychological Science, 16,* 123–127.

Gaulin, S. J. C., & McBurney, D. H. (2001). *Psychology: An evolutionary approach.* Upper Saddle River, NJ: Prentice-Hall.

Gauthier, I., & Curby, K. M. (2005). A perceptual traffic jam on highway N170 interference between face and car expertise. *Current Directions in Psychological Science, 14,* 30–33.

Gawronski, B., Rydell, R. J., Vervliet, B., & De Houwer, J. (2010). Generalization versus contextualization in automatic evaluation. *Journal of Experimental Psychology: General, 139,* 683–701. doi: 10.1037/a0020315

Gazzaniga, M. (1999). The interpreter within: The glue of conscious experience. *Cerebrum, 1*(1), 68–78.

Gazzaniga, M. S. (1992). *Nature's mind.* New York: Basic Books.

Gazzaniga, M. S. (1995). Consciousness and the cerebral hemispheres. In M. S. Gazzaniga (Ed.), *The cognitive neurosciences* (pp. 1391–1400). Cambridge, MA: MIT Press.

Ge, X., & Natsuaki, M. N. (2009). In search of explanations for early pubertal timing effects on developmental psychopathology. *Current Directions in Psychological Science, 18,* 327–331. doi: 10.1111/j.1467-8721.2009.01661.x

Gehar, D. R. (2009). *Mastering competencies in family therapy.* Belmont, CA: Brooks/Cole, Cengage Learning.

Geier, A. B., Rozin, P., & Doros, G. (2006). Unit bias: A new heuristic that helps explain the effect of portion size on food intake. *Psychological Science, 17,* 521–525.

Geipert, N. (2007, January). Don't be mad: More research links hostility to coronary risk. *Monitor on Psychology, 38*(1), 50–51.

Gel, S., Gohl, E. L. K., Sailor, K. A., Kitabatake, Y., Ming, G., & Song, H. (2006). GABA regulates synaptic integration of newly generated neurons in the adult brain. *Nature, 439,* 589–593.

Geller, B. (2006, October 16). Early use of methylphenidate: The jury on neuronal effects is still out. *Journal Watch Psychiatry.* Retrieved from http://psychiatry.jwatch.org/cgi/content/full/2006/1016/2.

Gelstein, S., Yeshurun, Y., Rozenkrantz, L., Shushan, S., Frumin, I., Roth, Y., Sobel, N. (2011). Human tears contain a chemosignal. *Science, 331,* 226–230. doi: 10.1126/science.1198331

Geraerts, E., Lindsay, D. S., Merckelbach, H., Jelicic, M., Raymaekers, L., Arnold, M. M.,.. Schooler, J. W. (2009). Cognitive mechanisms underlying recovered-memory experiences of childhood sexual abuse. *Psychological Science, 20,* 92–98. doi: 10.1111/j.1467-9280.2008.02247.x

Gerhart, B. (2005). The (affective) dispositional approach to job satisfaction: Sorting out the policy implications. *Journal of Organizational Behavior, 26,* 79–97.

German, T. P., & Barrett, H. C. (2005). Functional fixedness in a technologically sparse culture. *Psychological Science, 16,* 1–5.

Gershoff, E. T. (2002b). Corporal punishment, physical abuse, and the burden of proof: Reply to Baumrind, Larzelere, and Cowan (2002), Holden (2002), and Parke (2002). *Psychological Bulletin, 128,* 602–611.

Gershoff, E. T. (2002a). Corporal punishment by parents and associated child behaviors and experiences: A meta-analytic and theoretical review. *Psychological Bulletin, 128,* 539–579. doi: 0033-2909/02/$5.00 DOI: 10.1037//0033-2909.128.4.539

Gertner, Y., Fisher, C., & Eisengart, J. (2006). Learning words and rules: Abstract knowledge of word order in early sentence comprehension. *Psychological Science, 17,* 684–691.

Gibson, E. J., & Walk, R. D. (1960, April). The visual cliff. *Scientific American,* pp. 64–71.

Gignac, G. E. (2006). Self-reported emotional intelligence and life satisfaction: Testing incremental predictive validity hypotheses via structural equation modeling (SEM) in a small sample. *Personality and Individual Differences, 40,* 1569–1577.

Gilestro, G. F., Tononi, G., & Cirelli, C. (2009). Widespread changes in synaptic markers as a function of sleep and wakefulness in drosophila. *Science, 324,* 5923 109–112.

Gill, R. E. (2006, January/February). *The National Psychologist, 15,* 1–2.

Gilligan, C. (1982). *In a different voice: Psychological theory and women's development.* Cambridge, MA: Harvard University Press.

Gilligan, C., Lyons, P., & Hanmer, T. J. (Eds.). (1990). *Making connections.* Cambridge, MA: Harvard University Press.

Giltay, E.J., Kamphuis, M.H., Kalmijin, S., Zitman, F.G., & Kromhout, D. (2006). Dispositional optimism and the risk of cardiovascular death: The Zutphen Elderly Study. *Archives of Internal Medicine, 166,* 431–436.

Giotakos, O., Markianos, M., & Vaidakis, N. (2005). Aggression, impulsivity, and plasma sex hormone levels in a group of rapists, in relation to their history of childhood attention-deficit/hyperactivity disorder symptoms. *Journal of Forensic Psychiatry & Psychology, 16,* 423–433.

Glasman, L. R., & Albarracín, D. (2006). Forming attitudes that predict future behavior: A meta-analysis of the attitude-behavior relation. *Psychological Bulletin, 132,* 778–822.

Glassman, A. H., Bigger, T., Jr, & Gaffney, M. (2009). Psychiatric characteristics associated with long-term mortality among 361 patients having an acute coronary syndrome and major depression: Seven-year follow-up of SADHART participants. *Archives of General Psychiatry, 66,* 1022.

Glickstein, M., Strata, P., & Voogd, J. (2009). Cerebellum: history. *Neuroscience, 162,* 549–559. doi:10.1016/j.neuroscience.2009.02.054

Godden, D. R., & Baddeley, A. D. (1975). Context-dependent memory in two natural environments: On land and underwater. *British Journal of Psychology, 66,* 325–331.

Godleski, S. A., & Ostrov, J. M. (2010). Relational aggression and hostile attribution biases: Testing multiple statistical methods and models. *Journal of Abnormal Child Psychology, 38,* 447–458. doi:10.1007/s10802-010-9391-4

Goebel, M. U., Trebst, A. E., Steiner, J., Xie, Y. F., Exton, M. S., Frede, S., et al. (2002). Behavioral conditioning of immunosuppression is possible in humans. *FASEB Journal, 16,* 1869–1873.

Goel, N., Banks, S., Mignot, E., & Dinges, D. R. (2010). DQB1*0602 predicts interindividual differences in physiologic sleep, sleepiness, and fatigue. *Neurology, 75,* 1509–1519.

Goldberg, L. R. (1993). The structure of phenotypic personality traits. *American Psychologist, 48,* 26–34.

Goldstein, I., Meston, C., Davis, S., & Traish, A. (Eds.). (2006). *Female sexual dysfunction.* New York: Parthenon.

Goldstein, R. B., Grant, B. F., Huang, B., Smith, S. M., Stinson, F. S., Dawson, D. A., et al. (2006). Lack of remorse in antisocial personality disorder: Sociodemographic correlates, symptomatic presentation, and comorbidity with Axis I and Axis II disorders in the National Epidemiologic Survey on Alcohol and Related Conditions. *Comprehensive Psychiatry, 47,* 289–297.

Golier, J. A., Yehuda, R., Bierer, L. M., Mitropoulou, V., New, A. S., Schmeidler, J., et al. (2003). The relationship of borderline personality disorder to posttraumatic stress disorder and traumatic events. *American Journal of Psychiatry, 160,* 2018–2024.

Golinkoff, R. M., & Hirsh-Pasek, K. (2006). Baby wordsmith: From associationist to social sophisticate. *Current Directions in Psychological Science, 15,* 30–33.

Gómez, R. L., Bootzin, R. R., & Nadel, L. (2006). Naps promote abstraction in language-learning infants. *Psychological Science, 17,* 670–674.

Gonsalves B. D., Cohen N. J. (2010). Brain imaging, cognitive processes, and brain networks. *Perspectives on Psychological Science, 5,* 744–752. doi:10.1177/1745691610388776

González, H. J., Vega, W. A., Williams, D. R., Tarraf, W., West, B. T., & Neighbors, H. W. (2010). Depression care in the United States: Too little for too few. *Archives of General Psychiatry, 67,* 37–46.

Goodwin, I. (2003). The relevance of attachment theory to the philosophy, organization, and practice of adult mental health care. *Clinical Psychology Review, 23,* 35–56.

Goodwin, R. D., Canino, G., Ortega, A. N., & Bird, H. R. (2009). Maternal mental health and childhood asthma among Puerto Rican youth: The role of prenatal smoking. *Journal of Asthma, 46,* 726–730. doi: 10.1080/02770900903072051

Gopnik, A. (2000, December 24). Children need childhood, not vocational training. *The New York Times Week in Review,* p. 6.

Gorchoff, S. M., John, O. P., & Helson, R. (2008). Contextualizing change in marital satisfaction during middle age: An 18-year longitudinal study. *Psychological Science, 19,* 1194–1200.

Gorman, C. (2007, January 29). 6 lessons for handling stress. *Newsweek,* pp. 80–85.

Gosling, P., Denizeau, M., & Oberlé, D. (2006). Denial of responsibility: A new mode of dissonance reduction. *Journal of Personality and Social Psychology, 90,* 722–733.

Gosling, S. D., Kwan, V. S. Y., & John, O. P. (2003). A dog's got personality: A cross-species comparative approach to personality judgments in dogs and humans. *Journal of Personality and Social Psychology, 85,* 1161–1169.

Gothold, J. J. (2009). Peeling the onion: Understanding layers of treatment. *Annals of the New York Academy of Sciences, 1159,* 301–312.

Gottesman, I. I. (1997). Twins: En route to QTLs for cognition. *Science, 276,* 1522–1523.

Gottesman, I. I., & Hanson, D. R. (2005). Human development: Biological and genetic processes. *Annual Review of Psychology, 56,* 263–286.

Gottfredson, L. S. (2003a). Discussion on Sternberg's "Reply to Gottfredson." *Intelligence, 31,* 415–424.

Gottfredson, L. S. (2003b). Dissecting practical intelligence theory: Its claims and evidence. *Intelligence, 31,* 343–397.

Gottfredson, L. S. (2004). Intelligence: Is it the epidemiologists' elusive "fundamental cause" of social class inequalities in health? *Journal of Personality and Social Psychology, 86,* 174–199.

Gottfredson, L. S., & Deary, I. J. (2004). Intelligence predicts health and longevity, but why? *Current Directions in Psychological Science, 13,* 1–4.

Gould, C. E., & Edelstein, B. A. (2010). Worry, emotion control, and anxiety control in older and younger adults. *Journal of Anxiety Disorders, 24,* 759–766.

Goymer, P. (2007). Genes know their left from their right. *Nature Reviews Genetics 8,* 652. doi:10.1038/nrg2194

Grabe, S., & Hyde, J. S. (2006). Ethnicity and body dissatisfaction among women in the United States: A meta-analysis. *Psychological Bulletin, 132,* 622–640.

Grace, A. A. (2010). Ventral hippocampus, interneurons, and schizophrenia: A new understanding of the pathophysiology of schizophrenia and its implications for treatment and prevention. *Current Directions in Psychological Science, 19,* 232–237. doi: 10.1177/0963721410378032s

Graham, J. R. (2006). *MMPI-2: Assessing personality and psychopathology* (4th ed.). New York: Oxford University Press.

Grant, B. F., Hasin, D. S., Blanco, C., Stinson, F. S., Chou, S. P., Goldstein, R. B., et al. (2006). The epidemiology of social anxiety disorder in the United States: Results from the National Epidemiologic Survey on Alcohol and Related Conditions. *Journal of Clinical Psychiatry, 66,* 1351–1361.

Grant, B. F., Hasin, D. S., Stinson, F. S., Dawson, D. A., Goldstein, R. B., Smith, S., et al. (2006). The epidemiology of DSM-IV panic disorder and agoraphobia in the United States: Results from the National Epidemiologic Survey on Alcohol and Related Conditions. *Journal of Clinical Psychiatry, 67,* 363–374.

Grant, B. F., Stinson, F. S., Dawson, D. A., Chou, P., Dufour, M. C., Compton, W., et al. (2004). Prevalence and co-occurrence of substance use disorders and independent mood and anxiety disorders: Results from the National Epidemiologic Survey on Alcohol and Related Conditions. *Archives of General Psychiatry, 61,* 807–816.

Gratz, K. L., Rosenthal, M. Z., Tull, M. T., Lejuez, C. W., & Gunderson, J. G. (2010). An experimental investigation of emotional reactivity and delayed emotional recovery in borderline personality disorder: The role of shame. *Comprehensive Psychiatry, 51,* 275–285. doi:10.1016/j.comppsych.2009.08.005

Gray-Little, B., & Hafdahl, A. R. (2000). Factors influencing racial comparisons of self-esteem: A quantitative review. *Psychological Bulletin, 126,* 26–54.

Grayson, M. (2010). Parkinson's disease. *Nature, 466,* 7310 suppl. pp. S3–S22. doi:10.1038/466S2a

Graziano, W., G., & Tobin, R. M. (2009). Agreeableness. In M. R. Leary & R. H. Hoyle (Eds.), *Handbook of individual differences in social behavior* (pp. 46–61). New York: Guilford.

Green, B. L., & Kenrick, D. T. (1994). The attractiveness of gender-typed traits at different relationship levels: Androgynous characteristics may be desirable after all. *Personality and Social Psychology Bulletin, 20*(3), 244–253.

Greenberg, S. H., & Springen, K. (2001, Fall/Winter). Keeping hope alive. *Newsweek Special Issue,* pp. 60–63.

Greenwood, A. (2006, April 25). Natural killer cells power immune system response to cancer. *NCI Cancer Bulletin, 3*(17). Retrieved from http://www.cancer.gov/ncicancerbulletin/NCI_Cancer_Bulletin_042506 /page4.

Greer, M. (2004a, April). General cognition also makes the difference on the job, study finds. *Monitor on Psychology, 35*(4), 12.

Greer, M. (2004b, July). Strengthen your brain by resting it. *Monitor on Psychology, 35*(7), 60–61.

Gregoire, C. (2010, January 25). Cohabitation and marriage in America—study: The state of our unions 2009—living together vs getting married. Retrieved from http://divorce.suite101.com/article.cfm/cohabitation_and_marriage_in_america_2009#ixzz0hySvsOSG.

Griffiths, S., Scott, H., Glover, C., Bienemann, A., Ghorbel, M. T., Uney, J., Bashir,. Z.I. (2008). Expression of long-term depression underlies visual recognition memory. *Neuron, 58*, 186–194. doi: 10.1016/j.neuron.2008.02.022

Griffo, R., & Colvin, C. R. (2009). A brief look at interactionism: Past and present. *Journal of Research in Personality, 43*, 243–244. doi:10.1016/j.jrp.2008.12.038

Grigoriadis, V. (2003, July 20). Smiling through the 30th, a birthday once apocalyptic. *The New York Times*, Section 9, pp. 1, 8.

Grimm, L. R., Markman, A. B., Maddox, W. T., & Baldwin, G. C. (2009). Stereotype threat reinterpreted as a regulatory mismatch. *Journal of Personality and Social Psychology, 96*, 288–304. doi: 10.1037/a0013463

Grob, G. N. (1996). *The mad among us: A history of the care of America's mentally ill*.Cambridge, MA: Harvard University Press.

Gross, J. (2007, March 21). Prevalence of Alzheimer's rises 10% in 5 years. *The New York Times*, p. A14.

Grossman, L. (2003, January 20). Can Freud get his job back? *Time*, pp. 48–51.

Grossman, P. (2008). On measuring mindfulness in psychosomatic and psychological research. *Journal of Psychosomatic Research, 64*, 405–408.

Gubbels, S. P., Woessner, D. W., Mitchell, J. C., Ricci, A. J., & Brigande, A. J. (2008). Functional auditory hair cells produced in the mammalian cochlea by in utero gene transfer. *Nature Online*. Retrieved from http://www.nature.com/nature/journal/vaop/ncurrent/abs/nature07265.html

Guéguen, N., Jacob, C., & Lamy, L. (2010). 'Love is in the air': Effects of songs with romantic lyrics on compliance with a courtship request. *Psychology of Music, 38*, 303–307. doi: 10.1177/0305735609360428

Guenther, R. K. (1998). *Human cognition*. Englewood Cliffs, NJ: Prentice-Hall.

Guilford, J. P., Christensen, P. R., Merrifield, P. R., & Wilson, R. C. (1978). *Alternate uses: Form B, Form C*. Orange, CA: Sheridan Psychological Services.

Guisinger, S., & Blatt, S. J. (1994). Individuality and relatedness: Evolution of a fundamental dialectic. *American Psychologist, 49*, 104–111.

Gunderson, J. G. (2007). Disturbed relationships as a phenotype for borderline personality disorder. *American Journal of Psychiatry, 164*, 1637–1640.

Gunderson, J. G. (2011). Borderline personality disorder. *New England Journal of Medicine*, 364, 2037–204.

Gunn, R. L., & Smith, G. T. (2010). Risk factors for elementary school drinking: Pubertal status, personality, and alcohol expectancies concurrently predict fifth grade alcohol consumption. *Psychology of Addictive Behaviors, 24*, 617–627. doi:10.1037/a0020334

Gunter, B., & McAleer, J. (1990). *Children and television: The one-eyed monster?* London: Routledge.

Gunter, R. W., & Whittal, M. L. (2010). Dissemination of cognitive-behavioral treatments for anxiety disorders: Overcoming barriers and improving patient access. *Clinical Psychology Review, 30*, 194–202. doi:10.1016/j.cpr.2009.11.001

Gupta, R., Warren, T., & Wald, A. (2007). Genital herpes. *The Lancet, 370*, 2127–2137.

Gustavson, C. R., & Garcia, J. (1974). Aversive conditioning: Pulling a gag on the wily coyote. *Psychology Today, 8*, 68–72.

Gustavson, C. R., Garcia, J., Hawkins, W. G., & Rusiniak, K. W. (1974). Coyote predation control by aversive conditioning. *Science, 184*, 581–583.

Gwaltney, C. J., Metrik, J., Kahler, C. W., & Shiffman, S. (2009). Self-efficacy and smoking cessation: A meta-analysis. *Psychology of Addictive Behaviors, 23*, 56–66. doi: 10.1037/a0013529

Gyatso, T. (2003, April 26). The monk in the lab. *The New York Times*, p. A29.

Haber, R. N. (1979). Twenty years of haunting eidetic imagery: Where's the ghost? *Behavioral and Brain Sciences 2*, 583–629.

Hafdahl, A. R., & Gray-Little, B. (2002). Explicating methods in reviews of race and self-esteem: Reply to Twenge and Crocker (2002). *Psychological Bulletin, 128*, 409–416.

Haider, B., Duque, A., Hasenstaub, A. R., &. McCormick, D. A. (2006). Neocortical network activity in vivo is generated through a dynamic balance of excitation and inhibition. *The Journal of Neuroscience, 26*, 4535–4545.

Haidt, J. (2008). Morality. *Perspectives on Psychological Science, 3*, 65–72. Doi: 10.1111/j.1745-6916.2008.00063.x

Halbreich, U., O'Brien, S., Eriksson, E., Bäckström, T., Yonkers, K.A., & Freeman, E.W. (2006). Are there differential symptom profiles that improve in response to different pharmacological treatments of premenstrual syndrome/premenstrual dysphoric disorder? *CNS Drugs, 20*, 523–547.

Hall, H. I., Song, R., Rhodes, P., Prejean, J., An, Q., Lee, L. M., et al. (2008). Estimation of HIV incidence in the United States. *Journal of the American Medical Association, 300*, 520–529. Retrieved from http://jama.ama-assn.org/cgi/content/abstract/300/5/520.

Halpern, D. F. (2004). A cognitive-process taxonomy for sex differences in cognitive abilities. *Current Directions in Psychological Science, 13*, 135–139.

Halpern, D. F., & LaMay, M. L. (2000). The smarter sex: A critical review of sex differences in intelligence. *Educational Psychology Review, 12*, 229–246.

Halpern, D. F., Benbow, C. P., Geary, D. C., Gur, R. C., Shibley Hyde, J., & Gernsbacher, M. A. (2007). The science of sex differences in science and mathematics. *Psychological Science in the Public Interest, 8*(1), 1–51.

Ham, L. S., & Hope, D. A. (2003). College students and problematic drinking: A review of the literature. *Clinical Psychology Review, 23*, 719–759.

Hamel, M., Shafer, T. W., & Erdberg, P. (2003). A study of nonpatient preadolescent Rorschach protocols. *Journal of Personality Assessment, 75*, 280–294.

Hamilton, B. E., Martin, J. A., & Ventura, S. J. (2009) Births: Preliminary data for 2007. *National vital statistics reports, 57* (12). Hyattsville, MD: National Center for Health Statistics. Retrieved from http://www.cdc.gov/nchs/FASTATS/.

Hamilton, E. A., Mintz, L,. & Kashubeck-West, S. (2010). Predictors of media effects on body dissatisfaction in European American women. *Sex Roles, 56*, 397–402, doi: 10.1007/s11199-006-9178-9

Hamilton, S. P. (2008). Schizophrenia candidate genes: Are we really coming up blank? *American Journal of Psychiatry, 165*, 420–423. doi: 10.1176/appi.ajp.2008.08020218

Hammond, D. C. (2007). Review of the efficacy of clinical hypnosis with headaches and migraines. *International Journal of Clinical and Experimenal Hypnosis, 55*, 207–219.

Hampton, T. (2008). Sleep deprivation. *Journal of the American Medical Association, 299*, 513. Doi: 10.1001/jama.299.5.513-c

Hampton, T. (2010). Parkinson disease insights. *Journal of the American Medical Association, 303*, 2129.

Hardy, S. A., & Raffaelli, M. (2003). Adolescent religiosity and sexuality: An investigation of reciprocal influences. *Journal of Adolescence, 26*, 731–739.

Hargreaves, D. A., & Tiggemann, M. (2009). Muscular ideal media images and men's body image: Social comparison processing and individual vulnerability. *Psychology of Men & Masculinity, 10*, 109–119. doi:10.1016/j.bodyim.2004.10.002

Harlow, H. F., & Harlow, M. K. (1966). Learning to love. *American Scientist, 54*, 244–272.

Harlow, H. F., & Zimmermann, R. R. (1959). Affectional responses in the infant monkey. *Science, 130*, 421–432.

Harlow, H. F., Harlow, M. K., & Meyer, D. R. (1950). Learning motivated by a manipulation drive. *Journal of Experimental Psychology, 40*, 228–234.

Harmison, R. J. (2006). Peak performance in sport: identifying ideal performance states and developing athletes' psychological skills. *Professional Psychology: Research and Practice, 37*, 233–243.

Harriger, J. A., Calogero, R. M., Witherington, D. C., & Smith, J. E. (2010). Body size stereotyping and internalization of the thin ideal in preschool girls. *Sex Roles, 63*, 609–620. doi: 10.1007/s11199-010-9868-1

Harris, A. H. S., Cronkite, R., & Moos, R. (2006). Physical activity, exercise coping, and depression in a 10-year cohort study of depressed patients. *Journal of Affective Disorders, 93*, 79–85.

Harris, A. H. S., Cronkite, R., & Moos, R. (2006). Physical activity, exercise coping, and depression in a 10-year cohort study of depressed patients. *Journal of Affective Disorders, 93*, 79–85.

Harris, J. L., Bargh, J. A., & Brownell, K. D. (2009). Priming effects of television food advertising on eating behavior. *Health Psychology, 28*, 404–413. doi: 10.1037/a0014399

Harrison, B. J., Soriano-Mas, C., Pujol, J., Ortiz, H., Lopez-Sola, M., Hernandez-Ribas, Deus, J., et al. (2009). Altered corticostriatal functional connectivity in obsessive-compulsive disorder. *Archives of General Psychiatry, 66*, 1189–1200.

Harro, J. Merenäkk, L., Nordquist, N., Konstabel, K., Comascoe, E., & Oreland, L. (2009). Personality and the serotonin transporter gene: Associations in a longitudinal population-based study. *Biological Psychology, 81*, 9–13. doi:10.1016/j.biopsycho.2009.01.001

Harshman, R. A., & Paivio, A. (1987). Paradoxical sex differences in self-reported imagery. *Canadian Journal of Psychology, 41*, 287–302.

Hartmann, E. (1998). *Dreams and nightmares*. New York: Plenum.

Hassert, D. L., Miyashita, T., Williams, C. L. (2004). The effects of peripheral vagal nerve stimulation at a memory-modulating intensity on norepinephrine output in the basolateral amygdala. *Behavioral Neuroscience, 118*, 79–88.

Haubensak, W., Kunwar, P.S., Cai, H., Ciocchi, S., Wall, N.R., Ponnusamy, R., et alJ. (2010). Genetic dissection of an amygdala microcircuit that gates conditioned fear. *Nature, 468*, 270. doi: 10.1038/nature09553

Havighurst, R. J. (1972). *Developmental tasks and education* (3rd ed.). New York: McKay.

Hawkins, D. I., Mothersbaugh, & Best, R. J. (2007). *Consumer behavior: Building marketing strategy* (10th ed.). Boston: McGraw-Hill/Irwin.

Haworth, C. M., Kovas, Y., Harlaar, N., Hayiou-Thomas, M. E., Petrill, S. A., Dale, P. S., et al. (2009). Generalist genes and learning disabilities: A multivariate genetic analysis of low performance in reading, mathematics, language and general cognitive ability in a sample of 8000 12-year-old twins. *Journal of Child Psychology and Psychiatry, and Allied Disciplines, 50*, 1318–1325.

Haynes, J.-D., & Rees, G. (2006). Decoding mental states from brain activity in humans. *Nature Neuroscience Review, 7*, 524–534.

Healy, M. (2010, October 5). *Americans are branching out sexually, survey finds.* Retrieved from http://www.latimes.com/health/la-sci-sex-survey-20101005,0,587370.story.

Heath, R. A. (2006). *The Praeger handbook of transsexuality: Changing gender to match mindset.* Westport, CT: Praeger Publishers.

Hebb, D. O. (1955). Drive and the CNS (central nervous system). *Psychological Review, 62*, 243–254.

Heffernan, V. (2011, January 9). Against headphones. *The New York Times Magazine*, pp. 16–17.

Hehman, E., Mania, E. W., & Gaertner, S. L. (2010). Where the division lies: Common ingroup identity moderates the cross-race facial-recognition effect. *Journal of Experimental Social Psychology*, 46, 445–448. doi:10.1016/j.jesp.2009.11.008

Heider, E. (1958). *The psychology of interpersonal relations.* New York: Wiley.

Heilbronner, C., & Berlin, I. (2005). Maternal smoking during pregnancy induces obstetrical and fetal complications but also has an impact on newborns, infants, children and adults. *European Journal of Obstetrics and Gynecology and Reproductive Biology*, 34(7 Pt 1), 679–686.

Heine, S. J., Kitayama, S., Lehman, D. R., Takata, T., Ide, E., Leung, C., et al. (2001). Divergent consequences of success and failure in Japan and North America: An investigation of self-improving motivations and malleable selves. *Journal of Personality and Social Psychology, 81*, 599–615.

Heinemann, L. A. J., Minh, T. D., Filonenko, A., & Uhl-Hochgräber, K. (2010). Explorative evaluation of the impact of severe premenstrual disorders on work absenteeism and productivity. *Women's Health Issues, 20*, 58–65. doi:10.1016/j.whi.2009.09.005

Helms, J. E. (1992). Why is there no study of culture equivalence in standardized cognitive ability testing? *American Psychologist, 47*, 1083–1101.

Helwig, C. C. (2006). Rights, civil liberties, and democracy across cultures. In M. Killen & J. G. Smetana (Eds.), *Handbook of moral development* (pp. 185–210). Mahwah, NJ: Erlbaum.

Henderlong, J., & Lepper, M. R. (2002). The effects of praise on children's intrinsic motivation: A review and synthesis. *Psychological Bulletin, 128*, 774–795.

Henrickson, H. C., Crowther, J. H., & Harrington, E. F. (2010). Ethnic identity and maladaptive eating: Expectancies about eating and thinness in African American women. *Cultural Diversity and Ethnic Minority Psychology, 16*, 87–93.

Henslee, A. M., & Coffey, S. F. (2010). Exposure therapy for posttraumatic stress disorder in a residential substance use treatment facility. *Professional Psychology: Research and Practice, 41*, 34–40. doi:10.1016/j.brat.2010.02.002

Hepper, P. G., Shahidullah, S., & White, R. (1990). Origins of fetal handedness. *Nature*, 347, 431.

Herbenick, D., Reece, M., Schick, V., Sanders, S., Dodge, B., Fortenberry, J.D. (2010). Sexual behavior in the United States: Results from a national probability sample of males and females ages 14–94. *Journal of Sexual Medicine*, 7 (suppl 5), 255–265. doi:10.1111/j.1743-6109.2010.02012.x

Hergenhahn, B. R. (1997). *An introduction to the history of psychology* (3rd ed.). Pacific Grover, CA: Brooks/Cole Publishing Co.

Heron, M. (2010) Deaths: Leading Causes for 2006 National Vital Statistics Reports, Volume 58, No. 14, March 31, 2010.

Herrington, J. D., Mohanty, A., Koven, N. S., Fisher, J. E., Stewart, J. L., Banich, M., et al. (2005). Emotion-modulated performance and activity in left dorsolateral prefrontal cortex. *Emotion, 5*, 200–207.

Herrup, K. (2010). Reimagining Alzheimer's disease—an age-based hypothesis. Journal *of Neuroscience, 30*, 16755–16762. doi: 10.1523/jneurosci.4521-10.2010

Herry, C., Ciocchi, S., Senn, V., Demmou, L, Müller, C., & Lüthi, A. (2008). Switching on and off fear by distinct neuronal circuits. *Nature* (online edition). Retrieved from http://www.nature.com/nature/journal/vaop/ncurrent/full/nature07166.html.

Hertz-Pannier, L., Chiron, C., Jambaqué, I., Renaux-Kieffer, V., Van de Moortele, P. F., Delalande, O., et al. (2002). Late plasticity for language in a child's non-dominant hemisphere: A pre- and post-surgery fMRI study. *Brain, 125*, 361–372.

Hetherington, E. M. (2006). The influence of conflict, marital problem solving and parenting on children's adjustment in nondivorced, divorced and remarried families. In A. Clarke-Stewart & J. Dunn (Eds.), *Families count:Effects on child and adolescent development* (pp. 203–237). Cambridge, UK: Cambridge University Press.

Hewstone, M., Rubin, M., & Willis, H. (2002). Intergroup bias. *Annual Review of Psychology, 53*, 575–604.

Higher Education Research Institute, UCLA Graduate School of Education & Information Studies (2011, January 26). *Incoming college students rate emotional health at record low, annual survey finds.* Retrieved from http://www.heri.ucla.edu/pr-display.php?prQry=55.

Hildebrandt, T., Alfano, L., Tricamo, M., & Pfaff, D. W. (2010). Conceptualizing the role of estrogens and serotonin in the development and maintenance of bulimia nervosa. *Clinical Psychology Review, 30*, 655–668. doi: 0.1016/j.cpr.2010.04.011

Hilgard, E. R. (1977). *Divided consciousness: Multiple controls in human thought and action.* New York: Wiley.

Hilgard, E. R. (1994). Neodissociation theory. In S. Lynn & J. W. Rhue (Eds.), *Dissociation: Clinical and theoretical perspectives.* New York: Guilford Press.

Hill, P. L., & Roberts, B. W. (2010). Propositions for the study of moral personality development. *Current Directions in Psychological Science, 19*, 380–383. doi:10.1177/0963721410389168

Hillman, J. (2008). Sexual issues and aging within the context of work with older adult patients. *Professional Psychology: Research and Practice, 39*, 290–297. doi: 10.1037/0735-7028.39.3.290

Hilmert, C. J., Kulik, J. A., & Christenfeld, N. J. S. (2006). Positive and negative opinion modeling: The influence of another's similarity and dissimilarity. *Journal of Personality and Social Psychology, 90*, 440–452.

Hilton, J. L., & von Hippel, W. (1996). Stereotypes. In J. T. Spence, J. M. Darley, & D. J. Foss (Eds.), *Annual Review of Psychology* (Vol. 47, pp. 237–271). Palo Alto, CA: Annual Reviews.

Hingson, R. W., Heeren, T., Jamanka, A., & Howland, J. (2000). Age of drinking onset and unintentional injury involvement after drinking. *Journal of the American Medical Association, 284*, 1527–1533.

Hingson, R. W., Zha, W., & Weitzmanet, E. R. (2009). Magnitude of and trends in alcohol-related mortality and morbidity among U.S. college students ages 18 to 24, 1998–2005. *Journal of Studies on Alcohol and Drugs, 16*, 12–20. doi:10.1146/annurev.publhealth.26.021304.144652

Hinrichsen, G. A. (2008). Interpersonal psychotherapy as a treatment for depression in later life. *Professional Psychology: Research and Practice, 39*, 306–312. doi: 10.1037/0735-7028.39.3.306

Hirst, W., Phelps, E. A., Buckner, R. L., Budson, A. C., Cuc, A., Gabrieli, J. D. E., . . . Vaidya C. J. (2009). Long-term memory for the terrorist attack of September 11: Flashbulb memories, event memories, and the factors that influence their retention. *Journal of Experimental Psychology: General, 138*, 161–176. doi: 2009-05547-001

Hobson, J. Allan. (1999). *Consciousness.* New York: Scientific American Library.

Hobza, D. L., & Rochlen, A. B. (2009). Gender role conflict, drive for muscularity, and the impact of ideal media portrayals on men. *Psychology of Men & Masculinity, 10*, 120–130. Doi : 10.1037/a0015040

Hoeksema van Orden, C. Y. D., Gaillard, A. W. K., & Buunk, B. P. (1998). Social loafing under fatigue. *Journal of Personality and Social Psychology, 75*, 1179–1190.

Hoelscher, C. (Ed.). (2001). *Neuronal mechanisms of memory formation: Concepts of long-term potentiation and beyond.* New York: Cambridge University Press.

Hoffman, D. D. (1999). *Visual intelligence.* New York: Norton.

Hoffman, R. R., Sherrick, M. F., & Warm, J. S. (Eds.). (1998). *Viewing psychology as a whole: The integrative science of William N. Dember.* Washington, DC: American Psychological Association.

Hoffman, S. G. (2000a). Self-focused attention before and after treatment of social phobia. *Behavior Research and Therapy, 38*, 717–725.

Hoffman, S. G. (2000b). Treatment of social phobia: Potential mediators and moderators. *Clinical Psychology: Science and Practice, 7*, 3–16.

Hofmann, S. G. (2008). Cognitive processes during fear acquisition and extinction in animals and humans: Implications for exposure therapy of anxiety disorders. *Clinical Psychology Review, 28*, 200–211.

Hofstee, W. K. B. (2003). Structures of personality traits. In T. Millon & M. J. Lerner (Eds.), *Handbook of psychology: Vol. 5. Personality and social psychology* (pp. 231–256). New York: John Wiley & Sons.

Hogan, J. (2007). A pattern of errors. In J. S. Nevid, *Psychology: Concepts and applications* (2nd ed.) (p. 368). Boston: Houghton Mifflin.

Holden, C. (2009, July). A face for Phineas Gage. *Science, 325*, p. 521.

Holden, C. (2010, February 26). Experts map the terrain of mood disorders. *Science, 327*, 1068. doi: 10.1126/science.327.5969.1068-a

Holland, A. S., & Roisman, G. (2010). Adult attachment security and young adults' dating relationships over time: Self-reported, observational, and physiological evidence. *Developmental Psychology, 46*, 552–557. doi: 10.1037/a0018542

Holland, R. W., Hendriks, M., & Aarts, H. (2005). Smells like clean spirit: Nonconscious effects of scent on cognition and behavior. *Psychological Science, 16*, 689–693.

Holma, K. M., Melartin, T. K., Haukka, J., Holma, I. A. K., Sokero, T. P., & Isometsä, E. T. (2010). Incidence and predictors of suicide attempts in DSM–IV major depressive disorder: A five-year prospective study. *American Journal of Psychiatry, 167*, 801–808.

Holroyd, K. A. (2002). Assessment and psychological management of recurrent headache disorders. *Journal of Consulting and Clinical Psychology, 70*, 656–677.

Holt, N. L., & Tamminen, K A. (2010). Moving forward with grounded theory in sport and exercise psychology. *Psychology of Sport and Exercise, 11*, 419–422. doi:10.1016/j.psychsport.2010.07.009. |

Holt, C. L., Clark, E. M., & Kreuter, M. W. (2001). Weight locus of control and weight-related attitudes and behaviors in an overweight population. *Addictive Behaviors, 26*, 329–340.

Hölzela, B. K., Carmody, J., Vangel, M., Congleton, C., Yerramsetti, S. M., Garda, T., et al. (2011). Mindfulness practice leads to increases in regional brain gray matter density. *Psychiatry Research, 191*, 36–43. doi:10.1016/j.pscychresns.2010.08.006

Holzinger, B., LaBerge, S., & Levitan, L. (2006). Psychophysiological correlates of lucid dreaming. *Dreaming, 16*, 88–95.

Holzman, L. (2009). *Vygotsky at work and play*. New York: Routledge/Taylor & Francis Group.

Hongpaisan, J., Sun, M.-K., & Alkon, D. L. (2011). PKC ε activation prevents synaptic loss, Aβ elevation, and cognitive deficits in Alzheimer's Disease transgenic mice. *Journal of Neuroscience, 31*, 630–643. doi: 10.1523/JNEUROSCI.5209-10.2011

Hopkin, M. (2008, May 5). Fat cell numbers stay constant through adult life. *Nature News*. Retrieved from http://www.nature.com/news/2008/080505/full/news.2008.800.html doi:10.1038/news.2008.800

Hopkins, W. D., & Cantalupo, C. (2008). Theoretical speculations on the evolutionary origins of hemispheric specialization. *Current Directions in Psychological Science, 17*, 2133–237. 10.1111/j.1467-8721.2008.00581.x

Hopko, D. R., Bell, J. L., Armento, M., Robertson, S., Mullane, C., Wolf, N., et al. (2007). Cognitive-behavior therapy for depressed cancer patients in a medical care setting. *Behavior Therapy, 39*, 126–36.

Horn, J. (2001). Raymond Bernard Cattell (1905–1998). *American Psychologist, 56*, 71–72.

Horn, J. L., & Noll, J. (1997). Human cognitive capabilities: Gf-Gc theory. In D. P. Flanagan, J. L. Genshaft, & P. L. Harrison (Eds.), *Contemporary intellectual assessment: Theories, tests, and issues* (pp. 53–91). New York: Guilford Press.

Horrell, S. C. V. (2008). Effectiveness of cognitive-behavioral therapy with adult ethnic minority clients: A review. *Professional Psychology: Research and Practice, 39*, 160–168. doi: 10.1037/0735-7028.39.2.160

Hossain, P., Kawar, B., & El Nahas, M. (2007). Obesity and diabetes in the developing world—a growing challenge. *New England Journal of Medicine, 356*, 213–215.

Hothersall, D. (1995). *History of psychology* (3rd ed.) New York: McGraw-Hill.

Houry, D. (2004). Suicidal patients in the emergency department: Who is at greatest risk? *Annals of Emergency Medicine, 43*, 731–732.

Houston, D. M., & Jusczyk, P. W. (2003). Infants' long-term memory for the sound patterns of words and voices. *Journal of Experimental Psychology:Human Perception and Performance, 29*, 1143–1154.

Hsee, C. K., Hastie, R, & Chen, J. (2008). Hedonomics: Bridging decision research with happiness research. *Perspectives on Psychological Science, 3*, 224–243. doi: 10.1111/j.1745-6924.2008.00076.x

Hu, F. B., Stampfer, M. J., Manson, J. E., Grodstein, F., Colditz, G. A., Speizer, F. E., et al. (2000). Trends in the incidence of coronary heart disease and changes in diet and lifestyle in women. *New England Journal of Medicine, 343*, 530–537.

Hu, M.-C., Davies, M., & Kandel, D. B. (2006). Epidemiology and correlates of daily smoking and nicotine dependence among young adults in the United States. *American Journal of Public Health, 96*, 299–308.

Huang, L, Galinsky, A. D., Gruenfeld, D. H., & Guillory, L. E (2011). Powerful postures versus powerful roles: which is the proximate correlate of thought and behavior? *Psychological Science, Psychological Science, 22*, 95–102. doi: 10.1177/0956797610391912

Hubel, D. H. (1988). *Eye, brain, and vision*. New York: Scientific American Library.

Hubel, D. H., & Wiesel, T. N. (1979). Brain mechanisms of vision. *Scientific American, 241*, 130–144.

Huber, R., Ghilardi, M. F., Massimini, M., & Tononi, G. (2004). Local sleep and learning. *Nature, 430*, 78–81.

Hudson, J. I., Hiripi, E., Pope, H. G., Jr., & Kessler, R. C. (2006). Prevalence and correlates of eating disorders in the National Comorbidity Survey Replication. *Biological Psychiatry, 61*, 348–358.

Hudson, J. I., Mangweth, B., Pope, H. G., Jr., De Col, C., Hausmann, A., Gutweniger, S., et al. (2003). Family study of affective spectrum disorder. *Archives of General Psychiatry, 60*, 170–177.

Huerta, M., Cortina, L. M., Pang, J. S., Torges, C. M., & Magley, V. J. (2006). Sex and power in the academy: Modeling sexual harassment in the lives of college women. *Personality and Social Psychology Bulletin, 32*, 616–628.

Huesmann, L. R. (2010). Nailing the coffin shut on doubts that violent video games stimulate aggression: Comment on Anderson et al. (2010). *Psychological Bulletin, 136*, 179–181.

Huesmann, L. R., Moise-Titus, J., Podolski, C.-L., & Eron, L. D. (2003). Longitudinal relations between children's exposure to TV violence and their aggressive and violent behavior in young adulthood: 1977–1992. *Developmental Psychology, 39*, 201–221.

Huey, E. D., Krueger, F., & Grafman, J. (2006). Representations in the human prefrontal cortex. *Current Directions in Psychological Science, 15*, 167–171.

Huff, N. C., Frank, M., Wright-Hardesty, K., Sprunger, D., Matus-Amat, P., Higgins, E., et al. (2006). Amygdala regulation of immediate-early gene expression in the hippocampus induced by contextual fear conditioning. *Journal of Neuroscience, 26*, 1616–1623.

Hull, C. L. (1943). *Principles of behavior*. New York: Appleton-Century-Crofts.

Hull, C. L. (1952). *A behavior system*. New Haven: Yale University Press.

Hunt, M. (1993). *The story of psychology*. New York: Anchor Books.

Huntjens, R. J. C., Peters, M. L., Postma, A., Woertman, L., Effting, M., & van der Hart, O. (2005). Transfer of newly acquired stimulus valence between identities in dissociative identity disorder (DID). *Behaviour Research and Therapy, 43*, 243–255.

Hustad, J. T. P., Barnett, N. P., Borsari, B., & Jackson, K. (2010). Web-based interventions for college student drinkers: A randomized controlled trial. *Addictive Behaviors, 35*, 183–189.

Huston, A. C., &. Wright, J. C. (1996). Television and socialization of young children. In T. M. MacBeth (Ed.), *Tuning in to young viewers: Social science perspectives on television* (pp. 37–60). Thousand Oaks, CA: Sage.

Hutchinson, J. G., & Williams, P. G. (2007). Neuroticism, daily hassles, and depressive symptoms: An examination of moderating and mediating effects. *Personality and Individual Differences, 42* (7), 1367–1378.

Hutchinson, J. G., & Williams, P. G. (2007). Neuroticism, daily hassles, and depressive symptoms: An examination of moderating and mediating effects. *Personality and Individual Differences, 42*, 1367–1378.

Hutchison, R. M., Chidiac, P., Leung, L. S. (2009). Hippocampal long-term potentiation is enhanced in urethane-anesthetized RGS2 knockoyut mice. *Hippocampus, 19*, 687–691.

Hwang, W.-C. (2006). The psychotherapy adaptation and modification framework: Application to Asian Americans. *American Psychologist, 61*, 702–715.

Hyde, J. S, Mezulis, A. H., & Abramson, L. Y. (2008). The ABCs of depression: Integrating affective, biological, and cognitive models to explain the emergence of the gender difference in depression. *Psychological Review, 115*, 291–313.

Hyde, J. S. (2005). The genetics of sexual orientation. In J. S. Hyde (Ed.), *Biological substrates of human sexuality* (pp. 9–20). Washington, DC: American Psychological Association.

Hyde, J. S., Lindberg, S. M., Linn, M. C., Ellis, A. B., & Williams, C. C. (2008). Gender similarities characterize math performance. *Science, 321*, 494–495. doi: 10.1126/science.1160364

Hyde, J.S. (2007). New directions in the study of gender similarities and differences. *Current Directions in Psychological Science, 16*, 259–263.

Hyde, Z., Flicker, L., Hankey, G. J., Almeida, O. P., McCaul, K. A., Chubb, S. A. P., et al. (2010). Prevalence of sexual activity and associated factors in men aged 75 to 95 years: A cohort study. *Annals of Internal Medicine, 153*, 693–702.

Hyman, R. (2010). Meta-analysis that conceals more than it reveals: Comment on Storm et al. (2010). *Psychological Bulletin, 136*, 486–490. doi: 10.1037/a0019676

Hyman, S. E. (2011). The meaning of the Human Genome Project for neuropsychiatric disorders. *Science, 331*, 1026. doi: 10.1126/science.1203544

In the year 2040—1.3 billion senior citizens. (2009, July 20). Retrieved from http://www.msnbc.msn.com/id/32007564/ns/health-aging/.

Inglehart, R., Foa, F., Peterson, C., & Welzel, C. (2008). Development, freedom, and rising happiness: A global perspective (1981–2007). *Perspectives on Psychological Science, 3*, 264–285. doi: 10.1111/j.1745-6924.2008.00078.x

Instant recall. (2000, February 14). *Newsweek*, p. 8.

International Schizophrenia Consortium, Purcell, S. M, Wray, N. R., Stone, J. L, Visscher, P. M., O'Donovan, M. C., et al. (2009). Common polygenic variation contributes to risk of schizophrenia and bipolar disorder. *Nature, 460*, 748–752. doi:10.1038/nature08185

Irwin, C. E., Jr. (2005). Pubertal timing: Is there any new news? *Journal of Adolescent Health, 37*, 343–344.

Isaacson, W. (2007). *Einstein: His life and universe*. New York: Simon & Schuster.

Isay, R. A. (1990). Psychoanalytic theory and the therapy of gay men. In D. P. McWhirter, S. A. Saers, & J. M. Reinisch (Eds.), *Homosexuality/heterosexuality:Concepts of sexual orientation* (pp. 283–303). New York: Oxford University Press.

Izard, C. E. (2007). Basic emotions, natural kinds, emotion schemas, and a new paradigm. *Perspectives on Psychological Science, 2*, 260–280.

Jacob, G. H., & Nathans, J. (2009, March). Color vision: how our eyes reflect primate evolution. *Scientific American*. Retrieved from http://www.sciam.com/article.cfm?id=evolution-of-primate-color-vision

Jacobi, C., Hayward, C., de Zwaan, M., Kraemer, H. C., & Agras, W. S. (2004). Coming to terms with risk factors for eating disorders: Application of risk terminology and suggestions for a general taxonomy. *Psychological Bulletin, 130*, 19–65.

Jacoby, L. L., & Rhode, M. G. (2006). False remembering in the aged. *Current Directions in Psychological Science, 15*, 49–53.

Jaffe, E (2007, May). Mirror neurons: How we reflect on behavior. *APS Observer, 20*(5), 20–23.

Jaffee, S., & Hyde, J. S. (2000). Gender differences in moral orientation: A meta-analysis. *Psychological Bulletin, 126*, 703–726.

Jahnke, C. J., & Nowaczyk, R. H. (1998). *Cognition*. Upper Saddle River, NJ: Prentice-Hall.

James, W. (1890/1970). *The principles of psychology* (Vol. 1). New York: Holt.

Jan, J. E., Reiter, R., J., Wasdell, M. B., & Bax, M. (2009). The role of the thalamus in sleep, pineal melatonin production, and circadian rhythm sleep disorders. *Journal of Pineal Research, 46*, 1–7. doi: 10.1111/j.1600-079X.2008.00628.x

Jang, K. L., Livesley, W. J., Ando, J., Yamagata, S., Suzuki, A., Angleitner, A., et al. (2006). Behavioral genetics of the higher-order factors of the Big Five. *Personality and Individual Differences, 41*, 261–272.

Janis, I. L. (1997). Groupthink. In R. P. Vecchio (Ed.), *Leadership: Understanding the dynamics of power and influence in organizations* (pp. 163–176). Notre Dame: University of Notre Dame Press.

Jankowiak, W. R., & Fischer, E. F. (1992). A cross-cultural perspective on romantic love. *Ethnology, 31*, 149–155.

Javier, R. (2010). Acculturation and changing roles. In J. S. Nevid & S. A. Rathus, *Psychology and the challenges of life: Adjustment and growth* (p. 336). Hoboken, NJ: John Wiley & Sons.

Jay, M. S. (2006). The tempo of puberty. *The Journal of Pediatrics, 148*, 732–733.

Jee, S. H., Sull, J. W., Park, J., Lee, S.-Y., Ohrr, H., Guallar, E., et al. (2006). Body-mass index and mortality in Korean men and women. *New England Journal of Medicine, 355*, 779–787.

Jefferson, D. J. (2005, August 8). America's most dangerous drug. *Newsweek*, pp. 41–48.

Jenkins, L., Myerson, J., Joerding, J. A., & Hale, S. (2000). Converging evidence that visuospatial cognition is more age-sensitive than verbal cognition. *Psychology and Aging, 15*, 157–175.

Jensen, M. P. (2008). The neurophysiology of pain perception and hypnotic analgesia: implications for clinical practice. *The American Journal of Clinical Hypnosis, 25*, 123–148.

Ji, D., & Wilson, M. A. (2007). Coordinated memory replay in the visual cortex and hippocampus during sleep. *Nature Neuroscience, 10*, 100–107.

Jiang, H., & Chess, L. (2006). Regulation of immune responses by T Cells. *New England Journal of Medicine, 354*, 1166–1176.

Joe, S., Baser, E., Breeden, G., Neighbors, H. W., & Jackson, J. S. (2006). Prevalence of and risk factors for lifetime suicide attempts among blacks in the United States. *Journal of the American Medical Association, 296*, 2112–2123.

Johansson, P., Høglend, P., Ulberg, R., Amlo, S., Marble, A., Bøgwald, K.-P., et al (2010). The mediating role of insight for long-term improvements in psychodynamic therapy. *Journal of Consulting and Clinical Psychology, 78*, 438–448. doi: 10.1037/a0019245

Johnson, C. K. (2010). *1 in 5 U.S. teens has hearing loss, new study says*. Retrieved from http://www.msnbc.msn.com/id/38742752/ns/health-kids_and_parenting/.

Johnson, D. F. (2000). Cultivating the field of psychology: Psychological journals at the turn of the century and beyond. *American Psychologist, 55*, 1144–1147.

Johnson, J. G., Cohen, P., Chen, H., Kasen, S., & Brook, J. S. (2006). Parenting behaviors associated with risk for offspring personality disorder during adulthood. *Archives of General Psychiatry, 63*, 579–587.

Johnson, J., Wood, A. M., Gooding, P., Taylor, P., & Tarrier, N. (2011). Resilience to suicidality: The buffering hypothesis. *Clinical Psychology Review, 31*, 563–591. doi:10.1016/j.cpr.2010.12.007

Johnson, M. K., Rowatt, W. C., Barnard-Brak, L. M., Patock-Peckham, J. A., LaBouff, J. P., & Carlisle, R. D. (2011). A mediational analysis of the role of right-wing authoritarianism and religious fundamentalism in the religiosity–prejudice link. *Personality and Individual Differences, 50*, 851–856. doi:10.1016/j.paid.2011.01.010

Johnson, S. C., Dweck, C. S., & Chen, F. S. (2007). Evidence for infants' internal working models of attachment. *Psychological Science, 18*, 501–502.

Johnson, W., Bouchard, T.J., McGue, M., Segal, N.L., Tellegen, A., Keyes, M., et al (2007). Genetic and environmental influences on the Verbal-Perceptual-Image Rotation (VPR) model of the structure of mental abilities in the Minnesota study of twins reared apart. *Intelligence, 35*, 542–562. doi:10.1016/j.intell.2006.10.003

Johnson, W., Nijenhuis, J. T. & Bouchard, T.J. (2008). Still just 1 g: Consistent results from five test batteries. *Intelligence, 36*, 81–95. doi:10.1016/j.intell.2007.06.001

Johnson, W., Turkheimer, E., Gottesman, I. I., & Bouchard, T. J., Jr. (2009). Beyond heritability: Twin studies in behavioral research. *Current Directions in Psychological Science, 18*, 217–220.

Johnston, L D., et al. (2010b). Monitoring the Future, National Survey Results on Drug Use: Overview of key findings, 2009 (NIH Publication No. 10-7583). Bethesda, MD: National Institute on Drug Abuse, May 2010.

Johnston, L. D., et al. (2010a) Marijuana use is rising; Ecstasy use is beginning to rise; and alcohol use is declining among U.S. teens. University of Michigan News Service: Ann Arbor, MI, December 14, 2010, http://www.monitoringthefuture.org.

Johnston, L. D., O'Malley, P. M., & Bachman, J. G. (2001). *Monitoring the future: National survey results on drug use, 1975–2000. Vol. II: College student and adults ages 19–40*. (NIH Publication No. 01-4925). Bethesda, MD: National Institute on Drug Abuse.

Johnston, L. D., O'Malley, P. M., Bachman, J. G., & Schulenberg, J. E. (2004). Monitoring the future: National survey results on drug use, 1975B2003. Volume II: College Students and Adults Ages 19B45 (NIH Publication No. 04_5508). Bethesda, MD: National Institute on Drug Abuse.

Jones, E. E. (1998). Major developments in five decades of social psychology. In D. T. Gilbert, S. T. Fiske, & G. Lindzey (Eds.), *The handbook of social psychology* (4th ed., Vol. 1, pp. 1–57). Boston: McGraw-Hill.

Jones, J. T., Pelham, B. W., Carvallo, M., & Mirenberg, M. C. (2004). How do I love thee? Let me count the Js: Implicit egotism and interpersonal attraction. *Journal of Personality and Social Psychology, 87*, 665–683.

Jonides, J., Lacey, S. C., & Nee, D. E. (2005). Processes of working memory in mind and brain. *Current Directions in Psychological Science, 14*, 2–5.

Jorgensen, G. (2006). Kohlberg and Gilligan: Duet or duel? *Journal of Moral Education, 35*, 179–196.

Joseph, J. E., Liu, X., Jiang, Y., Lynam, D., & Kelly, T. H. (2009). Neural correlates of emotional reactivity in sensation seeking. *Psychological Science, 20*, 215–223. doi: 10.1111/j.1467-9280.2009.02283.x

Joyce, N., & Baker, D. B. (2008, July/August). The early days of sport psychology. *Monitor on Psychology, 39*(7), 28–29.

Judge, D. E. (2007, February 1). Explaining the decline in teen pregnancy. *Journal Watch Women's Health*. Retrieved from http:// womens-health.jwatch.org/cgi/content/full/2007/201/4?qetocAPN/.

Judge, T A., & Cable, D. M. (2004). Income: Preliminary test of a theoretical model. *Journal of Applied Psychology, 89*, 428–441.

Judge, T. A., & Ilies, R. (2002). Relationship of personality to performance motivation: A meta-analytic review. *Journal of Applied Psychology, 87*, 797–807.

Judge, T. A., Heller, D., & Mount, M. K. (2002). Five-Factor Model of personality and job satisfaction: A meta-analysis. *Journal of Applied Psychology, 87*, 530–541.

Jung, J., Forbes, G. B., & Chan, P. (2010). Global body and muscle satisfaction among college men in the United States and Hong Kong-China. *Sex Roles, 63*, 104–117. doi: 10.1007/s11199-010-9760

Jussim, L., & Eccles, J. S. (1992). Teacher expectations II: Construction and reflection of student achievement. *Journal of Personality and Social Psychology, 63*, 947–961.

Just, N., Abramson, L. Y., & Alloy, L. B. (2001). Remitted depression studies as tests of the cognitive vulnerability hypotheses of depression onset. A critique and conceptual analysis. *Clinical Psychology Review, 21*, 63–83.

Kabat-Zinn, J. (2003). Mindfulness-based interventions in context: Past, present, and future. *Clinical Psychology: Science and Practice, 10*, 144–156.

Kagan, J. (1997). Biology and the child. In W. Damon (Editor-in-Chief) & N. Eisenberg (Vol. Ed.), *Handbook of child psychology: 5th ed., Vol. 3. Social, emotional, and personality development* (pp. 177–236). New York: John Wiley & Sons.

Kahneman, D., & Klein, G. (2009). Conditions for intuitive expertise: A failure to disagree. *American Psychologist, 64*, 515–526.

Kahneman, D., & Deaton, A. (2010). High income improves evaluation of life but not emotional well-being. *Proceedings of the National Academy of Sciences*, 107, 16489–16493.

Kahneman, D., & Frederick, S. (2005). A model of heuristic judgment. In K. J. Holyoak & R. G. Morrison (Eds.), *The Cambridge handbook of thinking and reasoning* (pp. 267–293). Cambridge, UK: Cambridge University Press.

Kahneman, D., Krueger, A. B., Schkade, D., Schwarz, N., & Stone, A. A. (2006). Would you be happier if you were richer? A focusing illusion. *Science, 312*, 1908–1910.

Kaiser, C. R., Vick, S. B., & Major, B. (2006). Prejudice expectations moderate preconscious attention to cues that are threatening to social identity. *Psychological Science, 17*, 332–338.

Kalechstein, A. D., & Nowicki, S., Jr. (1997). A meta-analytic examination of the relationship between control expectancies and academic achievement: An 11-year follow-up. *Genetic, Social, and General Psychology Monographs, 123*, 27–56.

Kandel, D. B. (2003). Does marijuana use cause the use of other drugs? *Journal of the American Medical Association, 289*, 482–483.

Kanin, G. (1981). *It takes a long time to become young*. New York: Berkley.

Kantrowitz, B., & Springen, K. (2003, September 22). Why sleep matters. *Newsweek*, pp. 75–77.

Kantrowitz, B., & Wingert, P. (1999, October 18). The truth about teens. *Newsweek*, pp. 62–72.

Kaplan, P. S. (2000). *A child's odyssey: Child and adolescent development* (3rd ed.). Belmont, CA: Wadsworth.

Kappe, R., & van der Flier, H. (2010). Using multiple and specific criteria to assess the predictive validity of the Big Five personality factors on academic performance. *Journal of Research in Personality, 44*, 142–145. doi:10.1016/j.jrp.2009.11.002

Karlsgodt, K. H., Sun, D., & Cannon, T. D. (2010). Structural and functional brain abnormalities in schizophrenia. *Current Directions in Psychological Science, 19*, 226–231.

Karremans, J. C., Stroebe, W., & Claus, J. (2005). Beyond Vicary's fantasies: The impact of subliminal priming and brand choice. *Journal of Experimental Social Psychology*, Retrieved from http://www.science direct.com.

Katon, W. J. (2006). Panic disorder. *New England Journal of Medicine, 354*, 2360–2367.

Kaufman, J. C., Agars, M. D., & Lopez-Wagner, M. C. (2008). The role of personality and motivation in predicting early college academic success in non-traditional students at a Hispanic-serving institution. *Learning and Individual Differences, 18*, 492–496.

Kay, A. B. (2006). Natural killer T cells and asthma. *New England Journal of Medicine, 354*, 1186–1188.

Kaye, W., (2009). Eating disorders: Hope despite mortal risk. *American Journal of Psychiatry, 166*, 139–1311. doi: 10.1176/appi.ajp.2009.09101424

Keating, C. F., Randall, D., Kendrick, T., & Gutshall, K. (2003). Do babyfaced adults receive more help? The (cross-cultural) case of the lost resume. *Journal of Nonverbal Behavior, 27*, 89–109.

Keller, M. C., Fredrickson, B. L., Ybarra, O., Côté, S., Johnson, K., Mikels, J., et al. (2005). A warm heart and a clear head: the contingent effects of weather on mood and cognition. *Psychological Science, 16*, 724–731.

Kelsoe, J. R. (2010). A gene for impulsivity. *Nature 468*, 1049–1050. doi:10.1038/4681049a

Kemeny, M. E. (2003). The psychobiology of stress. *Current Directions in Psychological Science, 12*, 124–129.

Kempton, M. J., Stahl, D., Williams, S. C. R., & DeLisi, L. E. (2010). Progressive lateral ventricular enlargement in schizophrenia: A meta-analysis of longitudinal MRI studies. *Schizophrenia Research, 120*, 54–62.

Kendler, K. S. (2005a). "A gene for . . .": The nature of gene action in psychiatric disorders. *American Journal of Psychiatry,162*, 1243–1252.

Kendler, K. S. (2005a). Psychiatric genetics: A methodologic critique. *American Journal of Psychiatry, 162*, 3–11.

Kendler, K. S. (2005b). "A gene for . . .": The nature of gene action in psychiatric disorders. *American Journal of Psychiatry, 162*, 1243–1252.

Kendler, K. S. (2005b). Psychiatric genetics: A methodologic critique. *American Journal of Psychiatry, 162*, 3–11.

Kendler, K. S., & Gardner, C. O. (2010). Dependent stressful life events and prior depressive episodes in the prediction of major depression: The problem of causal inference in psychiatric epidemiology. *Archives of General Psychiatry, 67*, 1120–1127. doi:10.1001/archgenpsychiatry.2010.136

Kendler, K. S., Myers, J. M., & Neale, M. C. (2000). A multidimensional twin study of mental health in women. *American Journal of Psychiatry, 157*, 506–513.

Kendler, K. S., Schmitt, E., Aggen, S. H., & Prescott, C. A. (2008). Genetic and environmental influences on alcohol, caffeine, cannabis, and nicotine use from early adolescence to middle adulthood. *Archives of General Psychiatry, 65*, 674–682.

Kennedy, S. H., Milev, R., Giacobbe, P., Ramasubbu, R., Lam, R. W., Parikh, S. V., et al. (2009). Canadian Network for Mood and Anxiety Treatments (CANMAT) clinical guidelines for the management of major depressive disorder in adults. *Journal of Affective Disorders, 117*, S44–S53.doi: 10.1111/j.1399-5618.2006.00432.x

Kenrick, D. T., Griskevicius, V., Neuberg, S. L., & Schaller, M. (2010). Renovating the pyramid of needs: contemporary extensions built upon ancient foundations. *Perspectives on Psychological Science, 5*, 292–314. doi:10.1177/1745691610369469

Kern, M. L., & Friedman, H. S. (2008). Do conscientious individuals live longer? A quantitative review. *Health Psychology, 27*, 505–512. doi: 10.1037/0278-6133.27.5.505

Kernberg, O. F. (1975). *Borderline conditions and pathological narcissism*. New York: Jason Aronson.

Kernberg, O. F., & Michels, R. (2009). Borderline personality disorder. *American Journal of Psychiatry, 166*, 505–508.

Kerns, K. A., & Richardson, R. A. (2005). *Attachment in middle childhood*. New York: Guilford.

Kerr, N. H., & Homhoff, G. W. (2004). Do the blind literally "see" in their dreams? A critique of a recent claim that they do. *Dreaming, 14*, 230–233.

Kerr, N. L., & Tindale, R. S. (2004). Group performance and decision making. *Annual Review of Psychology, 55*, 623–655.

Kesebir, P., & Diener, E. (2008). In pursuit of happiness: Empirical answers to philosophical questions. *Perspectives on Psychological Science, 3*, 117–125. Doi: 10.1111/j.1745-6916.2008.00069.x

Kessler, R. C., Berglund, P. A., Demler, O., Jin, R., & Walters, E. E. (2005). Lifetime prevalence and age-of-onset distributions of DSM-IV disorders in the National Comorbidity Survey Replication (NCS-R). *Archives of General Psychiatry, 62*, 593–602.

Kessler, R. C., Chiu, W. T., Demler, O., & Walters, E. E. (2005). Prevalence, severity, and comorbidity of 12-month DSM-IV disorders in the National Comorbidity Survey Replication. *Archives of General Psychiatry, 62*, 617–627.

Kessler, R. C., McGonagle, K. A., Zhao, S., & Nelson, C. B. (1994). Lifetime and 12-month prevalence of DSM-III-R psychiatric disorders in the United States: Results from the National Comorbidity Survey. *Archives of General Psychiatry, 51*, 8–19.

Keysers, C., Wicker, B., Gazzola, V., Anton, J.-L., Fogassi, L., & Gallese, V. (2004). A touching sight: SII/PV Activation during the observation and experience of touch. *Neuron, 42*, 335–346.

Khaw, K. T., Wareham, N., Bingham, S., Welch, A., Luben, R., & Day, N. (2008). Combined impact of health behaviours and mortality in men and women: the EPIC-Norfolk Prospective Population study. *PLoS Med, 5*(1), e12. http://medicine.plosjournals.org/perlserv/?request=get-document&doi=10.1371/journal.pmed.0050012.

Kiecolt-Glaser, J. K., Bane, C., Glaser, R., & Malarkey, W. B. (2003). Love, marriage, and divorce: Newlyweds' stress hormones foreshadow relationship changes. *Journal of Consulting and Clinical Psychology, 71*, 176–188.

Kiecolt-Glaser, J. K., Marucha, P. T., Atkinson, C., & Glaser, R. (2001). Hypnosis as a modulator of cellular immune dysregulation during acute stress. *Journal of Consulting and Clinical Psychology, 69*, 674–682.

Kiecolt-Glaser, J. K., McGuire, L, Robles, T. F., & Glaser, R. (2002). Emotions, morbidity, and mortality: New perspectives from psychoneuroimmunology. *Annual Review of Psychology, 53*, 83–107.

Kiecolt-Glaser, J. K., Preacher, K. J., MacCallum, R. C., Atkinson, C., Malarkey, W. B., & Glaser, R. (2003). Chronic stress and age-related increases in the proinflammatory cytokine IL-6. *Proceedings of the National Academy of Sciences, 100*, 9090–9095.

Kiefer, A. K., & Sekaquaptewa, D. (2007). Implicit stereotypes and women's math performance: How implicit gender-math stereotypes influence women's susceptibility to stereotype threat. *Psychological Science, 18*, 13–18.

Kiehl, K A., Bates, A. T., Laurens, K. R., Hare, R. D., & Liddle, P. F. (2006). Brain potentials implicate temporal lobe abnormalities in criminal psychopaths. *Journal of Abnormal Psychology, 115*, 443–453.

Kieseppä, T., Eerola, M., Mäntylä, R., Neuvonen, T., Poutanen, V.-P., Luoma, K., Tuulio-Henrikssona, A., Isometsä, E. (2010). Major depressive disorder and white matter abnormalities. *Journal of Affective Disorders, 120*, 240–244. http://www.sciencedirect.com/science/journal/01650327http://dx.doi.org/10.1016/j.jad.2009.04.023

Kiesner, J. (2009). Physical characteristics of the menstrual cycle and premenstrual depressive symptoms. *Psychological Science, 20*, 763–770.

Kihlstrom, J. F. (2005). Is hypnosis an altered state of consciousness or what? *Contemporary Hypnosis, 22*, 34–38.

Kilgore, K., Snyder, J., & Lentz, C. (2000). The contribution of parental discipline, parental monitoring, and school risk to early-onset conduct problems in African American boys and girls. *Developmental Psychology, 36*, 835–845.

Killingsworth, M., A, & Gilbert, D. T. (2010). A wandering mind is an unhappy mind. *Science, 330*, 932. doi: 10.1126/science.1192439

Kim, B. S. K., Brenner, B. R., Liang, C. T. H., & Asay, P. A. (2003). A qualitative study of adaptation experiences of 1.5-generation Asian Americans. *Cultural Diversity and Ethnic Minority Psychology, 9*, 156–170.

Kim, H. S., & Sherman, D. K. (2007). "Express yourself": Culture and the effect of self expression on choice. *Journal of Personality and Social Psychology, 92*, 1–11.

Kim, J. J., & Jung, M. W. (2006). Neural circuits and mechanisms involved in Pavlovian fear conditioning: A critical review. *Neuroscience and Biobehavioral Reviews, 30*, 188–202.

Kim, K. H. (2005). Can only intelligent people be creative? A meta-analysis. *Journal of Secondary Gifted Education, 16*, 57–66.

Kimchi, R., & Peterson, M. A. (2008). Figure-ground segmentation can occur without attention. *Psychological Science, 19*, 660–668. doi: 10.1111/j.1467-9280.2008.02140.x

Kim-Cohen, J., & Gold, A. L. (2009). Measured gene–environment interactions and mechanisms promoting resilient development. *Current Directions in Psychological Science, 18*, 138–142. doi: 10.1111/j.1467-8721.2009.01624.x

Kimura, D. (1992). Sex differences in the brain. *Scientific American, 267*(3), 118–125.

King, D. E., Mainous III, A. G., & Geesey, M. E. (2008). Adopting moderate alcohol consumption in middle age: Subsequent cardiovascular events. *American Journal of Medicine, 121*, 201–206.

King, D. E., Mainous, A. G., Carnemolla, M., & Everett, C. J. (2009). Adherence to healthy lifestyle habits in US adults, 1988–2006. *American Journal of Medicine, 122*, 528–534.

King, J. W., & Suzman, R. (2008). Prospects for improving cognition throughout the life course. *Psychological Science in the Public Interest, 9*, i –iii. doi : 10.1111/j.1539-6053.2009.01033.x

King, S., St-Hilaire, A., & Heidkamp, D. (2010). Prenatal factors in schizophrenia. *Current Directions in Psychological Science, 19*, 209–213. doi: 10.1177/0963721410378360

Kinsey, A. C., Pomeroy, W. B., & Martin, C. E. (1948). *Sexual behavior in the human male*. Philadelphia: W. B. Saunders.

Kinsey, A. C., Pomeroy, W. B., Martin, C. E., & Gebhard, P. H. (1953). *Sexual behavior in the human female*. Philadelphia: W. B. Saunders.

Kirp, D. L. (2006, July 23). After the Bell curve. *The New York Times Magazine*, pp. 5–16.

Kirsch, I. (1996). Hypnotic enhancement of cognitive-behavioral weight loss treatments: Another meta-reanalysis. *Journal of Consulting and Clinical Psychology, 64*, 517–519.

Kirsch, I. (2004). Conditioning, expectancy, and the placebo effect: Comment on Stewart-Williams and Podd (2004). *Psychological Bulletin, 130*, 341–343.

Kirsch, I., & Lynn, S. J. (1995). Altered state of hypnosis: Changes in the theoretical landscape. *American Psychologist, 50*, 846–858.

Kisilevsky, B. S., Hains, S. M. J., Lee, K., Xie, X., Huang, H., Ye, H-H., et al. (2003). Effects of experience on fetal voice recognition. *Psychological Science, 14*, 220–224.

Kissane, D. W., Grabasch, B., Clarke, D. M., Smith, G. C., Love, A. W., Bloch, S., et al. (2007). Supportive-expressive group therapy for women with metastatic breast cancer: Survival and psychosocial outcome from a randomized controlled trial. *Psycho-Oncology, 16*, 277–286.

Kitayama, S., Duffy, S., Kawamura, T., & Larsen, J. T. (2003). Perceiving an object and its context in different cultures: A cultural look at new look. *Psychological Science, 14*, 201–206.

Klar, A. J. S. (2003). Human handedness and scalp hair whorl direction develop from a common genetic mechanism. *Genetics, 165*, 269–276.

Klass, P. (2011, March 8). On the left hand, answers aren't easy. *The New York Times,* pp. D1, D6.

Kleinman, A. (1987). Anthropology and psychiatry: The role of culture in cross-cultural research on illness. *British Journal of Psychiatry, 151,* 447–454.

Kleinspehn-Ammerlahn, A., Riediger, M., Schmiedek, F., von Oertzen, Timo, T., Li, S.-C., et al. (2011). Dyadic drumming across the lifespan reveals a zone of proximal development in children. *Developmental Psychology, 47,* 632–644. doi: 10.1037/a0021818

Kliegel, M., Mackinlay, R., & Jäger, T. (2008). Complex prospective memory: Development across the lifespan and the role of task interruption. *Developmental Psychology, 44,* 612–617. doi: 2008-02379-026

Klinesmith, J., Kasser, T., & McAndrew, F. T. (2006). Guns, testosterone, and aggression: An experimental test of a meditational hypothesis. *Psychological Science, 17,* 568–571.

Kluger, J. (2003, October 26). Medicating young minds. *Time Magazine Online,* Retrieved from http://www.time.com/time/magazine/ article/0,9171,1101031103-526331,00.html.

Kluger, J., & Masters, C. (2006, August 28). How to spot a liar. *Time Magazine,* pp. 46–48.

Knafo, A., Iervolino, A. C., & Plomin, R. (2005). Masculine girls and feminine boys: Genetic and environmental contributions to atypical gender development in early childhood. *Journal of Personality & Social Psychology, 88,* 400–412.

Knoblauch, S. (2009). From self-psychology to selves in relationship: A radical process of micro and macro expansion in conceptual experience. In W. Coburn & N. Vanderhide (Eds.), *Self and systems, Annals of the New York Academy of Sciences, 1159,* 262–278.

Knoedler, A. J., Hellwig, K. A., & Neath, I. (1999). The shift from recency to primacy with increasing delay. *Journal of Experimental Psychology: Learning, Memory, and Cognition, 25,* 474–487.

Knutson, B., Rick, S., Wimmer, G. E., Prelec, D., & Loewenstein, G. (2007). Neural predictors of purchases. *Neuron, 53,* 147–156.

Kobasa, S. C. (1979). Stressful life events, personality, and health: An inquiry into hardiness. *Journal of Personality and Social Psychology, 37,* 1–11.

Kobasa, S. C., Maddi, S. R., & Kahn, S. (1982). Hardiness and health: A prospective study. *Journal of Personality and Social Psychology, 42,* 168–177.

Kodl, M. M., & Mermelstein, R. (2004). Beyond modeling: Parenting practices, parental smoking history, and adolescent cigarette smoking. *Addictive Behaviors, 29,* 17–32.

Koenigs, M., Young, L., Adolphs, R., Tranel, D., Cushman, F., Hauser M., et al. (2007). Damage to the prefrontal cortex increases utilitarian moral judgments. *Nature, 446,* 908–911.

Kohlberg, L. (1969). *Stages in the development of moral thought and action.* New York: Holt, Rinehart and Winston.

Kohlberg, L. (1981). *The philosophy of moral development.* San Francisco: Harper & Row.

Köhler, W. (1927). *The mentality of apes.* New York: Harcourt Brace.

Kohn, N. W., Paulus, P. B., & Choi, Y. (2011). Building on the ideas of others: An examination of the idea combination process. *Journal of Experimental Social Psychology, 47,* 554–561. doi:10.1016/j.jesp.2011.01.004

Koko the gorilla calls for the dentist. (2004, August 8). *Cable News Network.* Retrieved from http://www.cnn.com/2004/US/West/08/ 08/koko.health.ap/index.html.

Kolata, G. (2010, August 28). Years later, no magic bullet against Alzheimer's disease. *The New York Times.* Retrieved from nytimes.com Koltko-Rivera, M. E. (2006). Rediscovering the later version of Maslow's hierarchy of needs: Self-transcendence and opportunities for theory, research, and unification. *Review of General Psychology,10,* 302–317.

Kölves,K., Ide, N., & De Leo,D. (2010). Suicidal ideation and behaviour in the aftermath of marital separation: Gender differences. *Journal of Affective Disorders, 120,* 48–53. http://dx.doi.org/10.1016/j.jad.2009.04.019

Komaroff, A. L. (2004, March 25). Sleep improves insight. *Journal Watch Psychiatry,* Retrieved from http://psychiatry.jwatch.org/cgi/ content/full/2004/325/10?qetoc.

Komaroff, A., & Lieberman, J. (2005, Summer). Silencing bad genes. *Newsweek Special Issue,* pp. 51–52.

Koolhaas, J. M., de Boer, S. F., & Buwalda, B. (2006). Stress and adaptation: Toward ecologically relevant animal models. *Current Directions in Psychological Science, 15,* 109–112.

Kopell, B. H., Machado, A. G., & Rezai, A. R. (2005). Not your father's lobotomy: Psychiatric surgery revisited. *Clinical Neurosurgery, 52,* 315–330.

Kosslyn, S. M., Thompson, W. L., Costantini-Ferrando, M. F., Alpert, N. M., & Spiegel, D. (2000). Hypnotic visual illusion alters color processing in the brain. *American Journal of Psychiatry, 157,* 1279–1284.

Koster, E. H. W., De Lissnyder, E., Derakshan, N., & De Raedt, R. (2011). Understanding depressive rumination from a cognitive science perspective: The impaired disengagement hypothesis. *Clinical Psychology Review, 31,*138–145. doi:10.1016/j.cpr.2010.08.005

Kotch, J. B., Lewis, T., Hussey, J. M., English, D., Thompson, R.,. Litrownik, A. J., . . . et al. (2008). Importance of early neglect for childhood aggression. *Pediatrics, 121,* 725–731. doi:10.1542/peds.2006-3622

Kounios, J. & Jung-Beeman, M. (2009). The Aha! moment: The cognitive neuroscience of insight. *Current Directions in Psychological Science, 18,* 210–216. doi: 10.1111/j.1467-8721.2009.01638.x

Kramer, A. F., & Willis, S. L. (2002). Enhancing the cognitive vitality of older adults. *Current Directions in Psychological Science, 11,* 173–177.

Krantz, M. J., & Mehler, P. S. (2004). Treating opioid dependence: Growing implications for primary care. *Archives of Internal Medicine, 164,* 277–288.

Kranzler, H. R. (2006). Evidence-based treatments for alcohol dependence: New results and new questions. *Journal of the American Medical Association, 295,* 2075–2076.

Krauss, R. M., Curran, N. M., & Ferleger, N. (1983). Expressive conventions and the cross-cultural perception of emotion. *Basic and Applied Social Psychology, 4,* 295–305.

Krebs, D. L., & Denton, K. (2005). Toward a more pragmatic approach to morality: A critical evaluation of Kohlberg's model. *Psychological Review, 112,* 629–649.

Krendl, A. C., Richeson, J. A., Kelley, W. M., & Heatherton, T. F. (2008). The negative consequences of threat: A functional magnetic resonance imaging investigation of the neural mechanisms underlying women's underperformance in math. *Psychological Science, 19,* 168–175.

Kretchmar, M. D., & Jacobvitz, D. B. (2002). Observing mother-child relationships across generations: Boundary patterns, attachment, and the transmission of caregiving. *Family Process, 41,* 351–374.

Kreuger, K. A., & Dayan, P. (2009). Flexible shaping: How learning in small steps helps. *Cognition, 10,* 380–394.

Kriegstein, A., & Alvarez-Buylla, A. (2009). The glial nature of embryonic and adult neural stem cells. *Annual Review of Neuroscience, 32,* 149–184. doi:10.1146/annurev.neuro.051508.135600

Kring, A. M., & Caponigro, J. M. (2010). Emotion in schizophrenia: Where feeling meets thinking. *Current Directions in Psychological Science, 19,* 255–259. doi:10.1177/0963721410377599

Kristensen, P., & Bjerkedal, T. (2007). Explaining the relation between birth order and intelligence. *Science, 316,* 1717.

Kros, C. (2005). Hearing: Aid from hair force. *Nature, 433,* 810–811.

Kruglanski, A..W., & Stroebe, W. (2005). Attitudes, goals and beliefs: Issues of structure, function and dynamics. In. D. Albarracin, B. Johnson, & M.P. Zanna (Eds.), *Handbook of attitude research.* New York: Guilford.

Ksir, C. J., Hart, C. L., & Ray, O. S. (2008). Drugs, society, and human behavior (12th ed). New York: McGraw-Hill.

Kübler-Ross, E. (1969). *On death and dying.* New York: Macmillan.

Kuehn, B. M. (2009). Antipsychotic risks. *Journal of the American Medical Association, 301,* 817.

Kuehn, B. M. (2011). Teen marijuana use on the rise. *Journal of the American Medical Association, 305,* 242. doi:10.1001/jama.2010.1927

Kuehn, B. M. (2011). Treatment is lacking for many us adults with mental illness or substance abuse. *Journal of the American Medical Association, 305,* 27. doi: 10.1001/jama.2010.1898

Kuhn, D. (2006). Do cognitive changes accompany developments in the adolescent brain? *Perspectives on Psychological Science, 1,* 59–67.

Kujawal, S. G., & Liberman, M. C. (2006). Acceleration of age-related hearing loss by early noise exposure: evidence of a misspent youth. *Journal of Neuroscience, 26,* 2115–2123.

Kumar, R., Birrer, B. V., Macey, P. M., Woo, M. A., Gupta, R. K., Yan-Go, F. L., et al. (2008). Reduced mammillary body volume in patients with obstructive sleep apnea. *Neuroscience Letters, 438,* 330–334. doi:10.1016/j.neulet.2008.04.071

Kuncel, N. R., Hezlett, A. A., & Ones, D. S. (2004). Academic performance, career potential, creativity, and job performance: Can one construct predict them all? *Journal of Personality and Social Psychology, 86,* 148–161.

Kupfersmid, J. (1995). Does the Oedipus complex exist? *Psychotherapy, 32,* 535–547.

Kurpius, S. E. R., Nicpon, M. F., & Maresh, S. E. (2001). Mood, marriage, and menopause. *Journal of Counseling Psychology, 48,* 77–84.

Kusnecov, A. W. (2001). Behavioral conditioning of the immune system. In A. Baum, T. A. Revenson, & J. E. Singer (Eds.), *Handbook of health psychology* (pp. 105–116). Mahwah, NJ: Lawrence Erlbaum Associates.

Kuyken, W., Watkins, E., Holden, E., White, K., Taylor, R. S., Byford, S., et al. (2010). How does mindfulness-based cognitive therapy work? *Behaviour Research and Therapy, 48,* 1105–1112.

LaFrance, M., Hecht, M. A., & Paluck, E. L. (2003). The contingent smile: A meta-analysis of sex differences in smiling. *Psychological Bulletin, 129,* 325–334.

LaFromboise, T. D., Albright, K., & Harris, A. (2010). Patterns of hopelessness among American Indian adolescents: Relationships by levels of acculturation and residence. *Cultural Diversity and Ethnic Minority Psychology, 16,* 68–76. doi:10.1037/a0016181

Lahey, B. B. (2009). Public health significance of neuroticism. *American Psychologist, 64,* 241–256. doi: 10.1037/a0015309

Lahey, B. B., Van Hulle, C. A., Keenan, K., Rathouz, P. J., D'Onofrio, B. M., Rodgers, J. L., et al. (2008). Temperament and parenting during the first year of life predict future child conduct problems. *Journal of Abnormal Child Psychology, 36,* 1139–1158. doi: 10.1007/s10802-008-9247-3

Lalumière, M. L., Harris, G. T., Quinsey, V. L., & Rice, M. E. (2005). Sexual interest in rape. In M. L. Lalumière, G. T. Harris, V. L. Quinsey, & M. E. Rice (Eds.), *The causes of rape: Understanding individual differences in male propensity for sexual aggression* (pp. 105–128). Washington, DC: American Psychological Association.

Lamanna, M. A., & Riedmann, A. (2005). *Marriages and families* (8th ed.). Belmont, CA: Wadsworth.

Lamberg, L. (2006). Rx for obesity: Eat less, exercise more, and—maybe—get more sleep. *Journal of the American Medical Association, 295,* 2341–2344.

Lambert, M. J., & Ogles, B. M. (2004). The efficacy and effectiveness of psychotherapy. In M. Lambert (Ed.), *Bergin and Garfield's handbook of psychotherapy and behavior change* (5th ed., pp. 139–193). New York, NY: Wiley.

Lambert, M. J., Hansen, N. B., & Finch, A. E. (2001). Patient-focused research: Using patient outcome data to enhance treatment effects. *Journal of Consulting and Clinical Psychology, 69,* 159–172.

Lambracht-Washington, D., Qu, B-X., Fu, M., Eagar, T. N., Stüve, O., & Rosenberg, R. N. (2009). DNA β-amyloid1-42 trimer immunization for Alzheimer disease in a wild-type mouse model. *Journal of the American Medical Association, 302,* 1796–1802.

Landhuis, C. E., Poulton, R., Welch, D., & Hancox, R. J. (2007). Does childhood television viewing lead to attention problems in adolescence? Results from a prospective longitudinal study. *Pediatrics, 120,* 532–537.

Lane, R. F., Raines, S. M., Steele, J. W., Ehrlich, M. E., Lah, J. A., Small, S., A. et al. (2010). Diabetes-associated SorCS1 regulates Alzheimer's amyloid-β metabolism: evidence for involvement of SorL1 and the Retromer Complex. *Journal of Neuroscience, 30,* 39. doi: 10.1523/JNEUROSCI.3872-10.2010

Långström, N., Rahman, Q., Carlström, E., & Lichtenstein, P. (2010). Genetic and environmental effects on same-sex sexual behavior: A population study of twins in Sweden. *Archives of Sexual Behavior, 39,* 75–80. doi: 10.1007/s10508-008-9386-1

Långström, N., Rahman, Q., Carlström, E., & Lichtenstein, P. (2008). Genetic and environmental effects on same-sex sexual behavior: A population study of twins in Sweden. *Archives of Sexual Behavior*. Published online, June 7, 2008. doi: 10.1007/s10508-008-9386-1

Lansford, J. E. (2009). Parental divorce and children's adjustment. *Perspectives on Psychological Science, 4,* 140–152.

Larsen, H., van der Zwaluw, C. S., Overbeek, G., Granic, I., Franke, B., & Engels, R. C. (2010). A variable-number-of-tandem-repeats polymorphism in the dopamine D4 receptor gene affects social adaptation of alcohol use: investigation of a gene-environment interaction. *Psychological Science, 21,* 1064–1068.

Latané, B., & Darley, J. M. (1970). *The unresponsive bystander: Why doesn't he help?* New York: Appleton-Century-Crofts.

Laughlin, P., Hatch, E., Silver, J., & Boh, L. (2006) Groups perform better than the best individuals on letters-to-numbers problems: Effects of group size. *Journal of Personality and Social Psychology, 90,* 644–651.

Laumann, E. O., Gagnon, J. H., Michael, R. T., & Michaels, S. (1994). *The social organization of sexuality: Sexual practices in the United States.* Chicago: University of Chicago Press.

Laumann, E. O., Paik, A., & Rosen, R. C. (1999). Sexual dysfunction in the United States. Prevalence and predictors. *Journal of the American Medical Association, 281*(6), 537–544.

Laumann, E. O., Paik, A., Glasser, D.B., Kang, J.-H., Wang, T., Moreira, E. M., et al. (2006). *A cross-national study of subjective sexual well-being among older women and men: Findings from the Global Study of Sexual Attitudes and Behaviors.* Retrieved from http://www.npr.org/documents/2006/apr/sex_ study/sex_study.pdf.

Lazarus, R. S. (1995). Toward better research on stress and coping. *American Psychologist, 55,* 665–673.

Lazarus, R. S. (1995). Vexing research problems inherent in cognitive-mediational theories of emotion and some solutions. *Psychological Inquiry, 6,* 183–197.

Lazarus, R. S. (2000). Toward better research on stress and coping. *American Psychologist, 55,* 665–673.

Leaper, C., & Ayres, M. M. (2007). A meta-analytic review of gender variations in adults' language use: Talkativeness, affiliative speech, and assertive speech. *Personality and Social Psychology Review, 11*(4), 328–363

Leckman, J. F., & Kim, Y. S. (2006). A primary candidate gene for obsessive-compulsive disorder. *Archives of General Psychiatry, 63,* 717–720.

LeDoux, J. (2003). The emotional brain, fear, and the amygdala. *Cellular and Molecular Neurobiology, 23,* 727–738.

LeDoux, J. E. (1994, June). Emotion, memory, and the brain. *Scientific American, 270,* 32–39.

LeDoux, J. E. (1996). *The emotional brain.* New York: Touchstone.

LeDoux, J. E. (2000). Emotion circuits in the brain. *Annual Review of Neuroscience, 23,* 155–184.

LeDoux, J. E. (2008). Amygdala. *Scholarpedia, 3*(4), 2698. Retrieved from http://www.scholarpedia.org/article/Amygdala.

Lee, L., Loewenstein, G., Ariely, D., Hong, J., Young, J. (2008). If I'm not hot, are you hot or not? Physical-attractiveness evaluations and dating preferences as a function of one's own attractiveness. *Psychological Science, 19,* 669–677. doi: 10.1111/j.1467-9280.2008.02141

Lees, A. J., Hardy, J., & Revesz, T. (2009). Parkinson's disease. *The Lancet, 373,* 2055–2066. doi:10.1016/S0140-6736(09)61557-9

Lehrer, P., Feldman, J., Giardino, N., Song, H.-S., & Schmaling, K. (2002). Psychological aspects of asthma. *Journal of Consulting and Clinical Psychology, 70,* 691–711.

Leiblum, S. R., Koochaki, P. E., Rodenberg, C. A., Barton, I. P., & Rosen, R. C. (2006). Hypoactive sexual desire disorder in postmenopausal women: US results from the Women's International Study of Health and Sexuality (WISHeS). *Menopause, 13,* 46–56.

Leibowitz, H. W. (1971). Sensory, learned, and cognitive mechanisms of size perception. *Annals of the New York Academy of Sciences, 1988,* 47–62.

Leichsenring, F., & Rabung, S. (2008). Effectiveness of long-term psychodynamic psychotherapy. *Journal of the American Medical Association, 300,* 1551.

Lemons, J. A., Baur, C. R., Oh, W., Korones, S. B., Stoll, B. J., Verter, J., et al. (2001). Very low birth weight outcomes of the National Institute of Child Health and Human Development neonatal research network, January 1995 through December 1996. *Pediatrics, 107,* 1.

Lepore, L., & Brown, R. (1997). Category and stereotype activation: Is prejudice inevitable? *Journal of Personality and Social Psychology, 72,* 275–287.

Leucht, S., Komossa, K., Rummel-Kluge, C., Corves, C., Hunger, H., Schmid, F., et al. (2009). A meta-analysis of head-to-head comparisons of second-generation antipsychotics in the treatment of schizophrenia. *American Journal of Psychiatry, 166,* 152–163. doi: 10.1176/appi.ajp.2008.0803036

Leue, A., Borchard, B., & Hoyer, J. (2004). Mental disorders in a forensic sample of sexual offenders. *European Psychiatry, 19*(3), 123–130.

Leutgeb, S. (2008, March 21). Detailed differences. *Science, 319,* 1623–1624. doi: 10.1126/science.1156724

LeVay, S. (2003). *The biology of sexual orientation.* Retrieved from http://members.aol.com/slevay/page22.html.

Leve, L. D., Harold, G. T., Ge, X., Neiderhiser, J. M., & Patterson, G. (2010). Refining intervention targets in family-based research: lessons from quantitative behavioral genetics. *Perspectives on Psychological Science, 5,* 516–526. doi:10.1177/1745691610383506

Leve, L. D., Kerr, D. C. R., Shaw, D., Ge, Z., Neiderhiser, J. M., Scaramella, L. V., et al. (2010). Infant pathways to externalizing behavior: Evidence of genotype × environment interaction. *Child Development, 81,* 340–356. doi: 10.1111/j.1467-8624.2009.01398.x

Levine, E. S., & Schmelkin, L. P. (2006). The move to prescribe: a change in paradigm? *Professional Psychology: Research and Practice, 37,* 205–209.

Levine, H. (2005, January 17). Another culprit to watch. *Newsweek,* p. 48.

Levine, L. E., & Waite, B. M. (2000). Television viewing and attentional abilities in fourth and fifth grade children. *Journal of Applied Developmental Psychology, 21,* 667–679.

Levine, M. (1994). *Effective problem solving* (2nd ed.). Englewood Cliffs, NJ: Prentice-Hall.

Levinson, D. J., with Darrow, C. N., Klein, E. R., Levinson, M. H., & McKee, B. (1978). *The seasons of a man's life.* New York: Knopf.

Levy, B. R, Slade, M. D., Kunkel, S. R., & Kasl, S. V. (2002). Longevity increased by positive self-perceptions of aging. *Journal of Personality and Social Psychology, 83,* 261–270.

Lewin, T. (2010, November 6). Many single mothers have a live-in partner, Census Bureau finds. *The New York Times,* p. A17.

Lewin, T. (2011). Record level of stress found in college freshmen. *The New York Times,* A1, A18.

Li, D., Morris, J. S., Liu, J., Hassan, M. M., Day, R. S., Bondy, M. L., et al. (2009). Body mass index and risk, age of onset, and survival in patients with pancreatic cancer. *Journal of the American Medical Association, 301,* 2553–2562.

Li, N. P., & Kenrick, D. T. (2006). Sex similarities and differences in preferences for short-term mates: What, whether, and why. *Journal of Personality and Social Psychology, 90,* 468–489.

Li, S. C. (2003). Biocultural orchestration of developmental plasticity across levels: The interplay of biology and culture in shaping the mind and behavior across the life span. *Psychological Bulletin, 129,* 171–194.

Li, W., Moallem, I., Paller, K. A., & Gottfried, J. A. (2007). Subliminal smells can guide social preferences. *Psychological Science, 18,* 1044–1049.

Liben, L. S., Susman, E. J., Finkelstein, J. W., Chinchilli, V., Kunselman, S., Schwab, J., et al. (2002). The effects of sex steroids on spatial performance: A review and an experimental clinical investigation. *Developmental Psychology, 38,* 236–253.

Liberles, S., D., & Buck, L. B. (2006). A second class of chemosensory receptors in the olfactory epithelium. *Nature, 442,* 645–650.

Lichta, R. W. (2010). A new BALANCE in bipolar I disorder. *The Lancet, 375,* 350–352. doi:10.1016/S0140-6736(09)61970-X

Lichtenbelt, K. D., Hochstenbach, R., van Dam, W. M., Eleveld, M. J., Poot, M., & Beemer, F. A. (2005). Supernumerary ring chromosome & mosaicism: Case report, investigation of the gene content, and delineation of the phenotype. *American Journal of Medical Genetics, 132,* 93–100.

Lien, M.-C., Ruthruff, E., & Johnston, J. C. (2006). Attentional limitations in doing two tasks at once: The search for exceptions. *Current Directions in Psychological Science, 15,* 89–93.

Lilienfeld, S. O., Kirsch, I., Sarbin, T. R., Lynn, S. J., Chaves, J. F., Ganaway, G. K., et al. (1999). Dissociative identity disorder and the sociocognitive model: Recalling the lessons of the past. *Psychological Bulletin, 125,* 507–523.

Lim, J., & Dinges, D. F. (2010). A meta-analysis of the impact of short-term sleep deprivation on cognitive variables. *Psychological Bulletin, 136,* 375–389. doi: 10.1037/a0018883

Limebeer, C. L., & Parker, L. A. (2006). Effect of conditioning method and testing method on strength of lithium-induced taste aversion learning. *Behavioral Neuroscience, 120,* 963–969.

Lindberg, S. M, Hyde, J. S., Petersen, J. L., & Linn, M. C. (2010). New trends in gender and mathematics performance: A meta-analysis. *Psychological Bulletin, 136,* 1123–1135. doi: 10.1037/a0021276

Linde, K., Allais, G., Brinkhaus, B., Manheimer, E., Vickers, A., & White, A. R. (2009a). Acupuncture for tension-type headache. *Cochrane Database of Systematic Reviews,* Issue 1. doi: 10.1002/14651858.CD007587

Linde, K., Allais, G., Brinkhaus, B., Manheimer, E., Vickers, A., & White, A. R. (2009b). Acupuncture for migraine prophylaxis. *Cochrane Database of Systematic Reviews,* Issue 1. doi: 10.1002/14651858.CD001218.pub2

Linville, P. W., & Fischer, G. W. (1993). Exemplar and abstraction models of perceived group variability and stereotypicality. *Social Cognition, 11,* 92–125.

Lippa, R. A. (2008). The relation between childhood gender nonconformity and adult masculinity–femininity and anxiety in heterosexual and homosexual men and women. *Sex Roles, 59,* 684–693. doi: 10.1007/s11199-008-9476-5

Lippa, R. A. (2009). Sex differences in sex drive, sociosexuality, and height across 53 nations: testing evolutionary and social structural theories. *Archives of Sexual Behavior, 38,* 631–651. doi: 10.1007/s10508-007-9242

Lipsman, N., Neimat, J. S., & Lozano, A. M. (2007). Deep brain stimulation for treatment-refractory obsessive-compulsive disorder: The search for a valid target. *Neurosurgery, 61,* 1–13.

Lipton, E. (2006, August 16). Faces, too, are searched as U.S. airports try to spot terrorists. *The New York Times,* pp. A1, A10.

Litt, M. D., Kadden, R. M., Cooney, N. L, & Kabela, E. (2003). Coping skills and treatment outcomes in cognitive-behavioral and interactional group therapy for alcoholism. *Journal of Consulting and Clinical Psychology,* 71, 118–128.

Little, A. C., Burt, D. M., & Perrett, D. I. (2006). What is good is beautiful: Face preference reflects desired personality. *Personality and Individual Differences, 41,* 1107–1118.

Littlejohn, S. W. (2002). *Theories of human communication* (7th ed.). Belmont, CA: Wadsworth.

Liu, I. C., Blacker, D. L., Xu, R., Fitzmaurice, G., Lyons, M. J., & Tsuang, M. T. (2004). Genetic and environmental contributions to the development of alcohol dependence in male twins. *Archives of General Psychiatry, 61,* 897–903.

Liu, R. T., & Alloy, L B. (2010). Stress generation in depression: A systematic review of the empirical literature and recommendations for future study. *Clinical Psychology Review, 30,* 582–593.

Ljótsson, B., Falk, L., Vesterlund, A. W., Hedman, E., Lindfors, P., Rück, C., et al. (2010). Internet-delivered exposure and mindfulness based therapy for irritable bowel syndrome—A randomized controlled trial. *Behaviour Research and Therapy, 48,* 531–539. doi: 10.1016/j.brat.2010.03.003

Loa, C. S. L., Ho, S. M. Y., & Hollon, S. D. (2008). The effects of rumination and negative cognitive styles on depression: A mediation analysis. *Behaviour Research and Therapy, 46,* 487–495. doi: 10.1016/j.brat.2008.01.013

Lobbestael, J., & Arntz, A. (2009). Emotional, cognitive and physiological correlates of abuse-related stress in borderline and antisocial personality disorder. *Behaviour Research and Therapy, 34,* 571–586. doi: 10.1016/j.brat.2009.09.015

Lockley, S. W., Cronin, J. W., Evans, E. E., Cade, B. E., Lee, C. J., Landrigan, C. P., et al. (2004). Effect of reducing interns' weekly work hours on sleep and attentional failures. *New England Journal of Medicine, 351,* 1829–1837.

Loeb, S., Fuller. B., Kagan, S. L., & Carrol, B. (2004). Child care in poor communities: Early learning effects of type, quality, and stability. *Child Development, 75,* 4765.

Loftus, E. F. (1997, September). Creating false memories. *Scientific American,* pp. 71–75.

Loftus, E. F. (2003). Make-believe memories. *American Psychologist, 58,* 867–873.

Loftus, E. F. (2004). Memories of things unseen. *Current Directions in Psychological Science, 13,* 145–147.

Loftus, E. F., Miller, D. G., & Burns, H. J. (1978). Semantic integration of verbal information into a visual memory. *Journal of Experimental Psychology: Human Learning and Memory, 4,* 19–31.

London-Vargas, N. (2001, July). Organizing a life's work: Finding your dream job. *TIP: The Industrial-Organizational Psychologist, Vol. 39*(1). Retrieved from http://www.siop.org/TIP/backissues/TipJul01/Jul01TOC.htm.

Loos, R. J. F., Lindgren, C. M., Li, S., Wheeler, E., Zhao J. H., Prokopenko, I., et al. (2008). Association studies involving over 90,000 people demonstrate that common variants near to MC4R influence fat mass, weight and risk of obesity. *Nature Genetics online.* Retrieved from http://www.eurekalert.org/pub_releases/2008-05/wtsi-sgl050108.php.

López-León, S., Janssens, A. C., J. W., Ladd, A. M. G.-Z., Del-Favero, J., Claes, S. J., Oostra, B. A., & van Duijn, C. M. (2008). Meta-analysis of genetic studies on major depressive disorder. *Molecular Psychiatry, 13,* 7772. doi: 10.1038/sj.mp.4002088

Lorenz, F. O., Wickrama, K. A. S., Conger, R. D., & Elder, G. H., Jr. (2006). The short-term and decade-long effects of divorce on women's midlife health. *Journal of Health and Social Behavior, 47,* 111–125.

Lorenz, K. (1966). *On aggression.* New York: Harcourt Brace Jovanovich.

Lorenzetti, V., Allen, N. B., Whittle, S., & Yücel, M. (2010). Amygdala volumes in a sample of current depressed and remitted depressed patients and healthy controls. *Journal of Affective Disorders, 120,* 112–119. doi: 10.1016/j.jad.2009.04.021

Lorenzo, G. L., Biesanz, J. C., & Human, L. J. (2010). What is beautiful is good and more accurately understood: Physical attractiveness and accuracy in first impressions of personality. *Psychological Science, 21,* 1777–1782. doi:10.1177/095679761038804

Lothane, Z. (2006). Freud's legacy—is it still with us? *Psychoanalytic Psychology, 23,* 285–301.

Love ballad leaves women more open to a date. (2010, June 18). *ScienceDaily.* Retrieved from http://www.sciencedaily.com/releases/2010/06/100618112139.htm.

Low, C. A., Stanton, A. L., & Danoff-Burg, S. (2006). Expressive disclosure and benefit finding among breast cancer patients: Mechanisms for positive health effects. *Health Psychology, 25,* 181–189.

Luborsky, L., Rosenthal, R., Digue, L., Andrusyna, T. P., Berman, J. S., Levitt, J. T., et al. (2002). The Dodo bird verdict is alive and well—mostly. *Clinical Psychology: Science and Practice, 9,* 2–12.

Lucas, R. E., & Donnellan, M. B. (2009). Age differences in personality: Evidence from a nationally representative Australian sample. *Developmental Psychology, 45,* 1353–1363.

Lucas, R. E., Clark, A. E., Georgellis, Y., & Diener, E. (2003). Reexamining adaptation and the set point model of happiness: Reactions to changes in marital status. *Journal of Personality and Social Psychology, 84,* 527–539.

Luczak, S. E., Glatt, S. J., & Wall, T. J. (2006). Meta-analyses of ALDH2 and ADH1B with alcohol dependence in Asians. *Psychological Bulletin, 132,* 607–621.

Ludwig, D. S., & Kabat-Zinn, J. (2008). Mindfulness in medicine. *Journal of the American Medical Association, 300,* 1350–1352.

Luijendijk, H. J., van den Berg, J. F., Marieke, J. H. J., Dekker, M. D., van Tuijl, H. R., Otte, W., et al. (2008). Incidence and recurrence of late-life depression. *Archives of General Psychiatry, 65,* 1394–1401.

Luo, S., & Klohnen, E. C. (2005). Assortative mating and marital quality in newlyweds: A couple-centered approach. *Journal of Personality and Social Psychology, 88,* 304–326.

Lupski, J. R. (2007). Structural variation in the human genome. *New England Journal of Medicine, 356,* 1169–1171.

Luria, A. R. (1968). *The mind of a mnemonist.* New York: Basic Books.

Luscombe, B. (2010, November 29). Marriage: What it's good for? *Newsweek,* pp. 46–56.

Lynn, R., & Harvey, J. (2008). The decline of the world's IQ. *Intelligence, 36,* 112–120. doi: 10.1016/j.intell.2007.03.004

Lynn, S. J., Boycheva, E., Barnes, S., Barretta, N., Barretta, P.,Geary, B. B., et al. (2008). To assess or not assess hypnotic suggestibility? that is the question. *American Journal of Clinical Hypnosis, 51,* 161–165.

MacGregor, J. N., Ormerod, T. C., & Chronicle, E. P. (2001). Information processing and insight: A process model of performance on the nine-dot and related problems. *Journal of Experimental Psychology: Learning, Memory, and Cognition, 27,* 176–201.

Maggiolini, A., Cagnin, C., Crippa, F., Persico, A., & Rizzi, P. (2010). Content analysis of dreams and waking narratives. *Dreaming, 20,* 60–76. doi: 10.1037/a0018824

Mah, K., & Binik, Y. M. (2001). The nature of human orgasm: A critical review of major trends. *Clinical Psychology Review, 21,* 823–856.

Maier, N. R. F. (1931). Reasoning in humans: II. The solution of a problem and its appearance in consciousness. *Journal of Comparative Psychology, 12,* 181–194.

Main, M. (1996). Introduction to the special section on attachment and psychopathology: 2. Overview of the field of attachment. *Journal of Consulting and Clinical Psychology, 64,* 237–243.

Maisto, S. A., Galizio, M., & Connors, G. J. (2008). (5th ed.) *Drug use and abuse.* Belmont, CA: Wadsworth Publishing.

Major, G. C., Doucet, E., Trayhurn, P., Astrup, A., & Tremblay, A. (2007). Clinical significance of adaptive thermogenesis. *International Journal of Obesity, 31,* 204–212.

Malamuth, N. M., Huppin, M., & Paul, B. (2005). Sexual coercion. In Buss, D. M. (Ed.). *The handbook of evolutionary psychology* (pp. 394–418). Hoboken, NJ: John Wiley & Sons, Inc.

Malle, B. A. (2006). The actor–observer asymmetry in attribution: A (surprising) meta-analysis. *Psychological Bulletin, 132,* 895–891.

Malouff, J., Rooke, S., & Schutte, N. (2008). The heritability of human behavior: Results of aggregating meta-analyses. *Current Psychology, 27,* 153–161. doi: 10.1007/s12144-008-9032-z

Manicavasgar, V., Parker, G., & Perich, T. (2011). Mindfulness-based cognitive therapy vs cognitive behaviour therapy as a treatment for non-melancholic depression. *Journal of Affective Disorders, 130,* 138–144 doi: 10.1016/j.jad.2010.09.027

Manini, T. M., Everhart, J. E., Patel, K. V., Schoeller, D. A., Colbert, L. H., Visser, M., et al. (2006). Daily activity energy expenditure and mortality among older adults. *Journal of the American Medical Association, 296,* 171–179.

Manne, S., Winkel, G., Zaider, T., Rubin, S., Hernandez, E., & Bergman, C. (2010). Therapy processes and outcomes of psychological interventions for women diagnosed with gynecological cancers: A test of the generic process model of psychotherapy. *Journal of Consulting and Clinical Psychology, 78,* 236–248 248. doi: 10.1037/a0018223

Manning, R., Levine, M. & Collins, A. (2007). The Kitty Genovese murder and the social psychology of helping: The parable of the 38 witnesses. *American Psychologist, 62,* 555–562.

Mansnerus, L., & Kocieniewski, D. (2004, August 14). Ex-aide says he was victim of McGreevey. *New York Times Online*. Retrieved from www.nytimes.com/2004/08/14/nyregion/14jersy.html.

Manson, J. E., Skerrett, P. J., Greenland, P., & VanItallie, T. B. (2004). The escalating pandemics of obesity and sedentary lifestyle a call to action for clinicians. *Archives of Internal Medicine, 164*, 249–258.

Marcia, J. E. (1980). Identity in adolescence. In J. Adelson (Ed.), *Handbook of adolescent psychology* (pp. 159–187). New York: Wiley.

Marcia, J. E., Waterman, A. S., Matteson, D. R., Archer, S. L., & Orlofsky, J. L. (Eds.). (1993). *Ego identity: A handbook for psychosocial research*. New York: Springer-Verlag.

Marion, I. J. (2005, December). The neurobiology of cocaine addiction. *Science Practice Perspectives, National Institute on Drug Abuse, 3*(1), 25–31.

Markel, H. (2003, September 3). Lack of sleep takes its toll on student psyches. *The New York Times, Science Times*, p. F6.

Markey, P., M., & Markey, C. N. (2010). Vulnerability to violent video games: A review and integration of personality research. *Review of General Psychology, 14*, 82–91. doi: 10.1037/a0019000

Marks, I., & Cavanagh, K. (2009). Computer-aided psychological treatments: Evolving issues. *Annual Review of Clinical Psychology, 5*, 121–141. doi: 10.1146/annurev.clinpsy.032408.153538

Markus, H. R., & Kitayama, S. (1991). Culture and the self: Implications for cognition, emotion, and motivation. *Psychological Review, 98*, 224–253.

Marsh, A. A., Elfenbein, H. A., & Ambady, N. A. (2003). Nonverbal "accents": Cultural differences in facial expressions of emotion. *Psychological Science, 14*, 373–376.

Martin, C. L., & Ruble, D. (2004). Children's search for gender cues: Cognitive perspectives on gender development. *Psychological Science, 13*, 67–70.

Martin, E. K., Taft, C. T., & Resick, P. A. (2007). A review of marital rape. *Aggression and Violent Behavior, 12*(3), 329–347.

Martins, A., Ramalho, N., & Morin, E. (2010). A comprehensive meta-analysis of the relationship between emotional intelligence and health. *Personality and Individual Differences, 49*, 554–564. doi: 10.1016/j.paid.2010.05.029 |

Maruyama, K., Sato, S., Ohira, T., Maeda, K., Noda, H., Kubota, Y., et al. (2008). The joint impact on being overweight of self-reported behaviours of eating quickly and eating until full: Cross sectional survey. *British Medical Journal, 337*, 2002. doi: 10.1136/bmj.a2002

Maslach, C, & Leiter, M. P. (2008). Early predictors of job burnout and engagement. *Journal of Applied Psychology, 93*, 498–512. doi: 10.1037/0021-9010.93.3.498

Maslow, A. H. (1943). A theory of human motivation. *Psychological Review, 50*, 370–396

Maslow, A. H. (1969). The farther reaches of human nature. *Journal of Transpersonal Psychology, 1*, 1–9.

Maslow, A. H. (1970). *Motivation and personality* (2nd ed.). New York: Harper & Row.

Maslow, A. H. (1971). *Farther reaches of human nature*. New York: Viking Penguin.

Maslow, A. H. (1987). *Motivation and personality* (3rd ed.; R. Frager, J. Fadiman, C. McReynolds, & R. Cox, Eds.). Boston: Addison Wesley.

Mason, M. F., Norton, M. I., Van Horn, J. D., Wegner, D. M., & Grafton, S. T., & Macrae, C. N. (2007). Wandering minds: The default network and stimulus-independent thought. *Science, 315*, 393–395.

Mason, P. T., & Kreger, R. (1998). *Stop walking on eggshells*. Oakland, CA: New Harbinger Publications.

Masters, W. H., & Johnson, V. E. (1966). *Human sexual response*. Boston: Little, Brown.

Masters, W. H., & Johnson, V. E. (1970). *Human sexual inadequacy*. Boston: Little, Brown.

Masuda, T., & Nisbett, R. E. (2001). Attending holistically versus analytically: Comparing the context sensitivity of Japanese and Americans. *Journal of Personality and Social Psychology, 81*, 992–934.

Matsumoto, D. (2004). Paul Ekman and the legacy of universals. *Journal of Research in Personality, 38*, 45–51.

Matsumoto, D., & Willingham, B. (2009). Spontaneous facial expressions of emotion in congenitally and non-congenitally blind individuals. *Journal of Personality and Social Psychology, 96*, 1–10. doi: 10.1037/a0014037

Matsumoto, D., Yoo, S. H., Hirayama, S., & Petrova, G. (2005). Development and validation of a measure of display rule knowledge: The Display Rule Assessment Inventory. *Emotion,5*, 23–40.

Matsumoto, D., Yoo, S. H., Nakagawa, S., & Multinational Study of Cultural Display Rules. (2008). Culture, emotion regulation, and adjustment. *Journal of Personality and Social Psychology, 94*, 925–937. doi: 10.1037/0022-3514.94.6.925

Matsumoto, K., Suzuki, W., & Tanaka, K. (2003). Neuronal correlates of goal-based motor selection in the prefrontal cortex. *Science, 301*, 229–232.

Matz, D. C., & Wood, W. (2005). Cognitive dissonance in groups: The consequences of disagreement. *Journal of Personality and Social Psychology, 88*, 22–37.

Mavor, K. I., Macleod, C. J., Boal, M. J., & Louis, W. R. (2009). Right-wing authoritarianism, fundamentalism, and prejudice revisited: Removing suppression and statistical artifact. *Personality and Individual Differences, 46*, 592–597.

Max, D. T. (2005, December 11). National smiles. *The New York Times Magazine*, p. 82.

Maxwell, J. S., & Davidson, R. J. (2007). Emotion as motion: Asymmetries in approach and avoidant actions. *Psychological Science, 18*, 1113–1119.

Mayer, J. D., Salovey, P., & Caruso, D. R. (2008). Emotional intelligence: New ability or eclectic traits. *American Psychologist, 63*, 503–517. doi: 10.1037/0003-066X.63.6.503

Mays, V. M., Cochran, S. D., & Barnes, N. W. (2007). Race, race-based discrimination, and health outcomes among African Americans. *Annual Review of Psychology, 58*, 201–225.

Mazzoni, G., & Memom, A. (2003). Imagination can create false autobiographical memories. *Psychological Science, 14*, 186–188.

Mazzucchelli, T., Kane, R., & Rees, C. (2009). Behavioral activation treatments for depression in adults: A meta-analysis and review. *Clinical Psychology: Science and Practice, 16*, 383–411. doi: 10.1111/j.1468-2850.2009.01178.x

McAdams, K. K., & Donnellan, M. B. (2008). Facets of personality and drinking in first-year college students. *Personality and Individual Differences, 46*, 207–212. doi: 10.1016/j.paid.2008.09.028

McBride, C. K., Paikoff, R. L., & Holmbeck, G. N. (2003). Individual and familial influences on the onset of sexual intercourse among urban African American adolescents. *Journal of Consulting and Clinical Psychology, 71*, 159–167.

McCabe, M. P. (2005). The role of performance anxiety in the development and maintenance of sexual dysfunction in men and women. *International Journal of Stress Management, 12*, 379–388.

McCarthy, B. W., Ginsberg, R. L., & Fucito, L. M. (2006). Resilient sexual desire in heterosexual couples. *Family Journal: Counseling and Therapy for Couples and Families, 14*, 59–64.

McCartney, K., Burchinal, M., Clarke-Stewart, A., Bub, K. L., Owen, M. T., Belsky, J., et al. (2010). Testing a series of causal propositions relating time in child care to children's externalizing behavior. *Developmental Psychology, 46*, 1–17. doi:10.1037/a0017886

McClelland, D. C. (1958). Risk-taking in children with high and low need for achievement. In J. W. Atkinson (Ed.), *Motives in fantasy, action, and society*. Princeton, NJ: Van Nostrand.

McClelland, D. C. (1985). *Human motivation*. Glenview, IL: Scott, Foresman.

McCrae, R. R. (2004). Human nature and culture: A trait perspective. *Journal of Research in Personality, 38*, 3–14.

McCrae, R. R., & Costa, P. T., Jr. (1986). Clinical assessment can benefit from recent advances in personality psychology. *American Psychologist, 41*, 1001–1003.

McCrae, R. R., & Costa, P. T., Jr. (1996). Toward a new generation of personality theories: Theoretical contexts for the five-factor model. In J. S. Wiggins (Ed.), *The five-factor model of personality: Theoretical perspectives*. New York: Guilford Press.

McCrae, R. R., & Terracciano, A. (2005). Personality profiles of cultures: Aggregate personality traits. *Journal of Personality and Social Psychology, 89*, 407–425.

McCrae, R. R., & Terracciano, A. (2006). National character and personality. *Current Directions in Psychological Science, 15*, 156–161.

McDougall, W. (1908). *An introduction to social psychology*. New York: Methuen.

McEvoy, P. M. (2008). Effectiveness of cognitive behavioural group therapy for social phobia in a community clinic: A benchmarking study. *Behaviour Research and Therapy, 45*, 3030–3040.

McGirra, A., Tousignant, M., Routhier, D., Pouliot, L., Chawky, N., Margolese, H. C., et al. (2006). Risk factors for completed suicide in schizophrenia and other chronic psychotic disorders: A case–control study. *Schizophrenia Research, 84*, 132–143.

McGovern, F. J., & Nevid, J. S. (1986). Evaluation apprehension on psychological inventories in a prison-based setting. *Journal of Consulting and Clinical Psychology, 54*, 576–578.

McHugh, R. K., & Barlow, D. H. (2010). The dissemination and implementation of evidence-based psychological treatments: A review of current efforts. *American Psychologist, 65*, 73–84. doi: 10.1037/a0018121

McKown, C., & Strambler, M. (2009). Developmental antecedents and social and academic consequences of stereotype-consciousness in middle childhood. *Child Development, 80*, 000–000. doi: 10.1111/j.1467-8624.2009.01359.x

McLean, L. M., & Gallop, R. (2003). Implications of childhood sexual abuse for adult borderline personality disorder and complex posttraumatic stress disorder. *American Journal of Psychiatry, 160*, 369–371.

McNally, R. J., & Geraerts, E. (2009). A new solution to the recovered memory debate. *Perspectives on Psychological Science, 4*, 126–134. doi: 10.1111/j.1745-6924.2009.01112.x

McVary, K. T. (2007). Erectile dysfunction. *New England Journal of Medicine, 357*, 2472–2481.

Mead, M. (1935). *Sex and temperament in three primitive societies*. New York: Dell.

Meaney, M. J. (2010). Epigenetics and the biological definition of gene × environment interactions. *Child Development, 81*, 41–79. doi 10.1111/j.1467-8624.2009.01381.x

Means-Christensen, A. J., Snyder, D. K., & Negy, C. (2003). Assessing nontraditional couples: Validity of the Marital Satisfaction Inventory—Revised with gay, lesbian, and cohabiting heterosexual couples. *Journal of Marital and Family Therapy, 29*, 69–83.

Medical News Today. (2011). *Are positive emotions good for your health in old age?* Retrieved from http://www.medicalnewstoday.com/articles/214442.php.

Mednick, S., Makovski, T., Cai, D., & Jiang, Y. (2009). Sleep and rest facilitate implicit memory in a visual search task. *Vision Research, 49*, 2557–2565. doi: 10.1016/j.visres.2009.04.011

Meeus, W. H. J., & Raaijmakers, Q. A. W. (1995). Obedience in modern society: The Utrecht studies. *Journal of Social Issues, 51*, 155–175.

Mehl, M. R., Vazire, S., Ramírez-Esparza, N., Slatcher,R. B., &. Pennebaker, J. W. (2007). Are women really more talkative than men? *Science, 317*, 82.

Melamed, S., Shirom, A., Toker, S., Berliner, S., & Shapira, I. (2006). Burnout and risk of cardiovascular disease: Evidence, possible causal paths, and promising research directions. *Psychological Bulletin, 132*, 327–353.

Meltzoff, A. N., & Gopnik, A. (1997). *Words, thoughts, and theories*. Cambridge, MA: MIT Press.

Melzack, R., & Wall, P. D. (1965). Pain mechanisms: A new theory. *Science, 150*, 971–979.

Melzack, R., & Wall, P. D. (1983). *The challenge of pain*. New York: Basic Books.

Menard, K. S., Hall, G. C. N., Phung, A. H., Ghebrial, M. F. E., & Martin, L. (2003). Gender differences in sexual harassment and coercion in college students: Developmental, individual, and situational determinants. *Journal of Interpersonal Violence, 18*, 1222–1239.

Mendes W. B. (2007). Social facilitation. In R. Baumeister & K. Vohs (Eds.). *Encylopedia of social psychology*. Thousand Oaks, CA: Sage.

Mendez, J. L., Fantuzzo, J., & Cicchetti, D. (2002). Profiles of social competence among low-income African American preschool children. *Child Development, 73*, 1085–1100.

Menza, M. (2006). STAR*D: The results begin to roll in. *American Journal of Psychiatry, 163*, 1123.

Merckelbach, H., Arntz, A., & de Jong, P. (1991). Conditioning experiences in spider phobics. *Behaviour Research and Therapy, 29*, 301–304.

Merckelbach, H., de Jong, P. J., Muris, P., & van den Hout, M. A. (1996). The etiology of specific phobias: A review. *Clinical Psychology Review, 16*, 337–361.

Merikangas, K. R., & Pato, M. (2009). Recent developments in the epidemiology of bipolar disorder in adults and children: Magnitude, correlates, and future directions. *Clinical Psychology: Science and Practice, 16*, 121–133. doi: 10.1111/j.1468-2850.2009.01152.x

Messinis, L., Kyprianidou, A., Malefaki, S., & Papathanasopoulos, P. (2006). Neuropsychological deficits in long-term frequent cannabis users. *Neurology, 66*, 737–739.

Meston, C., M, & Buss, D. M. (2007). Why humans have sex. *Archives of Sexual Behavior, 36*, 477–507.

Metcalfe, J. (1986). Feelings of knowing in memory and problem solving. *Journal of Experimental Psychology: Learning, Memory, and Cognition, 12*, 288–294.

Meyer, G. J. (2000). Incremental validity of the Rorschach Prognostic Rating Scale over the MMPI Ego Strength Scale and IQ. *Journal of Personality Assessment, 74*, 365–370.

Meyer, G. J., Finn, S. E., Eyde, L. D., Kay, G. G., Moreland, K. L., Dies, R. R., et al. (2001). Psychological testing and psychological assessment: A review of evidence and issues. *American Psychologist, 56*, 128–165.

Meyer, I. H. (2003). Prejudice, social stress, and mental health in lesbian, gay, and bisexual populations: Conceptual issues and research evidence. *Psychological Bulletin, 129*, 674–697.

Meyer, P., Saez, L., & Young, M. W. (2006). PER-TIM interactions in living drosophila cells: An interval timer for the circadian clock. *Science, 311*, 226–229.

Meyer-Lindenberg, A., Buckholtz, J. W., Kolachana, B., Hariri, A. R., Pezawas, L., Blas, G., et al. (2006). Neural mechanisms of genetic risk for impulsivity and violence in humans. *Proceedings of the National Academy of Sciences, 103*, 6269–6274.

Meyers, L (2007, February). "A struggle for hope." *Monitor on Psychology, 38*(2), 30–31.

Meyers, L. (2005, November). Psychologists back increased parity, prescriptive authority and professional access. *Monitor on Psychology, 36*(10), 42–43.

Meyers, L. (2007, February). "A struggle for hope." *Monitor on Psychology, 38*(1), 30–31.

Michael, Y. L., Carlson, N. E., Chlebowski, R. T., Aickin, M., Weihs, K. L.,Ockene, J. K., al. (2009). Influence of stressors on breast cancer incidence in the Women's Health Initiative. *Health Psychology, 28*, 137–146. doi: 10.1037/a0012982

Mikolajczak, M., Gross, J. J., Lane, A., Corneille, O., de Timary,P., & Luminet, O. (2010). Oxytocin makes people trusting, not gullible. *Psychological Science, 14*, 1072–1074. doi: 10.1177/0956797610377343

Milgram, S. (1963). Behavioral study of obedience. *Journal of Abnormal and Social Psychology, 67*, 371–378.

Milgram, S. (1974). *Obedience to authority*. New York: Harper & Row.

Miller, A. G. (2009). Reflections on "Replicating Milgram" (Burger, 2009). *American Psychologist*, 64, 20–27.

Miller, G. (2007). Hunting for meaning after midnight. *Science, 315*, 1360.

Miller, G. (2009). Sleeping to reset overstimulated synapses. *Science, 324*, 22. doi: 10.1126/science.324.5923.22

Miller, G. (2011). Why loneliness is hazardous to your health. *Science, 331*, 138–140. doi: 10.1126/science.331.6014.138

Miller, G. E., Chen, E., & Zhou, E. S. (2007). If it goes up, must it come down? Chronic stress and the hypothalamic-pituitary-adrenocortical axis in humans. *Psychological Bulletin, 133*, 25–45.

Miller, J. G., & Bersoff, D. M. (1992). Culture and moral judgment: How are conflicts between justice and interpersonal responsibilities resolved? *Journal of Personality and Social Psychology, 62*, 541–554.

Miller, M., Azrael, D., & Hemenway, D. (2004). The epidemiology of case fatality rates for suicide in the northeast. *Annals of Emergency Medicine, 43*, 723–730.

Miller, S. L., & Maner, J. K. (2010). Scent of a woman: Men's testosterone responses to olfactory ovulation cues. *Psychological Science, 21*, 276–283. doi: 10.1177/0956797609357733

Mindlin, A. (2009, November 2). Children watch more TV than ever. *The New York Times*, p. B3.

Minerd, J., & Jasmer, R. (2006, April). Forty winks or more to make a healthier America. *MedPage Today*. Retrieved from http://www. medpagetoday.com/PrimaryCare/SleepDisorders/tb/3009.

Minzenberg, M. J., Laird, A. R., Thelen, S., Carter, C. S., & Glahn, D. C. (2009). Meta-analysis of 41 functional neuroimaging studies of executive function in schizophrenia. *Archives of General Psychiatry, 66*, 811–822.

Mischel, W. (1970). Sex-typing and socialization. In P. H. Mussen (Ed.), *Carmichael's manual of child psychology* (3rd ed.). New York: Wiley.

Mischel, W. (1973). Toward a cognitive social learning reconceptualization of personality. *Psychological Review, 80*, 252–283.

Mischel, W. (2009). From personality and assessment (1968) to personality science, 2009. *Journal of Research in Personality, 43*, 282–290. doi: 10.1016/j.jrp.2008.12.037

Mitka, M. (2000). Psychiatrists help survivors in the Balkans. *Journal of the American Medical Association, 283*, 1277–1228.

Mitka, M. (2009). College binge drinking still on the rise. *Journal of the American Medical Association, 302*, 836–837.

Miyamichi, K., Amat, F., Moussavi, G., Wang, C., Wickersham, I., Wall, N. R., . . . Luo, L. (2010). Cortical representations of olfactory input by trans-synaptic tracing. *Nature*, Published online. Retrieved from http://www.hfsp.org/frontier-science/awardees-articles/cortical-representations-olfactory-input

Moffitt, T. E., Caspi, A., & Rutter, M. (2006). Measured gene-environment interactions in psychopathology concepts, research strategies, and implications for research, intervention, and public understanding of genetics. *Perspectives on Psychological Science, 1*, 5–27.

Mollica, R. F., Henderson, D. C., & Tor, S. (2002). Psychiatric effects of traumatic brain injury events in Cambodian survivors of mass violence. *British Journal of Psychiatry, 181*, 339–347.

Monahan, K. C., Steinberg, L., & Cauffman, E. (2009). Affiliation with antisocial peers, susceptibility to peer influence, and antisocial behavior during the transition to adulthood. *Developmental Psychology, 45*, 1520–1530. doi: 10.1037/a0017417

Monk, C. S., Telzer, E. H., Mogg, K., Bradley, B. P., Mai, X., Louro, H. M. C., et al. (2008). Amygdala and ventrolateral prefrontal cortex activation to masked angry faces in children and adolescents with generalized anxiety disorder. *Archives of General Psychiatry, 65*, 568–576.

Monroe, S. M. & Reid, M. W. (2009). Life stress and major depression. *Current Directions in Psychological Science, 18*, 68–72. doi: 10.1111/j.1467-8721.2009.01611.x

Monti, P. M., Binkoff, J. A., Abrams, D. B., & Zwick, W. R. (1987). Reactivity of alcoholics and nonalcoholics to drinking cues. *Journal of Abnormal Psychology, 96*, 122–126.

Montorsi, F., Adaikan, G., Becher, E., Giuliano, F., Khoury, S., Lue, T. F., . . . Wasserman, M. (2010). Summary of the recommendations on sexual dysfunctions in men. *Journal of Sexual Medicine, 7*, 3572–3588. doi: 10.1111/j.1743-6109.2010.02062.x

Montpetit, M. A., Bergeman, C. S. (2007). Dimensions of control: Mediational analyses of the stress–health relationship. *Personality and Individual Differences, 43*, 2237–2248.

Moon, C., Cooper, R. P., & Fifer, W. P. (1993). Two-day-olds prefer their native language. *Infant Behavior and Development, 16*, 495–500.

Moore, D. R. & Heiman, J. R. (2006). Women's sexuality in context: Relationship factors and female sexual functioning. In I. Goldstein, C. Meston, S. Davis, & A. Traish (Eds.), *Female sexual dysfunction*. New York: Parthenon.

Moore, D. S., & Johnson, S. P. (2008). Mental rotation in human infants: A sex difference. *Psychological Science, 19*, 1063–1066. doi: 10.1111/j.1467-9280.2008.02200

Moracco K. E., Runyan C. W., Bowling, J. M., & Earp, J. L. (2007). Women's experiences with violence: A National study. *Women and Health, 17*, 3–12.

Moreno-De-Luca, D., Mulle, J. G., Kaminsky, E. B., Sanders, S. J., Myers, S. M., Adam, M. P., . . . Ledbetter, D. H. (2010). Deletion 17q12 is a recurrent copy number variant that confers high risk of autism and schizophrenia. *American Journal of Human Genetics, 87*, 618–630. doi: 10.1016/j.ajhg.2010.10.004

Morgeson, F. P., & Humphrey, S. E. (2006). The Work Design Questionnaire (WDQ): Developing and validating a comprehensive measure for assessing job design and the nature of work. *Journal of Applied Psychology, 91*, 1321–1339.

Morin, C. M. (2010). Chronic insomnia: Recent advances and innovations in treatment developments and dissemination. *Canadian Psychology, 51*, 31–39. doi: 10.1037/a0018715

Moriya, J., Kakeda, S., Abe, O., Goto, N., Yoshimura, R., Hori, H., et al. (2010). Gray and white matter volumetric and diffusion tensor imaging (DTI) analyses in the early stage of first-episode schizophrenia. *Schizophrenia Research, 116*, 196–203.

Morley, S., Williams, A., & Hussain, S. (2008). Estimating the clinical effectiveness of cognitive behavioural therapy in the clinic: Evaluation of a CBT informed pain management programme. *Pain, 137*, 467–468. doi: 10.1097/YCO.0b013e3283252d5a

Morrato, E. H., Druss, B., Hartung, D. M., Valuck, R. J., Allen, R., Campagna, E., et al. (2010). Metabolic testing rates in 3 state medicaid programs after FDA Warnings and ADA/APA recommendations for second-generation antipsychotic drugs. *Archives of General Psychiatry, 67*, 17–24.

Morris, W. L., Sinclair, S., & DePaulo, B. M. (2006). The perceived legitimacy of civil status discrimination. Manuscript submitted for publication.

Morris, W. N., Miller, R. S., & Spangenberg, S. (1977). The effects of dissenter position and task difficulty on conformity and response conflict. *Journal of Personality, 45*, 251–256.

Moser, M., Franklin, S. F., Handler, J., (2007). The nonpharmacologic treatment of hypertension: How efective is it? An update. *The Journal of Clinical Hypertension, 9*, 209–216.

Mosher, W. D., Chandra, A., & Jones, J. (2005). *Sexual behavior and selected health measures: Men and women 15–44 years of age, United States, 2002. Advance data from vital and health statistics, No. 362.* Hyattsville, MD: National Center for Health Statistics.

Motivala, S. J., & Irwin, M. R. (2007). Sleep and immunity: Cytokine pathways linking sleep and health outcomes. *Current Directions in Psychological Science, 16*, 21–25.

Motl, R. W., Dishman, R. K., Saunders, R. P., Dowda, M., Felton, G., Ward, D. S., et al. (2002). Examining social–cognitive determinants of intention and physical activity among black and white adolescent girls using structural equation modeling. *Health Psychology, 21*, 459–467.

Mulder, R. T., Frampton, C. M. A., Luty, S. E., & Joyce, P. R. (2009). Eighteen months of drug treatment for depression: Predicting relapse and recovery. *Journal of Affective Disorders, 114*, 263–270. doi:10.1016/j.jad.2008.08.002

Multiracial America is fastest growing group. (2009, May 28). Retrieved from http://www.msnbc.msn.com/id/30986649/.

Munakata, Y., McClelland, J. L., Johnson, M. H., & Siegler, R. S. (1997). Rethinking infant knowledge: Toward an adaptive process account of successes and failures in object permanence tasks. *Psychological Review, 104*, 686–713.

Munsey, C. (2008, October). The dangers of turning 21. *Monitor on Psychology*, p. 10

Munsey, C. (2010, October). Does marriage make us happy? *Monitor on Psychology*, pp. 20–21.

Murakoshi, H., Wang, H., & Yasuda, R. (2011). Local, persistent activation of Rho GTPases during plasticity of single dendritic spines. *Nature, 472*, 100–104. doi: 10.1038/nature09823

Murray, D. J., Kilgour, A. R., & Wasylkiw, L. (2000). Conflicts and missed signals in psychoanalysis, behaviorism, and Gestalt psychology. *American Psychologist, 55*, 422–426.

Murray, H. A. (1938). *Explorations in personality.* New York: Oxford University Press.

Murstein, B. I., & Mathes, S. (1996). Projection on projective techniques pathology: The problem that is not being addressed. *Journal of Personality Assessment, 66*, 337–349.

Muscatell, K. A., Slavich, G. M., Monroe, S. M., Gotlib, I. H. (2009). Stressful life events, chronic difficulties, and the symptoms of clinical depression. *The Journal of Nervous and Mental Disease, 197*, 154–160. doi: 10.1097/NMD.0b013e318199f77b

Must, A., Kõks, S., Vasar, E., Tasa, G., Lang, A., Maron, E., et al. (2009). Common variations in 4p locus are related to male completed suicide. *NeuroMolecular Medicine, 11*, 13–19. doi: 10.1007/s12017-008-8056-8

Muzzatti, B., & Agnoli, F. (2007). Gender and mathematics: Attitudes and stereotype threat: Susceptibility in Italian children. *Developmental Psychology, 43*, 747–759.

Nahas, Z., Anderson, B. S., Borckardt, J., Arana, A. B., George, M. S., Reeves, S. T., & Takacs, I. (2010). Bilateral epidural prefrontal cortical stimulation for treatment-resistant depression. *Biological Psychiatry, 67*, 101–109. doi:10.1016/j.biopsych.2009.08.021

Nakagawa, T., Sakurai, T., Nishioka, T., & Touhara, K. (2005). Insect sex-pheromone signals mediated by specific combinations of olfactory receptors. *Science, 307*, 1638–1642.

Nappi, R. E., Wawra, K., & Schmitt, S. (2006). Hypoactive sexual desire disorder in postmenopausal women. *Gynecological Endocrinology, 22*, 318–323.

Nasrallah, H. A., Keshavan, M. S., Benes F. M., Braff, D. L., Green A. I., Gur, R . . . Correll, C. U. (2009). Proceedings and data from The Schizophrenia Summit: A critical appraisal to improve the management of schizophrenia. *The Journal of Clinical Psychiatry, 70*, Suppl 1, 4–46.

National Cancer Institute (NCI), National Institutes of Health (2009). *SEER stat fact sheets.* Retrieved from http://seer.cancer.gov/statfacts/html/all.html

National Cancer Institute (NCI), National Institutes of Health (2010c). *Melanoma.* Retrieved from http://www.cancer.gov/cancertopics/types/melanoma.

National Cancer Institute (NCI), National Institutes of Health. (2009b, October 22). *Human papillomavirus (HPV) vaccines.* Retrieved from http://www.cancer.gov/cancertopics/factsheet/Prevention/HPV-vaccine.

National Cancer Institute (NCI), National Institutes of Health. (2006, August 22). *New study shows that being overweight at middle age can be harmful.* Retrieved from http://www.cancer.gov/newscenter/pressreleases/BMImortality.

National Cancer Institute (NCI), National Institutes of Health. (2010b). *Skin Cancer.* Retrieved from http://www.cancer.gov/cancertopics/types/skin.

National Cancer Institute, National Institutes of Health, U.S. Department of Health and Human Services. (2010a). *2008–2009 annual report: President's Cancer Panel: Reducing environmental cancer risk: What we can do now.* Bethesda, MD: Author.

National Institute of Mental Health (NIMH), National Institutes of Health (2001). *Seeing our feelings: Imaging emotion in the brain* (NIH Publication No. 01-460). Bethesda, MD: Author.

National Institute on Drug Abuse, U.S. Department of Health and Human Services, National Institutes of Health. (2004, November). *Research Report Series: Cocaine abuse and addiction.* NIH Publication No. 99-4342.

National Institutes of Health (NIH). (2003). *HIV/AIDS, severe mental illness and homelessness.* Retrieved from http://grants.nih.gov/ grants/guide/pa-files/PA-04-024.html.

National Science Foundation (2008, June 6). Plastic brain outsmarts experts: Training can increase fluid intelligence, once thought to be fixed at birth. *ScienceDaily.* Retrieved from http://www.sciencedaily.com/releases/2008/06/080605163804.htm.

National Science Foundation. (2004, April). *Science and engineering degrees, by race/ethnicity of recipients: 1992–2001* (NSF 04-318, Division of Science Resources Statistics). Arlington, VA: Author.

National Survey of Sexual Health and Behavior (NSSHB). (2010). *Findings from the National Survey of Sexual Health and Behavior. Journal of Sexual Medicine, 7,* Supplement 5.

National Women's Health Information Center, U.S. Department of Health and Human Services, Office on Women's Health. (2009, August 10). *Genital herpes.* Retrieved from http://www.womenshealth.gov/faq/genital-herpes.cfm#b.

Nawrot, M., Nordenstrom, B., & Olson, A. (2004). Disruption of eye movements by ethanol intoxication affects perception of depth from motion parallax. *Psychological Science, 15*, 858–865.

Negy, C., & Snyder, D. K. (2000). Relationship satisfaction of Mexican American and non-Hispanic white American interethnic couples: Issues of acculturation and clinical intervention. *Journal of Marital and Family Therapy, 26*, 293–304.

Neisser, U., Boodoo, G., Bouchard, T. J., Jr., Boykin, A. W., Brody, N., Ceci, S. J., et al. (1996). Intelligence: Knowns and unknowns. *American Psychologist, 51*, 77–101.

Nelson, D. L., & Gibbs, R. A. (2004). The critical region in trisomy 21. *Science, 306*, 619–621.

Nelson, J. C., Mankoski, R., Baker, R. A., Carlson, B. X., Eudicone, J., M. Pikalov, et al. (2010). Effects of aripiprazole adjunctive to standard antidepressant treatment on the core symptoms of depression: A post-hoc, pooled analysis of two large, placebo-controlled studies. *Journal of Affective Disorders, 120*, 133–140. doi: 10.1016/j.jad.2009.06.026

Nelson, T. D. (2002). *The psychology of prejudice.* Boston: Allyn and Bacon.

Nemiah, J. C. (1988). Psychoneurotic disorders. In A. M. Nicholi, Jr. (Ed.), *The new Harvard guide to psychiatry* (pp. 234–258). Cambridge, MA: Belknap Press.

Nestoriuc, Y., & Martin, A. (2007). Efficacy of biofeedback for migraine: A meta-analysis. *Radiology Source, 128*, 111–127.

Nestoriuc, Y., Rief, W., & Martin, A. (2008). Meta-analysis of biofeedback for tension-type headache: Efficacy, specificity, and treatment moderators. *Journal of Consulting and Clinical Psychology, 76*, 379–396. doi: 10.1037/0022-006X.76.3.379

Nettelbeck, T., & Wilson, C. (2005). Intelligence and IQ: What teachers should know. *Educational Psychology, 25*, 609–630.

Nevid, J. S. (1984). Sex differences in factors of romantic attraction. *Sex Roles, 11*, 401–411.

Nevid, J. S. (2010). Implicit measures of consumer response: The search for the Holy Grail of marketing research. Introduction to Special Issue. *Psychology and Marketing, 27*, 913–910. doi: 10.1002/mar.2036

Nevid, J. S., & Rathus, S. A. (2007a). *Psychology and the challenges of life: Adjustment in the new millennium.* (10th ed.). New York: Wiley.

Nevid, J. S., & Rathus, S. A. (2007b). *Your health.* Mason, OH: Thomson Custom Publishing.

Nevid, J. S., & Rathus, S. A. (2010). *Psychology and the challenges of life: Adjustment and modern life* (11th ed.). New York: Wiley.

Nevid, J. S., & Sta. Maria, N. (1999). Multicultural issues in qualitative research. *Psychology and Marketing, 16*, 305–325.

Nevid, J. S., Rathus, S. A., & Greene, B. (2006). *Abnormal psychology in a changing world* (6th ed.). Upper Saddle River, NJ: Prentice-Hall.

Nevid, J. S., Rathus, S. A., & Greene, B. (2008). *Abnormal psychology in a changing world* (7th ed.). Upper Saddle River, NJ: Prentice-Hall.

Nevid, J. S., Rathus, S. A., & Greene, B. (2011). *Abnormal psychology in a changing world* (8th ed.) Upper Saddle River, NJ: Prentice-Hall.

New therapies for prevention and treatment of Alzheimer's Disease identified. (2011, January 11). *ScienceDaily.* Retrieved from http://www.sciencedaily.com/releases/2011/01/110112110739.htm.

Newbern, J. M., Li, X., Shoemaker, S. E., Zhou, J., Zhong, J., Wu, Y., et al. (2011). Specific functions for ERK/MAPK signaling during PNS development. *Neuron, 69*, 91. doi: 10.1016/j.neuron.2010.12.003

Newman, M. G., & Llera, S. J. (2011). A novel theory of experiential avoidance in generalized anxiety disorder: A review and synthesis of research supporting a contrast avoidance model of worry. *Clinical Psychology Review, 31*, 371–382. doi:10.1016/j.cpr.2011.01.008

Nguyen, H.-H.D., & Ryan, A. M. (2008). Does stereotype threat affect test performance of minorities and women? A meta-analysis of experimental evidence. *Journal of Applied Psychology, 93*, 1314–1334. doi: 10.1037/a0012702

Ni, X., Chan, K., Bulgin, N., Sicard, T., Bismil, R., McMain, S., et al. (2006). Association between serotonin transporter gene and borderline personality disorder. *Journal of Psychiatric Research, 40*, 448–453.

NICHD Early Child Care Research Network. (1997). The effects of infant child care on infant-mother attachment security: Results of the NICHD study of early child care. *Child Development, 68*, 860–879.

Nicholson, R. A., Mouton, G. J., Bagby, R. M., Buis, T., Peterson, S. A., & Buigas, R. A. (1997). Utility of MMPI-2 indicators of response distortion: Receiver operating characteristic analysis. *Psychological Assessment, 9*, 471–479.

Nicolosi, A., Laumann, E. O., Glasser, D. B., Brock, G., King, R., & Gingell, C. (2006). Sexual activity, sexual disorders and associated help-seeking behavior among mature adults in five anglophone countries from the Global Survey of Sexual Attitudes and Behaviors (GSSAB). *Journal of Sex & Marital Therapy, 32*, 331–342.

NIDA Notes (2004, December). 2003 survey reveals increase in prescription drug abuse, sharp drop in abuse of hallucinogens. *NIDA Notes, 19(4)*, 14.

Niiya, Y., Ellsworth, P. C., & Yamaguchi, S. (2006). Amae in Japan and the United States: An exploration of a "culturally unique." *Emotion, 6*, 279–295.

Nisbett, R. (2003). *Geography of thought*. New York: Free Press.

Nitschke, J. B., Sarinopoulos, I., Oathes, D. J., Johnstone, T., Whalen, P. J., Davidson, R. J., et al. (2009). Anticipatory activation in the amygdala and anterior cingulate in generalized anxiety disorder and prediction of treatment response. *American Journal of Psychiatry*. Retrieved from http://ajp.psychiatryonline.

Noftle, E. E., & Robins, R. W. (2007). Personality predictors of academic outcomes: Big Five correlates of GPA and SAT scores. *Journal of Personality and Social Psychology, 93*, 116–130.

Nolen-Hoeksema, S. (2008). It is not what you have; it is what you do with it: Support for Addis's gendered responding framework. *Clinical Psychology: Science and Practice, 15*, 178–181.

Nolen-Hoeksema, S., Morrow, J., & Fredrickson, B. L. (1993). Response styles and the duration of episodes of depressed mood. *Journal of Abnormal Psychology, 102*, 20–28.

Nolen-Hoeksema, S., Wisco, B. E., & Lyubomirsky, S. (2008). Rethinking rumination. *Perspectives on Psychological Science, 3*, 400–424.

Noonan, D. (2006, June 6). A little bit louder, please. *Newsweek*, pp. 42–45.

Norcross, J. C., Karpiak, C. P., & Santoro, S. O. (2005). Clinical psychologists across the years: The division of clinical psychology from 1960 to 2003. *Journal of Clinical Psychology, 61*, 1467–1483.

Norlander, T., Erixon, A., & Archer, T. (2000). Psychological androgyny and creativity: Dynamics of gender-role and personality trait. *Social Behavior and Personality, 28*(5), 423–435.

Nosek, B. A., Banaji, M. R., & Greenwald, A. G. (2003). Math male, me female, therefore math ≠ me. *Journal of Personality and Social Psychology, 83*, 44–59.

Novak, S., Nemeth, W. C., & Lawson, K. A. (2004). Trends in medical use and abuse of sustained-release opioid analgesics: A revisit. *Pain Medicine, 5*, 59–65.

Novotney, A. (2009, February). Dangerous distraction. *Monitor on Psychology, 40*(2), 3236.

Novotny, A. (2008, July/August). A competitive, slowly growing field. *Monitor on Psychology*, 39(7), 66.

Nowak, A., Vallacher, R. R., & Miller, M. E. (2003). Social influence and group dynamics. In T. Millon & M. J. Lerner (Eds.), *Handbook of psychology: Vol. 5. Personality and social psychology* (pp. 383–418). New York: John Wiley & Sons.

NYC Department of Health and Mental Hygiene. (2010). *Tobacco control*. Retrieved from http://www.nyc.gov/html/doh/html/smoke/smoke.shtml.

O'Connor, A. (2004b, March 23). Dreams ride on Freud's royal road, study finds. *New York Times*, p. F5.

O'Neil, J. (2003, February 4). Jog your memory? At the gym? *The New York Times*, p. F6.

O'Boyle, E. H., Humphrey, R. H., Pollack, J. M., Hawver, T. H., & Story, P. A. (2010). The relation between emotional intelligence and job performance: A meta-analysis. *Journal of Organizational Behavior*. Retrieved from http://crossroadscalifornia.com/wp-content/uploads/2010/09/Study-EQ-and-Job-Performance.pdf

Ohi, K., Hashimoto, R., Yasuda, Y., Yoshida, T., Takahashi, H., Iike, N., et al. (2010).The chitinase 3-like 1 gene and schizophrenia: Evidence from a multi-center case-control study and meta-analysis. *Schizophrenia Research, 116*, 126–132.

Ojemann, G. A., Schoenfield-McNeill, J., & Corina, D. P. (2002). Anatomic subdivisions in human temporal cortical neuronal activity related to recent verbal memory. *NatureNeuroscience, 5*, 64–71.

Olshansky, S. J., Passaro, D. J., Hershow, R. C., Layden, J., Carnes, B. A., Brody, J., et al. (2005). A potential decline in life expectancy in the United States in the 21st century. *New England Journal of Medicine, 352*, 1138–1145.

Olson, J. M., & Maio, G. R. (2003). Attitudes in social behavior. In T. Millon & M. J. Lerner (Eds.), *Handbook of psychology: Vol. 5. Personality and social psychology* (pp. 299–326). New York: John Wiley & Sons.

Olson, J. M., Vernon, P. A., & Harris, J. A. (2001). The heritability of attitudes: A study of twins. *Journal of Personality and Social Psychology, 80*, 845–860.

Olson, M. A., Crawford, M. T., & Devlin, W. (2009). Evidence for the underestimation of implicit in-group favoritism among low status groups. *Journal of Experimental Social Psychology, 45*, 1111–1116. doi:10.1016/j.jesp.2009.06.021

Oncken, C. A., & Kranzler, H. R. (2003). Pharmacotherapies to enhance smoking cessation during pregnancy. *Drug Alcohol Review, 22*, 191–202.

Ong, A. D. (2010). Pathways linking positive emotion and health in later life. *Current Directions in Psychological Science, 19*, 358–362. doi: 10.1177/0963721410388805

Ong, J. C., Shapiro, S. L., & Manber, R. (2008). Combining mindfulness meditation with cognitive-behavior therapy for insomnia: A treatment-development study. *Behavior Therapy, 39*, 171–182. doi: 10.1016/j.beth.2007.07.002

Onion, A. (2000, September 12). *Mind games: Subliminal ads mostly ineffective, but Americans think otherwise*. Retrieved from http://abcnews.go.com/sections/science/Daily News/subliminal000912.html.

Oquendo, M. A., Friend, J. M., Halberstam, B., Brodsky, B. S., Burke, A. K., Grunebaum, M. F., Malone, K. M., & Mann, J. J. (2003). Association of comorbid posttraumatic stress disorder and major depression with greater risk for suicidal behavior. *American Journal of Psychiatry, 160*, 580–582.

Oquendo, M. A., Hastings, R. S., Huang, Y., Simpson, N., Ogden, R. T., Hu, X. Z., et al. (2007). Brain serotonin transporter binding in depressed patients with bipolar disorder using positron emission tomography. *Archives of General Psychiatry, 64*, 201–208.

Ormerod, T. C., MacGregor, J. N., & Chronicle, E. P. (2002). Dynamics and constraints in insight problem solving. *Journal of Experimental Psychology-Learning, Memory, and Cognition, 28*, 791–799.

Ornstein, R. E. (1973). *The psychology of consciousness*. New York: Penguin Books.

Ortega, A. N., Rosenheck, R., Alegria, M., & Desai, R. A. (2000). Acculturation and the lifetime risk of psychiatric and substance use disorders among Hispanics. *Journal of Nervous and Mental Disease, 188*, 728–735.

Orth, U., Trzesniewski, K. H., & Robins, R. W. (2010). Self-esteem development from young adulthood to old age: A cohort-sequential longitudinal study. *Journal of Personality and Social Psychology, 98*, 645. doi: 10.1037/a0018769

Ortigue, S., Bianchi-Demicheli, F., Patel, N., Frum, C., & Lewis, J. W. (2010). Neuroimaging of love: fMRI meta-analysis evidence toward new perspectives in sexual medicine. *The Journal of Sexual Medicine*, 7, 3451–3552. doi: 10.1111/j.1743-6109.2010.01999.x

Osborne, A. F. (1963). *Applied imagination: Principles and procedures of creative problem solving*. New York: Scribners.

Ostir, G. V., Berges, I. M., Markides, K. S., & Ottenbacher, K. J. (2006). Hypertension in older adults and the role of positive emotions. *Psychosomatic Medicine, 68*, 727–733.

Ostler, K., Thompson, C., Kinmonth, A. L. K., Peveler, R. C., Stevens, L., & Stevens, A. (2001). Influence of socio-economic deprivation on the prevalence and outcome of depression in primary care: The Hampshire Depression Project. *British Journal of Psychiatry, 178*, 12–17.

Ottersen, O. P. (2005). Neurobiology: Sculpted by competition. *Nature, 434*, 969.

Ouellette, S. C., & DiPlacido, J. (2001). Personality's role in the protection and enhancements of health: Where the research has been, where it is stuck, how it might move. In A. Baum, T. A. Revenson, & J. E. Singer (Eds.), *Handbook of health psychology* (pp. 175–194). Mahwah, NJ: Lawrence Erlbaum Associates.

Overstreet, N. M., Quinn, D. M., & Agocha, V. B. (2010). Beyond thinness: The influence of a curvaceous body ideal on body dissatisfaction in Black and White Women. *Sex Roles, 63*, 91–103. doi: 10.1007/s11199-010-9792-4

Overton, W. F. (1997). *Developmental psychology: Philosophy, concepts, and methodology*. New York: Oxford University Press.

Oyserman, D. (2008). Racial-ethnic self-schemas: Multidimensional identity-based motivation. *Journal of Research in Personality, 42*, 1186–1198.

Oyserman, D., Coon, H. M., & Kemmelmeier, M. (2002). Rethinking individualism and collectivism: Evaluation of theoretical assumptions and meta-analyses. *Psychological Bulletin, 128*, 3–72.

Oz, M. (2003, January 20). Say "om" before surgery. *Time*, p. 43.

Pacemaker for brain may ease mental illness. (2008, November 12). Retrieved from http://www.msnbc.msn.com/id/27684083/.

Pacheco-Lopez, G., Niemi, M. B., Kou, W., Harting, M., Fandrey, J., & Schedlowski, M. (2005). Neural substrates for behaviorally conditioned immunosuppression in the rat. *Journal of Neuroscience, 25*, 2330–2337.

Packer, D. J. (2008). Identifying systematic disobedience in Milgram's Obedience experiments: A meta-analytic review. *Perspectives on Psychological Science, 3*, 301–304. doi: 10.1111/j.1745-6924.2008.00080.x 1

Pagani, L. S., Fitzpatrick, C., Barnett, T. A., & Dubow, E. (2010). Prospective associations between early childhood television exposure and academic, psychosocial, and physical well-being by middle childhood. *Archives of Pediatrics & Adolescent Medicine, 164*, 425–431.

Palfai, T. P., & Weafer, J. (2006). College student drinking and meaning in the pursuit of life goals. *Psychology of Addictive Behaviors, 20,* 131–134.

Pallier, C., Kouider, S., & De Gardelle, V. (2008). An fMRI study of subliminal priming of spoken words. *The Journal of the Acoustical Society of America, 123,* 3580. doi: 10.1121/1.2934684

Pampaloni, I., Sivakumaran, T., Hawley, C. J., Al Allaq, A., Farrow, J., Nelson, S., et al. (2009). High-dose selective serotonin reuptake inhibitors in OCD: A systematic retrospective case notes survey. *Journal of Psychopharmacology.* Retrieved from http://jop.sagepub.com/cgi/content/abstract/0269881109104850v1.

Pancsofar, N., & Vernon-Feagans, L. (2006). Mother and father language input to young children: Contributions to later language development. *Journal of Applied Developmental Psychology, 27,* 571–587.

Papadatou-Pastou, M., Martin, M., Munafò, M. R., & Jones, G. V. (2008). Sex differences in left-handedness: A meta-analysis of 144 studies. *Psychological Bulletin, 134,* 677–699. doi: 10.1037/a0012814

Paris, J. (2008). *Treatment of borderline personality disorder: A guide to evidence-based practice.* New York: Guilford Press.

Park, A. (2011, March 7). Healing the hurt. *Time,* pp. 64–71.

Park, A., Sher, K. J., & Krull, J. L. (2008). Risky drinking in college changes as fraternity/sorority affiliation changes: A person-environment perspective. *Psychology of Addictive Behaviors, 22,* 219–229. doi: 10.1037/0893-164X.22.2.219

Park, A., Sher, K. J., Wood, P. K., & Krull, J. L. (2009). Dual mechanisms underlying accentuation of risky drinking via fraternity/sorority affiliation: The role of personality, peer norms, and alcohol availability. *Journal of Abnormal Psychology, 118,* 241–255. doi: 10.1037/a0015126

Park, D. C., Lautenschlager, G., Hedden, T., Davidson, N. S., Smith, A. D., & Smith, P. K. (2002). Models of visuospatial and verbal memory across the adult life span. *Psychology and Aging, 17,* 299–320.

Park, J., & Banaji, M. R. (2000). Mood and heuristics: The influence of happy and sad states on sensitivity and bias in stereotyping. *Journal of Personality and Social Psychology, 78,* 1005–1023.

Parke, R. D. (2004). Development in the family. *Annual Review of Psychology, 55,* 365–399.

Parke, R. D. (2004). Fathers, families, and the future: a plethora of plausible predictions. *Merrill-Palmer Quarterly, 50,* 456–470.

Parke, R. D., & Buriel, R. (1998). Socialization in the family: Ethnic and ecological perspectives. In W. Damon (Editor-in-Chief) & N. Eisenberg (Vol. Ed.), *Handbook of child psychology: 5th ed., Vol. 3. Social, emotional, and personality development* (pp. 463–552). New York: John Wiley & Sons.

Parker, G., Gladstone, G., & Chee, K. T. (2001). Depression in the planet's largest ethnic group: the Chinese. *American Journal of Psychiatry, 158,* 857–864.

Parker, J. D. A., Duffy, L. M., Wood, L. M., Bond, B. J., & Hogan, M. J. (2005). Academic achievement and emotional intelligence: Predicting the successful transition from high school to university. *Journal of First-Year Experience and Students in Transition, 17,* 67–78.

Parker-Pope, T. (2009, January 13). A problem of the brain, not the hands: Group urges phone ban for drivers. *The New York Times,* p. D5.

Parloff, R. (2003, February 3). Is fat the next tobacco? *Fortune,* pp. 51–54.

Parsons, B., Allison, D. B., Loebel, A., Williams, K., Giller, E., Romano, S., et al. (2009). Weight effects associated with antipsychotics: A comprehensive database analysis. *Schizophrenia Research, 110,* 103–111.

Parsons, T. D., & Rizzo. A. A. (2008). Affective outcomes of virtual reality exposure therapy for anxiety and specific phobias: A meta-analysis. *Journal of Behavior Therapy and Experimental Psychiatry, 39,* 250–261.

Part of the brain that tracks limbs in space discovered. *ScienceDaily* (July 19, 2010). Retrieved from http://www.sciencedaily.com/releases/2010/07/100715123406.htm.

Pascalis, O., deHaan, M., Nelson, C. A., & de Schonen, S. (1998). Long-term recognition memory for faces assessed by visual paired comparison in 3- and 6-month-old infants. *Journal of Experimental Psychology:Learning, Memory, and Cognition, 24,* 249–260.

Pasupathi, M. (1999). Age differences in response to conformity pressure for emotional and nonemotional material. *Psychology and Aging, 14,* 170–174.

Pate, J. L. (2000). Psychological organizations in the United States. *American Psychologist, 55,* 1139–1143.

Patterson, C. J. (2009). *Lesbian & gay parents & their children: Summary of research findings.* Retrieved from http://www.apa.org/pi/lgbc/publications/lgpsummary.html.

Patterson, D. R., & Jensen, M. P. (2003) Hypnosis and clinical pain. *Psychological Bulletin, 129,* 495–521.

Patton, G. C., et al. (2002). Cannabis use and mental health in young people: Cohort study. *British Medical Journal, 325,* 1195–1198.

Paul, P. (2005, January 17). The power to uplift. *Time Magazine,* pp. A46–A48.

Paulos, J. A. (2009, December 12). Mammogram math. *The New York Times Magazine,* pp. 19–20.

Payne, J. D., & Kensinger, E. A. (2010). Sleep's role in the consolidation of emotional episodic memories. *Current Directions in Psychological Science, 19,* 290–295. doi:10.1177/096372141038397

Pearson, H. (2006, September 18). Distaste for sprouts in the genes. *News@ Nature.com.* Retrieved from http://www.nature.com/ news/2006/060918/full/060918-1.html.

Pedersen, D. M., & Wheeler, J. (1983). The Mueller-Lyer illusion among Navajos. *Journal of Social Psychology, 121,* 3–6.

Pengilly, J. W., & Dowd, E. T. (2000). Hardiness and social support as moderators of stress. *Journal of Clinical Psychology, 56,* 813–820.

Penner, L. A., Dovidio, J. F., Piliavin, J. A., & Schroeder, D. A. (2005). Prosocial behavior: Multilevel perspectives. *Annual Review of Psychology, 56,* 365–392.

Peplau, L. A. (2003). Human sexuality: How do men and women differ? *Current Directions in Psychological Science, 12,* 37–40.

Pepper, T. (2005, February 21). Inside the head of an applicant. *Newsweek,* pp. E24–E26.

Perello, M., Sakata, I., Birnbaum, S., Chuang, J.-C., Osborne-Lawrence, S., Rovinsky, S. A., Zigman, J. M. (2009). Ghrelin increases the rewarding value of high-fat diet in an orexin-dependent manner. *Biological Psychiatry, 67,* 880–888. doi: 10.1016/j.biopsych.2009.10.030

Peres, J. (2007, July 31). The 237 reasons to have sex. *Chicago Tribune.* Retrieved from http://tinyurl.com/2mg5k5.

Peretz, I., & Zatorre, R. J. (2005). Brain organization for music processing. *Annual Review of Psychology, 56,* 89–114.

Perlis, M. L., Jungquist, C., Smith, M. T., & Posner, D. (2008). *Cognitive behavioral treatment of insomnia: A session by session guide.* New York, NY: Springer.

Perry, W. (2003). Let's call the whole thing off: A response to Dawes (2001). *Psychological Assessment, 15,* 582–585.

Pesant, N., & Zadra, A. (2004). Working with dreams in therapy: What do we know and what should we do? *Clinical Psychology Review, 24,* 489–512.

Peters, E., Hess, T. M., Västfjäll, D., & Auman, C. (2007). Adult age differences in dual information processes: Implications for the role of affective and deliberative processes in older adults' decision making. *Perspectives on Psychological Science, 2,* 1–23.

Petersen, J. L, & Hyde, J. S. (2010). A meta-analytic review of research on gender differences in sexuality, 1993–2007. *Psychological Bulletin, 136,* 21–38.doi: 10.1037/a0017504

Peterson, B. E., & Duncan, L. E. (2007). Midlife women's generativity and authoritarianism: Marriage, motherhood, and 10 years of aging. *Psychology and Aging, 22,* 411–419.

Peterson, M. A. & Skow, E. (2008). Inhibitory competition between shape properties in figure-ground perception. *Journal of Experimental Psychology: Human Perception and Performance, 34,* 251–267. doi: 10.1037/0096-1523.34.2.251

Petrova, P. K., Cialdini, R. B., & Sills, S. J. (2006). Consistency-based compliance across cultures. *Journal of Experimental Social Psychology, 43,* 104–111.

Pettigrew, T. F., & Tropp, L. R. A. (2006). A meta-analytic test of intergroup contact theory. *Journal of Personality and Social Psychology, 90,* 751–783.

Petty, R. E., & Briñol, P. (2008) Persuasion: From single to multiple to metacognitive processes. *Perspectives on Psychological Science, 3,* 137–147. doi: 10.1111/j.1745-6916.2008.00071

Petty, R. E., Wegener, D. T., & Fabrigar, L. R. (1997). Attitudes and attitude change. *Annual Review of Psychology, 48,* 609–647.

Pew Social Trends. (2010, November 18). *The decline of marriage and rise of new families.* Retrieved from http://pewsocialtrends.org/2010/11/18/the-decline-of-marriage-and-rise-of-new-families.

Pezdek, K., & Lam, S. (2007). What research paradigms have cognitive psychologists used to study "false memory," 'and what are the implications of these choices? *Consciousness and Cognition, 16,* 2–17.

Phelps, E. A., Ling, S., & Carrasco, M. (2006). Emotion facilitates perception and potentiates the perceptual benefits of attention. *Psychological Science, 17,* 292–299.

Phillips, S. T., & Ziller, R. C. (1997). Toward a theory and measure of the nature of nonprejudice. *Journal of Personality and Social Psychology,* 72, 420–434.

Piaget, J. (1952). *The origins of intelligence in children.* New York: International Universities Press.

Pierce, R. C., & Kumaresan, V. (2006). The mesolimbic dopamine system: The final common pathway for the reinforcing effect of drugs of abuse? *Neuroscience and Biobehavioral Reviews, 30,* 215–238.

Pierre, M. R., & Mahalik, J. R. (2005). Examining African self-consciousness and black racial identity as predictors of black men's psychological well-being. *Cultural Diversity and Ethnic Minority Psychology, 11,* 28–40.

Pietschnig, J., Voraceka, M., & Formann, A. K. (2011). Female Flynn effects: No sex differences in generational IQ gains. *Personality and Individual Differences, 50,* 759–762.

Pincus, A. L., Lukowitsky, M. R., Wright, A. G. C., & Eichler, W. C. (2009). The interpersonal nexus of persons, situations, and psychopathology. *Journal of Research in Personality, 43,* 264–265. doi:10.1016/j.jrp.2008.12.029

Pink, D. (2003, December 14). Gratitude visits. *The New York Times Magazine,* p. 73.

Pinker, S. (1994). *The language instinct.* New York: William Morrow.

Pinker, S. (2003). Language as an adaptation to the cognitive niche. In M. H. Christiansen and S. Kirby (Eds.), *Language evolution* (pp. 16–37). New York: Oxford University Press.

Pittman, T. S. (1998). Motivation. In D. T. Gilbert, S. T. Fiske, & G. Lindzey (Eds.), *The handbook of social psychology* (4th ed., Vol. 1, pp. 549–590). Boston: McGraw-Hill.

Plaks, J. E., & Higgins, E. T. (2000). Pragmatic use of stereotyping in teamwork: Social loafing and compensation as a function of inferred partner-situation fit. *Journal of Personality and Social Psychology, 79*, 962–974.

Plaza, M., Gatignol, P., Leroy, M., & Duffau, H. (2009). Speaking without Broca's area after tumor resection. *Neurocase, 9*, 1–17.

Pliner, P. H., Hart, H., Kohl, J., & Saari, D. (1974). Compliance without pressure: Some further data on the foot-in-the-door technique. *Journal of Experimental Social Psychology, 10*, 17–22.

Plomin, R., & Haworth, C. M. A. (2009). Genetics of high cognitive abilities. *Journal of Behavior Genetics, 39*, 347–349. doi: 10.1007/s10519-009-9277-9

Plomin, R., & McGuffin, P. (2003). Psychopathology in the postgenomic era. *Annual Review of Psychology, 54*, 205–228.

Plomin, R., & Petrill, S. A. (1997). Genetics and intelligence: What's new. *Intelligence, 24*, 53–57.

Plomin, R., DeFries, J. C., Craig, I. W., & McGuffin, P. (Eds.). (2003). *Behavioral genetics in the postgenomic era*. Washington, DC: APA Books.

Plous, S. (1996). Attitudes toward the use of animals in psychological research and education. *American Psychologist, 51*, 1167–1180.

Poldrack, R. A. (2010). Mapping mental function to brain structure: How can cognitive neuroimaging succeed? *Perspectives on Psychological Science, 5*, 753–761. doi:10.1177/1745691610388777

Polinko, N. K., & Popovich, P. M (2001). Evil thoughts but angelic actions: Responses to overweight job applicants. *Journal of Applied Social Psychology, 31*, 905–924.

Pollack, A. (2004a, January 13). Putting a price on a good night's sleep. *The New York Times*, pp. CF1, F8.

Pollick, A. S., & de Waal, F. B. M. (2007). Ape gestures and language evolution. *Proceedings of the National Academy of Sciences, Online Edition*. doi: 10.1073/ pnas.0702624104

Poropat, A. E. (2009). A meta-analysis of the five-factor model of personality and academic performance. *Psychological Bulletin, 135*, 322–338. 10.1037/a0014996

Posthuma, D., & de Geus, E. J. C. (2006). Progress in the molecular-genetic study of intelligence. *Current Directions in Psychological Science, 15*, 151–155.

Potkin, S. G., Guffanti, G., Lakatos, A., Turner, J. A., Kruggel, F., Fallon, J. H., et al. (2009, August 7). Hippocampal atrophy as a quantitative trait in a genome-wide association study identifying novel susceptibility genes for Alzheimer's disease. *PLos One*. Retrieved from http://www.plosone.org/article/info:doi/10.1371/journal.pone.0006501;jsessionid=8C9F392B696757818A7FF8EC8D7016EE

Powers, M. & Emmelkamp, P.M.G. (2008). Virtual reality exposure therapy for anxiety disorders: A meta-analysis. *Journal of Anxiety Disorders, 22*, 561–569.

Powers, M. B., Halpern, Powers, M. B., Halpern, J. M., Ferenschak, M. P., Gillihan, S. J., & Foa, E. B. (2010). A meta-analytic review of prolonged exposure for posttraumatic stress disorder. *Clinical Psychology Review, 30*, 635–641. doi:10.1016/j.cpr.2010.04.007

Premack, D. (1971). Language in chimpanzees. *Science, 172*, 808–822.

Pressman, S. D., & Cohen, S. (2005). Does positive affect influence health? *Psychological Bulletin, 131*, 925–971.

Price, M. (2009a, January). The left brain knows what the right hand is doing. *Monitor on Psychology*, 40(1), 60–63.

Price, M. (2009b, January). Lateral of the sexes. *Monitor on Psychology*, 40(1), 62.

Price, M. (2009c, December). More than shelter. *Monitor on Psychology, 40*(11), 59–62.

Price, T. S., & Jaffee, S. R. (2008). Effects of the family environment: Gene-environment interaction and passive gene-environment correlation. *Developmental Psychology, 44*, 305–315. doi: 10.1037/0012-1649.44.2.305

Priebe, N. J., & Ferster, D. (2010). Neuroscience: Each synapse to its own. *Nature, 464*, 1290–1291. doi:10.1038/4641290b

Prochaska, J. O., & Norcross, J. C. (2010). *Systems of psychotherapy* (7th ed). Brooks/Cole, Cengage Learning.

Proffitt, D. R. (2006). Distance perception. *Current Directions in Psychological Science, 15*, 131–135.

Provine, R. R. (2004). Laughing, tickling and the evolution of speech and self. *Current Directions in Psychological Science, 13*, 215–218.

Prudic, J., Olfson, M., Marcus, S. C., Fuller, R. B., & Sackeim, H. A. (2004). Effectiveness of electroconvulsive therapy in community settings. *Biological Psychiatry, 55*, 301–312.

Pruessner, M., Iyer, S. N., Faridi, K., Joober, R., & Malla, A. K. (2011). Stress and protective factors in individuals at ultra-high risk for psychosis, first episode psychosis and healthy controls. *Schizophrenia Research, 129*, 29–35.

Puighermanal, E., Marsicano, G., Busquets-Garcia, A., Lutz, B., Maldonado, R. & Ozaita, A. (2009). Cannabinoid modulation of hippocampal long-term memory is mediated by mTOR signaling. *Nature Neuroscience, 12*, 1152–1158. doi:10.1038/nn.2369

Qaseem, A., Snow, V., Denberg, T. D., Casey, D. E., Jr., Forciea, M. A., Owens, D. K., et al. (2009). Testing and pharmacologic treatment of erectile dysfunction: A clinical practice guideline from the American College of Physicians. *Annals of Internal Medicine, 151*, 639–649.

Qaseem, A., Snow, V., Denberg, T. D., Forciea, M. A., Owens, D, K., & the Clinical Efficacy Assessment Subcommittee of the American College of Physicians (2008). Using second-generation antidepressants to treat depressive disorders: A clinical practice guideline from the American College of Physicians. *Annals of Internal Medicine, 149*, 725–733.

Querfurth, H. W., & LaFerla, F. M. (2010). Alzheimer's Disease. *New England Journal of Medicine, 362*, 329–344.

Quinn, P. C., & Liben, L. S. (2008). A sex difference in mental rotation in young infant. *Psychological Science, 19*, 1067–1070. doi: 10.1111/j.1467-9280.2008.02201

Quinn, S. (1987). *A mind of her own: The life of Karen Horney*. New York: Summit Books.

Rabasca, L. (2000, March). Listening instead of preaching. *Monitor on Psychology, 31*(3), pp. 50–51.

Rabin, R. C. (2008, May 13). For a sharp brain, stimulation. *The New York Times*, p. H4.

Radel, M., Vallejo, R. L., Iwata, N., Aragon, R., Long, J. C., Virkkunen, M., et al. (2005). Haplotype based localization of an alcohol dependence gene to the 5q34? aminobutyric acid Type A gene cluster. *Archives of General Psychiatry, 62*, 47–55.

Raeburn, P. (2005, February 20). The therapeutic mind scan. *New York Times Magazine*, pp. 20–21.

Rahman, A. A., Lophatananon, A., Brown, S. S., Harriss, D., Anderson, J., Parker, T., et al. (2010). Hand pattern indicates prostate cancer risk. *British Journal of Cancer, 104*, 175–177. doi:10.1038/sj.bjc.6605986

Raine, A. (2008). From genes to brain to antisocial behavior. *Current Directions in Psychological Science, 17*, 323–328. doi: 10.1111/j.1467-8721.2008.00599

Ransohoff, R. M. (2007). Natalizumab for multiple sclerosis. *New England Journal of Medicine, 356*, 2622–2629.

Rapee, R. M., Gaston, J. E., & Abbott, M. J. (2009). Testing the efficacy of theoretically derived improvements in the treatment of social phobia. *Journal of Consulting and Clinical Psychology, 77*, 317–327. doi: 10.1037/a0014800

Raskin, N. J., Rogers, C. R., & Witty, M. C. (2008). Person-centered therapy. In R. J. Corsini & D. Wedding (Eds.) (8th ed.), *Current psychotherapies* (pp. 141–186). Belmont, CA: Thomson Higher Education.

Ratiu, P., & Talos, I. F. (2004). The tale of Phineas Gage, digitally remastered. *New England Journal of Medicine, 351*, e21.

Rawe, J., & Kingsbury, K. (2006, May 22). When colleges go on suicide watch. *Time*, pp. 62– 63.

Rawson, N. E. (2006). Olfactory loss in aging. *Science of Aging Knowledge Environment, 5*, p.6.

Ray, O., & Ksir, C. (1990). *Drugs, society, and human behavior* (5th ed.). St. Louis: Times Mirror/Mosby.

Raya, S., Nizamie, S. H., Akhtar, S., Praharaj, S. K., Mishra, B. R., & Zia-ul-Haq, M. (2011). Efficacy of adjunctive high frequency repetitive transcranial magnetic stimulation of left prefrontal cortex in depression: A randomized sham controlled study. *Journal of Affective Disorders, 128*, 153–159. doi:10.1016/j.jad.2010.06.027

Raymond, J. (2000, Fall/Winter). The world of the senses. *Newsweek Special Issue*, pp. 16–18.

Raz, A., Zigman, P., & de Jong, V. (2009). Placebo effects and placebo responses: Filling the interstices with meaning. *PsycCRITIQUES*, 54(33). Retrieved from http://psycnet.apa.org/index.cfm?fa=search.displayRecord&uid=2009-10507-001

Read, J. P., Wood, M. D., Kahlera, C. W., Maddock, J. E., & Palfaid, T. P. (2003). Examining the role of drinking motives in college student alcohol use and problems. *Psychology of Addictive Behaviors, 17*, 13–23.

Reardon, L. E., Leen-Feldner, E. W., & Hayward, C. (2009). A critical review of the empirical literature on the relation between anxiety and puberty. *Clinical Psychology Review, 29*, 1–23. 10.1007/978-0-387-74753-8

Reas, D. L., & Grilo, C. M. (2007). Timing and sequence of the onset of overweight, dieting, and binge eating in overweight patients with binge eating disorder. *International Journal of Eating Disorders, 40*, 165–170.

Redick, T. S., Calvo, A., Gay, C. E., & Engle, R. W. (2011). Working memory capacity and go/no-go task performance: Selective effects of updating, maintenance, and inhibition. *Journal of Experimental Psychology: Learning, Memory, and Cognition*, 37, 308–324. doi: 10.1037/a0022216

Reece, M. Herbenick, D., Schick, V., Sanders, S. A., Dodge, B., & Fortenberry, D. (2010). Sexual behaviors, relationships, and perceived health among adult men in the United States: Results from a national probability sample. *Journal of Sexual Medicine*, 7 (suppl 5), 291–304. doi: 10.1111/j.1743-6109.2010.02009.x

Reece, M., Herbenick, D., Schick, V., Sanders, S.A., Dodge, B., & Fortenberry, J.D. (2010). Sexual behaviors, relationships, and perceived health among adult men in the United States: Results from a national probability sample. *Journal of Sexual Medicine*, 7 (suppl 5), 291–304.

Reed, G. (2008). Birth of a new breed of supertaster. *Chemical Senses, 33*, 489–491.

Rees, P. M., Fowler, C. J., & Maas, C. P. (2007). Sexual function in men and women with neurological disorders. *The Lancet, 369*, 512–525.

Reese-Weber, M. (2000). Middle and late adolescents' conflict resolution skills with siblings: Associations with interparental and parent-adolescent conflict resolution. *Journal of Youth and Adolescence, 29*, 697–711.

Reese-Weber, M., & Marchand, J. E. (2002). Family and individual predictors of late adolescents' romantic relationships. *Journal of Youth and Adolescence, 31,* 197–206.

Reifler, B. V. (2006). Play it again, Sam—depression is recurring. *New England Journal of Medicine, 354,* 1189–1190.

Reinberg, S. (2009, January 12). Lack of sleep linked to common cold. *WashingtonPost.com.* Retrieved from http://www.washingtonpost.com/wp-dyn/content/article/2009/01/12/AR2009011202090.html.

Reiner, W. G., & Gearhart, J. P. (2004). Discordant sexual identity in some genetic males with cloacal exstrophy assigned to female sex at birth. *New England Journal of Medicine, 350,* 333–341.

Reinisch, J. M. (1990). *The Kinsey Institute new report on sex: What you must know to be sexually literate.* New York: St. Martin's Press.

Reis, H. T., & Aron, A. (2008). Love: What is it, why does it matter, and how does it operate? *Perspectives on Psychological Science, 3,* 80–86. doi: 10.1111/j.1745-6916.2008.00065.x

Reiss, D. (2010). Genetic thinking in the study of social relationships: Five points of entry. *Perspectives on Psychological Science, 5,* 502–515. doi:10.1177/174569161038351

Reiss, D., Neiderhiser, J. M., Hetherington, E. M., & Plomin, R. (2000). *The relationship code: Deciphering genetic and social influences on adolescent development.* Cambridge, MA: Harvard University Press.

Reitz, C., Honig, L., Vonsattel, J. P., Tang, M.-X., & Mayeux, R. (2009). Memory performance is related to amyloid and tau pathology in the hippocampus. *Journal of Neurology, Neurosurgery, and Psychiatry, 80,* 715–721. doi:10.1136/jnnp.2008.154146

Renner, M. J., & Mackin, R. S. (1998). A life stress instrument for classroom use. *Teaching of Psychology, 25,* 46–48.

Renoux, C., Vukusic, S., Mikaeloff, Y., Edan, G., Clanet, M., Dubois, B., et al. (2007). Natural history of multiple sclerosis with childhood onset. *New England Journal of Medicine, 356,* 2603–2613.

Rescorla, R. A. (1967). Pavlovian conditioning and its proper control procedures. *Psychological Review, 74,* 71–80.

Rescorla, R. A. (1988). Pavlovian conditioning: It's not what you think it is. *American Psychologist, 43,* 151–160.

Rescorla, R. A. (2009). A theory of Pavlovian conditioning: Variations in the effectiveness of reinforcement and nonreinforcement. In D. Shanks (Ed.), *Psychology of learning.* Thousand Oaks, CA: Sage.

Rettner, R. (2010, May 17). *People are happier, less stressed after age 50.* Retrieved from http://www.msnbc.msn.com/id/37195913/ns/health-aging/.

Reuter, M., Frenzel, C., Walter, N. T., Markett, S., & Montag, C. (2010). Investigating the genetic basis of altruism: The role of the COMT Val158Met polymorphism. *Social Cognitive and Affective Neuroscience.* Retrieved from http://scan.oxfordjournals.org/content/early/2010/10/28/scan.nsq083.full.pdf, doi: 10.1093/scan/nsq083

Rey, J. M., & Tennant, C. C. (2002). Cannabis and mental health: More evidence establishes clear link between use of cannabis and psychiatric illness. *British Medical Journal, 325,* 1183–1184.

Reyna, V. F., & Farley, F. (2006). Risk and rationality in adolescent decision making implications for theory, practice, and public policy. *Psychological Science in the Public Interest, 7,* 2–44.

Reynolds, C. A., Barlow, T., & Pedersen, N. L. (2006). Alcohol, tobacco and caffeine use: Spouse similarity processes. *Behavior Genetics, 36,* 201–215.

Reynolds, C. F., Dew, M. A., Pollock, B. J., Mulsant, B. H., Frank, E., Miller, M. D., et al. (2006). Maintenance treatment of major depression in old age. *New England Journal of Medicine, 354,* 1130–1138.

Rhoades, G. K., Stanley, S. M., & Markman, H. J. (2009). The pre-engagement cohabitation effect: A replication and extension of previous findings. *Journal of Family Psychology, 23,* 107–111.

Ribeiro, S., & Nicolelis, M. (2004). Reverberation, storage, and postsynaptic propagation of memories during sleep. *Learning and Memory, 11,* 686–696.

Ricciardelli, L. A., McCabe, M. P., Williams, R. J., & Thompson, J. K. (2007). The role of ethnicity and culture in body image and disordered eating among males. *Clinical Psychology Review, 27,* 582–606.

Richardson-Jones, J. W., Craige, C., Guiard, A., Stephen, A., Metzger, K., Kung, H.,et al. (2010). 5-HT1A autoreceptor levels determine vulnerability to stress and response to antidepressants. *Neuron, 65,* 40–52. doi:10.1016/j.neuron.2009.12.003

Richtel, M. (2009, December 7). Promoting the car phone, despite risks. *The New York Times,* pp. A 1, A20.

Richter, L. M. (2006). Studying adolescence. *Science, 312,* 1902–1905.

Rief, W., Nestoriuc, Y., Weiss, S., Welzel, E., Barsky, A. J., & Hofmann, S. G. (2009). Meta-analysis of the placebo response in antidepressant trials. *Journal of Affective Disorders, 118,* 1–8. doi:10.1016/j.jad.2009.01.029

Rieger, E., Van Buren, D. J., Bishop, M, Tanofsky-Kraff, M., Welch, R., & Wilfley, D. E. (2010). An eating disorder-specific model of interpersonal psychotherapy (IPT-ED): Causal pathways and treatment implications. *Clinical Psychology Review, 30,* 400–410. doi:10.1016/j.cpr.2010.02.001

Rieger, G., Linsenmeier, J. A. W., & Bailey, J. M. (2009). Childhood gender nonconformity remains a robust and neutral correlate of sexual orientation: Reply to Hegarty (2009). *Developmental Psychology, 45,* 901–903.

Rimmele, U., Hediger, K., Heinrichs, M., & Klaver, P. (2009). Oxytocin improves social recognition in humans. *The Journal of Neuroscience, 29,* 38–42.

Rind, B., & Strohmetz, D. (1999). Effect on restaurant tipping of a helpful message written on the back of customers' checks. *Journal of Applied Social Psychology, 29,* 139–144.

Ripley, A. (2005, March 7). Who says a woman can't be Einstein? *Time,* pp. 51–60.

Riso, L. P., duToit, P. L., Blandino, J. A., Penna, S., Dacey, S., Duin, J. S., et al. (2003). Cognitive aspects of chronic depression. *Journal of Abnormal Psychology, 112,* 72–80.

Roberts, A., Cash, T. F., Feingold, A., & Johnson, B. T. (2006). Are black-white differences in females' body dissatisfaction decreasing? A meta-analytic review. *Journal of Consulting and Clinical Psychology, 74,* 1121–1131.

Roberts, B. W., Walton, K. E., & Viechtbauer, W. (2006a). Patterns of mean-level change in personality traits across the life course: A meta-analysis of longitudinal studies. *Psychological Bulletin, 132,* 1–25.

Roberts, B. W., Walton, K. E., & Viechtbauer, W. (2006b). Personality traits change in adulthood: Reply to Costa and McCrae (2006). *Psychological Bulletin, 132,* 29–32.

Roberts, B., W., Smith, J., Jackson, J. J., & Edmonds, G. (2009). Compensatory conscientiousness and health in older couples. *Psychological Science, 20,* 553–559. doi: 10.1111/j.1467-9280.2009.02339.x

Roberts, S. (2007, January 16). 51% of women are now living without spouse. *The New York Times,* pp. A1, A18.

Rodgers, R. F., Salès, P., & Chabrol, H. (2010). Psychological functioning, media pressure and body dissatisfaction among college women. *European Review of Applied Psychology, 60,* 89–95. doi:10.1016/j.erap.2009.10.001

Rodriguez, J., Umaña-Taylor, A., Smith, E. P., & Johnson, D. J. (2009). Cultural processes in parenting and youth outcomes: Examining a model of racial-ethnic socialization and identity in diverse populations. *Cultural Diversity and Ethnic Minority Psychology, 15,* 106–111. doi: 10.1037/a0015510

Roemer, L., & Orsillo, S. M. (2003). Mindfulness: A promising intervention strategy in need of further study. *Clinical Psychology: Science and Practice, 10,* 172–178.

Roger, V. L. (2009). Lifestyle and cardiovascular health: Individual and societal choices. *Journal of the American Medical Association, 302,* 437–439.

Rogers, C. R. (1951). *Client-centered therapy: Its current practice, implications, and theory.* Boston: Houghton Mifflin.

Rogers, C. R. (1961). *On becoming a person.* Boston: Houghton Mifflin.

Rogers, C. R. (1980). *A way of being.* Boston: Houghton Mifflin.

Roisman, G. I., & Fraley, R. C. (2008). A behavior-genetic study of parenting quality, infant attachment security, and their covariation in a nationally representative sample. *Developmental Psychology, 44,* 831–839. doi: 10.1111/j.1467-8624.2006.00965.x

Ronksley, P. E., Brien, S. E., Turner, B. J., Mukamal, K. J., & Ghali, W. A. (2011). Association of alcohol consumption with selected cardiovascular disease outcomes: a systematic review and meta-analysis. *British Medical Journal, 342,* 671. doi: 10.1136/bmj.d671

Rosch, E. (1975). Cognitive representation of semantic categories. *Journal of Experimental Psychology: General, 105,* 192–223.

Rosch-Heider, E., & Olivier, D. C. (1972). The structure of the color space in naming and memory for two languages. *Cognitive Psychology, 3,* 337–354.

Rosen, R. C., & Laumann, E. O. (2003). The prevalence of sexual problems in women: How valid are comparisons across studies? Commentary on Bancroft, Loftus, and Long's (2003) "Distress about sex: A national survey of women in heterosexual relationships." *Archives of Sexual Behavior, 32*(3), 209–211.

Rosen, R. C., Fisher, W. A., Eardley, I., Niederberger, C., Nadel, A., & Sand, M. (2004). Men's Attitudes to Life Events and Sexuality (MALES) Study. *Current Medical Research Opinion, 20,* 607–617.

Rosenberg, K. D., Sandoval, A. P., Hedberg, K., & Hedberg, K. (2010). Television and video viewing time among children aged 2 Years—Oregon, 2006–2007. *Journal of the American Medical Association, 304,* 1662–1667.

Rosenfeld, M. J. (2010). Nontraditional families and childhood progress through school. *Demography, 47,* 755. doi: 10.1353/dem.0.0112

Rosenkoetter, L. I., Rosenkoetter, S. E., & Acock, A. C. (2009). Television violence: An intervention to reduce its impact on children. *Journal of Applied Developmental Psychology, 30,* 381–397. doi:10.1016/j.appdev.2008.12.019

Rothbart, M. K., (2007). Temperament, development, and pesonalty. *Current Directions in Psychological Science, 16,* 207–212.

Rotter, J. B. (1990). Internal versus external control of reinforcement: A case history of a variable. *American Psychologist, 45,* 489–493.

Roy, A. K., Shehzad, Z., Margulies, D. S., Kelly, A. M., Uddin, L. Q., Gotimer, K., et al. (2009). Functional connectivity of the human amygdala using resting state fmri. *NeuroImage, 45,* 614–626. doi:10.1016/j.neuroimage.2008.11.030

Roy-Byrne, P. (2010, August 2). How do antidepressants increase suicide risk in the young? *Journal Watch Psychiatry.* Retrieved from http://psychiatry.jwatch.org/cgi/content/full/2010/802/2

Roy-Byrne, P. (2007, January 2). *Behavioral treatment for chronic insomnia*. Retrieved from Workshttp://psychiatry.jwatch.org/cgi/content/ full/2006/1229/3?qetoc.

Roy-Byrne, P. (2009, January 12). With a little help from my friends: The happiness effect. *Journal Watch Psychiatry*. Retrieved from http://psychiatry.jwatch.org/cgi/content/full/2009/112/1.

Roy-Byrne, P., Craske, M. G., Sullivan, G., Rose, R. D., Edlund, M. J., Lang, A. J., et al. (2010). Delivery of evidence-based treatment for multiple anxiety disorders in primary care: A randomized controlled trial. *Journal of the American Medical Association, 303*, 1921–1928.

Rozin, P., Bauer, R., & Catanese, D. (2003). Food and life, pleasure and worry, among American college students: Gender differences and regional similarities. *Journal of Personality and Social Psychology, 85*, 132–141.

Rubenzahl, L. (2011). The bright spots of kids' TV. *Scientific American*, 304, 28–28.

Rubin, K. H., Bukowski, W. M., & Laursen, B. (Eds.) (2009). *Handbook of peer interactions, relationships, and groups*. New York: Guilford.

Rubin, K. H., Burgess, K. B., & Dwyer, K. M. (2003). Predicting preschoolers' externalizing behaviors from toddler temperament, conflict, and maternal negativity. *Developmental Psychology, 39*, 164–176.

Rudman, L. A., Ashmore, R. D., & Gary, M. L. (2001). "Unlearning" automatic biases: The malleability of implicit prejudice and stereotypes. *Journal of Personality and Social Psychology, 81*, 856–868.

Rupp, R. (1998). *Committed to memory: How we remember and why we forget*. New York: Crown.

Rusanen, M., Kivipelto, M., Quesenberry Jr, C. P., Zhou, J., & Whitmer, R. A. (2010). Heavy smoking in midlife and long-term risk of Alzheimer disease and vascular dementia. *Archives of Internal Medicine, 171*, 333–339. doi:10.1001/archinternmed.2010.393

Rushton, J. P., & Bons, T. A. (2005). Mate choice and friendship in twins: Evidence for genetic similarity. *Psychological Science, 16*, 555–559.

Rutledge, P. C., Park, A., & Sher, K. J. (2008). 21st birthday drinking: Extremely extreme. *Journal of Consulting and Clinical Psychology, 76*, 511–516. doi: 10.1037/0022-006X.76.3.511

Ryan, D.H., & Kushner, R. (2010). The state of obesity and obesity research. *Journal of the American Medical Association, 304*, 1835–1836. doi:10.1001/jama.2010.1531

Ryan, R. M., & Deci, E. L. (2000). Self-determination theory and the facilitation of intrinsic motivation, social development, and well-being. *American Psychologist, 55*, 68–78.

Rydell, R. J., Rydell, M. T., & Boucher, K. L. (2010). The effect of negative performance stereotypes on learning. *Journal of Personality and Social Psychology,* 99, 883–896. doi: 10.1037/a0021139

Sadeghniiat-Haghighi, K., Aminian, O., Pouryaghoub G., & Yazdi, Z. (2008). Efficacy and hypnotic effects of melatonin in shift-work nurses: Double-blind, placebo-controlled crossover trial. *Journal of Circadian Rhythms, 6*,10. doi:10.1186/1740-3391-6-10

Sahin, N.T., Pinker, S., Cash, S. S., Schomer, D., & Halgren, E. (2009). Sequential processing of lexical, grammatical, and phonological information within Broca's area. *Science, 326*, 445–449.

Sakai, K. L. (2005). Language acquisition and brain development. *Science, 310*, 815–819.

Salmon, P. (2001). Effects of physical exercise on anxiety, depression, and sensitivity to stress. A unifying theory. *Clinical Psychology Review, 21*, 33–61.

Samalin, N., & Whitney, C. (1997, December). When to praise. *Parents Magazine*, pp. 51–55.

Samuels, Y., Wang, Z., Bardelli, A., Silliman, N., Ptak, J., Szabo, S., et al. (2004). High frequency of mutations of the PIK3CA gene in human cancers. *Science, 23*, 554.

Sánchez-Ortuño, M. M., & Edinger, J. D. (2010). A penny for your thoughts: Patterns of sleep-related beliefs, insomnia symptoms and treatment outcome. *Behavior Research and Therapy, 48*, 125–133. doi:10.1016/j.brat.2009.10.003 Sandell, M. A., & Breslin, P. A. S. (2006). Variability in a taste-receptor gene determines whether we taste toxins in food. *Current Biology, 16*, R792–R794.

Sandlin-Sniffen, C. (2000, November 2). How are we raising our children? *St. Petersburg Times*. Retrieved from http://www.psycport. com/news/2000/11/02/eng-sptimes_floridian/eng-sptimes_floridian_071015 _110_905256867409.html.

Sasaki, S., Sata, F., Katoh, S., Saijo, Y., Nakajima, S., Washino, N., et al. (2008). Adverse birth outcomes associated with maternal smoking and polymorphisms in the N-nitrosamine-metabolizing enzyme genes NQO1 and CYP2E1. *American Journal of Epidemiology, 167*, 6. doi: 10.1093/aje/kwm360.

Sauerland, M., & Sporer, S. L. (2009). Fast and confident: Postdicting eyewitness identification accuracy in a field study. *Journal of Experimental Psychology: Applied, 15*, 46–62. Retrieved from http://www.allacademic.com/meta/p228794_index.html>

Saulny, S. (2011, February 10). In a multiracial nation, many ways to tally. *The New York Times*, pp. A1, A17.

Savage-Rumbaugh, S., Shanker, S. G., & Taylor, T. J. (1998). *Apes, language, and the human mind*. New York: Oxford University Press.

Saxe, R., Carey, S., & Kanwisher, N. (2004). Understanding other minds: Linking developmental psychology and functional neuroimaging. *Annual Review of Psychology, 55*, 87–124.

Sayim, B., Westheimer, G., & Herzog, M. H. (2010). Gestalt factors modulate basic spatial vision. *Psychological Science, 21*, 641–6444. doi: 10.1177/0956797610368811

Sbarra, D. A., & Nietert, P. J. (2008). Divorce and death: Forty years of the Charleston Heart Study. *Psychological Science, 20*, 107–113.

Scarmeas, N., Luchsinger, J. A., Schupf, N., Brickman, A. M., Cosentino, S., Tang, M. X., et al. (2009). Physical activity, diet, and risk of Alzheimer disease. *Journal of the American Medical Association, 302*, 627–637.

Scerri, T. S., Brandler, W. M., Paracchini, S., Morris, A. P., Ring, S. M., Talcott, J. B., Monaco, A. P. (2010). PCSK6 is associated with handedness in individuals with dyslexia. *Human Molecular Genetics, 20*, 608–614. doi: 10.1093/hmg/ddq475

Schachter, S. (1971). *Emotion, obesity, and crime*. New York: Academic Press.

Schachter, S., & Singer, J. E. (1962). Cognitive, social, and physiological determinants of emotional state. *Psychological Review, 69*, 377–399.

Schafer, R. B., & Keith, P. M. (1990). Matching by weight in married couples: A life cycle perspective. *Journal of Social Psychology, 130*, 657–664.

Schaffer, A. (2007, August 28). Not a game: Simulation to lessen war trauma. *The New York Times Science Section*, pp. 5, 8.

Schaubroeck, J., Jones, J. R., & Xie, J. L. (2001). Individual differences in utilizing control to cope with job demands: Effects on susceptibility to infectious disease. *Journal of Applied Psychology, 86*, 265–278.

Scheier, M. F., Carver, C. S., & Bridges, M. W. (1994). Distinguishing optimism from neuroticism (and trait anxiety, self-mastery, and self-esteem): A re-evaluation of the Life Orientation Test. *Journal of Personality and Social Psychology,* 67, 1063–1078.

Schenkman, L. (2010, November 11). Daydreaming is a downer. *Science*. Retrieved from www.news.sciencemag.org.

Schick, V., Herbenick, D., Reece, M., Sanders, S. A., Dodge, B., Middlestadt, S. E., et al. (2010). Sexual behaviors, condom use, and sexual health of Americans over 50: Implications for sexual health promotion for older adults. *Journal of Sexual Medicine*, 7 (suppl 5), 315–329. doi: 10.1111/j.1743-6109.2010.02013.x

Schmahl, C., & Bremner, J. D. (2006). Neuroimaging in borderline personality disorder. *Journal of Psychiatric Research, 40*, 419–427.

Schmidt, N. B., Richey, J. A., Buckner, J. D., & Timpano, K. R. (2009). Attention training for generalized social anxiety disorder. *Journal of Abnormal Psychology, 118*, 5–14. doi: 10.1037/a0013643

Schmitt, B., Gilovich, T., Goore, H., & Joseph, L. (1986). Mere presence and social facilitation: One more time. *Journal of Experimental Psychology, 22*, 242–248.

Schmitt, D. P. (2003). Universal sex differences in the desire for sexual variety: Tests from 52 nations, 6 continents, and 13 islands. *Journal of Personality and Social Psychology, 85*, 85–104.

Schneiderman, N., Antoni, M. H., Saab, P. G., & Ironson, G. (2001). Health psychology: Psychosocial and biobehavioral aspects of chronic disease management. *Annual Review of Psychology, 52*, 555–580.

Schooler, C. (2007). Use it—and keep it, longer, probably: A reply to Salthouse (2006). *Perspectives on Psychological Science, 2*, 24–29.

Schramke, C. J., & Bauer, R. M. (1997). State-dependent learning in older and younger adults. *Psychology and Aging, 12*, 255–262.

Schredl, M., Fuchedzhieva, A., Hämig, H., & Schindele, V. (2008). Do we think dreams are in black and white due to memory problems? *Dreaming, 18*, 175–180.

Schroeder, S. A. (2007). We can do better—improving the health of the American people. *New England Journal of Medicine, 357*, 1221–1228.

Schultz, C. C., Koch, K., Wagner, G., Roebel, M., Schachtzabel, C., Gaser, C., et al. (2010). Reduced cortical thickness in first episode schizophrenia. *Schizophrenia Research, 116*, 204–209.

Schulz, K. F., Altman, D. G., Moher, D., & Fergusson, D. (2010). CONSORT 2010 changes and testing blindness in RCTs. *The Lancet, 375*, 1144–1146. doi:10.1016/S0140-6736(10)60413-8

Schwab, A.P. (2009). Putting cognitive psychology to work: Improving decision-making in the medical encounter. *Social Science & Medicine, 67*, 1861–1869.

Scientists answer ticklish question. (2000, September 11). Retrieved from http:// www.cnn.com/2000/HEALTH/09/11/tickle.mechanism. reut/index.html.

Scribner, R. A., Mason, K. E., Simonsen, N. R., Theall, K., Chotalia, J., Johnson, S., et al. (2010). An ecological analysis of alcohol-outlet density and campus-reported violence at 32 U.S. colleges. *Journal of Studies on Alcohol and Drugs, 71*, 184.

Searle, J. R. (1996). *Dualism: Descartes' legacy. The philosophy of mind: The Superstar Teachers Series* [Audiotape]. Springfield, VA: The Teaching Company.

Segal Z.V., Bieling; P., Young,. T., MacQueen, G., Cooke, R. Martin, L., et al.. (2010). Antidepressant monotherapy vs sequential pharmacotherapy and mindfulness-based cognitive therapy, or placebo, for relapse prophylaxis in recurrent depression. *Archives of General Psychiatry, 67*, 1256–1264.

Segall, M. H. (1994). A cross-cultural research contribution to unraveling the nativist/empiricist controversy. In J. Lonner & R. Malpass (Eds.), *Psychology and culture* (pp. 135–138). Boston: Allyn & Bacon.

Segall, M. H., Campbell, D. T., & Herskovits, M. J. (1963). Culture differences in the perception of geometric illusions. *Science, 139*, 769–771.

Segall, M. H., Campbell, D. T., & Herskovits, M. J. (1966). *The influence of culture on visual perception.* Indianapolis: Bobbs-Merrill.

Seifert, K. L., & Hoffnung, R. J. (2000). *Child and adolescent development.* Boston: Houghton Mifflin.

Seifert, K. L., Hoffnung, R. J., & Hoffnung, M. (2000). *Lifespan development* (2nd ed.). Boston: Houghton Mifflin.

Selby, E. A., & Joiner, T. E., Jr. (2009). Cascades of emotion: The emergence of borderline personality disorder from emotional and behavioral dysregulation. *Review of General Psychology, 13,* 219–229. doi:10.1037/a0015687

Seligman, M. E. P. (1973). Fall into helplessness. *Psychology Today, 7,* 43–48.

Seligman, M. E. P. (1975). *Helplessness: On depression, development, and death.* San Francisco: Freeman.

Seligman, M. E. P. (2003, August). *Positive psychology: Applications to work, love, and sports.* Paper presented at the meeting of the American Psychological Association, Toronto, CA.

Seligman, M. E. P., Steen, T. A., Park, N., & Peterson, C. (2005). Positive psychology progress: Empirical validation of interventions. *American Psychologist, 60,* 410–421.

Sellbom, M., Graham, J. R., & Schenk, P. W. (2006). Incremental validity of the MMPI-2 Restructured Clinical (RC) Scales in a private practice sample. *Journal of Personality Assessment, 86*(2), 196–205.

Seltzer, L. J., Ziegler, T. E., & Pollak, S. D. (2010). Social vocalizations can release oxytocin in humans. *Proceedings of the Royal Society B: Biological Sciences,* published online. doi: 10.1098/rspb.2010.0567

Seo, D., Patrick, C. J., & Kennealy, P. J. (2008). Role of serotonin and dopamine system interactions in the neurobiology of impulsive aggression and its comorbidity with other clinical disorders. *Aggression and Violent Behavior, 13,* 383–395. doi:10.1016/j.avb.2008.06.003

Serfaty, M. A., Haworth, D., Blanchard, M., Buszewicz, M., Murad, S., & King, M. (2009). Clinical effectiveness of individual cognitive behavioral therapy for depressed older people in primary care: A randomized controlled trial. *Archives of General Psychiatry, 66,* 1332–1340.

Seshadri, S., Fitzpatrick, A. L., Ikram, A., DeStefano, A. L., Gudnason, V., Boada, M., et al. (2010). Genome-wide analysis of genetic loci associated with Alzheimer disease. *Journal of the American Medical Association, 303,* 1832–1840.

Seyfarth, R. M., & Cheney, D. L. (2003). Signalers and receivers in animal communication *Annual Review of Psychology, 54,* 145–173.

Shadish, W. R., Matt, G. E., Navarro, A. M., & Phillips, G. (2000). The effects of psychological therapies under clinically representative conditions: A meta-analysis. *Psychological Bulletin, 126,* 512–529.

Shafran, R., Clark, D., M., Fairburn, C. G., Arntz, A., Barlow, D. H., Ehlers, A. M., Williams, J. M. G. (2009). Mind the gap: Improving the dissemination of CBT. *Behaviour Research and Therapy, 47,* 902–909. doi:10.1016/j.brat.2009.07.003

Shane, S., Nicolaou, N., Cherkas, L., & Spector, T. D. (2010). Genetics, the Big Five, and the tendency to be self-employed. *Journal of Applied Psychology, 95,* 1154–1162. doi: 10.1037/a0020294

Shanker, S. G., & Savage-Rumbaugh, E. S. (1999). Kanzi: A new beginning. *Animal Learning and Behavior, 27,* 24–25.

Sharpee, T. O., Hiroki, S. Kurgansky, A. V., Rebrik, S. P., Stryker, M. P., &. Milleet, K. D. (2006). Adaptive filtering enhances information transmission in visual cortex. *Nature, 439,* 936–942.

Shaw, B. A., Liang, J., & Krause, N. (2010). Age and race differences in the trajectories of self-esteem. *Psychology and Aging, 25,* 84–94. doi: 10.1037/a0018242

Sheard, M., & Golby, J. (2007). Hardiness and undergraduate academic study: The moderating role of commitment. *Personality and Individual Differences, 43,* 579–588.

Shedler, J. (2010). The efficacy of psychodynamic psychotherapy. *American Psychologist, 65,* 98–109. doi: 10.1037/a0018378

Shepherd, G. M. (2006). Behaviour: Smells, brains and hormones. *Nature, 439,* 149–151.

Sher, L. (2005). Suicide and alcoholism. *Nordic Journal of Psychiatry, 59,* 152.

Sherman, D. K., Kim, H. S., & Heejung, S. (2005). Is there an "I" in "team"? The role of the self in group-serving judgments. *Journal of Personality & Social Psychology, 88,* 108–120.

Sherman, J. W., Stroessner, S. J., Loftus, S. T., & Deguzman, G. (1997). Stereotype suppression and recognition memory for stereotypical and nonstereotypical information. *Social Cognition, 15,* 205–215.

Sherman, R. A., Nave, C. S., & Funder, D. C. (2010). Situational similarity and personality predict behavioral consistency. *Journal of Personality and Social Psychology, 99,* 330–343. doi: 10.1037/a0019796

Shneidman, E. S. (1996). *The suicidal mind.* New York: Oxford University Press.

Shoulberg, E. K., Sijtsema, J. J., & Murray-Close, D. (2011). The association between valuing popularity and relational aggression: The moderating effects of actual popularity and physiological reactivity to exclusion. *Journal of Experimental Child Psychology,* in press doi:10.1016/j.jecp.2011.03.008

Siegle, G. J. (2008). Brain mechanisms of borderline personality disorder at the intersection of cognition, emotion, and the clinic. *American Journal of Psychiatry, 164,* 1776–1779.

Siegler, I., Bosworth, H. B., & Poon, L. W. (2003). Disease, health, and aging. In R. M. Lerner, M. A. Easterbrooks, & J. Mistry (Eds.), *Handbook of psychology: Vol. 6. Developmental psychology* (pp. 423–442). New York: John Wiley & Sons.

Silbersweig, D., Clarkin, J. F., Goldstein, M., Kernberg, O. F., Tuescher, O., Levy, K. N., et al. (2008). Failure of frontolimbic inhibitory function in the context of negative emotion in borderline personality disorder. *American Journal of Psychiatry, 164,* 1832.

Silverman, L. H. (1984). Beyond insight: An additional necessary step in redressing intrapsychic conflict. *Psychoanalytic Psychology, 1,* 215–234.

Simmons, R. G. (1991). Presidential address on altruism and sociology. *Sociological Quarterly, 46,* 36–46.

Simms, L. J. (2007). The Big Seven model of personality and its relevance to personality pathology. *Journal of Personality, 75,* 65–94.

Singer, N. (2010, November 14). Making ads that whisper to the brain. *The New York Times,* p. BU4.

Singer, T., Verhaeghen, P., Ghisletta, P., Lindenberger, U., & Baltes, P. B. (2003). The fate of cognition in very old age: Six-year longitudinal findings in the Berlin Aging Study (BASE). *Psychology and Aging, 18,* 318–331.

Singleton, R. A. Jr., & Wolfson, A. R. (2009). Alcohol consumption, sleep, and academic performance among college students. *Journal of Studies on Alcohol and Drugs, 70,* 355.

Sink, M. (2004, November 9). Drinking deaths draw attention to old campus problem. *The New York Times,* p. A16.

Sleek, S. (1997, October). People's racist attitudes can be unlearned. *APA Monitor, 28*(9), 38.

Slijper, F. M., Drop, S. L. S., Molenaar, J. C., & de Muinck Keizer Schrama, S. M. P. F. (1998). Long-term psychological evaluation of intersex children. *Archives of Sexual Behavior, 27,* 125–144.

Sloan, D. M., & Marx, B. P. (2004). A closer examination of the structured written disclosure procedure. *Journal of Consulting and Clinical Psychology, 72,* 165–175.

Slutske, W. S. (2005). Alcohol use disorders among US College Students and their non-college-attending peers. *Archives of General Psychiatry, 62,* 321–327.

Smart Richman, L., Pek, J., Pascoe, E., & Bauer, D. J. (2010). The effects of perceived discrimination on ambulatory blood pressure and affective responses to interpersonal stress modeled over 24 hours. *Health Psychology, 29,* 403–411.

Smetana, J. G., Campione-Barr, N., & Metzger, A. (2006). Adolescent development in interpersonal and societal contexts. *Annual Review of Psychology, 57,* 255–284.

Smith, A. E. M., Msetfi, R. M., & Golding, L. (2010). Client self rated adult attachment patterns and the therapeutic alliance: A systematic review. *Clinical Psychology Review, 30,* 326–337. doi:10.1016/j.cpr.2009.12.007

Smith, C. O, Levine, D. W., Smith, E. P., Dumas, J., & Prinz, R. J.(2009). A developmental perspective of the relationship of racial–ethnic identity to self-construct, achievement, and behavior in African American children. *Cultural Diversity and Ethnic Minority Psychology, 15,* 145–157. doi: 10.1037/a0015538

Smith, D. B. (2009, Autumn). The doctor is in. *The American Scholar.* Retrieved from http://www.theamericanscholar.org/the-doctor-is-in/.

Smith, E. R. (1998). Mental representation and memory. In D. T. Gilbert, S. T. Fiske, & G. Lindzey (Eds.), *The handbook of social psychology* (4th ed., Vol. 1, pp. 391–445). Boston: McGraw-Hill.

Smith, K. (2010). Settling the great glia debate. *Nature, 468,* 160–162. doi:10.1038/468160a

Smith, M. L., Glass, G. V., & Miller, T. I. (1980). *The benefits of psychotherapy.* Baltimore: Johns Hopkins University Press.

Smith, M. T., & Perlis, M. L. (2006). Who is a candidate for cognitive-behavioral therapy for insomnia? *Health Psychology, 25,* 15–19.

Smoller, J. W., Paulus, M. P., Fagerness, J. A., Purcell, S., Yamaki, L. H., Hirshfeld-Becker, D., et al. (2008). Influence of RGS2 on anxiety-related temperament, personality, and brain function. *Archives of General Psychiatry, 65,* 298–308. doi: 10.1097/CHI.0b013e3181908c2c

Smyth, J. M., & Pennebaker, J. W. (2001). What are the health effects of disclosure? In A. Baum, T. A. Revenson, & J. E. Singer (Eds.), *Handbook of health psychology* (pp. 339–348). Mahwah, NJ: Lawrence Erlbaum Associates.

Snowden, R. V. (2009, February 25). Even moderate alcohol use increases risk of certain cancers in women. *ACS News, Press Release.*

Snyder, C. R., & Lopez, S. J. (2007). *Positive psychology: The science and practical explorations of human strength.* Thousand Oaks, CA: Sage Publications.

Soa, C. Y. C., Leung, P. W. L., & Hung, S.-F. (2008). Treatment effectiveness of combined medication/behavioural treatment with Chinese ADHD children in routine practice. *Behaviour Research and Therapy, 46,* 983–992. doi:10.1016/j.brat.2008.06.007

Society for Neuroscience. (2005). *Pain: Making a difference today.* Retrieved from http://web.sfn.org/content/Publications/BrainResearchSuccessStories/BRSS_Pain.pdf.

Soto, C. J., John, O. P., Gosling, S. D., & Potter, J. (2011). Age differences in personality traits from 10 to 65: Big Five domains and facets in a large cross-sectional sample. *Journal of Personality and Social Psychology, 100,* 330–348.

Soto, J. A., Levenson, R. W., & Ebling, R. (2005). Cultures of moderation and expression: emotional experience, behavior, and physiology in Chinese Americans and Mexican Americans. *Emotion, 5,* 154–165.

Soussignan, R. (2002). Duchenne smile, emotional experience, and autonomic reactivity: A test of the facial feedback hypothesis. *Emotion 2*, 52–74.

Spanos, N. P. (1994). Multiple identity enactments and multiple personality disorder: A sociocognitive perspective. *Psychological Bulletin, 116*, 143–165.

Spearman, C. (1927). *The abilities of man*. New York: Macmillan.

Spector, P. E. (2005). *Industrial and organizational psychology: Research and practice* (5th ed.). New York: John Wiley & Sons.

Spence, I., Yu, J., J. Feng, J., & Marshman, J. (2009). Women match men when learning a spatial skill. *Journal of Experimental Psychology: Learning, Memory, and Cognition, 35*, 1097–1103.

Sperry, R. W. (1982). Some effects of disconnecting the cerebral hemispheres. *Science, 217*, 1223–1226.

Spiegel, D. (2006). Recognizing traumatic dissociation. *American Journal of Psychiatry, 163*, 566–568.

Springen, K., & Kantrowitz, B. (2004, May 10). Alcohol's deadly triple threat. *Newsweek*, pp. 90–92.

Springen, K., & Seibert, S. (2005, January 17). Artful aging. *Newsweek*, pp. 56–65.

Springer, S. P., & Deutsch, G. (1993). *Left brain, right brain* (4th ed.). New York: Freeman.

Staddon, J. E., R., & Cerutti, D. T. (2003). Operant conditioning *Annual Review of Psychology 54*, 115–144.

Stambor, Z. (2006a, April). Both sexes seek attractiveness in one-night stand partners. *Monitor on Psychology, 37*(4), 12.

Stambor, Z. (2006b, April). Extraversion, agreeableness linked to happiness in orangutans. *Monitor on Psychology,* 37(4), p. 10.

Standing tall is key for success: "Powerful postures" may trump title and rank. (2001, January 6). *ScienceDaily*. Retrieved from http://www.sciencedaily.com/releases/2011/01/110106145257.htm.

Stansfeld, S. A., Clark, C., Cameron, R. M., Alfreda, T., Head, J., Haines, M. M., et al (2009). Aircraft and road traffic noise exposure and children's mental health. *Journal of Environmental Psychology, 29*, 203–207. doi:10.1016/j.jenvp.2009.01.002.

Staw, B. M., & Cohen-Charash, Y. (2005). The dispositional approach to job satisfaction: More than a mirage, but not yet an oasis. *Journal of Organizational Behavior, 26*, 59–78.

Steele, J. R., & Ambady, N. (2006). "Math is hard!" The effect of gender priming on women's attitudes. *Journal of Experimental Social Psychology, 42*, 428–436.

Steenhuysen, J. S. (2010, November 18). *Nearly 1 in 5 Americans had mental illness in 2009*. Retrieved from http://www.msnbc.msn.com/id/40263028/ns/health-mental_health.

Stein, J. (2005, January 17). Is there a hitch? *Time Magazine*, pp. A37–A40.

Stein, M. B., & Stein, D. J. (2008). Social anxiety disorder. *The Lancet, 371*, 1115–1125. doi:10.1016/S0140-6736(08)60488-2

Stein, R. (2010, May 14). Low-quality child care can have lasting impact. (2010, May 14). Retrieved from http://www.msnbc.msn.com/id/37147870/ns/health-more_health_news/

Steinberg, L. (2007). Risk taking in adolescence: New perspectives from brain and behavioral science. *Current Directions in Psychological Science, 16*, 55–59.

Steinhauer, J. (1995, July 6). No marriage, no apologies. *The New York Times*, pp. C1, C7.

Steptoe, A., & Diez Roux, A. V. (2008). Happiness, social networks, and health. *British Medical Journal, 337*, 2781. doi: 10.1136/bmj.a2781

Steptoe, A., Wardle, J., & Marmot, M. (2005). Positive affect and health-related neuroendocrine, cardiovascular, and inflammatory processes. *Proceedings of the National Academy of Sciences, 102*, 6508–6512.

Sternberg, E. M. (2000). *The balance within: The science connecting health and emotions*. New York: W. H. Freeman & Co.

Sternberg, R. J. (1988). Triangulating love. In R. J. Sternberg & M. J. Barnes (Eds.), *The psychology of love*. New Haven: Yale University Press.

Sternberg, R. J. (1997b). The triarchic theory of intelligence. In D. P. Flanagan, J. L. Genshaft, P., L., & Harrison (Eds.), *Contemporary intellectual assessment: Theories, tests, and issues* (pp. 92–104). New York: Guilford Press.

Sternberg, R. J. (2001). What is the common thread of creativity? Its dialectical relation to intelligence and wisdom. *American Psychologist, 56*, 360–362.

Sternberg, R. J., & Grigorenko, E. L. (2008). Ability testing across cultures. In L. A. Suzuki & J. G. Ponterotto (Eds.), *Handbook of multicultural assessment* (3rd ed., pp. 449–470). San Francisco: Jossey-Bass.

Sternberg, R. J., Grigorenko, E. L., & Kidd, K. K. (2005). Intelligence, race, and genetics. *American Psychologist, 60*, 46–59.

Sternberg, R., J., & Weis, K. (Eds.). (2006). *The new psychology of love*. New Haven, CT: Yale University Press.

Stewart, A. J., & McDermott, C. (2004). Gender in psychology. *Annual Review of Psychology, 55*, 519–544.

Stickgold, R., & Wehrwein, P. (2009, April 27). Sleep now, remember later. *Newsweek*, p. 56.

Stockdale, M. S., Gandolfo Berry, C., Schneider, R. W., & Cao, F. (2004). Perceptions of the sexual harassment of men. *Psychology of Men and Masculinity, 5*, 158–167.

Stolberg, S. G. (2001b, May 10). Blacks found on short end of heart attack procedure. *The New York Times*, p. A20.

Stolzenberg-Solomon, R. Z., Adams, K., Leitzmann, M., Schairer, C., Michaud, D. S., Hollenbeck, A., et al. (2008). Physical activity, and pancreatic cancer in the National Institutes of Health-AARP Diet and Health Cohort. *American Journal of Epidemiology, 167*, 586–597.

Stone, A. A., Schwartz, J. E., Broderick, J. E., & Deaton, A. (2010). A snapshot of the age distribution of psychological well-being in the United States. *Proceedings of the National Academy of Sciences*, doi:10.1073/pnas.1003744107

Stone, J., Lynch, C. I., Sjomeling, M., & Darley, J. M. (1999). Stereotype threat effects on black and white athletic performance. *Journal of Personality and Social Psychology, 77*, 1213–1227.

Stone, J., Smyth, R., Carson, A., Lewis, S., Prescott, R., Warlow, C., & Sharpe, M. (2006). La belle indifférence in conversion symptoms and hysteria: Systematic review. *British Journal of Psychiatry, 188*, 204–209.

Storandt, M., Kaskie, B., & Von Dras, D. D. (1998). Temporal memory for remote events in healthy aging and dementia. *Psychology and Aging, 13*, 4–7.

Story, P. A., Hart, J. W., Stasson, M. F., & Mahoney, J. M. (2009). Using a two-factor theory of achievement motivation to examine performance-based outcomes and self-regulatory processes. *Personality and Individual Differences, 46*, 391–395. doi:10.1016/j.paid.2008.10.023

Stout, D. (2008). A history of modern experimental psychology: From James and Wundt to cognitive science. *Canadian Psychology, 49*, 179–180.

Strata, P., Thach, W. T., & Ottersen, O. P. (2009). New insights in cerebellar function. *Neuroscience, 162*, 545–548. doi:10.1016/j.neuroscience.2009.06.047

Strauss, J. L., Hayes, A. M., Johnson, S. L., Newman, C. F., Browne, G. K., Barber, J. P. et al. (2006). Early alliance, alliance ruptures, and symptom change in a nonrandomized trial of cognitive therapy for avoidant and obsessive–compulsive personality disorders. *Journal of Consulting and Clinical Psychology, 74*, 337–345.

Strayer, D. L., & Drews, F. A. (2007). Cell-phone-induced driver distraction. *Current Directions. in Psychological Science, 16*, 128–131.

Strenziok, M., Krueger, F., Deshpande, G., Lenroot, R. K., van der Meer, E., & Grafman, J. (2010). Fronto-parietal regulation of media violence exposure in adolescents: a multi-method study. *Social Cognitive and Affective Neuroscience*, published online. doi: 10.1093/scan/nsq079

Stricker, G., & Gold, J. R. (1999). The Rorschach: Toward a nomothetically based, idiographically applicable configurational model. *Psychological Assessment, 11*, 240–250.

Strohmetz, D. B., Rind, B., Fisher, R., & Lynn, M. (2002). Sweetening the till: The use of candy to increase restaurant tipping. *Journal of Applied Social Psychology, 32*, 300–309.

Stuart, R. B. (2004). Twelve practical suggestions for achieving multicultural competence. *Professional Psychology: Research and Practice, 35*, 3–9.

Suarez-Almazor, M. E., Looney, C, Liu, Y.F., Cox, V., Pietz, K., Marcus, D. M., Street, R. L. (2010). A randomized controlled trial of acupuncture for osteoarthritis of the knee: Effects of patient-provider communication. *Arthritis Care & Research, 62*, 1229–1236. doi: 10.1002/acr.20225

Substance Abuse and Mental Health Services Administration (SAMHSA). (2005). *Overview of findings from the 2002 National Survey on Drug Use and Health* (Office of Applied Studies, NHSDA Series H-21 DHHS Publication No. SMA 03-3774). Rockville, MD: Author. Retrieved from http:// www.nida.nih.gov/NIDA_notes/NNvol19N5/Study.html.

Substance Abuse and Mental Health Services Administration (SAMHSA). (2006). *2004 National Survey on Drug Use & Health: Detailed tables*. Retrieved from http://www.drugabusestatistics.samhsa.gov/NSDUH/2k4nsduh/2k4tabs/Sect1peTabs1to66.htm#tab1.1b.

Substance Abuse and Mental Health Services Administration (SAMSHA). (2010a). *Results from the 2008 National Survey on Drug Use and Health: National Findings*, Updated 2010. Retrieved from http://oas.samhsa.gov/NSDUH/2K8NSDUH/tabs/toc.htm

Substance Abuse and Mental Health Services Administration. (SAMHSA) (2010b). *Results from the 2009 National Survey On Drug Use And Health: National Findings*. Office of Applied Studies, NSDUH Series H-38A, HHS Publication No. SMA 10-4586. Rockville, MD: Author.

Sugita, M., & Shiba, Y. (2005). Genetic tracing shows segregation of taste neuronal circuitries for bitter and sweet. *Science, 309*, 781–785.

Sullivan, C. (2006). Women and men in management. *Gender, Work & Organization, 13*, 96–98.

Sullivan, M. J. L., Martela, M. O., Tripp, D. A., Savard, A., & Crombez, G. (2006). Catastrophic thinking and heightened perception of pain in others. *Pain, 123*, 37–44.

Sulloway, F. J. (2007). Birth order and intelligence. *Science, 316*, 1711–1712.

Sun, S. S., Shume, S., Schubert, C. M., et al. (2002). National estimates of the timing of sexual aturation and racial differences among US children. *Pediatrics, 110*, 911–919.

Suzuki, K. (1991). Moon illusion simulated in complete darkness: Planetarium experiment reexamined. *Perception and Psychophysics, 49*, 349–354.

Swami, V., & Furnham, A. (2008). *The psychology of physical attraction*. New York: Routledge.

Swann, A. C., Lijffijt, M., Lane, S. D., Steinberg, J. L., & Moeller, F. G. (2009). Trait impulsivity and response inhibition in antisocial personality disorder. *Journal of Psychiatric Research, 43*, 1057–1063. doi:10.1016/j.jpsychires.2009.03.003

Sweatt, J. D. (2010). Epigenetics and cognitive aging. *Science, 328*, 701–702. doi: 10.1126/science.1189968

Sweeney, C. (2009, July 29). Banking on a chemical reaction. *The New York Times*, p. E3.

Swendsen, J., Ben-Zeev, D., & Granholm, E. (2010). Real-time electronic ambulatory monitoring of substance use and symptom expression in schizophrenia. *American Journal of Psychiatry, 168*, 202–209. doi: 10.1176/appi.ajp.2010.10030463

Szanto, K., Mulsant, B. H., Houck, P., Dew, M. A., & Reynolds, C. F. (2003). Occurrence and course of suicidality during short-term treatment of late-life depression. *Archives of General Psychiatry, 60*, 610–617.

Tackett, J. L., Waldman, I. D., & Lahey, B. B. (2009). Etiology and measurement of relational aggression: A multi-informant behavior genetic investigation. *Journal of Abnormal Psychology, 118*, 722–733.

Takahashi, M., Shimizu, H., Saito, S., & Tomoyori, H. (2006). One percent ability and ninety-nine percent perspiration: a study of a Japanese memorist. *Journal of Experimental Psychology: Learning, Memory, and Cognition, 32*, 1195–1200.

Takahashi, Y. (1990). Separation distress of Japanese infants in the strange situation. *Research and Clinical Center for Child Development, 12*, 141–150.

Talarico, J. M., & Rubin, D. C. (2003). Confidence, not consistency, characterizes flashbulb memories. *Psychological Science, 14*, 455–461.

Tanaka, A., Koizumi, A., Imai, H., Hiramatsu, S., Hiramoto, E., & de Gelder, G. (2010). I feel your voice: Cultural differences in the multisensory perception of emotion. *Psychological Science, 19*, 1259–1262. doi: 10.1177/0956797610380698

Tandon, R., Keshavan, M. S., & Nasrallah, H. A. (2008). Schizophrenia, "just the facts" what we know in 2008. 2. Epidemiology and etiology. *Schizophrenia Research, 102*, 1–18.

Tandon, R., Nasrallah, H. A., & Keshavan, M. S. (2009). Schizophrenia, "just the facts" 4. Clinical features and conceptualization. *Schizophrenia Research, 110*, 1–23. doi:10.1016/j.schres.2009.03.005

Taylor, R. D. (2010). Risk and resilience in low-income African American families: Moderating effects of kinship social support. *Cultural Diversity and Ethnic Minority Psychology, 16*, 344–351. doi: 10.1037/a0018675

Taylor, S. E. (2007). Social support. In H.S. Friedman & R. C. Silver (Eds.), *Foundations of health psychology*. New York: Oxford University Press.

Taylor, S. E., Klein, L. C., Lewis, B. P, Gruenewald, T. L., Gurung, R. A., & Updegraff, J. A. (2000). Biobehavioral responses to stress in females: Tend-and-befriend, not fight-or-flight. *Psychological Review, 7*, 411–429.

Taylor, S., Jang, K. L., & Asmundson, G. J. G. (2010). Etiology of obsessions and compulsions: A behavioral-genetic analysis. *Journal of Abnormal Psychology, 119*, 672–682. doi: 10.1037/a0021132

Teachman, B. A. (2006). Aging and negative affect: The rise and fall and rise of anxiety and depression symptoms. *Psychology and Aging, 21*, 201–207.

Teachman, B. A., Marker, C. D., & Clerkin, E. M. (2010). Catastrophic misinterpretations as a predictor of symptom change during treatment for panic disorder. *Journal of Consulting and Clinical Psychology, 78*, 964–973. doi: 10.1037/a0021067

Teasdale, T. W., & Owen, D. R. (2008) Secular declines in cognitive test scores: A reversal of the Flynn Effect. *Intelligence, 36*, 121–126. doi:10.1016/j.intell.2007.01.007

Teens' brains hold key to their impulsiveness. (2007, December 3). Retrieved from http://www.msnbc.msn.com/id/21997683/.

Telecommuting has mostly positive consequences for employees and employers, say researchers. (2007, November 19). American Psychological Association Press Release. Retrieved from http://www.apa.org/releases/telecommuting.html.

Tellegen, A., Lykken, D. T., Bouchard, T. J., & Wilcox, K., J. (1988). Personality similarity in twins reared apart and together. *Journal of Personality and Social Psychology, 54*, 1031–1039.

Terrace, H. S. (2005). Metacognition and the evolution of language. In H. S. Terrace & J. Metcalfe (Eds.), *The missing link in cognition: Origins of self-reflective consciousness* (pp. 84–115). New York: Oxford University Press.

Tervaniemi, M., Kruck, S., De Baene, W., Schröger, E., Alter, K., & Friederici, A. D. (2009). *European Journal of Neuroscience, 30*, 1636–1642. doi: 10.1111/j.1460-9568.2009.06955.x

The BALANCE Investigators and Collaborators. (2010). Lithium plus valproate combination therapy versus monotherapy for relapse prevention in bipolar I disorder (BALANCE): A randomised open-label trial. *The Lancet, 375*, 385–395. doi:10.1016/S0140-6736(09)61828-6

The fearless SM: Woman missing amygdala. (2010, December 17). *NeuroscienceNews.com*. Retrieved fromhttp://neurosciencenews.com/sm-fearless-woman-missing-amygdala/

The Lancet. (2011). No mental health without physical health. *The Lancet, 377*, 611. doi:10.1016/S0140-6736(11)60211-0

Think positive, live longer (2002, July 28). *MSNBC.com.* Retrieved from http://www.msnbc.com/news/786749.asp.

Thompson, I. M., Tangen, C. M., Goodman, P. J., Probstfield, J. L., Moinpour, C. M., & Coltman, C. A. (2005). Erectile dysfunction and subsequent cardiovascular disease. *Journal of the American Medical Association, 294*, 2996–3002.

Thompson, P. M., Hayashi, K. M., Simon, S. L., Geaga, J. A., Hong, M. S., Sui, Y., et al. (2004). Structural abnormalities in the brains of human subjects who use methamphetamine. *Journal of Neuroscience, 30*, 6028–6036.

Thompson, R. A. (1997). Early sociopersonality development. In W. Damon (Editor-in-Chief) & N. Eisenberg (Vol. Ed.), *Handbook of child psychology: 5th ed. Vol. 3: Social, emotional, and personality development* (pp. 25–104). New York: John Wiley & Sons.

Thompson, R. A., Easterbrooks, M. A., & Padilla-Walker, L. M. (2003). Social and emotional development in infancy. In R. M. Lerner, M.A. Easterbrooks, & J. Mistry (Eds.), *Handbook of psychology: Vol. 6. Developmental psychology* (pp. 91–112). New York: John Wiley & Sons.

Thompson, R. R. (2005). In search of memory traces. *Annual Review of Psychology, 56*, 1–23.

Thompson, S. (1995). *Going all the way*. New York: Hill and Wang.

Thompson, T. (1995). *The beast: A journey through depression.* New York: Putnam.

Thomson, E., Hanson, T. L., & McLanahan, S. S. (1994). Family structure and child well-being: Economic resources vs. parental behaviors. *Social Forces, 73*, 221–242.

Thoresen, C. J., Kaplan, S. A., Barsky, A. P., Warren, C. R., & de Chermont, K. (2003). The affective underpinnings of job perceptions and attitudes: A meta-analytic review and integration. *Psychological Bulletin, 129*, 914–945.

Thorndike, E. L. (1905). *The elements of psychology*. New York: Seiler.

Thurstone, L. L., & Thurstone, T. G. (1941). Factorial studies of intelligence. *Psychometric Monographs, 94*(2).

Tienari, P, Wynne, L. C., Läksy, K., Moring, J., Nieminen, P., Sorri, A., et al. (2003). Genetic boundaries of the schizophrenia spectrum: Evidence from the Finnish adoptive family study of schizophrenia. *American Journal of Psychiatry, 160*, 1587–1594.

Tienari, P., Wynne, L.C., Sorri, A., Lahti, I., Laksy, K., Moring, J., et al. (2004). Genotype-environment interaction in schizophrenia spectrum disorder. *British Journal of Psychiatry, 184*, 216–222.

Tierney, J. (2007, August 28). A world of eloquence in an upturned palm. *The New York Times Science Section*, pp. 1, 4.

Tiggemann, M., & Miller, J. (2010). The Internet and adolescent girls' weight satisfaction and drive for thinness. *Sex Roles, 63*, 79–90. doi: 10.1007/s11199-010-9789-z

Tindle, H. A., Chang, Y.-F., Kuller, L. H., Manson, J. E., Robinson, J. G., Rosal, M. C., et al. (2009). Optimism, cynical hostility, and incident coronary heart disease and mortality in the women's health initiative. *Circulation, 120*, 656–662. doi: 10.1161/CIRCULATIONAHA.108.82y

Tobacco use in the USA. (2010, September 18). *The Lancet, 376*, 930. doi:10.1016/S0140-6736(10)61433-

Tohidian, I., & Tabatabaie, S. M. M. (2010). Considering the relationship between language, culture and cognition to scrutinize the lexical influences on cognition. *Current Psychology, 29*, 52–70. doi: 10.1007/s12144-010-9072-z

Tolin, D. F. (2010). Is cognitive-behavioral therapy more effective than other therapies? A meta-analytic review. *Clinical Psychology Review*, doi:10.1016/j.cpr.2010.05.003

Tolman, E. C., & Honzik, C. H. (1930). Introduction and removal of reward, and maze performance in rats. *University of California Publications in Psychology, 4*, 257–275.

Tomlinson, K. L., Tate, S. R., Anderson, K. G., McCarthy, D. M., & Brown, S. A. (2006). An examination of self-medication and rebound effects: Psychiatric symptomatology before and after alcohol or drug relapse. *Addictive Behaviors, 31*, 461–474.

Toomey, R., Lyons, M. J., Eisen, S. A., Xian, H., Chantarujikapong, S., Seidman, L. J., et al. (2003). A twin study of the neuropsychological consequences of stimulant abuse. *Archives of General Psychiatry*, 60, 303–310.

Topolinski, S., & Reber, R. (2010). Gaining insight into the "Aha" experience. *Current Directions in Psychological Science, 19*, 402–405. doi: 10.1177/0963721410388803

Torpy, J. M., Burke, A., E., & Golub, R. M. (2011). Generalized anxiety disorder. *Journal of the American Medical Association, 305*, 522.doi:10.1001/jama.305.5.522

Traish, A. M., Goldtein, I., Munarriz, R., & Guay, A. (2006). Roles of androgens in women's sexual function & dysfunction: What have we learned in sex decades? *Current Women's Health Reviews, 2*(1), 75–86.

Tran, A. G. T. T., & Lee, R. M. (2010). Perceived ethnic–racial socialization, ethnic identity, and social competence among Asian American late adolescents. *Cultural Diversity and Ethnic Minority Psychology, 16*, 169–178. doi: 10.1037/a0016400

Treanor, M. (2011). The potential impact of mindfulness on exposure and extinction learning in anxiety disorders. *Clinical Psychology Review, 31*, 617–625. doi:10.1016/j.cpr.2011.02.003

Treutlein, J., Cichon, S., Ridinger, M., Wodarz, N., Soyka, M., Zill, P., et al. (2009). Genome-wide association study of alcohol dependence. *Archives of General Psychiatry, 66*, 773–784.

Trevarthen, C. (1995). Mother and baby—Seeing artfully eye to eye. In R. L. Gregory et al. (Eds.), *The artful eye* (pp. 157–200). New York: Oxford University Press.

Triandis, H. C., & Suh, E. M. (2002). Cultural influences on personality. *Annual Review of Psychology, 53*, 133–160.

Troxel, W. M., Matthews, K. A., Bromberger, J. T., & Sutton-Tyrrell, K. (2003). Chronic stress burden, discrimination, and subclinical carotid artery disease in African American and Caucasian women. *Health Psychology, 22*, 300–309.

Trunzo, J. J., & Pinto, B. M. (2003). Social support as a mediator of optimism and distress in breast cancer survivors. *Journal of Consulting and Clinical Psychology, 71*, 805–811.

Trzesniewski, K. H., Donnellan, M. B., & Robins, R. W. (2003). Stability of self-esteem across the life span. *Journal of Personality and Social Psychology, 84*, 205–220.

Trzesniewski, K. H., Donnellan, M. B., Moffitt, T. E., Robins, R. W., Poulton, R., & Caspi, A. (2006). Low self-esteem during adolescence predicts poor health, criminal behavior, and limited economic prospects during adulthood. *Developmental Psychology, 42*, 381–390.

Tucker-Drob, E. M., Rhemtulla, M., Harden, K. P., Turkheimer, E., & Fask, D. (2011). Emergence of a gene × socioeconomic status interaction on infant mental ability between 10 months and 2 years. *Psychological Science, 22*, 125–133. doi:10.1177/0956797610392926

Tun, P. A., & Lachman, M. (2008). Age differences in reaction time and attention in a national telephone sample of adults: Education, sex, and task complexity matter. *Developmental Psychology, 44*, 1421–1429. doi: 10.1037/a0012845

Turati, C. (2004). Why faces are not special to newborns: an alternative account of the face preference. *Current Directions in Psychological Science, 13*, 5–8.

Turkington, C. (1996). *12 steps to a better memory*. New York: MacMillan.

Turnbull, C. (1961). *The forest people*. New York: Simon & Schuster.

Turner, J. A., Mancl, L., & Aaron, L. A. (2006). Short- and long-term efficacy of brief cognitive-behavioral therapy for patients with chronic temporomandibular disorder pain: A randomized, controlled trial. *Pain, 121*, 181–194.

Tustin, K., & Hayne, H. (2010). Defining the boundary: Age-related changes in childhood amnesia. *Developmental Psychology, 46*, 1049–1061. doi: 10.1037/a0020105

Tweney, R. D., & Budzynski, C. A. (2000). The scientific status of American psychology in 1900. *American Psychologist, 55*, 1014–1017.

Twenge, J. M. (2009). Change over time in obedience: The jury's still out, but it might be decreasing. *American Psychologist, 64*, 28–31.

U.S. Census Bureau. (2010, November 10). *U.S. Census Bureau reports men and women wait longer to marry*. Retrieved from http://www.census.gov/newsroom/releases/archives/families_households/cb10-174.html.

U.S. Department of Health and Human Services (USDHHS). (2001). *National Household Survey on Drug Abuse: Highlights 2000*. Retrieved from www.samhsa.gov.

U.S. Department of Health and Human Services (USDHHS). (2010, December) *Results from the 2009 National Survey on Drug Use and Health*. Retrieved from http://oas.samhsa.gov/NSDUH/2k9NSDUH/MH/2K9MHResults.pdf.

U.S. Department of Justice (2006). *Criminal victimization in the United States. Statistical Tables, 2003*. Office of Justice Programs. Bureau of Justice Statistics. Retrieved from http://www.ojp.usdoj.gov/bjs/abstract/cvus/rape_sexual_assault.htm.

U.S. Department of Justice.(2006). *Criminal victimization in the United States. Statistical Tables, 2003*. Office of Justice Programs. Bureau of Justice Statistics. http://www.ojp.usdoj.gov/bjs/abstract/cvus/rape_sexual_assault.htm.

U.S. Preventive Services Task Force. (2009). Folic acid for the prevention of neural tube defects: U.S. Preventive Services Task Force recommendation statement. *Annals of Internal Medicine, 150*, 626–631. Retrieved from http://www.ahrq.gov/clinic/uspstf09/folicacid/folicart.htm.

U.S. Surgeon General, U.S. Department of Health & Human Services (USDHHS). (2010). *How tobacco causes disease: The biology and behavioral basis for smoking-attributable disease: A report of the Surgeon General*. Washington, D.C. USDHHS.

Uhl, G. R., Drgon, T., Liu, Q.-R., Johnson, C., Walther, D., Komiyama, T., et al. (2008). Genome-wide association for methamphetamine dependence: Convergent results from 2 samples. *Archives of General Psychiatry, 65*, 345–355.

Uhlmann, E., & Swanson, J. (2004). Exposure to violent video games increases automatic aggressiveness. *Journal of Adolescence, 27*, 41–52.

Umaña-Taylor, A. J. (2004). Ethnic identity and self-esteem: examining the role of social context. *Journal of Adolescence, 27*, 139–146.

Unsworth, N., & Engle, R. W. (2007). The nature of individual differences in working memory capacity: Active maintenance in primary memory and controlled search from secondary memory. *Psychological Review, 114*, 104–132.

Unsworth, N., Heitz, R. P., & Parks, N. A. (2008). The importance of temporal distinctiveness for forgetting over the short term. *Psychological Science, 19*, 1078–1081. doi: 10.1111/j.1467-9280.2008.02203.x

Unsworth, N., Spillers, G. J., & Brewer, G. A. (2010). The contributions of primary and secondary memory to working memory capacity: an individual differences analysis of immediate free recall. *Journal of Experimental Psychology: Learning, Memory, and Cognition, 36*, 240–247. doi:10.1037/a0017739

Unützer, J. (2007). Late-life depression. *New England Journal of Medicine, 357*, 2269–2276.

Urry, H. L., & Gross, J. J. (2010). Emotion regulation in older age. *Current Directions in Psychological Science, 19*, 352–357. doi:10.1177/0963721410388395

Vacic, V., McCarthy, S., Malhotra, D., Murray, F., Chou, H.-H., Peoples, A., Sebat, J. (2011). Duplications of the neuropeptide receptor gene VIPR2 confer significant risk for schizophrenia. *Nature, 471*, 499–503. doi:10.1038/nature09884 n press.

Vaitl, D., Birbaumer, N., Gruzelier, J. Jamieson, G. A., Kotchoubey, B., Kübler, A. et al. (2005). Psychobiology of altered states of consciousness. *Psychological Bulletin, 131*, 98–127.

Valla, J. M., & Ceci, S. J. (2011). Can sex differences in science be tied to the long reach of prenatal hormones?: Brain organization theory, digit ratio (2D/4D), and sex differences in preferences and cognition. *Perspectives on Psychological Science, 6*, 134–146. doi:10.1177/1745691611400236

Vallea, M. F., Huebner, E S., & Suldo, S. M. (2006). An analysis of hope as a psychological strength. *Journal of School Psychology, 44*, 393–406.

van den Akker, A. L., Deković, M., Prinzie, P., & Asscher, J. J. (2010). Toddlers' temperament profiles: stability and relations to negative and positive parenting. *Journal of Abnormal Child Psychology, 38*, 485–495. doi: 10.1007/s10802-009-9379

Van der Heijden, K. B. (2007). Effect of melatonin on sleep, behavior, and cognition in ADHD and chronic sleep-onset insomnia. *Journal of the American Academy of Child and Adolescent Psychiatry, 46*, 233–241.

Van der Heijden, K. B. (2007). Effect of melatonin on sleep, behavior, and cognition in ADHD and chronic sleep-onset insomnia. *Journal of the American Academy of Child and Adolescent Psychiatry, 46*, 233–241.

Van der Oord, S., Prins, P. J. M., Oosterlaan, J., & Emmelkamp, P. M. G. (2008). Efficacy of methylphenidate, psychosocial treatments and their combination in school-aged children with ADHD: A meta-analysis. *Clinical Psychology Review, 28*, 783–800. doi:10.1016/j.cpr.2007.10.007

van Praag, H. (2008). Neurogenesis and exercise: past and future directions. *NeuroMolecular Medicine, 10*, 1535–1084. doi: 10.1007/s12017-008-8028-z

Vandell, D. L., Belsky, J., Burchinal, M., Steinberg, L., Vandergrift, N., & NICHD Early Child Care Research Network (2010). Do effects of early child care extend to age 15 years? Results from the NICHD Study of Early Child Care and Youth Development. *Child Development, 81*, 737–756.

Vandell, D. L., Belsky, J., Burchinal, M., Steinberg, L., Vandergrift, N., & NICHD Early Child Care Research Network (2010). Do effects of early child care extend to age 15 years? Results from the NICHD Study of Early Child Care and Youth Development. *Child Development, 81*, 737–756.

Vargha-Khadem, F., Gadian, D. G., Copp, A., & Mishkin, M. (2005). FOXP2 and the neuroanatomy of speech and language. *Nature Reviews Neuroscience, 6*, 131–138.

Vasquez, M. J. T., & Jones, J. (2006). Increasing the number of psychologists of color: Public policy issues for affirmative diversity. *American Psychologist, 61*, 132–142.

Vecchio, R. P. (1997). *Leadership: Understanding the dynamics of power and influence in organizations*. Notre Dame: University of Notre Dame Press.

Veilleux, J. C., Colvin, P. J., Anderson, J., York, C., &. Heinz, A. J. (2010). A review of opioid dependence treatment: Pharmacological and psychosocial interventions to treat opioid addiction. *Clinical Psychology Review, 30*, 155-166155-166. doi:10.1016/j.cpr.2009.10.006

Veltri, C. O., Graham, J. R., Sellbom, M., Ben-Porath, Y. S., Forbey, J. D., O'Connell, C., et al. (2009). Correlates of MMPI-A scales in acute psychiatric and forensic samples. *Journal of Personality Assessment, 91*, 288–300.

Verhaeghen, P. (2003). Aging and vocabulary scores: A meta-analysis. *Psychology and Aging, 18*, 332–339.

Verkuyten, M. (2005). Ethnic group identification and group evaluation among minority and majority groups: Testing the multiculturalism hypothesis. *Journal of Personality and Social Psychology, 88*, 121–138.

Vetter, I., Kapitzke, D., Hermanussen, S., Monteith, G. R., & Cabot, P. J. (2006). The effects of pH on beta-endorphin and morphine inhibition of calcium transients in dorsal root ganglion neurons. *The Journal of Pain, 7*, 488–499.

Victor, S. B., & Fish, M. C. (1995). Lesbian mothers and the children: A review for school psychologists. *School Psychology Review, 24*(3), 456–479.

Visser, B.A., Ashton, M.C., & Vernon, P.A. (2006). Beyond g: Putting multiple intelligences theory to the test. *Intelligence, 34*, 487–502.

Visser, P. S., & Cooper, J. (2003). Attitude change. In M. Hogg & J. Cooper (Eds.), *Sage handbook of social psychology*. London: Sage Publications.

Vitiello, M. V. (2009). Recent advances in understanding sleep and sleep disturbances in older adults: growing older does not mean sleeping poorly. *Current Directions in Psychological Science, 18*, 316–320. doi: 10.1111/j.1467-8721.2009.01659.x

Volbrecht, M. M., & Goldsmith, H. H. (2010). Early temperamental and family predictors of shyness and anxiety. *Developmental Psychology, 46*, 1192–1205. doi: 10.1037/a0020616

Von Békésy, G. (1957, August). The ear. *Scientific American*, pp. 66–78.

von Hippel, W. (2007). Aging, executive functioning, and social control. *Current Directions in Psychological Science, 16*, 240–244.

Vrij, A., Granhag, P. A., & Porter, S. (2010). Pitfalls and opportunities in nonverbal and verbal lie detection. *Psychological Science in the Public Interest, 11*, 89–121. doi: 10.1177/1529100610390861

Vuilleumier, P., & Huang, Y.-M. (2009). Emotional attention: Uncovering the mechanisms of affective biases in perception. *Current Directions in Psychological Science, 18*, 148– 152. doi: 10.1111/j.1467-8721.2009.01626.xVygotsky, L. S. (1978). *Mind in society: The development of higher psychological processes*. Cambridge, MA: Harvard University Press.

Vygotsky, L. S. (1986). *Thought and language*. Cambridge, MA: MIT Press. (Original work published 1934.)

Wadden, T. A., Berkowitz, R. I., Womble, L. G., Sarwer, D. B., Phelan, S., Cato, R. K., et al. (2005). Randomized trial of lifestyle modification and pharmacotherapy for obesity. *New England Journal of Medicine, 353*, 2111–2120.

Wade, N. (2007, May 1). Among chimps and bonobos, the hand often does the talking. *The New York Times*, p. F3.

Wade, N. (2011, January 11). Depth of the kindness hormone appears to know some bounds. *The New York Science Times*, p. D1, D2.

Wadsworth, S. J., DeFries, J. C., Fulker, D. W., & Plomin, R. (1995). Cognitive ability and academic achievement in the Colorado Adoption Project: A multivariate genetic analysis of parent/offspring and sibling data. *Behavior Genetics, 25*, 1–15.

Wager, T. D. (2005). The neural bases of placebo effects in pain. *Current Directions in Psychological Science, 14*, 175–179.

Wagner, K. D., Ritt-Olson, A., Chou, C.-P., Pokhrel, P., Duan, L., Baezconde-Garbanati, L., et al. (2010). Associations between family structure, family functioning, and substance use among Hispanic/Latino adolescents. *Psychology of Addictive Behaviors, 24*, 98–108. doi: 10.1037/a0018497

Wagner, U., Gais, S., Haider, H., Verleger, R., & Born, J. (2004). Sleep inspires insight. *Nature, 427*, 352–355.

Wagstaff, G. F., & Frost, R. (1996). Reversing and breaching posthypnotic amnesia and hypnotically created pseudomemories. *Contemporary Hypnosis, 13, 191–197.*

Wagstaff, J. (2006, September 29). Facial non-recognition: At least there's one thing humans are better at than computers. *Wall Street Journal Online*. Retrieved from http://online.wsj.com/article/SB115948110655577171.html?modtechnology_featured_stories_hs.

Waismann, R., Fenwick, P. B. C., Wilson, G. D., Hewett, T. D., & Lumsden, J. (2003). EEG responses to visual erotic stimuli in men with normal and paraphilic interests. *Archives of Sexual Behavior, 32*(2), 135–144.

Waldman, I. D., Weinberg, R. A., & Scarr, S. (1994). Racial-group differences in IQ in the Minnesota Transracial Adoption Study: A reply to Levin and Lynn. *Intelligence, 19*, 29–44.

Walker, E., Shapiro, D., Esterberg, M. & Trotman, H. (2010). Neurodevelopment and schizophrenia: Broadening the focus. *Psychological Science, 19*, 204–208. doi: 10.1177/0963721410377744

Walker, M. P., & Stickgold. R. (2006). Sleep, memory, and plasticity. *Annual Review of Psychology, 57*, 139–166.

Walker, R. (2008, October 5). Team Speedo USA parka. *The New York Times Magazine*, p. 22.

Wallace, D. S., Paulson, R. M., Lord, C. G., & Bond, C. F. (2005). Which behaviors do attitudes predict? Meta-analyzing the effects of social pressure and perceived difficulty. *Review of General Psychology, 9*, 214–227.

Waller, B. M., Vick, S.-J., Parr, L. A., Bard, K. A., Pasqualini, M. C. S., Gothard, K. M. et al. (2006). Intramuscular electrical stimulation of facial muscles in humans and chimpanzees: Duchenne revisited and extended. *Emotion, 6*, 367–382.

Wallis, C. (2005). The new science of happiness. *Time Magazine*, pp. A3–A9.

Wallston, K. A. (2001). Conceptualization and operationalization of perceived control. In A. Baum, T. A. Revenson, & J. E. Singer (Eds.), *Handbook of health psychology* (pp. 49–58). Mahwah, NJ: Lawrence Erlbaum Associates.

Walsh, B. T., Fairburn, C. G., Mickley, D., Sysko, R., & Parides, M. K. (2004). Treatment of bulimia nervosa in a primary care setting. *American Journal of Psychiatry, 161*, 556–561.

Walsh, T., Casadei, S., Coats, K. H., Swisher, E., Stray, S. M., & Higgins, J. (2006). Spectrum of mutations in BRCA1, BRCA2, CHEK2, and TP53 in families at high risk of breast cancer. *Journal of the American Medical Association, 295*, 1379–1388.

Wamsley, E. J., Tucker, M., Payne, J. D., Benavides, J. A. & Stickgold, R. (2010). Dreaming of a learning task is associated with enhanced sleep-dependent memory consolidation. *Current Biology, 20*, 850–855. doi: 10.1016/j.cub.2010.03.027

Wang, L., McCarthy, G., Song, A., W., & LaBar, K. S. (2005). Amygdala activation to sad pictures during high-field (4 tesla) functional magnetic resonance imaging. *Emotion, 5*, 12–22.

Wang, P. S., Lane, M., Olfson, M., Pincus, H. A., Wells, K. B., & Kessler, R. C. (2005). Twelve-month use of mental health services in the United States: Results from the National Comorbidity Survey Replication. *Archives of General Psychiatry, 62*, 590–592.

Wang, Q., Bowling, N. A., & Eschleman, K. J. (2010). A meta-analytic examination of work and general locus of control. *Journal of Applied Psychology, 95*, 761–768. doi: 10.1037/a0017707

Wang, S. S. (2011, April 19). New guidelines for spotting Alzheimer's. *The Wall Street Journal*, p. D4.

Ward, D., & Lasen, M. (2009, January 31). An overview of needs theories behind consumerism. Retreived from http://mpra.ub.uni-muenchen.de/13090/

Ward, T. B. (2004). Cognition, creativity, and entrepreneurship. *Journal of Business Venturing 19*, 173–188.

Ward, T. B. (2007). Creative cognition as a window on creativity. *Methods, 42*, 28–37.

Ward, T., Smith, S. & Vaid, J. (Eds.). (1997/2001). *Creative thought: an investigation of conceptual structures and processes.* Washington, DC: American Psychological Association.

Wargo, E. (2006, July). How many seconds to a first impression? *APS Observer, 19*(7), 11.

Wargo, E. (2008, May). Talk to the hand: New insights into the evolution of language and gesture. *APS Observer, 21*(5), 16–22.

Warner, M. B., Morey, L. C., Finch, J. F., Gunderson, J. G., Skodol, A. E., Sanislow, C. A., et al. (2004). The longitudinal relationship of personality traits and disorders. *Journal of Abnormal Psychology, 113*, 217–227.

Warren, G., Schertler, E., and Bull, P. (2009). Detecting deception from emotional and unemotional cues. *Journal of Nonverbal Behavior, 33*, 59–69. doi: 10.1007/s10919-008-0057-7

Watanabe, H., & Mizunami, M. (2007). Pavlov's cockroach: Classical conditioning of salivation in an insect. *PLoSOne*, 2(6), e529.

Watson, D., & Clark, L. A. (2006). Clinical diagnosis at the crossroads. *Clinical Psychology: Science and Practice, 13*, 210–215.

Watson, J. B. (1924). *Behaviorism*. New York: W. W. Norton.

Watson, J. B., & Rayner, R. (1920). Conditioned emotional reactions. *Journal of Experimental Psychology, 3*, 1–14.

Webster, G. D. (2009). The person-situation interaction is increasingly outpacing the person-situation debate in the scientific literature: A 30-year analysis of publication trends, 1978–2007. *Journal of Research in Personality, 43*, 278–279. doi:10.1016/j.jrp.2008.12.030

Wechsler, D. (1975). Intelligence defined and undefined: A relativistic appraisal. *American Psychologist, 34*, 135–139.

Wechsler, H., & Nelson T. F. (2008). What we have learned from the Harvard School of Public Health College Alcohol Study: Focusing attention on college student alcohol consumption and the environmental conditions that promote it. *Journal of Studies on Alcohol and Drugs, 69*, 481–490.

Wegner, D. M., Wenzlaff, R. M., & Kozak, M. (2004). Dream rebound: The return of suppressed thoughts in dreams. *Psychological Science, 15*, 232–236.

Weis, R. (2002). A parenting dimensionality and typology in a disadvantaged, African American sample: A cultural variance perspective. *Journal of Black Psychology, 28*, 142–173.

Weiss, A., Bates, T. C., & Luciano, M. (2008). Happiness is a personal(ity) thing. *Psychological Science, 19*, 205–210. doi: 10.1111/j.1467-9280.2008.02068.x

Weiss, A., King, J. E., & Perkins, L. (2006). Personality and subjective well-being in orangutans (Pongo pygmaeus and Pongo abelii). *Journal of Personality and Social Psychology, 90*, 501–511.

Weisz, J. R., Jensen-Doss, A., & Hawley, K. M. (2006). Evidence-based youth psychotherapies versus usual clinical care: A meta-analysis of direct comparisons. *American Psychologist, 61*, 671–689.

Wells, B. E., & Twenge, J. M. (2005). Changes in young people's sexual behavior and attitudes, 1943–1999: A cross-temporal meta-analysis. *Review of General Psychology, 9*, 249–261.

Westen, D., & Gabbard, G. O. (2002). Developments in cognitive neuroscience: 1. Conflict, compromise, and connectionism. *Journal of the American Psychoanalytic Association, 50*, 53–98.

Whitchurch, E. R., Wilson, T. D., & Gilbert, D. T. (2011). "He loves me, he loves me not . . ." Uncertainty can increase romantic attraction. *Psychological Science, 22*, 172–175. doi: 10.1177/0956797610393745

White, H., R., Fleming, C. B., Kim, M. J., Catalano, R. F., & McMorris, B. J. (2008). Identifying two potential mechanisms for changes in alcohol use among college-attending and non-college-attending emerging adults. *Developmental Psychology, 44*, 1625–1639. doi: 10.1037/a0013855

White, J. K., Hendrick, S. S., & Hendrick, C. (2004). Big five personality variables and relationship constructs. *Personality and Individual Differences, 37*, 1519–1530.

White, K. S., Brown, T. W., Somers, T. J., & Barlow, D. H. (2006). Avoidance behavior in panic disorder: The moderating influence of perceived control. *Behaviour Research and Therapy, 44*, 147–157.

Whorf, B. L. (1956). Science and linguistics. In J. B. Carrroll (Ed.), *Language, thought, and reality: Selected writings of Benjamin Lee Whorf.* Cambridge, MA: MIT Press.

Widiger, T. A. (2005). Five factor model of personality disorder: Integrating science and practice. *Journal of Research in Personality, 39*, 67–83.

Wilcox, L. M., & Duke, P. A. (2003). Stereoscopic surface interpolation supports lightness constancy. *Psychological Science, 14*, 525–530.

Wilcox, W. B. (2010). *The state of our unions. The National Marriage Project.* University of Virginia. Retrieved from http://www.virginia.edu/marriageproject/pdfs/Union_11_25_09.pdf.

Willcox, B. J., He, Q., Chen, R., Yano, K. Masaki, K. H., Grove, J. S., et al. (2006). Midlife risk factors and healthy survival in men. *Journal of the American Medical Association, 296*, 2343–2350.

Williams, L. E., & Bargh, J. A. (2008). Experiencing physical warmth promotes interpersonal warmth. *Science, 322*, 606–607. doi: 10.1126/science.1162548

Williams, M. A., & Mattingley, J. B. (2006). Do angry men get noticed? *Current Biology, 16*, R402–R404.

Willingham, D. T. (2007). *Cognition: The thinking animal* (3rd ed.). Upper Saddle River, NJ: Pearson/Prentice Hall.

Willis, J., & Todorov, A. (2006). First impressions: Making up your mind after a 100-ms exposure to a face. *Psychological Science, 17*, 592–598.

Wills, T. A., & Cleary, S. D. (1999). Peer and adolescent substance use among 6th–9th graders: Latent growth analyses of influence versus selection mechanisms. *Health Psychology, 18*, 453–463.

Wilson, R. S., & Bennett, D. A. (2003). Cognitive activity and risk of Alzheimer's disease. *Current Directions in Psychological Science, 12*, 87–91.

Winerip, M. (1999, May 23). Bedlam on the streets. *New York Times Magazine*, pp. 42–49.

Winerman, L. (2005, July/August). Figuring out phobia. *Monitor on Psychology, 36*, 96–98.

Winerman. L. (2006, January). Brain, heal thyself. *Monitor on Psychology, 37*(1), 56–57.

Wingert, P., & Brant, M. (2005, August 15). Reading your baby's mind. *Newsweek*, pp. 33–39.

Wingert, P., & Kantrowitz, B. (2007a). *The complete guide to menopause*. New York: Workman Publishing Company.

Wingert, P., & Kantrowitz, B. (2007b, January 15). The new prime time. *Newsweek*, pp. 38–50, 53–54.

Wiseman, R., & Watt, C. (2006). Belief in psychic ability and the misattribution hypothesis: A qualitative review. *British Journal of Psychology, 97*, 343–338.

Witte, T. K., Timmons, K. A., Fink, E., Smith, A. R., & Joiner, T. E. (2009). Do major depressive disorder and dysthymic disorder confer differential risk for suicide? *Journal of Affective Disorders, 115*, 69–78. doi:10.1016/j.jad.2008.09.003

Wixted, J. T. (2004). The psychology and neuroscience of forgetting. *Annual Review of Psychology, 55*, 235–269.

Wixted, J. T. (2005). A theory about why we forget what we once knew. *Current Directions in Psychological Science, 14*, 6–9.

Wolff, T., Witkop, C., T., Miller, T., & Syed, S. B. (2009). Folic acid supplementation for the prevention of neural tube defects: An update of the evidence for the U.S. Preventive Services Task Force. *Annals of Internal Medicine, 150*, 632–639.

Wood, J., M., Lilienfeld, S. O, Nezworski, M. T, Garb, H. N., Allen, K. H., & Wildermuth, J. L.. (2010). Validity of Rorschach Inkblot scores for discriminating psychopaths from nonpsychopaths in forensic populations: A meta-analysis. *Psychological Assessment, 22*, 336–349. doi: 10.1037/a0018998

Wood, W., & Eagly, A. H. (2002). A cross-cultural analysis of the behavior of women and men: Implications for the origins of sex differences. *Psychological Bulletin, 128*, 699–727.

Woods-Giscombé, C. L., & Lobel, M. (2008). Race and gender matter: A multidimensional approach to conceptualizing and measuring stress in African American women. *Cultural Diversity and Ethnic Minority Psychology, 14*, 173–182.

Wratten, N. S., Memoli, H.,, Huang, Y., Dulencin, A. M., Matteson, P. G., Cornacchia, M. A., et al. (2009). Identification of a schizophrenia-associated functional noncoding variant in NOS1AP. *American Journal of Psychiatry, 166*, 434–441. doi: 10.1176/appi.ajp.2008.08081266

Wray, H. (2010). *On second thought*. New York: Crown.

Wray, N. R., Middeldorp, C. M., Birley, A. J., Gordon, S. D., Sullivan, P. F., Visscher, P. M., et al. (2008). Genome-wide linkage analysis of multiple measures of neuroticism of 2 large cohorts from Australia and the Netherlands. *Archives of General Psychiatry, 65*, 649–658.

Wright, S. C., Aron, A., McLaughlin-Volpe, R., & Ropp, S. A. (1997). The extended contact effect: Knowledge of cross-group friendships and prejudice. *Journal of Personality and Social Psychology, 73*, 73–90.

Xu, J., & Roberts, R. E. (2010). The power of positive emotions: It's a matter of life or death—Subjective well-being and longevity over 28 years in a general population. *Health Psychology, 29*, 9–19. doi: 10.1037/a0016767

Yager, J. (2011, January 10). Real-time study of substance use and psychotic symptoms. *JournalWatch Psychiatry*. Retrieved from http://psychiatry.jwatch.org/.

Yaggi, H. K., Concato, J., Kernan, W. N., Lichtman, J., H., Brass, L. M., & Mohsenin, V. (2005). Obstructive sleep apnea as a risk factor for stroke and death. (2005). *New England Journal of Medicine, 353*, 2034–2041.

Yan, L. L, Daviglus, M. L., Liu, K., Stamler, J., Wang, R., Pirzada, A., et al. (2006). Midlife body mass index and hospitalization and mortality in older age. *Journal of the American Medical Association, 295*, 190–198.

Yang, Q., She, H., Gearing, M., Colla, E., Lee, M., Shacka, J. J. & Mao, Z. (2009). Regulation of neuronal survival factor MEF2D by chaperone-mediated autophagy. *Science, 323* (5910), 124–127. doi: 10.1126/science.1166088

Yatham, L. N. (2011) A clinical review of aripiprazole in bipolar depression and maintenance therapy of bipolar disorder. *Journal of Affective Disorders, 128*, S21–S28.

Yonkers, K. A., O'Brien, P. M. S., & Eriksson, E. (2008). Premenstrual syndrome. The *Lancet, 371*, 1200–1210. doi:10.1016/S0140-6736(08)60527-9

Yücel, M., Solowij, N., Respondek, C., Whittle, S., Fornito, A., Pantelis, C., et al. (2008). Regional brain abnormalities associated with long-term heavy cannabis use. *Archives of General Psychiatry, 65*, 694–701.

Yunger, J. L., Carver, P. R., & Perry, D. G. (2004). Does gender identity influence children's psychological well-being? *Developmental Psychology, 40*, 572–582.

Zajonc, R. (1965). Social facilitation. *Science, 149*, 269–274.

Zajonc, R. B. (1980). Feeling and thinking: Preferences need no inferences. *American Psychologist, 35*, 151–175.

Zajonc, R. B. (1984). On the primacy of affect. *American Psychologist, 39*, 117–123.

Zalewska, A. M. (2010). Relationships between anxiety and job satisfaction–three approaches: 'Bottom-up', 'top-down' and 'transactional.' *Personality and Individual Differences, 50*, 977–986. doi:10.1016/j.paid.2010.10.013

Zautra, A. J., Davis, M. C., Reich, J. W., Nicassario, P., Tennen, H., Finan, P., et al. (2008). Comparison of cognitive behavioral and mindfulness meditation interventions on adaptation to rheumatoid arthritis for patients with and without history of recurrent depression. *Journal of Consulting and Clinical Psychology, 76*, 408–421. doi: 10.1037/0022-006X.76.3.408

Zeelenberg, R., Wagenmakers, E.-J., & Rotteveel, M. (2006). The impact of emotion on perception: bias or enhanced processing? *Psychological Science, 17*, 287–291.

Zeidan, F., Martucci, K. T., Kraft, R. A., Gordon, N. S., McHaffie, J. G., & Coghill, R. C. (2011). Brain mechanisms supporting the modulation of pain by mindfulness meditation. *Journal of Neuroscience, 31*, 14. doi: 10.1523/JNEUROSCI.5791-10.2011

Zentall, T. R. (2010). Justification of effort by humans and pigeons: Cognitive dissonance or contrast? *Current Directions in Psychological Science, 19*, 296–300. doi:10.1177/0963721410383381

Zernike, K. (2007, January 21). Why are there so many single Americans? *The New York Times*, Section 4, pp. 1, 4

Zhang, W., & Luck, S. J. (2009). Sudden death and gradual decay in visual working memory. *Psychological Science, 20*, 423–428.

Zhong, C. B. (2010). You are how you eat: Fast food and impatience. *Psychological Science, 2*, 619–22. doi: 10.1177/0956797610366090

Zickler, P. (2006, October). Marijuana smoking is associated with a spectrum of respiratory disorders. *NIDA Notes, 21*(1), 12–13.

Zigler, E., & Styfco, S. J. (1994). Head Start: Criticisms in a constructive context. *American Psychologist, 49*, 127–132.

Zimbardo, P. G. (1975). On transforming experimental research into advocacy for social change. In M. Deutsch & H. Hornstein (Eds.), *Applying social psychology: Implicaitions for research, practice and training*. Hillsdale, NJ: Erlbaum.

Zimbardo, P. G., Haney, C., Banks, W. C., and Jaffe, D. (1973, April 8). The mind is a formidable jailer: A Pirandellian prison. *The New York Times Magazine*, Section 6, pp. 38 ff.

Zubin, J., & Spring, B. (1977). Vulnerability—A new view of schizophrenia. *Journal of Abnormal Psychology, 86*, 103–126.

Zucker, A. N., Ostrove, J. M., & Stewart, A. J. (2002). College-educated women's personality development in adulthood: Perceptions and age differences. *Psychology and Aging, 2*, 236–244.

Zucker, K. J. (2005a). Gender identity disorder in children and adolescents. *Annual Review of Clinical Psychology, 1*, 467–492.

Zucker, K. J. (2005b). Gender identity disorder in girls. In Bell, D. J., Foster, S. L., & Mash, E. J. (Eds.), *Handbook of behavioral and emotional problems in girls: Issues in clinical child psychology* (pp. 285–319). Kluwer Academic/Plenum Publishers.

Zuckerman, M. (1980). Sensation seeking. In H. London & J. Exner (Eds.), *Dimensions of personality*. New York: John Wiley & Sons.

Zuckerman, M. (2004). The shaping of personality: Genes, environments, and chance encounters. *Journal of Personality Assessment, 82*, 11–22.

Zukow-Goldring, P. (1997). A social ecological realist approach to the emergence of the lexicon: Educating attention to amodal invariants in gesture and speech. In C. Dent-Read & P. Zukow-Goldring (Eds.), *Evolving explanations of development: Ecological approaches to organism-environment systems* (pp. 199–250). Washington, DC: American Psychological Association.

Zuroff, D. C., & Blatt, S. (2006). Therapeutic relationship in the brief treatment of depression: Contributions to clinical improvement and enhanced adaptive capacities. *Journal of Consulting and Clinical Psychology, 74*, 130–140.

Zvolensky, M. J., Kotov, R., Antipova, A. V., & Schmidt, N. B. (2005). Diathesis stress model for panic-related distress: A test in a Russian epidemiological sample. *Behaviour Research and Therapy, 43*, 521–532.

Zweigenhaft, R. L. (1970). Signature size: A key to status awareness. *Journal of Social Psychology, 81*, 49–54.

Name Index

Note: Italicized page numbers indicate illustrations of the person.

I

J

K

Subject Index

Note: Italicized page numbers indicate figures, tables, and charts.

D

(Continued)